W9-CTW-640

Contemporary
Literary Criticism

Guide to Gale Literary Criticism Series

When you need to review criticism of literary works, these are the Gale series to use:

If the author's death date is: **You should turn to:**

After Dec. 31, 1959
(or author is still living)

CONTEMPORARY LITERARY CRITICISM

for example: Jorge Luis Borges, Anthony Burgess,
William Faulkner, Mary Gordon,
Ernest Hemingway, Iris Murdoch

1900 through 1959

TWENTIETH-CENTURY LITERARY CRITICISM

for example: Willa Cather, F. Scott Fitzgerald,
Henry James, Mark Twain, Virginia Woolf

1800 through 1899

NINETEENTH-CENTURY LITERATURE CRITICISM

for example: Fedor Dostoevski, Nathaniel Hawthorne,
George Sand, William Wordsworth

1400 through 1799

LITERATURE CRITICISM FROM 1400 TO 1800
(excluding Shakespeare)

for example: Anne Bradstreet, Daniel Defoe,
Alexander Pope, François Rabelais,
Jonathan Swift, Phillis Wheatley

SHAKESPEAREAN CRITICISM

Shakespeare's plays and poetry

Antiquity through 1399

CLASSICAL AND MEDIEVAL LITERATURE CRITICISM

for example: Dante, Homer, Plato, Sophocles, Vergil,
the Beowulf Poet

Gale also publishes related criticism series:

CHILDREN'S LITERATURE REVIEW

This series covers authors of all eras who have written for the preschool through high school audience.

SHORT STORY CRITICISM

This series covers the major short fiction writers of all nationalities and periods of literary history.

ISSN 0091-3421

Volume 61

Contemporary Literary Criticism

Excerpts from Criticism of the
Works of Today's Novelists, Poets,
Playwrights, Short Story Writers, Scriptwriters,
and Other Creative Writers

Roger Matuz
EDITOR

Cathy Falk
Mary K. Gillis
Sean R. Pollock
David Segal
Bridget Travers
Robyn V. Young
ASSOCIATE EDITORS

Gale Research Inc. • DETROIT • NEW YORK • LONDON

STAFF

Roger Matuz, *Editor*

Cathy Falk, Mary K. Gillis, Sean R. Pollock, David Segal,
Bridget Travers, Robyn V. Young, *Associate Editors*

Susanne Skubik, *Assistant Editor*

Jeanne A. Gough, *Production & Permissions Manager*
Linda M. Pugliese, *Production Supervisor*
Suzanne Powers, Maureen A. Puhl, Linda M. Ross, Jennifer Van Sickle, *Editorial Associates*
Donna Craft, James G. Wittenbach, *Editorial Assistants*

Victoria B. Cariappa, *Research Manager*
H. Nelson Fields, Judy L. Gale, Maureen Richards, *Editorial Associates*
Jennifer Brostrom, Paula Cutcher, Alan Hedblad, Robin Lupa, *Editorial Assistants*

Sandra C. Davis, *Permissions Supervisor (Text)*
Josephine M. Keene, Kimberly F. Smilay, *Permissions Associates*
Maria L. Franklin, Michele Lonoconus, Camille P. Robinson,
Shalice Shah, Denise M. Singleton, Rebecca A. Stanko, *Permissions Assistants*

Patricia A. Seefelt, *Permissions Supervisor (Pictures)*
Margaret A. Chamberlain, *Permissions Associate*
Pamela A. Hayes, Lillian Quickley, *Permissions Assistants*

Mary Beth Trimper, *Production Manager*
Marilyn Jackman, *External Production Associate*

Art Chartow, *Art Director*
C. J. Jonik, *Keyliner*

Laura Bryant, *Production Supervisor*
Louise Gagné, *Internal Production Associate*

Contents

Preface   vii

Acknowledgments   xi

Authors Forthcoming in *CLC*   xv

Preface

Named "one of the twenty-five most distinguished reference titles published during the past twenty-five years" by *Reference Quarterly,* the *Contemporary Literary Criticism (CLC)* series has provided readers with critical commentary and general information on more that 2,000 authors now living or who died after December 31, 1959. Previous to the publication of the first volume of *CLC* in 1973, there was no ongoing digest monitoring scholarly and popular sources of critical opinion and explication of modern literature. *CLC,* therefore, has fulfilled an essential need, particularly since the complexity and variety of contemporary literature makes the function of criticism especially important to today's reader.

Scope of the Series

CLC presents significant passages from published criticism of works by creative writers. Since many of the authors covered by *CLC* continually inspire critical commentary, writers are often represented in more than one volume. There is, of course, no duplication of reprinted criticism.

Authors are selected for inclusion for a variety of reasons, among them the publication or dramatic production of a critically acclaimed new work, the reception of a major literary award, revival of interest in past writings, or the dramatization of a literary work as a film or television screenplay. The present volume of *CLC* includes:

☞ Award-winning dramatists María Irene Fornés, an influential force in off-Broadway theater; Larry Gelbart, author of *City of Angels,* which garnered several Tony Awards in 1990; and George F. Walker, two-time recipient of the Canadian Governor General's Award.

☞ Stephen King, author of many popular works of horror, and Sue Townsend, who wrote the best-selling *Adrian Mole Diaries.*

☞ Anthony Burgess and Thomas Bernhard, widely regarded as major figures in contemporary literature.

Perhaps most importantly, works that frequently appear on the syllabuses of high school and college literature courses are represented by individual entries in *CLC.* Ernest Hemingway's *The Sun Also Rises,* Jack Kerouac's *On the Road,* and Zora Neale Hurston's *Their Eyes Were Watching God* are examples of works of this stature represented in *CLC,* Volume 61. Attention is also given to several other groups of writers—authors of considerable public interest—about whose work criticism is often difficult to locate. These include mystery and science fiction writers, literary and social critics, foreign writers, and authors who represent particular ethnic groups within the United States.

Format of the Book

Altogether there are about 500 individual excerpts in each volume—with approximately seventeen excerpts per author—taken from hundreds of book review periodicals, general magazines, scholarly journals, monographs, and books. Entries include critical evaluations spanning from the beginning of an author's career to the most current commentary. Interviews, feature articles, and other published writings that offer insight into the author's works are also presented. Students, teachers, librarians, and researchers will find that the generous excerpts and supplementary material provided by *CLC* supply them with vital information needed to write a term paper, analyze a poem, or lead a book discussion group. In addition, complete bibliographical citations facilitate the location of the original source and provide all of the information necessary for a term paper footnote or bibliography.

A *CLC* author entry consists of the following elements:

• The **author heading** cites the form under which the author has most commonly published, followed by birth date, and death date when applicable. Uncertainty as to a birth or death date is indicated by a question mark.

- A **portrait** of the author is included when available.

- A brief **biographical and critical introduction** to the author and his or her work precedes the excerpted criticism. The first line of the introduction provides the author's full name, pseudonyms (if applicable), nationality, and a listing of genres in which the author has written. Since *CLC* is not intended to be a definitive biographical source, *cross-references* have been included to direct readers to these useful sources published by Gale Research: *Short Story Criticism* and *Children's Literature Review*, which provide excerpts of criticism on the works of short story writers and authors of books for young people, respectively; *Contemporary Authors*, which includes detailed biographical and bibliographical sketches of nearly 95,000 authors; *Something about the Author*, which contains heavily illustrated biographical sketches of writers and illustrators who create books for children and young adults; *Dictionary of Literary Biography*, which provides original evaluations and detailed biographies of authors important to literary history; and *Contemporary Authors Autobiography Series* and *Something about the Author Autobiography Series*, which offer autobiographical essays by prominent writers for adults and those of interest to young readers, respectively. Previous volumes of *CLC* in which the author has been featured are also listed in the introduction.

- The **excerpted criticism** represents various kinds of critical writing, ranging in form from the brief review to the scholarly exegesis. Essays are selected by the editors to reflect the spectrum of opinion about a specific work or about an author's literary career in general. The excerpts are presented chronologically, adding a useful perspective to the entry. All titles by the author featured in the entry are printed in boldface type, which enables the reader to easily identify the works being discussed. Publication information (such as publisher names and book prices) and parenthetical numerical references (such as footnotes or page and line references to specific editions of a work) have been deleted at the editor's discretion to provide smoother reading of the text.

- A complete **bibliographical citation** designed to help the user find the original essay or book follows each excerpt.

New Features

Beginning with Vol. 60, *CLC* has incorporated two new features designed to enhance the usability of the series:

- A list of **principal works**, arranged chronologically and, if applicable, divided into genre categories, notes the most important works by the author.

- A **further reading** section appears at the end of entries on authors who have generated a significant amount of criticism other than the pieces reprinted in *CLC*. In some cases, it includes references to material for which the editors could not obtain reprint rights.

Other Features

- A list of **Authors Forthcoming in *CLC*** previews the authors to be researched for future volumes.

- An **Acknowledgments** section lists the copyright holders who have granted permission to reprint material in this volume of *CLC*. It does not, however, list every book or periodical reprinted or consulted during the preparation of the volume.

- A **Cumulative Author Index** lists all the authors who have appeared in *CLC, Twentieth-Century Literary Criticism, Nineteenth-Century Literature Criticism, Literature Criticism from 1400 to 1800, Classical and Medieval Literature Criticism*, and *Short Story Criticism*, with cross-references to these Gale series: *Children's Literature Review, Contemporary Authors, Contemporary Authors Autobiography Series, Contemporary Authors Bibliographical Series, Dictionary of Literary Biography, Something about the Author, Something about the Author Autobiography Series, Yesterday's Authors of Books for Children*, and *Authors & Artists for Young Adults*. Readers will welcome this cumulated author index as a useful tool for locating an author within the various series. The index, which lists birth and death dates when available, will be particularly valuable for those authors who are identified with a certain period but whose death date causes them to be placed in another, or for those authors whose careers span two periods. For example, Ernest Hemingway is found in *CLC*, yet a writer often associated with him, F. Scott Fitzgerald, is found in *Twentieth-Century Literary Criticism*.

- A **Cumulative Nationality Index** alphabetically lists all authors featured in *CLC* by nationality, followed by numbers corresponding to the volumes in which they appear.

- A **Title Index** alphabetically lists all titles reviewed in the current volume of *CLC*. Listings are followed by the author's name and the corresponding page numbers where the titles are discussed. English translations of foreign titles and variations of titles are cross-referenced to the title under which a work was originally published. Titles of novels, novellas, dramas, films, record albums, and poetry, short story, and essay collections are printed in italics, while all individual poems, short stories, essays, and songs are printed in roman type within quotation marks; when published separately (e.g., T.S. Eliot's poem *The Waste Land*), the title will also be printed in italics.

- In response to numerous suggestions from librarians, Gale has also produced a **special paperbound edition** of the *CLC* title index. This annual cumulation, which alphabetically lists all titles reviewed in the series, is available to all customers and will be published with the first volume of *CLC* issued in each calendar year. Additional copies of the index are available upon request. Librarians and patrons will welcome this separate index: it saves shelf space, is easy to use, and is disposable upon receipt of the following year's cumulation.

A Note to the Reader

When writing papers, students who quote directly from any volume in the Literary Criticism Series may use the following general forms to footnote reprinted criticism. The first example pertains to material drawn from periodicals, the second to material reprinted from books:

[1]Anne Tyler, "Manic Monologue," *The New Republic* 200 (April 17, 1989), 44-6; excerpted and reprinted in *Contemporary Literary Criticism,* Vol. 58, ed. Roger Matuz (Detroit: Gale Research, 1990), p. 325.

[2]Patrick Reilly, *The Literature of Guilt: From 'Gulliver' to Golding* (University of Iowa Press, 1988); excerpted and reprinted in *Contemporary Literary Criticism,* Vol. 58, ed. Roger Matuz (Detroit: Gale Research, 1990), pp. 206-12.

Suggestions Are Welcome

The editors welcome the comments and suggestions of readers to expand the coverage and enhance the usefulness of the series. Please feel free to contact us by letter or by calling our toll-free number: 1-800-347-GALE.

Acknowledgments

The editors wish to thank the copyright holders of the excerpted criticism included in this volume, the permissions managers of many book and magazine publishing companies for assisting us in securing reprint rights, and Anthony Bogucki for assistance with copyright research. We are also grateful to the staffs of the Detroit Public Library, the Library of Congress, the University of Detroit Library, Wayne State University Purdy/Kresge Library Complex, and the University of Michigan Libraries for making their resources available to us. Following is a list of the copyright holders who have granted us permission to reprint material in this volume of *CLC*. Every effort has been made to trace copyright, but if omissions have been made, please let us know.

COPYRIGHTED EXCERPTS IN *CLC*, VOLUME 61, WERE REPRINTED FROM THE FOLLOWING PERIODICALS:

Authors Forthcoming in *CLC*

To Be Included in Volume 62

Martin Amis (English novelist, critic, and short story writer)—Amis employs a flamboyant prose style in satirical novels that castigate hedonism in contemporary society. Criticism in this entry will focus on *Einstein's Monsters*, a short story collection, and *London Fields*, which is widely considered Amis's most ambitious novel.

John Berryman (American poet and critic)—A key figure in the group of American poets known as the "Middle Generation," Berryman expanded the boundaries of post-World War II poetry with his intense, confessional verse and his imaginative adaptations of various poetic forms and personae. The recent publication of Berryman's *Collected Poems* has revived interest in the work of this influential poet.

Anthony Burgess (English novelist, essayist, and critic)—Considered among the most important novelists in contemporary literature, Burgess is a prolific writer best known for his dystopian novel *A Clockwork Orange*. His work, which covers a vast range of topics, frequently explores the conflict between free will and determinism and the role of the artist in society.

Henry Dumas (American short story writer and poet)—Considered an author of extraordinary talent, Dumas did not achieve critical recognition until after his death in 1968. His posthumously published collections *Ark of Bones* and *Goodbye Sweetwater* emphasize the African heritage of black Americans as he chronicles their divergent experiences in the rural South and the industrial North.

Lorraine Hansberry (American dramatist)—The first African-American woman to win the New York Drama Critics Circle Award, Hansberry is best known for *A Raisin in the Sun*. This acclaimed play about a black working-class family's attempt to move into a white neighborhood will be the focus of her entry.

Tony Hillerman (American novelist)—Valued for their accurate and evocative depictions of Native American life on reservations of the Southwest, Hillerman's popular and critically respected mystery novels feature Navajo tribal policemen who employ both modern crime-fighting methods and ancient Navajo philosophy.

Margaret Laurence (Canadian novelist and short story writer)—One of Canada's most prominent contemporary writers, Laurence is respected for her "Manawaka" works, a series of four novels and a volume of short stories that examine Canadian social and historical issues through their evocation of small-town Manitoba life.

Cynthia Ozick (American short story writer and novelist)—Ozick is praised for her intricate, poetic fiction that incorporates magical elements within narratives concerning Jewish identity. This entry will focus on Ozick's recent works, *The Messiah of Stockholm* and *The Shawl*.

Sylvia Plath (American poet and novelist)—Considered one of the most powerful poets of the post-World War II era, Plath examined conflicts relating to her familial, marital, and career aspirations. This entry will concentrate on her autobiographical novel *The Bell Jar*, which portrays a young woman's struggles with despair and her attempts to assert a strong female identity.

Thomas Pynchon (American novelist and short story writer)—A preeminent author of postmodern works best known for his celebrated novel *Gravity's Rainbow*, Pynchon has attracted renewed critical interest with the publication of *Vineland*, his first novel in seventeen years.

Christy Brown (Irish autobiographer and poet)—Crippled from birth by cerebral palsy, Brown is recognized for his celebrated autobiography *My Left Foot*, which was adapted into an Academy Award-winning film. Brown also wrote several novels, including *Down All the Days* and *A Shadow on Summer*, as well as numerous volumes of poetry.

Albert Camus (Algerian-born French novelist and essayist)—Awarded the Nobel Prize in 1957, Camus is renowned for writings that defend the dignity and decency of the individual and assert that one can transcend absurdity through purposeful actions. This entry will focus on his novels.

Tess Gallagher (American poet and short story writer)—Gallagher won acclaim for her direct yet subtle approach to family relations and the passage of time in two recent publications, *Amplitude: New and Selected Poems* and *The Lover of Horses and Other Stories*.

Shelby Hearon (American novelist and short story writer)—Described as a "female Larry McMurtry," Hearon sets much of her fiction in Texas or surrounding locales and presents strong and colorful female protagonists.

Joseph Heller (American novelist)—Heller is a popular contemporary satirist whose provocative blend of farce and tragedy is most often applied to the absurd machinations of large bureaucracies. His entry will focus on his most famous work, *Catch-22*, an irreverent portrayal of American armed forces during World War II.

Elia Kazan—(Turkish-born American filmmaker and novelist)—An award-winning director of such films as *A Streetcar Named Desire*, *On the Waterfront*, and *A Face in the Crowd*, Kazan also drew attention for several novels he wrote following his film career.

Boris Pasternak (Russian poet and novelist)—Awarded the 1958 Nobel Prize in Literature, which he was forced to decline under political pressure, Pasternak is best known for his novel *Dr. Zhivago*, an account of the Russian Revolution, but is equally respected for his complex, mystical poetry.

Upton Sinclair (American journalist and novelist)—A leading figure in the Muckraking movement, a term denoting the aggressive style of exposé journalism that flourished in the United States during the early 1900s, Sinclair aroused international furor with his best-selling novel *The Jungle*. Exposing exploitative, unsanitary, and hazardous conditions in American meat-packing plants, *The Jungle* is considered an exemplary work of social protest literature.

Gloria Steinem (American nonfiction writer and editor)—Among the most well-known leaders of the contemporary feminist movement, Steinem cofounded *Ms.* magazine and wrote essays that influenced the personal and political lives of many women. Her best-known works include the essay collection *Outrageous Acts and Everyday Rebellions* and her feminist biography of Marilyn Monroe.

Tom Stoppard (English dramatist)—A leading playwright in contemporary theater, Stoppard examines moral and philosophical themes within the context of comedy. Often described as "philosophical farces," his plays frequently draw upon Shakespeare's works to examine modern concerns, as in his his acclaimed work *Rosencrantz and Guildenstern Are Dead*, which will be the focus of Stoppard's entry.

Nicholson Baker

1957-

American novelist and short story writer.

Baker has garnered critical acclaim for his unconventional first novel, *The Mezzanine*. Largely devoid of plot, action, and characterization, this work consists primarily of the labyrinthine thoughts of Howie, a detail-obsessed young businessman. The central event of the novel is Howie's escalator ride to the mezzanine level of his workplace after eating lunch and purchasing shoelaces. This uneventful premise inspires myriad flashbacks, digressions, footnotes, lists, charts, and ruminations by Howie on the minutiae of daily existence, and such ordinary objects as milk cartons, vending machines, ice cube trays, and paper towel dispensers are invested with an aura of wonder. Thus, Baker implies that seemingly trivial aspects of contemporary life possess great significance. Steven Moore commented: "[The narrator of *The Mezzanine*]—a Proust of the commonplace, a yuppie Tristram Shandy—links his own emotional history with recent technical advances by way of hundreds of analogies, metaphors, and fanciful comparisons that are so apt, so insightful, and often so amusing that I felt I was seeing the world I live in for the first time—as trite as that may sound."

Baker's second novel, *Room Temperature,* also focuses on the digressive musings of a man involved in a generally unremarkable activity—the feeding of his baby. As in *The Mezzanine,* Baker elaborates on this seemingly mundane plot to create numerous inventive similes and metaphors about the marvels of material objects and nature, often provoked by the protagonist's remembrance of events past and present.

PRINCIPAL WORKS

NOVELS

The Mezzanine 1988
Room Temperature 1990

BARBARA FISHER WILLIAMSON

[*The Mezzanine*] is the most daring and thrilling first novel since John Barth's 1955 *The Floating Opera,* which it somewhat resembles. It is innovative and original, words that usually translate into tedious to read, but it is never tedious. It is wonderfully readable, in fact gripping, with surprising bursts of recognition, humor, and wonder.

The entire action of the novel takes place during a 30-second ride on an escalator from the ground floor of an office building to its mezzanine, where the narrator works. During this ride, the narrator describes the events of his just-finished lunch hour along with numerous digressions. He has just purchased a new pair of shoelaces. His laces have both independently broken in the last two days, a coincidence that intrigues and irritates him and leads him into much speculation

on the rubbing and wearing of surfaces as they come into contact with other surfaces. Most of his digressions are about the things of modern daily life: vending machines, plastic straws, aluminum popcorn poppers, staplers, paper towels. The descriptions of these things are more detailed, precise, and beautiful than a reader could imagine, verbal ballets of incredible delicacy. . . .

Many of these descriptions appear in tightly printed footnotes at the bottom of the page. Lists, including one on the relative frequency of thoughts during a year, interrupt the narrative. Thus, instead of a flowing chronology of events, a reader is confronted with an extraordinary and idiosyncratic train of thought. This novelistic tradition, which began with *Tristram Shandy,* is gracefully extended here.

In tiny droplets along the way, the narrator dispenses a few facts about himself. He is 23 years old on the day of the escalator ride, although he was born in 1957. He is tall, wears glasses always and ear plugs often. His name is Howie. He grew up in Rochester. His parents are divorced, and he has a girlfriend (a word he finds inadequate) he refers to only as L. Several of his co-workers seem to avoid him. His boss answers his one question with a cutting, sarcastic reply. He says he has no friends. Is he mad? Is his acute sensitivity to things and his complete neglect of people a form of madness? Have

1

corporate life, fast food, and convenience stores driven him nuts? Does the fragmentation of modern life lead to this?

While these questions occur to a reader, they don't press on him. Finally a reader doesn't care if Howie is mad or not, he's such wonderful, eccentric, unusual company, provides such a fresh new way of seeing and reflecting on the world.

Howie says of Boswell, Lecky and Gibbon, great footnote writers of the past. "They knew that the outer surface of truth is not smooth, welling and gathering from paragraph to shapely paragraph, but is encrusted with a rough protective bark of citations, quotation marks, italics, and foreign languages, a whole variorum crust of 'ibid.'s' and 'compare's and 'see's' that are the shield for the pure flow of argument as it lives for a moment in one mind." Howie gives the flow as it lives for a moment in his mind, ending with the exhilarating discovery that the shoelace-breaking problem has been tackled and perhaps solved by a Polish researcher, whose study he has found by chance.

And then abruptly the ride is over, the escalator has reached the mezzanine. Howie steps off, and the reader stands bereft, longing for more, looking back fondly "down the great silver glacier to the lobby."

Barbara Fisher Williamson, "Young Man Descending An Escalator," in Book World—The Washington Post, *November 13, 1988, p. 7.*

DAVID GATES

Here's the plot [of *The Mezzanine*]: Howie, a young businessman, buys shoelaces at a CVS store on his lunch hour. The subplots? He chats with a secretary, goes to the john and eats a cookie. And thinks about things: the squiggly mark you make after "and 00/100" when writing checks, the lines of dust that never quite disappear when you ply the broom and dustpan. We ask art to hold the mirror up to life: isn't this how most of our days really go?

And just because this is a first novel, don't think it's fraught with romantic anguish over the dreariness of dailiness. Howie once reflects that he's "not nearly the magnitude of man I had hoped I might be," but that's just another thought, like his thought about whether or not he should put his hand on the handrail that the man just finished polishing. Nor is this a tragicomedy of tedium like Samuel Beckett's *Molloy*. . . . When Baker is funny (as in the men's room episode), he's more like Bruce Jay Friedman. Most of *The Mezzanine*, though, simply pays open-eyed, open-ended attention to "the often undocumented daily texture of our lives." It never switches on the rhetoric to bathe details in fake luminosity; it peddles no unifying vision. Some readers may have a problem with that: art, they'll say, must do more. More than show us our lives afresh? Maybe in Baker's next book. But most writers never get *this* far.

David Gates, "A Plot That's Completely Out to Lunch," in Newsweek, *Vol. CXIII, No. 1, January 2, 1989, p. 61.*

DREW JEWETT

Near the end of *The Mezzanine,* a young man called Howie sits in a public plaza outside an office building during his lunch hour. He has been eating a chocolate-chip cookies and drinking from a carton of milk. He has also been reading a Penguin Classics edition of Marcus Aurelius's *Meditations,* thrilled by the sentence, "Manifestly, no condition of life could be so well suited for the practice of philosophy as this in which chance finds you today!" Rising to enter the building and ride the escalator to his job on the mezzanine level, he carefully places the empty milk carton and cookie bag on an overflowing trash container. "A bee rose up from a sun-filled paper cup," he observes, "off to make slum honey from some diet root beer it had found inside."

The escalator ride that awaits Howie is the central narrative event in *The Mezzanine,* a first novel by Nicholson Baker. . . . The ride will depend on batteries of flashbacks and footnotes, as Howie ruminates on such matters as the likelihood of two shoelaces breaking within a day of each other, the evolution of stapler design, the advantages of paper versus plastic drinking straws, and the possibility that the dying off of brain cells is not such a bad thing. This landslide of trivial obsessions serves as Howie's diet root beer—the basis for a slum philosophy adaptable to his condition of life. That the bee has better chances is beside the point—Baker is much more concerned and impressed with the diligence of Howie's quest.

How it sits with the reader is another question. Baker's ornate flashback structure withholds the catalytic tableau I've outlined above until the very end of the novel. The escalator ride and its footnoted onslaught of petty analyses begin on the first page, and we're as likely to find ourselves mired in minutiae as our diligent hero is. (pp. 5-6)

Granted, Howie's obsessions take on certain themes that support his quest for a practical philosophy. One is the notion of the individual among an ordered many: paper towels in lavatory dispensers, Pez tablets in their plastic elevators, cardboard cups stacked in vending machines, and escalator steps that emerge temporarily from an unbroken plane. He also flirts with symbols of binding and connection: knots, from shoelaces to those on shirt-laundry packages, are favored subjects of discussion. But even when Howie comes closest to self-awareness, sensing his own mediocrity as "the sort of person who stood in a subway car and thought about buttering toast," he plunges immediately into luxurious reflections on the variables of slicing raisin toast and the fastest methods of opening paper bags.

Baker's fluid, occasionally beautiful prose is well suited to the stylistic choices he has made. His rhythms are impeccable, and his graceful swells of exuberance have a surprisingly pleasant impact in the navel-gazing world he has defined. But *The Mezzanine's* lack of development casts a self-consciously literary pall over the whole endeavor; for all his trouble, Baker only shadows the achievements of his stylistic predecessors. . . . Baker's footnotes only extend his narrator's mania, ceaselessly returning to what has already been established. It's a useful trick for defining character, but it long overstays its welcome. A well-crafted bore is still a bore.

The sense that Baker isn't playing fair, that he's only showing off, sets in early in *The Mezzanine* and drags on till the subtle, false moment of hope Baker throws Howie on the final page. Just as Howie works on a mezzanine—not a whole story up, a place not even serviced by elevators—his quest for meaning is suspended between childhood fixations and real progress. But Howie at least gets to ride an escalator; we have to climb Baker's maddening hills of beans. (p. 6)

Drew Jewett, in a review of "The Mezzanine," in
VLS, *No. 71, January/February, 1989, pp. 5-6.*

ROBERT PLUNKET

I love novels with gimmicks. By that I mean novels that are told not through plain old narrative but rather through some enormously complicated technical stunt. The list of great ones is not long; *Tristram Shandy* comes to mind, and Nabokov's brilliant *Pale Fire,* a story told entirely in footnotes. I would even include Patrick Dennis's vastly underrated *Little Me.* Gimmick novels are often parodies, but this is not essential—just look at *Ulysses,* which I consider the ultimate gimmick novel.

The Mezzanine, a first novel by Nicholson Baker, a short story writer, is a definite contribution to this odd little genre: it has no story, no plot, no conflict. When somebody describes it to you it sounds stupid (which, by the way, is a characteristic of all good gimmick novels). Yet its 135 pages probably contain more insight into life as we live it than anything currently on the best-seller lists, with the possible exception of *The Frugal Gourmet Cooks American.* . . .

The Mezzanine is a very funny book about the human mind, in particular that part of the mind that processes the triviality of daily events that seem to have no importance but end up occupying so much of our existence. A few of the issues it deals with in depth (and I mean *depth;* he goes on for pages and pages, he even uses footnotes that go on for pages and pages). . . .

Gimmick novels are often narrated by an eccentric, and Howie certainly fills that bill. Though unremarkable on the surface—there is a girlfriend occasionally alluded to, plus an upper-middle-class set of parents—he leads such an intense inner life that he is compelled to make charts and equations concerning his thought processes. At one point he figures out what thoughts are childish thoughts and what are adult thoughts; at another he compiles a list of things he thinks about regularly and how many times a year he thinks about them. . . .

What makes Howie's ruminations so mesmerizing is the razor-sharp insight and droll humor with which Mr. Baker illuminates the unseen world. Take his description of the odd, tantalizing atmosphere of a discount drugstore, where they sell "important and secretive" products:

> Men and women eyed each other strangely here—unusual forces of attraction and furtiveness were at work. Things were for sale whose use demanded nudity and privacy. . . . You slip by a woman reading the fine print on a disposable vinegar douche kit. She feels you pass. *Frisson!*

Granted, you have to be in the right mood for this sort of thing (that's the reason they sell drinks at comedy clubs). And granted, *The Mezzanine* never transcends its gimmick to become more than a dazzling skit. But there is a first-rate comic mind at work here, so let's be thankful he's chosen to toil in the salt mines of fiction rather than making a fortune writing for David Letterman.

Robert Plunket, "Howie and the Human Mind," in
The New York Times Book Review, *February 5, 1989, p. 9.*

STEVEN MOORE

This wonderful novel [*The Mezzanine*] begins at the bottom of the escalator a young man rides to the mezzanine level where he works, and ends at the top of the escalator a minute or so later. His circumstances at the time of that ride—returning from lunch with a bag containing new shoelaces, carrying a Penguin paperback of Marcus Aurelius's *Meditations* . . .—provide the contents of the novel: what he had for lunch, why he needed new shoelaces, why he likes Penguin paperbacks, etc., all conveyed in reminiscences, digressions, footnotes (some as long as three pages), lists, and charts.

A mundane, even tedious subject for a novel? Not in this case, for Baker's delightful attempt to document "the often undocumented daily texture of our lives" also encompasses mini-histories of technical advances and human ingenuity in our time, from the workings of the escalator he rides to a celebration of perforation. At the end of a long footnote on "another fairly important development in the history of the straw," the narrator writes: "An unpretentious technical invention—the straw, the sugar packet, the pencil, the windshield wiper—has been ornamented by a mute folklore of behavioral inventions, unregistered, unpatented, adopted and fine-tuned without comment or thought." Giving voice to this mute folklore, the narrator—a Proust of the commonplace, a yuppie Tristram Shandy—links his own emotional history with recent technical advances by way of hundreds of analogies, metaphors, and fanciful comparisons that are so apt, so insightful, and often so amusing that I felt I was seeing the world I live in for the first time—as trite as that may sound. (pp. 249-50)

Steven Moore, in a review of "The Mezzanine," in
The Review of Contemporary Fiction, *Vol. IX, No. 2, Summer, 1989, pp. 249-50.*

BRAD LEITHAUSER

Although Nicholson Baker's *The Mezzanine* might reasonably be described as a novel about a man who purchases a pair of shoelaces, the book's likable narrator, whose name is Howie, would probably protest that his story is far more action-packed than that. In the penultimate chapter Howie reflects on the range of activities he has presented to the reader:

> Chance found me that day having worked for a living all morning, broken a shoelace, chatted with Tina, urinated successfully in a corporate setting, washed my face, eaten half a bag of popcorn, bought a new set of shoelaces, eaten a hot dog and a cookie with some milk.

Needless to say, this is not a novel taut with suspense. Nor does it provide—prospective readers should early be advised—much in the way of plot development, disclosure of character, or emotional interplay.

What the book is, triumphantly, is a celebration. As it follows Howie through his notably—even spectacularly—uneventful lunch hour, *The Mezzanine* sings praises to seemingly humdrum minutiae, with especially keen-eyed attention given to the mechanical marvels of modern life. Baker is capable of lavishing hundreds, even thousands of words on a paper towel dispenser, a stapler, the perforations on a reply coupon, ice cube trays, drinking straws, milk containers, vending machines, a urinal, or an escalator handrail. Nearly all these miniatures are dexterously and wittily delineated, and now and then, engineering a little miracle of blended exactitude and fancy, he manages to bring an everyday (and hence unnoticed) object into so pristine a focus that we see it as though for the first time. . . .

By electing to string the plot of this, his first novel, on something so tenuous as a shoelace—and a frayed shoelace at that—Baker boldly wagers everything on the proposition that his observational powers are in themselves sufficient to bind a novel securely. It's a sucker's bet—as Baker must have known. He has undertaken a job that is at once brutally taxing and easily dismissed; he is like the poet who commences a lengthy and elaborately formal piece of light verse, fully aware that if he once stumbles he will be spurned as clumsy and that even if he manages to pull off his feat, many will reject it as that contradiction in terms, a "mere tour de force."

Well, Baker does pull it off, and I know of no other first novel since Steven Millhauser's *Edwin Mullhouse* (1972) that offers so winning a mixture of charm, intelligence, and out-and-out weirdness. Millhauser's novel purported to be the biography of a great American writer who died at the age of eleven. It was at once a parody of academic hagiography, a mystery story, and a gruesome meditation on the parasitism of literary scholarship. What held it together—and what holds together *The Mezzanine*—was a core of jubilation. Ostensibly an elegy, *Edwin Mullhouse* was actually a eulogy for the vividly pigmented joys of an American childhood. When Millhauser approached the subject of crayons, or playgrounds, or television cartoons, his prose thumped with life.

The kinship between the two novels deepens once one perceives that Howie's office, for all its sophisticated, high-tech trappings, is a sort of kindergarten. Howie is not so much working as playing at working. In a book that relishes detail of every sort, his duties are never defined. Howie himself cannot quite believe that he and his fellow workers . . . have entered the corridors of the "Big Kids." And if the world of contemporary fiction is overpopulated, at the moment, by young men who cannot quite accept that they have crossed the threshold into adulthood and its grown-up responsibilities, few of them can boast Howie's salvational gift for wonder. His is a wide-eyed amazement that doesn't blink; he sees far more than the adults around him ever will.

The Mezzanine asks to be read slowly, in brief, intense interludes. I had the bad luck to begin it (and almost to abandon it) on a transatlantic flight, where its quirky finenesses were steadily eroded by the grinding of the jet engine; this book is many things, but it is not a page-turner. And even under the best reading conditions, it occasionally seems designed to illustrate how fine is the line that separates admiration from vexation. Baker works hard to slow the reader down. The book comes thickly footnoted, and there are times when the little trickling rivulet of its narrative feels damned by the boulder-sized masses of type lodged beneath it. Baker is demanding in his vocabulary as well. *The Mezzanine* abounds with words of a sort for which—even if they are recognized—one would probably hesitate to venture a pronunciation during, say, an academic dinner: microscopy, vibratiuncles, cotyledonary, bungee, remorid. . . .

All the more impressive, then, is Baker's control over what he does. His baroque vocabulary rings true. He is a precisionist. And he succeeds in bringing the twin strains of his novel—the slender narrative, the outsize footnotes—to diver-

gent but appropriate termini. His final footnote is an inspired collocation of improbabilities which concludes with a reference to an article in a technical journal (a *Polish* technical journal) concerning "abrasion resistance and knot slippage resistance of shoelaces." The narrative, by contrast, drifts off with a gentle, genial wave of the hand.

Having finessed his way through a remarkable debut, Nicholson Baker, who was born in 1957, ought to feel entitled to exult momentarily and not to fret overmuch about his next performance. His readers, however, will naturally speculate about what might follow so eccentric a première. Where will he go from here? . . .

The Mezzanine may well turn out to be the start for Baker of a splendidly unpeopled architecture. Or—perhaps more beguiling still—there's the possibility that in time he will manage to introduce into his microscopically tactile environment various forces that are not isolable under any magnifying lens—fears, confusions, allegiances, carnal desires, spiritual misgivings.

In an exuberant, extended footnote that serves as tribute to Frederick Mennen, the inventor of Jiffy Pop popcorn, Howie speaks of a newly exploded kernel as "potentiated cellulose." One is left to wonder what lively, outflung shapes Nicholson Baker will take as he potentiates.

Brad Leithauser, "Microscopy," in The New York Review of Books, *Vol. XXXVI, No. 13, August 17, 1989, p. 15.*

WALTER NASH

Nicholson Baker's *The Mezzanine* is a book about the mind electrically at odds with vacancy and repose; about the astonishing turbulence in the little grey cells of little grey people like you, and me, and Howie, who at lunchtime quits his office on the mezzanine floor and goes down the escalator to the street, to buy milk and cookies and a new pair of shoelaces. On the way we follow the movement of his mind through a conveyor-belt meditation, rigorous as a Zen discipline, zany as a Disneyland dance, on the everyday mechanics of things contemplated most minutely in particular. What things? Oh, just ordinary things, you know, things counter, original, spare, strange, spring-loaded, gear-driven, fully automated and packaged for your all-American convenience, that sort of thing. Howie's central preoccupation is with the working life of shoelaces and the rival hypotheses (there are two contenders) which may be adduced to explain not only how they come to break but also how one shoelace will snap within days of the other.

This is the argumentative mainstream, into which, however, flow frequent tributaries in the form of disquisitions on earplugs, date-stampers, staplers, shirt packagings, milk cartons, and men's rooms where you suffer the exquisite ignominy of keeping your water while all around you (especially the senior executives) are bountifully losing theirs. I should intone here a manifold and multi-conglomerate 'et cetera', because the foregoing list hardly begins to mention the things upon which the solitary Howie thinks, opines, and ungainsayably ratiocinates. He is falling-down-drunk with data, like a PhD student, and elaborates his observations with maniac footnotes which grow longer and longer, until they begin to outbalance the main text. . . .

Well, but the point? A point not to be overlooked is that one of the objects Howie carries with him on his lunchtime excursion is a copy of the *Meditations* of Marcus Aurelius, in which he reads that mortal life is 'transient and trivial . . . yesterday a drop of semen, tomorrow a handful of spice and ashes'. Howie denies this with an emotional intensity not apparent elsewhere in the book: 'Wrong, wrong, wrong! I thought. Destructive and misguided and completely untrue!' Wrong, wrong, wrong, we may assume, because for Howie everything in mortal life—shoelaces, shopping bags, escalators, et cetera, everything palpable and divinely unabstract—is of such peculiar and complicated interest that nothing can be trivial. Life is too full to be fobbed off with abstractions and aphorisms. Had Howie been a Romantic poet, he might have hymned the particular significance of daisies and lesser celandines: being a modern metropolitan man, he wanders lonely as a cloud, musing on vending machines and paper-towel dispensers. These blessed forms locate the mind's unending, self-delighting play. This is worth thinking about, though whether it adds up to a novel I do not know. I found myself repeating Dogberry's phrase, 'most tolerable and not to be endured': meaning, I suppose, that I congratulate Mr Baker on a brilliant performance and hope he will not want to repeat it.

Howie is an oddly elusive creation; his mind is recorded in every tremor of its movement, and yet—perhaps because his relationships with others are barely adumbrated—we miss a personality, and are thus obliged to forgo one of the pleasures of novel reading, the extension of one's acquaintance through interesting situations, the amusing discovery of a how-d'ye-do as we come to know Him and Her.

Walter Nash, "Turbulence," in London Review of Books, *Vol. 11, No. 21, November 9, 1989, pp. 22-3.*

JULIAN LOOSE

Like his earlier *The Mezzanine,* Baker's ostensible narrative [in *Room Temperature*], Mike feeding his baby, is spectacularly uneventful. A part-time technical writer and reviewer of TV commercials, Mike's one act of "abject, charmless, filthy stealth" is nose-picking in the nuptial bed. When he confesses this habit to his wife the thrilling intimacy of the moment—like his wife's revelation that she searches for reading material ("often a specialized work of reference") to take to the bathroom—is cherished as "one of those powerful, marriage-reinforcing confidences".

Mike's talent is for quirky analogies which display his outsize vocabulary. As the baby sucks at her bottle he rhapsodises on such matters as an air-pump filling a car tyre, Robert Boyle's *General History of the Air,* the "uvularly hoisted" voice of Pee Wee Herman, the vacuum in an unopened jar of peanut butter, childhood breath-holding contests, playing the French horn, and the "addictively sickening" taste of a sucked Bic pen. Mike has a theory that twenty minutes of anyone's mental ruminations contain enough proliferating connections to cover "every pet theory, minor observation, significant moment of shame or happiness", and somehow these fascinating reveries on material objects do add up to an entrancing evocation of a common man's uncommon inner life.

The novel makes such a playful virtue of its slightness that it is easy to overlook Baker's large-scale ambition: to take the "stiff-jointed prose" that we have inherited from the 17th century and revitalise it with the "genetic fund of replenishing counterexample and idiosyncratic usage" of an earlier, Jacobean digressiveness of style. We are so entertained by his capacious sentences, which accommodate everything from aircraft design to Stravinsky, that we are entirely persuaded that Baker has succeeded. We only resent the economy of his means, and wish that Mike could continue to direct his speculations "frictionlessly in any direction".

Julian Loose, "Dream-Time in America," in New Statesman & Society, *Vol. 3, No. 95, April 6, 1990, p. 38.*

WENDY LESSER

Everyone who read Nicholson Baker's marvelous first novel, *The Mezzanine,* wondered what he could possibly do for an encore. Packed with fascinatingly digressive footnotes on everything from the shape of staplers to the buoyancy of straws, *The Mezzanine* was a brief, Swiftian, Proustian tale about a seemingly unremarkable lunch hour in the life of a big-city office worker, as well as an impressively precise commentary on the nature of memory, the esthetics of industrial design, the boredom of white-collar work and the sources of life's small, sustaining pleasures. It was a whole book seemingly made up of the best parts of Updike, those moments of acutely described visceral perception that remind us what it's like to live in late-20th-century America.

The good news is that *Room Temperature* is written in approximately the same style as *The Mezzanine* (minus, alas, the footnotes). But perhaps that's really the bad news. For, as Mr. Baker points out near the beginning of this new novel, too much similarity between dissimilar objects invites "a tricky lateral sort of comparison, in which the two terms threaten to be insufficiently disparate in some respects for the connection to work properly, as if you said that the sun was in some way or other like the moon." Where *The Mezzanine* was filled with breathtaking similes, this book (as the above example suggests) tends more toward the labored discussion of similes. Many of the endearing virtues of Mr. Baker's earlier narrator—his intense inward focus, his philosophical dilettantism, his willingness to expose himself to our ridicule, his physical awkwardness—have here become irritating characteristics.

Part of the problem is what, in a more standard novel, might be called the plot. *Room Temperature* focuses on an afternoon in the life of a young Boston-area father, who sits at home giving a bottle to his baby daughter and allows numerous incidents from his past and present to crowd through his head. But parenthood is, novelistically speaking, a poor choice of occupation for Mr. Baker's idiosyncratic Everyman. It is at once more universal and less representative than office work: we all meander mentally when in the fugue state of baby-feeding, but the timeless love people feel in response to their infants tells us very little about our particular moment in history. . . .

The novel's many oblique comments on its narrative technique suggest that Nicholson Baker is probably his own best critic. Consider, for example, the following passage, in which the narrator is talking about a photo he once saw of a pair of frogs, one cloned from the other. Both frogs were complete, but the "artifical" sibling had "a disturbing and somehow gastrointestinal pallor. . . . The artificial frog permanently influenced my theory of knowledge: I certainly believed . . . one's whole life could be reconstructed from any single twenty-minute period . . . but you had to expect that a version of your past arrived at in this way would exhibit, like the unhealthy pale frog, certain telltale differences of emphasis. . . . The particular cell you started from colored your entire re-creation." Perhaps, with *Room Temperature,* Mr. Baker just picked the wrong cell. Or maybe the conditions in the petri dish (recent *succès d'estime,* pressure to produce again quickly) were not conducive to healthy growth. Whatever. Next time out, I hope, Nicholson Baker will begin with a whole new animal.

> *Wendy Lesser, "Peter Lorre Does a Handstand," in* The New York Times Book Review, *April 15, 1990, p. 17.*

Thomas Bernhard

1931-1989

Dutch-born Austrian novelist, dramatist, autobiographer, short story writer, poet, critic, and scriptwriter.

Considered one of the most original German-language prose stylists to emerge after World War II, Bernhard earned a reputation as an intellectual *enfant terrible* for his emphasis on philosophical pessimism and his vituperative attacks upon values, institutions, and cultural and political figures of modern Austria. Writing in a musical yet tumultuous style in which atonality and dissonance serve to reflect the emotional states of his characters, Bernhard often focuses on withdrawn, compulsive men obsessed with utopian ideals of artistic perfection who are offered no hope of religious, aesthetic, or political transcendence. Compared to Franz Kafka, Peter Handke, and Samuel Beckett for his vision of isolation and despair, Bernhard often dwells on such subjects as physical and mental illness, death, cruelty, and decay. While his works often comment upon what he termed his "love-hate" attitude toward Austria, he chose to reside in that country throughout his life, and many critics have noted a contradiction between his preoccupation with hopelessness and failure and his prodigious literary output. Although notorious for the contempt he visited upon those who offered him literary prizes, Bernhard received many major awards, including the Bremen Prize, the Georg Büchner Prize, and the Austrian Prize for Literature.

Raised in Austria and southeastern Bavaria during the Depression, Bernhard witnessed both the rise of Nazism and the aftereffects of World War II. Born to the unmarried daughter of a liberal couple who were also unmarried, he inherited his mother's surname as she had that of her own mother. Bernhard was largely cared for by his maternal grandparents, especially his grandfather, Johannes Freumbichler, a respected but impoverished novelist who introduced him to a pessimistic view of existence influenced by his reading of such authors as Michel Montaigne, Arthur Schopenhauer, Blaise Pascal, and Friedrich Nietzsche. A chronic bedwetter, Bernhard was publicly humiliated by his mother during his childhood and was eventually sent to a boarding school for disturbed youths in Salzburg, where he was able to discern no difference between the school's Nazi supervision and the Catholic administration which replaced it following World War II. At eighteen years of age, Bernhard developed a form of lung disease that was considered terminal, and in 1949 came close to death. Bernhard also contracted tuberculosis while recovering in a sanatorium, an experience that resulted in a permanent hatred and distrust of the medical establishment.

In 1951, Bernhard determined to study music and acting in Vienna. He attended the Mozarteum in Salzburg a year later and in 1956 graduated with his thesis on Antonin Artaud and Bertolt Brecht. His initial writings, including several short narratives as well as three volumes of melancholy poetry, *Auf der Erde und in der Hölle, In hora mortis,* and *Unter dem Eisen des Mondes,* drew scant critical attention. During the 1970s, Bernhard published several volumes of memoirs esteemed for their insights into his life and works; these books include *Die Ursache: eine Andeutung,* a bitter account of his

experiences in boarding school; *Der Keller: eine Entziehung,* about his subsequent employment as a grocer's apprentice in a postwar housing development for the poor and outcast in Salzberg; *Der Atem: eine Entscheidung* and *Die Kälte: eine Isolation,* in which he recounts his struggle against lung disease and the Austrian public health system; *Ein Kind,* about his childhood experiences with poverty and overcrowding; and *In der Höhe: Rettungsversuch, Unsinn,* a report on his young adult life. The first five of these volumes were translated into English and published in 1985 as *Gathering Evidence: A Memoir.*

Bernhard attained literary prominence with his first major work of fiction, *Frost.* Written in epistolary form, this novel is related through the journals of a young doctor who travels to a remote rural region of contemporary Austria. There he is overcome by nihilistic views of an aging and cynical artist who possesses an acute awareness of the slow and absolute approach of death. In Bernhard's next novel, *Amras,* two brothers who accidentally survived a suicide pact they had formed with their parents retreat to an isolated tower, one of many buildings in Bernhard's fiction suggestive of the lost grandeur and incipient decay of modern Austria. This work, which introduces the intellectual characters typical of Bernhard's ensuing fiction, focuses on events leading up to the suicide of the younger brother, a musically-gifted epileptic, and the mental collapse of the elder brother. Using disease and mental illness as metaphors for the inherited distress of the past, Bernhard comments upon the frailty of art and intellect in modern Austria.

In Bernhard's next major novel, *Verstörung* (*Gargoyles*), the son of a physician accompanies his father on his daily rounds, where he is confronted with human misery in the form of neglect, insanity, deformity, and disease. The book's culminating section, generally regarded as a *tour de force* of contemporary fiction, consists of a monologue spoken by the doctor's final patient, the misanthrope Prince Saurau, who figuratively destroys the world through his solipsistic outpouring of rage and disgust at decayed human values. Although some critics faulted Bernhard's angry, rhythmic prose style, *Gargoyles* was highly popular in Europe. Bernhard's next novel, *Das Kalkwerk* (*The Lime Works*), focuses on Konrad, a middle-aged eccentric who becomes obsessed with writing a nonfiction book on the subject of hearing. Long after Konrad moves to an isolated lime works to complete his study, the book remains unwritten, and he inexplicably kills his invalid wife. Many critics commended the temperate tone of *The Lime Works,* which Bernhard achieved through the use of an impartial narrator who constructs the story from gossip, hearsay, and supposition. D. A. Craig commented: "*Das Kalwerk* must rank as one of the finest and most worthwhile German novels of today through its single-mindedness, its most individual style, and, in places, its crazy humour."

The protagonist of Bernhard's next novel, *Korrektur* (*Correction*), is modelled on philosopher Ludwig Wittgenstein. Roithamer, who is consumed with a passion for impeccable architecture, conceives of the perfect house for his beloved sister. However, she dies following the building's completion and, able to see only the flaws in his work, the artist commits suicide. George Steiner called the novel "one of the towering achievements of postwar literature," and Richard Gilman observed: "*Correction* is something exceedingly rare among novels of recent years: a paradigm of consciousness and not simply a product. That it's a consciousness of despair and hopelessness doesn't mean the book induces them in us. Bernhard has said that 'the art we need is the art of bearing the unbearable,' and his novel joins that small group of literary works which nobly help us to do that." In *Beton* (*Concrete*), Bernhard centers on a self-obsessed musicologist who hopes to begin a work of scholarship on composer Mendelssohn. While vacationing in Spain, the protagonist encounters a Bavarian woman whose husband has committed suicide due to financial difficulties. Although he overcomes his personal failures through contact with her misery, the protagonist feels guilty about his inability to help her. Visiting the man's grave two years later, the musicologist discovers the widow's name next to her husband's, along with the word "suicide." In *Der Untergeher,* the death of Glenn Gould, a successful concert pianist, prompts his colleagues—a pair of failed pianists—to confront their limitations. When one commits suicide, the narrator, who has given up music to become a writer, notes the fulfillment of Gould's prophecy that the man was an "Untergeher," or one destined for decline.

Bernhard's next novel, *Holzfällen: eine Erregung* (*Woodcutters;* published in Great Britain as *Cutting Timber*), is set at a dinner party attended by leading Austrian cultural figures. The narrator, a successful writer, contemplates his own life and limitations as well as those of the guests, his former

friends. Like the child Hedvig, who kills herself for the sins of her parents in Henrik Ibsen's play *The Wild Duck,* the protagonist of this work sacrifices himself for society. Many readers identified autobiographical elements and similarities between characters and actual contemporary artists; for example, composer Gerhard Lampersberg, for whom Bernhard had written a libretto in the late 1950s, accused the author of slander, provoking a scandal in the German and Austrian press that led authorities to temporarily halt the book's sale in both countries. In his next novel, *Alte Meister* (*Old Masters*), Bernhard addresses his perennial theme of the artist's quest for flawlessness. This work focuses on an eighty-two-year old Austrian music critic who has visited Vienna's Museum of Art History every other day for thirty-two years in hopes of discovering latent defects in the works of the great masters that would enable him to renounce his pursuit of artistic perfection. *Auslöschung: ein Zerfall,* Bernhard's last major work of fiction, centers on an Austrian intellectual living in self-imposed exile in Rome who attempts to reject his family's heritage of collusion with the Nazi past by turning over his inherited family estate to the Jewish community of Vienna.

Beginning in the late 1950s, Bernhard developed a reputation as an avant-garde dramatist. His many successful plays are influenced in part by the German Expressionist theater of Frank Wedekind and August Strindberg. Written in unrhymed free verse, these works are usually surreal in atmosphere and eschew plot development and characterization in favor of compelling icons and situations that become gradually intensified and elaborated. Bernhard's first drama, *Ein Fest für Boris,* reflects the influence of absurdism and the Theater of Cruelty in its blackly humorous story of a birthday party attended by a group of legless characters in wheelchairs. After presenting the hostess's husband, Boris, with long underwear and boots, the guests discuss their various maladies as Boris pounds a drum. No one notices that he has died until the drama's end. *Die Jagdgesellschaft,* a parody of Anton Chekov's drama, *The Cherry Orchard,* concerns a playwright who informs a general wounded in combat that he has lost any possibility of holding political office, that his wife is an adulteress, and that he is dying of an incurable illness.

In *Die Macht der Gewohnheit* (*The Force of Habit*), one of Bernhard's few full-length dramas to be translated into English, an elderly ringmaster with a wooden leg commands a caravan of musically-illiterate circus performers to rehearse Schubert's *Trout Quintet.* At the play's conclusion, he listens jealously to a perfect rendition of the piece on the radio. *Heldenplatz,* one of Bernhard's last plays, prompted heated controversy by claiming many contemporary Austrians harbor anti-Semitic sentiments. This work focuses on a Jewish professor who leaves Germany in 1938 after the rise of Nazism and commits suicide upon his return to the country in the present day. Although some critics have faulted Bernhard's plots and characterizations as two-dimensional or undeveloped, Martin Esslin commented: "Bernhard's theatre is essentially a *mannerist* theatre. If his characters are puppets, all the greater the skill with which they perform their intricate dance; if his subject-matter is venom and derision, all the more admirable the perfection of the language in which the venom is spat out, the intricacy of the patterns it creates."

(See also *CLC,* Vols. 3, 32; *Contemporary Authors,* Vol. 85-88, Vol. 127 [obituary]; and *Dictionary of Literary Biography,* Vol. 85.)

PRINCIPAL WORKS

POETRY

Auf der Erde und in der Hölle   1957
In hora mortis   1958
Unter dem Eisen des Mondes   1958
Ave Virgil   1981

NOVELS

Frost   1963
Amras   1964
Verstörung   1969
   [*Gargoyles,*   1970]
Das Kalkwerk   1970
   [*The Lime Works,*   1973]
Korrektur   1975
   [*Correction,*   1979]
Beton   1982
   [*Concrete,*   1984]
Der Untergeher   1983
Holzfällen: eine Erregung   1984
   [*Woodcutters,*   1987; published in Great Britain as *Cutting Timber,*   1988]
Alte Meister   1985
   [*Old Masters,*   1989]
Auslöschung: Ein Zerfall   1986

PLAYS

Ein Fest für Boris   1968
Der Ignorant und der Wahnsinnige   1972
Die Jagdgesellschaft   1974
Die Macht der Gewohnheit   1974
   [*The Force of Habit,*   1976]
*Der Präsident   1975
Die Berühmten   1976
Minetti: ein Portrait des Künstlers als alter Mann   1977
Immanuel Kant   1978
*Vor dem Ruhestand   1979
Der Weltverbesserer   1979
Am Ziel   1981
Über allen Gipfeln ist Ruh: ein deutscher Dichtertag um 1980   1981
Der Schein trügt   1983
Heldenplatz   1988

**MEMOIRS

Die Ursache: eine Andeutung   1975
Der Keller: eine Entziehung   1976
Der Atem: eine Entscheidung   1978
Die Kälte: eine Isolation   1981
Ein Kind   1982
Wittgensteins Neffe: eine Freundschaft   1982
   [*Wittgenstein's Nephew: A Friendship,*   1986]
In der Höhe: Rettungsversuch, Unsinn   1989

SHORT FICTION

An der Baumgrenze   1969
Midland in Stilfs   1971
Der Wetterfleck   1976
Der Stimmenimitator   1978

OTHER

Die Rosen der Einöde   (ballet sketch)   1959

Prosa   (prose)   1967
Ungenach   (prose)   1968
Ereignisse   (prose)   1969
Watten: Ein Nachlass   (prose)   1969
Der Italiener   (screenplay)   1971
Der Kulterer   (screenplay)   1974
Die Stücke: 1969-1981   (omnibus of plays)   1983

*These plays were translated and published in 1982 by Performing Arts Journal Publications as *The President & Eve of Retirement.*

**The first five of these works were translated and republished in 1985 as *Gathering Evidence: A Memoir.*

GITTA HONEGGER

Following the long-winded sentence structures of Bernhard's earlier stories and novels (*Frost, Amras, Verstoerung* [*Gargoyles*], *Das Kalkwerk* [*The Lime Works*], *Midland in Stilfs, Ungenach, Watten, Gehen* and more) becomes an archeological dig in a horrifying landscape of decay and death for fragmented traces of the human mind, minds literally broken, captured at their breaking point in states of extreme tension, when the names of people, objects, landscapes become physically threatening, contagious, where the sign has more power than the signified and there is no more dividing line between outer and inner realities. The writing itself is located in what Foucault calls the "frontier situation" shared by the madman and the poet, the one "alienated in analogy," the other searching beneath the named differences for the language of resemblance, "where their words unceasingly renew the power of their strangeness and the strength of their contestation."

It is dangerous territory, to be sure, and Bernhard is constantly testing, challenging its most extreme consequences, fully if defiantly aware that they may finally catch up with him, the writer/poet as well. Most of his prose pieces introduce two or more "languages" through an elaborate system of quoting. There is the author quoting a narrator as he quotes the actual central figure, usually a dead person, driven to death by an overriding obsession (illness in this context is an obsession too) which led to madness and frequently suicide. The thought process culminating in total collapse is revealed in letters, journals, notes and personal conversations until the narrator's voice merges with the quoted voice to the point where he becomes the impersonator of a dead man's mind. The process in these novels and stories is profoundly theatrical: the narrator, by elaborately quoting another, no longer functions as the conventional story teller, but rather as performer, "impersonator." Appropriately enough, one collection of Bernhard's short satirical tales is entitled *Der Stimmenimitator* (literally: "The Imitator of Voices," whose English equivalent is an impersonator. Incidentally, the *Stimmenimitator* of one of the stories can imitate many different voices, but not his own). The author himself is, of course, the supreme performer—of all the voices introduced by him, which is to say, ultimately, of himself. Only by an extreme act of artistic consciousness—the consciousness of the performer who is able to distance himself from what he impersonates, most importantly from himself—can he save himself from succumbing to the madness of his voices.

All of Bernhard's writing takes the form of monomaniacal soliloquies, bravura performances of the mind which is both tragic hero and sole spectator in this drama of life that is a tragedy for the subject, and becomes a grotesque comedy for his "other," who is watching himself perform the futile struggle against his limitations, his better knowledge. *Is it a Tragedy? Is it a Comedy?* is the title of one of Bernhard's stories. It is the key to his philosophy and aesthetics. If the question sounds banal, Bernhard would be the last one to deny it. On the contrary, its banality is quite to the point in his vision (and personal experience) of life, where the tragic hero becomes a clown (as such as much a cliché as any other theatrical convention), when observed in action, in performance.

The place of action is always Austria. More specifically, it is the landscape between Salzburg, where Bernhard grew up and Gmunden, where he has been living for the past twenty years. Overshadowed by looming mountains, darkened by damp forests, peopled by stuporous, brutal peasants and pompous, equally stupid representatives of the educated, so-called "civilized" classes (notably doctors, his favorite targets), Bernhard's Austria is invariably outlined in clusters of outraged superlatives racing each other from deepest despair to the heights of deadly derision, from biblical to satirical wrath. In his theater of the mind, it is not a naturalistic landscape, but a set, a "foreign body," its persistent exaggerations linked to the other world like malignant tumors from a virus which has infiltrated the brain from outside.

No one, least of all the writer himself, is safe from contagion. We are all part of the disease, be it specifically cultural or basically human, a tragic predicament, no doubt, but ultimately a comic spectacle as our efforts to protect ourselves from it are the surest symptoms of our contamination. There is no way out. Teutonic predilection for *Weltschmerz,* pathos and the commonplace? Yes, of course, except that in Bernhard's world these aspects are already part of a performance and, in the process, subject to exaggeration which invariably leads to ridicule. Moreover, with his characteristic obsessive insistency Bernhard in his most recent work does not shy away from the ultimate consequence: self-parody. For Bernhard, the writer who has won the most prestigious literary awards as the twentieth century visionary of doom, successor to Kafka in the pantheon of Middle-European literary geniuses and subject of an ever increasing body of secondary literature, this may seem an outrageous act of self-destruction. But it is totally consistent with his radical theatrical philosophy, a particularly Austrian sensibility which links him to such desperately funny satirists as Johann Nestroy and Karl Kraus and the self-deflating, deadly serious irony of Ludwig Wittgenstein, who begins his *Tractatus logico-philosophicus* with a quote from Nestroy and ends it with the complete negation of everything he said before.

> "The question is not 'How do I write about Wittgenstein?' but rather: "Is it possible for me to be Wittgenstein for just *one* moment without destroying either him (W) or me (B)?"
> (Thomas Bernhard [in a letter to Austrian writer Hilde Spiel])

Ludwig Wittgenstein has haunted the imagination and challenged the craft of Austria's post-war generation of writers from Ingeborg Bachmann to Peter Handke. But while Handke attempted to apply Wittgenstein's logical positivism directly to his writing, Bachmann and Bernhard share a much deeper affinity to the source of Wittgenstein's philosophy, to

Wittgenstein as "metaphysical subject" who cannot be described because he is situated at the frontier between the speakable and the unspeakable. It is Wittgenstein, the mystic, as Bachmann pointed out, who truly opened up new, dangerous territory, precisely that vast field of silence, closed to the philosopher's discourse, which the poet must dare to transgress. It is here that Bernhard must meet Wittgenstein in full knowledge of the philosopher's rigorous critique of language and its possible consequence for the writer, namely self-annihilation. Wittgenstein's genius, his full impact on our century, as Bernhard (and Bachmann before him) understands so well, lies in the consciously sustained dialectic of his failure: if the positivist thinker failed the mystic, it is the latter's unthinkable silence that finally eclipses the philosopher's most brilliant achievement.

Approaching Wittgenstein ("Is it possible for me to be Wittgenstein. . . . ?") in Bernhard's dramaturgy of the mind is a performance act: he must enter a particular state of mind (the stage) and look into the mechanism of its thought processes (the rhythmical foundation of theater: music/text) with its built-in self-destructive power which may not spare the intruder (performer: the red shoes dancing their dancer to death): he may be exposed as a phony (impersonator/impostor) or completely lose all sense of personal self in his attempted identification with another—Wittgenstein as "metaphysical subject" (the "soul" of the stage character behind a "voice") which at best is never more concrete than the "focal vanishing point behind the mirror of his language".

Bernhard's novel *Correction*—generally acknowledged as a seminal masterpiece of twentieth century literature—is a triumph totally in tune with the legacy of Wittgenstein's spirit, precisely because it is *not* about Wittgenstein, although it is quite possibly the most accurate approximation of the philosopher's uncompromising temperament and intellectual/spiritual integrity. Bernhard's language originates in the same cultural/geographical space as Wittgenstein's. But in response to that space, which is to say, in response to itself, it transforms all regional, biographical and temperamental similarities between Wittgenstein, Roithamer, the book's central figure and Bernhard himself. They become correspondences which designate the cultural as mental space which contains both the origin and destruction of thought in its struggle to achieve perfection and verification through matter. The house in the shape of a perfect cone that Roithamer, the Austrian born Cambridge scientist, builds for his beloved sister in the middle of the forest which is their native landscape, is to be the perfect expression of his sister's nature, that is, of his, Roithamer's complete understanding of his sister, hence the perfect expression of both himself and his sister. It is the mystic's age-old attempt to reconcile all differences: between spirit/matter, inside/outside: the cone as shelter and monument, male/female: as a sign of total penetration (perfect understanding) as well as enclosure (home/womb) incestuous/self-love, self/other, through the triumph of the spirit that has completely penetrated the other and given birth to itself in a perfect expression of their joint nature. This is impossible since all matter (including man's biological self) is part of nature, hence subject to decay and death. Perfection in accordance with nature can therefore only be achieved through illness (both physical and mental, since the mind is part of nature as well) in death. All that is left in the end is the empty space: "The end is not process. Clearing." The clearing is the site both of the cone (in the forest) and its origin and destruction (in the mind). Only that space is left intact. It marks the survival of Bernhard, the writer/poet as author of this particular book. But the victory is only temporary, as Bernhard would be quick to point out not with self-pity, but with that profound sense of irony which so often is mistaken for nihilistic black humor. It is the awareness that death is only deferred through the act of writing in the space which also contains his (B's) destruction.

> Am I right in saying
> that what you write
> has to do with philosophy
> even though you call it comedy
> Or am I right in saying
> that what you write is comedy
> while you insist
> that it is philosophy

"*Ist ja alles ein Theater*" is a popular Austrian expression which implies much more than its English translation: "Everything's just theater." It stands for an entire *Lebenseinstellung,* an attitude toward life, which accepts the fun and futility, the illusion as well as the vanity and perversity of all our efforts in view of the fact that the final curtain will come down for good. The traditional Austrian *gestus* accompanying this statement is a shrug which takes the edge off any pathos that might arise from all too reverential associations with Shakespeare's famous "*All the world's a stage . . . *"

In this spirit the theater has provided Bernhard with a theoretical basis for his philosophy and aesthetics and with a perspective on himself as writer, survivor, clown: tireless performer and spectator of himself. Therefore it should come as no surprise that besides a substantial body of prose literature, Bernhard has also written about 15 plays. What might be more surprising is his repeatedly expressed disgust with theater, which goes beyond his more obvious attacks on the present state of the theater and is frequently aimed at himself. But such an attitude is also totally consistent with his unrelenting self-investigation in the context of his philosophy. Theater as an idea, as a philosophical challenge, is quite different from theater as a practiced artform or, as he calls it, an "entertainment mechanism." A theatrical performance, in its original attraction, must hold the same promise for Bernhard as the cone did for Roithamer: Thought turned into matter, the temptation of the perfect expression (embodiment) of self in another. Only that theater, by its very nature, quickly exposes the illusory nature of all such attempts and in its temporality makes a mockery of all claims to permanence. If thought seeks its expression in a medium that already renders reality as an illusion, it is one step further removed from its aim and doomed to failure from the start. In this sense theater becomes the perfect sign for failure. No wonder Bernhard jumps on it with masochistic self-disgust (and joy) as the most useful (and delightful and despicable) model for his philosophy, which, performed on stage, must naturally imply the mockery of itself. (pp. 58-60)

The most equivocal, deceitful aspect of theatrical convention is language: an actor who pretends to be another speaking spontaneously, actually quotes a text that pretends to quote that most elusive original, called "character." Bernhard's theatrical language never attempts to create the illusion of spontaneity. On the contrary, a language based on quotes is his most essential means of characterization which points to the deadly traps of culture and tradition. His characters are always quoting, whether they speak a literary, "theatrical" language, or express themselves in commonplaces, phrases

and slogans, all of which are part of their cultural history. Moreover, the language they are locked into also carries the traditional mode of delivery so that very often it is the language which incites the emotion rather than the other way around, as is common in naturalistic, "psychological" drama. His built-in critique of the use of language makes its most effective, chilling point in the play *Eve of Retirement,* which shows how fascist rhetoric has succeeded in perverting so-called "traditional values" passed on through generations in popular idioms and sayings and stubbornly persists today in the most "innocent" use of language. Bernhard's theater demonstrates the process of mortification of a society which is solely animated and eventually destroyed by a historical mechanism which has long been cut off from its source and is kept in motion on the strings of language which activate their desperate speakers like pitiful marionettes.

Bernhard doesn't exclude himself from the process. While in his earlier plays the prevailing mood is an ominous, if often grotesque sense of tragic despair over this human predicament, his later plays reveal more and more how the fatal mechanism eventually takes hold of the writer himself. He is locked into it by his own language, trapped as it were, in his own texts. Several of his recent plays contain ironic reflections of the legend he himself has become. But self-parody, self-quotes are more than in-jokes or symptoms of a writer who has run dry or simply exploits his proven technique. Even if they are that too, they are necessarily part of a writer who is honest enough (or shameless enough as he may put it) not to claim that he can place himself outside his culture. . . .

[*Appearances Are Deceiving*] shows how the mechanism of language, like the lives of its speakers, is slowly coming to a halt, burning itself out "like cigarettes left burning in an ashtray" as Bernhard himself described it recently. It is much quieter, gentler, more openly compassionate and vulnerable than anything he had written before. For the first time the ironies are touching rather than cruel as they point to the writer who is playing out the familiar strategies of his own language (his life) until there is, like for Beckett's R [the reader in *Ohio Impromptu*] "nothing left to tell."

> If I hadn't actually lived through everything that
> led up to my present existence, I would have proba-
> bly invented it and come up with the same results.

In the second part of *Don Quixote,* notes Michel Foucault [in *The Order of Things*], Cervantes' text turns back upon itself and becomes the object of its own narrative. Don Quixote meets people who have read the first part and recognize him. He has become the book and what he is (represents) must correspond with the way he is read. Don Quixote's truth, according to Foucault, is not in the relation of the words to the world, but in the complex relationship of verbal signs between themselves. The "disappointed" fiction (*la fiction déçue*) of the great epic romances has brought out the representative power of language.

Similarly, Bernhard's earlier work keeps reappearing in his later work. As much as he himself has become text through his earlier books, he makes himself the object of his later work which, aside from five autobiographical books about his youth [*Die Ursache, Der Keller, Der Atem, Die Kälte, Ein Kind*], contains more and more of what we can now recognize as "biographical" elements. But those, too, have emerged exclusively from his earlier texts. It seems relatively easy to track him down through his many repetitions, thematic obsessions, stylistic patterns and essentially the same mind driving itself again and again into the same excruciating tension. But with his reclusive life-style and personality which covers itself in his rare public appearances through skillful "autoperformances" (clownish exaggerations of his "literary" image, layered masks of impenetrability), he makes sure that his biography is never anything but *fiction déçue*, text interacting with text from which he, Bernhard, like Don Quixote, emerges as yet another—still the same—book. (p. 61)

Gitta Honegger, "Wittgenstein's Children: The Writings of Thomas Bernhard," in Theater, *Vol. XV, No. 1, Winter, 1983, pp. 58-62.*

DENIS CALANDRA

The nearest one could come to categorizing Bernhard would be as a bitter and austere writer within the tradition of the absurd. His vision is solitary and uncomfortable; his relative success with theatre audiences in Germany may attest both to the middle class German's penchant for self-criticism to the point of self-hatred, as Thomas Mann once put it, and perhaps, as Handke quipped in the late sixties, to the latent masochism of the theatre-going public. The images in the social mirror Bernhard offers his public are among the most severe to be found on today's German language stage.

Thomas Bernhard, two years younger than Heiner Müller, had his early schooling during the Nazi years in a Catholic seminary (he has said he hardly noticed the difference when the Nazis left) and drew from his experience of the war era his general conclusions about the capacity for society, and mankind, to destroy itself. There is no equivalent in Bernhard's thinking to Müller's faith in the force of revolutionary change, or any other kind of progress. Bernhard relentlessly meditates on intellectual torpor, physical deterioration and death; his vision is sharply misanthropic. He has written 'In the dark everything becomes clear', and it is into that dark side of his own mind that he invites readers and audiences.

He has expressed admiration for the sheer hopeless idealism of his communist uncle and socialist grandfather, but the object of their utopian longings left no strong imprint on him. (Salary, and not ideology, is apparently what led him to work briefly as a reporter for a socialist newspaper.) Liberation is possible only in the imagination and for the individual. Implicitly, only the practice of art gives value to life, and given the number of plays in which either despairing or failed and ridiculous artists have prominent parts (**The Ignoramus and The Madman; The Force of Habit; Minetti; The Famous Ones**) even here Bernhard's vision is bleak. The absurd chasm between man's perception of his capabilities and reality is a constant theme of his work.

In his semi-autobiographical novel **The Cellar—A Withdrawal** (1976; 'semi' in that he refuses to classify and separate details of his 'imaginative' and 'real' lives in the fictions he has created out of his experience) Bernhard describes his grandfather in the post-war years:

Day after day, I know, he'd lock himself in, and his wife, my grandmother, waited for the shot from the pistol he'd lain on the desk, at night under his pillow, she feared this shot, he had threatened all of us, again and again, he had no money and not the least bit of strength, starved like the rest of us, he

knew now, two years after the war had ended, in the bitterest of times once again, nothing more than hopelessness.

The style of the passage is typical of Bernhard's work: a possessed mind in a rush of thought, which proceeds through contradictions and conflicting emotions as if by the inertia of its own forward motion. Several pages further in the novel the old man takes up his daily task, at 3 a.m., 'his struggle with the impossible, with the total hopelessness of writing'. For many of Bernhard's characters, as for himself, the last words of Beckett's *The Unnamable* are appropriate: 'You must go on, I can't go on, I'll go on.'

Bernhard has kept writing, quite prolifically. . . . (pp. 140-42)

The situations in Bernhard's first two plays are typical of his work. In *A Feast For Boris* a birthday party is thrown by a wealthy crippled woman ('The Good One') for her deformed, legless husband Boris; in the final torment, witnessed by thirteen fellow cripples and objects of the 'Good One's' charity, he is given a present of boots and long underwear. In *The Ignoramus and The Madman* (1972) an opera singer and surgeon are juxtaposed as two absurd 'specialists': the doctor talks incessantly about the details of autopsy, while the soprano prepares for a performance as the *Queen of Night* in *The Magic Flute*. Her drunken father listens to the doctor through much of the play, which ends with the daughter coughing spastically while she cancels further engagements. In virtually all of Bernhard's plays normal human values are turned inside out: philanthropy is sadism in *A Feast For Boris* while unique skill and beauty are fatuous narrow mindedness and affectation in *The Ignoramus and The Madman.* Positions of power, whether in personal or social terms, are always seen as loathsome.

More than one critic has noted the misanthropy of this author as having a special Austrian cast to it—shaped in part, it would seem, from the self imposed isolation of his remote mountain village where Bernhard, like numerous characters he has invented, resides. One thinks of reclusive characters in Adalbert Stifter's fiction—also a favourite of Handke's—in this context.

Among his contemporaries, Bernhard bears comparison with the younger Austrian Handke. Both authors' works derive in part from the Austrian stage tradition of dark humour and bitter satire in the nineteenth-century playwrights Nestroy and Raimund—the latter of whom, like Adalbert Stifter, took his own life. Linguistic patterns and repetition with variations are important structural features of both Bernhard's and Handke's plays, though Bernhard shows less interest in formal experiment in each work.

The musicality of the virtually unpunctuated long speeches in his plays may derive from Bernhard's early training in music, and its dependence on the specifics of the German language may explain why his plays have not enjoyed great success in translation. (pp. 142-43)

Bernhard's attitude toward language and communication (and his interest in Wittgenstein) overlaps with Handke's, as does his idea of the artist in society. Both playwrights are clearly in the romantic tradition which sees the artist as isolated and writing for his own sake, out of private need. Bernhard's contempt for the idea that the writer can effect any but personal changes even goes further than Handke. One could take the statement in *The Cellar* as typical: 'I speak a language which only I understand, no one else, just the way everyone understands his own language, and those who think they've understood, they're idiots and charlatans.' While he considers actors totally ignorant about his writing, he carries the idea to an extreme when he concludes that neither could he explain or interpret his own work: he just does it, by compulsion.

Bernhard leaves his texts unpunctuated so that the reader or actor can find his own suitable tempo or rhythm: the dramatic scripts are, to use his own word, 'skeletons', to be fleshed in by others. One actor who has played the lead in a number of Bernhard premieres (the author carefully restricts the rights of his plays for particular directors and actors) is Bernhard Minetti. In a piece actually titled *Minetti* (1976), about an ageing actor waiting to be interviewed for *Lear,* the producer never shows up, and the final image of the play is Minetti sitting on a park bench while snow gradually blankets his body. In an interview by Claus Peymann (the director with whom he frequently collaborates on Bernhard scripts) Minetti described the typical situations in the plays as balanced between comedy and tragedy, and the typical characters as Hamlet-like, because they think aloud but do very little. Bernhard's extremely long speeches are especially challenging to an actor, according to Minetti. He must determine the movements of the character's consciousness from the outline Bernhard provides; choices must be made as to which spoken words are merely private reflection, which are less controlled emotional outbursts, and finally, which are uttered for the sole purpose of evoking responses from others on stage. Like Shakespeare's, Bernhard's plays are virtually devoid of 'stage directions'.

When I saw the premiere performance of *The World Reformer* ([Bochum] 1980, directed by Claus Peymann) Minetti's acting itself seemed part of Bernhard's total concept. One might call it 'ironic' acting, in keeping with one of the playwright's chief literary resources. *The World Reformer* presents, in two parts, the portrait of a misanthrope, a crotchety philosopher, nearly seventy years old, upon whom the academic worthies of Frankfurt University are about to bestow an honorary degree. (In *Immanuel Kant* [1978] Bernhard has the philosopher, his servant, and his parrot travel to New York University under the delusion that he is to receive a similar award: he is greeted by men in white coats.) The world reformer lives with an elderly concubine, whom he mistreats: at one point in the Bochum performance she tightened the knot on his tie while he gazed into her eyes, mocking her to take revenge in the very act of serving him: 'if only you knew how to tighten it—it makes you hateable—you wait'. After accepting the Frankfurt degree, he peremptorily orders the entire visiting party (including the mayor and vice-chancellor) out of his house. The self-mockery of the world reformer parallels the self-mockery of Bernhard the 'writer'. Minetti in the [Peymann] production, rolling his eyes after lines like the following, actualized the thought in performance:

> All roads unavoidably lead
> to perversity
> and absurdity.
> We can only improve the world
> if we destroy it [rolled eyes]
> Or do you think they understood my tractatus. [quizzical]

The acting itself transcends the banality of despair in the text.

The difficulty with Bernhard's plays is that they do not contain the range of possibilities of the classics of absurdist theatre. They are similar in theme to Beckett plays and have such features in common as images of crippled humanity or petty daily frustrations expressed through standard comic business (shoelaces that keep coming undone, hats that will not stay on), but they lack breadth of vision, or liberating humour. A Beckett prop usually has several levels of significance; for Bernhard such things are often flat and simple.

The cultured premiere audience at *The World Reformer* was certainly responding as much, or more to the performer as to the play, when Minetti rambled through a catalogue of remarks debunking the idea of culture and cultural institutions. (An additional irony for the German audience, Bernhard Minetti is a living cultural institution. His work dates back to the heyday of Weimar Republic theatre when he worked with such greats as Jessner.) Bernhard's mockery extends to the cultural ritual of attendance at highly subsidized world premieres. The Bochum audience laughed heartily at itself in Minetti's rambling monologue. . . . (pp. 144-46)

Bernhard constructs his plays around such monologues, and shows disregard for realistic dramatic construction. When Handke toys with dramatic convention it is usually for a purpose, and he often displays a surrealist's sense of humour: wanting to underscore a 'meaningful event' in *They Are Dying Out* Handke calls for a garbage can lid to be thrown to the floor backstage. Bernhard's contempt for 'meaning' and for normal dramatic practice is expressed more nakedly. To clear the stage for a soliloquy in *The World Reformer* Bernhard has a phone ring from the wings, wastes no words on plausibility or rationalization in terms of plot, and off goes the extraneous character.

A recent play, *Before Retirement* (1979), offers insight into how facets of German history and social reality achieve dramatic form in Bernhard's work in comparison to that of his contemporaries. Georg Hensel [in *Frankfurter Allgemeine Zeitung,* July 2, 1979] described this 'comedy of the German soul' as his most elegant play: 'three performers, animated with Strindberg psychology, in a mythical situation, bedecked with Nazi emblems and packed with relevant political material.' Rudolf Höller, a former deputy commandant of a concentration camp, and currently a high ranking official of the West German judiciary, lives with his two sisters. Clara, crippled by an American bomb blast in the last days of World War II, has left-wing sympathies, and loathes her brother, while Vera clings adoringly (and incestuously) to him. Höller has traditionally celebrated Himmler's birthday, but on this October 7th his guests have deserted him, so he puts on his SS uniform, drinks himself into a stupor, and threatens to shoot Clara. He collapses from a heart attack, Vera puts on a recording of Beethoven's Fifth Symphony (Höller had earlier said 'Music makes it all bearable') before welcoming the Jewish doctor; her bitter ironic penultimate lines accuse Clara: 'You're guilty / with your silence / you with your eternal silence.'

The thematic material of the play could be the substance of any number of post-World War II German plays; but whereas someone like Heiner Müller forces the audience to face the brutalities of German history and its continuing present influence, Bernhard's satirical thrust leads to a general misanthropy. The grotesque details of Höller's birthday party—reminiscing on Himmler's humanitarian act of saving Höller's life; leafing through a photo album which juxtaposes the trivial (holiday snaps) and the horrid (snaps of condemned Hungarian Jews); the 'demon's' love of music; the endless intoning of 'good German' clichés about duty and hard work—are not so much exposés, as they are illustrations of Bernhard's world view. While in the late seventies the issue of ex-Nazis in high-ranking West German government positions was a real one, Bernhard sees both the fact of reinstated Nazis and the idea of effectively changing things by exposing them as equally absurd. He has explained (*Der Spiegel,* 23 June 1980) that such people as these 'are in me, just as they are in everyone else.' Even the idea of environmental protection, a topical subject in the seventies, finds its way into Bernhard's play: Höller draws strength from the conviction that his hero, Himmler, was also concerned with the environment. 'If Himmler hadn't lived / right where our house stands / there would have stood a poison gas factory.' Himmler had rescued Höller, and now Höller fights to preserve the natural landscape (and would like to rid it of Jews and Americans, too). The satire is aimed at *homo sapiens,* rather than at any particular ruling group; there is no point in exposing corruption; it is as ubiquitous as it is amorphous.

In Franz Xaver Kroetz's play *The Nest* a working class character learns he has been unknowingly poisoning a lake at the bidding of his boss (and for extra pay); the results are nearly tragic. But something is learned about pollution and responsibility, and a change of consciousness results. No wonder that Kroetz, who once shared a literary prize with Bernhard, expresses contempt for the Austrian's work. The two represent opposite directions in contemporary German theatre. Bernhard's work is *sui generis,* both part of and aloof from the contemporary scene. (pp. 148-50)

> Denis Calandra, *"Private Visions: Thomas Bernhard and Butho Strauss," in his* New German Dramatists, *Grove Press, Inc., 1983, pp. 139-61.*

HARRIETT GILBERT

Thomas Bernhard's *Concrete* is only half satisfactory. It has, apparently, been proclaimed a 'despairing indictment of our society'—yet the one-dimensional, anti-intellectual, anti-artistic, 'concrete' world against which the novel rails is nothing but a worn-out cliché, with little resemblance to 'our' or to anyone's society. The attack, being aimed at a delusion, can only fall flat on its face.

As a study of *personal* sterility, however, the book does have the neurotic integrity to drag the reader along (a process assisted by the fact that it has neither paragraphs nor chapter breaks). For ten years, the narrator, Rudolf, has been researching the life of Mendelssohn Bartholdy. That he hasn't yet started to *write* the life, he blames on either his ill health (a condition that the reader must doubt) or the claimed interference of his sister. Set entirely in Rudolf's unreliable head—as he tries to talk himself into the work we can see he will never begin—the book is a deft illustration of one kind of madness. Where it fails is in its attempt to create, from this, a metaphor for modern life.

> Harriett Gilbert, *"Truth Games," in* New Statesmen, *Vol. 107, No. 2768, April 6, 1984, p. 35.*

SVEN BIRKERTS

[*The essay excerpted below originally appeared in* The New Republic, *August 13-20, 1984.*]

Among Nietzsche's posthumously published notes we find the following: "Let us consider this idea in its most terrifying form: existence as it is, without meaning or goal, but inescapably recurrent, without a finale into nothingness . . . Those who cannot bear the sentence, There is no salvation, *ought* to perish." Serving up that "existence as it is" has long been one of the main activities of modernist literature, especially in Europe, but the sternly enjoined "ought" has proven thorny even to the most fire-hardened pessimists. The organism manifests a striking sort of obstinacy when its own cessation is at issue. What our masters show us, by and large, is man in a state of deadlock, unable to bear the sentence and unwilling to perish. Beckett's "I can't go on, I'll go on" more or less sums it up.

But the Austrian novelist Thomas Bernhard has made it his special program to restore to Nietzsche's proposition its cutting edge. Putting to one side the matter of eternal recurrence, he asks: is an existence without meaning or goal—he does not doubt that this is its true character—bearable or not? If it is, then what is the toll exacted from the psyche? If it is not . . . From the first, Bernhard's novels, *Gargoyles* (1970), *The Lime Works* (1973), *Correction* (1979), and *Concrete* (1984), have explored the options with an unflinching gaze. Konrad in *The Lime Works* endures his hellish life—poverty, paralysis of creative will, a crippled, importuning wife—for as long as he can. When he reaches the end of his tether, when his reserves are gone, he shoots the woman in the head and lapses into catatonia. In *Correction,* Roithamer, the philosopher, struggles to achieve the perfect integration of his life and his thought; at last he concludes that he has done everything that he can, and must, do, and hangs himself in a clearing in the forest. Possibilities of redemption or reclamation are nowhere suggested.

Concrete is very much of a piece with the earlier works. The same thematic elements are present, though in different groupings, and the investigation of the psyche's response to the "impossible" nature of existence proceeds apace. Even the narrator, Rudolph, is instantly recognizable. Obsessed, depressed, loathing himself and others, he is but the latest carrier of Bernhard's acetylene torch. (pp. 77-8)

Rudolph is repressed, narcissistic, obsessive-compulsive. We are hardly surprised when we learn . . . that he is incapable of putting pen to paper to begin his masterwork. To call him "blocked," however, would be to attach a simplifying epithet to what is, in fact, a total paralysis of soul. Rudolph is not obstructed by some malfunctions in part of his being—his being itself is a knot. And as Bernhard's narrative proceeds, we begin to register the dimensions of his crisis, its self-consuming circularity.

Rudolph is a master at displacing and shifting blame; he is unable to stare his demon in the face. He cannot begin his treatise, he insists, because he lives in dread of his older sister. She preys on his weakness. He has only to decide to begin and she will promptly appear on his doorstep. Her unannounced visits—the very possibility of them—assault his nerves and destroy his composure. And what a sister! Projected through the enlarging mechanism of his neurosis, she is like some horrible two-dimensional cutout—loud, domineering, crass, the very incarnation of bourgeois philistinism. Against such a visitant all of Rudolph's delicacy and refinement must shrink away.

As readers, though, we have an advantage of objectivity. True, she is an irritating, self-important creature; but she is not nearly the harpy that her brother makes her out to be. The contrast between images underlines for us the severity of the malaise. Her negative attributes—which Rudolph conflates with those of his culture—loom larger as his condition worsens. . . . (p. 79)

Lacerating relationships supply much of the central tension in Bernhard's work. Invariably his withdrawn, compulsive males are pitted against small-minded, intractable women. Not in a sexual way, though—the men are too disembodied for that; the opposition is, if this is possible, even more primary. Everything in the female psyche exists for the sole purpose of affronting the man. And this state of affairs is as necessary as it is intolerable. Konrad serves and placates his wife even as he reviles her; Roithamer continues to visit his crude, shrewish mother long after it is clear to him that nothing but pain could ever result from their contact. These characters are so far removed from the daily human commerce that they can only feel their reality in the presence of an adversary. As to why it should always be a woman—a mother, wife, sister— Bernhard gives no clue. Nothing in the work suggests the origin or etiology of this primal face-off. It is simply presented as the state of things. As readers, we feel at times unwelcome, as if we have arrived by mistake at the site of some incomprehensible private exorcism.

Meanwhile, Rudolph, riding the swell of his vituperations, realizes that he cannot endure another winter in his village of Peiskam. And his sister urges him on: "If you don't get away soon, you'll go to pieces and die." He tantalizes himself with images of the island of Palma. There, away from everything, free of his sister and his life-sapping culture, he will work. Nothing will prevent him. Making a decision, though, and following it through are two very different things for Rudolph. His character makes it all but impossible to act. Time and again he gets himself to the brink, has his papers and medicines all packed and ready, only to back down. . . . Bernhard is aware of the possibilities for humor in Rudolph's indecisiveness:

> I was caught up once more in my own personal comedy. I'd changed course, and once again it was simply a laughing matter or a crying matter, depending on how I felt, but since I wanted neither to laugh nor to cry, I got up and checked whether I had packed the right medicaments. I had put them in my red-spotted medicine bag. Had I packed enough prednisolone, spironolactone and potassium chloride? I opened the medicine bag, looked inside, and tipped out the contents on the table by the window.

Bernhard's style, with its peculiar recursive throb, its controlled clause repetitions, is wonderfully suited for recapturing the myriad forms of psychic hypertrophy. In *The Lime Works* the relentless circularity mimes the process of a mind that is no longer in control of its own momentum ("his wife had spoken to him about a pair of mittens she was making for Konrad, she had been working on this one pair of mittens for six months, because she unravelled each mitten just before she had finished knitting it"). In *Correction,* on the other hand, the insistent hammering of clauses, not so different from the above, is used to project the extreme difficulty of

thought. Roithamer (very much a Wittgenstein figure) and his narrator, who is also a philosopher, proceed by way of repetitions because thought cannot hope to penetrate reality in any other way—truth is not to be caught on the wing. Stylistically conjoined in this way, "genius" and madness look like the heads and tails on a spinning coin.

But Rudolph is neither genius nor madman—quite—and to transmit his particular condition, Bernhard loosens the weave of his prose somewhat. Sentences are shorter and jumpier and are paced to suggest the erratic movements of a psyche bent upon hiding from itself. Phrase repetitions are manipulated in symphonic fashion: they give us the crescendo and diminuendo of uncontrollable nervous activity.

After interminable and, for the reader, infuriating vacillations, Rudolph finally does travel to Palma. He arranges himself in his hotel room, puts his papers in order—and is no more able to work than he was before. Only now, away from his sister, he has removed his main excuse for inactivity. By escaping to freedom he has painted himself still further into a corner. But he cannot see this. For Rudolph the future remains an inexhaustible fund of propitious moments—the miracle is certain to happen.

At this point, Bernhard inserts a curious flashback. Rudolph is in Palma on a previous visit. Walking in the town one day, Rudolph meets a young German woman named Anna Hardtl who promptly tells him her tragic story: her husband just recently jumped/fell to his death from their hotel window. Rudolph listens intently while she traces for him the events of their life together, and he accompanies her when she goes to look for the grave in the nearby cemetery. The whole circumstance somehow seems to gratify his own morbidity. We steel ourselves for some dark broodings. But no—quite unexpectedly, in the course of a long sentence, we recall that years have passed, that Rudolph is now in Palma a second time. It is a disturbing switch. So little has changed. The unfortunate Anna is a memory, but everything else remains as before: Rudolph is still ailing, his book is still unwritten . . .

Nevertheless, years do not pass without some mark. In the interval since he was last in Palma, Anna's story has worked its way into his system. And as Rudolph walks along the familiar streets, the spell is renewed. One morning he wakes up possessed by her image. "I must go to the cemetery as quickly as possible," he tells himself. In three breathless sentences he is there, standing in front of the stone. He sees that there is a new plaque and that Anna's name has been engraved under her husband's. "Suicido," explains the porter. Rudolph rushes back to the hotel in a taxi—"I drew the curtains in my room," writes Rudolph, "took several sleeping tablets, and woke up twenty-six hours later in a state of extreme anxiety."

Concrete ends with a spasm. We are pitched out into uncertainty. Are we to trust the momentum of the last pages, to assume that Rudolph hurries to throw himself from the window? It would be consonant with Bernhard's belief—that durability is finite in the face of pain. What's more, the logic of events fits well with Camus's insight about suicide, that a single event, a straw, is enough to trigger a person who has been steadily, imperceptibly "undermined" by life.

On the other hand, recalling Nietzsche's formulation, we may also venture the opposite: that Anna's strength of character, the purity of her despair, enabled her to grasp her situation and act upon the imperative, and that it is Rudolph's tragedy to be without that strength. We can imagine without difficulty how he drags himself forward from day to day, as before, pushing his stake to the next square, waiting for the next—redeeming—turn of the roulette wheel. Bernhard has calculatedly left us to our own devices. He has expressed the expected exclamation point down to make a tensely bent question mark.

Reading through Bernhard's novels consecutively, one begins to remark, and later enlarge upon, a problematic paradox. As we have seen, the concerns are dark ones and the conclusions unrelievedly bleak. Madness and suicide dance attendance upon exacerbated consciousness; there is no relief except through self-deception. Whatever our own biases might be, we set them apart while the writer performs. But here is the crux: writing is, by its very nature, an effort at the redemption of pain. So long as it continues, it intimates that redemption is possible. The statements Bernhard makes are, in a sense, contradicted by the fact of their being made. We feel, and respond to, the authorial presence behind the projected voices. But it is difficult to hear the writer keep saying, "I can't go on," without eventually muttering, "But you do." As Shakespeare understood, "The worst is not so long as we can say: This is the worst."

Still, we must concede that Bernhard's is a very real and impassioned despair, and that the novels, even though they move within a confined locus, have emblematic force. Konrad, Roithamer, and Rudolph, in their production or paralysis, represent what Susan Sontag has called "the artist as exemplary sufferer." Their torments are caused, in part, by the conditions of the modern social order, and their invectives are not wholly off the mark. What Rudolph writes on the eve of his departure for Palma could just as well have been set down by Konrad or Roithamer:

> If I go away, I said to myself, sitting in the iron chair, I shall be leaving a country whose utter futility depresses me every single day, whose imbecilities daily threaten to stifle me, and whose idiocies will sooner or later be the end of me, even without my illnesses. Whose political and cultural conditions have of late become so chaotic that they turn my stomach when I wake up every morning, even before I am out of bed. Whose indifference to intellect has long since ceased to cause the likes of me to despair, but if I am truthful only to vomit . . . in which everything that once gave pleasure to so-called thinking people, or at least made it possible for them to go on existing, has been expelled, expunged and extinguished, in which only the most primitive instinct for survival prevails and the slightest pretention to thought is stifled at birth.

This is not lament—this is rage. We can only guess at its deeper origins, though the relationships depicted in the novels may give us a clue. Where rage of this intensity is directed outward, we often find the sociopath; where inward, the suicide. Where it breaks out laterally, onto the page, we sometimes find a most unsettling artistic vision. (pp. 80-4)

Sven Birkerts, "Thomas Bernhard," in his An Artificial Wilderness: Essays on 20th-Century Literature, *William Morrow and Company, Inc., 1987, pp. 77-84.*

JOHN UPDIKE

Mr. Bernhard's particular contribution to the armory of the avant-garde, and a daunting one, is the elimination of paragraphs, so that the bitter pill of his writing is administered as steadily as an I.V. drip, and solid page follows solid page as if in an album of Ad Reinhardt's black paintings.

However, his sentences make lucid sense. Trained as a musician, he writes for the ear, and in *Concrete* the voice of the narrator flutters on and on, unravelling in a fascinating comedy of self-incrimination. The narrator's name is Rudolf, and he is writing these "notes," it turns out, in Palma, on Mallorca. But most of the action (if you can call it that) occurs in Rudolf's country estate of Peiskam, where his delicate nervous system is recovering from a visit by his sister and he is trying to sit down at last to "a major work of impeccable scholarship" upon the composer Mendelssohn. Rudolf, who lived in Vienna for twenty years, was active in musical circles there and may even have published a critical article or two but has long since retired to Peiskam; there he fulminates, takes medicine, stalls, and becomes more and more of a recluse, seeing on a regular basis only Frau Kienesberger, his housekeeper. He is, we eventually learn, forty-eight years old and for most of his life has been dependent on medicine: "I myself owe everything to chemicals—to put it briefly—and have done for the last thirty years." A life so fruitless and self-indulgent requires money: "Basically I have no right whatever to lead the life I do, which is as unparalleled—and as terrible—as it is expensive." His wealth is inherited, and rouses his prose to one of its few surges of enthusiasm:

> My sister's business sense, which is her most distinctive trait, though no one would suspect it without knowing her as well as I do, comes from our paternal grandfather. It was he who made the family fortune, in the most curious circumstances, but at all events, however he did it, he made so much money that my sister and I, the third generation, still have enough for our existence, and all in all neither of us leads the most modest existence. . . . In fact, even though I am the most incompetent person in all so-called money matters, I could live for another twenty years without having to earn a penny, and then I could still sell off one parcel of land after another without seriously impairing the estate and thus lowering its value, but that won't be necessary, and it's absurd to contemplate it in view of the fact that I have only a very short time left to live, thanks to the incessant and inexorable progress of my illness.

Devotees of modern literature have met Rudolf's type of neurasthenic, self-doubting, hypercritical, indecisive, and demanding personality often before—in the letters and works of Kafka and Proust above all, but also in the luxuriant nervous systems and imaginations of Henry James, Virginia Woolf, and Thomas Mann. These all, of course, got down to work, and it is doubtful whether Rudolf ever will; but the artistic sensibility, and a certain power of fascination, are his. His diatribes have a swing to them—Austrian politics become "all the horror stories emanating from the Ballhausplatz, where a half-crazed Chancellor is at large, issuing half-crazed orders to his idiotic ministers [and] all the horrendous parliamentary news which daily jangles in my ears and pollutes my brain and which all comes packaged in Christian hypocrisy." The suggestion that he get a dog to relieve his solitude prompts a magnificent caricature, not without truth, of the global dog situation:

> The masses are in favour of dogs because in their heart of hearts they are not prepared to incur the

strenuous effort of being alone with themselves, an effort which in fact calls for greatness of soul. . . . If the dog has to go out, I have to go out too, and so on. I won't tolerate this dog comedy, which we can see enacted every day if we only open our eyes and haven't become blinded to it by daily familiarity. In this comedy a dog comes on the stage and makes life a misery for some human being, exploiting him and, in the course of several acts, or just one or two, driving out of him all his harmless humanity.

Sudden aphorisms dart from Rudolf's freewheeling discourse: "Everyone is a virtuoso on his own instrument, but together they add up to an intolerable cacophony." "Everyone wants to be alive, nobody wants to be dead. Everything else is a lie." His own maneuvers—changing rooms, arising at a certain hour—to minimize his discomforts and secure a foothold in which he can begin writing his book have the beguiling energy of Kafka's nameless hero's futile efforts to secure his "Burrow." These movements and the shifts of his monologue suggest less Pascal's motions of Grace than what Nathalie Sarraute described as "numerous, entangled movements that have come up from the depths," and whose "restless shimmer" exists "somewhere on the fluctuating frontier that separates conversation from sub-conversation." Rudolf's sister exists in his discourse as elusively as a sea monster in deep waters: she first appears to be a vulgar ogress whom he detests, but as he goes on, and describes her active life as a real-estate agent among the very rich, we see her as a normally dynamic woman of a certain set and style, faithfully trying to tease and goad her neurotic little brother into something like her own health. He does not hate her; he loves her, with the resentful adoration the ineffective feel for the effective, an emotion given its classic expression in Kafka's "Letter to His Father." Rudolf goes Kafka one better, however, in finally identifying with his sister, for all his protests against her: "We're both like this: for decades we've been accusing each other of being impossible, and yet we can't give up being impossible, erratic, capricious and vacillating."

And, just when the reader has resigned himself to another Beckettian study of total inertia and claustrophobic captivity, Rudolf manages to get himself out of fogbound Peiskam and to Palma. There he describes the scenery, the relative warmth, his agonies of recuperation after the adventure of the flight, and a story told to him over two years ago, during his previous visit to Mallorca, by a stranger, a Bavarian named Anna Härdtl, whom he and a local friend met on the street. Her tale, of a young woman's rather pedestrian misadventures with marriage and an ill-advised appliance shop, was as relevant as a shaggy-dog story to Rudolf's normal concerns, but he listened and now relates it, briskly and circumstantially, in his normally self-obsessed "notes." On his present visit to Palma, his memory of Anna Härdtl causes him to visit the local cemetery, where all the tombs are of concrete, giving this book its title. The hardness of Palma concrete contrasts with the soft fog and musty furniture of Peiskam, and, though Rudolf ends in his usual, typically modernist state of "extreme anxiety," he has been brought, for an interval, to think of somebody else's troubles. (pp. 97-100)

"In the end we don't have to justify ourselves or anything else," Rudolf writes. "We didn't make ourselves." . . . Relief from what Ibsen, in *The Wild Duck,* called "the claim of the ideal" is being prescribed. "Oh, life would be quite tolerable, after all," Ibsen's Dr. Relling concludes, "if only we could be rid of the confounded duns that keep on pestering us, in our poverty, with the claim of the ideal." Clearly enough, Rudolf's ardent wish to write a great "life" of Mendelssohn is preventing him from getting the first word onto paper; perfectionism is the enemy of creation, as extreme self-solicitude is the enemy of well-being. (p. 100)

John Updike, "Ungreat Lives," in The New Yorker, *Vol. LX, No. 51, February 4, 1985, pp. 94-101.*

D. J. ENRIGHT

On the jacket of [*Concrete*], the Austrian writer Thomas Bernhard is likened to Kafka and Beckett, while reviewers are quoted as linking him with Broch, Strindberg, and Musil. Whether these constitute sure-fire recommendations is a matter of opinion. Are we certain we need another Kafka? Or that we want another Beckett or Strindberg (or even Broch)? We could never hope for (what is he doing here?) a second Musil. In the event it is Beckett, though a more loquacious Beckett than we have met of late, whom Bernhard comes nearest to.

Not that the reader should worry too much about this cloud of elevated comparison: all he will need is an overflowing and impregnable stock of compassion, or else a very odd and insatiable sense of humor. Or, one had better add (though this supposes a rather less than common reader), a taste for sheer technical skill, in this case evinced in brio, a vivacious passivity, or a kind of confident dash that doesn't actually go anywhere but wriggles a lot.

Rudolf, the narrator of *Concrete,* has for ten years been planning "a major work of impeccable scholarship" on the composer Mendelssohn. He is, by his own account, gravely ill, but resolved to begin writing at last. "We must be alone and free from all human contact if we wish to embark upon an intellectual task!" He cannot start until his sister, a domineering and destructive force, has left him to return to Vienna. She is "anti-intellectual" and has already put a stop to projects of his on *Jenufa,* on *Moses and Aaron,* on Rubinstein, and on "Les Six." "People exist for the sole purpose of tracking down the intellect and annihilating it." (Mind you, Rudolf believed he needed to have his sister with him; he did ask her to come.) Why, his sister married her husband only in order to drive him away to Peru—and (which appears to be worse) when she travels by sleeper she takes her own sheets, on principle.

Now she has gone, but Rudolf still cannot write that opening sentence. "We need someone for our work, and we also need no one": unhappily, at any given time we never know which. He couldn't eat breakfast when his sister was present, and now he can't stand eating breakfast alone. His large house, out in the countryside, is like a morgue. He can't sit at his desk, he hasn't the strength, the postman will knock at the door, a neighbor will come by; perhaps he has overdone his research into Mendelssohn, publishing anything anyway is "folly and evidence of a certain defect of character," though he intends to publish his work notwithstanding, it will be his most successful or his least unsuccessful; but before he publishes it he has to write it.

This state of animated paralysis, sustained through 153 chapterless and unparagraphed pages of print as though to oblige the reader to swallow it all down at one go, is enacted (if that's the right word) again and again, in differing situations.

Since he has no friends—he used to have friends in Vienna but they have died of madness or by their own hand—his sister has advised him to keep a dog for company. She herself doesn't need one because she has lovers, counts and barons who are useful to her in her real-estate business. But he has always hated dogs, and what sort of dog ought it to be, and who would look after it? And look at Schopenhauer, who was ruled not by his head but by his dog. People are ruined by their dogs, "they would rather save their dog from the guillotine than Voltaire," indeed wars are caused by dogs because of their influence over politicians and dictators, the biggest and most expensive tombstone ever seen (not in America, as you might expect, but in London) was erected to the memory of a dog. . . . It seems Rudolf doesn't much fancy dogs.

His sister has also suggested that he should take a holiday—clearly the one thing Rudolf isn't short of is money—and so round we go in rings once more. It would be good to get out of Austria—Austria comes in for several pages of tirade, not particularly interesting, or convincing, since anyone in a bad mood could say much the same about whatever country he was living in—and if he went anywhere it would have to be Palma. But how can he think of setting out for Palma when his physical condition doesn't allow him to walk two hundred yards from his house?

To drive the notion out of his head, he contrives to walk to his nearest neighbor, a cavalry officer from World War I. In what, after the canine indictment, is the book's most plainly amusing passage, the old man reveals the arrangements he has made to bequeath his property. He has no intention of leaving anything to the Church or the state welfare service, both of which stink, or (how could he?) to any person he knows. So he sends for a London telephone directory and picks a name out of it at random: "Sarah Slother," whoever she may be, shall inherit.

The visit has the contrary effect, it inspires Rudolf; and he finds himself dusting off his suitcases, packing them, and unpacking them to make sure he has included the right medicines as well as the Mendelssohn material. He *will* go to Palma, for two or three or four months. "I have all my life, as I know, been a man of quick decisions." (Either this novel is innocent of irony or it consists of nothing else.) Having come to this decision, he starts to feel that his house isn't as bad as he has been making out, in fact it's a marvelous, comfortable house, not in the least like a morgue, so it's hardly worth making the tremendous effort to leave it. *"Habe nun, ach, Philosophie, Juristerei und Medicin durchaus studiert."* In the succeeding bout of introspection Rudolf presents himself as a sort of sickbed Faust:

> I talked myself into studying mathematics, then philosophy, but it wasn't long before I conceived a distaste for mathematics and philosophy, at least for the mathematics taught at the university, as well as for the philosophy that is taught there but in fact can't be taught at all.

He has studied at Innsbruck and Graz as well as Vienna (does he hate Vienna because his sister lives there? Is he unjust toward his sister because she lives in Vienna?), and he would have gone to Oxford or Cambridge except that he couldn't endure the English climate.

Suddenly something promises to happen. Rudolf has reached Palma, to be laid low by the sharp rise in temperature. But he will start on his book, "if not today, then tomorrow; if not tomorrow, then the day after, and so on." Hope springs eternal in this despairing breast. In the meanwhile he remembers a young woman, Anna Härdtl, whom he had met on his previous visit to Palma, two years earlier. Anna's story is truly tragic. She had persuaded her husband to start an electrical business in a suburb of Munich; the rash enterprise flopped, and they fled to Majorca for a short, cheap holiday. On the fifth day her husband either fell or threw himself from the hotel balcony and was found dead on the concrete below. He was buried huggermugger in a concrete tomb which bore only the name of an old woman, a complete stranger. There was nothing to be done about Anna, Rudolf tells himself; she was one of those millions of "luckless creatures who can't be rescued from their misfortune."

Is this the significance of the book's title, we wonder? That whereas Rudolf suffers in the abstract, Anna's sufferings are concrete? Rudolf observes that when we meet someone like her, we tell ourselves that we are not as badly off as we had believed. "The fact is that we immediately use someone who is *still more* unfortunate than we are in order to get ourselves back on our feet." And you see, he may not be writing on Mendelssohn, but at any rate he is writing the notes that comprise *Concrete*. But no, we suspect we were being sentimental and simpleminded. Looking for a message, for a moral! Isn't the relentless and ingenious portrayal of neurosis, paranoia, multimonomania, enough for us? Rudolf walks out to look again at the tomb in which the young husband was laid and finds that the old woman's name has disappeared and the plaque now bears Anna's name as well as that of her husband. It must be that she has killed herself. He goes back to his hotel, takes several sleeping tablets, and—in the closing sentence—wakes up twenty-six hours later "in a state of extreme anxiety," the state in which, fearing his sister might suddenly return to the house, he began. A stiff peg of whiskey should suffice for most readers. (p. 31)

D. J. Enright, "Calling Dr. Angst," in The New York Review of Books, *Vol. XXXII, No. 5, March 28, 1985, pp. 31-2.*

WALTER ABISH

Thomas Bernhard is by far the most disturbing and original literary figure to have emerged in postwar Austria. At 54 he has produced a remarkable body of work, over 30 books of fiction and drama that focus with an immeasurable singlemindedness on the ill will, the continual betrayal and the self-doubt that inexorably motivate his characters to contemplate their self-destruction.

Now ranked with the foremost world authors, Mr. Bernhard writes novels that continue to incur a certain resistance on the part of the reader, for to read him is to enter a hazardous emotional maze singularly devoid of affection, love or pleasure not marred by the intrusion of death. The utter nihilism of a comment such as, "The dead are more attractive than those who haven't yet reached that stage," by an eccentric aristocrat discussing suicide with his physician in *Gargoyles,* one of Mr. Bernhard's earlier novels, exemplifies not only the recklessness with which the author's often distraught characters tend to expose their innermost thoughts, but also their all-pervasive lack of expectation. Whatever writing may actually mean for Mr. Bernhard, one can read into it an indubitable delay, the postponement of an implacable ending of which his characters are all too aware.

The compelling, obsessional flow of the text inherently serves to energize the calamitous narrative. In no other author is language, as an entity, so forcefully charged with the urgency of life and also committed to opposing, in effect, what it has been enjoined to create—namely, the omnipresence of death and its ensuing silence. Everything impedes clarity, everything ominously predicts disintegration: the landscape, an inhospitably wooded or mountainous Austrian terrain; the curiously inbred characters that people Mr. Bernhard's early rural novels such as *Gargoyles, The Lime Works,* and the masterly *Correction,* in which the narrator sifts through the papers left behind by his friend, a reclusive scientist who took his life after having built for his sister an idealized building, a cone-shaped house in the center of a forest, only to conclude that his undertaking was aberrational.

Mr. Bernhard's characters are morbid, self-engrossed, suicidal. Though these exasperating figures loom larger than life, with their state of unrest greatly magnified, they remain strikingly distant, not unlike that mysterious group of massive heads assembled on Easter Island. As readers we are in the relentless grip of Mr. Bernhard. One marvels at the consistency of his austere vision. In every case it is a life with little if any reward. Only the totally unscrupulous and desensitized can be said to achieve anything, and their success invariably comes at the expense of those incapable of fending for themselves. The victims do not expect or invite pity but, at most, a mild contempt.

In his most recent novels Mr. Bernhard has shifted to an urban setting, and the social quandaries within that spoiled, "civilized" atmosphere of the city, for the most part Vienna, are more self-centered and the display of malice, if anything, more mannered and codified. It is altogether fitting that the elderly former cavalry officer in *Concrete* should derive an exquisite pleasure from his decision to bequeath his property not to relatives but to someone whose name he had picked at random out of the London telephone book.

Everyone is emotionally unstable, not least the first-person narrators who, in these later novels, display traits (one might call them symptoms) that bear a disconcerting resemblance to Mr. Bernhard's acerbic self-portrait in *Gathering Evidence.* This is not to say that the author is writing about his "self" in the novels, but that each text to some degree receives its instruction from an autobiographical impulse. Death, his central theme, is a measure of life's energy; what is measured is the ability to stave off self-destruction. Death encapsulates an esthetic, an Austrian morbidity, and its embrace, its avoidance, its rituals permeate the author's remarkable memoir, which in one volume brings together the five separately published autobiographical books that cover Mr. Bernhard's childhood—really a failure of childhood—from the age of 8 to his early adulthood and near death at 18.

The five-part memoir appropriately begins with an act of supreme independence, a forever memorable moment of self-assurance and folly, when the young Thomas Bernhard, without any prior experience, mounts his guardian's bicycle and euphorically sets off in the direction of his aunt in Salzburg, almost covering the 20 miles, a journey that predictably ends in disaster. An exaggeration? That's immaterial. What we have is the author gazing at his past and thereby assessing the emergence and authenticity of his later rebellion. For someone like Mr. Bernhard, who readily concedes his role as troublemaker and flatly asserts, "I still am a troublemaker, with every breath I draw and in every line I write," the mem-oir is a means of waging an unremitting vituperative war on his unresolved past—on a father who died a violent death in 1943, never having set eyes on or acknowledged the existence of his illegitimate son; on a mother who longed to secure a foothold in the middle class; on his destitute family, which never considered itself a family; on the abhorrent institutions of learning that first were dominated by ferociously authoritarian Nazi instructors and then, following the war, by intensely doctrinaire Roman Catholics. The struggle is an endless one.

Mr. Bernhard selectively organizes this past in a way not inconsistent with the duplicitous and joyless world of his novels. Yet what he describes is not entirely free of pleasure. To begin with, there is the pleasure of excelling as a runner in school, though characteristically the author offers his boundless fear of losing as the reason for his success. Then there is the pleasure of music and his foolhardy determination despite a serious lung ailment to become a singer. Finally, during his enforced stay in the hospital he immerses himself in Verlaine, Trakl and Dostoyevsky.

What is missing, what appears to have been excised as if its mere mention might serve as an antidote to death, is sexuality. Equally curious is the absence of any mention of play in his childhood. Mr. Bernhard appears to exist in a world without games. His friends are few. . . .

Mr. Bernhard dwells on his failures: "My escape from the grammar school, my apprenticeship, my musical studies—all of them symptoms of my disobedience—came to assume in my own eyes all the dimensions of madness and grotesque megalomania." His escape from school leads him by choice to work in the cellar grocery of a housing project in the most disreputable and forsaken part of Salzburg. The outsider, the doomsman, in Mr. Bernhard cannot fail to respond to the opprobrium of the tenants—these undesirable fellow outsiders—who by simply living in the project had been shunned by the city under as well as following the Nazi regime. Finally Mr. Bernhard is no longer being tested. The housing project becomes his limbo, his selected failure. By neglecting his health he ultimately is able to escape into illness—by no means an unfamiliar escape for the writer-to-be. Emerging from a coma, he finds himself in a hospital's death ward, where he is given the last rites. Around him patients are dying like flies.

Somehow he survives the doctors, the treatments. His subsequent "escape" is to a sanitarium where he promptly contracts tuberculosis. More treatments, more surgery. Yet his mind is set on becoming a singer. Secretly he takes lessons from a woman organist in the village and sings in the church choir. As a musician, which he is at heart, Mr. Bernhard has brilliantly orchestrated these fiercely critical stages of his life. An apt summation of the memoir, composed as poignantly as Mahler's "Kindertotenlieder," is the author's observation: "I feel as though I were a diviner in my own mind." He concludes with: "My character is made up of all characters put together; my desires consist of all desires put together; and the same is true of my hopes and fears and desperations. There are times when only dissembling can rescue me and others when openness is called for."

Walter Abish, "Embraced by Death," in The New York Times Book Review, *February 16, 1986, p. 12.*

MICHAEL FEINGOLD

"A record like the present one," Thomas Bernhard writes, late in *Gathering Evidence,* "must naturally always be made in the knowledge that it is likely to be attacked or denounced, or quite simply dismissed as the product of a deranged mind. The writer must guard against letting himself be irritated by such a reaction or by the prospect of it, however ridiculous it may be. After all, he is used to having everything he says or writes attacked and denounced and dismissed as madness. . . . When he is dealing with facts he has no interest in opinion, from whatever quarter it comes. He is not for one moment prepared to alter his conduct or his way of thinking and feeling and thus become untrue to his own nature, even though he is of course aware that nothing can ever be more than an approximation of the truth . . . "

Aside from being an excellent specimen of Bernhard's neck-or-nothing torrent of prose (and of the fluid, slightly cloggy way David McLintock's translation catches it), this contradictory assemblage of burning paranoid pessimism, doughty integrity, and hapless ironic shrugs sums up the 55-year-old Austrian writer's vision of his place in the world. Spiky, contentious, an implacable believer in the hopelessness of all human activity, he is driven both to create literature and to mock it out of existence, to record life, laugh at it, weep over it, critique it and savage it by turns—all in a glorious stew of endless, self-readjusting German sentences, the variety and intricacy of which are the best possible arguments against the total negativity they seem to preach. Though gloom is Bernhard's native element, always the first thing seized on by skeptical critics, he's chiefly a comic, at times even a joyous, writer. His cascades of prose can have the same exhilarating effect as a whirlpool bath or a toboggan ride.

A block of his text that opens with the most dire prognostications can usually be relied on to turn itself upside down three or four times, contemplating its forebodings from a variety of angles, before rising to some tentative conclusion, by which time the next topic has delicately adumbrated itself, like a distant horn sounding a new theme in the coda of a symphonic movement. To recount the plot of a Bernhard novel or play without the aid of these twisty, spellbinding chains of words is no use: If the catalogue of misfortunes involved doesn't reduce a listener to either numbness or hysterical laughter, it suggests that the author is a morbid, self-pitying injustice collector, indeed a sort of lunatic. Bernhard, as the credo above implies, has grown inured to the misunderstanding that takes his subject for his tone, his views for his quality.

In fact the miseries he enumerates, like his pessimistic opinion of everything under the sun, are to him simply factual instances, notes on the scale with which he composes. Music, his first love and intended profession, determines the form of his works, and frequently their major theme as well: The driven hero of his novel *The Lime Works* is trying to write a treatise on human hearing; the narrator of *Concrete* is planning a definitive study of Mendelssohn. One play, *The Fool and the Madman,* takes place backstage at a performance of *The Magic Flute;* another, *Celebrities (Die Berühmten),* is a scathing attack on opera-world egos, set in a conductor's villa at the Salzburg Festival (which commissioned the work and then rejected it, triggering one of the numerous literary scandals that have dogged Bernhard's tracks). Maddest of all Bernhard's obsessive heroes is Caribaldi, the circus ringmaster of his comedy *Force of Habit,* who wants his troupe to

replace their routines with Schubert's "Trout" Quintet. "We don't want our lives," he says at one point, "but they must be lived. / We hate the Trout Quintet / but it must be played."

Given his steady output, which now comprises seven novels and over 15 plays, Bernhard may seem to be merely marketing despair, like an eccentric Austrian factory set up in Salzburg to churn out Beckett instead of bric-a-brac. Some of the reasons behind his life-hating, and even his "Trout" Quintet-hating, attitudes are offered in *Gathering Evidence,* a fat one-volume compendium of the five fragmentary memoirs Bernhard has devoted to various stages of his childhood and adolescence. It makes an ideal starting point for anyone sufficiently fascinated by the wheeling flights of Bernhard's prose to look past his reductive philosophy at his multifaceted art. Besides being his most accessible work in any form, this nightmarish account gives important clues, both psychological and historical, to the source of his pitch-dark vision, widening its scope to take in the whole society around him: The darkness he evokes may be unremitting, but it is both lively and populous as well. If his misery detests company, it still can't help setting a whole worldful in motion.

Born in 1931, Bernhard was illegitimate, the unwanted offspring of a freethinking Viennese couple's stolid, beautiful daughter by a local no-good, who immediately deserted her and never acknowledged the child. Rather than face the gossipmongers of the small Upper Austrian town where she lived, she snuck off to Holland; it was a year before she could summon up the courage to tell her parents. She boarded the infant Thomas with a wet-nurse who lived on a fishing boat in Rotterdam harbor. "I am told . . . that while I was on the trawler my face was covered with ugly boils, since there was an incredible stench and impenetrable fumes." At last she confessed to her parents (who, being freethinkers, welcomed her with open arms), and she brought the baby back, in a laundry hamper, to Austria.

Bernhard sees his mother's dim, obstinate drive for respectability as a defense against her charismatic, freewheeling father, a minor novelist and philosopher who would become the most significant influence on his grandson's life: The rebel son of a prosperous peasant family, he had renounced his inheritance to meander across Europe; his wife was a Nora Helmerish refugee from an arranged marriage with an older man. By the time of his grandson's birth he was living hand to mouth, off his wife's midwifery and his daughter's drudgery as a domestic servant. Cynic, anarchist, and village eccentric, he provided the affection and tutelage that sustained Bernhard through his childhood, teaching him to think, to love the arts, and to regard most other human institutions with loathing or suspicion. "Grandfathers are our teachers, our real philosophers," writes Bernhard. "They are the people who pull open the curtain that others are always closing."

In other ways, the curtain was pulled tightly shut. Bernhard's mother, who never let him forget that he was the great shame of her life, frequently whipped him as well as berating him verbally: *"You're the cause of all my unhappiness. Damn you! You've destroyed my whole life. . . . You're the death of me. You're a nothing. I'm ashamed of you. You're as useless as your father."* Eventually she married, and had two other children by a man apparently as stolid as herself. Her husband never formally adopted Bernhard, who refers to him throughout, stiffly, as "my guardian" or "my mother's husband." Unsurprisingly, the unloved child developed a streak of violent fantasy early on. . . .

School—after one short, idyllic period of living with his grandparents in the country—was also hell: The only activities Bernhard admits to enjoying were geography and, later, running—both modes of escape. (The latter did briefly lift his odd-man-out status by making him a local athletic champion.) As if the small-town stuffiness of Upper Austria during the Depression wasn't bad enough, the one job his "guardian" could find forced the whole family to move across the border to an equally small town in Bavaria. This put his grandfather, who had the cultivated Austrian's traditional contempt for everything German, in a state of perpetual ire. And the Hitler era was no time to be either a foreigner or an anarchist-cynic in rural Bavaria, motherland of fundamentalist bigotry. Thomas found himself despised as not only a bastard and a weirdo but a suspicious foreigner: "Going to school was like going to the scaffold, except that my ultimate decapitation was endlessly postponed."

Under the additional pressure of intense parental fear, he was shoved into the *Hitlerjugend.* . . . He became a chronic bedwetter, a new source of embarrassment and guilt that reached its apex, or perhaps nadir, when he was sent away for a "change of air," at what turned out to be a home for maladjusted children, in Thuringia, far to the north. Here he was publicly humiliated by having his stained bedsheets displayed every morning in the mess hall at breakfast, of which he was naturally deprived as part of his punishment. (p. 45)

The adolescent Bernhard divided his time between repressing his fear of the sadistic school headmaster, a devout Nazi, and watching Salzburg get gradually reduced to rubble and cemeteries: "The city had become gray and ghostly, and it seemed as though the only goods transported through the streets were consignments of coffins." The cynicism with which he naturally received any attempt to educate him under such circumstances was reinforced in 1945: Amid universal privation, with thousands dying of hunger and exposure, food, clothing, and shelter at a premium, and the pervasive stench of decomposed bodies oozing from the bombsites, the Nazi school magically turned back into a Catholic one, virtually unchanged, with a kindly priest replacing the jackbooted headmaster, and a cross where the picture of Hitler had hung.

Like the stench, Bernhard's bitterness became all-engulfing. . . . (pp. 45-6)

Hopelessness, however, could not prevent the 15-year-old Bernhard from taking action to escape. Among the many small triumphs, joys, and gestures of love that flash their rushlights across the dark landscape of *Gathering Evidence,* none is more heartening than the third of its five sections, "The Cellar," Bernhard's account of how one day he simply turned his back on school and discovered his independence through the most menial and unrespectable of jobs—hauling sacks, as a grocer's assistant, in a tiny basement grocery in Salzburg's seediest welfare housing project. The *lumpen* denizens of the project earn his respect and compassion for making the best of their doomed lives, just as he earns theirs by subjecting himself to the work and becoming a part, if an eccentric one, of the community. . . . (p. 46)

The last two segments, "Breath" and "In the Cold," are set successively in the terminal ward of a fetid local hospital, where he tests his own will to survive while watching the mostly elderly patients die off one by one, and in a mountain

sanitarium, where he is cured of his pleurisy but, with true Bernhardian inevitability, contracts tuberculosis. Though filled with horrific medical torments described in detail—like the sensation of having one's thorax punctured, then watching a pickle jar fill to the top with yellowy mucus drained from one's lungs—these closing sections are by no means the least pleasant in the work. Taking on the deranged assurance of a topsy-turvy *Bildungsroman,* they alternate a serenely mature tone, a growing acceptance of death and fate, with a mordant comic sense that finds delight in every grotesquery of the medical routine. . . .

During the two years of his illness, Bernhard loses both his grandfather and his mother, and his confinement provides long meditative opportunities for him to reevaluate their influence on him. He reconciles himself to both, as he does to death and to the unending human failure he sees around him. Perhaps most importantly, his lung condition forces him to give up singing, the vocation with which he has played cat-and-mouse since childhood, and begin writing: In the manner of Bernhard's tragicomic fictional paradoxes, this simultaneous account of the unmaking of a child and a society has all along, subliminally, also been the tale of a creative artist's nurturing and growth, a five-movement symphony of reminiscences working through the theme of childhood torment till it transforms into the resplendent coda of a calling discovered. Even its horror and bleakness are expressed through the delicacies of a music which the author may hate as a burden, but which he is nonetheless bound to go on creating, and which even the most reluctant reader may find gripping and beautiful. (p. 46)

Michael Feingold, "Bernhard's Bad Boyhood," in The Village Voice, *Vol. XXXI, No. 11, March 18, 1986, pp. 45-6.*

GEORGE STEINER

It was on the streets of Vienna, prior to 1914, that Adolf Hitler supped his fill of the racial theories, hysterical resentments, and anti-Semitism that were to make up his demonology. When Nazism came home to Vienna, in the spring of 1938, the welcome accorded it exceeded in fervor even that which it had received in Germany. Phantom forms of National Socialism, a scarcely diminished pulse of anti-Semitism, and a singular brew of obscurantism, partly ecclesiastical, partly rural, continue to characterize the climate of consciousness in the Austria of Kurt Waldheim. It is this witches' caldron which provokes the implacable indictments and satires of Thomas Bernhard. . . .

Bernhard is principally a writer of fiction—of novels, short stories, and radio plays. Prolific and uneven, he is at his best the foremost craftsman of German prose after Kafka and Musil. *Amras* (not yet translated into English); *The Lime Works,* the still untranslated *Frost* created a landscape of anguish as circumstantial, as closely imagined, as any in modern literature. The black woods, the rushing but often polluted torrents, the sodden, malignant hamlets of Carinthia—the secretive region of Austria in which Bernhard leads his wholly private life—were transmuted into the locale of a small-time inferno. Here human ignorance, archaic detestations, sexual brutality, and social pretense flourish like adders. Uncannily, Bernhard went on to extend this nocturnal, coldly hysterical vision into the high reaches of modern culture. His novel on Wittgenstein, *Correction,* is one of the towering achievements of postwar literature. His *Der Untergeher* (untranslated), a fiction centered on the mystique and genius of Glenn Gould, searches out the manic powers of music and the enigma of a talent for supreme execution. Musicology, erotic obsession, and the keynote of self-contempt distinctive of Bernhard give compelling strength to the novel *Concrete.* Between these peaks lie too many fictions and scripts imitative of themselves, automatically black. Yet even where Thomas Bernhard is less than himself the style is unmistakable. Heir to the marmoreal purity of Kleist's narrative prose and to the vibrancy of terror and surrealism in Kafka, Bernhard has made of the short sentence, of an impersonal, seemingly officious syntax, and of the stripping of individual words to their radical bones an instrument wholly fitted to its excoriating purpose. The early novels of Beckett will give the English reader some approximation of Bernhard's technique. But even in the most desolate of Beckett there is laughter.

Born in 1931, Bernhard spent his childhood and adolescence in pre-Nazi and Nazi Austria. The ugliness, the strident mendacity of that experience have marked his entire vision. From 1975 to 1982, Bernhard published five studies in autobiography. They span the period from his birth to his twentieth year. Now assembled into a continuous sequence, these memoirs make up *Gathering Evidence.* They recount the early years of an illegitimate child taken in, brought up by eccentric grandparents. They chronicle Bernhard's hideous school years under a sadistically repressive system, run first by Catholic priests, then by Nazis, then again by priests, the evident point being that there is little to choose between the two. The section called "The Cellar" narrates in paralyzing detail the young Bernhard's experiences in Salzburg when the city was being bombarded by the Allied Air Forces. The immediate postwar years were an oasis for Bernhard, who became an apprentice and a shop assistant to a Viennese grocer and witness to the temporary discomfiture of the Nazis, now so suddenly and surprisingly converted to democracy. Running errands for his dying grandfather, the old anticlerical and anarchic tiger whom Bernhard loved as he had loved no one else near him, the eighteen-year-old falls ill. He is consigned to a hospital ward for the senile and the moribund. (Such wards will become perennial in his later novels and in the inspired book—part fact, part invention—*Wittgenstein's Nephew.*) In the ward, Bernhard contracts tuberculosis. On the threshold of adult life, he finds himself under sentence of death. It is both in constant expectation of the fulfillment of that sentence and in defiance of it that he will escape into the armed citadel of his art. (p. 92)

Doctors are licensed torturers no less than teachers. Their contempt for the inner life of the patient, for the complex needs of the dying is exactly proportionate to their arrogance, to their lofty but hollow claims to expert knowledge. Bernhard's minute account of near-suffocation during injections of air into his chest is, intentionally, unbearable. It stands for a larger allegory of strangulation: by family circumstances, by schooling, by political servitude. He writes,

> The professor turned up at the hospital immediately and explained to me that what had happened was *nothing out of the ordinary.* He kept on repeating this emphatically, in an excited manner and with a malignant expression on his face which carried a clear hint of menace. My pneumothorax was now ruined, thanks to the professor's debate over his

luncheon menu, and something new had to be devised.

A worse, even more brutal intervention follows.

Within this "world-wide insanity," the insanity of Austria is by far the most loathsome. Bernhard lashes out at Austria's unctuous burial of its thoroughly Nazi past; at the megalomaniacal provinciality of Viennese culture; at the morass of superstition, intolerance, avarice in which the Austrian peasant or mountain-dweller conducts his affairs. Bernhard anathematizes a country that has made a systematic practice of ignoring, humiliating, or banishing its greater spirits, be they Mozart or Schubert, Schoenberg or Webern; an academic establishment that refuses to honor Sigmund Freud, even posthumously; a literary-critical code that exiles Broch and Canetti and relegates Musil to near-starvation. There are numerous precincts of hell, traced by human stupidity, venality, and greed. Vienna and Salzburg are the worst. In the province of Salzburg alone, two thousand human beings, many of them young, attempt suicide annually. A European record, but hardly, if we are to believe Bernhard, adequate to the motives: "The inhabitants of the city are totally cold; meanness is their daily bread and squalid calculation their characteristic trait." In a very recent novel, *Old Masters,* the palm of infamy is bestowed, beyond right of appeal, on the "stupidest," "most hypocritical" of all cities, which is Vienna.

The trouble with hatred is its shortness of breath. Where hatred generates truly classic inspiration—in Dante, in Swift, in Rimbaud—it does so in spurts, over short distances. Prolonged, it becomes a monotone, a blunted saw buzzing and scraping interminably. The obsessive, indiscriminate misanthropy in Bernhard, the around-the-clock philippics contra Austria threaten to defeat their own ends. He does not concede the fascination and genuine mystery of the case. The country, the society, that he so rightly chastises for its Nazism, for its religious bigotry, for its risible self-satisfactions happens also to be the cradle and setting for much of what is most fertile, most significant in all of modernity. The culture that spawned Hitler also bred Freud, Wittgenstein, Mahler, Rilke, Kafka, Broch, Musil, the Jugendstil, and what matters most in modern music. Excise Austria-Hungary and interwar Austria from twentieth-century history and you will lack not only that which is most demonic, most destructive, in that history but also its great springs of intellectual and aesthetic energy. You will lack the very intensities, the self-lacerating violence of spirit, that produced a Kraus and a Bernhard. What was once central to Europe became central to Western civilization. There are so many obvious ways in which American urban culture today, and particularly American Jewish urban culture, is a coruscating epilogue to fin-de-siècle Vienna and to that dynamo of genius and neurosis defined by the Vienna-Prague-Budapest triangle. To that heartland, mere hatred is a one-eyed guide. (p. 93)

George Steiner, "Black Danube," in The New Yorker, *Vol. LXII, No. 22, July 21, 1986, pp. 90-3.*

GARY INDIANA

Thomas Bernhard doesn't so much tell a story as chew one to pieces, distributing parts of it to various interlocutors, shuffling narrative time backward and forward in the space of a phrase or a sentence. The compulsive quality of his prose, its simulation of nervous chatter, its stress on the ultimate inaccuracy of narrative—these qualities have led most English and American critics to link Bernhard with Samuel Beckett. I think this tendency ought to be resisted; Bernhard's repetitions serve a very different purpose than Beckett's, and his characters inhabit a more palpable geopolitical continuum.

Despite their eccentric construction, Bernhard's recently re-issued novels, *Gargoyles* (1967) and *The Lime Works* (1970) are essentially linear narratives. In the episodic *Gargoyles,* a doctor describes a sequence of rural house calls he makes with his son. *The Lime Works* has a circular structure, opening with news of the murder which the rest of the book leads up to; the overall tale is pieced together by an insignificant figure, an insurance salesman who haunts the local inns trying to sell policies.

Both books are set in upper Austria, Bernhard's native territory, an archipelago of wretched towns and villages, full of unregenerated Nazism, "where Catholicism waves its brainless sceptre." In this miserable setting, peasant ignorance and provincial eccentricity are underscored by the steady encroachments of the consumer society, and the residue of Austrian high culture persists, pervertedly, in the lives of various individuals. Bernhard's main characters are usually autodidacts who have gone batty in splendid isolation, their meager contact with society both wholly unprofitable and endlessly irritating. All of Bernhard's novels describe twisted projects of self-improvement and ruined, or ruinous, aspirations, usually redolent of megalomania and delusions of grandeur. His narratives depict the contours of obsessed consciousness, perceived from both inside and outside. Often a friend or acquaintance of the narrator has gone mad or killed himself; the exposition begins in an external vantage-point and gradually enters the disintegrating mind under examination.

It's important in Bernhard's novels that some "objectivity," however specious, occasionally interrupts the ruminative, tireless, malcontented *ipsissima verba* of his fictional surrogates; even in *Concrete,* which maintains the first-person mode throughout, the first and last sentences identify the text as the writing of a "character," with the phrase "writes Rudolf." Bernhard means to offer a provisional version of events, to stress the margin of the unknowable that remains even after the staggering self-revelations of his creatures.

Bernhard tends to attack his themes in bizarre, elliptical strokes; *Gargoyles* achieves an unexpected symmetry by apparent indirection. At the outset, the narrator intends to discuss important family matters with his father: his mother's early death, his sister's most recent suicide attempt. He reports having written a long letter to his father about all this. However, before they can talk, an innkeeper turns up at their door; the innkeeper's wife has been assaulted (fatally, it turns out) by a drunken miner. Doctor and son travel to the inn, take the woman to the hospital, then visit a succession of distressed and dying patients in the countryside.

The relatively unexplored pathology of the narrator's family suffuses the overt pathologies that doctor and son encounter. Frau Ebenhöh, a widow whose brother was a murderer and whose son is a semi-retarded brute, languishes in terminal illness while reading *The Princess of Cleves,* a bust of Schubert standing near her bed; a nameless industrialist lives in a state of marriage with his half-sister, writing an immense philosophical treatise that he tears up as he goes along; Krainer, a potentially homicidal cripple, fills his room with defaced engravings of famous composers; and most grotesquely, the nephews of a deceased miller have decided to slaughter the miller's aviary of exotic birds. . . .

Gargoyles's odyssey culminates at Hochgobernitz Castle, where a deranged insomniac, Prince Saurau, regales the doctor and his son with a spectacular hundred-page monologue. The three walk along the inner castle walls, as if marooned in the first act of *Hamlet.* Prince Saurau's speech is a relentless torrent of psychological analysis verging on uncontrollable mania; it tears apart everything from the Austrian forestry service to the diseased relations between fathers and sons, in the Prince's case characterized by hereditary suicide. Like the doctor, the Prince has received a long letter from his son, a letter enumerating the son's plans to liquidate the father's estate, written as if the Prince had, like *his* father, already committed suicide.

Here the real subject of *Gargoyles* breaks through the surface of densely anecdotal description. In a destroyed culture, the past liquidates itself or is liquidated by its progeny; the stuff of culture is powerless against political and social ruin. . . .

In *The Lime Works,* provincial degeneration has an almost Chekhovian side effect of hysterical delusion. We immediately learn that Konrad, who bought the old lime works five years before, has killed his invalid wife with a shotgun she kept strapped to the wheelchair; local gossip, from which the narrator pieces together his story, offers conflicting versions of the crime. . . .

As *The Lime Works* arches back in time, Konrad is revealed as an obsessed dilettante who has lived off an inheritance for several decades. Sometime in the middle past, he decided to write the definitive work on auditory phenomena, *The Sense of Hearing,* a book only his burgeoning insanity qualifies him to write. He believes the old lime works is the ideal location in which to carry on his experiments, employing "the Urbanchich method." With his wife confined to her room, Konrad sells off their possessions to underwrite his research, turns the lime works into a heavily barricaded fortress, severs contact with friends and relatives, and proceeds to use his wife as a guinea pig for increasingly torturous auditory tests. . . .

Like many less maniacal Bernhard characters, Konrad cannot get any writing done. He is constantly on the verge of beginning, "has the whole book in his head," from moment to moment feels the writing urge welling up inside him; then someone knocks at the door, or Hoeller the lime works manager starts chopping wood, or his wife asks him to fetch a glass of cider from the cellar. Konrad's life is a series of maddening interruptions. Most of *The Lime Works* is an intricate unfolding of symbiotic craziness; as Konrad's torture of his wife becomes unremitting, she develops an elaborate repertoire of distractions, interruptions, and humiliations, ultimately forcing him to see his lifelong scientific project as an unrealizable, daft chimera.

The details of Konrad's final crack-up are offered as multivocal speculations. It's implied, for instance, that Konrad's hearing fails him several times just before the murder, that the murder itself may have been a gun-cleaning accident. In the penultimate passage, the babble of narrative doubles back on itself, further loosening the "progressive" version of Konrad's madness. . . .

Bernhard's strategy is revelatory; his novels restlessly worry bits of information, rehash events, play back snippets of speech and touches of character, until a completed picture locks into place, the last jigsaw piece snaps into its jagged niche.

Gary Indiana, "Gloom with a View," in The Village Voice, Vol. XXXI, No. 39, September 30, 1986, p. 56.

MARTIN CHALMERS

In German-Speaking Europe, Thomas Bernhard is both celebrated and notorious. Considered to be one of the most outstanding contemporary authors, his work and his public life have also been an unceasing provocation and insult to his surroundings. The objects of his disgust and mockery include most Germans, nearly all Austrians ('The Austrian is through and through national socialist and Catholic by nature . . . '), doctors (and especially psychiatrists), actors (and especially actors in some of his own plays), producers, publishers, subsidised writers, civil servants and politicians. He has frequently been taken to court for libel. He is entirely unreasonable, immoderate and *ill*-mannered. The Waldheim debacle can only have fuelled and confirmed his prejudices.

For more than 20 years, Bernhard has maintained an enviable output of novels, stories, plays and autobiography, despite his own judgment that 'to publish anything is folly and evidence of a certain defect of character'. It is a body of work which is extraordinarily unified, both in its themes—illness, dying, isolation, the punishment of familial relationships, the inability of language to communicate—and in its frequently labyrinthine discourse.

In an early story, Bernhard describes a man just released from prison: 'Like those of all [who are] subordinated, excluded, his speech was clumsy, everywhere open, comparable to a body full of wounds, in which anyone at any time can scatter salt . . . ' Bernhard has been determined to avoid such vulnerability in his work, even though his own body has been repeatedly vulnerable to illness. In *Wittgenstein's Nephew* he writes: 'When I rebel or resist, when I have to take arms against the world's outrageousness, I do not wish to be the loser, to be annihilated by it.'

It would be wrong to see Bernhard as a 'political writer'; the radical or reformer cannot take any more comfort from him than the conservative Catholics of Austria. It would also be mistaken to take his art of hyperbole entirely at face value. Like a great comic or clown, his tragedy can always turn into comedy, even if grotesque, and vice versa. And despite the grimness of Bernhard's themes and the perfection of his prose readers will frequently find themselves taken unawares by laughter: 'This was the fourth crime this year in these parts she said, and reminded Frau Edenhöh of the strangled potter, the throttled schoolmistress, both from Ligist, and Horch, the Afling furrier, who had been shot. Unpacking the bread and butter, she said: "It's the sultry weather.' " . . .

Bernhard has no time for a sentimental view of the goodness of nature, of nature as health. Such a sentimentality is based on an ignorant sense of superiority. Illness is as much nature as health; is, indeed, the 'fist-sized tumour' in Bernhard's thorax at the beginning of *Wittgenstein's Nephew.* Perhaps the most consistent of Bernhard's provocations is to confront the illness, death and incapacity which the late 20th-century sensibilities have tried to ban from (everyday) life. . . .

Bernhard's style [in *The Lime Works* (1973) and *Gargoyles*

(1967)] is at first sight perhaps somewhat strange. He composes and arranges rather than plots his work. There is little description, characterisation, direct speech or action; he proceeds by making an incident or insight the theme for variation and modulation before leading into the next theme. It is a very musical approach to the writing of prose. The spiralling sentences, which exclude any other reality except their own, which allow no objective position, are a product of a scepticism of the truth expressible in language. At the same time it produces writing which, even in translation, is a pleasure to read aloud, which is always capable of surprise. . . .

[*Wittgenstein's Nephew* is] much lighter than the earlier novels—perhaps surprisingly, since its subject is a friend dying—much closer to the conventional material of autobiography and memoir. The writing rage comes as less of an attack and is moderated by tenderness and regret. Paul Wittgenstein, nephew of the famous philosopher and, like him, despised by a wealthy family, was one of the few Austrians who could share the extremity of Bernhard's abstentionism and match his mental and physical pain. And yet as Paul dies, Bernhard, the narrator, like the other former friends, is unable to cope with it, and participates in the discrimination against the sick by the healthy. Perhaps, he tries to argue with himself, he does not visit Paul out of a desire to avoid embarrassing his friend.

Like virtually everything Bernhard has written it is remarkable, not least for its outrageous comic scenes (the scandal that Bernhard achieves on accepting a state literary prize, for example; a futile chase through the Austrian countryside for a foreign newspaper). And the more one reads, the more each individual work grows in force and reverberates with the others. However, much, much more still remains to be translated of Bernhard's unique work on our unending 'last days'.

Martin Chalmers, "An Illness Called Austria," in New Statesman, Vol. 113, No. 2915, February 6, 1987, p. 27.

FRANCIS KING

The Paul Wittgenstein of this brief memoir [*Wittgenstein's Nephew*] is not the celebrated pianist—brother of the no less celebrated philosopher, Ludwig—who, having lost an arm in the first world war, commissioned composers as various as Richard Strauss, Ravel and Britten to write for him works which he then performed with an aplomb and brilliance far beyond the capacity of most two-handed executants. This Paul is a nephew, celebrated, if at all, as a 'character' in Vienna, but nonetheless regarded by the author, for reasons never wholly substantiated, as a man as intellectually remarkable as either of his distinguished uncles.

The memoir opens in 1967, when the two men, already friends, are dangerously ill in adjoining pavilions (as the translation has it) of the same hospital. The author appears to be dying after the removal of a fist-sized tumour from his thorax. Wittgenstein has been confined in a strait-jacket after yet another of the nervous breakdowns that have afflicted him, with increasing ferocity, after the age of 35. It has often been said of Bernhard that he is obsessed with illness and mortality, and these first pages, describing his fellow patients, most of them doomed and all of them suffering acutely, project that obsession. How accurate is his account? When the mental patients strayed from their pavilion into the other one, were they really driven back, screaming, by attendants with rubber truncheons? When in the open space between the two pavilions, the chest patients dropped tissues, did squirrels really snap them up, to race into the trees with them? Certainly these images, like many others in the book, have a morbid power.

Friends of the pianist Wittgenstein (who, oddly, is never once mentioned) have reported that he could at once identify any three or four bars from any score presented to him at random. (His philosopher brother shrugged off this ability—'If you are learned, you are learned'.) Bernhard presents the younger Paul as having the same kind of musical erudition. Other consuming interests are motor-racing—in his prime, he himself is a racing-driver, and in later years he entertains such champions as Jackie Stewart and Graham Hill in his house outside Vienna—and sailing. His madness at first manifests itself in what appears to be no more than eccentricity, as when he gives away large sums from his rapidly diminishing fortune to undeserving strangers or hires a taxi to drive him from Vienna to Paris and back again. Slowly, his periods of insanity become more and more frequent and violent, his family wish to have less and less to do with him, and he sinks deeper and deeper into poverty, solitude and despair.

The author certainly evokes one's pity for this man of outstanding talents and—during his periods of insanity—no less outstanding charm. What he does not succeed in doing is to persuade one, as he clearly intends, that here was a man of unacknowledged genius. 'The one, Ludwig, was *possibly* more philosophical, while the other, Paul, was *possibly* crazier; but it may also be that we believed the one, the philosophical Wittgenstein, to be a philosopher only because he put his philosophy down on paper and not his craziness, and the other, Paul, to be a lunatic merely because he had suppressed and not published his philosophy and only displayed his madness.' The antithesis is a neat one; but little that one reads supports it.

As so often, this memoir really tells one more about its author than its subject. When Paul—whom Bernhard has claimed to be his closest, perhaps even his only, friend—eventually trails, bereft of his wife and mortally ill, through the streets of Vienna in canvas shoes, a shopping bag in either hand, Bernhard, so far from seeing what he can do to help him, hurries away in the opposite direction, hoping that he has not been noticed. 'We avoid those who bear the mark of death,' he writes. Later, realising that this is hardly excuse enough for his conduct, he confesses: 'I am not a good character, I am not, quite simply, a good man.' One guesses that here is one of those people who believe that, if one says 'Oh God, what a shit I am!' with sufficient vehemence, that absolves one from doing anything about being less of one. The memoir contains two bizarre accounts of what happened when Bernhard, who says that he disapproves of prizes—those who give a prize to an author are merely 'spitting on him'—went to receive two prizes in Austria. Clearly he believes that on each occasion everyone behaved monstrously to him, but to the reader it is his behaviour which, if not monstrous, is reprehensible. (pp. 35-6)

Francis King, "*More About Its Author than Its Subject,*" in The Spectator, *Vol. 258, No. 8274, February 7, 1987, pp. 35-6.*

NICHOLAS EISNER

Because of the concentration on illness, madness and death in his work as a whole, Thomas Bernhard and his work have until recently often been classified—and dismissed—as nihilistic, without further thought being given to the matter. As can be seen from a reading of any of Bernhard's texts, whether prose or drama, nihilistic is a suitable, but nevertheless incomplete, classification of this product. It is incomplete because the ease with which the nihilism is perceived leads one to suspect that it is perhaps a façade covering something else and that Bernhard might well be a poseur, "a literary figure excelling in brilliant but destructive artistry using nihilism as an expedient" rather than a "true nihilist who bases his beliefs on valid data about the world surrounding him," as A. P. Dierick has suggested [in *Modern Austrian Literature* (Vol. 12, 1979)]. And, from a similar perspective, Martin Esslin has observed that, as far as Bernhard's plays are concerned, although the themes are the same as those of his prose works, there is an atmosphere of ambivalence about them [see *CLC,* Vol. 32]. This, combined with certain changes in style resulting from the move from prose to drama, produces what Esslin calls "a strangely disturbing effect" and leads one to question the grimness and nihilism which otherwise dominate. This is especially so when one considers the complexities and ironies of Bernhard's work, which are more fully developed and thus more easily perceived in his plays than in his prose works. However, it seems to me that although Esslin pinpoints an essential element of Bernhard's plays he does little more than observe that the audience willingly subjects itself to a stream of ridicule from Bernhard. This would make Bernhard simply an aggressive and cynical writer. In performance, however, his plays have a sly, humorous air about them which belies this conclusion. Such observations raise questions regarding the contrast between the nihilism and the irony in these plays. And upon examination of this contrast we encounter an interesting and, to my knowledge, as yet overlooked feature of Bernhard's plays. It seems to me that the ambivalence and disturbing effect of these plays is not only carefully engineered to place the audience in an unusual situation, but that Bernhard has also developed a form of theatre which is in keeping with trends in (post-modern) writing in recent years which I shall examine more closely later.

The main point to note about the nihilism of Bernhard's plays—as of his prose—is that it is derived essentially from a highly repetitive style of language, which does not allow the development of plot, character and genuine dialogue. In addition to this linguistic device are the dramatic ones of portraying grotesque situations and of using visibly oppressive settings. The continued concentration on these elements and the fact that Bernhard has consistently used the same style for all of his published work has led Esslin to suggest that Bernhard is indulging in a form of mannerism. He defines mannerism as the predominance of technique over content, in which "how" becomes more important than "what." This predominance of form or technique over content definitely seems to be the case with Bernhard. As far as drama is concerned, this means that it is no longer simply a literary genre, but in its very form is a physical presentation of an idea ("eine dargestellte Idee")—or in other words, the form is the idea. Consequently, Bernhard's figures are merely "verkörperte Funktionen," (personified functions) used to illustrate the concept which generates them. What they are and what they say is entirely subordinated to a concept which extends beyond each individual play and which governs Bernhard's dramatic production as a whole. As such they are instruments in a performance and exposition of an idea or technique—a metaphor which is given concrete form in the figures and instruments of the play *Die Macht der Gewohnheit* (*The Force of Habit*). Once it is accepted that the structure is more important than the content we can see that the nihilism of Bernhard's work—at least on the level of the expression of a personal philosophy of "Weltanschauung"—is hard to take seriously.

This is especially so when one considers the ironies surrounding his work, particularly his plays. These ironies, which seem as intentional as the static form of the monologues which dominate the plays, soften the harsh impressions of grimness and gloom which Bernhard goes to such lengths to create, so much so, in fact, that one begins to question both the purpose behind the plays and their artistic seriousness. (pp. 104-05)

Bernhard's work seems to fit into the category known as metafiction—or, more appropriately for the plays, "metadrama"—in which the conventions of narrative form are made the narrative's focal subject. In a metadrama this refocalisation is the result of the text self-consciously and systematically declaring its status as a (dramatic) artifact. In other words, it makes clear that it is a *performance* of a prepared text by a group of actors who have either rehearsed or performed this text previously. Such a performance draws attention not only to the involvement of many people beyond the actors on the stage, but also to the very nature of drama and the cultural phenomenon of theatre-going itself. (p. 106)

[The] presence of irony in these "nihilistic" plays is contradictory and results in a sense of uncertainty—a tension of opposition; the mannerism involved in the creation of this nihilism is clearly self-conscious and appears to be structured according to a set literary programme, and as a result of the combination of these two features we begin to see the "game" Bernhard is playing in which he seems to be toying with, or teasing, his audience. And as further evidence of the metadramatic and game-like nature of Bernhard's plays we can see that they embody another feature common in metafiction—self-reflexiveness. This is most obvious in the passages depicting or discussing the artist's own creative experience, but is also involved in the use of general and self-referential parody. In this last respect we can see the title figures of the plays *Immanuel Kant* (1978) and *Der Weltverbesserer* (*The World Reformer,* 1979) as (ironic) references to Bernhard himself. In the play *Immanuel Kant* the title character is not the Kant of historical fame but a madman who is celebrated as a great philosopher. And in *Der Weltverbesserer* the title figure is celebrated for his treatise on the improvement of the world, but as he himself tells us he seems to have been badly misunderstood because his plans call for the destruction of the world before it can be improved. As can be seen, there appears to be a strong element of self-irony on Bernhard's part in these two plays. Both figures are misunderstood in a similar way to which he has been generally misunderstood, but in reverse: Whereas the Kant of the play is mad, Bernhard is not, and although the "Weltverbesserer" calls for the destruction of the world, Bernhard does not. However, these are similar to accusations which have been levelled at Bernhard himself. What better way to mock his accusers than to write more plays generated by their accusations, and thus further increase his literary fame? In similar vein the title of the play *Der Schein trügt* (*Appearances are Deceptive,* 1983) can

also be seen as evidence of his sense of having been misinterpreted, although it begins to appear that he wanted this to happen in the first place as it seems to be a vital part of the whole concept. Further irony is to be found in the titles of the plays *Vor dem Ruhestand* (*Eve of Retirement,* 1979), *Am Ziel* (*At One's Goal,* 1981) and *Über allen Gipfeln ist Ruh* (*Rest Beyond the Peaks,* 1981). The irony here lies in the optimism hinted at in these titles. Such optimism contrasts strongly with the nihilism which is often observed in Bernhard's work and which is to be found primarily in the continual struggle against fear and despair. Therefore, these titles would seem to be highly ironic because it simply is not possible to achieve any respite from the torments of life in his world—and none is shown in these plays.

However, the most striking irony has to do with the theme of communication and seems to encompass his work as a whole. Bernhard's "nihilism" is a concept which is well worked out, and it rests largely on the problems of language as our main means of communication. As I mentioned above, Bernhard's figures are constantly struggling against fear and despair. One of the main reasons for this is that they are unable to discuss this with those around them and thus relieve their pain because language disguises the truth. Therefore, the figures must continue suffering in isolation as they are unable to communicate. According to Bernhard this is a universal phenomenon and all he is doing in his work is to portray this reality. However, although Bernhard constantly denies the possibility of communication in his work as well as in interviews and speeches, he not only publishes "in steter Folge" (in constant succession) but is also commercially successful both as an author and a playwright. This would seem to indicate that he is communicating to at least some of his readers and audience on some level or other, otherwise he would have been rejected long ago. In fact, this potential for understanding his work is actually built-in by Bernhard, despite his claims to the contrary.

One of the features of his work which is clearly meant to be understood is, of course, the irony itself. For example, in the play *Die Macht der Gewohnheit* (*The Force of Habit,* 1974) we have the recurrent phrase "Morgen in Augsburg" (Augsburg tomorrow). Esslin points out that this phrase carries four separate overtones within the play itself, and one which goes beyond this particular play. Within the play the phrase is used in the following ways: as an indication of the transitoriness of the present situation and of hope for the future; contempt for Augsburg as a filthy second-rate provincial city; a threat to the ringmaster Caribaldi's grand-daughter; and as the final line in the play an admission of hopelessness and defeat. But beyond the confines of the play itself we have a further meaning, one which refers to Bernhard's basic dramatic concept. For, as Esslin notes, Augsburg is Brecht's home town and thus "exemplifies an epic theatre of plot and meaning, everything that Bernhard's theatre emphatically tries *not* to be." None of these first four overtones can be felt unless we understand the rest of the play, and the fifth requires an understanding of drama history and dramatic theory. However, while this fifth overtone is less obvious, all five must be understood if they are to be effective. In fact, if the play is to be effective at all, then at least the first four must be understood—a requirement that would appear to be expected by Bernhard. As such he is contradicting himself (consciously, it seems). While he claims on the one hand that communication is not possible, on the other he implants these ironic overtones in his plays which need to be understood for these plays to be successful.

A further example of irony and the possibility of understanding it is to be found in the play *Der Präsident* (*The President*, 1975). In this play the dictatorial President of the title drinks a toast to Metternich, in apparent reference to the Austrian arch-reactionary. However, to a German-speaking audience there is a further (ironical) meaning, for Metternich is also a brand of champagne—presumably the kind the President is drinking as he makes the toast. Again, although this second meaning will only be understood by those in the know, it *can* be understood and is clearly meant to be.

By way of contrast, a phrase which can be understood by everyone and not just by those in the know is the final line of *Immanuel Kant*—"Sie haben mich erkannt" (They have recognised me/They have seen through me). In this play the title character is not the Kant of historical fame but a madman who is celebrated as a great philosopher and who is on his way to America to have his eyes operated on. Yet when he arrives in New York, instead of being met by doctors who are to operate on his eyes as expected, he is met by doctors from a mental hospital who take him away to their asylum. Kant's final line, therefore, is not only loaded with irony and ambiguity, but also refers back to the play itself and makes clear the true nature of Kant's "philosophy" and of the play as a whole. For this Kant is unquestionably a madman but is revered as a great philosopher because he makes such profound statements as:

> Alles was ist
> ist
> alles was nicht ist
> ist nicht
> Die Welt ist die Kehrseite
> der Welt
> Die Wahrheit ist die Kehrseite
> der Wahrheit
>
> (Everything that is
> is
> everything that is not
> is not
> The world is the flip side
> of the world
> Truth is the flip side
> of the truth)

The play is full of such statements, which Esslin calls a "deliberate flood of derisive nonsense," and which he feels are there to test the audience's capacity to remain solemnly interested in the play. Consequently, the final line can be seen as a jibe at the audience for having sat out this performance, but a jibe which depends on their having (or not having!) understood the rest of the play. The other figures in the play accept Kant as a great philosopher because of his "profound" statements. Clearly they are fools and are mockingly treated by their creator, Bernhard. By analogy, if the audience accepts Kant's supposed philosophical greatness on the strength of what they hear and see during the performance, then Bernhard is mocking them too. However—and this is the point Esslin makes—if the audience understands that Kant is mad, but waits until the end for confirmation of this, then Bernhard is also mocking them for having sat through the rest of the performance. It is this toying with the audience that finally undermines Bernhard's nihilism and makes one question the seriousness with which his plays are received and which

leads us to a further re-assessment of Bernhard's play complex.

In this respect Esslin feels that the public is being confronted with a mass of horror which it believes is a reflection of itself and, because it is inclined to take such things seriously, ignores the possibility of irony and is blissfully unaware of the joke being played on it. From this perspective it seems that Bernhard goes to great lengths to create a performance of such stunning grimness that, as Herbert Gamper says [in *Thomas Bernhard*], the members of the audience will be left at the end "wie erschlagen" (as if thunderstruck), and "reglos in ihren Sesseln" (motionless in their seats), while he sits watching them, laughing at their failure to see the deception being played on them. Consequently, because of this radical alteration in the focus of these plays, they are not simply plays in the usual sense, but what Gamper calls "Theatertheater" in which the whole process of a dramatic performance—including the audience's reaction—is made the actual subject of the play, and in which the conventions and artificiality of such a performance are laid bare for examination.

This, of course, is highly metadramatic. But to support this observation we have to be able to find examples not only of elements of a "game" resulting from Bernhard's playfulness, but also of such a "laying bare" of the conventions and artificiality of a theatrical performance. For this we can turn to the figure of the playwright in *Die Jagdgesellschaft* (*The Hunting-Party*, 1974), who, as we shall see, is engaged in the same activity as Bernhard when he creates him and the play itself. Within the play it is the function of the playwright figure to reveal to the General the realities of the latter's existence. Working in tandem with this is an awareness on the part of the General that the playwright is turning his life into a play—which is, of course, the one the audience is now seeing. Thus the playwright is doing exactly what Bernhard claims to be doing in his plays—revealing to his audience that life is made up of illness, madness and death. Consequently it comes as no surprise when we are told that the playwright is in the process of writing a play about a similar hunting-party—one that will presumably be entitled *Die Jagdgesellschaft.* As Esslin says, there can be no doubt that this playwright clearly represents Bernhard himself. Further confirmation of this self-representation is to be found in the fact that the play this figure is writing is one in which "improbable horrors are accumulated for an audience who will take them for tragedy while they are in fact parody, farce." Again, it comes as no surprise that this is exactly what *Die Jagdgesellschaft* is. The "improbable horrors" which accumulate in this play all concern the General—his sight is failing, he loses his political office as a member of the Government, has his beloved wood cut down because it is diseased, learns of his wife's adultery, and hears that he is incurably ill. But, although it appears to be a tragedy, this play is actually a savage parody—of Chekhov's *The Cherry Orchard*. This combination of internal self-reflexivity and external parody puts into question, if not completely destroys, the ostensibly tragic nature of this play. It is also an extremely metadramatic combination.

A similar mix of "traditional" dramatic elements combines in *Die Macht der Gewohnheit* to produce a somewhat different effect to that of *Die Jagdgesellschaft*. The basic situation of this play is obviously ridiculous—a group of circus artists attempting a perfect rendition of Schubert's *Forellenquintett* (*Trout Quintet*) in a circus caravan—and the possibilities of the situation are played out to the full. Therefore we have the ever-hopeful, but desperately resigned phrase "Morgen in Augsburg" recurring throughout, plus the slapstick of the clown's hat falling off and the forcing of the lion-tamer to play the piano with bandaged hands after having been mauled by his animals. As has been noted by some critics, the presence of so many humorous elements weakens the horror of the play, but such criticism ignores the fact that it purposely carries the mood of the play into the realm of the absurd. However, to class Bernhard's plays as absurd is to miss what seems to me to be both their purpose and their most interesting feature. Like so many of Bernhard's plays *Die Macht der Gewohnheit* focusses on artists and one aspect of the artistic process—in this case performance. What is so remarkable about this particular play is that it is about one type of artist, the circus performer, attempting perfection in another artistic field, music, but which in turn is being performed in the theatre by yet another type of artist, an actor. It is this telescoping of the layers of performance, this sense of *mise en abyme* (also present in *Die Jagdgesellschaft*), which is important here and which adds to the metadramatic nature of Bernhard's play complex. (pp. 106-11)

Although they do not all contain such clear-cut examples, many of Bernhard's plays do seem to be made up of several internal layers plus some external ones. Therefore, the particular text in question is like a Chinese box which not only has many ever smaller ones inside it, but is itself also contained within many ever larger ones. Our smaller boxes are the internal references of the text (such as the playwright writing the play in which he is presently appearing, in *Die Jagdgesellschaft*) and the larger ones are the intertextual references (such as to *The Cherry Orchard* or *King Lear*) and, extending beyond that, the whole concept of drama, literature and, especially in the case of Bernhard, to the theatrical nature of life itself. Therefore, in this structure of Chinese boxes the members of the audience are no longer passive observers of a performance of a dramatic text, but have been drawn into a never-ending cycle of active participation. It is only when we distance ourselves from Bernhard's texts that we can see the whole process: Bernhard plays out the "game" so consistently and successfully that we must do this to see the whole process from start to finish—from the commencement of writing, through the actors' rehearsals, to the actual performance—which includes the procedure of people buying tickets and going to the theatre, etc.—and beyond, to the critical response to this performance. All of this becomes the subject of Bernhard's plays, not just what is printed in the text. Consequently, the audience is just as much the subject of each performance as the text itself. This means that it will have difficulty in interpreting the play it is attending because it is too close to this deceptive core to have a broad enough critical perspective to assess the whole. Because of this the audience tends to come to the conclusion that Bernhard is (deadly) serious and to say that his nihilistic plays are a metaphor for man's tragic condition. However, if we step back and look more deeply into the ironies and structural layers of these plays, we can see that this reaction has been carefully engineered by Bernhard: It is the result of what Esslin calls the serious-minded "consumers of culture" having been unwittingly drawn into the centre of the "game," from which position they can only superficially interpret his theatrical work. As such, Bernhard cannot be classed as a nihilist. Prankster would be more apt, for he has perfected a form of drama in which the audience is no longer a passive observer, but is the active subject and victim of a gigantic hoax. (pp. 111-12)

Nicholas Eisner, "Theatertheater/Theaterspiele: The Plays of Thomas Bernhard," in Modern Drama, *Vol. XXX, No. 1, March, 1987, pp. 104-14.*

IRVING MALIN

This remarkable novel [*The Lime Works*] begins with three dots. We are plunged into the middle of things. We discover that Konrad has murdered his wife. But the murder is a mysterious event—the townspeople cannot agree on the causes, on the psychology of Konrad and his victim. Thus from the opening of the novel we are informed subtly that reality is fictional, that even hideous acts cannot be explicated, that psychology and sociology are limited guides.

The matter is more complicated. We learn (or overhear) that Konrad is a hypersensitive expert, that he is (has been) trying to write a book about *The Sense of Hearing*. We recognize that "hearing" resembles "reading" and "interpretation." The very fact that the townspeople gossip about—or, better yet, *read*—Konrad in contradictory ways demonstrates that they resemble Konrad; they also cannot establish the correct construction, meaning, significance. The irony is great because there is double vision—it appears that Konrad is a "character" in their fictions and that they are "characters" in his mind. Reality melts—we cannot interpret Konrad (and his "odd" doubles) in any solid, enduring way.

Bernhard is, of course, the creator of Konrad and the townspeople. He refuses to give us simple dialogue, paragraphs, spaces. His paragraphs are long, convoluted ones that enclose the various events (or interpretations). He forces us to become obsessive detectives, to become hypersensitive to every word. His dense style deliberately encircles us. Therefore he "creates" victim-readers; we parallel his characters.

There are reasons for these mirrors of perception. We realize that we are reading a text, that we are listening to an obsessive voice. We cannot get out. Nor can we enter. There is a subtle game. We become so careful that we are accomplices in experience. Yet we are also alone—as is Konrad—because our interpretations vary. If I read the text in a certain way—this way!—I am trapped in my special "lime works."

Bernhard recognizes Wittgenstein as a hero. (Konrad refers to the philosopher several times.) Language—overheard or overread—is never in accord with reality. "Reality" is a word; "murder" is a word. Such words can never be understood by the crowd. The individual is trapped by language—his special text. I destroy Bernhard's novel because I conform it to my needs; I, like Konrad, am a killer—criticism is, if you will, destruction. How different is it from Konrad's actions?

Bernhard refers to Francis Bacon, the painter. (Konrad owns a painting.) Bacon, like Wittgenstein, mutilates existence. His figures are viewed from perverse perspectives, odd angles. His art is one of dislocation.

The Lime Works is a noble achievement. It is beautifully cruel. It murders and creates us. (pp. 196-97)

Irving Malin, in a review of "The Lime Works," in The Review of Contemporary Fiction, *Vol. VII, No. 2, Summer, 1987, pp. 196-97.*

MICHAEL FEINGOLD

The dinner party you never wanted to go to—you know, the one at which you loathe all the guests on sight, the food is pure swill, and the hosts are creeps from your past whom you just ran into again by regrettable coincidence—is one of the basic experiences of Western civilization. Still, nobody had pinned it definitively on paper till Thomas Bernhard, the great pessimist-rhapsodist of contemporary German literature, wrote *Woodcutters.* As chronicled by Bernhard's usual narrator, a mistrustful, embittered "I," the after-theater supper at the center of this short novel makes an evening at Madame Verdurin's (the previous record holder in the field of ghastly dinner parties) look as jolly as the Artists' and Models' Ball.

As in many of Bernhard's previous novels and plays, culture—the set of art objects and artistic conventions in which a civilization mirrors itself—is the source of the hero's distress: The party-givers are a horrid couple named Auersberger, the wife a dilettante singer from a wealthy family, the husband a seedy, alcoholic composer manqué whom the narrator once admired as a "successor to Webern" and a "Novalis of sound." The link that brings "I" to their house despite his distaste is a dead woman, Joana, an ex-lover of the narrator's whom he met through the Auersbergers and who has now hanged herself—a failed actress and dancer who, unlike the Auersbergers, has succeeded in recognizing her failure and removing herself from mediocrity.

The murky connection between a woman's pitiful death and a cultural excursus of some kind is a recurring theme in Bernhard, and particularly makes *Woodcutters* a mirror-image of his last novella, *Concrete,* in which the woman is a stranger to the narrator, her death occurs at the end rather than the start of the story, and the cultural delving it disrupts is personal rather than public (the "I" of *Concrete,* a musicologist, has gone to an off-season resort island to tackle his much-postponed study of Felix Mendelssohn). Using the news of Joana's death, the Auersbergers have persuaded the "I" of *Woodcutters* to attend a supper in honor of a popular actor, currently being celebrated for his performance as Hjalmar in a production of *The Wild Duck*—a play in which, not coincidentally, an interfering fool's misplaced idealism causes a confused young girl to commit suicide.

This last little mirror-game is one of many buried in the dense text of *Woodcutters,* which, as usual with Bernhard, is an unparagraphed flow of long, complex sentences, alternating a Jamesian stateliness and reserve with headlong rushes of compulsive, hysterical outrage, just as the narrator's moment-by-moment excruciations at the supper party alternate with his recollections of Joana's small-town funeral and the subsequent meal at the local tavern. (pp. 4-5)

The Auersbergers and their other guests—all pilloried by Bernhard, a gallery of insect specimens impaled on the pins of his loathing—are those who have given up, who've let their art settle into the muddle of a compromise with life. . . . The beauty of Bernhard is that he never compromises, never makes peace with life. "I" is last seen running "without knowing why," away from these ex-friends of the 1950s into "the dangerous, benighted, mindless eighties," where he will purge himself of the nightmarish dinner party by writing it out. Far from settling Bernhard's account with life, this act only created a new debit: *Woodcutters* was pulled off the market for a time, when it first came out in Austria, because one of Bernhard's victims recognized his portrait, and thought it sufficiently insulting to sue for libel. Countersue, one should really say, since Bernhard's works are really an ongoing indictment of life, more and more richly detailed and beautifully phrased, for being everything that we know it shouldn't be and is. Only in the pure, fierce isolation of his art can he get justice. (p. 5)

Michael Feingold, in a review of "Woodcutters," in VLS, No. 63, March, 1988, pp. 4-5.

MARTIN CHALMERS

The settings of Thomas Bernhard's recent novels are much more recognisably contemporary than those of earlier masterpieces like *Gargoyles* and *The Lime Works*. . . . Instead of an archaic rural Austria, the milieu is modern, urban Vienna, and the material the novels draw on is more evidently autobiographical.

There are risks in this shift. The targets of Bernhard's outrageous invective and withering observation of human weakness have become more identifiable and less universal. His towering scorn and disgust are sometimes in danger of overbalancing, when its objects are the puny figures of Viennese arts and letters.

The narrator of *Cutting Timber* [published in the United States as *Woodcutters*] finds himself condemned to attending an "artistic dinner party". It takes place on the evening after a funeral. The dead woman, who committed suicide, had been a friend both of the narrator and the hosts. The novel consists of a single, obsessive, hyperbolic monologue reflecting on the course of the dinner party, the funeral and the relationship between the narrator himself, the dead woman, the hosts and some of the other guests.

He accuses himself of a failure of nerve in accepting an invitation to an occasion he was bound to hate. From the security of a wing chair, he castigates the avarice and vanity of everyone present. However, the reader is on shaky ground in believing anything the narrator says—so often does he reverse statements and turn them back on himself. Finally, he behaves just as hypocritically as every other guest.

It would be equally unwise to collapse into one the identities of narrator and author. Nevertheless, some artists, including friends of Bernhard, recognised themselves in certain of the descriptions, objected to the characterisations—and took him to court. Bernhard is obviously determined to go to some lengths to avoid being absorbed into the artistic establishment.

The attacks on the pretentions of an artistic life overshadowed by the giants of Viennese traditions (the drunken host, who takes to waving his lower denture about at one point, is a minor follower of Webern) and on the links between art and social climbing are not so central to this novel as might at first appear. More searching are the considerations of our inability to cope with death and the erosion of the rituals that used to accompany it. A large place, too, is taken by reflections on friendship: the suddenness with which ties of apparently lifetime importance can be broken and replaced by indifference; how regret can turn to hatred.

The narrator even displays a degree of tenderness in his regard for the dead woman, Joanna. Her life had fallen apart when the male artist, with whom she had lived and who she "scared out of mediocrity", had left her. More unexpectedly, perhaps, the novel itself also concludes on a note of tenderness, even optimism.

The activities of walking and running have always been important within Bernhard's writing. A quality of his prose is a constant, almost physical attempt to outrun the constraints of words and the constraint of bodily frailty. This aspect assumes an almost celebratory charge at the end of **Cutting Timber.** Having been the last to leave the party (perhaps to be a more convincing liar in expressing his thanks to the hostess) the narrator begins to run towards the city centre:

> . . . and I ran and ran and ran, as if now in the eighties I were once more escaping from the fifties and into the eighties, into these dangerous and helpless and brainless eighties . . . and I reflected while running now through the inner city that this city was nevertheless my city and always would be my city and that these people were my people and always would be my people and I ran and ran . . .

> *Martin Chalmers, "He Who Dines and Runs Away," in* New Statesman, *Vol. 116, No. 2981, May 13, 1988, p. 34.*

PARUL KAPUR

"Nothing matters," exclaims an acquaintance Thomas Bernhard encounters by chance on a Salzburg street, twenty-five years after he first knew him. Bernhard, the acclaimed Austrian novelist and playwright, recalls in his autobiography **Gathering Evidence** the nostalgic lunch he shares with the man, now a drunken bare-chested construction worker. The worker recounts the miserable deaths of his mother and sister, as well as others Bernhard knew as an apprentice clerk in a grocery at the Scherzhauserfeld Project, a Salzburg ghetto where the workman lived as a boy. Nothing matters, concludes the toothless pneumatic driller. Bernhard agrees it's a "a nice, clear, concise handy phrase" because, indeed, "in the end nothing matters. The cards come down, one after the other."

Criticized for his nihilism, his scathing views on human affairs, Bernhard provides in **Gathering Evidence** some justification—the justification of experience—for the despair that permeates his latest novel, **Woodcutters.** (p. 16)

It is society—the savage and civilized art world of Vienna—and its undoing of the individual that is at the heart of **Woodcutters.** A nameless narrator, a successful exiled writer—temporarily repatriated to Vienna—isolates himself at a dinner party where, for the length of the novel, he condemns his hosts, the other guests, and himself, assailing a social structure that crushes its artists. The gathering takes place on the same day the partygoers have buried an old friend, Joana, a once prominent actress-dancer who has ended as an alcoholic and suicide. The hosts, however, name the occasion an *"artistic dinner,"* one they have planned in honor of an actor enjoying success in Ibsen's *The Wild Duck,* at the city's Burgtheater. The notion of an *artistic dinner* (narrator's emphasis) and an artistic life, in general, is for the fictional observer, behind whom Bernhard looms large, a pathetic pretension and falsification. Ruminating on Joana's funeral in her home village, he observes that "all these *artistic people* had seemed grotesque. Their *artistic preoccupations* and their *artistic ac-*

tivity made them seem somehow unnatural, at least to me; they had an *artificial way of walking, an artificial way of talking; everything* about them was artificial, whereas the cemetery itself was the most natural place in the world." And this artificial world of posture and ambition and manners, like the most primitive society, demands human sacrifices.

Sitting mute among the guests, maintaining a hostile silence as he invokes and dissects the past, the narrator recalls how the country girl Elfriede Slukal rechristened herself with the exotic pseudonym Joana upon coming to the city. She draped herself in fantastic Roman and Egyptian evening gowns, establishing herself as a socialite, and eventually relinquished her own quest for fame to promote her husband, a tapestry artist who achieved international renown as a result of her prodigious efforts. Having won a reputation he had never imagined possible, the tapestry artist—selfish and ungrateful as any human being—left Joana, who, subsequently abandoned by her friends too, slid into drink and despair. Suicide has claimed several of his friends, too, remarks the Burgtheater actor in a postdinner conversation. And a former lover of the narrator's, mocked for her literary pretensions and meager output—she's titled the "Virginia Woolf of Vienna"—notes that the suicide rate is higher among Austrians than among any other Europeans. Illness spreads through the society as well, the narrator informs us, remarking on his own lung disease, heart ailment, and nervous debility. Physical illness, though, is only a symptom of a wider social malaise. Bernhard's artists are particularly susceptible to social poisons, to a political state that rewards creative mediocrity and suppresses genius, resulting in "the degenerate intellectual life of Austria."

The narrator laments the course taken by many of his old friends, who, in their pursuit of state prizes and money, eventually prostitute their talent and their mission to create *art* in the grand European sense. And those who begin with money, like his well-to-do host Auersberger, a composer of unfulfilled promise, lapse into a comfortable bourgeois lassitude. They extend their patronage only to assuage boredom or deflect from their domestic misery. The narrator even insinuates that Auersberger seduced him as compensation for the financial and social support he provided the young writer. Though the critique offered by Bernhard's fictional alter ego sometimes dissolves into mere ranting, and though we are at times exasperated by his peevishness—he is petty enough to attack even the middle-class habit of offering predinner snacks—the narrator irresistibly draws us into an exotic European society, foreign to us because of its very cohesiveness and closure, an anachronistic world whose mannered beauty belies its viciousness. Bernhard writes of the Vienna of the 1980s, but for those dwelling in a fissured future-oriented society, who live outside any European sense of society, the very name *Vienna* belongs to the last century or to the dawn of this one. Bernhard's world seems to belong to the luridly bright street scenes of the Expressionist Ernst Kirchner, to his pink- and green-faced bourgeois grotesques, which were painted nearly eighty years ago, and not in Austria, but in Germany next door. Despite the narrator's obsessions, which spin around the nucleus of Joana's suicide, the social atmosphere is denser here than in Bernhard's earlier fictions, where the domain is more narrowly psychological.

An object of the narrator's unrelenting ridicule, the Burgtheater actor is a farcical figure—his absurdly late arrival at the party keeps the guests waiting for dinner until well past midnight—who exemplified the lowest type of artist in this unbroken monologue that, typically of Bernhard, swings between parody and pathos. Surprisingly, though, a simple wish the actor expresses catapults him to the stature of a *"momentary philosopher"* in the narrator's eyes. "The forest, the virgin forest, the life of a woodcutter—" the actor cries, "that has always been my ideal." This sentimental desire is absurdly regarded by the narrator as the point of the actor's "philosophical metamorphosis." It is a wish of the most superficial of men for a natural—a genuine—life. And in Bernhard's view the farcical is another face of the tragic; the sentimental other voice of the truth. In this fiction as in life, the tone in which something is spoken may bear a meaning deeper or different from the sum of the words. We hear the way a phrase is said—for instance the affectation of *artistic dinner*—through Bernhard's habit of italicizing. His playwright's ear registers the peculiar brittleness or sincerity of a thought or sentence, and when he duplicates these nuances in italicized print, we do not so much read the text as hear it speaking to us. Bernhard's cunning is his sense of hearing; his art is about the power of speech and of thought endowed with a voice.

Though they might have wound up an irritating tic, Bernhard's recurrent italicized phrases and passages instead awaken the text with sound. And though the unbroken rush of the narrator's opinions, insults, and ruminations might have submerged the reader in pessimism, it is diverted just in time by self-satire and self-incrimination. (pp. 16, 18)

Ibsen's *The Wild Duck*—in which the celebrated Burgtheater actor ironically plays a small role—is a name that echoes through the text and establishes a presence of its own. The tragic drama about the child Hedvig sacrificing herself for the lies of her parents—of the world—casts a line directly into Bernhard's own preoccupations with the fate of an individual at the hands of society. The narrator's old friend Joana is broken by the very people whose friendship she coveted. But Bernhard, casting a colder eye than other writers who have pitted an individual against a cruel world—writers as divergent as Dickens and Flaubert and Edith Wharton—observes a law of indifference at work. Those who let themselves be destroyed might, in different circumstances, under a favorable balance of power, have squashed others. The victims of Vienna are its victimizers as well. The only thing to be done about such perversity, the narrator raves, is to chronicle it. And we have his testament in our hands. (p. 19)

> *Parul Kapur, "Done In by Society," in* The American Book Review, *Vol. 10, No. 3, July-August, 1988, pp. 16, 18, 19.*

TOM WILHELMUS

That the artist may not have known himself and may dramatize that unknowing is the intriguing conception of **Woodcutters,** a recently-translated novel by the acclaimed Austrian novelist Thomas Bernhard. Bernhard's novels are compulsively autobiographical, and this novel, in particular, is preceded by scandal, delayed in publication because of a suit brought by one of Bernhard's acquaintances who claims to have been slanderously portrayed in it.

The novel is the record of a late-night artistic dinner party at the home of the Auersbergers, one of Vienna's literary elite, following a performance of Ibsen's *The Wild Duck.* The guests comprise a small salon who decide the fate of Viennese art but who are more adept at manipulating business, social, and governmental agencies than producing work themselves. At least this is the opinion of the narrator, ensconced in a wing chair from which he observes the others and their participation in a gathering that to him seems a sordid and ridiculous farce:

> Because they've made a name for themselves, won a lot of prizes, published a lot of books, and sold their pictures to a lot of museums, because they've had their books issued by the best publishing houses and their pictures hung in the best museums, because they've been awarded every possible prize that this appalling state has to offer and had every possible decoration pinned to their breasts, they believe they've become something, though in fact they've become nothing.

As a result, "Vienna is a terrible machine for the destruction of genius," he thinks. "An appalling recycling plant for the demolition of talent."

Part of the pleasure of reading such a work comes from our cherished conviction that indeed artistic careers *are* fostered in this manner—making us even more willing to believe that in this case the novel actually is a thinly disguised *roman à clef.* We are also more willing to believe that the narrator has shunned his former friends for twenty years and has only come to the party because he accidentally met them that day on the way to the funeral of a mutual acquaintance. On the other hand, I am told the literary dinner party is a familiar convention of Austrian literature, and these characters seem more like types than portraits—including the narrator who is far from a sympathetic creation. Thus, depending upon the quality of David McLintock's translation, even the tediousness of the style appears intentionally alienating, and the text, comprised of 181 repetitive, circular, and sometimes boring pages takes on the quality of a tour de force.

The plot of the novel turns on the arrival of the actor for whom the party is being given. At first the narrator is repelled, once again, by a man who appears equally shallow and egotistical, a poseur mouthing the words of others. Nonetheless, as the evening progresses, the actor wins the narrator's grudging respect as a person who also suffers from the oppressive artificiality of these surroundings and wishes for something more natural: *"The forest, the virgin forest, the life of a woodcutter."* This phrase transforms the actor in the eyes of the narrator, "from a gargoyle into a philosophical human being," and this transformation, along with the memory of the dead mutual friend, awakens a brief and highly-qualified admission that "Vienna, which I found detestable and had always found detestable, was suddenly once again the best city in the world."

Personally, I find **Woodcutters** as persuasive—and perhaps finally as sympathetic to its countrymen—as Joyce's "The Dead." Both works contain the same sense of isolation and hatred of pretense, the same dread of social gatherings, the same memory of warmer and more hospitable times, and the same longing for what is passionate and natural. Both contain the same reconciling force of the dead who bind the characters together, however briefly, in mutual sympathy. (pp. 554-56)

> *Tom Wilhelmus, "Knowing," in* The Hudson Review, *Vol. XLI, No. 3, Autumn, 1988, pp. 548-56.*

FURTHER READING

Anderson, Mark. "Notes on Thomas Bernhard." *Raritan* 7 (1987): 81-96.
    Relates the inventive prose style in Bernhard's fiction with his focus on death, insanity, and cruelty, and argues that political and satirical elements in Bernhard's stories negate charges that his work is aloof and nihilistic.

Barthofer, Alfred. "The Plays of Thomas Bernhard: A Report." *Modern Austrian Literature* 11, No. 1 (1978): 21-48.
    Overview of Bernhard's drama.

Brokoph-Mauch, Gudrun. "Thomas Bernhard." In *Major Figures of Contemporary Austrian Literature,* edited by Donald G. Daviau, pp. 89-116. New York: Peter Lanf Publishing, Inc., 1987.
    Critical and biographical overview, alternately focusing on Bernhard's poetry, prose, and drama.

Chambers, Helen. "Theatre Checklist No. 12: Thomas Bernhard." *Theatrefacts* 3, No. iv (1976): 2-11.
    Provides descriptions of Bernhard's plays.

Cook, Bruce. "The Sorrows of Young Writers." *Book World—The Washington Post* (26 August 1984): 7, 9.
    Review of Bernhard's *Concrete* and Peter Handke's *The Weight of the World.*

Craig, D. A. "The Novels of Thomas Bernhard: A Report." *German Life and Letters* 25 (July 1972): 343-353.
    Overview of Bernhard's novels.

Demetz, Peter. "Thomas Bernhard: The Dark Side of Life." In his *After the Fires: Recent Writings in the Germanies, Switzerland, and Austria,* pp. 199-212. San Diego: Harcourt Brace Jovanovich, 1986.
    Discusses Bernhard's career and assesses his place in contemporary German-language literature.

Dierick, A. P. "Thomas Bernhard's Austrian Neurosis: Symbol or Expedient?" *Modern Austrian Literature* 12, No. 1 (1979): 73-93.
    Considers whether or not Bernhard's bleak depiction of life in Austria accurately reflects conditions in that country.

Fetz, Gerald. "Thomas Bernhard and the 'Modern Novel.' " In *The Modern German Novel,* edited by Keith Bullivant, pp. 89-108. Leamington Spa: Berg Publishers Ltd., 1987.
    An overview of Bernhard's first eight novels and analysis of his place in contemporary German-language literature. In his later novels, Fetz contends, "a Berhardian vision emerges which is not nearly so exclusively dark or apparently hopeless as that which prevails in the earliest ones."

Innes, C. D. "Dialogues." In his *Modern German Drama: A Study in Form,* pp. 235-59. Cambridge: Cambridge University Press, 1979.
    Discusses Bernhard's plays, often comparing them with those of German dramatist Peter Handke.

Kearns, Nancy. Review of *Force of Habit,* by Thomas Bernhard. *Theatre Journal* 37 (December 1985): 493-495.
    Comments on a rare American production of a Bernhard play, and analyzes the play's exploration of semantic problems and political issues.

Modern Austrian Literature 21 (1988).
    Special issue devoted entirely to Bernhard.

Plaice, Stephen. "Need for Exaggerations." *The Times Literary Supplement* No. 4357 (3 October 1986): 1088.
    Discussion of Bernhard's novel *Auslöschung.*

Malcolm Bradbury

1932-

(Born Malcolm Stanley Bradbury) English novelist, critic, short story writer, editor, dramatist, scriptwriter, and essayist.

Bradbury is esteemed for both his literary criticism and for his satirical novels about academic life. A university professor and one of England's most respected authorities on the modernist tradition in novels, Bradbury incorporates his knowledge of literature and college life into his fiction. Through irony, wit, and deft mimicry of fashionable attitudes and speech mannerisms, he treats what he terms "the problems of liberalism and moral responsibility" pervasive in academia. Although essentially a writer of realistic fiction, Bradbury increasingly displays in his novels a preoccupation with the artificiality of fiction and a self-reflexiveness characteristic of postmodern literature.

Some critics have compared Bradbury's first novel, *Eating People Is Wrong,* to Kingsley Amis's *Lucky Jim* for its comic depiction of the spiritlessness of English provincial university life. *Eating People Is Wrong* focuses on the midlife crisis of conscience that a British professor experiences when his liberal humanist values are challenged by younger colleagues and students. In his next novel, *Stepping Westward,* Bradbury lampoons disparities between English and American culture. The protagonist, a liberal, socially awkward British novelist invited to become writer-in-residence at an American college, discovers that the vulgar, anarchic, and self-aggrandizing nature of American universities repulses and intimidates him. Consequently, he returns to his family in England six months earlier than planned. *The History Man,* generally considered Bradbury's finest novel, satirizes radical liberal excesses prevalent on college campuses in the 1960s, as embodied in an ambitious sociology professor whose plots to change the world stem more from greed than altruism. According to Bradbury, this work is written in the present tense and composed largely of dialogue in order to "[diminish] the sense of historical or personal rootedness, making the world instantaneous."

Bradbury's next novel, *Rates of Exchange,* concerns the culture shock experienced by a meek professor of linguistics during a lecture tour in the imaginary Eastern European police state of Slaka. Through his experiences in a foreign country where grammar and monetary systems continually change and through his affair with a Slakan female novelist, the professor learns the value of cultural differences. In the novella *Cuts,* the story of a reclusive experimental author's bewildering experience with a crass television company serves as the pretext for a scathing indictment of the British government's drastic reduction of social programs in 1986. *Mensonge: Structuralism's Hidden Hero* is a spoof of Structuralism, a school of critical thought that originated in France in the 1960s.

Bradbury is regarded as one of England's preeminent scholars of modernist literature. *The Social Context of Modern English Literature* is intended as a modernist handbook that examines the intellectual responses of writers to historical and cultural changes. In *Possibilities: Essays on the State of the*

Novel, Bradbury advocates naturalism but also calls for a flexible approach to what he terms the "new problematics of realism." *The Modern World: Ten Great Writers* analyzes representative works by authors that in Bradbury's opinion epitomized literary modernism, including James Joyce's *Ulysses,* Virginia Woolf's *Mrs. Dalloway,* and Fedor Dostoevski's *Crime and Punishment.*

(See also *CLC,* Vol. 32; *Contemporary Authors,* Vols. 1-4, rev. ed.; *Contemporary Authors New Revision Series,* Vol. 1; and *Dictionary of Literary Biography,* Vol. 14.)

PRINCIPAL WORKS

NOVELS

Eating People Is Wrong   1959
Stepping Westward   1965
The History Man   1975
Rates of Exchange   1983
Cuts   1987
Mensonge: Structuralism's Hidden Hero   1987

CRITICISM

Evelyn Waugh   1964

What Is a Novel? 1969
The Social Context of Modern English Literature 1971
Possibilities: Essays on the State of the Novel 1973
Saul Bellow 1982
The Expatriate Tradition in Modern American Literature 1982
The Modern American Novel 1983
No, Not Bloomsbury 1988
The Modern World: Ten Great Writers 1988

OTHER

Who Do You Think You Are?: Stories and Parodies 1976
Unsent Letters: Irreverent Notes from a Literary Life (humor) 1988

RICHARD TODD

[The essay excerpted below, originally delivered as a lecture, was slightly revised by the critic.]

Malcolm Bradbury published *The History Man* in 1975. It was his third novel, but the first for ten years. In consequence, at the time of its appearance, Bradbury was probably better known as a critic and essayist, since the two earlier novels were becoming hard to find. *The History Man* was successful enough to appear in paperback a couple of years after its hardback publication, and its success has resulted in attention being drawn once again to the two earlier novels, to the extent that the paperback publishers of *The History Man* have taken the step of reissuing them. The first, entitled *Eating People is Wrong*, had originally appeared in 1959, when Bradbury was in his late twenties, and the second, *Stepping Westward*, in 1965.

We might consider for a moment what it is about *The History Man* that has provoked this gratifying retrospective interest in Bradbury's fiction. The earlier novels are different enough from this third one to justify the action of the paperback publishers, but all three share recognizable characteristics. All three are concerned with academic life, and with some of the social and moral issues which life in such a community seems to raise. All three contain a central male figure, around whom events occur. Here we can make one or two distinctions. These male figures are of varying degrees of effectuality. Those of the two earlier novels—Stuart Treece in *Eating People is Wrong*, and James Walker in *Stepping Westward*—are both characterized by a certain diffidence in the face of the decision-making, as well as by a sense of impracticality. This seems to be summed up in the way in which neither man can drive. More importantly, I think, both Treece and Walker allow events to happen around them; in this, they seem characteristic, in Bradbury's novelistic world, of the academic *liberal*. The male characters in *The History Man* who most readily spring to mind when the word "liberal" is mentioned, the characters who are most inclined to let things happen around them, who show respect for things as they are, include Professor Marvin and Henry Beamish. Howard Kirk is utterly different, in being both highly practical and quite intolerant to things as they are; he is surrounded by descriptions of growth, of movement, of change, of action. In the case of Henry Beamish, diffidence and impracticality have been transformed into a hideous kind of proneness to

accident, which provides a constant source of reference in the novel. We shall shortly see that Bradbury himself feels that the idea of accident is an important and necessary consequence of the moral viewpoint of his novel.

To return briefly to the earlier novels, Treece is on his own ground, as head of the English department of a provincial university in Britain. Walker's case is somewhat different, since his liberalism is set against the radicalism of several of his American colleagues—Walker, an allegedly "angry young man", is invited as a Creative Writing Fellow to an American mid-West campus. Walker's visit is in fact more than partly the result of an attempt by a clever East Coast graduate, Bernard Froelich, to radicalize both the campus and, indirectly, Walker himself. This seems to me interesting in the context of *The History Man.* I think we can see in *Stepping Westward* the beginnings of the theme of radical exploitation, of a desire to push events along rather than just let them happen, which is central in *The History Man.* Readers of *Stepping Westward* may feel, as I do, that Froelich is in many respects a prototype of Howard Kirk. This would allow us to feel that the earlier novels provide a useful introduction to *The History Man* for certain rather specific reasons. The "liberal-radical" opposition is given a particular perspective in *Stepping Westward,* and this is a sharper critique of the liberal academic standpoint which we find in *Eating People is Wrong.* In *The History Man* the perspective of the previous novel is entirely altered, and the radical viewpoint triumphs, destroying the liberal. Bradbury has not attempted to disguise his hostility towards the radical standpoint, either within the text or outside it; we are therefore justified in calling *The History Man* a satire. Though at times character approaches caricature, particularly in the persons of Howard Kirk and some of the extremer radicals surrounding him, we would have (I think) to admit that the satire is kept in check, and is not allowed to deteriorate into polemic.

In a recent essay, Bradbury has referred to his novel as "a novel about de-humanization". I quote at greater length from this essay:

> The central figure, Howard Kirk, the radical sociologist who, four years after the revolutionary season of 1968, when onerous reality seems wonderfully to lift, tries to sustain his transforming passion in an inert world. But he believes that privacy is over, and the self is no more than the sum of the roles that it plays. Howard acts . . . in a world where speech-acts and ideas cannot affix themselves to a sense of value in action or history, passivity is the norm. Accidents become important, and so do happenings, those chance events which arise when we give a party or juxtapose students in a classroom. There are no purposeful plots, except Howard's; he plots in a plotless world, hoping to serve the radical plot of history. The dominant tense is the present, diminishing the sense of historical or personal rootedness, making the world instantaneous . . .

There is a lot of interest here, but the point I hope to have made is that *The History Man* does not stand alone in Bradbury's novelistic development, although it is radically different from its predecessors. It should rather be seen as meditating on matters which have emerged from the earlier novels.

One thing which Bradbury stresses in this essay ["**Putting in the Person: Character and Abstraction in Current Writing and Painting**"] is the deliberate way in which he has *not* attempted to enter into the psychology or consciousness of his characters in *The History Man.* The characters, as he puts it, "manifest themselves by their speech and their actions". Indeed, there is a very large proportion of dialogue. There is also a sense of narrative detachment, perhaps even of inscrutability, though I think we may be able to define this quality more closely as we proceed. Certainly Bradbury's portrayal of his characters in this novel contrasts with the way in which we are allowed into the minds of those in his earlier novels. We become observers; in this novel the narrator stands in a new relation to his material. He seems to know nothing beyond what he can observe, or (as at certain moments) beyond what he says Howard can tell him. (The narration of the potted history of the Kirk's transformation into "new people" in chapter two—how, in fact, they became "Kirks"—seems to be of this second kind.) What we see from Howard's actions is the way in which the plot of the novel is actually the same as Howard's plot. Gradually this becomes the same as Howard's view of history, and once that point is reached, Howard and the narrator part company, and the narrative comes to an end. This raises the question of who is in charge of the conduct of this novel: is it the narrator, or is it Howard? The question is a complicated one, because it could be argued that at least at one point in the novel the narrator becomes one of the characters. This may remind us of Bradbury's interest in a modernist novelist for whom an awareness of "the plot of history" was extremely sophisticated. This novelist is Ford Madox Ford, and in an essay on Ford Bradbury writes of "the aloof or detached narrator, presenting the novel 'without passion', and with a guiding selectivity". This notion of "guiding selectivity" seems a useful description of the effect of the narrative of *The History Man.*

With this idea of guiding selectivity in mind, we might notice briefly how the novel encompasses the autumn term, which provides a useful way of "beginning" and "ending" it. We notice the flashback in chapter two which explains how the Kirks became Kirks; we also have the flashback of the rest of the autumn term which is incorporated into the last chapter. The term begins and ends with a party, and all this makes us think, by means of selectivity, in what ways history might be said to repeat itself.

The flashback of the last chapter contains the result of one of the most spectacular pieces of Howard's radical plot-making. This is the projected visit of Professor Mangel. Mangel, of course, never materializes; however, what matters about the near-revolution surrounding this non-event is that it is something which Howard sets up. It is on the first day of the term that Howard begins to spread the rumours that Mangel—who holds controversial views on genetics and race—is coming to lecture at Watermouth University. We see quite clearly that Howard needs the kind of tension and pressure which such rumour will provide, in order to survive. Howard first mentions Mangel's name to his colleague Moira Millikin, and immediately afterwards we see him leaning against the metal wall of the lift "looking like a man who is no longer looking for someone or something." Eventually, during a magnificent Departmental meeting, the Sociology Department is manoeuvred into issuing Mangel an invitation to come and lecture. All the time this is happening, the narrator seems to be close to Howard, following him around. Perhaps the only moments of speculation in the novel come from one of its most sympathetic characters, Flora Beniform; yet she disappears before the last chapter, and while she remains in the book she is observed too, particularly on the occasions

when she and Howard go to bed together. In this way the narrative enacts for us, at times, the subject of Howard's recent book, on which there is much silent comment: *The Defeat of Privacy*.

The last chapter also reveals, by means of flashback, the fate of George Carmody, the reactionary English student who attempts, with his camera, to spy on Howard's sex-life. Earlier, Carmody has almost attained significance as he has moved into a position of being able to blackmail Howard, but we find that, in consequence of the general atmosphere of radicalism that Mangel's non-visit—Howard's plot—has aroused in the University, Carmody has fled in total humiliation. Carmody has in fact proved to be what Howard describes him as: he is "an historical irrelevance".

This shows something of the way in which the novel's events are "guided" and "selected" to form Howard's plot. Howard might be described, in fact, as an eager impresario of the events at Watermouth University. In this he is demonstrably quite different from Stuart Treece and James Walker: to these ineffectual, pleasant liberals "things happen"; Howard Kirk—even more radically than Bernard Froelich—"makes things happen".

Let us return for a moment to the case of the invitation which the Sociology Department at Watermouth University is forced into issuing Mangel, an invitation, which is defended by Dr Zachery. His reasons for defending it are worth quoting:

> "Professor Mangel and myself have a background in common; we are both Jewish, and both grew up in Nazi Germany, and fled here from the rise of fascism. I think we know the meaning of this term. Fascism, and the associated genocide, arose because a climate developed in Germany in which it was held that all intellectual activity conform with an accepted, approved ideology. To make this happen, it was necessary to make a climate in which it became virtually impossible to think, or exist, outside the dominant ideological construct. Those who did were isolated, as now some of our colleagues seek to isolate Professor Mangel." There are many murmurs round the table from the sociologists, all of them are deeply conscious of having definitions of fascism they too could give, if asked. "May I continue?" asks Zachery. "Fascism is therefore an elegant sociological construct, a one-system world. Its opposite is contingency or pluralism or liberalism. That means a chaos of opinion and ideology; there are people who find that hard to endure . . ."

No-one will fail to miss the relevance of the distinction which Zachery draws here—and one of its consequences is to bring about the fulfilment of that part of Howard's plot which involves issuing the invitation to Mangel.

Zachery's distinction also provides us with terms in which to consider the attitudes which characters in the novel hold towards history itself, or rather, in view of what I was saying at the beginning, to the fiction we call "history"—and, indeed, to plots, extend to novels, including this one. Howard radicalizes the world of the fiction, in which he appears, by means of his plot-making, he creates a "one-system world". Bradbury himself, in the essay I have just referred to, writes of the novel's main representative of the other, the "liberal", "pluralistic" standpoint in a way which shows his disappointment. He says of the book: "There is one ostensibly sympathetic character, who speaks for humanism; she is a deception to the readers." (pp. 164-70)

We first meet Miss Callendar at the party which opens the term for the Kirks and everyone else, and when Howard first speaks to her, we discover what we may already be gathered from two previous conversations which we have overheard at this party. Miss Callendar does not fit into the radical sociological set of most of the guests; her views and values might, in contrast, be described as "liberal" (if not, to the sociologists, "unliberated"); she dresses differently; she has a certain hard critical intelligence. It turns out that she is a new lecturer in the English department at the university. Now we also discover that she hasn't actually been invited to Howard's party. She says:

> "I was brought by someone who's gone." "Who is that?" asks Howard. "He's a novelist," says the girl. "He's gone home to write notes on it all."

Whether or not this is actually true, it certainly sets up an association which the attentive reader may well recall later.

Having introduced Miss Callendar to the Kirks' house by taking her to a party there, any novelist could, I suppose, remain reasonably confident that a man with Howard's sexual reputation would try to get to know her. But during the party itself she does remain fairly elusive. She manages to avoid the increasingly sexual atmosphere of its later stages, and detaches herself as most of the remaining people are pairing off. Among them is Howard, who seduces—or is seduced by— one of his students, Felicity Phee, in his study; he has discovered her there in the act of defeating his privacy by reading his unfinished MS. Her reason for doing this is that she has made Howard her object of research, her special option. Barbara has also disappeared—with whom remains uncertain, though it is suggested to Howard the next day that her partner has been Dr Macintosh. Shortly after all this, Henry Beamish causes a disturbance, heard only by those who are not busy. We are told that Henry "has put his left arm through and down" the window in the guest bedroom, "and slashed it savagely on the glass." Fortunately he is discovered by someone, and then Flora Beniform, who has just arrived, takes charge. The next day the question is raised as to whether Henry has made a suicide attempt. The question is left unresolved. The narrative's description is too neutral to be helpful. Henry has cut his *left* hand, and Flora feels that no-one would have acted as Henry did if his intention were really serious. However, it is also uncertain whether Henry realizes that his wife Myra is contemplating leaving him—an action which she continues to contemplate, with varying degrees of conviction, throughout the rest of the book. And, of course, Henry's life seems beset by the accidental. So the question of his motive in cutting his hand remains something which the other characters, and we as readers, can only guess at.

However, on the morning after the party, Howard is able to make a further attempt to get to know Miss Callendar since he sees her waiting at a bus-stop, and offers her a lift. After a little hesitation she accepts. Howard discovers a little more about her, but not much more, since she is—as she says—a very private person. Despite Howard's assurances that the concept of privacy is outmoded, she is unwilling to tell him where she lives. . . .

We will see that her reservations prove well-founded. For the time being, however, Howard has to be content to express his wish, quite unreservedly, to go to bed with her. She is sophis-

ticated enough not to express shock or surprise at this proposal, while at the same time declining it fairly gracefully. Later we will come to know what we may already be guessing—that she has sexual needs which may indeed require fulfilment, and which cannot forever be ignored or sublimated behind a protective facade of intelligent, slightly brittle academic chat. This raises a problem we should not underestimate. I believe we must, as readers of this novel, strongly resist the temptation simply to "place" Howard as a trendy sociologist, and Miss Callendar as simply representing opposition to all that Howard stands for. In doing so, we will ignore Miss Callendar's needs. Bradbury seems to me to raise very seriously in this novel some of the problems have to do with the morality of the liberal novelist. Do we want to hang on to Miss Callendar as the one "ostensibly sympathetic character", or are we prepared to relinquish our hold on her, and allow her to find her own way, to discover for herself where her needs and requirements lie? Which of these two alternatives actually involves *manipulating* the character of Miss Callendar? And equally, how are we to take Bradbury's own remark, quoted earlier, that Miss Callendar is "a deception to the reader"?

I am trying to suggest that we have here a moral paradox which so puzzles the liberal novelist that he has been dramatized and introduced into the narrative. As one of its very minor characters, he attempts to show, ineffectually as it happens, where his sympathies lie. But his failure seems to me to be a statement of the paradox: who manipulates Miss Callendar? Why is she not a free agent, as (in a true liberal fiction) she should be?

The results of the novelist's initial act of interference continue: later in the day, Howard succeeds where he had earlier failed, and invites Miss Callendar out to dinner. Her view of Howard's view of her (an assessment with which Howard agrees) seems revealing:

> "I think I know what your interest is in me. I think you regard me as a small, unmodernized, country property, ripe for development to fit contemporary tastes. You want to claim me for that splendid historical transcendence in which you feel you stand."

We only find out about the innocence of the dinner evening indirectly, and it is after this point that the destinies of Howard and Miss Callendar become intermingled with that of the student George Carmody. Carmody is a kind of "historical offence":

> He is an item, preserved in some extraordinary historical pickle, from the nineteen-fifties or before; he comes out of some strange fold in time.

The liberal Professor Marvin recognizes more complexity in Carmody's case than does Howard, and Miss Callendar is even prepared to grant that he is a person, with a background that ought to be looked into. But Carmody goes wrong when he attempts to substantiate his thesis that his persistent failure in Howard's classes (he is reading English, with Sociology as one of his subsidiary subjects) is, as he puts it, a consequence of his possessing neither a left-wing head nor female genitals. By contrast, Felicity Phee possesses both of these requirements. Carmody collects very full evidence, including photographs, of Howard's various sexual exploits. Marvin is forced to concede that Carmody has "a certain capacity for research. If only he could have harnessed it to better use."

It is at this point that Howard begins his final assault on Miss

Callendar's privacy. She is Carmody's tutor in English, and Howard wishes to discuss with her the delicate situation which has arisen as a result of Carmody's actions, since Howard's job is now, he feels, at some risk. Howard tries to find her at her office in the English department, and here we have the novel's one direct encounter with its reluctant impresario, the "novelist":

> The doors have bright nameplates; Howard inspects them as he walks. Then, before one labelled "Miss A. Callendar" he stops, he knocks. There is no response, so he knocks and waits again. The door of a room adjoining opens a little; a dark, tousled-haired head, with a sad visage, peers through, looks at Howard for a little while, then retreats. The face has a vague familiarity; Howard recalls that this depressed-looking figure is a lecturer in the English department, a man who, ten years earlier, had produced two tolerably well-known and acceptably-reviewed novels, filled, as novels then were, with moral scruple and concern. Since then there has been silence, as if, under the pressure of contemporary change, there was no more moral scruple and concern, no new substance to be spun. The man alone persists; he passes, nervously through the campus, he teaches, sadly, he avoids strangers. Howard knocks on this man's door; hearing no reply, he opens it. The novelist is not immediately visible; he sits out of the light, in the furthest corner, hunched over a typewriter, looking doubtfully up at his visitor. "I'm sorry to disturb you," says Howard, "but I'm looking for Miss Callendar. Do you know where she is?" "I don't think I do," says the man. "You've no idea?" asks Howard. "Well, I thought she'd better go home," says the man, "she's in a very upset state." "Well, this is a very urgent matter," says Howard, "I wonder whether you'd give me her address." "I'm afraid I can't," says the man. "It's very important," says Howard. "Miss Callendar's not easy to find out about," says the novelist, "she's a very private person." "Do you know her address?" asks Howard. "No," says the man, "no I don't." "Ah, well," says Howard, "if you want to find things out about people, you always can, with a little research. A little curiosity." "It's sometimes better not to," says the man. "Never mind," says Howard, "I'll find it." "I wish you wouldn't," says the novelist. "I will," says Howard, going out of the room and shutting the door.

I have quoted this at some length because in my account of the novel it is a very crucial passage. There are one or two details, such as the two novels published ten years earlier, and even the sad, tousled-haired visage, which suggest that we are perhaps to see this as what has elsewhere and in another context been called [by Frank Kermode] a "reticent signature" by the author. The "novelist" is reluctant to pass on information about Miss Callendar. It is as if he is regretting having set the ball rolling by having introduced Miss Callendar to the Kirk circle—yet novelists are always arranging encounters of this kind; they cannot help, in this sense, being impresarios. *This* novelist is unwilling, it seems, to allow the acquaintance to proceed further, since knowing Howard (though Howard doesn't seem to know him very well) the novelist can be fairly certain of the outcome, and doesn't like what he sees. In other words, he is unwilling to relinquish Miss Callendar to the forces of radicalism, yet this relinquishment has been implicit in the very act of writing his novel. The moral paradox is a very poignant one.

If we accept this view of the novel's "novelist" as reluctant impresario, foreseeing and regretting the consequence of an act of creative rashness in having introduced Miss Callendar and Howard, some larger patterns begin to emerge from the fiction as a whole. We might notice, in passing, the rather fine contrast between the "novelist" and Howard; the novelist reluctantly, and perhaps even unwittingly, plays the same role in relation to Miss Callendar as Howard does in relation to Mangel. Both—for whatever reason—exercise the use of power. And Howard will now show a tenacity and dedication to researching Miss Callendar's address—and defeating her privacy in so doing—that had shocked him when applied to his own privacy by Carmody.

Anyway, Howard manages to track down Miss Callendar at her home address. Like George Carmody, Howard has "a certain capacity for research", and he has finally managed to find her name and address on the bookshop list. His excuse for coming to visit her is that he wants to tell her a story. I suppose it would be fair to summarize her reservations about stories in this way: that much depends on the way you tell them. This will—I hope—have been evident already; I've been giving an account of the "story" of *The History Man* which has been slanted in a particular direction, as all accounts must be. My account has been constructed in the way it has because I am trying to suggest a particular interpretative possibility. In fact there are one or two occasions in the novel itself where we can see this process actively at work. I have in mind, for instance, the difference between Flora's story and Henry's story (about Henry and the broken window) on the day after the first party of the term. The "point" about these two versions is that it's important for our view of the end of the novel that we never know (but can only guess) which is the truer version. Or we might think of Henry's account of his "uncontentious" staff-meeting, which has included the invitation to Mangel. Of course to Howard (and, as it happens, to the narrator) the invitation to Mangel has made the meeting quite contentious; but the narrator has been very selective in his account of this meeting, and Henry may be quite right—from *his* point of view.

Howard and Miss Callendar, then, begin discussing Howard's story of Carmody's blackmail attempt, and they compare it with Carmody's story of the same events. Miss Callendar sums up the matter like this:

> "It shows how different a story can be if you change . . . the angle of vision." "Angle of vision!" says Howard, "That man's followed me everywhere, tracked my movements, photographed me through curtains, and then built a lie out of it. He's a fine angle of vision." "An outside eye's sometimes illuminating," says Miss Callendar, "and of course, as Henry James says, the house of fiction has many windows. Your trouble is you seem to have stood in front of most of them.

So far, Miss Callendar seems to have had the upper hand, perhaps, quite simply, because she is more intelligent, and a better reader, than Howard. But now things change—Howard tempts her down from her theoretical perch, and begins to persuade her that she has to accept, for quite practical reasons, one or other version of the story. She must choose between Howard and Carmody. It isn't simply that Howard's career is at stake; Howard persuades Miss Callendar that the kind of critical scepticism which she is attempting to maintain just is not possible. By not accepting Howard's version, she will implicitly be moving towards Carmody's version, and so towards his lifestyle and his standards. This may be shrewder than Howard knows. It very shortly becomes clear that Miss Callendar's needs, especially her sexual needs, are such that the prospect of a permanent identification with Carmody's conservative, life-denying standards is not tolerable to her. The logic of Howard's argument may be spurious, but this isn't important; what matters is that Miss Callendar is caught at a particular moment of weakness, perhaps, in her own history, and Howard delivers a rhetorical blow which, at this moment, is so devastating that she cannot withstand it:

> Howard says: "Freud once gave a very economical definition of neurosis. He said it was an abnormal attachment to the past." Miss Callendar's face is very white; her dark eyes stare out of it. "I don't want this," she says, "I can't bear this."

The suddenness of Miss Callendar's capitulation is troubling because we are not certain how far it is to be seen in moral terms, and how far in artistic terms.

So, by what is perhaps a spurious rhetoric Miss Callendar is seduced. Her sexual experience appears to have been very limited; now she is one of Howard's conquests, and when we next meet her, her changed identity and role will be reflected in the way she will have become Annie Callendar. She is, in Bradbury's words, "a deception to the reader". I must stress the paradox here: what has brought about the deception can be traced to the activities of the reluctant impresario. If the "novelist" hadn't brought her to the Kirks' party, there is no reason to believe that events would have taken this turn, or at least, not at this particular stage. Howard is fairly convinced that she would have allowed herself to be conquered sooner or later; and, as Annie puts it, Howard has "helped [historical] inevitability along a little." But inevitability in this book is a very suspicious concept. Still, the "novelist" has helped it along too, and what I have been trying to suggest is that the activities of ineffectual liberalism have here played their part in Annie's betrayal. This is one of the implications behind James Walker's "kindness to things as they are"; to the liberal, life *is* messiness and contingency, although it may be virtuous morally, and even artistically, to believe in what contingency implies.

Finally, then, how does the passive tolerance of the liberal standpoint allow us to see the ending of *The History Man*?

We haven't followed Barbara Kirk around with anything like the same persistence as that with which we've followed Howard during the course of the novel. But we have been with her on her visit to London—this is the same weekend which Howard has spent (offstage, though on photographic film) "helping" Felicity Phee. During this weekend, Barbara has spent her time with the actor, Leon, and towards its end Leon breaks the news that his company will be going on a five-month tour to Australia and the United States. After this, we see less of Barbara, but she is becoming less relevant, now, to Howard's plot, since it is soon after this weekend that he conquers Annie Callendar. Still, while Howard and Barbara are planning the final party, and reflecting upon the term's events, there is an outburst from Barbara:

> "The more we go into this," says Barbara, "the more I feel the last thing we need is a party. I think it's a very doubtful celebration." "You thought that last time," says Howard, "and it cheered you up." "My God, Howard," says Barbara, "what in hell do you know about my cheerfulness or my misery? What access do you have to any of my feelings? What do you know about me now?" "You're fine," says Howard. "I'm appallingly miserable," says Barbara.

Like most miserable people, she won't say why she feels like this. We don't find out, either, though we can attempt to guess. I do think, however, that in this context, the last paragraph of the novel—in which Barbara puts her hand through the upstairs window—is an extremely resonant one. It is true that the parallel with the earlier incident with Henry springs immediately to mind, and helps to round off the novel; still, many questions remain, and because they are difficult and in the end impossible to answer, I can best give an idea of what they seem to me to be.

Was Henry's "accident" an accident, a suicide attempt, or a call for attention? All three possibilities are raised at one time or another, but left as possibilities. The doubt remains because the various accounts of the incident don't tally, and what the narrator offers is, as I've said, phrased so neutrally that it's impossible to guess from the narrative alone. Many readers would probably find Flora Beniform's account the most plausible—but is this not simply because she comes across as probably the most sensible and practical thinker in the book? She suggests that it was "a *minimal* suicide attempt. A gesture to say, look at me, think of me. The trouble is, we're busy people, none of us have time." She goes on to point out that it was Henry's left hand that went through the window and that she has checked that Henry is right-handed. Flora's reasoning might seem to be applicable to Barbara too. Barbara, however, puts her right hand through the window, but we don't, I think, know whether she is right-handed or not, nor, indeed whether this is something which matters to her in the same way as it matters to Henry. Henry, like Howard, writes books; earlier, we have seen that Barbara means to. Furthermore, Barbara is—it seems—getting little sexual attention in a book which is not remarkable for abstinence. Leon is away; Howard has Annie Callendar; and Felicity Phee, who has had Howard last time, has Dr Macintosh this (and Flora's guess is that it is Dr. Macintosh whom Barbara had last time). But we know only a little about what Barbara has been thinking throughout the term. Looking back over this term we remember that she says she has been feeling bad at the beginning of term, and that the solution would be a weekend in London. There aren't any more weekends now that Leon is away; there is, as she says, "nothing there . . . nothing at all there." Howard admits to Flora Beniform on the day after the first party that Barbara "is a bit depressed . . . but that's just the price of a dull summer. She needs a bit of action."

Perhaps one of the narrator's rare moments of insight is worth quoting here: "The plot of history; it serves them, and it matters to them, but somehow is doesn't quite give them all now." The plot is, of course, a radical plot for the Kirks, and Barbara does seem to realize, more than does Howard, a sense of dissatisfaction with it. Barbara is clearly affected by the news of Henry's accident when Myra rings her up, and she has been very upset to hear of the suicide of the man her friend Rosemary has been living with. What particularly affects her here is the note he has left behind: "This is silly." It seems that she begins to apply this message to much of her former radicalism; it would describe Howard's prescription for all problems, "revolt as therapy", and his attempts to liberate their children from "corn-flake fascism". Ironically, of course, she provides the radical solution herself—the novel ends on "a bit of action". Since she is not discovered by the time the narration falls silent, we do not know whether this radical solution has solved anything or not. The novel ends, in other words, not just on a note of radicalism, but on a kind of existential question-mark. The uncertainty has been contributed to by the novel's reluctant impresario, and he does not stay for an answer to the question which the narrative, by its silence, raises. In this novel, Malcolm Bradbury has subjected to very particular scrutiny the cliché that history repeats itself, and it is with this claim that I therefore conclude. (pp. 173-82)

> *Richard Todd, "Malcolm Bradbury's 'The History Man': The Novelist as Reluctant Impressario," in* Dutch Quarterly Review of Anglo-American Letters, *Vol. 11, No. 3, 1981, pp. 162-82.*

J. R. BANKS

David Lodge and Malcolm Bradbury are contemporaries, friends and friendly rivals in both literary criticism and original writing. Their last few novels have tended to run in parallel, and they both make brief appearances in the other's pages. [*Small World* and *Rates of Exchange*] are both about academic travel, but there the resemblance ends. Bradbury's novels are centripetal, Lodge's centrifugal. Bradbury's books are about small groups of people who talk incessantly, brilliantly, who are continually grounded, frustrated, immobilised; in Lodge's they hardly stop moving to talk, parting, flying round the globe and recombining in fresh combinations in vast daredevil aeronautical displays before shooting off in different directions.

Although Bradbury's four novels (unlike Lodge's) are all closely related to the academic scene, he seems to have been taken more seriously as an original voice by the critical establishment. Though it reads gauchely today, *Eating People is Wrong* (1959) was seen as a more weighty, even if not wholly 'angry', follow-up to Kingsley Amis's *Lucky Jim* (1954); while *The History Man* (1975), with its portentous Goya dust-jacket, hit the headlines at just the right moment, echoing popular disquiet about the permissive society, 'sociology' and the new universities. (Its limited cast and single-campus setting also made it ideal television material.) Bradbury is a superb stylist, with a splendid ear for dialogue, as the stories and parodies in *Who do you think You Are?* (1976) amply demonstrate. Yet he is surprisingly ill at ease with structure, pacing and plot. *Stepping Westward* (1965) is a strangely shapeless book, and the struggle at the end of *The History Man* to marry a novel of ideas with a well-rounded comic plot lets the book down badly.

The same is true of *Rates of Exchange.* The plot is perfunctory, and fizzles out lamely at the end. The basic idea, of a timid British academic visiting a Communist country on a lecture tour, is promising, and the other main characters—his interpreter, an embassy man, a former student and so on—all come vividly to life. The broken English they talk is never-endingly inventive and very funny, but page after page of it eventually becomes wearisome. The settings—hotels, restaurants, trains and big squares (presided over by portraits of the great ideological heroes, Marx, Lenin and Wanko) are plausible, and one never feels (as occasionally with Lodge) that one is eavesdropping on academic in-jokes. The result is funny,

but it never shocks—as *The History Man* did in places—or even surprises. (p. 79)

> *J. R. Banks, "Back to Bradbury Lodge," in* Critical Quarterly, *Vol. 27, No. 1, Spring, 1985, pp. 79-81.*

ROBERT S. BURTON

As its title suggests, ***Rates of Exchange*** centers on the metaphor of trading values on the international currency market; Bradbury writes in his author's note that "like money, this book is a paper fiction, offered for exchange." The novel's protagonist, linguistics professor Angus Petworth on a lecture tour through a fictional East European state, repeatedly asks for the going rate of exchange but never obtains an absolute value due to continuing upheavals in that country's economy. Other values, besides monetary, are simultaneously changing: the native language has its suffixes altered overnight from -uu to -ii, Petworth's name is given different pronunciations (Petwit, Pervert, Patwat, Pumwum) by his various acquaintances, and an alluring "batik-clad, magical realist novelist" explains her brief relationship with Petworth in terms of a sexual dialectic: "I make you a certain kind of man, you make me a certain kind of woman." In these circumstances, Petworth realizes he is in "a difficult world, a place of false leads and harmful traps" where he is in need of a reliable guide "to bring shape to the shapeless, names to the unnamed, definition to the undefined."

Like the other protagonists in Malcolm Bradbury's novels (with the notable exception of Howard Kirk in *The History Man*), Petworth finds his peculiarly British brand of mild-mannered liberalism (the narrator taunts, "He is a man to whom life has been kind, and he has paid the price for it" inadequately prepares him for the unstable, shifting values of his new surroundings. . . . Bradbury endows Petworth with a gift of knowledge that none of his other characters, however, possessed: an understanding of theoretical linguistics, particularly semiotics and speech-act theory. This knowledge does not make Petworth's task of understanding the spoken language of his hosts any easier, but it does give him insights into his surroundings at a "deep structural" level. Thus, Petworth is often found reflecting on the universal qualities of human systems and organizations, from plane travel ("Plane travel makes all life alike; yet inside likeness there is difference", to universities' lecture-halls, cafeterias, stairwells, even students are—despite some differences in detail—"always rather much the same,"). Petworth follows the most basic signs and is able to complete his perilous journey to the East European city of Slaka and return to home and domesticity; at the end of the novel, he is found in London airport "following the signs, the words, the arrows, that lead him out, through the green channel that means nothing to declare, into the Heathrow concourse; where, at the barrier, he sees, waving at him, his dark wife."

Where Petworth fails to communicate effectively, where he stumbles frequently over "false leads and harmful traps," is at the "surface" level of human behavior and language-use; he feels threatened by foreign words and expressions, the mannerisms of foreign speakers, the behavior of people from an alien culture. Bradbury's importance as a comic novelist seems to thrive at this level. Commenting on the satirical art of C. S. Lewis, Aldous Huxley, and Evelyn Waugh, he provides a valuable insight into his own fiction:

The sense of the contingent nature of contemporary action, the feeling of a loss of logic running through society and history . . . , produces a sense of authorial displacement. The result is a species of comedy that turns neither on compassion or, in any direct sense, nostalgia, but on the immediate field of action seen by a distanced, confident narrator as a conditioned farce.

Certain key phrases here particularly apply to Bradbury's last two novels, *The History Man* and *Rates of Exchange,* where contingency and loss of logic are seen as bases of the contemporary condition by a narrator who seems cooly detached or displaced from the immediate field of action; the result is a succession of long paragraphs detailed with different objects and voices taken from modern life and written in an "historical present" tense that has now become a distinctive trademark of the Bradbury style. (pp. 101-03)

In his prefatory Author's Note, Bradbury jokes with the reader, "I'll be your implied author, if you'll be my implied reader"; besides being a playful allusion to Wayne Booth, the statement also sustains the post-structuralist assertion that meaning and value are not inherent in texts but are continually negotiated between reader and writer.

Bradbury's fictions, however, are not riddled with Nabokovian layers of elusive meanings. His first two novels are conventional in style and content; even *Rates of Exchange* treasures the fixed, stable value of liberal moralizing. . . . Each of his novels features at least one character who is obsessed with an intransigent political ideology.

If *Rates of Exchange* blends both post-modernist and conventional literary principles with great comic effect, it is because Bradbury becomes both a self-conscious and a self-effacing narrator. He foregrounds himself, paying tribute to the post-structuralist assertion that his novel is a verbal structure and a system of signifiers, but just as quickly he withdraws behind Petworth, his protagonist, to nudge him on and strike up a moral stance, holding the fiction up more conventionally as a mirror to the world. Bradbury recounts, at the beginning of the novel, a legend told of a local Slakan patron saint whose decimated corpse, being weighed in gold, could not tip the balance of scales until a little old widow woman stepped forward to add her tiny gold coin. "Of the story, you may make what you like," Bradbury comments, and then goes on to speculate how "Christian theologians . . . Marxist aestheticians . . . folklorists . . . (and the) more fashionable thinkers of the Structuralist persuasion" would interpret the story; but "if you were to ask me," he continues "I would probably pause for a moment, lighting my pipe to give an appearance of critical sagacity, think a little, and then suggest . . . that it is a typical Slakan fable about rates of exchange." He is both self-conscious and self-effacing here for at the same time as he brings attention to himself (as the armchair critic whose common sense repudiates the ideologically-bound theorists), he also demeans himself (as the stereotypical pipe-smoking, pseudo-intellectual).

A few pages later he again adopts the voice of common sense by claiming he will not be forced into making an interpretation of his novel because "I am a writer, not a critic; I like my fictions to remain fictions." This deliberately misleading statement and self-effacing posture conceal and illuminate a liberal humanist stance that Bradbury more explicitly adopts in his criticism where he argues that a closed ideology or critical formula (such as Christian theology, Marxist aesthetics,

Structuralism, and the kind of sociology practiced by Howard Kirk in *The History Man*) neglects the energies and creative curiosity that have gone into the shaping of a society or a novel. Clearly, he does not wish his fictions purely "to remain fictions" (in that playful arena of anti-meaning cherished by the "more fashionable thinkers of the Structuralist persuasion"); neither does he wish having his novel locked into unambiguous meaning by over-hasty critical interpretation.

This ambivalence helps to further explain Bradbury's stance toward his protagonists in *Rates of Exchange.* Petworth is conceived on two levels. On one level, he represents Bradbury's acknowledgment of post-structuralist theory, functioning as a verbal construction consciously manipulated by the author, clearly not a real-life character but a playful tool of fiction. On another level, Petworth is a realistic character who seems to share many of Bradbury's own liberal views, doubts, and uncertainties. He is the author's mouthpiece—a real person whose ideas and beliefs are meant to be taken seriously and sympathetically. On this level, Bradbury identifies with his protagonist's ability to open-mindedly absorb the plurality of voices and events that circulates around him.

Bradbury's criticism, at this point, offers another useful insight into the stylistic eclecticism of *Rates of Exchange.* Commenting on the heterogeneity of the post-World War Two British literary scene in *Possibilities: Essays on the State of the Novel,* he detects a "turning away from symbolist and formalist separation, as well as from a traditional humanistic moralism"; this turning away has "tended to bring realism and experiment oddly close together." (pp. 103-05)

Bradbury's own fiction attempts to creatively demonstrate what his criticism sets out as its underlying principle: that what is currently issuing out of Britain is not a single strain of fiction but a plurality of styles and voices. It seems to me that Bradbury is right there in the middle of the hubbub, analyzing as a critic and closely observing and absorbing as a fiction-writer. Like Professor Treece [protagonist of *Eating People Is Wrong*], he may be bewildered by all the commotion; like James Walker [protagonist of *Stepping Westward*], he may at times yearn for the vast open spaces of a foreign country; however, like Angus Petworth, he is able to read the signs clearly and ultimately find his way back to a home rooted in a stable domestic and literary tradition, from which standpoint he writes conventionally moral fictions mixed with stylistic ingenuity. (p. 105)

Robert S. Burton, "A Plurality of Voices: Malcolm Bradbury's 'Rates of Exchange'," in *Critique: Studies in Modern Fiction, Vol. XXVII, No. 2, Winter, 1987, pp. 101-06.*

ANDREW DAVIES

Cuts is a satirical farce about television, rather along the lines of [Evelyn Waugh's] *Scoop.* The Boot figure, Henry Babbacombe, is a harmless and obscure academic who sits in a shed inventing solipsistic fictions which 'fall somewhere between Eco and Endo'. By a quirk of fate (his agent happened to be having it off with the Head of Production for all of one crucial week . . . ah, those were the days!) he is plucked from obscurity to write a major serial which is going to recoup the fortunes and reputation of Eldorado TV and its chairman Lord Mellow (the Lord Copper figure).

Lord Mellow is good value: 'I like quality. I said so at the Edinburgh Festival, and now I'm stuck with it.' And Henry, despite his total ignorance of the genre, is contracted to deliver the quality product. Before his first draft has got beyond four pages, it is being developed, treated, exploited, rewritten, co-financed, cast, recast, location-scouted (Bradbury's lists are infectious) and sold worldwide by Lord Mellow's vast team of creative talent, all brilliant, resourceful, mindless, terrified people. 'The rewrites?' says Henry. 'How can he be doing the rewrites? I haven't even done the writes yet.' In no time at all Henry finds that he has written, or at least has his name on, a 13-episode blockbuster, with mountains in the background, short scenes, tight muscles, and climactic climaxes. He has forgotten who he was or what he used to believe. He has become part of the machine.

All this is sharp, knowing, and in its odd way uncomfortably accurate. Working in television does actually feel like this sometimes. But it would be naive to assume that realism, even of the satirically farcical kind, is what Bradbury is after here. His hero doubts the existence of external reality, seeks in his work to compete with the world rather than trying vulgarly to imitate it. His novels are 'paradigmatically intertextual and parodically postmodern,' noted for their refusal of the concept of character. Clearly Bradbury is nudging us into the correct posture for a reading of his own work.

Well, *Scoop* will have to do for intertextuality. As for the concept of character, Bradbury doesn't exactly refuse it point-blank. The—what shall we call them? Personae? Puppets?—have names, and physical attributes, so that we can tell them apart. . . . The more elaborately drawn figures, like Lord Mellow himself, or Sir Luke (an octogenarian theatrical knight), have a rich whiff of *Spitting Image* about them; which is apt, because ultimately everyone in this world is jerking in response to the Money on the Street.

How far Bradbury is competing with the world rather than vulgarly imitating it, is a knottier problem. The text is scattered with 'real' names: *Jewel in the Crown*, the Groucho Club, Harold Pinter, John Updike. Lighting cameramen behave like lighting cameramen, and make-up girls behave like make-up girls, though the electricians don't seem to be staying in the best hotel. So far, so lifelike. But in other ways Bradbury is boldly competing with the world, not in the manner of Eco, or Endo, or Beckett, or Marquez, or Llosa, but in the sturdy traditions of English wish-fulfilment. . . . (pp. 38-9)

Bradbury is also in competition with the techniques of television: his scenes are bravely and unfashionably lengthy, their muscles defiantly slack, and the climaxes . . . well, he never seems quite sure whether he's finished or not. Short as the text is, it might perhaps be improved by one or two, well . . . No. *Cuts* will make a smashing 13-part TV blockbuster. (p. 39)

Andrew Davies, "1986 and All That," in The Listener, *Vol. 117, No. 3007, April 16, 1987, pp. 38-9.*

OLIVER HARRIS

Set in the summer of 1986, with Thatcher's Britain performing 'a kind of national hara-kiri', [*Cuts*] dramatises an intersection of financial cuts on the university campus and editorial cuts in celluloid. These economies and liberties connect through the academic and media careers pursued by un-

known author and Morris Traveller driver, Henry Babbacombe. Commissioned by Eldorado Television to write a blockbuster series called 'Serious Damage', Babbacombe airs doubts about his script's lack of aesthetic teeth: 'I feel it could be missing something . . . Some element of experimentalism, some sense of surprise, some . . . difference.' Not only could the same easily be said of Bradbury's novella, but perhaps Babbacombe also realises the ironic appropriateness of their works' titles, since he inhabits a comic-strip reality where nothing is serious enough to suffer damage, or fleshed-out enough to feel the bite.

That no blood should flow from Bradbury's *Cuts* suggest the limits of the man who 'has his pulse on the finger of contemporary society'. That account of his ironic role was made some 20 years ago in *All Dressed Up and Nowhere to Go:* 'I was,' wrote Bradbury, the essayist of phogeydom, 'not an angry young man . . . But I was a niggling one, an uneasy figure struggling in my Englishness, fighting to get out.' As retrospective self-descriptions go, the image of Bradbury the niggling victim in sporting jackets fits suitably. For he has always been at his best when engaging the absurdities of liberalism at its historical turning points, each of his novels deliberately addressed to its respective decade.

Following *Rates of Exchange* (1983), *Cuts* seems intended as a mid-decade update. Accordingly it records news headlines on Chernobyl, AIDS and all the other topical crises that test the mettle of Englishness. But the same struggle to escape the national character that made Bradbury contempory in the 1960s leaves him out of step now; his passéist formula that 'it is better to live in the past than to live nowhere at all' has itself become passé, pre- rather than post-modern. Underneath the journalistic bulletins that punctuate the story, behind Bradbury's latest in literary in-jokes (lisping references to 'Woland Barthes', etc) moves an uneasy conservative spirit. The comedy of *Cuts* is reactionary, recycling once-funny jokes into stereotypes and exploiting the stock figures of English humour at its most hackneyed—the common cleaning lady with her silly malapropisms, the funny speech habits of those funny foreigners, the dozing Lords, bombastic theatrical Knights and randy women sporting unlikely names.

Overworking such gags and belabouring the verbal play on its title with tiresome éclat *Cuts* descends at times to shere puerlity. When the Vice Chancellor of Babbacombe's university plans to privatise its posts to include 'the Durex Chair of French Letters', it isn't even undergraduate laughter, but the smutty giggles of schoolchildren that is solicited. It is as if Bradbury the traditional novelist must now fight to escape Bradbury the modern critic not only by undercutting the values of enlightened liberalism and sophisticated academe, but also by parodying the bankruptcy, of fiction itself. (pp. 30-1)

Oliver Harris, "Worn-Out Blade," in New Statesman, *Vol. 113, No. 2925, April 17, 1987, pp. 30-1.*

TERRY EAGLETON

A typical ploy of the English academic novel is to bounce a dog-eared liberal humanist off a hard-boiled technocracy, allowing each to put the other into satirical question while the author disappears conveniently down the middle. Sparrow versus Zapp, Birmingham versus California, criticism against theory, mandarin modernism against brutalized postmodernism: these stark antagonists, irresolvable in content, have to make do with a coyly flirtatious liaison in the very forms of such fiction as an old-style literary realism tarts itself up with the odd structuralist device. Malcolm Bradbury's novella *Cuts* adheres faithfully to this model in its dominant metaphor: the title alludes at once to Thatcherite austerity, hence to the liberal conscience, and to the manipulative world of the media, as the surreal empire of Eldorado TV packages its consumerist fictions in a glass tower high above the human devastation of a northern industrial city.

The link between these worlds is Henry Babbacombe, a crumpled cross between David Lodge's Philip Sparrow and one of Raymond Briggs's grotesque innocents, catapulted by error from his humble post as extra-mural literature lecturer to a mammoth scriptwriting assignment with Lord Mellow, Eldorado's megalomaniac proprietor. Babbacombe is a wimp, Mellow a swine, and the rest of us live with Malcolm Bradbury somewhere in the middle, grinning wryly at both. Since grinning wryly at your own ineffectualness is part of the stock-in-trade of liberal humanism, indeed the best these days it seems able to muster, this middle is not such a impartial place as it looks. The whole model is deeply consoling, and works just as deftly when you transplant it to the current contentions between humanist criticism and literary theory. . . .

In a brilliantly witty essay entitled **"Writer and Critic"** [in *No, Not Bloomsbury*], Bradbury conducts a schizoid dialogue between the creative and critical aspects of himself, noting how the literary theorist in him is at war with the imaginative writer. Since Bradbury is not in fact a literary theorist, the rest of us can be forgiven for not having noticed this particular conflict. The dialogue in question is utterly disingenuous, since Bradbury treats literary theory, in these essays and elsewhere, in the facetious, civilizedly philistine manner common to English middle-class liberals. The idea that he is somehow on both sides of this debate simultaneously is mere rhetorical sleight-of-hand, and the middle, once more, rather further towards one side than the other. . . .

Bradbury is a humane rather than an ideological critic, which explains why in these essays he goes astonishingly easy on the sexism of a well-known English novelist, implicitly equates political radicalism and Thatcherite materialism, and elsewhere in his work refers politely to late capitalism as "modernization".

The submerged parallel between Eldorado TV and contemporary theory, however, doesn't really work. For Eldorado's products are of course drearily realist affairs, and the literature associated with contemporary theory is of course avantgarde. Bradbury thus makes Babbacombe, quite improbably, an experimental writer, to sustain the contrast with the aesthetics of Lord Mellow. This move, in the manner of the English academic novelist-critics, seeks to appropriate modernism to humanism, an operation which, as *Scrutiny* well enough revealed, unfortunately can't be carried off. A postLeavisian liberal humanism may trick itself out in modernist dress, and even dip the odd delicate toe into the swamps of post-structuralism; but it cannot go the whole theoretical hog, whatever the critic in Bradbury might like to think he is doing, since what such theory has to deliver is the bad news that modernist anti-humanism is not after all compatible with English empiricism. The strategy, then, is to hover sardonically in a rapidly shrinking middle, implicitly equating a commodified mass culture with Marxist, feminist and poststructuralist theory, so as to ward off the unsettling insight that the latter might after all have something useful to say about how to dismantle the former.

Terry Eagleton, "Undistributed Middle," in The Times Literary Supplement, No. 4393, June 12, 1987, p. 627.

BERNARD BERGONZI

Malcolm Bradbury, like John Bayley, is a critic who works in a university. But whereas Bayley does his best to ignore or conceal the system he is part of, Bradbury frequently focuses on it. One should say, more accurately, "systems", since he rotates hats rapidly: he is a Professor of American Studies, a critic, a reviewer, a novelist, an editor, a prize judge, a TV script-writer. Bradbury's most famous novel, **The History Man,** was about systems and how to work them, and the same preoccupation is apparent in his new collection of essays, **No, Not Bloomsbury.** It is a substantial volume, focusing on modern British writing, particularly fiction. . . .

Bradbury is much given, in the words of the old pop song, to "Talking About My Generation" and, quite apart from its other qualities, **No, Not Bloomsbury** provides a useful guide to the progress of English fiction since the 1950s, at the end of which decade Bradbury published his first novel, **Eating People is Wrong.** But the best and most revealing essay is the introductory one called **"Writer and Critic"**, in which Bradbury considers the relations between imaginative writing and literary criticism in the present phase of our culture, and then gives the discussion a quasi-autobiographical turn by showing how he deals with these two aspects of his own literary persona. This is a splendidly witty essay, which acknowledges that the relationship is basically schizophrenic, and concludes by seeing it as a difficult but reluctantly persisting marriage. The discussion relates interestingly to parts of Bayley's, as when Bradbury remarks:

> "Writers do not really want to be analysed and put on record. They simply want to be totally and entirely *understood,* wordlessly valued for their irreducible perfection. In this, of course, they are just like the rest of us."

Bradbury's tone is evasive. He is ready to make jokes about the current gurus of the academy, but what Bayley resists, Bradbury tends to accept, as the way things are. In practice, the division within himself between the critic and the writer seems to be one that he can live with quite comfortably.

This opening essay is followed by two others of general literary speculation, on the relations between contemporary writing and painting, and on the present as an "age of parody". They are full of interest and ideas, though intermittently marred by Bradbury's tendency to work at a vulnerably high level of cultural generalisation. The rest of the collection is arranged in a loosely literary-historical way to discuss British writing from the 1940s to the present.

Bradbury's arguments are conducted, it seems to me, in terms of two different schemata, which do not work together very easily. The first is concerned with modernism and its aftermath, implicitly in terms of an entropic running-down; the entropy model is noticeable in post-modernist fiction. In this perspective the neo-Realistic British writing of the 1950s—the era of the Movement and the Angry Young Men—represents decline, a collapse after the high energies of modernism had been expended, a return to convention and a regressive sense of the past.

This was the way unsympathetic critics saw it at the time, and in places Bradbury comes close to this view; he is a great respector of modernism and has no inclination to diminish its achievements. Nevertheless, his loyalty to his generation provides another and conflicting model, which represents the 1950s as a period when strong if insular literary talents emerged in England. (p. 43)

The clash is illustrated in the juxtaposition of two essays. One is on Malcolm Lowry, applauding *Under the Volcano,* a long-gestated masterpiece of modernist fiction, appearing, improbably, in the late 1940s. The following essay is a sympathetic and admiring study of C. P. Snow and William Cooper, whose work embodied the spirit of the '50s: opposition to literary modernism, a concern for man as a social being, and traditional concepts of character and story-telling. Snow and Cooper are unlikely to have had much time for Lowry, but Bradbury writes of them all in the same broadly approving tone. Undoubtedly his ideas have changed and developed during the many years in which these essays were written, but they are reprinted without dates of publication, and have been revised in the attempt to create a seemingly homogeneous and sustained study, but without concealing shifts in attitude.

"I have never much liked realism", he remarked in a recent piece, which is not what he used to say. An explicit dialogue between the Bradbury of the '50s and the Bradbury of the '80s might have made a lively way of dealing with the problem. Some of his best studies do in fact hint at such a dialogue, when they discuss novelists who first made their reputations in the '50s and have continued to develop creatively ever since, moving in the process from ostensible realism and social comedy to pastiche, fantasy, and a consciousness of the terrors and disturbances that undermine the safe existence of "man in society" on the 1950s model. Kingsley Amis and Angus Wilson are notable examples, on both of whom Bradbury writes well. The implicit parallel with his own development as a novelist is unmistakable.

One essay, inserted rather incongruously among the studies of novelists, is on F. R. Leavis, seen as a major contributor to that by now somewhat mythicised cultural climate of the 1950s: insular, provincial, non-conformist, empirical, decent, down-to-earth. Bradbury writes admiringly of Leavis, who influenced his own origins as a critic, as he did so many of that generation. But by now he is far from being a Leavisite critic. Bradbury's literary sympathies are so broad as to exclude very little, and he avoids making unfavourable judgments where possible, generally preferring exposition and interpretation to evaluation. . . .

Some of Bradbury's criticism reads rather like a publicity handout for modern English fiction, in a deeply un-Scrutineering spirit; the model may be partly that of the British Council lecture delivered in foreign parts, where the lecturer aims to tell the audience in straightforward terms about "what has been going on lately in the novel", and at the same time to provide some discreet patriotic hyping of the product. He is given to curiously formulaic accolades, which have the invariability of epic diction: "Iris Murdoch is unmistakably one of our great contemporary novelists"; "Muriel Spark is one of our finest and surest modern novelists"; on John Fowles, "I consider him one of our great writers"; "Burgess

is one of our most likeable writers"; on William Golding, "one of our greatest postwar novelists"; on D. M. Thomas, "one of our best contemporary writers".

This formulaic tendency is related to another, in that Bradbury's critical prose tends to the condition of the rapid list, whether of proper names, or attributes, or concepts, usually illustrative of the present or pending condition of our culture. This does not make for good writing, and suggests little of the acute linguistic sensitivity that marks *Rates of Exchange,* or the parodies in *Who Do You Think You Are?* In a vigorous, personal piece about the problems of working for television Bradbury remarks of the medium: "Out of it all comes a little that is good, a fair amount that is bad, and a general level of technical competence so impressive that it is quite often hard to tell the difference." This makes, sharply and accurately, the kind of point that tends not to be often made in his writing on fiction. Here, as elsewhere in the book, we are hearing the voice of the Writer rather than the Critic. On the whole, the Writer writes better. (p. 44)

Bernard Bergonzi, "A Quiet Place: 'Readers' vs. 'Students'," in Encounter, *Vol. LXIX, No. 2, July-August, 1987, pp. 40-5.*

LAURENCE LERNER

The death of the author poses a tricky problem for those authors who are still alive. If it is language that speaks and writing that writes; if the individual writer has lost his autonomy and become a dispersed subject through which linguistic and social codes transmit themselves; and if the function of thought is now to deconstruct the concepts necessary for thinking, so that (in the words, if they are his words, of Henri Mensonge [hero of *Mensonge*]) there is not only no philosophical object of attention, but also no agent capable of doing the philosophising; and if the classical distinctions between literature and philosophy, between narrative and theory, between thinking and joking, are all called into question . . .

I keep saying 'if', but we are surrounded by people who do believe these things—or rather, if they really believe them, they are not people who believe them, but vehicles through which the ideas are transmitted in texts that tirelessly undermine their own status. So perhaps we should say *since* the author is dead and the individual has become a dispersed subject, etc, there are problems for the person who sits down at his/her desk to put words onto a hitherto blank page. What will the book be 'about' if there is no extra-textual reality? Will it be a novel or a work of theory?

Enfin Malherbe vint. The situation was waiting for Malcolm Bradbury. In [*Mensonge*], Bradbury has invented the figure of Henri Mensonge, who changed the face of modern philosophy by writing a book on fornication as a cultural act, published by the Imprimerie Kouskous in Luxembourg, in a minute edition of which no two copies are alike and all are now unobtainable. Since then Mensonge has preserved an absence more magnificently total than any deconstructor has yet managed. (p. 29)

It would be nice to think that Bradbury in his turn was invented by Mensonge, as a persona to speak through while remaining silent, so indulging in the deconstructive act of having one's chocolate cake and eating it—well, not 'it', but a text, fictitious like all texts, in which 'cake' is a lexeme brought into being by the existence of culinary discourse.

I would love to think this, and so (in some moods) would Bradbury, but it won't work. Bradbury is no Mensonge, he lives (extra-textually) in Norwich, and wrote not only this book but lots of others, some of them novels (stories, that is, about people who never existed) and others literary criticism (discussions, that is, of books which exist and tell stories about people who never existed). This means that he belongs to that interesting modern species, the academic novelist, with his two selves, one sober, scholarly and salaried, the other inventive, irresponsible and either very rich or very poor. One problem for the members of this species is whether to keep the two selves as separate as they can, or to blend them constantly, to write fiction that sounds like criticism, criticism that sounds like narrative, and parody that differs only by the lifting of an eyebrow from what it parodies.

The latter has always been Bradbury's method. His novels are about academics, his comic writing glides in and out of his own critical style. It is obviously a dangerous method: self-parody can be a means of saving others the trouble. (pp. 29-30)

But as well as dangers the method has great opportunities— or rather one great opportunity, when it comes to making fun of post-structuralism. For deconstruction has discovered what satire has always known, that the most devastating sub-version comes not from those who merely fear and dislike what they attack, but from those who fear what they love, who understand and admire what they also believe to be impossible. Swift is far more deadly on the Houyhnhnms than he is on the pedants of Laputa. Bradbury himself has claimed that he is far closer to his own Howard Kirk [of **The History Man**] than are those readers who find Kirk merely despicable. And out of Bradbury's own ambivalence towards modern criticism comes the most effective satire that it has yet received. I have heard old-fashioned academics raise easy laughs from like-minded audiences by quoting bits of decon-structivist jargon. I have heard earnest deconstructors use the jargon to admiring, gullible audiences. But I have had to wait for Malcolm Bradbury to find the undermining from within, the tiny displacement that makes the whole thing plausible and absurd. This is not only the best satire of deconstruction, it is the best thing Bradbury has written. (p. 30)

Laurence Lerner, *"Somebody's Best Book Yet,"* in The Spectator, *Vol. 259, No. 8303, September 5, 1987, pp. 29-30.*

JOHN LANCHESTER

Mensonge is an expansion of an article originally published in the *Observer* on April Fool's Day, 1984. It comes with a bogus index and bibliography and an afterword by David Lodge, written in the persona of Michel Tardieu, the fictional Professor of Structuralist Narratology from Lodge's novel *Small World* (Tardieu claims to have once had a glimpse of Mensonge, perhaps at 'one of Samuel Beckett's increasingly brief first nights'). As well as being an account of Mensonge's 'life' (about which nobody knows anything) and 'work' (just the one very short, unobtainable book) *Mensonge* is a jokey potted history of Structuralism, starting with Saussure and going through to 'our "post-modern condition"—a state of affairs where, in the wake of the Holocaust and in an era of

terrible nuclear anxiety, we not only lose all hope in techno-logical, human and social progress but start wearing green Liberty scarves as well'.

The non-relation of Post-Structuralism to common sense and its close thematic counterpart, the paradox of the jogging De-constructionist, are the source of much of the comedy in *Mensonge.* The book also allows the reader to feel the kind of pleasure which comes from being sufficiently in the know to get its jokes. The sentences tend to contain their comic component in a facetious little kick at the end: for instance, Bradbury says of Post-Structuralism that it is 'the philosophy that goes along with everything else we know so well now— our chiliasm, our apocalypticism, our post-humanist scepti-cism, our metaphysical exhaustion, our taste for falafel'. *Mensonge* depends on an attitude of sympathetic scepticism towards the ideas it describes, and in that sense it is a very British contribution to the Structuralist and Post-Structuralist *paideuma*. After all, a reader genuinely hostile to Deconstruction might not have much time for Mensonge the thinker, but he or she would be unlikely to have much sympathy either for the Post-Modernist trickery of *Men-songe* the book. The blurb hints that *Mensonge* is targeted on the 'Thinking Person's' Christmas stocking, and that seems about right for it. If it is an unsatisfactory book to sit down and read at a sitting, that is, perhaps, because of its length, and also because of the unremittingness of the face-tious humour it employs: I could not help thinking that Bor-ges would have dealt with a fictional Mensonge in ten pages and without wisecracks, though not of course without hu-mour. Not that Bradbury can be blamed for not being Borges: but it is probably true that *Mensonge* would have been a fun-nier book if it contained fewer jokes. (pp. 10-11)

John Lanchester, *"Absent Authors,"* in London Re-view of Books, *Vol. 9, No. 18, October 15, 1987, pp. 10-11.*

LORRIE MOORE

Henry Babbacombe, the writer-protagonist of Malcolm Bradbury's new novel, **Cuts,** has no need to search for El-dorado; it has come looking for him. Eldorado is a British television company aiming to insure its solvency and future with a blockbuster "miniseries". . . .

It wants a drama with "love and power and tenderness and glory, and a lot of mountains in the background." It wants "love and power. Past and present. Tears and laughter." It wants "love and feeling, ancient buildings and contemporary problems." It wants "contemporary reality, strong hero, ele-gant locations." It wants "something that's art, but is also life at its deepest and most telling." It wants "a lush foreign loca-tion where you can get malt whisky." It wants "epic." It wants "tragic." It wants "cheap."

In a quaint and decorous moment Eldorado decides it also wants a writer—someone brilliant and postmodern, with a "decidedly bushel-hidden light." Someone with a rumbling stomach. That week, it so happens, Henry Babbacombe's agent is sleeping with an Eldorado executive, and it is sug-gested that Eldorado give Babbacombe a try.

As for Babbacombe, he desires no such thing. He lives con-tentedly and alone in a tiny northern hill village, where he teaches evening classes on "Sex and Maturity in the English Novel" and the somewhat more popular "Fiction and the

Farm." During the day he writes obscure, Beckettian novels in the garden shed of his backyard. . . . When he is summoned to the glass high-rise of Eldorado Television, he is baffled but he goes, bringing with him on the train a pile of student essays on *Middlemarch.*

After that, circumstances conspire to urge Babbacombe into accepting Eldorado's offer. . . . When he returns to his provincial university to discuss with the head of his department the possibility of a leave of absence, Babbacombe is given a grim speech about university financial problems. Already the college has had to rely on private endowments in an unprecedented manner, as in "the Kingsley Amis Chair of Women's Studies." The chairman, whose problems before the cuts had always been either of fornication or of plagiarism, is now obliged to get rid of two staff members. . . .

Henry Babbacombe has given his chairman the perfect opportunity. The chairman must consider the impact of crass television work on the reputation of his faculty. . . . Envy and budget cuts team up, and Babbacombe is fired from his academic Eden—his life of quiet eccentricity and bold indifference to reality, his world of sooty Gothic buildings papered with announcements of essay competitions on "whether there should be a third sex." He is plunged instead into the dark farce of a scriptwriting career.

What ensues is riotous if predictable misadventure. In the world of script collaboration, Babbacombe is the prototypical literary naïf: a country cousin, sans feck, sans hap, sans hope. Without his knowledge or consent the setting of the series switches continents weekly. Eldorado personnel begin the rewrites before Babbacombe has finished the "writes." Eldorado titles Babbacombe's script "Serious Damage," and truly it is that. His literary ambitions in abeyance, Babbacombe, wooed with kiwi fruit, becomes a kind of emissary of his own incapacitated self, a venturer if not adventurer into the heartless illogic of commercial television. It is a world that believes all problems are problems of "notional casting." It is a world in which an obscure Beckettian novelist is asked to work up a totally spurious death scene, and does so, setting a new "standard in rigor mortis."

To add injury to insult, the urban landscape Babbacombe encounters is one wrought by privation, privatization, moral calamity. Lovemaking is "staccato and short. . . . It was wise not to touch someone who might have touched someone else who in turn had touched someone else. . . . Sex was being replaced by gender." And tenderness is pruned to tender—wedges and slivers of the diminishing national pie. Says the omniscient narrator of *Cuts,* "The only pleasure left to make life worth living, if it was at all, was money, poor little paper money, which was trying to do all the work."

Malcolm Bradbury is the author of an impressive array of critical works (including books on Evelyn Waugh and Saul Bellow) and of the novels *Eating People Is Wrong, The History Man* and *Rates of Exchange.* What he has given us in *Cuts* is once more a depiction of man as historical performer, this time in a satirical romp through Thatcher England. "It was a time for getting rid of the old soft illusions, and replacing them with the new hard illusions."

Mr. Bradbury has milked his title for all it is worth, and it is worth much. If he has left us feeling a bit severed at the end, it may have been one cut too many, but we get the authorial joke. There is so much fun, fury and intelligence in this little novel, one can forgive its insistent cartoonishness

or those rare moments when the wit is less rapier than spoon. If the insidious world of television—as literary subject or sociological context—manages by its very nature to preclude the writing of great literature, that would be this modest book's point. Mr. Bradbury has succeeded in doing what the social satirist must do: to amuse trenchantly, leaving in the throat "a strange taste rather like a rancid kiwi fruit."

> Lorrie Moore, "Give Me Epic, Give Me Tragic, Give Me Cheap," in The New York Times Book Review, October 18, 1987, p. 9.

ANN HULBERT

Margaret Drabble's long and ironic novel [*The Radiant Way*] about the early years of Margaret Thatcher's reign reads like a fat book with a thin book inside, dying to get out. Malcolm Bradbury's short and satiric novel [*Cuts*] about the Thatcher government's maturity shows what the thin book might have looked like.

The books' origins may help account for their physiques. Drabble was at work revising *The Oxford Guide to English Literature* when Thatcher began revising just about everything else in Britain during the first half of the '80s. Not surprisingly, Drabble was thinking big by the time she surfaced from the classics in 1984. What the decade needed was a Dickens or a George Eliot—an ambitious, imaginative social portraitist. . . . [The] time had come to undertake the state-of-England novel, and Thatcher's conservative revolution conveniently seemed to call for a large canvas.

Bradbury's inspiration was more direct and modest. In 1985 he was busy at the BBC, working on an elaborate television dramatization of one of his novels. As filming was about to start (after trips to Turkey and other extravagances), funding was cut off: the Thatcher ax had struck close to home. But the fiasco wasn't a complete waste. When his publisher proposed that he produce a short novel in four months, Bradbury was ready. Why not try a send-up of Thatcherite austerity, at screenplay length, set in the TV industry?

Cuts is just that. But it is also, uncannily, a send-up of the long-winded anti-Thatcherite sensibility of Drabble's novel. The premise of Bradbury's book is that the best way to treat Lady Rigour's revolution is to give it a taste of its own medicine; the heartless, straitened times don't deserve—and can't inspire—a spacious, grandly ironic novel. His compact "screenplay," peopled by caricatures and propelled by a preposterous plot, is more than simply clever parody. Bradbury conveys a mood of dazed disorientation; it feels dark when his book is over. (p. 38)

Bradbury sets out to dramatize the comic abnormality of all the ax-wielding in England in a book that reads like a mock revision of Drabble. He cuts her five years to three months, focusing on the summer of 1986, when government austerity was at its peak and the Big Bang was around the corner—when regulations limiting London's banks would be cut, to revive the City as an international financial center. He cuts back geographically as well: where Drabble shuttled between London and "Northam, that figurative northern city," he sets his story all in a "great sad northern city," where gleaming gentrification and decay are juxtaposed.

Bradbury also cuts down on protagonists, and makes them contrasting caricatures. The CEO of Eldorado Television and the lecturer in the Department of Extra-Mural Studies who star in Bradbury's plot call to mind Drabble's Charles and Brian. But Lord Mellow and Henry Babbacombe are not stereotypes striving to be rounded, they are triumphantly flat and extreme: the tyrannical TV mogul is the worldly entrepreneur and the hapless professor is the innocent dreamer. It's a tried and true pairing for the story about illusion and disillusion with reality that Bradbury, like Drabble, sees in the Thatcher revolution.

But where Drabble ironically titles her grim book after an idealistic TV documentary (and a child's primer), Bradbury takes his title straight from the cutting room floor. He presents rushes of unreality, and they turn out to be not only entertaining but revealing. His focus is on the rich and renovated, a dimension of the Thatcher revolution missing from Drabble's drama of the crumbling middle. Offering the devastating view from the inside, Bradbury captures the frenetic confusion of those who do the cutting as well as of their victims.

Eldorado Television is housed in a tall glass building that looms over a bleak region, which "all the same . . . offered many stories of bleak human truth, set against good grainy locations." Low-budget productions have been the company's specialty, but Lord Mellow has decided in the summer of 1986 that the "moment has come to try for the peaks." It's time to produce a high-quality show that will attract all the "floating money [in London] that's begging to invest in the right-quality artistic package," as well as worldwide co-production money—a series that will end up on prime-time American TV. (p. 41)

Henry Babbacombe, a "decidedly bushel-hidden light," as the head of his department calls him, is plucked from his teaching post at a provincial university in a dispiriting hill village to save the day for Eldorado. His previous literary work "falls somewhere roughly between Eco and Endo" and is best characterized, he explains, not by subject but by color; "I'm afraid I doubt the existence of an external reality," he says, and describes his latest book as yellow. Happily working all day in his shed on his Beckettian novels, Henry has no reason to know anything about reality. But now, suddenly a "great model of Thatcherite enterprise" (as his department head wryly salutes him, before firing him), he's plunged into it.

Or is it fantasy? Bradbury nimbly plays off of the convergence of Henry's and Eldorado Television's tenuous holds on reality. For although Henry is totally flummoxed by the strange project he embarks on, he also fits in. "I see it as essentially puce" is his contribution to the first script consultation he attends at Eldorado, which doesn't deter the rest of the staff in the slightest, because they'd never planned to pay him any attention anyway. The writer is only one cog in the mad machinery that goes into making "Serious Damage," as the series is to be called. Bradbury has a great time exposing the heartless, brainless havoc of script composition: while everyone is busy cutting whatever everyone else has written, locations are scouted, costumes made, actors hired, money spent. The point is that the crazy splicing and splurging in the studio conjure up the ravages in the real world. The story, in the end, really is puce.

It veers, for a while, toward a sunnier, more conventional color. In a panoramic passage that sounds remarkably like Drabble, except that here the satire sails rather than sinks, Bradbury elaborates on the relation between Eldorado's drama and Thatcher's serial:

> Manufacturing industry was declining, jobs for the young were disappearing, financial speculation was increasing, and everyone was waiting for the Big Bang. Rape and child-murder were increasing; crime-figures escalating, the centres of great cities deteriorating. Sex was lethal, smoking abhorrent, drinking dangerous, food destructive, and indeed the only pleasure left to make life worth living, if it was at all, was money, poor little paper money, which was trying to do all the work. It was a serial that Henry watched intermittently, glancing at its banal horrors, its bland tragedies, its half-apocalyptic messages, its unstructured and chaotic plots.

Given this backdrop, Henry understood "why people might actually want to watch a tale of reassuring characters, traditional and solid houses, established customs, sunlit lawns, sentimental feelings, flowing nostalgia, and an all too happy ending—the sort of tale that somehow, as he worked along with the team at Eldorado, 'Serious Damage' was showing every sign of becoming."

Due to last-minute cuts, however, the teamwork unravels. When one of the two stars collapses, Henry is sent to rework the script. Now "he had some deep cuts to make himself," and as he tries to write around the empty spaces, his original aspiration toward puce is realized: cold darkness intrudes. "Perhaps it didn't really need to be about anything at all, or not in the sense of about that is usually about. Lots of events happened, but they happened disconnectedly, obscurely, just as in his novels"—just as in real life. Bradbury closes the circle: Henry's arcane vision of an atomized world and the chaotic reality of an atomized world have converged in the surreal serial.

In the end, the whole series is cut, so we never know exactly how Henry has handled those banal horrors, bland tragedies, half-apocalyptic messages, and chaotic plots that have pressed in upon him. But it's quite clear that he, like his creator, would have avoided Drabble's difficulties. In striving for encompassing realism, Drabble succumbed to the radical confusion of the Thatcher decade. The prime minister shook up the country; the novelist tried to assemble the pieces on her canvas—and prose proved more unwieldy than politics. Drabble earnestly monitors the mood of the times, but she never manages seriously and fully to imagine it. The irony she counts on to mark her distance from the chaos only makes everyone's bewilderment seem inconsequential; it doesn't inspire the sympathy needed for an ample portrait of a disoriented country.

Henry skirts such dangers, airily announcing his anti-realist stance early on: "Naturally as a maker of fictions I believe the world is a fiction. . . . I am competing with the world, not trying vulgarly to imitate it." As literary theory, this entrepreneurial spirit of competition turns out to produce fiction that is peculiarly well-suited to the fractured age. The prime minister has exercised a free hand, slicing and splicing; so has Bradbury, seizing an opportune moment for a cutting farce. (p. 42)

Ann Hulbert, "Maggiemarch," in The New Republic, *Vol. 197, No. 24, December 14, 1987, pp. 38, 40-2.*

OLIVER CONANT

[*Cuts*] is assuredly a "good read" (the originally English lo-cution is especially apt here), but it is a slighter effort [than Bradbury's previous novels]; indeed, it is in some respects the slightest of his fictions to date. In the first place, it is really a novella. Then there is the principal subject, British com-mercial television, and the cheerfully off-hand manner in which it is treated. The characters are without exception one-dimensional, and the briskly constructed plot is confined to the level of farce.

Given such limitations, the variety and ambitiousness of the satire in *Cuts* is remarkable, well beyond the reach of many novels twice its length. The author undertakes no less than a comprehensive accounting of the symptoms, major and minor, of what he would have us believe is England's "ulti-mate state of decline." Besides the surprising vulgarity of commercial British TV, the symptoms include postmodern architecture, nouvelle cuisine, Thatcherite retrenchment, provincial academics, avant-garde writers, and provincial ac-ademics who are also avant-garde writers. Bradbury is at mo-ments capable of an almost Dickensian scorn for the selfish cant of Tory politicians, and for the newer, American-inspired forms of money worship.

At the center of *Cuts* is Henry Babbacombe, a lecturer in En-glish and drama at a small university in the north of England where, because of fiscal austerity, "they were cutting almost everything." He is also a writer who is "virtually unknown even to himself." In a gloomy shed at the bottom of his cot-tage garden on the moors, hard by the "tiny and depressing hill-village" of Smallby, he produces what his department head refers to as "strange and solitary fantasies." . . .

The machinery that will propel this pure, obscure soul into the hectic world of television is set in motion when the pugna-cious Lord Mellow, chairman of the board of Eldorado TV—"one of the smaller and more remote of the independent pro-gramme companies"—addresses his cowering staff in the company's headquarters. Eldorado's franchise is up for re-newal, and he announces that it needs a "high quality drama" to ensure this.

Lord Mellow is fed up with the customary prize-winning seri-als, such as *Brideshead Revisited* or *The Jewel in the Crown.* He wants no more End of Empire stories, no more Great Houses. . . . To write the series he has in mind, Mellow in-sists on "someone new and original who delivers scripts on time and isn't off on a yacht with Bertolucci when you need him for rewrites."

Out of the blue, Henry—whose agent happens at the time to be sleeping with a strategically placed woman at Eldorado—is informed he is to be that someone. He is flattered but uncer-tain. Mightn't it compromise his integrity? Lord Mellow's people are counting on him to write something with "believ-able characters," something that has "reality." He doesn't be-lieve in characters, nor, as a good disciple of Umberto Eco, is he particularly keen on the concept of reality. . . . And how can he possibly produce all he is expected to—10 epi-sodes of 50 minutes each—before the next semester begins?

The last problem, at least, is solved when Henry learns that he has been—what else?—cut from the university staff. So he proceeds to pound out on his Remington portable a script containing no action, no dialogue, and stage directions de-scribing "an atmosphere of indescribable menace" and "an atmosphere of intellectual confusion." After much team ef-fort and many rewrites, the script finally resembles what Lord Mellow desires. Henry's teleplay, called *Serious Dam-age* (the name, along with most of the plot and characters, is supplied by the Eldorado staffers) ends up a schlocky mul-tigenerational saga, featuring reassuring characters, elegant locations and an all too happy ending.

Much of the best comedy in *Cuts* comes from the carefully established contrasts between Henry's old and new worlds: between his grouchy old department head, who has always thought that "genitals are a great distraction to scholarship" and the luscious script girl Cynthia Hyde-Lemon, ever eager to work on Henry's climaxes; or between the hard, lonely cre-ating in the garden shed and the more congenial collaborative effort of writing for television. Ultimately, one suspects, Henry is happier working for Eldorado TV. He is thrilled by the belief that this vast and intricate organization, with its de-partments of design and transport and casting and locations and finance, is laboring to bring his words, his vision, before the great British public.

Occasionally the jokes in *Cuts* fall a little flat. It is perhaps too predictable, for example, that the French structuralist at Henry's university should have named his daughters Langue and Parole. And the caricature of the avant-garde sensibili-ty—is there really such a thing anymore?—is less, well, cut-ting than some of the other thrusts. At times Henry's pro-nouncements make him sound more like a Gilbert and Sulli-van esthete than a contemporary writer. Lord Mellow and his subordinates at Eldorado are about as cartoonish as the news-paper magnates in Evelyn Waugh's equally slight novel *Scoop,* the apparent source of part of the premise for *Cuts.* In short, this is not the great satiric novel on England's cur-rent plight that someday someone—maybe Bradbury—will write. Still, it is great fun. (p. 21)

Oliver Conant, "John Bull's Decline," in The New Leader, *Vol. LXXI, No. 1, January 11-25, 1988, pp. 20-1.*

ANDREW SHELLEY

"*La Mort de L'Auteur*" is the occasion for Malcolm Brad-bury's Arthurian quest for the mythical Henri Mensonge [*Mensonge*], author of *La Fornication comme acte culturel.* "The significance of the non-significance" of M. Mensonge, according to M. Bradbury, is to have drawn attention to the illogicality of Deconstruction:

> "If the author was dead, it was still necessary to have a Deconstructionist author who could explain this to us."

Barthes lived up to the death of the author by being run over by a laundry van in 1980. Mensonge out-Barthes Barthes by not existing in the first place. As he says (the "translation" is Bradbury's):

> "You must understand that the 'fact' of my exis-tence would negate what my text *as text* is saying."

Mensonge's non-existence makes him the most important fig-ure in de-, pre-, and post-structuralist thought, claims Brad-bury. (pp. 45-6)

Mensonge's absent presence, or present absence, allows a di-rect "dissemination of authority" to Mensonge's readers, who thus become his authors. Bradbury offers an illuminating summary of some exceedingly difficult passages in *La Fornication,* whose main thesis is that the whole of human thought, in postulating "an illusory metaphysical vagina", is based upon "a phallusy". He also presents us with a fascinating insight into the origin of Cubism—that it occurred when Picasso resolved to paint Gertrude Stein's portrait—and a revisionist reinterpretation of Marx, "who showed how history worked, if we followed the instructions properly". (p. 46)

Andrew Shelley, "The Word & The World: Literary Theory, Critical Práctice," in Encounter, *Vol. LXXX, No. 4, April, 1988, pp. 42-7.*

DAVID WRIGHT

[*Unsent Letters*] is an entertaining collection of put-downs and take-offs: in effect Malcolm Bradbury's burlesque *curriculum vitae* plus Bluffer's Guide to novel-writing and the groves of Academe. It's an on-target critique of contemporary universities, writing, writers' lives, wives—and, come to think of it, of life as lived—a mix of light-handed, lethal drollery and grassroots commonsense that puts one in mind of Oscar Wilde's dictum: 'Criticism is the highest form of autobiography.' Not that one is bound to swallow, without a shovelful of salt, quite all that Mr Bradbury lets slip, with admirable comic gravity, concerning the various dolours and delights he has experienced as novelist. Eng Lit don, visiting lecturer in America, peripatetic conference-attender, television scriptwriter, etc. But one is left convinced of the impressionist truth of these anecdotes, if not of their factual veracity. (p. 33)

Mr. Bradbury's strategy has been to concoct letters addressed to fictional—and on occasion non-fictional—representative figures in the academic, literary, and publishing worlds in which he has moved, or at any rate glissaded, during the last 30 years: letters that he (as one may well believe) never got round to posting. Some of the addressees are pests—eg. the Mittel-european student seeking information for a thesis, the would-be writer who wants to get started.

> There is an old saw that says that every one of us has one novel in us, and I can personally attest that this is true—since what they do when they have written it is to pack it in a parcel and send it to me. No, they are started all right . . . for the truth is that most of the books that are written are never published, just as most of the books that are published are never written.

Realistic, not to say disillusioned, advice is handed to aspirants for university posts:

> Our present political masters regard British universities in much the same way that Henry VIII regarded the monasteries. My own university, far from looking for new people, is paying distinguished colleagues considerable sums to depart.

As for writers:

> A good writer is someone with a mind so fine that no idea can violate it, someone on whom no impression is lost, and someone who also has a relative, friend, or lover who happens to work in the editorial department of one of our leading publishing houses. . . . People do not want books about the kind of life you lead. No point in depressing them

unnecessarily. . . . Any great artist knows that the reading public he is appealing to is posterity, which, by definition, has not arrived yet, causing cash-flow problems.

(pp. 33-4)

One could go on picking the plums out of Mr Bradbury's enjoyable pudding, which contains among other things good take-offs of Auden and Alan Pryce-Jones, much relevant advice to writers' wives (and to the husbands of writers' wives), and particularly to those contemplating taking up the academic life:

> British universities do accept and study writers, but with one stern proviso I was not prepared to accept: they must be dead first. American universities seem to have the opposite attitude, filling their campuses with errant poets and wandering novelists, who write their work in one room and teach it in the next, so short-circuiting many of the problems of reaching an audience.

(p. 34)

David Wright, "A Miscellany of English Pros," in The Spectator, *Vol. 260, No. 8341, May 21, 1988, pp. 33-4.*

ELLEN CAROL JONES

Unsent Letters is Malcolm Bradbury's letter to the world that never wrote to him: a collection of letters of the Moses Herzog "Dear Nietzsche" type, written not to the famous dead but to the famous never alive—Nabokov's Charles Kinbote, Bradbury's own Nathalie Pelham Barker, for example—and the famous still alive—Rushdie. The collection is collective, representative, all-purpose, intended to post(pone) any and all issues that Bradbury or his correspondents may address. It is itself one large "Wissenschaft" letter, that representative missile from abroad that the desperate scholar sends: "If your books are funny, please tell me where, and send me your ontology of the comedic and your theoretiks of the humoristic, and how you like to compare yourself with Aristotle, Nietzsche, Bergson and Freud." (p. 385)

Bradbury founds his ontology of the comedic and theoretiks of the humoristic in irreverence, particularly toward the pretensions of academia, as his epistolary lay-person's guide to conferences, complete with a sample multipurpose conference paper, and his university novels, . . . bear witness. . . . One of the unsent letters, **"Inspeak: Your Streetwise Guide to Linguistics and Structuralism,"** written to a Semiotic Enquirer, purports to answer those questions raised by his most wicked satire yet of the postmodern condition of the university, the *fin de siècle* philosophies of posthumanist scepticism, in *My Strange Quest for Mensonge.* But the very *presence* of the new philosopher who calls all in doubt, Henri Mensonge—indeed, the very representation of his *voice* in the text of the letter or the letter of the text—give the lie to the ontological necessity (or anti-ontological necessity) of his absence in the novel itself. By his absence Mensonge remains the purest instance of the death of the author, living proof of Roland Barthes's famous comment that "linguistically the Author is never more than the instance writing." (p. 386)

Ellen Carol Jones, in a review of "Unsent Letters: Irreverent Notes From a Literary Life," in Modern Fiction Studies, *Vol. 35, No. 2, Summer, 1989, pp. 385-86.*

FURTHER READING

Widdowson, Peter. "The Anti-History Men: Malcolm Bradbury and
David Lodge." *Critical Quarterly* 26, No. 4 (Winter 1984): 5-32.
    Examines numerous similarities in the fiction and criticism of
    Bradbury and Lodge.

Alexander Buzo

1944-

(Born Alexander John Buzo) Australian dramatist, scriptwriter, and novelist.

Regarded as among Australia's most popular and controversial dramatists, Buzo is best known for his comedies of manners that expose the personal inadequacies of outwardly successful middle-class characters. Influenced during the late 1960s by such absurdist playwrights as Samuel Beckett and Eugéne Ionesco, Buzo was among the first of the "New Wave" Australian dramatists who explored social dynamics through surrealism, stereotypes, and stylized dialogue. Peter Fitzpatrick observed: "Buzo's subject is the hollowness of a generation; his method often seems Dickensian in the way caricatured superficiality is at once a satiric tactic and a moral consequence of the kind of society that is satirized. . . . Both ideas and relationships are shown as debased by a kind of verbal overkill, but the extravagance of language is Buzo's." While his later plays feature naturalistic, psychologically complex characters, Buzo has sustained the sardonic moral and sociological observations which first distinguished his work.

Buzo gained prominence with his one-act play, *Norm and Ahmed,* in which a middle-aged shopkeeper casually engages a Pakistani student in conversation at a bus stop. However, the Australian's glib speech steadily degenerates into verbal then physical violence when he attacks the student after offering his hand in parting. Due to its profane language, *Norm and Ahmed* became embroiled in a controversial censorship test case that eventually upheld the right of authors to freedom of expression. Critics have since lauded the play as a perceptive portrait of the fear and alienation underlying stereotypical Australian masculinity. *Rooted,* Buzo's next work, centers upon Bentley, an ambitious civil servant who speaks only in television commercial slogans and bureaucratic jargon. As the play progresses, Simmo, an omnipotent, offstage character, sends his henchmen to mercilessly interrogate Bentley before claiming his possessions, career, and family. Often compared to Harold Pinter's play *The Birthday Party,* *Rooted* garnered praise as an indictment of society's superficial standards of success and happiness. In his subsequent works *The Front Room Boys,* which examines the ritualized patterns of domination and subservience in a large corporation, and *The Roy Murphy Show,* a comic portrait of behind-the-scenes pandemonium during a television sports broadcast, Buzo continues to use stylized visual or verbal images to illuminate pervasive social patterns.

With *Macquarie,* Buzo shifts away from the grotesque stereotypes emblematic of "New Wave" dramatists toward more realistic, psychologically complex protagonists. While retaining the heightened imagery of Buzo's early plays, *Macquarie* presents an intricately developed portrait of Lachlan Macquarie, the early nineteenth-century governor of New South Wales whose liberal policies led to his downfall at the hands of conservative landowners. Buzo also focuses more closely upon personal relationships in *Tom,* an examination of an oil industry executive's failing marriage, and in *Coralie Lansdowne Says No.* Considered one of Buzo's most successful

dramas, *Coralie Lansdowne Says No* centers upon the title character, an acerbic, independent woman who, dismayed by the prospect of a solitary future, marries a boorish yet dependable bureaucrat. Critics praised the play as an incisive portrait of a woman who successfully reconciles her idealistic concept of love with the reality of human imperfection.

In later plays, Buzo further explores the romanticism of seemingly jaded characters. *Martello Towers* portrays Edward and Jennifer Martello, an estranged couple who arrive simultaneously at the family cottage with their lovers. Although initially disconcerted by this unexpected encounter, Edward and Jennifer realize that their present companions are inadequate substitutes for one another and reconcile. In *Makassar Reef,* underlying hostilities and attractions surface between a disparate group of vacationers to Indonesia, while *Big River* focuses upon a turn-of-the-century Australian woman who regrets having compromised her family relationships for personal gain. While some critics contended that these plays lacked the experimental vitality of Buzo's early productions, others agreed with John McCallum, who asserted that "Buzo is moving towards a new stylistic lightness, but he is using what is by now a very complex tool to analyse the relationship between individuals and the social *milieu* within which they have to survive. He is using romanticism theatrically to give an ostensive definition of moral attractiveness, 'niceness', in his characters, and so is pointing the way to one of the means which his audiences can use to understand and come to terms with their world."

In addition to his plays, Buzo has written the novel *The Search for Harry Allway,* a satirical portrait of a young journalist who becomes immersed in the cultural complexity of Sydney during her investigation of a man's disappearance.

(See also *Contemporary Authors,* Vols. 97-100 and *Contemporary Authors New Revision Series,* Vol. 17.)

PRINCIPAL WORKS

PLAYS

Norm and Ahmed   1968
Rooted   1969
The Roy Murphy Show   1971
Macquarie   1972
Tom   1972
Batman's Beachhead   1973
Coralie Lansdowne Says No   1974
Martello Towers   1976
Makassar Reef   1978
Big River   1980
Vicki Madison Clocks Out   1980

NOVEL

The Search for Harry Allway   1986

T. E. KALEM

Absurdist playwrights like Ionesco and Pinter have taken as their special province the psychic discordance—both funny and unnerving—that occurs when words are out of sync with reality, as in a dubbed movie. This is at the root of *Rooted,* the first full-length play by Australia's Alexander Buzo. . . . Buzo is no tracing-paper mimic; he is linked to Ionesco and Pinter by an intuitive kinship of mind, spirit and talent.

The play's hero, Bentley, speaks ad copy. He is the adjunct of his possessions, the stereo set, transistor and white antiseptic machine for nonliving that he calls his "home unit." He adores his wife though she makes him a voyeur to his own cuckolding. He has unquestioning faith in his friends, though they are parasitic phonies. Perishing in a snowdrift of optimistic clichés, Bentley loses all—home, wife, job, future.

In the wings, and never seen, is a devil *ex machina,* Simmo, a man who strip-mines simple souls like Bentley. Buzo tells us that the meek do not inherit the earth, and that the power-brutes who do pocket only cinders. Rarely has black comedy been more lavish in its laughter.

> *T. E. Kalem, "Aussie Absurdist," in* Time, *New York, Vol. 99, No. 7, February 14, 1972, p. 60.*

ROSLYN ARNOLD

[*This essay was originally given as a paper at a conference on Australian drama arranged by the Drama Studies Unit, Sydney University, in August 1974.*]

The use of four-letter words, abusive terms and ribald imagery is a feature of the Australian drama currently attracting attention here and overseas. This aggressive use of language may be the feature of the plays remembered by the audience after other features have been forgotten, but its role is not so superficial. It strikes down into the preoccupations and motivations of the characters, sheds light on social rituals, and raises questions about contemporary Australian life and the traditions informing it. Certainly verbal aggression, physical violence, shallow personal relationships and ambivalent attitudes to authority can be found in many societies, but the plays of [David] Williamson and Buzo seem to reflect a situation that is distinctive, if not unique.

In a comment reported on the back of . . . *Three Plays* (1974), David Williamson has claimed that

> There is an awful Australian uniqueness, and for the first time the Australian theatre is getting down to the business of finding out what it is.

This "awful Australian uniqueness" manifests itself in the aggressive language and uncommitted or unfulfilling relationships shown in the plays being discussed. And while the language is often witty and funny, it defines the limitations of the characters and points to a deeper malaise in the audience if it is accepted at face value. A fear of aloneness is exposed in both the male and female characters. (p. 385)

Norm and Ahmed . . . encapsulates some of the attitudes and failings which make up this "awful Australian uniqueness". At midnight, Norm (the average Australian, as his name suggests) strikes up a conversation with Ahmed, a young Pakistani student, as they both wait at a bus-stop. Norm is lonely, and by a series of provoking questions manages to draw Ahmed into a kind of communication with him. Not only is the Australian vernacular with its clichés, forthright statements, and slangy references to "piss-pots", "boongs" and "poofters" faithfully reproduced by Norm, but juxtaposed with the stilted, over-formal phrases of Ahmed, it is shown to be essentially inadequate in meeting Norm's deepest needs for expression. If we accept that language helps humans to communicate their needs, desires and feelings then Norm's failure becomes rather pitiable, and the glibness of his speech is deceptive.

Norm hates the apparent articulateness of Ahmed, and he tries to explore his attitude to the new Australian in his conversation. What he reveals is a stereotyped prejudice cloaked in false friendliness. His language is adequate for reflecting on past experiences, and expressing prejudice, but totally inadequate for the more difficult task of self-analysis, or for establishing any kind of mutual relationship with the man he has cornered.

It comes as a shock at the end that Norm bashes Ahmed with a blow and the outburst "fucking boong", but on reflection, it is artistically right that Norm should act this way. A closer analysis of the play, particularly of Norm's shifts in language, and his increasing sense of frustration and alienation from the alien, anticipate his outburst. What is more shocking about the ending is the realization that in spite of the apparent cathartic effect of such language, it is ultimately futile and frustrating unless coupled with physical aggression. In fact Norm recognizes this himself, and the tension increases with the use of his self-provoking language.

It is significant that Norm had to tell Ahmed about the "old perv" he saw in Centennial Park: "He was having a tug in the gutter, going at it hammer and tongs. He must have been hard up, eh?" In his own conversation Norm is trying to find a similar relief, but his orgasm is one of destructive violence. (pp. 385-86)

This play raises to consciousness one of the dilemmas of being Australian. For all the supposed friendliness and warmth extended to newcomers (a traditionally outback ideal) there is fear and suspicion of challenging relationships, or threateningly close human contact either physical or verbal. Norm assured Ahmed "But anyway, Ahmed, that's just another reason why you should settle down here—there's no language barrier". The language barrier is more subtle and insidious than Norm realizes. When the language of tenderness or compassion is ignored or feared then the barrier between people is impregnable. Norm tried to smash it with his fist, but he only reinforced it.

If it *is* of the Australian tradition to fear the alien, then this play dramatizes that fear, and challenges our responses to change, or at least understand, an attitude which is destructive and self-limiting, whatever its origins might be.

In the introduction to . . . the three plays *Norm and Ahmed, Rooted,* and *The Roy Murphy Show,* Katharine Brisbane says of the language Buzo so accurately records: "It rises from a deep inability to make steady moral decisions". She adds "But what, in Buzo's observation, the outback friendliness hides is an urban terror of proximity, involvement and responsibility—a way of using words to not listen, not learn and not understand". This might be a universal human failing but I suggest that it is an integral part of that "awful Australian uniqueness" which both Buzo and Williamson expose in their plays. Actually few of the plays show situations which demand of the characters a steady moral decision and this might be an area for future development in Australian plays. While I agree fully with the critic's recognition of "the deep inability to make steady moral decisions", I feel that the point might be too subtly made in the plays, and so escape a theatre audience's notice. It is too valuable an observation to be lost, but the central concerns of Buzo's . . . plays so far involve observing people trying to cope with existing circumstances, not people trying to change these circumstances. *Coralie Lansdowne Says No* moves towards the dramatic analysis of a woman trying to make "a steady, moral decision". Just how "steady" that decision was is one of the teasing qualities of the play. (pp. 387-88)

[Buzo's plays] are realistic and artistic portraits of social (or anti-social) behaviour to which . . . [he feels] sufficiently committed, to present dramatically. The modern urban settings of these plays extend and update the Australian tradition. When transferred from the bush to the city, the ideal of mateship is still worshipped, not because it is valued as a potentially mutually-supportive relationship, but out of an inordinate sense of fear should man find himself alone. It is the degree to which aloneness is feared that is particularly Australian, and it seems to be related not only to geographical factors, but to uncertainty about personal, and national worth. It would be too simplistic to suggest that Australians are still universally suffering from a national inferiority complex; nevertheless, the fact that the Ocker image, the Barry McKenzie and Paul Hogan image, can still be perpetuated and applauded by Australians, reflects a complacency about our international image. While Buzo's and Williamson's picture has few attractive features to show us of our society, at least they do not endorse the scene they portray, and their art does improve our cultural standing. A recognition of shortcomings is a step towards maturity, and past values like mateship do need to be understood and re-assessed. The invisible Simmo in *Rooted* exercises a powerful tyranny over the other characters because his supposed qualities as a strong, successful dominant male are never questioned by his subjects. Similarly, fears of inferiority and exposure dominate other characters' behaviour leading to aggressive conduct and the very rejection by others which they initially feared so irrationally. The self-fulfilling prophecy is a tyrant.

While [Buzo and] the new playwrights are not the first to isolate the mateship theme or the violence theme for examination, they are the first to relate these themes to the same social and educated classes as make up their audiences. For the first time in Australian literature we hear the upper middle-class educated characters using language we used to believe belonged to the uneducated working class. Such a belief is now a myth. Aggressive language ignores class barriers. To re-apply Norm's comment "there is no language barrier here", it is possible to comment that it is not education, or class position which makes one a more fully realized human being, unless it is coupled with sensitivity, self-awareness, self-esteem and an ability to communicate fears, hopes, joys, success and failure to others. (pp. 389-90)

[As Buzo's plays demonstrate], insulting witty comments are only momentarily funny, and when they are the whole measure of a man's capacity to express himself, the characters become stunted, pitiable, and emotionally impotent. The security blanket of abuse is poor protection against the total demands of human interaction.

Aggressive language is not always overtly defensive. In *The Roy Murphy Show,* Buzo shows his skill in capturing the slick hysterical language of the television sports show. Roy, the commentator, has very creditably overcome a speech impediment which affects his pronunciation of "r" and proves himself master of all the trite phrases, glib generalizations, and inflated terms of congratulation which are an essential speech pattern on such a show.

He is quickly established as the big-hearted, broad-minded, versatile, competitive personality who reflects the viewers' expectations on the "wide and wonderful world of Rugby League". He assures his father-in-law Sir Roland (Sir Role, to Roy) and owner of the TV Channel, "I have never deceived your daughter, and the very thought of indulging in adulterous intrigue is one which I find repugnant to my sensibilities. Photographs of me and a bird having a . . .". If he could really sustain the tone of false moral indignation even under pressure, he might even be plausible, but adept as he is at hurling phrases at his listeners, his language is a poor defence under pressure.

The familiar tone of self-righteousness ("The Rugby League public is sick and tired of pig-in-poke attitudes of these dog-in-the-manger deadheads on the board of directors of the S.C.G. Trust") has the breathless pace of a church litany, and with its false moral certitude, it becomes comic. Personal attacks on Roy are vehemently countered, from the security of the TV studio, with a barrage of abuse which borrows phrases from all jargons.

> Quite apart from invoking the pot and kettle syndrome, yes, syndrome, this piddling, puerile, pusillanimous, pen-pushing, pie-eating Pariah, yes piddling, has stepping to the lowest depths of denigration and besmirching by taking umbrage and dudgeon at a certain alleged speech defect of mine which has long since disappeared . . . my speech impediment has been completely ewadicated . . . without a twace . . .

The subtleties and complexities of speech defeat Roy, but he is a temporary master of inappropriate vocabulary. When speech fails him, he can resort to blowing a raspberry. Roy meets his match when he encounters someone with an equal talent for mouthing the meaningless phrase. Charles, the import from Britain, establishes his superiority with slick observations which Roy might envy. "I feel I am rapidly approaching an understanding of the sort of quintessential contemporary high campery of the Antipodean mentality." Just what this quintessence is, is suggested by the unquestioned public acceptance of the sports-gods marketed by the media with as much verbal-packaging as the material products they promote on their shows. Sports-heroes are big business, and the only enterprise needed is a talent for verbosity, and a Roget's *Thesaurus* of synonyms. Roy finally talks himself out of his job, but he goes down fighting back with all the clichéd phrases he has ever used before, delivered this time with his speech-impediment in full play.

Inarticulateness is not a national trait, but neither is the purposeful, appropriate use of language in a variety of contexts. Nor is the effective use of silence given the recognition it deserves although Sandy, the girl in **Rooted,** knows its value and uses it to advantage. (pp. 392-94)

In spite of the wordiness of Buzo's Roy, there is an artistic merit in his dialogue which relates to the total impact of the play. A transcript of a sports commentary is actually rather boring and repetitive. In the play, there is subtle control exercised by the author and he reveals an acute ear for the colourful and character-defining vernacular of his characters. Aggressive language is seen as self-defeating when used relentlessly or inappropriately, and the characters who believe in it implicitly or out of necessity, are always vulnerable and limited.

It would be naive to suggest that verbal aggression alone is a unique feature of all Australians, or that it is the fundamental style of all the modern playwrights. It is the degree to which it is used unselectively and inflexibly by the characters in the plays, which makes the point that these characters retard their development by their defensive use of language.

Aggression is often concealed, too, under the guise of humour. In greeting the Italian Vittorio, Robbo in Buzo's **The Front Room Boys** mockingly warns him "That's an unlucky desk you got there, mate".

> VITTORIO. What do you mean?
> ROBBO. The last bloke who sat there jumped out of the window one lunch time and killed himself. University graduate, he was. Stained the pavement something terrible.
> GIBBO. I remember that day. He jumped one hour before the start of the Melbourne Cup.

A wealth of commentary on Australian fears, prejudices and preoccupations is conveyed in that exchange, and simultaneously the characters preserve their individuality. A wholly cynical sense of humour, with threatening undertones, is the mark of a rather jaundiced personality. While this might be a shortcoming shared by many people there is a distinctively Australian language pattern conveyed in that dialogue. While the context is a public-service office, the point made here goes beyond the immediate context, recalling Williamson's phrase "the sardonic sense of humour". There is nothing self-conscious or stereotyped about the speech-patterns Buzo constructs. In fact, in laughing at the characters portrayed in Australian plays, one might overlook the self-implicating result of such identification with the characters.

It is not particularly difficult to isolate and comment on the use of aggressive language in Buzo and Williamson, as the subject dictates itself. What is difficult is relating the topic to the Australian tradition. If we recognize that these writers are different from their predecessors, and different from each other and other modern playwrights (that is, they do have individuality) then it suggests that the Australian tradition is changing, as is Australian society. (pp. 394-95)

> *Roslyn Arnold, "Aggressive Vernacular: Williamson, Buzo and the Australian Tradition," in* South-*erly, Vol. 35, No. 4, December, 1975, pp. 385-96.*

T. L. STURM

[*This essay was originally published in* Southerly *in September, 1975.*]

On the surface, Alexander Buzo's plays seem to provide obvious evidence for the widely held view that recent Australian drama is the expression of a new spirit of national self-consciousness. The new playwrights, in this kind of argument, are seen as linked in their desire to explore contemporary Australian life critically: probing its myths (consumerism, status and the like), its middle-class values and lifestyles, its obsessions, its violence; re-examining Australian history in a new spirit of iconoclasm; and capturing the rhythms of Australian speech with a new directness and vitality. At one level, Buzo's plays can be made to fit this sociological pattern: Australian racism (**Norm and Ahmed**); the drive for success and status (**Rooted**); patterns of power and subservience among 'white collar office employees' in a large Sydney business enterprise (**The Front Room Boys**); the Australian obsession with sport (**The Roy Murphy Show**); liberalism in Australian history (**Macquarie**); the lifestyle of young executives-on-the-make (**Tom**); contemporary Australian ecological issues (**Batman's Beachhead,** a reworking of Ibsen's *An Enemy of the People*); and most recently, the portrayal of a young Australian woman's rebellion against the stereotyping pressures of her environment (**Coralie Lansdowne Says No**).

Buzo has, however, persistently rejected descriptions of his plays which define them in exclusively Australian terms, limiting them to one level of expressiveness—especially the view which makes him out to be a social satirist making savage attacks on 'the Australian way of life'. [According to Margaret Jones, 'Buzo] says his plays are not about attitudes but about people. One of his characters may turn out to be a mate, or another an Australian hedonist, but he is not making overt judgments about them.' When **The Front Room Boys** was published in 1970, Buzo felt constrained to add an author's note drawing attention to misinterpretations:

As is usual with Australian plays, *The Front Room Boys* was immediately branded by some people as 'experimental' and 'about the Australian way of life'. The play is not experimental and is not about the Australian way of life, whatever that may be.

Interviewed in 1974, after his return from a trip to England and the United States, where plays of his own were being staged, Buzo criticised English patronage of Australian playwrights and the influence of the comic 'Bazza McKenzie' stereotype on the way English audiences saw Australians, making it impossible for Australian characters on stage to be taken seriously. He preferred the American reception of his plays, which placed them in the context of absurdist playwrights like Ionesco, Beckett and Pinter. Despite his reservations about such an approach, it at least indicated a climate in which Australian plays were taken seriously. And in the same interview he again dissociates his plays from 'Australianist' approaches:

> Some people regard my plays as documentaries on the Australian way of life and that disturbs me. . . . My plays are meant as works of fiction. *Coralie* is absolute fiction intended to work on the audience's imagination.

In another interview of 1973 (discussing yet again the persistent label of 'social satirist' attached to his plays) he describes himself as 'an imagist with a personal style of surrealism':

> The majority of my audiences probably think my plays are comedies anyway, and it sounds a bit pretentious to talk in terms of absurdism and realism. But I am not a social writer in that I'm not just writing about Australia. I prefer to think of my plays as set in Australia in the same way as Tennessee Williams's are set in America. I am not overly concerned with the Australian way of life.

Playwrights like Buzo . . . have now achieved substantial *oeuvres* of their own, each with its characteristic identity and concerns. It is becoming much less obvious than it appeared several years ago that their work can be contained within any single definition of the 'new drama'; and in any case, they are unlikely ever to have seen themselves in such terms, as constituting a 'movement'. The real history—in terms of the actual dramatic practice of individual playwrights, actors and directors, and of the organisation of theatre—is . . . one of conflict, diversification and the injection of new ideas from overseas. From this perspective, the differences between David Williamson's demand for 'a meticulously naturalistic acting style' (linked with his feeling that Australia has 'a wealth of types, subcultures and lifestyles awaiting exploration') and Buzo's interest in imagism, surrealism and the methods of the cinema, may turn out to be of greater importance than any superficial connection derived from a comparison of so-called Australian content in their plays. It may be superficially true that Buzo's *Macquarie* can be linked with *The Legend of King O'Malley* and other historical plays as part of a new Australian historical self-consciousness; but Buzo's own comment, that his play 'is not a product of the current mania for history-in-vaudeville', might suggest that he wrote it in opposition to the prevailing trend. . . . As a final example, there is Buzo's interesting statement of a preference for living in Sydney rather than in Melbourne: "There is nothing there to stimulate my imagination. Melbourne has ideas but there is something bizarre about Sydney; you get so many images, so many changes of mood.' Apart from *Batman's Beachhead* (which is a special kind of play in any case) all of Buzo's plays

are set in Sydney, with a very immediate sense of urban or suburban locale. Buzo's comment suggests that there might be a direct connection, between the imagistic or cinematic formal elements in his plays and his experience of life in Sydney, which could in turn be related to writers like Slessor, whose sense of Sydney was very similar. This might provide a much more fruitful analysis of the 'local' surfaces of his plays than any approach through the more abstract conceptions of their 'Australian' content, which necessarily ignores the possibility of urban diversity and conflict as an influence on Australian writers.

Buzo's comment that he prefers to think of his plays as set in Australia 'in the same way as Tennessee Williams's are set in America', indicates that he does not *primarily* think of them as 'Australian' at all, but as probing more 'universal' concerns through the lives with which he happens to be familiar, in Sydney. His plays are built on an extraordinarily acute observation of these lives—especially, of individual mannerisms and characteristic rhythms and patterns of speech. But his dramatic methods are not primarily realistic, and in this he is ultimately very different from Pinter (with whom he has occasionally been compared), and also from David Williamson, whose plays combine a vigorous Australian naturalism with the sophistication of playwrights like Pinter and Albee. Buzo *was* influenced by Pinter and Albee in his early plays—in *Norm and Ahmed* (which has surface similarities to *The Zoo Story*), and in *Rooted* (which is reminiscent, at some points, of Pinter's *The Homecoming*). Yet even *Norm and Ahmed,* which depends so much on the meticulous naturalism of its characterisation and dialogue, contains oddly suggestive, surrealistic images in its setting and lighting. The details may seem innocent enough, explicable in naturalistic terms: the building site with its scaffolding and white protective fence, the bus stop, the garbage can, the play of light and shadow throughout against a dark background, the time of the action (marked out by the striking of the clock at midnight and one a.m.). But they also create a sinister visual environment for the action. It may be over-interpreting to suggest that the building site with its white fence is a symbol of white Australian society in the making and that Norm, prowling suspiciously in front of it, is in a sense its self-appointed guardian, on the lookout for those, like Ahmed, whom he fears might be trying to get in. What the details do suggest, however, is that the play is not simply making its point in documentary or verbal terms—that in fact the visual images may be designed to cut across the verbal effects. The violence which ends the play—which some have objected to as insufficiently motivated—is in theatrical terms more a product of sinister visual qualities than of purely verbal elements. In fact at a purely verbal level it might seem as if Norm is gradually being persuaded to modify his attitudes by Ahmed's evident reasonableness. The play does not, however, offer us a discussion of racism, but a disturbing image of it as a compulsive, irrational force in Norm's behaviour, beyond the appeal of the merely verbal.

Naturalism is also prominent in Buzo's most recent play, *Coralie Lansdowne Says No,* though in this play also other non-naturalistic conventions are at work. It is a more tightly structured play than any he has written; and the characterisation of Coralie Lansdowne, which provides its dramatic centre, is the fullest he has so far achieved. Buzo allows himself an unusual measure of identification with her feelings and problems. Ken Horler, the director of the first production of the play, comments rather oddly in his preface to the published version of the play:

> We are prevented from responding even to Coralie with direct sympathy by the character's own capacity for self-analysis: like many of Alexander Buzo's most successful characters, she is articulate beyond the demands of naturalistic theatre.

Coralie's articulateness, her capacity for self-analysis, *is* the decisive naturalistic feature of the play, and it differentiates her from the main characters in Buzo's other plays. Characters like Norm, Bentley and Sandy, the Front Room Boys (with the exception, perhaps, of Jacko), Roy Murphy and even Macquarie possess little capacity for self-analysis. There is a considerable gap—often, even, a clinical detachment—between the author's (and audience's) understanding of them, and the way they see themselves; though this does not mean, as some of Buzo's less sympathetic reviewers have implied, that he is making overt moralistic judgments about his characters, presenting them in over-formularised black-and-white terms, or lacking in sympathy for their situations and predicaments. Coralie Lansdowne, on the other hand, is cast very much in the mould of Maggie in *Cat on a Hot Tin Roof* and Martha in *Who's Afraid of Virginia Woolf?* Robust and sensitive, intelligent and witty in her grasp of social hypocrisies, a nervous mixture of aggressiveness and vulnerability, she faces difficult personal decisions about the direction of her life now that she is moving into her thirties. Wary of being exploited, she is in a situation where none of the available options is perfect. It is a measure of the strength of Buzo's sympathies, and of his success within the naturalistic conventions he makes use of, that most of our attitudes to the other characters in the play are either the same as Coralie's or strongly coloured by her reactions.

Except, perhaps, at the end. Much of the discussion of the play, when it was first performed, focused on the play's conclusion, an ambiguous ending in which Coralie appears to succumb to the pressures she has been struggling against, settling for marriage to a Canberra public servant described by one of the other characters as 'an *apparatchik* of the emotions'. Endings invariably pose special problems in naturalistic plays, since they expose the artificial, or fictional, nature of the conventions which have been designed, throughout, to naturalise the stage action, creating an illusion of real life. The play *has* to end; the naturalistic illusion demands that the characters live on, as if real. The ending of *Coralie Lansdowne Says No* is no exception to the rule. In one sense it might be possible to see only a simple irony in the title, and read Coralie's Yes to Stuart Morgan as a capitulation and self-betrayal. But the possibility of a further irony, over and above the superficial one, is also hinted at in the final sequence of the play: Coralie's sudden convulsion (hardly explicable in naturalistic terms), which Ken Horler interpreted as 'a rejection of Stuart Morgan and his world'; Dr. Salmon's enigmatic exit line, addressed to Stuart ('That's the least of your worries'); and the final line of the play, spoken by Coralie to an apprehensive husband—'You'll do.' It is in the nature of plays like this that speculation can never be finally resolved, and that the author refrains from making direct judgments. The ambiguity—so recurrent in this type of play as to itself have the force of a convention—thrusts us back into the central conflicts of the play, and leaves us with the questions they raise.

Coralie Lansdowne's character is given its complexity by what is gradually revealed about her past, and by the range of perspectives in which other characters see her. None of the other characters in the play fully understands her; in fact, it is typical of the mode itself that there is always an ironic distance between each character's partial view of her, which is coloured by the particular emotional or sexual claims each makes on her, and the view of her which the play as a whole constructs. Coralie's inner conflict throughout the play is centred on the dilemma of reconciling the different aspects of herself brought into play by the various relationships in which she is involved. In another sense too (and in this the play is reminiscent of *Summer of the Seventeenth Doll*) it is a problem of tailoring an illusory romantic idealism—her sense of herself as 'a high-flying bird', her ambition to be 'brilliant in life'—to a real world in which none of the alternatives is perfect. Her decision to marry Stuart Morgan is, inevitably, a compromise, but a compromise which offers her at least a fighting chance of retaining the kind of personal autonomy she wants. It is the *least* compromising alternative, faced as she is by the emptiness of Peter York's urbane, modishly radical lifestyle and Paul Coleman's egotistic masculinity, by the sterile careerism of her sister Jill and the tragic marriage of Anne Coleman.

However, despite the unusually rich vein of naturalism which Buzo develops in the course of the play, its basic conventions are those of sophisticated romantic comedy, a genre with a long tradition behind it. Buzo manipulates these conventions with a great deal of flair: the comedy of sophisticated dialogue based on witty repartee and malicious innuendo, conversational gambits charged with trenchant humour or bitchiness, topical satire and in-jokes; and the romantic elements in the action itself, with its central issue of who, among her three jealous suitors, the heroine will settle for, and the subsidiary complications this introduces into the lives of the other characters. Much of the energy of the play derives from Buzo's exploitation of such conventions for more serious purposes. The shock of Anne Coleman's suicide, introduced at a relatively early point in the play, establishes a tragic undercurrent to the comic surface, undercutting the conventions themselves. The same kind of questioning occurs at the end of the play, where what one might normally think of as a comic-romantic resolution to the play's tension—the device of a happy marriage—becomes a source of uncertainty and ambiguity. And there are other suggestive or 'poetic' features which complicate the comedy and the naturalism: the exotic atmosphere of decadent affluence and physical deformity—the closest Buzo gets in this play to a surrealistic effect—which provides the background of the action and an image of the destructive pressures against which Coralie's robust vitality is pitted. Coralie herself makes these connections in a brief, effective, introspective scene (Scene Four), which in its intensity also cuts across the comic conventions. It is one of the rare moments in Buzo's plays where he allows a character a degree of 'romantic' involvement, emotional empathy, with landscape and seascape. It has parallels, in other contexts, in Elizabeth Macquarie's feeling for the beauty of Sydney's physical landscape in *Macquarie;* more pathetically, in Bentley's stunted emotions, as they struggle to express themselves through seascape in *Rooted;* and in Jacko's comic-pathetic calendar fantasies in *The Front Room Boys.* The absence of physical nature as a vital force in the lives of most of Buzo's characters is generally associated with emotional stuntedness, with energies repressed and channelled into the drive for affluence and status. Coralie, Elizabeth Macquarie, Bentley and Jacko are all to a degree isolated characters, struggling at such moments to express an authentic sense of self denied them by society.

Coralie Lansdowne Says No, with its combination of naturalism and romantic comedy, is a new departure in Buzo's work, suggesting interesting possibilities for the future. In earlier plays like *Rooted, The Front Room Boys, The Roy Murphy Show,* and *Macquarie* (on the surface, a rather different play from the other three) Buzo's own description of himself as 'an imagist with a personal style of surrealism' is more relevant. They are all plays which reject the conventions of realism in favour of a more swift-flowing, imaginative conception of the possibilities of theatre, allowing freer play to his flair for comic or zany or grotesque situations, his sense of the absurd and farcical, his uninhibited delight in the comic resources of language, and in particular (in *Macquarie*) his sense of theatre as a visual medium with a wide range of possibilities for exploiting different levels and intensities of physical action. Some of the surface effects in *Rooted* suggest Pinter's characteristic brand of realism—the longish monologues of Bentley and Sandy, in which obsessions and fears are half-recognised, half-rationalised; and the play's sense of the habitual confusions and uncertainties of speech, conveyed through comic dialogue and through the characters' fumbling efforts at self-expression. Bentley, for example, oscillates between a pompous bureaucratic jargon associated with his public service ambitions and the in-group clichés and slang of his mates. His inability to develop a personal speech reflects his failure to achieve a personal identity. One might, I suppose, be able to see such effects as implying a project for social satire, but only incidentally, in that many of the obsessions the play deals with happen to be about status, sexual prowess, and affluence. The total effect has less to do with 'social satire on the Australian way of life', however, than with providing a theatrical image, or series of images, of the way people are driven by obsessions and illusions.

The play's action is framed within the two poles represented by the absent characters, Simmo and Hammo: success and power on the one hand, defeat and humiliation on the other. Bentley's history in the course of the play is a downward spiral, a gradual loss of self-esteem; other characters are in varying degrees of ascendancy; all are engaged in a competitive struggle, a conflict of egotisms. Some critics have spoken of the play, rather loosely, as too rigidly schematic—a criticism which might be relevant if the play's mode were naturalistic. In fact the play offers no solutions, certainly no political formulae, for the issues it raises and probes. As in *Norm and Ahmed,* its images are conveyed only partly in verbal terms. . . . Surrealist effects in the play—Sandy's voice answering Bentley through his tape-recorder (the material symbol of his sense of status 'speaking' directly of the failure of his personal life); the 'choric' passages in which Bentley's friends ritually engulf him in cliché; the scenes without words in which apparently mundane details take on a strange quality of visual tableau—all reveal aspects of Bentley's humiliation and defeat which at a purely verbal level he is never able to admit.

Similarly, in *The Roy Murphy Show,* the general effect lies less in its aspect of social documentary (though its hilarious mimicry of the mannerisms of the actual sports commentators on which it is based is so brilliantly accurate as to make one suspect that Buzo was using material from a 'live' programme), than in the vivid theatrical images provided by the paraphernalia of the television studio itself: characters re-sponding puppet-like to the light which informs them that they are on screen, aggressions and rivalries beneath the surface of the exchanges, frenzied behind-the-scenes activity as Roy Murphy juggles telephone conversations with his wife, his mistress and his boss in the moments when he is not on screen. The collapse of the show itself—from the relative order in which it opens to the frantic disorder in which it ends—carries with it the disintegration of Roy Murphy's own hopes and ambitions, under pressures which are only precariously kept in control in the earlier stages. The comic device of intruding the 'real' world into the 'fictional' world of the television image provides a central dramatic metaphor of the process: a revelation of personal pressures undermining the precarious fictions on which one's public image, or social identity, is based.

An analogy has sometimes been drawn between Buzo's theatrical methods and the art of the cartoonist or comic strip illustrator—with its technique of caricature, its exaggeration of surface mannerisms in gesture and speech, its simplification of structural outlines. The analogy is helpful, provided that it is not distorted (in Buzo's case) into a criticism of the plays as vehicles of simplistic doctrinal messages. A cartoonist's view of the world may be more or less complex—and Buzo's carefully structured plays do not carry simple messages, or enforce black-and-white judgments. Where the comic strip or cartoon analogy is most relevant, I think, is in the immediacy of the effects they make possible: the creation of unusual visual or verbal images which by the suddenness of their impact illuminate a situation or event. This imagist perception of things is related to Buzo's interest in the free-flowing succession or juxtaposition of images characteristic of cinema and television—the kind of technique exploited in both *The Roy Murphy Show* and *The Front Room Boys.* Buzo also mentions cinema and television in commenting upon the dramatic method of *Macquarie:*

> The present generation that we are attracting to the theatres was brought up on cinema and television. They are used to fast-moving and quick-cutting scene changes. I think the stage has the potential to be quicker moving; at one moment in *Macquarie,* five things are going on at the same time.

The difficulties which arise from the kind of fast-moving imagistic technique which Buzo employs in *The Roy Murphy Show* and *The Front Room Boys* have to do with the demands it makes on the actors themselves, who not only have to cope with sudden or difficult transitions between naturalistic and non-naturalistic styles, but often with the sheer physical difficulty of performing complicated actions at great speed and with split-second timing. There is also the problem of establishing a convincing dramatic momentum, and a clearly defined background against which the images can function. A mere assembly of images, without a beginning, middle and end, would fail to sustain dramatic interest once the novelty wore off. *The Front Room Boys* is less successful from this aspect, despite the sheer inventiveness of the dramatic ideas behind many of the scenes and the comic gusto of the dialogue. The play's energies tend to become diffused and its action repetitive because of the need to maintain the twelve-part structure—one scene for each month of the year. The central dramatic device of ritual cycle, seasonal rhythm and sacrificial scapegoat is firmly established within the space of three or four scenes—and its potential for development, within the confines of day-to-day office routine (where the accent is on mindless conformity and subservience) is severely limited.

Later scenes seem less a progressive development of earlier ones than a simple restatement of their basic idea, though there is a great deal of ingenuity in the effort to diversify the action, to create local interest in the rivalries and comic exchanges between different characters, and to make each scene the source of some new insight into the way 'the rhythms of modern life' can be seen as a grotesque parody of the spontaneous tribal rhythms of more primitive times.

In *Macquarie,* however, the necessary background is provided, ready-made, by Australian history itself, in the life of Macquarie during the turbulent twelve-year period of his rule as Governor of New South Wales (1810-1821). In shifting from contemporary to historical subject matter Buzo allows himself less scope for the kind of imaginative comic dialogue, mixed with absurdity and farce, which gave many of the scenes of *The Front Room Boys* their vitality. On the other hand, by focusing the action on the strong figure of Macquarie, there is a considerable gain in cohesion. There is a firm dramatic centre to the play, freeing the author's imagination to develop a range of exciting theatrical effects without tending to diffuseness—striking visual images, spectacle, fast-moving changes of scene and action, static moments of tableau, simultaneous actions presented in counterpoint, which collapse disparities of time and place and provide powerful dramatic ironies, establishing visual connections between events, situations and characters superficially different. The combination of a strong central dramatic momentum—based on the pattern of rise and fall in Macquarie's fortunes—with the controlled play of such a variety of fast-moving visual impressions, probably owes a great deal to the collaborative activity of playwright, actors and director. . . . And Buzo's fascination with Australian history—which he studied as a student at the University of New South Wales—obviously lies behind his interest in the play's subject. What is more interesting about it is its dramatic method, the *way* the problems of presenting history on the stage are approached, and the implications of such an approach for historical method itself.

Central to the play's dramatic method is its rejection of naturalism, and with this the positivist idea of historical study as the painstaking objective accumulation of documented facts. Historical perspective, the play implies, involves an interaction of present and past. We view history selectively through contemporary eyes: it is as much an illumination of contemporary problems as it is a recovery of the past. *Macquarie* deliberately asserts its character as a selective interpretation of historical events, seeking an answer to the question which Polski, the liberal-minded history lecturer, has set his third-year students, and which he announces in the opening lines of the play: 'In What Ways Did the Rise and Fall of Governor Macquarie Illustrate the Classic Liberal Dilemma?' The play's basic theme, then, is not an exclusively Australian one, although obviously at one level of the action an interpretation of Australian history is involved. The 'classic liberal dilemma' is a worldwide one. Examples of modern liberals which Buzo mentioned in an interview about the play were Alexander Dubcek and Senator McGovern; they are 'stranded (like Macquarie) midway between the forces of conservatism and revolution.' . . . (pp. 323-35)

The interaction of past and present is embodied in the play by presenting two actions—historical and contemporary—in counterpoint to each other throughout. Polski serves as a narrator to the main action, providing the audience with the minimal factual information necessary to grasp the chronological movement of events, and occasionally spelling out in simple terms the significance of a particular scene. But he is also a liberal caught in a similar dilemma to Macquarie, pressured to conform by a conservative university bureaucracy and unwilling to identify himself with the radical programmes of student and Black Power militants. The connections between Polski and Macquarie are made not only in terms of parallel actions (Polski agreeing to withdraw his 'critical article' from the university magazine, in the same way as Macquarie withdraws his petition to Bathurst under pressure from Bigge, and later abjectly signs Macarthur's reactionary programmes into law), but also by having the same actors involved in both actions in such a way as to suggest a continuity of political and social roles. Ellis Bent, Macquarie's Judge-Advocate, reappears as the professor of Polski's department, and the brutalised convict, working-class and Aboriginal characters of the historical action reappear in contemporary radical, working-class and white-collar roles. Perspectives are merged, also, in the play's conclusion, which presents Macquarie ironically through the dramatic image of a modern political interview on television, as he attempts to explain and justify his policies and fend off awkward questions.

The play's method throughout is to create a succession of sharply defined images of its central ideas. It is not a detached catalogue of historical details. It selects events, occasionally cobbles separate incidents into a single episode, and sometimes creates quite imaginary situations (like the Hogarthian tavern scenes) in order to give a sense of colour and vitality to the period, and more especially to emphasise the importance of pattern, bringing out strong contrasts between Macquarie's pragmatic reformism and those (like MacNaughton, Marsden and the Bents, representing the power of the military, propertied Christianity and the judiciary) who have a vested interest in preserving a system based on class, property and privilege. An additional dramatic image is provided by Bathurst, Colonial Secretary in England, strategically located at one side of the stage, the representative of a well-intentioned but bumbling and ignorant official colonial policy which nevertheless exercises considerable power over the events which unfold at the centre of the stage. Two opposed versions of 'human nature' are also built into the play's central contrast: Macquarie's naively optimistic belief in the goodness of human nature, which makes him vulnerable to the political maneuvring of his opponents, and Marsden's Christian belief in the innate depravity of human nature, which provides the ideological justification for his (and others') authoritarian attitudes to the convicts and Aborigines. The implications of this contrast, in terms of the power struggle which develops between Macquarie and the Marsden clique, are spelt out by Polski at the end of Act One, an ominous tableau in which Macquarie, apparently on the ascendant, works at his desk unaware of the forces which are conspiring to defeat him (Jeffrey Bent and Bathurst 'laugh and joke' on one side, and Marsden and MacNaughton, above, 'stroll slowly across, conversing earnestly'):

> The main trouble with being a liberal is that you tend to play by the rules of the system you are trying to reform, whereas your opponents, who uphold the system, feel no such constrictions on their freedom.

The swift-moving episodic character of the play (often no more than the briefest of sketches merging into or cutting across each other) allows it to develop as a sequence of images, each illustrating some central idea or character trail, e.g. corrupt justice, the boisterous squalor of the tavern, a political sermon preached at a funeral, backstage chicanery and manipulativeness. The vigorous momentum which sustains the action is possible only in terms of the simple, permanent set marked off into spaces capable of accommodating a variety of quick transitions, with the aid of simple stage properties. 'Upper' action, taking place on the raised platform, includes episodes of a ceremonial or official nature: set speeches like Macquarie's arrival speech and his valedictory address; Marsden's funeral oration; the official opening of the Aboriginal Institute (a parody of the opening of the Sydney Harbour Bridge); the flogging of the convict Joe by McNaughton. At other times the upper space simply signifies open space, by contrast with the enclosed spaces (rooms, offices) below; a place, that is, where characters can stroll, look at the scenery, converse casually, or plot, and make entrances and exits to and from the lower space. The lower space with two tables, below the raised platform, serves as Macquarie's office, or for tavern scenes, or for the dinner party at the Governor's residence. The upper and lower centre spaces—the arena of the historical action set in Australia—can be used either in isolation from each other or to develop two actions contrapuntally, especially in episodes illustrating the increasing tensions in Macquarie's situation. In addition there are the acting spaces left and right—the areas of contemporary action involving Polski, and of British colonial policy, seen in action in the figure of Bathurst—and these spaces offer further possibilities for contrapuntal and triple-puntal effects. Conceived in this way, the stage becomes an extremely fluid medium, making for swift transitions in time and space, from Australia to England, from past to present.

Because the play is primarily concerned to depict characters in representative social or political roles, and examine the political effects of their actions through the ways these roles interact and come into conflict, there is little naturalistic emphasis on issues of personal motivation or temperament. All that is required (as in **The Front Room Boys**) is a minimal suggestion of identifying personal qualities: MacNaughton's brutality, Marsden's fanaticism, Elizabeth Macquarie's civilised intelligence and sympathies, Greenway's headstrong enthusiasms, Macarthur's aristocratic aloofness. The exception is Macquarie himself, whose character is presented in a number of different perspectives. Unlike the other characters, who remain fixed in their social or political roles throughout, Macquarie's character is allowed to develop and change in response to the changing situation in which he is involved. Although he is initially aloof and pompous, with a trace of egotism in his temperament, something of his repressed humanity and warmth shows through on less formal occasions (in conversation with Campbell or Greenway, or at the wedding of Mabel and Joe). As well as his determination and vision, we see his naivety and his tendency to bluster and over-react when things go wrong. Yet despite the sympathy for Macquarie which this kind of mixed human portrayal inevitably creates, Buzo resists the temptation to romanticise him in the later stages of the play, as he becomes increasingly isolated, increasingly a victim of political forces beyond his control. In fact, at the end of the play, under the pressure of defeat and frustration, his personal vanity reasserts itself; he remains an obstinate, rather pathetic figure, not fully aware of the nature of the forces which have brought about his downfall. By ending his play in this way, Buzo leaves the audience with the issue of the 'classic liberal dilemma' raised in the play's open-

ing lines, and with the problem of finding their own solution to it. (pp. 335-38)

T. L. Sturm, "Alexander Buzo: An Imagist with a Personal Style of Surrealism," in Contemporary Australian Drama: Perspectives since 1955, *edited by Peter Holloway, Currency Press Pty. Ltd., 1981, pp. 322-39.*

PETER FITZPATRICK

Alex Buzo and David Williamson have a number of qualities in common. Among the 'new generation' of playwrights whose work began to appear in the late 1960s, they were the first to be granted the token of legitimacy that went with performance in commercial and subsidized theatres; their developing 'professionalism' was marked by their writing for film—Buzo's **Rod** (1971) and co-authorship of **Ned Kelly** (1968), and Williamson's screenplays for *Stork, Libido, Peterson, The Removalists, Eliza Fraser* and *Don's Party*. They share a preoccupation with the values and life-styles of their own generation, the Hughie Cook generation grown up to a place in the suburbs. And they are both very particular in locating their plays.

Buzo knows his Sydney, and the people of his plays are often fixed quite precisely (for a Sydney audience especially) by the areas in which they live or to which they aspire. Their locations suggest a concentration on increasingly 'trendy' and sophisticated groups of people; from the garish white unit in **Rooted** (1969) which is Bentley's stepping stone . . ., to the 'sparsely and tastefully furnished harbourside flat' in **Tom** (1972), to the attractive house 'in the Bilgola-Palm Beach area' in **Coralie Lansdowne Says No** (1974) and the 'well designed and furnished' holiday house at Pittwater, in **Martello Towers** (1976). Williamson's Melbourne settings also draw on the local knowledge of his audience to define a particular corner of society; his plays reflect, less specifically than Buzo's, the general tendency of recent Australian drama to move further away from working-class settings and idioms to the affluent and articulate groups which make up its audience.

Each has a 'good ear', too, and has been able from the beginning to supply for Australian audiences the shock and delight of hearing themselves speak. The lasting value of successful mimicry, though, depends on its purpose, and the degree to which it informs rather than simulates reality. And it is in their treatment of the vernacular that the differences in interest between the two are striking. Williamson's language is racy and economical, but as a general rule its familiarity is its strength. His concern is predominantly sociological and psychological—it is with the analysis of recognizable groups of people and the strategies and power struggles which mark their interaction. It is important that the plays should be convincingly realistic, since in the accuracy of their social observation lies a kind of guarantee for the validity of their conclusions. (pp. 98-9)

Buzo's people characteristically speak a good deal better than any off-stage equivalents. While his plays are well laced with clichés, the clichés are heightened either by 'unnatural' rhythmic emphasis or, increasingly, by juxtaposition with other more exotic and exploratory orders of language. The method remains partly satiric, in the relationships drawn between the words of the play and known social models; but the bright and bitchy conversations of Buzo's people expose more than the pretensions of young Australian trendies. The angle of interest is moral rather than sociological, concerned with the way people act in relation to the ideas which might give value to their lives, rather than in relation to others in their group and their society. Buzo's plays are unapologetically stylish, and his is a theatre not of illusion but display.

These generalizations do not apply to all of Buzo's plays— *Norm and Ahmed* and the historical play 'in plain English' *Macquarie* are exceptions, and the other plays are sufficiently diverse to require some adjustment of the terms to individual cases. But it is important to establish a context for the formal licence of so much of Buzo's work. Reviewers have sometimes found his work wanting by quite inappropriate naturalistic criteria; or more often have approached it with expectations of formal consistency which may be equally disappointed. A number of commentators, for example, noted the shift in *Martello Towers* from extravagant five-door farce to vaguely analytical comedy of manners; there is a comparable change of mood, marked by some fading of the exuberant wit of the dialogue, in *Coralie Lansdowne Says No.* The process has been seen often as a symptom of a lapse in control, or Buzo's confusion about the kind of play he wanted to write. Such criticism not only begs some important questions, but obscures the way that the process is part of the point of both plays, in its exposure of the relationship between bright, complacent surfaces and hollow, threatening centres. Formal variations like the virtual soliloquies in *Tom* and *Rooted,* the music hall routines in *The Front Room Boys,* and the shifting time scales and multiple acting areas in *Macquarie,* need to be viewed similarly in terms of their immediate and thematic effectiveness, rather than simply as different from what one was led to expect.

Buzo's plays commonly offer the logical satisfactions of a linear plot (the way that Bentley in *Rooted* is relentlessly stripped of home unit, stereo, wife, job and mates is the clearest of them); but his comparative lack of interest in the psychological development of the individual in his plays tends to make these processes more interesting for their representativeness or their place in a pattern than they are in themselves. The structural symmetry to which Richard Wherrett, the play's first director, draws attention in *Martello Towers,* is one instance of the way a sense of shape becomes a quite immediate part of the impact of Buzo's work:

> Considered formally, the play introduces us in three successive duologues to three ill-matched couples; it then opens out to embrace and exploit the permutations and combinations of the situation; and in the second half the pattern is reversed as each character departs singly and the play is resolved in another sequence of three duologues . . .
> I found this formality very satisfying, and aimed to heighten it with a formal pattern of movement and physical composition.

The couples in *Tom, Rooted,* and *Coralie Lansdowne Says No* interchange in similar ways to draw attention both to the fecklessness of their culture and the theatrical style of the piece. The cavalcade of the seasons in *The Front Room Boys* provides the strongest impression of formality, with its twelve-monthly-parts tour of the office calendar from the stories of bowls and beach parties in January to the November Melbourne Cup broadcast and the embarrassing Christmas party; Pammy's litany of worthy causes for the office collection intensifies the sense of ritual, and the repetitiveness of a plot that is more circle than straight line.

Buzo's plays are full of talk, and typically the energies are in the play of language rather than in direct dramatic action. Often the real confrontations in Buzo's plays are between individuals and faceless systems. The back room boys, the top oil-men in *Tom,* the omnipotent unseen Simmo in *Rooted,* are forces to be talked about endlessly, but never confronted or resisted. These are comic-strip antagonisms between mighty powers and the little guy, but they resolve themselves with the certainty of realpolitik. The plays are set up in a series of snapshot impressions of a predictable and repetitive process, charted for the most part with a cooly detached burlesquing spirit.

The sheer delight in language in Buzo's work deflects the line of trenchant moral criticism a little, but these plays remain, very disturbingly, black comedy. Buzo's subject is the hollowness of a generation; his method often seems Dickensian in the way caricatured superficiality is at once a satiric tactic and a moral consequence of the kind of society that is satirized. Buzo, like Hibberd and Williamson, raises the problem of the parasitism of the satirist, and the artist's fascination with qualities that may be repellent to him, for the focus of Buzo's satire is the stylish surface from which the plays take their life; the jargons of the whole range of pretensions are its targets, and its comic means. Both ideas and relationships are shown as debased by a kind of verbal overkill, but the extravagance of language is Buzo's.

The relation between verbal stereotype and the integrity of personality has a more familiar emphasis in *Norm and Ahmed,* the play which first brought Buzo's name into prominence and became a watershed in the recurrent debate about censorship in Australia. Norm Gallagher seems offered as a caricature of the traditional qualities of the Australian male, and his garrulity offers plenty of the pleasures of parody against the stilted correctness of Ahmed. The casual racism of his references to 'boongs', 'Krauts' and 'Gyppos' is the only clear sign of verbal menace, but the violent hostility which surfaces shockingly at the end is intimated in some of Norm's gestures—the savagery with the cigarette packet, the over-zealous demonstration of wartime commando tactics, and the circling movements which accompany his 'friendly' interrogation.

The extremity of the violence (and the new order of language introduced after it in the offhand 'Fuckin' boong') is quite unexpected, though; its theatrical shock value rests precisely in its lack of any developed connection with the substance and mood of what goes before. A kind of incipient Fascism is demonstrated in Norm's smug assumptions of superiority and his unquestioning submissiveness to 'higher authorities', but the relation between this knowledge and what we see tends to be left to audiences to fill in, from their experiences of the habits of Australian drivers, football crowds and the like.

Within the bounds of the one-actor, though, Buzo accomplishes quite a lot. Its strength in the theatre relies not simply on the sensational close, but on a very assured control of the rhythms of tension and relaxation in the dialogue. There are easy laughs for the educated middle-class in Norm's curious affectation of 'good conversation' through cliché . . . and in familiar kinds of ignorance ('Arts, eh? What, bit of a painter, are you?'); and most of all in the religion of Emoh Ruo, where one can almost hear the whistling s's of Humphries' Sandy Stone in Norm's idylls among the frangipannis and hydrangeas, and his memories of 'dear Beryl':

. . . She was a lovely woman, a real beauty in her day. Jet-black hair, sparkling eyes, and an ear for music. Played a good game of bowls in her twilight years . . . It's the good times I miss. Ahmed, those magic moments that make life seem worthwhile. Like the time we danced all night at the Bronte R.S.L. Yes I really miss dear old Beryl with her happy laugh, her way with kids, her curried eggs on toast of a winter's night . . .

Even in Norm domestic sentiment carries a little genuine pathos, for all the familiar sorts of laugh at his expense.

What is new in Buzo's dramatization of an old stereotype is the fear and narrow hostility underneath the domestic complacency, and, especially, the obsequiousness behind the proud anti-authoritarianism. Norm's pride in having actually had a drink with the managing director, and his shame about his trade-unionist father who fought for the I.W.W. ('Wobbly bastards!') is one aspect of the cannon-fodder conservatism that makes his passion for law and order a murderous one. Though 'bloody dignitaries' and 'mug coppers' can expect no kowtowing from Norm ('I don't take no crap from no one'), he feels that they are entitled, respectively, to 'a little bit of respect' and 'a fair go'. Buzo's exposure of what lies behind Norm's fake egalitarianism takes the play beyond audience-indulging parody into an image of horror which challenges some old complacencies.

In *The Roy Murphy Show* (1971) Buzo has great fun with the jargon and rituals of T.V. football panels, and the chaos of giveaways, contests, abuse and pointless predictions builds to a farce of manic proportions. There is something of the student revue about it, though, particularly in the place of its audience; it is an exception to a shift in Buzo's work after *Norm and Ahmed* which brings the use of parody progressively nearer to the people likely to attend a Buzo play in the subsidized theatres.

The people of the later plays tend to be quite wealthy, talkative, humorous—they are educated without being distinctively intelligent, materialistic and yet very naive about some things. They are offhand and 'liberated' about sex, but often painfully inept in their relationships. They live in sunny, self-indulgent bliss, but while a host of superficial goals and enthusiasms are accessible to them all, some are faced with the crisis of value that can accompany a fashionable ennui. Poor old Bentley is the first of them, with his sad little bout of the existentialist dilemma in *Rooted:*

> GARY. Just assert yourself a bit. Throw your weight around. Remember, in this life it's up for grabs. You've got to go out and get it.
> BENTLEY. I'd like to go out and get it, but I don't know where it is.

In the later *Martello Towers,* the ironist Edward offers his sister a more worldly-wise version of the same hopelessness:

> VIVIEN. No, bugger it! Why should I miss out on everything?
> EDWARD. There's *nothing* to miss out on. I'm telling you.

Most of the talkers, though, are dedicated to social success. They seem no more than the sum of their affectations. For the men in particular, the maintenance of a suitable image is related to a new kind of go-getting work-value; for the oil executives in *Tom* business drive seems interconnected with vi-

rility, as Tom's versatility and Ken's 'thrust' are lauded by the Stallion company wives.

The Front Room Boys (1969) looks at the jockeying of its junior clerks fairly whimsically; Thomo, Robbo, Gibbo, Jacko, Presto and the new boy Vittorio ('funny name to give a bloke, that's all I can say', says Thomo) run like rats about a wheel for the anonymous back-roomers and the grim intermediary Hendo, but have some fun on the way. The play works on the ideas of mechanized behaviour familiar in farce and offers a number of slapstick routines, not only in the office revue, but in visual jokes; Vittorio throws the portrait of the Duke of Edinburgh out the window, and moments later the glaring Hendo appears with the portrait around his neck like a ruff. There is plenty of gratuitous fun at the expense of this authority figure, of a kind unthinkable with the all-powerful Simmo in *Rooted.* There are more good laughs at the expense of Robbo, the archetypal 'mate' and anthology of Australiana, who opened up the Northern Territory, bowled Don Bradman for a duck, etc. etc.; and Presto, whose name is closest of all to that of a traditional clown, provides a fund of knock-about antics.

However, there is an uncomfortable edge to some of the jokes. The 'collective liturgy' of the office 'whip-round' through which Pammy leads the boys is great fun as they intone the engagements of all the Raelenes, the family events of the Barries, and the disastrous career of Donnie Dixon (new gear box, new surfboard, and funeral). But its effect is to relate that catalogue of births, copulations, and deaths, and the network of private relationships it implies, to the repetitious routines of the office; and to contrast the linear time of individuals with what seems the eternal recurrence of corporations. And *The Front Room Boys* has the first of Buzo's little men who say no; Jacko comes to see the madness in their method, and becomes less and less one of the boys in becoming more and more a critic of exploitative systems and their pointless rituals.

Bentley in *Rooted* is an unwilling drop-out. He accepts all the indexes of status appropriate to a young public servant in a hurry, and rejoices in having the worth of his possessions confirmed by his mates. He sees Simmo's takeover of Sandy and the unit as a violation of ownership. . . . (pp. 99-103)

Bentley works hard to conform in everything, and from the ritual 'chug-a-lug' of 'the old Resch's' to the M.G.B. sports car he gives a passable version of the required role of the rogue male in the sharp suit. But he is a born loser. . . . There are delicate intimations of an inner Bentley, in wistful accounts of morning walks in sunlight and by water to which nobody listens; but of course when Bentley 'dangles' from the willows, he falls in.

Simmo, on the other hand, is born winner, an all-Australian success; every man would like to be Simmo, every woman would like to be his girl. By the end of the play Simmo Enterprises owns them all, except Bentley whom it crushes. (pp. 103-04)

Simmo's dramatic ancestors are among Pinter's inexplicably powerful and disruptive outsiders. But this superman is too big for the stage, and the curtain falls just before he joins the satellites at his birthday party. Buzo's game with the Godot device is not aimed simply at deceptive suspense, though. Quite apart from the certainty of disappointment in a fleshly Simmo, *Rooted* is a play much concerned with the substance of images, and to give substance to Simmo's would upset its sociology.

Rooted still seems Buzo's tightest and most assured play; the satire is narrower here, the logic simpler than in *Coralie Lansdowne Says No* and *Martello Towers,* which have rather more interesting ambitions at the cost of some effectiveness in the theatre. *Rooted* is held in perfectly consistent focus, as a kind of moral burlesque. At the same time, though, it is a transitional play for Buzo. The interest in the mateship myth which is marked in *Norm and Ahmed* leads to the sequence in *Rooted* where Gary tells Bentley he has to go; Bentley's mates have thoughtfully packed his bag, and included some rissole and pineapple sandwiches for his journey:

> GARY. Look, Bentley, old mate, we've been good mates for years, and I've always tried to do the right thing by my mates . . . I'm a bloke who always does the right thing by a bloke . . .

The hollowness of the concept is reflected in the vacuous language; Robbo, in *The Front Room Boys,* gives the definitive statement in his eulogy to Thomo—'he's a good bloke and he does the right thing by the other blokes who do the right thing by a bloke they know is a bloke who'll always do the right thing by a bloke . . .'

The new preoccupation is with the jargon of trendy role-playing. Bentley's exit in this play has to be a silent one, since all his language is bound up with a stereotype to which he can no longer pretend; all its material symbols have been taken away from him. This interest in verbal affectation as the sign of the absence of meaning in the characters' lives is further developed in Buzo's next play, *Tom.* It results, though, in a play which is disappointingly wordy and diffuse. Perhaps the lesson is that the method of the comedy of manners, with its air of detachment and preoccupation with style, demands an appropriately stylish container; *Tom* does not give the kind of formal satisfactions which might compensate for a lack of interesting people by drawing attention to its art.

We have moved up the scale of corporation men to the big wheels of the oil industry, but the characters in *Tom* are seen in familiar terms. It is a world of back-stabbers, of 'bugged' and tape-recorded conversations, where Stephen would rather be thought guilty of breaking in for Tom's wife than Tom's briefcase, and where passionate living seems confined to the frenzied urgency of the business crisis. Stephen's arty claptrap is an extension of Richard's in *Rooted;* his aesthetic is in keeping with the media-image culture:

> STEPHEN. . . . It's become suicidally ridiculous to continue operating with Augustinian metaphors of human identity and motivation in the age of lunar exploration and genetic engineering. Traditional notions of "freedom" and "individuality" are deftly absurd in the face of the inevitable shaping matrix of organized behavior.
> SUSAN. Crap.

The exchange is symptomatic of the new preoccupations which are evident in *Tom.* It fixes the relationship between the dehumanizing forces of the culture and the dehumanizing methods of the satire, but at the same time it offers the first signs of an articulate resistance—Susan, who claims (not completely convincingly) a heroic self-containment at the end, foreshadows Buzo's more complex romantics, Coralie Lansdowne and Edward Martello. And that exchange marks a new procedure, too; this juxtaposition of a very sophisticated jargon with a blunt vernacular produces some odd and striking tonal effects in *Tom* and its successors.

Tom, the troubleshooter, who carefully fosters the image of dedicated outsider through a commitment to sea-wine and a studied line in coarse dismissiveness, provides some of these moments. But he is not always verbally in keeping with his image as 'tough guy in an effete milieu'. Tom manages to keep up with Susan in the cleverness of his abuse ('An independent clinging vine! A liberated leech!'). She, while capable of great sharpness (she suggests a biography of Tom to be titled 'A Foetus Preserved'), can also wallow in banal repetitions in her complaints about toothache and Tom's infidelity. The co-existence of verbal poverty and ingenuity in her speech is nicely caught when she yells at Tom, 'You bloody great ape! You simian imbecile!'

This interest in sliding registers, and the incidental delights of some of the verbal effects, seems the central thrust of the play. It shares with *Coralie Lansdowne Says No* and *Martello Towers* its focus on a particular generation (all the people in *Tom* are in their mid-twenties) and a style of living to which the advertising men urge us all to aspire. Its structure is similarly controlled by shifts and resolutions in personal relationships; Tom starts the play married to Susan, who has an affair with Stephen whose wife Angela pursues Tom, who is pursuing Carol, the wife of Ken in whom Angela shows a passing interest; at the play's end Susan and Tom are separated, each having affirmed the irrelevance of the other. Unlike the later plays though, *Tom* stays on the surface with its clever talkers.

Not that the more recent plays are altogether conclusive in their probing. *Coralie Lansdowne Says No* exposes some private vulnerability behind the roles its people play, but the forms it takes remain mysterious. Anne Coleman, wishy-washy and pregnant, is the most striking of those who seem smooth enough on the surface but evidently paddle like hell underneath. At the end of scene one she responds with a strained smile at finding her husband Paul in Coralie's bedroom; early in scene two, several days later, we pick up in the course of conversation the fact that she threw herself off the cliff that night.

At the centre of the play, of course, are the limits of Coralie's self-possession. Jill draws the simple dichotomy within two lines, when she describes her sister as a 'bloody bitch' and 'a cream puff', and Coralie concedes as much to Stuart:

> STUART. Just look at yourself. What are your choices?
> CORALIE. I'm a . . . I'm a . . . high flying bird . . .
> STUART. What a pathetic illusion. All you've done, all your life, is describe a small spiral inside a vacuum. A collection of tiny arcs. How much longer can you go on?
> CORALIE. (*weakly*) No . . .

Stuart's cave-man psychology is triumphant. This time the 'pipsqueak' public servant gets the girl, and this time the play ends not with a separation but a marriage. It is not an unqualified romanticism—after some giggling over the wedding gifts a mysterious ailment hits Coralie, and only the timely arrival of a one-legged doctor removes the possibility of an even more gratuitous death and lurches the play into grotesque comedy again. With this last confirmation of Coralie's vulnerability, and the defensiveness of her old aggressive self-sufficiency, the closing touch seems apt enough:

> (. . . *she looks around the room slowly and calmly and then her eyes come to rest on* STUART. *They stand there, looking at each other. Silence.*)
> CORALIE. You'll do.
> (STUART *looks at her apprehensively. Silence.*)

From one point of view this is understated, from another realistic. It is a welcome adjustment of the earlier impression that under Coralie's tough exterior beats a heart of pure marzipan; for Coralie *is* a high-flier, a dramatic figure of great vitality, and the apparent vindication of Stuart's denial of that seems simplistic and unfair to her. The last line is at once a recognition of Stuart's worth and of her own needs, and it implies a challenge. It confirms that Coralie's dependence is not a conversion to frilly aprons, and that the new relationship is no miracle cure, but humanly difficult and possible.

The energy of the play is still in its bright facades though. The rest remains rather murky, in Coralie's apprehensions at turning thirty, and the shudders of 'night over my shoulder' that recall the black wind that haunts Mag in **Big Toys;** and these intimations of mortality are given a special context by the sunburnt cripples of Palm Beach. Her personal crisis is related to the distinctive experience of a generation by a number of verbal signposts—for the educated children of the late 1950s and early 1960s they extend from snatches of Lesley Gore and Brenda Lee to the odd piece from Yeats. There is a vaguely 'in-group' quality about **Coralie Lansdowne Says No,** which matches the sense that this is not a play in which the dramatist stands well away from his subject; at least, not all the time.

A standard of verbal agility is set in the play's opening moments:

> PETER. . . . I thought you were going to a seance at that clairvoyant's place this evening.
> CORALIE. It was cancelled because of unforeseen circumstances.

It defines something of the style of the group, in which clever conversation is competitive and the effort is to make the details of a life into an interesting script. They listen to each other, but for cues rather than information:

> PETER. You drift through life, aimless, rootless—
> CORALIE. That I have never been.
> PETER. Flippant, smart-arsed,
> CORALIE. I'm sorry.
> PETER. Apologetic.
> CORALIE. Oh shut up. [*She laughs*]

It is hard to get away with pretension or verbal inadequacy in such company. The art of the send-up is second nature to them all; to Coralie especially, who emerges as Buzo's first genuine parodist in her nice mimicry of Anne's constant 'which was beaut' and impersonal pronouns. Keeping people laughing with her is one way to guarantee a personal distinctiveness while preserving a distance.

While no-one in this play is contained by the fairly simple verbal stereotypes of **Tom** and **Rooted,** their talk is by no means brilliantly individual. The way Peter, Stuart, and Anne observe in turn that 'the tree is of course fabulous' suggests the languid quality of their enthusiasms, and more importantly something mechanical about their cleverness. But certainly they seem to have control over a number of lan-

guage roles, and are quite discriminating in their use of the cruder vernacular. Paul in particular enjoys the role of the ocker male, especially in male company ('Jesus! Surrounded by smart farts. Here, let's all get pissed'), but the shift in language is just radical enough to keep an air of parody.

The most characteristic aspect of their cleverness is a form of *bon mot*, a rapid barbed pigeonholing of people and places; it aims for the maximum brightness with the least apparent effort, and again Coralie is its best exponent. Anne is categorized with a characteristic blend of flashy polysyllables and vigorous colloquialism:

> . . . She's English, a gaminesque harridan from some provincial ghetto called Finsburystead-upon-Harrowfordgate or something. Two swans and a marmalade factory—it's very picturesque. Doesn't stop her from being slightly on the smarmy side, though. She's a film buff—always rushing off to see *Man's Favourite Sport* or discussing Guilt in Fritz Lang. Am I being unkind?

The line of wit is Buzo's trademark, and one has the sense that he shares his characters' excitement about verbal display. It is outside the norms of naturalistic dialogue, and comfortably so for the first half of the play. The difficulty comes with the shift in mood of the second half, in which the play seems to be pushing closer to the familiar territory of naturalism with its probing of the motives and choices of its heroine. This shift is not as clear as that in **Martello Towers,** nor is there quite as much effort to dull the surface of the dialogue to accommodate it. But it is there, and it involves some sort of moral review of the earlier conversational style. In this light the artificiality of the talk comes to be seen not simply as a set of entertaining routines, nicely blending mimicry with adventurousness, but as a symptom. Coralie says no to a deceptive self-possession which keeps others at bay by tartly stereotyping them and herself; and she says no to Peter and Paul, who are taken in by the mask and find it desirable. Stuart may oversimplify in his determination to bring the high-flier down to earth, but the secret of his success is his refusal to believe that Coralie's style is either real or adequate. The movement of the play seems to be toward a corroboration of that judgment.

Coralie Lansdowne is a moral play and a stylish play, but there is a certain conflict between those elements. The self-consciousness of its talkers inhibits the front-on conversation, and ensures that some of Coralie's reasons for saying yes to Stuart remain unexamined. The same limits apply to **Martello Towers,** where Edward is so accomplished an ironist that there is some tension between his style and the play's happy ending, in which Edward and Jennifer decide to have a second try at their marriage. Buzo wrote a neat retort to those who found this resolution unsatisfying in a post-script to the play:

> They found it shocking and degrading that a husband and wife should reaffirm their love for each other, but I think any reasonably ambitious play should confront its audience with disturbing unpalatable facts, such as the existence of love.

But the problem goes deeper than the advocacy of unfashionable virtues, if that is what they are. It is implied in Edward's wry announcement that 'Our separation is on the rocks'. The manner of the dialogue precludes emotional exposure or analysis—an ironist like Edward can make any commitment look like an affectation, and the tendency of his habit of parody is to empty important words of their meaning. Buzo's only recourse in bringing him to an acknowledgement of his dependence and setting up a relationship which might meet it is the *Coralie Lansdowne* tactic—the new relationship simply happens, with a minimum of talk about why and how it should. The lesson seems to be that, among clever people, the less said the better.

The play sets up some straightforward aunt sallies in the first act. Francesca is one, with her social work. . . . Lonnie, the 'radical rock radio' man who is 'into' women's rights is an even larger target, and there are some very easy laughs at his expense:

> LONNIE. You two girls sit down. *I'll* serve lunch. (*To* EDWARD) You've got a lot of nerve, expecting women to be your servants. They weren't put on earth to change nappies and slice up salami, tiger, so you just wake up your fuckin' ideas.
> JENNIFER. It might be easier if I served lunch, Lonnie.
> LONNIE. Righto.

Buzo is very skilled at this sort of thing, and in the farce-action of the first act with its stagey comings and goings through doors and French windows there are plenty of laughs.

Edward is very good at parody too, and can always find the right cliché to put down pretension. He nicely undercuts the enthusiasm of Lonnie and Jennifer for a film:

> JENNIFER. I loved that bit at the mental asylum. The hands at the window.
> LONNIE. Yeah, the whole bit made a really good point—
> EDWARD. That the insane are more sane than the so-called sane?
> LONNIE. How did you know?
> EDWARD. Oh, let's just say I'm an old hand-at-the-window man. God, it sounds great! Let's have a drink.

He stops all conversation on the script with the same tactic ('I thought it was rich in quaint juxtapositions. How are the dogs running?'; when challenged about his rudeness to Lonnie he replies 'It's a cry for help'. In all this we have a very strong impression of intellectual rank-pulling, but no clear notion of what, if anything, Edward thinks is worth taking seriously.

The second act offers some likely-looking answers. In the slightly disruptive farce cameos of the visits of his father and mother-in-law there are a number of gestures about a coming-to-terms-at-last with parental expectation; with some tempting, but slightly glib, treatment of the familiar theme of the man between cultures, in the form here of the first generation Australian. And the vaguely erotic suggestions of his relationship with his sister Vivien are brought into the open, and dismissed. None of this 'explaining' works very well, though. The force that sustains the second act, and which makes *Martello Towers* one of the most interesting of recent Australian plays, is Buzo's capacity to make Edward convincingly intelligent. The directions remain rather vague, but Edward's effort to rid himself of automatic self-protective irony is absorbing, and is handled with some subtlety.

Edward is not the only character who is the victim of self-conscious role-playing, of course. Even Lonnie, fumbling absurdly about who he is . . . is saying something about himself; moments later he gives a biographical tirade covering at least three of the people he has been. And more pointedly, Vivien's scorn of herself when young—'I was obsessed with superficial image-making'—is hard to leave at face value. The levels of irony at work in *Martello Towers* entitle us to ask whether a hostility to superficial image-making might not be a form of superficial image-making.

Martello Towers in some ways is an attempt to have the best of both forms—the question of why this collection of ill-matched and embarrassed couples chose to stay at all, for example, is first rendered irrelevant by the farce action of Act One, and then answered by the underlying tensions which become evident in Act Two. The sense that neither the farce model nor the closely observed darker comedy can contain Buzo's interest in the situation is, of course, a very good reason for the combination. The way that the experience of the first act works to qualify that of the second is still a constraint, but there is a deliberateness about the shifts in tone here, and about facing the problems it raises, which is lacking in *Coralie Lansdowne Says No.*

The line of wit seems to have petered out in Buzo's most recent play, *Makassar Reef* (1978). There is some clever talking here, but not much is expressive; and the dialogue has little of the energy that marks the play's predecessors. Partly this is because of the personality of Weeks Brown, its principal agent. Weeks, an economist soaking up the Indonesian sun and gin for the want of anything else to do, is engaging enough. But in keeping with his own self-assessments, he doesn't really matter, as Coralie Lansdowne or Edward Martello matter. Weeks' self-consciousness is ultimately devoid of their strength and irony—'I don't know where I am' and 'What a mess I've made' are about as far as he can go past flippancy.

The superficiality in *Makassar Reef* though has less to do with satire than picturesqueness, and that seems the other cause of the play's forgettable style. There are some diverting bits of local colour, and some touches of Hollywood exotica for good measure; an odd assortment of types and accents drift together like the people of *Casablanca* for some fleeting romance and intrigue, while around them flit sinister locals like Karim of the Sidney Greenstreet suit and smuggler Silver of the Peter Lorre cringe. There is little room for development of the play's emotional conflicts. Its final image, of Weeks standing helplessly before the cage-bed to which Beth has tricked him into returning, has some elements of real horror; but they are weakened by the lack of substantiation of his improbable love for Wendy, the sensible 'older woman'. *Makassar Reef* leaves one feeling that Buzo is careless of his characters, but has great enthusiasm for Makassar.

It also offers some confirmation that *Martello Towers* took Buzo's fascination for self-consuming cleverness in dialogue about as far as it could valuably go. His contribution to theatre in Australia is distinctive in a number of ways. The best of the plays are not content to rest in stereotype, and offer more scope to females and sophisticates than most of their contemporaries; and they show a delight in formal pattern and bravura language which gives his work an unmistakeable individuality. He has also shown a readiness for formal experiment; now that there are strong signs that it is needed, there are interesting terms for speculation as to where it might take him next. (pp. 104-11)

Peter Fitzpatrick, "Alexander Buzo," in his After

"The Doll": Australian Drama since 1955, *Edward Arnold (Australia) Pty. Ltd., 1979, pp. 98-111.*

JOHN McCALLUM

Alexander Buzo is in the curious, and no doubt frustrating, position of being an established playwright, with ten more or less successful plays to his credit, who is still often not taken seriously, and whose deeply humanitarian purpose is often ignored. Since he first began his stormy relationship with the critics . . . with **Norm and Ahmed** twelve years ago, he has on several occasions reluctantly but forcefully launched himself into what he has called 'the dreaded world of theory' to explain his position. He has now something of a reputation for bringing to bear on his critics the same wit he gives his characters. There is an image of Buzo—alone, isolated, ensconced in the Martello Towers of his artistic integrity and moral purpose—encircled by the 'plangent whingers', 'splenetic hacks' and 'empty pseuds' who write about him and fail to understand him. It is an image perfectly represented by his leading characters—Bentley, Jacko, Macquarie, Tom, Coralie Lansdowne, Edward Martello and Weeks Brown—who are all in their way similarly embattled. Like them (or at least the last three) he seems to cloak a deep-seated romantic humanitarianism in a mantle of dry wit and cynicism. This is obviously not a new thing in 'the Australian character', but in Buzo it is particularly sophisticated. It is perhaps not surprising, then, that he should be misunderstood in a country with a very slight tradition of stylish playwriting.

All of Buzo's early group of plays, up to and partly including **Tom** (1972), which seems a transitional work, show their principal characters as victims, at first unconscious, of an amoral and dehumanising society. Buzo himself has called them his 'angry' plays, when he thought that 'a playwright's function was to change society's thoughts'. Since then he has modified this view, as we shall see, and the style of his plays has subsequently changed, but up until **Tom** the dramatic emphasis is firmly on the social situations within which individuals find themselves.

These social situations are evoked, very wittily, by the use of the cliches and platitudes of the Australian idiom and Australian life. . . . Many reviewers, in fact, responded simply to the 'Australian-ness' of the plays, interpreting them as satirical social documentaries. Buzo himself denied this. . . . At a seminar at the University of New South Wales in 1976, he said his plays were fiction, not documentary sociology, and extended the point to apply to **Tom** and **Coralie Lansdowne Says No** (1974) which had by then appeared and met with a similar response. In *Theatre Quarterly* he wrote:

> As a playwright I saw myself as working essentially in fiction, creating images rather than in-depth think-tank investigative probes. Were our mores changing in the technocratic residue of a once-and-future colonial heritage? I couldn't care less.

The 'images' of the plays are all concerned with characters who struggle to express their humanity in the face of a surrounding moral vacuity, and to find a sense of personal value which may have some hope of enduring. From **Norm and Ahmed** to **Big River** (1980) there is a huge development in the self-awareness of the characters, and in the evocation of the social and historical context within which they struggle; but this central concern remains the same.

Norm and Ahmed, a fairly simple play, shows the way in which Norm uses cliches and platitudes to express (and attempt, unsuccessfully, to come to terms with) his feelings of loneliness and alienation. (The cliches and platitudes are, naturally enough, Australian, but they are not the play's subject.) His speech about life's 'simple pleasures' ('Put me amongst the hydrangeas and I'm at peace with the world') shows him groping to find the genuine feeling under the cliche; and his choked, almost tearful, breaking off is surely genuine, even if instantly masked by a fresh outburst of conventionalities.

Similarly, **Rooted** (1969) shows Bentley's painful struggle to come to terms with a social situation which not only alienates him, but, quite surreally, tries to destroy him. He is only fitfully aware of what is going on. The real destructive influence of his social environment is not the loss of flat, wife and job, but the fact that he has few means of expressing his humanity other than the ocker and the public-service jargon given him by his friends and colleagues. So Bentley, the character, assumes the style of the society which Buzo is criticising; but a certain authorial distance allows us to see the man behind the social stereotype. Already in Bentley we have the beginnings of the self-awareness which is to make Edward Martello and Weeks Brown such powerful characters. Any character who is given such a speech as Bentley's about his swim in the rock pool is not being satirised. The fact that we see this side of him makes all the more moving his later inability to transcend the cliches of his life. The society which tries to destroy Bentley only succeeds in driving him out—which makes the ending oddly optimistic in the face of what happens to him. The play has taken some trouble to set up the strength of silence, particularly through Sandy, and so Bentley's silence at the end is eloquent.

Jacko, in **The Front Room Boys** (1969), is also groping for an awareness of the way the system ignores the human needs of, in this case, a group of office-workers. **Macquarie** (1972) shows the dilemma of conscience of a small-l liberal trying to reform an amoral society. His weakness, and his particular form of victimisation, are summed up by Polski when he says,

> The main trouble with being a liberal is that you tend to play by the rules of the system you are trying to reform, whereas your opponents, who uphold the system, feel no such constrictions on their freedom.

The society happens to be colonial New South Wales, but, as Buzo has himself pointed out, the liberal could as easily have been McGovern, Dubček, or Whitlam.

In **Tom,** the rapacious and morally and emotionally bankrupt oil-men who surround Tom and Susan are still the focus of attention, and supply a great deal of the wit and energy of the play. For the first time, however, we have two characters who do not assume the valueless attitudes of their friends. Tom merely bends in the wind, but the play focuses on Susan's loneliness and pain in a way new to Buzo. The play perhaps does not go far enough in this; but it is sufficiently marked to make **Tom** a significant turning point in Buzo's writing.

In 1973, just before **Coralie Lansdowne** appeared, Buzo stated in an interview, 'I'm more concerned now with individuals in Australian society, rather than how society forms individuals'. In **Coralie Landsdowne, Martello Towers** (1976) and **Makassar Reef** (1978) the dramatic focus has shifted away from the social *milieu* of the characters onto the leading individuals themselves. There is still a strong sense of a world outside, but it is retreating away over the water which by now has begun to surround Buzo's settings. In *Coralie Lansdowne* we are aware of the wealthy cripples who live around her, but the French windows of her retreat look out over the Pacific Ocean—and the ocean claims the life of Anne, whose sense of personal value is at her first entrance already very faint. Perched in her eyrie, Coralie is alone, surrounded by people who don't live up to her high-flying ideals and who aren't, except for Stuart, aware of her pain. The pain is manifested theatrically by her very real feelings of guilt about Anne's death.

In *Martello Towers* the characters are shifted to an island in Pittwater, completely surrounded by water in which lurk the dreaded oyster beds which eventually gash Vivien. Edward Martello is central, but not alone. Jennifer, like Bentley, uses the jargon of the vacuous ones, but unlike him she comes to her senses within the play. Vivien feels the vacuity from the outset but moves along with it, generally in control of her pain. With both of them Edward has moments where valuable intimacy peeps through his normally thick layer of self-protective irony:

> EDWARD. Just don't get yourself mucked around, if you can swing it.
> VIVIEN. I think I deserve credit, for stopping short of, 'I'm not a kid any more.'
> EDWARD. Look—
> VIVIEN. It's all right. I'm glad someone's interested, anyway.
> EDWARD. (*stroking her hair*) You could say that.

When his separation from Jennifer goes on the rocks his emotion almost, but not quite, overwhelms his wit:

> EDWARD. An unsuccessful separation. Sometimes I despair of ever becoming fashionable.
> JENNIFER. I hated it, being like all those frightful people who can't sustain adult communication for more than five minutes and dress up their boring neuroses with ideological finery. I think they're wet and naff and totally dull.
> EDWARD. Let them eat brown rice.
> JENNIFER. There'll still be just the two of us when we're eighty.
> EDWARD. Yes.
> JENNIFER. It'll be a porch and jasmine affair by then. And I'll refuse to give advice to anyone under seventy. There's no such thing as advice. There's no prescription and I'm so glad I found out. Hey, what's this?
> EDWARD. (*wiping his eyes*) It's okay.
> JENNIFER. Teddy, Teddy, hey come on. You're the apostle of good taste.
> EDWARD. Yes, it's disgraceful, I know. I always get depressed when I wear brown shoes.

Here we see the beginnings of the romantic sensibility which matures into full-blown romantic comedy in *Makassar Reef* and *Big River.* Buzo has often said that he is on the side of 'niceness', that in an amoral society people being nice to each other is one of the few hopes they have. He wrote that at about the time *Tom* appeared.

> I became more concerned with human relationships, desperation, psychological cruelty, aloneness, pursuit, anguish, and Congreve-style comedy. I also saw myself as a defender of niceness.

In *Martello Towers* we see for the first time not only the nice characters banding together, but also the problems they themselves have in relation to each other. There is a slight sourness at the end of the play—Edward cannot altogether retreat both into the family and into his marriage at the same time. In *Makassar Reef,* barely before the dramatic focus on individuals has been introduced, we are shifting again—this time to concentrate on the bonds, weak and strong, which the nice people forge with each other, and the compromise and sadness which these shifting relationships entail.

At the same time that Buzo's dramatic concerns are changing, his style is developing. His earlier surrealism is being modified to a heightened realism; his images are softening and being absorbed more subtly into the fabric of the play's action; his verbal skill is developing into a sophisticated wit, and although his characters are still non-naturalistically articulate, the humour of the dialogue is somehow less authorial. There was a feeling in the early plays that the characters speaking the funny lines were not in on the joke. The effect of this, for many reviewers, was that the witty style became a barrier to a full appreciation of what Buzo was actually using his characters for; so that Peter Fitzpatrick could argue, with some justification, that *Tom,* for example, 'stays on the surface with its clever talkers.'

By the time of *Coralie Lansdowne,* and particularly *Martello Towers,* the wit of the characters is an integral part of *their* style, not merely Buzo's, and is part of their struggle to come to terms with their moral and personal anxieties. Buzo has written,

> [Edward] is an educated 'rake' who is, in keeping with the style of the play, articulate beyond the demands of naturalism. I conceived Edward as a wholly serious character whose wisecracks stem from pain, but most people see him as a 'funny man'.

The dialogue with Jennifer, quoted above, surely indicates the extent to which Edward uses his wit self-protectively. He turns his wit on himself when he rather ruefully admits this:

> LONNIE. I'm getting bad vibes from your old man.
> JENNIFER. Why do you have to be so rude?
> EDWARD. It's a cry for help.

Jennifer empties her glass over his head. Edward replies by emptying his glass over her head, as if to say, 'I meant it'. Even Lonnie, whose speech is a very clever and funny parody of the jargon of the 'radical rock radio' DJ, is using the jargon to hide an inner directionlessness. Of this he is himself painfully aware, as his final speech demonstrates quite movingly.

Another element of the barrier of style is a supposed stylistic promiscuity, whereby we are said to get frightfully confused about what sort of play we are watching—as Buzo moves from farce to romantic comedy to drama within, for example, *Martello Towers.* It was the critical response along these lines to *Martello Towers* which led Buzo to write his best-known attack on the critics, in the *National Times.* He wrote:

> A few splenetic hacks have complained that it's against the rules to mix styles like this but I think they should appreciate that the theatre is a practical place where what works in rehearsal and in performance with an audience can be deemed to have worked full stop.

In fact the 'mixing of styles' is simply a carelessness about *genre,* something we surely accepted some forty years ago when we accepted that there could be such a thing as 'black comedy'. *Martello Towers* is perfectly coherent stylistically—it simply moves from a light-hearted mood to an increasingly serious one. If the early farcical scenes are contrived, then the later, quite serious reconciliation scene is equally so.

The wit remains in the later scenes of course, and the seriousness lies in what is taking place underneath it, between the characters. There is, in fact, a subtext. By *Big River,* it is beginning to become the dominant action of the play.

Finally, in regard to stylistic development, what used to be seen as a cold, clinical surface (although as I have suggested it concealed a warm humanist interior) is now merely dry, brittle and slightly distant. The inner pain of the characters springs to the fore more often and more strongly, particularly in Buzo's next play, *Makassar Reef,* where the sudden outbursts of overt feeling, in the context of the dry wit, are very powerful. So much of the resonance of the dialogue is contextual that it is difficult to quote, but examples are the early scene in which Beth forces Weeks to agree to return to Australia, and so confronts him painfully with the mess of his past; and the later scene in which Camilla and Wendy are discussing when they shall leave:

> WENDY. I don't know! I don't know that and I don't know myself any more. If I could say when we're leaving it would mean I've come to an understanding. But there's no understanding. Years of introspection mean nothing. A lifetime of pounding temples comes to nothing. I'm not equipped. I simply don't know where I am. If that makes me derelict in your eyes, and I suspect it does, then that makes it even worse.
> WEEKS. It can't be all bad. After all, I'm in love with you.
> WENDY. No! I didn't hear that. It wasn't said.
> (CAMILLA *jumps on* WEEKS, *punching him.*)
> CAMILLA. You bastard! You great big bastard!

Weeks' rather flippant declaration is a trigger which explodes Wendy's suppressed love, and both Wendy's and Camilla's insecurity about their future.

Makassar Reef is still a very stylish play, of course. The surface style is a 'romantic adventure story' of intrigue in the tropical north, or far east, depending on whether you are Weeks or Wendy. The atmosphere is that of *Casablanca.* The world beyond is evoked more richly than ever—be it Weeks' Australia, or Wendy's Geneva or Silver's Bali—all of these places over the water which in this play is literally lapping around the set (at least in the Seattle production). There is an even stronger feeling of isolation from this terrifying outside world than in *Martello Towers.* Underneath the style lies the same study of people seeking stability in love, and relationships, in the face of the ugly, valueless world outside. By now the images (the water, the triangular black sails, the cage around the bed, the sordid political and criminal intrigue of the subplot) are fully integrated into the action, instead of standing out slightly self-consciously, like Coralie's tree. The play shows people coming to terms with their past, in order that, like Beckett's characters, they might go on. . . . Buzo is in this play exploring the specific moral decisions which people have to make in their lives, if they are to satisfy themselves without hurting other people. Wendy has made a grand plan for a new start in life, but she has largely ignored her daughter's needs and has not allowed for the sudden resurgence of passionate love provoked by Weeks. Weeks himself is having his 'last flicker out of bounds', but has failed to

consider the suffering this will cause Wendy. It is a sign of the generally sad atmosphere of compromise which pervades the play that Beth's final, and in a way quite morally responsible (considering the future) promise to Weeks, that she has not made love with Perry, is known by the audience to be a lie.

And yet throughout this there is a gentle world-weariness and a lightness of touch, which seems to have deceived many people. The lack of a tradition of stylish playwriting, and the consequent dearth of directors with a feeling for style, may have something to do with it. In itself, there is no reason why Buzo should not write a romantic comedy with underlying serious concerns. In any case, it is certainly not a question of 'admirable restraint' . . . but rather of the refreshing formality and stylishness with which a very strong play is constructed.

With *Big River* this trend is confirmed. It is in some ways a very old-fashioned play. It confirms that Buzo's interests are moving towards the compromise and desperation of his characters in their relationships with each other, and yet it returns to focus, like the earlier plays, and particularly *Coralie Lansdowne,* on a strong central character, Adela Learmonth. Adela, however, knows what she wants and gets it. The compromises she makes along the way, and her doubts about the value of her goal, give the play, again, a sadness which affects our response to the resolute and rather grim 'party-girl' atmosphere. In the process of getting what she wants she distances herself from Monica and Hugh, develops a new but sadly distant relationship with Charles, and hurts her sister Olivia:

> CHARLES. Just a minute, Livvie. I want to tell Adela that I love her very much and that I wish her all the best for her future happiness.
> OLIVIA. What an extraordinary thing to say.
> ADELA. Thank you, Charles. I love you very much, too. (*She kisses him.*)
> OLIVIA. Well, I'm going out to watch the fireworks. (CHARLES *grabs* OLIVIA's *arm.*)
> CHARLES. Livvie. I didn't mean to hurt you.
> OLIVIA. How was I hurt? You've all gone mad. But that doesn't hurt me at all.

The irony is no longer even the characters', but true dramatic irony. Adela's doubts about the value of her success, in the closing moments of the play, shed a new light on our attitudes to all the moral decisions she has made.

Big River also brings a new historical and geographical strength to the evocation of the world outside the Learmonth home. It shows a pioneer society in decline, about to be replaced by the new Federation; and it shows a rural society in decline, as the children move towards the city. The water is now the Murray River, just down the slope from the house. At one dark moment it throws up, by threatening to overflow its banks, the branding irons with which Ben and Leo have their savage fight, but generally it is placid, not moving the branch of dead leaves which Adela throws into it. 'The river has stopped,' she says.

In *Makassar Reef* and *Big River* Buzo is moving towards a new stylistic lightness, but he is using what is by now a very complex tool to analyse the relationship between individuals and the social *milieu* within which they have to survive. He is using romanticism theatrically to give an ostensive definition of moral attractiveness, 'niceness', in his characters, and so is pointing the way to one of the means which his audiences can use to understand and come to terms with their world. (pp. 60-9)

John McCallum, "Coping with Hydrophobia: Alexander Buzo's Moral World," in Meanjin, Vol. 39, No. 1, April, 1980, pp. 60-9.

ALEXANDER BUZO (INTERVIEW WITH GEOFFREY SIRMAI)

[This interview originally took place on November 25, 1985.]

[Sirmoi]: Alex Buzo, one of the things that has been noted about your work in particular is that what is said by your characters is not nearly so significant as the way in which it is said. Katherine Brisbane noted in her introduction to your **Three Plays** *that "Mr. Buzo is unique amongst present Australian writers in that he is a stylist in the first instance." Do you agree that style is your principal theatrical weapon?*

[Buzo]: Yes I do. To paraphrase Oscar Wilde, I think content is the last refuge of the unimaginative. There's an interesting debate over whether people get involved with the content because they haven't got the style or because they really "believe in" the content. Take structure for instance. My approach to structure is an aesthetic one. I set out **Martello Towers** by opening with three duologues then expanding onto permutations of eight and closing again with three duologues; thus you get a formal aesthetic pattern. With the works of people who are more involved with content or naturalism, the structure tends to be what the story dictates. There's quite a gulf between the people who write naturalistic content-oriented plays and stylists like myself. That's not to say that the style is purely an end in itself; I hope that the plays I write are saying something reasonably logical. It's just that they're more a product of style than substance.

You are very much a product of the "New Wave"—the rise of popular Australian theatre of the early seventies. Jack Hibberd's description of the new Australian theatre as aiming to "jolt and agitate within a context of sheer local enjoyment, a whirl of community and awareness of a shared heritage" implies the sort of love of all things Australian, a celebration, if you like, of Australian institutions and personalities, that we see illustrated in his plays and in many others of the same vintage. Your view of Australian culture is much harsher—not so much celebrating as flaying our sacred cows. Why the departure from New Wave parochialism?

It's strange how many people think I have an adversary position to society. Wherever you go, you find people apologizing for everything because they think that writers in general—and perhaps me more than some—are critical. I think how that comes about is that there's usually a layer of what you might call ingratiation, or some kind of apology for what's about to come in most plays, whereas that layer is absent in mine. I don't think my plays are any more stringent than most but perhaps the others just lead into it more gently.

Perhaps then, if your style is absurdist and in that way subversive of naturalistic conventions, it seems to pull at the heart of what people expect and if that is, as you say, "unapologetic", then it must come across as being true.

That's very true. If people don't get what they expect, or even get something just a little different from what they expect, they get very upset.

The use of language in your plays is one of those "unapologet-

ic" barbs that is aimed at an empty cultural life, but also turns upon itself, so that we're left with a sort of metalinguistic irony. Is that a fair comment?

Yes. . . . In the early plays the characters aren't aware of what they're saying; what they're saying "gives them away" in a sense. By the time we get to 1974, Coralie Lansdowne is more conscious—and so is Edward Martello. I can't give you a complete answer to the question because of the change that came about around then. With **Martello Towers** the language is so tightly strung that I couldn't go any further in that direction.

There certainly was a big change between **Martello Towers** *and* **Makassar Reef.**

Yes, with **Martello Towers** if you changed one word it would be like popping a string on a guitar or a tennis racquet, it's just pulled so tight.

Then this was the end of a process that the earlier plays were charting?

In a way, yes, **Martello Towers** was a culmination of a certain use of language and a type of observation.

So the absurd and very funny rush of words from Lonnie in **Martello Towers** *is the last sign of that style?*

Yes. I thought I'd taken that as far as it would go.

I'd like to ask you about influences on your development and as a prelude to that, may I put to you something written by Beckett in one of his "Dialogues", where he posits that the modern artist has "nothing to express, nothing with which to express, no power or desire to express, together with the obligation to express." This sort of paradoxical bind suggests an emptiness at the core of Absurdism. Is that a relevant insight for your work?

Well there is certainly a big difference between the absurdism of the European writers and absurdism in a new country like Australia. At the heart of European absurdism is a pessimism about the collapse of civilization in the twentieth century, particularly over the Second World War, and a kind of defiant wonder that life still goes on. In Australia it's quite different, and the absurdism derives from the fact that we're looking at a young country that at times defies description. The absence of morality or more particularly, tradition, gives it that absurd edge. The writer's position then becomes a very difficult one, as it must be.

But isn't there a sort of despair, black humour at least, in the empty ritual of **The Front Room Boys** *or the hollow pretensions of the characters of* **Rooted?**

Well, they're certainly not full of boundless optimism! (*he laughs*) I first conceived the idea for **The Front Room Boys** when I was working in an office where there was this Swiss calendar on the wall and as you would imagine, everything was out of sync . . . everything seemed just out of reach; on a treadmill. I think the play is more tantalizing in its absurdity. It's saying that life for the wage-earner puts everything, perennially, out of reach. The odd thing was, when **Rooted** was shown on TV an extraordinary number of people said, "Oh, it's so dark and unsettling! Is Simmo going to come and get me?" and all that sort of thing. I was surprised, frankly.

Then that wasn't your intention?

Not completely. A lot of people didn't find it funny either. I think it's hilarious (*laughter*). . . . (pp. 80-2)

It seems to me that the most absurd—and entertaining—elements of **Rooted** *that I enjoyed in the text and in live performance, were lost on TV and that it tended to naturalism with only confusing moments of absurdity.*

Oh, I think **Rooted** is rigged so that it never becomes naturalistic; the nature of the Simmo thing and Bentley's position see to that. I was very happy, incidentally, with the actor who played Hammo, with his brief appearances in an overcoat. (p. 83)

Getting back to influences, it seems that many passages of your plays make parodic references to works of the European Absurdists, especially Beckett, Pinter and Ionesco. Was this intentional?

I was strongly influenced by them, certainly. They were major influences on all young theatre people of the '60s.

How about Simmo in **Rooted?** *He seems to be a throwback to the* Godot *device . . .*

Well, one of the 'rules' of playwriting is that you should never have a main character always off-stage. Beckett changed that with *Waiting for Godot*. The characters in **The Front Room Boys,** for instance, are living on the fringe, well outside the power or central dynamo of society. So by having Alan White on one side and Barry Anderson on the other with the rest of the "back-room boys" all on the far side of the divide, the absurdity of existence in that tiny area was heightened. The off-stage becomes nearly as important as the on-stage. In **Rooted,** there was this trinity of unseen characters, Davo, Hammo and Simmo, each representing different things, with Bentley torn between wanting to be a Davo and a Hammo and never really approaching Simmo who is that "all-powerful god". The use of off-stage characters is a reaction against naturalism. As soon as you base a play on an ordinary person, they seem to become the centre of the universe and the play takes place in their living room; there's an embargo on off-stage characters. But it just doesn't seem to resonate. My intention is to have some concern for what's happening outside that room. These powerful figures are supposed to work on the audience's imagination. Whether it's successful or not I don't know. Some people say Simmo was so real for them; others say, "you really went on a bit with that Simmo business". Then of course you get the hardy types who wanted Bentley to stop being a wimp and biff Simmo. Presumably they would also have torn a few strips off Godot for unpunctuality.

Another similar theme is the unreliability of memories, as in **Rooted** *where Bentley and Richard argue, rather unconvincingly, about what actually happened in the past—was Hammo's sister called Doreen or Susan for instance. Doesn't this suggestion of the unreliability, even insignificance, of history, go back to Beckett?*

Yes. There was that play *The Old Tune*, that Beckett translated, about two old men failing to remember . . .

And Godot's *Vladimir and Estragon can't really be sure even of what happened the day before.*

Yes. Pinter too has a lot of that sort of thing. It was an influence, certainly, though I can't remember why.

You mention Pinter. His sense of menace and in particular the

malevolence of inanimate objects as in The Dumb Waiter, *seems to come through in your work. . . . Pinter was a strong influence then?*

Yes, very much so.

The interrogation scene in **Rooted,** *where Richard and Diane corner Bentley with a cavalcade of advice, seems very much to derive from Pinter's* The Birthday Party . . .

Yes, I remember I showed the play to Clive Donner who directed the film of *The Caretaker* and he said how strongly I seemed to be influenced in that way. He said, "It's not a steal, but it's a fair old nod." (*laughter*) That was his exact expression.

The link with Ionesco seems to be the strongest, especially on the stylistic and linguistic levels, where you evoke similar rhythms of absurd dialogue. For example, the non-sequitur of the passage in **Rooted** *where Bentley, Richard and Diane each talk about the effects of different alcoholic drinks without any apparent reference to what the others are saying. All this seems to hark back to something like* The Bald Primadonna.

(*laughter*) Yes it does! That was certainly an influence. . . . There's no question that that dislocation of thought and language derives from Ionesco.

And the long monologues; Sandy raving about the dry-cleaner for instance?

I use that in **Macquarie** too. Aesthetically, I've always loved his monologue, one person giving a long speech and another coming in with one line at the end, or something similar. I think I got that from a film called *Inside Daisy Clover*. There's a scene by the pool between Christopher Plummer and Natalie Wood where he just goes into this monologue and she doesn't say a thing at all. I think I modified that. In **Macquarie,** Macquarie has this big speech to Marsden and at the end all he says is, "Will that be all?" You've got Macquarie running out of puff. I was all for using that device in a couple of TV scripts I was doing at the time, but they said, "Oh, you can't do that, it's too big a swadge of dialogue. The audience won't pay attention to that!" And you know . . .

Snip, snip, snip?

Exactly. They must have thought the collective I.Q. of the country was about 20. But I remain addicted to that technique. I used it in **Coralie** too with Coralie's long monologue which ends up, "You'll have to treat me well."

. . . Which seemed to be a watershed moment of the play.

Well, it's where she says, "Yes", really. It's a verbal contract between her and Stuart.

And Sandy's use of the cutting single line at the end of someone else's pretentious or empty monologue is the same sort of thing?

Yes. Rhythmically it's effective too in that the audience gets caught up in a monologue and then you cut it.

There's also a circular dialogue isn't there, when characters get caught on a track and eventually only manage to get off it with difficulty?

That's an old established comedy technique which you can also use in naturalism, although not to the same extent. It's just the combination of the absurd feel of the thing plus some old-fashioned comedy. Beckett does much the same with the hat business in *Godot*. That's the kind of thing where things go in threes or fours—you need to set up a pattern clearly enough before you can get a laugh through breaking it.

Is your work subversive do you think?

There's a funny thing to do with recognition and reality in plays. What I wanted to do was get together things that are recognizable, things that I've observed, and place them in a different context which does subvert an audience's expectations. So the effect is not reassuring. If audiences are not reassured, then they find everything traumatic. So I question the degree to which I'm considered "subversive". They're getting something that they're not used to and they just over-compensate. A lot of it is insecurity. People think, "Oh, God! He's having a go at us", whereas what's on view may just be questioning and certainly not saying, "This is WRONG WRONG WRONG! Change your way of life!"

Perhaps this over-reaction from audiences is a product of their having been accustomed to a diet of bland naturalism, where their expectations and beliefs are consistently confirmed. I'm reminded of Stephen Sewell's response to the branding of his work as "political", where he says that all *plays are political and the fact that his stand out only reflects the extent to which the general ideological fare has been one-sided. Is this what's happening with your work on the stylistic level?*

Very possibly. My recent experience of that was with television where they get this diet of naturalism all the time. All these endless mini-series based on reconstructed fact. (pp. 83-7)

Are TV audiences, or I suppose more particularly, directors and producers, becoming more sophisticated in their view of dramatic forms? Can your work be rendered more truly in the foreseeable future?

I don't know. A few years ago, I would have said, "Oh, of course." But the 1980s have been a really odd decade; it's as if the '60s and '70s never happened. We all thought in the '60s that we'd gone a step further—taken Absurdism and Realism on to a new style and that people would go on from that. They did for a while, but now . . .

*Did you perhaps enter a cul-de-sac? After all, you admit that post-***Martello Towers,*** around 1976, there was a drastic change in your work, for one.*

Yes, I suppose it's quite possible. (p. 87)

Returning to the social, philosophical function of absurd theatre, Richard Coe said of Ionesco:

> *Every now and then there comes an instant of lucidity, of self-discovery, when his characters try to speak to us of their real existence. And these are the moments when the terror of absurdity reaches its highest pitch of intensity, for only then do we realize that, between the total and the sham reality, there is, in the last analysis, no effective contrast. The choice . . . is between an intolerable recognition of the absurd and an equally intolerable refusal to admit it.*

It seems to me that such a statement could just as easily refer to Buzo characters, for example, that passage you talked of a moment ago, where Coralie, returning late at night from a party, has a sort of existential debate with herself as Stuart listens passively. Would you agree with that analysis?

Mm, yes. There's a wrangle within her and she's got to the very edge of her particular existence and she just has to decide whether she's going to jump over the edge or find her way back. And that is probably the predicament you mentioned. Realizing the absurdity of existence, or refusing to acknowledge it.

Is it surprising then that people are disturbed by a play that you protest is light in its theme, when moments like that occur and Coralie talks as she does there about "feeling night" over her shoulder? Isn't there something subversive there despite the apparent resolution we witness?

I don't think anyone will ever feel completely comfortable with it, but if the director of a play like *Coralie* pushes all the right buttons, you can take the audience through a rainbow, a complete experience. That's what I aim for. Certainly the blackness, the satire and the rest of it are there, but they're in the context of the rest of the play's insights. I've seen audiences really knocked out by performances where there's been that balance between the comedy and the drama; where the director has understood that these are comedy-dramas. That's the wonderful thing that Absurdism achieved: the complete mixture of comedy and drama which hadn't before existed. People tend to exaggerate only the one element of my plays—though quite often it's the production that's to blame. (p. 88)

There's that moment at the very end where after Coralie has had a quite inexplicable respiratory attack, and Stuart tells the doctor that this is a bad start to a honeymoon, the doctor replies in a sort of absurd but underneath it all rather menacing way, "That's the least of your worries" and exits.

(*laughter*) Yes, well some people found that unsettling. I think he's just saying that you've got all your lives ahead of you and life is full of traps and things . . .

People shouldn't read too much into that then?

Oh, I think the point of it is that a man without a leg is saying it. He's saying that this isn't the biggest problem you're likely to face.

Isn't it a bit like the Fire Chief's exit line in The Bald Primadonna *where the couples are saying to him, "Goodbye, have a nice fire!" and he stops tensely and replies, "Let's hope so . . . for everyone's sake . . ."?*

(*laughter*) Yes, that probably was something I absorbed. It's hard to put your finger on exact influences, but certainly *The Bald Primadonna* was a play I'd read, seen, studied and admired.

Was Jean-Claude van Itallie's American Hurrah *another such osmotic influence? I'm thinking in particular of its portrayal of social ritual.*

Oh sure, I thought that was the best of that type of theatre. *The Front Room Boys* was very much influenced by that. There was a group called "The Human Body" that was doing something in the PACT theatre and lots of their stuff was based on ceremonies and rituals. I didn't like it much, but I thought that if you could take the strength they had of a group of people throwing up their energy in a ritual ceremonial way and add to it a literary context—give them words—it could work. But in *The Front Room Boys* there was a definite attempt to include all those rituals that exist in our society. End-of-year revues are popular in offices; Christmas parties; Melbourne Cup days. All the rituals of society are reproduced in the play and given a sort of theatrical basis.

You've recently turned to the novel with **The Search for Harry Allway.** *Is the form of the novel a better vehicle for absurdity and the sort of verbal games you obviously delight in?*

Yes. Part of it also is that I had a series of bad productions. (pp. 89-90)

Are you aware when you write of the curious contradiction of the chaotic world of absurdity where, if there is any order at all, it's a malevolent order (Buzo laughs) straining against the determinism that feeds your use of stereotypes? I'm thinking of the almost inexorable drive of the novel whereby Prue follows the clues blindly but confidently to her quarry. Also the way that when she meets a "Westy", its name must *be Karen, just as Prue, being herself a "type",* must *drive a blue Honda Civic (with a sun-roof, of course!).*

Well, when I'm writing in that style, I just know that you can't have a main character who's hugely introspective, interested in exercising free-will and full of self-analysis because it's a . . .

Real downer?

(*laughter*) Yes. There's a style that precludes that. Prue has got to be the sort of character who's a little bit blinkered, otherwise the style wouldn't work. If she had that other dimension to her, she wouldn't get into those predicaments. The novel would have finished on page two if she hadn't been disposed to be that kind of character. There's an Odyssey format. The route she takes is the "golden triangle": Sydney, Ulladulla and Canberra and she meets "types" along the way. There are the two "Karens", both the Westy and the South Coast one, the Passionate European Woman . . .

"Erky" people?

(*laughter*) Not all of them erky, but a fair proportion of them, it has to be said. Like the characters in **Rooted.** While the theatre is, as I believe it is now, in a temporary eclipse, I'll work through the novel. As soon as things change in the theatre, or if I can make them change, I'll go back to the play. (pp. 90-1)

[The younger playwrights are] different from the form and style you started with . . .

Yes, although I was interested in what John McCallum said in reference to that in his introduction to my last book of plays, **The Marginal Farm** and **Big River.** He said that history had a very important role in both the works of these younger writers and those two plays of mine. I suppose that's inevitable in a young country like ours, where if the present is absurd, perhaps history can provide the answers.

Is this connection between your recent works and the plays of the new young writers like Nowra and Sewell then a recognition that your personal watershed after **Martello Towers** *was a reflection of a wider cul-de-sac in Australian drama and that the "New New Wave" has begun a new phase, a new direction in our theatrical tradition?*

That could well be so. There's obviously a much larger vision in this new work, epic even. All the other ground has been covered. And perhaps, our history could have a lot to do with why that's so. (p. 91)

Alexander Buzo and Geoffrey Sirmai, in an interview in Southerly, *Vol. 46, No. 1, March, 1986, pp. 80-91.*

FIONA GILES

[A morgue is] featured in Alex Buzo's first work of prose fiction, *The Search For Harry Allway,* which is published in the course of a successful playwrighting career. Yet this is a . . . simply cheerful satire, neatly structured and with a happy, though surprising ending. . . .

The search of the title is conducted by the young, underreaching journalist, Prue Foster, an apprentice and virginal Modesty Blaise who, in her mission to find the missing pools winner Harry Allway, seeks also (or *really*) the accoutrements of a clean and conventionally middle-class life. This sounds more serious than it is, as the search provides a simple narrative structure that enables a series of comic encounters between Prue and what she calls the "Awful Types" of Sydney. It is not what she sees so much as what she rejects (as well as the simple-minded expressions of her rejection) that provides much of the humor. Thus, while some of the satire spills over herself, it is not really middle-class Australia but only its pretenses that are being attacked.

Because Prue's quest is also the professional journalist's search for a story, Buzo presents a parody of both highminded but vacuous journalism and the expediently twisted plots of detective fiction, and lightly points to a more serious scrutiny of the sources of information in our world. But principally, with his use of comic-strip characterization and his interest in physical detail, the narrator is concerned efficiently to diminish his cast of Sydney's urban Left, who likewise depend on a few choice props and behavioral packages. It is the style that might have resulted from mixing Margaret Atwood with Raymond Chandler.

The anatomy of Awful Types that Prue's search gradually maps at times rests on a rather flimsy narrative base comprised of a series of disappointed 'leads', but any potential thinness in this device is saved by the ludicrously unexpected and implausible resolution of the mystery. Like its ending, the book's portraits and epigrammatic observations are both deflationary and amusing. Take, for example, Prue's jaded recognition that "most television news stories consisted of people walking in and out of doors carrying briefcases" or her attack on the "affectations" of one Awful Type, the "Gutsy Lady", whose habit of rolling her own cigarettes under the pressure of Prue's questioning "was the modern equivalent of Victorian ladies pretending to faint".

While there is a consistent ironic distance between the prudish Ms Foster and the narrator, one of the nicer touches of Buzo's satire is that Prue's militantly unhip niceness is amiably tolerated. That she is "Nice" is paradoxically one of the few things she regrets about herself, but the one left to stand as an inoffensive advantage in what is ultimately depicted as an only mildly polluted world. Prue sees men principally as an army of sexual harassers, for example, but instead of marching them to the tribunal she is content to exploit and, she imagines, to devastate. Such is the nature of the entertainment: ideologically sound but loosely committed. And despite the caricature, Buzo provides a refreshing image of a heroine whose flaws are simple and with whom, as her vices amount only to being middle class and having a weakness for

vermouth and Toblerone, at least some of us may indulgently
identify. (p. 80)

Fiona Giles, "Comic Cuts," in Overland, No. 102,
April, 1986, pp. 79-80.

Gillian Clarke

1937-

Welsh poet, editor, and essayist.

Strongly rooted in Welsh heritage and landscape, Clarke's poetry features traditional Celtic metric and sound patterns that enliven otherwise spare, almost conversational, poetry. Clarke's work is characterized by meticulous observations regarding a distinct range of subject matter, including her family, their home, and Welsh culture. Noting that Clarke's gender is evident throughout her work, critics often contrast the tone of her poems with the anger or bitterness some associate with contemporary feminist poets. Clarke has been commended for drawing insightful connections between occurrences in the civilized and the natural worlds. Her literary models are the Romantic poets of the nineteenth century as well as William Butler Yeats and such older contemporaries as R. S. Thomas and Seamus Heaney. Welsh poet and critic Michael Hulse has written: "[Clarke's] poetry is arrestingly filled with quiet beauty and clear insight, with visionary celebration and elegiac power, and reveals a writer wedded to the world and the word in equal measure."

From the publication of her first collection, the chapbook *Snow on the Mountain,* Clarke has been perceived as a mature, skillful, and insightful poet. Relying less on imagery and metaphor than in her later poetry, the pieces in *Snow on the Mountain* were praised for the emotional honesty with which Clarke depicts her relationships with her children, husband, home, and country. While the paucity of imagery was faulted by some critics, others felt it lent predominantly polite, domestic pieces a much-needed authority. Clarke's first full-length collection, *The Sundial,* was well received in Wales and helped extend her reputation throughout Great Britain. Including work from *Snow on the Mountain, The Sundial* continued Clarke's exploration of the role of women in a distinctly Welsh setting. Critics remarked that Clarke's growing confidence in the power of metaphorical language evoked that landscape in exquisite detail.

Letter from a Far Country, her second major collection, was also praised for these attributes. The acclaimed title poem begins a meditation on the nature of women's lives with the question men have directed at those who claim equality, "Where are your great works?" Clarke answers in the remaining forty-three stanzas with an account of the many and varied projects that occupy the day of a housewife in rural Wales. Some critics commented that although Clarke begins from a strong feminist stance, the tone of "Letter from a Far Country" is remarkably serene yet persuasive in its implicit assertion that the "great works" of women comprise the human race itself. The publication of Clarke's *Selected Poems* inspired commentators to remark upon the evolution of her skills and her steadfast dedication to celebrating her heritage as both a woman and a native of Wales. *Letting in the Rumour,* Clarke's most recent effort, traces the source of her poetic preoccupations to her bond with her ancestors.

(See also *Contemporary Authors,* Vol. 106 and *Dictionary of Literary Biography,* Vol. 40.)

PRINCIPAL WORKS

POETRY

Snow on the Mountain   1972
The Sundial   1978
Letter from a Far Country   1982
Selected Poems   1985
Letting in the Rumour   1989

PETER ELFED LEWIS

It is no accident that the modern literary renaissance in Wales has coincided with a resurgence of cultural and political nationalism. Welsh poets, those using English and those writing in Welsh, have found that the contemporary plight of Wales—the erosion of a traditional and distinctive way of life and of a language, and the determined effort by a minority to salvage as much as possible of both in the face of the anonymous uniformity being spread by the neocapitalist Attilas of our Eurocracy—has provided them with a theme almost worthy of epic treatment. This explains the public nature of much present-day Anglo-Welsh poetry (that of Raymond Garlick for example), but even poets whose work is as apparently non-nationalistic and a-political as Gillian Clarke's are often as conscious of their Welshness and as committed to Wales as those writing explicitly 'committed' poetry. (p. 52)

During the last few years Gillian Clarke has rapidly become known to readers of Anglo-Welsh poetry, and has been acclaimed as one of the most talented of the younger Welsh poets. To describe her as a woman-poet may therefore seem both condescending and unfair, the kind of discrimination attributable to male prejudice, but her work, unlike that of Marianne Moore or Denise Levertov for example, is immediately recognizable as a woman's. Much of her poetry [collected in *Snow on the Mountain*] is 'domestic' in that it is about her family (**"Community"**), her children (**"Catrin"** and **"The Sundial"**), her relationship with her husband (**"Two Working"** and **"Beech Buds"**), and their primitive cottage retreat deep in the Cardiganshire countryside (**"Blaen Cwrt"**). At first sight the range and content of her work seem extremely limited, even though she does explore these areas of experience with unflinching emotional honesty, as in her fine analysis of the mother-daughter relationship in **"Catrin"**. But what gives her best poems an extra dimension and makes the word 'domestic' an inadequate description is the way in which she relates her personal concerns to the wider patterns of the natural world. In **"Birth"**, for example, her own experience of childbirth is linked with that of a cow she watches giving birth to a calf in a field, and in **"Beech Buds"** she describes her developing relationship with her husband in terms of the opening of the buds into leaves:

> From the hard,
> Brittle wood came tenderness and life, numerous
> Damp, green butterflies, transparently veined,
> Opening like a tree that is alive.

In some of her poems one is as aware of the land and the sky and the cycle of the seasons as of the 'domestic' microcosm contained within them, while in **"Storm Awst"** and **"In a Garden"** her private life is almost completely abandoned for a direct treatment of the external yet constantly impinging world of natural forces:

> It is hardly Spring. The flowers sing in cold soil.
> There are patches of snow still. But it is promised.
> We have a future and are not shadow people.
> The moving stream, the swelling bud, nothing can halt.

The strengths and weaknesses of Gillian Clarke's writing are exemplified in this stanza from **"In a Garden"** consisting of six laconic sentences that modulate without jarring from the austere utterance of the first to the high rhetoric of the sixth featuring asyndeton and anastrophe. Her style is often as spare and sinewy as this, there rarely being any trace of verbal fussiness in her work and imagery frequently being conspicuous by its absence, but she runs the risk of lapsing into prosaicness and unfortunately does so in a number of poems. In such cases (the first stanzas of **"Baby-Sitting"** and **"Journey"** for example) any element of imagery or rhetoric seems strained, as though she is trying to impose a poetic effect on material not capable of bearing its weight. To sum up, Gillian Clarke has found her subject-matter but is still struggling to develop her own poetic voice. It is a pity that so many of her poems should bring to mind other poems and poets that make hers look comparatively undistinguished. **"The Fox"** recalls Ted Walker's considerably finer 'Easter Poem', and **"Storm**

Awst" is reminiscent of Ted Hughes's more vivid and powerful 'Wind'. But despite all their differences, especially in content, it is R. S. Thomas in particular that one can hear in these poems, but an R. S. Thomas firing on three cylinders or not in the right gear. (pp. 54-5)

Peter Elfed Lewis, "Varieties of Welsh Experience," in Stand Magazine, *Vol. 14, No. 4, 1973, pp. 52-6.*

JOHN MOLE

Gillian Clarke has a gift for conveying the tense intimacy of family life. She is particularly good at defining those moments when a mother is confronted fiercely by her child's separate identity, from birth ("the tight / Red rope of love which we both / Fought over") onward through the growth of personality:

> She used to fling her anguish into
> My arms, staining my solitude with
> Her salt and grimy griefs. Older now
> She runs, her violence prevailing
> Against silence and the avenue's
> Complacency, I her hatred's object.

Gillian Clarke has dedicated her first collection, *The Sundial,* to her children, and although it would be quite wrong to consider her as being mainly preoccupied with domestic themes, some of her most attractive poems—such as **"Sailing"**, **"Swinging"**, **"Nightride"** and the brilliantly chilly **"Baby-Sitting"**— set the family, as a frail and precious unit, in wider contexts of time and movement: "All day he told the time to me. / All day we felt and watched the sun / Caged in its white diurnal heat, / Pointing at us with its black stick."

Elsewhere, in her exploration of the Welsh hill country, its history, landscapes and community life, she shows herself as possessing the power to strike memorable images which are both exact and richly sensuous: "Sweet surreptitious smells, like tar and sweat / And dusty arms, and pollen on my knees", "the stretched / Sea, tensing to crease at its rim", "My fire of nettles crackles / Like bees creeping in a green / Hive . . .". Several of the poems do not amount to much more than an accumulation of resonant particularities moving towards a short, dramatic concluding sentence—leaving one with the impression of a skilled landscape artist manoeuvring her detail into allegorical perspectives—but the best of them, like **"Waterfall"**, are both dazzlingly immediate in their imagery and intelligently worked through as metaphors of experience:

> Closer to crisis the air put cold silk
> Against our faces and the cliffs streamed
> With sun water, caging on every gilded
> Ledge small things that flew by mistake
> Into the dark spaces behind the rainbows.

John Mole, "High Tension Lines," in The Times Literary Supplement, *No. 3996, November 3, 1978, p. 1291.*

ANNE CLUYSENAAR

Although the referential scope of [Gillian Clarke's] work is not wide—I mean by this that she doesn't include the contemporary reverberations of her subjects, in biology, for instance, or physics—it has the accuracy and relevance of observation that many people have praised recently in Flora

Thompson's *Lark Rise to Candleford.* Those who enjoyed, and that is the right word, her work as it appeared in *Poetry Introduction 3* will find all those poems in [*The Sundial*] plus many new poems in the same vein. **"Harvest at Mynachlog"** is one of these and it illustrates her evocative powers and the unobtrusive control she exercises over language. Women who have followed the mechanical bailer for hours stop at "the far/field edge, mothy and blurred in the heat" to take tea.

> We talk
> Of other harvests. They remember
> How a boy, flying his plane so low
> Over the cut fields that his father
>
> Straightened from his work to wave his hat
> At the boasting sky, died minutes later
> On an English cliff, in such a year
> As this, the barns brimming gold.
>
> We are quiet again, holding our cups
> In turn for the tilting milk, sad, hearing
> The sun roar like a rush of grain
> Engulfing all winged things that live
> One moment in the eclipsing light.

Through the narrative structure (only skimmed in the quotation) the emotion is created and placed. The tooling of minutiae of sound and rhythm is at once natural and indicative of the artistic pressure that issues more obviously in the relationship between the tilting milk, the roar of the sun, the rush of grain, blending the bountiful and the awesome, to which the women are linked by their holding out of cups (*holding, hearing* is a small underlining of this). There is a literalness about *eclipsing light* which is enlivened by the paradox, and the ambiguity of "that live / One moment" has nothing merely clever about it. Apparently reckless phrases, such as "barns brimming gold", appear as a sort of poets' shorthand, a means of referring without strain, or impairment of the narrative flow, to traditional connotations which are relevant to the poem's treatment of the theme of harvest. The more one reads Gillian Clarke, the more pleasure one receives from the quietness of her skill.

Anne Cluysenaar, in a review of "The Sundial," in Stand Magazine, *Vol. 20, No. 3, 1979, p. 74.*

PRISCILLA ECKHARD

Gillian Clarke is an immensely tough poet. By which I do not mean that she is difficult: on the contrary, many of her images and much of her diction have a startling directness and simplicity. Gillian Clarke's toughness would appear to be in the bone, and it manifests itself not only in her absolute refusal to be anything other than honest:

> I am sitting in a strange room listening
> For the wrong baby. I don't love
> This baby. . . .
>   If she wakes
> She will hate me. . . .
>
> To her I will represent absolute
> Abandonment. For her it will be worse
> Than for a lover cold in lonely
> Sheets.
>
>   ("Baby-Sitting.")

but also in the way in which she is now using the line-breaks as an adjunct to syntax.

It has been pointed out before, with reference to her first collection, **Snow on the Mountain,** that Gillian Clarke's writing is given the quality of image by her syntactical exploration. In this second book *The Sundial* she appears to be doing more, and to be using her trade's syntax to carry her in and out of the shifting technical illusions of metaphor. She has always had, and in her more recent work appears to be expanding, a particularly direct relationship with image. In Gillian Clarke's work image, idiosyncratically, is the means by which observation and thought is made more understandable, reduced to its barest form, and made of immediate human need. (pp. 69-70)

Priscilla Eckhard, "Directness and Indirection," in Poetry Review, *Vol. 69, No. 1, July, 1979, pp. 69-72.*

JOHN MOLE

I admired Gillian Clarke's previous collection, **The Sundial,** but found rather too many of her vivid, sensuous nature poems marred by neat, moralistic codas. **Letter from a Far Country** trusts more in the power of metaphor to teach through revelation, and is a various, impressive book. ["**Letter from a Far Country**"], written for radio, explores the role of the home-centered wife and mother "who ought to be / up to her wrists in marriage" in the context of place and history, those "dead grandmothers" who

> . . . haul at the taut silk cords;
> set us fetching eggs, feeding hens,
> mixing rage with the family bread,
> lock us to the elbows in soap suds.
> Their sculleries and kitchens fill
> with steam, sweetness, goosefeathers.

From wrists to elbows, as the sense of history and restless disquiet intensifies throughout a poem which is—paradoxically—also a celebration. Gillian Clarke is best, though, as in her earlier work, at making her reader aware of what she calls "the otherness of pain." That is the farthest country of all. It crowds her poems with intimations, and she looks resolutely in its direction.

John Mole, "Respectable Formalities," in Encounter, *Vol. LX, No. 4, April, 1983, pp. 69-75.*

DICK DAVIS

Like Margaret Atwood and Adrienne Rich, Gillian Clarke writes about what it is to be a woman—but there the resemblance ends. Where they are strident she is *sotto voce,* where they accuse she examines, where they celebrate an angry apartness, a willed contemporaneity, she looks for community and the presence of what has preceded her. . . . ["**Letter from a Far Country**"] opens falteringly, but we soon submit to its hypnotically persuasive cadences; it is a 'letter' on womanliness addressed to the past, a meditation on what stays, is rooted and persists over generations. There is no gaudiness in her poetry; instead, the reader is aware of a generosity of spirit which allows the poems' subjects their own unbullied reality.

Her themes are large—the proximity of life and death, the interaction of individual and family, loss and the lapse of time—but we come on them, as it were, accidentally while watching birds or visiting a neighbour or sightseeing. And, similarly, her language has a quality both casual and intense, mundane and visionary. [*Letter from a Far Country*] is a moving and impressive collection from a poet who should be better known. (p. 24)

Dick Davis, "Violence in the Garden," in The Listener, *Vol. 109, No. 2807, May 5, 1983, pp. 24-5.*

ANNE STEVENSON

At the end of the 1960s it looked as if the predominent tone of women's poetry for the next forty or fifty years was going to be obsessively Medean. Vengeance, self-immolation, man-hating and blood were the themes of the angry women who followed Sylvia Plath, taking from her brilliant, feverish example those elements best calculated to sustain her note of hysteria. Now, in the 1980s, the overall mood seems calmer.

Gillian Clarke's title poem **"Letter from a Far Country"** is a paean of praise to the women of her Welsh past, to their selfless devotion to cooking, clothing, babies, husbands, nature and order. Coming as it does in the wake of the Women's Movement and domestic rebellion, the poem (indeed, the whole book) has the force of a counter-revolution; yet it is a peace offering, a celebration. In the poet's own words, it is her "letter home from the future, / [her] bottle in the sea which might / take a generation to arrive."

The ambiguity of such a declaration must be deliberate. The poem is being sent to the poet's ancestors from *their* future, but it is also a poem written to the poet's descendants in *the* future. Time, it suggests, is in any case cyclical and repetitious in women's lives:

> The chests and cupboards are full,
> the house sweet as a honeycomb.
> I move in and out of the hive
> all day, harvesting, ordering.
> You will find all in its proper place,
> when I have gone.

If such an image of eternal domesticity seems idealized to the thinking of contemporary pre-packaged society, it still rings true as a picture of conditions in rural Wales. Time moves slowly in that country, where faces and farms change little:

> My grandmother might be standing
> in the great silence before the Wars.
> Hanging the washing between trees
> over the white and red hens.

Such lyrical linkings of nature, memory and laundry are distinctive and moving, despite the hovering shade of Mrs. Ogmore-Pritchard who, oddly enough, does not strike a dissonant note. The **"Wedding Wind"** purity of

> The sea stirs restlessly between
> the sweetness of clean sheets,
> the lifted arms,
> the rustling petticoats . . .

is off-set by:

> (In the airing cupboard you'll see
> a map, numbering and placing
> every towel, every sheet.
> I have charted your needs.)

Hearing the gulls "grieve at our contentment", asking their "masculine question, 'Where are your great works?' ",

Clarke is momentarily drawn into resentment: "They [the gulls] slip their fetters and fly up / to laugh at the land-locked women. / Their cries are cruel as greedy babies." But the girl who stays home "to mind things" has her own compensations: "our perfect preserves . . . jams and jellies . . . tiny onions imprisoned / in their preservative juices . . . the recipe for my best bread." Like Adrienne Rich in the impressive finale to "Transcendental Etude", Gillian Clarke makes much of the patchwork of women's lives which persist as one endless and ageless "great work", pointing up the (literal) fruitlessness of the vertical *Putsch*.

The whole *Letter from a Far Country*—the title poem together with the others—breathes an air of satisfactoriness and completeness which can only be attributed to the excellence of the poetic performance. With their charged language and unmistakable feminine bias, the poems are like positive inversions of Plath's: persuasive, apparently irrefutable, written with impeccable skill. There is, of course, an element of romance about such a view of things. It could be a man's vision, too, this woman's domain—idyllic, pastoral, a place of timeless mothering and love.

If there were a single phrase to describe this kind of poetry, it would have to reverse Keats's notion of "negative capability". One might speak instead of *projective* capability (disregarding Olson's quite different notion of Projective Verse). That is, some poets have the ability to project in language overwhelming images of their own state of mind, whether it be Sylvia Plath's skull-moon and hell-mouthed poppies, or Gillian Clarke's foetus in a chalk pebble and cornucopia of lambs between the horns of a dead ram. Such poetry may be easier to read than more investigative verse, which seeks to discover the reality of objects on their own terms; but no good poems are easy to write, and Gillian Clarke's ring with lucidity and power:

> Boisterous in its bone
> cradle, a stone-breaker,
> thief in its mother's orchard,
> it is apple round.

This is Welsh poetry with a vengeance, the relationship of sound between the *b*'s and *o*'s reinforced by the elemental imagery.

Clarke's work is both personal and archetypal, built out of language as concrete as it is musical. . . .

Anne Stevenson, "In and Out of Time," in The Times Literary Supplement, *No. 4189, July 15, 1983, p. 757.*

ADAM HOPKINS

When Gillian Clarke sent a poetry manuscript to the Carcanet Press in the spring of 1981, it was accepted in eight days. A year and a half later, on publication of the book, English readers might have felt justifiable surprise at the appearance, without preliminary fanfare, of a fully mature British poet writing in a clear and passionate voice and with great lyrical assurance. Peter Redgrove, in the *Guardian,* hailed the long, title poem, **"Letter from a Far Country,"** in terms of possible greatness within the feminist canon.

So where has Gillian Clarke been hiding? The answer is that she hasn't been hiding at all but lives in Wales where she has been recognised for some years as a powerful and expressive poet. . . .

"Letter from a Far Country" was written on commission for BBC Radio Wales—a task, says Gillian Clarke, which seemed easy enough when the deadline was 12 weeks off. In the event, though, it was composed entirely during the final week of the commission and delivered by hand, steaming, on the day it was due.

> "I wrote it in a terrible rage," she says, "in great anger against the things and people that stopped me having enough time to write—the children, the house, the need to earn a living. I'd just had 12 people for Christmas and it was rage that gave me the energy to sit up five nights in a row.

> I started each night where I'd left off the night before but without knowing what I was going to write. I thought it was a protest poem. It was only when I finished that I realised I had not made a protest but a celebration.

What is celebrated in the poem, as well as lamented, is the work of women, the work that imprisons them, work in the house, work supplying men with food and clothes and particularly the labours of motherhood. All is described with profound ambivalence, with a mixture of yearning and satisfaction and at the same time a sense of absolute loss.

"I had the census list for the parish I love best in West Wales," she says.

> It was very noticeable that the poor were largely women and they were poor because they were women, because they were unsupported or had a child outside marriage. . . .

> Of course, I wouldn't compare our plight today in any way with the plight of women 100 years ago, but I felt the history of the women in my poem could begin there. So I would write in anger, but I could hear the voice that was writing the poem becoming tender with the memories of real life.

> The women had to do all this work. My own grandmothers had to be hardworking women. But suddenly I could remember the smell of the methylated spirits burning in the ice-cold back kitchen of my North Wales grandmother's farm, singeing the stubble off a goose, and the air full of goose feathers, and so the poem became tender with the pleasure of that memory.

Much the same mechanism was at work over the treatment of motherhood.

> It's what caused me the greatest distress and grief of my life. I feel as if I had no time to be grown-up. Within 18 months of having my first job I was married and pregnant. That was the end of full-time work. I was trapped by a pram, and have been trapped ever since.

But she has, she says, an important and close relationship with each of her three children, now aged from 22 down to 16. "They had me, not the other way round. They are all in my mind all the time." And unquestionably, the tenderest lines of all in **"Letter from a Far Country"** are reserved for motherhood and the nursing of distressed babies at night. . . .

One of the strengths behind her writing is that her own family story is an exact mirror of a large part of the social history of modern Wales.

Both sets of grandparents were country people and Welsh-speaking. Her paternal grandfather was a railwayman and moved to industrial Llanelli to take promotion. He died young, leaving his wife with four children to raise in urban hardship. The child who was to become Gillian Clarke's father escaped to sea as a boy. He became a wireless engineer and was recruited as such, there being not many wireless engineers with Welsh, to BBC Wales in Cardiff in its early days.

And so the cycle was completed in two generations—from Cardiganshire to coal country and on to the city. He sent his daughters to college and didn't teach them Welsh. Gillian, for her part, has learned it as an adult.

The consciousness that her experience is not exceptional helps to give her a strong sense of community against which to write. There is also the matter of the special, or rather, the ordinary, status of the poet in Wales.

In most circles in the Principality you don't have to apologise for being a poet nor need you feel set apart. There are occasions in North and West Wales where all those interested, whether mere versifier or eisteddfod bard, gather together to read out their poems. For Gillian Clarke all this is deeply important.

Her belief that poetry can be widely enjoyed is matched by the directness of what she writes. She believes in full-stops, commas, and Jane Austen and she says of her own work: "If my 16-year-old son doesn't know what it means I go away and rewrite it." It's not, she says, a rejection of modernism. "I just positively do what I do and other people do it differently. I think I would be failing if readers did not understand."

> *Adam Hopkins, "A Terrible Rage, Melting Slowly into Tenderness," in* The Guardian, *August 26, 1983, p. 9.*

MARY KINZIE

> "There are infinite things on earth; any one of them may be likened to any other."
>
> —Jorge Luis Borges

The work of Anglo-Welsh poet Gillian Clarke is serious, delicate, and on the whole, wonderfully fresh. She is both a poet of place and a painter of psychological landscapes, and those points at which portrait and projection merge are often disturbing in their power. *Letter from a Far Country* is a volume of meditations on the solitudes that penetrate and surround domestic existence in a rural village. The poet's method is associative, and although association may be said to have its own logic, it is perhaps not various and coherent enough by itself to organize an entire poetics. It may be that the adjustment of surfaces to show symbolic layering, albeit interesting, is both arbitrary and overly analytic, microscopic, abstract at the small end of the scale. This is Clarke's limitation; working against it, she gives pleasure by her acute and sensitive observation and, more crucial traits, by her good sense and tact.

In [*"Letter from a Far Country"*] Gillian Clarke is abstract in a second and more expansive sense, for she assumes as primary the woman's obligation, corroborated in all the ballads where the minstrel boy leaves the maid behind, to pass the time while she stays put. Because "There's always been time on our hands," acts of revery, such as sea-gazing, are bound to feel very different for the women of the countryside than for the men of whom the world makes outwardly more strenuous demands. On the "white page" presented by the sea's forbidding surface to the brooding imagination of the speaker, a cormorant flickers, then is "as suddenly gone / as a question from the mind" as the bird dives to its quarry; surfacing again much later, "the cormorant breaks the surface / as a small, black, returning doubt." The bird as it were "interrogates" the speaker, not merely with the threat of harm, but also with the temptation to fly. In fact, throughout the title poem, the physical world is ominous and memorious, reflecting the yearning that comes over the inhabitants of Clarke's world, even among the objects of repose: "A stony track turns between / ancient hedges, narrowing, / like a lane in a child's book. / Its perspective makes the heart restless."

Not only is the hilly coastal country ancestral, it is for Clarke "essentially feminine"—by which the author reminds us that this is a history—loose, episodic, impressionistic—of the women in her family and parish, who practiced the housewifely tasks required by the men who worked the fields and mines. And although at many points in the past, as the following passage suggests, craft and culture, distaff and plough, were nominally balanced, the poet permits the deepest reverberations of the heart to commend the former, while the relation between the sexes is subtly torn by the imagery of mill-blade, shuttle, beak, and knife which troubles the domestic weave. A hundred years ago:

Water-wheels milled the sunlight
and the loom's knock was a heart
behind all activity.
The shuttles were quick as birds
in the warp of oakwoods.
In the fields the knives were out
in a glint of husbandry.

The quick birds to which the moving shuttles are compared exist, naturalistically, outside the comparison as well: they are the tutelary spirits of the women in cottages who yearn for the open air and open road, yet are intimidated by the risk of something that repays their yearning from the other side of its satisfaction:

From the opposite wood the birds
ring like a tambourine. It's not
the birdsong of a garden, thrush
and blackbird, robin and finch,
distinguishable, taking turn.
The song's lost in saps and seepings,
amplified by hollow trees,
cupped leaves and wind in the branches.
All their old conversations
collected carefully, faded
and difficult to read, yet held
forever as voices in a well.

In this, the darkening labyrinth of the folk tale, the birds cannot sing clearly enough for us to distinguish them; their messages—their very species—are lost in echoes, dampened by leaf mold and decay in the forest. This haunting sense of meaning lost and confounded, of fibres and family traits subtly broken down, of emptiness that may once have been actual conversation, suggests a negative outcome for restless desire. Yearning is fulfilled not in freedom but in enchantment, a state bewitched and hollow whose music is a wild tambourine, an indistinguishable jangling.

Not all of the female figures are at the same pitch of discontent; some are creatures of absolute, willing domesticity. While recognizing the cost in thought and inwardness of a life thus devoted, Clarke respects this motive, recognizing even in herself the urge to launder, fold, label, measure, and make. But the associational contours of her home-thoughts are aligned with the hive, the field, the sea, and the gemstone in such a way that claustrophobia is avoided: "The chests and cupboards are full, / the house sweet as a honeycomb. / I move in and out of the hive / all day, harvesting, ordering"; "the saucers of marmalade / are set when the amber wrinkles / like the sea if you blow it."

But poverty, isolation, or unguessed-at fear and rage drive others to the brink. One woman, "who had everything," divests herself of all her clothes and jewelry and then drowns herself:

she is shaking the bracelets
from her hands. The sea circles
her ankles. Watch its knots loosen
from the delicate bones
of her feet, from the rope of foam
about a rock. The seal swims
in a collar of water
drawing the horizon in its wake.
And doubt breaks the perfect
white surface of the day.

The doubt that plunged and surfaced with the cormorant presents itself again: is this the solution to bondage?—to swim out in the iridescent "collar of water" toward the horizon? The question is irksome because idle: we are too ignorant of the character whose life and suicide put the question to us. A nimbus of Pre-Raphaelite mist keeps the woman's face indistinct, while Pre-Raphaelite taste arranges her limbs in a flattering drowning pose. The poet distracts us with secondary facts from realizing the lack of primary ones.

Organization is more forceful in the memoir **"Llŷr,"** in which Shakespeare's *King Lear* alerts the young protagonist both to her language and to her betrayals to come. The poem, naturally, is in blank verse, the form that so transparently registers both literary conventionality and independence. Seeing a performance of *Lear,* the speaker learns the meaning of "little words," "All. Nothing. Fond. Ingratitude." Clarke's feeling for rural Wales opens a new dimension on the play, picking up these hints of tragic sentiment between father and daughter, played out among storms and breakers:

The landscape's marked with figures of old men:
The bearded sea; thin-boned, wind-bent trees;
Shepherd and labourer and night-fisherman.
Here and there among the crumbling farms
Are lit kitchen windows in distant hills,
And guilty daughters longing to be gone.

The tableau presented by the daughter's cottage lights is one of many excellent uses of metaphorically resonant descriptive detail in **Letter from a Far Country.** The poems about mowing are especially deft. The hay being carted back to barns along narrow lanes gets caught in the branches, betokening a hurt to everyone who inadvertently makes this connection: "Men in the fields. / Loads following the lanes, / strands of yellow hair caught in the hedges." In a second poem, after the grain is cut down, the height of the fields does indeed appear to have "fallen": "You know the hay's in / when gates hang slack / in the lanes. These hot nights / the fallen fields lie open"—again, a subtle sexual humiliation seems built into the seasons and shapes of things. In another poem, the writer recaptures something of a skaldic feeling as, driving along an industrial dump in a rough storm, she has a near-collision with a swooping heron. She calls him, quite credibly, an "archangel / come to re-open the heron-roads . . . where wind comes flashing off water / interrupting the warp of the snow / and the broken rhythms of the blood." All three are bright moments within average poems, but they show great flair.

In more completely realized works, it is not the radiant *apercu* but a tougher consciousness that connects and controls. In several, Clarke again turns to other poets to frame the conditions of insight. Reading Wordsworth to a ward of mentally ill adults, she reports how a heretofore mute laborer rises to his humanity as he breaks a half-century of silence to recite with her, verbatim, from memory, "The Daffodils" ("They flash upon the inward eye / Which is the bliss of solitude"). The occasion is risky, but the poet manages to control it: "The nurses are frozen, alert; the patients / seem to listen. He is hoarse but word-perfect. / Outside the daffodils are still as wax." In a companion poem, in the geriatric ward, an old woman with a young mind mesmerizes the speaker, who is reading from *The Merchant of Venice*. The gentle, undiscriminating rain, of course, ironically links the famous speech of Portia ("The quality of mercy is not strained; / It droppeth as the gentle rain from heaven / Upon the place beneath") to the grim, bare weather of Wales, which is also, as we heard in the *Lear* poem, the weather of age, remorse, and grief:

"Mrs Frost"

Turning my head a moment
from the geriatrics' ward
I see the bare wood bowed
quietly under the rain,
mists rising in silence.

Her white head is lowered
to her one good shaking hand,
clear thoughts rising from a body
ninety-two years old and done-for,
waiting to look up, blue, blind,

from another century
when I stop reading. Portia
perfectly remembered, just
and gentle in her mind and mine.
The undiscriminating rain

brisk as nurses, chills the wood
to the bones as night comes on.
In the beaded silks of rain
the trees feed secretly
while she, not sleeping, remembers.

The music of **"Mrs Frost,"** so understated, is almost entirely a matter of assonance (long *i* in the first three stanzas, short *i* and long *e* in the last) and of short free-verse lines that tend to bracket three or four stresses together while slightly altering the rhythms (note the difference between the last two lines, both nominally three-stress: the penultimate so insistent and raw, the last so delicate and recessional). The music and diction, which emphasize in such unemphatic ways, avoid the two patent dangers of the subject, yammering and pontificating; we are given to estimate perfectly the dilemma of Mrs. Frost and thus to respect the courage of her continued mental application.

In some respects, Gillian Clarke's resources are most deeply

tapped by a suite of summer poems called **"A Journal from France."** Perhaps a change of scene put the speaker in a clearer relation to her traveling companion than they had enjoyed at home, or perhaps there is a seasonal principle at work. I also wonder whether the associative mind—or the kind of temperament that is drawn to revery—isn't more at home in France than Great Britain? At any rate, Clarke's **"Kingfishers at Condat"** unmistakably shows the vivid, unmistakable coloration of the impressionists. In the "village silence / of gold-dust and evening heat," a motorcycle gang has buzzed into view. Loud, bright, and mechanical, the cyclists are also omens of a nature turned perverse: "Their bikes wait in the courtyard, / blue as mallard, glittering flies." In the countryside beyond, where the poet and friend had earlier been swimming, life swells and, quietly, commands: "The river / moves its surfaces, its reedy / stirrings and sudden glitter / rushing under the bridge." Then as night falls, and the cyclists, to everyone's relief, explode off through the trees—as the river cools under a greener dusting of gold—"there!"

> under the bank where it's dark, blue
> as fire the kingfishers are hunting,
> blue as storm, iridescent, alive
> to the quoit on the surface
>
> where the fish rises. Dragonfly
> blue crackling down the dark vein
> of the riverbank, as quick
> and as private as joy.

The iridescent tear-shaped thoraxes of the motorcycles are naturalized—realized—in the long blue bodies of the kingfishers, in the metaphoric dragonfly, and in the blue-gold rings made by the touch of the feeding fish to the river's silken surface. In visual and linguistic suggestion alive with physical pleasure, the poet mingles drops of water, drops of color and paint, tapering globes of body, organ, and eye, into a superbly satisfying descriptive lyric. It is description, furthermore, that also presses toward feeling and response; the lovers' privacy is like a painting's in being an intimacy of and in this place, conscious of caressing just these shapes. (pp. 40-1)

Mary Kinzie, "Pictures from Borges," in The American Poetry Review, *Vol. 12, No. 6, November-December, 1983, pp. 40-6.*

SIMON RAE

Much of Gillian Clarke's poetry is set in rural Wales and expresses a preoccupation with the countryside and the people who farm it. She writes a quietly effective poetry, which at the birth of a calf for instance, delights in 'satisfaction / falling like a clean sheet around us'. [*Selected Poems*] contains her excellent meditation on previous generations of women, **"Letter from a Far Country"**, which was first broadcast on Radio 3. She writes well about death and bereavement, and two of the more recent poems concern suicides. In **"Suicide on Pentwyn Bridge"**, she traces 'the parabola' of the unknown man's death 'in the brown / eyes of this wife week after week', while **"Shearing"** records the unwitting recording of an unsmiling sheep-shearer's last afternoon:

> Next day, still in my camera not smiling
> he died in a noose in his own barn
> leaving Hywel his moon-eyed dog.

(p. 133)

Simon Rae, "Telling Stories," in London Magazine, n.s. Vol. 25, Nos. 5 & 6, August & September, 1985, pp. 129-33.

JOHN MATTHIAS

[Gillian Clarke is a poet] whose work feels to an outsider fully committed to its engagement with Welsh tradition, history, community, family life, and the genius of the place. Roland Mathias's successor as editor of *The Anglo-Welsh Review,* Clarke, while adequately represented in the anthology [*Anglo-Welsh Poetry: 1480-1980*], makes a far better showing in [her *Selected Poems*]. This is in part because there is room for **"Letter From a Far Country,"** a poem originally written, like Dylan Thomas's *Under Milkwood,* for the radio. The poem is valuable for a good number of reasons, not the least of which is its concern for the history and experience of women in a western rural parish where Clarke writes her apologia to "husbands, fathers, forefathers," calling it her "letter home from the future, / [her] bottle in the sea." Greedy circling gulls put to her their "masculine question:" "Where," they ask, "are your great works?" And from the daily, ordinary routines of obscure women—wives, mothers, and grandmothers—Clarke constructs her reply:

> It is easy to make of love
> these ceremonials. As priets
> we fold cloth, break bread, share wine,
> hope there's enough to go round.

As is the case with modern English poetry, Anglo-Welsh poetry does not seem to have produced many poems of merit written by women about the lives of women. This is an impressive instance of one such poem (there are others in [*Selected Poems*]), and one applauds with equal enthusiasm its clear vision and accomplished craftsmanship. (p. 184)

John Matthias, "Not for Sale in USA," in Another Chicago Magazine, *No. 16, 1986, pp. 177-86.*

TONY CURTIS

Gillian Clarke's *Selected Poems* includes almost all her published poems to date. In the last fifteen years she has published two successful books, the first, *Sundial,* being the best-selling collection published in Wales for many years. This was followed by the well-received *Letter From A Far Country* from Carcanet in 1983.

Her themes are constant, her destinations fixed. An early poem such as **'Blaen Cwrt'** establishes the search for roots, in the country and in the Welsh language, to which Gillian Clarke has committed herself in moving from suburban Cardiff to the eponymous 'Remote Dyfed Cottage':

> It has all the first
> Necessities for a high standard
> Of civilised living: silence inside
> A circle of sound, water and fire,
> Light on uncountable miles of mountain
> From a big, unpredictable sky,
> Two rooms, waking and sleeping,
> Two languages, two centuries of past
> To ponder on, and the basic need
> To work hard in order to survive.

We feel that the poet has earned the right to the moralising, even hectoring, address of these concluding lines by her fine realisation of details earlier in the poem. I would, however,

question the implicit value-judgements which are at other times loaded on Wales in Gillian Clarke's work. These seem to be very much influenced by R. S. Thomas (generally a much more instructive model for post-war Anglo-Welsh poetry than Dylan Thomas). In **'Harvest at Mynachlog'** and the more recent **'Fires on Llŷn',** for example, her use of 'England' and 'English' seems heavy-handed when considered in the full context of her work. The poem which lapses most completely into both nationalist and Romantic stereotypes is **'Miracle on St. David's Day',** when daffodils wave in mute admiration of an insane Welshman's recital of Wordsworth's poem. I would rather stress the justly-lauded title poem from *Letter from a Far Country* and the very fine lyrical pieces such as **'Ram', 'Choughs'** and **'The Water-Diviner'.** The influence of both Heaney and Hughes is clear, but it has been properly assimilated and informs some of her best work.

Of the new poems in this volume, **'Syphoning the Spring'** and **'Overheard in County Sligo'** are fine additions to her repertoire. **'Hare',** written for her friend Frances Horovitz, is an emotionally transcendent piece of the highest order. The *Selected Poems* as a whole display a poet with the craft and the sensibility to claim herself an international reputation. (pp. 63-4)

Tony Curtis, "Common Ground," in Poetry Review, *Vol. 75, No. 4, February, 1986, pp. 62-5.*

TONY CURTIS

Gillian Clarke first published in 1970, encouraged by her husband who, redeeming a poem in draft from her wastepaper-basket, sent it to Meic Stephens. Stephens' response was positive and Gillian Clarke threw herself into the writing of poetry with enormous energy. She wrote and published very frequently through the 1970s, also becoming Reviews Editor for *The Anglo-Welsh Review* and then succeeding Roland Mathias as editor in 1976. Gillian Clarke was quickly established as a leading Welsh poet and her first full-length collection *The Sundial,* published by Gomer Press in 1978, has proved the most successful book of poetry from a publisher in Wales for many years. Her *Selected Poems* encourages one to consider the development of a poet over fifteen years, working in Wales to considerable effect in terms of critical acclaim, audience response and book sales.

The commitment to poetry, for Gillian Clarke, was linked with her growing recognition of the importance of Wales to her life. Living in suburban Cardiff, she was spiritually inhabiting a more rural, Welsh-speaking world to the west. The act of writing involved in the deepest sense a confrontation and acceptance of her essential Welshness. In 1970 the context of publishing in Wales and the concern to voice Welsh issues, to proclaim a specific Welsh identity, provided a receptive ground for Gillian Clarke's growth as a writer. In a recent interview she acknowledges this:

> My loss of Welsh has been a very strong tension in my writing. But English is my mother tongue, and it is the tongue I was educated in. But being a woman and Welsh and therefore in two senses not wholly ready to count myself as one of the grown-ups, not easily able to feel I was permitted to be myself, to be a writer, an artist, I was a very late developer. Many women, particularly in Wales, are late developers as writers. I didn't begin writing properly until I was thirty, by which time I had long been

learning Welsh. So, while I grew through childhood and adolescence without Welsh, I already knew a lot of Welsh before I began to write openly. I began to write and to post poems because of the existence of the Welsh magazines written in English, like *The Anglo-Welsh Review, Poetry Wales,* and others. Those magazines gave me a sense of my own ability to join the ranks of the writers within them, writers who seemed to be giving me, written down, my own world.

That process, as a woman and as a writer, has been steady and determined. Gillian Clarke's themes remain constant, her destination fixed. She still works under the influence of Yeats, the Romantic poets and, of her contemporaries, Ted Hughes and Seamus Heaney especially. The influence of Hughes and Heaney is clear in much of her best work; but these poems *are* her best work because she has learned from and assimilated, rather than merely imitated, those poets. It would be crude misrepresentation to assign the birth and death imagery of poems such as **"Scything," "Ram"** and **"Welsh Blacks"** to Hughes alone; just as it would be churlish to credit Seamus Heaney for **"The Water-Diviner"** or **"Chalk Pebble".** Still, these two powerful poets inform Gillian Clarke's work as they do many of their contemporaries and it is interesting to compare Gillian Clarke's work with Hughes' 'Thought Fox' and its mystical aesthetics; her use of the Welsh language with the poems from Heaney's *Wintering Out,* and his own fascination with the elements and the poet's need to name them in poems such as 'The Diviner' and the 'Shelf Life' sequence from *Station Island.*

Whilst she has been swayed and carried on by the musicality of Yeats, Gillian Clarke, unlike Tripp and Garlick, has avoided the direct voicing of political concerns. She is not a poet of instant responses and, though she has written to commission, notably from the B. B. C. and the R. S. C., one cannot imagine her producing work such as R. S. Thomas' *What is a Welshman?* or the protest poems of Raymond Garlick in the early 1970s. She is far less direct than her contemporary Sally Roberts Jones. Sally Jones does not have the lyrical strength of Gillian Clarke, but she has constantly addressed herself to the matter of Wales. Like Raymond Garlick and John Tripp, Sally Jones' arrival from London in the 1960s was a significant opting into a Welsh identity. In poems such as 'Community', 'Language Protest, Llangefni' and 'Tryweryn' her concern for the survival and integrity of a Welsh Wales is clear. It is interesting to compare 'Tryweryn' with Gillian Clarke's **"Clywedog".** Where Sally Jones is angry and ironical—

> All's for the best—rehoused, these natives, too,
> Should bless us for sanitation and good health.
> Later, from English cities, see the view
> Misty with hiraeth—and their new-built wealth.

Gillian Clarke is lyrical and ironical—

> And walls a thousand years old.
> And the mountains, in a head-collar
> Of flood, observe a desolation
> They'd grown used to before the coming
> Of the wall-makers. Language
> Crumbles to wind and bird-call.

All this is not to say that her poetry is merely content to hold a traditional, lyrical ground in a pastoral landscape. Her long poem **"Letter From a Far Country"** succeeds as a feminist polemic where more directly aggressive voices have repelled those they would seek to change. Her work as a whole also exists against, and contributes to, a Wales that is, for her, as for R. S. Thomas, the core of everything that she knows. To this end she is driven by the need to reclaim a lost heritage that is encoded in a language to which she must lay claim; an inheritance that may only be realised by the continuing act of naming. . . . Over the last ten years more and more of her time has been spent away from Cardiff, renovating and finally, in 1984, fully occupying a cottage remotely placed in Dyfed, in one of the most strongly Welsh-speaking areas of Wales.

There is an appropriateness, even an inevitability, in that move. The cottage, Blaen Cwrt, had been the setting and the subject of one of her strongest early poems. This describes and celebrates the renovation of the place, "Some of the smoke / Rises against the ploughed, brown field / As a sign to our neighbours in the / Four fields of the Valley that we are in". A claim is being made to enter that community, to turn one's back on the "brochure blues or boiled sweet / Reds" and opt for "Nettles tasting sour and the smells of moist / Earth and sheep's wool". Nettles in Gillian Clarke's work are more likely to be those of Edward Thomas than John Ormond. The much-maligned Georgian qualities exemplified in Thomas' work have been more constructive than the modernism of Eliot and Pound as far as Anglo-Welsh poetry is concerned.

Just as Edward Thomas in celebrating the rural life of pre-war England protested the immorality and absurdity of the Great War's carnage, so Gillian Clarke's creation of a rural landscape in the west of Wales serves to underline implicit arguments concerning the way she feels we, especially we who wish to call ourselves Welsh, should conduct ourselves. **"Blaen Cwrt"** is a place where "air spins", smoke "curls like fern"; where there is "a thick root". Images build up an impression of an organic, holistic state of being and, in response, even "Our fingers curl on / Enamel mugs of tea, like ploughmen". The poem closes with a summation of the qualities of Blaen Cwrt that has the weight and some of the naiveté of a manifesto.

> It has all the first
> Necessities for a high standard
> Of civilised living: silence inside
> A circle of sound, water and fire,
> Light on uncountable miles of mountain
> From a big, unpredictable sky,
> Two rooms, waking and sleeping,
> Two languages, two centuries of past
> To ponder on, and the basic need
> To work hard in order to survive.

Gillian Clarke is not only drawing a parameter around the physical and imaginative territory which she wishes to occupy, she is dedicating herself here to the the task of poetry and the cause of her Wales with a crusading zeal. It is a zeal which is predicted in the dislocation which urban life has occasioned and in this respect she is following in the steps of R. S. Thomas (she literally does this in **"Fires on Llŷn"**). But where Thomas' landscape is a harsh tutor, testing and undermining any easy belief in a benevolent creator, Gillian Clarke's nature, while it can be instructive in its constant offerings of mortality, is closer to Wordsworth's maternal Nature. Bones, eggs, skulls, proliferate in Gillian Clarke's poems, but they are seized upon as *objets trouvé*: the ram's "helmet" skull could be "a vessel for blackberries and sloes" until the "Night in the socket of his eye" insists a harsher lesson. "Sheep's

Skulls" are sought like mushrooms and it is only later that one assumes a closer significance—

> On the rose
> Patina of old wood it lies
> Ornamental in the reflection
> Of a jar of wheat stalks.

There is a sense in which Nature, and natural truth is "out there"; one brings it back to one's world, the security of one's day to day living, where it resonates and disturbs.

In her treatment of this nature of Wales, this instructive landscape, Gillian Clarke involves even her sense of her womanhood. Her long title poem from *Letter from a Far Country* is set in motion from an immediate, urban, domestic situation, but from that life in the Cardiff suburb of Cyncoed the poet projects herself out and back into a quite different

> . . . landscape. Hill country,
> essentially feminine,
> the sea not far off.

Blaen Cwrt is now an

> . . . innocent smallholding
> where the swallows live and field mice
> winter and the sheep barge in
> under the browbone . . .

which holds the secret of its former owner's suicide. Again and again it is Nature's revelation of our mortality which quickens the impulse to shape one's life to a natural cycle.

In the earlier **"Harvest at Mynachlog"** the same point is underlined, though on this occasion there is no questioning of the woman's role and the farmer's son who flashed through "the boasting sky" over those same fields in a previous year

> . . . died minutes later
> On an English cliff.

That "English" seems in itself to be inconsequential, perhaps arbitrary. However, it does fit into a pattern of derogatory comparisons between England and Wales which underpin Gillian Clarke's poetry.

In **"Fires on Llŷn"**, written in 1984, the poet walks on the Llŷn peninsula in North Wales receptive to the special resonances of that area and linking them with the violent history of the almost-visible Ireland across the sea. She has explained in some detail the poem's genesis:

> Many things which seemed unconnected were in my mind when I wrote it, though I was only aware of some of them. The year I was born, 1937, three men, out of deep-felt belief that what they were doing was right and in what they saw as the interests of peace and of their small country, Wales, set fire to an R. A. F. bombing school in North Wales, in Llŷn, the north-west peninsula which reaches far out into the Irish Sea. The Welsh poet R. S. Thomas lives in Llŷn, and about five years ago I heard him interviewed on the radio and he said that he believes in God because sometimes he finds the form of a hare on the mountainside, and although the hare has gone the form is still warm. He called it God's absence. It is an idea which has occupied me ever since. In the Llŷn peninsula more and more of the houses and farms are becoming holiday cottages, occupied for only a few weeks every year, while many local people are homeless. In the past few years anger about this, and about the breaking-

up of Welsh speaking communities, has taken a frightening turn—holiday cottages are burned down in what the media have called 'The Arson Campaign'.

What is clear from that is the poet's awareness of wider, and often specifically political, events which are subsumed into her work more often than might be generally assumed.

In **"Fires on Llŷn"** the sanctity of the land's end at Uwchmynydd is broken by the thoughtlessness of "Three English boys":

> Over the holy sound Enlli
> is dark in a ruff
> of foam. Any pebble or shell
> might be the knuckle-bone
> or vertebra of a saint.
>
> Three English boys throw stones.
> Choughs sound alarm.
> Sea-birds rise and twenty thousand saints
> finger the shingle
> to the sea's intonation.

Those English boys, by their casual actions, set in motion a line of imagery and cross-reference that links the two Celtic countries, both with histories of subjugation by the English. The "fires" at the poem's end are explained as the sun's flash upon windows rather than the work of the Welsh-language militant arsonists, but the poem has by that time established a complexity of fearful associations, and guilt, and anger. In more senses than one the poet has been playing with fire. In what way can the "sea's mumbled novenas" convincingly resolve the multiplicity of social and political dilemmas which the poem has touched upon?

"Miracle on St. David's Day" loads even more spiritual weight onto Wales. The poet is conducting a writer's visit to an asylum. She establishes some sense of her audience of inmates in rather clumsy, generalised terms—

> I am reading poetry to the insane.
> An old woman, interrupting, offers
> as many buckets of coal as I need.
> A beautiful chestnut-haired boy listens
> entirely absorbed. A schizophrenic
>
> on a good day, they tell me later.
> In a cage of first March sun a woman
> sits not listening, not seeing, not feeling.
> In her neat clothes the woman is absent.

Included in this introduction to the inmates is the central subject of the poem, "A big, mild man" with "labourer's hands". It is this "big, dumb labouring man" who rocks to the rhythm of the poems and then, affected, transported by the sound, he rises to recite Wordsworth's 'The Daffodils'. The poem becomes significant as a positive act of memory, a lucid evocation of his past, his lost innocence. The fact of his utterance too is a moment of clarity focussed in his fogged brain.

The incident, it cannot be denied, was a remarkable one; it underlines the power of poetry, albeit learned by rote "Forty years ago, in a Valleys school", to touch areas of our emotional needs which the mind, even a healthy mind, can work hard to avoid. However, in her re-creation of the incident and her weighting of the elements in the poem, Gillian Clarke overloads the piece. The title makes a claim for our patron saint's intervention which is, to say the least, unquestioning. The risk she takes in quoting surely the most frequently-quoted lines in English poetry is obviously a calculated one, but just as obviously, it must finally appear as heavy-handed.

The poem closes with a transcendent image of daffodils that are, by now, the flower of poetry itself, "their syllables / unspoken", the spirit of nature animated by "the big, dumb, labouring man's" act of speech, and the emblem of Wales (courtesy of Lloyd George). It is as if the daffodil were being made to function as does T. S. Eliot's rose:

> And all shall be well
> All manner of thing shall be well
> When the tongues of flame are in-folded
> Into the crowned knot of fire
> And the fire and the rose are one.
>   "Little Gidding"

But that triumphant conclusion to the *Four Quartets* stands on the achievement of those quartets, and the body of Eliot's poetry as a whole. **"Miracle on St. David's Day"** has not earned its ending, and, again, one is asked to accept a set of corollaries from its Welsh setting that may, in fact, be far from acceptable.

This poem, which opens so effectively—its first stanza pointing out "the rumps of gardeners between nursery shrubs"—manages, remarkably, to proceed to its transcendent resolution with no further sense of irony. That irony would have helped to press the intriguing elements of the story and the descriptions of its setting into a more acceptable form. Gillian Clarke's work may not be consciously, or even obviously, politically-charged, but, in fact, her entire aesthetic is heavily weighed by passionate convictions regarding Wales, and presupposes such feelings in her audience. (pp. 110-18)

> Tony Curtis, "Grafting the Sour to Sweetness:
> Anglo-Welsh Poetry in the Last Twenty-Five Years,"
> in Wales, the Imagined Nation: Studies in Cultural
> and National Identity, edited by Tony Curtis, Poetry Wales Press, 1986, pp. 99-126.

MICHAEL HULSE

Because it has been done so well and so often by so many, a poetry based on natural description and response to the small everyday incidents of rural life invites failure in our time. It invites either the humdrum and dull, or the intense and bombastic. (Robert Minhinnick's is sometimes the latter pitfall.) To write firmly and steadily to a clarity of vision, with neither over-reaching pretensions nor inconsequential gabble, requires a poet of exceptional touch and tact, and in her *Selected Poems* Gillian Clarke proves quite beautifully to be that poet.

> At last the women come with baskets,
> The older one in flowered apron,
> A daisied cloth covering the bread
> And dappled china, sweet tea
> In a vast can. The women stoop
> Spreading their cups in the clover.
>
> The engines stop. A buzzard watches
> From the fence. We bury our wounds
> In the deep grass: sunburnt shoulders,
> Bodies scratched with straw, wrists bruised
> From the weight of the bales, blood beating.

This is Gillian Clarke's typical tone: an almost iambic, un-

rhymed line, conversationally enjambed, lightly held together with alliteration, arranged in tidy sentences that are plainly content with conventional syntax and barely want more than to relax and talk. As the physical work begins, the language too takes on a more physical texture: it is thicker, the syllables jostle somewhat, and it seems that we are having our attention drawn to the word "blood", not in any menstrual, feminist way but because this poem, **"Harvest at Mynachlog"**, is about the physical awareness of being alive, and it is therefore right to speak of the blood. After two stanzas that describe bale-making and stacking, **"Harvest at Mynachlog"** continues:

> We are soon recovered and roll over
> In the grass to take our tea. We talk
> Of other harvests. They remember
> How a boy, flying his plane so low
> Over the cut fields that his father
>
> Straightened from his work to wave his hat
> At the boasting sky, died minutes later
> On an English cliff, in such a year
> As this, the barns brimming gold.
>
> We are quiet again, holding our cups
> In turn for the tilting milk, sad, hearing
> The sun roar like a rush of grain
> Engulfing all winged things that live
> One moment in the eclipsing light.

These final lines resemble those modulated up-beats that so inspiringly transform the conclusions to many of Philip Larkin's best poems, but in Gillian Clarke, just as nothing that has gone before is strongly stated, so too the conclusion is left unassertive and modest. "One moment in the eclipsing light": it is a lovely phrase, but in fact it is itself eclipsed by the tale told in the two previous stanzas, where a language both imaginatively fresh ("the boasting sky") and reassuringly familiar ("the barns brimming gold") has created a vivid scene for us. The focus of the poem, so involved with the experience of physical living, is on a memory of death; and it is in fact apt, then, that when the reapers (death and the reapers!) are "quiet again" (what, after all, is there to say?) the poem too quietens.

"Harvest at Mynachlog" is from *The Sundial*, published in 1978, and in its calm quietness establishes the tone that remains most characteristic of Gillian Clarke. (It also, incidentally, hints at what elsewhere can become a somewhat tiresome tic: Clarke's Housmanian penchant for rural deaths, particularly suicides.) But **"Harvest at Mynachlog"** would not prepare us for the vivacious rhyming thump of a newer poem, **"Overheard in County Sligo"**; or for the exacter observation Clarke devotes to birds in **"Curlew"**, **"Choughs"**, **"Buzzard"**, **"Kingfishers at Condat"**, **"Heron at Port Talbot"**, **"Bluetit and Wren"** and **"Tawny Owl"**; or for the command of longer structure in the remarkable meditative title poem of *Letter from a Far Country* (1982). Nor does it prepare us for the knack Gillian Clarke apparently learned between the first and second books (I suspect from Sylvia Plath) of allowing a measure of doubt and instability into a scene of industry and contentment, merely through the texture of description:

> As we eat crushed strawberry ice
> under a bee-heavy vine
> we watch for the seamstress to come.
> Through the open doorway we hear
> her chatter, see her Singers

glint with gold roses in the dark room.

(Is it only the twofold repetition of "dark" later in the poem—once in the final line—that persuades us that the **"Seamstress at St Leon"** is getting something of the treatment Plath meted out to those who gathered in the innocent name of bee-keeping? Surely there is something more, in the sinister glint of the Singer roses, in the very expectancy of the cadences?) The calm quietness of **"Harvest at Mynachlog"** is present as a ground tone throughout Clarke's poetry, but beyond it there is a variousness all the subtler for being achieved within limited scope.

Drawing obliquely but powerfully on what we think to be the spirit of Wales, Gillian Clarke's major authority is found in her religious writing. Catholic without tears, it gladly celebrates **"St Thomas's Day"** or a **"Miracle on St David's Day"**, recreates the **"Tawny Owl"** through a unified, metaphysical system of imagery from the Mass, and constantly seeks the symbolism of flame and light. One lovely poem from the second collection, **"The Water-Diviner"**, shows that almost mystical point where Christian faith and love of the natural world meet in Clarke; the word *"dwr"* is Welsh, meaning "water".

> His fingers tell water like a prayer.
> He hears its voice in the silence
> through fifty feet of rock
> on an afternoon dumb with drought.
>
> Under an old tin bath, a stone,
> an upturned can, his copper pipe
> glints with discovery. We dip our hose
> deep into the dark, sucking its dryness,
>
> till suddenly the water answers,
> not the little sound we know,
> but a thorough bass too deep
> for the naked ear, shouts through the house
>
> a word we could not say, or spell, or remember,
> something like *"dwr . . . dwr"*.

The same scene described by Wordsworth would have swerved into the mystical pointlessness of pantheism; Gillian Clarke seems all the stronger because, beginning with the image of prayer (and indeed of the rosary, the telling of the beads), she asserts from the outset that the presence of powerful natural forces is a confirmation of belief, rather than a cause for doubt. A similar scene described by Seamus Heaney, in a poem from his first collection, is altogether slighter since it shifts our attention to the role of the diviner as a man with an unusual gift, and hints rather clumsily that in this he resembles others with special gifts (such as poets, perhaps)—in this way Heaney's poem has a dimension of self-admiring that is absent from Gillian Clarke's clear and modest sonnet.

Gillian Clarke writes in English, but draws occasionally upon the Welsh language, and on Welsh history and legend, and has a vital sense of the Welsh land and people. Her poetry is arrestingly filled with quiet beauty and clear insight, with visionary celebration and elegiac power, and reveals a writer wedded to the world and the word in equal measure. (pp. 82-3)

Michael Hulse, "Two Welsh Poets: Gillian Clarke and Tony Curtis," in Quadrant, *Vol. XXXII, Nos. 1 & 2, January & February, 1988, pp. 81-4.*

JOHN LUCAS

Gillian Clarke's [*Letting in the Rumour*] has four or five poems whose grace is matched by and won from the intractability of matter, as in **"Seal"**, which refuses the easy current of feelings it may seem to set in motion: "When the milk-arrow stabs she comes / water fluent down the long green miles. / Her milk leaks into the sea, blue / blossoming in an opal." The language holds sentiment at bay: it sounds lovely, but "In two days / no bitch-head will break the brilliance / listening for baby-cries. / Down in the thunder of that other country / the bulls are calling and her uterus is empty."

This may be minor poetry, but it has a regard for its subject without which style becomes trivially fetishistic. Clarke does become trivial when she claims that attention to nature red in tooth and claw happens on bare hills, not where people are: "The cities can forget on days like this / all the world's wars" (**"In January"**). No, they can't. **"Neighbours"** is a much better poem, about the post-Chernobyl world where "In the democracy of the virus and the toxin / we wait". And as we wait, we make poems. As Luther famously said: "Even if the world should end tomorrow, I still would plant my apple tree." (p. 34)

John Lucas, "Hallo to the Art of Poetry," in New Statesman & Society, *Vol. 2, No. 65, September 1, 1989, pp. 33-4.*

MARK WORMALD

Two of the more notable achievements in recent British poetry have also been the quietest. Hugo Williams's *Writing Home* and Gillian Clarke's *Letter from a Far Country* focused on home and the individual's place in it. Both also resorted to the same metaphor: the poem as letter home. . . . [Clarke's] letter home was more ambivalent [than Williams's], an exercise in projecting herself into an emancipated future which she could never, finally, inhabit. She was a woman writing in English in a patriarchal world of Welsh, and the combined weight of tradition, present experience and her own frustration fascinated her into immobility. In *Letting in the Rumour,* her new collection, Clarke redefines her own position, and her attitudes to her past. Not much in her situation seems to have changed since the publication of her *Selected Poems.* . . .

The difference is that Clarke is now in a mood to track down myths, to reconcile her own situation with the past she has inherited. In her *Letter,* a glance back revealed a woman of her grandmother's generation "up to her wrists in marriage . . . looking coldly from the old world" as a seal stares through the surface of an encircling, imprisoning sea. Letting in the rumour, however, from her own present and her family's past, allows the poet to contain and so defuse the threat of this obscure inheritance. Seal and pup now "caress as humans do": generations meet and exchange houses, losses, confidences. Clarke lives in her ancestors' future, where lanes "[lead] everywhere": through the same small radio she receives topical Russian and timeless Welsh, "glasnost, / golau glas" (this latter the blue air of her valley). And, though she is "Housewife" still, her language enables her to exert some sort of control over her local, global world: cleaning the windows,

> With a warm cloth I clear hills,
> a tractor ploughing, fields whose names

> I know. In their bracelets of hot water
> my wrists root.

"Slate Mine" sees her employing the same powerful mono-syllables to more morally ambiguous effect; as she throws a slab of slate into the pit,

> My cast slate panics
> through generations of silence,
> such a long wait
> for the sound of drowning.

It is only with the final, beautifully rendered section of the book, another long poem, **"Cofiant"** (the Welsh for biography), that the sources of this ambiguity are tracked down to her family's past. From it the mine, the sea and the radio all well resonantly up. Against this, the poet's own experience remains valid, and different; but there is real enlightenment, for the reader and for Clarke herself, in the revelation of the origin of her preoccupations.

> *Mark Wormald, "Tracking Her Sources," in* The Times Literary Supplement, *No. 4513, September 29-October 5, 1989, p. 1065.*

Lucy Ellmann
1956-

(Born Lucy Elizabeth Ellmann) American novelist and critic.

In her acclaimed first novel, *Sweet Desserts,* Ellmann focuses on Suzy Schwarz, an unhappy and vulnerable young woman living in London and attempting to complete her thesis in art history. Embroiled in a lifelong rivalry with her older sister and a strained relationship with her father, both of whom are art historians, Suzy appeases her emotional needs by indulging in food and sex and by maintaining a sardonic attitude, which is reflected in the droll, often acerbic tone of the narrative. *Sweet Desserts* is structured in the form of a collage, juxtaposing Suzy's chaotic lifestyle with reminiscences of such events as her mother's death, the family's move to Great Britain when she was thirteen, and incidents that exacerbated her antagonism toward members of her family. Items drawn from popular culture, including ads, recipes, and instructions, are interspersed throughout the narrative, revealing the effects of mass media upon the individual. College and popular culture are also integral to Suzy's thesis, which explores how these elements contribute to artistic detachment. In addition to receiving generally positive reviews, *Sweet Desserts* won *The Guardian* Fiction Prize for best first novel of 1988.

(See also *Contemporary Authors,* Vol. 128.)

LESLEY CHAMBERLAIN

For Suzy, protagonist of Lucy Ellmann's short autobiographical first novel [*Sweet Desserts*], life "as per usual" alternates between empty sex and a full stomach. Her mother is dead, and when her father remarries fashionable, elegant Saskia the disappointment drives the teenage daughter to an excess of food and a permanent duffel coat. Daddy comments she would feel better in herself if she finished her thesis and lost some weight. Nothing improves in her early twenties. She fridge-hovers, vomits, couples hungrily and greedily takes advice about her personal problems. Ellmann has given us a painful account of how the consumer world eats its dithering prey. The metaphor is ironic since Suzy the big eater would dearly like to be swallowed whole by some passion. When her man abandons their post-love-making to eat yoghurt she lies alongside him yearning to be a milk culture. Her elder sister Fran, sexier and more successful, sends along cast-off boyfriends and gets the better jobs.

The vacant round of bulimic days and nights is relieved by the author's fresh thoughts on how to write about it. Suzy's art-history thesis is not much of a comfort to her, but the fragments we read illuminate the unexpectedly gripping way Ellmann has written her story. Depicted by "the withdrawal method", it's a classic account of dissatisfaction:

> This study will trace the theme of the artist's non-participation in the art-making process, through his/her use of borrowed materials, often merely stuck onto the canvas with glue. The spectator is

left to await the artist's return like a bewildered dog at a graveside: hence the claim that Art is Dead.

The young woman who can't give her life beauty and shape disfigures her body from the inside to fill up the space, while from the outside her existence looks like a collage of views from women's magazines, instructions from cookery books and opinions from newspapers. Though she hates it she can't find other props. The narrative includes fragments of diets and recipes and comment on Princess Di's latest outfit and ends with an index, ironically underpinning the pseudo-rational, pseudo-orderly discourse of the commercial environment which has invaded Suzy's personality. It's a fake, flat, passionless world, which is driving Suzy to self-destruction. One of the merits of this intelligent book is that it bubbles with ideas under the dejected, consumerish surface. It is also a knowing put-down to all claims that life is good in the gap between adolescence and early middle age.

Lesley Chamberlain, "Filling the Space," in The Times Literary Supplement, No. 4454, August 8-12, 1988, p. 891.

MAUREEN FREELY

There are two kinds of expatriates, the consenting adults, who decide they would be better off in a foreign country, and the unconsulted children they drag along with them. The heroine of **Sweet Desserts** belongs to the second category—as does the author, who is the late Richard Ellmann's daughter.

Arriving in Oxford at the age of 13, Suzy Schwartz is not impressed. Why no boys at Oxford High? Why so little heat coming out of the radiators and why no plugs on new electrical appliances? Why are the English, so reserved in person, so loud and gregarious when they discuss tubers on the radio? Why do they eat lardy cake? And why can't *she* go back to live in Illinois? Suzy decides not to adjust. She does badly in her 'O' levels and hangs on to her American accent. When her kind-hearted, absent-minded, world-famous father, does not object she resorts first to shoplifting and then, along with her older sister Franny, to secret eating.

Her father, a Rubens expert, has often confessed in print to being repelled by fat women. But even Suzy's expanding waistline does not lessen his affection. His advice remains common-sense: 'You know, you'd be a lot happier if you lost some weight.' Sister Franny takes heed and moves on to academic successes and multi-national boyfriends, while Suzy drags her feet through an indifferent art course, an unsuccessful marriage, and a host of unsatisfying love affairs. Although she finds happiness in motherhood, she still depends on Mother's Pride, which she consumes behind locked doors by the loaf. ('I had no use for friends—my life was centered around the fridge, the bread box, and a few of the kitchen cupboards.') Her eating becomes all the more desperate when she discovers that her father is fatally ill.

In a normal novel, there would have been a heart-rending conclusion in which father and daughter arrived at an understanding. Here, thank God, there is no such thing. Lucy Ellmann is too intelligent for cheap insights and sentimental resolutions. She chooses instead to be true to the emotional moment. This is, therefore, a wild book, in which angst-ridden confessions are interrupted by excerpts from cook books, authoritarian healthy-eating guides, pretentious theses on modern art, officious radio sex advice shows, diaries, suicide notes, and pauses for American ice cream and Rich Tea biscuits. Even the index breaks the rules:

> 'Aloofness, *see* inhabitants of the British Isles . . . Boyfriends, Franny's hand-me-down, *see* less of . . . Cakes, angel-food, 136; crumb, 15-16; eccles, 41; lardy, 41 . . . Impressionism, the Courtauld's expert on, nausea associated with, 63 . . . Tomaatto, *say* tomatoe.'

The story may be depressing and familiar, but thanks to its spirited author, it is funny in spite of itself—and refreshingly unguarded. Hopefully it is the first of many.

Maureen Freely, "Loafing About," in The Observer, *August 18, 1988, p. 41.*

JOHN SUTHERLAND

Lucy Ellmann has written a slim but stylish first novel. The matter of **Sweet Desserts** is easily summarised, though summary destroys the odd angling of the narrative. This is a daughter's novel, but told ostensibly from a sister's point of view. At the emotional centre of the story is an internationally-renowned American professor. History of art is his field and Rubens his specialism. Professor Schwarz establishes his reputation at the University of Illinois in Champaign-Urbana, where the heroine Suzy is born in 1956. She has an older sister, Fran. In 1970, Schwarz takes up a chair at Oxford and becomes even more renowned. Trailing in his academic baggage train are his two daughters. The professor also has two wives. The first dies of a stroke in America in the Sixties, and makes only a very faint impression on the narrative. The second does not get on well with her foster-daughters and, like her predecessor, features only remotely in the story. The professor finally dies, agonisingly, of muscular dystrophy, Lou Gehrig's disease. It may, or may not, bring the sisters together.

The story is told, with studious off-handedness, by the least-regarded member of the Schwarz family: Suzy, the younger, duller and constantly out-rivalled sibling. Even before birth she is upstaged by a young Fran who responds to her mother's pregnancy with a first (phony) suicide attempt. Having failed to abort Suzy, Fran reacts to her birth by silence and bed-wetting. She gets the desired paternal sympathy: 'Her father told her he too had wet the bed as a child; his mother hung the stained sheets out of his window so the neighbours would know (an Old World cure). Fran sat on his lap and he confided in this small, wet, troubled person.' Suzy does not sit on her father's lap.

Later, the rivalry between the sisters tones down into more acceptable forms of rivalry which can be lived with, or at least survived. Fran becomes an academic over-achiever in the same Rubens field as her father, accepting his belief that 'scholarship is the only antidote to emotional turmoil.' Her line, in opposition to his patriarchal belletrism, is fiercely feminist, attacking the master's abuse of his '*mater*ials'. As a postgraduate at Essex, she sleeps with her teacher and does well. She publishes, lands good jobs in British and American universities, becomes a deconstructionist and has a state-of-the-art computer. Suzy by contrast is an academic dud. She is writing a history-of-art PhD thesis on collage which itself remains obstinately fragmentary. She consoles herself with food; 'eating disorder' becomes her criticism of life. Deep-down, she wants to become a roly-poly Rubens woman.

There are a few childhood snapshots. The sisters collaborate on a story about sisters that naively reflects their differences. A five-year-old Suzy runs away from home, leaving a note: 'Dear Mommy, I am running away. I hope you don't mind me taking a sandwich. Love Suzy.' But she is recovered four blocks away, 'wondering where to go, since she had already reached the boundary of her usual zone'.

The remainder of the novel skips over Suzy's 30 years of life, weaving elaborations on the set pattern of outshone sister and insufficiently-loved daughter. Her first, painfully unconsummated love affair in Illinois is stage-managed by Fran. As a young Yank at Oxford High School in 1970, Suzy is wretchedly unhappy. She writes her last will and testament, and finds Franny reading it with relish. Her father remarries a gorgeous fashion consultant who 'clearly considered me a large blob on her horizon, as did I'. She reacts by shoplifting and is put on probation. In 1973, she is sent to Italy by her father, to study Italian. Franny directs her to one of her former lovers, a middle-aged lecher who takes 'the unexciting and unnoticed gift' of Suzy's virginity in between spouting lively Italian into his telephone. After investigating 'another orifice or two, he dumped me at a bus-stop outside Florence.

I've always associated the event with Napoleon.' Suzy finally lands up in Ulysses Road, North London, co-habitating with another of Fran's cast-off lovers, Jeremy, a Courtauld post-graduate. She gets pregnant (astonished by the fact that she should matter enough to be fertile) and they marry. But it doesn't work. He batters her, she leaves with her daughter, Lily, and no means of support. Battles with the DHSS, British central heating and British Telecom ensue.

The last, most affecting section of *Sweet Desserts* deals with the father's protracted illness. Suzy can keep the suffering at bay only by telling herself the Jewish jokes that he used to tell his girls. When, eventually, he dies, Suzy wants to murder his doctor, while Fran, 'full of the mysteries of death', plays a dignified part in the family bereavement. At Oxford, six months later, Fran and Suzy get together for Christmas: 'I give her some nice ear-rings which she likes, and a star-fish potholder. She fails to give me a copy of her latest book, but offers instead a pair of naughty knickers that don't fit. Later that afternoon we watch *La Traviata* on TV together, and weep.'

The power of *Sweet Desserts* lies in its passive-aggressive tone of voice (a kind of slyly snide bleat), interspersed, in the manner of a collage, with scraps from diet sheets, popsongs, newspaper headlines, school reports, family letters and post-mortems. The novel contrives to be both bitter and amusing. It is, as its publishers claim, a very successful debut. But it is nevertheless difficult to read it without some uncomfortable twinges. The narrative accords so closely to publicly-known facts about the author's family that one can't help feeling it would have been proper, as with Sylvia Plath's *Bell Jar*, to publish the work (at least initially) under a pseudonym. (p. 27)

John Sutherland, "Flights from the Asylum," in London Review of Books, *Vol. 10, No. 15, September 1, 1988, pp. 26-7.*

MICHIKO KAKUTANI

Suzy Schwarz, the heroine of Lucy Ellmann's sharp first novel [*Sweet Desserts*]—which which won Britain's prestigious Guardian Fiction Prize—is living in London and supposedly completing her Ph.D. on the art of collage. Titled "The Withdrawal Method: The Absence of the Artist's Touch in Collages and Ready-Mades," her thesis is concerned with artists' use of collage as a means of achieving distance, and disguising their own involvement in the creative process. Suzy foresees a future lecturing on such topics as "Aloofness, From Chardin to Christo," "Artistic Absence and Abstinence," "Fake Ready-Mades, From Oldenburg to Louise Nevelson."

Suzy's own story, appropriately enough, takes the form of a collage as well: childhood reminiscences and descriptions of her current adventures in England are juxtaposed with pointedly absurd newspaper clippings, recipes, ad copy and passages from textbooks. It's a defensive method, as we've been told, enabling Suzy (and her creator) to hide their vulnerability behind a posture of detachment, and it's a method complemented by the acerbic, even sarcastic, tone of much of this novel. Major events—the breakdown of a marriage, the death of a parent—virtually happen offstage, sandwiched in between jokes and bits from popular songs; and by the time we've learned all about Suzy's failed romances and eating dis-

orders, we've also learned how to make a flower out of marzipan, how to "eat for health, strength and efficiency," how to build a workbench, how to deal with the English phone company.

No doubt these seemingly irrelevant asides are supposed to show us something about the zaniness of contemporary life, while at the same time italicizing Suzy's alienation—her tendency to dwell on trivia and her penchant for trying to pass the time by reading "personal ads, TV guides, problem pages, recipes, technical handbooks and junk mail." Yet if a couple of the quotations used as found objects are fairly witty, most of them are employed in a coy and willfully arty manner. Empty post-modern gestures, they distract the reader from Suzy's story, rather than enriching it.

It is when Ms. Ellmann sticks to her main narrative that she demonstrates her many skills as a writer: an unsentimental eye for the incongruities of modern life; a bawdy sense of humor; and a distinctive voice, by turns angry and regretful, poetic and dyspeptic. In a few lines, she conjures up the American suburb where Suzy and her sister, Franny, grew up: a wealthy Illinois town, where all the houses have front-yards and backyards, porches and attics, and lawns spotted with buttercups. England, where the family moves when Suzy is a teen-ager, is described in considerably less idyllic terms. . . .

A food addict, [Suzy] is constantly stuffing herself with cookies and peanut-butter-and-jelly sandwiches, bread and other goodies; and she soon balloons, distressingly, in size. Her sister, Franny, appears to be similarly obsessed with food. Suzy explains their eating disorders as a kind of revenge on their father, a famous scholar with a repugnance for Rubens and his large women.

In fact, Franny and Suzy's father—who bears something of a resemblance to Ms. Ellmann's own father, the well-known Joyce scholar Richard Ellmann, who died in 1987—plays a pivotal role in their lives. In the wake of their mother's death, the two girls vie for his attention—a struggle only exacerbated by his illness. Unable to live up to his expectations, and overshadowed by her sister's success, Suzy drifts angrily from day to day, . . .

In the last chapters of the book, as Suzy's father lies dying of a neurological illness, Ms. Ellmann shifts gears, exchanging the flippant tone that has informed so much of the novel for a darker, more lyric mode. Refusing any sort of easy, happy ending, she shows us, with brutal honesty, the mixture of fear, anger, self-pity and guilt that a parent's death can engender. We see Suzy attempt to run away from her father's illness, try to deny her love with fits of self-indulgence, and we see her, finally, attempt to come to terms with his death. It is in these last few pages of the book that Ms. Ellmann demonstrates that she is not merely a clever collage maker, but a gifted writer capable of exploring the tragedies as well as the absurdities of family life.

Michiko Kakutani, "Food and Sex as Substitutes for a Father's Love," in The New York Times, *June 6, 1989, p. C19.*

CAROL ANSHAW

Unlike the parent-child relationship, which is de facto emotionally tethering, the connections between siblings run from the most fragile, easily snipped threads, to submerged trunk lines, to—when the current flows just right—a great rush, a heady counterpartnership, what Springsteen calls up in the line "Nothin' feels better than blood on blood."

Of course, he's talking about brothers. Sisters are a trickier deal; fewer avenues are open to them for easy camaraderie or direct competition. Also, starting early on, the culture presses a girl to identify herself by how she is seen. She forms herself by gathering reflective information from all other women, but most especially from the one standing so adjacent to her, looking so much like her. The sisters in . . . [*Sweet Desserts*] use each other in these ways, come at each other from these oblique angles. And move together uncomfortably joined, holding each other at arm's length, yet unable to let go.

Suzy and Franny are mostly rivals. Both are fat girls—secret snackers, binge eaters, habitués of the space just in front of the open refrigerator. One is bulimic (although not very successfully—she's still fat). Their spirit of *bon appetit* extends to sex. Franny passes on her used boyfriends to Suzy, who supplements these rejects with quickies on trains and a wrong number she turns into a Mr. Right Enough. Professionally, both sisters follow in the footsteps of their father, a noted art historian. Franny publishes widely while Suzy keeps busy with avoiding her dissertation. (If you're looking for a *clef* to the *roman,* Lucy Ellmann writes on art for *The Times Literary Supplement* and is the daughter of Richard Ellmann, the late literary biographer.)

The book is played in a droll key, counterpointed with jazzed-up mechanics—narrative clips that cut back and forth between points of view, present and past, first and third person, and alternate with pasted-in bits of this 'n' that—recipes, medical advice, personals ads. These work better when they seem to be non sequiturs, worse when they are designed to be telling (a sexual misadventure followed by the line "I can't get no satisfaction").

The central aspect of Franny and Suzy's relationship is envy—Suzy's of Franny's success, Franny's of Suzy's becoming married with baby. None of this emotion is investigated, only presented. And I suppose in real life emotion does go pretty much uninvestigated, and envy is one of the purely dumbest and least considered in our repertoire, but still. In this book, emotion isn't even felt, by the reader or the writer. It's a simulated emotion-grained veneer concept. Naugafeeling.

Individual passages do show Ellmann in possession of a wry talent. . . . But the book as a whole lacks aspiration, as though the author didn't bother to show up to write it, just phoned it in. In the end, the novel, like Suzy, is still working on its thesis. Although packed with literary pretensions, *Sweet Desserts* is not really very different from those thicker novels in which (usually) three sisters (or college roommates) go on to suffer through difficult, troubled lives, until they finally reach the heartbreaking denouement in which they openly rue their choices and tearfully covet each other's.

> Carol Anshaw, "Twisted Sisters: Tales of the Ties that Bind," in VLS, No. 76, July, 1989, p. 29.

RICHARD EDER

It is not the character that stands out in this essentially one-character novel about an impulsive, clever and put-upon young woman. Suzy, an American living in England and embarking upon an assortment of ill-fated experiments to discover life, sex and her brain, is a familiar sort of klutz, though a classy and hand-dipped one.

It is not the story, and it is not the discoveries. They are first-novel discoveries. They are good ones and they have essentially been discovered before, though not, of course, on the typewriter of Lucy Ellmann. It is important for first-novel writers to have their characters make such discoveries. Then they can go on to write second novels, and in the case of Ellmann, this is likely to be an excellent idea.

Because there is something about *Sweet Desserts* that does stand out. It is the raving turn of a sentence here and there; a sentence that won't lie down as you are led through it, but humps up, twines around your ankle, fixes you with a round eye, and whispers an invitation to meet somewhere later.

Suzy and Fran, her older sister and perpetual rival, live in an Illinois college town until their early teens. After their mother dies of a stroke, their father, an art historian, gets an appointment at Oxford, and they move to England. . . .

In the early pages, Fran, as baby and child, is the star; Suzy darts in and out of her shadow. From the start, Ellmann's sentences wriggle like grass-snakes. Here is a glimpse of Fran, at 2, trying in vain to get the attention of her mother, who is pregnant and dozing on the porch.

> The little girl sits down again encircled by nonplused toys, and crosses her legs. Minutes pass and a few bugs.

To claim attention, she wanders the neighborhood sneaking other kids' toys; among them, 36 pairs of dolls' shoes. Her mother has to lock her in her room at nap time. "The two wept in their separate enclaves," Ellmann writes, "absorbing the fact that Franny had become an enemy." . . .

After these few delicate and pointed pages, the book shifts to Suzy in her married life in London. Fran, so appealing and spiky, has become all spike; a disagreeable, bossy adult, one more among the personages and furnishings that agitate Suzy's tale of universal put-down. We miss Fran; perhaps the book would be stronger if it had stayed with her. Perhaps that will be the second book.

Still, Suzy is appealing, particularly in her marriage trap. She goes on food binges, with special emphasis on bread. To bolster her sexual self-esteem, she buys specialized pornographic magazines that feature fat women.

The marriage to Jeremy, a discarded lover of Fran's, provides a whole cluster of wriggling sentences. He is English, idle, fussy, self-absorbed and a leech. Occasionally he condescends to make love, retiring immediately afterwards with an individual portion of yogurt. Suzy is grateful but "envies the yogurt."

When she finds herself pregnant, they get married and go on a one-night honeymoon to a dreary rural inn. "We consummated the business of the day. I went to sleep. Jeremy lay awake contemplating minor faux pas he'd committed." The next day, they take a walk in the park at Blenheim "past a dead body that wasn't discovered until a few days later." Ellmann, who tells us on the jacket flap that she was taken to

England at 13 "against her will" and still lives there, makes English awfulness a thing of beauty.

Lily, her baby, gives Suzy her first dose of self-confidence as well as the gumption to leave Jeremy. She then embarks on a series of sexual adventures and a tentative career—following in her father's and Fran's footsteps—as an art writer.

The adventures are mostly misadventures; they reinforce Suzy's klutziness but they also drag the book down. . . .

The sex, if not the aftermaths, is unfailingly protracted and marvelous ("We fit together like two wandering continents"). Even if Suzy's adventures are told with humor and irony, they remain a woman's stud-fantasies, and they drain the book as well as Suzy. They serve to point up her comic disarray, but that is just the trouble. Ellmann has turned her live character into a hapless doll, and her writing turns to comic decoration.

It is often appealing decoration but the writing lacks the sting it had earlier. Snippets of magazine household hints and advice columns are interjected every so often. It gives a nice sense of a world full of meaningless instructions, but it wears out. So do the flat and irritating jokes inserted ever so often. Telling bad jokes is more hapless decor; it says: You can look at me—I'm no threat.

By the time a harder note is introduced with the terminal illness of Suzy's and Fran's father, this too seems like a decoration. *Sweet Desserts* doesn't fizzle, exactly, but it loses its way. In part, though, this is a tribute to the burning and delicate anarchy with which it started; we want it sustained and it isn't.

Richard Eder, "The Beauty in British Awfulness,"
in Los Angeles Times Book Review, *July 2, 1989,*
p. 3.

DAVID FINKLE

If there's a graduate student out there preparing a dissertation on "The Importance and Meaning of Food to Women in Contemporary Fiction," Lucy Ellmann's *Sweet Desserts* is a novel to know about. In it, two sisters named Fran and Suzy Schwarz both turn into secret eaters as they grow up in Champaign-Urbana, Ill. (where, as children, they lose their mother to a cerebral hemorrhage), move to Oxford, England (where their art historian father has accepted a position), become art historians themselves and trundle to London and back to the United States according to what happens to the ineffectual men they live with, marry and separate from. Ms. Ellmann's theory is that women's overeating has to do with repressed desire for and anger at men. Whether or not this makes the psychology just a little too simple, Ms. Ellmann keeps it funny by setting the two sisters against a father whose main claim to scholarly fame is his hatred for Rubens. Lucy Ellmann's own father was the biographer Richard Ellmann, so this may be an autobiographical exercise. But it is also a tribute to his devotion to Oscar Wilde, at least in the sense that the younger Ellmann writes with grace, grit and a gift for the epigram. *Sweet Desserts,* which won Britain's Guardian Prize for a first novel, is a book that looks to achieve its effects through the accumulation of unchronological recollections interrupted by snippets of magazine self-help tips, recipes and quotations from *King Lear,* with the aim of driving home just how disjointed Suzy's life is. But in scanting Fran's experiences, in giving mere glimpses of other characters, Ms. Ellmann has made the not uncommon mistake of thinking that skimpy lives can be adequately represented in a book of skimpy length.

David Finkle, in a review of "Sweet Desserts," in
The New York Times Book Review, *July 2, 1989,*
p. 12.

Nissim Ezekiel

1924-

Indian poet, dramatist, editor, and critic.

A leading English-language Indian poet, Ezekiel is best known for his concise, traditional verse that intimately examines such subjects as self-understanding, urban life, and the existence of God. Born in Bombay to Jewish parents, Ezekiel attended Catholic and Presbyterian schools before traveling to Great Britain, where he lived from 1948 to 1952. While noting that Ezekiel's verse draws primarily upon the British Modernist tradition, critics discern the influence of his diverse cultural and religious experience on the rational humanism of his poetry, which transcends conventional European and Indian values. Occasionally faulted as derivative, Ezekiel's work has nevertheless garnered praise for its thoughtful, complex examination of spiritual and worldly existence. Linda Hess commented: "[Ezekiel] is a poet of the city, Bombay; a poet of the body; and an endless explorer of the labyrinths of the mind, the devious delving and twisting of the ego, and the ceaseless attempt of man and poet to define himself, and to find through all 'the myth and maze' a way to honesty and love."

Ezekiel acknowledges that his first collection of verse, *A Time to Change and Other Poems,* is strongly influenced by the work of T. S. Eliot and William Butler Yeats. While combining secular and religious imagery, this volume confirms Ezekiel's commitment to poetry as an aesthetic and moral credo. In his subsequent collections, *Sixty Poems* and *The Third,* Ezekiel chronicles his struggle to achieve inner peace amidst a tumultuous reality. For example, the autobiographical poem "What Frightens Me" explores the process by which the poet overcomes psychological barriers through art. With *The Unfinished Man: Poems,* Ezekiel published what many critics considered to be his most successful metrical poems, including "Jamini Roy," an iambic exercise dedicated to the craft of this Indian folk artist, and "A Morning Walk," which uses an intricate rhyme scheme to capture Bombay's contradictory scenes of opulence and squalor. Adil Jussawalla asserted that *The Unfinished Man: Poems* is "the most perfect book of poems written by an Indian in English. . . . [This is] Ezekiel at his most honest and lyrical best."

In *The Exact Name: Poems, 1960-1964,* Ezekiel moves away from the tightly structured, traditional poetics of his earlier works toward a more experimental free verse. While containing many of Ezekiel's best-known poems—"In India," "Paradise Flycatcher," and "Night of the Scorpion"—this collection also features the often anthologized "Poet, Lover, Birdwatcher." Regarded as among Ezekiel's finest achievements, this piece delineates his poetic ideal of disciplined yet alert observation. Continuing in this experimental mode, Ezekiel's next book of verse, *Hymns in Darkness,* contains poems distinguished by what commentators describe as an increasing sophistication and emotional openness. Christopher Wiseman observed that Ezekiel's poetic voice, "once liberated from formal shackles, has continued to strengthen and deepen, modifying itself perfectly to areas of experience ranging from the mystical to the most realistically social. His new technical ability is an instrument of power and confidence,

capable of many dimensions of tonal variation. Above all, it is his *own* instrument."

In addition to poetry, Ezekiel has written several plays, including *The Sleepwalkers,* a ritualistic farce concerning the arrival of a callous American to India; *Nalini,* in which two men debate whether the female title character exists outside their sexual fantasies; *Marriage Poem,* an examination of an aging husband's self-doubt; and *Song of Deprivation,* an experimental drama featuring two lovers who actively involve the audience in their affair. Although dismissed by some reviewers as inaccessible, these dramas drew acclaim as incisive portraits of moral and spiritual vacuity.

(See also *Contemporary Authors,* Vols. 61-64.)

PRINCIPAL WORKS

POETRY

A Time to Change and Other Poems 1952
Sixty Poems 1953
The Third 1958
The Unfinished Man: Poems 1960; also published as *The Unfinished Man: Poems Written in 1959,* 1965

INDER NATH KHER

Nissim Ezekiel's poetry may be viewed as a metaphoric journey into the heart of existence; into the roots of one's self or being which embodies the mythic as well as the existential dimensions of life. This endless quest for identity, intertwined with the search for a poetics, provides Ezekiel with the sense of creative continuity in his own life. Through juxtaposition of art and life he envisions a state of harmony between the fountain of inner life and the landscape of outer world. Thus, from the existential-esthetic view-point, his poetry represents a structure of imaginative reality in which all the dichotomies of life are encompassed, in which contraries exist side by side, and in which the encountering self seeks resolution out of the tension caused by opposing forces in nature and in the heart of man. This creative structure of reality is an emblem of a continual process which reveals itself through myriad names and forms, relations and themes, failures and realizations. Such a process is embodied most fully in the poems contained in *The Unfinished Man* (1959) and *The Exact Name* (1965).

"Enterprise" (*The Unfinished Man*) deals with the subject of pilgrimage, Ezekiel's metaphor for life and the movement toward its spiritual meaning. The persona or the "I" of the poem goes through an initial experience of elation and the sense of endurance on such a journey:

> It started as a pilgrimage,
> Exalting minds and making all
> The burdens light. The second stage
> Explored but did not test the call.
> The sun beat down to match our rage.
>
> We stood it very well, I thought,
> Observed and put down copious notes
> On things the peasants sold and bought.
> The way of serpents and of goats,
> Three cities where a sage had taught.

But soon the "differences" arise "On how to cross a desert patch" in this primitive hinterland. Intellectual opinions and arguments lead to disintegration and disillusionment. The "copious notes" do not assist in resolving the enigma of life, and "A shadow falls on us—and grows." The journey loses its symbolic significance; it becomes merely topographical. The urge and enthusiasm for the inner meaning wear out:

> We noticed nothing as we went,
> A straggling crowd of little hope,
> Ignoring what the thunder meant . . .

The pilgrims ignore "the thunder" which is symbolic of illumination, and which is related to man's longing for the higher world. And when the goal is reached it does not provide with any sense of accomplishment or fulfillment. . . . The entire purpose and meaning of the pilgrimage is missed. But this does not refer to the failure of the metaphor itself; only the pilgrims who are basically city-dwellers have failed to perceive the nature of the calling. However, the failure on the part of the pilgrims proves paradoxical; their shame and torment lead to the realization which the poet reveals in the last line of the poem:

> Home is where we have to gather grace.

Ezekiel implies here that "grace" or redemption can be obtained through life, in the very act of living in the world. But in so far as "Home" is a metaphor for the self, redemption has to be won also through the private landscape of one's psyche or mind. Both these realms, the outer and the inner, are essential to human growth and fulfillment. Without commitment to life in the world and without journey into the abyss of one's being, the metaphoric pilgrimage of Ezekiel's esthetic vision remains incomplete, though as an everlasting possibility. (pp. 17-18)

Linda Hess informs us: "He (Ezekiel) is a poet of the city, Bombay; a poet of the body; and an endless explorer of the labyrinths of the mind, the devious delving and twisting of the ego, and the ceaseless attempt of man and poet to define himself, and to find through all 'the myth and maze' a way to honesty and love." But we will do well to remember that Ezekiel's poetry dramatizes the tension between the urban and the primal; there is no compromise with the city on its purely mundane terms. It is only through an esthetic strategy or the syncretic vision that he reconciles the opposites; in this metamorphic process the city develops its own primitive roots from within. And it is in this primitive city that the urban artist, Jamini Roy, succeeds and "His all-assenting art survives." The artist is successful because

> He started with a different style,
> He travelled, so he found his roots.
> His rage became a quiet smile
> Prolific in its proper fruits.
>
> A people painted what it saw
> With eyes of supple innocence.
> An urban artist found the law
> To make its spirit sing and dance.
>   (**"Jamani Roy,"** *The Unfinished Man*)

By travelling *within* the self the artist discovers his primordial roots which are also the roots of the city. In this journey his "rage" for meaning is transformed into "a quiet smile," indicating that the artist eventually achieves an awareness of his blissful role, which makes him highly prolific. His art subsumes the realities of existence as seen through the imagination. By finding the primeval law of all life he makes "its spirit sing and dance." But for the city man who is caught up in the phantasmagoria of sex and power there is no redemption; at his best, he has a dim recognition of that part of his being which dreams of higher levels of existence. . . . [The persona of **"Urban"**] is passionately attached to the city and its worn-out tracks of custom and habit. He is always at a great distance from the "hills" which symbolize the loftiness of spirit. His river of life is dry, and "the winds lie dead" in his path, meaning that he is devoid of the creative breath which has the power of regeneration. He does not perceive the rebirth of the skies each morning; nor does he feel the reclining fingers of "the shadows of the night" on his eyes. In other words, he does not experience the life-death continuum within himself. There is no place for sun and rain in his closed system, indicating that he lacks light or warmth, as well as the fertilizing power or creativity. And thus, "His landscape has no depth or height." Even when he "dreams of morning walks, alone, / And floating on a wave of sand," his mind turns its course "Away from beach and tree and stone," images of movement, growth, cohesion and harmony, and he loses himself "To kindred clamour close at hand," or in the confused noise of the city.

By contemplating the contemporary human condition, and by focussing on the urban through an ironic mode of perception, Ezekiel seems to be drawing our attention toward the pastoral or the primordial. As stated earlier, in Ezekiel's esthetic vision the primordial and the urban are integral. His poetry enacts this myth in a variety of ways. But as long as the city man lacks perception of this imaginative reality he is bound to remain incomplete or unfinished, and he will continue to suffer from "The pain of his fragmented view." In **"A Morning Walk"** (*The Unfinished Man*) we witness exactly such a person who is

> Driven from his bed by troubled sleep
> In which he dreamt of being lost
> Upon a hill too high for him

The experience of being "lost" is dialectical, because it is by *losing* oneself in the spirit, symbolized here in the hill of the dream, that one *finds* oneself. However, the city man does not heed the voice of his dream, and

> His native place he could not shun,
> The marsh where things are what they seem

His existence is without "light," and the "Barbaric city" of his habitation, which is "sick with slums," cannot prove to be a source of grace, in spite of its "million purgatorial lanes." Turning away from the unconscious, dream world, which Jung calls "the hinterland of man's mind," the city dweller suffers from the consequent loss of the perceiving power. . . . (pp. 18-20)

[However, by] bringing the protagonists of his poems close to the ironic awareness of their situation Ezekiel suggests the possibility of redemption. From this point of view, his art is highly therapeutic. As a result of this esthetic therapy, he finds several of his poetic characters on the threshold of a new awakening, a mental state in which self-analysis plays a major role. For instance, the protagonist of **"Case Study"** (*The Unfinished Man*) discovers through self-examination that "Whatever he had done was not quite right." He looks back at his "foolish love affair," a fatal political involvement, damned marriage, and the compulsive habit of never sticking to one job. Although he tries to defend himself by saying that "he never moved / Unless he found something he might have loved," his friend, the "me" of the poem, advises him against the stultifying pattern of his life, and warns: "The pattern will remain, unless you break / It with a sudden jerk." Similarly, in **"Event"** (*The Unfinished Man*) the persona experiences revulsion against the sexual love of a woman in whose presence he cannot define his true self. The woman idealizes him, but she hardly understands him. . . . The lovers in **"Marriage"** (*The Unfinished Man*) also come to the bitter realization that their relationship had relied too heavily on sexual intercourse, and that they had murdered their spirituality. . . . (p. 21)

[Such] failures and self-analyses contain the directive toward some meaningful action. Paradoxically speaking, the poems succeed as failures, because without the failures one may not perceive the dichotomy at the heart of existence itself. The action which is generated by these poems manifests itself in the form of an ecstatic love, in an existential plunge into the world, and in the prayer for a poetics. **"Love Sonnet"** (*The Unfinished Man*) realizes the possibility of *love* in which the lovers respond to each other with both body and soul, and also get involved with the world without any trepidation:

> The café, on the hill, among the birds,
> Could house a passing cloud.
>   The city's lights
> Are coming on.
>   You and I wait for words;
> Our love has formed like dew on summer nights.
> The wind has ruffled up our hair:
> We look in consort at the distant sea,
> And feel it turbulent and salty there,
> A passionate and perpetual mystery.
>
> Floating down the hill, as on a cloud,
> Proud as lovers are, inarticulate,
> We lose ourselves in mingling with the crowd,
> Not unafraid of this ambiguous fate. . . .

In this poem the hill on which the lovers meet is not very remote from the city lights. There exists a tangible relationship between the urban and the primitive, the worldly and the spiritual. In a state of perfect harmony, the lovers look down from the hill "at the distant sea" which they perceive as a "passionate and perpetual mystery." The sea symbolizes the flux between life and death. With this imaginative awareness the lovers descend the hill in the manner of floating on a cloud, and their mingling with humanity is achieved without any dissonance, though they express fear at their ambivalent destiny—this fear or terror pervades the heart of creation itself. **"Commitment"** (*The Unfinished Man*) embodies the theme of action as an existential imperative:

> When, with sudden smile, the visions come
> Inviting us to sweet disaster,
> We envy saints their martyrdom
> And press the accelerator.
>
> At once we know that we must leap,
> Although we have not looked ahead,
> Lake falsely calm and mountain steep,
> But we are wiser than the dead.

Through the "visions," action or involvement assumes the form of a religious passion; even disaster looks "sweet" to a man of commitment. The saints obtain their spiritual stature through sufferings; they never betray any sign of fear in the face of existential dangers. It is by envying the paradoxical fortune of a saint that we can quicken the process of our own growth. Doing this we discover the urgent need to "leap" into action and commitment with the world, though our path may be strewn with enormous difficulties. This is the only way *to be*, to exist and become whole, and to look "wiser than the dead" who cannot perceive at all. **"Morning Prayer"** (*The Unfinished Man*) reveals what the poet needs for this type of commitment. The poet asks for privacy and inaccessibility but "only of the soul," and further prays to God:

> Restore my waking time
> To vital present tense,
> And dreams of love or crime
> To primal quiescence.

God grant me certainty
In kinships with the sky,
Air, earth, fire, sea—
And the fresh inward eye.

Whatever the enigma,
The passion of the blood,
Grant me the metaphor
To make it human good.

This is what I referred to earlier as the search for a poetics.
The poet wishes to live in the "vital present tense" which constitutes eternity, and in which everything culminates. He
wants his dreams of love and violence to remain dormant and
silent in the primal consciousness or the unconscious until
they are transformed into forms of meaningful actions. He
seeks absolute relationship with the elements of air, earth, fire
and water—these elements symbolize the central points of
man's material as well as spiritual existence. He entreats to
be gifted with "the fresh inward eye" which will enable him
to have a true perception of things. And finally, he urges God
to bestow upon him the energizing metaphor with which he
hopes to re-create the enigma and the tension of existence for
the benefit of humanity.

Ezekiel's prayer has been answered: he has received the gifts
of the inward eye and poetic power, and a great deal more
besides. He tells us about this bestowal in a number of esthetic modes which dramatize not only the character of the gifts
but also what he has become through them. In **"Two Images"**
(*The Exact Name*) he briefly records the moment of initiation, or the manner in which he received the gifts:

From the long dark tunnel
of that afternoon, crouching, humped,
waiting for the promised land,
I peeped out like a startled animal
and saw a friend flapping his angelic wings.
I welcomed him.

From this moment onwards, the poet gains in spiritual
strength and perspective. He accepts life with all its evil and
good; he does not reject anything. . . . By accepting both
good and evil one eventually transcends them. Those who fail
to see or do not wish to see the relationship between evil and
good lead a life of pretence. In **"A Conjugation"** (*The Exact
Name*), Ezekiel proposes an end to a life of dishonesty and
pretension and, by implication, suggests a life of simplicity
and harmony. In **"Platonic"** (*The Exact Name*) he celebrates
the virtue of simplicity which takes one beyond "the reach
of all but praise or love." In the presence of a simple person
who is the true mirror, who defies the limitations of time and
space, and whose face carries a perennial dawn, the poet discovers his own identity, and addresses himself to it in a firm
and authentic manner:

You have the tone of voice for true or false,
A sense of season, place and element.
Your sunniness is not to be obscured
By people, gods, or ghosts within the blood:
You quietly burn and find the fire good.

With this quiet burning in his heart, and the sunniness on his
face, the poet moves toward "the invisible landscape of love,"
where he learns the precise value of ambivalence, and corrects his former view of words:

The spring was late
but I was impatient.
I used too many words,

and now I know:
There is a point
in being obscure
about the luminous,
the pure musical
phases of living
which ought to be
delicately improvised
and left alone.

(**"In Retrospect,"** *The Exact Name*)

Obtaining this new dimension of complexity or clarity, and
the power to improvise experience, the poet touches and
plays with the hair of his beloved and consummates himself
through her thoughtful love without a word. . . . [Through
sexual union] the male persona comprehends the dual aspects
of the female form. The beast of sex is now perceived as myth
and dream. The imaginative perception of love transforms
the male-female relationship into a ritual, and makes them
whole. (pp. 22-5)

Induced by the inner voice, the poet or the lover leaves "the
safer paths of men," and spontaneously "rides into a marsh
to see the Grail" (**"Perspectives,"** *The Exact Name*). The
quest for the Grail represents the search for "one's inner ad-
hesions" or the primordial source of happiness. Ezekiel looks
for this original centre by plunging *into* the marsh of reality.
However, this poetic plunge *into* existence constitutes, paradoxically, a movement away from all existence. The pragmatic world where the "mundane language of the senses sings /
Its own interpretations" (**"Philosophy,"** *The Exact Name*),
is metamorphosed into "the primal landscape in which God's
mills furiously turn and myths meander like rivers through
a topography of pain." Possessing his Grail or being possessed by it, the poet moves confidently toward the act of improvisation. He tells us the secrets of poetic creation; its
method and process, its objects and rewards, in one of the
most beautiful poems, **"Poet, Lover, Birdwatcher."** . . . (p.
25)

[In the poem's] complex symbolic construct, several of Ezekiel's themes and concerns blend into one another. The poem
reveals the nature of the poetic perception through the network of a highly fecund metaphor in which the images merge
into each other like lovers in the act of love. The poet or the
birdwatcher begins by defining the mood in which all those
who study birds or women must place themselves—birds or
women symbolize freedom, imagination, love and creativity.
A posture of stillness is recommended, because it is in stillness that one listens to the stirrings of the soul, a necessary
prerequisite to the study of freedom and creativity. That is
why the best poets always wait for words from the centre of
stillness before they articulate their experience. This exercise
in waiting is analogous to the patient lover or the birdwatcher's act of "relaxing on a hill / To note the movement of
a timid wing." At the end of this wait, the poetic word appears in the concrete and sensuous form of a woman "who
knows that she is loved," and who surrenders to her lover at
once. In this process, poetry and love, word and woman become intertwined. But this "slow movement" of love and poetry, which shows no irritable haste to arrive at meaning,
does not come by easily. In order to possess the vision of the
rarer birds of his psyche, the poet has to go through the "deserted lanes" of his solitary, private life; he has to walk along
the primal rivers of his consciousness in silence, or travel to
a far off shore which is "like the heart's dark floor." The
image of "thorny" ground refers to the arduous nature of the

poet's mission. It is only after he has gone through this travail that he is able to see the birds or words of poetry in the form of the women who "slowly turn around" not only as "flesh and bone" but also as "myths of light / With darkness at the core." The poet, then, gloats on the slow curving movements of the women, both for the sake of their sensuousness and the apocalypse they bring. He creates his poetry out of these "myths of light" whose essential darkness or mystery remains at the centre of creation itself. But the poet finds the greatest sense or meaning in his own creativity which eventually liberates him from the "crooked, restless flight" of those moments when he strenuously struggles to find the poetic idiom. The poetry which releases the poet from suffering is the medium through which the deaf can hear and the blind see. It is this kind of poetry in which mythology becomes "a structure of human concern," to use Northrop Frye's phrase. And it is this kind of poetry which becomes the true voice of the poet in **"Poetry Reading"** (*The Exact Name*) where the poet's friends "hear him read and be applauded":

> He raised his voice. An image fell
> Like silver coin upon the floor.
> We listened to its echo swell
> That message from another shore.
>
> Where he, released from worldly things,
> Was dumb before the sight he saw:
> His demons wore angelic wings—
> The monstrous truths of moral law.
>
> Against those demons who can win?
> He drank, he drugged himself, he went
> With wives and whores galore. In sin
> And song he spelt out what they meant.

The poet, when "released from worldly things," though not from his *concern* for the human, apprehends his true identity or being. This moment of apprehension makes him dumb or inarticulate; for it is in this moment that he receives the shock of recognition, and discovers both evil and good at the heart of his own being. He sees his demons or the inner ghosts wearing angelic wings, and in this mysterious combination perceives the "truths of moral law," which govern the whole existence. In the initial dread of this perception, the poet calls these truths "monstrous" or absurd. But on being reconciled to the demonic angels or the angelic demons of his being, he drinks, gets intoxicated with the vision, and goes out, metaphorically speaking, with wives and whores simultaneously. What this whole experience *means* is, then, communicated in "sin" and "song" of the poet. The poet's sin constitutes *action* which brings him close to the awareness of his being, and his song constitutes *poetry* which brings us the reverberating "message from another shore." This shore is the abyss of the human heart, which contains the esthetic vision of Nissim Ezekiel. (pp. 26-7)

Inder Nath Kher, " 'That Message from Another Shore': The Esthetic Vision of Nissim Ezekiel," in Mahfil, *Vol. VIII, No. 4, Winter, 1972, pp. 17-28.*

CHETAN KARNANI

For most Indian-English poets, poetry tends to go to two extremes. Either it is a bourgeois dream as in the case of Chaman Revri or it is bohemian practice as in the case of Shasti Bratha. Ezekiel has avoided both the extremes by refusing either to wallow in sloppy sentiment or by becoming a full-time poet in the art for art's sake tradition of Walter Pater. In-

stead, he has followed a healthy mean between these two extremes. While doing many other odd jobs . . . he has continued to show remarkable dedication to the lofty rhyme. Since 1962, he has been Professor of English in a College affiliated to the University of Bombay but his interest in poetry continues unabated.

No other Indian-English poet has shown the ability to organise his experience into words as competently as Ezekiel has done. Unlike other amateurs, aristocrats and philistines of Indian-English verse, he has shown remarkable ability to give his poems a certain finality of form. In this, he has believed in Yeat's dictum that poets, like women, "must labour to be beautiful." In his **"Poet, Lover and Birdwatcher,"** he rightly says that "the best poets wait for words" like an ornithologist sitting in silence by the flowing river or like a lover waiting for his beloved till she "no longer waits but risks surrendering." . . . It is characteristic of Ezekiel to say that the mere warmth of human emotions is not enough for the creation of great poetry unless the heavens grant that greatest gift of genius—the ability to perceive new resemblances. Such a gift enables him to look at the folk art of Jamini Roy with fresh wonder: "The birds are blue aristocrats / Who make my childhood crystallise." The last word shows his rare gift in bringing the word evocatively alive in a new context.

The city of Bombay has to thank one poet who has avoided its burning passion and refused to be 'an active fool.' Ezekiel has managed to create his own Lake Isle of Innisfree: "He dreams of morning walks alone / And floating on a wave of sand." Still, he manages to put up with "kindred clamour close at hand." (pp. 166-67)

What impresses one about Ezekiel is his remarkable sincerity. He is always himself, within his range. His poems are generalisations of his own intimately-felt experiences. His stark bluntness can be seen from the way he describes that complex relationship called **"Marriage"**, wherein the initial excitement—"Our love denied the primal fall"—is followed by a feeling of satiation: "The same thing over and over again." The paradoxical pleasure is summed up in the last three lines: "Why should I ruin the mystery / By harping on the suffering rest / Myself a frequent wedding guest."

Like another distinguished writer, R. K. Narayan, he is unpretentious yet disciplined. Also like Narayan, he avoids the dilettantism and philistinism of Mulk Raj Anand, the pretentiousness and pose of Raja Rao. No intricate symbolism or far-fetched mythology haunts Ezekiel's work, and yet the thing clicks. He believes neither in the bogus repetition of P. Lal nor in the shock tactics of A. K. Ramanujan, yet he creates an authentic effect. His poetry is simple, introspective and analytical. . . . [He] treats poetry as a first-hand record of life's growth.

In these days, if we understand a poem, we get suspicious about its value. . . . At such a time, it is to Ezekiel's credit that he has resisted the temptation to be obscure. His elegance and his communicative efficiency may not please the lovers of Pound and Eliot. His poetry arises from a simple self-questioning attitude. . . . (pp. 167-68)

Ezekiel loves simplicity in poetry as the most important virtue. Hence he chooses to speak from the heart to the heart. His love of the genuine and the authentic is expressed in these words:

> These I have dwelt upon, listening to rain,

And turning in, resolved
That I must wait and train myself
To recognise the real thing,
And in the verse or friends I make
To have no truck with what is fake.

This is true because, in verse, he can occasionally inspire and console in his characteristically aphoristic wisdom: "Not all who fail are counted with the fake."

Ezekiel has believed in the Yeatsian dictum that poetry is essentially a method of organising oneself through words. As a verbal experience, every poem of his shows the gift not only for subtle organisation but also the ability to bring a commonplace word evocatively alive in a new context. (p. 169)

Ezekiel's great achievement lies in the fact that he has avoided—to use his own phrase from the poem **"The Company I Keep"**—"monumentality of vanity" which Indian-English poetry pursues. Instead, he has tried to be authentically Indian without having the faults of his fellow practitioners of verse. Ezekiel is essentially a serious poet. Yet, his experiments in the levity and frivolity of Indian English have retained their own flavour. **"A Very Indian Poem in Indian English," "Goodbye Party for Miss Pushpa"** and **"Irani Restaurant Instructions"** are characteristic products of his love of the Indian soil. He has believed with Yeats that "All that we did, all that we said or sang / Must come from contact with the soil, from that / Contact everything Antaeus-like grew strong." It is because of this belief that he has written many poems which are the characteristic products of the Indian environment. The typical strength of his poetry arises from the fact that he has his ideas firmly rooted in Indian soil. (pp. 169-70)

[Why] he approves of [Indian artist] Bhupen Khakar gives us some idea of Ezekiel's role in Indian-English poetry. He rightly says: "To be in the swim of the contemporary art movements and at the same time to assert a racial heritage that is dormant is a way of being new which, in my opinion, has an absolute value. It opens a vein of creative responsibility." This is equally true about Ezekiel's own achievement in poetry. He has been alive to every new experiment made in the West, yet he has retained characteristic Indianness of his own. (pp. 170-71)

In keeping with the contemporary aesthetic, Ezekiel does not like poetry which involves direct self-expression. He believes that in the poetry of Dom Moraes, slickness has occasionally become a substitute for depth. After all, Ezekiel's own ability to organise himself in verse marks him out as a different poet from the romantic attitudinising of Dom Moraes. The latter gives the impression of having turned his autobiography into his poetry. A large number of poems in his selection *poems* (1955-1965), give the impression as if he has worked certain key passages of his Autobiography *My son's father* into the poetic mould. Ezekiel does not like such direct self-expression. . . . On the other hand, Ezekiel's poetry sometimes illustrates Eliot's dictum of an 'escape from personality.' Because, Moraes's poetry is the direct self-expression of his personality, hence he does not give any idea of growth. While Ezekiel's poetry is the record of the various stages in the journey of his life: "The middle of his journey nears / Is he among the men of straw / Who think they go which way they please."

It is on this account that Ezekiel has been cautious and disciplined in his expression. I agree with David McCutchion who has rightly commented that Ezekiel

> belongs with Thom Gunn, R. S. Thomas, Elizabeth Jennings, Anthony Thwaite, and others like them. He has their cautions, discriminating style, precise and analytical, with its conscious rejection of the heroic and passionate as also of the sentimental and cosy. The technique is immaculate: rhymes, and carefully varied yet regular rhythms, lines that run over with a poised deliberateness. But behind the casual assurance one senses the clenched fist, the wounded tenderness.

Ezekiel does not allow himself the luxury of Moraes' smooth and bland style. Ezekiel's poetry contains some fine aphoristic wisdom born out of the fact that "the best poets wait for words". He writes slowly with his eye fixed steadily on the object. He is always in the pursuit of the exact name. (pp. 171-72)

Ezekiel not only borrowed the title of his major work *The Unfinished Man* from Yeats but also like the great Irish poet, he aspired to have 'the right mastery of natural things.' In the process of realising this aspiration, he wrote 'the book of the people.' He treated his poems as a source of remaking himself. Hence, all his felt thoughts in their sensuous richness give us a shock of recognition because he says what we feel. Thus, the later Yeats who talked of "Warty lads / That by their bodies lay" finds a similar honest echo in Ezekiel's line: "The use of nakedness is good." Ezekiel has always tried to say what all people experience. The following lines are a characteristic example of this aspiration of his art: "Always the body knows its nakedness / The first baptism is not in water / But in fire."

In our time, each major English-speaking country can claim a poet who has made his region memorable through the use of that common foreign tongue—the English language. America with her Robert Lowell, Canada with Irving Layton, Australia with A. D. Hope, Ireland with Austin Clarke and Scotland with Hugh Macdiarmid. Ezekiel, in his own modest way, has tried to express the Indian ethos through the English language. His aspiration has been to give expression to the genius of the soul of India. Hence, he has never shown any desire to go and settle abroad. He is a poet of the city, Bombay, and remains rooted in that metropolitan soil. Except for a few short spells abroad, he has always remained in India. He has said it explicitly:

I have made my commitments now.
This is one, to stay where I am,
As others choose to give themselves
In some remote and backward place.
My backward place is where I am.

But one can't escape the impression that Ezekiel has remained backward because he belongs to the 'backward place.' As the God-father of Indian-English poetry, he doesn't have to feel that tough sense of competition that other poets have to face in some parts of the world. This has tended to inhibit his art because it has given him an undesirable sense of complacency. . . . This has tended to create a certain smugness which is not an ideal condition for the creation of great poetry. He suffers from certain sense of insularity in so far as he has few rivals in India. . . . His later poetry has shown a marked decline because flattery—a too common phenomenon in India—has spoilt him. Considering his talent and his mastery of the craft, he gives the impression that he has failed himself. Though it is to his credit that he is still hopeful that he will do full justice to his talent.

When Suresh Kohli asked him about the influences on him, Ezekiel gave a characteristic reply: "A clear influence is no proof of a poem's merit. Quite the contrary I was not influenced by Yeats after *The Unfinished Man,* nor by Eliot and Pound after *Sixty Poems* . . . All this talk about influences may be of some value only when I write really good poetry during the next ten years or so, which I certainly hope to do." If this is so, then the best is yet to be. It is to the credit of Ezekiel that he has outgrown the early influences on him and discovered his own authentic voice. He has rightly said: "It is possible to be a good minor poet, without major delusions." This modestly, sums up his own special effort. He has extreme distrust of theorising. Most Indian poets start placing themselves even before the first collection is out. But after five collections, Ezekiel continues to devote himself to the muse in the hope that the days to come will enable him to write something even better than *The Unfinished Man.*

But the real trouble is: Does Ezekiel whole-heartedly devote himself to poetry? He tends to get distracted into too many extra-curricular activities. He is not only seriously interested in art criticism but also in L.S.D., parapsychology, Hindu mysticism and many other subjects. . . . I have a suspicion that Ezekiel has not been the sort of poet he should have been because he has not shown whole-time, persistent application to the task. Contrary to his expectations, his recent poetry has showed a marked decline. One reason is that he exposes himself to bad poetry [as an editor] and the argument against bad poetry is that it incapacitates us for the appreciation and the writing of good poetry. But Ezekiel seems to prefer human interest to personal achievement. It is on this account that he can't resist the temptation to edit a new journal. (pp. 173-76)

In the days to come, how good a poet Ezekiel becomes depends partly on how successfully he is able to synthesise his diverse interests. But as it is, Ezekiel's criticism of Jehangir Sabavala applies in his case as well. His charge that Sabavala's art is harmonious without having anything to harmonise; and that it lacks tension, is equally true about his own recent poetry. To quote Ezekiel: "Where turmoil is bypassed, complacent stereotypes replace the unsettling function of ideas, and pictorial beauty hides the absence of resolved tension." His own poetry is, likewise, full of 'complacent stereotypes.' It is bland and smooth, without intellectual turmoil and without any struggle to reconcile opposites. It lacks that heroic effort which was Yeats' ideal: "When I was young / I had not given a penny for a song / Did not the poet sing it with such air / That one believed he had a sword upstairs?" Ezekiel has aspired for the simple and the sublime, rather than the intricate and the beautiful.

In the article on Sabavala, Ezekiel goes on to speak the truth bluntly: "The personality projected in his paintings is that of the socialised, bourgeois-adjusted individual, undisturbed by the elemental forces of life and nature, remote from conflict, contradiction, tragedy and turbulence, within the psyche and outside." It is precisely the absence of this turmoil and turbulence which makes Ezekiel's recent poetry read like occasional verse. He was great in *The Unfinished Man* where he had tensions to reconcile; but in most other poems, in *The Exact Name* and later, he is too matter-of-fact and pedestrian to make any profound or permanent appeal. Poems like **"Virginal," "A Warning"** and **"A Woman Observed"** give the impression of superficiality because he does not have much to say and because he has no tensions to reconcile. It is the grand old daddy of Indian-English literature talking platitudes to his children. But in all this, Ezekiel now seems to believe in the Indian, rather than the Western, view of literature. For us, the function of literature is to give joy 'Ananda' rather than catharsis. So why believe in Aristotle, when our own theorists like Abhinav Gupta have given us *rasanubhava.* After all, joy is nearer to our hearts than purgation. The more Ezekiel has lived in India, the more he has tended to believe—to use the classification of Edmund Burke—in the sublime rather than in the beautiful.

This is all the more surprising because Ezekiel started as a rebel with a total distrust of the Indian tradition. He did not like the sing-song manner, the so-called lyrical stuff of Sarojini Naidu. About Toru Dutt, Ezekiel said that as far he is concerned, "the interest of Toru Dutt's poetry is severely limited." Finally, he did not even like the high priest of Indian-English literature, Aurobindo Ghosh. . . . Against this background, Adil Jussawalla has given a very balanced statement about the achievement of Ezekiel:

> Compared to the loose horrors of our early Romantics it is even an important achievement, for Ezekiel is perhaps the first Indian poet consistently to show Indian readers that craftsmanship is as important to a poem as its subject matter. It would be a pity if the clean straightforward line he has used so successfully in the past were abandoned for the muddier metronomics of his latest work.

It is unfortunate that Ezekiel treated the singing line as a luxury in his later poetry. He aspired to a different sort of structure and to the musical phrase. This was not arbitrary. He had some feeling for the units separately and the whole within which the units functioned. Nevertheless, Ezekiel failed to create the impact of his early verse. . . . A. Alvarez rightly commented in the introduction to his Penguin anthology *The New Poetry* (1962): "Since about 1930 the machinery of modern English poetry seems to have been controlled by a series of negative feedbacks designed to produce precisely the effect Hardy wanted." Hardy was right in predicting the futility of *verse libre.* His own and Yeats' example showed that one can still write grandly 'on the old themes in the old styles.' But after 1965, Ezekiel gradually decided to give up this practice. If he persists with his muddy metronomics, the result may not be happy. Because, temperamentally, he still seems to be in the tradition of the last romantics who choose for their theme "Traditional sanctity and loveliness; / . . . whatever most can bless / The mind of man or elevate a rhyme." But for this sense of musical delight, provided by metre and rhyme, Ezekiel's poetry loses its dancing quality.

About many poems that Ezekiel wrote after *The Unfinished Man,* one can only recall the profound statement of Paul Valery: "Certain states of mind, called poetic, produce poems; other states would lead to a proposition." Ezekiel's later poetry has all the weakness of propositions. It suffers from an uncertain groping rhythm. Its ways are arbitrary and tentative. He seems to be finding his way along without knowing any settled destination. It is surprising that Ezekiel accused William Carlos Williams of looseness of structure, but subsequently he committed the same mistake himself.

The fact that Ezekiel was master of the traditional forms could even be seen in *The Exact Name.* After the success of Eliot's Sweeney poems, he wrote an abab rhyme scheme with the calm self-assurance of a master. Poems like **"Poetry Reading," "Art Lecture," "Event"** are written with remarkable success in this rather difficult form. The fact that Ezekiel had a brilliant mastery of prosody could be seen from all the poems written in **The Unfinished Man.** (pp. 177-80)

Besides his mastery of prosody, Ezekiel has cultivated a restrained conversational style. His mastery of tone and ironic control strongly suggest Dryden. Also, like that great master of English poetry, he has maintained remarkable purity of diction in his verse. In this respect, he is closer to Johnson and Goldsmith than to any one else. He has shunned the vast romantic excesses; instead, he has maintained admirable restraint in his expression. (p. 181)

Whether in religion or in politics, Ezekiel has not been fascinated by any particular dogma or ideology. In this flexibility, he has tended to believe in Keats' dictum: "What shocks a moral philosopher, delights the chameleon poet." In **The Third,** the poem on **"Prayer"** jostles side by side with those on erotics. It is on this account that Ezekiel is a poet who has worked within various traditions. He is a Jewish Maharashtrian who chose not to write in Marathi because he was educated in English medium schools. As far as Judaism is concerned, it is at present very imperceptible in his poetry. He refers to himself as 'a mugging Jew among the wolves.' Likewise, his references to Buddhism are as peripheral as those to Christianity. . . . Ezekiel tends to use these traditions as his intellectual framework. Otherwise, in his beliefs, he has maintained remarkable freedom from any rigidity or orthodoxy. The reason for this is to be sought in the fact that in his scale of values, Ezekiel is very close to that grand old man of poetry, Robert Graves. David McCutchion rightly said: "Robert Graves . . . rejected the visionary for the real, politics for human relationships, lyricism for the rugged truth." What Robert Graves did long ago, Ezekiel has done with renewed vigour and freshness now.

It is a pity that in India, we do not read poetry; we merely talk about it. Ezekiel has no faith in unnecessary theorising. That is why the high quality of his poetry runs parallel to the tartness of his replies in P. Lal's questionnaire. He had the courage to say: "The Indo-Anglian background is undoubtedly not a very helpful one, but it is up to writers to make the best possible use of it. Good writing has often been done in the worst possible cultural conditions." Ezekiel has not frittered away his energies on whether Indians can or cannot write in English, or on an another pompous question, whether they can change and recreate the English language. He has settled down to the task of writing poetry instead of bothering about these futile, theoretical questions. This is as it should be. Most Indian-English poets are bothered more about 'commitment' or "the recreation of language' than about the writing and reading of great poetry. . . . If literature is to progress in India, we should put certain moratorium on unnecessary theorising which does not have the corresponding practice to match that theory. In this respect, Ezekiel's example has been a very helpful one to aspiring Indo-Anglian poets. He, more than any one else, has tried to create the right sort of environment in which the arts can thrive.

His achievement is all the greater because he has not only been a competent critic but also a devoted poet. William Walsh was right when he said: "Ezekiel's poetry more than that of any other of these writers seems to be generated from within and to have within it a natural capacity for develop-

ment. It is intellectually complex, mobile in phrasing, fastidious in diction, and austere in acceptance." (pp. 182-84)

Chetan Karnani, in Nissim Ezekiel, *Arnold Heinemann Publishers (India) Private Limited, 1974, 192 p.*

FRITZ BLACKWELL

[In an interview conducted in 1972], Nissim Ezekiel stated that he was then "at work on some new plays" and felt "a loss of interest in the first lot," though his interest in them, he went on, "may revive later." Earlier in his remarks he stated that he did not "think too badly" of his plays, but also did not "think very highly of them either."

In light of this, if not outrightly presumptuous, it is at least premature to reach any critical conclusions. As Ezekiel himself put it in the interview: "I've been writing poetry for more than twenty years, while my plays were all written in 1968, quite recently. It is too early for me to start making comments on them." Perhaps in time, with any revisions and some new plays, penetrating critical assessment on his plays can be made, whether merely as a separate corpus of works, or in relation to his poetry, or in relation to other Indo-Anglian drama. . . .

Nevertheless, even with the reservations, it could be of some profit to note the common dramatic outlook and methodology in four of his readily accessible plays: [**Nalini, Marriage Poem, The Sleepwalkers,** and **Song of Deprivation**]. . . . All are short; the longest (which Ezekiel referred to as "the full-length one" in the interview), though three acts is only about forty-five pages. . . . (p. 265)

All exhibit a stylistic approach which frankly admits itself as theatre. One, **The Sleepwalkers,** subtitled An Indo-American Farce, is ritualistic in tone, opening with a parody of The Lord Prayer: "Give us this day our daily American," followed by a lengthy listing of the kinds of daily American: "Our American Town Planner," "Our American Traffic Control Expert," and so on. All characters, except, significantly, a bearer, wear masks; and, according to the directions at the start of the play, the director "should seek to 'type' them and avoid individuality." At one point the eight Indians in the play (again, not including the bearer), do "a circular sleepwalk" around the four Americans; here, elsewhere, cliches are effectively used—effectively, due in a large part to the ritual style of the play. . . . The play is humorous, but at the same time uncomfortable—I'm sure to Indians as well as to Americans.

Two others, **Nalini,** subtitled A Comedy in Three Acts, and **Song of Deprivation,** subtitled A Comic Morality in One Act for the Non-existent Underground Theatre in India, have the characters admit at the end of the play that they are, indeed, in a play. This is done somewhat more effectively in **Nalini.** The two male characters are trying to decide which Nalini— the girl of their sexual fantasies, an object, or the actual person, who refuses to be objectified—is real. They call for the front bell to ring, which is to signal Nalini's entrance. It does not ring, then, finally, "a violent ring fills the auditorium and resounds in it." Wondering who did it, one character tells the other that "it couldn't be the stage manager. He's a gentleman." The other replies that "it couldn't be the author, either. He's a gentleman too." One declares, "That was no ordinary bell, more like some natural force." The other replies,

"Some historical force." They continue their roles, having another drink and discussing whether to go to the movies; yet, they maintain their recognition of their theatrical position, yelling out orders to whoever is offstage controlling the electricity. Of course exactly the opposite of what they request is done.

In *Song of Deprivation,* which involves a phone conversation between the only two characters, two ultra-mod, sexually-oriented lovers, "He" and "She," the characters finally recognize and acknowledge the presence of the audience, hide from them behind screens, and remove the only stage prop—another screen—which separates them. They continually tell the audience to go away, obviously for reasons of privacy. It is probably meant to be for reasons of effect as well, but one would have to see the play to determine whether or not it is an effective device; on paper it does not seem so. . . . (pp. 265-66)

In both plays the admission of the play as a play, suspending reality as it were, strikes one as more of a recognition on the part of the characters than a conscious, or at least effective, theatrical approach. Certainly it is not Brechtian, wherein the audience from the beginning is made aware, and continually reminded, that the play is just that—a play. It could also be contrasted to other Indian plays in which the audience is alerted at the start of the style of approach to be used. . . . (p. 266)

Since the audience itself is not involved in the breaking of the "illusion" in *Nalini,* the effect is not disastrous; but it certainly seems so in *Song of Deprivation.* There is no "theatrical illusion" to break in *The Sleepwalkers,* as it starts in a ritualized manner—with immediate suspension of any sense of realism. In *Marriage Poem* the theatrical illusion, though by no means purely "realistic," is maintained to the end.

Yet each of the four plays is an effective expose of reality, of the hollowness people contrive for themselves. In *Nalini* it involves two young advertising executives who are such simply because they can be nothing else. They also "are Indian by accident of birth," neither fish nor fowl, and reminiscent of Ezekiel's poem of the Indian figure with the Cezanne slung around his neck. They are unable to cope with a woman as a person, but only as "women," and do not really know each other as individuals; their lives—life, perhaps, as there's little to distinguish between them—are not only hollow, but repetitious: "Another drink, another girl, another party, another sales conference, another exhibition, another play to be produced with all those stirring ideas in it, another visit from you and friends like you, another record on the gramophone"; even their lines are repetitious, as is eminently shown in one character's self-description, first to his friend, then repeated to the girl. At least one of the two realizes the situation, but appears unwilling, if even at all able, to do anything about it. Their situation seems even more pitiable than that of Beckett's two tramps: they are not even waiting for anything.

Marriage Poem, aptly subtitled A Tragi-comedy, is an effective treatment of the familiar marriage-at-the-menopause; not the woman's, but the man's—and consequently the marriage's. The intentional melodrama is reinforced by continuous background music which, as the opening stage directions say, is "heard softly . . . when the dialogue is going on and . . . loudly at every pause." The wife has the ubiquitous next-door-neighbor to complain to, and the husband "the other woman" for sympathy. Whether either is real or merely

imaginary is intentionally unclear, as each appears in dream-like sequences, fading in and out; of course, the actual physical reality of either is irrelevant. What is important is the existence of the children, who knock on the door at the end, the husband saying, "The children," the wife, "Our children." There is also another couple, bringing out the frustrations and weaknesses of the primary couple. (pp. 267-68)

[These] characters are not important as individuals, but as clear types. In all four plays the characters are distinctly and purposely types, for it is the situation that is central and dominant. There is no psychological development; these are not plays of individual character analysis, and that is most clearly seen in the typing involved in *The Sleepwalkers.*

The play involves a reception for a visiting American publisher and his wife, grossly (and unfortunately, typically) ignorant about India, and equally as grossly ignorant and uncaring about their ignorance. It is a rich play, and powerful. All the obvious tritenesses and cliches are employed—but as art, not propaganda. There is an American publisher, whose first lines are, "Hi, folks. Call me Ed." There's the inveterate writer in Hindi, "India's national language," who's done "one hundred and eighty-seven short stories in Hindi. Also, four hundred and seventeen poems. In Hindi I am one of the well-known writers." He is counter-balanced by Miss Ganguly, who does Family Planning plays for the villagers, and observes that "Bengali has the most advanced literature in India . . . according to foreign observers." Then there is the professor (with the silent wife) who points out the spiritual and cultural richness of India, which is in contrast to American materialism (and who also has not revised his lectures—which are actually his college notes—in twenty years). There is the typical reference to the Ford Foundation and the Rockefeller Foundation in relation to the population problem, with the suggestion (by the American) that they might "agree to finance a night-club in every Indian village," in order to provide a form of entertainment besides that of copulation. . . . (p. 268)

The American couple flies off to see "the real India"—more writers, followed by a visit "to the Gir Forest for a glimpse of the lions there," while the Indians resume (and also close the play with) the "Give us this day our daily American" litany.

The intent of the playwright is obvious, and needs no comment other than to say that it is a testimonial to his talents that what could easily have been heavy-handed and trivial has been handled with such deftness, irony, and humor.

The fourth play, *Song of Deprivation,* reveals contemporary hollowness no less than the other three, although with less of the dramatic rapidity and lightness of touch which makes the other three so effective. It involves the same use of repetition, of triteness, and of cliche, but perhaps in too unstructured a manner (it must be most difficult to dramatically structure a phone conversation of such length), and falls apart at the end with a suddenly out-of-character (for both the girl and the play) idealistic speech by the female, and the attempt to use the audience as a theatrical device. But there are some effective lines, revealing the characters' mindlessness and obsession with trivia (including sexual trivia—while obviously adult their vicarious attitude seems almost teen-agerish; a sort of Frankie Avalon and Annette Funicello for the seventies—or at least the late sixties).

The hollowness inherent in the plays, and the playwright's

careful manipulation of the characters as types so that the situation dominates, are reinforced by and allow for a third characteristic: an expose of not merely a mindlessness, but an anti-thought outlook characteristic of contemporary society. This underscores *Song of Deprivation:* the characters seem to view life as a beach party, with the fun spoiled by grandmother and society; they speak of freedom, but are completely unconcerned with responsibility. Indeed, for them freedom means merely license. (p. 269)

There are a number of places in *Nalini* where thought is denigrated. One of the male characters, asking, "Why should we be mere spectators of life?" (a line and outlook, incidentally, too much like that expressed by the girl toward the end of *Song of Deprivation* to be coincidental), answers himself: "One can break out and find a new pattern, a direct, fresh knowledge of life through action, through impulsive, bold action. I don't mean we shouldn't think. We *should* think about it, afterwards." The girl asks, "After we have acted?" and he replies, "Yes, after we have acted." She asks then how one knows "when to act," and he replies that "the time to act is always now" (of course, he himself takes no action). Later he refers to himself as "not an intellectual." He condemns Nalini to his friend: "She has ideas, damn her. . . . She's an independent woman, with the intelligence of a man and the determination of an orthodox Indian mother-in-law. She's a living insult to me and to you, to all of us. Damn her." His friend laughs, "I understand. You made advances to her and she turned you down." His code, and final justification for his job—and perhaps his existence—is that "everybody in the profession dresses well. I can't stand people who don't dress well." Yet even his self-analyses, or more correctly, self-observations, are rejected by his friend: "Well, I must be going. I'm not an intellectual. I don't understand all these big questions, and your big answers." The "big questions" with the "big answers" are merely a series of admissions that exemplify his hollowness—and his hollowness as a type; it's not a Freudian individual analysis, but a social comment:

> We are modern only as it suits us, but we don't fight for the modern against the dying and the dead. We are liberal only as it suits us, but we don't fight for the liberal against the orthodox and the tyrannical. We are advanced only as it suits us, but we don't fight for the advanced against the backward and the primitive. We are progressive very cautiously, without ever confronting the forces that pull this country down. We are Indian by accident of birth, we are . . . (*here he is interrupted, his friend impatient*).

Perhaps the major point of *Marriage Poem* is the hollowness that develops in a marriage in which thought dies. On the one hand there's the problem that arises when a wife comes to know a husband too well—at least as conceived by the husband: "No more mystery in him, no more prospect of the unpredictable. Every weakness clearly seen, every strength seen through for the fraud it is." Yet, when the wife of the secondary or supporting couple observes that "husband and wife always think differently," her husband objects that it's true "only to the extent that any two persons think differently, if they think at all." And that is the heart of the problem, "if they think at all." Usually they don't, or at least in this play.

After the second couple leaves, the wife of the central couple says, "You never want to say anything to your wife. But when visitors come, you know how to talk. What long speeches!" She summarizes what he had said, dismisses it as

"rubbish," and asks what it all means. He tells her she wouldn't understand. She sneers no, but that Malati—the other woman—"understood it, of course." "I'm sure she did." "Why are you so sure?" "She's an understanding woman, that's why." "Every woman is an understanding woman, except your wife." Throughout the play, again and again, they agree to quit quarreling, only to resume in a few lines. But it is not with any such rational solution that the play ends, but with the arrival of the children, who seem to be all that cements their marriage.

The anti-thought characteristic is most obviously displayed in *The Sleepwalkers*—in the rhythmic opening and close, the mindless cliches, the bits of trivia, the title itself. It is blatantly—but effectively—developed in the descriptions of and references to the American magazine which the publisher wishes to issue in India. . . . It is called *Blank*. It has "lots of pictures and things," few words. Its publisher explains it . . . :

> Let me put it this way. We live today in one world. We are all human, even the communists. Yet we are all divided and unhappy. What is the chief cause of division and unhappiness? Thinking. If we discourage thought, we shall decrease unhappiness. . . . In my magazine, there is no thought. We only describe. We don't say something is good and something else is bad. We merely report it. We present it. We tell our readers what is going on. They can be up-to-date, without thinking. The very latest in everything is reported, what is, what does. We flow along. We are happy or at least contented. We eat, we drink, we see, we hear, we touch. Life is happening all the time, and we happen with it. We don't analyse. We don't separate one thing from another. We don't make any distinction between what is important and what is unimportant. That makes for discomfort. Everything that happens is important and unimportant. They merge, they become one. We merge with it. We are with it, we swing along. We happen. In that way we discourage ideas.

The Hindi writer suggests that his stories "are perfectly suitable" for the magazine, as, "My critics say that they are totally without thought." Someone else observes that "a magazine without thought will be popular with Indian women." The professor points out that it is an Indian ideal "to transcend thought, to reach a state of mind where thought is unnecessary," to which the American publisher replies, "We Americans find that too high for us. We prefer to be below thought, not above it."

Perhaps the crux of this and the other plays is expressed by the American publisher when asked his magazine's central technique: "The person is depersonalized, treated as a thing, something to which something happened."

It is the situation—or, as in *Nalini,* some "force"—that depersonalizes, results in thoughtless types; man becomes a thing, "something to which something happened."

Yet it is man's hollowness, thoughtlessness—literally—that makes the situation. While he may appear a mere cog, it is by his own, and his fellow's, doing. (pp. 269-71)

[A] final word should be said about the over-all technical or esthetic quality of these plays. In an article relating his experiences as one of five judges for "The Sultan Padamsee Award", which offered Rs. 5000 "for the best full-length play in English by an Indian," and drew eighty-three entries, Ezekiel noted:

Reading the plays had provided invaluable insight into the minds of a representative cross-section of Indians who speak, read and write mainly or exclusively in English. It had also revealed in a drastic way the complex difficulties of playwriting, the technical hurdles to be crossed, the relentless exposure of weaknesses in the writer's inner knowledge of the stage and its conditions, the extensive demands on the author's familiarity with the speech habits of the prototypes of the characters in real life.

One could apply all this in regard to Ezekiel's own plays, though they would come out, I'm sure, far stronger in regard to his criteria than the vast majority of the plays submitted for the award. For that matter, on the whole they would rank high in comparison with other Indian plays available in English, whether written in it, or translated from other languages. (p. 272)

Fritz Blackwell, "Four Plays of Nissim Ezekiel," in Journal of South Asian Literature, Vol. XI, Nos. 3 & 4, Spring-Summer, 1976, pp. 265-72.

CHRISTOPHER WISEMAN

The Exact Name is a fascinating volume of poetry, not only for its quality and its evidence of a major extension of the poet's themes, but because of its pivotal position in the development of Ezekiel's craftsmanship and poetic techniques. In this collection we can see a poetic in transition; a new voice slowly making itself heard as an important poet tries to cast off derivative techniques and break away from forms which are beginning to stifle and constrict him in a damaging way. *The Exact Name* embodies three distinct voices or styles representing the old, the transitional and the new, and in this paper I hope to show, by a technical examination of some of the poems, the development of new techniques and the strong thrust towards a new and personally viable poetic.

Prior to *The Exact Name,* Ezekiel's poetry is notable for an extreme technical formality. In this, of course, he was merely reflecting the conventions of the 1950's, when most poets of the English-speaking world were obsessed with low-toned poetry, carefully worked in traditional metrical and stanzaic forms. Auden, Empson, Graves, Yeats, Frost were looked to for inspiration and imitation; sestinas, villanelles and many kinds of traditional forms were rediscovered and employed. The fastidious use of meter, rhyme and stanza-form was highly appropriate for the understated ironic modes which were so typical of the 1950's; the influence of American West Coast and Black Mountain poets was still an unworrying distant echo, exotic but by no means threatening to the poetic mainstream.

Not surprisingly, Ezekiel's poetry of this period fits squarely into this convention with strong meters, formal stanza structures and regular rhyme. It is my contention, however, that he is never completely happy in this style, that it often restricts and limits him, and that his own real voice is often suppressed. It is, I think, significant that Ezekiel never experimented with traditional forms to the extent that most British or American poets did, seeming to be content with strict accentual-syllabic patterns and relatively straight-forward stanza-forms, and, for all his obvious innate talent, many of his earlier poems suffer from an almost mechanical rigidity, a monotony of sound which deadens and weighs down the bright buoyancy of his content.

We may usefully look at *The Unfinished Man* (1959) for examples of this "old" style. All ten poems are exactly regular in form. All are fully rhymed, all are written in regular stanzas and iambic meter. Most poets, when using strict forms, rely heavily on variations to give rhythmic power and subtlety, especially through the employment of foot-substitutions, run-on lines and half-rhymes. The patterns of meter, stanza and rhyme become norms against which variations are sounded, moving away from and back towards the pattern in a creative tension. What we miss in *The Unfinished Man* is sufficient variety. In good poetry, prosody articulates the movement of feeling, and the total meaning of a poem includes the meaning of its rhythmic structures as these trace and define emotional and psychological processes. In these poems Ezekiel's sound patterns are astoundingly rigid. Very few foot-substitutions—even of the common trochee and anapest—vary the heavy iambic pulse, and this heaviness is emphasized by the fact that he uses many fewer run-on lines than most poets. For example, "Jamini Roy" has not one foot-substitution. The poem consists of sixty-four iambic feet one after the other with only six run-on lines out of sixteen, making the sound ponderous and insistent. This is heightened by the use of two-line end-stopped sentences, where the syntax reinforces the stilted effect instead of playing dynamically and expressively against the metre and the line breaks. . . . [The poem] is reduced in power by the clumsy rigidity of its sound; a mechanical application of form which functions as a constricting claustrophobic force.

Similarly, "Case Study," with its very tight rhyme scheme (a b a b b) suffers from a startling inflexibility, especially in the use of metre. Let us consider the last stanza:

He came to me and this is what I said:
"The pattern will remain, unless you break
It with a sudden jerk; but use your head.
Not all returned as heroes who had fled
In wanting both to have and eat the cake.
Not all who fail are counted with the fake."

We notice immediately the weakness, even triteness, of lines 1 and 5, which seem little more than mechanical fillers of the metrical form. We cannot help hearing, too, the plodding regularity of the iambic feet, again completely unrelieved by substitution, and only salvaged temporarily by the enjambement after line 2. The inflexible sound is exaggerated even more by the number of monosyllabic words—forty-four out of fifty-two in this stanza—which pound the meter into the ear with massive force. In a thirty-line pentameter poem there are only three minor foot-substitutions, only two rhymes which are not full and strong. Again I have to suggest that the ambitious content of the poem is restricted by the clumsiness of the technique; the psychological subtleties of the "case study" are crudified and coarsened by the unyielding shape into which Ezekiel has forced them.

The Unfinished Man suffers throughout from such technical problems. "Urban" is marred by an unnatural rhyme-forced inversion and archaic diction at its climax. . . . "A Morning Walk"—potentially a fine poem—contains a second stanza of some awkwardness, in terms of meter, end-stopping and forced rhyme. "Love Sonnet," better in its use of foot-substitutions, has one awkward line of only four feet in its pentameter structure. "Commitment"—a regular tetrameter poem—starts with confused sound properties as the first stanza opens with a pentameter line and ends with a trimeter. And so on. When one compares these poems with the metrical poetry of, say, Philip Larkin or Auden, it is clear that Ezekiel is just not using the regular forms with any degree of subtlety or variety; that the forms are, in fact, constricting and limiting the content, not energizing it; that they are being applied mechanically instead of being employed as useful norms against which to play dynamic variations of pace, shape and sound. In these poems, the rhythm of developing feeling is too often distorted and held in check. However, in the five or six years subsequent to the publication of *The Unfinished Man* we can see a fascinating attempt by Ezekiel to break away from this formal straitjacket and discover his own real voice.

It is interesting that the epigraph in *The Exact Name,* from Jiménez, contains the lines "Let my word be / The thing itself / Newly created by my soul," which, although not specifically referring to poetic technique, bears strongly upon the importance of formal renewal. The need for the word to be closely correlated to experience and deeply personal and individualized implies a language and technique less artificial, participating more intensely with life and perception, and it is towards this that the poetry in *The Exact Name* moves, however slowly and, at times, falteringly.

I have suggested that in *The Exact Name* we find three kinds of style—the "old," which I have discussed briefly above; a transitional style, where there is a clear attempt to loosen the ties of exact form; and a new style, where the poet's own voice finally breaks through. It is my intention to concentrate on transitional poems and those in the new style in order to demonstrate the significant changes taking place in Ezekiel's work at this time.

Eight of the twenty poems in *The Exact Name* are in the "old" style and show, to a large degree, the deficiencies of technique I have suggested as characteristic. These poems are **"Philosophy," "Poetry Reading," "Virginal," "Love Poem," "Platonic," "Perspective," "Fruit"** and **"Art Lecture."** None of them, with the exception of **"Art Lecture,"** is quite as rigid or technically inflexible as the poems of *The Unfinished Man,* but they all share many of the same problems, especially in the area of metrical monotony. Admittedly, some of them, especially **"Love Poem"** and **"Philosophy,"** are interesting and quite successful. But there still remains a suspicion that the forms are not quite natural, that the poet's own voice is being sacrificed to a literary convention assumed by habit. There is a throttled quality about many of these poems; a sense of feeling held too tightly in check and swelling impotently and painfully in its bonds. The discovery of techniques which can shape and release feelings in their own natural forms is by now essential, and in the other poems of this volume we can clearly see that discovery being made.

The transitional poems here are characterized by a greater or lesser degree of movement away from insistent regularity of meter, rhyme, syntax and stanza structure. We find examples of blank verse and free verse for the first time, and under the pressure of new and excited content, we discover much more life and exhilaration in the forms being used. It is as if the old forms can no longer contain the eruption of new visionary and social insights, and the sudden new confidence of a personal and important subject matter gives the poet the strength to abandon previously comforting but increasingly sterile habits.

The transitional poems vary from those which are regular but which use more flexibility and variation to those which break from regular patterns. **"Poet, Lover, Bird-Watcher"** belongs to the former category. Here we have a poem based on a standard iambic pentameter line, in two closely rhymed ten-line stanzas, but strongly hinting at a new kind of straining at the shackles of the form. This is a justly celebrated poem, containing a beautifully worked set of images moving, as the title suggests, on three interpenetrating levels. The rich quiet density of the texture is most impressive and is helped by a new, but still minor, breaking of the formal pattern. For instance, in the twenty lines we find ten run-ons—a far higher proportion than in most of the poet's traditional poems—which allows the syntax much more scope in defining pace and emphasis, and in following emotional and intellectual rhythms in a natural way. The sentences are much longer than usual, exactly embodying the urgent but meditative movement of the experience. At the beginning of the second stanza the pentameter breaks as something of the poet's visionary and metaphoric intensity takes over:

> The slow movement seems, somehow, to say much more.
> To watch the rarer birds, you have to go
> Along deserted lanes and where the rivers flow
> In silence near the source, or by a shore
> Remote and thorny like the heart's dark floor. . . .

Here line 1 has five-and-a-half feet and line 3 has six feet; the run-ons and the juxtaposition of short and long sentences provide a rhythmic tension and a sense of feelings and perceptions moving inevitably forward through complexity towards resolution, helped, not hampered, by the metrical pattern. The spondaic substitution of "the heart's dark floor" draws attention to this striking central image as well as enlarging the poem's sound properties in a powerful way.

"Paradise Flycatcher," a poem of the highest quality, also demonstrates the pull away from regularity under the urgent promptings of content. In this, one of the most fully realized of Ezekiel's poems, sound is used as a potent expressive agent and traditional form only as a sustaining and flexible skeletal binding. The poem has two stanzas, one of eleven and one of ten lines—in itself a departure from regularity. The iambic base is enriched by variation; the five-foot norm established in the first two lines, is quickly departed from, and the poem, in fact, contains eleven lines of five feet, six of four feet, two of six feet and two of three feet. The meter throughout is unobtrusive, functioning as a controlling agent but never drawing attention to itself by settling on an insistent patterned regularity. Run-on lines and syntactical variation add to the sound variety. There is no regular rhyme in the poem; instead Ezekiel uses repeated assonance as a unifier of sound and tone. (pp. 241-44)

Similarly, we see the use of emblematic colors throughout. Sustaining the poem's pseudo-narrative are the colors—white, green, black, green, red, white, chestnut; in the epigraph white and green—which perform a key role in the developing symbolism, leading strongly to the climactic lines "It lay with red and red upon its white, / Uncommon bird no longer, in the mud." The languorous exoticism and highly-colored beauty are reduced finally to the reality, the noncolor of mud and mortality. The esthetic vision becomes earthed in the most basic elements, buried in the ground and in the mind. Throughout the poem this contrast is developed and released into perception. Dream, air, flight and color oppose, merge with and finally assimilate mud, earth and burial, and this is done technically through sound and emblematic image.

I called the development of this poem a pseudo-narrative and this aspect seems to me the most significant contribution of the technique. Throughout, Ezekiel deliberately confuses time and place, dream and reality, symbol and concept in a fruitful and vital act of apprehension. Past and present are mingled with a purpose. We have, in the epigraph, the record of a present reading of a book about a past event which itself recalls an event even further in the past. The first stanza of the poem is in the present tense, although the awakened sleeper has, just previously, been dreaming of birds. The bird observed in the present reminds him of past readings about Indian birds. In the second stanza the tense switches to past, as the bird's predecessor is recalled, until the poem resolves in the present tense which seems to contain now both past, present, and, by strong implication, the future. The actual place of the poem is never specified. It is the garden described in the epigraph, perhaps; certainly the casurina tree links the epigraph with both stanzas of the poem. But it is a place both past and present, in dream as well as in reality. Thus time and place seem to be the same in art (the book), in dream, in the past and in the present. The dislocation of time and space is, of course, a classic symbolist technique where symbols are unanchored and move freely in and out of dream and reality, time and eternity, striving to define themselves away from the logic and causality associated with time and place. The questions which may be posed here by the literal mind—How many birds are there? What is the relationship between the "I" of the poem and the bird-watcher in the epigraph? Is the experience real or imagined, literal or symbolic?—become ultimately irrelevant as the dynamic confusion of tense, of imagined and personally apprehended reality, gives us not confusion but one great simultaneous act of perception removed from the sanctions of time and place, transcending the barriers between conscious and unconscious levels of experience. Like music, the poem exists in one time only—the time it takes to read. It is "legend come alive" and the techniques of the poem, its sounds, colors and recurrent images, its dislocation of time and space, dream and reality, permit this transcendence. The urgency of the vision, the content, have forced Ezekiel into a superb and instinctive use of form of a far higher order than anything he has previously achieved. His "old" style could never have permitted such a strenuous exploration of the shifting and elusive boundaries of perception, nor come to the kind of inclusive knowledge, nonfactual but deeply felt, which is implied at the poem's end. And yet **"Paradise Flycatcher"** must be considered a transitional poem which retains strong affinities to the "old" style by the use of a strong iambic base and a certain formality of language and construction.

"Night of the Scorpion" demonstrates a deliberate attempt at formal innovation by using a loose, seemingly free-verse narrative structure. This poem is much more relaxed and open-worked than Ezekiel's formal poetry, with a new quality of natural colloquialism in diction and tone. . . . We notice in the poem the abandonment of capitals at the start of each line, the dramatic casualness of the recalled crisis, the long paragraph set off abruptly from the three-line climax, all of which give **"Night of the Scorpion"** a new feel, a new appearance, a sense of unhurried lucid progression through time. And yet the poet is only partially able to escape old habits. On closer inspection the apparently free verse is not very free as regular iambic lines keep insisting upon their own pat-

tern, and the casual flow of the newly-loosened sound is several times violated and made awkward as the metrical pulse appears and tries to assert itself. . . . Of the forty-eight lines, fifteen are fairly regular tetrameters and seven are pentameters. The result is less than satisfactory, being too regular for good natural free verse and too free for good formal verse. It is as if Ezekiel, iambic rhythms running instinctively in his mind after years of metrical writing, cannot quite make the complete break into the free verse he clearly aspires to. "Night of the Scorpion" remains an interesting and very valid poem, containing a fascinating tension between personal crisis and mocking social observation, but the discrepancies of form confuse the tone, which swings between the natural and colloquial reporting of experience and a more removed literary formality. And yet, for all the problems, a real voice is heard in this poem, with its own rhythms and cadences. . . . We are already a long way from *The Unfinished Man.*

Another important transitional poem is **"In India,"** where, instead of attempting a whole poem in a new style, Ezekiel breaks it into four sections of varying degrees of formal freedom, and lets each section play against and modify the others. Section 1 gives us a classic example of the transitional state between formal and free verse. . . . [It] is neither fully regular verse nor fully free. The first nine lines are based on a three foot pattern, predominantly in trochaic rhythm, but including iambs, a trochee and occasional missing syllables, while the last three lines are tetrameters with a strongly iambic base. The whole section forms one long sentence, driven forward by the list of suffering humanity observed by the seeking eye and climaxing with the observer's own presence and reaction. For all its uncertainty, the form remains appropriate for this guided tour of repression and lifeless squalor. The absence of rhyme speeds the movement from line to line and allows the syntax to force us onward through the lines without permitting us a place to stop, to forget, to catch our breath. This section is effective, then, on this level, but again I wonder about the handling of form, as the poem has neither the full varied strength of free verse nor the sustaining framework of patterned formality.

Section 2 of **"In India"** is more effective as Ezekiel deploys an over-formal, jingling form as an ironic reinforcement of his meaning. . . . The repetition of "prayers" in every stanza, the contemptuous repeated "boys" (reminiscent of Empson's "Just a Smack at Auden"), the boorish, childish behavior of the various religious and racial groups, are all instruments of cutting, almost sneering satire. This is a strong section—though stanza 3 is weaker than the others—where form itself becomes an instrument of satirical meaning.

Sections 3 and 4 break from the more formal characteristics of the first sections. Section 3 is another transitional poem, ostensibly in free verse, but once again plagued by the insistent eruption of iambic feet and regular lines. . . . These lines, so regularly iambic, squat rather indigestibly among freer, more flexible sound patterns, and even give an annoying hint of rhyme ("kiss," "is" and, later, "success") in a poem which has no place for it. Clearly no genuinely free verse can exist with this level of metrical regularity asserting itself. Perhaps the pungent irony and self-awareness of this section would have been strengthened by a more natural pattern of diction and sound.

This we find in Section 4, which is the first example we have seen of Ezekiel's "new" voice. Suddenly, and confidently, an impressive strength and individuality displays itself in this final section, undamaged by any extraneous remnants of formal prosody, and the result is a poem of great strength and interest, acid in its satire and spontaneous and natural in its sound. . . . Only the capital letters at the beginning of each line remind us of the "old" style. Otherwise, the form embodies the concreteness of the content, effortlessly allowing the emergence of the vicious understated satire:

> Certainly the blouse
> Would not be used again.
> But with true British courtesy
> He lent her a safety pin
> Before she took the elevator down.

Here the concluding iambic pentameter does not intrude, nor does it hint at patterns trying to assert themselves, but works with justness and finality because of the energy and variety of the lines leading up to it. In terms of technical development, **"In India"** is highly interesting, containing in microcosm Ezekiel's struggles to free himself from restriction, and concluding with a breakthrough. (pp. 245-49)

To change a style, a voice, a tone in a major and dramatic way does not come easily to a poet, implying, as it does, far more than a surface tinkering with words and lines. It necessitates new ways of looking at the world, new and strange rhythms of thought and feeling, and, often, new kinds of subject matter which insist upon their own particular shapes and sounds. As I have tried to show, Ezekiel found the process difficult, but **The Exact Name** does contain examples of the new style he is struggling towards. We have already noted the last section of **"In India"** and may, at this point, usefully examine **"Two Images"** and **"In Retrospect"** as examples of achieved form in the new free style.

In **"Two Images"** the form echoes and fortifies the poem's content. The sudden vision of "a friend flapping his angelic wings"—an image of redemptive possibility from a place in the "long, dark tunnel"—is a welcoming of new life, of a visionary transcendent dimension. The form, too, with its springy confidence, implies new beginnings away from the dark tunnel of obsessive traditionalism. Nowhere here do we feel restrictions. The tone is consistent, the handling of the syntax—each section of the poem being one long sentence—the cunning juxtaposition of the two images without comment, the overlapping circles of meaning as the angelic wings link meaningfully with the "fluttering fly" at the poem's end, all these show a new technical sureness. The voice is simple, natural and individual:

> Fish-soul in that silent pool
> I found myself supported
> by the element I live in,
> but dragged out. . . .

This does not read like broken-up metrical verse; it has its own rhythms, spare and confident, which emody unobtrusively the existential concerns of freedom and imprisonment with which the poem involves itself.

But it is **"In Retrospect"** which proves more clearly that a breakthrough has been made. Here Ezekiel's new voice rings out, clear and trenchant. . . . In this poem, the rhythm moves with the mind and feelings, the line-breaks and the syntax play with and against each other, the voice is personal, dramatic and strong, sensitive to nuances of feeling and attitude and to wide tonal coloring. Nowhere do we find the arbitrary literariness which characterises Ezekiel's earlier work.

The short lines, the sinewy free verse, the flexibility of syntax and tone are here perfectly appropriate, assuming into themselves without strain the impulse of the experience and allowing it to find its own shape, its own potency. Comparing **"In Retrospect"** with, say, **"Art Lecture"** or **"Poetry Reading"** is to compare two utterly different kinds of technical constructs, two completely different approaches to experience.

It is not within the scope of this paper to consider what Nissim Ezekiel has been writing since the publication of **The Exact Name;** suffice to say it demonstrates the consolidation and development of the new technical freedom he gained with such difficulty in that collection. His own voice, once liberated from formal shackles, has continued to strengthen and deepen, modifying itself perfectly to areas of experience ranging from the mystical to the most realistically social. His new technical ability is an instrument of power and confidence, capable of many dimensions of tonal variation. Above all, it is his *own* instrument.

The Exact Name is the record of a revolution in an important poet's technique where he learns, with much difficulty, to abandon styles inherited from others and to create his own style for his own purposes. Some poets write better in traditional forms than in free forms. It is my contention that this is not the case with Nissim Ezekiel, who is rarely completely comfortable with regular meter and rhyme and uses it too rigidly and inflexibly, often allowing it to dominate and distort his content. His discarding of these forms was clearly not easy, and the problems are obvious in the transitional poems of this volume, but the break was essential to his development as a poet and it is in **The Exact Name** that the dramatic breakthrough occurs. (pp. 250-51)

> *Christopher Wiseman, "The Development of Technique in the Poetry of Nissim Ezekiel: From Formality to Informality," in* Journal of South Asian Literature, *Vol. XI, Nos. 3 & 4, Spring-Summer, 1976, pp. 241-52.*

J. BIRJE-PATIL

The career of Nissim Ezekiel is the history of new poetry in India, written in English, but as its seminal expression his work is informed by a sense of what Professor Cleanth Brooks calls 'the shaping joy' rather than Dionysian frenzy. It is a career that unfolds a talent in control of its destiny and deriving its force from a cultural encounter. Ezekiel's poetry can be viewed as a reincarnation of English poetry, incorporating aspects of his own country's intellectual traditions. It is not a self-consciously staged revolt by a 'professional' Indian, intent upon vindicating his Indianness by repudiating an established order. This lack of self-consciousness, the deliberately cultivated separateness one finds in some African poetry with a tribal focus, and the absence of rhetorical and illconcealed atavism of poets who flaunt their Indianness, make Ezekiel's poetry immediately relevant to us. This relevance is an attribute of fine intelligence and discriminating craftsmanship rather than the continuities flowing from Ezekiel's Judaic heritage and Western upbring. It is true that these two have probably made inheritance possible, so far as the English tradition is concerned, in place of the somewhat hectic process of succession, which invariably expends its energy on bi-cultural and bi-lingual controversies. This freedom from self-defeating schizophrenia has given Ezekiel time to refine his technique, so that he is able to make the poet in him available in terms of process as well as product. Ezekiel's poetry evolves from English, but it constitutes a revolt against the incipient romanticism and vapid narcissism which had for long made it impossible for Indian poetry in English to be a criticism of life.

Nissim Ezekiel's image as a pioneer in modern Indian poetry is sustained by his insight which compelled him to see, as Eliot did when he turned to La Forgue and Hulme, that the modern spirit can truly express itself only through aesthetic and metaphysical discontinuities. These stem from unprecedented cultural changes. . . . [It] was necessary for the modern Indian to make a clean break with the past freighted with pseudophilosophic claptrap and puerile nationalistic pieties. In the absence of pre-independence urgencies, these only camouflaged widespread hypocrisies.

> The district authorities
> at Balasore
> admitted they had failed
> but they claimed they could not have done better.
> Nature, they said,
> had conspired against them.
> 'Write the truth', they said,
> 'in your report'.
> And so I did.

"The Truth About The Floods" works at a certain level. Despite its apparent starkness, the ironic counterpoints lend it authenticity. A race addicted to futile gestures is relentlessly exposed and yet the pity that abject poverty distils is not eluded.

"The Truth About The Floods" hardly reveals the truth about Ezekiel. It does not represent him at his best because in the really excellent poems he has written, finely wrought integral images fuse the world of intuition and discourse, the inner and outer realms. Ezekiel's voice grows more ironic and detached as he develops, and one notices a distinct tilt toward social concern. Though never expressed stridently or programmatically, this has been gathering increasing intensity in his recent poetry.

Ezekiel's development as poet is difficult to categorize in temporal phases. However, it is possible to locate a few landmarks where significant changes seem to have occurred. It is customary to talk about influences while discussing a poet's early work. Critics have evoked Eliot and Auden among the chief influences on Ezekiel. Was there any poet writing in the early fifties who had not absorbed something of Eliot or Auden unconsciously? To hear echoes and determine the extent of the so called influence is to indulge in amateur sleuthing. . . . The poet with whom Ezekiel is most frequently yoked together is Auden. The reasons are rather obvious. Ezekiel's dexterity in handling rhyme and his commitment to formality in execution seem almost to invite the comparison. . . . There might be certain stylistic affinities between Auden and Ezekiel but such correspondence notwithstanding, there are important differences which are often overlooked. Ezekiel's later poetry does reflect greater social concern, yet the poems from *A Time To Change* written at a time when Ezekiel might quite conceivably have come under Auden's influence, reveal an altogether different sensibility. . . . [The] social and political underpinning of Auden's poetry is either missing or appears in a muted form in *A Time To Change*. Indeed, if it were not for Ezekiel's almost imperious need for formalizing contingency to the point where affective centres get thickly encrusted with self-

directed irony, Ezekiel of this period could be easily characterized as a confessional poet. Poems like the "The Double Horror," "The Worm," "An Affair," "A Word for the Wind," "Planning," "The Stone," "The Crows" and also some of the poems from *Sixty Poems* lend themselves easily to that kind of interpretation.

As in the confessional poetry of Robert Lowell and Sylvia Plath, Ezekiel speaks directly without the mediation of a persona. The poet himself is the undisguised speaker, the subject matter is self, and a cross-fertilizing relationship is established between art and the poet's personal life. Why then should he not be classified as a confessional poet? Perhaps the main reason for not assigning the name to his poetry, is the absence of morbid obsessions and neurotic contretemps which make at least some confessional poetry difficult to read. And though Ezekiel's poetry lacks Auden's well-formulated social vision, he keeps reaching out to other people. The sense of being a victim in the grip of unseen forces and the solipsistic orchestration of the poet's catatonic state of mind, associated with confessional poetry, are missing from Ezekiel's earlier poetry. Not many of the poems in the volume may be remarkable but the sincerity of the mind which produced them and the urge to define a personal agony, not through romantic posturing but in terms of radical paradox, lend them an artistic elegance rarely found in first collections.

> Seeking
> The pure invention or the perfect poem

at a time when "The Flute Player of Brindaban" had got everyone ecstatic must have required courage as well as imagination of a high order. The true significance of Ezekiel's early poems lies in their being attempts at relating poetry to contemporary reality. From the start, Ezekiel's poetry reveals a keen perception of his function as poet in a particular time and place. The early poetry bears the unmistakable stamp of a poet's quarrel with himself. But sometimes the abstemiously maintained neutrality of tone leads to a certain flatness. As long as the inner and outer landscapes are held in balance, as in a poem like "A Morning Walk" when he sees

> A million purgatorial lanes,
> And child-like masses, many tongued,
> Whose wages are in words and crumbs.

The poem engages us because an impulse is shaped to encompass a whole range of experience. Where the focus is narrower, it is not the starkness of a landscape but the sheer predictability of some of the lines trapped by rhyme which creates a sense of aridity. The starkness of "Drawing Room," a later poem, does not destroy semantic space. But the narrative literalness of "An Affair" prevents the release of resonance. In "The Worm" shades of Lawrence's *Snake*—the conclusion reached is trite because it is arrived at too pat, as though it were predetermined. However, in the later poetry there is a constant feeling of language being assimilated to experience instead of the other way around. In "From A Long Distance," with the image of a poet exploring reality and the illusion of a poem being written even as the poet grasps the nettle, a sort of ambient space is created: aesthetic distance does not blur the experience. This gives us a perspective on the speaker who sees himself at once as a predacious victim and spectator, the hunted and the hunter.

> I see myself enhanced, and also small.

And yet the true victim is

> perched upon your fear like a bird
> That has flown from a long distance,
> A mere prologue to a longer flight.

Against some of these later poems the earlier ones appear to be monotonously predictable. In **"Planning"** for instance the word 'ground' is followed by 'round' and 'beer' dogged by 'fear'. Fortunately, the realization that

> The best poets wait for words

embodied in **"Poet, Lover, Birdwatcher"** came pretty soon. The poem possesses a sort of flawless energy. There is a sense of being released into a kind of equilibrium whereby the craft of the poet and the birdwatcher stand in quiet apposition.

> The hunt is not an exercise of will
> But patient love relaxing on hill
> To note the movement of a timid wing.

The conversational style drops words into relevant places with descriptive ease and one feels that the

> The slow movement of the poem itself
> seems, somehow, to say much more.

and so what would seem like a sudden heightening of language appears to be totally spontaneous. . . . Shortcircuiting a great deal of mythologizing with the help of a few quotidian objects Ezekiel links separate activities through what might be identified as Orphic phenomena. But Orphic gestures are avoided and the two basic areas of human experience superintended by Eros and Orpheus are explored in terms of an ornithological metaphor. The latter also stresses the primeval nature of these experiences and their pervasive quality. Once we arrive at the crossroads of the senses the creative faculty begins to shape and order.

> Until the one who knows that she is loved
> No longer waits but risks surrendering
> In this the poet finds his moral proved
> Who never spoke before his spirit moved.

In the dissolving act, polarities are suspended and we move back and forth between the created world and creation until the temporal sphere intersects the still centre and stasis is achieved. . . . But the still centre is not an abstraction but a vortex where the polarities are resolved and the work becomes an allegory of poetic creation. . . . Ezekiel's sagacity in avoiding spurious linguistic complexity as a younger poet deserves special mention. But sometimes his unwillingness to extend himself imaginatively toward a world of reference beyond mere facticity warps his vision. . . . It is unfair to belittle a poet's earlier attempts in the light of his later achievement but I wish to demonstrate that his later strengths flow from his earlier struggle to master the craft of writing. Besides, at least some of his earlier weaknesses stem from an almost pathological dread of the large gesture. Large gestures, when controlled with the subtlety he is eminently capable of, have produced some of the most brilliant poems ever written by an Indian. In **"Minority Poem"** which is my favourite, concern for self emerges not as self-indulgence but as unmediated perception. Here mimesis becomes a matter of painstaking artistry which transforms the oppressive feeling of claustration into integral images of great power. The vision of 'her guests' dying 'visibly' in Mother Theresa's arms spreads itself from the centre of the poem until it touches reality at all levels. Words do not give off quaintness nor is their

force released through strange or fanciful juxtapositions. The originality is not located in an unusual syntactic manipulation but in the poet's unique perception.

> And you, uneasy
> orphan of their racial
> memories, merely
> polish up your alien
> techniques of observation,
> while the city burns.

The out-of-the-way is made available with immediacy but not dramatized in a facile manner nor trivialized through over exposure.

From *A Time To Change* onwards Ezekiel's poetry seems to have organized itself around three different patterns. First there are poems about low pressure events and incidents opening out to reveal a strongly realized archetypal force beneath the apparently casual encounters which develop from them. The second type is characterized by a discontinuous simultaneity when time is fractured and past and present telescoped to catch the self, striving to rearrange itself with images plucked from the factitious world. These poems constitute his finest achievement. The third type is where impelled sense of commitment to India, Ezekiel does not allow his self to violate the factitious universe and lets his pattern emerge from different modes of squalor which combine in a meaningful way.

Let us examine those three patterns with specific reference to certain poems. To the first category belong poems like **"Nakedness," "What Frightens Me . . . ," "Platonic,"** and **"Transparently."** If the intensity of violence which is 'in excess the fact' in certain confessional poetry, makes one recoil in distaste from it, the narrowing of thematic scope and stylistic orthodoxy of the poetry of the first category in Ezekiel, prevent one from participating in the experiences they evoke, their craftsmanship notwithstanding. The experience is clinically insulated. Perhaps Ezekiel was aware of this dilemma when he wrote them. (pp. 198-206)

On the other hand, one of his earlier poems entitled **"Speech and Silence"** with the lucidly delineated apprehension that

> . . . a man
> Is purified through speech alone

with the concluding lines reminiscent of Eliot's meditation on words from "East Coker," embodies a poignant vision of the artist's alienated universe:

> If speech is truly speech, silence
> A whisper of eternity.
> Integral with the inner self
> Becomes the public spoken word
> Emerging from the silence which is not articulation,
> But rather speech that needs no words,
> Being obedience to the word.

In this significant second category, I place poems like **"In India," "Night of the Scorpion," "Poet, Lover, Birdwatcher," "Paradise Flycatcher," "Island," "London,"** and **"Minority Poems."** I must add that each of these poems is distinguished by its own specially evolved form, each is different in tone, and in each one of them the subject-object dichotomy is maintained with a varying degree of balance. Yet, the polarities projected by the poet generate a sense of *la vie en parole,* that is, life acquiring a meaning even as the poet speaks. Consider that most celebrated of Ezekiel's poems,

"Night of the Scorpion." Moving, because unpretentious in sentiment, the simple touching slice-of-life affair, with the incantatory ramifications of a distant crisis with all its affective tints held intact, takes us into its drama with a homely gesture. Ezekiel has always avoided esoteric symbolism and even in "Night Of the Scorpion" where evil is symbolized by the scorpion, the occult overtones do not evoke a hermetic world. Casuistry is delicately held at bay and even when the peasants begin to ululate liturgically

> May he sit still, they said
> May the sins of your previous birth
> be burned away tonight, they said

we feel that language is released from its usual function as social discourse. Acquiring a liturgical lilt it soars and flows with a deliquescent locomotion. Folk psychology is dramatised without letting it degenerate into a spectacle of barbarous ritual which in fact would work against the touching homeliness of the situation involving a mother. The ritual of exorcism as well as scientific scepticism are subjected to gentle irony and the terrors of the actual event buried in the memory reappear in the form of intimations of parental mortality. The sceptical, rationalist father

> . . . even poured a little paraffin upon the bitten toe and
>   put a
> match to it. I watched the flame feeding on my mother.

Ezekiel's ability to recover the optimum significance from every familiar situation is most evident here. It is amazing how many different perspectives he is able to offer while moving along a reminiscent tract. The lethal quality of the scorpion's sting is indicated through a contrapuntal movement of sounds and words. The peasants' voices rising in crescendo are paralleled by the groans emanating from the twisting form on the mat. The discreteness of self-indulgent ritualism and the helplessness of the individual who suffers is depicted through controlled irony. . . . We are made to participate in the ritual as well as suffering through a vivid evocation of the poison moving in the mother's blood. The cinematically amplified

> giant scorpion shadows

of the peasants buzzing

> like swarms of flies

create a sense of communal participation which reinforces the exquisite irony reflected in the maternal sentiment

> My mother only said
> Thank God the scorpion picked on me
> and spared my children.

One believes Ezekiel when he says that although he admires the way William Carlos Williams writes poetry, he does not want to write poetry like his. . . . Form does not regress into myth even in a poem like "Night Of The Scorpion." And Dr K. D. Varma's otherwise perceptive article offers a rather procrustean reading of Ezekiel's poetry in relation to myth. Varma's interpretation with its stress on the post-lapsarian urban scene visualized by him and Ezekiel's alleged 'Romantic nostalgia' for the lost home which is the vision before the fall, sounds somewhat imposed. I cannot think of any poem in which Ezekiel is seen expressing regret over a lost Eden. The sense of sin is nowhere corrosive and when expressed it gets attenuated and modified by a self-directed irony. (pp. 206-09)

In Eliot, the City is the *urbs aeterna* declined into *li'monde cité*, a model derived from Virgil and Dante, of *imperium* in its metropolitan manifestation. . . . Ezekiel's Bombay is located in the present and like Williams's Paterson it lacks the historical dimension. In fact, for both Williams and Ezekiel, their respective cities as well as their poems are expressions of the same agitations and unrealized experience. To talk about the mass man, sulking in his anonymity in the bowels of a monstrously callous metropolite would be to labour the obvious. It is fascinating to find out what is distinctive in Ezekiel's treatment of Bombay. In a special sense it is different from Williams's treatment of his city. For Bombay is a hybrid colonial city and in it are incarnate all the tensions and horrors generated by a cultural encounter gone sour. It is peopled by a race spawned by itself. Ezekiel's originality lies in his projection of Bombay as a metaphor which defines the alienation of the modern Indian intellectual, brought up in the Judaeo-Christian and Greco-Roman traditions and being forced to come to terms with a culture whose response to life is controlled by a totally different metaphysics.

Ezekiel is a man without a past trapped in a city that has no past and where there is only an illusion of order derived from its colonial genesis. Both poet and city are creations of the same historical forces. The city is as much within him as without. It is this apprehension which makes Ezekiel's city poems unique. The island and the poet are synonymous as symbols of alienation from the living world and both are sudden eruptions on a scene lacking the fertilizing tensions of a long and healthy tradition. . . . [In Ezekiel's poetry, there is] a sense of simultaneous genesis and concomitant—inner and outer—squalor, rather than a feeling of inhabiting a 'fallen city with all the symptoms of a mass culture that devours its own creator'. The fragmented self occasionally experiences a sense of quarantined terror and it inadvertently cries out for help. But it has trained itself to keep its own counsel. And the evil that menaces is not external but is something projected by the modern man's own tortured self. This is a peculiarly western realization. The peasants in "Night of the Scorpion" fight an evil which they think is a force which has lodged itself into the human self and can be discarded. For Ezekiel as for the modern alienated intellectual the forces that terrorize are those which represent his other self, the self that is decapitated. Like an actor wearing a hideous mask depicting some unspeakable horror the poet tries to remove it only to discover that like the picture of Dorian Gray the horror is etched on the face itself. . . . [Although] his consciousness recognizes that he is an inhabitant of a city on the brink of collapse his damnation becomes the only certitude which offers at least a temporary respite. Therefore he accepts his infernal citenzenship stoically. . . . For Ezekiel the city is not a mere manifestation of an abstract horror but a natural habitat. His immersion into its specificity is a condition of life although from the viewpoint of conventional morality such an existence is tantamount to damnation.

Consciousness must recognize its nothingness in order to give shape to its being. It is in this manner that Ezekiel's poetry reflects his existential preoccupations.

> There's no other way
> except to burn
> your bridges, bury your dead.
> ("The Poet Contemplates His Inaction") (pp. 209-11)

Perhaps V. S. Naipaul's *An Area of Darkness* intensified an awareness that had already been festering within and which he had avoided confronting squarely. I do not know whether **"Background, Casually"** was written before or after he had read *An Area of Darkness* but there he asserts his Indianness once again.

> I have made my commitments now.
> This is one: to stay where I am,
> As others choose to give themselves
> In some remote and backward place.
> My backward place is where I am.

> (p. 211)

The commitments Ezekiel has made have certainly added a new dimension to his poetry and as long as he manages to reconcile the claims of his 'commitments' and his art, he continues to produce readable poems. But what about poems like **"The Truth About the Floods"?** We began with this poem and to it we return. The poem has a persona, a newspaper reporter and his report serves as the thematic base for the poem. I appreciate that social concern must find its place in the writing of poetry. Unless one is totally insensitive to what goes around, one cannot help noticing the suffering caused by natural calamities and accompanied by 'the law's delay and the insolence of office'. And yet I must express my reservations about this sort of writing because despite the distance achieved through cool understatement and the satiric refrain stressing bureaucratic obtuseness, the poem lacks imaginative space and resonance. The incident gets isolated as a single event. Every good poem unites us with our past and presses us toward a future. The life of this poem ends with its physical end. Incidentally I should like to relate the last point to Ezekiel's very amusing poems in Indian English. The voice one hears in **"The Truth About the Floods"** is a stranger's and not the poet's as we have come to recognize it. The best of Ezekiel's poetry includes all his contradictions, his concerned side as well as his primal being. In the writing of this poem his whole being does not seem to have been brought into play. The poem reads well and makes a certain impact but since the situation is inherently tragic, it is difficult to ascertain the difference in the quality of impact made by the poem and by the original report itself. Its writing represents to me the very reverse of Ezekiel's customary procedure. Writing for Ezekiel remains essentially an art, and here art is turned into a handmaiden of commitment.

That he who taught a whole generation of younger poets to transform unambiguous social concern into significant form should have foregrounded the former, can, I believe be attributed to an aberrant impulse. At his best, as in **"Paradise Flycatcher"** or **"Minority Poem,"** everything that is in the process of forming and dissolving is caught between instants. The continual passage of future into past as in

> The line one flashes at the watcher
> Chestnut wings; the dead is buried in his mind

allows the pure notion to emanate with all the interior cadences of the mind, claiming for the poem a place among the poetic achievements of our time. (pp. 211-12)

> J. Birje-Patil, *"Interior Cadences: The Poetry of Nissim Ezekiel," in* The Literary Criterion, *Vol. XII, Nos. 2-3, 1976, pp. 198-212.*

SATYANARAIN SINGH

As one of the foremost Indian poets in English, Ezekiel has attracted considerable critical attention from scholars in India and abroad. In range of interests and depth of sensibility, he remains unsurpassed in Indo-English poetry to-day. He has a philosophic mind and, although a poet of many themes, operating at different levels, there is discernible in his recent poetry—with greater clarity and definiteness—a distinct sense of direction, an emphasis and an orientation. The description of Ezekiel as a pilgrim with a sense of commitment and of his poetry as 'a metaphoric journey into the heart of existence' is a perceptive indication of the direction of his genius. As such, it would be fruitful to evaluate his poetry from this point of view. Ezekiel's insistent urge for commitment has been recognised, but there is need to focus upon this and define its nature more precisely. The poems written between 1970-1975 add an important dimension to this and thus provide a significant perspective for understanding more clearly the course and movement of his entire poetry. In confining myself to his recent poetry, with particular reference to his poems written from 1956 to 1975, to **Hymns in Darkness** and to **Poster Prayers,** my purpose is to analyze Ezekiel's distinctive slant for spiritual themes and to explore the nature of his inquiry into the science of Being—beyond the merely economic, moral and biological man.

Although a keen student of religion, Ezekiel is too humanistic to be an adherent of any particular creed. He would most willingly submit to experience uninhibited by set opinions or dogmas, and work his way to real knowledge. (pp. 48-9)

He would rather court follies and mistakes, learn from experience, and forge ahead zealously in the adventure of living than play safe. (p. 49)

In the existential arena of the world man is essentially a lonesome being pitted against unknown adversaries. He has to face new challenges, drawing upon his own inner reserves of strength. Rather than assiduously search for solutions to life's problems in scriptural texts, or depend upon the ready-reckoners supplied by priests or gurus, he would be 'a man withdrawn into himself', developing the energy and resilience to choose his course of action. 'Sometimes I cry for help / but mostly keep my own counsel' **("Island").**

> If nothing else, I'll keep my nerve,
> refuse the company of priests,
> professors, commentators, moralists,
> be my own guest in my own one-man
> lunatic asylum. . . .

> **"A Small Summit"**

The 'one-man lunatic asylum' is expressive of a deep sense of isolation from people who are insensitive to individual needs and responses. In his poem **"A Comment",** Ezekiel quotes Kenneth Barnes in *What I Believe:* 'The world is a place to be at home in . . . into which we can be reborn time after time as new possibilities open up, new kinds of experience come to us.' In commenting on this belief, Ezekiel voices the constraints and compulsions of fast industrial living on a sensitive and thinking mind. To him, the world is too big to be a home and in the overcrowded cities or slums, a single room is the only thing he can call his own—the true home of his affections. The abstract ideal of universal brotherhood fails to move him. How can he love mankind without even getting to love his family and his neighbours? 'A single room / is all I can love, / or the equivalent of a single room / where love is made in one form or the other, but not the world of history, / no, decidedly not' **("A Comment").**

In keeping with his limitations and capacities, Ezekiel would set modest goals without striking attitudes or finding refuge in escapist aesthetics: 'To be reborn is simply, / perhaps, to take the next step / that had to be taken, / timely, in joy, / or overdue and sad' (**"A Comment"**). His rebirth is quietly to take the next step without much fuss and have the courage to accept the consequences of his action.

The question of the individual ranged against establishment assumes a sharp and strident note when the poet has to cross the hurdles set by code ethics, or grapple with fossilized tradition. Ezekiel's poetry discloses a constant dialectic between an individual's yearning for spiritual growth and the constraints of institutionalized religion, his quest for deeper fulfilments and the iron-cast framework of organised opinion. Ezekiel's own statement recognises the presence of such schism and tension in moulding his poetry: 'I am not a religious or even a moral person in any conventional sense. Yet, I've always felt myself to be religious and moral in some sense. The gap between these two statements is the existential sphere of my poetry.'

The poet's aversion to sham and hypocrisy in the field of art and religion stems from his faith in genuineness as the cardinal virtue of the seeker. The complacent smugness and self-righteous stupor of bogus Godmen and fake artists disgust him. . . . (pp. 49-51)

Poetry does not consist merely in exhibiting one's linguistic skills, or in sedulously aping popular imagist patterns, or in formal virtuosity and craftsmanship without 'the shudder of genuine feeling'.

> I am tired
> of irony and paradox
> of the bird in the hand
> and the two in the bush
> of poetry direct and oblique,
> of statement plain or symbolic
> of doctrine or dogma—
>
>   **"Theological"**

In his flair for how to say, the writer almost forgets what he says, and we have a flashy surface without dimension and depth, a hollow experience stuffed with words—not the inevitable expression issuing out of intense feeling. Ezekiel is repelled at the morbid expression of sickly imagination. . . . (pp. 51-2)

One cannot fail to discern in Ezekiel a persistent note of discontent with the poet's vocation. If poetry amounts to voiding the heart in words without imperatives to action, the poet cannot be a genuine seeker, modulating his lifestyle in terms of his developing convictions. He does not appear isolated from the happenings around him. He is involved in them. His poetry crosses life at several points and at different levels, and its artistic worth does not suffer in the process. What Ezekiel distrusts, however, is the hiatus between words and deeds, between his poetic faith and actual life.

Ezekiel is, however, irked by an inherent sense of inadequacy while making firm decisions in the context of his life.

> In silence is no safety
> nor in the indulgence of speech.
> I have to act
> Despair is not my normal climate.
> Yet all I end up with is mumbling
> poetry, and a thousand helpless books.
>
>   **"Chronic"**

In a self-castigating vein, the poet breathes out his insufficiency:

> Compared to my mind,
> rocks are reasonable,
> clouds are clear.
> It makes me mad
> but that is how it is.
> How many times
> have I felt free?
> How many times spontaneous?
> It's fantastic
> what a slave
> a man can be
> who has nobody
> to oppress him
> except himself
>
>   **"Transparently"**

A victim of impulses and indecision, the poet's worst oppressor is his own self and yet this oppressing self is also the source of his poetry.

The poet struggles to control the Hamlet-streak in his personality which has a penchant for ruminating on all-inclusive solutions to life's varied problems. He yearns to identify the dilemma and settle for its resolution. . . . (pp. 52-3)

He prays for stamina and strength to rid himself of self-deception, think transparently, and act with promptness and conviction. . . . (p. 54)

Ezekiel is most unconventional in his conception of God. In the *Poster Poems* entitled **"The Egoist's Prayers"**, he does not conceive of God in terms of His Olympian aloofness, or as an awesome, supernatural reality. There is in Ezekiel a Blakean strain of humanising God. He speaks to God casually and informally like a friend and often his expression is inflected with banter and irony. Adverting to the *Gita's* famous doctrine about disinterested action, the devotee craves God's indulgence over his inability to suppress entirely his appetite and hunger for the fruit of action:

> No, Lord,
> not the fruit of action
> is my motive.
> But do you really mind
> half a bite of it?
> It tastes so sweet
> and I'm so hungry.
>
>   **"Poster Poems—4"**

Alluding to the Biblical word about God's chosen men enjoined to execute His will, he does some bishop-baiting by his 'blasphemy' in asking God to spare him from such activity as he has his own wishes to fulfil. He might, however, oblige provided God's will coincides with his:

> Do not choose me, O Lord,
> to carry out thy purposes,
> I'm quite worthy, of course,
> but I have my own purposes.
> You have plenty of volunteers
> to choose from, Lord.
> Why pick on me, the selfish one?
>
> O well, if you insist,
> I'll do your will.
> Please try to make it coincide with mine.
>
>   **"Poster Prayers—9"**

The poet seeks to explore the true and the false in the Self and to understand the ambiguities of virtue and vice. The question of evil engages him in his poem **"Crow"**. The crow's 'caw caw' symbolises his sense of inherent sin and evil. Would it be right to hate the crow—its weird blackness and its repulsive croaking sound—while nursing the crow in one's self? It requires readiness and courage to subdue the bird, or prepare oneself to succumb to its total domination. (pp. 54-5)

He is sceptical of deliverance, whether through faith in God's grace or through man's overweening confidence that he is the master of his fate. He underscores the need for humility and sincerity and constant application of the questioning mind. (p. 55)

Salvation is a question neither of belief nor of unbelief. We are all subject to life and mortality. It is given only to earnest and assiduous seekers to discover reality and its mysteries.

In the quest for inner stability and strength, the seeker does gain by impatient efforts at knowledge or irritable reaching after results. He would learn and cultivate 'The gentle art of leaving things alone'—not 'mock the grace of living with small analysis'. He would behold the tranquil process of creativity and growth as in **"Lawn"**:

> A silence in the depth
> A stir of growth
> an upward thrust
> a transformation
> Botanic turmoil
> in the heart of earth
>
> **"Lawn"**

This has a Biblical strain: 'Consider the lilies of the field, how they grow; they toil not, neither do they spin: And yet . . . even Solomon in all his glory was not arrayed like one of these . . . ' ('Matt. 6: 28-34') and what Keats termed in his celebrated phrase as 'deligent indolence'!

The capacity for complete self-exposure could be attained only if one could strip the mind of all masks and shed all falsities and pretensions. 'At first it is cold, I shiver there, / later comes a touch of truth, / a ferment in the darkness / finally a teasing light' **("Tribute to the Upanishads")**. The seed has to break its identity in order to sprout and bloom into a sapling. It has to give itself up to dissolution—rot and die into new life. Shorn of the trappings of egoism, the self is now sufficiently mature to receive the truth. The poet evokes this idea in the erotic metaphor of the lover's consummation in his poem **"The Sensuality of Truth"**.

> Freshen for me, Lord,
> Every hackneyed truth,
> And make her open
> Like a virgin
> To her lover.
> Nervously, but with the first thrill
> of making it at last.
>
> **"Poster Prayers—8"**

Finally an attempt at defining the nature of Ezekiel's commitment. The poet is drawn with varying degrees of impulsion towards his desired objects: self, family, society and God:

> He has seen the signs, but
> has not been
> faithful to them
> where is the fixed star of my seeking?
> It multiplies like a candle in the eyes of a drunkard.
>
> **"Hymns in Darkness"**

Such a confession, while suggestive of his different loves, points also to the central dilemma at the heart of his work. I am using the analogy of the concentric circles of self, family and society to help understand the poet's chief concern more closely and concretely. In his search for a larger identity, he longs to merge with and then transcend one by one the confines of self, family and society. But his progression is not charted outward from circle to circle but is a journey inward into the centre of the being from where he could choose to rise to maximum expansion—which would embrace, and not reject, all his other concerns:

> I don't want to be
> the skin of a fruit
> Or the flesh
> or even the seed
> which only grows into another
> wholesome fruit
> What there is within the seed
> that is what I need to be.
>
> **"Tribute to the Upanishads"**

One who gets nearer to his true self, gets nearer his fellow-men: 'I close the door and sit alone / in kinship with the world / I am near everybody / being near myself alone' **("Happening")**.

It is in one's awareness of Being and in the realisation of the primal power of self that the multiplicity of lights gets fused into a 'steadfast radiation', and the apparent diversities and contradictions are resolved into harmony. Ezekiel aspires for commitment to this ideal, setting the way for the pilgrim's progress.

To venture a few observations on Ezekiel's growing philosophical concerns in relation to his receptivity to different kinds of experience, and on his poetic form and technique. In my article on 'Ramanujan and Ezekiel', I tried to define the nature of Ezekiel's poetic mind and method:

> If I generalise that in Ramanujan, the image outruns the idea while in Ezekiel the idea eludes the image, it is only to identify, too crudely perhaps, the individual note of each writer. With Ezekiel the idea—in the sense of an alert and thoughtful response to a life-situation—appears central to his method. . . . Ezekiel is gifted with a thinking mind and shows promise of greater poetry if he is a little more of an artist and—to adapt Keats's words, 'loads every rift of his song with ore.'

While Ezekiel's subsequent poetry in its marked orientation towards spiritual themes has grown in vitality and strength, such a trend may have the effect of attenuating his appetite for varieties of experience and restrict the range and scope of his interest in life. Perhaps the verve and energy of art consists in the capacity of the artist to cultivate 'the knowledge of contrast, feeling for light and shade, all that information necessary for a poem'. The human landscape of our country provides for the artist enough sense of contrast resulting from socio-economic disparities, religious exploitation and bureaucratic despotism. Although Ezekiel has shown an awareness of these diverse problems, his preoccupation with religious experience may tend to distance him from the pressures and tensions of his time and place, and from the joys and woes of existence around him.

In technique and workmanship, his forte lies not in realising himself through images or symbols or in employing conventional artistic devices, but through a precise and imaginative articulation of experience in words: 'The best poets wait for words . . .' (**"Poet, Lover, Birdwatcher"**). (pp. 56-9)

The form of a short poem, in my opinion, appears too narrow for expressing the nuances and intricacies of a spiritual experience. The use of a slightly larger canvas like Keats's "Odes" may perhaps be a more adequate and effective medium for the organisation of Ezekiel's meditative self-explorations. (p. 59)

> Satyanarain Singh, *"Journey into Self: Nissim Ezekiel's Recent Poetry,"* in Indian Poetry in English: A Critical Assessment, *edited by Vasant A. Shahane and M. Sivaramkrishna, The Macmillan Company of India Limited, 1980, pp. 48-60.*

NISSIM EZEKIEL (INTERVIEW WITH FRANK BIRBALSINGH)

[This interview originally took place on June 3, 1986.]

[Birbalsingh]: *I notice that some critics use the word "cynical" about your writing. I think you represent Indian ways ironically. You ridicule various things—mimicry, ignorance, the modern Indian ethic—as in* **"Goodbye Party for Miss Pushpa T.S."** *I have met Indians who react defensively to that poem.*

[Ezekiel]: Yes, and sometimes angrily. They resent it.

Yet the speech patterns are correct, and the whole sense of mimicking western habits and manners. Those seem to be accurate observations. There is no malice in them.

There may even be a streak of malice, I don't know. I would not defend myself against it. I would say that there is a faithfulness of temperament.

I would imagine the temperament has to do with your Jewish background and the Hindu environment?

It may be a combination of factors. But, after all, other people have reacted in different ways to the same situation in which I am. I do not find scores of people in my community or in allied communities in India responding in the same way I do.

I read somewhere that you had rejected religious belief at some stage of your career. What has been your attitude to Hinduism?

I don't think I have ever sat down to completely define my attitude to Hinduism, Judaism, Christianity, or any other set of beliefs. Although people who are critical might apply the word "cynicism" to me, I think "skepticism" would be more accurate.

There are characteristic themes in your poems—evanescence, separation, loss. Throughout, you describe human experience as inadequate or limited. It may be difficult to say exactly where that comes from. But I get a feeling of absolute honesty from your poetry, as if your only aim is to get at the truth—the exact thing. This encourages self-questioning. Is this what you mean by "skepticism?" Nothing works out. Nothing pleases you in the end.

No. It is not that nothing pleases me. Some things please me more than others; but I would be inclined to say that if one is not cautious, and if one overlooks the consequences throughout history of things that have pleased, then such things can go to extremes. People misinterpret their responses to events; and things can go wrong again. I could be pleased, and at the same time be cautious.

It is more caution than anything else?

It is a fear of over-interpretation, let us say, of a particular event or happening, and flinging oneself into it and saying, "Ah, now we've got it, the truth at last." Such convictions and beliefs have led in the past to fanaticism, violence, and war. (pp. 130-31)

That skepticism, or distrust of settled views, the questioning of certainties, is represented fairly consistently throughout your writing. But you are now sixty-one years old, and have been writing for more than forty years. Has your sekpticism changed over the years?

It develops or may be modified as I go along, but I do not think I have abandoned it altogether at any stage, and jumped to final conclusions about the nature of existence, the cosmos, and life.

You have always distrusted certainties of any kind—religious, political, and economic?

Yes, and distrust does not cancel out trust, in my view. It is a strengthening of trust by saying to oneself that if it is really trust, then it must stand up to the most acute cross-questioning, not only by other people, but by oneself. I do not have to sit in front of an opponent and hear him demolish my views. I can be my own opponent. Yet I cannot destroy everything. I know I must work out values and basic attitudes, without assuming that these constitute a general truth which I can sell to everybody.

Your poetry reflects this tension between opposites.

I would accept that description.

However we define the opposites, whether as physical/spiritual, or as immersion/detachment, there is a fundamental pattern of statement and counter-statement which works against confident revelations in your poetry.

But I don't think it leads me to despair. It leads me often enough to humor and irony, to statements of paradox and so on. If there is an occasional sense of despair, that is for me a passing thing.

I do not find despair in your poems. There is an appreciation of transience and contradiction; but as you say, there are sustaining elements, like humor and irony, which suggest that, whereas you observe contradictions, your attitude to them is not passive. It is not positive either.

It is not positive either. But it does not make me feel, "Oh, well, since all these contradictions do exist, suicide is the only way out." (p. 131)

One subject I have been circling around is the relationship of your work to the tradition of Indian writing as a whole. Am I missing something of India and the Indian reality in your work which I would get from Umashankar Joshi, for example, writing in Gujarati? Is this a relevant question?

Yes, absolutely, and the majority of critics of Indo-English writing would assert it at all costs. They almost take it for granted that outstanding or even second-order writers in Punjabi, or Tamil, or Bengali are more Indian, naturally, because they use the mother tongue. Not writing in English means that their environment, their setting, their normal sensibilities are more Indian than those of an Indian writer in English. I have never really accepted this, but I have not rejected it either, because it seems to have some validity, depending on how far claims for such validity are carried. . . . [Most Indian critics] tend to have a basically negative view of the whole enterprise of Indian writing in English.

What is their justification for that?

That Indians really should not write in English. If they confront me, they say: "Why the hell do you not write in your mother tongue?" without grasping the historical situation which makes writing in the mother tongue impossible for me. In other words, I would have to stop writing altogether. And I prefer to go on writing in the language which happens to be the one in which I feel and think and live. What can I do about it? (pp. 131-32)

Is not your subject largely urban?

I do not see that "urban" is a condemnation or a limitation. Most of the critics who use the word in that sense live in the cities.

One likes to think of an artist taking a more comprehensive view of human issues and life, making penetrating analyses. I wonder whether your subject is not too severely circumscribed by being restricted to the educated, urban environment of modern India.

Unfortunately, this phrase which you have just used is not chosen to describe but often only to dismiss. For me, a writer's subject is only the starting point. Many outstanding Indian writers have gone back to the village they have lived in and written a whole novel about life in that village. We don't say that is circumscribed. We say it is wonderful. Whatever the writer knew under his skin was used. He did not write about life in the big town because he did not know it. He knew life in his own village; he was more at home there, and his characters are more real. To say "urban" is no more criticism than to say "rural."

I think there are political questions which enter here. Following colonialism and the subjugation of one nation by another, people tend to have a natural sympathy for the oppressed nation whose peasants, toiling on the land, appear more desirable as a subject of art than the concerns of the oppressor.

I see that as sentimentality, and also a bit of hypocrisy. We have the equivalent of the rural masses in the big cities. It is not as if every one living in the urban centers is rich, educated, and speaks English. A real urban area in India is a very mixed place. First of all, the proletariat cannot be left out, and then from that class to the bourgeoisie, you get various other classes and groups, including the poorest of the poor, who are neither proletarian nor bourgeois, and are still as poor as the rural masses. They also work hard and struggle for survival. They have responses which can be very human. It is amazing to see people living on the pavement, laughing frequently and enjoying life. You can come to false conclusions about that; but it suggests one mode of survival.

I was really asking about your feeling about politics. You do not write poems about the suffering of the proletariat and call for political reforms?

There are references or allusions to such suffering, or politics may be mentioned; but I think to go beyond that is to enter the field of political writing or journalism. A lot of that kind of poetry becomes journalese.

You can have genuine poetry in it.

You must have some justification for it in what you have done. You should not say to other people, "Do this," if your own life does not vindicate it.

Yes, but your own observations of human poverty or suffering do not seem to evoke political solutions.

No. They are part of the scene. I would not see a justification for myself to make it more than that unless there was something in my life or career which would give me the authority to say so or do it. I am pointing out that in a lot of the things we say and do, there is some authority which comes from the kind of life we live. One has to be careful about this, otherwise scores of voices are suddenly pleading on behalf of the poor, and it seems a meaningless kind of chorus.

Since we are talking mainly about Indian writers in English, can I ask for your opinions of some of these writers? Is it the same to read [Ruth Prawar] Jhabvala as [R. K.] Narayan?

No, Narayan is an Indian writer and Jhabvala is not. Jhabvala's situation is that she is Jewish, from Poland via England. She had an English education, married a Parsee, came to India, and lived here for twenty years. I would put her among those to be taken seriously as writers or critics about India, but not as an Indian. After all, we do divide and subdivide writing in English by Indians, and separate that writing from what may be called "Anglo-Indian" writing, which is not a correct phrase because it should be "Indo-English" writing. So if an Englishman comes to India and lives here for three or four years and produces a novel, and then goes to Australia or New Zealand or Canada, then for me he is not necessarily to be dismissed. It is only when you come to categories and classes and groups that it is essential to make these distinctions. Maybe that person is the greatest writer who has ever written about India, but he is still not an Indian writer. (pp. 132-34)

That makes your position all the more subtle, because you are not an outsider like Jhabvala.

No, I am an Indian national. I was born in India; my tribe of the Jewish community has lived in India for 2,000 years. If I had rejected my Indianness, which some Indian writers obviously have done, and if I had decided that I am so much of an outsider that I have to settle down in London or New York, and then, even if I did write about India, I don't know if I could be regarded as an Indo-English writer. . . .

I think a lot has to do with the beginning, with the formative stages, of sensibility. That problem is in the West Indies, too. V. S. Naipaul remains West Indian, no matter how long he lives in England. His attitude toward India is that of someone who has been alienated by his West Indian experience.

Incidentally, I do not consider the word "alienation" by itself as a label of condemnation. A lot of Indian critics use the word "alienation" as if that settles the issue. Since they have identified someone as alienated, there is no reason to praise him for anything Indian. This is too negative for my purposes. If an author does not feel quite the way those around him seem to feel, and if he then tries to give that perception a certain shape and form, I would respect him for it. (p. 134)

There is a good critical piece on your versification by Christopher Wiseman [see excerpt above], who talks about the growth of your technical skill and your use of the regular line.

The essay assumes that my early poetry is all of one kind, and that the later poetry is free verse, whereas the fact is that I have written both kinds of verse from the very beginning. Even in the earliest poems, written in college and school, which were never published, I always attempted both.

Wiseman is a little too schematic in saying you began in one way, then progressed to another.

Academics sometimes love to do that.

It makes a good argument. But I agree with you. The strong iambic base Wiseman talks about has always been present in your poetry. One thing I like is your conversational lucidity, an impression of talking informally and with clarity. Others have also noted that you do not delve into legends, myths, symbols, and other forms of dense, complex, or obscure writing. Did you consciously work against recondite allusiveness? When you began writing, surely that was all the rage?

An obscure poem is not necessarily bad or good. It all depends on what the characteristics of that obscurity are within a particular poet's work. I think all I can say is that whenever I wrote, from my point of view, a successfully obscure poem, then studied it, I would say, "What game am I playing? How did I fall into this trap? Is it impossible to rewrite this poem and clarify it?" So I would rewrite it and I invariably found that I could clarify it.

Why did you want to clarify it?

Because I could say what I wanted to say without using the fashionable idiom of the time.

So it is your own personal liking for clarity and lucidity?

Others might use obscurity profoundly, but I can't. I can only use clarity, and hope that that clarity is also profound. If it is not, the poem is at least clear, and that is enough.

Have people accused you of simplification because of the clarity?

Yes, of not being profound, and if the conversational tone is obvious, and clear, then they say it is oversimplification. I would not reject that criticism, by the way, because I am not so sure about the qualities of my own poems as to feel that they are worth reading. I would say that such criticism should be taken seriously, and the poem should be read again. Is it as bad as it seems, or has the critic prejudices of his own, which lead him to consider the poem bad *because* it is simple?

Some of Blake's poems are none the worse for being simple. But I want to ask about your reading of Rilke and T. S. Eliot?

Rilke and Eliot both influenced me, although I soon understood the difference between being influenced in the right and in the wrong sense. I did not want to write like Rilke.

Become an imitator only?

Yes, an echo. If someone were to say, "Ah, but in these poems in an early book, there are echoes of Rilke or Eliot," I would agree. This does not mean that I produced a whole poem which is nothing but Rilke. If there were some poems like that, I don't think I published them.

Your poems invariably identify limited aspects of the world, without being angry or vehement. There is mockery without malice, and I immediately think of Chaucer, who is remarkable in being able to indict almost the whole of fourteenth-

century English society and appear to enjoy it. He seems delighted by human foibles and frailties.*

I studied Chaucer only up to the M. A. stage, and rarely read him again during the rest of my life. He was probably not taught to us very well either, so I must have done that minimum reading necessary to pass an examination.

You are able to convey sympathy for the subject, for the person who is made to look ridiculous. I would not agree at all with those people who see you as putting down other Indians.

I regret it very much when I hear that kind of response. There is a linguistic, political, and social nationalism in India which can also be very strong in the various regions. Each language goes through that phase, when it insists on its own identity and also puts down all other identities. If I mention the search for identity and then lay a great deal of emphasis on finding my own, then I have to realize that, in entirely different cultural and historical situations, you may also search for your identity, which may turn out to be very different from mine. (pp. 136-37)

V. S. Naipaul argues that, especially for post-colonial people, it is difficult, if not impossible, to achieve identity in the modern world.

I think it suits Naipaul, because it is his answer to his own problems. But I can think of almost any regional Indian writer—a Bengali, or a Tamil—ultimately deciding, quite painfully and slowly, that he is a Tamil or whatever, and nothing can shake him out of that. Everything else he has to relate to will be in terms of his being Tamil or Bengali. I would respect such a person's Bengaliness or Tamilness.

There seems to be an ongoing tension between this need for group identity, based on culture, or race, or geography, or something, and the opposite reaction that one belongs nowhere.

Both extremes are normal.

I suppose we all function within those two extremes.

I don't think everything I write or say or do should absolutely and unconditionally have what I have discovered to be my identity. That would suggest psychological insecurity. I would prefer to claim that nine times out of ten my being human is more important than anything else in the whole world. (pp. 137-38)

Nissim Ezekiel and Frank Birbalsingh, in an interview in Journal of South Asian Literature, *Vol. 22, No. 2, Summer-Fall, 1987, pp. 130-38.*

FURTHER READING

Beston, John B. "An Interview with Nissim Ezekiel." *World Literature Written in English* 16, No. 1 (April 1977): 87-94.
    Discussion in which Ezekiel addresses his Indian heritage, religious beliefs, and poetic influences.

Edgington, Norman Ross. "Nissim Ezekiel's Vision of Life and Death." *Journal of South Asian Literature* 22, No. 2 (Summer-Fall 1987): 139-45.

Maintains that in Ezekiel's poetry "death remains a thought and life is a joy to be celebrated."

Garman, Michael. "Nissim Ezekiel: Pilgrimage and Myth." *Journal of South Asian Literature* XI, Nos. 3-4 (Spring-Summer 1976): 209-22.

Explores Ezekiel's synthesis of classical poetics and contemporary issues.

Kohli, Suresh. "Nissim Ezekiel." *Mahfil* VIII, No. 4 (Winter 1972): 7-10.

Brief interview with Ezekiel.

Kumar, Shiv A. "Poster Prayers of Nissim Ezekiel." *Journal of South Asian Literature* XI, Nos. 3-4 (Spring-Summer 1976): 263-64.

Examines those poems in which Ezekiel questions the existence of God.

Taranath, Rajeev. "Nissim Ezekiel." *Quest* 74 (January-February 1972): 1-17.

Discusses the poetry which Ezekiel published following *The Exact Name*.

Verghese, C. Paul. "The Poetry of Nissim Ezekiel." *Indian Literature* XV, No. 1 (March 1972): 63-75.

Examines the stylistic and thematic innovations of Ezekiel's metrical poetry.

Penelope Fitzgerald

1916-

English novelist, biographer, and journalist.

Fitzgerald writes carefully plotted novels in spare, witty prose, delineating interactions and subtle tensions among groups of characters who work together or reside in a small community. She utilizes varied settings of time and place, vividly evoking period detail and peculiar issues and customs. Her diverse, often eccentric characters cope with sudden conflicts in their lives and relationships. Anne Duchêne observed that Fitzgerald's fiction "has a natural authority, is very funny, warm, and gently ironic, and full of tenderness towards human beings and their bravery in living."

Fitzgerald's first novel, *The Golden Child,* is a mystery set in an art museum where a prized exhibit is discovered to be a forgery and a well-known explorer is murdered. Fitzgerald exposes human foibles and deception resulting from struggles for power and authority among museum staff members. In *The Bookshop,* a woman attempts to bring higher culture to a decaying Suffolk village by opening a bookstore in a quaint, old building. Her efforts are opposed and eventually overcome by a society matron who wants the building for other purposes. Fitzgerald recreates the political climate of the late 1950s, including the debate over whether Vladimir Nabokov's controversial novel, *Lolita,* should be sold in Great Britain. *The Bookshop* also features humorous incidents involving eccentric local characters or poltergeists that haunt the bookstore. In *Offshore,* for which she won Britain's prestigious Booker Prize, Fitzgerald draws upon personal experience to detail comraderie and conflicts among members of a community of houseboat dwellers on the Thames River. Peter Kemp observed: "The book's happenings are appropriate to the world portrayed. Little eddies of disturbance bring the boat-dwellers bumping together or swinging further apart. Some are drifters; one sinks; others lose their moorings. It is all very deftly done, with both language and perceptions bracingly precise."

Fitzgerald also draws upon personal experience in *Human Voices,* which revolves around activities at the British Broadcasting Corporation (BBC) during the 1940 Nazi air offensive against England. The novel examines the importance of truth in public communications and private relationships as it depicts BBC staff members who must provide moral uplift to their beleaguered listeners. *At Freddie's* centers around the efforts of a drama school proprietress to keep her business financially solvent. Many of the characters in this novel are actors who experience confusion between their actual lives and their theatrical roles. Fitzgerald's concern for sense of place and its effect on character are important elements in her next two novels, *Innocence* and *The Beginning of Spring. Innocence,* which is set in Florence, Italy, chronicles the lives of the Ridolfis, a decaying aristocratic family, and the Rossis, a working-class family. Through the courtship and marriage of Chiari Ridolfi and Salvatore Rossi, Fitzgerald examines various themes relating to innocence and the influence of family history as she develops allegorical implications through allusions to fables and legends. C. K. Stead praised *Innocence* as "a work of strange, muted power and intelli-

gence." *The Beginning of Spring* is set in an English community in Moscow during the early twentieth century. While describing customs and period detail to recreate the social atmosphere prior to the Russian Revolution, Fitzgerald focuses upon the confusion and unhappiness experienced by an Englishman abruptly abandoned by his wife. Typical of Fitzgerald's fiction, *The Beginning of Spring* is a comedy of manners with an ambiguous conclusion, as a small group of well developed characters experience conflict, tensions, and change while reacting to unexpected and perplexing events.

(See also *CLC,* Vols. 19, 51; *Contemporary Authors,* Vols. 85-88; *Contemporary Authors Autobiography Series,* Vol. 10; and *Dictionary of Literary Biography,* Vol. 14.)

PRINCIPAL WORKS

NOVELS

The Golden Child 1977
The Bookshop 1978
Offshore 1979
Human Voices 1980
At Freddie's 1982
Innocence 1986

The Beginning of Spring   1988

BIOGRAPHIES

Edward Burne-Jones: A Biography   1975
The Knox Brothers   1977
Charlotte Mew and Her Friends   1984

JOHN MELLORS

The Golden Child is an entertainingly witty mystery, based improbably but ingeniously on Herodotus 4,174, a description of a backward African people, the Garamantes. 'The Museum' is holding an exhibition of the gold treasures of Garamantia. But is there a Curse of the Golden Child? Or is there a more mundane explanation of the deaths by defenestration and shock that threaten to cause a scandal 'which will destroy the credibility of the Museum, perhaps indeed of all museums'? Penelope Fitzgerald enjoys herself immensely destroying the credibility of the pompous and ambitious officials, whose voices betray 'the pride and bitter jealousy' that are 'the poetry of museum-keeping'.

The plot is as complicated and hard to unravel as the ball of golden twine that figures among the treasures, but for those who never did care who killed Roger Ackroyd there is enough pleasure to be derived from the author's jokes and the fun she has with her characters. Rochegrosse-Bergson—'one had to be a very clever man to produce such nonsense as antistructural anthropology'—is a self-styled 'philosopher-criminal'; he lives in Paris on the Rue Baron de Charlus. The director of the museum 'was very familiar to the public as the result of his lengthy TV series, *What is Culture?*, in which he had appeared in close-up against all the better-known works of art in western Europe'. I particularly admired the choice of food by a pregnant woman taken to dinner in a Bloomsbury restaurant once called 'Lytton Strachey Slept Here': snails, tripe cooked in cream, and suet-pudding with treacle.

> John Mellors, "Anon Events," in The Listener, *Vol. 98, No. 2528, September 29, 1977, p. 410.*

EMMA FISHER

A middle-aged widow sets up a bookshop in a small town in Suffolk. The house is haunted by poltergeists. At first business is slow but it picks up when she orders 250 copies of *Lolita*. A General's wife wants the house for an Arts Centre and eventually, by scheming and pressurising, gets it, and the widow leaves town humiliated. It sounds like nothing, but Penelope Fitzgerald [in *The Bookshop*] has made it into a solid and satisfying piece of human life, and is able to convince the reader that every action in it matters, however small—the same consolation as can be found in Jane Austen, though the two writers are not alike. Over it, though not obtrusively, rises a faint mist of parable: the town is Hardborough, the nearest rival town Flintmarket; Florence Green's name suggests hope and courage in taking on this stony ground; the villainess, Mrs Gamart, makes art look silly—'How can the arts have a centre?' asks Mr Brundish, on Florence's side but ineffectual because he is a hermit; and she is also wily in the art of getting what she wants, though the author assures us that she did not directly suggest to her MP

nephew that he get the new Act passed which empowers the Council to buy up the house. The effect is not as Bunyanesque as this might make it sound. The style is understated but exact, and the crystalline and amused observation of small country town people, speech, ways, animals and landscapes gives continuous pleasure, especially the 1950s bookshop interior, with the boy who comes in every day after school to read another chapter of *I Flew with the Fuhrer*. Mr Brundish is a delight—unused to conversation, he speaks his thoughts out loud, saying to Mrs Gamart 'You had better offer me something. The bitch cannot deny me a glass of brandy,' and 'Either this woman is stupid, or she is malevolent'.

Which is she? The only flaw in the book is Mrs Gamart's motivation. She sometimes stands for misguided do-gooders—'She did not know that morality is seldom a safe guide for human conduct'—yet her machinations are surely immoral enough to have alerted even her. Her desire to be important is plausible; but would she have wanted an Arts Centre that much? And would it have made her important? And would the Old House have been such a good place for it? One is not absolutely sure why Deben's fish shop would not have done instead. Still, villains with poorly explained motives are not necessarily weak. . . . Mrs Green can get the better of the supernatural; the poltergeists do not deter her because she knows how far they can go. Elsewhere human beings are divided into exterminators and exterminatees, and as an exterminator Mrs Gamart is kept properly in the background and allowed to work. (pp. 22-3)

> Emma Fisher, in a review of "The Bookshop," in The Spectator, *Vol. 241, No. 7844, November 4, 1978, pp. 22-3.*

BLAKE MORRISON

[*The Bookshop* is set] in Suffolk in 1959. The date is important, for in that year *Lolita* appeared in England: the 250 copies in Florence Green's new bookshop sell like hot cakes, but further distress the influential locals opposed to her venture. It's only a matter of time before she gets the chop. The rise and fall of a country bookshop makes pretty thin material for a novel, even if (as here) that shop is fortunate enough to be haunted by 'rappers' (poltergeists) and to have a splendidly precocious 11-year-old helping behind the counter. Worse, we are by the end being expected to supply a sentimental response to Florence's victimisation by the local bigwigs. But initially the author's sharp insights make for a refreshingly disenchanted view of life on the Laze. (p. 631)

> Blake Morrison, "Looking Backwards," in New Statesman, *Vol. 96, No. 2486, November 10, 1978, pp. 630-31.*

PETER KEMP

Like her last work, *The Bookshop*, [*Offshore*] concentrates on a small community. The one in *The Bookshop* was precariously clinging to the marshy edge of Essex. The one here bobs up and down in barges on Battersea Reach. Boat-dwellers, sometimes afloat and sometimes aground, are the novel's subject. Amphibious in their life-style, these 'tideline creatures' have not found a permanent niche in life, don't fully fit in anywhere. They are 'creatures neither of firm land nor water': correspondingly, their situations and their personalities are half and half.

The book's happenings are appropriate to the world portrayed. Little eddies of disturbance bring the boat-dwellers bumping together or swinging further apart. Some are drifters; one sinks; others lose their moorings. It is all very deftly done, with both language and perceptions bracingly precise. There is also an enthralling fund of information about life upon the Thames (where the author herself once lived on a barge). The book is very strong on fact: and riverside artists for whom composition has taken priority over know-how are mildly guyed in an entertaining scene where a child from the barges wanders round the Tate. (p. 387)

Peter Kemp, "Snakes on the Grass," in The Listener, *Vol. 102, No. 2629, September 20, 1979, pp. 386-87.*

EMMA FISHER

Penelope Fitzgerald prefaces her new novel about houseboat-dwellers on the Thames with a slyly apposite quotation from Dante; it comes from the point where Dante asks Virgil why some of the damned are suffering on a greasy marsh, lashed by wind and rain, rather than inside the infernal city itself. Virgil explains that they are less offensive to God because they have only been incontinent, not deceitful or violent. The only violent character in [*Offshore*] is Harry, a sinister criminal who uses the houseboat of Maurice, a sympathetic male prostitute, as a repository for stolen goods, emerging only now and again from the mysterious city, and eventually assaulting with a spanner one of the well-intentioned water-dwellers. Nenna, existing penuriously with her two daughters aged six and 12 and longing for the return of her hopeless husband, is incompetent rather than incontinent, though she does, after a funny and pathetic journey in pursuit of the husband, spend one night with the stiff, correct Richard, who lives a fantasy Navy life on his shipshape boat and drives his upper-class wife to drink. The apparent muddle of life is both captured with detailed preciseness and discreetly shaped into a tale wherein one can ask what was who's fault, though the water-dwellers are innocents and their greatest sins seem to be indecision, white lies, or too much self-reproach. The pleasures and hazards of their position are tangibly recreated, and the two daughters are splendidly particular, especially in the social comedy of their encounters with the shore world.

Emma Fisher, in a review of "Offshore," in The Spectator, *Vol. 243, No. 7891, October 6, 1979, p. 30.*

P. H. NEWBY

Human Voices is about the BBC in the summer and autumn of 1940, when French troops camped in London parks, the Concert Hall in Broadcasting House was turned into a dormitory and the Blitz started. . . . [Fitzgerald] is an individual, witty and trusting writer—trusting because she assumes that readers are as alert as she is. The tone of voice is important. In a conversation about music one of her characters is told that emotion must never intrude. 'If you have strong feelings, let us say personal affection, do not let it attach to the music.' This sounds something like the discipline Penelope Fitzgerald herself writes under, and it does not imply coldness. On the contrary. The control is there because the current of feeling runs so strongly.

She is also a writer who cherishes absurdities. For example,

the Head of Supply and Equipment is worried about his responsibilities if the United States and all of Central and South America, 15 countries in all, declare war on Germany. 'All of them are going to want representation at the BBC'—and he will be expected to provide the equipment: carpets, chairs, desks, typewriters and, what are quite unobtainable, steel filing cabinets. What is he to do? Jeff Haggard, Director of Programme Planning, advises him to pray for a negotiated peace. . . .

The story turns on the relationship between this Jeff Haggard, a cold, efficient type, and Sam Brooks, who runs Recorded Programmes and is so obsessed with the job that he appears to view the threatened invasion as no more than an opportunity for recording the sounds of a tank division moving up a sand and shingle beach. Haggard protects him from the consequences of this single-mindedness from time to time. Brooks's department is known as the Seraglio because he has recruited so many young women into it. They are expected to listen to his troubles and to his clumsy flattery but not to have feelings or troubles of their own. Unexpectedly, one of these girls, 17-year-old Annie, falls in love with him and, to his consternation, tells him so. It is a predicament Haggard cannot help him in, partly because he declines to get mixed up in such an affair but mainly because he mistakes a huge, unexploded bomb for a parked taxi and tries to open its door.

There are a number of set pieces, some just funny like the abortive broadcast of a defeatist French general, some funny and touching like the celebratory dinner at Prunier's where Brooks improvises an engagement ring out of a piece of wire and a red currant, and one funny but black; this is an account of a girl in labour in the Concert Hall cubicle normally reserved for the Senior Announcer. But it is Annie who gives the novel its heart. In the handling of this honest and vulnerable character Penelope Fitzgerald uses the control that seems to shut out emotion only to involve the reader more. She creates appealing characters out of the simplest fairy-tale material. Annie sees life steadily and is unafraid; not a Beauty, perhaps, but then Brooks, though intolerable, is not completely the Beast. If all the elements in this short novel do not quite cohere there is enough vitality and good humour to make up for it.

P. H. Newby, "BBC Seraglio," in The Listener, *Vol. 104, No. 2681, October 2, 1980, p. 445.*

BRIAN MARTIN

Once again we are offshore in Penelope Fitzgerald's novel *Human Voices,* this time not moored in Battersea Reach, but aboard Broadcasting House in 1940 as it steers a course through Langham Place. Working there 'suggested more strongly than ever a cruise on the Queen Mary' and in its curving corridors there are 'sudden shipboard meetings and even collisions'. Its crew, mostly known by the initials of their positions (RPD is the Recorded Programmes Director), organise the broadcasting and scatter 'human voices into the darkness of Europe'.

Penelope Fitzgerald's writing has a fine economy and a constant flow of gentle, whimsical humour reminiscent of Muriel Spark at her best. Sam Brooks, the RDP, whose office girls constitute 'his seraglio' is described as the man 'who means everything he says at the time'. He and his colleagues are the

BBC, loyal to the truth: 'As an institution that could not tell a lie, they were unique in the contrivances of gods and men since the Oracle of Delphi.'

Some of her set pieces are very funny, but at the same time moving. An Anglophile French general supposedly broadcasting to rally England to the Free French unexpectedly calls for Englishmen to surrender, 'Give in when the Boche comes. Give in,' and he refers to 'the courageous drunkard whom you have made your Prime Minister'. Fortunately the DPP (Director of Programme Planning) had met the old boy in the corridor beforehand and had speedily pulled the plugs on him. DPP's prescience on this occasion does not save him though from the novel's amusingly macabre and almost fairytale ending.

Brian Martin, "A Taste of Drains," in New States-
man, Vol. 100, No. 2585, October 3, 1980, p. 24.

FRANCIS KING

The ability to pace herself with the finesse of an Olympic gold-medalist is something that Penelope Fitzgerald happily possesses. She began her writing career late, with a book on Edward Burne-Jones and an admirable biography, at once discreet, sympathetic and informative, of her remarkably diverse Knox father and uncles. These were followed by a slight but accomplished detective story, **The Golden Child. The Bookshop** first indicated that here was a novelist out of the ordinary. **Offshore** won the Booker Prize and, though I have a feeling that she took amiss my comment in this journal that the theme of its successor, **Human Voices** was 'a storm in a powder-compact', that account of life in the wartime BBC evoked my admiration, freely expressed, for its fun, pathos and elegance. With **At Freddie's,** she has both extended her territory and consolidated it. It is a true and strong work.

Within the novel itself, Mrs Fitzgerald's ability to pace herself is also instantaneously evident. (p. 24)

Freddie (theatre-people will have no difficulty in guessing her real-life prototype) once worked for Lilian Baylis, from whom 'she studied the craft of idealism, that is to say, how to defeat materialism by getting people to work for almost nothing.' Little else is known about her. Like her youthful protégés, who, true actors, are forever constructing their own realities, so she is forever constructing hers. It seems that once she knew the worst of poverty. But was that in Peterborough or St Petersburg? Perhaps she was an actress in her youth, but her walk, feet splayed outwards and head held high, suggests a former dancer. To be 'Freddie'd' is to be cajoled, conned or bullied into doing what Freddie wants of you. Even Noel Coward allows himself to be 'Freddie'd', briefly and buoyantly accepting the role of former pupil that she thrusts on him, though there is no evidence that he ever studied for even a day at her school.

This character, shafts of dazzling light piercing intermittently through a self-created opacity, is a wonderful original. Mrs Fitzgerald is scarcely less successful with the children, half angels and half monsters, whom Freddie trains for Shakespeare, *Peter Pan* and the pantomimes. 'The ambition of all children is to have their games taken seriously,' Mrs Fitzgerald comments at one point. It is also the ambition of all actors—though Mrs Fitzgerald works too subtly to establish that parallel except by constant implication. The characters of her book, like people in real life, are rarely wholly themselves. Sometimes consciously, more often unconsciously, they assume the roles that circumstances and stronger personalities force on them. This let's-pretend is at its most insidiously pernicious when her child actors are acting at being child actors.

The one exception is a young, unqualified Irishman who teaches general subjects at the school, falls in love with his only other academic colleague, and at the end of the book is dismissed by her when she gives him 'a hug and a kiss, as one does to a colleague, or to the inconsolable'. (Those last four words, turn what might have otherwise been a banale simile into a mysteriously arresting one—in a manner typical of Mrs Fitzgerald). This man 'could only be himself and that not very successfully.' But, having this rare ability—even if to him it seems a disability—he has achieved something that the more successful and happier people around him (the girl, the girl's actor lover, Freddie herself, the businessman eager to put money into the school, the pupils) have none of them achieved.

Mrs Fitzgerald's evocation of the ephemerality of the theatre is immensely moving since, by implication, it is also an evocation of the ephemerality of life itself. Actors and audience, mirror images of each other, come together and something briefly is created between them and then, for all eternity, is lost. 'The extravagance of that loss was its charm'—another unexpected redemption of the commonplace.

Mrs Fitzgerald describes one of her characters as 'a man who kept his eye on things, rather than listening to them.' She too, keeps her eye, severe yet forgiving, on things; but she never loses her capacity to listen to the still, sad music that sounds, faint but constant, beneath them. (pp. 24-5)

Francis King, "Gold-medalist," in The Spectator,
Vol. 248, No. 8020, March 27, 1982, pp. 24-5.

JOHN SUTHERLAND

Freddie's is the Temple Stage School, off Covent Garden, and Penelope Fitzgerald's [*At Freddie's*] is also set in the 1960s. . . . In the absence of any authorial note, I assume that the school and its head ('Freddie'—Frieda Wentworth) are historical. If there were no generous memorial motive behind this novel, then it's hard to see why it was undertaken and hard to forgive its broad sentimentality. Freddie is portrayed as one of the lovable prehistoric monsters of English theatrical history, a similar specimen to Lilian Baylis, with whom she served an apprenticeship and from whom she learned 'the craft of idealism, that is to say how to defeat materialism by getting people to work for almost nothing'. Around the depiction of this absurd person two sub-plots are woven. There is a love conflict for Hannah, a young Catholic teacher forced to choose between a charming, drunken, false-hearted actor and a fellow teacher (Irish, but Protestant) who is the antithesis of the acting type: literal, honest, humourless. At the juvenile level, there is rivalry among two of Freddie's pupils to fill the part of Prince Arthur in *King John*. One boy is crude but magnetic and destined for stardom; the other is finer-grained, a true Thespian. Their opposition is less interesting than Fitzgerald's sharply accurate evocation of an old-style West End production of Shakespeare, footlights and all, before the RSC and the National Theatre came along to rule the roost. I don't think she did herself justice in choosing this subject for her novel. But many of her customarily deft good things can be found here. Particularly good is the reconstruction of a Lyons tea shop, in which the lovers take their parting, genteelly clutching the statutory cup, quarter full of grouts and cold tea, to ward the tablewipers off:

> At Lyons, the females, if escorted, sat at a table and 'kept the place' while the males queued for what was needed and carried it back, as their remote forbears had done, with difficulty. During this process the tea overflowed into saucers. Later the sugar, which was only put out on every fourth table, had to be borrowed and exchanged. There was always a good deal of apologising at Lyons.

(p. 19)

John Sutherland, "Nationalities," in London Review of Books, *Vol. 4, No. 8, May 6-19, 1982, pp. 18-19.*

VALENTINE CUNNINGHAM

The power of the past to connect with the present affects Penelope Fitzgerald with loving wryness rather than perturbation [as evidenced in *Innocence*]. The strange array of dwarf statues adorning the country house of the Florentine Rudolfis was erected by some loving ancestors for their midget daughter as part of a well-intentioned fiction of a shrunken world. It misfired, and the statues remain as reminders that kindness can be misplaced. Ill-judged kindnesses still afflict the Rudolfis in the post-war years of Italian reconstruction, when the novel is set. And helping proves only a hindrance even if you're from other families or other traditions, as are Chiara Rudolfi's briskly organising schoolfriend, the large English girl Barney, or the man Chiara marries, impoverished, touchy, devoted Doctor Rossi.

Innocence bustles along most agreeably. It's warm with gossip, fluently organised, and unexpectedly knowledgeable about things Italian (and commendably modest about its wide range of reference). Penelope Fitzgerald garners in English snobberies and absurdities with the same joyous appreciation that marks her account of the Italians' hectic to-ings and fro-ings—all soured menials, mothering aunties, machinating monsignors, faded counts, and Vespas. Things here, especially mouldering mansions, tend to fall gloriously apart. But this is the pleasing sort of novel in which the innocence of a family's victims will see them through, if not quite to happy endings, at least to survival.

Valentine Cunningham, "Skulls Beneath the Skin," in The Observer, *September 7, 1986, p. 26.*

ANNE DUCHÊNE

[*Innocence*] is by far the fullest and richest of Penelope Fitzgerald's novels, and also the most ambitious. Her writing, as ever, has a natural authority, is very funny, warm, and gently ironic, and full of tenderness towards human beings and their bravery in living; and it also has several new elements.

For one thing, she forsakes drab English settings for Florence, which she evidently knows well, and the change has been refreshing: exotic new detail, a quickening of energy in the story, and above all a sense of tremendous physical presence in the writing, in surface-textures and sensuousness. Then, too, and startlingly, the large promise of the title is underpinned by overt admissions of allegory. The book opens

by telling the legend of the Villa Ricordanza, where in the sixteenth century a girl was mutilated to protect her from the world, unknown but adjudged unfriendly. In other words, she suffered at the hands of a loving "innocence" unable to see the world in anything but its own terms; innocence at its most obtuse, and capable of cruelty.

La Ricordanza is owned by the Ridolfi family, impoverished patricians who cannot afford to live there any more. They live now in a flat in the Piazza Limbo—no trouble with *that* name; nor with sensing the association of La Ricordanza with memory, reminding, bringing back to the heart. Their third property is a farm, Valsassina—"sasso" is a stone, in Italian—where a lonely, silent nephew, Cesare, farms the hard land, and struggles to recover the lost right to call its wine *classico*.

These labels do not make for abstraction. Florentine life is observed going on with Florentine vigour all round the focal theme; the sense of place, of people belonging to place, and of people working, is very intimate and happy. Pallid passages—visits to London, to English expatriates in Tuscany, to a literary party in Rome—occur when the action moves too far away from its resonant Ridolfi centre.

The head of the family, the elderly count, Giancarlo, has honed his detachment to a virtually seamless urbanity, and decided to "outface the last part of his life, and indeed of his character, by not minding about anything very much", though he understands acutely everything he does not deliberately evade. He lives with his sister, Maddelena, once married to an English bird-watcher, and his daughter, Chiara, aged eighteen.

Chiara returns from her English convent school, and falls into love, as into water or fire, with a very poor (but promising) young doctor from the south. . . . Happily, Salvatore, the doctor, responds totally; he is as galvanic and intellectual an innocent as Chiara is an animal, instinctive one. Salvatore was traumatized at the age of ten when his loyal, poor, communist father took him to see the dying Gramsci in a clinic in 1936: he swore on the spot never to become emotionally dependent on anyone. This awkward stance he tries to maintain, even after marrying Chiara, but always feels at a disadvantage: "a serious thinking person had no defence against innocence because he was obliged to respect it, whereas the innocent scarcely know what respect is, or seriousness either". He rides a Vespa, and has violent intellectual arguments in the street.

The title refers to more than lack of respect and seriousness, however; and little is made of the cruel fable at the book's outset. The lovers are cruel, certainly, but to each other, and on the whole rather enjoyably. They cannot, on that account, assume the status of hero and heroine. For one thing, everyone else is cast in a much more heroic mould.

The title, in fact, can be seen as cheering; the author is giving innocence a hard, long look at last. It has been the primary concern of all her novels. *Offshore*, the 1979 Booker Prize winner, about people on Thames barges, was awash with innocence of all the commoner kinds; later books—notably *At Freddie's*—suggested that too much clear-eyed innocence, which stops short of noticing anyone else's impulses or motives, might lure even such a clever writer as this into self-indulgence and the *fauxnaïf*.

Now, however, she has embraced innocence in its every

sense, not only in its lamb-and-petticoat extension, but as meaning unacquainted with evil, as having done no evil, and as not intending to do any. It may indeed mean unknowingness, in the young; but it means unhurtfulness when one is older.

Anne Duchêne, *"Do No Evil, Mean No Evil,"* in The Times Literary Supplement, No. 4354, September 12, 1986, 1986, p. 995.

FRANCIS KING

Clearly it must have been a visit to the Villa Valmarana that inspired Penelope Fitzgerald to create [in **Innocence**] her La Ricordanza, a similar villa outside Florence, in which a noble family, the Ridolfi, have lived, in increasing obscurity, for many generations.

Back in the 16th century a Ridolfi, himself a midget, marries a midget and has a midget daughter by her. As a companion for this daughter, from whom he wishes to conceal the truth of the family abnormality, he brings into the villa, sealed off from the outer world, another midget girl. But unaccountably, soon after her arrival, this newcomer begins to grow with remarkable celerity. The Ridolfi girl, devoted to her new companion and wishing to spare her the ignominy (as she sees it) of realisation of her monstrous size, then out of compassion decides that it would be better for her if she were to be blinded and have her legs amputed at the knees. This grim fairy-tale announces the theme on which the rest of the novel is a series of often brilliant and always fascinating variations. When love impels us to attempt changes in others, what all too often results is grotesque mutilation and therefore unhappiness for all.

Anyone who lived in Florence (as I did) in the Fifties will marvel at the authenticity with which Mrs Fitzgerald brings that period of tentatively burgeoning hope and confidence to life. . . . Mrs Fitzgerald is particularly successful with her Ridolfi, their Italian blood thinned by the passing of centuries as much as it has been diluted by foreign marriages. Impractical, impoverished and for the most part idle—the exceptions are one member of the family who is a Monsignore and another who runs the estate—they are sadly ill-equipped to survive in the post-war world.

Curiously, Mrs Fitzgerald's one failure of characterisation is her heroine, Chiara, the daughter of the family. When she writes of her, it is as though a sculptor were kneading a piece of clay with increasing frenzy and frustration, never quite succeeding in breathing life into it. In contrast, the penniless neurologist from the Mezzogiorno, Salvatore, with whom Chiara makes what appears to be a certain misalliance, is a wholly credible, if also almost wholly unlikeable, creation.

What has made him unlikeable—it is here that we have an example of love resulting in mutilation—is, on the one hand, the devotion of a mother who insisted on naming him after the Saviour, and, on the other, the influence of a father constantly dreaming of an Italy, such as the left-wing martyr Antonio Gramsci envisaged, of *Liberazione* and *Umanitá*. In first migrating to the prosperous north, then opting for a life of science, and finally marrying into the minor aristocracy, Salvatore has constantly attempted to repudiate his peasant inheritance. . . .

The book contains some splendid set-pieces. The most vivid of these is when the ten-year-old Salvatore is taken by his father to the Clinica Quisiana in Rome, to visit Antonio Gramsci, who has been transferred there from prison when known to be terminally ill from spinal tuberculosis. Mrs Fitzgerald is unsparing here—'Salvatore had seen deformed animals, and dead bodies of both people and animals, but never anything as ugly as comrade Gramsci. Ugliness is a hard thing to forgive at the age of ten.' She is also extremely moving.

There are times in this book when she seems to be searching for a path from which she has inadvertently wandered, and other times when her pace grows a little weary. But, all in all, this is, in equal measure, a work of moral, intellectual and emotional richness.

Francis King, *"Cutting People Down to Size,"* in The Spectator, Vol. 257, No. 8253, September 13, 1986, p. 33.

LESLEY CHAMBERLAIN

Whatever a few hopeful rationalists maintain to the contrary, to many Western sensibilities Russia remains a mysterious place. In [**The Beginning of Spring**] its people are imbued with unpredictable emotions, intermittent religious sensibility and an instinctive mendacity. It is an enlightening backdrop against which to view Frank Reid, an expatriate printer by trade and something of a pillar of the English community in Moscow at the turn of the century. Reid is decent, a mild sceptic, not dull, honest with his three bright children and a conscientious employer. His decency doesn't disappear when his wife Nellie suddenly leaves him without explanation. . . .

The women servants weep when he announces that Nellie has left; they invoke God's mercy, yet claim to be atheists; the children's Russian teacher goes into hiding, sure that she will be blamed for the mistress's departure. Even the messenger who has brought the news from Nellie has lied, and his colleagues in the household have told a few gratuitous untruths on his behalf so he can have a rest and a drink in the kitchen. Things are much the same with Frank's business colleague, the Moscow merchant Arkady Kuriatin, who lies and repents at regular intervals without obvious reason. . . .

But the English in their own understated way are just as deceptive and unpredictable. What is irresistible in this account of a few weeks of confusion and loss in the life of a middle-aged man is the buoyant happiness of its atmosphere none the less, and the subtle emotional symmetry of the tale. Selwyn Crane, another expatriate, is a Tolstoyan disciple, moralist and mawkish poet, also Reid's most uncommercial accountant. Quietly he and Frank accuse each other of cruelty, of seduction, of misuse of their fellow men. Frank is not keen on Selwyn's poems but sees their merit: he gives a copy of *Birch Tree Thoughts* to the gun-toting student. Some truth about human nature lies in the midst of all the male characters in this book, just as some truth about love is hinted at through the diverse behaviour of the children and the women. Nellie, whom we never see, has left behind her a trail of devotion and good sense. Her eldest daughter clings to a rationality beyond her years when she writes to her mother of "irresponsibility"; the toddler Annushka, meanwhile, is ready to love even the daft and feckless Uncle Charlie. But one thing is certain: the men, even the holier-than-thou Selwyn, will always be alert to the sexual possibility.

This modest drama of relationships unfolds against a background of daily joys: wind-up telephones which are still miraculous, motorcar rides which are still a treat enjoyed at the excursionists' peril, the bizarre workings of the Russian police bureaucracy, and the untended dacha in the countryside, with its stores of dried mushrooms and pickled vegetables. The novel is strong on the domestic character of an era usually viewed through political events: Stolypin has been shot dead in a Moscow theatre; revolution hangs in the air.

With interest in Russia now so fashionable, a delicate, intelligent and readable piece of fiction like this cannot fail to please. It would only be a pity if popularity diverted attention from the high quality of Penelope Fitzgerald's writing, which must make *The Beginning of Spring* one of the outstanding novels of the year.

Lesley Chamberlain, "Worried, Norbury," in The Times Literary Supplement, *No. 4460, September 23-29, 1988, p. 1041.*

ANITA BROOKNER

[In *The Beginning of Spring*] Penelope Fitzgerald has produced a real Russian comedy, at once crafty and scatty. This is all the more remarkable since she is one of the mildest and most English of writers. Mild, yes, but there is authority behind those neat, discursive and unresolved stories of hers, of which the most typical is her last novel, *Innocence.* She seems innocent herself but she knows exactly what she is doing, and if the novels appear to ramble or to end inconsequentially we may take this as proof of her good faith, for only in fiction is the neat tight ending available: life itself refuses to conform. She has introduced a one line conclusion to the present novel, but this does not contradict the farcical aspect of what has gone before, as Frank Reid puzzles over the disappearance of his wife, Nellie, discovers that she had a lover, falls in love himself, and is thwarted but perhaps also relieved when Nellie returns.

But the novel is only superficially about Frank and Nellie, about Lisa, the mysterious governess and her unexplained tryst at midnight in the forest (this struck me as taking inconsequence a little too far), and about Selwyn, cost accountant, follower of Tolstoy, lover and friend. The novel is about Moscow, and not only about Moscow, but about Moscow in 1913. With astonishing virtuosity Mrs Fitzgerald has mastered a city, a landscape, and a vanished time, as she sets up her story of Frank Reid's printing works. (p. 29)

This is all the more of a triumph in that the novel refuses to make too much capital out of this reconstitution. Penelope Fitzgerald is clearly in love with Russia, but she can hardly have known it in 1913, when ramshackle structures still impeded the sidewalks and students were automatically suspect and servants abounded. Yet her Moscow is probably essentially unchanged since early days, for she is not interested in politics but in customs. Indeed, in spite of the need for both internal and external passports and the threat of expulsion for foreigners if they become awkward, this is a peaceful, 'maternal' city, traditional, kindly, shabby and affectionate. Thus all that is familiar in our haziest notions of a literary Russia—from Chekhov, even from Turgenev—is brought before us in defiance of the more recent vogue for novels of dissidence, with their emphasis on state corruption. And yet Penelope Fitzgerald's Russia seems authentic.

Hers is a Moscow in which certain ceremonies—the break-up of the ice, the unsealing of the windows—herald the beginning of spring. There is a whole section on the composition of a birch forest which in other hands would be a flagrant digression. But the author makes no concessions to our expectations of what a novel should be about or how it should proceed: she is simply recreating a time and a place and she does this with complete success. (pp. 29-30)

Character is not stressed but suggested: Mrs Graham at the English Chaplaincy, smoking her roll-ups of rough shag, Miss Kinsman, the deranged governess, Kuriatin, the double-crossing associate fall into place quite naturally. Only Lisa Ivanovna, brought in to look after the children, fails as a character, largely because her activities are unexplained. What exactly was she doing in the forest at midnight? Has a note of mysticism crept in, or is this some strange political ritual? An association between Lisa and a student is posited but left vague. In fact everything is vague but confident, elusive, unclear, and almost absent in comparison with the fabric of the city and its inhabitants. And it is a city utterly lacking in logic yet simple in character. Although deals are struck and bribes taken, the image of the city as 'maternal' (the word is repeated) is very strong.

I am suggesting that Mrs Fitzgerald has written something remarkable, part novel, part evocation, and that she has done so in prose that never puts a foot wrong. She is so unostentatious a writer that she needs to be read several times. What is impressive is the calm confidence behind the apparent simplicity of utterance. *The Beginning of Spring* is her best novel to date. (p. 30)

Anita Brookner, "Moscow Before the Revolution," in The Spectator, *Vol. 261, No. 8360, October 1, 1988, pp. 29-30.*

MARGARET WALTERS

Penelope Fitzgerald has always seemed a quintessentially English novelist, low-key, exquisitely perceptive, and with a notable feeling for place—the seedy houseboats on the Thames in *Offshore,* or the mean little Suffolk town that dominates *The Bookshop.* Her latest novel, *The Beginning of Spring,* is a surprise, and something of a *tour de force.* Its subject is Moscow just before the Revolution: 'dear slovenly Moscow, bemused with the bells on its four times forty churches, indifferently sheltering factories, whorehouses and golden domes, impeded by Greeks and Persians and bewildered villagers and seminarists straying onto the tramlines, centred on its holy citadel but reaching outwards with a frosty leap across the boulevards to the circle of workers' dormitories and railheads, where the monasteries still prayed, and last to a circle of pigsties, cabbage patches, earth roads, earth closets, where Moscow sank back, seemingly with relief, into a village.' The great messy city, muddling towards its destiny, is conjured up in a vivid and astonishing detail: the narrow back-streets with their seedy basement workshops; the crowded markets and railway stations; the exuberantly noisy club where the merchants drink tea and vodka; the vast dark river choked with broken ice and rubbish.

Penelope Fitzgerald's hero is a quiet, thoughtful Englishman, Frank Reid, born and brought up in the city and running a small printing business inherited from his father. The tragicomedy of Frank's domestic difficulties is played out, often ironically, against this enormous, turbulent backdrop. At the start of the novel, his English wife Nellie has upped and left him without a word of explanation: she had apparently intended to take her three children with her, but left them behind at the Alexandrovna station. We never know much about Nellie, always 'a jumper up and walker about', though there's a wonderfully telling glimpse of the girl Frank met and married when he was back in England learning the trade: a 26-year-old schoolteacher desperate to escape a spinster's existence. We understand Nellie a little better through her 14-year-old daughter Dolly, captured in all her spiky individuality in just a few scenes. Deeply hurt by her mother's departure, Dolly copes by plunging back into the routine of her next day's homework, and offers a sad, precocious explanation of the way Nellie abandoned them. 'After all, she's never had to look after us before . . . She had to send us back, we weren't a comfort to her.' Later, picking up on some of the advanced ideas around her, she informs her father that 'the mistake she probably made was getting married in the first place.' Dolly sees more of what's going on than anyone else, though she has learned to keep her own counsel.

The Reid family troubles are acted out on a very public stage, with servants and neighbours and colleagues throwing themselves into the fray. The merchant Kuriatin welcomes the children, but they're scared and shocked by his 'half-savage' household, and by the way rough-and-tumble games with a bear cub turn vicious. The English community is even less help. The chaplain's sharp-tongued wife is always on the look-out for the least hint of scandal; an out-of-work English governess, lonely and half-crazed, pursues Frank through the streets to offer her services. Nellie's brother Charlie helpfully makes the long journey to Moscow, but has no real news of Nellie, and wanders round wide-eyed and enthusiastic about their 'Arabian Nights' existence. And Frank's dotty colleague Selwyn, a gratingly benevolent devotee of Tolstoy and author of *Birch Tree Thoughts,* consoles Frank with the notion that loss, like poverty, is 'matter not for regret but rejoicing'. Frank can't take the pretentious Selwyn seriously, and that's one of his mistakes: he's much more implicated in Nellie's departure than he admits, and it's Selwyn who changes their lives, for good or bad, by finding Lisa Ivanovna to look after the children.

Fitzgerald writes affectionately about the everyday routines in the house and at the printing-press, but we're aware, all the time, of currents below the placid surface, of tiny discrepancies glimpsed from the corner of the eye and not fully understood, or awkward feelings not put into words. The city Frank loved as a child is changing fast: it is the new electric trams which break the silence in the early morning—not the cows leaving their stalls in the side-streets. Reidkas still use hand-presses, and there are loving descriptions of the routines and rhythms of the compositors, or the annual ritual blessing of the office icon. But everyone is nervous when a pistol-brandishing student breaks into the works and the Police start taking a closer interest in the firm: a couple of Frank's best men talk about emigrating, while his ambitious new accountant insists that the future is with big firms using hot metal. When he dismisses hand-printing as a relic from the past 'associated now with Tolstoyans and student revolutionaries', Frank has a sudden vision of activists beavering away all over the city, in 'garrets and cellars, in cowsheds, bath houses and backyard pissoirs, hen coops, cabbage patches, potato stacks—small hand-presses . . . spirited away to another address at the hint of danger. He imagined the dissi-

dents, on Moscow's a hundred and forty days a year of frost, warming the ink to deliver one more warning. Printer's ink freezes readily.' Are those dissidents inhabitants of the past, or the future? Frank, a practical man, doesn't ask many questions. But he's made preparations for an emergency departure, in the sad knowledge that, though he doesn't quite belong in Russia, he'll never be at home anywhere else.

It's Lisa Ivanovna, the joiner's daughter, the girl from the men's handkerchief counter in a department store, the governess, who represents the unknown future. With her 'pale broad, patient, dreaming Russian face', she brings order and calm back to the house: the children love her, and, inevitably, Frank finds himself desperately attracted to her. But she's something else as well. The bitchy chaplain's wife, not really meaning it, implies that she could easily be some kind of revolutionary. We begin to suspect that, for once, her malice has weaselled out the truth. But Fitzgerald resolutely refuses to spell anything out: we see Lisa's intelligence and humour, but we are denied any insight into her inner world. There's just one, tantalising glimpse of her other life. When Lisa and the children go to Frank's dacha during the spring thaw, Dolly follows her to a mysterious meeting deep in the birch forest. Very briefly, we're allowed to eavesdrop on history in the making: anything more would demand a different kind of writing, and a very different kind of novel.

Penelope Fitzgerald's fiction works by indirection, by hints and suggestions, and it leaves unresolved ambiguities. The image that dominates the novel is the coming of spring, the thaw. In Frank's earliest childhood, when the family still lived at the factory, he would become delightedly aware of a small 'protesting voice, the voice of the water, when the ice melted under the covered wooden footpath between the house and the factory . . . once it had begun to run in a chattering stream, the whole balance of the year tilted over.' As a man, he has more complicated reactions: he knows the dirt and discomfort brought by the melting ice, its destructive power, and the 'inconceivable amount of rubbish' that chokes the river as the ice breaks up. But, like the servants and the children, Frank feels released as the house is unsealed and the outer windows, at last, flung wide. 'Throughout the winter the house had been deaf, turned inwards, able to listen only to itself. Now the sounds of Moscow broke in, the bells and voices, the cabs and taxis which had gone by all winter unheard like ghosts of themselves, and with the noise came the spring wind, fresher than it felt in the street, blowing in uninterrupted from the northern regions where the frost still lay.' There's a feeling of optimism on the last pages, a feeling that the spring may imply rebirth, new ways of living, a freedom from personal or political repression. But with her characteristic cool integrity, Penelope Fitzgerald refuses to commit herself, and she leaves us with a whole series of questions, about Frank's marriage, about his future, and about the great changes coming to the country he loves. (p. 20)

Margaret Walters, "Women's Fiction," in London Review of Books, *Vol. 10, No. 18, October 13, 1988, pp. 20-1.*

RICHARD EDER

Spring is most violent where winter is most implacable. The foreground of [*The Beginning of Spring*], set in Russia in 1913, is the passage from a frozen March to the mud, snow-melt, prodigious budding and patchy blue of April. In the background is another changing weather: the erratic pulse of a revolution sprouting underneath the czarist ice.

Between these two weathers wander Fitzgerald's comical innocents, an assortment of English expatriates living in St. Petersburg. Each has appropriated various bits of Russia and has got them, to various degrees, wrong. Their blithe myopia can't quite make out the unpredictable shifts of the Russians around them, caught in their tempestuous double equinox.

Fitzgerald is one of the most gifted and elusive of living English writers. She writes with humor and an apparently gentle absurdity; there is something grave behind. Her books are archaic smiles, the corners turned down, devoid neither of compassion nor of distance.

Her theme is the English theme; which always and ever is that of a world in decline. Fitzgerald's decline lies not in politics, economics or morals, but in a dwindling sense of reality. She will place her English in houseboats, as in *Offshore,* or abroad, as in this book and in *Innocence,* set in Italy. They never quite touch ground.

The Russians in *The Beginning of Spring* move with a sense of incipient tragedy, though they can be very funny while doing it. The English interpret the ground tremors not as tragedy but as unreliability.

The grave comedy of *Spring* centers around Frank Reid, the most innocent of the expatriates. He is a good and just man, but he is always catching up with what is going on. He is neither weak nor foolish; it's simply that the world at the turning of the seasons is moving faster and worse than he is.

Everything eludes him. He comes home one day from the printing factory he inherited from his father to find a messenger sipping tea in his kitchen. The messenger has been summoned to pick up a letter for him from his wife, Nellie. Frank is told why a messenger is needed to deliver a letter within the same house. He gets a reasonable answer, but it is the reasonableness of *Alice in Wonderland.*

Nellie writes that she has left with their three children. A theatrical approach being expected by the servants, Frank makes a dramatic announcement of the news. Theatrically, they weep and exclaim, although they have just helped her pack. . . .

Why Nellie has left and where she has gone is a mystery until the end of the book. It is not a mystery anyone bothers much about; the real question is how Frank and the children will manage. The question serves to introduce an assortment of characters offering consolation or help.

There is Selwyn, Frank's English assistant. He writes poetry, wears a Russian peasant blouse under his frock coat and is a disciple of Tolstoy. Tolstoy tells him he is boring but not to mind about it.

Selwyn will go through various transformations; the lack of clarity about just what he is up to moves along the book's slender plot. He begins by telling Frank that his loss is a cause for rejoicing. "No it's not," Frank replies. "What a good man," one of the servants says of Selwyn afterwards. "Always on his way from one place to another searching out want and despair."

Mystic Russia, courtesy of Selwyn, is one of Frank's crosses. Another is the hearty and marginally sincere embrace of Kuryatin, a friend and business associate. Kuryatin takes the

children into his household but the arrangement lasts barely an afternoon. . . .

Selwyn produces Lisa, a young woman from the country whom he claims to have met weeping at the handkerchief counter of the local department store. Frank hires her as governess and falls in love. But she is connected with the underground; before long, she has to flee the country. Here as always, Selwyn's role is unfathomable.

A whole tangle of elusive schemes and subplots takes shape around Frank. The secret police appear, the printing press is in danger, and spring advances more and more disruptively.

Frank sees, but only dimly. He is not a dim man, though, in fact, he is a kind of patient hero. If his sight is fuzzy, it is a comic English fuzziness, but it is also something more. The world is shifting in its cloud of unreliability, and the dust gets in his eyes.

Fitzgerald has written a lovely book; a comedy lit by writing so precise and lilting that it can make you shiver, and an elegy that nods at what passes without lamentation or indifference.

Richard Eder, "A Morris Dance at Russian Easter," in Los Angeles Times Book Review, *April 23, 1989, p. 3.*

ROBERT PLUNKET

What is it that makes a good old-fashioned comedy of manners just about the most satisfying reading there is? For many people—certainly me—a few days spent immersed in a tiny domestic atmosphere, full of characters as ordinary (and as weird) as my own friends, with their schemes, self-delusions and operatic emotions, is the literary equivalent of a whole pint of rum raisin ice cream.

But for all the pleasure it gives, the comedy of manners remains a vastly underrated art form. It is considered a little too shallow, a little too polite to be taken all that seriously. Look at E. M. Forster. His purported masterpiece, *A Passage to India,* is thought to be the height of profundity; to me, it's just another long-winded book about a trial. But his first novel, *Where Angels Fear to Tread*—now there's a book you can read over and over.

The United States has never been very good at turning out comedies of manners, but the form still flourishes in England, where there is a whole new stream both of heirs and innovators to the tradition. One of the best, only recently familiar to American readers, is Penelope Fitzgerald, who won Britain's Booker Prize in 1979 for *Offshore.* Her latest book, *The Beginning of Spring,* is a very good comedy of manners. But old-fashioned? Hardly.

It begins with a group of concerns that would tempt the pen of Forster himself. A middle-class British family is domiciled in a most un-British country, in this case, Russia. It is 1913, the tail end of the Edwardian age. The head of the household, Frank Reid, runs a printing business that was established by his father. Frank was born in Russia, unlike his wife, who hails from Norbury, a few miles south of London. Nellie, a difficult, headstrong woman whose favorite expression is "I'm not going to be got the better of," has headed back home to England. Why did she leave? Is she coming back? No one—most of all Frank—seems sure. But one thing is certain.

Arrangements must be made about their three young children.

Frank is a decent, honorable man, somewhat of a loner in spite of the masses of humanity who depend on him. . . . He is a modest and self-effacing hero, and this is definitely his book, but much of the bite and sparkle belong to the secondary characters.

These include Frank's management accountant, Selwyn Crane, who, if he were around today, would be into channeling and health foods. . . .

Selwyn may not quite be the do-gooder he seems, but, like all of Frank's friends and neighbors, he enters enthusiastically into the problem of what to do with the children. One possibility is to engage the dowdy but determined Muriel Kinsman, at loose ends in Moscow after being let go from her position as governess to a provincial family following a number of unfortunate incidents, including "the matter of the valerian drops" and the mysterious "matter of the bath house." Fortunately, Miss Kinsman is sent back to England, and a beautiful young peasant girl named Lisa Ivanovna gets the job instead.

Another trait Ms. Fitzgerald shares with Forster is the ability to create characters from other cultures that are so deftly drawn they become as believable as her slightly flaky British expatriates. The Russians in *The Beginning of Spring* are an exuberant bunch, from the vast and unruly family of the merchant Kuriatin to the student radical Volodya, who sneaks into the Reid Press one night, ostensibly to print a manifesto on "universal pity."

But with Forster there was always an unbridgeable gap between the two cultures. When someone tried to cross it, the results were at first comic and then disastrous. This is certainly not the case with Ms. Fitzgerald. Her British and her Russians meet as social and emotional equals; in fact, Frank and his family are so assimilated into their adopted country that their life style (to use a most un-Edwardian word) is almost entirely Russian. And it is this slightly exotic atmosphere—daily life in pre-Revolutionary Moscow, with its housekeeping rituals, the blessing of the office ikon and a visit to the family dacha—that gives *The Beginning of Spring* its rhythms and much of its charm. . . .

I hope I'm not giving the impression that Ms. Fitzgerald is merely a clever imitator of the masters. She and her characters have their own agenda; its priorities are the timelessness of human nature and the possibility of love. She is that refreshing rarity, a writer who is very modern but not the least bit hip. Ms Fitzgerald looks into the past, both human and literary, and finds all sorts of things that are surprisingly up to date. Yet as *The Beginning of Spring* reaches its triumphant conclusion, you realize that its greatest virtue is perhaps the most old-fashioned of all. It is a lovely novel.

> *Robert Plunket, "Dear, Slovenly Mother Moscow,"*
> *in* The New York Times Book Review, *May 2,*
> *1989, p. 15.*

JONATHON PENNER

[*The Beginning of Spring*] is (to begin with) a remarkably vivid portrait of prerevolutionary Moscow. Rarely do invention and research yield anything so like memory:

Once you were off the main streets you had to know (since it could scarcely be explained) the way. Street names soon ran out. You were faced by towering heaps of bricks and drain-pipes, or a lean-to which encroached on the pavement, or a steaming cowshed whose rotten planks seemed to breathe in and out under their own volition.

The novel opens with a situation at once absurd and frightening. Frank Albertovitch Reid is a Russian-born Englishman, the proprietor of a printing company, a man more gifted with decency and energy than with imagination. One day he comes home to find his wife gone. Her mysterious letter awaits him; so, ridiculously, does the hired messenger who should have delivered it to his office. Calmly sipping tea in the kitchen, the self-satisfied messenger is an unexpected flourish of invention, typical of the creative generosity that appears throughout.

Left with three children, a houseful of servants, a business to run and his heart's wound; Frank works to preserve the little world while, in the great world outside, the shadow of 1917 is already falling. The political cataclysm that we (but not the characters) know is coming adds tension, dramatic irony and a sense of scale.

Yet the great charm of this book rests on detailed observation, minute insight and the wit that close attention yields. (p. 1)

Complementing this power of attention is an inspired daring. Contrasting scenes are brilliantly juxtaposed: in one, we meet ladies who, asked to help with a domestic crisis, are grieved that they will be needed only briefly, for "out of sheer tenderness of heart they liked every emergency to go on as long as possible"; and in the next we see a dancing bear, soaked with vodka, incinerated atop a dining-room table.

Consider, as an epitome of Fitzgerald's daring, a single sentence (grammatically it isn't even that). Here Frank recalls the first time he and his wife made love: "These sudden decisions of Nellie's—but Frank could really only remember one, in her bedroom in Longfellow Road, that hot afternoon, with just enough breeze, after Frank had drawn the blinds, to make the tassel at the end of the blind-cord tap against the window." How that verbal pathway follows the inward spiral of awareness, narrowing to the single startling, inevitable and numinous detail that means—at the level of feeling—everything!

The novel loses force when the author becomes an authority—glossing exotics like "*listofka, slievanka, vieshnyovka* and *beryozovitsa,* the liqueurs of the currant-leaf, plum, cherry and birch-sap"; or offering *sententiae* that apply to the world at large, not just the world of the story: "Middle-aged poets, middle-aged parents, have no defences."

A larger problem is the case of mysticism that falls over the book's last pages. A peasant girl, daughter of a carpenter (the symbol is made unmissable by the placing of crucial events at Easter) with whom Frank falls in love, proves able to summon apparitions. The symbolic level of the book, implied at once in the title, becomes obtrusive, as seasonal change, political change, religious resurrection and sexual arousal are linked pointedly and bluntly.

But this is a novel that somehow bears even its flaws with grace. For many readers, its charm, intelligence and energy will compel unconditional love. "Life makes its own corrections," says a philosophical Moscow sledge driver, and so, in this case, does art. (p. 14)

Jonathon Penner, "Moscow on the Eve," in Book World—The Washington Post, *June 11, 1989, pp. 1, 14.*

María Irene Fornés

1930-

Cuban-born American dramatist.

Fornés is among the pioneering avant-garde dramatists who created the off-off-Broadway forum during the 1960s. Unlike most of her contemporaries, she continued working in small, non-commercially oriented theaters for over twenty-five years. In 1972, Fornés helped to found the New York Theater Strategy—an organization that produced the work of experimental American playwrights—and served in various roles, from bookkeeper to president, until the league dissolved in 1979. Fornés's works have earned her an unprecedented seven Obie Awards, the highest recognition for off-Broadway productions, a tribute to her dedication to the non-Broadway theater. Her 1982 Obie was a commendation for sustained achievement. Despite her accomplishments, Fornés has not received significant public attention. Her plays are neither widely reviewed nor have they been subject to numerous interpretations, perhaps because critics are unable to categorize Fornés's constantly evolving, experimental style. Fellow dramatist Lanford Wilson commented: "She's one of the very, very best—it's a shame she's always been performed in such obscurity. Her work has no precedents, it isn't derived from *anything.* She's the most original of us all."

Fornés was born in Cuba and came to the United States in 1945. She began a career as a painter but decided to devote her life to playwriting after attending Roger Blin's 1954 Paris production of Samuel Beckett's *Waiting for Godot.* Of the performance, Fornés said: "I didn't know a word of French. I had not read the play in English. But what was happening in front of me had a profound impact without even understanding a word. Imagine a writer whose theatricality is so amazing and so important that you could see a play of his, not understand one word, and be shook up. When I left that theater I felt that my life was changed, that I was seeing everything with a different clarity." The surrealistic elements of Beckett's writing influenced Fornés's early plays, which are unconventional in their structure, dialogue, and staging. Eschewing plot and character development, her works often explore emotions in human relationships through symbolism rather than realism, and at times contain both brutality and slapstick humor. Critics praise Fornés for her subtle social criticism and economy of style. Susan Sontag asserted: "Fornés has a near faultless ear for the ruses of egotism and cruelty. Unlike most contemporary dramatists, for whom psychological brutality is the principal, inexhaustible subject, Fornés is never in complicity with the brutality she depicts." Sontag added: "[Her] work has always been intelligent, often funny, never vulgar or cynical; both delicate and visceral."

In her first important play, *Tango Palace,* Fornés presents ill-fated male lovers who enact such roles as father-son and teacher-pupil. They gradually become engaged in a metaphysical power struggle that ultimately ends in murder. *The Successful Life of 3: A Skit for Vaudeville,* a romantic spoof for which Fornés received her first Obie Award, features characters named He, She, and 3, who meet in a doctor's office and become involved in a love triangle. Their archetypal relationship is delineated through a series of short, unrelated

sketches in which the sense of disconnection helps explain the dynamics of their love. Bonnie Marranca commented: "*The Successful Life of 3* represents Fornés at her comic best. This beautifully orchestrated piece, with its crisp, precise dialogue, peculiar internal logic, and short, cinematic takes is a wonderful display of comic anarchy."

Fornés's next Obie Award-winning play, *Promenade,* contains perhaps her strongest social criticism. In this comedy of manners, two guileless, lower-class prisoners, 105 and 106, escape from their jail cell in quest of the evil they know to exist in the world, but have never seen. Their flight leads them to direct confrontation with the wealthy for the first time, and 105 and 106 learn that the rich are cruel, while the poor are "rich" in spirit and kindness. However, unable to pinpoint evil because they cannot identify it, the uncorrupted prisoners willingly return to the "freedom" of their cell. Another of Fornés' favorite satirical targets is popular culture, and she often employs ironic reversal to illustrate the influence it has on the American psyche. In *Molly's Dream,* for example, a waitress falls asleep on the job and dreams herself into melodramatic movies of the 1940s. Fornés parodies and mocks the romantic conventions of the era, as Molly refuses to break into song when music swells dramatically and she interrupts a torch song about abusive love to explain the implausibility of the situation in her actual life.

Fefu and Her Friends marks a change for Fornés to a somewhat more conventional approach to drama. With this pivotal work, Fornés begins to emphasize realistic, three-dimensional characters rather than symbolic and surreal action. The play revolves around eight female friends who have gathered at a New England country home for a reunion weekend in 1935. Wrought with tension, however, the characters eventually become violent, and their frenzy culminates in murder. Innovative staging highlights this Obie Award-winner, which John G. Kuhn described as "a mature play, ripe with nuance and mystery." Scenes in Act II take place in different rooms simultaneously; the audience, which is split into groups, physically moves from room to room. Several critics believe that the play's action, viewed in no particular sequence, stresses the redundant lives of women in a chauvinistic society. Through a blend of quick humor and stream-of-consciousness dialogue, Fornés illuminates the concerns and social ills of the Depression era from a female perspective. *Mud*, also grounded in realism, is set on an Appalachian farm, where Mae, her husband Lloyd, and Henry, who becomes Mae's lover after her husband is accidentally crippled, live in gloom and ignorance. After Mae learns that knowledge and communication are the keys to power, she prepares to leave the stifling farm, but the inarticulate Lloyd kills her.

Fornés treats the themes of sexual politics and the failure of communication in other plays as well. *The Danube* centers upon Paul and Eve, whose difficulty communicating is punctuated by the broadcasting of a foreign language instruction tape following each argument. The title character in *Sarita* is an adolescent Cuban girl from the South Bronx who harbors a self-destructive, unrequited love for a young man. Confused by contradicting Cuban and American values and unable to stay away from the boy, Sarita ultimately stabs him to death. *The Conduct of Life,* an Obie Award-winning play, focuses on the personal and sexual life of Orlando, a Latin American soldier whose duty is torturing prisoners for his military government. Rather than showing the audience the particulars of the captain's job, Fornés conveys his heartless temperament by depicting his violent relationship with his wife, whom he harasses and ridicules, and his twelve-year-old female servant, whom he rapes and enslaves. Through the link between Orlando's private and public lives, Fornés comments on the brutality of political oppression. *The Conduct of Life* received critical praise for its avoidance of didacticism and for its strong theatrical impact. Another Obie Award-winning play, *Abingdon Square,* is set in New York City in 1905 and conveys the sense of stagnation felt by Marion, a fifteen-year-old girl married to a middle-aged man. Marion escapes her confining world through sexual fantasies. When a young man helps her discover her true self, she begins to acknowledge the importance of her own needs and desires.

(See also *CLC,* Vol. 39; *Contemporary Authors,* Vols. 25-28, rev. ed.; *Contemporary Authors New Revision Series,* Vol. 28; and *Dictionary of Literary Biography,* Vol. 7.)

PRINCIPAL WORKS

PLAYS

The Widow   1961
Tango Palace   1963

The Successful Life of 3: a Skit in Vaudeville   1965
Promenade   1965
The Office   1966
The Annunciation   1967
A Vietnamese Wedding   1967
Dr. Kheal   1968
Molly's Dream   1968
The Red Burning Light; or, Mission XQ3   1968
The Curse of the Langston House   1972
Dance   [with Remy Charlip]   1972
Aurora   1974
Cap-a-Pie   1975
Washing   1976
Fefu and Her Friends   1977
Lolita in the Garden   1977
In Service   1978
Eyes on the Harem   1979
Evelyn Brown: A Diary   1980
A Visit   1981
The Danube   1982
Mud   1983
No Time   1984
Sarita   1984
The Conduct of Life   1985
Art   1986
Lovers and Keepers   1986
The Mothers   1986
The Trial of Joan of Arc on a Matter of Faith   1986
Abingdon Square   1987
And What of the Night   1989
Hunger   1989

OTHER

Promenade and Other Plays   (play collection)   1971; revised 1987
María Irene Fornés: Plays   (play collection)   1986

ROSS WETZSTEON

In the alliterative spirit of the title of Maria Irene Fornés's new play, ***Fefu and Her Friends,*** let me call it a flawed but fascinating and frolicsome feminist fable. Hilarious in its analysis of affairs, touching in its depiction of relationships, and Fornes knows the difference between the two, it contains long passages of lovely writing, one stunning coup de theatre, insufficient characterisations, and questionable conclusions (I'd dispute her contention that sexuality is physical for men, spiritual for women, and heartily, and with a touch of male panic, protest her apparent conviction that women can only be fulfilled in isolation from men).

My main objection to the piece, though, is that the symbolic denouement (something about killing the beast within, you know) has no independent 'realistic' literal level but has to be 'translated' from validity, it doesn't stand by itself on a symbol into critical analysis in order for its meaning to be understood. Effective symbols have to *be* before they can *mean*.

One of Fornés's own devices demonstrates the point. In the second act, the audience is divided into four groups, each of which sees four separate scenes in different order. The meaning here, of course, and the action and its meaning interrelate appropriately, is that women's lives in a chauvinist society are to a large degree random and repetitive and can be seen in any sequence. A familiar image came to mind—'women's work' is like washing dishes, for they're only washed in order to be used and then washed again, an endless, stultifying cycle. 'Man's work', on the other hand, grows out of what they've done in the past and has consequences for their future, and in the very structure of her play Fornes has made a provocative feminist argument. (pp. 36-7)

> *Ross Wetzsteon, in a review of "Fefu and Her Friends," in* Plays and Players, *Vol. 24, No. 11, August, 1977, pp. 36-7.*

EDITH OLIVER

Fefu and Her Friends is about a gathering of eight women, in 1935, at the house in New England of a woman called Fefu. The action takes place all over the house and in the garden, and the members of the audience leave their seats and, in groups, move from room to room, backstage and upstairs and down, where the characters, in twos and threes, discuss matters of general and intimate concern to women (or Women; the theme is what the heroine calls "the passion of friendship"). There is no plot, but there are episodes—in one of them, for example, a love affair that has come to an end is renewed; in another, somebody who is paralyzed and in a wheelchair sneaks into the living room on foot to remove a sugar bowl—and there is a strain of mysticism throughout. The idea of a mobile audience is original and, for a while, delightful. In the early, best scenes, *Fefu* has a notional, lyrical charm and humor that bring to mind Gertrude Stein's *In Circles*. Miss Fornés is a subtle, stylish writer, but she can also be a distressingly whimsical one. As for the evening as a whole, I must say with regret that I ran out of steam before she ran out of play.

> *Edith Oliver, in a review of "Fefu and Her Friends," in* The New Yorker, *Vol. LIII, No. 49, January 23, 1978, p. 46.*

HAROLD CLURMAN

Maria Irene Fornes's *Fefu and Her Friends* is a play that floats. There is hardly any situation: a group of women speak at random—in the air. Some of what they say is well said; odd though clear (or vice-versa), with an occasional resemblance to automatic writing. Much of it is just that, *writing*, not dialogue: it does not often *sound* on the stage. What the audience receives is the impression of a series of prose poems strung together. The effect is "circular," like a drifting haze.

Eight women friends—of unknown background—are gathered in a New England house in 1935. (I am not sure why this specification is called for.) The hostess, a woman somewhat older than the others, opens the play with the line, "My husband married me to have a constant reminder of how loathsome women are." She adds to two of her startled guests, "It's true that women are loathsome." Of Fefu's husband one woman comments, "He's crazy. They drive each other crazy. They are not crazy really. They drive each other crazy."

There is constant talk—to the point of obsession—about women and sexuality. There is ambiguity in this, revulsion and fascination.

Men have sexual strength. Women have to find their strength, and when they do find it, it comes forth with bitterness . . . with chattering to keep themselves from making contact, or else, if they don't chatter, avert their eyes, like Orpheus . . . as if a god once said 'and if they shall recognize each other, the world will be blown apart'. . . .

Another friend is a woman paralyzed by a bullet fired at a deer. Alone in her bed she hallucinates on the subject of "Women are evil. Woman is not a human being. . . . Unpredictable, therefore, wicked and gentle and evil and good which is evil. . . . If a man commits an evil act, he must be pitied. The evil comes from outside him, through him and into the act. Woman generates the evil herself. . . ." and on and on.

A sense of guilt—induced perhaps by some (unmentioned) religious upbringing—hovers in the atmosphere, with a homosexual nuance. Though I must note that a scene and a speech of delicate tenderness between two women who have been lovers is one of the best in the play. With all the sophistication in attitudes and conversation, there are playful descents into childish silliness. The troubled ambiance is discomfiting, so that finally we are almost ready to acquiesce to an amused quip about, "Everyone ended by going to the psychiatrist."

The mixture of elements—symbolism, abstracted or semi-surrealistic discourse, stream-of-consciousness rumination and hysteria along with quirks of humor—keep one, by turn, alert and dazed. Movement is created by having the audience (in divided sections) proceed to different places or settings—a living room, a lawn, a study, a bedroom, a kitchen. There is no intermission, the flow is continuous, except for the time it takes to get from one place to the other. We vaguely overhear bits of one scene being played for one part of the audience while we listen to another. The result is a feeling of simultaneity of action. This contributes to the play's overall style and certainly relieves the danger of being irritated by a teasing nebulousness. . . .

I doubt that it was a good idea for the author to direct her play. She likes her lines too well—some of them are eloquent after a particular literary fashion—but their delivery is often made deliberate enough to become exasperating. This may possibly be a calculated ploy, for the play itself teeters on the edge of several different modes.

There is today a cult of the imprecise. It flirts with the so-called unconscious. Addicts will find *Fefu and Her Friends* especially beguiling. To others I say, "Beware!"

> *Harold Clurman, in a review of "Fefu and Her Friends," in* The Nation, New York, *Vol. 226, No. 5, February 11, 1978, p. 154.*

MARTIN DUBERMAN

Irene Fornés's new play, *Fefu and Her Friends,* has drawn either raves or pans, almost nothing in between. The raves have predominated. Michael Feingold, the often astute chief critic of the *Village Voice,* wrote one of them: "*Fefu* is the only essential thing the New York theater has added to our cultural life in the past year." I must assume that a compound of languor and stilted disconnection is the essential ingredient "our cultural life" has gained—for that is all I can find in *Fefu.* The characters suffer from endemic malaise, but its source is shared neither among themselves nor with us ("What is wrong?" "Everything"). The predominant form of communication is windy monologue, punctuated by yawn-inspiring pronouncements ("Hallucinations are real, you know").

Fornés is known in the theater world for her generosity, for the long hours she has spent trying to get other playwrights produced. For that reason alone, I'm glad she had a hit (*Fefu* was the hottest Off-Broadway ticket in town). Fornés is also known as a strong feminist. I'm much less glad (as a fellow traveler) that her play is being promoted as a "feminist statement." For I fail to see its contribution in that regard—and think it's more likely to be a disservice. Fornés's women are given to pondering such propositions as "If people are swept off their feet, are the feet left behind?" or to portentously announcing that "a woman's entrails are the heaviest things on earth." To be sure, these are *Thirties* feminists—but we are listening to them in the Seventies. The complacent foolishness of much of what they do and say may not be the least important reason so many established male critics have found so much to cheer about. (pp. 83-4)

Martin Duberman, "The Great Gray Way: The Period Pieces of the Future," in Harper's, *Vol. 256, No. 1536, May, 1978, pp. 79-80, 83-7.*

JOAN LARKIN

In *Fefu and Her Friends,* eight friends, eight diverse, high-spirited women come together for a weekend in 1935. Each is struggling to use her gifts, her capacity for love, her uniqueness. Fefu is their center and their host. Her friends love, but fear for, her "light," which is endangered by her demons: loneliness, self-hate, self-destructiveness. In the first act, she shoots at her offstage husband with a rifle she hopes is loaded only with blanks; later she tells how she fears to close her door against a cat that fouls her kitchen with diarrhea.

Fefu's—women's—predicament is made literal in the character of Julia, who, in fact, dominates the play. In her hallucinations and inability to walk, Julia manifests the ways Fefu—and all strong and beautiful women, playwright Maria Irene Fornés implies—is crippled and cut off from her power.

In the second act, the audience is split into four groups and conducted one after another into the interior of the exquisitely executed set: in the kitchen we sit—witnesses rather than remote spectators—watching two women deal with their finished love affair. In the backyard, during a game of croquet, we overhear Fefu's bravado and her pain. In the bedroom we sit, literally surrounding Julia's bed, and share her haunted visions of women's visceral loathsomeness. (p. 28)

When all the audience groupings have experienced each of the four scenes, we have a sense of the texture of time that the theater has never given us before. And we have seen each character at a different stage of recognition of Julia's truth of women's condition.

Fefu's conviction that Julia can really walk is dramatized in a chilling moment. After her passionate accusation and Julia's quiet denial, Fefu gives way to despair. She rushes offstage, where we hear an explosion from the gun she has been aiming at her husband; she returns holding in her arms a dead rabbit, symbolic of women's old condition of helplessness. At the same instant, Julia dies. Since we do not see Fefu, having

"killed" the crippled Julia in herself, free to grow in spirit, the resolution seems incomplete and unsatisfying in its abrupt reliance on purely symbolic action. This feeling lingers, despite the regular post-play discussions during which Fornés shares her intent with the audience.

Fefu left me torn, deeply moved, but critical and dissatisfied. I love the play for its intimacy, for the beauty and economy of its language, for the dignity and intelligence of its women characters, for their respect, tenderness, and passion. But I am disappointed to see women yet again as sacrificial victims who cannot endure their strength. In the end I find that the images in the play that remain strongest are those of women's self-loathing. Not that in our writing we must deny our demons—but I fear, finally, that this play loves them more than our powers. (pp. 28, 32)

Joan Larkin, in a review of "Fefu and Her Friends," in Ms. *Vol. VI, No. 12, June, 1978, pp. 28, 32.*

RICHARD EDER

In a way, it is female subjugation and male fear that Maria Irene Fornes is getting at in [*Eyes on the Harem*], her comical-explosive vaudeville about the degenerate low points in the 600-year dynasty of the Turkish Ottomans.

Only in a way: her way, in fact. To draw a straightforward feminist lesson from such extreme examples as the infant Sultan Murad, who shot 10 passersby each day with his little arquebus; or Ibrahim, who drowned his entire harem because one of its inhabitants might have been unfaithful, or Abdul Hamid, who believed his clothes were poisoned—this would be ponderous as well as farfetched.

Miss Fornes's *Eyes on the Harem* is often farfetched, but it is hardly ever ponderous. Miss Fornes, one of the more interesting playwrights around, proceeds by glints and flashes.

Taking outrageous liberties with these quakey Ottoman potentates, she seems to be as interested in the images they raise as in the ideas they may or may not suggest. Take care of the fables, she is saying—hers are disassembled and lunatic—and the morals will take care of themselves. In *Eyes on the Harem,* a bumpy but occasionally quite wonderful patchwork, Miss Fornes is often as not at cross purposes with herself, and the better for it.

Miss Fornes, who is the director as well as the author, conducts an absurd tour back and forth through the domestic history of the Ottomans. There is a deliberate fragmentation of chronology and tone. . . .

The first of the play's sketches is set in 1909, and we see a starved-looking, straggly bearded Sultan Abdul Hamid. It is the terminal stage of the dynasty. Sultan hides inside a ridiculous frock-coat. He is terrified of everything: of visitors who might kill him (he keeps his hand on a gun in his pocket so that he can shoot them first, and once he shot a daughter by mistake), of poisoned clothes and, above all, of women. Occasionally a black-clad woman passes through the room, sending him into hysterics. . . .

Some of the sketches are very funny. Incongruity is their cornerstone; some build on it for a complex mixture of comedy and seriousness, others never really take off. There is a delightful, ironic fashion show. One performer poses seductively in a green sari; she is followed by others in increasingly cumbersome and grotesque outfits, and their efforts at striking the same winsome poses are devastating.

The finest sequence is a series of conversations among three heavily veiled women, sitting on a square of cloth. They talk, half wistful, half unbelieving, about a future where they will be allowed to eat in public, go unveiled, and wear—a delicate irony—outrageous clothes.

The conversation is comic, and so is the seemingly ludicrous chorus of "Meet Me in St. Louis" which they periodically break into. ("We will do the hootchie-kootchie; I will be your tootsie-wootsie."). Imperceptibly the conversation grows in pain. Their talk of freedom takes on fear; one reads Byron out loud, and suddenly another weeps. The song repeats, each time slower and more sadly.

It is a hallucinatory moment; an extraordinary progression from comedy to seriousness, an audacious and successful theatrical rendering of a complex vision of feminine history.

A great deal of *Eyes on the Harem* is nowhere up to this. Some of the playfulness is private and tedious; we are being played at, not with. The reading out of Ottoman histories is not always effective; a prayer sequence, performed more or less straight, seems to accomplish little; and ludicrousness is often exercised for its own sake. Also, I wonder whether some of the comical outrageousness might be more troublesome to those for whom Turkish history is personal history.

At its weakest, *Eyes on the Harem* is childish. At its strongest, the childishness grows into something that is funny, provocative and sometimes magical.

> Richard Eder, "The Fear of the Ottomans," in The New York Times, *April 25, 1979, p. C17.*

EDITH OLIVER

Eyes on the Harem is an eccentric work by Maria Irene Fornés, a poet and a fierce feminist, which is a collage of music, movement, tableaux, and a playful, poker-faced irony that is so strong it verges on sarcasm as the six members of the cast read or recite brief lives of the sultans and brief passages from the history of the Ottoman Empire—all of unspeakable, unimaginable cruelty, especially to women. Especially but not entirely; the men suffered, too. (There is one horrifying passage, clinical and grisly, on different types of eunuchs.) Still, the women bore the brunt of the cruelty: a whole harem drowned because one of the sultans suspected one of his wives of infidelity—that sort of thing. The friskiness of much of the performance (directed by Miss Fornés), though appropriate—that's the kind of show it is—grows tiresome after a while, but there is one scene near the end that is eloquent and beautiful. Three harem women, heavily veiled and costumed, speak in whispers about possible reforms promised by the ruler and then—first laughing and later quietly crying—sing "Meet Me in St. Louis," making the most of "We will dance the hoochee koochee." That scene, breaking from the prevailing mood into a mood all its own, is indelible.

> Edith Oliver, in a review of "Eyes on the Harem," in The New Yorker, *Vol. LV, No. 12, May 7, 1979, p. 131.*

MEL GUSSOW

A Visit written and directed by Maria Irene Fornes, is a quaint, impossibly cute musical trifle about a licentious weekend in the country. The impulse is to titillate; the impact is the opposite.

The year is 1910, and a nubile coed pays a visit to a family in Lansing, Mich., and becomes the key link in a sexual roundelay. She is easily seduced by hosts and houseguests, male and female, upstairs and down, and in milady's backyard. Demurely she unbuttons herself for her sundry tempters while an offstage trio tinkles music of the tea-time variety. The lyrics by Miss Fornes deal with such unpromising subjects as red ink and zucchini.

Humor is supposed to arise from the juxtaposition of lascivious behavior and ornate dialogue. For example, the co-ed's statement, "I like embroidery—cross stitch and back stitch," is uttered with all the innuendo of an invitation from Mae West.

The men in the play are outfitted with dildos in plain sight (and even one woman has one). . . . The landscape is single-mindedly priapic. The play quickly succumbs to coyness and redundancy as the characters rendezvous in predictable sequence, producing a kind of domino effect.

In Act II, after an unamusing interlude about crickets copulating on a clean tablecloth, there is an iota of anthropormorphic inventiveness. As [one character] reads from a scholarly tome on insect sexuality—a subject that touches bottom as a source for comedy or drama—[two other characters], without embarrassment, simulate the mating habits of grasshoppers and locusts. By the time they get to wasps, all passion has been spent, and the actors, exhausted, simply listen to the textbook description. This mime could have a future as a visual aid in high school biology.

> Mel Gussow, "Around the House," in The New York Times, *December 30, 1981, p. C8.*

BONNIE MARRANCA

Fornes's plays are whimsical, gentle and bittersweet, and informed with her individualistic intelligence. Virtually all of them have a characteristic delicacy, lightness of spirit, and economy of style. Fornes has always been interested in the emotional lives of her characters, so human relationships play a significant part in the plays (*The Successful Life of 3, Fefu and Her Friends*). She apparently likes her characters, and often depicts them as innocent, pure spirits afloat in a corrupt world which is almost always absurd rather than realistic (*Fefu and Her Friends* is the exception). Political consciousness is present in a refined way.

Fornes's characters have rich fantasy lives (*Tango Palace, Aurora*) which tend to operate according to their own laws of time and space. Small wonder the structure of playacting frequently shapes her plays (*Tango Palace, Red Burning Light, A Vietnamese Wedding*). And if the entire play isn't constructed as an "entertainment" there is, nonetheless, always some sort of inner theatre or "turns" for the actors (*Molly's Dream*).

Sometimes the characters parody film stars or scenes from films; at other times the dramatic structures spring from American "popular" forms such as vaudeville, burlesque, and musical comedy. High camp, too, provides much of the fun in Fornes's comedies, which reflect an idiosyncratic wit. There is also plenty of word play and reversals of cliches and conventions (**Dr. Kheal**).

Frequently, however, the warmth and good humor in these plays is counterpointed by large doses of irony or melancholy (**Promenade**). For Fornes's character's relationships just don't seem to turn out the way they do in the movies (**Molly's Dream**). Human nature has its way of intruding, and games and playacting end all too quickly.

An early play, **Tango Palace,** is entirely based on game—or role—playing. In a room cluttered with furniture, swords, masks, teapots, a mirror, vase, guitar, whip, and a Persian helmet—with a shrine set in one wall and the door bolted shut—two men enact their love-hate ritual. The older, Isidore, has a half-man, half-woman appearance; the other, Leopold, is a young, handsome man in a business suit.

In this "no exit" land where they make their home the two men create a world of totally fictionalized reality. . . . They enact seducer-seduced, masculine-feminine, teacher-pupil, father-son roles to suit their needs, and create fantastical situations in which to play out their dramas. For Isidore, especially, it is a metaphysical attempt to penetrate the mystery of existence. At various times Isidore, who lives in a completely aestheticized world, is a salesman, dancer, sadist, warrior, dueler, matador, teacher. Each "scene" he introduces has its own set of gestures and its own dialogue. (pp. 53-4)

For a time Leopold serves as Isidore's willing pupil but, unwilling to merge art and life (as Isidore has), he becomes corrupted by knowledge and begins to take their playing seriously. The end of the play, in the scene where the two men metamorphose into beetles, reflects Leopold's loss of innocence. It remains for him to kill Isidore. Overwhelmed by impulse, Leopold stabs him: he is the criminal and Isidore the saint, the eternal innocent. When Isidore at the play's end appears among clouds dressed as an angel and carrying a stack of cards, his presence symbolizes the eternal human struggle. The cards are yet new variations on this theme. Fornes's ill-fated lovers are victims of the universal dance of death, their relationship begun, metaphorically, with the erotic tango we see them dance at the beginning of the play.

Fornes's **The Successful Life of 3** is an entirely different sort of play, rooted less in a metaphysical realm than in reality. Still, one would hardly call this "skit for vaudeville," which playfully romps across logical borders of time and space, realistic. In this zany, romantic parody He, She, and 3, who meet in a doctor's office, appear in a series of ten short scenes (or vignettes) over a period of approximately sixteen years. She is sexy and young but dumb; He is handsome but a loser; 3 is middle-aged and frumpy but a successful anti-hero. He to 3: "I'm very annoyed. I have all the brains and the looks and it's you who goes South with your squeaky voice and sweaty hands and makes all the money." Fornes offers several versions of He, She, and 3—together, or two at a time—in a string of short sketches which endlessly surprise with their off-center lunacy. Here is part of one conversation:

> SHE. Weddings are a pain in the neck.
> 3. Why do you want one then?
> SHE. (*thinks with a stupid expression*)
> HE. Don't you see she doesn't know?
> 3. Yes, I see.
> SHE. The Andrew sisters are all married.

> HE. Do you like brothers too?
> SHE. Not so much.
> HE. Did you see *The Corsican Brothers?*
> SHE. That's not brothers. That's just Douglas Fairbanks playing twins. It's not the same.

In this play events turn out just fine, but completely opposite of what one would expect. The lives of these characters are presented to us as a microcosm of human communication in all its wonderful craziness and imperfectability. If ironic reversals rule their lives it is because they are such natural comedians—simply lovable cartoon characters.

The Successful Life of 3 represents Fornes at her comic best. This beautifully orchestrated piece, with its crisp, precise dialogue, peculiar internal logic, and short, cinematic takes is a wonderful display of comic anarchy. Forget about conventional observations of time and place; they don't exist for these successful three. The pacing is at times rigid, at other times rapid, but the overall rhythm of this tightly structured piece is as smooth as the story is unbelievable.

Characters fall in and out of relationships and conversations, at times imitate postures of film actors—all with a deadpan attitude disarming in its ease. Little do they know, these characters who are continually talking about going to the movies, that their own life together is a movie in itself.

In the scene when 3 has organized a revolt and broken out of jail this exchange occurs:

> 3. . . . The guys are coming presently.
> HE. What kind of idiot are you that says presently?
> 3. No idiot. I'm the Alec Guinness type gangster.

Later on 3 will wear a Zorro costume in a scheme to steal from the rich to give to the poor. (pp. 54-6)

The characters who inhabit this comic landscape are innocents, archetypal Fornes heroes, who simply want to be left alone to live out their lives in splendid disarray. At the end of the play they sing a "Song to Ignorance," a joyful celebration of their idiosyncratic individuality, and their obliviousness to the mundane world around them. (p. 56)

In **Promenade** two young prisoners, 105 and 106, escape from their cell (a metaphor for their lower-class surroundings) and go on a journey. They dine with the rich, become involved at the scene of a car accident, experience war on a battlefield, and are reunited with their mother, before returning willingly to their home in jail. Total innocents, the two young men are uncorrupted by their experiences in the world. When their mother asks them at the end of the play, "Did you find evil?" they reply in the negative: they didn't find evil because they can't identify it. It is because 105 and 106 are pure in spirit, ruled by their own emotional lives, that they can turn their backs on the rich and their riches, and the cruelties of life. They simply refuse to recognize them, finding more "freedom" in their cell. The Servant, on the other hand, who earlier in the adventure was on their side—in a hilarious scene she dresses up and parodies the rich crowd's manners and conversations to prove "Money makes you dumb"—eventually succumbs to the allure of wealth and goes off with the rich. The prisoners, on the other hand, have "rich" inner lives which makes them free.

Promenade has the *joie de vivre,* the disregard for external logic and spatial convention, the crazy-quilt characters that one associates with the plays of Gertrude Stein. It also has some of the charming French insouciance of an early surrealist play like Cocteau's *The Marriage on the Eiffel Tower*. Characters talk at cross purposes yet all the while revealing an inner logic and offering witty, perceptive comments on manners and mores. One has only to read the speeches in the Banquet scene to see Fornes making fun of the trivial concerns and flightiness of the rich. And in the Battlefield sequences they repeat their callousness by regarding the bombing as an aesthetic event (much like Shaw's insipid characters in *Heartbreak House* who equate bombs with a Beethoven symphony), and construing a Maypole dance by using soldiers' head bandages as ribbons. In *Promenade* the upper classes are shown at play; the lower classes fight their battles for them. Social criticism is never far from Fornes's plays, many of which are sprinkled throughout with her comments on class struggle, and this play is no exception.

The satire seems almost effortless because the playwright's touch is so playful and laid back. Yet Fornes makes her point, and there's no confusion as to whose side she is on in this comedy of manners. Much of the satire in *Promenade* derives from comic inversion. The song lyrics comment ironically, in Brechtian fashion, on the narrative rather than acting as show-stopping numbers or changes of mood. For example, the Servant sings:

> A lot of satisfaction
> Produces happiness.
> And the source of satisfaction
> Is wealth.
> Isn't it?
> All that a man possesses
> Displaces discontent.

It is also the Servant, who in the first part of the play served as its choral figure (before her corruption), who declares: "Isn't it true that costumes change the course of life?"

Promenade offers the highlights of Fornes the absurdist, Fornes the entertainer—a host of looney characters in an insane, wonderful story that is even moralistic! The language is short and to the point, with lots of rhythms and plays on words. The playwright's fascination with American "popular" forms is also evident—in the vaudeville "turns" in the Mayor's party scene, in the car accident sequence where two cases of mistaken identity are prompted by a switch of clothes, and in general by her lovable overturning of musical comedy convention and use of "bits" from movie comedy. (pp. 56-7)

In *Molly's Dream* Molly, too, escapes her ordinary surroundings. In a Western-style saloon Molly, a waitress, falls asleep at her job after reading a piece of Western genre fiction in a popular magazine. She dreams herself into a world of handsome strangers and romance, but like *The Successful Life of 3* the play evolves as romantic parody. In her dream play Molly does not walk off into the sunset with her dream guy, Jim—whose sexuality, incidentally, is embodied in the "Hanging Women" draped about him. And John, a cowboy who enters the saloon, is transformed into a vampire lover and then a Superman—fantasies which include his Shirley Temple-like partner.

The play easily moves into a high camp parody of old (mainly forties) movies, with Molly doing takes on film stars. Brandishing a top hat, she puts one foot up on the bar and her elbow at her knee and speaks in a German accent: she is Marlene Dietrich. At other times she relives a moment from *Morocco*, paraphrases a famous line from *Casablanca* ("Mack, play something amusing, Sam"), recalls conventions from tropical island movies (people drinking absinthe), and sings a torch song, "My Man." But here she adds a comic counterpoint to the tune: "I don't really let anyone beat me." (Molly isn't so dead to the world that she's lost consciousness!)

Here again is a Fornes character dreaming herself into a "role": she and those around her are continually transformed into figments of her subconscious. Sexual rivalry, seduction, macho convention, and unrequited love—the realities of heterosexual relationships—all find their way into this bittersweet dream world. Fornes entertains us by presenting her themes in old movie and song images which demonstrate how much popular culture influences the American psyche.

The forties ambience, however, is presented not for nostalgic purposes but to serve as a playful critique of the "old" notion of romance. The songs in this piece, like those in *Promenade,* fulfill an ironic function; more often than not they gleefully satirize romantic convention. One song is entirely comprised of the word "Bang." And, at one moment when the music starts up, Molly says wistfully, "No. I'm not breaking into song. The moment is too sad." Here Fornes is deliberately jolting audience expectations shaped by the conventions of the very form she is subverting. *Molly's Dream* is a good example of Fornes's ironic reversal of popular cultural forms. It is a musical comedy gone awry at all the "great" moments.

Quite a different kind of play, *Dr. Kheal* is a brief monodrama in the absurdist mode, acted by a nutty professor for the delight of his (invisible) students. On the surface *Dr. Kheal* appears as a simple exercise which mocks academic pretensions, but on closer inspection it reveals itself to be a much more detailed investigation about the way people think; the strange Kheal grows into a mad genius. Kheal's "lecture" is comprised of fragments of his reflections on a variety of topics which include poetry, ambition, speech, beauty, and love. But the play imitates no ordinary classroom situation. (pp. 58-9)

What Fornes does is create for Kheal a series of anecdotes, examples, and riddles which he uses to make his "pupils" look beyond the meaning of a word, beyond accepted notions of abstract concepts and reflexive reactions to convention. Kheal is illustrating the difference between received knowledge and knowledge gained from personal experience. The lesson in all of this is that what we experience around us is enough to teach us if we use our natural rational powers. *Dr. Kheal,* while not having the full sweep of the more accomplished plays, provides a helpful insight into the way Fornes thinks about life.

A Vietnamese Wedding uses role-playing and social convention, two staples of her drama, in a more directly political way. This reenactment of a Vietnamese wedding ceremony has audience members "play" the wedding party as the rituals of the ceremony are directed and explained by "readers" or "hosts" (Fornes herself and three other performers). In this short piece Fornes manages to outline a social-political-cultural context for marriage among the Vietnamese. By its simplicity, it shows the universality of certain cultural rituals. *A Vietnamese Wedding* is not a play but a celebration of the graceful ritual of Vietnamese cultural life. The piece itself was originally a gracious gesture of protest presented as part of "Angry Arts Week" in 1967, a cumulative opposition by various artists to the war in Viet Nam. (p. 59)

[*The Red Burning Light Or: Mission XQ3* is a surrealistic,

black comedy which] makes use of circus and vaudeville techniques, television cliches, and officialese to parody American attitudes. The play is constructed as a kind of sideshow—with a general as circus barker—illustrating American racism, imperialism, and colonialist views in a series of comic spoofs.

While the play has highly comic moments, its real message is in the end diluted by the broad comic structure. There is simply too much happening in *Red Burning Light* for it to sustain itself. But the real problem is due perhaps to another reason: Fornes's characteristic light touch is not well suited to protest themes and bitterly mocking satire. She works best in modes like *The Successful Life of 3* and *Promenade,* whose form and subject matter are more attuned to her whimsical satirical manner.

Aurora is a historical fantasy with a parade of characters dressed in contemporary, medieval, and Renaissance costume. Parodying the revenge tragedies of Jacobean drama, it features duels, suicides, alchemy, and hypnosis, and an Angel of Death spouting Communist theory. What robs the play of success is a lack of specificity as to its intentions, and a muddled line of dramatic action that introduces symbols and metaphors without clarification.

Fornes appears to be suggesting the death of one world order and the birth of another, but the play is too symbolical and abstract—and its political line too obtuse—to put its message across clearly. What is significant about *Aurora* is the planned simultaneity of action in the last two scenes, which are witnessed by an audience in sequence. This pattern of action points to a development that shapes Fornes's most recent play, *Fefu and Her Friends,* which has simultaneous scenes in its center section. (pp. 59-60)

Fefu and Her Friends is set in 1935 in a country home where eight women gather to discuss an educational project they plan for some future (unidentified) event. The play has no plot in the conventional sense, and the characters are presented as fragments. Though there is much about them that Fornes keeps hidden, the play—seeming at first like realism—is purposely set in the realm of the mysterious and abstract. By setting the play in a home, and then offering a narrative that subverts realistic conventions, Fornes plays ironically with domestic space, and the notion of domestic drama.

Fefu doesn't tell one story but offers a number of stories as it unfolds in a series of encounters between the women, all of them different personalities reflecting different points of view about human relations. What is strikingly unconventional about the play is the environmental structure Fornes devised to isolate the separate realities of the characters. *Fefu* is divided into six scenes—the first and last take place in the living room, the others in the kitchen, the bedroom, study, and lawn. The audience is together only for the first and last scene, and is split into four different groups during the middle scenes, which run simultaneously, (the actresses must play these scenes four times each performance). In each of the different spaces, the mood and relationships of the characters change, so that the environmental concept functions thematically as well as structurally.

The play opens with Fefu's provocative statement, "My husband married me to have a constant reminder of how loathsome women are." Immediately it brings the play into the world of women and how they think about themselves. There are no men in *Fefu* but their presence is felt—in the odd game Fefu plays with her husband, whom she occasionally shoots at from the living room doors overlooking the lawn, and in Julia's nightmarish speech on the status of women in society.

Deeply feminist in its perspective and guiding spirit, *Fefu* is primarily a play about women, about their certain way of being in the world. In its analytical approach to metaphysical questions and precision of thought, it far surpasses the trivialities which frequently pass today as feminist art. Very much a play of contemporary culture—a work which probably wouldn't have been made before the women's movement—it reflects the growing personal approach to theatre. Yet *Fefu* remains non-rhetorical and non-ideological which is a tribute to Fornes's willingness to let her characters speak for themselves. The dialectic between the private world of the characters, as filtered through the author's own private inner life, and the public theatrical space they act it out in, is so outrageously ironic it is downright subversive. Fefu, an independent, bright, older woman who serves as the ironist of the proceedings, is the most fascinating member of the group. Julia, the strange, paralyzed young woman in the wheelchair, is the thematic key to the play, and in a long, painful monologue (the bedroom scene) she catalogues all the hateful attitudes about women propagated by Western culture, in cliches that are comically and tragically grotesque.

The symbol of oppression in the play, Julia talks of "judges," "repenting," and a "prayer" she must say about the evil of women. If she gave in to the reactionary forces of male-dominated society—and her physical paralysis is emblematic of her mental paralysis—Fefu is still fighting them, even though by the end of the play she is approaching Julia's vision. When in the final scene of the play Fefu aims out the window at her husband and kills a rabbit instead, blood mysteriously appears on Julia's forehead. Fefu accepts at last that Julia is "dead" to the feminist struggle.

Fefu has its lightheartedness, too. In fact there is a concerted effort on the part of Fornes to show the spontaneous, affectionate way of women among women. By setting the play in 1935, she has admitted in interviews, she avoids feminist dogmatism and the overly analytical, excessive psychologizing of contemporary characters who refuse to accept things at face value, reinterpreting instead a casual gesture or remark to the point of exhaustion. Fefu and her friends are warm and open with each other, but a sense of decorum and privacy prevails.

Though almost nothing about the past of the characters is known, they reveal themselves in several different situations. There's the high-spirited bohemianism of Emma, who regales Fefu during their game of croquet with her hilarious account of heaven's "divine registry of sexual performance." And there's lovely Paula—with her calculation that all love affairs last seven years and three months—suddenly jolted by the presence of a former lover, Cecilia, the intellectual of the group. The study scene between Cindy and Christina is one of casual, affectionate moments passed in the study of French lessons. As the audience travels to the different rooms in the house, they seem to be eavesdropping, as it were, on the women.

In *Fefu* Fornes has discovered a wonderfully intelligent and pleasurable way to explore the politics of consciousness. She has simply let her characters be themselves—not mothers, daughters, wives, or sisters. One has only to compare Clare Boothe Luce's *The Women* to see how much the image of women has changed on the American stage.

Aside from its innovative treatment of subject matter, *Fefu* can make a claim to being one of the few experimental plays written in the seventies—which has not been a decade noted for experimentation in playwriting (texts of avant-garde groups excepted). Because of the play's environmental concept, the experiential factor of the theatrical performance is very strong, drawing the audience into an active intimacy with the actors who, in the middle scenes, appear in cinematic close-up. What appears on the surface to be a realistic play becomes (like its contemporary counterpart in painting) super realism in performance due to the filmic intensity of the scenes.

Fefu and Her Friends has the delicacy of tone and economical style of Fornes's earlier plays; the keen intelligence has always been there. What makes this play stand apart—and ahead—of the others is, more than the inclusiveness of the experiment in text and performance, the embodiment of a deeply personal vision.

It is encouraging to find Maria Irene Fornes speaking in a more revealing voice. She is an immensely intelligent and witty woman who, up until now, has only teased us with her intelligence. Though not a few of her non-realistic plays—*The Successful Life of 3* and *Promenade,* in particular—are stunning stylistic realizations, this new move into realism reflects a generosity of spirit and self-assuredness that makes its presence more commanding than the others.

Fornes is one of the few contemporary experimenters in playwriting who doesn't suffer from self-indulgence, and she has a refinement of technique and expression that most others lack. If she continues in this more personal approach to drama, we have much to look forward to. (pp. 60-3)

Bonnie Marranca, "Maria Irene Fornés," in American Playwrights *by Bonnie Marranca and Gautam Dasgupta, Drama Book Specialists, 1981, pp. 53-63.*

GAYLE AUSTIN AND MARIA IRENE FORNÉS

On May 1, 1983, the New York Times *Magazine published a cover story, "Women Playwright: New Voices in the Theater" by Mel Gussow. It mentioned a number of contemporary American women playwrights (a "new generation of dramatists"), but focused on Marsha Norman, whose play* 'night Mother *had just won the Pulitzer Prize for Drama. Her photograph also appeared on the cover of the magazine.*

Reaction to the article in the theatre community was immediate and intense; especially among women. Gussow's generalizations, acts of commission and omission, his lack of historical and critical perspective, brought on an avalanche of opinions, feelings, and alternative views. Performing Arts Journal invited a number of people to respond to the issues raised in the article, and to pursue other issues related to women in the arts.

Some of these respondents address the article itself; most take off on the idea of women and playwriting and run in their own directions. We hope these responses will continue and expand the dialogue in many new areas of thought, namely, how the culture perceives women as artists, problems unique to women working in theatre, the definition of a "women's aesthetic" and "feminist play," new forms evolving to express women's concerns, and politics in the cultural establishment. (p. 87)

[Maria Irene Fornés]: I have been thinking about the question of identifying with the opposite sex, not just observing the opposite sex but being one with it. The question of identification is of great interest, as it is through identification that we learn to become whole human beings. The experience of others becomes our own. And our experience endows details that we observe in the lives of others with a depth that benefits our understanding. We do not share a lifetime with any other person so in order to know, to begin to know, anything about others we must refer to our own experience continuously. This may be what is called thinking; it is so completely a part of our existence. We are one with the rest of humanity and that is not a choice. It is what we are. We are one with the kind ones and the beautiful ones and the talented ones, but we are also one with the victims of crimes and with the murderers.

Compassion is of course a result of identification, and so is hatred. My intention is not necessarily to promote kindness to the opposite sex but something ultimately more interesting, which is that any human being is a member of our species and if we do not allow our imagination to receive the experiences of others because they are of a different gender, we will shrivel and decay, and our spirit will become a dry prune and we will become ill and die and we will not go to heaven because in heaven they do not allow dry prunes.

When my play *Fefu and Her Friends* was done there were discussions of the play after each performance and so I became aware of how these audiences were thinking about the play. I began to notice that a lot of the men looked at the play differently from the women. They wanted to know where the men in the play were; they wanted to know whether the women were married. They insisted on relating to the men in this play, which had no male characters. If the name of a man was mentioned that was the person they wanted to identify with. There was a man who thought the play was about Phillip (he is the husband of the central character and he never appears on stage nor is he very much talked about). Women learn from the time they are very young to identify with men. If they see a movie with a soldier fighting in a battlefield they identify with the soldier. If he mentions the girlfriend back home they don't identify with the girlfriend because they are identifying with the subject matter, the action, the theme of the film—not the gender.

This, besides being a problem for men, is a problem for women because if they write a play where a woman is the protagonist men get all confused. They cannot make heads or tails of it. The only answer they have is that it is a feminist play. It could be that it is a feminist play but it could be that it is just a play. We have to reconcile ourselves to the idea that the protagonist of a play can be a woman and that it is natural for a woman to write a play where the protagonist is a woman. Man is not the center of life. And it is natural when this fact reflects itself in the work of women.

The question of personal vision and imagery is for me more important than gender. It could well be that you have the images of a dog; then the important thing is that your work be dog-like. A lot of men are extremely delicate and feminine, and they will write as they experience the world. When we start respecting imagery and sensibility, which are unique, the gender of the writer will be the last thing we will think of. (pp. 90-1)

Gayle Austin and Maria Irene Fornés, in two excerpts from "The 'Woman' Playwright Issue," in

Performing Arts Journal, *Vol. VII, No. 3, 1983, pp. 87, 90-1.*

MARIA IRENE FORNÉS [INTERVIEW WITH ALLEN FRAME]

[Frame]: *How did you start directing your own work?*

[Fornés]: Having a play directed by someone else is like going to a religious school when you're a child, you listen and obey. When you write a play you are in such intimate relationship with it. This is yours, you created these characters. Even more than you created them, they came to you. Because in the process of creating a character or a world, one has to be humble, one has to allow for the play's images to take over. That's why I say it comes to you, it has befriended you, and if you are wise enough, you receive it. You have this very profound connection with it, and suddenly somebody who doesn't know anything about it (who immediately starts reading the play thinking, "What do I want to do with it?") comes and starts working on it and tells you how he is going to do things. . . . They think they understand and they go and tell the actor what you're talking about, and you hear it and it's not the same. Now isn't that absurd? Writers either suffer it or they direct. That they have to learn how to direct. Now the unfortunate thing is that nobody tells playwrights that they cannot just go and direct. They first have to learn acting, not to become actors, but to know what the process is. Not only that but they should take classes with different teachers so they know different techniques and ways of approaching it. They should take a couple of directing classes. Writing a play is not enough. Playwrights don't think, "I am not going to suffer this anymore. I'm going to find out how to do it and then do it." They say, "I'm not going to suffer this anymore. *I'm* going to do it." Then they start doing it and from the beginning they don't know what to do, and then they give up . . . You don't lose anything by learning. . . .

I thought your staging. . . . of **Fefu and Her Friends** *was ingenious. These women come together in the first act for a college reunion at Fefu's house. There is a realistic set. Then in second act, the audience is divided into 4 groups and led to 3 other sets in the backstage area and then the scenes take place in each of these areas as well as in the living room simultaneously, performed 4 times until each audience group has seen all 4 scenes. And the scenes are of the same length so that each audience group is ready to move at the same time. And you see characters leave the room occasionally and go into the scene of another room while that other scene is actually taking place. I found that the meaning inherent in this staging, what you experience from those shifts of perspective, to be as powerful as anything that was actually in the text.*

Well, that's what happens. That's a result. Maybe unconsciously, but certainly there are all kinds of things that happen everytime you make a move on stage or you make a decision which is the result of other moves. I don't think anyone can anticipate. The reason why the four scenes in *Fefu* happen the way they happen is completely accidental—*not* accidental because I saw the possibility and realized it. It had to do with a performing place I wanted to rent at the time when I had just finished the first act and I was putting together the second. I was putting together the play using many different kinds of writing that I had done. Some of these monologues had nothing to do with the play but were just things I wrote, and I was feeding them into the play. I started also looking

for a place to rent because at the time I was managing director of Theatre Strategy, a group of experimental playwrights, and I had to find a place for the plays to be performed, and the person who was assisting me said, "There is a loft on Lower Broadway advertised in the newspaper as a performing place. Would you like to look at it?" Now that place when I saw it was a wonderful place, but I didn't think it was right for performance because the ceiling was too low and there were columns in the center which meant we couldn't use the whole width of the loft and then we'd have to build bleachers so everybody could see. But I loved the way it looked so the person who ran the place took us to the front, it had been a factory, and the windows were all the width of the place and plants were all over, and I said, "Oh, this looks like a sun room in Fefu's house." And then he said, "Will you come to my office?" And there was this division and another division he called the green room and then the large performance area and on the other end of it was another partition he had made, and he had a beautiful little office there, Victorian furniture, beautiful desk. And when we sat down I said, "This could be Fefu's library." And then it hit me, and I thought I could do the play—the following scenes—in different places. And I said to him, "If I do the play here, can I use the whole place?" and he said, "Yes, would you like to see the kitchen?" And I said, "Kitchen!" He was wanting to turn the place into a theater but what he was mostly doing was catering.

When I worked with the actresses in **Fefu** in these spaces it was one of the most beautiful directing experiences for me because I was sitting with them right in the room. And it would be only us—whoever was in the scene and me sitting there. And it was more real to me than anything. Because when there's a set and you're on a stage, you're further away. I would be sitting at the table with them. There was a table in this kitchen. Or in the study, I would be sitting in a chair, and it was completely quiet. There was total silence. To me that silence was necessary. If I had at that point written down stage directions which would have been forever binding, I would have said, "It's important that the rooms be totally isolated so that there's no sound at all." Now when I was trying to synchronize the scenes, the sound of the other scenes was too loud, so we started putting curtains and blankets on the windows and the doors. My aim would have been to isolate the sound completely. Since we were not successful, there was a little bit of sound that drifted through it. It was actually the audience then that said, "What a wonderful thing that you hear the other conversations faintly. And sometimes you recognize lines, and sometimes they're lines you've heard, and sometimes they're lines you know you're going to hear." So you think, "Oh, my God! Of course!" But I didn't know that. And I think when you deal with a play that's completely a new form you know a little about it, and you say, "Yes, this is how it should be done," because from what you see it's exciting, but then you don't anticipate many many other things.

There's a heightened reality in your work that's almost super-real. In **Mud** *the writing was so compressed, so spare, that the play achieved an intensity that seemed super-real. One critic interpreted the story as a post-apocalyptic situation. The setting actually looked like something from the Depression era, but the terms of the play were so bleak and unpromising that the situation almost appeared to be a futuristic nightmare.*

I understand seeing that, but I didn't intend it. My plays are clean. Most plays have four, five vital moments in the play and the rest of the play is just getting to it. It's just fill. I don't know why, whether it's just to create the sense that it's real or that you have to spend two hours to experience the power (you have to see not just snapshots). But I find it very boring. I go to sleep when I see plays like that, and I go to sleep writing it. I would just actually fall asleep at the typewriter and would not be able to finish a scene written like that. What's different now is that my work is much more emotional and connected to story. Because of that and the fact that the air around it is clean, it's very strange. It reminds me a little bit of Edward Hopper's paintings—where there's something very real about the situation, it's very mundane, but the air is always so clean you feel there's something wrong.

It's different from the "magic reality" of a lot of Latin American writers whose structure is also looser.

You mean the novelists?

Yes.

The Latin American artist is almost always a surrealist, whether it be painters, artists, or poets. I don't know that they ever see themselves as being surrealists. That's just how they conceive art. Art is something you don't just reproduce—what you see everyday doesn't seem to be inspiring to them. But you do something with it so that it's not bound by the law of reality. My work has always had that influence. I've never felt that it was necessary at all to write realistic plays. Moreover, the work that I'm doing now is much more based on reality than my work before. (p. 28)

I find it bold of you to express your own sense of despair through a situation of poverty in Appalachia, as you did in **Mud.** *My guess is your experience is nothing like the dire deprivation of those three characters. Were you criticized for this?*

I grew up during the depression in poverty. No. But when I did a shorter version of it . . . last year there was a critic who said I treated men like pigs. And I was shocked by that because first of all I think these three people are wonderful. I think if you're going to call the men pigs then call them all pigs because they're all quite brutal in some way and quite tender in another sense. But the men are not anymore piggish than she is. They have a bigger heart than she has. She's more self-centered, more ambitious, in a way harder than they are. The three of them are trying to survive as best they can. And they're not bad people. That critic is anticipating that I'm going to write a play which has a feminist point of view, maybe because I wrote *Fefu* which is a pro-feminine play rather than a feminist play. I think Mae is a sexist role reversed. If Mae were a young *man* who wants to go to learn and was married to this slightly mentally retarded woman, and he would say, "Woman, you sleep on the floor, now this other woman who has a third grade education is going to come to the house and sleep in my bed, you go sleep on the floor," then they would think that that guy was a son of a bitch and these two women are hardworking, honorable women who are victimized by this devil of a person. Now because Mae is a *woman* and these other two are *men*—you know what I mean? I think *Mud* is a feminist play but for a different reason. I think it is a feminist play because the central character is a woman, and the theme is one that writers usually deal with through a male character. The subject matter is—a person who has a mind, a little mind, she's not a brilliant person, but the mind is *opening,* and she begins to feel obsessed with it, and she would do anything in the world to find the light. And some people can understand that as a subject matter only if it were a male character wanting to find

that. It has nothing to do with men and women. It has to do with poverty and isolation and a mind. This mind is in the body of a female. . . .

One thing I liked about **Danube** *was the use of the frequently changing backdrops. It seemed as though you were making a reference to the passing pageantry of theater. They rolled up and they rolled down, and they were in direct contrast to the style of the play, which made them almost satirize proscenium theater with curtain and lavish backdrops. It was like an intellectual comment on . . .*

What is the comment?

A reference to theatrical convention.

What is the reference, though?

Theater's use of illusion. You used the painted backdrops to express an obvious illusion while you used the foreign language tapes to break down the illusion of their speech, interrupting it between lines with the tapes.

But the idea of illusion. Is that something that is presented as a mistake, as false?

No, when I say satire, that's not right. It was humorous *to see the incongruousness of an experimental play about the end of the world using these backdrops, which were a throwback to an old kind of theater. You could say you were celebrating a tradition rather than satirizing it.*

Yes, that is it. To me the quality of those language tapes has the same quality as those backdrops, which is a kind of innocence. I just loved those tapes, the little skit they make for a language lesson. And I long for that innocence. To me the loss of that innocence and over-sophistication is a crime against humanity. It's like a violation of the personality or the environment with pollution.

In your work you often juxtapose beauty and horror.

Right. And innocence . . . A lot of people have said to me about *Mud* and *Sarita,* that they like it, they feel very much, but they feel at the very end there is a hole. "What are you saying?" they ask. "That there's no hope?" One of the critics said of *Mud* that it's saying there's no way out. I wasn't saying any such thing. Even though *Sarita* has a tragic ending—she kills her lover and then goes crazy and to a mental institution—I'm not saying any such thing! I'm showing what could *happen. Precisely.* I'm giving them an example of what is *possible.* There are works, though, in which you feel the writer is relishing in the despair, in the pain. And now, how can you tell the difference between one and the other? It's something you feel in your heart. You know the writer doesn't have to show the good side. It doesn't have to be there. It's in the spirit of the work and you know in the spirit of the work immediately whether the writer is just relishing in pain. Maybe it is that these people who want the uplifting message right in the character's lives rather than in the spirit of the play—maybe it is that they can't tell the difference in those that are relishing in pain and those that are talking about goodness. (p. 30)

Maria Irene Fornés and Allen Frame, in an interview from Bomb Magazine, *Fall, 1984, pp. 28-30.*

BONNIE MARRANCA

Ever since *Fefu and Her Friends* Maria Irene Fornes has

been writing the finest realistic plays in this country. In fact, one could say that *Fefu* and the plays that followed it, such as *The Danube* and now *Mud,* have paved the way for a new language of dramatic realism, and a way of directing it. What Fornes, as writer and director of her work, has done is to strip away the self-conscious objectivity, narrative weight, and behaviorism of the genre to concentrate on the unique subjectivity of characters for whom talking is gestural, a way of being. There is no attempt to tell the whole story of a life, only to distill its essence. Fornes brings a much needed intimacy to drama, and her economy of approach suggests another vision of theatricality, more stylized for its lack of exhibitionism. In this new theatricality, presence, that is, the act of being, is of greatest importance. The theatrical idea of presence is linked to the idea of *social being* expressed by character. The approach is that of a documentary starkness profoundly linked to existential phenomenology.

Fornes's work goes to the core of character. Instead of the usual situation in which a character uses dialogue or action to explain what he or she is doing and why, her characters exist in the world by their very act of trying to understand it. In other words, it is the characters themselves who appear to be thinking, not the author having thought.

Mud, which has as its center the act of a woman coming to thought, clarifies this process. Here is a poor rural trio, Fornes's first lower depths characters, which consists of Mae, Lloyd and Henry, all who lead lives devoid of any sense of play or abandonment; their lives are entirely functional. Each of them exists in varying relations to language—Mae through her desire to read and acquire knowledge realizes that knowledge is the beginning of will and power and personal freedom; Henry, who becomes crippled in an accident during the course of the play, must learn again how to speak; Lloyd, barely past the level of survival beyond base instincts, has no language of communication beyond an informational one. *Mud* is the encounter of the characters in seventeen scenes which are separated by slow blackouts of "eight seconds," the story of struggles for power in which Henry usurps Lloyd's place in Mae's bed, and Lloyd kills Mae when she eventually walks out on Henry and him and their destitute existence. The violence committed in this play is the violence of the inarticulate. (pp. 29-30)

What Fornes has done in her approach to realism over the years, and *Mud* is the most austere example of this style to be produced in the theatre on this side of the Atlantic, is to lift the burden of psychology, declamation, morality, and sentimentality from the concept of character. She has freed characters from explaining themselves in a way that attempts to suggest interpretations of their actions, and put them in scenes that create a single emotive moment, as precise in what it does not articulate as in what does get said.

She rejects bourgeois realism's cliches of thought patterns, how its characters project themselves in society; she rejects its melodramatic self-righteousness. Though her work is purposely presented in a flat space that emphasizes its frontality, and the actors speak in a non-inflected manner, it is not the detached cool of hyper-or super-or photo-realism, but more emotive, filled with content. Gestures, emptied of their excesses, are free to be more resonant. *The Danube* resounds with the unspeakable horror of nuclear death precisely because it is not named.

Mud's scenes seem, radically, to be a comment on what does

not occur in performance, as if all the action had happened off stage. Her realism subtracts information whereas the conventional kind does little more than add it to a scene. She turns realism upside down by attacking its materialism and in its place emphasizing the interior lives of her characters, not their exterior selves. Hers is not a drama infatuated with things, but the qualities that make a life. Even when Henry buys Mae lipstick and a mirror in which to see herself, the moment is not for her a cosmetic action but a recognition of a self in the act of knowing, an objectification, a critique of the self.

There is no waste in this production. Fornes has always had a common sense approach to drama that situates itself in the utter simplicity of her dialogue. She writes sentences, not paragraphs. Her language is a model of direct address, it has the modesty of a writer for whom English is a learned language. She is unique in the way she writes about sexuality, in a tender way that accents sexual feelings, not sex as an event. It is a bitterly sad moment when Henry, his body twisted, his speech thick with pain, begs Mae to make love to him: "I feel the same desires. I feel the same needs. I have not changed." Emotion is unhidden in her plays. Just as language is not wasted, so the actors don't waste movements. Each scene is a strong pictorial unit. Sometimes a scene is only an image, or a few lines of dialogue. This realism is quotational, theatre in close-up, freeze frame. Theatre made by a miniaturist: in *The Danube* an acted scene is replayed in front of the stage by puppets, creating a fierce honorableness in its comment on human action. It is not imperialistic in its desire to create a world on the stage invested with moral imperatives, it is interested only in tableaux from a few lives in a particular place and time. Each scene presents a glimpse of imagery that is socially meaningful.

The pictorial aspect of this realism signifies an important change in theatrical attitudes towards space. It brings about a reduction of depth and a flattening of the stage picture which allude to a new pictorialism in drama. Whereas traditional realism concerned itself with a confined physicality determined by "setting," the new realism is more open cosmologically, its characters iconic. That is one of the reasons why this emotive, aggressive realism is rooted in expressionist style. (Expressionism keeps realism from becoming melodrama.) It is not coincidental that contemporary painting should also turn to expressionism after a period of super-realism, in order to generate an approach to emotion, narration and content. If styles change according to new perceptions of human form and its socialization, then painting and theatre, arts that must continually revise their opinions of figuration, should follow similar directions in any given period. Today, the exaggerated theatricality in everyday life has brought painting and theatre closer together.

The new realism would be confined by mere setting, which is only informational, it needs to be situated in the wider poetic notion of "space" which has ontological references. In the ecology of theatre, setting is a closed system of motion while space is more aligned to the idea of landscape which influences theatre, not only in writing but in design, as a result of now regarding the stage as "performance space." The very idea of space itself indicates how much the belief that all the world's a stage has been literalized. The concept of theatrical "space" alludes to the global repercussions of human action, if only metaphorically.

In recent years Fornes has become such a self-assured director that the movement in her productions seems nearly effort-less, totally inhibiting actorly artificiality. She doesn't force her actors' bodies on us in an attempt for them to dominate space. She leaves spaces on the stage unused. She makes the actors appreciate stillness as a theatrical idea, they are con-siderate toward other theatrical lives. And Fornes acknowl-edges the audience by giving them their own space and time in the productions. In *Mud* the short scenes and blackouts emphasize this attitude toward reception. They leave room for the audience to enter for contemplative moments. The au-thorial voice does not demand power over the theatrical expe-rience. It is not territorial. There is room for subjectivity, as a corrective to evasive objectification, on the part of all those involved in the making and witnessing of the event. *Fefu and Her Friends* is the play that most literally invites the audi-ence into the playing space—there were five of them to be exact—and for this Fornes created a style of acting that seemed, simply, a way of talking, it was so real.

Fornes has found her own stage language, a method of dis-course that unites play, actor and space in an organic whole that is always showing how it thinks, even as it allows for fragments of thought, unruly contradictions. One of the char-acteristics of Fornes's plays is that they offer characters *in the process of thought.* Her characters often question received ideas, conventions, the idea of emotion, even how one en-gages in thought. "What would be the use of knowing things if they don't serve you, if they don't help you shape your life?" asks Mae, an only partially literate woman who yet is dignified with a mind, however limited in its reach. All thought must be useful to characters and find meaning through life itself, to allow life its fullest expression. *Mud* is imbued with a feminism of the most subtle order, feminism based on the ruling idea that a free woman is one who has autonomy of thought. So, it does not matter to the play that Mae is murdered because the main point has already been made: Mae is free because she can understand the concept of freedom.

On one level, Fornes's plays equate the pleasure of thinking with the measure of being. That so many of her plays, *Dr. Kheal, Tango Palace, Evelyn Brown,* besides those already mentioned here, to one degree or another deal with the acqui-sition of language, alludes to what must surely be one of her consistent interests: the relationship of language to thought to action. The dramatic language is finely honed to exclude excessive qualifiers, adjectives, clauses. Sentences are simple, they exist to communicate, to question. There is a purity to this language of understatement that does not assume any-thing, and whose dramatic potential rests in the search for meaning in human endeavor. That is why the human voice, as an embodiment of social values, has so significant a place in this kind of writing.

Fornes's work has a warm delicacy and grace that distinguish it from most of what is written today. Apart from her plays there is little loveliness in the theatre. And yet I must stop to include Joseph Chaikin and Meredith Monk in this special group of artists for they also reflect this "loveliness" of pres-ence. Loveliness?—a humanism that guilelessly breathes great dignity into the human beings they imagine into life, and so propose to reality.

Working for more than twenty years in off-Broadway's un-heralded spaces, Fornes is an exemplary artist who through her writing and teaching has created a life in the theatre away from the crass hype that attends so many lesser beings. How

has she managed that rare accomplishment in this country's theatre—a career? What is admirable about Fornes is that she is one of the last of the real bohemians among the writers who came to prominence in the sixties. She never changed to fit her style to fashion. She has simply been busy writing, experi-menting, thinking. Writers have still to catch up to her. If there were a dozen writers in our theatre with Fornes's wis-dom and graciousness it would be enough for a country, and yet even one of her is sometimes all that is needed to feel the worth of the enormous effort it takes to live a life in the Amer-ican theatre. (pp. 30-4)

> *Bonnie Marranca, "The Real Life of Maria Irene Fornés," in* Performing Arts Journal, *Vol. VIII, No. 1, 1984, pp. 29-34.*

CATHERINE A. SCHULER

Along with Sam Shepard, Megan Terry, and a few others, Maria Irene Fornes is a survivor. With the possible exception of Shepard, playwrights who led the avant-garde theatre of the 1960s are no longer fashionable. Many of them have mel-lowed with age, turned to more lucrative activities, or com-promised their early radicalism in the hopes of cultivating a larger popular audience. And who can blame them? Living from hand to mouth, depending on foundation and federal grants, minimal royalties, and brief paid visits to university theatre and English departments is an exhausting and precar-ious business. Given the financial, emotional, mental, and even physical strain of a prolonged creative life in avant-garde theatre, it is hardly surprising that many playwrights whose names were so familiar in the 1960s and early 1970s have dropped from sight. Thus it was with particular pleasure that I discovered the recently published volume of four new plays by Maria Irene Fornes, and they attest to Fornes's con-tinuing commitment to the ideals of the decade that saw the first productions of her work. Indeed, despite all of the obsta-cles, she may be one of the last true icons of the avant-garde. (p. 514)

[*Maria Irene Fornes: Plays*] includes *Mud, The Danube, The Conduct of Life,* and *Sarita,* and while each has a particular story to tell, perhaps the most striking feature about them is the collective consistency with which they reflect Fornes's preoccupation with the struggle for human intimacy. In her world, men and women hunger for physical and emotional contact, but the desperate search for connection brings only violence, pain, and suffering.

Fornes is wary of the feminist label; apparently she has had the misfortune to be severely criticized by the truest of true believers who reject any play, novel, story, or poem that fails the test of ideological purity, works that do not present their readers with idealized images of women warriors triumphing over oppression and discovering the goddess within them-selves. I am puzzled by this reaction to Fornes's work. As a feminist, I read these plays with a mounting sense of horror—but my response was engendered not by ideological impurity, but rather by their disturbing reality.

Three of the plays, *Mud, The Conduct of Life,* and *Sarita,* treat the politics of sexual subordinance and domination, and while this has been popular thematic material in works by women for the last fifteen years, rarely has a woman writer tackled the relationships between men and women with the violence that we have come to accept and rationalize in the works of male authors like Norman Mailer and Henry Miller. This is, however, sexual violence as experienced from a woman's point of view—and the perspective is remarkably dissimilar from that of most male authors regardless of how sensitive (or insensitive) they may be to issues of sexual politics. Where sexual violence is usually tinged with eroticism in stories authored by men, in Fornes's work, this particular image of intimacy is a prison constructed both by the women themselves and by the men who would sacrifice them to fanatical pursuit of their physical and emotional satisfaction. In each play, a woman is held in bondage by two factors: her own irrational desire for intimacy that focuses on an inappropriate object, and the seemingly universal male demand for the total subordination and submission of women. Ultimately, the futile attempts by these women to extricate themselves from fundamentally sado-masochistic situations have one of two consequences: death or insanity. In *The Conduct of Life,* a whimpering twelve-year-old is held in bondage and raped repeatedly by an adult male who tries to convince himself and her that this is pleasurable activity. In the meantime, his wife, knowing all the while of his abuse to the child and having experienced his emotional abuse herself, continues to "love" him. In *Mud* and *Sarita,* two spirited young women are dragged down from their dreams of self-improvement and self-realization by men for whom autonomous existence is impossible. These are themes that surface in Fornes's most widely read and performed work of recent years, *Fefu and Her Friends,* but in the three plays under consideration here, we have a taste of sexual politics in the raw. Perhaps this is what disturbs not only some feminists, but many women and men who continue to grasp at the straws of romantic sexual mythology.

Although *The Danube,* the fourth play in this collection, presents similar motifs, it is gentler in content and more radical in form. Once again, an initially loving relationship is torn apart by the frustrating inability to communicate, a situation symbolized very effectively by playing foreign language tapes after exchanges by the central characters, Paul and Eve. Their attempts to understand each other are as futile and frustrating as the often humorous attempts by strangers from foreign countries who, having no knowledge of the other's language, cannot communicate even the simplest ideas. . . . Perhaps men and women speak in languages so foreign that mutual understanding, satisfaction, and harmony are ultimately impossible.

My brief descriptions of these plays may make them seem like ideological feminist diatribes. They are not. They work on many levels, but I find the sexual political plane most interesting. What is fascinating is that Fornes co-opts themes that have been popular for centuries in literature by male authors, and reintroduces them to us from an alternative point of view. If to express a female perception of reality—a perception that is radically different from dominant traditions, is ideological, then perhaps we must re-evaluate standard definitions of ideological literature. The plays in this volume are eminently readable, well worth production, and Fornes's unique voice has long deserved a wider audience. (pp. 514-15)

Catherine A. Schuler, in a review of "Maria Irene Fornés: Plays," in Theatre Journal, *Vol. 38, No. 4, December, 1986, pp. 514-15.*

MEL GUSSOW

White walls, tall French doors, spare furniture, a feeling of elegant coolness in early-20th-century New York—this could be the setting for a Merchant-Ivory film. Against the pristine background, Maria Irene Fornes tells a story swirling with undercurrents of sexuality. In *Abingdon Square* what appears to be languid is actually stifling. The leading character, a 15-year-old, seeks sanctuary and security married to a much older man. Over a period of years, she frees herself from bondage of several kinds.

Ms. Fornes has directed the play in her signature impressionistic style. Episodes, some silent and as brief as blackouts, divided by bursts of music, are designed to accumulate into a group portrait of a time, place and sensibility. Thematically and atmospherically, the work is intriguing, but even as Ms. Fornes's directorial attentiveness continues, the play itself becomes languid. There are arid stretches and lifeless events. The second act drifts to an anticlimatic conclusion.

Early in the play, [15-year-old Marion] announces that she is drowning in vagueness, that she has no character. As we watch, she gathers awareness, dreaming about adventure (adultery) before it actually occurs. [Marion's character] is marked by awakening passion. In one scene, for example, she retreats to an attic, where she finds an orgasmic delight in reciting Dante.

However, other characters remain vague. In several cases, roles have been arbitrarily split in two. The heroine's aunt and cousin, though divided by age, occupy a similar position in the play—as the wife's sounding board and buffer. Her two seducers could have been merged into one; the first seduction is so fleeting that some theatergoers may not be aware of the man's individual identity.

Only two subsidiary characters, the husband and his teenage son from a previous marriage, achieve a modicum of definition. . . . [The husband] is an exact figure of business-minded complacency. He is remote not only from his child bride, but also, as he says, from all knowledge of her "obligations" to him and their household. . . .

[Marion's stepson is] youthfully impetuous and, in terms of temperament as well as age, a far more appropriate romantic match for his stepmother. . . .

As a period piece, *Abingdon Square* maintains a kind of Jamesian reserve—as strong, late-afternoon light catches a character in an extended thought or a moment of *ennui*. Ms. Fornes sometimes holds these pictures for an extra beat, as if she is taking a time exposure. . . . [She] captures the mood of a lost way of life. It is in her role as director that Ms. Fornes has come closest to realizing her intention as a playwright.

Mel Gussow, "Fornés's 'Abingdon Square'," in The New York Times, *October 17, 1987, p. C16.*

MARIA IRENE FORNÉS [INTERVIEW WITH KATHLEEN BETSKO AND RACHEL KOENIG]

[Betsko and Koenig]: *Did you see your first plays in Europe?*

[Fornés]: I'd seen some plays here, but I didn't go to the theater often because it was expensive and I didn't like to plan things. Sometimes I would buy the ticket in advance and miss the play! At that time, there was something peculiar to me about going to theater, something forbidden. The first play that amazed me (I thought it was the most powerful thing of all—not only in theater but in painting, film, everything!) was Beckett's *Waiting for Godot*. I saw the play in Paris and I didn't understand a word of the French, but I left the theater as if I'd been hit over the head. I understood every moment of it. That play had a profound influence on me. When I returned from Europe, I started writing. That was 1959.

Had you done any writing previously?

In a way. I had been translating some letters that I brought over from Cuba. Letters that had been written to my great-grandfather from a cousin who lived in Spain. These letters told the whole story of their lives. At first I was just translating them for myself, not for anyone else to read. I wanted to understand something about that whole world. Then I became completely obsessed with the idea of writing a play. I thought about it day and night. It wasn't as if I thought, "I want to be a playwright"; it was just something I needed to do. For nineteen days I did nothing but write the play. Each day I called in sick to work. I would wake up in the morning and go directly to the typewriter. That was *Tango Palace* (1963). I had never experienced such an obsession in my life. Never. I could not eat . . . there wasn't anything that I preferred to do. It was like a door opened, and I entered into a world. If anything, I was afraid I would never come back. I could not *stop* writing. I loved it, it was such a thrill. I started writing late; I was around thirty. I had never thought I would write; as I said, I was an aspiring painter. But once I started writing it was so pleasurable that I couldn't stop. (pp. 154-55)

Do you feel that playwrights should educate themselves about directing and acting techniques?

I think every playwright needs to. First of all, you are not a good playwright unless you do all of those things. There are many reasons why playwrights, given the opportunity, might not *want* to direct: Perhaps they don't like dealing with so many people, or they're impatient; maybe they prefer somebody else to do it. If it's the playwright's choice and they prefer not to direct I don't think they have to. But to say they cannot direct! At the Padua Hills Theater Workshop where I go every summer you don't need to ask permission to direct your own play. On the contrary, if you don't want to direct, you have to *find* a director. We don't tell people, "You must direct" . . . they just do. It's like making your own sandwich. Because of this, the students see from the start that they *can* direct their own plays.

Are women playwrights more intimidated by the idea of directing their own work because of the traditional notion of the director being the "father" of the production?

I don't think so, because the playwright is the "woman" of the theater.

Whether the playwright is male or female?

Yes. The playwright is the woman and the director is the husband. Lanford Wilson pointed that out to me. I was explaining about how, as a playwright, you feel that someone is taking you out to have a "nice day" in a "nice place." The idea is "You be a nice girl and I'm going to take care of you." I thought that was because I am a woman, and Lanford said, "I feel the same way. I feel I am a girl; I have to be nice to this guy who is going to do nice by me; he's going to choose

the right actors for my play because I don't know what I'm doing. I am very talented, but I don't really understand anything." I thought, "Well, perhaps it is because Lanford is not forceful enough." But then I was on a panel with another playwright who had had several plays on Broadway, and who had done quite a lot of commercial work. He looked like a business man, a big-shot executive. The panel was discussing the position of the playwright and this man, who was so masculine, so firm and definite with his white shirt and proper suit and strong voice, said that he understood the position of women in society because as a playwright, he was treated as a woman. So I am assuming that the playwright is the woman of the theater.

I do think it's more difficult for women directors than male directors. First of all, a producer has to believe that as a director, you will be in charge, that you will be able to control the cast, the crew, the production. In my case, they never would believe that I could control anything, and it's true. I don't have any control over anything *except* my art. I never say, "*You* go there!" But I work with people who believe in my work and then I have a power that is almost hypnotic. . . . My first directing experience, *Molly's Dream* (1968) at New Dramatists, was essentially a reading—there were no reviews or publicity, and only five performances. It wasn't until later that I directed something finished, and then I had to work with lighting designers, etc. But I do have a good eye, and that's important. I was able quickly to ask for what I wanted and when the light designers would show me something, I knew whether it was good or not. I remember what a surprise it was to work with them.

Did your new understanding of the technical side of theater affect your writing? Did it open your imagination?

Yes. For instance, you have to find out what lights are all about or you may destroy scenes. But you see, I was a painter before. The stage for me is a very beautiful place, nice to look at. And space is very important. I'm very picky with actors. I will keep on positioning them—a little to the left, no, three inches more . . . —because for me, it's as important as focusing a camera. You reach a point, pass it, go back a little and ZING! it's in focus.

Is this how the photographic freezes between scenes evolved in your play Mud *(1983)?*

I did the play in Padua Hills, outdoors, and I could not have blackouts because I had scheduled myself in daylight time. The freezes were a way to change scenes. I kept them in the New York production because there was something about the freezes that I liked.

What about the monochromatic quality? . . .

The drab color also had to do with the original daylight production, which started when the sun was about to set and ended when the light became gray. The light changed during the performance, and the audiences always felt that it was deliberate because later in the play, everything becomes gray. The direct sunlight also created a quality. In the New York production, the clothes were drab and the set was white. The costume designer made the character Lloyd's clothes streaky, dirty. At some moment in rehearsal I felt he looked like a painting. I said to the designer, "Let's go with this . . . " and she gave Harry and Mae's costumes the same look.

Would you discuss the eroticism in your work?

That really began to happen with *A Visit,* which was an attempt to do something erotic. There is sexuality in the earlier work, like *Successful Life of Three* (1965), but it's more cartoonish. I don't like *A Visit* too much now, because it was composed from other people's writing and I violated their intentions. It was something I did in a playful way, almost like a party piece for friends. People have wanted to publish it and I have had some offers for productions, but I have refused. I was using material from Victorian novels, and I found there was something hot about the emotions in them. I took sections and made a collage of other people's writings. This completely changed the authors' meanings. I turned their Victorian words into something erotic. The men wore porcelain phalluses and the women porcelain breasts. The designer who made them put a little blue line around the tip of the penises and nipples. It was mischievous, playful, and I think it was my way of breaking through a kind of shyness about erotic things—because one always feels shy. To do something all the way out, like *A Visit*—which was completely erotic and completely bold, although it was in good taste because I don't like pornography—freed me.

I think, too, that as you get older you become freer sexually. When you are young you are afraid if you write something like *A Visit* people will call you on the phone and say, you know . . . (laughter). But when you get older, you don't care. First of all, nobody calls you on the phone (laughter). I feel that the older I get, the more shameless I feel. And in a sense, more pure. For instance, I am more interested in my work now. When I was younger, I was more interested in romance. The hours and hours I would spend being tormented by somebody or trying to pursue someone, fantasizing or imagining what the words meant. Now I watch that in others and it seems like rather odd behavior. Not that I am indifferent to love or romance. I am just not obsessed. I have more time to concentrate. I watch young people and it's endless, constant, they are like little animals, like dogs in heat. I think my writing is more passionate now, because when you are younger there is a fear of exposure and you protect yourself.

A play is so hot, so passionate; the Greeks, Shakespeare, opera have hot, hot passions, but very little sexuality. Today, sexuality is dealt with in pornography, in a cold, obscene way. The possibility of sexual drama is something unexplored. I am freer to examine these passions now because of the workshop. Many of the exercises, the meditations I do, are intended to work in a visceral way. I employ exercises to root the writer into their own organism, their own humanity, rather than the intellect. Writing is an intellectual process, so it is good to *root* the process into your stomach, your heart, your bowels. It is difficult sometimes for the younger women in the workshop. They are in a room of Hispanic men. Because of my age, I set an example: Whenever something erotic comes up in my own work, I read it. At first they all go, "Whoo . . . " It may be better for the younger women not to read when something erotic comes up in their work because it's true, when women are younger, they have to put up with the guys saying "Hey, baby . . . " But when I read my erotic passages aloud as an example, as a possibility in writing, at least I have given my female students permission to be fully *present* as writers, even if they choose not to read that material out loud. It may be that because of these exercises my own writing is becoming more erotic. Even so, I don't think, "Oh, here comes the erotic scene." I just write a scene of Harry (*Mud*) eating soup one day, and a scene where he is sexually aroused and masturbating the next.

After I had written the erotic scenes for *Mud* and *Sarita* I realized that the sexuality is very unconventional. They are not scenes that represent a typical sexuality, they are special moments, and those moments are theatrical. I probably owe—and I say *owe* because I think it's something important that has come into my writing—those strong sexual scenes to *A Visit.*

Do you believe there is a female aesthetic in drama?

How could there possibly not be? Not only is there a women's aesthetic, each woman has her own aesthetic and so does each man. It's like saying "Is there a Hispanic aesthetic?" Of course there is. Your aesthetic is different from mine—each person has their own universe—but how could we, as women, have nothing in common? That's not possible. We are different from a man, who is not a woman, who has never had a menstrual period in his life.

Do you feel that a gender bias may exist in theater criticism, are women's plays often accused of being poorly structured "non-plays" when the playwrights may have intentionally broken form?

You have to remember that we are dealing with theater and theater is the backward art. Theater is one hundred, two hundred years behind the times. There was an American girl living in Paris who wanted to translate *Promenade,* and have it produced in France. She came to New York to meet me and during her visit she went to (the) Lincoln Center (Branch of the New York Public) Library to read some old reviews of the play. She was amazed when she discovered that *Promenade* was considered an avant-garde piece. I told her, "It's because we are backward in the theater." If *Promenade* connects to anything, it's with movies of the thirties, popular art from the thirties—which is commercial! When the play was done in 1965, and then again in 1970, it was called "The musical of the seventies" to warn people that they were going to see something odd. I am sure people *still* consider that play odd.

I have a discussion every night after the performance of *The Danube* at The American Place Theater (1984). I love doing it because I like to hear what audiences think. It's not pleasant, often the response is "What does it mean?" or "Why didn't you make it clear?" or "I'm *depressed.*" The triumph came just last night. A woman (one of those who said earlier that she did not understand the play) said, "Frankly it is *excruciating.* Could you tell me why anyone would produce this play?" I was glad that (artistic director) Winn Handman was there; I let him explain why he produced it. After a few more comments, the discussion closed and the same woman said in praise, "This is really an important play and I have to tell you that the images are so powerful." She was quite honest, even though what she said was contradictory. I think at first she felt, "If this doesn't tell me a clear story it is not theater. If this doesn't conform to everything I've seen previously in theater, then the playwright must have made a mistake." Perhaps when she heard the other comments she realized that her notion of theater was not necessarily what theater is; other things count also.

Are the public discussions required by The American Place Theater or do you routinely attempt after-play discussions with the audience?

They are set up by The American Place. Usually the playwright is asked to participate in a few of the discussions, but writers often feel as if they are being attacked, they feel defensive. There are times when the criticism is unanimous and harsh, and I have also felt from time to time like saying "You didn't like the play? Too bad!" But for the most part I like to hear what the audience has to say because you seldom get a chance to find out what people think about your work. (pp. 159-64)

What do the more conventional critics find disturbing in your work?

I was thinking about it just today. I wanted to discuss it with my students. I was thinking about what makes conventional theater. Let's say you were interested in doing a play that would be accepted by large numbers of people. What is it, then, that you should concentrate on? I realized that what makes my plays unacceptable to people is the form more than the content. My content is usually not outrageous. I think it's mild! *The Danube* is a play about a nice family that is being destroyed. Why don't nice middle-class people feel, "Oh, those poor darlings! That nice boy Paul and his girlfriend Eve, they were so good to their father and he loved them and this thing came along and destroyed their nice home . . . how terrible." That is the story of that play. I think people are sometimes afraid and suspicious. They don't know what bomb you have planted in your play. There is no reason for that. *Fefu and Her Friends,* although it has very profound things in it, is a middle-class play. It is about nice middle-class girls from Connecticut, not about people saying "Let's destroy the world." It's mild. What makes people almost vicious must be the form. Because there are many plays that have outrageous things going on, but they have a conventional structure so people don't care. Isn't that curious?

In a recent Performing Arts Journal *symposium, you stated, "We have to reconcile ourselves to the idea that the protagonist of a play can be a woman." Would you elaborate?*

Even women are not aware of how important that is. Some women feel they must write plays in which there is a feminist statement, that they must attempt to clarify a situation in which there is prejudice against women. But they want to see situations where a woman is at a disadvantage and then becomes a victor. They are not interested anymore in seeing cases of women who suffer or succumb. I see their point. It's nice to see the person you are rooting for win all the battles, but at the same time, it is a little childish. I don't believe that the artist, the creator, is saying, "This character has perished, therefore all humanity will perish." I am very sad when I see a film or read a story in which the character I'm identifying with dies. But I don't feel that something has been killed inside of me because the character died. My ability to see their death as unnecessary is intact regardless of the pain I may feel about their death. I believe when you portray an unnecessary death, you are speaking on behalf of the person's life, the person's prime.

Would you discuss that in terms of the female protagonist in **Mud,** *who is shot by one of her lovers at the end of the play? One critic said the message of the play was directed towards women: "Don't try, they'll never let you get away with it." This critic felt it was quite a despairing play.*

I see Mae differently than many people did. I love her very much, I'm completely identified with her, but she is *not* an angel. I wrote the last scene just the way I saw it. At the end of the story, Mae is after something; she is learning, and that is so dear you cannot blame her for it. *Mud* is not an anti-male play that says men are pigs. It is also not a feminist message play about how Mae tries to liberate herself from these two men who will not let her develop. They are not keeping her down. She can leave any time she wants. It isn't that she is a brilliant woman. She says that she has a difficult time remembering things, she can't pass the tests at school. I think if she had got away she would probably have come back to Henry and Lloyd. She loves them, they love her, that's their life. When Lloyd shoots her it is not because he doesn't want her to get away and develop herself. It's because she is leaving and he would die without her. He must not let her do this. I think that when you write you must really open your eyes and see: Is it true that they would not let her get away? Does Lloyd's response grow out of the play? Of course it does. Of course Lloyd is very annoyed in the beginning that she is pursuing her studies. But it is not this annoyance that leads him to kill her. I don't think Mae really would have improved herself if she got away. What's wonderful about Mae is her love for knowledge. Knowledge is the beloved thing. She is not an artist, she worships art and wants to go where she can visit museums, et cetera. There is something noble and beautiful in this aspect of her character and I don't think it has been dealt with in plays or in fiction. Mae is a pursuer of angels, it doesn't mean she wants to *be* an angel, to grow wings and have magic powers.

In terms of the question about the female protagonist, I feel that what is important about this play is that Mae is the central character. It says something about women's place in the world, not because she is good or a heroine, not because she is oppressed by men or because the men 'won't let her get away with it,' but simply because she is the *center* of that play. It is her mind that matters throughout the play, and the whole play exists because her little mind wants to see the light, not even to see it because she wants to be illuminated, but so she can revere it. It is because of that mind, Mae's mind, *a woman's mind,* that that play exists. To me that is a more important step toward redeeming women's position in the world than whether or not *Mud* has a feminist theme, which it does not. The theme is just a mind that wants to exist and has difficulties. The difficulties have nothing to do with gender, but the fact that this mind is in a woman's body makes an important feminist point. I believe that to show a woman at the center of a situation, at the center of the universe, is a much more important feminist statement than to put Mae in a situation that shows her in an unfavorable position from which she escapes, or to say that she is noble and the men around her are not.

What did you mean when you said, "It is impossible to aim at an audience when writing a play?"

It's impossible because you can never predict the audience reaction. People think they are writing a comedy and then nobody laughs. If nobody laughs, it's not a comedy. That's why many plays fail. People spend millions of dollars to put plays on Broadway. If people knew what would succeed, none of those plays would fail.

You have said that you would be willing to spend your entire life in poverty and struggle in order to be a working playwright. Have you had to make sacrifices in order to devote yourself to writing for the theater?

I haven't made sacrifices, really. It's not as if I chose writing as a career to make money. There *are* people who can write ad copy or soap operas, I couldn't, I would die. I might be able to do it technically, but I could not spiritually. I feel I've never had any choice. When I'm not doing something that comes deeply from me, I get bored. When I get bored I get distracted, and when I get distracted, I become depressed. It's a natural resistance, and it insures your integrity. You die when you are faking it, and you are alive when you are truthful. I consider myself lucky to have been able to survive financially doing what I want to do. Sometimes it's been very, very tight, and sometimes it's been scary because I've had to go into debt. Still, I don't consider it a sacrifice. (pp. 164-67)

Maria Irene Fornés, Kathleen Betsko and Rachel Koenig in an interview from Interviews with Contemporary Women Playwrights, *by Kathleen Betsko and Rachel Koenig, Beech Tree Books, 1987, pp. 154-67.*

RUIS WOERTENDYKE

The image of women in American plays has been a limited one. Though there seems to be a large variety of roles, the vast majority of them live lives that revolve around men. The unfortunate effect of this characterization is that it establishes women as either saint or sinner; virgin or whore; for man or against him. (p. 264)

The saintly image includes married women who are honest, sensitive, and completely devoted to their husbands and families like Linda in *Death of a Salesman* and Mrs. Antrobus in *The Skin of Our Teeth,* as well as the women who refuse to compromise their ideals for anything but the perfect man like Rose Maurrants in *Street Scene,* Peggy Grant in *Front Page,* and Miriamne in *Winterset.*

The sinning women in American plays are innumerable and can be found in all the above plays, most of Tennessee Williams, Sam Shepherd, Edward Albee, William Saroyan, William Inge, Clifford Odets, and others. We are sympathetic to many of them like Blanche in *A Streetcar Named Desire* and Babe in *Crimes of the Heart* and some of them even get off without punishment: Amy in *They Knew What They Wanted,* Laura Reynolds in *Tea and Sympathy,* and Kitty Duval in *The Time of Your Life.*

Maria Irene Fornes, though not apart from this practice, sheds new light on the character of American women. She does this . . . simply by showing us the world from a woman's point of view. As a consequence, Marion in *Abingdon Square* is both virgin and whore but reminds us more of Tom than Laura (*The Glass Menagerie*) and more of Joe than Amy (*They Knew What They Wanted*). Marion is a young woman who must escape her limited and confining home to enter the outside world and search out the visions of her imagination in order to discover her true self. Stated as such, the play seems like the standard "find yourself" story with a reversal of sexual roles, but Marion is not a woman in a man's role like Regina in *The Little Foxes,* or Harriet Craig in *Craig's Wife:* she is a girl growing into a woman and though she ends as the standard woman in love with her husband, the excursion through her awareness is not stereotypical and sheds much light on woman's sexuality and the role men play in forming that sexuality.

Juster, Michael's widowed father, befriended Marion when her parents died, and is to be her husband. She wants to be a good and loving wife and mother even though she has no idea what that means. When she asks Juster what her married obligations will be, he tells her that she must "run the house" but has no idea how: when he was born his mother ran it, when he married his wife ran it, and when she died the housekeeper took it over. Juster is a kind and good man who has no idea what a woman does with her life. The roles of gender are clearly and firmly established in 1905.

Marion, good Victorian Christian that she is, learns to run the house and does very well until her libido begins to raise its exciting and mysterious head. At first she is satisfied by creating an imaginary affair in her diary and sharing that fantasy with Michael. She creates a dark eyed poet with a delicate face and sensitive hands named F., but it soon ceases to fulfill her need and she allows herself to be taken by a young, virile glazier who is doing repairs on the house. A pregnancy results from that single morning's coupling and Juster is pleasantly surprised that he is to become a father again. Obviously Marion and Juster have sex but in a very funny scene when he is reading about flowers, bees, stigmas, and golden pollen, it is clear that his idea of sex is more scientific than sensual—not exactly the kind of image that excites a newly awakened sexuality.

She meets a dark eyed man named Jonathan, who she calls Frank, after the imaginary lover in her diary. Though a small point, it becomes a very significant detail that strongly effects our perception of the play. Marion does not fall in love with Jonathan but with her own image of an idealized man; not with his sexuality but with the compulsion to fill her own needs. It is not long before she becomes entrenched in an affair with this projected fantasy and not long before she realizes this young man is incapable of taking care of himself. She begins smoking, drinking, is discovered by Juster, thrown out of the house, and not allowed to see her baby. If the play ended here, it would merely be another piece about a fallen woman, but old and gentle Juster cannot repress his conflicting passions of love and betrayal. He does not know on whom to use his pistol, however, and loses his self-assured identity. He reminds us of Marion when she was first becoming aware of her sexuality. She is "drowning in vagueness" and does not know who she is, and does not know how to stop what she feels. Juster feels the same things, but unlike Marion, he has been too long immersed in his image of himself and cannot break the social mold that has formed him. Instead of shooting someone, he has a heart attack. Marion instinctively goes to him and realizes she has a very deep love for this dying, old man. She has returned to where she began, knowing the place for the first time. Not such an unusual story, but Ms. Fornes shows us the restrictions of our gender roles and dissolves the stereotypes that have so long littered our stages. She makes us fully aware that women's actions are based on women's needs, and not on the overpowering appeal and superiority of men. (264-66)

Ruis Woertendyke, in a review of "Abingdon Square," in Theatre Journal, *Vol. 40, No. 2, May, 1988, pp. 264-66.*

JOHN WILDERS

Although the style and construction of *Abingdon Square* are strikingly original, the story it tells is one of the oldest in literature. The tale of the old man whose young wife proves unfaithful to him has been treated by authors as diverse as Chaucer, Wycherley, Flaubert, Tolstoy and Lawrence. The interest of this recent play by Maria Irene Fornes, a Cuban-born dramatist who works in New York, arises not from its plot, familiar and predictable as it is, but from the way she has treated it.

Whereas in *The Country Wife* Wycherley used the tale to reveal the sexual pursuits of Restoration London, Fornes has created a quite different emphasis by placing it in the sober, stable environment of early twentieth-century New York (not far, one imagines, from James's *Washington Square* with which the play has some similarities). Moreover the husband, Juster, far from being a figure of fun, is a kindly, prosperous, good-natured business man of regular habits, who has brought Marion up with his own son, Michael, and marries her not out of sexual desire but because it seems the logical thing to do when his first wife dies. When the high-spirited Marion forms a secret liaison with Frank (who bears a significant resemblance to Michael), and is then made pregnant by a handsome workman, our sympathy goes out both to the husband who sees the act as a monstrous betrayal, and to the wife whose marriage supplies her with no outlet for her youthful, romantic energies and is filled with remorse for what she has done. Fornes passes no judgment on either party in a marriage which initially seemed reasonable but which was actually doomed from the start. When, just before her husband's death, Marion's love for him revives, a situation more often used for its comic potential comes close to tragedy.

Fornes's desire to withhold censure expresses itself in the construction of **Abingdon Square,** which consists of a sequence of very short, significant episodes, some no longer than two or three minutes: Marion and Michael dancing ragtime to the gramophone as Juster, returned from the office, looks on approvingly; Marion seated on Frank's knee in their secretly rented apartment. The style of the dialogue is similarly non-naturalistic: the characters explicitly declare their feelings and convictions directly to the audience and are always recognizably characters in a play. Fornes can be verbally eloquent and she makes use of an expressive visual language. . . . [The elegant furniture] is arranged with geometrical orderliness and the characters group themselves as though for a series of family portraits expressing the formality of their daily life. Hence the slightest departure from this norm—as when Frank, the lover, lolls back in a chair—assumes an extraordinary significance. Music is also used dramatically, notably at the opening of the second act when Marion simply stands facing the audience as Mahler's "Ich bin der Welt abhanden gekommen . . . " is played. In her silence she expresses the maturity and desolation contained in the song. . . .

Fornes hints that the breakdown of the marriage reflects the collapse of an established, traditional way of life (Marion's downfall coincides with the entry of America into the First World War and on his final appearance Michael is in uniform, the silent embodiment of doomed youth.) This is, however, essentially a domestic tragedy, understated in style and impeccably performed.

> *John Wilders, "A Doomed Match," in* The Times Literary Supplement, *No. 4541, April 13-19, 1990, p. 396.*

FURTHER READING

Cummings, Scott. "Seeing with Clarity: the Visions of Maria Irene Fornés." *Theater* XVII, No. 1 (Winter 1985): 51-6.
    Interview in which Fornés discusses her changing style and the language, realism, and feminism of her plays.

Fornés, María Irene. "I Write these Messages that Come." *The Drama Review* 21, No. 4 (December 1977): 25-40.
    Offers insight into Fornés' writing habits and the backgrounds of her works.

Wetzsteon, Ross. "Irene Fornés: the Elements of Style." *The Village Voice* XXXI, No. 17 (29 April 1986): 42-5.
    Examines Fornés' fluctuating career up to *The Conduct of Life.*

Larry Gelbart

1923-

American scriptwriter and dramatist.

A prominent comedy writer for stage, film, radio, and television, Gelbart is best known to popular audiences as one of the creators of "M*A*S*H," an innovative television comedy series that is often called a classic of the medium. Praised as ingenious and engrossing, Gelbart's scripts often blend wry, witty satire with elaborate puns and vaudevillian one-liners. Alone or in collaboration with other writers, he has written several popular and critically-acclaimed films, including *Oh, God!* and *Tootsie.* Gelbart's Broadway credits include such respected works as *A Funny Thing Happened on the Way to the Forum, City of Angels,* and *Mastergate: A Play on Words.*

Gelbart began his distinguished career at age sixteen, writing for radio's "The Fanny Brice Show." At eighteen, he was hired for Sid Caesar's television comedy hour, collaborating with writers Neil Simon, Carl Reiner, Mel Brooks, and Woody Allen. After winning an Emmy award for his contributions to Art Carney's television specials, Gelbart ventured into theatrical comedy with his first play, *The Conquering Hero,* which he adapted from the film *Hail the Conquering Hero.* A slightly sarcastic commentary on motherhood, war, and the U. S. Marine Corps, the play received generally unenthusiastic reviews. In partnership with writer Burt Shevelove, Gelbart next developed a Broadway musical, *A Funny Thing Happened on the Way to the Forum.* This play, for which Gelbart received an Antoinette Perry (Tony) Award, is loosely based on the bawdy comedies of Plautus, an ancient Roman dramatist. Hailed by some critics as one of Broadway's best musicals, the show combines stock Roman characters and situations with the raucous humor of American vaudeville. Gelbart also earned praise for his play *Sly Fox,* a comic farce about greed set in nineteenth-century San Francisco and based on Ben Jonson's Elizabethan drama *Volpone.*

Gelbart returned to television in 1971 as chief writer for a new television series involving doctors in an American mobile army surgical hospital behind the front lines of the Korean War. Adapted from the film of the same title, "M*A*S*H" initially drew a small viewing audience but eventually became immensely popular and earned a reputation as one of the medium's most intelligent, poignant, and comical programs. Although the show's excellence derived from collaborative efforts, Gelbart is often described as the show's original guiding force, for he is credited with directing many of its episodes as well as writing ninety-seven of the show's early scripts. For these pieces, Gelbart received his second Emmy award.

After five years of writing for "M*A*S*H," Gelbart left the show to develop other projects, including a critically acclaimed but commercially unsuccessful television series, "United States." A half-hour show that concentrated on the realities of contemporary marriage and eschewed such standard situation comedy conceits as an accompanying laugh-track, jokes placed at predictable intervals, and simple plots resolved in twenty-four minutes, the program lasted less than half a season. Characterized by clever dialogue, sexual frank-

ness, and psychological insight, "United States" was lauded by critics, who often commented that the show's sophisticated format limited its popular appeal.

In *Mastergate,* Gelbart satirizes the Iran-contra scandal that occurred during the Reagan administration, mocking the obfuscating rhetoric often used by indicted officials. Set in a congressional hearing room, Gelbart's play features arrogant military officers, fatuous politicians, and slick newscasters, all of whom perpetuate the use of inscrutable jargon. For example, sworn witnesses, in their pursuit of "future and probable deniability," practice "selective honesty" through "responditorial redundancy" and "non-denial denials." Gelbart decries the use of doublespeak not only for its deceptive intent, but also for its corrosive effect upon the English language. Although some critics commented that Gelbart's view of the Iran-contra scandal was either dated or less ludicrous than the actual proceedings, many lauded the play as intelligent, accurate satire and parody. Frank Rich concluded: "When *Mastergate* is funny, it is very funny. When it is not, it still stands up for a patriotic integrity beyond the understanding of the clowns who parade across its national stage."

City of Angels, a musical that lampoons 1940s Hollywood detective films, earned acclaim from critics. Structured as a movie within a play, the comedy centers on Stine, a New

Yorker who has moved to Los Angeles to write the film adaption of his first novel, a prototypical detective mystery. In the play's central narrative, Stine argues with imperious movie moguls, defends his battered artistic integrity, and continually rewrites his script, which features the author's "hard-boiled" alter-ego, Stone. Simultaneously, on a separate set composed entirely in the black and white hues of film noir, Stone and other film characters enact Stine's evolving script; when Stine decides to rewrite a scene, the film cast moves and speaks backwards, as if Stine were rewinding his vision of the film. As Stine crafts his script, he assimilates colleagues into his film, and many of his friends appear as characters in the movie sequences, transcending the boundary between the author's reality and his fictional creation. While some reviewers noted that Gelbart's satiric target, 1940s Hollywood, has often been parodied, most deemed *City of Angels* fresh and animated, praising Gelbart's adroit wit and stylish innovation. Edwin Wilson observed: "Hollywood is held up to hilarious ridicule by author Larry Gelbart. . . . Mr. Gelbart, one of the cleverest wordsmiths working today, not only captures the spirit of film-noir, he delivers one knockout punch line after another."

[See also *CLC,* Vol. 21 and *Contemporary Authors,* Vols. 73-76.]

PRINCIPAL WORKS

SCREENPLAYS

The Wrong Box   1966
Not With My Wife, You Don't   1966
Oh, God!   1977
Movie, Movie   1979
Tootsie   [with Murray Schisgal, Elaine May, and others]
    1982

PLAYS

The Conquering Hero   1960
A Funny Thing Happened on the Way to the Forum   [with
    Burt Shevelove]   1961
Sly Fox   1976
Mastergate: A Play on Words   1989
City of Angels   1989

TELEVISION SCRIPTS

"Your Show of Shows"   1953-55
"M*A*S*H"   1972-1977
"United States"   1980

HOWARD KISSEL

If you think the title is funny, you'll probably enjoy *Mastergate.* If you find it adolescent, which I'm afraid I do, stay home and read Mark Twain on politics.

Larry Gelbart's attempt to satirize contemporary political ineptitude has the subtitle "a play on words." For much of the evening, *Mastergate* is indeed that.

Gelbart is skillful at lampooning current Washington gobbledygook, as when a character declares to a Senate investigating committee. "My involvement was strictly limited to the extent of my participation," or when another speaks of "future and probable deniability."

He also understands the bureaucratic mentality, as when he has a witness say, "I'm not cleared to have that kind of curiosity, sir."

At times he engages in word play for its own sake. A witness is asked a standard forensic question, "Do you recall your appearance at that time?" and answers, "I think I looked much the same as I do now."

This cleverness grows tiresome after about 10 minutes. Moreover, when one of the witnesses says, "Ethics and morality aside, I was aware that I had a higher obligation to do as I was ordered," it sounds a bit stale.

The plot of *Mastergate* concerns an attempt by the CIA to take over a film studio and use its production of a war film as a conduit to get arms to Central America. This might have made a nice "Saturday Night Live" skit but . . . it is not a very satisfying piece of theater.

This is yet another case of reality far outstripping fiction. Gelbart's unraveling of a potentially funny situation has none of the suspense or the amusement of actual congressional investigations. They hinge, after all, on Character. Gelbart's situations are entirely stereotyped and predictable. . . .

"It could probably be shown by facts and figures that there is no distinctly native American criminal class except Congress," Twain wrote a century ago. The Executive branch has outstripped the Legislative in this area. They do it more interestingly than Gelbart.

Howard Kissel, "D.C. Satire Misfires in 'Master-
gate'," in Daily News, *New York, October 13, 1989.*

CLIVE BARNES

When did we last have a thoroughly partisan political play on Broadway? You have to go back to Gore Vidal's *An Evening with Richard Nixon* in 1972 or Jay Broad's *Red, White, and Maddox* in 1969, to find Broadway revealing anything like a political streak, let alone a political conscience.

For this reason alone—and there are funnier ones—Larry Gelbart's *Mastergate,* a self-styled "play on words," . . . would be welcome.

And for much of the time—before it fizzles out at the end—this parody of congressional hearings from Watergate to Irangate has some riotously ribald moments. . . .

The fascinating reality of . . . these congressional hearings—I became an addict of them, as, obviously, did Gelbart—was comic enough, and the playwright really hasn't had to distort that reality by anything much more than a little shrewd exaggeration.

Gelbart is obviously almost as appalled at the onslaught upon our always fragile language as on any mayhem dealt to the basically resilient U.S. Constitution.

He has a lovely comic ear for the wilder bureaucratic excesses of gobbledegook, sensing out the dangers of George Orwell's newspeak and doublethink, but also painfully exulting in such seemingly harmless evasions as "compliance of the non-variety" instead of a "no!"

The virtues of the piece are evident, and Gelbart . . . has made the most of them.

Yet it remains more an extended (relentlessly extended, in fact) revue sketch than a play, and the joke has started to fade well before the end, where the author tries, without much success, to provide a knock-out, cataclysmic, *Dr. Strangelove* ending.

Thus it proves an evening more of incidental belly laughs ending in a belly flop rather than a sustained evening of satire—and for that matter the satire is perhaps a little too gentle-natured for the good of its corrosive potential.

I laughed a lot—sometimes wryly, sometimes explosively—but I was not instructed or surprised. . . .

Unfortunately—when all is said and laughed—[*Mastergate*] is a brief evening that would have been even better even shorter.

Clive Barnes, "Satirical Swipe at Petty Politics," in New York Post, *October 13, 1989.*

FRANK RICH

How do you write a truthful play in which everyone is a liar? Set it on Capitol Hill, of course. In *Mastergate,* Larry Gelbart's excoriating satire of the Iran-contra hearings, the witnesses before a Congressional committee aspire only to be "steadfastly evasive and selectively honest," and they don't even succeed at that. They speak in nonsensical double talk and official bureaucratese redolent of such past Gelbart writings as Sid Caesar's shtick and television's **"M*A*S*H."** As Maj. Manley Battle—a lunatic amalgam of Oliver North, Alexander Haig and Joseph Heller's Major Major—says, "I prefer to call a spade by its code word."

Yet Mr. Gelbart, unlike his obfuscating characters, speaks the harsh truth. *Mastergate* isn't subtitled "A Play on Words" for nothing. Its subject is not just Washington's scandals but the destruction of language that accompanies those scandals, for language is the first casualty of official mendacity. American voters have now lived through two decades of "pacification programs," "modified limited hangouts," "stonewalling," "non-denial denials" and other euphemisms for covert criminal actions or their subsequent cover-ups. What has this relentlessly corrupt coinage done to our society? Mr. Gelbart, mad as hell and unable to take it anymore, has written a comedy in which the laughter derives almost entirely from the linguistic pratfalls taken by public officials to avoid taking responsibility for their betrayal of the public trust. . . .

Officials testify about their nonparticipation in "non-discussions" and applaud the ally of San Elvador for practicing "a democratic form of government that's been run by its army for the past 40 years." . . . To thicken the smoke screen separating citizens from the facts, *Mastergate* has another overlay of falsehood provided by the fatuous gavel-to-gavel coverage of Total News Network. It's part of Mr. Gelbart's point that the fictive media event, or in the historian Daniel Boorstin's phrase, "the pseudo-event," and the actual news event have blurred into a single impenetrable morass. Everyone is showboating for the camera, whether in Congressional tribunals or in the real or faked battle scenes that have brought war, from Tet on, into our living rooms each night. . . .

Mastergate, however smart, is not the Broadway show its venue suggests but a sketch—and one that feels stretched to fill 90 minutes. There are times when Mr. Gelbart's compulsive wordplays, whether malapropisms or pun-ridden proper names, run off into wheel-spinning overdrive, and there are a few missed satiric opportunities that might have served in their place. It seems a waste to have a television correspondent who sounds exactly like Diane Sawyer and not have fun with her real-life counterpart's role as a press officer in the waning days of the Nixon White House. Nor does Mr. Gelbart, a co-author of *Tootsie* and a veteran of show-biz wars, get all the juice out of the Hollywood corruption that makes the budget-padding of *Tet!, the Movie* echo *Heaven's Gate* as much as Watergate.

By outliving Oliver North's trial and the front-page prominence of figures like George Shultz and William Casey, *Mastergate* has also lost immediacy since its premiere. . . . Satire can have the shelf life of yesterday's newspapers. But if *Mastergate* leaves the audience a bit unsatisfied especially by its lack of resolution, that is consistent with the Iran-contra affair itself, which refuses to follow the well-made scenario of Watergate. As Theodore Draper wrote in *The New York Review of Books* over the summer, "Without a full disclosure of the President's responsibility, the [North] trial took on the appearance of *Hamlet* without the Prince." In [the October 16, 1989 issue of *The New Yorker*], Frances Fitz-Gerald similarly likens the scandal, with its shuffled events and shredded subplots, to "modernist drama": "The simple, old-fashioned questions cannot be answered directly, and the most serious questions have jokes for answers."

Mr. Gelbart has sharpened those black jokes and demands that we take seriously the "squandered lives and laundered dollars" that are their constant punch lines. *Mastergate* concludes with an angry warning of "the next, inevitable WhateverGate," with its fresh crowd of "photo-opportunistic nobodies who grab the limelight before either being sent on to jail or up to higher office." And with Noriegate and HUD-gate looming, the warning sticks. When *Mastergate* is funny, it is very funny. When it is not, it still stands up for a patriotic integrity beyond the understanding of the clowns who parade across its national stage.

Frank Rich, "Casualties of Officialdom: Language and Truth," in The New York Times, *October 13, 1989, p. C3.*

LINDA WINER

The time is the Morning After. The place is Washington, D.C. The action is relentless and there is no intermission. As Larry Gelbart's *Mastergate* has such fun reminding us, there are no intermissions in political shamelessness. In our permanent joint crisis of language and leadership, it is always the Morning After something.

Mastergate, Gelbart's "play on words" . . . , is a one-joke extended sketch that, unfortunately, never manages the leap to dramatic—much less philosophical—revelation of much we didn't already know. Nevertheless, the joke is a very good one, performed with deadpan delight by deft imitators who appreciate the sweaty attraction of top-rank political sleaze.

The setting is a congressional hearing, with regards to Watergate and you-know-what-other-gate, complete with ominous foreshadowings of "gates" forever more. The situation is political, but the target is also lingual. Like most of America, Gelbart was addicted to the Iran-contra hearings—you remember, the ones with plausible deniabilities, crisis preplanning groups, related obfuscations and flat-out doublespeak howlers.

So Gelbart listened to the hearings, created a few political mendacities of his own and then, apparently, couldn't stop. His 95-minute send-up is loaded—make that stuffed—with compulsive wordplay. Eventually, such nonstop cleverness becomes predictable and the attacks start flattening into word games, but until then the momentum is positively giddy.

Much of the writing is priceless. Gelbart, for starters, created TV's **"M*A*S*H"** and co-wrote **A Funny Thing Happened on the Way to the Forum** and **Tootsie.** Trust him to dream up senators who wish to "broadly narrow down the scope," a telegenic military hero who is "gung holier than thou," a witness who is "not cleared for that kind of curiosity" and hearings that ask "what did the president know and does he have any idea that he knew it?" . . .

[**Mastergate**] is, visually, a three-ring circus, with questions fielded from both sides of the audience, witnesses on the stage, backed by an inspirational American history mural, TV monitors overhead. Tables of witnesses and press are peopled with real people and real dummies, in a montage of dark suits and briefcases and self-importance. For gavel-to-gavel coverage, there is the obligatory camera-hogging blond TV reporter. Behind each witness is a generic wife . . . [with] long-suffering little-woman posture or, in the case of the vice president's wife, a grandmotherly twinkle.

Basically, Mastergate—don't say it fast—is the scandal of "governmental self-abuse" in which the CIA bought a Hollywood studio called Master Pictures. Under the guise of making a $1.3 billion film called *Tet: the Movie,* the CIA funnelled weapon money to Los Otros in the Central American country of San Elvador—next door to Ambigua, which, of course, is under Soviet influence. Thus, Gelbart is able to combine little digs at Hollywood in his Washington lampoon: Some of the movie's huge cast is explained as "catering." . . .

Gelbart, who also has a musical, *City of Angels,* opening on Broadway this fall, has updated **Mastergate** a bit since ART, adding references to HUD and staged news footage on the networks. Still, with Reagan back in Hollywood, Bush in the White House and Ollie on the lecture circuit, the lampoon seems slightly dated.

Mastergate is cutting, without really drawing blood. It is entertaining and absurd, but not insane enough to compete with the parody of values we've seen in Washington in the '80s. Some have argued that real events of the last decade have made satire almost impossible. **Mastergate** doesn't disprove that theory. But it's a pleasure to see a playwright playing politics with originality and wit. Considering the lack of political theater outside Washington lately, we need the laughs.

Linda Winer, "Gelbart's Mash Note to Washington," in Newsday, *October 13, 1989.*

JOHN SIMON

Don't expect too much from [**Mastergate**]. This "play on words"—as Larry Gelbart calls his send-up of congressional investigations in which linguistic ineptitude and dishonesty of utterance mirror the mindlessness and corruption in high places—has its ear to the ground-down and stomped-upon language (and morals) of the tribe. But something is missing. . . .

Perhaps it is the format. Ninety plotless minutes are too much for a skit and too little for a dramatic event. There is something here of every political nightmare visited on us from the gates of ivory (*Odyssey,* XIX) to Irangate and aid to the *contras.* And it is all neatly worded: "What did the president know, and does he have any idea that he knew it?" "Let me emphatisize," "Publicity is a small price to pay for security," "I don't intend to take up more time today than I will. . . . I just have one or two questions that I don't quite understand," "I believe that this particular shoe fits like a glove, Sir," "You can't put history on hold; there's no snooze button on the American dream," and, inexhaustibly, on and on.

But, worse luck, the parts are bigger than the whole. For one thing, there is no payoff. Correctly, Gelbart has the farce turn surreal (as it does in life), but he does it too early. As a result, the final irruption of the superreal is robbed of its shock value. And though he tries to, he cannot spread the guilt and folly evenly: Those in the eye of the TV cameras get it in the neck, but those who do the televising and those who consume it get off barely nicked and scot-free, respectively. And the tone is not always right. "I can see no point in waking the president every five minutes of his working day" may be to the point, but to have, a bit later on, "Each and every one of them [the contributors to *los otros,* as the *contras* are dubbed here] had his picture taken napping with the president" doesn't top, merely topples the joke. So, too, "No one else is in the position not to know as much as the president didn't" reprises a gag I've quoted earlier, only with diminished returns.

Actually, the bold strokes in **Mastergate** are less effective than the quick little jabs. "Senator Knight's Committee on Hindsight and Déjà Vu" is much less telling than "a prayer breakfast in the War Room" or "If you could think of me as a human being rather than a lawyer." Sometimes the testimony is too witty, such as this about a major tax evader: "That is my conviction based on several of his own." At other times, the wordplay falls flat. . . . (p. 165)

Yet there are also priceless moments, as when a congressman questioning a heavily decorated witness misreads a question about the medals the latter earned "during two hours of duty in Vietnam." The witness corrects him—"Two tours of duty"—and everybody grins sheepishly, as if the lapse, though egregious, were not unconscionable. Splendid, too, are the wives who exchange with their falsely testifying husbands glances or hugs of authentically supportive conjugal tenderness, particularly touching as enacted before millions of voyeurs glued to the tube. And the nomenclature is nifty: Chief Counsel Shepherd Hunter, Representative Oral Proctor, and so on.

But there is something a mite sophomoric about it all—a satire that slashes about without cutting to the quick; self-indulgent jesting that offers inadvertent indulgences to sinners. Yet, I repeat, there are also bull's-eyes, e.g., "That is the spectrum of his range" and "How many people were present at the meeting?" "If you include me, two." Finally, however, it takes an older, more entrenched tradition of political satire to make its targets and its audiences hurt not only when they laugh. The true satirist does not gloat at his own jokes, does not throw rabbit punches, and does not stick in balloons reading SPLAT! and CRUNCH! (pp. 165-66)

John Simon, *"Satiric Gelbart, Satanic Durang,"* in New York Magazine, *Vol. 22, No. 42, October 23, 1989, pp. 165-66.*

WALTER KERR

[In Larry Gelbart's **Mastergate,** both] stage *and* auditorium are abuzz with the hypertense comings and goings of TV cameramen, committee members, lawyers and witnesses as proceedings get underway in Washington for an investigation into everything that's gone wrong with our Government. . . .

[As the play begins], a stentorian voice pierces the void with a promise that the hearings are going to be fair and square, with no predispositions, no persecutions. "We are not looking for hides to skin nor goats to scape," is what the man says.

The audience is caught off guard. It has laughed, but it wasn't ready for that particular laugh. That laugh doesn't really say anything about Irangate, or contras, or numbered bank accounts, does it? But it *was* funny, wasn't it? Though it's early on to be asking such a question, what exactly is this satirical comedy throwing darts at?

Well, of course it's about politics in some sense: politics we've been through, politics long since satirized by every stand-up and sit-down-a-minute comedian in the funny business. When a witness is asked a question that causes him to wince and clench his teeth before he squeeks out, "I believe that's one of the things I don't know anymore," we have no trouble summoning up perfectly real names, names whose bearers have suffered severely from just this planned aphasia. There's a laugh in that line, too—a bit grimmer, perhaps—but the joke is unmistakably a political joke. Real politics.

As we bubble along into the heart of the evening, however, we begin to notice that we seem more and more to be using politics as background, as milieu, not as target. Mr. Gelbart isn't arguing Irangate or any Gate of his choice all over again; he's taken all that for granted. What he's really after is the damage, possibly irreparable, that all Gates have done to language—to words, syntax, *meaning*.

"Anything that follows will come after," we hear a senator say, and suddenly, unmistakably, we have wandered into *Alice in Wonderland,* where words do indeed mean what their speakers mean them to say. I love that line. It is so stately, so firmly in control of itself, so treacherously confident. So deliciously, utterly empty. (p. 45)

When a man on life supports must be interviewed in a hospital, his responses will necessarily be delayed; short bursts of Muzak are heard during the gaps. "A former podiatrist and his band of foot soldiers" are ready for any eventuality; an actor who strangely resembles Vice President Bush remembers them "leading the attack on Pearl Harbor." "You seem like a nice young man, Mr. Lamb," purrs the chairman to a witness, the witness takes a moment to reflect, then soberly

replies, "Yes, sir, I do." Possibly the most honest statement of the evening, and the most ambiguous.

Mastergate isn't a play; it is an extended burlesque sketch of a kind that may not have been heard in these parts since the close of Weber and Fields's Music Hall. Neither is it soliciting any votes. Well, not too earnestly. It is about a terrible loss of meaning through the manipulation of syntax and the defiant abuse of words.

A tragedy, if you will. And very, very funny. (pp. H5, H38)

Walter Kerr, *"Of Passion, Politics and Other People's Money,"* in The New York Times, *November 19, 1989, pp. H5, H38.*

HOWARD KISSEL

I want to be very positive about *City of Angels.* Not because I enjoyed it. But because I know the American musical is in trouble and I know critics are credited with its perilous condition. And just because I didn't have a good time, why should I assume you won't?

Maybe you'll admire Larry Gelbart's cleverness more than I did. Maybe you won't grow as tired of his plot as quickly as I did. It's the story of a young New York writer in Hollywood in the '30s doing a screen adaptation of his best-selling crime novel.

Maybe you won't feel that trundling back and forth between the writer's personal life and his screenplay, which often reflects that life, is as tiresome as watching a lazy game of tennis. Maybe, because you haven't already seen two spoofs of Hollywood detective movies this year, you'll be more charmed than I was by the contrived parody of the Raymond Chandler style.

There may be some things we can agree on. Gelbart, who knows Hollywood all too well, has adroitly lampooned the producers' mentality. "I'm your biggest fan," his maniacal producer tells the young writer. "I've read a synopsis of everything you've ever written."

But I fear you won't find any of the other characters any more interesting or attractive than I did. Ultimately they're all paper-thin. . . .

Maybe you've never seen a sendup of Hollywood before. Maybe this will strike you as fresh. Don't let me stop you.

Howard Kissel, *"Little Hope for Fallen Angels,"* in Daily News, *New York, December 12, 1989.*

FRANK RICH

There's nothing novel about show-stopping songs and performances in Broadway musicals, but how long has it been since a musical was brought to a halt by riotous jokes? If you ask me, one would have to travel back to the 1960's—to *Bye Bye Birdie,* **A Funny Thing Happened on the Way to the Forum,** *How to Succeed in Business Without Really Trying* and *Little Me*—to find a musical as flat-out funny as *City of Angels,* the new show about old Hollywood. . . .

This is an evening in which even a throwaway wisecrack spreads laughter like wildfire through the house, until finally the roars from the balcony merge with those from the orchestra and the pandemonium takes on a life of its own. Only the fear of missing the next gag quiets the audience down. To make matters sweeter, the jokes sometimes subside just long enough to permit a show-stopping song or performance or two to make their own ruckus at center stage.

Since the musical's principal creators are the writer Larry Gelbart and the composer Cy Coleman—pros who worked separately on *Forum* and *Little Me* early in their careers—the exhilarating result cannot really be called a surprise. Yet Mr. Gelbart and Mr. Coleman, invigorated with the try-anything brio of first-time collaborators half their age, bring the audience one unexpected twist after another. Only the territory of *City of Angels* is familiar: the late 1940's Hollywood romanticized in hard-boiled detective fiction and ruled by tyrannical studio moguls who seemed to give nearly every movie a title like *Three Guys Named Joe.*

To take comic possession of the entire sprawling cultural landscape—to mock not just the period's movies but also the men behind the movies—Mr. Gelbart stages a two-pronged satirical attack. His hero, Stine, is a novelist trying against considerable odds to turn his own book, *City of Angels,* into a screenplay that will not be an embarrassing sellout. But as Mr. Gelbart tracks Stine's travails in the film industry—where the "envy is so thick you can cut it with a knife lodged in every other back"—he also presents the hard-knock adventures of Stone, the Philip Marlowe-Sam Spade-like private eye of Stine's screenplay in progress and . . . a comic shamus who is the stuff that dreams are made of.

There is no end to the cleverness with which the creators of *City of Angels* carry out their stunt of double vision, starting with a twin cast list (a Hollywood Cast and a Movie Cast) in the Playbill. [The] extraordinarily imaginative set design—maybe the most eloquent argument yet against coloring old movies—uses the lush black-and-white of a pristine Warner Brothers print for the Stone sequences and candied Technicolor for Stine's off-camera adventures. Because the Stine and Stone narratives have their ironic parallels—fiction's thugs and temptresses often resemble Hollywood's movers and shakers—the *City of Angels* actors frequently play dual roles, shifting continually between color and black-and-white settings and characters. In one spectacular turn that rocks the second act, the winning Randy Graff, as a loyal secretary to both Stone and Stine, leaps across the color barrier to belt out her blues as the other woman in two male lives. (p. C19)

With occasional injections of stock period film, *City of Angels* recreates the swirling flashbacks, portentous tracking shots and swift dissolves of movies like *The Maltese Falcon* and *The Big Sleep* even as it wallows in the kitschy glamour of nouveau-riche Bel Air mansions where the conversation is "never at a loss for numbers."

Mr. Gelbart's jokes come in their own variety of colors. As in his screenplay for *Movie Movie,* he is a master at parodying vintage film genres—in this case finding remarkably fresh ways to skewer the sardonic voice-over narration, tough-guy talk and heavy-breathing imagery ("It's as though I was hit by a wrecking ball wearing a pinky ring") of the Chandler-Hammett film noir. But the funniest lines in *City of Angels* may well be those that assault the movie business—as personified by Buddy Fidler, an egomaniacal producer and director at Master Pictures, the same fictional studio that Mr. Gelbart accused of money-laundering in his Iran-contra satire, *Mastergate.*

There are no angels in this show's Hollywood. Next to Fidler's self-serving Goldwynisms—"You can tell a writer every time: words, words, words!" he complains—the mixed metaphors of Stone's narration and the obfuscating double talk of the *Mastergate* politicians almost make sense. . . . Fidler congratulates himself on his philanthropic largess while destroying Stine's script in the interests of commerce or blacklist-era political cowardice. As he revises, the rewrites are carried out in the black-and-white flesh on stage, complete with mimed rewinding of the footage bound for the cutting-room floor. "You're Nothing Without Me" goes the title of the high-flying duet for Stine and Stone, but, in Mr. Gelbart's jaundiced view, the writer and his fictional alter ego are both nothing next to the greedy bully with casting approval, screenplay-credit envy and final cut. (pp. C19, C23)

> Frank Rich, *"40's Hollywood Doubly Mocked in Gelbart's 'City of Angels',"* in The New York Times, December 12, 1989, pp. C19, C23.

EDWIN WILSON

There is a great moment at the end of act one of *City of Angels* that brings the modern American musical slam-bang against Pirandello, the Italian playwright who was fascinated with the relationship of reality to fiction and life to art. . . .

[In *City of Angels*], Stine, a young novelist turned screen writer, has created a hard-boiled private eye named Stone, the hero of a detective movie in the Raymond Chandler mold. The character is giving Stine trouble, and at the close of the first act when both men—the real and the reel one—are on stage, an angry Stine turns to Stone and sings, "You're nothing without me, without me you're nothing at all." Of course this is true: Stone is a fictional creation of Stine's and would not exist without him. But then the film detective turns on his creator and sings the same lyric to him: "You're nothing without me, without me you're nothing at all." Suddenly we realize that this is equally true: In a very real way, a writer has his truest existence in the characters he creates. Seeing the two performers on stage, hurling these truths at each other in song, brings this Pirandellian idea home in a way even the master himself would have approved.

This unexpected revelation is only one of many surprises in *City of Angels.* The time of the story is the late 1940s. Stine has written a novel that a Hollywood mogul, Buddy Fidler, plans to direct as a movie. The novelist's wife accuses him of selling out, and quickly beats a retreat back to her job in New York. Stine, however, is convinced he can retain his integrity as he turns his detective story into a screenplay.

The script concerns a tough-guy private eye who is hired by the sexy wife of a millionaire to find his missing daughter Mallory. No sooner has Stone taken the job than two tough guys in broad-brimmed fedoras, one towering and the other tiny, accost him in his bungalow and give him the beating of his life. Naturally he survives, just the way Sam Spade and Philip Marlowe always did. . . .

In the end the film mogul, Buddy Fidler, does completely take over the movie, and Stine realizes he has been both corrupted and betrayed. But he recovers his integrity just in time. Meanwhile Hollywood is held up to hilarious ridicule by author Larry Gelbart. *City of Angels* is a writer's revenge on Hollywood—and what sweet revenge it is. Mr. Gelbart, one of the cleverest wordsmiths working today, not only captures the spirit of the film-noir, he delivers one knockout punch line after another. The material is familiar, but served with such relish you may think you're seeing it for the first time.

Edwin Wilson, "Broadway Gets Bitchy," in The Wall Street Journal, *December 18, 1989.*

WILLIAM A. HENRY, III.

The ballad throbs to a climax, the two singers look at each other in a confession of mutual need, and the title line of mock-bragging devotion, "You're Nothing Without Me," reverberates from the rafters. All in all, a classic first-act finale—except that in this musical the characters who vow undying fidelity are a nerdy novelist turned screenwriter and the hard-boiled detective he has created on page and celluloid.

That quirky, funny, oddly thrilling moment epitomizes the twofold cleverness of *City of Angels*. . . . The show pays honest homage to the pop-culture traditions of stage, cinema, radio and recording studio (especially those of the '40s, when it is set), yet brings them together in a fashion that feels fresh and new. Nostalgia plus novelty is a notoriously volatile cocktail, but *Angels* has the impeccably elegant fizz of champagne.

Perhaps its most remarkable attainment is that the premise and structure, which sound inordinately egghead when described, are easy to grasp in performance. The action begins with the detective, a rumpled knight of the tenderloin who lives by a code of honor in a world of thugs and well-heeled thieves. Moments later the story shifts to the office (coyly labeled a "cell") where his creator labors as a hireling of a movie tycoon more crass, smug and fascinatingly awful than any envisioned by Nathanael West. As the tycoon lays down the law (no social criticism, no politics, no hint of kinky sex), the money-struck young writer peevishly retypes his scenes—and, in an inspired bit of playfulness, that action causes his characters to move and speak jerkily backward, as if a film were being rewound, until they are back in position to perform the new bowdlerized version.

As the script unfolds, it becomes clear that the characters in the detective plot are all based on the people around the writer at the studio—indeed, the same actors play both sets of roles. This connection leads to countless comic effects. In the splashiest, the perennially disappointed "other woman" of both plot lines switches characters, costumes and locales in mid-song, all without missing a beat of her ferociously funny lament, "You Can Always Count on Me."

The detective plot borrows classic elements from the likes of *The Big Sleep* and *The Long Goodbye:* a missing girl who turns up, clad only in a sheet and beckoning for comfort, on the detective's flophouse bed; the sultry wife of a rich, infirm old man, who fibs as automatically as other people breathe; the detective's torch-singer ex-girlfriend, now reduced to offering more private entertainments; and a spooky guru bilking the faithful. Librettist Larry Gelbart cheerily exploits these clichés without sneering at the genre. In telling the Hollywood side of the story, however, he is at times as snide as in his just closed satire of Iran-*contra*, **Mastergate**. . . .

City of Angels is that rarest of things on Broadway these days, a completely original American musical, not imported, not adapted from something else and not a recycling of bygone songs. Coming at the end of a decade of almost nonstop doomsaying, it proves that Broadway's signature style of show is, in the right hands, as viable and valuable as ever.

William A. Henry III, "Hello Again to the Long Goodbye," in Time, *New York, Vol. 134, No. 26, December 25, 1989, p. 92.*

JACK KROLL AND MAGGIE MALONE

There's a miracle on Broadway—an *American* musical, with American jazz rhythms, American wisecracks, an original American script not based on English poems or French novels. It's got singers who don't think they're in an opera, singing songs that aren't about the Weimar Republic or the reign of Louis Philippe. The miracle is *City of Angels,* and the chief miracle workers are composer Cy Coleman and writer Larry Gelbart. . . .

City of Angels may be a sign that the American musical is at last fighting back against the wave of imports that have taken over the Broadway stage during the '80s.

City of Angels dares to break this pattern by going back to American basics: It's smart, swingy, sexy and funny. Gelbart's book is a double spoof: of the private-eye novel and its movie counterpart in the '40s. He creates two interlocking worlds: the real world of his detective-story writer named Stine, and the movie that Stine is writing for his gumshoe named Stone. What could have been a Stine-Stone rhinestone becomes in Gelbart's hands a gem of craftsmanship. . . .

Heavy breathers may want more social significance, but *City of Angels* is a welcome reminder that musicals used to be called musical comedies.

Jack Kroll with Maggie Malone, "The Battle of Broadway," in Newsweek, *Vol. CXV, No. 2, January 8, 1990, pp. 62-3.*

Kate Grenville

1950-

Australian novelist and short story writer.

Grenville is best known for satirical works that expose the machinations of power underlying conventional male-female relationships. A feminist, Grenville often presents her characters' relative empowerment through their use of language, depicting, for example, a domineering male as a person who verbally abuses others, or an oppressed female as one who has trouble using and understanding words. Grenville was a film editor in Australia and England before she became a writer, and her prose technique has been called cinematic for its reliance on juxtaposition of short vignettes, dialogue, and imagery rather than straightforward narration. In addition, Grenville's interest in the relationship between history and literature is evident in nearly all her fiction. Constance Markey commented: "Grenville possesses a rare and beautiful gift for words, a delicacy of description, and an awareness of nature rare to present-day fiction. These qualities, plus an abiding intuition of life's eternal conflicts, distinguish her as a writer of great strength and sensitivity."

Grenville's first book, *Bearded Ladies,* is a collection of short fiction featuring women of all ages who come to realize their inability to comply with society's ideal of femininity. *Lilian's Story,* Grenville's first novel, demonstrates her interest in history and introduces silence as an extended metaphor for oppression. A fictionalized life of a street-person who roamed Sydney in the 1930s and 1940s, this novel traces the cause of Lilian's descent into homelessness and apparent lunacy to her painful childhood. Lilian's memories of this time, comprising the majority of the novel, are haunted by her tyrannical father's abuse and her mother's failure to protect her. Lilian becomes obese in order to defend herself against her father's verbal and physical attacks, an ineffectual retreat that further sets her apart from others. Despite the gloomy premise of *Lilian's Story,* most critics found it a predominantly humorous depiction of the freedom to be found in eccentric behavior.

In *Dreamhouse,* Grenville's second novel, Louise and Rennie, a glamorous couple from London, spend a summer in a dilapidated villa in Tuscany. The narrative is filtered through Louise, whose anger and confusion regarding her marriage create an atmosphere of tension and imminent disaster. The eventual exposure of Rennie's homosexuality frees Louise to abandon the relationship and repair her self-esteem. Critics commended the complexity of Grenville's characters and the sensuous imagery of sinister decay that pervades the Italian landscape, symbolizing the relationships depicted. *Joan Makes History* was commissioned in honor of Australia's bicentennial. The story of a woman whose ambitious plans dissolve as an inconvenient pregnancy and an early marriage narrow her prospects provides the framework for the center section. This portion of *Joan Makes History* comprises a series of dreams or fantasies depicting the lives of twelve other women named Joan throughout Australia's history, including the first female convict to be sent to the colony, and the wife of one of its governors. A fictional rendering of revisionist history, this novel asserts the ultimate significance of the small, everyday actions of ordinary people.

(See also *Contemporary Authors,* Vol. 118.)

PRINCIPAL WORKS

Bearded Ladies (short stories) 1984
Lilian's Story (novel) 1984
Dreamhouse (novel) 1986
Joan Makes History (novel) 1988

PUBLISHERS WEEKLY

With [Kate Grenville's *Bearded Ladies*], a vibrant Australian voice speaks of universal concerns. The "ladies" we meet are bearded by virtue of their personalities and pursuits, the soft skin of their femininity roughened with the effort of moving away from conventional behavior and expectations. Sandy, traveling alone to India, wanders into a native quarter where the children jeer at her dilemma: "You boy or gel?" A younger Sandy, leader of her gang, about to raid the house of an eccentric old woman who lives alone, is apprehended by the woman herself, with an offer of cookies and milk—and a

Swiss army knife. An aspect of the same girl, now a teenager, goes to visit an aunt who harangues her about propriety, only to reveal a sexual shiftiness far less acceptable than the act she is cautioning against. The concluding story is a paradigm for much that has gone before: a woman is trapped in a marriage to a posturing, ineffectual Ph.D. candidate, trapped as well in a crumbling Italian villa symbolic of her husband's insubstantiality. . . . [*Bearded Ladies*] is a collection to be savored as much for the colloquial ease of the writing as for the hypocrisy it exposes.

A review of "Bearded Ladies," in Publishers Weekly, *Vol. 226, No. 21, November 23, 1984, p. 67.*

JOANNA MOTION

Kate Grenville's *Bearded Ladies* are contemporary Australian women. Their chief defence against restraining influences is the long-distance air ticket. It takes them to India, to North America and, lingeringly, to "shuffling through the tired old pack of Europe". The book is a collection of fourteen stories, mostly about women who find themselves out of step with their surroundings and respond by slipping away from other people's expectations.

The women come in all ages as well as all geographies: a child discovering the costs of vanity; a sixteen-year-old testing the contradictions of adult behaviour; disenchanted lovers; stale wives. A traveller's tale out of bedsit-land provides a wry dissection of her compatriots on the Athens coach. "**Meeting the Folks**" is a devastating display of condescension as offensive weapon, practised by a glamorous-tatty French mother and son. In "**No Such Thing as a Free Lunch**", cultural differences are not enough to stop two women meeting in complicity against their male companions. Most characteristically, Grenville's women acquiesce in the illusions men wrap them in, but make a point of telling the truth to themselves. She writes powerfully, particularly in "**Making Tracks**" and "**Country Pleasures**", of the panic-stricken claustrophobia of a deteriorating love affair. One or two of the stories read almost like exercises, technical testings-out. Kate Grenville shouldn't worry; she can do it.

Joanna Motion, "Patterning the Stuff of Life," in The Times Literary Supplement, *No. 4307, October 18, 1985, p. 1173.*

ELIZABETH WARD

[Grenville's novel, *Lilian's Story,* begins:] "It was a wild night in the year of Federation that the birth took place. Horses kicked down their stables. Pigs flew, figs grew thorns . . . *A girl?* the father exclaimed, outside in the waiting room, tiled as if for horrible emergencies." So Lilian Una Singer introduces her story, giving notice that we had better expect somebody special, different, fatally marked by her origins, as well as somebody whose femaleness is going to be an issue.

Kate Grenville's first novel, which won the Australian/Vogel Literary Award, is in fact a rousingly feminist work, but a pleasant rarity in that genre, a novel in which feminist politics are entirely subsumed by art: *Lilian's Story* is good fiction first, ideology (and one or two other things, such as biography and history) only a distant second. Grenville admits that her exuberant study of an eccentric woman was inspired by the

life of the notorious Sydney baglady, Bea Miles, who in the '30s and '40s was a familiar figure on the city's streets, button-holing passers-by, commandeering taxis and giving public recitations of Shakespeare for a shilling. The original version of Grenville's book was actually entitled "Bea's Story." But Grenville has made no attempt to *document* Bea Miles' life. Leaving aside the obvious parallels, such as taxis, Shakespeare, wartime Sydney and demagogic father-figures (Bea's father was W.J. Miles, a well-known anti-Semite and fascist), *Lilian's Story* is a work of pure dramatic imagination.

Life for the child Lilian is a desperate business. Her father, Albion Singer, is a mustachioed, oversexed, Victorian brute, obsessed with facts. "*Your father is a gentleman, and is writing a book,*" her mother tries to explain, in the italicized dialogue which Grenville uses effectively throughout to place and distance remembered conversation. Mother herself is a lady, in lilac and lavender and grey, but takes refuge from her husband's rages and sexual demands in headaches, camphor on red flannel and, eventually, a genteel madness. Little Lilian has more spunk, struggling to comprehend: "In my early paintings, I drew his head as a square brown box on his shoulders, and drew the facts coming out of his mouth. *What are those lines, Lilian?* Miss Vine asked at school. Has he been speared, dear? and I would have to try to explain, *Those are Father's facts, Miss Vine.*"

Father prevails, his cruel neuroticism deflecting every life in the household into further neuroses: Mother retires for good to her favorite wicker-chair on the verandah, stop-watch in hand, timing the ferries as they steam across the bay; Lilian's younger brother, John, folds in his earlobes, pretending to be deaf, takes up the tuba as the only instrument large enough to hide in, and becomes a vegetarian to drown out the sound of his father's voice: ". . . while we all became greasy from mutton, John crunched his way through entire bunches of celery, heads of lettuce, raw green beans, apples that sprayed juice, anything loud. *John!* Father would exclaim, *I cannot hear myself think!*"

And Lilian grows enormously fat, at first to pad herself against her father's beatings, much later as a deliberate statement of nonconformity. "Clothed in my bulk, I was free to try for other kinds of admiration and other kinds of attention . . . *I would be a mediocre pretty girl,* I said. *And I am too arrogant to be mediocre.*" Bright, she also arms herself with Shakespeare, memorizing enough for a lifetime before her father drowns "William" in the bay. (Indeed, though it is not stated, Lilian's fatness comes to seem as much a Falstaffian as a feminist strategy, something she positively exults in.)

But always the shadow of Albion Singer looms. "There was a space in my vision of the world that Father filled and blocked like a great rock at the mouth of a cave, and behind that rock, locked in, I whimpered and shrieked for something I longed for and would never have." The novel climaxes at mid-point, with what one can only assume is the rape of Lilian by her father, a scene as chilling for what it omits as for what it includes. The brown buttons of Father's cardigan "made a small tinny noise like rats' feet as he took it off and let it drop to the floor." Then no details but more sounds. "*No!* I heard myself cry with a feeble piping sound. *No! No!* The house gave back only silence, and the panting of the desperate machine that was Father."

The shock of this incident unhinges Lil altogether "I cowered in (my) flesh, my self shrunk to the size of a pea" and after an episode of exhibitionism, a memorable scene in which Lil marches naked through a country pub, all her fat shaking, her father has her committed to the "loony bin." But despite her (real) outward symptoms of psychosis, Lilian as we have come to know her is not "loony" at all, rather a human being reacting with great dignity to circumstances of intolerable pain. So we experience the unraveling of her life from this point on as an unexpected illumination: how tenuous is the line which divides "us" from "them" and how dull it sometimes is on the right side of the line.

Philosophically, *Lilian's Story* owes a lot to Patrick White, whose visionary women have long been at odds with conformist society. In matters of style, however, Kate Grenville is an original. A professional film editor, she writes in brief, cinematic scenes like a series of thoughts made visible. Yet the book has more to recommend it than an interesting technique. it has this truth, that "the story of all our lives is the story forward to death," and this lesson, that it is possible to face death as Lilian does, crying to her last taxi-driver, *"Drive on, George . . . I am ready for whatever comes next."*

> Elizabeth Ward, "A Woman of Independent Spirit," in Book World—The Washington Post, September 7, 1986, p. 9.

JAMES PURDY

[*Lilian's Story*] is a work of considerable beauty and power. Written in the first person in a sumptuous style, it flows easily, unobstructedly from the birth of its heroine, Lilian Una Singer, to her old age and approaching death (the time is the early half of this century). *Lilian's Story,* Kate Grenville's first novel, has an uncompromising vision behind it, and is told with honesty and virtuosity.

Lilian suffers from being fat as a girl and fatter still as a woman, but though her sense of herself is painful, she is alive with her grasp of the absurdity and rapture of life. We laugh with Lil at times, but we never laugh at her, because she is a fully realized fictional creation. So are all the characters around her: Lil's broken, ruined mother, a woman of lilac and lavender, with countless corsets, who believes in conversation so long as it does not involve communication, love or truth; Lil's bestial, miserly father, Albion, with his mustaches and squeaking, shiny boots; her blinking, spoiled, tuba-playing brother (he is favored in a family that looks down on girls): compassionate, boozing Aunt Kitty, the only one who truly cares for Lil; the mad old maid, Miss Gash, who wears clothes covered with postage stamps.

Like a silent, sluggish but steadily flowing river, the story of the fat girl moves inevitably through the various stations of her life, resembling as it goes a silent movie in its visual insistence, and adumbrated like those old films with titles to introduce each short section and jog the reader on to the next vivid progression of contretemps and disaster.

Fat as Lil is, beaten and ashamed by any and all, she remains indomitable and unbowed, upright and unfazed indeed, her fat itself comes to be a kind of strength of being, a true aura, the authentic envelope of her soul.

Either because of her obesity or in spite of it, Lil draws certain young men to her; two care enough to become her beaus. F. J. Stroud—Frank—a pale, skinny boy with thin wrists and

a laugh shrill like a cry for help, is to be in one sense the permanent love of her life. He pretends to be the son of a diamond merchant but is actually poor as Job. And then there is Duncan, who wears white flannels, blushes purple and calls Lil his "mate."

Furiously jealous that his daughter has been able to attract young men, Lil's father drives her two suitors away, spoiling the one proposal of marriage offered to her. Since her beaus are not "real men," he says, he must initiate her into true sexuality. Running from her father's advances, Lil takes to escaping from "incest house" and becomes a night wanderer, first on foot, until her feet are calloused, unfeeling, unrecognizable, and then on a broken-down bicycle. When she refuses to give up her night excursions, Albion commits her to an asylum. She is rescued from the "loony-bin" by her faithful, if slightly dotty, Aunt Kitty.

Freed from the asylum, and then freed again by the deaths of her mother and father, Lil Singer finds herself in, if possible, an even more hostile world than the family or the hospital. Authority in general is against her, and she clashes with bus drivers, policemen, judges, and is sent to jail. She becomes a public outlaw, a famous offender. No longer young, she discovers her old beau Frank, who has taken to drink. Together they find a kind of late solace, living on the beach in the protection of each other's arms.

Thus the story of Lil Singer is coming to an end. But she has remained herself through all vicissitudes, unrepentant, in her own way victorious.

> James Purdy, "Lunacy among the Teacups," in The New York Times Book Review, September 7, 1986, p. 27.

KATHERINE BUCKNELL

Natives of Sydney might recognize the central character in *Lilian's Story* as Bea Miles, a large, loony woman who used to jump into their taxi cabs and recite Shakespeare at them, then go home at night to sleep in the park. In her first novel, Kate Grenville imagines a past life for this woman (familiar in some form to us all), whom she calls Lilian Singer. The narration is direct and simple, well suited to presenting childhood and adolescence. Grenville's descriptions are eccentric but concise, and make vivid the conflict between Lilian's useful desires and the restraints of genteel family life. But as *Lilian's Story* develops, its simplicity seems increasingly a limitation; the range of tones narrows, themes and images are repeated, and the novel becomes relentlessly depressing.

From birth, Lilian does not matter: not to her vague, invalid mother, still less to her nervous, authoritarian father. She is determined to have it otherwise, and will do anything for attention. She stands on her head; she swings upside down from the jacaranda tree shrieking "Father, look!", but he just leaves her swinging there. So Lilian turns to eating, and this becomes a form of rebellion. Her growing bulk defies her father's beatings: "there is too much flesh for him now".

Sadly, Lilian's insatiable appetite—for attention and for food—disables her for life. At school she is resented, laughed at and bullied. As a young lady she fails to attract the suitors to whom her parents look for relief. So her father sends her to university. There, Lilian blooms. She has girlfriends and boyfriends; she thrills to the pleasures of mutual affection and physical love. . . .

Disgusted by her, Lilian's father sends her to the "loony-bin" where she spends ten frighteningly serene years grasping at the attention of inmates and nurses. Eventually she is rescued, and forces herself on people she meets in the street. At first it's prostitutes and tramps, eventually it's bankers and housewives. Lilian assures herself that they'll always remember and tell their families and friends about the public scenes into which she traps them. Nothing would have made her happier than to have Kate Grenville write this novel about her; whether we can be happy reading it is another matter.

Katherine Bucknell, "Attention-Seeker's Tale," in
The Times Literary Supplement, *No. 4358, October 10, 1986, p. 1130.*

KATE GRENVILLE [Interview with Gerry Turcotte]

[Turcotte]: *Where are some of the places you travelled to, and how did they get incorporated into your writing?*

[Grenville]: Some of them never have been. The first place I travelled to, and the one that made the biggest impact of all, was India, and I've never been able to write about that. England is the one I wrote about a lot. But I had uncomfortable feelings with England. It was so culturally familiar that I felt an awkward love/hate thing for it. So Europe—continental Europe—was actually what got the fiction going. I wrote about France, where I lived for a while, and Italy, where I lived for a shorter time, although I never wrote about those places while I was living in them. It seemed necessary always that there should be a kind of lag between leaving a place, and writing about it. And I haven't yet written about America except in a few short stories.

Places are states of mind for me, at least when I write about them. Remembering a place is like a smell, a shorthand way of remembering a whole mood. When you're travelling you're very open, observant, sensitized, so when you write about foreign places you can bring a heightened perception to them, a highly charged mood. That extreme sensitivity is numbed by habit and a settled life. It forces me to write a different sort of fiction now I *am* settled, and to find another way to get that high level of energy. (p. 286)

How useful was the creative writing programme you followed in Colorado?

It was the most useful thing I ever did. In those two years I learned what it would have taken me years to learn by trial and error; I might never have learned it. . . . I'd never been in a place that could not just dissect texts, but also somehow relate them to what you were doing in your own writing work. That was a terrific thing, to read Wordsworth and Shakespeare, and in discussion to see that you could actually see where Shakespeare had met a narrative problem, for example, and how *he* had got around it, or how Wordsworth had got around the paradox of, for example, trying to compress experience into a sort of simultaneity, when the written word is of its nature linear—to see how they had confronted similar problems to the ones I was starting to encounter myself. That was incredibly stimulating. My teachers were very good too. Most of them were academics with doctorates who also published fiction or poetry. I had always known somehow that revision was the key to writing. But it wasn't until

I was forced to read undergraduate stories in the course of teaching there, and see what they were trying to do, where they had failed, and then try to suggest what they might do in revision to fix it . . . that kind of honed an ability to see the things as a whole, and to take it apart and put it back together again. I think a lot of writers know how to do that by themselves, but I didn't.

When I wrote in London—I wrote most of **Bearded Ladies** in London (and a lot of those are *painfully* experimental)—I was floundering around on my own, reading Hawkes and Burroughs, and those sorts of writers trying desperately to get out of that boring English, grammatically correct, "well-made story" writing tradition that I'd been brought up in. And at the same time I was hostile to a lot of it. I remember when someone gave me a copy of *The Blood Oranges*, a John Hawkes novel—I sort of *flung* it back at him saying "What kind of rubbish is this? Call this a novel? Call this writing?" It took me a long time to come to terms with that. During the time in Colorado, people were saying, "Look, it doesn't matter if you don't like it, it doesn't matter that you're hostile, the thing is, can you use it?" They were vultures on the literature of the world, and that was a revelation to me—that you didn't look at writing in terms of "Is it good or is it bad?" or "Is it great or is it minor?"—that the most useful question was not "Do I like it?" but "What can I learn from it?"

Did you find that your anger with formulaic writing, and your need to break out of it, conjoined with a growing feminist thought?—in a story like **"Blast Off"**, *for example, where the form is so innovative and complements the message.*

Yes. That was *exactly* the motivation. When I left Australia and started writing seriously, I felt that there were huge gaps in human experience—female experience—that had never been written about, and that there was no way you could write about them in conventional terms. It somehow just wasn't adequate to talk about them in terms of the conventional, and in nice neat language. The forces operating—anger, frustration, pain, loneliness—couldn't be written about truthfully in neatly ordered fiction. That would trivialize them. It would also blunt the shock that I wanted readers to feel—the shock of recognizing truths that had been hidden. I was obsessed with photographing the way things really were, in fiction. Necessarily that brought in the way people's minds really worked and the way they really used words. I loathed—I still loathe—that kind of tidy "dialogue" that's nothing like the way people talk, so it was a kind of anger, and a kind of frustration with the conventions that forced me to look for new ways . . . not that what I was doing was all that new, of course. (pp. 287-88)

Once in conversation with me you mentioned that you found your first story in **Bearded Ladies** *too easy; that its narrative structure was too pat. How much do you consider the structure of your stories, symbolic or otherwise, before you write? And I say the stories, because you've already said that in regard to something like* **Lilian's Story** *it was the absence of structure which made its composition exciting. Is there a difference between your short story approach and your novel approach?*

I had one particular professor in Colorado who used to talk about "closure", and was very rude about the stories I brought with me because he said, "You know, Kate, they're full of closure", and the way he talked about it, he was sort of saying I was constipated. So I got very angry with him, because my idea of a well-made story was what he was calling closure. But he forced me to try another approach, and I did. Before that I'd been thinking, "Okay, here is something I want to say", and tried to think of a conventional structure to say it in. At the same time, though, I was fighting against that convention. I wanted to do it the right way and yet I was impatient with doing it the right way. The way I worked reflected that conflict. Usually I'd start a story without knowing where it was going to end, without a very clear notion of structure, but I wouldn't feel relaxed in the writing until I had worked out what the end was going to be. And then with a great sigh of relief I could fit it all into that structure and end-point. The one called **"Slow Dissolve"**, which I don't think is a terribly good story, is a real closure story. I remember that I actually worked backwards, from the ending to the beginning of that story, and I think it shows. The whole story funnels down to a rather lame ending, where the guy, after this big build-up of how wonderful he is, turns out to be a bit of a turd. If I'd adopted a more open-ended approach there would have been greater possibilities for complexity, subtlety, ambiguity. The first two novels I wrote—unpublished—were written in the "closure" mode, planned out with chapter synopses and all that. They were boring to write and boring to read. Since then I've tried to steer some middle course between closure and chaos, allowing the material to gradually discover or mould the structure it's happiest in.

Is this what resulted in your providing an extra chapter for the American edition of **Lilian's Story**, *or were there other pressures?*

The editor in New York suggested that Lil got too old and too mad too suddenly. At a purely structural or aesthetic level, she was saying that a transition was missing, and when I reread the section I decided I agreed. (pp. 289-90)

I remember reading an interview you gave in 1984 in which you called **Lilian's Story** *and* **Bearded Ladies** *comedies. The comic is undoubtedly a strong part of your writing, but its effectiveness, it seems, emerges from its juxtaposition with a darker vision. In* **Lilian's Story**, *for example, you continually play the nightmarish off against the humorous. How consciously do you use this chiaroscuro effect?*

It's conscious only in the sense that if I write something that looks flat to me, I feel it will be more interesting if I can juxtapose it with something contrasting. I get bored with it if it's only one thing. It's not conscious in that I plan it in advance. I just try to keep it surprising.

Dreamhouse *has a distinctly Gothic feel about it. You use so many conventions of the Gothic genre—the haunted or decrepit house, the landscape imagery which is almost Radcliffean, the hints of incest certainly. How much of the Gothic genre which appears in your writing is deliberately aimed at?*

It's deliberate in retrospect, if you can put it that way. I suppose I could say that for the first draft, nothing is conscious, nothing is deliberate, and after that it probably does become more conscious. When I saw, in the first drafts of **Dreamhouse**, that I had all those elements, then it was easy to think, "Well, here is a convention I can play off." And I had always liked the Gothic fiction that I'd read; I had always found it very interesting. So at that point, I followed it more consciously. It's a funny kind of groping process, and it's very hard to say just where thought takes over from instinct. (pp. 290-91)

Despite the lack of obvious quoting, there is a lot of Shake-speare in **Lilian's Story**. *Particularly* The Tempest. *How did you use Shakespeare? It seems almost to be a structural usage? How did it surface?*

It surfaced, like most things I do, by accident. I had written a fair bit of **Lilian's Story,** and I'd run out of steam a bit. I remembered that one of the ways that I had started **Lilian's Story** was by stealing bits of other writers. For example, the very first thing I ever wrote of **Lilian's Story** was a direct steal of a letter from Jane Austen to somebody or other in which she says something about "we sat around at night inventing a few hard names for the stars". I thought this was such a beautiful phrase and a lovely idea that I wrote it at the top of a sheet of that funny yellow paper that you buy in America, and started to write a whole scene from it, which is now in the book. And that gave me the idea that when you're a bit stuck you can go to fairly unlikely sources, and if you can just find the right one, you can pinch a bit, and then work off it, so when I ran out of steam with **Lilian's Story,** when I was back in Australia, I thought about the real Bee Miles. You know, her life had been Shakespeare, so I flipped through his work. Now, *The Tempest* happens to be the first play in my collection of Shakespeare, and I'd never read it, but I did then (because it was the first one in the book), and I realized that, among other things, it was about fathers and daughters, and also about the magic of storytelling. And I was starting to see those ideas as central to **Lilian's Story.** It was also full of these great phrases that I could pinch, so I didn't really bother to look any further than *The Tempest*; it was the one.

Increasingly, The Tempest *is being read in regard to its colonial/imperial concerns, with Caliban and Ariel representing indigenous colonial figures, and Prospero an imperial power. I notice a similar preoccupation with this colonial/imperial dialectic in your work. In* **Lilian's Story,** *for example, the section "Long to Reign Over Us" criticizes the imposition of decontextualized and useless imperial values on Australian children, and in a recent article you also discuss British attitudes toward Australians as being condescending and so forth. Do you see this as a major focus of your work?*

At the literal, political level it's one factor, though not a major focus. One of the big things for me about living overseas was the realization of what a handicap we labour under in this country, of being a colony, and specifically of being an English—a British—colony, in the sense that even now publishing agreements limit our access to American writing, for example. But at a less literal level the idea of colonialism as a metaphor is very central.

Do you see the idea of colonialism—or of cultural imperialism—as a corollary of male imperialism? That is, were you making a deliberate parallel between cultural oppression and individual, sexual oppression—between, say, Lilian and her father?

A book that I read in England which had a big effect on me was *Damned Whores and God's Police* by Anne Summers about women in Australia. Among other things, she draws a parallel between the position of a colonized country like Australia and the "colonized" position of women. That got me thinking about the colonial relationship as a metaphor for many kinds of relationships, of which, of course, the parent-child one is the most obvious. The father in **Lilian's Story** is called Albion, naturally, because he is in that oppressive imperial/colonial relationship with his daughter. So yes, I did see it as a parallel.

The feminist perspective is much stronger in **Lilian's Story** *than in* **Bearded Ladies** *or* **Dreamhouse.** *Was this intentional or inevitable?*

A lot of people actually find it the other way around, because **Bearded Ladies** is more obviously angry, and it's more obviously and pointedly anti-men . . . they actually find **Bearded Ladies** far more feminist. In fact, some of them accuse me of softening on my feminist stance, because they see **Lillian's Story** as "less feminist".

How do you feel about that? Do you agree?

No. I think it's an evolution. I'm as much a feminist now as when I wrote **Bearded Ladies.** But feminism, like any other process of thought, is going to change if you go on thinking. So **Bearded Ladies** is the sort of angry place where feminism actually begins, when you suddenly *see* how the world is really working, which is why I was obsessed with that sort of photographic clarity—people *must know* this is what's really happening underneath the nice rhetoric of romance. By the time I wrote **Dreamhouse,** which came next chronologically, I was beginning to see that women were very much accomplices in that you couldn't just blame the men, as I had earlier. So, the character Louise is a pretty nasty piece of work, and she is much at fault. It takes two, in that relationship, to make it such a disaster. By **Lilian's Story,** I was even able to see that everybody is simply a part of the process, part of the system. Men and women are all trapped, though the cages look different, and women are often in a whole series of cages, not just one.

It seems to me your focus has shifted to societal rather than gender-related victims, which is a nicely tempered and important movement.

I think as long as you're focusing on one part of the system, no matter how true that might be, the possibilities for changing the system are very limited, because you're not seeing *why* the cogs are intermeshing the way they are. Having done the photograph, I'd like to be able to draw the circuit-diagram now. (pp. 292-94)

One of the most effective stories in **Bearded Ladies** *surfaces again in* **Lilian's Story.** *Miss Spear in* **"The Test Is, If They Drown",** *reappears as Miss Gash. What makes the accounts powerful, I think, is the betrayal which takes place, but more than this, the betrayal of allies in a world which has provided too few. In your eyes, were these characters always similar? And was the betrayal difficult to portray?*

They certainly were similar. I was very conscious that I was reworking that story. I'm niggardly. I believe in recycling. That must be fairly obvious, actually. And it seemed to me that that was a successful story, one that needed a weightier context. It's tossed off as a fairly funny story in **Bearded Ladies,** but for me the idea of betrayal is very central, and deserved a more substantial treatment.

Lilian's Story *is really about the suppression of personal language isn't it? Lilian's, John's, the mother's. Even Duncan, Joan and F.J. Stroud are outcasts and so voiceless. Is that a preoccupation of yours?*

Yes, very much. The book I'm writing now is about a person telling a hitherto untold story. As well as people telling those untold stories, I'm interested in the storytelling process in general, the way that a story becomes a substitute for what really happened, and the fact that if you have control over the story, then you have control over the truth. That's really the thing that Lilian's interested in, and it is very much what Joan is doing in the book I've just finished. The person who tells the tale has a sort of immortality. The story is going to live forever, where the person who doesn't isn't going to. So, whoever tells the story wins in the long run. It's the ultimate revenge of those who've been rendered voiceless.

Can you say something about **Joan Makes History?** *Joan, obviously, is a carry-over from* **Lilian's Story.** *How important is a knowledge of the earlier character to an understanding of* **Joan Makes History?**

I've tried to make it so that it's quite independent. Lilian only appears in one scene in **Joan,** and she has a few cameo roles. So it's not that important. But it would be nice if people read them together. Faulkner is another person I could add to my collection of writers I admire, and I'm very drawn to the idea of building up a whole enormous canvas of books that are quite independent, but if you read them all, they enrich each other.

So you toyed with the idea of creating a fictional community, like Faulkner's Yoknapatawpha, or Margaret Laurence's Manawaka?

In a way, that's what I'm starting to do, in a small way—I wouldn't put myself in the same bus as Faulkner!—because Lilian and Joan are connected. And the book that I plan next is Father's book, so that's also going to be connected. But they're not quite as focused as a unit as Faulkner's novels were.

Lilian's Story *and* **Joan Makes History** *are both pseudo-historical treatments. What is your concept of history?*

I'm having great trouble with that at the moment   with **Joan.** Writing a book is the way I learn things. It seems the only way I can *think* is to doodle with words. I used to have a fairly simplistic view that history was a sanitized version of things that happened, and that you were asked to accept them as the truth, whereas, really, it was just one historian's version of things. In other words, the knowledge that the story is never going to be transparent . . . there is no such thing as a true history; there is always only a perception of history, a story. As a result, I had contempt for the real facts of history, but now that I've actually read a bit of history in the course of doing **Joan Makes History,** I think that as well as having to be very sceptical about what you read, you do actually have to read it. In the same way, for years I never read the newspapers because I said it's all a pack of lies, or at least it's just their point of view. Well, now I do, because somehow you have a social responsibility, to learn to read the lines—the lies—or around them [*laughs*]. Or to read enough different lies that you can build up a vision of something that might be closer to the truth. (pp. 295-96)

In the article **"The World is Round Like an Orange"** *you talk about the "first Australians" and "we invaders", obviously distinguishing between Aborigines and white settlers. I'm curious to know if* **Joan Makes History**—*despite beginning at the time of Cook's voyage—deals with Aboriginal peoples and issues.*

Yes it does. It's been a source of great discomfort to me, great unease, the Aboriginal element. I felt very strongly writing this history that I wanted to put in at least some of the groups that had been left out—mainly the women, but also the Aborigines—and there are a lot of other groups that I haven't put in; you can't put in everything. There are two sections in the book where Joan actually is an Aboriginal woman. She projects herself into that persona. And there are various other times where there are Aboriginal characters, and I feel uneasy about that, because I think . . . I imagine Aborigines reading it and getting very angry, and saying, "Look, here is yet another invader not only taking our country but telling our story as well."

Perhaps the critique you'll get for writing from a male perspective?

Exactly, yes, and on the one level you can argue, as I did about the male perspective, that every character that you write about is fictional. You read fiction with a kind of contract between the reader and the writer, that this is the writer's view of what something might be, it doesn't claim to be "fact". And in a way, any kind of person in the world is raw material for a fiction writer. You shouldn't have to censor yourself, that's true, but at the same time you can't ignore the context—all the outrages we still inflict on the Aborigines. I hope that what I've done with *Joan* is not misunderstood. (p. 297)

You mentioned once that you had written close to a hundred pages of Lilian's father's story. You're obviously planning to return to it—what kind of problems do you see coming up with that new perspective?

One problem will be to resist the obvious, which is always the problem in writing anyway: to overcome my own set of stereotypes about how men in general, or a particular kind of man, might think. But in another way you have to make that leap for any fictional character, so the fact that he's a man is just one more different thing. I was never fat, so I had to imagine that for Lilian—imagine a whole world view for her that I don't really have. Actually, the biggest problem with it, to be truthful, is trying to ignore the voices in my head of the critics and the reviewers, who'll say, you know, "Look at this woman, thinking she can write about a man", and the most difficult thing is to try not to even think about that, and to just write what I feel to be the truth . . . what should be written. (p. 298)

Kate Grenville and Gerry Turcotte, in an interview in Southerly, *Vol. 47, No. 3, 1987, pp. 284-99.*

CONSTANCE MARKEY

Dreamhouse is indeed about dreams, though not necessarily sweet ones. Less to do with fancy than with fact, it takes a hard look at the duplicity of human nature. Wryly, it pokes at the hypocrisy of personal relationships, especially marriage, exposing the self-deceit and prim conventions that often mask honest emotion. If the book's title does not immediately expose this irony, then the first page certainly does.

Surface events tell us that Louise and her professor husband, Rennie, are bound for a serene sabbatical in Italy, where he will complete a brilliant scholarly dissertation destined to bring them both success and happiness. Yet, even in the second paragraph, Louise, the narrator, blurts out her dissatisfaction with all that ought to please her. With disarming candor, she confesses her growing fear that "Rennie's vanity" and her "greed" will not "survive a foreign summer, alone

with each other," and without the distracting "parties" and "glitter" left behind them in London.

But she need not worry. Solitude, much less peace of mind, is out of the question. Soon their rustic woodland cottage, already overrun by mice, pigeons and other wildlife, is to be invaded by more primitive powers in the shape of Rennie's "friend" Daniel and his adult children, Hugo and Viola. This mysterious threesome will ultimately undo the precarious balance of the couple's marriage and teach them the painful truth about themselves. . . .

Before the reader's eyes, a modern version of a pagan mythology unfolds, a tableau not accidently set in the ancient hills of Rome and Etruria. A fresco of life today still deliberately recalls a brightly painted Botticelli canvas crowded with leering satyrs, sprightly nymphs, lush green foliage and sexual innuendo. This provocative fable lures the reader in pursuit of the characters as the story rushes toward a stunning and unexpected conclusion. It is a novel impossible to put down.

Titillating might be a good word to describe *Dreamhouse* but it would not do the novel justice. Author Grenville is into something here that is more essential than lust, and that is lust for life. Boundless freedom is both a driving force and a source of anxiety in her works. In fact, this tension between Victorian restraint and individual liberty was already a crucial theme in the Australian author's earlier prized work *Lillian's Story.*

In a different way, both novels by this brilliant new writer tackle the same existential questions. Is conformity worth the price of freedom? Or more specifically, is Louise's image of traditional womanhood (or Rennie's idea of manhood, for that matter) worth salvaging if it spells the loss of personal fulfillment? Wisely, Grenville does not decide these dilemmas for the reader.

Nor does she let philosophy interfere with poetry. Grenville possesses a rare and beautiful gift for words, a delicacy of description, and an awareness of nature rare to present-day fiction. These qualities, plus an abiding intuition of life's eternal conflicts, distinguish her as a writer of great strength and sensitivity.

Constance Markey, "Lust for Life," in Chicago Tribune—Books, *November 8, 1987, p. 5.*

MOLLY PEACOCK

Louise, "a striking secretary with lovely legs and little future," has married Rennie, "a vain man with a thick orange moustache . . . soon to be a professor with an income and a position." They have left London to spend the summer in a crumbling Tuscan farmhouse belonging to Rennie's sinisterly well-dressed mentor, Daniel. In Italy Rennie will complete (and Louise will type) his dissertation on "Malthus and the Doctrine of Necessary Catastrophe." This necessary catastrophe slowly impends throughout Kate Grenville's psychologically acute and very tightly written second novel, *Dreamhouse.* Louise is a shockingly passive heroine, yet she possesses, probably because of her self-absorption, fiercely active powers of observation. Her mistake has been to marry Rennie, and it is a catastrophe because, in doing so, she has denied both their true natures.

The novel becomes a kind of deprivation chamber because

Louise's outward life is dispossessed by her own personality. The reader as well is deprived of narrative fullness and development because Kate Grenville has constructed the novel depending heavily on the repetition of short pieces of information. While this serves her genius for capturing states of feeling, it depletes the quality of the narrative experience. *Lilian's Story,* Ms. Grenville's first novel, was full of richly peculiar and moving details of a girl's Australian childhood. In *Dreamhouse* the author directly counters this technique by removing the characters' backgrounds. Louise is sent, without a family history, without, it seems, even a previous life, into an unknown landscape with a slightly known, very politely hostile man. She lives almost entirely inside her own feelings, and the predominant feeling here is rage. . . .

The scenes of lovemaking—Louise masturbates as Rennie turns his back—are deliberately empty, made more horrifying by the blunt, sensually palpable language. Ms. Grenville employs every image to serve her main character's confused, angry, deprived state, the primary image being the shattered Italian farmhouse/dreamhouse. . . . The novel usually ignores the incongruities of Italian- and English-speaking cultures, but they are often felt because those elements which usually give fiction a physical stability, the sense of place which houses and landscape provide, are seriously askew. This is literally foreign territory for the writer, who lushly described Australian landscape and solidly realized houses, porches and gardens in *Lilian's Story.*

The collapsing villa occupies a place across the valley from another, much more comfortable house also belonging to the effeminate mentor, Daniel. Long divorced from his Italian wife, Daniel lives in London; the comfortable house is occupied by his two sensuous, mysterious grown children, Hugo and Viola, who coolly rebuff Louise and Rennie and who, according to the peasant who delivers their bread, are engaged in an incestuous affair.

Putting brilliant details on a blank canvas, Ms. Grenville exchanges some of the major devices of fiction for the modes of poetry—image and repetition. The picture of a sickening strand of saliva glistening in a mouth occurs in many permutations. The recurrence of such imagery wraps the novel tighter and tighter around the reader, just as Louise's emotional claustrophobia, which she is unable to express to her husband or to any other character, winds tighter and tighter around her psyche.

When Daniel arrives in midsummer, he discovers Louise and Rennie living among decayed beams and mouse droppings and insists that they move into his own house, where the three of them become invading visitors to Hugo and Viola. In more solid architecture all is less stable, for the atmosphere is sexually charged, with varied combinations of the three men and two women advancing toward and retreating from one another. All the characters are without humor and all seem to be defined by a simple aspect of appearance: Rennie's orange mustache; Hugo's leering beauty and obsession with taxidermy; Viola's dark, asymetrically cut hair and wordlessly efficient housekeeping; Daniel's suspiciously effete clothing, and, of course, the slender legginess of Louise herself.

Her hatred of Rennie's sexual rejection—an *entire* rejection because she is defined by the single characteristic of her beauty—is finally purged by her comprehension of Daniel's sexual designs on Rennie. Once she is struck with relief at the possibility of her husband's homosexuality, the discovery of his true nature allows her to possess her own; there is a bath of self-discovery and forgiveness.

The five go off on a midsummer night's retreat to a monastery notorious for the homosexuality of its monks. It is here that Daniel finally seduces Rennie—or *something,* since Louise never really learns from him what happened—and here that Hugo's bisexuality becomes apparent as well. Kate Grenville is extremely good at capturing how undermining it is to be with someone of confused sexuality. She is also spectacular at evoking the feeling of not understanding veiled signals. . . .

Despite the novel's frailties, Ms. Grenville's language has a powerful kinesthetic energy. Here she describes the frescoes of the monastery cloister:

> A figure that appeared in several scenes was a devil who wore only red tights and a drift of drapery. The saints and the women holding their ham-like babies had the wooden faces of bad actors, but the devil was so real that he looked as if he was about to turn and complain from his small rose-like mouth.

Yet because she chooses strategies that work against the complexity of the characters, *Dreamhouse* becomes thin. It is like the frescoes she describes: there can be some bad acting, but the devil is real.

Molly Peacock, *"Pairing Off in Tuscany,"* in The New York Times Book Review, *November 22, 1987, p. 24.*

HARICLEA ZENGOS

Dreamhouse, Kate Grenville's second novel, gives her readers a rather unpleasant narrator in Louise Dufrey. Louise is a woman willingly trapped in a marriage of convenience. She admits that her husband, Rennie, is nothing more than financial security, a man "soon to be a professor with an income and a position," while she "could never be anything wealthier than a striking secretary with lovely legs and little future." . . . That Louise does not try to escape is particularly frustrating to the reader—her greed and laziness stand in her way—but she must discover unconventional possibilities to take the place of her stiflingly conventional life. Louise, in fact, must discover her "dreamhouse."

To complete without disturbances or disruptions his dissertation on Malthus and the doctrine of necessary catastrophe (and this is the sense the reader gets, that some catastrophe is inevitable in this novel) Rennie's mentor, Daniel, offers to share his remote Tuscan villa for the summer. Louise imagines the house to be the stuff of dreams: "A *villa:* I heard that word and became languorous with visions of balustrades, a view of blue water, cool white wine, bare feet on marble." But the house is a nightmare of dirt and decay: Mice nest in the mattresses, beams and ceilings creak with age and strain, birds roost in the roof. The villa seems to inspire Rennie, who labors on his dissertation while Louise plays the faithful wife and devoted typist/amanuensis—and hates every minute of it. . . . The work leaves Louise with too much time to contemplate the ruin of her marriage. The run-down villa is much like her marriage; for both, the "final collapse was only a matter of time." Louise realizes that, while her greed chains her to Rennie, his vanity binds him to her. He appreciates

Louise as a possession, enjoying the way people admire his beautiful wife—"slim like a model." . . .

Grenville has described *Dreamhouse* as a "malevolent and cruel book in some ways," and most of this cruelty emanates from Daniel and his son, Hugo. Louise finds Daniel's family, which includes the mysterious daughter, Viola, sinister yet seductive. Daniel is a suave manipulator. When he chooses not to ignore Louise, he patronizes her, and Rennie, mimicking his mentor, joins in on these backslapping male-only activities. From his father, Hugo inherits a love of cruelty; he keeps a collection of stuffed birds, "all with vicious beaks and threateningly fanned wings," which he shows Louise with sadistic delight. Viola remains an aloof figure, the "nutty sister," as Rennie pegs her. Louise's anger towards this family ("I was sick of laughing at things that were not funny, hated this house and our hosts, and wished I could roar out a yodel of rage and up-end the table") turns to a strange fascination, and ultimately one of them opens up new possibilities for change in her life; one of them directs Louise to her "dreamhouse."

With a less talented writer, *Dreamhouse* could have been yet another ordinary novel concerning the dissolution of a marriage. But with Grenville nothing is ever ordinary; small yet significant details betray her extraordinary talent as a novelist. Her plotting is intricate yet economical. Each chapter is short and dense, ending with a cliff hanger. . . . The novel is tension-packed, suspenseful, and full of mystery. And by what seems like a trademark (if one recalls the italics of *Lilian's Story*), Grenville chooses not to use much dialogue, allowing the reader to see the novel's world mostly through the angry eyes of Louise. As in *Bearded Ladies,* a sustained anger is present in *Dreamhouse,* mostly directed at the men.

Grenville's first novel, *Lilian's Story,* was published to major acclaim, winning the Australian/Vogel Literary Award for an unpublished manuscript by a young writer and a Patrick White endorsement: "It is a pleasure to be able to praise a true novelist." *Dreamhouse,* a worthy follow-up of extraordinary wit, vision, and imagination, proves not that Grenville is up-and-coming but that she has arrived.

> Hariclea Zengos, "A Woman Full of Greed," in Belles Lettres: A Review of Books by Women, *Vol. 3, No. 6, July-August, 1988, p. 5.*

ELIZABETH WARD

"What a big thing this business of history is, and what absurd bits and pieces make it up!" exclaims Joan—daughter, wife, mother, Everywoman—towards the end of Kate Grenville's newest and least conventional novel [*Joan Makes History*].

If this is a novel, you ask, then what's all the chatter about history? The truth is that Grenville, widely praised as a fiction writer both in her native Australia and abroad, may be really a closet historian. Her first book, *Lilian's Story,* was based on the life of a Sydney bag-lady and now, in her third, Kate seems at least as interested in making history as Joan is. But this is not an "historical novel," so much as a novel whose principal character—Joan—is History personified, sashaying through its pages in the skirts (or undergarments) of Imagination. . . .

Kate Grenville, who used to work as a professional film editor, employs a highly imaginative splicing technique to weave a double plot: the story of a contemporary Australian Joan, born to an immigrant couple in 1901, the year of Federation, whose life is narrowed down by successive hard choices; and, alternating with hers, the stories of a whole string of historical Joans, whom the modern Joan either dreams, imagines or remembers (it doesn't matter which, the point being that Joan, like Whitman, contains multitudes):

> I thought my story was one the world had never heard before. I loved and was bored, I betrayed and was forgiven. I ran away and returned . . . There was not a single joy I could feel that countless Joans had not already felt, not a single mistake I could make that had not been made by some Joan before me.

Contemporary Joan is a bit of a rebel, "plain as a plate," but with dreams of a brilliant career. She kicks spiritedly at the traces of male dominance, but is finally brought by loneliness, pregnancy and an unexpected attachment to her own child to throw in her lot with a good, if undistinguished, man. The lives of the earlier Joans follow, in composite, a similar trajectory. Captain Cook's unsung wife; a female convict arriving with the First Fleet; a brazen young hussy of an aboriginal girl encountering white invaders on the beach; a pioneer wife happened upon by a strolling artist in the bush (later, in a case of art imitating art, she will be immortalized in a famous Australian painting, now in the Art Gallery of New South Wales); a washerwoman; the wife of a governor; and the wife of an itinerant Depression "swagman": all these Joans, too, experience the disappointment of failed, or scaled-down, expectations. . . .

It is a good many years since Australian historians, like their colleagues elsewhere, began to jettison the notion of their discipline as a mere record of heroic deeds, and to think of it as a matter of piecing together the lives of ordinary people. No doubt there was and is a political edge to much of this latter-day history, which often seems as blinkered and partisan and faddish as the old-fashioned history of powerful white males that it deplores. But where Kate Grenville comes in is in putting flesh on the dry ideological bones of the new enthusiasms, reminding the skeptics why it *is* important to be passionate about the fates of ordinary people.

If this makes the novel sound intolerably preachy, it should be said that *Joan Makes History,* with its rapid cinematic glimpses of women "frowning into the tiny square of life caught in the glass of [Grenville's] viewfinder," is consistently, surprisingly, engaging to read. The Joans are enormously likable, despite their collective tendency to philosophize. And Kate Grenville has a real gift for imagery, for the telling, casual details that capture, Strachey-like, the essence of a vanished time or a place.

Kate Grenville has made it her business in this purposeful *jeu d'esprit* of a novel to re-imagine Australian history. She takes the familiar legends and icons and landmarks and works of art and turns them on their heads, giving us thereby a view from the underside, not the pretty one of the official chronicler but the cynical one of the sock-washer and the pantrymaid and the helpmeet. Yet Grenville is no ideologue: despite the hardball feminist politics of *Joan Makes History,* her apparent conclusions—that maternity is destiny, for example—are refreshingly unexpected. Perhaps it is just this quality of independent judgment that makes her as good an historian as she is a novelist.

Elizabeth Ward, "Keeping Up with the Joans," in
Book World-The Washington Post, *November 20,*
1988, p. 7.

JUDITH FREEMAN

What Kate Grenville has chosen to do in *Joan Makes History,* her third novel, is to tell stories about Australia's history by creating an Everywoman named Joan—who is really 12 different women, present at various historical moments, who give accounts of their lives at those times.

These are stories within a larger, main story. The 12 historical tales are really the imaginings of a 20th-Century woman named Joan, who has believed herself capable of doing something great, making history in some way, but instead watches her life take on more ordinary dimensions. In between chapters revealing her life are accounts of the "other" Joans, the historical Joans whose tales she imagines: Joan as an explorer (wife of Captain Cook) and prisoner of the Crown (thief banished to new penal colony), hairdresser and frontier tree-chopper, washer-woman, lady of leisure, half-breed and bareback rider, photographer's assistant, mother and wife of the mayor.

Modern Joan is conceived in the hold of a boat by parents emigrating from Transylvania, just as the boat arrives in Sydney. She is raised by these dark foreign parents who do not speak the language of the new land and therefore don't know enough to say "Fine weather for ducks" when folks say, "Wet enough for you?"

Taunted as a "filthy Hun" during the war, Joan's father changes their name. No longer Joan Radulescu, she watches her father cross out her old name in her school books and write in her new one: Joan Redman. It is an act of deceptively violent obliteration.

In her private fantasies, Joan imagines herself becoming someone important. But instead, during her first years at college, she makes love in the Botanical Gardens one night, becomes pregnant by Duncan, sees her life set on an irreversible course that does not include making history so much as making babies and perfect scones.

If this sounds like an ordinary story, it is and it isn't. Things take a very quirky turn. When Duncan and Joan come in from the country to attend the annual big livestock show, she decides to abandon him and hides behind bottles of pickled peas in the Agricultural Hall until she's sure she's given him the slip.

Traveling to another town, and now on her own, she works menial jobs. She also decides to become a man, that is to cross-dress for a period of time, exploring the feeling of power that comes from such a disguise, until she wearies of it and longs for Duncan.

In the end, this Joan does not "make history." She returns to Duncan, becomes the forgiven wife and settles into a life of domesticity and child-rearing. Recognizing he is a very good man, she is "filled with the love that has no choice."

This is really more a collection of stories connected by the idea that we are reading history from the perspective of the women who never make the history books, the ones who cooked dinner, washed socks, and swept floors, those "who will melt away like mud when they die," the people who do

"things that would look silly in a book. Nobody would make a statue out of them." She is talking about "every new generation dancing in the shadow of history's grief," precisely because the grief is forgotten.

If this sounds slightly confusing, it is, intitially at least, and yet, once the structure of [*Joan Makes History*] is comprehended, these are delightful stories of women's adventures and conquests.

The history of the world is the male version. It seems perfect that Grenville has made Joan not an individual but an archetype of the "whole tribe of humanity keeping the generations flowing along," the women and the workers.

Judith Freeman, "An Everywoman Named Joan,"
in Los Angeles Times, *December 18, 1988, p. 9.*

NANCY WILLARD

"History is not the past, but the present made flesh," wrote Kate Grenville in her first novel, *Lilian's Story.* That statement might stand as an epigraph to her third novel, *Joan Makes History.* The history and setting here are again Australian, but more than faith in the present power of history connects these books. The only daughter of Hungarian immigrants, Joan Redman appears in the last half of *Lilian's Story,* involved in a passionate friendship with mad, wealthy Lilian Singer. A bold, independent young woman, Joan has no patience with her studies at the university. When she discovers she is pregnant by Duncan, a fellow student, Joan marries him and promptly vanishes·from the story.

This disappearance from history, this trading destiny for domesticity, haunts all three of Kate Grenville's novels. The young wife in her second, *Dreamhouse,* discovers she is not pregnant and reflects on her freedom: "There were decisions to be made, now that I was restored to myself." In *Joan Makes History,* the narrator rails against "having had my destiny nipped in its bud, and . . . my history prematurely snatched away from me by this tiny thief within." (p. 7)

Between the chapters showing Joan Redman's life stand 11 scenes, ranging from 1770 to 1901, in which those other Joans star: the wife of Captain Cook, who claimed Australia for Britain in 1770; a convict sent to Botany Bay in 1788 who jumps ship so that her feet will be "the first to soil the new land"; a laundress during the gold rush of 1851; the wife of the colonial governor in 1855. With dazzling skill, Ms. Grenville interweaves their stories. Society offers the same destiny to them all: "I was a woman, so my prospect was to be a wife." Joan the aborigine asks the new settlers to cut her hair like a man's; Joan Redman, the rebellious student, cuts her own hair. Joan the washerwoman sees small tragedies rise and froth in the suds: the unexpected pregnancy, the hasty marriage.

Their stories make one story, told in different voices, and Ms. Grenville avoids the pitfall of making it all sound like a feminist tract. No matter whose life she is narrating, her writing is as pithy as a proverb. "Feet were my first friends." "Pants altered my heart." "I wished not to marry history, but to make it." And, on the superiority of aborigines over colonists: "They . . . seemed to have managed without two sets of themselves, one in chains and one in silk."

What links the Joans is their wish to "make my mark," as

Joan the aborigine puts it. *"I was not born for this kind of small beer,"* says Joan the wife of the colonial governor, who imagines leading armies or "droves of inflamed poets." The wary reader asks, Is this destiny or daydreaming? The present-day Joan plans many histories for herself: *"I will be a great writer"; "I will be Prime Minister."* A miscarriage gives the present-day Joan the chance she wants. Acting on impulse, she leaves her husband—and the scene is wrenching—by disappearing into the crowd at an agriculture fair, from which she watches Duncan's despair and recalls the life she has given up: "the life of scones, the life where preserved quinces mattered."

Unable to make history as a woman, she dresses as a man and becomes "Jack, a woman of destiny." What she finds in her new life is not what she looked for; to be loved and to love in return is a kind of history too, and the men who make large visible histories walk a lonely path. . . . She returns to Duncan, who forgives her. Now she can have both her marriage and her destiny.

Or can she? In the last chapter, Ms. Grenville uses a conventional device to show Joan and Duncan hastening toward old age: the image of time passing through family snapshots. Their daughter goes off to the university, and Joan learns that "history was always out there waiting to be made not by parents, who had had their go at it, but the children of those parents." There she stands, tea towel in hand, washed up on the shore where the tide of life has come and gone. Her destiny, it seems, is to confront her own mortality. "I saw that although I had chosen to be that most invisible of creatures, the wife and mother . . . mine was the history not of an individual, but of the whole tribe of humanity."

Would that Ms. Grenville had given us a less subdued portrait of Joan here, going less gently into that good night. More admirable than suburban resignation is the triumph of mad Lilian at the end of *Lilian's Story*: "The story of all our lives is the story forward to death. . . . *Drive on. . . . I am ready for whatever comes next."*

But these flaws are as small as a cracked pane in the window of a castle. Kate Grenville is a powerful storyteller, right down to the last sentence: "Stars blazed, protozoa coupled, apes levered themselves upright, generations of women and men lived and died, and like them all I, Joan, have made history." (pp. 7, 9)

Nancy Willard, "The Nameless Women of the World," in The New York Times Book Review, *December 18, 1988, pp. 7, 9.*

GERRY TURCOTTE

> As a woman . . . I have always felt that the metaphor for what was happening to me in moments of danger was suffocation, smothering, drowning, sort of being washed away and not being able to speak and being . . . negated in that way . . . the ultimate oppression.
>
> —Kate Grenville

> In a world where language and naming are power, silence is oppression, is violence.
>
> —Adrienne Rich

Kate Grenville's small body of work reflects a decided preoccupation with language as self-creation. Her work, therefore, exhibits a fascination in, as well as a fear of, the possibilities of language, and traces the lives of her characters within this context as they strive to discover their own voice. It can be argued, in fact, that some of the stories in *Bearded Ladies,* much of *Dreamhouse* and most of *Lilian's Story* are largely sustained metaphors for the act of self-creation through self-expression, and that the prevailing theme of her work is the quest to survive silencing. Grenville's fiction, however, examines the idea of oppression not only in respect to women's history and literature, but also in regard to other forms of cultural oppression, at the personal and the group level, and at the national and the international level. Similarly, her depiction of oppression almost as a speech/rape metaphor suggests a type of imperialism which threatens not only women, but also races, outcasts, and societies. Grenville's fiction is wide in scope, and is a topical and complex examination of political silencing. She represents these acts of political aggression as violent acts against language, an idea which culminates as a rape metaphor in *Lilian's Story.*

The current trend in post-colonial criticism, fiction, and poetry is toward a concept of the self as language. Accordingly, the primary need would seem to be, as Simon During has suggested, "to hear oneself speak." The linguistic metaphor reflects many concerns, including: the threat of imperial monoliths subsuming colonial identities into themselves; the danger of a similar subjugation of feminine identity by the masculine agent; and the suppression of other marginalized groups, such as migrants and aborigines (or even less categorically distinct groups—such as "social misfits") by dominant centralizing bodies. In each case, the metaphor of "silenced language" is appropriate, and is often applied. (p. 64)

Grenville's work addresses all these issues to varying degrees, and does so in a similarly language-oriented manner. In her work can be seen an insistence on language which has as its point to underline the role of language in various "political arenas," including those suggested by the imperial/colonial, the central/marginal, and the male/female dialectics.

In *Lilian's Story,* for example, much is made of Miss Vine who attempts to inculcate British values in her students while denigrating all that is Australian. In the work, the difficulty faced by social misfits is soberly related through the stories of Stroud, Duncan, and Joan. Ultimate patriarchal domination is suggested through Lilian's father, as well as by other representatives of the masculine order, who rape women (both metaphorically and actually), in an attempt to subdue them to their authority. The effect of the rape, as will be shown, is to rob women of their ability to speak.

Grenville has pointed to the influence of two texts which stress or work with the idea of colonization on several levels: Anne Summers' *Damned Whores and God's Police,* and Shakespeare's *The Tempest.* In a recent interview [see excerpt above] Grenville stated that Summers' book first suggested to her the parallel between the colonization of land and of women. Summers' work argues that women are in fact a colonized sex in a political, not merely a metaphorical, manner: "To say that women are a colonized group is no metaphor. It is a salient political description of women in industrialized countries like Australia, if not of all women everywhere." She goes on to say, "The colonization of women contains the four elements which are present in the colonization of a continent or a tribal people. These are (1) invasion and conquering, (2) cultural domination, (3) divide and rule, and (4) the extraction of profits." Grenville has admitted that this work "had a big effect" on her; she was particularly drawn to Summers' idea of colonial relationships and how women enter into this relationship. (pp. 65-6)

Another work which provides a similar depiction of the various levels of colonial oppression, and which also includes the father/daughter paradigm, is Shakespeare's *The Tempest* which functioned as an impetus for the writing of *Lilian's Story.* As noted in the *Southerly* interview, *The Tempest* has been widely read in regards to its colonial/imperial concerns, with Caliban and Ariel representing indigenous colonial figures, and Prospero an imperial power. It is also "about fathers and daughters, and also about the magic of storytelling." More importantly, both *The Tempest* and *Lilian's Story* are about who, ultimately, gets to tell the story, and so reflect, implicitly, the masculine/feminine dilemma earlier described since so often the female account is given—even dictated—by the male. A concomitant of finding a voice, therefore, is the need to tell one's own story. By making articulation the ultimate goal and achievement in her work, Grenville provides a powerful focus for the many types of oppression with which she is concerned, not the least of which is sexual. (p. 66)

Words are a fixation with Grenville, and the theft of them, or their suppression, a major focus. Grenville herself has suggested that her turn to writing was impelled by a shyness which impeded her ability to speak: "I was always a bit shy and inarticulate. . . . Writing was like a private revenge: you could go away and get it all down on paper, and no one could interrupt you . . . they sort of had to listen to you." By becoming a wordsmith, she was able to express herself, to find a voice. It is small wonder, then, that so many of her characters attempt a similar goal, and that their success or failure to achieve it is articulated in precisely these terms.

In **"Rosalie's Folly,"** for example [collected in *Bearded Ladies*], a husband's betrayal is signalled by a simultaneous disintegration of "language," more accurately, Rosalie's refusal to confront her husband's infidelity results in her losing her ability to read and understand everyday language. Grenville cleverly implies that there is an interconnectedness between language and personal honesty. As long as Rosalie is dishonest with herself—endorsing the husband's lies, and, as it were, his language—she finds that the language she deals with loses all stability. (p. 67)

It is no coincidence that Grenville opens [**"Rosalie's Folly"**] with an invasion of the most personal kind. Martin's "voice slides into her sleep . . . until she wakes up." Not only does Martin's intruding voice suggest the insistent imposition of the masculine over the feminine voice, but also, his words display the cruel hypocrisy of the patriarchal language: Martin's words are encomia to his lover, which he utters in his uninterrupted sleep. As Rosalie struggles increasingly to deny their import, her own command of language deteriorates:

> GROUP URGES PUBLIC PROBE a headline sniggers. The Venereal Heating Centre tries to take her by surprise. A bus roars past advertising Hell Tours and a man with a limp goes into an On-The-Spot Hell Bar. . . . Then there's the Cobra Hotel where the desk clerk sits under a neon sign that says DECEPTION.

It is this last word which makes her panic, but even her attempts to run are impeded by the tactile world associated with her, so that "her coat wraps itself around her legs and

flaps in front trying to stop her." Rosalie cannot escape herself. As she rushes home in midday to her empty house, her own anger—her silenced language—threatens to spill out. Rosalie's denial of its expression is reflected in her own inability to breathe properly while she withholds speech; in fact, she realizes that "she's been forgetting to breathe." This is one of the first appearances of Grenville's penchant to parallel the idea of asphyxiation with a metaphor of aphasia. To accept the masculine voice, it seems, means to compromise the feminine. The story concludes with Rosalie confronting her husband, on the verge of speech—perhaps even of outburst. Fittingly, the story's last word is "speak." **"Rosalie's Folly,"** like *Bearded Ladies* itself, is about learning how to speak after a long, enforced silence.

Similarly, **"Dropping Dance,"** Grenville's contribution to the *Room to Move* anthology [edited by Suzanne Falkiner], describes an inarticulate, unexpressed and so frustrated woman, who finally discovers the value of her own "space." The metaphor used to describe this discovery is the woman's ecstatic run down the face of a mountain in complete isolation. It is a discovery of the value of private space—of a space of one's own—which is expressed linguistically: "She felt as though she had invented a language and was writing it on the air." The woman has escaped the need to seek a mate, and has escaped the constraints of a masculine world which requires so much compromise.

Dreamhouse, too, looks at the importance of secret or private languages, but introduces more clearly and sinisterly than *Bearded Ladies,* the concept of negative voice; that is, of language as a divider, and as a weapon. This notion is suggested early in the novel through an unexplained pun which is designed to connote language's multiple meaning, as well as the darker side this plurality can contain. When Rennie and Louise ask for directions to the town they cannot find, they are told, *"a sinistra, sempre sinistra."* The Italian is translated as "left, always left," but it can also mean "sinister, always sinister," a reading which takes on more credence when it is remembered that the line is spoken by an old crone with a cleaver, on a deserted road. The gothic world of the villa which the couple soon enter into complements the sinister side even further and prepares the way for the lexical instability to follow.

Like *Bearded Ladies* and *Lilian's Story, Dreamhouse's* focus on language is deliberate and to the point: it is used to stress the relationship of language to power, identity, and oppression. (pp. 67-8)

Often, power works on the premise of security, and control on the ability to undermine that security. Such, then, is the nature of many of the language games played throughout [*Dreamhouse*]. Daniel, for instance, continually disorients Louise by making statements which are highly suspect—as in wanting to make love to his own daughter—but cleverly presenting them so that she is uncertain of their precision, and to her alone so that she cannot verify their truth through witnesses. The statements leave Louise shaken, and Daniel is able to pursue her husband without fear.

Security is further compromised by the secret languages used by the various groups throughout the novel. Domenico speaks an incomprehensible Italian which Louise cannot decipher; Hugo and Viola speak a kind of code which denies to Rennie and Louise (although particularly the latter) any understanding of their motives; and Daniel's mysterious asides have already been mentioned. . . . Language is a tool used by the powerful (or power-hungry) and the inarticulate are constantly in danger.

The focus of the novel, then, seems to be the drive to discover a comparable language which will define place and self. To make the point, the novel not only focuses on the experiences of the wordsmiths, but also on those of the inarticulates. It is in this last instance, moreover, that Grenville's examples are most effective; when portraying the silent victims. The birds destined to be embalmed by Hugo fly desperately but silently against their wire tethers; the lobster which Daniel forces Louise to watch in the boiling water scrambles silently in its agony along the pot's side; the quiet, resigned mouse in the mattress silently endures Louise's cruelty as she presses the plastic cover over its body (an unsettling scene which reveals Louise's own need for power); and, finally, Louise's own quiet endurance of her husband's violent intercourse which not only bruises her buttocks and tears her anus, but also forces her to question her own importance in the relationship, and by extension, her own identity: "Each time, I wondered who it was he was thrusting into, behind his tightly-squeezed closed eyes."

In **Dreamhouse,** Grenville uses the idea of voice as a metaphor for complicity and control, and as long as Louise is a victim of other people's languages she is incapable of asserting any influence over her own life. In fact, Louise is not only controlled by others, but also she spends most of the novel transcribing another person's "story": Louise types Rennie's drafts of his dissertation on Malthus, a symbol both of the predominance of his own intellectual interests and of the suppression of her personal goals in favour of her husband's. Louise cannot surface from the fictions of other peoples' stories until she herself begins to write and acknowledge her own. It is only once Louise and Viola establish a dialogue together that the reader realizes Viola's former actions and language were, like Rennie's dissertation, imposed upon her. Their dialogue creates a language and with this voice the two women finally break out of the masculine world. The novel ends with Louise's departure from her husband, whose shouting, crying and begging voice is ineffectual in changing her plans: "nothing could stop me now."

Dreamhouse is about the discovery of personal voice—of a feminist voice—and ends, fittingly, with the description of a postcard Louise has written to Viola which says simply, "*Dear Viola . . . I am coming back.*" The novel's closing line, "There was nothing more I could think of that needed to be said," offers a final, positive picture of the possibilities of linguistic reappropriation, and underscores the crucial need for such measures to be taken before the recreation of the self can be possible. Viola and Louise have established a dialogue independent of the masculine linguistic codes and can at last converse—and live—unobstructed by the latter's oppressive influence.

It is in **Lilian's Story,** however, that the focus on language and on the silencing metaphor is most sustained. (pp. 69-70)

Lilian's home environment is revealed to function according to a sound/silence binary, with the control of each resting with the father. Albion Singer's ability to control language—and hence people—is suggested by his capacity to "silence": "I had not finished, had hardly begun . . . when Father began to shout back at me, *No, no, no, no, no!* until I was silent." His own world reflects the silence he would impose on

others. Although his study is "a silent and dusty place," however, Grenville makes clear that masculine silence is not an absence or a denial of speech, but a threatening, imminent voice. Albion's ubiquitous silent world belies the power of speech, and reflects his ability to *choose* whether or not he will speak. That even Albion's silence is a voice can be seen early in the story when Lilian enters her father's study. Here, the reader is told, Lilian is *deafened* by the facts and figures which are kept therein, and which symbolize her father's calculating world. Lil raises her voice to counter the father's and "hum[s] into the silence in a brave way," but her voice quickly proves the weaker: "I could not keep up my humming in the face of these facts and was frightened at the way the silence roared in my ears when I stopped." Accordingly, when her transgression into her father's world is discovered, she is punished with the very same facts she could not countenance; she is forced to listen while her father describes his "research," a recitation which "drowns" everything, even "the sounds of washing up." Tellingly, the patriarch's words are not only a form of guidance and prescription, they are a form of punishment as well.

The stress on the importance of language as a means to social power is also extensively developed in **Lilian's Story.** Grenville is concerned that the self-validating myths or codes which dominating groups develop in order to secure their position of power within society actually function to alienate and to destroy weaker individuals who are unable to come to terms with a variety of "languages." Those who are incapable of switching easily between various dialects as a situation demands, people such as Lilian and her Aunt Kitty, are ostracized by the powers that be. (pp. 70-1)

Those who choose not to conform, who abandon the social languages without first securing a confident personal voice, end up like Aunt Kitty, surrounded by musty air, dying plants on window sills and a garden comprising rockeries, cacti and sand. When Lilian visits, her aunt desperately searches her memory for an appropriate social phrase: "*I am glad to see you, Lilian,* Aunt Kitty said at last, remembering how language worked." Her recollection, however, is short-lived for it no longer operates in society; nor, however, has it been replaced by a vital personal language. Curiously, it takes Lilian's misfortune—her incarceration in the asylum by her father's treachery—to inspire Aunt Kitty with a cause. This personal voice, to speak metaphorically, not only frees Lilian, but also defeats Albion and returns to Aunt Kitty a positive sense of self. The conquest, however, comes too late for Aunt Kitty. Society, Grenville seems to say, tolerates no deviants, and only the strong survive the exile.

Mere survival, however, is often a singularly unattractive alternative. F. J. Stroud, for example, uses conventional language as a defence, though he certainly fails to conform to society's norms. When a gardener at the university objects to Stroud's defacing the garden, the latter retaliates with a barrage of Latin "until the gardener was driven to snort *bloody dagoes,* and walked off." Still, although Stroud's strength allows him to use the system's language for his own ends, and although he has an independent nature, he is still pushed to the margins of society where he lives in poverty. He has the gift of languages, but he chooses to cultivate the wrong ones, so that Albion can still refer to Stroud (and Duncan), as those "wordless boys." Without accepted speech, true power is impossible.

Throughout **Lilian's Story,** then, it is the inarticulate who are shown to be outcasts. At Rick's party, John and Lilian are made to sit at a table separate from the "accepted" children; it is significant that they are seated not only with "George with the webbed fingers and toes," but also with "wordless Gwen," suggesting that in the eyes of society, the inarticulate are just as despised as the deformed. Elsewhere, after Lilian's failure to impress her friends with the goat's-head tile, Grenville uses another example of the suffocation metaphor (so prevalent in her fiction) to demonstrate how, in the power hierarchy, the authority figures control by abrogating the ability to express oneself. When Rick doubts Lil's word that she did in fact discover the tile, the denial of the statement's veracity results in her being thrown in the dust and suffocated: "Kevin's knee in my back was squeezing all the air out of my lungs so I could not call out, and the dust in my mouth tasted of failure, and heroism gone wrong." Significantly, the heroic deed is attributed to John, who, as a *male* outcast, is nonetheless considered less of a threat by the predominantly masculine power structure. Lilian's subsequent ostracism is related in similar terms of suffocation: "I could not fail to notice the silence gathering around me." Ursula's accusation that Lil has lied makes Lil gag: "I could have choked on that scone . . . [it] muffled the words so that even I was hardly convinced," that is, of the truth of her earlier claim.

John's response to the conflict is to feign deafness—to block out hurtful words. But again, Grenville makes clear that even a non-statement can be a "position," that is, a political act. Lilian interprets as heroic John's refusal to denounce her verbally (even by remaining uninvolved): "It would have been easy for him to join all those who called out after me, but behind his thick glass John was still brave. He did not join, nor did he not join, but took off his glasses and . . . said, *What? What?* so many times that even shouting Rick lost interest in the end." John, in fact, is one of the most creative of the outcasts. He develops various methods of resistance to verbal pressure such as folding his ears over to keep out sound, taking off his glasses lest they impart some visual information, and, cleverest of all, eating only raw vegetables, "entire heads of celery, bunches of lettuce, raw green beans, apples that sprayed juice, anything loud," in order to block out his father's tirades. His tactics often prove quite successful: "*John!* Father would exclaim, *I cannot hear myself think!*" Just as John retreats into the shell which his noisy vegetables create, so Lilian retreats into a world insulated by fat: "I knew there was too much flesh for Father now," she avers. The defensive nature of these gustatory strategies is suggested by the vignette's witty title, "Three Types of Crustacean." Grenville uses the heading to ensure that the idea of retreat behind various personal defences is not misunderstood. Albion Singer mentions snails in general in the vignette, that is, one type of crustacean; it is left to the reader to discover that John and Lilian, inurned in their own worlds of noisy vegetarianism and obesity, are the other two.

If authority depends on certainty to consolidate its reign, it remains true that the slightest uncertainty can threaten to topple even the most perdurable power. The mutable nature of words and information is shown to be potentially lethal when mishandled, even by the Prosperos of the world, and Albion Singer himself finally succumbs to uncertainty and is "silenced by [his own] facts." Albion's downfall is the result of his eccentric and futile attempt to order and coordinate too rigorously this language which he commands. The extent of his downfall is cleverly hinted at by the paralleling of Albion's new status with his wife's former position. Where Mrs.

Singer once lived in a sombre "room of whispers" and seemed never to complete a sentence when talking to her husband ("*Gently, Albion, she did not mean*"), Albion is suddenly thrust into a "darkened room" of his own. The *coup de grace* comes when Mrs. Singer herself *directs* a carpenter to seal him in. Earlier, there were "*no doors*" in the Singer house, suggesting that Albion would tolerate no barriers to exclude his prying authority. As soon as he takes sick, however, a door is tightly fitted on his room, one which not only prevents him being disturbed, but also prevents him from gathering any information about the world outside.

Albion quickly reappears following his breakdown, however, and, like Lazarus (indeed the vignette bears this name), he knows no slow recovery, "no convalescence." Predictably, his immediate effect is on language. Mrs. Singer, who had known a brief personal renaissance during his absence, suddenly loses her command of language: "*We must give thuds,* she said, but I knew she meant *thanks.*" John, who had abandoned his "loud" vegetables during his father's illness, returns to his noisy diet. As Lilian points out, "Father's voice was all around us in the house again." Nevertheless, the illness has not left Albion totally unaffected; rather, his approach to language has undergone a slight transformation: "There were no more facts now, but many questions." Despite the change, however, Albion's purpose and use of language remain unchanged: he uses words to reinforce his own position and to subordinate others. Inevitably, this challenge is directed at identity. When John, for example, fails to answer his father's tirade of questions correctly, Albion retaliates by questioning John's very name. The tactic works, at first, to question and then to deny John's identity: "*My name is John Singer,* said poor John," at last, "and Father lost interest." Nothing is left for John but to leave the house and spin himself round and round until he is physically sick, and mercifully insensate.

Thus far the paper has suggested that dominating forces use the suppression of voice to gain power. Two almost concurrent passages in *Lilian's Story* demonstrate Grenville's intent to represent this silencing of voice as a physical oppression, even as a type of rape. The first scene results from Albion's discovery that Lilian and Duncan sit in trees and talk, highly irregular behaviour that embarrasses the patriarch. Naturally, the habit is a form of protest by the two "misfits"—it is a time for daydreams, snippets of Shakespeare and swear words which are normally taboo. Albion's attempt to chastise Lilian for her propensity to go "*Up a tree with a lout from the bush*" and of "*Showing the world your drawers,*" takes the form of a linguistic challenge; he expresses doubt in his daughter's ability to quote Shakespeare. Lilian responds by quoting Shakespeare at length, a recitation which borders on the hysteric; the greater the father's ridicule becomes, the more feverish her delivery: "I could not stop, but felt my mouth shaping word after word, faster and faster, and on those hated pink roses saw page after page slipping over, thick with words." Lilian has fixed her eyes on the rose bushes outside her father's study and has blocked out his ridicule with words. Albion immediately recognizes that although Lil can indeed recite Shakespeare, she is offering him out of context, without the sanitizing and legitimizing tenets of an accepted framework. Her father's attempt to stop her recitation becomes merely "a distant interruption to the words [which] it was vital to keep reading from the roses." Albion Singer's only alternative is to suppress this language, and in a gesture both comical and suggestive, he takes Lilian's collected Shakespeare and "drowns" the book.

It is important to note that the drowning episode precedes by only a score of pages the father's heinous attack on Lilian's body, a concurrence which suggests just how closely Grenville associates the suppression of private language with the act of rape. Indeed, Albion Singer's attack precipitates Lilian's loss of speech, so that the young woman is unable even to tell her mother of the invasion: "I could not start the sentence that would tell her what had happened. My mouth and tongue were *someone else's now* and even the words that rose into my mind *had nothing to do with me*" (emphasis added). The effect of Albion's attack is related in terms similar to Anne Summers' description of imperial colonization cited earlier, and consolidates strongly the speech/rape metaphor so often described in Grenville's fiction, but in no place as strongly emphasized.

The rape scene marks a turning point in the narrative. Until this point the tone of the work has been light. Although Lilian displayed a dismay with her family and social situation, there has still been a sense of resigned acceptance tinged with hearty humour which mitigated the extent of the oppression. Lilian, one sensed, could never fully be defeated. Following the rape, this strength is put into question. Where once she was a misfit, she is now an inarticulate outcast, incapable even of using the false words of "social phrases" and accepted dialogue: "all the words [she] had ever learned did not seem enough, or the right ones." Lilian can no longer "make the words come" for anyone; not her mother, father, or friends. Even her once protective obesity has become "Too Much Skin," and all physical contact becomes unbearable. Lilian's father has invaded the "shell" of her defences, and she can no longer keep out the world. Her only recourse is to determine a language for herself, and at last the novel begins to focus on the truly positive, truly necessary, processes of self-definition.

Lilian's "recovery" begins with a break from society, a purgative retreat into the Australian "Bush." Here she not only sheds accepted conventions completely (by swimming in the nude, or walking through a town naked), hence rejecting authoritative frameworks, but also she re-educates herself and learns a new language, one tied closely to her Australian landscape, and her colonial roots. Instead of reading the hated "cultivated roses"—symbols of establishment's order—Lilian spends her "hours reading the scribbles on gum-trunks" and is "sometimes within a dream of understanding everything." It is only in the wild, where pro- and prescriptive masculine authority is absent (though not always, even here), that Lilian finally moves toward a personal rebirth. Her return to the city, therefore, is followed by an outright rejection of patriarchal authorities such as her father and the university.

If Lilian's "purgation rite" signals a turn in the text toward personal (and Australian) self-assertion, it is nonetheless merely an indication of *potential*, rather than a description of a *fait accompli*. Grenville continues to stress the danger of the speech/rape threat in two chilling scenes which document masculine power plays to great effect, and emphasize further the correlation between linguistic and physical oppression. It is significant, moreover, that metaphors for such oppression should entail descriptions of Lilian's incarceration by masculine agents.

When Albion Singer realizes that his cowardly attack has been unsuccessful in controlling his daughter, he has her committed to an asylum. Lilian is taken away by "silent smiling men" who crush her "back against the leather of the seat" of the car "leaving [her] no air to speak with." In the institution, Lilian finds herself "locked into [her] lonely self" and is unable to "make anyone hear." Again, self-expression becomes the goal toward which Grenville's protagonist moves, and from which she is restrained. Lilian's earlier triumph in the bush, however, has not been lost; she transforms her thoughts into a linguistic apotheosis of sorts and discovers, in the process, that she is a poet:

> I amazed myself at such times by the way the words poured out of my mouth with such ease, and my mind created them so effortlessly it seemed they had always been there. *I am a great poet . . . I am Shakespeare.*

Lilian's declaration is crucial at this point. Earlier, Shakespeare had continually been a symbol of "otherness," of an external voice which she learned in order to conform. Even her readings in the tree represented a displacement of self rather than an appropriation of her oppressors' language. Here, for the first time, Lilian *becomes* Shakespeare, and reforges his words into a lexicon of self. Lilian's belief that she is Shakespeare is not a delusion, but a fact. She has taken the bard's words and stripped them of their codes and referents and has replaced them with her own systems of codification. Having done so, Lilian no longer trembles before her father's "loud" visits. Rather she sits contentedly and listens as he uses "only loud simple words as if I had lost my vocabulary as well as my mind." Insanity, Grenville suggests through her character, is a register of social expectations, while language is a register of self.

Grenville further stresses the linguistic importance of the confrontation between daughter and father (as well as the extent of Lilian's personal linguistic progress), by having Albion challenge her with fictions of his own creation. Albion's approach, it seems, is through a falsification of the mother's story, one which he has denied completely. He tells Lil that her mother has taken up the study of "*epistemology*" and "*is becoming fluent in Swahili.*" While Father creates "more and more outlandish details," trying to regain his power and position as story-teller, Lilian silently makes up her "own versions of Mother," suggesting, perhaps, the retaking of female experience by women, and also attesting to Lilian's growth as a story-teller in her own right. Shortly after this, Aunt Kitty and Lilian succeed in defeating Albion, and Lilian emerges from the institution.

The idea of the speech-assault as a sexual attack is reinforced in a second incarceration scene, one added by Grenville for the American edition of *Lilian's Story*. The scene begins with Lilian's arrest for causing a disturbance, and plays on many earlier leitmotifs already mentioned. As she is placed in the police wagon, for example, she is described as "suffocated," a metaphor for institutional oppression which not only surrounds its victims with "poisonous air" but also robs one totally of name and identity. For instance, it is not until Lilian is released from the van that she "remembered who [she] was." Even the taking of statistical information is rendered in terms which make it sound uncomfortably like a physical attack, an imposition of the masculine over the feminine will (the policemen, after all, are men). Lilian's first "instinct" when asked her name and height is "to clutch at my particulars and not let him have them." But she is quickly coerced into yielding them. The policeman's moving finger across the arrest record ("His finger ran down the form again") connotes fondling, an idea that is reinforced by the multiple references to the man's "pocked-looking" tongue. The degrading nature of the experience is also clearly stressed:

> The . . . policeman . . . made a great show then of leaning over the counter to look me up and down and said, *Well, Harry, what kind of build is it would you say, I would say build stout, eh.* They all laughed, and I wanted to shrink in shame, and I was beginning to loathe these men, who were . . . taunting me and loving it.

The only way Lilian can reassert her hold on herself is to retrieve possession of her physical self. In the moment after her police photo has been taken, when the policeman has relaxed his grip, Lilian turns her back on the men and lifts her "old black skirt" and "confronts" them with "the fact of my large bottom." The choice of words is interesting. Her display is a "fact" and a "confrontation." Robbed of the power of taking—of controlling—the men are reduced to silence. Lil's act does not abase or deny her; rather it demonstrates clearly that it is she who controls herself, that it is she who commands her body, her own private space. As soon as the policemen lose this control they no longer enjoy themselves: "there was no leering and no mockery . . . I had wiped the laughter off their faces, and taken back the centre." Lil describes her victory in linguistic terms; she has muted them, "having silenced them and proved my power." If there was ever any doubt that Grenville uses power and speech concomitantly, this new chapter certainly lays these to rest. The court scene, where words "bounce in front" of her, and the prison, where she is again robbed of her voice, are but temporary holds. Once she leaves the prison, "some of [her] being and voice returned," a comment which echoes Lil's earlier statement after she left the asylum. In that case, internment caused her temporarily to "mislay" her words. This time, speech is recovered more quickly, perhaps because she has recognized the centre, and is intent on reclaiming it for herself.

Before approaching a conclusion it is important to examine a final aspect of Grenville's oppression metaphor. It is useful to look at the imperial/colonial dialectic which is most in evidence in the Miss Vine passage of *Lilian's Story,* and which makes clear the connection between the various types of oppression described earlier in the paper.

The first suggestion that there is a parallel between personal and societal imperialism is found in the fact that Lilian and white Australia are born at the same time: "It was a wild night in the year of Federation that the birth took place." The parallel birth raises the possibility that each is, in fact, a colony, which implicitly suggests the presence of an imperial control. The theme is developed more extensively in a passage entitled "Long To Reign Over Us" where Grenville uses the British Loyalist teacher to comment on British attitudes toward Australia, as well as to underscore the importance of the story-teller's position in the creation, or destruction, of personal identity. Miss Vine's crucial position as speaker—as story-teller—empowers her not only to describe history, but also to rewrite it when it does not suit the desired British model: "Joan of Arc was hurried over in the history book, being against the English, and Boadicea was just a witch in woad." Grenville's cynical and unflattering depiction of Miss Vine reflects her own suspicion of historians and of their role

in falsifying the picture dishonestly by "embed[ding] an attitude . . . deeply but pretend[ing] not to." (pp. 73-9)

Miss Vine, in *Lilian's Story,* values everything which reinforces a notion of "there"; after all, she is from Kent and makes a point of saying that she hates how Australian birds laugh. But there is more than this. She is comfortable with the part of British history which can be objectified and discussed independently of the self, particularly when the self is rooted in Australia: "She was on steadier ground with Henry [the Eighth]. *A man of enormous vitality and eccentric tastes,* she read from the books. . . . *He married six times.*" When it comes to history which forces reflection on the self, Miss Vine is less comfortable. Queen Elizabeth's celibacy touched too closely on Miss Vine's awareness of her own unmarried state, and her ability—and willingness—to answer questions about her is limited.

English history, moreover, becomes a way of condemning or denying Australia: "She was pleased to explain just why *the sun never sets on the British Empire.* . . . But she did not wish to *hold up the whole class* for questions such as mine." Lilian's questions are concerned with the present—with "here"—or with those practical details which make realistic and approachable the earlier, imperial tales. Lilian wants to know where bathrooms were invented, what King Arthur died of "*exactly,*" and why words do not mirror precisely their apparent meaning ("*Why is it called suffrage, Miss Vine? Does it hurt?*"). Henry the Eighth . . . represents those exterior artefacts which deny the value of local artefacts, of local history. Placed in the hands of the authority figure, the view of "there" subsumes the possibility and viability of "here" by denying the latter's traditions, and by refusing it expression. When Lilian draws the Lady of the Lake according to an Australian model—"as a portrait of Miss Gash"—the teacher is scathing in her condemnation: "*I said to use your imagination, Lilian, I did not say to use your sense of humour.*" One can use the old world to interpret and rewrite the new, this seems to suggest, but never the opposite.

That Lilian herself recognizes the connection between Australian independence and her own is suggested much later in *Lilian's Story.* Seated in a theatre, Lilian decides to assert herself; she begins "to love defiance and being the centre of almost any kind of attention . . . I belonged to myself then." Her act of defiance, it turns out, is to refuse to stand for the British National Anthem: "If it had not been someone else's National Anthem playing when the red plush curtain jerked apart, I might not have minded, but I did not fancy foreign bombast." Naturally, she is chastised by an old man, a representation of patriarchal, British imperialist values: "*The Anthem, young lady,*" he calls and then, "*Show some respect, girlie.*" The noun he chooses suggests the same disparaging masculine regard for women that the British representatives display toward the colonies. Later, the race motif is unequivocally recalled through Lilian's father's wartime activities and his comment "*you are an example of the degeneracy of the white races. . . . You are sterile and degenerate.*" Grenville never lets the reader forget that the discrimination she has targeted as masculine chauvinism is comparable with racism and imperial arrogance of all kinds. (pp. 79-80)

Grenville has gone to great pains to end [*Lilian's Story*] on a positive note. This fact alone is significant. It not only suggests the triumph of the main character's language quest, but also a positive prognostic for individuals and societies; it is a hopeful vision predicted upon the precondition that individuals recognize the need to tell their stories, and that authority figures recognize that the marginalized must "take back the centre."

Grenville's portrayal of the linguistic nature of self-definition and of the imminent threat of "rape" which attends any power relationship, accounts for her insistence on the importance of story-telling (both personal and cultural) as apotheosis. It is, in fact, the single most important goal of most of her characters. In *Lilian's Story,* for example, the hermit "witch"—Miss Gash—writes songs "about her own dramas;" Lilian's mother writes down ferry crossing times in her private diaries, perhaps devising an eventual escape; Lilian's father compiles clippings on misfits and losers, together with facts and figures, in an effort, it seems, to reconcile the world to himself; John Singer's collection of hands is an attempt to create a world in which no one else will be interested, and so leave alone; and Lilian, the grand story writer, begins by composing a tale of tiles, and when this fails, reinvents Shakespeare so that he is indigenously Australian, and irrevocably Lilian. Everyone in *Lilian's Story* is intent on telling the tale. It is only when they—women, race, culture, nation—have begun to "take back the centre" and make it themselves, that they can become a part of history, or, more specifically, that they can *rewrite* it to include the excluded. That, no doubt, will be Joan's accomplishment in the forthcoming *Joan Makes History,* and it is certainly Lilian's triumph in *Lilian's Story.* As she herself points out in the vignette called "Fame": "My story was beginning to have a part in the stories of others." But the effort is not a solipsistic one. True linguistic freedom, Grenville suggests, will inspire others, will liberate the suffocated voices. In "Poets Abound," Lilian's recitation frees a Slav taxi driver's "thick phlegmy language" and allows the "Exile" with the "snarled language" to confidently admit, as Lilian had earlier, that *"I am a poet";* and Lilian, though disbelieving him, is "pleased that [her] exam-

ple had inspired him into a flight of invention." It is suggested through such incidents that invention—story-telling—is the only power which will allow transcendence of pain, isolation, suffocation, even death.

That the telling of self is also a cultural metaphor is made clear in the closing pages where Lil and Stroud create a family in the stormwater channel and, in a tentative but inspired way, reinvent the world; that is, they "invented a few hard names for the stars." The renaming process may suggest a return to a prelapsarian, or Ovidian, Golden Age, or to the colonial habit of legitimizing an alien landscape by giving it a familiar name. Here, however, the renaming process means more than this; it is also a way of giving birth to the self. The characters seem to be at a neo-colonial stage, where the imperial labels are discarded and the new land is rewritten according to the story-teller's needs. The rewriting of self into a new world is treated as a colonizing metaphor by Lilian herself, who says, "Like the others of long ago, we who sat on this dark beach had been slowly transported, by the nature of our lives and the choices we had made, to the stern lip of another land. The privilege of the first ones has always been to impose names of their own invention on the new world." As always, the metaphor suggests the importance of an assertion of individual language, not simply in order to rewrite oneself into history ("my name will live"), but also as a check against the ultimate oppression earlier mentioned, which is to have one's story (and story-telling right) removed or appropriated. (pp. 81-2)

Gerry Turcotte, " 'The Ultimate Oppression': Discourse Politics in Kate Grenville's Fiction," in World Literature Written in English, *Vol. 29, No. 1, Spring, 1989, pp. 64-85.*

Joe Haldeman

1943-

(Born Joseph William Haldeman; has also written under pseudonym Robert Graham) American novelist, short story writer, and editor.

One of the most acclaimed authors of speculative science fiction to have emerged during the 1970s, Haldeman usually addresses such themes as war, guilt, the inevitability of fate, and the necessity of maintaining a strict moral code in opposition to humanity's predominant amorality. Writing in a terse, crafted style, Haldeman generally sets his works in near-future societies and centers on characters who attain self-awareness as a result of their moral opposition to the corrupt and uncaring systems they purportedly represent. According to Algis Budrys, "Joe Haldeman exemplifies all that is best about the new science fiction writers. . . . [He] is educated in hard science yet very much aware of the liberal arts academe, and equipped with considerable storytelling powers in addition to an ability to create dramatic ideas."

Haldeman received a bachelor of science degree in physics and astronomy from the University of Maryland in 1967. Drafted into the United States Army the same year, Haldeman served as a combat engineer in the central highlands of Vietnam but was severely wounded in combat and received an honorable discharge in 1969. He later attended the University of Iowa, where he received his Masters of Fine Arts in English, and devoted himself to full-time writing after attending the Milford writers' conferences conducted by Damon Knight in the early 1970s. Haldeman described his first novel, *War Years,* as "a fictionally-extended version of my own combat diary," maintaining that "the main reason for writing it was to set down as accurately as possible the details of that experience." While atypical of his ensuing work in its lack of science fiction elements, the book achieved moderate critical success.

Haldeman attained widespread popular and critical recognition for his first science fiction novel, *The Forever War,* for which he received both a Hugo Award from the World Science Fiction Convention and a Nebula Award from the Science Fiction Writers of America. Although the novel initially attracted scant critical attention, *The Forever War* eventually emerged as Haldeman's most frequently debated work. In many ways a parable of the American government's involvement in Vietnam, *The Forever War* revolves around a near-future society manipulated by its military-industrial complex into declaring war on the Taurans, a distant race of alien telepaths. The novel's protagonist, William Mandella, is sent with his platoon into enemy territory, where plans to capture a single alien for medical experiments result in the accidental slaughter of many innocent Taurans. Tortured by guilt, Mandella and his lover, a female soldier, are transported around the universe on various missions while aging at a very slow rate. After two years of elapsed time they return to Earth, where twenty-six years have passed. Their sense of culture shock is compounded when they learn that two-thirds of the world's population is unemployed by choice and one-third has become homosexual to cope with the moral dilemma of overpopulation. Rejected by society as a violent misfit, Man-

della fights for several hundred more years. As the novel concludes, humanity is developed into a race of clones capable of reconciling their differences with the Taurans, an essentially harmless race, by means of telepathy.

Haldeman's next science fiction novel, *Mindbridge,* juxtaposes third-person narration with excerpts from such sources as diaries, newspapers, and government reports to depict two "Tamers" who ascertain whether certain alien planets are suitable for colonization. After discovering a creature resembling a sea urchin that is capable of imparting its telepathic abilities, the pair avert misunderstandings with an aggressive race of alien beings by means of telepathy. Haldeman's next novel, *All My Sins Remembered,* focuses on the theme of guilt in its portrayal of Otto McGavin, a member of a futuristic spy network in a predominantly Spanish-speaking galaxy, who suffers from having committed over forty assassinations, supposedly to preserve the galaxy's "Charter of Confederación." Haldeman's first short fiction collection, *Infinite Dreams,* contains the story "Tricentennial," for which Haldeman received a Hugo Award. In this tale, Haldeman offers a dystopian view of the United States on the 3000th anniversary of its Independence. Although critics agree that Haldeman's short stories are generally less effective than his novels, Joan Gordon commented of Haldeman's next collection, *Dealing*

168

in Futures: "[If] any criticism can be levelled against his writing it is that the craft is so meticulous, the telling so compact, that the reader wishes for a little sloppy expansion once in a while."

Haldeman's next major novel, *Worlds: A Novel of the Near Future,* combines the ordinary and the fantastic in its depiction of the year 2084, when the world has been ravaged by conventional and bacteriological warfare and revolution is imminent. This novel is related from the perspective of Marianne O'Hara, a promiscuous student of political science from a colony within a hollowed, orbiting asteroid known as New New York, who visits Earth to study political science. As World War III commences, Marianne becomes involved with a radical group. Algis Budrys commented: "What I brought away mostly from *Worlds* was a sense of contact with literacy and, of all rare things, mercy." In the novel's sequel, *Worlds Apart: A Novel of the Near Future,* Marianne helps refugees from the war on Earth to relocate in New New York and attempts to locate a lover from the previous novel. Her lover is living in a region dominated by the Mansonites, young people condemned to short lives by a deadly plague, who have formed a cult around the historical figure of Charles Manson.

Haldeman's later novels explore the effects of revolutionary inventions upon humanity. In *Tool of the Trade,* he combines espionage and science fiction to portray a professor of psychology who spies for the Soviet secret police. After discovering a mind-controlling device, the professor attempts to save the world from disaster. Although the novel's ending was faulted by some critics as predictable or unconvincing, several praised Haldeman's portrayal of the book's title character. *Buying Time* concerns a life-extending procedure known as the Stileman process by which human beings may attain immortality providing they pay one million pounds, renounce their possessions at the time of each renewal, and repeat the treatment every ten to twelve years. The novel largely revolves around the attempted assassination of a new candidate, who resists an elite group of "immortals" seeking control of the world and the Stileman process.

In addition to his science fiction novels, Haldeman has also written the adventure novels *Attar's Revenge* and *War of Nerves* under the pseudonym Robert Graham. His novels *Planet of Judgment* and *World without End* employ characters from the popular television series "Star Trek." A former editor of *Astronomy* magazine, Haldeman has also edited several anthologies of science fiction stories, including *Study War No More* (1977), *Body Armor: 2000* (1986), and *Supertanks* (1987).

(See also *Contemporary Authors,* Vols. 53-56; *Contemporary Authors New Revision Series,* Vol. 6; and *Dictionary of Literary Biography,* Vol. 8.)

PRINCIPAL WORKS

NOVELS

War Year 1972; revised, 1977
The Forever War 1974
Attar's Revenge [under the pseudonym Robert Graham] 1975
War of Nerves [under the pseudonym Robert Graham] 1975
Mindbridge 1976

All My Sins Remembered 1977
Planet of Judgment 1977
World without End 1979
Worlds: A Novel of the Near Future 1981
Worlds Apart: A Novel of the Near Future 1983
There Is No Darkness [with Jack Haldeman] 1983
Tool of the Trade 1987
Buying Time 1989

SHORT FICTION COLLECTIONS

Infinite Dreams 1978
Dealing in Futures 1985

GEORGE DAVIS

Military tacticians know that very young men make very good foot soldiers. Nations as different as China and Israel know that their national survival may depend on how well they persuade their children to accept a romantic-heroic view of death. One wonders how many German children would have marched off to war if so much of German literature had not softened them up for it; or how many Japanese youths would have volunteered for kamikaze raids if their childhoods had not been so full of the folklore of heroism. . . .

It is hard to tell why *War Year* is being marketed as a children's book, unless this is a way of excusing shortcomings that are really not too great. The book contains an excellent description of the day-to-day life of a grunt in Vietnam. It is a hard, realistic piece of writing, full of more "dirty" words than most mothers would want their 12-year-olds to read. Haldeman seems to believe that the first step toward destroying innocence . . . is to destroy the innocence of language.

War Year follows 19-year-old John Farmer through his full tour, from the first enemy attack until he is twice wounded but home safe in Oklahoma facing an uncertain future. It reads like a G.I. diary: this is its strength and may be regarded as its chief weakness, for there is no sense of growing involvement with a developing story. We are drawn forward by our desire for details of the ground war in the Central Highlands, where the VC attacks and vanishes without a trace into the jungle.

We learn from *War Year* how it feels to dig trenches in 130-degree heat, and to march in undergrowth so thick it could hide an ambush as close as five feet away. We learn what real combat death is like: its odor is sickly-sweet, the body begins to rot in less than an hour, the hands and face discolor, the uniform swells like a balloon, the eyes and mouth are often open and full of ants—and the skin is cold and soggy to the engineers on burial detail.

> *George Davis, in a review of "War Year," in The New York Times Book Review, May 21, 1972, p. 8.*

BERNARD BERGONZI

[Two] rewarding and accomplished novels are James Park Sloan's *War Games* and Joe W. Haldeman's *War Year.* They have obvious things in common; they are both brief first-person narratives, with similarly terse titles. But in other respects they are interestingly contrasted: a powerfully direct narrative thrust in Haldeman as against obliquity and irony in Sloan. Haldeman tells the story of a nineteen-year-old Oklahoman's one-year tour of duty in Vietnam serving in the engineers; he sees a good deal of action, is twice wounded and survives. Two of his buddies are not so lucky. Hemingway looks like Mr. Haldeman's most obvious model, and that influence becomes too overt at the very end when the narrator, John Farmer, decides not to write to his dead friend's parents:

> I smoked a couple of cigarettes and then felt ashamed and got the letter out of the wastepaper basket and smoothed it out and put it in a safe place. But what I could tell them wouldn't help, them or me, so I never answered the letter and I told myself that New York was too far away to visit.

But mostly the narrative carries absolute conviction in its own terms; Mr. Haldeman catches the way serving soldiers talk and move and respond to each other with a fidelity that is harsh but never inhumane. There is something paradoxical in trying to use a word like "beautiful" of a text where there is so much blood and obscenity, but it somehow seems appropriate. (p. 87)

> Bernard Bergonzi, "Vietnam Novels: First Draft," in Commonweal, Vol. XCVII, No. 4, October 27, 1972, pp. 84-8.

MARTIN LEVIN

The technology involved in [the interplanetary campaign described in **The Forever War**] is so sophisticated that the book might well have been accompanied by an operator's manual. But then, all the futuristic mayhem is plugged into human situations that help keep the extraterrestrial activity on a warm and even witty plane. Earthlings are at war with inhabitants of the planet Aldebaran, and our attention is directed to one William Mandella, an infantryman guarding a distant collapsar on a remote planet. In the 700 years that the war lasts, Mandella rises from private to major. He also ages about two years, a quirk of the space-time factor that someone has to explain to me someday. Anyhow, while the earth soldiers and the space creatures are decimating one another's ranks with everything from spears to lasers, things are changing back home. Mr. Haldeman compresses atavism and irony into a vastly entertaining trip. (pp. 33-4)

> Martin Levin, in a review of "The Forever War," in The New York Times Book Review, March 23, 1975, pp. 33-4.

JOE HALDEMAN [INTERVIEW WITH DARRELL SCHWEITZER]

[Schweitzer]: *Was* **The Forever War** *in any way a response to* [Robert Heinlein's novel] Starship Troopers?

[Haldeman]: No. That's interesting . . . I got seventy pages into it before somebody pointed out that I had stolen plot, all of the characters, all of the hardware from *Starship Troopers.* It hadn't occurred to me. I was writing what I considered to be a science fiction extension of my own Vietnam novel, and it turned out to follow the form of *Starship Troopers,* at least the first half, very closely.

Were you aware of Starship Troopers *at this time? Had you read it?*

Oh, I'd read it three or four times. I was not thinking of it while I was writing my own book, though.

I gather that your attitudes are the opposite of Heinlein's, since your novel isn't a glorification of war.

Well, I wouldn't be so simplistic about it. I have little enough sympathy for the attitude expressed in *Starship Troopers,* and I'm not sure Heinlein would be a hundred percent sympathetic with it either. Heinlein expressed a reasonable way to fight a certain kind of war with a certain kind of population backing it, and I did the same sort of thing. I think that my type of population is closer to what I see as a 1970's reality, and his is closer to what he sees as a 1940's reality. I don't think that the population of today would support the army going out for a *Starship Troopers* kind of war, not without a lot of conditioning.

What do you mean—the population wouldn't support it?

What makes a war? Taxes. You need money to fight it, and Heinlein had everyone essentially all behind it. Now, they grumble and growl, especially if they aren't veterans, but they do pay their taxes to keep the soldiers in the field. What I had was a population that didn't know any better and was led by the nose.

Isn't that the way it always is?

Not to that extent. I tried to make a case for projected Madison Avenue techniques taking over the government, and they were able to program people to support a total war, just to not question at all.

Well, you have a war, which seems to me at least in the outset to be justifiable.

Well, it would be justifiable if it were on Earth, but not when you consider the tremendous expense involved. In reality, if the Taurans had attacked 400 light-years away, most likely the voters would say, "Well, we won't go there anymore. We'll go someplace else."

How do you know they're not going to attack somewhere else?

Well, I tried to build that into the book, that you can't really tell where someone came from when he pops out of a collapsar, so they couldn't just trace your track back, and find your home planet, and attack it. They always had the alternative of retreating, and they never chose to use it.

Do you think that an interstellar war would ever be really practical?

No. Wars are fought for economic reasons, and it's been demonstrated adequately, at least to me, that it costs too much to move products from star to star, even with the ideal star drive. There wouldn't be a reason for fighting a war. The only thing you could exchange is information.

Meaning you could not pull a profit?

Right.

How about fighting over a planet?

Who would we be fighting against?

Somebody else who wants the same planet.

Who is 'else'? There are lots of planets, theoretically, and I don't see it. You just move on to another planet.

What about consideration of distance? Suppose the ideal colonizable planet is relatively close, and somebody else wants it? Can you actually envision any of this happening?

I can't really. The thing is, an interstellar endeavor in the first place involves so much money and so much energy that it would almost have to be international, and the idea of saying this planet is American or this planet is French, or Russian, or Spanish, or Chinese, or something is absurd, because no single country has enough money to do that sort of thing. And I think we're sophisticated enough now, at least in that piece of the pie, that no single country would try to colonize another planet. (p. 26)

Well, since way back when, whenever an explorer comes to a new place he plants his country's flag and claims it. Was the New World any farther away or harder to get to in the Sixteenth Century than another planet would be in the future?

Oh, it was a lot closer. All they really had to do was get enough food for three or four ships, and enough clowns they could knock on the head and put on the ship to sail it, and follow the winds. No, it was not that great an investment in terms of gross national product, whereas to get to another star, unless we find some way whereby you can stand on a magic square and go there, is too large an investment.

In **The Forever War** *you are postulating relatively cheap star travel.*

In fact I say that it costs less to send a hundred people to another star than it costs to send three clowns to the moon. I had to do that to make a war possible.

Doesn't this mean that when the war is possible the economic reasons all start to fall into place and work?

Yes, but I used pseudo-science. There is no way that you can get to another star without expending the energy. I had to do that to make it all possible. But science didn't generate the story; the story generated the pseudo-science.

As it traditionally does. I've heard Ben Bova talking about the idea of using black holes as tunnels through space.

Yeah, you know I discovered that, and I mean "discovered" in big strong quotes, before the first paper came out about it, because I needed it for my story, and I guess about twelve months after I wrote the story this guy from Yeshiva University came out in *Science,* and said "Well, black holes will make worm holes through space-time, and perhaps we can go from star to star that way."

I don't see how you can do it without getting squashed to a few random molecules by the gravity involved.

That's a thing I tried to bring out in **The Forever War.** You have a question, "How does this work?" and everybody says, "I don't know." The thing is the tidal forces. When you're close to the event horizon of a black hole, the difference between the forces at the front of your ship and the tail of your ship is so great that there is no material that can stand that kind of a torsion, and it would simply wrench itself apart. And everybody in **The Forever War** says, "Well, I wonder how it does that?" "I don't know, but it does it." (pp. 26-7)

[It seems that scientists] all read science fiction and come up with these things to order.

They come up with things, and so many science fiction writers are writing and making so many shotgun predictions that every once in a while one comes true. . . .

How do your Vietnam experiences go into this?

Not directly. In the first part of **The Forever War** I was trying to do a parallel with the American involvement in Vietnam, and then the story took over, and just went its own way. But oddly enough, a reader in India got in touch with me and showed me chapter and verse how the *last half* of the book followed American involvement. I had written it before we had quit the war, and the whole thing followed in a metaphorical way. Well, he was right, and I was simply drawing on the only war that I have experienced, and so that was my psychological background for the thing and I subconsciously followed it. But I stopped doing it consciously after the first fifty pages or so.

Were you in combat?

Oh, yeah.

I notice it reads like Vietnam in a few places. The first planet they land on is swampy. Was that deliberate or did it just come out that way?

I wanted to make it the usual army fuckup. That is, that they had spent years training to land on an icy ball of rock, and the first planet they get to is not at all like that. And here they are all prepared to fight on this cryogenic nightmare, and instead it's sort of a subtropical jungle. They're walking around in their suits and they'd be better off with an air mask. . . .

Why did you start writing science fiction?

Oh, for the same reason most people do. It was what I had always read for pleasure and I felt I knew it. You know, perhaps interestingly, I didn't feel like I could write science fiction when I started writing, and so I wrote maybe four or five mystery stories, and they didn't work at all. None of them were any good, just coming back with rejection slips. Then finally I screwed my courage to the stick and wrote some science fiction. I took a creative writing course at the University of Maryland, and I wrote three science fiction stories and *sold* two of them, so I knew I could do it. (p. 27)

Did you have any intent to write any type of science fiction, then, in reference to the "new wave" controversy that was going on then?

No, I just write what I would like to read, and some of it is fairly new wave. My next novel, **Mindbridge,** is not a straight story at all, although it can be read as a straight story if somebody just wants to be entertained. I think that's the first function. I am an entertainer, like a tap dancer, and if I don't do that I'm failing somewhere.

Do you see the writer as artist or as paid entertainer?

I don't see the two roles as irreconcilable. If you're a good enough craftsman you can be both an entertainer and an artist. Rembrandt's paintings, for example, are tremendously interesting to look at. There's a Rembrandt right here at the National Gallery; I could spend hours looking at it. Now I don't know painting from shit, but the people are there and the stories are written in their faces. When he was doing that, he was telling a story, and he did it beautifully. I know if I were a painter I could go through and analyze the pigments and the positions he put the people in, and everything like that. You can work at both levels. I don't see that there's any kind of contradiction at all. In fact I think quite the opposite. I read so much *dumb* stuff. Now I have a Master's degree in English, and I'm not a stranger to "new wave" writing. In fact "new wave" in science fiction writing is half a century behind the avant garde in American literature.

What does the term "new wave" mean to you? No two people define it the same.

"New wave" to me means incomprehensible arty writing, and the people who can do it well come over into my camp.

When they're not incomprehensible—

Oh no, no. The thing is, the new wave was good because the old-liners adapted the techniques of the young turks, and the young turks got the entertainment values from the oldtimers, and now, of course, it has all levelled out, and the field itself has benefited tremendously from it. The thing is you can sit down and write a science fiction novel with your toes. You just have to have a neat story. You can dictate the fucking thing and sell it. And people have been doing that—you know there are some people who have been in the field for forty years, who have done nothing else. And now come the young turks, the new wave, whatever you want to call it, who say, wait, wait, it makes a difference how you put the words together. It makes a difference in the rhythm. A novel is not simply saying how wonderful it is up here in the future. A novel has to have human characters. And so they started thinking seriously and you've got—Oh, Jesus, Bob Silverberg suddenly started becoming a novelist instead of a craftsman. . . . (pp. 27-8)

What are your writing methods like?

Oh mechanically, they're fairly gonzo. I get up at three in the morning and I run a mile, get some exercise, and I take a shower, hot, as hot as I can stand it, then gulp down a half a quart of orange juice, and brew some Expresso coffee, the strongest I can take, because I find that I can't sit and drink coffee all day long. That's bad for me. I pour myself about four cups of this and chug it down while reading the paper, yesterday's paper it turns out, because we don't get it early enough and I don't get time to read it otherwise, and I get hyper and up and everything, and I go to the typewriter and I sit there and either write or stare at it for six or seven hours. When my wife gets up I quit work. (p. 29)

Do your ideas come to you consciously, or do they just creep in from the back of your head somewhere?

They percolate out. I never sit around thinking, "What will I write?" Gordy Dickson turned me on to a great process. You know, when you've finished a story or a book, when you sit down at the typewriter the next morning, rather than sit or bitch, "What am I going to do?" you start typing, anything, random letters, words, whatever, just keep typing, make yourself not take your hands off the keys. Keep typing, keep typing, and out of boredom you start to get a story. I've never had to type more than a half a page single-spaced before a story starts, and by the time I've reached the end of my legal-sized paper I have half the story outlined. Then I just sit down and write it. It's a magic, magic thing if you can actually get into it.

Can you actually get a good story that way?

Yeah. Almost everything I've written that way has worked. . . .

Do you find it destructive to talk about a story before you write it?

Yeah. In fact I almost killed my next novel that way. I was sitting down with a bunch of young writers. We had a workshop situation and I was hyper, and we went downstairs to the local beer parlor and sat. For four hours I talked. You know you can't shut up a writer once he starts. And I gave them chapter and verse, things I hadn't even thought of, about the novel I was planning to do. I gave them the whole plot from the first chapter to the last, and they would ask me questions and I would answer them and things like that, and I got home and I thought, "Shit, I don't have to write this anymore." Essentially what's happening is I have to write a whole other novel. I just blew ten thousand dollars in one afternoon.

Why do you think it works that way?

It works that way, I think pretty precisely because you have to keep surprising yourself. If you know what you're going to do, it's not fun. (p. 30)

Joe Haldeman and Darrell Schweitzer, in an interview in Science Fiction Review, *Vol. 6, No. 1, February, 1977, pp. 26-30.*

GERALD JONAS

[As evidenced by his novel *Mindbridge,* Haldeman] writes of faster-than-light travel and shape-changing aliens. But for all his technical expertise—Haldeman is editor in chief of *Astronomy* magazine—his book leaves no clear image in the reader's mind. The plot revolves around the discovery on some distant planet of a telepathic but deadly creature that turns out to be the key to a brighter future for mankind. The writing is as up-to-date as yesterday's press release; interspersed between chapters of third-person narration are excerpts from diaries, newspapers, government reports, fictitious reference books, and so on.

Haldeman knows exactly what he is doing. The disjointed chronology, the fragmented style, the brittle persona of the principal character serve to distance the reader from the action. Apparently, Haldeman is afraid that if the reader catches a glimpse of the narrative machinery at work the game is up. Such fears have a way of becoming self-fulfilling prophecies. (pp. 24-5)

Gerald Jones, in a review of "Mindbridge," in The New York Times Book Review, *February 27, 1977, pp. 24-5.*

ALGIS BUDRYS

Joe Haldeman exemplifies all that is best about the new science fiction writers. Two steps beyond Dickson's generation, one beyond Niven's, he is educated in hard science yet very much aware of liberal arts academe, and equipped with considerable storytelling powers in addition to an ability to create dramatic ideas. That is not to say he's slicker and quicker than the Old Breed, whatever that is, but that even when he's mediocre he has a broad selection of resources to carry him over the doldrums.

Mindbridge follows on *The Forever War,* which established Haldeman's reputation in a flurry of critical acclaim and the Nebula award. In retrospect, *Forever War* had only one major extrapolative idea—war across Einsteinian distances at time-bending speeds—and the rest was good writing about human nature perceptively observed. The idea was not totally original with Haldeman, by a long jump, but his making a central theme of it was new enough.

In contrast, *Mindbridge* has two central ideas, of which the first is totally original as far as I can determine; I was sorry to see it turn into a minor gimmick in support of the second. And not only does *Mindbridge* have two—no, come to think of it, somewhere near three—central ideas, it also has a pyrotechnical narrative technique. The result is less, not more, for all that it is an interesting less.

The not-quite idea is interstellar travel by The Levant-Meyer Translation, an effect discovered very early in the 21st century when a freak electrical discharge happened to hit an electron microscope focused on a crystal of calcium bromide. . . . The L-M Translation enables Earth to send suitably armored exploration teams to stars within a spherical area beginning about 10 light years from Earth and ending at 115 light years, the distance of Achernar. Objects picked up on these expeditions return ("slingshot") to their native places, without announcement, let, or hindrance, after a time, and Terrestrial objects taken to alien locations do the same. . . . This latter feature is a legitimate extrapolation of the original premise here, which is no wilder than the one Isaac Asimov used to get the little tailor from today's Earth to that of the Galactic Empire. (pp. 39-40)

The idea this leads us to . . . is Class A. The expedition to Groombridge 1618's second planet doesn't find much except mud and scrub, but it does come up with a small aquatic creature which, *when* touched by any two people, enables them to read each other's minds.

The creature has no plans or purposes of its own; it is simply a bridge, and is utterly passive. It does kill anyone who attempts to harm it, and it kills the first person to touch it. It kills them with a speed that varies inversely with their natural teleperceptive talent, and it is effective as a bridge in direct relation to the order in which various individuals have touched it, weighted by their natural teleperceptive talent. In order for the bridge to become useful, it must first be touched by someone for the valid suicide permit, and then touched by the two persons who are going to use it . . . before it slingshots back, of course. And it is, as you can see, not a Sirius bridge; it is a Groombridge bridge. And it turns out, as noted, that the author's only real use for it in the story is to use it as a translation device when we encounter a truly vicious race of intellectually superior shape-changers.

So now we have two ideas which began clearly, showed immense dramatic possibilities, and were quickly foundered by auctorial second-thoughts, footnotes, loophole clauses, and elaborates which turn out to be hog-ties. Any attempt to develop them is thrown aside when it comes time to deal out the essentially dull old idea that we shall encounter an alien race which has no regard for us, is possessed of incredible cruelty, and moves with numbing swiftness to the attack. Too late—far too late—it turns out that this is not so. They're a wise old race that we've misunderstood, and which has per-

haps misunderstood us. But this twist on the idea, and a lame twist it is, comes after descriptions of physical damages that would sicken a connoisseur of packing plants. I can see what Haldeman intended, and its essential worth. I cannot see that he had his narrative under sufficient control to pull it off.

What *Mindbridge* is is a second novel, (third, but his first was non-SF, and apparently autobiographical) and the number of good second novels in this field is quite small, especially when the first was well-received. There's a lot of pressure to be more inventive, more innovative, more "well-rounded" with one's talent; there is the search for one's limits, which of course goes on forever, but in the sophomore writer it tends toward a ringing denial of limits.

All to the good, really, in the long run. Haldeman we shall have with us for a nice long time, and grateful for it. One feature of *Mindbridge* stands out as a sign of great hope, and that is how well Haldeman has worked with the essentially clumsy pastiche technique. There is little straight narrative; we are given the contents of file folders, statistical summaries, historical anecdotes, bills of lading, etc., from which the narrative emerges. There are thus 53 chapters in this 186-page book. Thank God, two of them, entitled "Crystal Ball," exist to tie up such loose ends as the (completely irrelevant) reason for the existence of the bridges, and the (dramatically sterile) outcome of our contact with the L'vrai. If they didn't, these questions could never be answered. But with the rest of it, Haldeman has cobbled up a tense, reasonably consecutive, and often engagingly witty means of telling a story that would look much worse if laid out in a straight line. That's resourcefulness, and I am not being a wiseacre when I cite it, and appreciate it. (pp. 40-1)

Algis Budrys, in a review of "Mindbridge," in The Magazine of Fantasy and Science Fiction, *Vol. 52, No. 4, April, 1977, pp. 39-41.*

T. A. SHIPPEY

Joe Haldeman's *Mindbridge* is almost homely in scale, following in essence the well-established pattern of the "Heinlein juvenile". An accident has given mankind a method of star-travel, a complex kind of emigration has started, but each new world has to be explored by the "Tamers"—and on one of these the elite of humanity come up against something they (literally) can't handle, a telepathy-inducing animal with an unbreachable capacity for self-defence.

The problems *it* creates tangle with those of star-travel itself and with the race of apparently murderous and invincible aliens who come barrelling into the middle of it all. But Haldeman has added one thing to the format, which is that he tells the story from many tangents and angles, filling the pages with carefully artless reports and letters and TV scripts and movement orders. It is a good hard-boiled way of telling a story about survival ethics, and the hero's background is well calculated as well: he is a kind of Edmund Gosse to his father's Philip—for his father had proved star-travel was impossible, as indeed anyone with the slightest streak of pessimism would agree. But science-fiction writers are optimists very nearly to a man, even in Hell, on uninhabitable Earth, or about to be swallowed by interstellar wolves.

T. A. Shippey, "Into Hell and Out Again," in The Times Literary Supplement, *No. 3930, July 8, 1977, p. 820.*

LEW WOLKOFF

[In *Infinite Dreams*], Haldeman has taken a dozen of his short stories and prefaced each with a brief essay on how it came to be. A story, as he shows, may have many sources. An editor suggests an idea that combines with something the writer has read or is interested in. The writer may experiment in short story form with a technique for later use in a longer work, or he may mimic another author's style. Finally, he may just write a story for his own amusement or for catharsis. There are stories in this collection for each of these reasons. In fact, Haldeman lists some *eighteen* reasons in the Afterword.

The essays also tell something of the man; his fear as a beginner facing a session of tough literary criticism, his writing habits, and his delight in just "goofing off" in libraries. There is also his recipe for perfect bacon. (Cook it when nude. You keep the heat down so it doesn't splatter, and it never burns.)

Oh, yes. Sandwiched between the essays are a dozen fine stories. Haldeman's range is wide. He moves easily from deep space in the Hugo-winning **"Tricentennial"** to within the human mind in **"A Mind of His Own;"** from the broad humor of **"The Mazel Tov Revolution"** to the supernatural terror of **"Armaja Das."**

For the stories, or the essays, or both, it is well worth reading. (p. 33)

Lew Wolkoff, in a review of "Infinite Dreams," in Best Sellers, Vol. 39, No. 1, April, 1979, pp. 32-3.

ALGIS BUDRYS

For admirers of the short story, I can do no better than to recommend Joe Haldeman's **Infinite Dreams.** Witty, graceful, often stinging, the pieces collected here are from the major media for short-length SF, including this magazine. They include such tricky constructs as **"Counterpoint"** and **"Juryrigged,"** some good funny things like **"All the Universe in a Mason Jar,"** and some creatively nasty thinking as in **"To Howard Hughes: A Modest Proposal,"** which I assume the gentleman in question did not take up.

Haldeman could still, at this comparatively advanced date since his debut, go in almost any direction within the SF pantheon. Nor is it automatically and necessarily true that the needs of SF readers would be best served if all SF writers were heavyweights. Furthermore, none of us can fairly be asked to become something other than what we might be. Still and all, it's comforting to know that the cadre of impressive talent among younger writers is not diminishing, and to think that people like Haldeman will be around for a long time to set high standards.

Whatever, this collection contains excellent, skillful entertainment. What it promises for the future is one thing; there is sufficient worth in what it delivers now. (pp. 28-9)

Algis Budrys, in a review of "Infinite Dreams," in The Magazine of Fantasy and Science Fiction, Vol. 57, No. 3, September, 1979, pp. 28-9.

MERRELL A. KNIGHTEN

Science fiction is a ghetto. It must be, for "everyone" says so, none more often and more vociferously than science-fiction writers themselves. This self-demonstrating verity aside, the hard evidence is everywhere abundant in payment practices, in advertising and publishing policies, and even within the practicing terminology of the students of the field. . . . (p. 167)

What is not so often mentioned—and should be—is that the prison is equally a fortress; ghetto writers, critics, and editors do much to perpetuate the ghetto as a defensive mechanism, and the denizens of the ghetto, with a very few notable exceptions, regard the mainstream, and particularly mainstream criticism, and most particularly academic criticism, with fear and loathing. The evidence of this scorn is likewise abundant, but perhaps an objective correlative will serve. Those familiar with Robert Heinlein's early short story "Coventry" will remember the tale's idealistic, pompous, and thoroughly unlikable protagonist who, exiled from society for his antisocial behavior and battered by his fellow outcasts into a new perception of self, is literally baptized in fire in his desperate attempt to return to society. Achieving rebirth (logically, for Heinlein, in a military hospital), the protagonist emphatically rejects his former occupation, with all its parasitic silliness, in favor of a career in military intelligence. That former occupation, some will remember, was literary criticism.

Heinlein's critical counterpart—within the ghetto—is Richard Geis, creator of *The Alien Critic* [later retitled *Science Fiction Review*] and columnist for *Galaxy* magazine. In a column written in 1974, Geis complained that more and more science fiction is being aimed at the "affected," "arty-farty," "intellectual" academic crowd. In 1975, Geis again objected to the academic study of science fiction: "Science fiction has become a property now, a territory, in academia, and as more teachers and professors stake out their acres and build their fences, science fiction will become another cemetery. . . ."

The vehemence of such objection seems likely to arise in large part from cruel experience. Kingsley Amis noted some years ago that science-fiction writers have good reason to resent mainstream criticism: "A new volume by Pohl or Sheckley or Arthur Clarke ought . . . to be reviewed as general fiction, not tucked away, as one writer put it, in something called 'Spaceman's Realm' between the kiddy section and the dog stories." Instead, as Jack Williamson observed more recently, "The mainstream critics have seldom made much sense about science fiction when they happened to notice it at all. . . ." (pp. 167-68)

[It] seems inevitable that the science-fiction community should face a certain difficulty in self-evaluation, and such has indeed been the case. The ghetto popularity of Joe Haldeman's *The Forever War* offers a convincing demonstration of this failure of judgment. Leonard Isaacs, reviewing the work in *Fantasy and Science Fiction*, finds quite a lot to praise and very little to deplore. Among other things, Isaacs admires the introductory technique, the "gritty realism," the "talent for verisimilitude," and the "near light-speed pace." Isaacs' only complaint is in the upbeat quality of the resolution (?), which even to Mandella, the protagonist, "sounded a little fishy."

A mainstream critic, however, might find more than a few fish in Haldeman's pond. The work has, of course, notable virtues—for instance, the sense of the ridiculous inherent in Mandella's discovery that he and a fellow male are the only heterosexuals on an otherwise gay planet, compounded by the discovery that the other hetero is in actuality an asexual cyborg, who is entirely plastic from the waist down.

Such virtues, however, are more often than not shadowed by the work's faults. The shock introduction Mr. Isaacs so much admires, for instance, is in fact more schlock than shock. "Tonight," says one of Mandella's instructors, "we're going to show you eight silent ways to kill a man." Mandella promptly falls asleep, noting only—in a bored cynicism incongruous with his later repugnance at killing aliens—that some of the techniques are demonstrated on (temporarily) live subjects. More to the point, the triteness of such collar-grabbing demands objection, which Isaacs fails to provide.

In spite of (or perhaps because of) the "light-speed pace," *The Forever War* consistently displays gaps in reasoning, implausible arguments, and papier-mâché motivations. The beginning of the 1,100-year war is blamed, wearily, on no fresher a villain than the military-industrial complex: "You couldn't blame it all on the military. . . . The fact was, Earth's economy needed a war and this one was ideal." Needless to say, this quaint cliché deserves a rest, particularly in a genre that prizes its originality.

Similarly, Mandella's promotion to command of a combat unit on the basis of his real-time years of service and the public relations value thereof, ignoring his recognized pacifism and his incompetence as a leader, deserves question. Admittedly, Mandella's public relations value as the oldest warrior is conceivable; it appears less than logical, then, to place him in command of a combat unit light-years away from the public he is expected to impress.

The ending of the war is even less convincing than its beginning. Returning to base with the battered remnants of his incredibly botched command, Mandella discovers that humanity has "progressed" beyond individuality into the infinitely replicated clone of a descendant of one of Mandella's casualties. Since, as it happily occurs, the enemy was already such a group organism, communications rapidly progressed from the "Me Tarzan, you Jane" stage to universally cloned brotherhood. There is no explanation as to why this communication became possible only after the cloning of mankind. "There were no words for it," Mandella *and the reader* are told, and "my brain wouldn't be able to accommodate the concepts even if there were words." Even Haldeman, perhaps embarrassed by this airy evasion, is moved to say, via Mandella, "It sounded a little fishy. . . ."

And the resolution? There is none, only an ending. The work fails decidedly, then, in its major premise, the pacifistic statement. Given Mandella's firm pacifism, the reader waits endlessly and fruitlessly for the act of rebellion—any act of rebellion—which will remove Mandella from the army's grip or at least deny its power over him. At a midpoint crisis, Mandella is tempted to suicide; instead, even knowing his incompetence, he accepts command of a combat unit and proceeds to make a series of non-decisions and wrong decisions which destroy his troops' faith in him and which cause, as a result of this distrust, a tremendous casualty rate. . . . (pp. 168-70)

Here then is neither growth nor decisive denial, but rather an undecided paralysis of will, a glorification through Mandella's eventual achievement of happiness not of pacifism but of passivity. The ghetto popularity of this work, in particular the fact that the Science Fiction Writers Association awarded it the 1975 Nebula Award for best novel, should be adequate demonstration of the gulf between science-fiction interests and mainstream standards. As Amis puts it, "Science fiction interests do not coincide with those of ordinary fiction,

though on occasion the two sets will overlap very considerably." Amis's theory of *idea as hero* pinpoints the difference nicely; put quite simply, content has for so long dominated science fiction's evaluative criteria that its readers have in years past been willing to overlook defects in style.

Every subgenre, of course, maintains with jealous rigidity its own particular conventions; . . . each and all are set into their conventions, conventions that relegate each to a ghetto precisely like that occupied by science fiction, . . . and when the individual work rises above the conventions of its subgenre (*The Ox-Bow Incident, The Spy Who Came in from the Cold*), it is, willy-nilly, "mainstreamed."

There, of course, waits the gulag gateway—and a problem. If science fiction would presume mainstream respectability (and the more bankable rewards of the mainstream), it must in its creation and in its critical modes submit to mainstream analytic criteria, a contortion that seems neither probable nor even desirable, for if it is to remain science fiction, it must also maintain its own unique features: "Both science fiction and the mainstream," says James Gunn, "will be stronger if science fiction retains its unique concepts. . . ."

A beginning, therefore, might be to recognize that the subgenre status of science fiction requires not a curtailing of critical judgment, but a redirecting of evaluative criteria; if science-fiction criticism is to have any real function beyond the mild self-entertainment of the critic, one part of that function must be the provision of appropriate evaluative tools.

The first of these tools might be an identification of those features—including, but perhaps not limited to, idea, setting, and scientific accuracy—where the demands of science fiction *exceed* those of the mainstream. These criteria are perhaps so obvious, once cited, as to require little comment; suffice it to note that the most successful science fiction has always been that concerned with an imaginative treatment of the "What if . . ." question, that depth and plausibility of detail in setting are prerequisite to a form that deals with future or alternate realities, and that scientific accuracy consistent with current knowledge (note, for instance, the recent plethora of "black hole" stories) is expected by an informed readership. Beyond the specific (and certainly demanding) requirements of the genre, however, exists further a body of aesthetic considerations appropriate to any work that pretends to the status of literature, no matter its genre, its intent, nor, ultimately, its own self-imposed and perhaps excusatory criteria. To such aesthetic imperatives—to depth and credibility of characterization, to plausibility of motivation, to logic of development and consistency of resolution, for instance—science fiction must also adhere, if it would in fact escape the ghetto. (pp. 170-71)

Merrell A. Knighten, "The Gulag Gateway: Critical Approaches to Science Fiction," in Extrapolation, *Vol. 21, No. 2, Summer, 1980, pp. 167-71.*

JOAN GORDON

Joe Haldeman's one collection of short stories [*Infinite Dreams*] demonstrates his performance in a form that to a great extent disallows his characteristic episodic structure. The traditionally tight order of a short story contradicts Haldeman's view of an essentially chaotic universe. This may be the reason why Haldeman feels more sure of his longer works and often writes his short stories for secondary motives. Many of his short stories are written to fit a narrow set of predetermined rules: to try out a technique or character for a novella or novel, or to satisfy editorial requirements. Such stories are intellectual games in which Haldeman doesn't always have a great deal at stake. When he writes a novel, he exposes his emotional and moral life enough to raise the stakes. Though Haldeman doesn't play a high-risk game in most of his short stories, they are still fun to read, he still plays skillfully, and once in a while he goes for broke. When his stories are particularly successful, they combine character study and strong moral stance with some of his most skillful writing. (p. 52)

The collection has several common motifs. The Washington, D.C. area keeps recurring as the locale for stories, and mathematicians appear in five of them. Less trivial recurrences include crippling and maiming, war, war's preludes and after-effects, the relentless inevitability of fate, and the importance of remaining moral in an amoral and chaotic universe. All these motifs have some sort of autobiographical origin. Though the individual stories are not always charged with high seriousness, the kinds of motifs that repeat themselves in the short pieces confirm what is important in the novels and to Joe Haldeman.

When Haldeman gives advice to struggling new science-fiction writers, he always suggests humorous science fiction. There is a dearth of funny science fiction but a constant market for it. Two of the stories in the collection, **"The Mazel Tov Revolution"** and **"All the Universe in a Mason Jar"** are written for laughs. **"The Mazel Tov Revolution"** involves very complicated financial finagling by an archetypically Jewish entrepreneur, which is to say that he speaks in Yiddish dialect, not that Haldeman is anti-Semitic. The story, written in the first person, is fast-paced, full of action, and machinations: it never goes beneath the surface of the politics and economics that structure the running of the plot. The chief charm, besides the chatty style and clever use of Yiddish hyperbole and understatement, lies in the fact that the story shows two nobodies who outsmart the ultimate multinational corporation. **"All the Universe in a Mason Jar"** is a local color story about moonshine in Florida, embellished with a retired mathematics professor, an alien, and his spaceship, which introduces familiar science-fiction elements. The incongruity of a saurian monster and a Florida moonshiner makes a successful entertainment.

Haldeman says his *metier* is the science-fiction novel, not the short story: often, in fact, the short stories are trial runs to test out techniques or characters he hopes to use in a novel. Or, once finished, some stories may suggest possibilities for a novel. Sometimes they don't point toward a novel at all, but represent a bit of pure research. *Infinite Dreams* contains examples of each sort of short story: the trial run, the suggestion, and pure research.

"To Howard Hughes: A Modest Proposal" is a trial run for *Mindbridge.* As he explains in the introduction to the story, Haldeman wanted to see if he could adapt Dos Passos' collage technique to a science-fiction novel. He knew it could be done, since John Brunner had done it in *Stand on Zanzibar* (1968) and *The Sheep Look Up* (1972). The question was if *he* could, and if he could do it in the boiled-down way he had in mind, limiting the scope to only a few characters instead of following many, as John Dos Passos and John Brunner had done. He wrote **"To Howard Hughes"** to find out.

Within a twenty-two page short story are twenty-four very short, nervous sections, usually dated, sometimes consisting of a document, a progress report, or quote from "the 2020 edition of Encyclopaedia Britannica." It is a collage of sorts, though it doesn't tell us a great deal of the world surrounding the plot (the world is our present one, the time in 1975, and it is narrowed down to trace only one chain of events). "This story was the test case, and I liked it, so I used the techniques for *Mindbridge,* which I think is my best novel, so far" (introduction to **"To Howard Hughes: A Modest Proposal"**). Having made the trial run, Haldeman went on to use the technique to trace not only several chains of events but also the central character in *Mindbridge.* The application was successful.

"Tricentennial" is a suggestion. It began inauspiciously—written to fit a cover illustration by Rick Sternbach for *Analog.* "Though it is one of my favorites, I've never done a story that was so thoroughly written to order" (introduction to **"Tricentennial"**). But the result was a short story spanning long centuries and employing the perspective of the wrong end of a telescope to show what might happen to an earth contemptuous of learning (contempt earns oblivion) and to people who fight against ignorance (they may have the chance to start over). The writing in **"Tricentennial"** is very strong, particularly the epilogue that uses Haldeman's colloquial style in a stately and poetic way:

> America itself was a little the worse for wear, this three thousandth anniversary. The seas that lapped its shores were heavy with crimson crust of anaerobic life; the mighty cities had fallen and their remains nearly ground away by the never-ceasing sand-storms.

He sets up repetitions, rhythmic phrasing, and inverted word order within the basic framework of plain and conversational language. (pp. 52-4)

"26 Days, On Earth" was more like pure research (or the casting out of a minor demon). The research hypothesis was "can I write an SF story in the manner of the twenty-two-year-old James Boswell?" The question for the writer-as-exorcist was "How can I shake the style of Boswell's *London Journal*?" By answering the second question—write a story—the first question was answered affirmatively.

Irresistible and negative fate motivates three of the stories: **"Counterpoint," "Anniversary Project,"** and **"Armaja Das."** We do not see this concept in blatant form in Haldeman's novels, though it is usually present in some ways. In each of the three stories, a life is predetermined, and not for the best. The individual cannot control his destiny and good works change nothing: destiny is a trap. In **"Counterpoint"** two children, born of the same father at the same moment to different mothers, are traced through their widely diverging lives to their simultaneous deaths. Wealth, brilliance, and love make no difference in determining their life spans. That has been predetermined.

In **"Anniversary Project"** a woman who briefly visits the far distant future returns to the present aware of everything that will happen to her. Seeing each moment of her future gives it the inevitability of predetermination, takes away the orderliness of sequential time, and constantly keeps before her all the tortures to which she has to look forward.

"Armaja Das" is no more cheery—here destiny is in the form of a gypsy curse that cannot be avoided, even by the unbeliever. It sets up a chain reaction that turns civilization into rubble. **"Armaja Das"** was written to order and, after some research on gypsy lore, "it was child's play to toss together gypsy curses, computer science, and minority assimilation into an 'ancient horror in modern guise'" (introduction to **"Armaja Das"**). The atmosphere is quite disturbing for a piece of child's play: the empathetic computer that dies to save a man and the carnage its kindness causes make the story more haunting than its seemingly casual birth would suggest.

The man who writes novels about war has also written many short stories on the subject. War was the single most influential and devastating thing to happen to Haldeman, an experience that remains even now in his mind, though writing and time have diminished much of the pain. Haldeman includes in *Infinite Dreams* three stories which center on war. **"To Howard Hughes: A Modest Proposal"** deals with threats of war. **"The Private War of Private Jacob"** with war itself, and **"A Mind of His Own"** with its after-effects.

"To Howard Hughes" suggests, in the form of an extrapolated example, that the way to implement disarmament successfully is for an outsider, who would have to be fabulously rich, to threaten atomic retaliation upon any government unwilling to cooperate. Like Swift's "A Modest Proposal," it is not meant to be a practical solution to a problem but to show readers how cruel humanity has been in its past attempts to solve its difficulties. In light of recent fears that people will indeed use nuclear weaponry for blackmail and recent revelations that private production of such bombs is quite possible, the story seems more prophetic than hyperbolic. It does show us how enmeshed such a horrific weapon has become in modern society—here the only way to eliminate it from the common catalog of warfare is to use it; the alternative to war is terrorism.

"The Private War of Private Jacob" is extremely short, a one-idea, one-gimmick story, but done with a powerful image. To love war one must be inhuman, so Haldeman shows soldiers led into war by happy robots. The story's central image of the sergeant laughing while shells burst and men die around him is a strong one; the notion that he or someone like him will always be there is stronger still.

"A Mind of His Own" is, as Haldeman reveals in his introduction to the story, the most autobiographical of the war stories in the collection. The protagonist Shays' injuries are extremes of the author's own, and his forbidding self-pity a disease Haldeman might have fallen victim to, a disease Haldeman watched take its course in a friend. War is not over when the treaties are signed and the fighting has stopped. Leonard Shays' mental and physical anguish are direct effects of war, and they will last him his lifetime.

"I had a friend who was suddenly and severely disabled, and he reacted in a human way, sliding into bitterness . . . driving away his family, then his friends, and then one day I left him too, in spite of knowing how he felt. Exit plaster saint" (introduction to **"A Mind of His Own"**). For Haldeman, who sees the world at large as amoral and formless, a strict moral code is the individual's salvation: it is *his* salvation. And the obligations of friendship are an important part of that code. Finding himself unable to meet his own standards (no matter how self-destructive and unreasonable it would have been to do so) diminished Haldeman's confidence in his spirit. As he

indicates in the introduction to the story, **"A Mind of His Own"** was meant to put the demon of his failure to rest. This Haldeman did by turning himself into his friend, thus sharing that friend's suffering; by showing how anyone would have left eventually, he justified his own leaving as a sane and reasonable act.

"A Mind of His Own" contains the recurring motif of crippling and maiming. Crippling is an outward sign of the damage that war inflicts upon the individual, but Haldeman uses versions and degrees of such crippling in other stories as well, especially in **"Juryrigged"** and **"26 Days, On Earth."** Physical disability traps the individual in the cell of his own body and makes him helpless in the face of attacks from outside: it violates his integrity. The protagonist of **"Juryrigged"** is powerless against the demands of his government or even of any individual who wants to use him. Jonathon Wu in **"26 Days"** can't defend himself against the bigoted attacks of small-minded people because his low-gravity, lunar muscles and bones carry too little weight on Earth.

Crippling mechanizes a person's movement, makes him rely upon mechanical devices, alienates him from the common run of mankind—he is unwillingly robbed of some of his humanity. The government that literally cripples L. Henry Kennem in **"Juryrigged"** dehumanizes him by turning him into a computer unit to help run his city. The government, in demanding complete control of Kennem's mind, robs him of a great portion of his humanity as surely as Otto McGavin's career as a spy dehumanized him in *All My Sins Remembered* and William Mandella's work as a soldier made him dream of being a machine in *The Forever War.*

In Haldeman's fiction, physical crippling may be an outward sign of inner limitations as well. Leonard Shays is more thoroughly crippled by his self-pity, anger, and refusal to cope than he is by his physical injuries. Jonathon Wu's arrogant adolescent assumption of superiority limits him more than the braces that support his wobbly limbs.

Haldeman says in his introduction to **"Summer's Lease"** that it is a story about scientific method, and so it is, in part. This story, written at ease and to an editor's specifications, is the best of the collection. Its characterization, landscape, style, and theme combine economically to create a vivid and moving piece of fiction. The protagonist, Lars Martin, stands as a strong individual whose integrity and love for knowledge single him out as a representative of both the value and the unpopularity of wisdom. The world in which Martin lives is a forgotten Earth colony, whose meteorological violence Haldeman carefully constructs so that it is believable and a vital element of the plot. The writing combines Haldeman's characteristically lucid setting forth of character, event, and theory with Biblical, metrical, and rhymed excerpts from the society's *Godbuk,* both a history and a myth. In choosing a document that should be the central work of the society and therefore its best representative, and that at the same time makes a moving contrast to the rest of the narrative, Haldeman gives this world conviction and reality in the reader's mind.

"Summer's Lease" is indeed about scientific method. Martin uses it slowly, carefully, thoughtfully, to discover the origins of his people and thereby determine how they might be spared the cyclical scourge of utterly destructive storms. Scientific method works, so eventually Martin knows enough of how his society started to begin working out a way to save it. Society finds him, with his knowledge and his offer for salvation, at best humorous and at worst a meddling nuisance. His work is ignored and he is manipulated, through an appeal to his kindness and his love for his people, into ignoring it too. The story honors the scientific method and the progress it makes possible, but it also condemns most of humanity for its cruel determination to remain ignorant. With almost no violence, in an essentially pastoral setting, this short story is Haldeman's most cynical. Hawthorne wrote of scientists violating men's souls to gain knowledge. Here people do the same to remain ignorant.

Infinite Dreams is a fair representation of Haldeman's short story career. He reveals his versatility, never bores, and occasionally shows great strength. His weaknesses are a certain looseness of organization, and, as a part of this looseness, a tendency to cover too much—too many characters, too many plots or plot fragments—at once. The stories often feel like stunted novels. "Summer's Lease," concentrating on one problem and one man while suggesting much more, is an exception. "Armaja Das" concentrates on one line of action and the evocation of one mood, following Poe's idea of unity in short stories: it too has integrity as a short story. "Tricentennial" is beautifully written, with the memorable Abigail Beamis and fascinating speculation, but it leaves much out that could be said: its episodes imply more story than Haldeman supplies, as if it were a moving outline of an invisible novel. (pp. 54-7)

Joan Gordon, in her Joe Haldeman, *Starmont House, 1980, 64 p.*

MICHAEL PAVESE

In the year 2084 our world, in particular the United States, is a mess. New York is dirty, dangerous and dolorous; Nevada is a haven for prostitutes and kidnappers, a lawless no-man's land; "idiotic sex farces" play on the "cube" or television; and power-hungry terrorists and madmen join radical organizations that put the world in a very precarious situation. So Joe Haldeman's science-fiction novel [*Worlds: A Novel of the Near Future*], which takes place in this "near future," is a curious combination of the familiar and the fantastic.

The Worlds of the title are orbiting, man-made settlements in space. They include, among others, Mazeltov (a Jewish community, of course), Devon's World (a world devoted to sexual pleasure, a kind of floating "Plato's Retreat") and New New York (a colony rich in "foamsteel" and tourism). The heroine, Marianne O'Hara, is an intelligent, promiscuous (in space promiscuity is encouraged) young New New York citizen. Born in space, she comes down among the "groundhogs" to do post-graduate study at N. Y. U. While on earth, she becomes involved with a variety of Earthies, including a bushy, young poet and a handsome, virile F. B. I. man. She also mixes in with one of those radical groups and after a series of adventures around the globe, finds herself in a very depressing denouement.

The story is told almost entirely from O'Hara's viewpoint. Her journals and letters are filled with interesting and amusing observations on culture, then and now. Hers is the character that comes the closest to having the breath of life in her; the other characters seem to be props, just part of the machinery. Haldeman's vision of the future is plausible and in-

volving and makes for enjoyable, fast-moving reading. His writing is efficient but artless, for the most part. But the main problem is that Haldeman states real human conditions, such as the meaningless sex bonanza on Devon's World and the violence of this world, without ever exploring them. The troubling components of the story only serve to push it further along. So the novel's effect is one of diversion and not enlightenment.

Michael Pavese, in a review of "Worlds: A Novel of the Near Future," in Best Sellers, *Vol. 41, No. 2, May, 1981, p. 47.*

ALGIS BUDRYS

[*Worlds*] is set in the very foreseeable future. Earth is poor, the orbital colonies are not quite rich but definitely in a far better position to obtain resources, revolution is brewing, and the ultimate results might be cataclysmic. Twenty-second century, says Haldeman. I'm not so sure, bearing in mind there were only fifty years between the War of 1812 and the Civil War.

In its beginnings, *Worlds* tends to remind one of *The Moon is a Harsh Mistress,* which is in many ways the best book Robert A. Heinlein ever wrote. So one braces a little to see Haldeman suffer by comparison. Haldeman is the heir apparent to later Pohl and middle Heinlein as the author of straightforward tales straitly told, but his peak hasn't arrived yet.

However, *Worlds* shifts away from this confrontation, concerning itself far more with events on Earth as seen through the eyes of what I think is a rather well-realized female protagonist. I'm not sure I like her that much as a person; she seems to be extending her childhood rather far into her lifetime. But she *is* a person, and that's harder for a male writer to do than it is for a female to turn the opposite trick. (Because *no one,* male or female, has that much experience of seeing realistically depicted females in fiction.)

In its movements across the face of a western world fragmented by 21st-century political and cultural events, the novel in fact depicts an even greater variety of worlds than exist in the space clusters. But certain human constants prevail, and what they result in is not at all pretty. Haldeman does not do a perfect job of this—begging all the award committees' pardon, he has yet to do a perfect job of any book—but there is a more-than-sufficient sense of the human condition in the job he does do. And as he says himself in *Worlds* the human condition is not fully knowable.

What I brought away mostly from *Worlds* was a sense of contact with literacy and, of all rare things, mercy. This seemed a very warm thing to have encountered. (pp. 55-6)

Algis Budrys, in a review of "Worlds," in The Magazine of Fantasy and Science Fiction, *Vol. 61, No. 2, August, 1981, pp. 55-6.*

TOM EASTON

Joe Haldeman's *Worlds* begins "a major SF trilogy," according to the cover blurb. Maybe. In an often offhand, flip style, he tells us what happens when Marianne O'Hara, sexually free daughter of an orbital colony (a World), goes to Earth to touch up her education. Amidst squalor and decadence, she falls in with the Third Revolution, finds love and love again, marries, is kidnapped, gets jammed in a crack when World War I—excuse me! I mean III, of course—begins, and, as Earth and Worlds boycott each other, she escapes homeward on the bow-wave of nuclear chaos. The world is dead. Long live the Worlds.

Clearly, with a change of venue to Europe, the book could have been written in 1915 or 1940, when the Grand Tour wound up every respectable Rich Kid's education and the Nihilists or Communists or Fascists were lying in wait like spiders. But it's still fun stuff, a quick read, even thought-provoking at times, despite the fact that Haldeman's future has been fondled by a good many SF hands. But what in the World will Haldeman do for an encore? This is a trilogy, remember?

(I couldn't resist that last. Sorry, Joe. Readers—let it be known that Earth is not totally destroyed, despite the book's back cover, and of course the Worlds offer plenty of scope for two—or more—additional volumes.) (pp. 164-65)

> *Tom Easton, in a review of "Worlds," in* Analog Science Fiction/Science Fact, *Vol. CII, No. 12, November, 1982, pp. 164-65.*

CHARLES PLATT

Haldeman's most recent novel *Worlds Apart,* volume two of his *Worlds* trilogy, steadfastly retains a focus on the near future—with limited success. Earth has been ravaged by nuclear war and bacteriological agents that persist in the biosphere and reduce average longevity to 20 years. Normal human life continues only in an enormous orbiting space colony, where, Haldeman suggests, a well-educated and nonviolent society would give rise to a socialist system allowing a paradoxically libertarian range of personal freedoms.

Worlds Apart is a capably told, sometimes eloquent novel, describing a decade in the career of an ambitious female politician in orbit, her one-time lover peddling medicine to devolved tribes on Earth, and a grab-bag of extraneous notions in between: a Manson-worshipping death cult, a starship with an anti-matter drive, a formalized ménage-a-trois, a hijacked space shuttle, an expedition into regressed Florida, a new science of behavioral conditioning, and more. This novel is so unfocused, so episodic, it can only be a deliberate experiment in form, as if Haldeman decided that art should imitate life—at the expense of orthodox narrative structure. I admire the courage to experiment, but in fact the passages that are most vivid are the ones that are most traditional in conception, depicting Haldeman's Florida home ground transformed as a post-holocaust landscape all too familiar to most science-fiction readers. The impact of computer technology is largely omitted, and advances in biology are almost completely overlooked. Haldeman is one of our most conscientious, technologically accurate writers; if he now has trouble building a complete picture of tomorrow, one wonders whether anyone else can do better.

> *Charles Platt, in a review of "Worlds Apart," in* Book World—The Washington Post, *December 25, 1983, p. 6.*

TOM EASTON

Just over a year ago I reviewed Joe Haldeman's *Worlds* by saying, in effect, that Joe was rewriting early 20th-century history with LaGrangian-type habitats as the U.S. and Earth as Europe [see excerpt above]. In *Worlds* he had Marianne O'Hara take the Grand Tour, visiting Earth to complete her education, and escaping just as nuclear holocaust began.

The second volume of the trilogy is now out, as *Worlds Apart: A Novel of the Near Future,* and I can't be a whole lot kinder to it. Marianne is home, embarking on her career track even as her World, New New York, absorbs refugees from other Worlds destroyed in the war, and tackles the forbidding task of survival independent of Earth. Thinking her Earthside lover lost forever and probably dead, she takes a pair of husbands. But Jeff Hawkings lives, and he has become a Healer in a region dominated by Mansonites who treat death as a sacrament. He is also one of the few adults in a world of children, for the war brought a plague upon age, Jeff's continued existence gives Haldeman a focus for frequent glimpses of the post-holocaust Earth. Unfortunately, his obviously satirical social commentary gooses only outdated sacred cows.

As New New York swipes a shuttle from an African spaceport to forestall an H-bomb surprise, drops plague vaccine, and delivers tools and seeds to survivors trying to rebuild, Marianne is there. Hers are the eyes of America on a post-War (I or II) Europe, her hand the hand of aid, her voice a superior tone of, "Isn't it nice that we live so far away and are above all that?"

I'm snide, but Haldeman makes this tone too explicit for me to feel very guilty about it. When New New York builds a starship, many of its people—including Marianne and her husbands—leave for Epsilon Eridani, and Marianne says, "We have our own concerns."

Worlds Apart is better than *Worlds.* It may even portray a fairly likely future, for "they" do say that history repeats. But I found it superficial and glib, without depth, with too few novel insights into people, history, or the future. And I might never have noticed these lacks if the book—or Haldeman's past work—hadn't seemed to promise more. There is nothing whatsoever *wrong* with the novel of sheer entertainment, unless we expect something else.

I expect the third volume of the trilogy will show us Marianne at Epsilon, building a new world, for she expects to live that long. She will be an elder leader then, and the story's protagonist may well be her daughter, born after departure from New New York. Perhaps there will be glimpses of the scene on and around Earth as well. Perhaps there will even be glimpses of the originality Haldeman once showed.

> *Tom Easton, in a review of "Worlds Apart: A Novel of the Near Future," in* Analog Science Fiction/Science Fact, *Vol. CIV, No. 3, March, 1984, p. 168.*

ALGIS BUDRYS

Some books are full of good prose, good incident, good characters, good background thought, and still, somehow, they fail to come together. They're maddening to read, because you can't quite put your finger on what's wrong; meanwhile, the good stuff keeps coming at you, and you wonder if perhaps it's just that you're terribly hard to please on this given day.

But maybe your instincts are right. Maybe this is, fundamentally, a book that fails despite its long catalog of excellences.

A sort of book we see a lot of is the panoramic "Future Historical," replete with incident and gritty detail, and within that genre we very much prize the Heinleinesque projective story—the tale of what will happen "if this goes on." We find, on reading a well-done example of the kind, that we have been given something to think about as well as to thrill to, and the combination of the two appealing effects is often cited as one of the special pleasures that SF can bring its readers.

Joe Haldeman dedicates **Worlds Apart** to a string of Robert Heinlein characters, which makes a very nice bow to the Grand Master's plainly visible influence. One could have had far worse models. But it may be that we have not yet assimilated all there is to know about how Heinlein makes characters work.

This is the second book in a projected trilogy, a sequel to **Worlds,** in which Earth-satellite dweller Marianne O'Hara, bright, postpubescent, but really quite young, came down dirtside for some not particularly glad research on the scruffy, noisy Earth of the 21st century, and unexpectedly found love—as well as the beginnings of maturity—with groundhog Jeff Hawkings. That book ended with World War III breaking out, and O'Hara barely getting on the last shuttle back up to New New York, her satellite-world, while Hawkings had to stay behind. This one picks up the tale almost immediately thereafter.

The problem, if there is one, is that it's the tale that gets picked up, not Marianne's tale or Jeff's tale, although they certainly figure frequently in the wordage.

Thanks in part to the choppy, episodic, viewpoint-switching style Haldeman seems to favor for his books, there is a curious distance between the reader and the story. Theoretically, that effect ought to lend a certain majesty to a diorama depicting times of great change. But it doesn't work here. For one thing, the chopping is too fine for the story's length; we cut in and out, sometimes so quickly that events become pro forma evocations of similar events in many other novels of this kind: The underhanded opposition on the ruling council, and the sabotage by the religious fanatics, for just two such. These are barely written at all; they're sketched-in, and you, the experienced reader, have to fill in the blanks. Which means there are no new insights, no surprises at all, in what thus becomes nothing more than stock red herrings.

This goes on. Although the story abounds with incidents of disaster and despair on Earth, mirrored in high-pressure situations on New New York as the overcrowded and marginal last surviving satellite—there is no running thread of reader involvement. I'm sure Haldeman thinks there is; doesn't he keep the focus tight on either O'Hara or Hawkings at nearly all times? Well, yes, but proximity, it seems, is not necessarily involvement. We stand by and watch, for instance, as a landing party including O'Hara makes a successful last-ditch effort to forestall a German terrorist plan to nuke New New York, and in reading through these scenes we come upon all sorts of dramatic pictures and subplot lead-ins. But we learn, soon afterward, that there was a plausible chance the German missile could have been stopped even if it had been launched, and if the nuke had detonated it might very well have done the satellite no damage. Haldeman educatively tells us so, thus informatively undermining himself as a storyteller.

We have meanwhile gotten involved with the two African children who stowed away on the shuttle. But one of them is dead, it turns out, and the other, though presented as a pitiable figure, just flicks offstage as soon as we learn she'll be researched for a vaccine to cure the deadly plague swirling round Earth. The result of a biowar virus gone very wrong, it maddens and then kills everyone older than twenty.

That vaccine, delivered to Earth, saves all sorts of lives and enables the beginning of a promising effort to teach the juvenile survivors how to farm, and thus how to break the hunter-gatherer life cycle into which they have all fallen. But when that, too, doesn't go quite as planned, O'Hara is yanked away from this possible involvement as well, and sent, irrevocably now, away from Earth as a high-ranking officer on humankind's first colonizing starship. And so she and Hawkings will apparently never meet again, despite the sporadic radio contacts that have occurred between them over the years of this . . . I was going to say "drama," but I would have misled.

There are, as noted, a great many dramatic events. Hawkings, one of the very few surviving adults on Earth, and the only sane one we ever see, wanders the ravaged southeastern states, racked by the acromegaly brought on by the hormone imbalance that preserves his life. He makes a precarious living by being Healer, an itinerant medico in a culture of vicious children, many of whom worship Charles Manson, few of whom have ever heard of the germ theory of disease, and almost none of whom understand the most elementary public health practices. (pp. 42-4)

The counterplaying and the echoing ironies inherent in this milieu fairly cry out for an artist's dedicated attention. But while Haldeman gives us scenes of death, destruction and suppuration, they are, like the rest of the incidents in this book, newsfilm bits; fast-cut short glimpses snatched from what ought instead to have been an unfurled tapestry of a desperate time.

In realizing that, I think, is where we begin to realize what's wrong. The thing that Heinlein does so well, when he does it well at all, is to not only isolate a break-point in history, but to also identify the exact people who are most involved. Heinlein speaks freely of writing to show what could rationally happen "if this goes on." He is a little more reticent about the dramatic need to answer the foreground question: "Whom does this hurt most?" But his successes are all based on casting his characters in that manner, either overtly or as it gradually dawns on the reader.

This is what **Worlds Apart** lacks. Everything else is there; the potentially fascinating characters, the picturesque settings, the realpolitik of life dirtside and skyside, the great perspectives of Earth's blasted horizons and the infinite stars. But O'Hara and Hawkings remain just people blown by the winds, hurtling across the scenery at the breakneck pace of a cut-rate tour.

In the case of O'Hara, there is an attempt to justify her centrality by having another character call her a "nexus"—where she goes, trouble inexplicably follows. In a novel about predestination, occult or otherwise paranormal powers, or Secret Masters persecuting Poor Willy, that might fly, as an opening proposition. But here, it is the sound of an author realizing that he is trying to assign all the dramatic burdens of a *War And Peace* to a middle-management functionary and a minor entrepreneur.

That, sadly, is what O'Hara and Hawkings are. She—despite repeated assurances that she had a lot on the ball, and despite the fact that upper management keeps sending her into crucial situations—is really a very ordinary sort of person who, despite a tendency to hand-wringing, appears to be anesthetic to deep emotions. She certainly keeps turning-in barely excusable performances in critical situations. He does only a little bit better, often letting weeks or years go by between effective moves.

They are neither one of them the stuff of heroes, and yet they are also not minor enough to enjoy the archetypical "strengths" of the salt-of-the-earth little people who carry Heinlein's spears for him. In short, they are very much like real people. But a vivid and convincing historical drama cannot have mere real people at its center. The fundamental problem here, in what turns out to be an over-intellectualized and over-worked piece of creation, is that Haldeman has remained remorselessly true to probability and life, to the fatal detriment of believability. (pp. 44-6)

Algis Budrys, in a review of "Worlds Apart," in The Magazine of Fantasy and Science Fiction, *Vol. 66, No. 3, March, 1984, pp. 42-6.*

GREGORY FEELEY

Two thirds of the way through his *Worlds* trilogy, Joe Haldeman has published his second story collection, *Dealing in Futures.* Most of the contents were published over the past five years, making them, unlike the stories in *Infinite Dreams,* the work of an already successful novelist. Haldeman confesses in his introductory notes to sharing the widespread prejudice that novels are more "serious" than stories, though he admits to knowing better. Given that, plus his incontestable observation that stories pay more poorly than novels, Haldeman continues to write them for a variety of reasons: the satisfaction of completing something relatively quickly, the ability to experiment without investing a year's work, an interesting assignment. Unlike the efforts of such writers as Harlan Ellison or Gardner Dozois, whose muses confine them to the shorter forms, Haldeman's later stories are essentially craftsmanlike productions, written with intelligence and wit if not passion.

Several are occasional pieces, commissioned by editors with sometimes a stipulated theme. A number of the others appear to have been written with some eye to the market, and though Haldeman claims that he saw how **"Blood Sisters"** was a *Playboy* story only after finishing it, the reader is likely to guess a lot sooner. The author's remarks about the genesis of each story prompt various observations (Haldeman writes as well on request as under his own impetus; humorous sf is rarely commissioned), and generally strengthen the impression of a good writer working competently within his chosen field, without trying to shake up things.

It is interesting to note that the only stories to contain genuine emotion are the two longest ones, **"Seasons"** and **"You Can Never Go Back."** The rest are variously funny, suspenseful, or horrific, but none can be considered moving in the way Haldeman's novels—and early stories—are. Any fan of Haldeman's novels will enjoy this book, though it will be the pleasures of honest craft, not art.

Gregory Feeley, "High-Tech Goes Haywire," in Book World—The Washington Post, *October 27, 1985, p. 6.*

JOAN GORDON

Joe Haldeman's prose—clean, sharp, moving, provocative, and telegraphic—is always a pleasure to read. His second collection of short fiction [*Dealing in Futures*] provides no exception. The book includes ten short stories, a novella, three poems, and an interpolated running commentary. Except for one poem and the commentary, all the pieces have been previously published, though it is a service to have them gathered up from the numerous magazines and anthologies where they first appeared. Joe is a slow writer and fans waiting for the third volume of his *Worlds* series will be grateful for this gathering of the fruits of his careful labor.

Although this collection is distinctively Haldeman, not only in style but in content (war, intrigue, bargains, and curses), it also shows the range of his skill. **"Blood Sisters"** and **"More than the Sum of His Parts"** are packed with (nonsexist) sex and violence. **"A Tangled Web"** and **"Seven and the Stars"** are effective light and humorous pieces. **"Seasons"** is a complex novella (I wish it were longer, a down-right novel) of anthropological SF. **"Lindsay and the Red City Blues"** is a creepy horror story and **"You Can Never Go Back"** returns us to the characters and world of *The Forever War.* The prose ranges from the straightforward to the experimental and from conversational to poetic, while retaining Haldeman's characteristic voice.

Haldeman links the stories with a commentary that discusses craft, sources, and connections. Besides "sucking you into the next story," the afterwords reveal something of the great care Joe takes in putting together a story. Indeed, if any criticism can be levelled against his writing it is that the craft is so meticulous, the telling so compact, that the reader wishes for a little sloppy expansion once in a while.

Joan Gordon, "Dealing and Winning," in Fantasy Review, *Vol. 9, No. 8, September, 1986, p. 24.*

GERALD JONAS

Tool of the Trade is a sharply written thriller based on a fantasy of power that most of us, I suspect, entertained at least once or twice during childhood. What if you had the ability to control other people's minds, to make them think and do exactly what you wanted? Would you use such power for personal gain or for the good of all humanity?

Nicholas Foley, a professor of psychology at M.I.T., accidentally discovers a mind-control device while conducting some experiments in hypnosis with his wife. His immediate reaction is to hide the discovery from everyone (including his wife). Foley has even better reasons than most to wonder whether the world is ready for such a breakthrough; he is in fact a K.G.B. mole so successful in his long masquerade as an American academic that he has grown unsure about where his loyalty belongs.

Resisting the temptation to tinker with history, Foley sits on his invention for years, using it only to snuff out an occasional mugger or dope dealer, who, according to his eccentric sense of morality, deserves to die. When his hand is finally forced by circumstances, he sets in motion an elaborate plan to save the world. Unfortunately, Mr. Haldeman lets the details of this plan divert attention from the fascinatingly flawed character he has taken some pains to create. I found Foley's ambivalences and hesitations far more intriguing than the slam-bang wish-fulfillment ending.

Gerald Jonas, in a review of "Tool of the Trade," in The New York Times Book Review, *June 7, 1987, p. 18.*

MARY TURZILLO BRIZZI

[*Tool of the Trade*] is a thoroughly elegant spy thriller which is nominally science fiction, but plausible enough that Haldeman could have placed it three years in the future. Haldeman's craft is so smoothly integrated that a lengthy discussion of the plot is unwise. The major premise involves an ultrasonic signal which compels obedience to voice commands. The hero, KGB agent Nick Foley, has invented a watch which broadcasts this signal. He keeps the device secret from both American and Soviet agents, but when his wife is kidnapped, he decides to use this "tool." Haldeman drops the hint that sooner or later Nick will encounter some one completely deaf to the signal, who will not obey. The implication teases the reader—like waiting for the proverbial second shoe to drop. It does drop, but at the least expected time.

The term "episodic" has been applied to Haldeman's earlier work, but *Tool of the Trade* is a seamless masterpiece of suspense. Everything in the novel works together to produce surprise after deft surprise, each more adroit than the last.

Haldeman's characters live, too. Nick shows motives so complex that no lesser writer could have sustained them in such a short novel. Like many of Haldeman's heroes, he is an "ethical killer," compelled to murder by circumstances beyond his control, but exhibiting almost Buddhistic detachment. Nick's wife Valerie is a thoroughly believable middle-aged woman, with guts, intelligence, and vulnerability. Haldeman also depicts a villain, called "the Scalpel," so detestable his wickedness has to be explained through psychological warping; he is a dynamic foil for the sympathetic characters.

Many of the themes of *The Forever War* are repeated in *Tool of the Trade:* contempt for Machiavellian governments manipulating their citizens without regard for individual or group welfare, the necessity of fighting for survival in an ethically chaotic world, the primacy of personal over political allegiances, and a desire for world peace. But this novel is even stronger in characterization and plotting, while Haldeman's genius for gadgetry fades into the background. As always, Haldeman's writing is extremely witty; if you like his fiction (and you should), you'll love this. (pp. 48-9)

Mary Turzillo Brizzi, "Elegant Espionage," in Fantasy Review, *Vol. 10, No. 6, July-August, 1987, pp. 48-9.*

TOM EASTON

Joe Haldeman's latest, *Tool of the Trade,* suffers from a problem common to that subgenre of SF that pretends to tell us how to save the world from its folly. The novel is well thought out (within its constraints). The main character, Nick Foley . . . is very well realized and the settings—Cambridge, Florida, Leningrad—ring true as they can only in the hands of one who has been there. Minor flaws include the KGB villain, "the Scalpel," who kidnaps Nick's wife and threatens her with lit cigarettes and razor blades; he is just too, too cli-

ched. Another is the rifle bullet that hits Nick in the chest and is then never mentioned again (shouldn't he at least say "Ouch!"?). Still another is the head cold that renders the villain conveniently deaf (as if bone conduction wouldn't work quite well enough in the context).

You can tell already, can't you? Even as I kvetch, you say to yourself, "Hey! This one sounds exciting! It must move right along, and it obviously has all the intrigue and mayhem anyone could possibly want." And you're quite right. There is a place for cliché villains, and when the story is moving fast enough, who's counting the bullet wounds? It's a good read, yes it is.

And I can't even say that the real problem—see my lead sentence above—gets much in the way. That problem is that if we, even for a moment, suspend our disbelief we promptly stop believing. We can't help thinking: If it's that easy to save the world, then how come we're still so miserable? Nick, quite by accident, discovers that a certain ultrasonic frequency has the effect of making people biddable. He has a tone generator built into his watch; thereafter he uses it to tell muggers to go shoot themselves, and they do. Eventually, both the KGB and the CIA catch on that he has something special, and the hunt is on. Foley must stay free until he can rescue his wife. Then he must get into position and tell the world's leaders exactly how to end the arms race. Finally, he must somehow keep his secret from falling into the hands of tyrants.

If at the end we decide it's all a crock, we can still say, "If only . . ." It's a good read, an enjoyable yarn, and told with all of Haldeman's considerable skill, but it *is* pure wish fulfillment.

Tom Easton, in a review of "Tool of the Trade," in Analog Science Fiction/Science Fact, *Vol. CIX, No. 2, February, 1989, p. 182.*

KATHY ROMER

Joe Haldeman has rehearsed a book with me that he thinks he wants to write. This book would be a retrospective about the making of his new science fiction novel-in-progress, whose working title is *The Long Habit of Living.* As he talked to me recently in a series of interviews, about this novel and his writing, I came to believe in paradoxes about the composing process and the mind of an artist at work. And I watched, first hand, as the still unfinished novel took shape and began to grow.

Joe has been a major writer of science fiction since he won both the Hugo and Nebula awards for *The Forever War* in 1975. He writes technologically-based stories of war and political intrigue that are always set in some future society. His main characters are usually at odds with the prevailing system, and easy to empathize with. Novels such as *Mindbridge, All My Sins Remembered,* the first two books of his *Worlds* trilogy [*Worlds* and *Worlds Apart*], and the short story collection, *Dealing in Futures,* are all written in a lean style bolstered with dialogue and action. . . .

I began my investigation into Joe's composing process with a meeting at his office at MIT. Joe is in his early 40s, and has short, curly hair and a pleasantly lined face. He always laughs a little when he smiles. He talked openly about a project he was considering: an analysis of the process of writing his new novel, whose working title is *The Long Habit of Living.* (p. 166)

Over the next several weeks, we met a few times at a quiet pub in Boston's Newbury Street. We began by talking about the writing of *Tool of the Trade,* his most recently completed novel, just published this spring. I thought a comparison of the usual methods of writing that he used for this book with the new methods he was trying for *The Long Habit of Living* would give us a context. Joe recalled the complicated plot of *Tool of the Trade,* an international spy-thriller, in a patient retelling that he seemed to enjoy. He is as good a storyteller in person as he is in print, maybe better.

Tool of the Trade is typical of his stories because it involves one person pitted against an uncaring system, an ordinary person with something special about him. That something special is the only science fictional element in this novel. But Joe feels that *Tool of the Trade* is also atypical because the main character is mentally unstable, and he succeeds, after a fashion, in the end. . . .

Joe is alone when he writes, both in the formal planning and in the storytelling. But before that, he's as public as anyone, soaking up the culture and talking about ideas. He mingles with scientists at MIT (Joe has degrees in physics and astronomy). He attends science fiction conventions where he parties with fans and has late night think tank sessions with fellow science fiction writers. (p. 167)

Joe also consciously studies style. Raymond Chandler claimed that he puts only a half page in the typewriter at a time, making himself write at least one sensory image on it. Joe has considered trying to put more images into his spare literary style, though, like Hemingway, he admires simplicity. At times Joe even talks with interviewers about his stories and methods. By the time he puts ideas to paper, there has been a community effort of sorts that gets synthesized through his unique thought process, and comes out as *The Forever War,* or *All My Sins Remembered,* or *Worlds*—all provocative successes given back to the community.

I questioned Joe about his solitary writing habits and learned that during this early morning writing time, he drinks tea, a little coffee, and lifts weights or does aerobics if he feels tired. . . . He has a Macintosh Plus with new software that's part of the experimental composing method for *The Long Habit of Living.* Since everything is tentative on a word processor, he feels he can "bail out" of a story up to about ten or fifteen pages if it isn't working.

This notion of tentativeness figures importantly in his process. He mentioned it several times, usually in the context of fooling around with something he didn't have to commit himself to in any way, playing with thoughts that he could make disappear with a light tap of a key, having fun at it. Joe's wife, Gay, can remember a time when he said he'd never have a computer. But coupling the creativity of storytelling with a new technological device is a modern paradox that many writers welcome. Joe uses a word processor for most of his writing now, though even that is changing with the new methods he wants to try. (pp. 167-68)

Joe revealed some of the frustration he feels with his old methods of writing, some of what might have been the catalyst for the changes he's incorporating now into the composing of his new novel. He spoke about old habits grown unsatisfactory.

I'd say more often than not, the first sentence I write is going to be the first sentence of the story, which is a failing. But that's part of the thing I'm trying to shake off. A person who feels that way is not taking advantage of having a word processor. You have to change your way of thinking so it's fluid to match the fluidity of the tool. Otherwise you might as well be hammering it out on a manual typewriter, chipping it in stone.

And this has been one of the biggest problems for Joe, the pace of his writing. He thinks it's too slow, and to him, a professional writer, time is money.

To sell novels, Joe writes outlines, and he uses them secondarily as a way out of a block. When he was writing *Tool of the Trade,* sometimes rereading a few pages before he began each morning, thinking more or less off the top of his head, he would often get stuck. "So I just changed to another (computer) file and started typing at random about the book to see whether I could break free, and that because sort of a plot outline. I wasn't doing an outline in a functional sense." But this wasn't wasted time. I began to see that Joe also used "outlines" to suggest to himself what he might do next. He doesn't usually outline to restrict himself to a story he's already figured out. Endings don't concern him. He'd rather not know them and spoil the suspense while he's writing. (pp. 168-69)

Still closer to the heart of his composing process were the reasons for his decision to experiment with different techniques. Many writers either don't want to analyze their styles and methods, or are too close to them to verbalize the problems. Joe admitted without hesitation that he's dissatisfied with how long it takes him to complete a novel, and with his style which he calls "too glib." He wants to consciously separate left brain planning from right brain storytelling, challenge himself by creating formal problems of composition to overcome, and stifle the critic in himself as he creates his story. Here was the writer standing outside his creative self and fearlessly evaluating his craft: the paradox of being both creator and critic. These two personas seem to inhabit Joe's mind in productive tension.

Writing in a genre often criticized for lack of depth, Joe is concerned about the literary quality of his writing and thinks perhaps it can be improved, or at least changed. He is a careful, deliberate writer who knows he produces clear prose, and writes page-turners. His evidence of that is his success at making a living as a science fiction writer, a feat not many achieve. Yet he sees himself in mid-life writing too easily and successfully with increasingly less artistic challenge, unless he provides that challenge for himself. This daring to change in the face of proven success is what sets Joe off dramatically from other, more contented writers. It is also what kept my inquiry into his process dynamic and full of surprises. (pp. 169-70)

Looking for ways to surprise his readers, and, I think, himself, sometimes takes the form of serious and vigorous inquiry into the nature of the novel itself as a form. This is the academic side of Joe, living in tandem with the writer. As far as I could see, the partnership is mutually beneficial. Joe's ideas and inspirations as a writer often spark an intellectual inquiry, which in turn shapes his writing. He reads foreign authors, like Yugoslavian Ivo Andric, to study particular story structures. Even as I asked him, he seemed to be trying to figure out what he wants to achieve.

If what I'm trying to do is reinvent for myself what a novel is, I ought to go back to those first people in each language and see what they invented in the first place. Like Richardson writing *Pamela*. Evidently he wanted to amuse people and also make a moral statement about sexual responsibilities. So he made up a form for it. So maybe I can make up a form for what I'm doing.

(p. 170)

One thing Joe loves to talk about is story ideas, especially possible futures. The idea for *The Long Habit of Living,* a complex novel about immortals a couple of hundred years in the future, came to him from considering an outrageous (according to Joe) statement Somerset Maugham once made that he had started all of his stories by putting a finger down at random in the Bible, and whatever word came up would lead to a chain of associations that became a story.

Joe tried the same trick with a thesaurus, and although he said the word he happened on was not inspiring, there was an interesting quotation under the column of synonyms: "The long habit of living indisposeth us for dying." He made a note of the quote, then wrote a chapter and filed it away for possible future use.

After completing the first two books of his *Worlds* trilogy, he got tired of living with the same characters for four or five years. Then he sold *Tool of the Trade* on the condition that he would deliver a second novel to the same publisher. So he took out the first chapter of *The Long Habit of Living* again and wrote a brief outline of the rest of the story, all of which the publishers accepted. From there things changed from their usual course.

There were superficial decisions that later put boundaries around the territory of the Muse. Joe decided that he wanted to write this novel in less than eighteen months. That's how long it took him to write *Tool of the Trade.* He settled on a six-pages-a-day goal, or 800 words, which is faster than his usual 500-words-a-day rate. When he finishes the first draft he'll go back and revise from the beginning. (pp. 170-71)

I was anxious to see where all this happened and, on invitation, was surprised to find Joe's study neat and spare, with a desk for the Macintosh and printer, an uncluttered bulletin board on the wall behind, and a small couch in a corner. Somehow I thought I'd have to wade through piles of books and papers, or at least empty coffee cups and beer bottles. But Joe looked as organized on the outside as he seems in his writing.

We went right to the word processor, and here Joe was at home, more relaxed even than during our interviews in the pub. He was almost animated showing me the latest software, bits of outline, segments of chapters, pointing out notes he had typed, telling himself to remember to include some particular detail. The word processing software was clearly a tool for planning. (p. 171)

The deliberate planning ended with the full outline, and Joe tried to separate for me the thinking process used for the planning from what happened next: creating the text. He explained to me that he enters a sort of "hypnotic" state when he writes. He experiences a leaving of conscious awareness and deliberate manipulation of words, characters and plot. "It's difficult to be analytical about it," he said, "because you're just sitting there being open to the cosmos, or whatever, and every now and then you tickle the keys."

I had it. This is when he tells the story. Joe thought that a lot of the creative writing of the text was subliminal and hadn't been planned at all. He recalled a Ph.D. dissertation that a graduate student wrote on his work, and how she found structural elements in *The Forever War* that amused him at first because he thought they necessarily meant he had planned them. "But on reflection I think the structures reflect something very basic about storytelling that I knew instinctively because of having read thousands of books, and I know what comes after something."

Joe's storytelling phase of writing changed when he began *The Long Habit of Living* to try yet another way of varying the literary quality of his prose. Instead of "tickling the keys," he is writing the novel longhand in a lined, beautifully bound blank book. He reached for the book next to the computer to show me page after page of small, flowing letters carefully made in thick, black ink. A manuscript. Even while he is in what he calls the hypnotic state, he can remember enough consciously to talk later about putting pen to paper. "I enjoy the craft aspect of actually writing out the book, the feeling of contact with the paper, physical contact with the words. I'm very conscious of forming the letters, of making my writing legible and artistic."

I wondered if the extent of this new outlining program was restricting Joe when he wrote the text, or making him feel that he couldn't go outside what he had planned. But he assured me there was invention in the longhand method. First he senses a change in rhythm from outline to text as the story "finds itself." Then he said, "I'm having to diverge. The writing is a process of discovery." (p. 172)

Joe said that for *The Long Habit of Living* he is trying not to let himself go back and rewrite, and so he thinks a lot of the longhand drafting is much worse than the text he produces in his usual ways. Gay disagrees, and says she thinks he's "going to be very surprised when he finishes at how little changing he's going to have to do." Joe plans to save revision until after the entire first draft is written, though he admits that he still catches himself mumbling sentences before he writes them down, and sometimes makes notes and arrows in the margins of the longhand book. Still, "in the spirit of giving the process a fair try," Joe intends to write the whole book using these new methods.

Though revising *The Long Habit of Living* was still a long way off, I asked him how he thought of that task for writers. He surprised me by saying,

> A lot of writers have fun blasting out their novel and then think that rewriting is torture. I think the writing itself is torture. By the time I finish the novel, the rest of it is roll up your sleeves, listen to the experts (editors), and realize that you're an expert too. That part of it is enjoyable literary labor. I don't mind it.

And here was another paradox, the enjoyment of what, for most, is the hardest, most tedious work.

He doesn't really mind the part of the writing that is torture either, or any part of the profession he's chosen, and succeeded at. He has the freedom to do what he wants to do on any day, invite an interviewer into his mental workshop, for instance, "not like a real job." But he takes living in what he calls a "shadowland between reality and fantasy" as seriously as if it were a "real job." And it looked hard enough to me. He told me finally that writing is simply his function, "and if I don't do my function for a couple of weeks, I get the existential heebie-jeebies."

I had reached a place in Joe's mind that I thought a writer wouldn't even be able to articulate, much less want to let me see. Though I am convinced that the Muse visits Joe regularly in a remote place that only the two of them know, I was most surprised to learn how aware he is of composing as a process that can be manipulated and changed to produce different results. Once the planning is finished, Joe dives in easily to where he meets the Muse, surfaces to give himself more direction, and returns happily to that place where the writing is "torture."

In a last interview, I sensed a summing up coming after we made a final sweep of the territory of change this new novel inhabits. Other writers might be content with success, but Joe says,

> I'm aware of a certain uneasiness about my writing in ways that disturb me. It's become too easy to solve various problems. And I don't want to wind up in a Hemingway/Heinlein trap of repeating myself and even satirizing myself unconsciously.

At a rewardingly close range, I have seen a successful writer who wants to break out of old routines and try for a new style, and maybe a surprise or two. I have seen both new word processing software and a longhand text shaping the new creation. I have seen an attempt to control the creative process consciously until that "hypnotic state" takes over, and awareness blurs, and something wonderful—and out of control—happens. And I have seen a careful writer secure enough to analyze his methods even as they evolve. (pp. 173-74)

> *Kathy Romer, "The Long Habit of Writing: Joe Haldeman," in* Extrapolation, *Vol. 30, No. 2, Summer, 1989, pp. 166-75.*

TED WHITE

Joe Haldeman's **Buying Time** is his first novel in more than five years, but those who saw in his early novels, like **The Forever War** and **Mindbridge,** the portents of a major science fiction novelist may conclude that Haldeman is only marking time with this book.

It begins with great promise. There is a life-extending process that must be renewed every 10 to 12 years, and costs no less than a million pounds for each treatment and that is addictive because to miss a treatment is to die quickly and unpleasantly. The process has been corrupted and one of the "immortals" is invited to join an inner circle. The novel quickly turns into a thriller, as the "immortal" in question goes on the run to escape assassination when he rejects the invitation.

As thrillers go, this one is good enough to be compulsively readable, but ultimately disappointing. Haldeman gives us a guided tour of the world and the nearby parts of the solar system approximately 100 years from now, and does his usual expert job of it. But he manipulates his protagonist unmercifully, keeping him on the run from one locale to the next until the book's weak conclusion.

Haldeman does as much as he can with a silly subplot in which the hero's girlfriend decides not to renew her treatments and to die at the respectable age of 100, only to change

her mind while off-planet and too far from a treatment center to reach it in time—but it can't disguise the fact that his protagonist, a can-do millionaire who climbs mountains and takes risks for fun, just runs from one hidey-hole to the next until ultimately he is caught, and never really has any workable plans or strategies. Luck and luck alone sees him through.

I found Haldeman's shifts from first- to third-person narration (and shifts of first-person narration between characters) obtrusive, his filler material (excerpts from newspapers, encyclopedias, etc.) sometimes unconvincing in tone or voice, and his placement of more than one character's actions or dialogue in a single paragraph clumsy craftsmanship. Yet Haldeman's innate storytelling talent kept me reading and left me with the wish when I'd finished the book that he'd kept its initial promise.

> *Ted White, "Love with the Proper Stranger," in* Book World—The Washington Post, *June 25, 1989, p. 8.*

DON D'AMMASSA

[In **Buying Time**], Dallas Barr is not exactly immortal, but he has been rejuvenated several times by the Stileman Process. Stileman set up an institute to return people to youthfulness up to a theoretical limit of one thousand years, but with a new treatment required every decade or so. The catch is that treatment costs $1,000,000 or your entire fortune, whichever is greater. Thus, every rejuvenated person starts over again as a relative pauper, and must earn a new fortune before his or her next treatment is due.

Shortly after emerging with his newly enlivened body, Ross discovers the existence of a secret society of "immortals", within which exists an even more secret society. Their goal is to use their influence and longevity to seize control of the world, and concomitantly, the Stileman process. Ross is reluctant to join, particularly when he draws unfortunate conclusions about a series of deaths, all of supposed immortals, in suspicious accidents. Complicating matters is the fact that one immortal appears to have succumbed to premature brain death, which might presage a general degeneration of everyone treated.

Accompanied by a fellow immortal and the electronically maintained personality of a third, Ross goes into hiding after several attempts on his life fail. Initially he travels the world seeking a refuge from his pursuers, but soon realizes that they control the news media and have enough power to extend their control anywhere he might hide on Earth. So instead they are forced to escape into space, taking refuge in the asteroid belt and the culture which has arisen there.

But the situation continues to boil toward explosion. The secret cabal appears to be taking control of the Stileman process, may already have planted one of their number as the next director of the institute. Nor are they as successful about concealing their identities, despite radically altered physical appearances, as they expected. Ross plots an elaborate failsafe method to alert people to what is really happening should he die, but a media blitz makes it unlikely that this tactic will succeed. (p. 39)

Haldeman's latest novel is a mixture of plots within plots, space travel and Earthbound chases and escapes, violence and character development. Ross is a reluctant hero forced for his own safety to act against the conspiracy, rather than an adventurer taking them on for the sheer joy of it. This makes him a more interesting protagonist and makes the story itself more plausible.

Stories in which the individual takes on the entire system frequently degenerate into wish fulfillment fantasies in which a chain of coincidence or unbelievable abilities on the part of the hero plays a key part in the outcome. Haldeman avoids these easy traps and instead has produced an evocative novel of the future, with a thoughtful, creative resolution to the conflict he has established. One of the best from one of the best. (pp. 39-40)

> *Don D'Ammassa, in a review of "Buying Time," in* Science Fiction Chronicle, *Vol. 10, No. 10, July, 1989, pp. 39-40.*

GERALD JONAS

[In *Buying Time*, Mr. Haldeman] takes a good idea and fails to develop it. This is all the more disappointing since Mr. Haldeman has distinguished himself in the past for the sensitive exploration of conventional science fiction premises, as in his fine post-holocaust novel *Worlds Apart.*

The title of his new novel is to be taken literally. In the second half of the 21st century anyone with a fortune in excess of $1 million can buy a complete (if temporary) "regeneration" from the Stileman Foundation; the process cleanses the flesh of its accumulated ills and restores the vigor of youth while leaving mind and memory intact. When you need another treatment (after a decade or so), the foundation will provide it on the same terms. The only catch: since you have to sign over all your worldly goods to the foundation each time, you have to keep creating new fortunes from scratch if you want to go on living.

One would expect the repeat winners in this life-or-death contest to be hard-hitting entrepreneurs and market manipulators in the mold of the age of Reagan. So it is hardly surprising when a group of "immortals" tries to take over first the foundation and then the world. Unfortunately, Mr. Haldeman chooses to tell this story from the point of view of two immortals, Dallas Barr and Maria Marconi, whose hearts are pure and whose motives are no more complicated than those of a pair of lovesick yuppies. This is not only incredible on the face of it but reduces plot development to a series of increasingly tedious confrontations between the Good Guys and the Bad Guys. All but buried among the shoot-'em-ups and macho posturings are some provocative near-future details and some trenchant observations on the nature of time, objective and subjective.

> *Gerald Jonas, in a review of "Buying Time," in* The New York Times Book Review, *July 2, 1989, p. 15.*

TOM EASTON

The last two Joe Haldeman novels to come my way didn't impress me tremendously. The skill of a master was there, yes, but the stories themselves made me think that he was taking it easy. Would he, I wondered on both my and your behalf, ever impress us again?

If you really wish an answer to that question, grab a copy of

Buying Time. The time is the mid-21st century. The gimmick is that just a few short years from right now, an absolutist idealist, Lord Stileman, will fund the development of a kind of immortality, based on a thorough medical reaming that must be repeated every 10 to 12 years. To prevent immortals from taking over the world, Stileman set it up so that whoever underwent the Stileman Process paid one million pounds or his or her entire assets, whichever was greater. Since the secret of gaining wealth, says Haldeman, is at least as much who and what you know as how much wealth you already have, this has certain effects on the lifestyles of the rich and famous.

Enter Dallas Barr, freshly rejuvenated and on the prowl for his next million. A fellow immortal tells him of a secret cabal with its eye on world "guidance" (*not* domination). When Barr rejects the offer of membership, assassins take aim at him. Happily, he has been around awhile, has learned to be properly paranoid about setting up boltholes, and has a pretty good idea of how to handle himself in a crisis. The bodies begin to accumulate. (p. 308)

Naturally enough, Barr flees, first on Earth, then into space, to the asteroids where he finds allies and the secret truth about the Stileman Process and gains a strong inkling of what the true nature of the cabal really is. Along the way, he finds a lost true love and nearly loses her again, and she in turn discovers unsuspected potentials in the Stileman-Processed body.

They win, of course. What experienced reader could have suspected otherwise? But getting there is all the fun, and the journey is Haldeman's way of telling us that absolutist idealists may seem to be offering beautifully logical, sane, well-designed ideas for the betterment of humanity, but there are many more pragmatic egotists just waiting to exploit the inevitable loopholes. Reality requires compromise. So does growing up.

I enjoyed this one, and I recommend it highly to you. It's Haldeman at or near the top of his form. (pp. 308-09)

> *Tom Easton, in a review of "Buying Time," in* Analog Science Fiction/Science Fact, *Vol. CX, Nos. 1 & 2, January, 1990, pp. 308-09.*

FURTHER READING

Gordon, Joan. *Joe Haldeman.* Edited by Roger C. Schlobin. Mercer Island, Wa.: Starmont House, 1980, 64 p.
    Analysis of Haldeman's fiction up to 1978. Includes commentaries on each of his novels as well as primary and secondary bibliographies. See excerpt above.

Hall, Peter C. " 'The Space Between' in Space: Some Versions of the *Bildungsroman* in Science Fiction." *Extrapolation* 29, No. 2 (Summer 1988): 153-59.
    Analysis of Robert A. Heinlein's *Starship Troopers,* Haldeman's *The Forever War,* and Orson Scott Card's *Ender's Game* as works that typify "the transition from inexperience and immaturity through the awakening of the sympathetic imagination."

McMurray, Clifford. "An Interview with Joe Haldeman." *Thrust* 11 (Fall 1978): 18-21.

Discussion in which Haldeman addresses such topics as his critical reception and writing method.

Ernest Hemingway

1899-1961

(Born Ernest Miller Hemingway) American novelist, short story writer, essayist, nonfiction writer, memoirist, journalist, poet, and dramatist.

The following entry presents criticism on Hemingway's novel *The Sun Also Rises* (1926). For discussions of Hemingway's complete career, see *CLC,* Vols. 1, 3, 6, 8, 10, 13, 19, 30, 34, 39, 41, 44, 50.

One of Hemingway's most celebrated works, *The Sun Also Rises* is widely recognized as a classic of twentieth-century American literature. Set against the backdrop of 1920s France and Spain, this novel portrays the sensual pursuits of "the lost generation" of American expatriates who were morally and spiritually devastated by World War I. Critics regard *The Sun Also Rises* as a significant point in Hemingway's career, as his stylistic and thematic concerns combine to achieve a power unequaled by his later works. Integrating such major themes as personal loss, disillusionment, tests of physical and emotional courage, and stoic resolve in the face of an apparently meaningless world, *The Sun Also Rises* also features Hemingway's economical use of dialogue and physical description to expose the inner lives of his characters. Conrad Aiken asserted: "[Hemingway] achieves an understanding and revelation of character which approaches the profound. . . . These folks exist, that is all; and if their story is sordid, it is also, by virtue of the author's dignity and detachment in the telling, intensely tragic."

Written while Hemingway worked as a journalist in Paris, *The Sun Also Rises* is based upon his 1925 visit to Pamplona, Spain, with his first wife and several friends, including Lady Duff Twysden, a striking British socialite to whom Hemingway had become strongly attracted after author Harold Loeb introduced them. While he and Lady Duff did not consummate their relationship, Hemingway threatened Loeb in Pamplona after learning of his brief affair with her. The trip ended on a further note of ill will when Lady Duff and her companion, an extravagant yet bankrupt British man, failed to pay their bills.

Like Hemingway, Jake Barnes, the terse, unemotional narrator of *The Sun Also Rises,* is an American reporter living in Paris. Rendered impotent by a wound suffered in combat, Jake is unable to consummate his love for Lady Brett Ashley, a reckless Englishwoman modeled after Lady Duff. Jake's condition, which comes to symbolize the sterility of the age, also sets him apart from the other characters, although he remains an informed, perceptive interpreter of their emotions and actions. Set in Paris, Book I of *The Sun Also Rises* follows several characters in frenetic pursuit of superficial affairs and diversions in the cafés and night clubs of the Left Bank. As the narrative begins, Jake introduces his tennis partner, Robert Cohn, who, like Loeb, is a successful Jewish novelist and amateur boxer. Suppressed by a possessive, insecure lover, Cohn confides his romantic desire for adventure and travel in Jake who, disabused by experience, dismisses these thoughts as worthless, a contrast that surfaces as a major theme in the novel. Critics perceive Cohn as inhibited by his

adherence to an obsolete Victorian idealism while Jake achieves a modicum of freedom by cultivating a personal code of behavior that requires an unemotional acceptance of a now meaningless world.

When Jake impulsively engages a Parisian prostitute with the "vague sentimental idea that it would be nice to eat with someone," he gently rebuffs her advances by revealing that he is "sick," to which she replies that indeed everyone is sick, an exchange that underscores the moral and spiritual malaise of post-war society. While dining with the prostitute, Jake is set upon by Cohn and several others who persuade him to come to a nearby jazz club. They are there only minutes before Brett arrives. Mannish in dress yet "built with curves like the hull of a racing yacht," she is at the center of the novel's action. After losing her fiancé in the war, she married and divorced an abusive British lord, and is now engaged to Mike Campbell, a failed Scottish businessman. Brett is often perceived as an amoral hedonist who signals the death of morality and romantic love. However, she is regarded by other commentators as a psychologically complex individual whose aggressiveness and frank sexuality herald the new independence of women in society. Enchanted by Brett, Cohn asks her to dance, but she declines, slipping away with Jake for a taxi ride instead. Alone together, Brett momentarily reveals her tormented love for Jake before resuming a light-hearted demeanor in the crowded atmosphere of another club.

A solemn undertone to the evening's revelry resurfaces when Jake lies awake in bed and his "hard-boiled" resolve is overcome by memories of the war. To calm himself, he thinks of Brett, but her drunken, late-night visit to his flat exposes once more the absurdity of their relationship. When she reappears the next evening, Jake asks Brett to live with him, a request that she rejects before announcing that she is leaving for a holiday in San Sebastian. For this visit, Brett also brings Count Mippipopolous, a mature Greek businessman who, like Jake, has cultivated a strategy for living in a world stripped of illusions. Having accepted the fallacy of a moral center, the Count exists upon the peripheries of sensation where "getting your money's worth" is his primary concern. Another person who has achieved a similar style is Jake's friend, Bill Gorton, who arrives in Paris at the opening of Book II. Considered one of the few positive characters of the novel, Bill attempts to buoy Jake's low spirits by offering to buy him a stuffed dog from a Parisian taxidermist, an example of a life philosophy based upon "a simple exchange of values."

With Bill now present, Jake makes arrangements for their trip to Pamplona for the bullfights at the festival of San Fermin. When they ask Mike Campbell and Brett, who has recently returned from her holiday, to meet them in Pamplona, Jake mentions that Cohn has been invited as well. Dismayed, Brett privately informs Jake that Cohn accompanied her to San Sebastian and that she has since broken off the liaison. Yet Cohn, who is still infatuated with Brett, declines Jake's later offer to cancel their arrangement. As their journey begins, Jake and Bill stop at Burguete in the Basque region of Spain, where fishing and male friendship dominate a peaceful interlude between the oppressive gaiety of Paris and the conflicts of Pamplona. Their humorous banter during this period also touches upon several of the novel's serious themes, including love, religion, expatriation, and the consequences of the war. After a week, Jake and Bill leave for Pamplona where they rejoin Mike, Brett, and Cohn.

On the first day, Jake renews his friendship with Montoya, the owner of their hotel, who correctly recognizes the American as a fellow *aficionado,* one who loves and deeply understands the ritual of bullfighting. Throughout the festival, Jake explains the intricacies of the sport to Brett and the others, sequences which are recognized as among the first detailed accounts of bullfighting in English. However, events in the ring are soon overshadowed by tensions between Mike and Cohn as they compete for Brett's attention. The situation is further complicated by her growing attraction to Pedro Romero, a talented young bullfighter as yet uncorrupted by his fame. When Brett confesses her feelings to Jake on the eve of the fiesta's conclusion, he introduces her to Romero and, in the eyes of Montoya, betrays his *aficion.* When Cohn learns of this from a drunken, vindictive Mike, he assaults Jake, knocking him unconscious. Upon reviving, Jake refuses the help of others and returns to the hotel wanting only to take a long bath, but finds that the plumbing will not work, symbolizing his inability to cleanse himself of his guilt.

The next morning at the bull ring, Jake learns that Cohn had fought with Romero after finding him with Brett, and that the young bullfighter, though badly beaten, had humiliated Cohn by refusing to be knocked down. Romero demonstrates this bravery once more when he performs superbly during the day's events. Another figure who commands Jake's attention is Belmonte, an aging matador who, despite his waning skills, retains his dignity in the ring. Many critics maintain that Romero and Belmonte epitomize Hemingway's definition of heroism, in that they conduct themselves well in defeat unlike men such as Cohn who "behave badly" when confronted with the harsh realities of life. Andrew Hook observed: "Romero supremely embodies the code in terms of which Jake himself tries to live. Romero does not fake or pose or evade; violence and death are the conditions he has accepted, and in face of them he creates the forms of his dangerous art. His is the ideal which Jake recognizes." At the conclusion of the bullfights, Jake discovers that Brett and Romero have run away together.

The brief third section of *The Sun Also Rises* recounts the aftermath of the fiesta. Mike and Bill leave Spain, following Cohn, who had returned to Paris after attacking Romero. Jake also departs, traveling alone to San Sebastian, where he swims and recovers from the events in Pamplona. There he receives a wire from Brett, asking him to come to Madrid immediately. Arriving on the express train, Jake learns that Brett has left Romero out of conscience, not wanting "to be one of these bitches that ruins children." She later tellingly observes that "it's sort of what we have instead of God." In the final scene of the novel, they take a taxi ride through the streets of Madrid and Brett laments, "We could have had such a damned good time together," to which Jake ironically replies, "Yes. . . . Isn't it pretty to think so?" Critics have variously interpreted this concluding moment as well as its relationship to the two quotes that preface the novel: "You are all a lost generation," attributed to Gertrude Stein; and a passage from Ecclesiastes that begins "One generation passeth away, and another generation cometh but the earth abideth forever . . . The sun also ariseth, and the sun goeth down, and hasteth to the place where he arose. . . ." While Jake and Brett epitomize the futility of their contemporaries as they, like the sun, return unchanged to the initial point of their hopeless love, the novel also sustains the promise of natural continuity and renewal through the advent of another generation unspoiled by war.

When *The Sun Also Rises* first appeared, American youth immediately responded to its cynical approach toward conventional social values by imitating the dress, speech, and attitudes of the characters. While F. Scott Fitzgerald characterized the novel as "a romance and a guidebook," critics maintain that through the understated narration of Jake, the moral and spiritual bankruptcy of Hemingway's characters becomes an eloquent testimony on modern times. John W. Aldridge observed: "[The] remarkable fact is that in telling as much or as little of the story as he did, Hemingway managed through his complex artistry to use words in such a way that we are allowed to see past them and to glimpse the outlines of the mysterious and probably tragic adventure that the words were not quite able to describe but were also not quite able to conceal."

(See also *Short Story Criticism,* Vol. 1; *Contemporary Authors,* Vols. 77-80; *Dictionary of Literary Biography,* Vols. 4, 9; *Dictionary of Literary Biography Yearbook: 1981;* and *Dictionary of Literary Biography Documentary Series,* Vol. 1.)

PRINCIPAL WORKS

NOVELS

The Torrents of Spring   1926
The Sun Also Rises   1926; also published as *Fiesta,* 1927
A Farewell to Arms   1929
To Have and Have Not   1937
For Whom the Bell Tolls   1940
Across the River and into the Trees   1950
The Old Man and the Sea   1952
Islands in the Stream   1970

SHORT FICTION COLLECTIONS

Three Stories & Ten Poems   1923
in our time   1924; also published as *In Our Time* [revised edition], 1925
Men without Women   1927
Winner Take Nothing   1933
Fifth Column and the First Forty-nine Stories   1939
The Snows of Kilimanjaro and Other Stories   1961
The Short Happy Life of Francis Macomber and Other Stories 1963
The Nick Adams Stories   1972
The Complete Stories of Ernest Hemingway   1987

OTHER

Death in the Afternoon   (nonfiction)   1932
Green Hills of Africa   (nonfiction)   1935
The Spanish Earth   (commentary and film narration)   1938
A Moveable Feast   (memoir)   1964
By-Line: Ernest Hemingway: Selected Articles and Dispatches of Four Decades   (nonfiction)   1968
88 Poems   (poetry)   1979
Ernest Hemingway: Selected Letters, 1917-1961   (correspondence)   1981

CONRAD AIKEN

It is rumored, with what accuracy I do not know, that Mr. Hemingway has at one time and another fought bulls in Spain as a mode of livelihood. Whether or not that is true, he writes of bull-fighting with extraordinary insight; he is clearly an expert. He is also, as clearly, *aficionado*—which is the Spanish term for a "fan." *Aficionado,* however, is a profounder word than fan, and suggests emotional intensities and religious zeals, not to mention psychotic fixations, which the baseball enthusiast does not dream of. If one likes bull-fighting, it has much the effect on one that half a course of psycho-analysis might have. One is thrilled and horrified; but one is also fascinated, and one cannot have enough. Perhaps the bull-fight only operates in this way on one who is too timid to descent into the ring himself—in which case one must absolve Mr. Hemingway from the charge of psychosis. Nevertheless, it is an interesting fact that his best short story, thus far, is a bull-fight story, **"The Undefeated,"** which in tragic intensity and spareness of outline challenges comparison with the very finest of contemporary short stories. And it is further interesting that in his new novel, ***The Sun Also Rises,*** the narrative works up to, and in a sense is built around, a bull-fight. More-

over, the story takes on, at this point, a force and tension which is nowhere else quite so striking.

This is not to suggest, however, that Mr. Hemingway's novel is lacking in these qualities, or that without the magnetism which the bull-fight exerts upon him he would be helpless. It has been apparent for some time that Mr. Hemingway is a writer of very unusual gifts; it has been merely a question as to what direction he would take. In ***The Sun Also Rises*** he takes a decided step forward and makes it possible for me to say of him, with entire conviction, that he is in many respects the most exciting of contemporary American writers of fiction. To say that his literary debts are obvious is not to mitigate this assertion in the slightest. He has learned something for Mr. [Sherwood] Anderson, and something, perhaps, from Mr. Fitzgerald's *Great Gatsby;* he may even have extracted a grain or two of ore from Miss Gertrude Stein—which is in itself no inconsiderable feat.

But in the accomplished fact his work is not in the least like the work of any of these writers. If one thing is striking about it, furthermore, it is its extraordinary individuality of style. His publishers say of him, with a discernment unusual in publishers, that he has contrived, in his novel, to present his people and his actions not as perceptible through a literary medium but as if immediate, and that is true. If once or twice in his story he slips into something of Mr. Anderson's cumbersome and roundabout explanatory method . . . these echoes are few and unimportant. His own method lies at the other extreme. He simply states; he even, as a general rule, can be said to understate. It almost appears that he goes out of his way, now and then, to avoid the descriptive or the expansive methods—one has the feeling that he is a little afraid of being caught with any sort of purple on his palette, whether it be of rhetoric or of poetry. The action, he seems to say, must speak wholly for itself.

This results, as might be expected, in quite extraordinary effect of honesty and reality. The half dozen characters, all of whom belong to the curious and sad little world of disillusioned and aimless expatriates who make what home they can in the cafes of Paris, are seen perfectly and unsentimentally by Mr. Hemingway and are put before us with a maximum of economy. In the case of the hero, through whose mind we meet the event, and again in the cases of Brett, the heroine, and Robert Cohn, the sub-hero, Mr. Hemingway accomplishes more than this—he achieves an understanding and revelation of character which approaches the profound. When one reflects on the unattractiveness, not to say the sordidness, of the scene, and the (on the whole) gracelessness of the people, one is all the more astonished at the fact that Mr. Hemingway should have made them so moving. These folk exist, that is all; and if their story is sordid, it is also, by virtue of the author's dignity and detachment in the telling, intensely tragic.

If one feature of ***The Sun Also Rises*** demands separate discussion, it is Mr. Hemingway's use of dialogue. The dialogue is brilliant. If there is better dialogue being written today I do not know where to find it. More than any other talk I can call to mind, it is alive with the rhythms and idioms, the pauses and suspensions and innuendoes and shorthands, of living speech. It is in the dialogue, almost entirely, that Mr. Hemingway tells his story and makes the people live and act. This is the dramatist's gift. . . . He clearly has the ability to make his story move, and move with intensity, through this medium. It is possible that he overuses this ability. One occasionally longs for a slowing down and expansion of the medium, a pause for more leisurely luxuriation in the instant, such as Mr. Hemingway only vouchsafes us in the fishing episode and in the account of the *fiesta* and the bull-fight. . . . [Henry James], despite his sins in this regard, somewhere remarked that dialogue, the most trenchant of the novelists' weapons, should be used as sparely as possible, to be kept in reserve, its force and edge unimpaired, for those scenes in which the action took a definite and decisive turn; it is above all in dialogue that climax should flower. In a sense, therefore, Mr. Hemingway gives us the feeling of finality and climax a little too often and thus deprives himself and his reader of that long curve of crescendo without which a novel lacks final perfection of form. His spareness and economy, his objective detachment, would be only the more effective for an occasional offset, and his canvas greatly richer.

Conrad Aiken, "Expatriates," in New York Herald Tribune Books, *October 31, 1926, p. 4.*

THE NEW YORK TIMES BOOK REVIEW

Ernest Hemingway's first novel, **The Sun Also Rises,** treats of certain of those younger Americans concerning whom Gertrude Stein has remarked: "You are all a lost generation." This is the novel for which a keen appetite was stimulated by Mr. Hemingway's exciting volume of short stories, **In Our Time.** The clear objectivity and the sustained intensity of the stories, and their concentration upon action in the present moment, seemed to point to a failure to project a novel in terms of the same method. . . . It is a relief to find that **The Sun Also Rises** maintains the same heightened, intimate tangibility as the sharter narratives and does it in the same kind of weighted, quickening prose.

Mr. Hemingway has chosen a segment of life which might easily have become "a spectacle with unexplained horrors," and disciplined it to a design which gives full value to its Dionysian, all but uncapturable, elements. On the face of it, he has simply gathered, almost at random, a group of American and British expatriates from Paris, conducted them on a fishing expedition, and exhibited them against the background of a wild Spanish fiesta and bull-fight. The characters are concisely indicated. Much of their inherent natures are left to be betrayed by their own speech, by their apparently aimless conversation among themselves. Mr. Hemingway writes a most admirable dialogue. It has the terse vigor of Ring Lardner at his best. It suggests the double meanings of Ford Madox Ford's records of talk. Mr. Hemingway makes his characters say one thing, convey still another, and when a whole passage of talk has been given, the reader finds himself the richer by a totally unexpected mood, a mood often enough of outrageous familiarity with obscure heartbreaks.

The story is told in the first person, as if by one Jake Barnes, an American newspaper correspondent in Paris. This approach notoriously invites digression and clumsiness. The way Mr. Hemingway plays this hard-boiled Jake is comparable to Jake's own evocations of the technique of the expert matador handling his bull. In fact, the bull-fight within the story bears two relations to the narrative proper. It not only serves to bring the situation to a crisis, but it also suggests the design which Mr. Hemingway is following. He keeps goading Jake, leading him on, involving him in difficulties, averting serious tragedy for him, just as the matador conducts the bull through the elaborate pattern of danger.

The love affair of Jake and the lovely, impulsive Lady Ashley might easily have descended into bathos. It is an erotic attraction which is destined from the start to be frustrated. Mr. Hemingway has such a sure hold on his values that he makes an absorbing, beautifully and tenderly absurd, heartbreaking narrative of it. Jake was wounded in the war in a manner that won for him a grandiose speech from the Italian General. Certainly Jake is led to consider his life worse than death. When he and Brett (Lady Ashley) fall in love, and know, with that complete absence of reticences of the war generation, that nothing can be done about it, the thing might well have ended there. Mr. Hemingway shows uncanny skill in prolonging it and delivering it of all its implications.

No amount of analysis can convey the quality of **The Sun Also Rises.** It is a truly gripping story, told in a lean, hard, athletic narrative prose that puts more literary English to shame. Mr. Hemingway knows how not only to make words be specific but how to arrange a collection of words which shall betray a great deal more than is to be found in the individual parts. It is magnificent writing, filled with that organic action which gives a compelling picture of character. This novel is unquestionably one of the events of an unusually rich year in literature.

"Marital Tragedy," in The New York Times Book Review, *October 31, 1926, p. 7.*

ALLEN TATE

[**The Sun Also Rises**] by the author of **In Our Time** supports the recent prophecy that he will be the "big man in American letters." At the time the prophecy was delivered it was meaningless because it was equivocal. Many of the possible interpretations now being eliminated, we fear it has turned out to mean something which we shall all regret. Mr. Hemingway has written a book that will be talked about, praised, perhaps imitated; it has already been received in something of that cautiously critical spirit which the followers of Henry James so notoriously maintain toward the master. Mr. Hemingway has produced a successful novel, but not without returning some violence upon the integrity achieved in his first book. He decided for reasons of his own to write a popular novel, or he wrote the only novel which he could write.

To choose the latter conjecture is to clear his intentions, obviously at the cost of impugning his art. One infers moreover that although sentimentality appears explicitly for the first time in his prose, it must have always been there. Its history can be constructed. The method used in **In Our Time** was *pointilliste,* and the sentimentality was submerged. With great skill he reversed the usual and most general formula of prose fiction: instead of selecting the details of physical background and of human behavior for the intensification of a dramatic situation, he employed the minimum of drama for the greatest possible intensification of the observed object. The reference of emphasis for the observed object was therefore not the action; rather, the reference of the action was the object, and the action could be impure or incomplete without risk of detection. It could be mixed and incoherent; it could be brought in when it was advantageous to observation, or left out. (p. 642)

In **The Sun Also Rises,** a full-length novel, Mr. Hemingway could not escape such leading situations, and he had besides to approach them with a kind of seriousness. He fails. It is not that Mr. Hemingway is, in the term which he uses in fine contempt for the big word, hard-boiled; it is that he is not hard-boiled enough, in the artistic sense. No one can dispute with a writer the significance he derives from his subject-matter; one can only point out that the significance is mixed or incomplete. Brett is a nymphomaniac; Robert Cohn, a most offensive cad; both are puppets. For the emphasis is false; Hemingway doesn't fill out his characters and let them stand for themselves; he isolates one or two chief traits which reduce them to caricature. His perception of the physical object is direct and accurate; his vision of character, singularly oblique. And he actually betrays the interior machinery of his hard-boiled attitude: "It is awfully easy to be hard-boiled about everything in the daytime, but at night it is another thing," says Jake, the sexually impotent, musing on the futile accessibility of Brett. The history of his sentimentality is thus complete.

There are certain devices exploited in the book which do not improve it; they extend its appeal. Robert Cohn is not only a bounder, he is a Jewish bounder. The other bounders, like Mike, Mr. Hemingway for some reason spares. He also spares Brett—another device—for while her pleasant folly need not be flogged, it equally need not be condoned; she becomes the attractive wayward lady of Sir Arthur Pinero and Michael Arlen. Petronius's Circe, the archetype of all the Bretts, was neither appealing nor deformed.

Mr. Hemingway has for some time been in the habit of throwing pebbles at the great. . . . The habit was formed in *The Torrents of Spring,* where it was amusing. It is disconcerting in the present novel; it strains the context; and one suspects that Mr. Hemingway protests too much. The point he seems to be making is that he is morally superior, for instance, to Mr. Mencken, but it is not yet clear just why. (pp. 642, 644)

Allen Tate, "Hard-Boiled," in The Nation, New York, Vol. CXXIII, No. 3206, December 15, 1926, pp. 642, 644.

LAWRENCE S. MORRIS

To anyone with an eye on what was coming, Ernest Hemingway's short stories in the volume, *In Our Time,* were the most stirring pages of imaginative prose by an American which appeared last year. This man was molding an idiom of his own to express his own way of feeling and seeing. Now comes his first novel, *The Sun Also Rises,* and it is clear that the shorter tales were merely a preparation. No one need be afraid any more that Hemingway's power is going to be limited to episodes. He has shown that he can not only state a theme, but develop it.

His approach to his job is so direct that it appears casual. Any café or hotel room will do him for a setting. He drops his characters in and lets them live. He does not explain them, as a less complete artist would. He does not label their motives with generalizations of love, hate, ambition. He watches their behavior. Seen from without, his people act in hard, direct ways; from within it is plain there is no direction whatever. They are stumbling through life like a man lost in a forest: attracted to this side by what appears to be a clearing, repelled when the clearing is found to be a marsh.

The essential characteristic of our time is that it is a period without a generalization. Without a mythology, if you prefer: we have inherited a hundred mythologies, and our minds flutter among them, finding satisfaction in none. The distress we are all acutely aware of comes from our failure to realize this fact emotionally. Intellectually we have cut down these frameworks into which our predecessors fitted experience. But we have received new information too fast to digest it. We have not yet reached the full realization that these familiar frameworks are gone from our minds; in practice we cling to their shadows and are hurt when they fail to support us. Until we are emotionally convinced that the old values are gone, we shall not begin to lay down our own generalizations. We have reached the stage—familiar in the history of cultures—where we must pass through Ecclesiastes before writing our Revelations. All contemporary art that is vital, that has its roots in our immediate problem, must seem destructive. It is concerned in realizing this desperate purposelessness by objectifying it.

The Sun Also Rises is one stride toward that objectification. The clear boundaries which were formerly assumed to define motives are gone. Very well: Hemingway will not try to make use of them, and will admit in his vocabulary only words which he himself has found solid. By this courageous self-denial—the mark of every genuine originality—he has achieved a style as close to his thought as the bone of which the skeleton is made is close to the skeleton; and firm with the firmness of packed sand and running water. The effect of this accuracy is a great gain in intensity. Between the lines of the hard-boiled narrative quivers an awareness of the unworded, half-grasped incomprehensibles of life.

The reader finds the characters of *The Sun Also Rises* gathered in Paris: an American newspaper correspondent; a Greek Count, with business experience in the Middle West; Cohn who had graduated from Princeton and written a book; an English bankrupt; and Brett, who was the pivot of the group. Brett was a young Englishwoman, who was getting a divorce from a man she had never loved, to marry another whom she did not love, either. The development of their relations is seen through the eyes of the newspaper correspondent, who had been rendered impotent by a wound received in the War—a brutally efficient symbol of "a lost generation." It was he whom Brett loved and who loved Brett. From Paris the group migrates to the Pyrenees and shares in a week's fiesta in a Spanish town. The peak of the fiesta is the bull fights; and Hemingway gives here the only account in English of a bull fight known to this reviewer, in which the emphasis is laid not on cruelty, but on the steely beauty of skill, the perfection of workmanship in the face of danger. A bull fight becomes a hard, beautiful dance, where an awkwardness means death. Amid the rioting of the fiesta and the clear, breath-taking scenes in the bull ring, the group of characters plays its little tragedy of futility.

Although Hemingway is objectifying the bewildered anguish of an aimless generation, he does not moon about it. His mind is masculine and imaginative. He loves all the hard, stinging experiences of the senses, he loves skill, he can laugh. He knows the intonations and obliquenesses of human speech. No other American, writing today, can match his dialogue for its apparent naturalness, its intimacy and its concealed power of revealing emotion. Ring Lardner's in comparison sounds framed and self-conscious. For something against which to measure the use of overtones in Hemingway's talk one must go to Joyce's account of a Christmas dinner in the Portrait of the Artist or—allowing for the greater intellectual scope and intensity of Joyce's mind—to the quarrel between Leopold Bloom and the Citizen in *Ulysses.* (pp. 142-43)

> *Lawrence S. Morris, "Warfare in Man and among Men," in* The New Republic, *Vol. XLIX, No. 629, December 22, 1926, pp. 142-43.*

JAMES T. FARRELL

Ernest Hemingway's first novel, *The Sun Also Rises,* has been generally heralded as the definitive account of a war-wearied lost generation. In the light of this interpretation it is interesting to note that this novel was published in 1927, and that the time of its action is 1925. For these years fall within the most hopeful period of the post-Versailles world. (p. 6)

It may seem paradoxical that in such a period a novel of war disillusionment, nihilistic in outlook, should have become an international success.

However, this paradox is only seeming. With signs of a return to world prosperity there were growing evidences of pacifism. In particular, the youth which had been too young to be in the trenches was deeply pacifistic. Disillusionment with the war was more or less accepted. Additionally, a re-examination of the character of disillusionment portrayed in *The Sun Also Rises* suggests that this mood has become a way of feeling and acting; in fact, a social habit. By 1925 those who had been morally unhinged or physically maimed during the war had had a number of years in which to make some kind of adjustment to the post-war world. The period of the first difficult readjustment had passed. Such, for instance, is the case of the chief protagonist in *The Sun Also Rises.* Jake Barnes, impotent as a result of wounds suffered on the Italian front, has more or less reconciled himself to his condition.

Whenever there is a widespread mood of disillusionment caused by an event as catastrophic as a world war, that mood is bound to be nihilistic and rather adolescent in character unless it serves as the basis for a radical and progressive political orientation which leads toward changing and bettering the world. This is illustrated in *The Sun Also Rises.*

The characters express their bitterness, their feelings of disenchantment, with calculated bravado. Their conversation is reduced to enthusiastic small talk about their escapades. And this talk, as well as their actions, is largely a matter of pose and gesture. They act like people who have not fully grown up and who lack the self-awareness to realize this: in fact, they possess no desire to grow up.

The Sun Also Rises influenced younger persons more widely than it did members of Hemingway's own generation. He may have reflected the feelings of many who fought in the war; but these men were finding some way of settling down and adjusting themselves in the Nineteen Twenties. They were writing, finding editorial jobs, launching themselves on careers which would win them Pulitzer prizes in poetry and so on. This novel struck deeper chords in the youth of the Twenties.

Hemingway's first books had hardly been published when he had imitators all over America; also boys and girls on campus after campus began to talk like Hemingway characters. One need not go into detail to describe certain features of the Twenties; these are too fresh in our minds. Suffice it to say that by and large younger people were revolting against the standards and conventions of their elders, against the accepted notions of middle-class society. At the same time they were nonpolitical in their revolt. Add to this the deep pacifism of the decade, and one can easily understand why this novel struck such chords of response among young people, why Hemingway suddenly became the influence he did at the time.

His influence was not merely superficial. It played a liberating and salutary role on those who would become the next generation of writers, and more numerically, of readers. The hopes of those days have now been proved fake by history. The nihilistic character of Hemingway's writing helped to free younger people from these false hopes. And although this novel (and many of his early stories as well) is set against a European background, Hemingway helped focus the eyes of younger people sharply on American life.

His writing was exciting and possessed of an extraordinary power of suggestiveness; it won the reader over to the feeling that he was being introduced into a sense of participation in the lives of very real men and women. His use of dialogue helped enormously to create this impression. Others, notably Ring Lardner, preceded him in exploring and revealing the literary possibilities of the use of American vernacular; but he used it with amazing skill and originality. His suggestiveness in conveying a sense of life, and his use of dialogue both tended to turn the attention of youth toward common American experiences and the speech expressing these on city streets and farms.

His influence, so widespread, has been, at the same time, one that seems quickly to have exhausted itself. Hemingway is a writer of limited vision, one who has no broad and fertile perspective on life. Younger writers were influenced, even seduced, by his moods. And they could grasp from him a sense of the great possibilities to be discovered in the true and simple treatment of common subject-matter and in the use of ordinary speech. But once they had learned these lessons, they had nothing left to gain from Hemingway.

The Europe described in *The Sun Also Rises* is a tourist's Europe of the Twenties. Cafes, restaurants, hotels, particularly of the Left Bank, are the setting. When the action shifts to Spain, it is to permit a magnificent description of bull fights and a fiesta. The mood and attitude of the main characters is that of people on a vacation. They set out to do what people want to do on a vacation, they have love affairs, drink, go fishing and see new spectacles. Written in the first person, the book embodies a spectator's attitude. Jake, the narrator, is a newspaper man: this is an occupation which naturally tends to develop the viewpoint of spectator. Jake is constantly looking at the other characters, at himself, at the scenery of Spain, at the bull fight, at everything which occurs or comes within his view.

The main characters have only a meager past. They are escaping from their past, and generally they do not even wish to talk or think of it. They live for the present in constant search for new and fresh sensations. They do not think; even Jake scarcely thinks about himself, or his own impotence. These people feel quite alike. They form a small clique, stoically accepting the ills of life.

Robert Cohn, however, is an outsider. He is with them because of his dog-like love for Lady Brett Ashley. Unlike the others, he is unable to drown his feelings in banalities, small talk and new spectacles. Cohn's difference from the others is one of the central points of the novel. This contrast is stated overtly when Lady Brett says that Cohn is "not one of us," and when Jake thinks that Cohn had behaved badly by pursuing Lady Brett. Focused against Cohn, Jake's simplified, stoical attitude is enforced more strongly. The attitude of Jake is one of the basic attitudes in Hemingway's writings.

Hemingway's realism is, by and large, one which deals with sensations, with shocks upon the senses. He has tended to reduce life to the effect which sights, scenes, experiences make upon the nervous system, and he has avoided complicated types of response. Herein, we find one of the major factors revealing his limitation as a writer.

In his most representative work he has saved himself from the crudities of simple behaviorism because of his gift of suggestiveness and his developed skill of understatement. The moral outlook in his work is on a plane of equal simplicity with his characters and subject-matter. It amounts to the attitude that an action is good if it makes one feel good. Such an outlook on characters and events suggests that development of greater understanding, broader range of feeling and sympathy, greater depth of imagination is practically precluded.

This has been the case in Hemingway's career. He arrived on the literary scene the absolute master of the style he has made his own; his attitudes were firmly fixed at that time. And he said pretty much what he had to say with his first stories, and his first two novels.

As a novelist, it is my opinion that the best of Ernest Hemingway is still to be found in *The Sun Also Rises.* Its freshness has not faded with time. It remains one of the very best American novels of the Twenties. (pp. 6, 14)

> James T. Farrell, "Ernest Hemingway, Apostle of a 'Lost Generation',*" in* The New York Times Book Review, *August 1, 1943, pp. 6, 14.*

PHILIP YOUNG

[*The Sun Also Rises*] reintroduces us to the hero. In Hemingway's novels this man is a slightly less personal hero than Nick [Adams of **"Big Two-Hearted River"**] was, and his adventures are to be less closely identified with Hemingway's, for more events are changed, or even "made up." But he still projects qualities of the man who created him, many of his experiences are still either literal or transformed autobiography, and his wound is still the crucial fact about him. Even when, as Robert Jordan of *For Whom the Bell Tolls,* he is somewhat disguised, we have little or no trouble in recognizing him.

Recognition is immediate and unmistakable in *The Sun Also Rises.* Here the wound, again with its literal and symbolic meanings, is transferred from the spine to the genitals: Jake Barnes was emasculated in the war. But he is the same man, a grown Nick Adams, and again the actual injury functions as concrete evidence that the hero is a casualty. He is a writer living in Paris in the twenties as, for example, Harry was; he was, like Nick, transplanted from midwestern America to the Austro-Italian front; when things are at their worst for him, like Fraser he cries in the night. When he refuses the services of a prostitute, and she asks, "What's the matter? You sick?" he is not thinking of his impotence alone when he answers, "Yes." He is the insomniac as before, and for the same reasons: "I blew out the lamp. Perhaps I would be able to sleep.

My head started to work. The old grievance." And later he remembers that time, which we witnessed, when for six months I never slept with the light off. He is the man who is troubled in the night, who leaves Brett alone in his sitting room and lies face down on the bed, having "a bad time."

In addition, Jake like Nick is the protagonist who has broken with society and with the usual middle-class ways; and, again, he has made the break in connection with his wounding. He has very little use for most people. At times he has little use even for his friends; at times he has little use for himself. He exists on a fringe of the society he has renounced; as a newspaper reporter he works just enough to make enough money to eat and drink well on, and spends the rest of his time in cafés, or fishing, or watching bull-fights. Though it is not highly developed yet, he and those few he respects have a code, too. Jake complains very little, although he suffers a good deal; there are certain things that are "done" and many that are "not done." Lady Brett Ashley also knows the code, and distinguishes people according to it; a person is "one of us," as she puts it, or is not—and most are not. The whole trouble with Robert Cohn, the boxing, maladroit Jew of the novel, is that he is not. He points up the code most clearly by so lacking it: he will not go away when Brett is done with him; he is "messy" in every way. After he has severely beaten up Romero, the small young bullfighter, and Romero will not give in, Cohn cries, wretchedly proclaims his love for Brett in public, and tries to shake Romero's hand. He gets that hand in the face, an act which is approved as appropriate comment on his behavior.

Cohn does not like Romero because Brett does. She finally goes off with the bullfighter, and it is when she leaves him too that she makes a particularly clear statement of what she and the other "right" people have salvaged from the wreck of their compromised lives. She has decided that she is ruining Romero's career, and besides she is too old for him. She walks out, and says to Jake:

> "It makes one feel rather good deciding not to be a bitch. . . . It's sort of what we have instead of God."

In early editions, *The Sun Also Rises* had on its title page, in addition to the passage on futility in Ecclesiastes from which the title is taken, Gertrude Stein's famous "You are all a lost generation." The novel provides an explanation for this observation, in addition to illustrating it in action. As in the story called **"In Another Country,"** the picture of the hero wounded and embittered by his experience of violence is broadened to include other people. Brett Ashley, for example, and her fiancé Mike Campbell are both casualties from ordeals similar to those which damaged Jake. Brett has behind her the very unpleasant death of her first fiancé; Mike's whole character was shattered by the war. (pp. 54-6)

The fact that characters in *The Sun Also Rises* are recognizable people, taken from "real life," does not contradict the fact that they are in this pattern. Various personages known to Paris of the twenties have thought that they recognized without difficulty the originals—Donald Ogden Stewart, Harold Stearns, Harold Loeb, Lady Duff-Twisden, Ford Madox Ford, and Pat Guthrie—and even Jake had his counterpart in actuality. But Hemingway, like most authors, has changed the characters to suit his purposes, and it is clear that whatever his origins, Jake, for instance, owes most to the man who created him, and is the hero.

He is the hero emasculated, however, and this must primarily account for the fact that he does not always seem entirely real. As he feels befits his status, he is largely a passive arranger of things for others, who only wants to "play it along and just not make trouble for people." But as narrator, at least, he is convincing, and if there is something blurred about him it helps to bring the participants into a focus that is all the sharper. Hemingway has always been good with secondary characters, finding them in a bright flash that reveals all we need know. Here, as he somehow manages to make similar people easily distinguishable, the revelations are brilliant. One remembers Brett and Cohn longest, for they get the fullest development, but Count Mippipopolous is wonderful, and wonderful too—save for their anti-Semitism, largely missing from the twenty-five cent edition, which advertises that "Not one word has been changed or omitted"—are Mike and Bill.

Chiefly it is Hemingway's ear, a trap that catches every mannerism of speech, that is responsible for the fact that these wastrels come so alive and distinct. That famous ear also caught a great many "swells" and "grands" that have dated—for slang is one thing almost certain to go bad with the passage of time—and some of the dialogue of camaraderie ("Old Bill!" "You bum!") is also embarrassing. But taken as a whole the talk is superb and, as a whole, so is the rest of the writing in the book. Hemingway's wide-awake senses fully evoke an American's Paris, a vacationer's Spain. Jake moves through these places with the awareness of a professional soldier reconnoitering new terrain. The action is always foremost, but it is supported by real country and real city. The conversational style, which gives us the illusion that Jake is just telling us the story of what he has been doing lately, gracefully hides the fact that the pace is carefully calculated and swift, the sentences and scenes hard and clean. This is true of the over-all structure, too: the book is informal and relaxed only on the surface, and beneath it lies a scrupulous and satisfying orchestration. It is not until nearly the end, for example, when Cohn becomes the center of what there is of action, that opening with him seems anything but a simply random way of getting started. This discussion of Cohn has eased us into Jake's life in Paris, and especially his situation with Brett. Suddenly the lines are all drawn. An interlude of trout fishing moves us smoothly into Spain and the bullfights. At Pamplona the tension which all try to ignore builds up, slowly, and breaks finally as the events come to their climax simultaneously with the fiesta's. Then, in an intensely muted coda, a solitary Jake, rehabilitating himself, washes away his hangovers in the ocean. Soon it is all gone, he is returned to Brett as before, and we discover that we have come full circle, like all the rivers, the winds, and the sun, to the place where we began.

This is motion which goes no place. Constant activity has brought us along with such pleasant, gentle insistence that not until the end do we realize that we have not been taken in, exactly, but taken nowhere; and that, finally, is the point. This is structure as meaning, organization as content. And, as the enormous effect the book had on its generation proved, such a meaning or content was important to 1926. The book touched with delicate accuracy on something big, on things other people were feeling, but too dimly for articulation. Hemingway had deeply felt and understood what was in the wind. Like Brett, who was the kind of woman who sets styles, the book itself was profoundly creative, and had the kind of power that is prototypal.

But for another generation, looking backward, this quality of the novel is largely gone out of it. The pessimism is based chiefly on the story of a hopeless love, and for Jake this is basis enough. But his situation with Brett sometimes seems forced—brought up periodically for air that it may be kept alive—as if Hemingway, who must have been through most of Jake's important experiences, but not exactly this one, had to keep reminding himself that it existed. And worse: though the rest of the pessimism rises eloquently out of the novel's structure, it does not seem to rise out of the day-to-day action at all. There is a gaping cleavage here between manner and message, between joy in life and a pronouncement of life's futility. Jake's disability excepted, always, the book now seems really the long *Fiesta* it was called in the English edition, and one's net impression today is of all the fun there is to be had in getting good and lost.

And yet *The Sun Also Rises* is still Hemingway's *Waste Land,* and Jake is Hemingway's Fisher King. This may be just coincidence, though the novelist had read the poem, but once again here is the protagonist gone impotent, and his land gone sterile. Eliot's London is Hemingway's Paris, where spiritual life in general, and Jake's sexual life in particular, are alike impoverished. Prayer breaks down and fails, a knowledge of traditional distinctions between good and evil is largely lost, copulation is morally neutral and, cut off from the past chiefly by the spiritual disaster of the war, life has become mostly meaningless. "What shall we do?" is the same constant question, to which the answer must be, again, "Nothing." To hide it, instead of playing chess one drinks, mechanically and always. Love is a possibility only for the two who cannot love; once again homosexuality intensifies this atmosphere of sterility; once more the Fisher King is also a man who fishes. And again the author plays with quotations from the great of the past, as when in reply to Jake's remark that he is a taxidermist Bill objects, "That was in another country. And besides all the animals were dead."

To be sure, the liquor is good, and so are the food and the conversation. But in one way Hemingway's book is even more desperate than Eliot's. The lesson of an "asceticism" to control the aimless expression of lust would be to Jake Barnes only one more bad joke, and the fragments he has shored against his ruins are few, and quite inadequate. In the poem a message of salvation comes out of the life-giving rain which falls on western civilization. In Hemingway's waste land there is fun, but there is no hope. (pp. 57-60)

Philip Young in his Ernest Hemingway, *Rinehart & Company, Inc., 1952, 244 p.*

MARK SPILKA

One of the most persistent themes of the twenties was the death of love in World War I. All the major writers recorded it, often in piecemeal fashion, as part of the larger postwar scene; but only Hemingway seems to have caught it whole and delivered it in lasting fictional form. His intellectual grasp of the theme might account for this. Where D. H. Lawrence settles for the shock of war on the Phallic Consciousness, or where Eliot presents assorted glimpses of sterility, Hemingway seems to design an extensive parable. Thus, in *The Sun Also Rises,* his protagonists are deliberately shaped as allegorical figures: Jake Barnes and Brett Ashley are two lovers desexed by the war; Robert Cohn is the false knight who challenges their despair; while Romero, the stalwart bullfighter, personifies the good life which will survive their failure. Of course, these characters are not abstractions in the text; they are realized through the most concrete style in American fiction, and their larger meaning is implied only by their response to immediate situations. But the implications are there, the parable is at work in every scene, and its presence lends unity and depth to the whole novel.

Barnes himself is a fine example of this technique. Cut off from love by a shell wound, he seems to suffer from an undeserved misfortune. But as most readers agree, his condition represents a peculiar form of emotional impotence. It does not involve distaste for the flesh, as with Lawrence's crippled veteran, Clifford Chatterley; instead Barnes lacks the power to control love's strength and durability. His sexual wound, the result of an unpreventable "accident" in the war, points to another realm where accidents can always happen and where Barnes is equally powerless to prevent them. In Book II of the novel he makes this same comparison while describing one of the dinners at Pamplona: "It was like certain dinners I remember from the war. There was much wine, an ignored tension, and a feeling of things coming that you could not prevent happening." This fear of emotional consequences is the key to Barnes' condition. Like so many Hemingway heroes, he has no way to handle subjective complications, and his wound is a token for this kind of impotence.

It serves the same purpose for the expatriate crowd in Paris. In some figurative manner these artists, writers, and derelicts have all been rendered impotent by the war. Thus, as Barnes presents them, they pass before us like a parade of sexual cripples, and we are able to measure them against his own forbearance in the face of a common problem. Whoever bears his sickness well is akin to Barnes; whoever adopts false postures, or willfully hurts others, falls short of his example. This is the organizing principle in Book I, this alignment of characters by their stoic qualities. But stoic or not, they are all incapable of love, and in their sober moments they seem to know it.

For this reason they feel especially upset whenever Robert Cohn appears. Cohn still upholds a romantic view of life, and since he affirms it with stubborn persistence, he acts like a goad upon his wiser contemporaries. As the narrator, Barnes must account for the challenge he presents them and the decisive turn it takes in later chapters. Accordingly, he begins the book with a review of Cohn's boxing career at Princeton. Though he has no taste for it, college boxing means a lot to Cohn. For one thing, it helps to compensate for anti-Semitic treatment from his classmates. More subtly, it turns him into an armed romantic, a man who can damage others in defense of his own beliefs. He also loves the pose of manhood which it affords him and seems strangely pleased when his nose is flattened in the ring. Soon other tokens of virility delight him, and he often confuses them with actual manliness. He likes the idea of a mistress more than he likes his actual mistress; or he likes the authority of editing and the prestige of writing, though he is a bad editor and a poor novelist. In other words, he always looks for internal strength in outward signs and sources. On leaving Princeton, he marries "on the rebound from the rotten time . . . in college." But in five years the marriage falls through, and he rebounds again to his present mistress, the forceful Frances Clyne. Then, to escape her dominance and his own disquiet, he begins to look for romance in far-off countries. (pp. 238-41)

Cohn's romanticism explains his key position in the parable.

He is the last chivalric hero, the last defender of an outworn faith, and his function is to illustrate its present folly—to show us, through the absurdity of his behavior, that romantic love is dead, that one of the great guiding codes of the past no longer operates. "You're getting damned romantic," says Brett to Jake at one point in the novel. "No, bored," he replies, because for this generation boredom has become more plausible than love. As a foil to his contemporaries, Cohn helps to reveal why this is so.

Of course, there is much that is traditional in the satire on Cohn. Like the many victims of romantic literature, from Don Quixote to Tom Sawyer, he lives by what he reads and neglects reality at his own and other's peril. But Barnes and his friends have no alternative to Cohn's beliefs. There is nothing here, for example, like the neat balance between sense and sensibility in Jane Austen's world. Granted that Barnes is sensible enough, that he sees life clearly and that we are meant to contrast his private grief with Cohn's public suffering, his self-restraint with Cohn's deliberate self-exposure. Yet, emasculation aside, Barnes has no way to measure or control the state of love; and though he recognizes this with his mind and tries to act accordingly, he seems no different from Cohn in his deepest feelings. . . . [At] best he is a restrained romantic, a man who carries himself well in the face of love's impossibilities, but who seems to share with Cohn a common (if hidden) weakness.

The sexual parade continues through the early chapters. Besides Cohn and his possessive mistress, there is the prostitute Georgette, whom Barnes picks up one day "because of a vague sentimental idea that it would be nice to eat with some one." Barnes introduces her to his friends as his fiancée, and as his private joke affirms, the two have much in common. Georgette is sick and sterile, having reduced love to a simple monetary exchange; but like Barnes, she manages to be frank and forthright and to keep an even keel among the drifters of Paris. Together they form a pair of honest cripples, in contrast with the various pretenders whom they meet along the Left Bank. Among the latter are Cohn and Frances Clyne, the writer Braddocks and his wife, and Robert Prentiss, a rising young novelist who seems to verbalize their phoniness: "Oh, how charmingly you get angry," he tells Barnes. "I wish I had that faculty." Barnes' honest anger has been aroused by the appearance of a band of homosexuals, accompanied by Brett Ashley. When one of the band spies Georgette, he decides to dance with her; then one by one the rest follow suit, in deliberate parody of normal love. Brett herself provides a key to the dizzy sexual medley. With a man's felt hat on her boyish bob, and with her familiar reference to men as fellow "chaps," she completes the distortion of sexual roles which seems to characterize the period. For the war, which has unmanned Barnes and his contemporaries, has turned Brett into the freewheeling equal of any man. It has taken her first sweetheart's life through dysentery and has sent her present husband home in a dangerous state of shock. For Brett these blows are the equivalent of Jake's emasculation; they seem to release her from her womanly nature and expose her to the male prerogatives of drink and promiscuity. Once she claims these rights as her own, she becomes an early but more honest version of Catherine Barkley, the English nurse in Hemingway's next important novel, *A Farewell to Arms.* Like Catherine, Brett has been a nurse on the Italian front and has lost a sweetheart in the war; but for her there is no saving interlude of love with a wounded patient, no rigged and timely escape through death in childbirth. Instead she survives the colossal violence, the disruption of her personal life, and the exposure to mass promiscuity, to confront a moral and emotional vacuum among her postwar lovers. With this evidence of male default all around her, she steps off the romantic pedestal, moves freely through the bars of Paris, and stands confidently there beside her newfound equals. Ironically, her most recent conquest, Robert Cohn, fails to see the bearing of such changes on romantic love. He still believes that Brett is womanly and therefore deeply serious about intimate matters. After their first meeting, he describes her as "absolutely fine and straight" and nearly strikes Barnes for thinking otherwise; and a bit later, after their brief affair in the country, he remains unconvinced "that it didn't mean anything." But when men no longer command respect, and women replace their natural warmth with masculine freedom and mobility, there can be no serious love.

Brett does have some respect for Barnes, even a little tenderness, though her actions scarcely show abiding love. At best she can affirm his worth and share his standards and perceptions. When in public, she knows how to keep her essential misery to herself; when alone with Barnes, she will express her feelings, admit her faults, and even display good judgment. Thus her friend, Count Mippipopolous, is introduced to Barnes as "one of us." The count qualifies by virtue of his war wounds, his invariable calmness, and his curious system of values. He appreciates good food, good wine, and a quiet place in which to enjoy them. Love also has a place in his system, but since he is "always in love," the place seems rather shaky. Like Jake and Brett and perhaps Georgette, he simply bears himself well among the postwar ruins.

The count completes the list of cripples who appear in Book I. In a broader sense, they are all disaffiliates, all men and women who have cut themselves off from conventional society and who have made Paris their permanent playground. Jake Barnes has introduced them, and we have been able to test them against his stoic attitudes toward life in a moral wasteland. Yet such life is finally unbearable, as we have also seen whenever Jake and Brett are alone together, or whenever Jake is alone with his thoughts. He needs a healthier code to live by, and for this reason the movement in Book II is away from Paris to the trout stream at Burguete and the bull ring at Pamplona. Here a more vital testing process occurs, and with the appearance of Bill Gorton, we get our first inkling of its nature.

Gorton is a successful writer who shares with Barnes a love for boxing and other sports. In Vienna he has helped to rescue a splendid Negro boxer from an angry and intolerant crowd. The incident has spoiled Vienna for him, and as his reaction suggests, the sports world will provide the terms of moral judgment from this point onward in the novel. Or more accurately, Jake Barnes' feelings about sports will shape the rest of the novel. For with Hemingway, the great outdoors is chiefly a state of mind, a projection of moral and emotional attitudes onto physical arenas, so that a clear account of surface action will reproduce these attitudes in the reader. (pp. 241-45)

[When] Barnes and Gorton approach "the good place," each item in the landscape is singled out and given its own importance. Later the techniques of fishing are treated with the same reverence for detail. For like Nick Adams [in **"Big Two-Hearted River"**], these men have left the wasteland for the green plains of health; they have traveled miles, by train and on foot, to reach a particular trout stream. The fishing there

is good, the talk free and easy, and even Barnes is able to sleep well after lunch, though he is usually an insomniac. The meal itself is handled like a mock religious ceremony. . . . A few days later, when they visit the old monastery at Roncevalles, this combination of fishing, drinking, and male cameraderie is given an edge over religion itself. With their English friend, Harris, they honor the monastery as a remarkable place, but decide that "it isn't the same as fishing"; then all agree to "utilize" a little pub across the way. At the trout stream, moreover, romantic love is given the same comparative treatment and seems sadly foolish before the immediate joys of fishing:

> It was a little past noon and there was not much shade, but I sat against the trunk of two of the trees that grew together, and read. The book was something by A. E. W. Mason, and I was reading a wonderful story about a man who had been frozen in the Alps and then fallen into a glacier and disappeared, and his bride was going to wait twenty-four years exactly for his body to come out on the moraine, while her true love waited too, and they were still waiting when Bill came up (with four trout in his bag). . . . His face was sweaty and happy.

As these comparisons show, the fishing trip has been invested with unique importance. By sticking closely to the surface action, Barnes has evoked the deeper attitudes which underly it and which make it a therapeutic process for him. He describes himself now as a "rotten Catholic" and speaks briefly of his thwarted love for Brett; but with religion defunct and love no longer possible, he can at least find happiness through private and imaginative means. Thus he now constructs a more positive code to follow: as with Nick Adams, it brings him health, pleasure, beauty and order, and helps to wipe out the damage of his troubled life in Paris.

Yet somehow the code lacks depth and substance. To gain these advantages, Barnes must move to Pamplona, which stands roughly to Burguete as the swamp in **"Big Two-Hearted River"** stands to the trout stream. In the latter story, Nick Adams prefers the clear portion of the river to its second and more congested heart:

> In the swamp the banks were bare, the big cedars came together overhead, the sun did not come through, except in patches; in the fast deep water, in the half light, the fishing would be tragic. In the swamp fishing was a tragic adventure. Nick did not want it. . . . There were plenty of days coming when he could fish the swamp.

The fishing is tragic here because it involves the risk of death. Nick is not yet ready for that challenge, but plainly it will test his manhood when he comes to face it. In *The Sun Also Rises* Barnes makes no such demands upon himself; but he is strongly attracted to the young bullfighter, Pedro Romero, whose courage before death lends moral weight to the sportsman's code.

So Pamplona is an extension of Burguete for Barnes: gayer and more festive on the surface, but essentially more serious. The spoilers from Paris have arrived, but (Cohn excepted) they are soon swept up by the fiesta: their mood is jubilant, they are surrounded by dancers, and they sing, drink and shout with the peasant crowd. Barnes himself is among fellow *aficionados;* he gains "real emotion" from the bullfights and feels truly elated afterwards. Even his friends seem like "such nice people," though he begins to feel uneasy when an argument breaks out between them. The tension is created by Brett's fiancé, Mike Campbell, who is aware of her numerous infidelities and who seems to accept them with amoral tolerance. Actually he resents them, so that Cohn (the perennial Jewish scapegoat) provides him with a convenient outlet for his feelings. He begins to bait him for following Brett around like a sick steer.

Mike's description is accurate enough. Cohn is always willing to suffer in public and to absorb insults for the sake of true love. On the other hand, he is also "ready to do battle for his lady," and when the chance finally comes, he knocks his rivals down like a genuine knight-errant. With Jake and Mike he has no trouble, but when he charges into Pedro's room to rescue Brett, the results are disastrous: Brett tells him off, the bullfighter refuses to stay knocked down, and no one will shake hands with him at the end, in accord with prep-school custom. When Brett remains with Pedro, Cohn retires to his room, alone and friendless.

This last encounter is the highpoint of the parable, for in the Code Hero, the Romantic Hero has finally met his match. As the clash between them shows, there is a difference between physical and moral victory, between chivalric stubbornness and real self-respect. Thus Pedro fights to repair an affront to his dignity; though he is badly beaten, his spirit is untouched by his opponent, whereas Cohn's spirit is completely smashed. From the beginning Cohn has based his manhood on skill at boxing, or upon a woman's love, never upon internal strength; but now, when neither skill nor love supports him, he has bludgeoned his way to his own emptiness. Compare his conduct with Romero's, on the following day, as the younger man performs for Brett in the bull ring:

> Everything of which he could control the locality he did in front of her all that afternoon. Never once did he look up. . . . Because he did not look up to ask if it pleased he did it all for himself inside, and it strengthened him, and yet he did it for her, too. But he did not do it for her at any loss to himself. He gained by it all through the afternoon.

Thus, where Cohn expends and degrades himself for his beloved, Romero pays tribute without self-loss. His manhood is a thing independent of women, and for this reason he holds special attractions for Jake Barnes.

By now it seems apparent that Cohn and Pedro are extremes for which Barnes is the unhappy medium. His resemblance to Pedro is clear enough: they share the same code, they both believe that a man's dignity depends on his own resources. His resemblance to Cohn is more subtle, but at this stage of the book it becomes grossly evident. Appropriately enough, the exposure comes through the knockout blow from Cohn, which dredges up a strange pre-war experience:

> Walking across the square to the hotel everything looked new and changed. . . . I felt as I felt once coming home from an out-of-town football game. I was carrying a suitcase with my football things in it, and I walked up the street from the station in the town I had lived in all my life and it was all new. They were raking the lawns and burning leaves in the road, and I stopped for a long time and watched. It was all strange. Then I went on, and my feet seemed to be a long way off, and everything seemed to come from a long way off, and I could hear my feet walking a great distance away. I had been kicked in the head early in the game. It was

> like that crossing the square. It was like that going up the stairs in the hotel. Going up the stairs took a long time, and I had the feeling that I was carrying my suitcase.

Barnes seems to have regressed here to his youthful football days. As he moves on up the stairs to see Cohn, who has been asking for him, he still carries his "phantom suitcase" with him; and when he enters Cohn's room, he even sets it down. Cohn himself has just returned from the fight with Romero: "There he was, face down on the bed, crying. He had on a white polo shirt, the kind he'd worn at Princeton." In other words, Cohn has also regressed to his abject college days: they are both emotional adolescents, about the same age as the nineteen-year-old Romero, who is the only real man among them. Of course, these facts are not spelled out for us, except through the polo shirt and the phantom suitcase, which remind us (inadvertently) of one of those dreamlike fantasies by the Czech genius, Franz Kafka, in which trunks and youthful clothes are symbols of arrested development. Yet there has already been some helpful spelling out in Book I, during a curious (and otherwise pointless) exchange between Cohn and another expatriate, the drunkard Harvey Stone. After first calling Cohn a moron, Harvey asks him to say, without thinking about it, what he would rather do if he could do anything he wanted. Cohn is again urged to say what comes into his head first, and soon replies, "I think I'd rather play football again with what I know about handling myself, now." To which Harvey responds: "I misjudged you. . . . You're not a moron. You're only a case of arrested development."

The first thought to enter Cohn's mind here has been suppressed by Barnes for a long time, but in Book II the knockout blow releases it: more than anything else, he too would like to "play football again," to prevent that kick to his head from happening, or that smash to the jaw from Cohn, or that sexual wound which explains either blow. For the truth about Barnes seems obvious now: he has always been an emotional adolescent. Like Nick Adams, he has grown up in a society which has little use for manliness; as an expression of that society, the war has robbed him of his dignity as a man and has thus exposed him to indignities with women. We must understand here that the war, the early football game, and the fight with Cohn have this in common: they all involve ugly, senseless, or impersonal forms of violence, in which a man has little chance to set the terms of his own integrity. Hence for Hemingway they represent the kinds of degradation which can occur at any point in modern society—and the violence at Pamplona is our current sample of such degradation. Indeed, the whole confluence of events now points to the social meaning of Jake's wound, for just as Cohn has reduced him to a dazed adolescent, so has Brett reduced him to a slavish pimp. When she asks for his help in her affair with Pedro, Barnes has no integrity to rely on; he can only serve her as Cohn has served her, like a sick romantic steer. . . . In the next book he will even run to her rescue in Madrid, though by then he can at least recognize his folly and supply his own indictment: "That was it. Send a girl off with one man. Introduce her to another to go off with him. Now go and bring her back. And sign the wire with love. That was it all right." It seems plain, then, that Cohn and Brett have given us a peacetime demonstration, postwar style, of the meaning of Jake's shell wound.

At Pamplona the demonstration continues. Brett strolls through the fiesta with her head high, "as though [it] were being staged in her honor, and she found it pleasant and amusing." When Romero presents her with a bull's ear "cut by popular acclamation," she carries it off to her hotel, stuffs it far back in the drawer of the bed-table, and forgets about it. The ear was taken, however, from the same bull which had killed one of the crowd a few days before, during the dangerous bull-run through the streets; later the entire town attended the man's funeral, along with drinking and dancing societies from nearby communities. For the crowd, the death of this bull was a communal triumph and his ear a token of communal strength; for Brett the ear is a private trophy. In effect, she has robbed the community of its triumph, as she will now rob it of its hero. As an *aficionado,* Barnes understands this threat too well. These are decadent times in the bull ring, marred by false aesthetics; Romero alone has "the old thing," the old "purity of line through the maximum of exposure": his corruption by Brett will complete the decadence. But mainly the young fighter means something more personal to Barnes. In the bull ring he combines grace, control and sincerity with manliness; in the fight with Cohn he proves his integrity where skill is lacking. . . . As one of these few remaining images of independent manhood, he offers Barnes the comfort of vicarious redemption. Brett seems to smash this as she leaves with Pedro for Madrid. To ward off depression, Barnes can only get drunk and retire to bed; the fiesta goes on outside, but it means nothing now: the "good place" has been ruined.

As Book III begins, Barnes tries to reclaim his dignity and to cleanse himself of the damage at Pamplona. . . . Then a telegram from Brett arrives, calling him to Madrid to help her out of trouble. At once he is like Cohn again, ready to serve his lady at the expense of self-respect. Yet in Madrid he learns to accept, emotionally, what he has always faintly understood. As he listens to Brett, he begins to drink heavily, as if her story has driven home a painful lesson. Brett herself feels "rather good" about sending Pedro away: she has at least been able to avoid being "one of these bitches that ruins children." This is a moral triumph for her, as Barnes agrees; but he can scarcely ignore its implications for himself. For when Brett refuses to let her hair grow long for Pedro, it means that her role in life is fixed: she can no longer live with a fine man without destroying him. This seems to kill the illusion which is behind Jake's suffering throughout the novel: namely, that if he hadn't been wounded, if he had somehow survived the war with his manhood intact, then he and Brett would have become true lovers. The closing lines confirm his total disillusionment:

> "Oh, Jake," Brett said, "we could have had such a damned good time together."
>
> Ahead was a mounted policeman in khaki directing traffic. He raised his baton. The car slowed suddenly pressing Brett against me.
>
> "Yes," I said, "Isn't it pretty to think so?"

"Pretty" is a romantic word which means here "foolish to consider what could *never* have happened," and not "what can't happen now." The signal for this interpretation comes from the policeman who directs traffic between Brett's speech and Barnes reply. With his khaki clothes and his preventive baton, he stands for the war and the society which made it, for the force which stops the lovers' car, and which robs them of their normal sexual roles. As Barnes now sees, love itself is dead for their generation. Even without his wound, he

would still be unmanly, and Brett unable to let her hair grow long.

Yet according to the opening epigraphs, if one generation is lost and another comes, the earth abides forever; and according to Hemingway himself, the abiding earth is the novel's hero. Perhaps he is wrong on this point, or at least misleading. There are no joyous hymns to the seasons in this novel, no celebrations of fertility and change. The scenic descriptions are accurate enough, but rather flat; there is no deep feeling in them, only fondness, for the author takes less delight in nature than in outdoor sports. He is more concerned, that is, with baiting hooks and catching trout than with the Irati River and more pleased with the grace and skill of the bull-fighter than with the bull's magnificence. In fact, it is the bullfighter who seems to abide in the novel, for surely the bulls are dead like the trout before them, having fulfilled their roles as beloved opponents. But Romero is very much alive as the novel ends. When he leaves the hotel in Madrid, he "pays the bill" for his affair with Brett, which means that he has earned all its benefits. He also dominates the final conversation between the lovers, and so dominates the closing section. We learn here that his sexual initiation has been completed and his independence assured. From now on, he can work out his life alone, moving again and again through his passes in the ring, gaining strength, order, and purpose as he meets his own conditions. He provides no literal prescription to follow here, no call to bullfighting as the answer to Barnes' problems; but he does provide an image of integrity, against which Barnes and his generation are weighed and found wanting. In this sense, Pedro is the real hero of the parable, the final moral touchstone, the man whose code gives meaning to a world where love and religion are defunct, where the proofs of manhood are difficult and scarce, and where every man must learn to define his own moral conditions and then live up to them. (pp. 246-56)

> *Mark Spilka, "The Death of Love in 'The Sun Also Rises',"* in Twelve Original Essays on Great American Novels, *edited by Charles Shapiro, Wayne State University Press, 1958, pp. 238-56.*

CARLOS BAKER

"A writer's job is to tell the truth," said Hemingway in 1942. He had believed it for twenty years and he would continue to believe it as long as he lived. No other writer of our time has so fiercely asserted, so pugnaciously defended, or so consistently exemplified the writer's obligation to speak truly. His standard of truth-telling has been, moreover, so high and so rigorous that he has very rarely been willing to admit secondary evidence, whether literary evidence or evidence picked up from other sources than his own experience. "I only know what I have seen," is a statement which comes often to his lips and pen. What he has personally done, or what he knows unforgettably by having gone through one version of it, is what he is interested in telling about. This is not to say that he has refused to invent freely. But he has always made it a sacrosanct point to invent in terms of what he actually knows from having been there.

The primary intent of his writing, from first to last, has been to seize and project for the reader what he has often called "the way it was." This is a characteristically simple phrase for a concept of extraordinary complexity, and Hemingway's conception of its meaning has subtly changed several times in the course of his career—always in the direction of greater complexity. At the core of the concept, however, one can invariably discern the operation of three esthetic instruments: the sense of place, the sense of fact, and the sense of scene.

The first of these, obviously a strong passion with Hemingway, is the sense of place. "Unless you have geography, background," he once told George Antheil, "you have nothing." You have, that is to say, a dramatic vacuum. Few writers have been more place-conscious. Few have so carefully charted out the geographical groundwork of their novels while managing to keep background so conspicuously unobtrusive. Few, accordingly, have been able to record more economically and graphically the way it is when you walk through the streets of Paris in search of breakfast at a corner café. . . . Or when, at around six o'clock of a Spanish dawn, you watch the bulls running from the corrals at the Puerta Rochapea through the streets of Pamplona towards the bullring:

> When I woke it was the sound of the rocket exploding that announced the release of the bulls from the corrals at the edge of town. . . . Down below the narrow street was empty. All the balconies were crowded with people. Suddenly a crowd came down the street. They were all running, packed close together. They passed along and up the street toward the bullring and behind them came more men running faster, and then some stragglers who were really running. Behind them was a little bare space, and then the bulls, galloping, tossing their heads up and down. It all went out of sight around the corner. One man fell, rolled to the gutter, and lay quiet. But the bulls went right on and did not notice him. They were all running together.

This scene [from *The Sun Also Rises*] is as morning-fresh as a design in India ink on clean white paper. First is the bare white street, seen from above, quiet and empty. Then one sees the first packed clot of runners. Behind these are the thinner ranks of those who move faster because closer to the bulls. Then the almost comic stragglers, who are "really running." Brilliantly behind these shines the "little bare space," a desperate margin for error. Then the clot of running bulls—closing the design, except of course for the man in the gutter making himself, like the designer's initials, as inconspicuous as possible.

The continuing freshness of such occasions as this might be associated with Hemingway's lifelong habit of early waking. More likely, the freshness arises because Hemingway loves continental cities, makes it almost a fetish to know them with an artist's eye, and has trained himself rigorously to see and retain those aspects of a place that make it *that place*, even though, with an odd skill, he manages at the same time to render these aspects generically.

As with the cities—and Hemingway's preference is for the Latin cities—so with the marshes, rivers, lakes, troutstreams, gulfstreams, groves, forests, hills, and gullies, from Wyoming to Tanganyika, from the Tagliamento to the Irati, and from Key West to the Golden Horn. "None can care for literature itself," said Stevenson, somewhere, "who do not take a special pleasure in the sound of names." Hemingway's love of names is obvious. It belongs to his sense of place. But like the rest of his language, it is under strict control. One never finds, as so often happens in the novels of Thomas Wolfe or the poetry of Carl Sandburg, the mere riot and revel of place-names, played upon like guitar-strings for the music they contain. Hemingway likes the words *country* and *land*. It is astonish-

ing how often they recur in his work without being obtrusive. He likes to move from place to place, and to be firmly grounded, for the time being, in whatever place he has chosen. . . . Wherever it is, it is solid and permanent, both in itself and in the books.

The earliest of his published work, descriptively speaking, shows an almost neoclassical restraint. Take a sample passage from *The Sun Also Rises,* not his earliest but fairly representative. This one concerns the Irati Valley fishing-trip of Jake Barnes and Bill Gorton:

> It was a beech wood and the trees were very old. Their roots bulked above the ground and the branches were twisted. We walked on the road between the thick trunks of the old beeches and the sunlight came through the leaves in light patches on the grass. The trees were big, and the foliage was thick but it was not gloomy. There was no undergrowth, only the smooth grass, very green and fresh, and the big gray trees were well spaced as though it were a park. "This is country," Bill said.

It is such country as an impressionist might paint almost exactly in the terms, and the subdued colors, which Hemingway employs. . . . [The] arrangement of the beech trees themselves, like the choice of the words, is clean and classical. The foliage is thick, but there is no gloom. Here is neither teeming undergrowth nor its verbal equivalent. The sage of Johnson's *Rasselas* advises all aspirant poets against numbering the streaks of the tulip or describing in detail the different shades of the verdure of the forest. Young Hemingway, still an aspirant poet, follows the advice. When he has finished, it is possible to say (and we supply our own inflection for Bill Gorton's words): "This is country."

For all the restraint, the avoidance of color-flaunting adjectives, and the plainsong sentences (five compound to one complex), the paragraph is loaded with precisely observed fact: beech wood, old trees, exposed roots, twisted branches, thick trunks, sunpatches, smooth green grass, foliage which casts a shade without excluding light. One cannot say that he has been given a generalized landscape—there are too many exact factual observations. On the other hand, the uniquenesses of the place receive no special emphasis. One recognizes easily the generic type of the clean and orderly grove, where weeds and brush do not flourish because of the shade, and the grass gets only enough light to rise to carpet-level. Undoubtedly, as in the neoclassical esthetic, the intent is to provide a generic frame within which the reader is at liberty to insert his own uniquenesses—as many or as few as his imagination may supply.

Along with the sense of place, and as a part of it, is the sense of fact. . . . Speculation, whether by the author or by the characters, is ordinarily kept to a minimum. But facts, visible or audible or tangible facts, facts baldly stated, facts without verbal paraphernalia to inhibit their striking power, are the stuff of Hemingway's prose.

Sometimes, especially in the early work, the facts seem too many for the effect apparently intended, though even here the reader should be on guard against misconstruing the intention of a given passage. It is hard to discover, nevertheless, what purpose beyond the establishment of the sense of place is served by Barnes's complete itinerary of his walk with Bill Gorton through the streets of Paris. The direction is from Madame Lecomte's restaurant on the Île St. Louis across to the left bank of the Seine, and eventually up the Boulevard du Port Royal to the Café Select. The walk fills only two pages. Yet it seems much longer and does not further the action appreciably except to provide Jake and Bill with healthy after-dinner exercise. At Madame Lecomte's (the facts again), they have eaten "a roast chicken, new green beans, mashed potatoes, a salad, and some apple pie and cheese." To the native Parisian, or a foreigner who knows the city, the pleasure in the after-dinner itinerary would consist in the happy shock of recognition. For others, the inclusion of so many of the facts of municipal or gastronomic geography— so many more than are justified by their dramatic purpose— may seem excessive.

Still, this is the way it was that time in Paris. Here lay the bridges and the streets, the squares and the cafés. If you followed them in the prescribed order, you came to the café where Lady Brett Ashley sat on a high stool at the bar, her crossed legs stockingless, her eyes crinkling at the corners.

If an imaginative fusion of the sense of place and the sense of fact is to occur, and if, out of the fusing process, dramatic life is to arise, a third element is required. This may be called the sense of scene. Places are less than geography, facts lie inert and uncoordinated, unless the imagination runs through them like a vitalizing current and the total picture moves and quickens. How was it, for example, that second day of the San Fermin fiesta in the Pamplona bullring after Romero had killed the first bull?

"They had hitched the mules to the dead bull and then the whips cracked, the men ran, and the mules, straining forward, their legs pushing, broke into a gallop, and the bull, one horn up, his head on its side, swept a swath smoothly across the sand and out the red gate."

Here are a dead bull, men, mules, whips, sand, and a red gate like a closing curtain—the place and the facts. But here also, in this remarkably graphic sentence, are the seven verbs, the two adverbs, and the five adverbial phrases which fuse and coordinate the diverse facts of place and thing and set them in rapid motion. If one feels that the sentence is very satisfying as a scene, and wishes to know why, the answer might well lie where it so often lies in a successful lyric poem—that is, in our sense of difficulty overcome. Between the inertness of the dead bull when he is merely *hitched* (a placid verb) and the smooth speed with which the body finally *sweeps* across the sand and out of sight, come the verbs of sweating effort: *crack, run, strain,* and *break.* It is precisely at the verb *broke* that the sentence stops straining and moves into the smooth glide of its close. The massing, in that section of the sentence, of a half-dozen *s*'s, compounded with the *th* sounds of *swath* and *smoothly,* can hardly have been inadvertent. They ease (or grease) the path of the bull's departure.

The pattern in the quoted passage is that of a task undertaken, striven through, and smoothly completed: order and success. (pp. 48-53)

The sense of place and the sense of fact are indispensable to Hemingway's art. But the true craft, by which diversities are unified and compelled into graphic collaboration, comes about through the operation of the sense of scene. Often, moving through the Latin language countries, watching the crowd from a café table or a barrera bench. Hemingway seems like a lineal descendant of Browning's observer in *How It Strikes a Contemporary.*

You saw go up and down Valladolid
A man of mark, to know next time you saw . . .
Scenting the world, looking it full in face.

(p. 54)

Carlos Baker, in his Hemingway: The Writer as Artist, *third edition, Princeton University Press, 1963, 379 p.*

EARL H. ROVIT

Within the entire canon of Hemingway's works—some seven novels, fifty-odd short stories, a play, and several volumes of nonfiction—*The Sun Also Rises* is something of a curious exception. Published in 1926 while Hemingway was still in his twenties and relatively unknown, it was his first serious attempt at a novel; yet, in spite of the fact that it was to be followed by such overwhelming commercial successes as *A Farewell to Arms* (1929), *For Whom the Bell Tolls* (1940), and *The Old Man and The Sea* (1952), most critics agree that *The Sun Also Rises* is his one most wholly satisfying book. Here Hemingway indelibly fixed the narrative tone for his famous understated ironic prose style. And here he also made his first marked forays into an exploration of those themes that were to become his brand-mark as a writer and which were to occupy him throughout his career. The pragmatic ideal of "grace under pressure," the working out of the Hemingway "code," the concept of "style" as a moral and ethical virtue, and the blunt belief or determination that some form of individual heroism was still possible in the increasingly mechanized and bureaucratic world of the twentieth century: these characteristic Hemingway notions deeply inform the structure of *The Sun Also Rises.* And while Hemingway was to develop these ideas at much greater length and with perhaps more drama in his subsequent work, they achieve a balance and a cogency in *The Sun Also Rises* which, it seems to me, he never really equaled again except in some of his short stories.

At the same time, while *The Sun Also Rises* is characteristically Hemingway, it is radically different from Hemingway's typical fictions. Indeed, it may be precisely in the area of its differences that it attains its special quality and pertinence as a major American novel. For there are subtleties of tone and meaning in *The Sun Also Rises* which suggest a profounder confrontation with the ambiguities of the modern "experience" than Hemingway was ever to sustain again. Hemingway himself regarded this work not as "a hollow or bitter satire, but a damn tragedy with the earth abiding forever as the hero." Without worrying about Hemingway's use of the academically sacred word, "tragedy," I think he may be correctly pointing his reader to the general area where the complexities of the novel come into focus. *The Sun Also Rises* is a novel about loss. Most of Hemingway's work is about loss; the loss of one's desires, one's loves, one's life. But *The Sun Also Rises,* alone among Hemingway's novels, begins with the loss as a "given," as a fatal limitation on open possibilities and opportunities. As in the best of the Nick Adams stories, *The Sun Also Rises* is concerned with that moral space which remains for man's occupancy after necessity has effected its inexorable curtailment on his freedom. And the concentrated passion which gives this novel its tautness of structure and its authority of statement is its exploration of that diminished measure of dignity and endurance which a man may still strive for even while he is a captive in the nets of bleak fatality.

When one considers the gallery of the popular Hemingway heroes—and how difficult it is to refrain from imposing Hemingway's own photogenic features on those of his heroic characters—the composite image can almost be stereotyped in Hollywood terms. . . . As Sean O'Faolain has pointed out, Hemingway's concept of heroism is almost unique in serious modern literature in the mere fact that, as it is presented, it is a convincing possibility. Far from being a passive pawn, the Hemingway hero succeeds in maintaining his own initiative and momentum in those isolated pockets of endeavor such as sports and war, which he carves out for himself in a dehumanized world. At the end, of course, he loses; the winner is allowed to take nothing, nothing except a sense of moral success in knowing that he has lost on his own and not on the world's terms. The typical background for the hero's exploits is a technicolor adventure world. . . . [These settings] are appropriately epic as both foil for and projection of the hero's ritual gestures in his dramatic dance with fate. Nor were the critics slow to attack the validity of Hemingway's fictional world. Dazzled by the exotic color and the Horatio Alger bravura with which Hemingway painted his version of moral struggle, they accused him of a variety of artistic and philosophical sins, ranging from the venial sin of romantic primitivism to the mortal sin of arrant commercialism. But this is to read Hemingway with a malicious premeditated selectivity. It is to ignore the marvelous classic restraint of his prose style. It is to fail to measure the qualitative difference between his heroic "heroes" and his typical narrator-protagonists. And it is almost wholly to disregard *The Sun Also Rises* as a work of art in itself, as well as a radical metaphor in terms of which Hemingway fashioned the most effective and influential elements of his work.

To be sure, *The Sun Also Rises* has been the most variously interpreted of all Hemingway's fiction. Critics have failed to agree on where, if at all, the base of values resides in the novel. They have argued the importance of Pedro Romero as a "code-hero"; they have disagreed on the goodness or badness of Lady Brett; and they are far from unanimous on the meaning of Jake's role or experience. The causes of these confusions would seem to be inherent in the novel itself and not in the subjective predilections of the critics; but in this case, at least, the confusions attest to the vitality rather than the incoherence of the work of art. On its most accessible level, *The Sun Also Rises* is a novel of deceptively casual surfaces, a seemingly realistic *roman à cléf*, narrated by Jake Barnes-Hemingway, which sketches several months in the lives of a not particularly prepossessing band of expatriated Bohemians in Paris in 1925. Nothing happens of much moment in the novel as the merrymakers drink, dance, arrange abortive liaisons, backbite, and generally fritter away their time in an empty irresponsible pursuit of joyless pleasure. The narration begins in the spring, builds up a small tension when Robert Cohn goes off to San Sebastian with Lady Brett, and comes to a climax at the final gathering and dispersion of the band in Pamplona for the July 6th Festival of San Fermín.

The critics who stress what Hemingway referred to as "the hollow or bitter satire" of the novel have had two options open to them. They can see the force of the novel's anger as directed against the characters in the novel who, for the most part, assume mawkish postures of self-pity and self-indulgence, while they excuse themselves from responsibility because they are all "a lost generation." From this viewpoint, *The Sun Also Rises* is a fictional extension of Hemingway's lifelong disgust with Bohemianism, tourism, amateurism, and lack of self-discipline. And certainly, narrated as it is by a character who stands off on the margins of the group, the novel supports this effect. The other option open to the critic of this persuasion is to view the satire in a larger, even a cosmic, dimension. The "dirty war" is the immediate historical antecedent behind the bombed-out lives of the expatriates. Jake Barnes has been rendered sexually impotent by his wound in the war. Brett Ashley's "true love" died of dysentery. The sustaining values of western civilization—religious, ethical, philosophical—have been exploded. The frenetic hedonism of the Bohemian group is only a desperate and hopeless complement to the futility and nihilism which the First World War has revealed as the essential element within which human beings have always lived when, for one reason or another, illusions are denied them. This critical view can treat the satire as historically contained—a condemnation of the shallow bourgeois Protestant ethic when it is tested by the absurd degradation of modern war; or, more ambitiously, as Hemingway's attempt to universalize the stark lessons of stoicism and philosophical resignation which have always ruled against man's attempts to impose transcendent meanings upon life. And again, the rhetorical resonance of the novel, as well as its ruthless, if muted, rejection of illusions, will offer a good deal to substantiate this position.

Probably, no interpretation will adequately capture the shifting nuances of meaning which generate the deeper energies in *The Sun Also Rises.* Satire, tragedy, even some variation of "romance" can find a supporting configuration in the novel, but only at the cost of deflecting the main thrust of the novel in an effort to make it amenable to the understanding. And the ultimate inconclusiveness of any interpretation will be almost entirely due to the ambiguous status of Jake Barnes. As the first-person narrator, he and only he is responsible for what the reader knows and what the reader can never know. But his reliability as a reporter is seriously affected by two factors: first, his inevitable physical and psychological passivity (unlike the popular Hemingway "hero," Jake is pre-eminently a man to whom things happen); and, second, his intense emotional involvement in the events that he describes, precisely because he is fighting as hard as he can to keep from succumbing to hysteria or despair. More than anything else, the novel is Jake's story, a blow-by-blow description, told from the inside, by a man struggling to catch his balance as he teeters on the edge of spiritual suicide. For Jake has already suffered his irreparable loss when the novel begins. Unusually responsive to physical sensation as are all Hemingway's heroes, Jake is continually beset by stimuli which mix a witches' brew of memory and desire in him. But he is not free to act upon his desires; the option of love is forever foreclosed in his life. *The Sun Also Rises* is a chronicle of Jake's attempt to live in a centerless world as a personality lacking a vital center. His dislocation is not single, but double, and it pervades his entire existence. Since Hemingway has chosen to locate the novel's viewing-point within a focus of such radical dislocation, we ought not to be surprised at the resultant confusion of interpretation because it is inherent in the internal dissociation of the narrative voice itself.

The point is that Jake cannot trust himself, nor can he even believe that he possesses or will ever possess a stable core of being which is potentially trustworthy. He must ignore his desires because they can only cause him anguish. He must try to bury his memories because they are only desires in a concealed guise. Even as he tries to maintain himself as a careful spectator in life, nurturing his epicurean satisfactions in the pleasures of trout fishing and watching bullfights, he finds himself acting the pander between Brett and Pedro Romero, and hence he betrays both his desired love and his hard-won *aficion*. He cannot trust himself because his grotesque wound has denuded him of man's most cherished illusion—the illusion that there is a center to one's life. It is in this context that Jake's often-quoted reflections during the fiesta should be interpreted:

> I thought I had paid for everything. Not like the woman pays and pays and pays. No idea of retribution or punishment. Just exchange of values. You gave up something and got something else. Or you worked for something. You paid some way for everything that was any good. . . . Either you paid by learning about them, or by experience, or by taking chances, or by money. Enjoying living was learning to get your money's worth. The world was a good place to buy in. It seemed like a fine philosophy. In five years, I thought, it will seem just as silly as all the other fine philosophies I've had.

> Perhaps that wasn't true though. Perhaps as you went along you did learn something. I did not care what it was all about. All I wanted to know was how to live in it. Maybe if you found out how to live in it you learned from that what it was all about.

This famous "exchange of values" philosophy is a movement from a concern with "essence" ("*what* it was all about") to a focus on "existence" ("*how* to live in it"). It is a movement which candidly rejects "centers" and transfers its interest to the peripheries of one's sensations. It suggests that life can be dealt with only as a system of transactions, a volatile sequence of energy-exchanges where the difference between life and death, value and worthlessness, being and nothingness, is dependent only on the capital reserve that is left in the credit column. And thus the structure of *The Sun Also Rises,* symmetrically but deceptively patterned in terms of the three acts of the classic bullfight, rests on a dynamically askew and radically dislocated, shifting basis.

This, it would seem, is the main source of the novel's strength and the root reason for Jake's moral success in achieving "a way to be" in the world. Without this eccentric focus, the novel would be little more than a banal variation of another "identity-quest," trite and pompous in its acquisition of platitudinous "truths." But Jake finds a different way out, or at least a viable technique of living within a world of inexorable loss. *Style* is what Jake resorts to after alcohol, religion, and philosophy have proved ineffectual in keeping him from crying at night in his room. Style of whatever kind is no more nor less than a manner, a system of rhythmic interrelationships, an achieved harmony of disparate movements, intentions, and effects. A "good" style is one which gives the impression of being inevitable and one which works; which, that is, accomplishes the job that it is set to do. And Hemingway's style in *The Sun Also Rises,* a style which is synonymous with Jake's voice, is the best documentation that we possess of Jake's success in working out for himself a psychological and spiritual balance without a center of gravity. Of all the characters in the novel, only he (and possibly Count Mippipopolous) achieve this order of style. Pedro Romero has an admirable style, of course, but it works only when he is fighting his bulls or Robert Cohn, and, at any rate, it is a "received," traditional style which is his by initiation and apprenticeship. Bill Gorton, Mike Campbell, and Brett also

possess a style of sorts; but it doesn't work particularly well for them, nor does it seem inevitable and natural.

The general life-style of the rootless expatriate world, as Hemingway presents it, is like that of an endless costume party where the drunks get drunker and the cheap finery gets shabbier and shabbier under the harsh lights. And Robert Cohn, of course, is the horrible example in the novel of precisely "the way *not* to be." In some sense Jake's alter ego, Cohn is sensitive, intelligent, and desperately eager to discover meaning and value in experience. However he is basically dishonest in his keeping of the accounts of his energy-transactions—the cardinal sin of an exchange-of-values philosophy is falsification—and his various styles (the romantic artist, the unrequited lover, the self-pitying martyr) are a succession of ill-fitting, secondhand gestures and responses which fool no one and fail to work at all. Only Jake has the self-discipline, the honesty, and the driving need to achieve a thin sleeve of freedom in recognizing and accepting the limitations of his condition. The prose style of *The Sun Also Rises* and the moral style which Jake successfully strives for are what give this book its power and continued relevance.

Hemingway was not to follow up this direction in his later work. Probably such an effort would have required an expense of psychic energy which no human being could have long sustained. Instead, he held on to the prose style which was Jake Barnes's achievement of a *moral* style, but he employed it to narrate the stories of men in the process of suffering loss. . . . Only in some of the magnificent short stories like **"Big Two-Hearted River"** (1925), **"In Another Country"** (1927), **"The Clean Well-Lighted Place"** (1933), and **"The Snows of Kilimanjaro"** (1936), stories, incidentally, in which the loss has occurred *before* the narrative begins, do we find that conjunction of prose style and moral style which Hemingway forged in *The Sun Also Rises,* seemingly as a last-ditch strategy to cope with a world stripped of illusions where *nada* is omnipresent and well-nigh omnipotent.

It would be well to remember here that as significant as the novel may have been in the development of Hemingway's work, *The Sun Also Rises* has enjoyed an importance of its own apart from Hemingway. What fortuitous conjunction of events it is that transforms a novel into a cultural document—what makes some works of art take on an additional life as expressions of an historical period or, indeed, a national life-style, we do not at all know. . . . At any rate, it is surely provocative to note that *The Sun Also Rises* was published within four years of such major American statements as Eliot's *The Waste Land,* Dreiser's *An American Tragedy,* and Faulkner's *The Sound and the Fury.* Certainly these four books are vividly independent, each pursuing its own content and creating its own form in terms of each individual author's unfathomable needs and artistic gifts. And yet there are curious similarities and parallels between these titles. If not one of them is a tragedy, still they all of them traffic surprisingly close to that mood of grotesque poignancy which may be the nearest our age can come to the spirit of the tragic. In Hemingway's and Eliot's works there is literal sexual impotence; in Dreiser's and Faulkner's books, a symbolic impotence is a major factor in the development of both plots. Further, all four books are, in their various ways, equally zealous at unmasking the social and metaphysical illusions which impose palpably false meanings on human experience.

Jake Barnes had suggested that "you paid some way for everything that was any good." "After such knowledge, what forgiveness?" asks Eliot's Gerontion, and, in a sense, all four of these books, foundering on the jagged intransigencies of payment and retribution, brood over the dark implications in those two statements: implications which challenge the very existence of moral impetus, responsibility, and the primal integrity of the human consciousness. The four authors differ greatly in the degree of intensity with which they suggest an ultimately nihilistic reality as the sole reality in the universe, and each, perhaps, offers his own tentative saving graces, but the void is frighteningly near to the surfaces of all of these texts. Most coincidentally of all, each of these books is fundamentally *uncentered* in a manner similar or analogous to the way *The Sun Also Rises* is uncentered. . . . [This] congruence of metaphor and structure in what are probably the four outstanding books of that great decade may indicate one reason why *The Sun Also Rises* has had a singular position among the scores of very good books that are part of the post-First World War disillusionment. These four works not only *reflect* the whirling frenzy of a culture in the midst of historical upheaval, but they also *project* metaphorical patterns of thought (specifically, those concerned with the most basic metaphor of all—the metaphor of man himself) that we are only now beginning to recognize and investigate with care.

Purely as a result of a geographical and a series of historical accidents, American culture has always been a "modern" culture; and its most basic and constant experience has been that of radical dislocation. Obviously this fact has been a source of both cultural strength and weakness. But one of the strengths has been the peculiar position accorded to the American writer within, as well as on the margins of, the western world. The American artist has enjoyed (or been burdened by) a special prescience, an almost preternatural and prophetic sensitivity to the major movements in modern life. Since his equilibrium has never come from traditionally supported bases of gravity, like a seismograph he has been inordinately receptive to the slightest of vibrations. . . . While Hemingway can be seen as at least a partial heir to that tradition, *The Sun Also Rises* is informed by an uncanny intuition of a new metaphor. As the Newtonian world-machine image of the eighteenth century gave way to the organic metaphor of the nineteenth century, so it is possible that the organic metaphor has already been supplanted by a new world-view, a view for which the most adequate metaphorical image may be that of explosion. If this is so, then it is likely that radically dislocated structures that are capable of functioning well, and personalities without a vital center that can maintain viable lives should have a special meaning for us today. And it is, finally, for this reason that *The Sun Also Rises* ought to continue to command our attention and provoke our thought. (pp. 303-12)

> *Earl H. Rovit, "Ernest Hemingway: 'The Sun Also Rises','" in* Landmarks of American Writing, *edited by Hennig Cohen, Basic Books, Inc., Publishers, 1969, pp. 303-14.*

TERRENCE DOODY

> In the morning it was raining. A fog had come over the mountains from the sea. You could not see the tops of the mountains. The plateau was dull and gloomy, and the shapes of the trees and houses were changed. I walked out beyond the town to look at the weather. The bad weather was coming in over the mountains from the sea.

With its insistent observation, simplicity, and repetitions this paragraph, which opens Chapter XVI of *The Sun Also Rises,* is a quintessential example of Hemingway's style, which we have honored because it has worked so well to recover for us (in Merleau-Ponty's phrase) "a naive contact with the world." Despite its naivete, however, Hemingway's style is not simply simple. And this paragraph of description is also a paragraph defining character. For it proceeds from the mouth of Jake Barnes, the novel's narrator, who makes it not because he is interested in giving a weather bulletin; but because at this point in the chaos of the fiesta at Pamplona, the weather is a certainty and getting it exactly gives Jake something, however incidental, to hold on to. It is an arresting paragraph because, as Edwin Muir says, Hemingway's power of "observation is so exact that it has the effect of imagination." For Hemingway, observation is an imaginative act, the issue of his style; but for Jake, who does not have "a style," it is something else. And this discrepancy is what raises problems about Jake's act of narration.

Other critics have seen certain difficulties in Jake's characterization. Earl Rovit, for instance, calls Jake a "particularly opaque first person narrator." Richard B. Hovey finds in Jake a psychological unreliability that makes his relation to Hemingway more ambiguous and revealing than we usually suppose it to be. Yet Rovit and Hovey, like most other critics, eventually affirm the formal success of Jake's narrative and, with E. M. halliday, praise Hemingway's solution to the problem of preserving a convincing immediacy in a retrospective narration. . . . Epitomizing Halliday's argument, Sheldon Norman Grebstein says: ". . . certainly the remarkable technical feature of the novel is the consistency and control of its narrative perspective and narrative voice." Grebstein goes on to say that one of the reasons Hemingway succeeds as well as he does is that "he deliberately avoids identifying the narrator at a precise point in time and space and thus minimizes the artificiality that sometimes attaches to the I-narratives of James and Conrad."

Grebstein's praise seems to beg the essential problem, however. The fundamental questions we ask about first person narrators deal with irony, reliability and distance. These are rhetorical categories, but their real concern is epistemological: what does the narrator know, how does he know, how fully do these constitute the meaning of the novel? Beneath these, there is another question, equally serious and moral as well as technical: how free is the narrator? By asking this question, we reverse the equation of distance in order to ask: how far away does the author allow his narrator to get? how specifically does he dramatize his narrator's autonomous capacity to make the narrative he makes? Successfully realized narrators who are placed "at a precise point in time and space," like James and Conrad's, have an autonomy that always makes them at least slightly "unreliable" simply because they are not the author of themselves nor the entirety of the fiction they inhabit. Now, we can all agree that Jake is not Hemingway himself, nor is he problematically unreliable in the way that, say, Gulliver is, and what Jake knows is certainly central to the meaning of *The Sun Also Rises.* Yet Jake remains a problem precisely because he has not been located in space and time, so he is never as far away from Hemingway as he should be and, therefore, never free enough to substantiate his own agency as the narrator. In *The Sun Also Rises,* Jake is more a function of the style than its source, and he finally gives to the style more than he gets from it because his voice and character are used to justify a vision of the world that Jake is never allowed to possess as his own.

What Jake does for the style is probably best exemplified in the variety of effects his voice can educe from the device of polysyndeton Hemingway uses so frequently. This polysyndeton Hemingway generally directs against the habits and assumptions of perception that organize experience into hierarchies of abstraction, value and time. For polysyndeton democratizes sensations and impressions; and in giving them all their equality, it preserves the primitive fullness and immediacy that is the hallmark of Hemingway's prose. In *The Sun Also Rises,* this democratizing effect is most patent in the landscape passages where the repeated use of *and* suggests peaceful slow time and an undiscriminating passivity, as the details of the scene accumulate themselves and compose Jake's mind while he travels from Paris in to Spain or up to the Irati fishing ground. To the arrival scene in Pamplona, however, these same *and's* are spoken in a more acctive voice that imparts a rush of enthusiasm to Jake's happy first impressions. (pp. 212-14)

A few pages later in the same chapter, *and* is "utilized" (as Jake would say) to conduct Jake's stream-of-consciousness as he tries to pray in the Pamplona cathedral. Though this next passage would never be mistaken for one of Joyce's, in 1926 Hemingway's style is still fresh enough to be more effective than embarrassing.

> I went inside. It was dim and dark and the pillars went high up, and there were people praying, and it smelt of incense, and there were some wonderful big windows. I knelt and started to pray and prayed for everybody I thought of, Brett and Mike and Bill and Robert Cohn and myself, and all the bull-fighters, separately for the ones I liked, and lumping all the rest, then I prayed for myself again, and while I was praying for myself I found I was getting sleepy, so I prayed that the bull-fights would be good, and that it would be a fine fiesta, and that we would get some fishing. I wondered if there was anything else I might pray for, and I thought I would like to have some money, so I prayed that I would make a lot of money, and then I started to think how I would make it, and thinking of making money reminded me of the count, and I started wondering about where he was, and regretting I hadn't seen him since that night in Montmartre, and about something funny Brett told me about him and as all the time I was kneeling with my forehead on the wood in front of me, and was thinking of myself as praying, I was a little ashamed, and regretted that I was such a rotten Catholic, but realized there was nothing I could do about it, at least for a while, and maybe never, but that anyway it was a grand religion, and I only wished I felt religious and maybe I would the next time; and then I was out in the hot sun on the steps of the cathedral, and the forefingers and thumb of my right hand were still damp, and I felt them dry in the sun. The sunlight was hot and hard, and I crossed over beside some buildings, and walked back along side-streets to the hotel.

In mixing Jake's memory and desire, this passage could have used some variety of tense and perhaps a more elliptical method for the transitions that are so earnestly consecutive. Nonetheless, the crudeness of the polysyndeton itself suggests very clearly the difficulty that self-consciousness causes in Hemingway's characters when they try to think. And the mo-

mentum the prose gathers enacts the motive, hidden in the passage's one ellipsis, that drives Jake from the church. When he discovers the holy water he has used to bless himself still on his hand, he begins to regain the control he has lost in thought by cataloguing the sensations that are always more certain.

Jake's voice also has an effect on Hemingway's style of conversation, which in *The Sun Also Rises* is characteristically laconic and very smart, and which is the least expressive literary technique ever to exert so great an influence on expression. What we tend to forget, unless we read Hemingway aloud, is that his conversation can also be very funny, as it is in the fishing episodes. But Jake is even capable of deliberate self-parody. In a passage he speaks to himself as he tries unsuccessfully to fall to sleep, not only does he comment on his own "hard-boiled" honesty, he even counters the flaccidity of the earlier stream-of-consciousness.

> What a lot of bilge I could think up at night. What rot, I could hear Brett say it. What Rot! When you are with English you got into the habit of using English expressions in your thinking. The English spoken language—the upper classes, anyway—must have fewer words than the Eskimo. Of course, I didn't know anything about the Eskimo. Maybe the Eskimo was a fine language. Say the Cherokee. I didn't know anything about the Cherokee either. The English talked with inflected phrases. One phrase to mean everything. I like them, though. I liked the way they talked. Take Harris. Still Harris was not the upper classes.

Hemingway does not often laugh at himself like this. . . . Yet because Jake Barnes is usually prevented from taking himself so seriously, he almost never succumbs to the portentousness that can inflate Hemingway's "simplicity."

When Jake does succumb, however, as he does in a paragraph in Chapter XVII, the fall is obvious and revealing.

> The bull who killed Vicente Girones was named Bocanegra, was Number 118 of the bull-breeding establishment of Sanchez Taberno, and was killed by Pedro Romero as the third bull of that same afternoon. His ear was cut by popular acclamation and given to Pedro Romero, who, in turn, gave it to Brett, who wrapped it in a handkerchief belonging to myself, and left both ear and handkerchief, along with a number of Muratti cigarette-stubs, shoved far back in the drawer of the bed-table that stood beside her bed in the Hotel Montoya, in Pamplona.

This passage is the most explicit statement of the absurdity Hemingway sees in a world where the sun does not seem to rise for anyone. The prose feels highly organized, with its hard turns, rapid accretion of detail, and sharp grade of declination, but the facts the first sentence juxtaposes so tightly have no causal connection at all. The bull that accidentally kills Vicente Girones is not for that reason then killed by Pedro Romero; the bull's name, number, and owner are pointedly irrelevant. On the other hand, the connections in the second sentence that are consequential are destructive. Brett's thoughtlessness reduces what is both a ritual trophy and a gift of love to the value of the random cigarette butts; and her use of Jake's handkerchief emphasizes his collusion in what he himself recognizes as Brett's corruption of Romero.

This paragraph sounds very different from the weather report, the arrival scene, the stream-of-consciousness; and for all its "significance," it sounds wrong. "A handkerchief belonging to myself" (which could have been "my handkerchief" without upsetting the rhythm of the line) is clumsier, more precious than it has to be; "in the Hotel Montoya, in Pamplona" is the kind of phrase that creates the invisible italics of a mannerism. These phrases heighten the effect, but cheapen the absurdity toward cynicism, and nowhere else in the novel is Jake so merely cynical. Moreover, nowhere else in the novel does he violate the chronology of the original events for the sake of such an effect. Jake could not have known about the bull's ear in the drawer until much later, until after Brett has left Pamplona with Romero. So while this paragraph may or may not be bad Hemingway, depending on your own taste, it is uncharacteristic of Jake Barnes, the narrator. And though Hemingway's intrusion here is slight, it points to the novel's central problem. Jake is most convincing when he is least self-conscious; yet because he is so unself-conscious about the whole of his narrative, he is hard to accept as the authoritative and autonomous source of the fiction his own voice delivers. As the paragraph about Bocanegra, which is so deliberately *written,* inadvertantly hints, Jake is possessed by a style that will finally not allow him any possession of himself.

All first person narratives require of the reader a certain suspension of disbelief. . . . If Jake were simply a passive behavioralistic register, there would be no problem; for then we could resign ourselves to seeing him as the medium through which events are made manifest and read *The Sun Also Rises* as something other than the novel of education that it is. Or if Jake were more completely dramatized in time, there would be no problem with the conclusions he draws in the paragraph about Bocanegra. But Hemingway wants it both ways. In order to preserve the famous immediacy, Hemingway cannot acknowledge that Jake's different perceptions have different styles of expression, which originate in Jake and for which he should have the authority. In other words, the prose changes, but Jake is not allowed to change it himself or see himself as changing. Time is denied, in effect, and with that denial Hemingway deprives Jake of both his freedom and his autonomy.

Jake seems to be at his most behavioralistic when he describes the Spanish street dancers in Chapter XV.

> In front of us on a clear part of the street a company of boys were dancing. The steps were very intricate and their faces were intent and concentrated. They all looked down while they danced. Their rope-soled shoes tapped and spatted on the pavement. The toes touched. The heels touched. The balls of the feet touched. Then the music broke wildly and the step was finished and they were all dancing up the street.

The dancer's gaze directs Jake's; responding to them first, he then sees and appropriates their dance, the music that orders it, and their career up the street. Though Jake does not give meaning to this dance in the way that he gives meaning to the weather, his response is not simply determined by it. No one else in the novel has the intensity of perception that allows Jake to see this dance so clearly; and in fact, his description of the dance comes in answer to Bill Gorton's unsatisfying generalization that "They dance differently to all the different tunes."

Jake's ability to see into the nature of things and to inform these things with his own values becomes even more apparent during the bullfights, which are at the center of the novel's meaning. Though he is no longer an able Catholic, Jake is an *aficionado* who has been confirmed by a laying on of hands, and he can see in the bullfights what most of the native Spanish spectators cannot: Belmonte's arrogant, classical integrity and Romero's act of romantic transformation. When he comes to describe Belmonte, Jake's paragraphs grow noticeably longer, and his narration is more fluent than it is anywhere else in the story. This next paragraph could not be more different than it is from the earlier stream-of-consciousness paragraph when Jake tries to pray in the Pamplona cathedral. The two paragraphs are exact thematic counterparts: Jake has difficulty praying, but no trouble at all in seeing the ritual that Belmonte both enacts and defies.

> Also Belmonte imposed conditions and insisted that his bulls should not be too large, nor too dangerously armed with horns, and so the element that was necessary to give the sensation of tragedy was not there, and the public, who wanted three times as much from Belmonte, who was sick with a fistula, as Belmonte had ever been able to give, felt defrauded and cheated, and Belmonte's jaw came further out in contempt, and his face turned yellower, and he moved with greater difficulty as his pain increased, and finally the crowd were actively against him, and he was utterly contemptuous and indifferent. He had meant to have a great afternoon, and instead it was an afternoon of sneers, shouted insults, and finally a volley of cushions and pieces of bread and vegetables, thrown down at him in the plaza where he had had his greatest triumphs. His jaw only went further out. Sometimes he turned to smile that toothed, long-jawed, lipless smile when he was called something particularly insulting, and always the pain that any movement produced grew stronger and stronger, until finally his yellow face was parchment color, and after his second bull was dead and the throwing of bread and cushions was over, after he had saluted the President with the same wolf-jawed smile and contemptuous eyes, and handed his sword over the barrera to be wiped, and put back in its case, he passed through into the callejon and leaned on the barrera below us, his head on his arms, not seeing, not hearing anything, only going through with it. When he looked up, finally, he asked for a drink of water. He swallowed a little, rinsed his mouth, spat the water, took his cape, and went back into the ring.

The long sustained lines of this paragraph are Jake's tribute to Belmonte's endurance and as firm in their expression as Belmonte is in his. But because Romero is doing something quite different in converting his bullfight into an act of tribute to Brett, Jake's description of him is appropriately different.

> Pedro Romero had the greatness. He loved bullfighting, and I think he loved the bulls, and I think he loved Brett. Everything of which he could control the locality he did in front of her all that afternoon. Never once did he look up. He made it stronger that way, and did it for himself, too, as well as for her. Because he did not look up to ask if it pleased he did it all for himself inside, and it strengthened him, and yet he did it for her, too. But he did not do it for her at any loss to himself. He gained by it all through the afternoon.

Jake is both uncertain and insistent here. The hesitancy and repetition of these sentences, the parallels of contrast, express and enforce the tension between Romero's discipline and his aspiration, between what he is doing in conformity with the rite and what he is doing beyond that as an offering to Brett. And we can feel Jake working as hard as Romero does to understand exactly what Romero is doing. Although he loves Brett desperately, Jake re-creates Romero's gift and makes its creation understood with a generosity even more impressive than his ability to see it in the first place.

Watching the bullfights forces Jake to face again the sad inadequacies of his situation and all the things Romero can do, for himself and for Brett, that Jake cannot. Still Jake loves the bullfights because they offer him an authentic, historic ritual—more meaningful than the Church, more permanent and communal than the fishing trip—that is the only mode he has to satisfy his need for order and control. When he describes Romero, he comes as close as he is allowed to describing himself and his own activity; for he too works within the discipline of an imposed style, without looking up, and gains from that fidelity a private strength. Jake's description re-enacts Romero's deed and gives it its personally expressive form—without which it would have meant something else and less, as it does to the native spectators. But it is impossible to tell whether Jake knows exactly what he is doing. For all his clarity of vision, he is opaque; but he is too old to be a Huckleberry Finn. He is, in fact, much closer to Nick Carraway, and he does for Romero what Nick does for Gatsby: he sees in Romero more than anyone else does and makes of that insight the definition of a hero, which entails a correlative definition of himself. But unlike Nick, Jake is finally deprived of that insight's ultimate personal advantage. (pp. 214-19)

[Jake] does not have Nick's freedom or distance. For Jake is only self-conscious enough to be suspicious of "all frank and simple people, especially when their stories hold together" and to be worried about how fair he is being to Cohn, whom he initially likes in spite of everything. These signs—and there are others like them—are fairly unexceptional notations of Jake's credibility, and they all come early in the novel, in Paris, long before Jake is required to face the bullfights. Moreover, Cohn is much less important as the test of Jake's honesty than he is as Jake's antagonist and anti-type. In *The Sun Also Rises,* Cohn absorbs much of the self-indulgence and sentimentality that later afflicts, and consecrates, so many of Hemingway's leading men. And what is most damning about Cohn is that he is a bad novelist, who profiteers on his popularity and who is described by Bill as a "great little confider. Jake, of course, is no confider at all. Only Brett knows his real pain, and only the unspecified reader has any access to Jake's thought. For though he is a writer by profession, Jake neither writes nor tells his narrative to anyone in particular, not even to himself. There is in *The Sun Also Rises* no formal recognition of the motive or the occasion of Jake's retrospect, nor beyond that is there any indication of his imaginative agency in producing the narrative, if even only for the purpose of his own self-discovery. So, we are asked to suspend our disbelief to the extent that we can accept the perfect paragraphs about Belmonte and Romero as coming from right off the top of Jake's head. And we are therefore led to conclude that Jake cannot be self-conscious without violating Hemingway's code. For if he were to solicit an audience, or commit his perceptual experience and moral education to a formal mode, Jake would apparently relinquish the integrity and self-control, with all their noble helplessness,

that Cohn relinquishes all the time by being so helpless in public. Art and morality are therefore at odds in *The Sun Also Rises,* and Jake's narrative is left formally suspended in the caesura between the many fine things Jake is supposed to be and the very few things he is allowed to do. Jake himself is left with only the bullfights and his "good behavior" because he does not have the novel he narrates. The only thing we see Jake write is a telegram.

Beyond all the familiar questions about Hemingway's indifference to history, culture and the mind, there is still the question of his personal *involvement* in his own art and how this affects the nature of his characters. In the case of Jake Barnes, the first answer to suggest itself is that Jake, despite his general reliability and clear virtue, is a profoundly ironic characterization: a portrait of the artist as an early middle-aged loser. For he has been given formidable powers of perception and a fine sense of language, but is left holding them in a situation that suggests they are insufficient and effete. Though this may be the case in fact, it does not seem to be the novel's intention, and there is nothing else in Hemingway's work or carer to support such a reading. For all his other interests in the sporting life, Hemingway speaks of the artist's vocation always with the utmost seriousness; and no one in the twentieth century fashioned a more public and romantic career *as a writer* than Hemingway did.

The second answer is that Hemingway does not realize what he is doing to Jake because he has not thought out the first person novel and its demands with enough care. This reading seems more defensible. Hemingway's most frequent mode of narration is the kind of omniscience he uses to tell the story of Nick Adams in **"Big Two-Hearted River."** In time and characterization, Nick Adams is close to Jake. Nick's retreat to a pastoral fishing ground and his need for personalized rituals are, like Jake's, the method of his post-war education in the discipline necessary to "live in it" (Jake's phrase). Nick, however, is not the narrator of his story. All of his experience and responses are presented through the intimately omniscient third person that Hemingway uses so well to close the distance between subject and object, reader and character. Nick need not be conscious of all the implications of his experience, nor its shape, because the style—Hemingway's style—does all the work of focus and exclusion necessary to convey the pressure Nick works through and against to achieve his self-possession. The power of **"Big Two-Hearted River"** results from our awareness that Nick endures his need to not think with such resolution, and our necessarily distant perspective on his enforced unconsciousness is essential to the poignancy we are made to feel in Nick's self-control.

Because Jake Barnes is the narrator, however, the style of *The Sun Also Rises* is supposedly his style. So, our experience of Jake and, therefore, our expectations of him are different. And immersed in his consciousness, we come to see that Jake's value and significance results precisely from his ability to understand the experience he undergoes. Unlike Nick Adams, Jake is not simply holding on and watching; for during the bullfights, he gives himself away to an experience that fosters in him not only a moral selflessness (which is why he pimps for Brett), but also the aesthetic impersonality that is the fundamental imperative of modernist literature. This impersonality is an ideal Hemingway honors in his definition of "the real thing, the sequence of motion and fact which made the emotion and which would be as valid in a year or in ten years or, with luck and if you stated it purely enough, always. . . . " (pp. 220-21)

Malcolm Cowley has said that "Hemingway himself sometimes seems to regard writing as an exhausting ceremony of exorcism"; and Philip Young has argued at length that Hemingway's stylistic austerity is his method of self-control. More recently, Alfred Kazin has concluded that for Hemingway the sovereignty of the storyteller himself is the *"matter* of fiction." The ultimate implication of these insights is that whatever integrity results from this way of writing is, first, the property of the artist himself and only secondarily the property of the artifact. Yet for Hemingway's most important contemporaries—Joyce, Faulkner, and Lawrence—the integrity of the artifact is what establishes the artist's sovereignty; and for them, style is not at all an exorcism, but the continual project of discovery, self-extension, and even transcendence. Consequently, Joyce, Faulkner and Lawrence have changed The Novel, while Hemingway's real and most enduring effect has been on the construction of the sentence.

Hemingway does not transcend himself in Jake Barnes because Jake is never free enough to move away and establish an autonomy that could rival Hemingway's own. Jake is held close and kept down as though Hemingway were competing with him. And it is this "competitive" need that Reynolds Price defines in his essay of homage, "For Ernest Hemingway," when he says:

> His early strategy is always, at its most calculated, an oral strategy. If we hear it read, it seems the convincing speaking-voice of this sensibility. Only on the silent page do we discover that it is an unidiomatic, as ruthlessly intentional as any *tirade* of Racine's. For behind and beneath all the voices of the actors (themselves as few in number as in Sophocles) rides the one real voice—the maker's. And what it says, early and late, is always this—"This is what I see with my clean keen equipment. Work to see it after me." What it does not say but implies is more important—"For you I have narrowed and filtered my gaze. I am screening my vision so you will not see all. Why?—because you must enact this story for yourself; cast it, dress it, set it. Notice the chances I've left for you: no noun or verb is colored by me. I require your senses." What is most important of all—and what I think is the central motive—is this, which is concealed and of which the voice itself may be unconscious: "I tell you this, in this voice, because you must share—*must* because I require your presence, your company in my vision. I beg you to certify my knowledge and experience, my goodness and worthiness. I mostly speak as *I.* What I need from you is not empathy, identity, but patient approving witness—loving. License my life. Believe me."

Price's insight has more drama and intensity than a critic usually allows himself. Yet it is, I think, absolutely right. "I mostly speak as *I.*" Although Hemingway's name cannot be easily corrupted into an adjective, his style is always his, unmistakably. And Hemingway's need for the reader's belief and confirmation is both his principal strength and his greatest weakness. His need gives his prose its lucidity and weight, but this same need has kept him in *The Sun Also Rises* from giving to Jake Barnes the free authority that would make the novel Jake's fiction. His courage, his honesty, and his generosity make Jake a convincingly good man—the hardest kind of character to do. But if Jake is to be pitied, it is because

Hemingway cannot give to him as much as Jake himself gives to Romero. Jake is so good, perhaps, that Hemingway cannot allow him to be quite true, lest we forget Hemingway himself is in charge of Jake and the author of the book.

Perhaps the final irony is, that of all Hemingway's imitators, Faulkner has used the Hemingway style with the most command. Yet the character who sounds most like a Hemingway narrator, limited to the immediate immutable present and unpossessed of himself, is Benjy Compson in the opening paragraphs of *The Sound and the Fury.* Without an explicit authority like Nick Carraway's, Jake remains, like Benjy, a brilliant observer but helpless. If Hemingway had known what he was doing to Jake and had done it on purpose, he would, perhaps, not have lost the reputation he has been losing, decade by decade, as we have come to understand the exigencies of the modernist novel and to shift our allegiances to Faulkner and Fitzgerald. A naive contact with the world does not provide us with "world enough and time." (pp. 222-23)

> Terrence Doody, "Hemingway's Style and Jake's Narration," in The Journal of Narrative Technique, *Vol. 4, No. 3, September, 1974, pp. 212-25.*

SAM S. BASKETT

In an early recognition of Hemingway's "literary" and "historical" accomplishment, John Peale Bishop observed in an essay taking its title from Emily Dickinson's "The Missing All," "It is the mark of the true novelist that in searching the meaning of his unsought experience, he comes on the moral history of his time." Hemingway studies over the years have further secured this recognition, particularly for *The Sun Also Rises.* Given what has become the critical consensus that this first novel somehow expresses the way it was in Hemingway's early time, there has been surprising disagreement about just what is revealed by the distinctly different experiences of Jake Barnes, Pedro Romero, Robert Cohn and Bill Gorton, each of whom has received consideration as the moral center of a work that has also often been read as having no moral center. These contradictory readings have not been easy to reconcile, supported as they largely are by seemingly convincing evidence. Yet the counterpointed experiences of the novel's principal characters do resolve into a clearly discernible moral pattern if they are brought into sharp "literary" and "historical" focus, a pattern that in part constructs the time's moral history as well as embodies it.

This is to say that the several lovers of Lady Brett Ashley fix upon her as an uncertain image of great value; to paraphrase the Lady herself, she is sort of what they have instead of God. To their image of her they make such overtures as the time and their individual capacities permit, overtures recalling the question Frost's oven bird "frames in all but words / . . . what to make of a diminished thing": for the value each affixes to Brett is a function of his value of himself and the life he is able to live. From these combined self-definitions emerges the "meaning" of the novel, the significance of which is most fully realized in the context of the patterns of a number of other authentic American "fictions" of the early twentieth century. (pp. 45-6)

In the consummate poem which now seems to epitomize the emerging "modern" era, T. S. Eliot's Prufrock describes a circumstance of chaos counterpointed by his desire for a center of meaning symbolized by the attracting power of woman. Thus, a central autobiography and a central poem of the time Hemingway inherited present a compelling version of the same image which dominates *The Sun Also Rises.* That image is also dominant in the novel which impressed Hemingway as an "absolutely first rate work" in May, 1925, two months before he began his own novel. In *The Great Gatsby,* he found a situation similar to the one he would employ, that of a woman idealized far beyond her "perishable" features controlling the world of her "high-bouncing lover" of the epigraph. In her depletion, Lady Brett Ashley, of course, is more akin to Daisy Fay, as she is finally realized, than . . . [to] Eliot's "one." How well both seemed to illustrate the extremity of the new age is apparent in Joseph Wood Krutch's *The Modern Temper,* published in 1929. The chapter "Love—or the Life and Death of a Value" describes a generation attributing to love "some of the functions of the God they had lost," although inexorably rationalism and physiology were stripping it of its "mystical penumbra." Krutch thus points to a major transformation in the treatment of Woman by Fitzgerald and Hemingway . . . [Eliot is] primarily concerned with Woman as symbolic of highest value, even if that symbol now seemed superseded or inaccessible. The two novelists, however, in a "time of troubles," were not only concerned with what R. P. Blackmur termed "a kind of irregular and spasmodic, but vitalized metaphysics," but also with "a broad and irregular psychology." Daisy is elevated to the role of goddess in Gatsby's romping mind, but she continues to exist, and ultimately *only* exists on a human psychological plane. In the presentation of several "visions" of Lady Brett Ashley, however, Hemingway was to hold in more ambiguous, if precarious, balance the perishable and transcendent, as a complex parade of lovers offer her their varied services in keeping with such value as love retains in their scheme of things.

Brett's complicated characterization is enigmatically voiced in both French and English by Jake's concierge: "that lady, that lady there is some one. An eccentric, perhaps, but quelqu'une, quelqu'une." Assuredly, Brett is "some one," in more than one language. As a type of the new woman of the 1920's, she radiates independence, intelligence and beauty. She sees through "rot," sharing with Jake a more profound appreciation of the "modern temper" than that of the other characters. Her appearance reflects the new idea of beauty, her short hair "brushed back like a boy's"—indeed, Jake claims proudly, "She started all that." In a striking image that suggests both her femininity and her impersonality, she is described as being "built with curves like the hull of a racing yacht, and you missed none of it with that wool jersey." Apparently her own woman, in only a few weeks she engages sexually with at least two men in addition to her fiancé. Under the gaiety of Mike's quip that their hotel is a brothel is the serious theme of Brett's debasement of sex. Half asleep, Jake can confuse her voice with that of Georgette, the *poule* he takes to dinner.

Yet in her feminine attractiveness, debased or otherwise, Brett remains essentially unfathomable, somehow apart, as Jake states expressly. She has a way of looking "that made you wonder whether she really saw out of her own eyes. They would look on and on after every one else's eyes in the world would have stopped looking." This is surely extraordinary seeing, both in relation to Brett and in relation to Jake as he sees Brett seeing. Jake immediately adds the ordinary, human dimension, however, appearing to recognize that the powers he attributes to her are illusory: "She looked as though there were nothing on earth she would not look at like that, and really she was afraid of so many things." But Brett, even when she is most "afraid," at least until the final scenes, is principally a contained figure to whom her suitors react, rather than a human being whose motives are susceptible to psychological analysis.

Brett's "mystical penumbra" is greatly intensified by a number of suggestions that she is more than "just personal," even to Jake, "my own true love. . . . [my only] friend in the world." In a passage of over one hundred words excised from the manuscript, Jake makes this dimension of their "own true love" even more explicit in an aside to his reader, disclaiming any psychological understanding of Brett or of his unbelievable passion for this person who determines his world. Perhaps Hemingway felt that enough evidence of Brett's strangeness remained in the novel, for there are many motifs suggesting her uniqueness, even apart from her magnification by her different lovers. For example, ironically enough, her promiscuity, which seems almost maternal, never casually salacious. . . . [She] acts for reasons not fully specifiable, at least as the data is given in the novel, but surely her motives go beyond simple self-gratification on any level, motives somehow related to the symbolic beauty of one who "started all that."

In another persistent motif, Brett seems to seek absolution for her actions through her compulsion to bathe, a persistence that expresses a desire for purification transcending cleanliness. But Brett's extraordinary qualities are most directly suggested in Pamplona, where on one occasion she walks through the crowd, "her head up, as though the fiesta were being staged in her honor." Earlier, on the afternoon of "the big religious procession" when "San Fermin was *translated* from one church to another," Brett is stopped inside the church because she is hatless. Clearly she is the wrong image for the church, too much a disheveled Venus to be allowed in the presence of the Virgin. Even appropriately attired, "I'm damned bad for a religious atmosphere. . . . I've got the wrong type of face." Outside, however, in the street that runs

> from the chapel into town. . . . lined on both sides with people keeping their place . . . for the return of the procession. . . . dancers formed a circle around Brett and started to dance. . . . They took Bill and me by the arms and put us in the circle. Bill started to dance, too. They were all chanting. Brett wanted to dance but they did not want her to. *They wanted her as an image to dance around"* [Italics added].

The interpretation is Jake's, of course, but Brett's actions here, as throughout much of the novel indicate that, try as she will to be merely a dancer, she possesses an aspect, however "wrong" that causes her to be an image "translated" from one sort of "church" to another—the otherwise empty space between the "chapel" and "town" around which a number of people dance in the absence of the return of "the big religious procession."

Six men in *The Sun Also Rises* offer Brett such love as they have: Bill Gorton, Count Mippipopolous, Mike Campbell, Pedro Romero, Robert Cohn and Jake Barnes. The first three listed are without illusions. . . . To them, there is no supreme value and Brett, far from incarnating such an ideal is a sexually tantalizing woman whom each in his own way wants to possess. It is easy to overlook the fact that at first Bill is much taken by her. Appreciative of the "Beautiful lady. . . . Going to kidnap us" before he has even met her, he responds to her spirited, openly flirtatious manner with a wittily veiled allusion to fornication and a promise to join her later. In only a few minutes, he has decided she is "Quite a girl," but on learning of her engagement to Mike he backs away, and there are no more charged exchanges, even rarely any conversation, between them. His immediate and total withdrawal expresses both his attitude toward Brett and his general approach to life. It is revealing that his friend Edna wishes that Bill had been present when Cohn fights Jake and Mike. "I'd like to have seen Bill knocked down, too. I've always wanted to see Bill knocked down. He's so big." Through the ironic code he tries to teach Jake, Bill remains "big" by limiting his risks, with Brett or anyone else. Having casually noticed the "Beautiful lady," he as casually dismisses her from his concern, despite an encouragement that would have fulfilled Cohn's greatest dreams, when he realizes love for her would not be an uncomplicated "exchange of values." And so he continues loveless, a quality apparent even in his relation with Jake, the person he is "fonder of . . . than anybody on earth." Ultimately, they don't really speak the same language. "You don't understand irony," he jeers at Jake jokingly, whereas Bill, entertaining, charming friend though he may be, lives through irony.

The count explains to Jake and Brett the "secret" of his enjoyment of life: "You must get to know the values." Having established his scheme in terms of what he can buy, he buys—champagne from his friend Baron Mumms, gourmet meals, a "housefull" of antiquities, eighteen eleven brandy, ladies with "class." Later, praying to "make a lot of money," Jake is reminded of the count. When Brett amusedly queries whether love has any place in his values,—a question in itself emphasizing her role in the novel—he responds that he is always in love. "That, too, has got a place in my values." Brett retorts, "You're dead," for she well understands that place: ten thousand dollars if she will go to Biarritz with him. To the count—who never "joke[s] people. Joke people and you make enemies"—love is obviously a serious business; it is either purchasable or not. With his love, as with his wine, the count does not intend "to mix emotions up" lest he will "lose the taste." Despite his impressive wounds, the count is hardly the hero much critical commentary has made of him.

Like Bill and the count, Mike sets a high value on his fiancée's sexual attractiveness: she, to him, is "a lovely piece." His emotions, of course, are involved to an extent precluded by Bill's irony and the count's accountant practicality, but they arise from his need for a mutual dependence, rather than any commitment to ideal worth. As Mike writes to Jake, "I know her so well and try to look after her but it's not so easy." Nor is it easy for Brett to look after Mike. . . . At the end, although she cannot bring herself to marry him, she plans to go back to Mike, and they doubtless will live in a brothel of sorts, alcohol and good-natured carelessness Mike's only defense against their mutual inadequacies in "looking after" each other.

Bill, the count and Mike remain unchanged by their "love" for Brett. Cohn, on the other hand, is vulnerable to passion and transformed by it. Boyishly cheerful, "he had been moulded by the two women who had trained him." His present "lady"—so designated four times in one page by Jake—had taken him in hand: "Cohn never had a chance of not

being taken in hand. And he was sure he loved her." "[L]ed . . . quite a life" by this demanding mistress, he is also the servant of a romantic imagination, stimulated by his reading of "splendid imaginary amorous adventures . . . in an intensely romantic land"—as a guidebook to what life holds in Jake's appraisal, "about as safe as it would be . . . to enter Wall Street direct from a French convent, equipped with a complete set of the more practical Alger books." In this unique figure facetiously suggesting an "exchange" of financial and religious values, Jake dramatically presents Cohn's danger, and his own as I will consider presently. It is a danger arising from utter commitment to a supreme value, all the more dangerous because so immaturely conceived, as opposed to the relative safety of the other "lovers" just discussed who contemplate a more or less "[s]imple exchange of values" for the fulfillment of their different ideas of satisfaction.

Cohn is thus by temperament recklessly ready for "amorous adventures" of greater intensity than that afforded by his liaison with Frances, who, even though she is unaware of Brett, describes what Cohn is looking for.

> I know the real reason Robert won't marry me. . . . It's just come to me. They've sent it to me in a vision in the Cafe Select. Isn't it mystic? Some day they'll put a tablet up. Like at Lourdes. . . . Why, you see, Robert's always wanted to have a mistress. . . . And if he marries me . . . that would be the end of all the romance.

The "mystic" vision. . . . is not Frances's, of course, but Cohn's; for from the first, he looks at Brett as Moses looked "at the promised land," a vision superseding his desire for romantic life in South America. He is ready to fight the next day when Jake calls her less than perfect. Cohn finds in her a certain indescribable "quality": "I shouldn't wonder if I were in love with her." . . . Faced with her profanation of what he regards as a sacramental union, he calls her Circe, but never denies her power over him, following her around "like a poor bloody steer," in Mike's drunken analogy. Cohn does not think of himself as a steer, however, and he ultimately does "battle for his lady love" until he is routed from the ambiguous world represented by Brett.

Concerned as he is with being a writer, Jake confesses in Chapter VI to a difficulty in showing Cohn clearly, giving as the reason, "I never heard him make one remark that would, in any way, detach him from other people" until he fell in love with Brett. Again, "If he were in a crowd nothing he said stood out." Yet manifestly Cohn does stand out for Jake—he begins his novel with him, is concerned to show him clearly and comes to be "blind, unforgivingly jealous of what had happened to him." One explanation, beyond jealousy, for Jake's blindness toward Cohn is that in him he may well see himself, both in his hopeless love and in the attitudes that make him vulnerable to such a love. Cohn has often been compared to Gatsby in his "romantic readiness," but in this respect neither is Jake totally unlike Fitzgerald's hero. The yacht image by which Jake first describes Brett suggests not only her feminine attractiveness, but a realm of inaccessible beauty, much as Dan Cody's yacht seen "over the most insidious flat on Lake Superior" represents to Gatsby "all the beauty and glamour in the world," the vision he was later to translate into Daisy's "white face." Jake's romantic readiness is in evidence throughout much of the novel. For example, he shares Cohn's interest in the "innocent occupation" of reading "romantic" books. Even if he does not take *The Purple Land* as "literally" as Cohn does, its "splendid imaginary amorous adventures" are his assessment; moreover, any possible irony in this description is undercut by his enjoyment of a similarly "sinister" book at Burguete, "a wonderful story" about a woman and "her true love" who waited twenty-four years for her husband's body to be recovered from a glacier. This protracted postponement of consummation mirrors Jake's spellbound attendance on his "own true love," revealing as it does that whether he fully realizes it or not he is in effect taking such a work as "a guide-book to what life holds" for him.

Of course, he does realize, particularly at night, that such "waiting" is unsatisfactory. "What do you do nights, Jake?" asks his fellow correspondent. What he does is to take a *"poule"* to dinner, having "forgotten how dull it could be." . . . More characteristically, Jake cries about what he cannot have. "It is awfully easy to be hard-boiled about everything in the daytime, but at night it is another thing." Decidedly, he is not "hard-boiled" with Brett. The two most obvious instances in which he seems to allow Brett to wrench the course of his life into her service are his taking her to Romero and his unquestioning obedience to her call at the end. But throughout the book, and over a considerably longer period than Cohn, he slavishly makes himself fully available to Brett, as she requires his services. Although in his "hard-boiled" moments Jake recognizes Brett "only wanted what she could not have," when they are first alone in the Paris taxi, he is unable to resist offering himself abjectly to her. . . . [Later], Jake summarizes his predicament: "I had the feeling of a nightmare of it all being something repeated, something I had been through and that now I must go through again." Although Brett is the most frustrating aspect of his life, he cannot do without her whenever she will suffer his attendance.

Irrevocably committed to his unavailing love, Jake is forced to see his attitude in perspectives provided by the calculating appraisal of the count, the lusty dependency of Mike, the romantic worship of Cohn, the passing interest of Bill. However, none of these "lovers" is able to function as his "tutor" . . . with the possible exception of Bill Gorton. The count, Mike and Cohn provide in their various ways clearly negative examples: ultimately, Jake is unable to take any of the three seriously as living a satisfactory life. Bill's stance is more problematical, especially since he is so convinced of its efficacy and since he so insistently concerns himself with what might be called "The Education of Jacob Barnes." When he arrives in Paris at the beginning of Book II, he immediately senses his friend's depression, and, without knowing the cause, light-heartedly undertakes a cure, continuing intermittently until he learns the dimensions of Jake's malaise at Burguete. Claiming to be on an extended spree, actually Bill is in complete control, and his barbed alcoholic prolixity turns out to be brilliantly pointed in their first scene together. As a writer, he first tells Jake a "travel story," moralizing "Injustice everywhere," a clear antidote to the self pity he must have discerned in him. He then takes another tack, this time as a "nature writer." Walking down the Boulevard, they come first to a statue of two men whom Bill identifies as inventors of pharmacy, and then to a "taxidermist." Bibulously inspired, he is up to the connection, urging Jake to buy "Just one stuffed dog" as a cure of sorts. "Certainly brighten up your flat. . . . Mean everything in the world to you. . . . Simple exchange of values. You give them money. They give

you a stuffed dog." Jake pretends to believe that Bill is drunk, but when Brett joins them and flirtatiously remarks, "You've a nice friend," he responds wryly, "He's all right. . . . He's a taxidermist," signalling his awareness that Bill has been trying to stuff him, to fill up his hollowness and "brighten up . . . [his] flat."

In this and ensuing conversations, Bill lays down a barrage of imperatives, functioning, as Morton L. Ross has noted, "very much as does the preacher in Ecclesiastes," his "sermon" consisting principally of "commandments" which he announces as "universal guides to action"; but it should be kept in mind he is only addressing Jake. Many of his instructions have often been read as facetious chatter, but even what seems mere badinage is charged with thematic significance. Whatever the degree of flippancy, his advice may be collected under four major precepts which are the basis of his life, the life he is urging on his best friend: Utilize a little; Never be Daunted; Show Irony and Pity; Do not Question. The reason for his instruction is obvious. For clearly Jake is not fully utilizing; he is often daunted; instead of showing irony and pity when he's "feeling" he is only "hard-boiled" in the daytime and self-pitying at night; and he continues to be "pretty religious."

Explicitly, Jake neither accepts nor rejects Bill's "commandments." In the Paris street scene, as noted, he evasively accuses Bill of being a hundred and forty-four drinks ahead of him. He is more relaxed at the Burguete inn, away from Paris and Brett, literally warming up to Bill's friendly advice, as echoes of Ecclesiastes, heretofore unnoticed, make clear. This feeling of warmth is quickly dispelled the next morning, however. Jake gets up early to dig fishing worms for both of them. Returning, he encounters a renewed ironic onslaught. "What were you doing? Burying your money? . . . You go out and dig some more worms and I'll be right down. . . . Work for the good of all! . . . Show irony and pity." Bill thus jibes that Jake is still not properly utilizing: the skilled fisherman uses flies; the knowledgeable buyer does not bury his money. Jake, unable to claim Bill is intoxicated in this instance, is reduced to retorting, "Oh, go to hell!" . . . At breakfast, however, under Bill's urging, he attempts to "Say something pitiful"; "Robert Cohn." Bill approves and extends his instruction. "That's better. Now why is Cohn pitiful? Be ironic," but Jake has had enough. "Aw, hell! . . . It's too early in the morning." At lunch Bill returns to his exhortation, giving his mock sermon,

> "Utilize a little, brother. . . . Let us not pry into the holy mysteries . . . with simian fingers. Let us accept on faith and simply say—I want you to join with me in saying—What shall we say, brother? . . . Let us kneel and say: 'Don't eat that, Lady—that's Mencken.' "

Jake attempts to "join" Bill repeating part of the lesson, "Utilize a little," in reference to a bottle of wine, although he ignores the other ironic reference to communion: "Don't eat that, Lady." and as Bill continues his anti-questioning preachment with the inspired conceit that Bryan, Mencken and he "all went to Holy Cross together—sacrilegious hilarity coupling simple fundamentalism, strident skepticism, traditional Catholicism and mocking irony—Jake is reduced again to accusing Bill of being "cock-eyed." His tutor, however, pushes on with sober understanding to Jake's two overwhelming questions: Brett and "what it was all about." For the first time Bill asks Jake directly, "Were you ever in love with [Brett]?'' and then, immediately, in an apparent *non sequitur*, "[A]re you really a Catholic?"

The two questions are closely related to Jake's condition, of course. The love he passionately desires to realize with Brett and the divine love of those who "have God. . . . [quite a lot]" are both unavailable to Jake. In this intimate scene he admits the dual source of his most fundamental "feeling," but despite this intimacy his answers are reserved. He admits to being in love with Brett, "Only I'd a hell of a lot rather not talk about it"; and he is "[t]echnically" a Catholic, although he disclaims any knowledge of what that equivocation signifies. Jake's brusqueness seals off Bill's probing, and he shifts from jabbing irony to sympathetic support, even to the extent of carrying the despised fishing worms.

How much of Bill's tutelage Jake finds acceptable is only gradually apparent. And two central episodes indicate that he must learn more profoundly from other sources: the fight with Cohn and the last day of bull fighting. In the Cohn encounter Jake pays the price of not following Bill's precepts, becoming in the latter's telling phrase, "Old Jake, the human punching-bag." His love for Brett has now led him to act as a "pimp" and then to try to fight Cohn. Quickly knocked unconscious, he is revived with "a carafe of water on my head" to find "everything looked new and changed. I had never seen the trees before. . . . It was all different." In this awakening, he is a way he has not been before; he still cares, but he is now more irreversibly aware of the unreality of his dream of Brett and all she represents to him. The experience is intensified by his recollection of the effects of another head "wound," of having been "kicked in the head" in a youthful football game and returning to full cognizance carrying his suitcase through his home town, only "it was all new. They were raking lawns and burning leaves. . . . It was all strange." Now in this similarly transformed world he has a feeling of carrying a "phantom suitcase," the baggage of his new awareness he must carry for the rest of his life, the burden of full consciousness that Bill is determined to avoid.

Stunned as he has been by Cohn, Jake must descend still further from his romantic expectations. After reluctantly shaking hands with his kindred adversary, he wants "a deep, hot bath to lie back in. . . . a hot bath in deep water" but, significantly, "the water would not run." More or less in a state of shock, still unable to cope with his feelings, he goes to bed. The next day, waking with "a headache" he must cope with even more: the articulation of his new awareness in the art form of the bull fight. Jake had loyally defended Bill's understanding of bull fighting to Montoya, who had merely repeated "But he is not aficionado like you." Montoya is astute in perceiving that Bill is an interested spectator rather than a passionate enthusiast. There are no knowledgeable exchanges between Bill and Jake at the fights as there had been in the "country" around Burguete; in fact, a number of comments reveal his limited appreciation. . . . Jake's appreciation of bull fighting as tragedy is on an entirely different plane, one prepared for by his observation on the second day of the fights. "Romero's bull-fighting gave real *emotion*," not "a fake *emotional feeling*, while the bull-fighter was really safe." Through this vocabulary, bull fighting is linked to Bill's song of "Irony and Pity," "When you're *feeling*. . . . When they're *feeling*" [All italics added]. The last day of the festival this motif is continued and charged with greater emphasis by the appearance of *sensation* three times on the same page, the only occurrences of the word as opposed to over forty instances of some form of *feeling*. With this underscoring, the concept of tragedy is specifically introduced.

> Belmonte, in his best days, worked always in the terrain of the bull. . . . This way he gave the *sensation* of coming *tragedy*. People went to the corrida to see Belmonte, to be given *tragic sensations*, and perhaps to see the death of Belmonte. . . . the element that was necessary to give the *sensation* of *tragedy*. . . . [Italics added].

Jake goes to the bull fights to see great matadors work "in the terrain of the bull" and thus to be given the traditional "tragic sensations" of pity and fear. What he must be struck by, however, is the pointed contrast with the way he had been living his life, in self pitying, futile aspiration, rather than "all the way up" as he had once characterized the life of the bull fighter to Cohn. "Everybody behaves badly," he tells Brett. "Given the proper chance, I'd be as big an ass as Cohn," and the "phantom suitcase" he now carries is part of his new recognition of himself in this light, in expecting from Brett, and from life, what he is not going to get. Romero, however, does not "behave badly" in or out of the ring, and as a bull fighter, through his "greatness" he enables his audience, including Jake, to experience the "sensations" of tragedy. Romero, in keeping with his name either as "pilgrim" or "pilot fish," provides Jake with a momentary vision of the stance he would like to be able to assume, not in the bull ring but in his entire life. In this sense Romero, in another dimension than Bill, serves as Jake's tutor.

But what of Romero outside the ring? There remains to consider him as Brett's lover. After saying that Romero had the "greatness," Jake adds, "he loved bull-fighting and I think he loved the bulls, and I think he loved Brett." . . . [He] performs for her in the bull ring, maneuvering the action in front of her, presenting her with the ear he is awarded for his triumph. But he is distinctly not a knight like Cohn, "ready to do battle for his lady love." His performance as a matador, as well as his fight with Cohn, is first of all for himself and only incidentally for Brett. He even has a bit of condescending humor as he presents the ear to her. " 'Don't get bloody,' Romero said, and grinned." He defines himself not primarily as Brett's lover as do Cohn and Jake, but as a bull fighter, with no commitment of any sort between himself and his vocation. Jake makes the distinction: "He loved bull-fighting . . . and I think he loved Brett."

In what way does he love her? After "a final look to ask if it were understood," he proceeds sexually in accordance with that understanding. His initial tentativeness arises both from his natural disbelief that this woman from what must seem another world is available, and also from his youth. . . . After Brett sends him away, she feels good at not ruining "children." And Romero, surely dimly understanding that he is out of his element, does go—back to *his* true love, bull fighting. . . . We do not fully know Romero's story, of course, but there is nothing in what we do know to suggest that Brett determines his world in the way she does that of Cohn and Jake: she is not his goddess. It is as impossible to consider his momentary expression of youthful male ardor for a sexually exciting woman as committed love as it is to understand how he has been read as fully heroic.

This is not to deny that he passes his first test of true "greatness" in the bull ring on the last day of the festival. But, as Cohn responded to Jake's rather rigid aphorism that only bull fighters live life all the way up, "That's an abnormal life."

What, to consider an example given dramatic focus in the novel, are we to make of Belmonte, a significant figure in Jake's education who has received little attention? Not one of Brett's lovers, he *is* Jake's unwitting tutor—an example of heroism, loving nothing, "going through his pain." Once, one of the greatest matadors, he can no longer live in his vocation "all the way up," providing an answer to Romero's youthful confidence, "I'm never going to die." . . . "[N]ot sure that there were any great moments," "He no longer had his greatest moments in the bull-ring." Where then, the phrasing seems to ask, does he have "his greatest moments"? Jake has just observed him in such a moment. Belmonte, having failed in the eyes of the crowd with his second bull, smiled contemptuously

> when he was called something particularly insulting, and always the pain that any movement produced grew stronger and stronger, until finally his yellow face was parchment color . . . he passed through into the callejon and leaned on the barrera below us, his head on his arms not seeing, not hearing anything, only going through his pain. When he looked up, finally, he asked for a drink of water. He swallowed a little . . . took his cape, and went back into the ring.

Observing such greatness as Belmonte can now achieve in the tragic human circumstance figured forth on the "parchment color" of death with which he, and Romero, as well as Belmonte are all ultimately faced, Jake is surely "given tragic sensations." Jake's identification with Belmonte is emphasized not only by the phrasing, "going through his pain," which recalls his earlier description of having been through a nightmare "that now I must go through again," but also by the fact that there is no indication that his perception of Belmonte's agony is shared or even perceived by anyone else—Bill, Brett or the crowd.

After the bull fights are over, it is not surprising that Jake, feeling "like hell," under Bill's ministrations gets "drunker than I ever remembered having been." Bill wants him thus to get over his "damn depression," that is to follow the advice he has been giving—to go through less pain. Jake has cause for his deepest depression. Brett has gone off with Romero, reinforcing the finality of his earlier "nightmare" that his dream has become. Also, in the same afternoon he has been "given" two different sets of "tragic sensations." He has experienced the classic tragic emotions evoked by Romero's public artistry transmuting the dangers of life to a higher form. But he has also identified with the private agony of Belmonte "looking at nothing," his "great moments" in the past. Jake recognizes that there are unlikely to be any "great moments" for him, that his life is to be in considerable part his going through a pain that will never be completely alleviated by pleasure, God, love or by any other opiate, reality or value. This recognition of himself and his world has not exhilarated him, but it has transformed him. . . . He now looks "strange" to himself in the mirror and his "world was not wheeling anymore. It was very clear and bright, and inclined to blur at the edges." Strengthened by this tragic perception of his life as he must live it, not the "abnormal" life of Romero, but the "normal" life of Belmonte, he is now able to rejoin Bill soberly, eat some proffered soup and start living his life as best he can, at the end of his line.

Jake has not thus facilely achieved tragic dimensions, but the issue of tragedy as opposed to therapy has been raised in the novel. Hemingway, of course, explicitly raised it himself, in two different letters shortly after publication. "It's funny to write a book that seems as tragic as that and have them take it for a jazz superficial story," and three days later, the book was not "a hollow or bitter satire, but a damn tragedy with the earth abiding forever as the hero." These remarks, together with the several references to tragedy in *The Sun Also Rises* . . . call attention to the movement of the novel, and the life of its narrator, in the direction of the tragic vision. At the beginning, Jake, in Rovitt's terminology, is the tyro, but by the end he has learned much from three tutors, Bill, Romero, and Belmonte; from the negative examples of Cohn, Mike and the count; as well as from the head blows of Cohn, Brett's lover most like himself. The extent of his development and its limitation, is apparent in the final scenes.

In Book III, which opens just after Jake's "world was not wheeling any more," it is "all over." Specifically, it is the fiesta that is finished, but more widely, it is the entire sequence of events that has wrought a change in Jake and his world, most particularly, his love of Brett. He says goodby to Bill in France, and Jake goes back to Spain, "recover[ing] an hour": they are in different countries and times. Jake proceeds steadily and quietly through the routine of his days in San Sebastian, seeming to gather strength from swimming in the "green and dark" water, from vistas of a "green mountainside" and "a green hill with a castle." . . . In San Sebastian, he sustains himself, unsupported by Bill's noisy camaraderie, and he seems more in control of his universe.

This serenity is put to test when Brett summons him to Madrid. At first, he seems in danger of reverting to the self-pitying attitude of Paris:

> That seemed to handle it. That was it. Send a girl off with one man. Introduce her to another to go off with him. Now go and bring her back. And sign the wire with love. That was it all right.

Here again is the familiar tone of helpless, desperate commitment. Jake seems ready to resume his dance around Brett's image, transfixed in a desire that can neither be denied nor satisfied—in effect endowing Brett with a "mystical penumbra" and making his worship of her serve for his "big religious possession." Jake is different, however, as a careful reading makes clear. Brett is now reduced to "a girl" in difficulty, and "love" is a "sign." For better and worse, Jake is no longer dancing around Brett's image in quite the same measures. Immediately after sending the telegram "I went in to lunch," not only an indication of his new equanimity, but an illustration of his determination to "utilize" as best he can, to be further shown in the climactic scenes in Madrid. These passages are carefully prepared for by Jake's journey to the "end of the line" through symbolic scenery intensified by the concentration of a number of images of elevation as well as by reverberations in the words . . . of portions of Section V of *The Waste Land*. . . . The "arid plain" is now behind Jake, and he is ready to set his lands in order by shoring up his ruins with such fragments as he has. He proceeds to exemplify in his actions and attitudes several of the commandments of his "nice friend," the "taxidermist." He takes Brett to Botin's, "one of the best restaurants in the world," where, as the name translates, he collects his "bounty" or "spoils of war" in a sumptuous meal. "I like to drink wine," he tells Brett, "I like to do a lot of things." Just how much he enjoys "utilizing a little" remains uncertain, but in sharp contrast to his behavior in Paris, he is "undaunted" in Brett's presence.

More significantly, as he "feels"—some form of the verb occurs seven times in two pages—he stabilizes his world with irony and pity. . . . All of his remarks to Brett, as well as all of his actions show attitudes designed to palliate the pain each is going through. In Paris, Jake had been the weaker of the two, but in Madrid, following some of Bill's instructions, he is much stronger. And so in the magnificently evocative last lines of the novel, he can sum up the growth he has achieved in his response to Brett's shallow *cri de coeur,* "we could have had such a damned good time together," with "Yes. . . . Isn't it pretty to think so?" Yet there is more to his response than irony and pity, for as he had signed his wire "with love," so this response also bears the mark of love. Jake now sees his love more clearly for what it is—even his comforting response is punctuated as a question. But in seeing his love in its diminishment, he still holds on to it, not desperately but with perspicacity. "Feeling" however diminished is preferable to calculated "simple exchange." Jake is now able to act for the first time as a Hemingway hero, having made his play, to back it up.

Bill had been concerned, of course, to get Jake not to make this play, the play for the love of Brett, the play for ultimate rather than simple "exchange." Aware that Jake could never have had a "damned good time" with Brett—with her his destiny would always be most likely that of the "human punching-bag"—Bill also believes that Jake's search for answers will be equally fruitless. In short, as a substitute for frustrated faith, human and divine, in whatever formula of precarious consubstantiation, he has recommended taxidermy and self-protection. Tutored as he has been by all of his experience of a world that is neither his own nor himself, and true to his own feelings, Jake, however, must make a more complicated play, a search for love as a value that transcends both utility and fantasy, even as Brett's mystery disperses under his more penetrating gaze.

By the final scenes in Madrid, Jake is able to hold himself steady in the paradox of wanting everything and having nothing except himself—Emily Dickinson's paradox of "The Missing All"—both states expressed in his absurd, magnificent passion for Brett, and captured in his final words. He is not yet a tragic hero pushing resolutely toward a victory of spirit against the inevitable defeat of circumstance, but he is at his own "boundary situation." If he is not, like Santiago, "beyond all the people in the world," he is farther out than he has been before. Much closer in time and situation to Nick Adams in **"Big Two-Hearted River,"** who "wanted to be a great writer," he is not yet ready to fish "In the swamp [where] . . . the fishing would be tragic. In the swamp fishing was a tragic adventure. Nick did not want it." Neither does Jake seem to "want it" as he holds himself tautly against the pressures of his life in the final scenes of the novel.

But Jake obviously does "want it." His experiences do not end in Madrid, in the taxi with Brett. They end with his seeking out the meaning of his impossible/possible love for Brett through the writing of *The Sun Also Rises.* . . . Recognizing that he may indeed have to live without the love of God, or any sufficient image thereof, the predicament cited as characteristic of the "modern temper" by Krutch, he still refuses to deny the attracting power of both. . . . Jake composes, in effect, his "love song"—the uniqueness distinguishing his human syllable from that of Brett's other lovers whom he knows in secret kinship. Faced with playing things as they are, he finally neither asserts in foolish desperation as Cohn, nor abdicates his full human responsibility as do the other lovers in their separate ways. Rather as the artist he set out to "create in honesty" a world in which he can live as a moral being. Bill had taunted him at Burguete with not knowing irony and pity, "And you claim you want to be a writer, too. You're only a newspaper man. An expatriated newspaper man." Bill is a writer, and a successful one; but he limits himself to "travel stories" and "nature-writ[ing]." Tragedy is beyond his reach. Jake, however, will not accept such limitations. Unlike Bill, and Cohn, another writer of limited vision, he really is ultimately concerned with "an abnormal life," one lived "all the way up." *The Sun Also Rises* is a record of how he attempts to learn to live that life. Seeing all around him, as well as inside himself, evidences of the death of value, Jake chooses, even in recognition of that extinction, to create his own "All"—*The Sun Also Rises*—and in the act of so doing comes on a "moral history" that at once follows the pattern of the age but also deepens and enriches its tragic colors. (pp. 46-69)

Sam S. Baskett, " 'An Image to Dance Around': Brett and Her Lovers in 'The Sun Also Rises'," in The Centennial Review, *Vol. XXII, No. 1, Winter, 1978, pp. 45-69.*

ANDREW HOOK

Hemingway remains a problem. Has any other modern writer so divided critical opinion? The difficulty is that there seems to be less than the usual room for discriminations of the good with reservations kind. Either Hemingway is a good writer—who in some novels and stories may well have written better than in others—or he is a sham, a phony, a charlatan. He believed that his first book, **In Our Time,** would be praised by highbrows and read by lowbrows. His fate has been to be read by all, praised and damned by either or both. Part of the problem is of course Hemingway the man. Towards the end of his own career, Fitzgerald came to feel he had been too much the man, too little the writer; in *The Crack Up* he suggests he had given too much of himself to life, too little to art. Hemingway seems never to have felt the need to choose between the two; unstintingly he gave himself to both. . . . The confusion of the two has always been one of the major impediments to a proper understanding of his art. Out of that confusion arose the damaging notion of Hemingway the inspired journalist, his art no more than a processing of his own life into artistic copy. In fact that problem is partly a result of his own success. . . . (pp. 49-50)

Hemingway the artist, and Hemingway the man, have, of course, much in common; Hemingway is no modern master paring his finger-nails, no fabulous artificer wholly detached from the world he creates. Yet man and artist are no substitute for each other; and dislike of the one should not mean rejection of both. . . . The case of **The Sun Also Rises** may be a specially difficult one, but that is all the more reason to adhere firmly to the general principle: it is the fiction, not the life, that is in the end the critic's proper concern.

Hemingway never denied that the characters in **The Sun Also Rises** were based on real people, but he did deny that the novel in any other substantial way transcribed his own or anyone else's life. In 1933 he wrote to Maxwell Perkins: '95 per cent of **The Sun Also** was pure imagination. I took real people in that one and I controlled what they did. I made it all up.' That he did make it all up is the point to remember.

Because once *The Sun Also Rises* has been disentangled from Harold Loeb, Duff Twysden, Pat Guthrie and the rest, it becomes very much easier to see it for what it is: the archetype, the purest and best of all Hemingway's fictions. . . . I would not want to suggest that after *The Sun Also Rises* Hemingway's career was a simple falling-off. There is truth in the suggestion that *The Sun Also Rises* and the early short stories go a long way towards defining both Hemingway's characteristic world and his characteristic treatment of it, and that thereafter Hemingway could only travel through that world rather than climb beyond it. And perhaps it is even true that in the '30s the strain was beginning to tell. But, ironically for a writer who seemed to pay such little tribute to time and history, Dos Passos's 'murderous forces of history', in the form of the Spanish Civil War and what came after, gave back his world to Hemingway. Papa had been right after all, and the sales of *For Whom the Bell Tolls* soon approached a staggering million copies.

The basic point holds nonetheless. *The Sun Also Rises* is a definitive statement. At the age of 26 Hemingway outlines to the attentive reader a vision of the world that he subsequently develops but never changes. Why it is possible to argue that *The Sun Also Rises* remains his finest novel depends upon the use of the word *outlines*. In the first novel outlines have not hardened into a fixed frame; they are still malleable, susceptible to pressure. At the end of *The Sun Also Rises* Jake Barnes is a defeated hero; but he is not defeated in the manner and style that Frederick Henry and later Hemingway heroes are defeated; and his heroism is of a different order to theirs. The difference is a crucial one, but after *The Sun Also Rises* there are no more Jake Barnes. (pp. 50-1)

Hemingway began writing *The Sun Also Rises* in Valencia on his twenty-sixth birthday, 21 July 1925. Only a month or two earlier he had been writing to Maxwell Perkins explaining that the novel form did not attract him. . . . Much later, in 1952, he told Bernard Berenson he had written *The Sun Also Rises* because everyone else his age had completed a novel, and he felt ashamed not to have done so. In any event, once begun, the writing of the novel went on at high speed. (pp. 51-2)

The novel that was published in October 1926 differed in only one major way from the completed manuscript version. After discussion with Fitzgerald, who had read and admired the manuscript, Hemingway decided to cut completely his first sixteen pages. 'There is nothing in those first sixteen pages', he wrote to Perkins, 'that does not come out, or is explained, or re-stated in the rest of the book—or is unnecessary to state.' With this excision of what had clearly been an introductory exposition concerning the major characters, Hemingway was satisfied. He was confident he had written a good novel: not as good as he hoped to write in the future, but good nonetheless. To Fitzgerald he wrote: 'Christ knows I want to write them a hell of a lot better but it seemed to move along and to be pretty sound and solid.'

Sound and solid was more or less precisely what the book's initial critics felt it wasn't. Inevitably Hemingway was disappointed by these early reviews, and equally inevitably he tended to suggest that the critics had not understood the book he had written. He was sure that his novel was sad, serious, tragic; hence his irritation at being told he had written 'a jazz superficial story' about unattractive people, or an 'amazing narrative of English and American after-the-war strays running up and down France and Spain in wistful wildness'. . . . In 1940, on the occasion of Fitzgerald's death, Westbrook Pegler, an American columnist not renowned for his liberal views, wrote that the event called to mind

> memories of a queer bunch of undisciplined and self-indulgent brats who were determined not to pull their weight in the boat and wanted the world to drop everything and sit down and bawl with them.

So much for the lost generation. Yet Pegler's view, or one much like it, continues to surface—in my teaching experience at least—in responses to *The Sun Also Rises.*

Hemingway himself, writing defensively to his mother who had been deeply offended by the book, was prepared to concede that the characters in his novel 'were certainly burned out, hollow and smashed'. But he insisted, as I've said, on his book's seriousness of purpose and tragic implications. He was willing to joke about the impotency theme; some subjects, he told Fitzgerald, were particularly good for novels—war is best of all, but love, money, and murder are also good. 'A dull subject I should say would be impotence.' That he was more than half serious though, is proved by a subsequent letter to Maxwell Perkins:

> Impotence is a pretty dull subject compared with war or love or the old lucha por la vida. I do hope though that *The Sun* will sell a tremendous lot because while the subject is dull the book isn't.

It was to Perkins too, of course, that Hemingway offered his most famous comment on the book's central meaning:

> The point of the book to me was that the earth abideth forever. . . . I didn't mean the book to be a hollow or bitter satire but a damn tragedy with the earth abiding for ever as the hero.

It is a strange comment. A sense of the natural permanence of things, of the earth abiding forever, is not in fact one of the major impressions created by the book. It may well be present, but is it as prominent as Hemingway's comment implies it should be? Perhaps Hemingway should have remembered what he had written to Sherwood Anderson over a year earlier:

> I get something out of bulls and the men that fight them, I don't know what. Anyhow I've got it all, or a big part of it, into the next book.

Whether or not the earth abideth in the novel, place is of immense importance in *The Sun Also Rises.* Rather than its formal division into three books, it is place that provides the novel with its basic structure. Paris, Burguete, Pamplona, San Sebastian, in that order, are geographical centres which focus and define the book's central meanings.

Paris, it has become a critical commonplace to insist, is Hemingway's version of the waste land that has emerged in the aftermath of the First World War. And it is true that a sense of sterility, both sexual and more general, of aimlessness and emptiness, of the failure and loss of values, is suggested by these opening chapters. But for Jake Barnes Paris is not all hopelessness and negativity. For Jake life in Paris is problematical; and in the first nine chapters of the novel the nature of Jake's problems is set out and developed: his hurt of course, his relationship with Brett and how he tries to cope with it, his relationship with Mike, Cohn, the Count, and the rest. Problems on every side. But Paris has its sweetness too: coffee and *brioche,* horse-chestnut trees, bridges across the Seine, work. Paris is life as it is: complex, difficult, unfulfilling, but endurable.

Burguete is a different world. The fishing trip with Bill Gorton (and Harris the Englishman) is an idyll, a pastoral interlude. Cohn, Campbell, and Brett, and all the problems and tensions they mean, have been left behind. Here in the hills nothing is messy. The weather is cold and clear like the water in which they fish. Relationships are easy and unforced; there is a purity of friendship and trust. The fishing itself is a delicate ritual. The nature with which the men are involved is approached in such a way as to be always on the point of transformation into sacramental metaphor. At night Jake feels good—in sharp contrast to his nights in Paris.

Burguete is high up, 1,200 metres above sea level. Higher still but visible are Roncevaux and the monastery at Roncevalles, with their suggestions of an heroic, religious idealism. . . . [Yet], Burguete provides no permanent alternative to Paris. The pastoral interlude can be no more than that. In the classical tradition the pastoral world offers an alternative, more ideal, set of values. For the visitor it provides refreshment, regeneration; but in the end the real world has to be faced again. So for Jake. Paris and its problems have been put aside, but they have not disappeared: the letter and telegram from Mike and Cohn signal as much. They will all meet in Pamplona.

Pamplona means fiesta. In Pamplona the worlds of Paris and Burguete come together and into collision. The festival of San Fermin provides Hemingway with an ideal setting for the crises and climax of his novel. Life during fiesta is extraordinary; colourful, explosive, dramatic. Fiesta is a time of release, of spontaneity and ritual, of passion, excitement, and intensity. Everything is speeded up, raised to a pitch. It is not only the Iruña café that is 'like a battlship stripped for action'. Inevitably, then, the Parisian problems blossom here insistently and violently: emotions spill over, antagonisms flare, frustrations and failures surface uncontrollably. Yet here too are images and experiences of a quite different order. The bull-ring at Pamplona presents a paradigm of ritualized, controlled and disciplined violence. Even more than Jake and Bill and the trout-fishing in the Irati river, Romero and his bulls in the Pamplona fiesta are a positive affirmation, a poised celebration of survival in a hostile and dangerous world. Pamplona juxtaposes Paris and Burguete; but rather than fusing them, fiesta finally blows them cruelly apart.

After the destructive emotional intensities and violence of Pamplona, Jake returns alone to San Sebastian. He swims in the quiet, cold sea in what is an act of ritual purification and refreshment. Restored, Jake is ready for the Hotel Montana in Madrid, and the renewed acceptance of Brett, his problems, and 'the old lucha por la vida'.

Because of his hurt, Jake is a character who knows a lot about life's problems. Because of his hurt, he is also a brilliantly-conceived narrator figure. His two roles as character and narrator fuse admirably in the first person narrative. Detachment, apartness, are imposed on Jake by his condition; but these limitations strengthen his position as a narrator. Unable to be wholly involved, he is in a better position to see things clearly and objectively. Jake's isolation (Hemingway is quite unable to conceive of a satisfactory sexual relationship not involving male consummation) thus contributes both to the method of *The Sun Also Rises* and to its meaning.

The notion of a narrator, at once within and without the story he is telling, Hemingway may have derived from Fitzgerald's use of Nick Carraway in *The Great Gatsby.* Conrad's Marlow, a familiar figure to both Fitzgerald and Hemingway, provides another obvious source. As for Jake's impotency, Hemingway explained in 1951 that the genesis of the idea lay in his own experience:

> It came from a personal experience in that when I had been wounded at one time there had been an infection from pieces of wool cloth being driven into the scrotum. Because of this I got to know other kinds who had genito urinary wounds and I wondered what a man's life would have been like after that if his penis had been lost and his testicles and spermatic cord remained intact. I had known a boy that had happened to. So I took him and made him into a foreign correspondent in Paris and, inventing, tried to find out what his problems would be when he was in love with someone who was in love with him and there was nothing that they could do about it.

Hemingway then goes on to repeat that he is not Jake Barnes. Despite these recollections—and it is noteworthy how little the novel is taken up with explorations of Jake's problems—the idea of Jake's impotency may have arisen from another, more literary source. During the Burguete interlude Jake and Bill joke about Jake's problem, referring to the mysterious hurt that kept Henry James out of the American Civil War. Michael Reynolds argues that in the early Paris years, largely through Pound's influence, Hemingway read a great deal more James than has been realized. There is no evidence of his having read *Portrait of a Lady;* but he may have done so, or Pound may have talked to him about the book which was one of his own favourites. The point is that Jake Barnes has not a little in common with Ralph Touchett. Perhaps it was the example of Ralph's debilitating illness, inhibiting a more active expression of his love for Isabel Archer, in association with his knowledge of James's own mysterious injury, which helped to make the impotency theme available to Hemingway.

Hemingway's formal success in *The Sun Also Rises,* however, is not simply a question of the device of Jake Barnes's physical condition. Jake's hurt, as we have seen, defines his character, as well as authenticating his position as objective narrator. And it is this integrity of roles as narrator and character which in turn produces the superbly achieved coherence of form and content, style and meaning, which is perhaps Hemingway's major aesthetic triumph in *The Sun Also Rises.* Jake's hurt has compelled him to come to terms with the pain and violence of living—the First World War has articulated that pain and violence on a grand scale—and his narrative style is the best index of how he has done so. The style is taut, economic, disciplined, unemotional, understated. Living is coped with in identical terms. The aesthetic mode is also a moral one; style is a way of living.

The other main characters in *The Sun Also Rises,* all of them products of the same world that has struck at Jake so damagingly, are judged by how far they approximate or fall short of Jake's style. Bill Gorton and Jake get on famously; Brett and Mike know what is required but lack the self-discipline to succeed; Robert Cohn's is an alternative, rejected style. An admirer of romantic prose, he behaves over Brett in a stereo-typed romantic fashion. In the heightened, dramatic world of fiesta, a collision between these styles is inevitable. But when it occurs this collision does not precipitate the central moral crisis of the book; Cohn's style is not allowed enough force for that. The pressure on Jake's style, which does produce that crisis, has a source other than Robert Cohn.

There has been fairly general agreement among Hemingway critics that the use of Jake Barnes as a first person narrator in *The Sun Also Rises* contributes immensely to the novel's success: the gains in immediacy, dramatic involvement, and the narrative enactment of a code of values, are clear. Nonetheless, it is possible to argue that Hemingway's use of the first person narrative procedure does leave him with some unresolved problems. For instance, he has not chosen to follow the example of James and Conrad, and provide an audience for his narrator's reminiscences—to whom then is Jake talking? (The same question can be asked of Nick Carraway in *The Great Gatsby*.) Much more important is the problem of whether Jake is sufficiently distanced from Hemingway himself. Is Jake given enough independent life as character and narrator, as Carraway is, or does he remain in bondage to his creator? Of course one agrees that Jake is not to be *identified* with Hemingway, but that hardly settles the question. Jake is a working journalist who wants to be a writer; but Hemingway does not dramatize him, say, as a writer with a particular vision which he wishes to communicate. He is presented simply as a man coping with his problems as well as he can, enjoying some aspects of life, unhappy about others. He is silent about *why* trout-fishing in the Irati river matters. About the purity of Romero's art as a bull-fighter, about the dangerous violence in terms of which the bull-fighter orders his art when he works 'in the terrain of the bull', about the moment of death when bull and bull-fighter are locked together in a single image—about all these things he is allowed to be eloquent, speaking either to Brett or directly to us. But about *why* bull-fighting is important in his own life, about the significant link between Romero's art and life and his own, he is silent. In an able essay Terence Doody has argued that it is the tight-lipped morality to which Jake subscribes which makes it impossible for him to be self-conscious about these matters [see excerpt above]. To talk about them would be to move too far towards Robert Cohn's style. Art and morality, that is, are at odds in *The Sun Also Rises*. But perhaps Mr. Doody expects too much. In his own words, Jake

> does for Romero what Nick does for Gatsby; he sees in Romero more than anyone else does and makes of that insight the definition of a hero, which entails a correlative definition of himself.

Is this not enough? Hemingway's art is always the art of absence, of the unstated. To succeed, such an art demands the collaboration of the reader; it is essential that the reader assent to the meaning Hemingway implies, to reassure him, as it were, that he is right. Hence no doubt his truculent, disbelieving response to those who do not see it his way, who see in *The Sun Also Rises* only the 'after-the-war strays running up and down France and Spain'. If this is true, then the crucial element in the paragraph from Reynolds Price's amazingly resonant essay on Hemingway, which Terence Doody quotes, is not 'I mostly speak as I.' But the sentences which follow:

> What I need from you is not empathy, identity, but

> patient approving witness—loving. License my life. Believe me.

There is a further difficulty in Doody's position. Like Mark Spilka, in another influential essay [see excerpt above], he assumes that Romero is the authentic hero of *The Sun Also Rises*, that it is through his definition of the heroism of the bull-fighter that Jake defines his own. To imply that this is the novel's final statement takes too little account of its closing movement. To that movement I wish finally to turn.

One of the finer qualities of *The Sun Also Rises* is its humour. After the scene in which Cohn knocks Jake cold and floors Mike Campbell, Bill's friend Edna asks, 'Does this happen every night at your fiestas?' In this novel, at least, Hemingway does not always take himself too seriously. One recalls the light-hearted exchanges between Jake and Bill at Burguete when, for example, Hemingway makes amusing hay with contemporary American nativist critics:

> 'You know what's the trouble with you? [says Bill] You're an expatriate. One of the worst type. Haven't you heard that? Nobody that ever left their own country ever wrote anything worth printing. Not even in the newspapers. . . .

> 'You're an expatriate. You've lost touch with the soil. You get precious. Fake European standards have ruined you. You drink yourself to death. You become obsessed by sex. You spend all your time talking, not working. You are an expatriate, see? You hang around cafés.'

> 'It sounds like a swell life,' I said. 'When do I work?'

Here the ironies are admittedly directed away from Hemingway himself. But the passage does show that Hemingway understands perfectly well that what he is trying to do can be fatally misunderstood. Jake can be even more self-critical. After one of the few, brief interior monologues that he is allowed, he dismisses his own train of thought comprehensively:

> That was a large statement. What a lot of bilge I could think up at night. What rot—I could hear Brett say it. What rot!

Not even bull-fighting is immune from criticism. After the rain has come, after the facade of fiesta geniality has cracked, and after Brett's destructive desire for Romero has been acknowledged, a Spaniard is gored during the running of the bulls. At this point, one might say, things are not going too well for Jake, but it is now that he has to listen to a Spanish waiter making some simple anti-bull-fighting points:

> 'You're not an aficionado?' 'Me? What are bulls? Animals. Brute animals.' He stood up and put his hand on the small of his back. 'Right through the back. A cornada right through the back. For fun—you understand.'

> He shook his head and walked away, carrying the coffee-pots.

Two men passing in the street report that the man is dead. That the earth may abide forever despite the death of Vicente Girones, does not wholly answer the waiter's criticism. That Brett leaves the ear of the bull that killed him, presented to her by Romero, in the drawer of her bed-table in the Hotel Montoya, along with her cigarette stubs, rather reinforces it.

All these may seem somewhat minor points, but cumulatively they suggest that in this first novel Hemingway is prepared to look critically at what he himself holds dear. When one reconsiders the situation in which Jake finds himself in the latter part of the novel, the same point suddenly becomes central to its meaning. Jake is in love with two things: with Brett and with bull-fighting and what it means to him. Brett may not be as unreliable as Daisy Buchanan, but there are hints from the beginning that she could threaten Jake and what he believes in. In the arrow-scarred Count Mippipopolous Brett claims to recognize 'one of us'. But the exchange that follows looks forward very precisely to the crisis in the novel she will in the end precipitate.

> 'You see, Mr Barnes, it is because I have lived very much that now I can enjoy everything so well. Don't you find it like that?'
>
> 'Yes. Absolutely.'
>
> 'I know,' said the count. 'That is the secret. You must get to know the values.'
>
> 'Doesn't anything ever happen to your values?' Brett asked.
>
> 'No. Not any more.'
>
> 'Never fall in love?'
>
> 'Always,' said the count. 'I'm always in love.'
>
> 'What does that do to your values?'
>
> 'That, too, has got a place in my values.'
>
> 'You haven't any values. You're dead, that's all.'
>
> 'No, my dear. You're not right. I'm not dead at all.'

Brett is wrong about the count. Like Count Greffi in *A Farewell to Arms,* who talks to Frederick Henry in terms very similar to these, he is certainly 'one of us'. But what is truly ominous in the exchange is the opposition that Brett sets up between love and values: because of course that is precisely the opposition she is going to create and act out in her affair with Romero. What Hemingway contrives so brilliantly, then, is a situation in which Jake's two loves—Brett and bull-fighting—come into unresolvable collision.

For Jake, Romero supremely embodies the code in terms of which Jake himself tries to live. Romero does not fake or pose or evade; violence and death are the conditions he has accepted, and in face of them he creates the forms of his dangerous art. His is the ideal which Jake recognizes. Yet the novel at no point questions the depth of Jake's commitment to Brett. It is not a subject to be talked about—not even with Bill; but it is the primary fact in Jake's emotional life. It underlies his attitude towards all the others, his concern and his revulsion. It explains why he finds it difficult to be hard-boiled at night. It explains, finally, the loyalty which determines his behaviour towards Brett herself.

By forcing Jake to choose between his loyalty to Romero and his loyalty to Brett, Hemingway is putting such pressure on the code of disciplined self-control that there can be no graceful outcome. Whatever course he follows, Jake cannot win; he loses either Brett or something crucial to his sense of his own worth and integrity. The point has just been underlined by Montoya's seeking advice from Jake over the matter of Romero and the American ambassador. Jake, Montoya, and Romero are on the same side—and Hemingway is there too. ('I get something out of bulls and the men who fight them. . . . ') Implicated in Brett's behaviour, Jake betrays a precious allegiance.

How does Hemingway expect us to understand this betrayal? What it means is that Jake chooses the impurities of love and life and relationship rather than the purity of moral integrity and personal honour. As we have seen, Terence Doody has argued that in *The Sun Also Rises,* art and morality come into collision. But in another sense art and morality (Romero and Montoya) are on the same side; it is life (Brett) that in the end subverts both. As so often in the endings of James's novels, here it is life which tragically resists the perfection of order which both art and morality strive to impose on it. Seen from this perspective, the definition of heroism in *The Sun Also Rises* becomes less obvious. Romero remains the code hero: knocked down by Cohn again and again, he refuses to admit defeat. But Romero is not the novel's hero. The Jake who responds to Brett's telegram from Madrid is also refusing to accept defeat, is also coming back for more. Jake's heroism, however, is of a more complex, even self-contradictory kind; it is gained at his own expense, and involves a continuing commitment to life and love even on the impossible terms that have been imposed on him. Jake gains or preserves nothing more dignified. Later Hemingway heroes accept defeat too, but they accept it within the logic of their own terms. Only in *The Sun Also Rises* does Hemingway risk challenging the very codes and values which his fiction as a whole will constantly celebrate. That is why the book is a triumph of art on the side of life. (pp. 52-63)

Andrew Hook, "Art and Life in 'The Sun Also Rises'," in Ernest Hemingway: New Critical Essays, *edited by A. Robert Lee, London: Vision Press, 1983, pp. 49-63.*

NINA SCHWARTZ

When Gertrude Stein called the group of expatriates in *The Sun Also Rises* "a lost generation," she identified the challenge this novel would continue to pose for its readers: how to make loss the source of some kind of gain. This challenge has not been particularly difficult to meet. Since the logical possibility of loss requires the prior possession of a presence or integrity, loss must also signify the possibility of recuperation. Critics have generally made the articulation of that second possibility their own imperative: whether this novel represents loss as personal or cultural—Jake Barnes's castration or the post-war disruption of national coherence—it does so to inscribe the promise of a particular kind of redemption. Leon F. Seltzer epitomizes the critical response to what he calls "the opportunity of impotence" in *The Sun Also Rises*:

> Impotence in *The Sun Also Rises* . . . describes, paradoxically, not man's deficiency but his amazing potentiality. For impotence can actually promote the scrupulously measured detachment that is itself the key to happiness—a happiness that can survive solely through the 'distanced involvement' with reality. . . . By not 'spending' almost the whole of his mental and emotional energies on a single love object, man may invest his abundant resources into wresting from reality its best possible bargain and, successful, satisfy his natural appetite for the infinite variety that life has—and has always

had—to offer. Such are the prerequisites to human fulfillment.

The "paradox" of impotence as Seltzer represents it would seem to be identical to the paradox of existential philosophy, whose influence on most readings of this novel is clear. Like Seltzer, existentialism requires that the individual "detach" himself from the artificial constraints of his external reality, embrace the terror of his own mortality, and thus discover that death is the author of his freedom. By acknowledging the limits of his power to effect the world—limits figured by his mortal contingency—the individual may paradoxically achieve a certain kind of authority over himself. Impotence is thus "prerequisite" to human fulfillment because it provokes the individual to repudiate the false conventionality of the life of "bad faith" and to choose self-consciously "the fate that governs his own values."

For all its posing as courageous realism, however, the existential project is a supremely romantic one that effectively returns man to the center of a humanistic universe. In locating the meaning of humanness in individual freedom and responsibility, existentialism divorces the subject from all forces of determination, except the inevitable death. All meaning is constituted by the individual; all the physical or material conditions of his life are inadequate to define him. However, it is precisely this rejection of the materiality of existence that has led contemporary critiques to locate existentialism's determination in the ideologies of traditional humanist idealism. The existentialist faces what he presumes to be the physical reality of death only to idealize it. In confronting the loss of absolute order to the world, he constructs a new absolute—absolute negation. (pp. 49-50)

Though it is true that Hemingway's novel incorporates the false dilemmas of existential philosophy . . . it just as seriously subverts those dilemmas by revealing the romanticism that sustains them. The novel inscribes the existential redemption of death and impotence within a dynamic fundamental to Western culture, the Oedipal complex and its institution of what Lacan calls the dialectic of castration and desire. Consider for example the parallels between the child's passing of the Oedipal complex and the existentialist's response to death. As the child enters the alienating world of language, he is forced to identify himself symbolically, by means of the "I," and thus "loses" the illusion of his autonomy produced by the mirror stage. To account for the loss of his unified ego, the child must make an interpretive leap: he decides that the father has taken the mother away because he possesses something she does not—the phallus. The child "invents" the Father to rationalize the loss he cannot avenge or overcome, but also to redeem the potential arbitrariness of the Father's greater power. It is this *méconnaissance* that will continue to determine all the subject's future relations to cultural power structures. By symbolically castrating himself, displacing his desire for the mother into his identification with the Father, the child ensures that he too may someday become a father. . . . Castration allows the subject to enter the Law of Fatherhood.

Similarly, the existentialist, faced with the death of God and the absence of immanent meaning in the world, imagines that the only obstacle to his own divinity is his immortality. He thus invents Death to account for his loss of power and to invest his otherwise meaningless life with its tragic significance. As the child's deferral of his bliss organizes his experience by directing it towards the eventual recuperation of autonomy,

so does the existentialist's "detour" of Death allow him to enter the Law of the Individual, to redeem the immanent meaning he had lost when God's death ensured his own. Renouncing God, that is, he becomes a god, just as the child "overcomes" the threat of the Father by imitating his master. Both existentialism and the castration complex thus function as strategies of deferral: both invent the possibility of a transcendent ego by defining the obstacle to autonomy as the signifier of what lies behind it.

What both the child and the existential hero fail to recognize is that the castration they attempt to overcome does not in fact exist: it is a *méconnaissance* produced by the binaries of Western culture, whose confirmation of the positive values of Life, Phallus, and Father depends upon the negatives of Death, Castration, and Child. Both strategies repress the arbitrariness of the subject's will to power by deferring it through a structure naturalized by culture. And, like both the child and the existential hero that he has come to represent, Jake Barnes depends upon similar strategies of deferral to transcend his impotence. Incorporating several modes of self-representation—the writing itself, the "affair" with Brett, the ritual of the bull-fight—Jake's narrative simultaneously exploits and exposes the strategies of deferral that underlie these and all signifying systems. What is crucial to the success of each mode is that the structure that supports its signifying power not be fully interpretable: it must exist as the promise of a meaning that cannot be adequately represented. Each system of self-representation thus preserves the illusion of a certain reserve or plenitude that can only be intuited from the signifiers that defer to and from the ineffable truth of Jake's self.

The narrative style is one manifestation of this strategy of deferral whereby truth is constituted through the assembly of lies, hints, or half-truths. Jake's writing, characterized by its understatement, evasiveness, and absence of subordination and transition, seems constantly to be withholding the very pieces of information essential to a true understanding of the story. Hemingway himself defined the motive of this style when he described its effects. Discussing another of his stories, **"Out of Season,"** he says "It was a very simple story . . . and I had omitted the real end of it which was that the old man hanged himself. This was omitted on my new theory that you could omit anything if you knew that you omitted and the omitted part would strengthen the story and make people feel something more than they understood." . . . [The] obvious omission of certain important facts makes the reader self-conscious of the writer's refusal to expose what he knows to be the truth. This style succeeds because it seduces the reader: by exposing, indeed producing a gap in the reader's knowledge, inscribing the reader as impotent slave to the master author, the story evokes the reader's desire to be like the author, to possess his knowledge and power. But to master his own impotence, the reader must acknowledge the inadequacy of the words he reads to represent the truth he wants to know; he must read "below the surface," a metaphor for reading that suggests the existence of an invisible true text beneath the deceptive one we see. The narrative thus becomes an entrance into the truth it hides, almost an initiation rite preceding membership in a secret club. The text becomes the means by which the reader earns his right to know the story's truth. However, as he fills in the narrative gaps so conveniently exposed to his view, the reader also becomes complicit with the text, committed to its ideal of a hidden truth. That he must temporarily castrate himself, defer his possession of that truth until he has earned it, legitimizes the mastery he hopes eventually to achieve.

The hidden truth of the novel is all the more seductive because it appears to be a deeply romantic one. The narrative's refusal to speak directly of the war and the wound, its evocation of those topics only as "the unspeakable," invests them with a potent and compelling fascination. When the hooker Jake picks up for "sentimental" reasons makes advances to him in a cab, his refusal is cryptic:

> She touched me with one hand and I put her hand away.
>
> 'Never mind.'
>
> 'What's the matter? You sick?'
>
> 'Yes.'

Sensitive readers will likely concur with Georgette's and Mark Spilka's interpretation of Jake's response: "Everybody's sick. I'm sick, too." By refusing to acknowledge the specificity of his wound—to *name* it—Jake effectively transforms it into a metaphor for the plight of modern man, "the venereal disease" Spilka defines as the death of love in the post-war world [see excerpt above].

A similar ellipsis occurs when the topic of the war arises. Georgette wants to know what's really wrong with Jake:

> 'I got hurt in the war,' I said.
>
> 'Oh, that dirty war.'
>
> We would probably have gone on and discussed the war and agreed that it was in reality a calamity for civilization, and perhaps would have been better avoided. I was bored enough.

Jake's reduction of the war to a series of tired clichés, the boredom that suggests serious understatement, serves paradoxically to elevate the war's significance. Its actual importance to Jake and to the world is so exaggeratedly minimized here that we know we are to take heed. That which cannot be spoken must be the center of Jake's and our concern. Jake's defamiliarization rescues both the war and the wound from their status as banal if unfortunate truisms; it is the omission of their real significance that makes these issues seem to be truth itself.

Jake's desire is clearly to withdraw from bondage to his wound. He wishes to avoid the culturally-determined significance of a castrated man. However, in retreating from the world that would make him a horrible joke (Jake?), the uncanny that can only be displaced by laughter, Jake still remains bound to the loss he would transcend. His strategic displacement of the literality of his castration allows him to invest that senseless mutilation with the function of an initiation into some fundamental truth. By making the wound serve him as the source of his mysterious and compelling tragedy, and as the source of his personal and narrative authority, Jake consequently serves the ideology that makes young boys want to go to war, to join the ranks of the initiated. (pp. 50-4)

[Yet], Jake's narrative is perhaps not so bound to the dominant ideology as I have suggested (and as many other critics have insisted, though not in so many words, and perhaps not critically). Or if the novel is bound to the ideology that valorizes war and its consequent mutilation as the initiation into

the horrific truths of manhood, it at least suggests the dependence of that ideology on strategically-constructed mysteries. The narrative's deferral of the truth it wishes to announce is part of a certain code of ethics. The suffering of these characters need never be directly spoken since it is simply betokened by their diversionary tactics: week-long drunks, multiple sexual escapades, financial profligacy, even a regular and ritualized confrontation with death. The foolish romantic Cohn, who speaks what all the others feel ("He can't believe it didn't mean anything") is mocked and finally ostracized for behaving badly when "He had a chance to behave so well." That is, given the perfect occasion for displaying his tortured stoicism, Cohn renounces his chance in favor of an expressivist mode. Cohn can't believe that his affair with Brett meant nothing and, in insisting upon its importance, he reveals that indeed it did mean nothing. The others, though, maintain the illusion that their suffering is significant by continually representing themselves as survivors of a tragedy they will neither name nor overcome. Brett's comment makes explicit what is suggested throughout the narrative: one can only "behave well" if one receives the opportunity to suffer stoically. One can only be tragic if one has experienced a significant loss. If one does not actually possess the deep secret whose denial bestows meaning and purpose on one's life, one can perhaps create that opportunity by manufacturing the loss, or at least its illusion.

Bill Gorton ironically but accurately characterizes the power of the secret when he catalogues the clichés about American expatriates: "You don't work. One group claims women support you. Another group claims you're impotent." Jake responds: "No . . . I just had an accident": " 'Never mention that,' Bill said. 'That's the sort of thing that can't be spoken of. That's what you ought to work up into a mystery. Like Henry's bicycle'." The allusion to Henry James, a writer who also had an "accident" and who mastered most consciously in his writing the power of the secret to evoke fascination and desire, suggests that Jake too participates, perhaps unconsciously, in the manufacture of mysteries as a means to power over others—and perhaps over himself as well.

Jake's exploitation of the power of omission presumes that the unconscious is a buried or hidden "depth" beneath the surface layer of consciousness. His notion of denial thus differs substantially from Freud's because Jake always assumes that he knows the truth that he omits. In fact, according to Freud, repression occurs not as "burial" but as disguise. Displacement, condensation, jokes and negation are all familiar modes of disguise by which the repressed may reside within consciousness in unrecognized form: "Thus the subject-matter of a repressed image or thought can make its way into consciousness on condition that it is *denied*." Jake's narrative, not surprisingly, explodes its own "false" unconscious by clearly enacting the motives for and the means of its mystification of the reader. Early in the story, Jake returns home after his reunion with Brett, a meeting that has evoked his doomed desire for her:

> Undressing, I looked at myself in the mirror of the big armoire beside the bed. That was a typically French way to furnish a room. Practical, too, I suppose. Of all the ways to be wounded. I suppose it was funny. I put on my pajamas and got into bed. I had the two bull-fight papers, and I took their wrappers off.

(pp. 54-5)

Though Jake denies his obsession with the wound when he calls it "funny," a remark intended perhaps to compel our admiration for his stoic forebearance, that obsession is clear: the room itself has become a shrine to the full presence of the missing god. Such is the complexity of Jake's relation to his mutilation. The loss of his capacity for a "normal" sexual life is truly a horror to him, but that horror is simultaneously cherished and exploited as the origin of Jake's new tragic specificity. The arbitrary pathos threatened by castration—having been literally "unmanned" in an accident—is redeemed because it provokes the dramatic performance of manliness. Jake's loss is thus a magnificent gain: like the existential hero, like Pedro Romero, he loves his enemy because it identifies him as a warrior. The end of the passage finds Jake rewrapping himself in his pajamas and his bed which he now shares with the unwrapped bull-fight papers. The presentation of the bull-fight now becomes the substitute object of Jake's frustrated sexual desire, identifying that strangely sexual ritual as another of Jake's means of self-representation.

More directly, however, the passage suggests the role of the dialectic of castration and desire in Jake's relation to Brett. In the never-consummated love affair, Jake once again redeems his castration by making it the source of his mastery of Brett, evoking in her a desire that he will never fulfill. . . . But though Jake may master Brett's desire, he does not master his own. . . . Jake cannot be satisfied with his capacity to control the desire of the other; he must continually evoke his own desire for her by sending her off with other men, "pimping" for her to create his own sense of loss and jealousy. Jake depends upon the presence of a third party, his rival, to maintain or mediate his desire; the lovers' discourse thus remains a stable source of desire and of the tragic identity inscribed by that desire.

Brett is of course the perfect love object precisely because she affords so many opportunities for rivalry and its consequent evocation of desire. Collecting lovers, finding pleasure in the growing ranks of her sexual conquests, Brett can nevertheless be counted upon to return to Jake, depending upon him to define her own otherwise sordid promiscuity as the result of her tragic desire for the only man she could never have. Brett's romantic history suggests that her desire has always depended upon a master/slave dynamic: she married her husband after "her own true love" had died, thus effectively mastering her desire. Michael, her present fiancé, is someone she "nursed," as he mentions in the context of her "looking after" the wounded Romero: "But she loves looking after people. That's how we came to go off together. She was looking after me." Similarly, her relationship with Jake began when she served as a nurse in the English hospital where Jake was sent after his injury. All her lovers, though, are too easily mastered, too easily made dependent upon her. Like the dead man, only Jake, her current "own true love," remains an appropriate object of desire since he allows the maintenance of their dialectic: she must continue to want him because he can never be possessed, and his love for her legitimizes their economic relation. (pp. 56-7)

It's fun to be in love when one will never have to risk the degeneration of the love relation, when one will never be forced to experience the lapse of desire in its "fulfillment." One thus feels one's love object to be a compulsion, the fated and necessary complement to one's being, rather than a manufactured and mediated occasion for the experience of desire.

The success of the relation depends precisely upon its capacity to withstand the threat of satisfaction. It thus perpetuates the delusion that the two are victims of a fate beyond their control. But the control they exert is nevertheless apparent:

> She was sitting up now. My arm was around her and she was leaning back against me, and we were quite calm. She was looking into my eyes with that way she had of looking that made you wonder whether she really saw out of her own eyes. They would look on and on after every one else's eyes in the world would have stopped looking.

From whose eyes could Brett look out at Jake so dependably if not from his own, her vision here determined by Jake's power to author her as one who desires. She can be counted upon to continue looking on "after every one else's eyes in the world would have stopped looking" because she is the stable mirror of his own image. After all, looking into Brett's eyes to see what she sees, Jake would of course see only his own reflection: he masters her by effecting her castration in imitation of his own.

Jake's fury at the homosexuals who accompany Brett to a nightclub becomes clearer when we recognize the power his castration confers on him. That rage is not resentment over the homosexual's willing abnegation of the conventional male sexuality Jake has been forced to sacrifice. Rather, it results from the serious threat the homosexual might pose to Jake's privileged relation to Brett. The homosexual is the only other male figure who might be able, like Jake, to evoke in Brett a desire that he would refuse to fulfill; indeed, the homosexual lover might even be preferable to Jake, who does not refuse to satisfy Brett's desire but is physically unable to do so. If anyone might displace Jake and his authority over Brett, it would be the homosexual man, so his response is fury over the "superior" composure of the gays.

What Jake requires in the way of an effective mediator to his own desire is someone who can temporarily replace him by becoming Brett's lover. Such a displacement is necessary because the temporary gratification of Brett's sexual desire will simply convince her that the true object of her desire is unpossessed. Brett's lover's sexual potency is thus requisite to ensure his impotence and Jake's continued mastery of her. He maintains his mastery by choosing the figures who will supplant him. . . . Brett's apparent willingness to give Jake up, for both their sakes, simultaneously ensures the preservation of their bond: her companion at San Sebastian will be Cohn, whom she has met through Jake and who is thus associated with her forbidden love. Cohn's displacement of Jake will only remind Brett of what she is denied and will thus guarantee her eventual return to her author.

Jake is even more clearly to be seen authoring Brett's desire for Romero. What might appear to be her "natural" fascination with the handsome boy who performs his dangerous task so gracefully is in fact a product of Jake's maneuvering. . . . Jake composes Romero's romantic persona. The matador is already clearly associated with Jake: the trip to Pamplona is Jake's yearly pilgrimage to his "holy land," and he is marked by Montoya as one who possesses the ineffable *aficion.* If Brett falls in love with Romero, it is at least partially in imitation of Jake's own passion for the boy. However, Jake carefully encourages Brett's interest:

> Brett sat between Mike and me at the barrera. . . .
> Romero was the whole show. I do not think Brett

saw any other bull-fighter. . . . I sat beside Brett and explained to Brett what it was all about. . . . I had her watch how Romero took the bull away from a fallen horse with his cape, and how he held him with the cape and turned him, smoothly and suavely, never wasting the bull. . . . She saw why she liked Romero's cape-work and why she did not like the others.

Brett can see no other bull-fighter because Jake will not allow her to. The parallels between Jake's mastery of Brett's vision and the matador's mastery of the bull reveal the particular strategy by which Jake transfers Brett's desire toward Romero: he makes her see the matador as the seductive master of the beast's desire.

The parallels suggest an even more curious link between the bull-fight and the affair with Brett, however. Jake's representation of the bull-fight depends upon and perpetuates the same mode of interpretation that underlies his representation of castration. Jake transcends his impotence, that is, only by repressing its textuality; now, he "naturalizes" the bull-fight. Brett instinctively recognizes the superiority of Romero's cape-work, Jake says, while he merely explains the technical skills involved in manifesting that superiority. The artifice of the cape-work, as absolute as the artifice of Jake's mastery of Brett, is denied when Jake identifies the ritual's conventions as mere tokens of the greater truths they hide. Depending upon both Brett and the reader to remain committed to the ideal of the hidden truth, Jake can thus represent the bull-fight as the formal and legitimizing account of his own struggles with castration.

Jake's representation of the ritual is, not surprisingly, fraught with the same sort of mysteries that we found in his constructions of the wound and the war. The ritual is a secret with something shameful attached to it, the disguised evidence of which provokes a desire for membership in its cult. . . . What is secret or shameful about the ritual cannot be spoken, however; it can only be figured by a very unpleasant, but certainly not a mysterious element of it: the goring of the horses during the fight. That horror, ostensibly a token of a deeper and more significant horror, is repeatedly referred to, though always in the form of a negative: " 'Don't look at the horses, after the bull hits them,' I said to Brett. . . . 'There's nothing but that horse part that will bother you, and they're only in for a few minutes with each bull. Just don't watch when it's bad'." Jake's insistent negation of the horses' importance grants their misery its symbolic status. By producing the illusion that something is omitted from the fight, displaced by the sacrifice of the horses, Jake also produces the illusion of the ritual's "secret" meaning.

Indeed, Jake suggests that there is no exact translation, in any language, for the bull-fight. . . . [He] implies that language is incapable of representing the totality of the bull-fight, that all the terms used to name it are evasions of its actual meaning. They may circle around the performance itself, evoking or suggesting aspects of it, but they cannot define what it really is. Only partial names can escape the repression that surrounds the fight and suggests its ineffability. The ritual is thus evoked precisely as the unnameable: the secret that is the ritual can be performed, but it is by nature alinguistic, primal, anterior to all representational systems. It is its own origin.

Jake wants us to feel the bull-fight as a constant and unchanging mystery that escapes the reduction of any language, even the language of the culture in which the ritual originates. In fact, however, the difficulty of translating the "meaning" of the bull-fight into another language lies in the fact that the Spanish signifiers *Corrida de toros* refer to other signifiers in the Spanish culture, signifiers that have taken on the status of signifieds; the Spanish signifiers to which the name of the ritual refers do not necessarily exist in Anglo-American culture. Again, it is by denying the cultural specificity of the ritual that Jake represents it as a fundamentally unchanging and essential mystery whose solution can only be intuited by the initiate.

One goes to the bull-fight to experience its secret as one's own, but Jake complicates the spectators' expectations when he describes Belmonte's failure to fulfill them:

People went to the corrida to see Belmonte, to be given tragic sensations, and perhaps to see the death of Belmonte. Fifteen years ago they said if you wanted to see Belmonte you should go quickly, while he was still alive. . . . When he retired the legend grew up about how his bull-fighting had been, and when he came out of retirement the public were disappointed because no real man could work as close to the bulls as Belmonte was supposed to have done, not, of course, even Belmonte.

Also Belmonte imposed conditions and insisted that his bulls should not be too large, nor too dangerously armed with horns, and so the element that was necessary to give the sensation of tragedy was not there, and the public . . . felt defrauded and cheated. . . . He had expected to compete with Marcial and the other stars of the decadence of bull-fighting, and he knew that the sincerity of his own bull-fighting would be so set off by the false aesthetics of the bull-fighters of the decadent period that he would only have to be in the ring.

The "tragic sensations" that one attends the fight to experience are a delicate commodity: they depend upon the illusion of the matador's natural and spontaneous daring. The goal of the ritual is a presentation of the matador's "sincerity," and the failure of that achievement leads to "decadence." Curiously, the terminology Jake employs here, evoking almost a Wordsworthian romantic aesthetic, conflicts with the earlier implication that the bull-fight is not a re-presentation, but a presentation of the thing itself. The supplementarity of the ritual that was previously denied is here acknowledged, but only as something that must be repressed if the bull-fight is to perform its intended function. Tragic sensations only occur if the matador's performance is good enough—that is, deceptive enough—to create the illusion of unstudied and natural courage.

The necessary but necessarily-denied artificiality of the ritual is also apparent in the matador's attitude toward his symbolic opponent. The relation of matador to bull is ostensibly one of rivalry, each desiring to master the other by destroying it. But in order for the matador's desire for mastery to be provoked by the bull—granted a legitimate ground in courage rather than in wanton destructiveness—the bull must be a particularly dangerous opponent. As Romero says, "The bulls are my best friends" because they make his bravery possible; it is the actual threat they pose to his life that invests his otherwise-artificial behavior in the ring with meaning. That real threat also provides the spectators with their opportunity for tragic sensations, as Belmonte's disappointing evasion of the threats reveals. Only a dangerous bull can make the matador a real master—of the bull, of the spectators, and of himself.

But the bull is oddly chosen to play its role in this allegory of man's confrontation with his own contingency: the animal is not a natural threat to man; it does not, like a lion or a wolf might, pose the wild hunter's threat to human domesticity. In fact, the bull is a domestic animal, and one that must be further "domesticated" for the purposes of the bull-fight. The animal, bred for a particularly unintelligent viciousness, must be *created* as the matador's enemy. If the bull is a token of anything in particular, then, it would have to be a pure but nevertheless *un*-natural physical energy or aggressivity devoid of either rationality or animal cunning. Or perhaps what the bull actually represents is the enormous resourcefulness of human narcissism, the ingenuity of which is demonstrated in this quite cunning transformation of a very strong and stupid beast into the terrifying and malignant enemy necessary to the warrior's existence.

According to the passage detailing Romero's mastery over the bull, the bull must actually be seduced into attacking the matador; all the elements of the fight involve goading, pricking, taunting the bull into making its direct attack on the matador rather than on some other figure in the arena. The bull's artificially-introduced aggressivity is initially without a particular object: it wants to destroy anything or everything or perhaps even nothing. . . . To make the bull attack him, the matador must behave in a curiously sexual, even "feminine" fashion: dressed in physically confining clothing—tight pants and heavily decorated tight jacket—carrying a large skirt-like cape, the matador performs a series of intricate dance-like steps in front of the bull, offering his body, teasing the animal into charging, and then at the last minute pirouetting away from the charge. The description of Romero's activity sounds suspiciously like that of a woman arousing a lover's desire: both forms of seduction involve offering the body, provoking the "pass," and then capriciously denying satisfaction until the "lover" has been sufficiently "worn down" by his own frenzied desire, readied for his final sacrifice to his beloved. Just as Brett's desire has been authored by her master-castrate, so is the bull made to desire the mastery of his own author. (pp. 58-64)

The relationship of matador to bull would seem to involve a bizarre sexual parody: the bull, made to play a role of conventionally aggressive masculinity, confronts the matador in the guise of feminine seductress. The two engage in a struggle in which the "man" apparently holds the advantage, but "woman" masters her rival by provoking his desire to master her. Here, the vulnerable passivity conventionally attributed to woman becomes her strength—her aggression, actually—against the man who goes "straight to the point" in this case, the point of the matador's sword:

> Out in the centre of the ring Romero profiled in front of the bull, drew the sword out from the folds of the muleta, rose on his toes, and sighted along the blade. The bull charged as Romero charged. Romero's left hand dropped the muleta over the bull's muzzle to blind him, his left shoulder went forward between the horns as the sword went in, and for just an instant he and the bull were one . . .

The matador—master as castrate as woman—fulfills for the "bull" what is precisely the desire of each subject: the gratification of his desire in the master's gratification of her own. The subject's desire for the master and his desire to be for the

master what she desires are fulfilled simultaneously: from behind the folds of the skirt (and some other "folds" might be imagistically evoked here) that veils the potentially horrifying absence, the master withdraws the phallus. But master and subject become one only at the cost of the "total expenditure": the end of the subject's specificity, the achievement of his *jouissance,* his return to his origin beyond the pleasure principle. And if the subject of this ritual is a particularly heroic one, if he defers this ultimate *jouissance* long and tragically enough, the highest compliment will be paid him in another manifestation of the total expenditure: a symbolic castration will occur in the cutting off of small appendages, like tail or ears, from his body. (p. 65)

Of course, this interpretation of the bull-fight is antithetical to everything the ritual is intended to stand for in Hemingway's novel, but that is what makes it interesting. What the ritual wishes to represent—humanness as some version of a hardy existential "machismo" engaging a mortal fate—represses another unwished-for representation: the mastery of culturally-defined masculinity by culturally-defined femininity. The signifiers of the ritual—matador and bull—are intended to refer to the given and thus necessarily true signifieds of man and nature, or man and death. What they in fact refer to are other signifiers, masculinity and femininity. The bull-fight is not a translation of an absolute code into cultural language; it is not the originary enactment of a taboo truth. It reveals what Jake's narrative has revealed throughout: that the subject is constituted by an imaginatively-constructed other who confers that subjectivity by threatening it. Whether that other is castration, death, the father, or the bull, the subject must produce his opponent in order to legitimize his own will to power.

The ritual of the bull-fight subverts more than just the integrity of the subject, existential or otherwise, however. Romero's transvestism suggests that, like Jake, the matador must behave "like a woman" to prove that he is a man. Jake's narrative would thus appear to define power as fundamentally "feminine." But this does not make sense: even if Brett possesses the power that Jake and Romero have, the novel does not represent her mastery of men as a victory over worthy opponents; it does not endorse her authority as it does Jake's and Romero's. The logical contradiction of "feminine power" could only be resolved if the male protagonist's transvestism were understood as the temporary but necessary deferral of his achievement of masculine autonomy; a woman's femininity, on the other hand, is a permanent and irredeemable "sentence" that cannot be transcended. In this sense, femininity figures the threat that the man must embrace to overcome. However, the bull-fight still poses one challenge to this particular resolution of its mysterious allegory: the matador may become a "woman" to prove his manliness, but the opponent he overcomes is "man." The question thus remains: why does the bull-fight depict the symbolic destruction of man by woman?

Perhaps we can account for this anomaly by recalling the multiplicity of the ritual's signifiers. The matador requires the artificially-constructed significance of the bull to signify something about himself. Similarly, both participants in the ritual figure a certain doubleness in themselves: the bull manifests the doubling of the binary human/animal, while the matador himself doubles the mutually-exclusive meanings of "male" and "female." He figures, that is, the coexistence of the structures of difference—male/female, aggressivity/passivity, reason/passion—that the patriarchy has divided into binaries to form its own "natural" basis. If the hierarchy of those polarized differences is now inverted so that the guise of femininity is associated with a certain kind of powerful aggressivity, the ritual may suggest a couple of things about the codes of patriarchal culture. That inversion indicates that the distinctions upon which the patriarchy depends are arbitrarily, or conventionally, ascribed to biological men and women; as Shoshana Felman has argued, " . . . the substitutions of woman for man and of man for woman, the interchangeability and reversibility of masculine and feminine manifests a discord which subverts the limits and compromises the coherence of each of the two principles."

Even more interestingly, however, the ritual may suggest *why* patriarchal culture has repressed the artificiality of its own category of castration. Again, to quote Felman, "If femininity becomes indeed a signifier of castration, it is by no means . . . the embodiment of *literal castration,* the literalization of the figure of castration . . . but rather . . . castration as a differential process of substitution, subverting, on the contrary, literality as such." "Castration" in this context still signifies a "loss" of sorts, but that loss must be understood as the power of certainty, of proper meaning, of literality. It is to repress the threat of this loss that the culture invents "castration" to signify the temporary deferral of such literality.

But in its dependence upon woman to signify a stable principle of castrated otherness—the permanence of a loss a man may transcend—the patriarchy invests her with a curious power that might be quite improperly employed, like the dagger, against the man who embodies the patriarchy's authority. If the bull-fight represents woman as the castrating enchantress, a version of the *vagina dentata,* it must suggest that the value of the phallus depends upon that toothy threat; it thus inscribes woman as author of the presence she threatens. But "she" is *already* a transvestite, a substitute signifier that can only refer to the presence she defers. According to the bull-fight, then, woman's power to destroy man is not quite the power to castrate him; it is rather the signifier's power to castrate the very mythos of castration. (pp. 65-7)

Nina Schwartz, "Lovers' Discourse in 'The Sun Also Rises': A Cock and Bull Story," in Criticism, *Vol. XXVI, No. 1, Winter, 1984, pp. 49-69.*

SUKRITA PAUL KUMAR

The Sun Also Rises projects Hemingway's well-formulated and sure-footed ideas on love and sex, incarnated in the various characters of the novel. In Brett Ashley around whom men revolve like satellites, Hemingway has portrayed the 'woman as hero' to adopt the striking phrase from Carolyn Heilbrun. Brett bears the burden of the novel's central action. She is defined so little by her sex and her role is not determined by her mere femaleness. Her tragedy lies not in her failure to remain encompassed within a pre-defined mode of existence but in the fact that except for Jake, she finds no man who could comprehend the multiplicity of her roles as a woman seeking the realization of her selfhood. . . . (p. 102)

'An extraordinary wench', Brett cannot look away, as any womanly woman may have done when "some rather awful things" happen to the horses at the bull-fight. Even her drunken fiance, Mike, can perceive that this is not because

she is not a sadist. As he says, she is 'just a lovely, healthy wench'. She apparently has the 'aficion' that normally only a man may have and she recognizes the 'real emotion' working behind Romero's bull-fighting. For romantics like Cohn, her unconventionality is thus of a Circe 'who turns men into swine'. She does 'just what she wants to' and probably it is just this illusion of confident cheer and security that attracts the men of an after-war sick world to her. Her 'masculine' attire and manner are not incongruous with her temperament whose complexity is symbolic of the social and psychological tensions of the time. She embodies in herself the heroic possibility of saving the society doomed by sexual polarization. And yet, unique in her energy and most unhypocritical in her denouncement of the hideous strictures of society, Brett is certainly not asexual or sexless. She is rooted in her 'womanliness' and the thrust of her personality makes it possible for her to realize her selfhood uninhibitedly. Robert Cohn, a 'wandering troubadour' and a case of 'arrested development' in the twentieth-century context, finds his 'golden-haired angel' in Brett. He is "proudly and firmly waiting the assault ready to do battle for his lady love" in the Pampiona brawl. Though this romantic knight has already been married once and has had a 'mistress' in Frances, he fails to see 'woman' as anything more than the 'Princess of Cleves'. His stubborn persistence to fit Brett's amorphous personality into the confines of chivalrous love and his curious belief that he has discovered his 'promised land' and a great love in his sexual interlude with Brett makes her appear like a *femme fatale* who has victimized Cohn with her destructive charms. In fact Cohn is a victim of his own illusions and an instrument of his own humiliation when he follows Brett around 'like a steer all the time' and becomes the butt of ridicule. What is merely a casual experience for Brett who spends a week-end with Cohn at San Sebastian becomes a very serious commitment for him and his personality crumbles at Brett's indifference. . . . (pp. 102-03)

Brett has no sympathies for self-deluded romantics. Such men have no significance in her search for a meaningful relationship. Mike Campbell, a down-to-earth realist who understands Brett perfectly, ridicules the sentimentality of Cohn and remains a faithful admirer of Brett without allowing himself to become a slave to the idea of being in love with her and thus suffer as Cohn does. Mike is brutally frank and forthright with himself and accepts Brett for whatever she is. . . . He knows perfectly well that Brett's amorous digressions from him are necessary for her restless and discontented temperament, resulting from her frustrated 'first love' and her marriage with the aristocratic Ashley. Mike and Brett 'came together' when Brett was 'looking after him'. Her tenderness and the capacity to care for others are a pointer towards the affirmation of her 'female' identity, which is generally ignored. But Mike is aware of it and he discerns Brett's personality in all its facets. He is however a dipsomaniac, a sick man, incapable of a full relationship with anyone. His personality has been corroded by the 'polymorphous-perverse' tendencies of the contemporary society. Though his morality sanctions a lot of freedom for Brett, he does suffer from pangs of uneasy jealousy when she gets passionately involved with Pedro Romero, the handsome young bull-fighter. But he suffers on the quiet and drinks himself to sleep. It is probably his very harmlessness and non-interference that is responsible for Brett's desire to get married to him. Also, Brett sees a fundamental likeness between Mike and herself. Both are, as she says herself, 'nice' and 'awful'.

Brett's initiative in approaching Romero stands conspicuous when compared to her other relationships. The impulsive Brett who has 'never been able to help anything' falls in love with Romero, the bull-fighter who showed her 'real emotion'. And, in order to retain her 'self-respect', Brett decides that she has got to do something which she really wants to do. She uses Jake to get to Romero even though it makes her feel 'such a bitch'. . . . She recognizes in Lawrentian terms, the 'impersonal' female principle in her desire to overcome her isolation through a relationship with Pedro Romero, who at once feels 'there was something between them'. Brett's short but powerful involvement with Romero gives a significant turn to the realization of her selfhood. The 'near-alcoholic' and the 'near-nymphomaniac' Brett, despite the overwhelming intensity of her emotion for Romero but in keeping with the integrity and 'benevolence' of her character, renounces him by deciding not to be "one of those bitches that ruins children". . . . In Brett the *femme fatale* acquires a more 'humanly' plausible role by balancing her superficial charms and passions with her cerebral powers. She is a sensitive, thinking woman whose aggressive 'femaleness' is sustained by an equally dominant conscience. Apart from curing her of the depression of the Cohn affair, her relationship with Romero and her subsequent 'renunciation', give Brett a heightened significance as a 'total woman'. She does not possess the 'conventionally' displaced and restrictive female consciousness that may have retarded her existence. The assertiveness of her personality rests on an alert human consciousness. Romero's suggestions confining her to conventional womanhood by altering her mode of hair and dress are of course outrageous to her. Nothing would make her become the prisoner of her gender, not even her passion for Romero. However, the realization of her sexual identity yields to her a happiness for which the Hemingway protagonists struggle all through their lives. Brett approaches 'sainthood' through her act of 'renunciation' and experiences moments of 'feeling good' which according to the Hemingway code is the same as being 'truly moral'.

Over Brett's affairs with Cohn, Mike and Romero, looms a very pressing and tragic love-relationship between Jake and Brett. In depicting Jake as a crucially victimized product of the war, one who has all the ingredients of genuine love but is physically wounded, Hemingway builds up the tragic strain in the novel. The tragedy lies in the disability of the otherwise strong man who suffers from acute loneliness in his inability to achieve the wholeness of a relationship with the other sex, despite his having found the right woman. Jake's alertness and sensitivity, combined with his tender feelings for her, keep Brett under his comprehending observation. Brett is not unaware of this. She is as much in love with him as he is and uses him, as a congenial Father Confessor on whose shoulders she wipes her tears and pours all her woes. . . . Jake is more stoical than Brett. He is not a sighing Werther and he cherishes his love for her as "an enjoyable feeling", whereas to Brett 'It's hell on earth', for she, of necessity, has to put constraints on her aggressive femininity in the only genuine and potential relationship she has discovered. But as Jake observes, she is in fact an idealist who desires to have only what she could not have, for which she suffers from a perpetual temperamental restlessness. Jake who is capable of a real male relationship, as is testified by his friendship with Bill, is also equally sincere in his sexless relationship with Brett. . . . Jake symptomizes rare qualities of friendship such as congeniality; sincerity, capacity to sacrifice for the other and a generous temperament. His relationship with Mike, Romero, Cohn, Bill and Brett emphasize all his innate 'noble' qualities. Each of them confides in his magnetic personality; which absorbs the 'suffering' of all. His healthy stoicism is a source of energy for the rest. His relationship with Brett is consistently powerful and meaningful through the end of the novel.

Though Jake suffers acutely to see Brett have an affair with either Cohn or Romero, he does seem at the same time to get vicarious pleasure out of her sexual adventures. In fact he himself becomes an instrument to convenience her meetings with Romero. Brett's diverse interpersonal relationships experienced through an alert consciousness make her a much richer personality. Towards the end of the novel when she meets Jake, she seems 'set-up' and a much more confident personality. She realizes that Mike who is "so damned nice" and 'awful' at the same time, is just her 'sort of thing'. Also she experiences deeply gratifying feelings as a 'substitute for God'. All the same, the novel ends on a rather ironical note:

> "Oh, Jake", Brett said, "we could have had such a damned good time together"
>
> "Yes", I said, "isn't it pretty to think so?"

This points towards the failure of an ideal male-female relationship due to the desexing of a war-victim. While Jake's answer to Brett is an evidence of his wisdom acquired through suffering, Brett's comment reminds one of D. H. Lawrence's theory of tension and 'dynamic counterpoint'. Jake and Brett gravitate towards each other, the attraction between them is augmented by an overpowering life-impulse but their inability to consummate their passion creates a sort of an innate chaos in their relationship. The need to lose their male-female polarities remains ungratified and the bitterness is a result of the unrealized Lawrentian 'moment of illumination'. They cannot recognize the 'vital reality' of the 'sacred' aspect of sex, of life through sex. Brett's ideal of 'good time' comes close to Lawrence's faith in the 'mysterious bio-chemical activity which is embedded in sensuality and which fructifies man's preconscious. Brett, however, is a model of the new emerging American woman who seems to have been given her due recognition at last. *The Sun Also Rises* celebrates her new female identity. It advocates a readjustment of man-woman pattern in the new context of the context of the confusion created by the overlapping masculinity and femininity. Though the novel is no specific alarm for a sexual revolution, it certainly recognizes the changing male and female roles. The novel paves the way for complete androgynous relationships through an acceptance and absorption of the new values as well as the new female ideal. (pp. 104-08)

Sukrita Paul Kumar, "Woman as Hero in Hemingway's 'The Sun Also Rises'," in The Literary Endeavour, *Vol. VI, Nos. 1-4, 1985, pp. 102-08.*

JOHN W. ALDRIDGE

As the sufficiently elderly among us may remember, Hemingway, by the time of his suicide in 1961, had become a public embarrassment. The trouble began a long time before, somewhere back in the years of his first international success, the years of African safari and *Death in the Afternoon,* when he had already begun to go slack and was indulging in celebrity exploits rather than the writing of good books. *The Old Man and the Sea* was received more with relief than with delight because it seemed a sign that the old Hemingway was still alive and sounding like himself. But then it had to be admitted that the book had no insides and was simply a synthetic imitation of Hemingway sounding like himself. *Across the River and into the Trees* had been just as bad as the disenchanted said it was, and it was ominously bad, for it proved that the writer could no longer tell the difference between himself and his public personality—undoubtedly because there had ceased to be any. (p. 337)

By 1961 all the signs seemed to agree that the usual posthumous decline in reputation would, in Hemingway's case, be redundant. There seemed to be no room for further decline. But what happened was something quite different and altogether unexpected. After the shortest eclipse recorded in recent literary astronomy, the Hemingway reputation began to shine with a brightness it had not displayed in decades, and it appeared that all the bad years and bad work had been magically purged from public memory. . . . There was pathos, even a hint of tragedy, in [his suicide], enough to set in motion a curious process by which a former fine writer become boring buffoon could be transformed in death into a species of martyred saint. Finally there was a vague something else—a sense that all the returns were not yet in, that there remained further questions as yet unanswered, some tantalizing, perhaps vindicating final truth still to be revealed.

Whatever the reasons, it can now fairly be said, twenty-five years after his death, that of the several gifted writers of his remarkable generation Hemingway is the one who still, in spite of everything, makes the strongest claim on our interest and curiosity. (pp. 337-38)

Since 1961 the sheer volume of critical and biographical information about Hemingway has reached the proportions of a corporate industry, with branches and subsidiaries spreading across the world into virtually every civilized country where his work has been translated and published. The immediate result has been to inflate still further the already overblown Hemingway legend and to elevate almost everything he wrote, both the best and the worst, to the status of holy scripture, while he himself is securely established as the imperial icon of American literature in the first half of the twentieth century. (pp. 338-39)

To extricate [his work] from the museums and restore them to life is an impossible task. But with a sufficiently vigorous exercise of imagination we can approach them once again and ask some of the first questions, the kind that, in our virginity of mind, we were once able to answer, and that all the subsequent celebrity has almost caused us to forget how to ask.

What was it then, and what is it now, that makes Hemingway so compellingly attractive as a writer; what is the nature and source of the very great pleasure we take in him when he is at his best, and the pain we feel when he is at his worst? To begin with the obvious—and accepting the pretense that we are reading him for the first time—let us say that Hemingway's initially most seductive attribute was and remains his powerful responsiveness to experience. That attribute is perhaps made more seductive by the fact that most of us since his time have found such responsiveness to be seriously diminished in ourselves. One reason is that our responses to the infinitely more complex and diffuse experiences of our present world have *had* to diminish if we are to retain our sanity. Another reason is that few of us today have, or have ever had, access to a clearly defined microcosmic world in which the things one feels, says, and does might take on the sacramental

importance they had for Hemingway in the first war, in Paris, and later in Spain. (p. 339)

One does not easily envy the life of any of our immediate contemporaries—the talent, perhaps, but not the life—as one so easily envies Hemingway's, particularly during the years when his talent was freshest and he was writing at the top of his form in those early stories and *The Sun Also Rises*—his first and, withal, still his best novel. He was young then, as we were young when we first read him. He was living, as we regrettably were not, in the most exotic city in Europe among some of the most remarkable personalities and gifted artists of the post-World War I era. And he brought to it all the highly sensitized perspective of the provincial midwestern tourist viewing with wonder and delight the hitherto undiscovered riches of foreignness.

He took the greatest pleasure—and gave us vicariously the greatest pleasure—in the hotels, bars, and restaurants of Paris; and with his quickly acquired inside-dopester knowingness, he appointed himself the official instructor in where and how to live wisely and well. He could recite the names of all the streets; he knew the exact location of all the good places and the best route to take to get to them; and he was on friendly terms with the best bartenders and waiters who worked in them. He had a wonderful eye not only for quality but for terrain, whether the topography of Paris or the landscape of Spain; and in sharing his knowledge with us, he schooled us in the ways of a world we did not know but desperately wished we did.

He also accomplished something far more significant for us and for literature. If he had not, then Scott Fitzgerald's well-known description of *The Sun Also Rises* as "a romance and a guidebook" might have been all that needed to be said. But in introducing us literally to the life of foreignness, Hemingway at the same time created the illusion that *every* element of life is in fact foreign, hence new and without precedent in the known experience of the past. Every element needs, therefore, to be carefully examined and tested to determine the degree of its authenticity. In order to live an authentic life and produce an authentic fiction, one has to proceed with the greatest caution and select only those experiences, express only those emotions, that have proved their validity because they have been measured against the realities of honest feeling and what one senses in one's deepest instincts to be true. The result in Hemingway's fiction is not a realistic reflection of a world but the literal manufacture of a world, piece by piece, out of the most meticulously chosen and crafted materials.

This world is altogether strange and perilous because it is without moral history and received standards of conduct. Characters therefore must move through it as if through enemy-held territory, learning how to live while trying to stay alive. To survive they need all the cunning and expertise they can muster. They must be sure that they know at all times exactly where they are, both geographically and in relation to others. They must also learn exactly how to behave so as to minimize the risk of becoming vulnerable to error and the dangerous consequences of losing self-control. They must fabricate, through constant study and trial, an etiquette that will enable them to know instinctively what is appropriate and what is not, so that they can maintain decorum under stress or siege. They must master the procedure for everything, the correct methods for carrying out their function—whether it is hunting, fishing, bullfighting, or eating and drinking. And above all they must know the cost of everything, not only the cost in money but the physical and emotional cost. To survive successfully is to learn how to get one's money's worth, the right return on the investment; hence one must be extremely careful to make only the *right* investments, those that will yield honest satisfactions and beneficial emotions rather than lead to the overinflation of specious values and destructive emotions.

The characters in *The Sun Also Rises* might all be seen to be morally measurable on the basis of whether or not they are wise enough to get their money's worth. Jake Barnes is one who is constantly preoccupied with cost. He tells us what meals cost in restaurants, how much it is proper to tip waiters and bellmen in order to be assured of a satisfactory return in attentive service, who borrowed how much from whom and whether the debt was promptly repaid (Mike Campbell borrows constantly and from everybody and never repays). In Bayonne after the disastrous end of the fiesta Jake is pleased to be back in France because there "everything is on such a clear financial basis. . . . If you want people to like you you have only to spend a little money." Earlier in Pamplona, while indulging in some drunken philosophizing, he concludes that "you paid some way for everything that was any good. I paid my way into enough things that I liked, so that I had a good time. Either you paid by learning about them, or by experience, or by taking chances, or by money. Enjoying living was learning to get your money's worth and knowing when you had it."

Count Mippipopolous has learned to get his money's worth and knows when he has. Robert Cohn does not know because he never understands the rate of exchange. His values have not been submitted to the test of actual experience and cannot be, for they have come out of books and romantic fantasy. He is therefore unable to see Brett for what she is, although exactly what she is never becomes altogether clear. Because of the count's wisdom about money as well as his arrow wounds, Brett identifies him as "one of us"—which he may or may not be, since he has already learned what she and Jake are still trying to learn: namely how to live decorously and well. Brett fails from the beginning because Jake's wound prevents her from fulfilling what she believes to be her true love for him. In compensation she has affairs, and she plans to marry Mike (about whom she does not appear to care very much), presumably because he will one day be rich. She has had an interlude with Cohn in San Sebastian, mostly because she was bored at the time, and she comes to despise Cohn because he is so obviously not "One of us" and refuses to believe that the affair did not mean anything.

Such values as Brett has are in limbo through the greater part of the novel and operate only momentarily and feebly when she decides to send Romero away. There is finally no hope for her, because she has been undisciplined and adrift for too long. She has never learned the value of anything, has given up or never taken control of her life, and so has passed into the control of random impulse and boredom. In the ultimate sense of the word Brett is *lost*. That is the poignant message behind Jake's closing remark about the prettiness of thinking things might ever have been different between them. Nor will things ever be different between her and Mike. He may inherit a fortune, but one can be sure that neither of them will get his money's worth because neither knows how to.

Hemingway's tight minimalist style, which is displayed in its purest form in *The Sun Also Rises,* is the precise verbal expression of the view of life that dominates and finally evaluates the action of the novel. If Hemingway believed—as he clearly did—that if the right, carefully selected experiences are chosen and only the proper emotions expressed, the result will be an absolutely authentic fictional world containing nothing that will ever ring false, then the language, chosen with equal care—so authentically simple and basic—is the perfect fastidious statement of the morally fastidious world it is designed to create. The vacant spaces between and behind the words, the strongly sensed presence of things omitted, become expressive of all the alternatives and elaborations, all the excesses and equivocations of language, that have been scrupulously rejected in the style's formation. The emphasis given to the individual words and phrases that seem so much larger than they are just because they have escaped rejection makes it appear that a verbal artifact is being constructed or salvaged, word by word, from a junk-heap of redundancy and imprecision. There are no moral or literary precedents to provide the style with foundation or scaffolding. Everything that manages, against great resistance, to achieve utterance is seemingly being uttered for the very first time in human history, is a kind of Ur-statement of primordial truth. It is a method whose ultimate effect is incantatory and catechistic, and what is being prayed to and propitiated is the demon god of flux and excess, that force of anarchy that drives most of the characters toward ruin and that it is the task of the language to redeem and convert into a force of artistic order.

Such a method, composed of a minimum of simple words that seem to have been squeezed onto the page against a great compulsion to be silent, creates the impression that those words—if only because there are so few of them—are sacramental, while the frequent reappearance of some of them in the same or in similar order at intervals through the text tends to give them idiographic value. Thus *nice* and the phrase *one of us* become the pervasive but hollow designations of moral judgment in the novel, and the hollowness is perfectly consonant with the theme. In a similar way, some of the characters become idiographs when a certain distinctive feature of their appearance or behavior is established in our minds as their identifying logo or psychological autograph—again because Hemingway describes them so sparingly that what little he does say about them takes on something of the quality of Homeric epithet. Thus Jake is personified by his impotence, Bill Gorton by his passion for stuffed animals, Brett by her mannish hats and hairstyle, the count by his arrow wounds, Robert Cohn by his romanticism. In each case, furthermore, the defining detail becomes revelatory of the character's dramatic role and thematic meaning, so that what begins as a novel of manners ends as a moral allegory about people who lack the moral substance even to follow the code of behavior that they profess to honor. Jake is unmanned and Brett is defeminized. Bill Gorton desires things that look like the real thing but are actually dead. The count has been wounded by arrows, which must make him as anachronistic as his fancy title and tastes supported by income from a chain of sweet-shops must make him ludicrous.

Brett with her title is also an anachronism, as is Mike, the stereotypical wastrel aristocrat with his stereotypical prospects of one day inheriting a fortune. And Cohn's romanticism, which is the central irritant in the novel, is yet another. All represent former sources of value that no longer have value. Cohn's sentimentalized vision of love belongs to that part of the nineteenth century that was supposedly killed in the first world war, and its resurrection in the aftermath can only mean trouble for people who are also resurrected casualties—stuffed human animals, to whom any feeling, when aggressively acted upon, is a threat to psychic harmony and the security of nonfeeling.

In his study of American modernism, *A Homemade World*, Hugh Kenner perceptively observes that "Hemingway's achievement . . . consisted in setting down, so sparsely that we can see past them, the words for the action that concealed the real action." Abundant evidence for this insight exists everywhere in *The Sun Also Rises.* Jake's strength as a character largely derives from his capacity for withholding information. We are constantly aware in the novel of the presence of what we are not told, of what Jake refuses to acknowledge and judge because it is too dangerous to make a judgment and thus bring the danger to the surface of consciousness. (pp. 340-43)

For the elaborately polite . . . [though] clearly traumatized characters of this novel, consciousness is so precarious and fragile that any kind of tension is to be feared and, if possible, ignored. One can safely respond to only the barest minimum of sensory stimuli—the look of the landscape, the physical pattern of an action especially when strictly ritualized, what people monosyllabically said to one another. But there must be little or nothing revealed about how anyone really felt, what deeper emotions were aroused by the various conflicts and confrontations. Part of the magic of the minimalist style is that we know almost nothing—and we scarcely miss knowing—about Jake's emotional state throughout the major part of the novel, nor do we know much of anything about the nature of the relationship between Brett and Mike and between Jake and Bill. This information is carefully withheld, or we are led to believe that it is revealed in actions that occur in the background or offstage. But the omissions make a statement that there is some acute unpleasantness here that cannot be directly confronted because it is a threat to psychic equilibrium and might cause a dangerous "flooding" of consciousness.

The dramatic movement of *The Sun Also Rises* has often been described as proceeding through a series of alternating scenes of conflict and recuperation from conflict. The fishing interlude in Burguette and Jake's holiday in San Sebastian both represent rest and curative periods following the stress-filled experiences, first of Paris, then of Pamplona. In both emotional decorum is almost fanatically maintained. Nothing is allowed to occur that might impose a strain or precipitate a crisis, and this is made easier to accomplish, significantly enough, by the fact that in Burguette there are only men without women—and in San Sebastian only one man alone in the good company of himself.

In both interludes attention is kept focused on matters of physical procedure: exactly how a fishhook is baited and with what, what kind of box lunch was provided by the hotel, just how cold the wine was, what dinner cost. And we are told just how Jake in San Sebastian went about putting his things away in his room and the movement she made as he went from the hotel to the beach and changed his clothes in a bathing-cabin, put on his bathing suit, and went swimming, then how he came out of the water, lay on the beach until he was dry, then went into the bathing-cabin, took off his suit, sloshed himself with fresh water, and rubbed dry. It is all as meticulously choreographed as the fishing routine in **"The Big Two-Hearted River"** and for the same reason—because

the real situation cannot be confronted, the real story cannot be told.

Gertrude Stein, in another of her famous pronouncements on Hemingway, said that there is in fact a real story to be told about Hemingway, one that he should write himself, "not those he writes but the confessions of the real Hemingway. . . ." Clearly Hemingway did not write it and could not because the real story was too deeply disturbing to tell, just as the young Nick Adams could not bring himself to enter the shadowy part of the river where it ran into the swamp—because "in the swamp fishing was a tragic adventure." But the remarkable fact is that in telling as much or as little of the story as he did, Hemingway managed through his complex artistry to use words in such a way that we are allowed to see past them and to glimpse the outlines of the mysterious and probably tragic adventure that the words were not quite able to describe but were also not quite able to conceal.

If the thing most feared is barely visible behind the language, the fear itself is barely controlled by the language. Language is a provisional barricade erected against the nihilism that threatens to engulf his characters, the nihilism that is always seeking to enter and flood the human consciousness. Hemingway at his best offered us a portrait that did not need to be painted of a condition we recognize everywhere around and within us, and he gave us as well our only means of defense against it—the order of artistic and moral form embodied in a language that will not, in spite of everything, give up its hold on the basic sanities, will not give up and let out the shriek of panic, the cry of anguish, that the situation logically calls for. That, and not any of the bravura exploits behind his celebrity, constituted his heroism, and that was the lesson in heroism he had to teach. Of his many qualities that was the one that most deserved, and continues to deserve, our admiration and loyalty. (pp. 344-45)

John W. Aldridge, " 'The Sun Also Rises'—Sixty Years Later," in The Sewanee Review, *Vol. XCIV, No. 2, Spring, 1986, pp. 337-45.*

SIBBIE O'SULLIVAN

It would be naive to say that **The Sun Also Rises** is a joyous book, or even a hopeful one; it is, of course, neither. Most often interpreted as a picture of post-war aimlessness and anomie, Hemingway's 1926 novel is usually said to be the bible of the Lost Generation, a modern-day courtesy book on how to behave in the waste land Europe had become after the Great War. However valid this interpretation may be, it is limiting and unduly pessimistic. It necessitates a particularly negative reading of the characters in the book and undervalues Hemingway's intuitive awareness of cultural and historical forces and the impact they have on personal relationships. Most damaging of all, the consensual interpretation fosters the harmful propagation of sexist stereotypes and ignores Hemingway's knowledge of and respect for the New Woman. Instead of reading **The Sun Also Rises** as the death of love, we can read it as a story about the cautious belief in the survival of the two most basic components of any human relationship: love and friendship. Examined this way, the novel is a rather extraordinary document that unites the two separate sexual spheres of the nineteenth century and in so doing breaks away from the moral imperatives of the Victorian age while demonstrating the possibility of love's survival in the more realistic but nihilist twentieth century.

The coaxial themes of love and friendship inform this book in such subtle ways that they are easily overlooked even though they are the forces which motivate the characters' behavior. In the case of Jake Barnes and Lady Brett Ashley they form the basis of their relationship. Too often this relationship is laid waste by stereotypical thinking. The cliché runs like this: Jake, unmanned in the war, is not only physically but spiritually impotent and allows himself to be debased by Brett, that "non-woman," that "purely destructive force." Such critical abuse is understandable when we realize that Brett is considered part of that long American tradition of the dark-haired, bad woman. She must be termed "promiscuous" and an "nymphomaniac" if her sexual behavior is to be explained at all. The mainspring of such a tradition is that "nice girls don't do it." But we've already seen in the short stories that Hemingway refuses to bind his female characters to such strictures. His women do "do it," and with relish.

Hemingway seems to take for granted that Brett is a sexually active woman. And though he did not consciously set out to create the New Woman, Hemingway's Brett is a fine example of one. (pp. 76-7)

[In the nineteenth century, the] emotional segregation of women and men had obvious consequences. It accounts for the intense relationships between female friends as well as the sad and deplorable conditions of many Victorian marriages. It burdened women with the preservation of all morals and manners, while it forced men to do homage to the unbending demands of progress. It safe-guarded the male ego by denying that "nice" women had erotic drives, thereby insuring male sexual adequacy. It interpreted any change in female behavior as a threat to male dominance; the new mannish behavior [of the 1920s] was particularly threatening because it called into question heretofore supposedly self-evident gender distinctions. Fear of women was, as Peter Gay points out, an international preoccupation of the nineteenth century.

But however fearful and discouraged at first, this mannish behavior of women had positive results. It helped to bring the two worlds of men and women closer together. And such bringing together had to be undertaken by women and actualized through a transformation of their behavior because it is less frightening for a woman to be masculinized than it is for a man to be feminized. Theron Ware discovered that the emergence of a man's sensual nature leaves him open to emotional and physical collapse, but Brett Ashley's deviant temperament gives her strength, determination, and resilience. The genius of Brett Ashley lies not in Hemingway's ability to create the Great American Bitch but in his ability to create woman as Friend.

The Sun Also Rises reflects the changing sex role patterns prevalent in Western society during the thirty years before its publication. In many ways this first novel is Hemingway's goodbye kiss to the Victorian ethos under which he was raised. As an expatriate, as a World War I veteran, as a young husband and father, and as an artist, Hemingway, since the age of eighteen, had lived an unconventional life. Living as he did in Europe he saw firsthand the shifting social structures that transformed the old order into the new. His sensibilities were equally attuned to both pre- and post-World War I mores. He was not so ignorant as to believe that 1918 had changed everything; it certainly had not changed Robert Cohn, the traditional, romantic, chivalric, and backward-looking character we meet when the book opens.

Cohn, of course, is a bridge figure. He lives in the waste land but does not adhere to its values. He represents the dual concepts of manly adventure and romantic love so important in the nineteenth century. When we meet him he is engaged to Frances Clyne, a woman with "the absolute determination that he [Cohn] should marry her." Though he wants to venture to South America and asks Jake Barnes, the book's narrator, to go with him, he physically silences Jake when Jake suggests in front of Frances that he and Cohn take a weekend trip to nearby Strasbourg. Frances, it seems, is the jealous type.

By focusing the first two chapters on Cohn and the dual concerns of romantic love and adventure, Hemingway establishes a backdrop against which the rest of the book is played. That backdrop becomes, as Cohn's daydream of South America fades, the conventional theme of courtship and marriage—in other words, the typical theme of the Victorian novel. Of course, conventional marriage does little to erode the rigid boundaries between men and women, and Robert and Frances act out scenes which accentuate, in a progressively negative manner, the worst attributes of both sexes. She becomes a nasty woman tremendously afraid of not being married, and he becomes a chump willing to take her verbal abuse lest he break into tears, as he habitually does whenever they "have a scene." The demise of this relationship is nothing less than a wicked parody of the engagement/marriage ritual itself. Fifty pages into the novel we see already that the old way offers nothing but anger and humiliation.

In Chapter II another Victorian ritual is enacted, but with a twist: Jake gets a prostitute but does not sexually use her. As he explains, "I had picked her up because of a vague sentimental idea that it would be nice to eat with some one." Jake's motive is not sexual fulfillment or an escape from a dull marriage bed, but companionship. Prostitute or not, Georgette is recognized by Jake as a fellow human being, not as a mere commodity to buy and discard. But however kindly Jake treats Georgette his actions still reflect the rigid gender roles of the nineteenth century. The underbelly of the conventional Victorian marriage was, after all, prostitution; the erotic restrictions placed on wives encouraged husbands to use whores for sexual release, experimentation, and erotic delight. Coming as it does after the parody of Victorian marriage that Robert Cohn and Frances Clyne represent, this chapter enacts the inevitable decline of such a relationship were it to go on. When Jake introduces Georgette to some acquaintances as his "fiancée" the connection between marriage and prostitution becomes unmistakable.

So far the male-female relationships fall within the scope of the typical Victorian ethos of courtship/marriage, and customer/prostitute. With the entrance of Lady Brett Ashley the focus shifts. Brett's arrival in Chapter III trumpets a new set of relationships. Since Brett is neither a wife nor a prostitute, it is fitting that she emerge from an environment alien to these two opposites; hence she arrives with a group of homosexual men. Her mannishness is thus established through this group, but since she quickly leaves that group and bonds with Jake we learn that her inclinations are orthodox and acceptable. We know that she is not a lesbian, and that her association with male homosexuals, instead of being a detriment, enhances her attractiveness.

As soon as Brett and Jake begin talking we realize theirs is no conventional relationship. Their dialogue bristles with familiarity. Jake asks, "Why aren't you tight?" and Brett answers by ordering a drink. The jabs continue:

"It's a find crowd you're with Brett," I said.

"Aren't they lovely? And you, my dear. Where did you get it?"

The "it," of course, refers to Georgette. As this exchange indicates, Brett and Jake share a public language (remember that Cohn is with them) that includes mild insult and sarcasm. It is a language in which the indefinite pronouns need not be identified. The verbal volley continues on the dance floor and in the taxi, where, alone at last, Brett confesses to Jake, "Oh, darling, I've been so miserable."

What we know so far about Brett's and Jake's relationship is this. First, as the dialogue reveals, Jake and Brett are friends. No matter what else their relationship may be it has a solid base in friendship; such benign verbal ribbing only takes place between friends. Secondly, they share a history. Reference to Brett's drinking habits and how out of character it is for Jake to pick up a whore indicate a more than superficial knowledge of each others' habits. Thirdly, Brett has control. She neatly declines two dances with Cohn and instigates her and Jake's departure. And fourthly, there seem to be two languages operating for them: public and private. It is by the latter that the truth is revealed.

And the truth isn't pretty. They are in love with each other but because of Jake's wound that love cannot be sexually fulfilled. . . . There is a sense of things being out of control; at the end of the taxi ride Brett is shaky, and later when Jake returns alone to his apartment he cries himself to sleep. When Jake leaves Brett it is at another bar and in the company of another man.

This pattern of public/private behavior shapes Brett's and Jake's relationship in an important way. Jake accepts Brett's need for public display, her need to breeze around Paris with as many men as possible. He also accepts her need to tell him about it privately. After she interrupts his sleep to recap her night's adventure with the Count, Jake comments to himself, "This was Brett, that I had felt like crying about." Though there is probably disgust in his voice at this point, there is also resignation, resignation that the woman he loves acts in such peculiar and unstable ways.

The ability to listen, the capacity to care, are not faculties belonging to Jake alone. Brett is also tender and solicitous in private moments. During her second visit to Jake with Count Mippipopolous, when she sees that Jake is a bit shaky, she sends the Count off to get champagne. As Jake lies face down on the bed Brett gently strokes his head. "Poor old darling. . . . Do you feel better, darling? . . . Lie quiet." Though her actions are kind and genuine, Brett does not allow this moment to blunt the truth. When Jake, perhaps succumbing to her touch, to her motherly devotion, asks, "Couldn't we live together, Brett? Couldn't we just live together?" she answers the only way she knows how:

"I don't think so. I'd just *tromper* you with everybody. You couldn't stand it."

"I stand it now."

"That would be different. It's my fault, Jake. It's the way I'm made."

When the count returns with the champagne all three go out and Jake and Brett talk once more in their public manner until out on the dance floor. Brett, in the privacy of Jake's arms, recites again what is fast becoming her litany, thus closing Book I: "Oh, darling, . . . I'm so miserable."

These two small scenes are interesting for what they tell us about how easily Brett and Jake merge the traditional sex roles. The two qualities of granting freedom and lending an ear that Jake exhibits in the first scene clash with the stereotypical image of the muscle-bound, closed-mouth husband/boyfriend who "doesn't want to hear about it." If Jake's attentiveness and meekness in the face of Brett's gallivanting seem in some ways feminine (Jake as the suffering wife?), then in the second scene Brett reenacts a particularly masculine ritual, characterized by the "line": "I love you babe, but I can't stay tied to one woman. I'm just that kind of man." Brett's version of this "line" is not delivered with any hint of bravado or cruelty as it has been delivered by men to countless women in books and movies, but as an assessment of, almost as an apology for her personality. What is striking about these role reversals is how easily and naturally they appear and reappear throughout the couple's interactions. Brett's behavior, especially, flows back and forth between being soft and caring, and hard and straight-forward. Jake has the ability to snap back after a painful relapse. Such flexibility is unthinkable in traditional relationships where sex roles are rigid. Robert Cohn and Frances Clyne do not have this kind of flexibility. One reason Brett leaves Romero at the end of the novel is that he demands that she conform to the rigid traditional female role.

If I over-emphasize that Jake's and Brett's departure from stereotypical male-female behavior is a positive dimension of their relationship, I do so because so many critics judge the couple's behavior in a negative way when measured against those stereotypes. Mark Spilka is one critic who is most ungenerous. In his essay "The Death of Love in *The Sun Also Rises*" [see excerpt above], Spilka sees Jake as emotionally impotent, as an emotional adolescent, and as a man of little integrity; according to Spilka, Jake has defaulted on his maleness. Brett fares no better. She is "the freewheeling equal of any man" who engages in the "male prerogatives of drink and promiscuity." She is a woman who allows her "natural warmth" to be replaced with "masculine freedom and mobility." Under such conditions, "there can be no serious love." Obviously Spilka identifies "serious love" with traditional male-female gender roles. Though he acknowledges the general damage to love wrought by World War I, he points specifically to the damage done when woman "steps off the romantic pedestal [and] moves freely through the bars of Paris, and stands confidently there beside her newfound equals." Such narrow-minded thinking not only oversimplifies a very complicated novel but blinds the reader to what demonstration of "serious love" there is in the book.

Hemingway has a much broader definition of love than Spilka does, and he examines it in many types of relationships and under many different conditions. (pp. 80-6)

There is no reason why Brett's and Jake's behavior should be gauged by traditional gender roles since those roles have been modified to suit the couple's needs. Brett is, after all, the New Woman, and her claim to sexual freedom, though irksome to the critics is both attractive and perplexing to her fellow characters. Jake cannot be the traditional man because he is impotent. Freed from the pressure to prove his worth through sexual intercourse, Jake must develop other means of asserting his personality.

Both Brett and Jake expect little of each other and have a relationship in which they agree to accept each other as they are. Early in the book Jake describes Brett's two worst habits to Robert Cohn: "She's a drunk," and "She's done it twice," referring to Brett's marrying men "she didn't love." Brett gives a clear self-assessment when she speaks of her intention to return to Mike: "He's so damned nice and he's so awful. He's my sort of thing." Because Jake accepts Brett as she is he has been able to maintain their relationship for as long as he has. We should remember that Cohn and Pedro Romero do not accept Brett as she is and therefore lose her. Brett, too, accepts Jake as he is. They can never be completely, physically united, and for a woman as sexually alive as Brett this loss is deep and sad.

At the end of Book I the boundaries have been drawn. Brett and Jake, the New Woman and the shattered veteran, conduct a relationship based on the honest assessment of each other's failings. In any other arms Brett's lament of "darling I'm so miserable" could pass for a comment on the progress of a particular night's activities, but in Jake's arms it is properly received for what it is: a statement about Brett's soul. This kind of emotional shorthand conveyed in private moments through a private language is the backbone of Jake's and Brett's relationship and a testament to its strength. Though imperfect, their friendship is imbued with the survival mechanisms of honesty, shared histories, and serious love.

Book II begins by depicting male-female friendships, first in Paris and then in Spain. In many aspects Jake's friendship with Bill Gorton is similar to his with Brett. Though they are frequently separated, the two men can quickly restore intimacy. Bill's retelling of his experiences in Vienna is not only some of the best dialogue Hemingway ever wrote, but a wonderful example of that familiar speech we first heard between Jake and Brett. (pp. 86-8)

Once Bill and Jake leave Paris they become more intimate; the pastoral Spanish setting invokes an even more private speech which allows them to discuss religion, literature, and personal problems such as Jake's impotency. (Though Jake's problems are not discussed at any length, and though his answers are frequently evasive or non-committal, the subject is mentioned often enough in a number of dialogues to warrant being designated a topic of conversation). Physical closeness is established by the freedom of movement between each other's rooms and by Jake watching Bill shave and dress. At one point, Bill even declares his love for Jake:

> Listen. You're a hell of a good guy, and I'm fonder of you than anybody on earth. I couldn't tell you that in New York. It'd mean I was a faggot.

Other examples of intense male interaction are the scenes with Wilson-Harris, the English angler Bill and Jake meet in Burguete, and with the aficionados in Pamplona. Wilson-Harris is very candid about how much he likes Bill and Jake. The sheer joy of buying his friends drinks almost overcomes

him. At one point he says, "I say Barnes. You don't know what this all means to me." When Jake and Bill leave to return to Pamplona, Wilson-Harris gives them each a present, a valentine of hand-tied fishing flies.

Not all male-male friendships are as successful as this. Once the characters are in Spain, Robert Cohn's presence grates on both Jake and Bill. Jake, of course, has reason to dislike Cohn because he recently vacationed with Brett. Jake is very forthright about his resentment:

> I was blind, unforgivingly jealous of what had happened to him. The fact that I took it as a matter of course did not alter that any. I certainly did hate him.

Bill's dislike seems rooted in prejudice: "Well, let him not get superior and Jewish." But even Jake and Bill cannot hold on to their hatred of Cohn for too long. Bill says to Jake:

> "The funny thing is he's nice, too. I like him. But he's just so awful."
>
> "He can be damn nice."
>
> "I know it. That's the terrible part."

This assessment of Robert Cohn is so similar to Brett's assessment of Mike ("He's so damned nice and he's so awful") that the parallel should not be overlooked. Appearing when they do, these assessments frame the events at Pamplona. They remind us that friendship holds both the promise of betrayal as well as of forgiveness.

Carlos Baker and others often divide the novel's characters into two groups: those who are solid, and those who are neurotic. Baker puts Jake, Bill, and Romero in the former category, and Cohn, Brett, and Mike in the latter. As fair as this division may seem on the surface, it belies the truth of human interaction and negates the web of friendship in which all the characters, at one time or another, are enmeshed. And what a complicated web it is. Throughout the fiesta the characters form new pairs or groups as they partake of the festivities. Everyone at one time or another shares the other's company. Of all the characters Brett seems most in control of choosing her companions. She maneuvers it so that, with one exception, she is never alone with Cohn. In contrast, she frequently asks Jake to go off with her alone, by now a rather predictable action.

Though Brett may behave consistently with Jake, she demonstrates new facets of her personality while interacting with others in the group. When we first see her in Pamplona she seems to have lost all patience with Cohn. "What rot . . . What rot . . . What rot" she keeps repeating in response to his self-aggrandizement. She is sufficiently irked to put aside the charm that was so evident in Book I. A few pages later, however, she's protecting Cohn from Mike's drunken barbs. . . . But even Brett has her limits as, a few pages later, she purposely scorns Cohn in order to make him go away: "For God's sake, go off somewhere. Can't you see Jake and I want to talk? . . . If you're tight, go to bed. Go on to bed." Knowing that such an outburst is out of character, Brett checks with Jake to see if she's done the impolite, but necessary thing: "Was I rude enough to him? . . . My God! I'm so sick of him!"

Jake says at one point to Brett, "Everybody behaves badly . . . Give them the proper chance." Not only does this foreshadow Jake's own bad behavior when he arranges for

Brett to meet Romero, but it explains everyone else's bad behavior as well. However, it does not excuse that behavior. When critics such as Baker define the moral norm of the novel as "the healthy and almost boyish innocence of spirit . . . carried by Jake Barnes, Bill Gorton, and Pedro Romero," he conveniently releases these three, already identified as the "solids," from responsibility for their actions. But if we look at the histories and current behavior of Jake, Bill, and Romero, we see that it is anything but boyish and innocent. There is nothing boyish about being in war and being wounded; nothing innocent about picking up whores, being blind drunk in Vienna, and defiling the code of the bullfighters by running off with an engaged woman. It is, however, boyish to think that one can get away with such things. But even boys discover there are consequences to such actions. Jake, for instance, suffers for pimping for Brett. Bill, who is good at bailing out strange boxers, is nowhere in sight when Cohn knocks out Mike and Jake. And it is doubtful that Pedro Romero can ever completely earn back Montoya's respect. Keeping these facts in mind, one reasonably concludes that the so-called "neurotics" behave in a better manner because they do not uphold false values and then act against them. Instead, they are consistent: Mike is consistently a drunk, so awful, so nice; Brett consistently exercises her right to sleep with whomever she wants and remains open and honest about it; and Cohn consistently acts like a "wounded steer," a sobriquet he earned early in the novel.

The separation of the group into two factions creates barriers if not as visible, surely, at least, as damaging as those erected between the sexes. Such barriers highlight how friends betray but not how they forgive one another. And in Brett's case, because she is grouped with the neurotics, she suffers under a double onus: she becomes the neurotic female, the "bitch," the "nymphomaniac." Clearly, it is the double standard and nothing else that permits the critics, both male and female, to criticize Brett for sleeping with Cohn and Romero while not criticizing Cohn and Romero for the same act. But Hemingway is not interested in erecting barriers but in destroying them. He does not see behavior as either male or female. Nor does he see passion as something solely inter-sexual. In *The Sun Also Rises,* bonding and passion occur in mysterious ways. There is no difference in the *intensity* of what Wilson-Harris feels for Jake and Bill and what Brett feels for Romero. Brett, however, is allowed the sexual expression of her intensity whereas Wilson-Harris would not be, even if his feelings were sexual. The bond that Jake establishes with Montoya is special because it is validated both by intensity and physical touch. Though this touch is not overtly sexual it certainly suggests sexuality because it is the symbol of a shared passion, just as the touching of sexual partners represents mutual passion.

The above relationships, considering their brevity, their passion, and the intensity of mutual attraction between their participants, would be like one-night stands or casual affairs, were they to exist in the sexual dimension. I am not suggesting that we belittle the effects of sexual union, or that Brett's escapade with Romero is as inconsequental as Wilson-Harris's fishing trip. What I am suggesting is that there are parallels between male bonding and heterosexual bonding which should not be overlooked, and that both forms of bonding are as easily established as they are destroyed. By removing the sexual barriers which unduly place the burden of bad behavior on sexually active women (as Jake points out the woman pays and pays and pays), we see that Brett's trans-

gression is no worse than Jake's; in fact, Brett's may have fewer repercussions. We can assume with good reason that Mike will take Brett back after her fling with Romero, but we are not as certain about a reconciliation between Jake and Montoya. True to form, Hemingway remains aloof in making clear any moral certainties. But one thing for certain is that Hemingway wants us to look at all the characters' behavior and not just Brett's. The structural parallels in the novel are too clear to ignore.

What seems to be more important than who does what to whom and why is the acceptance of the mysteries of behavior, and of bonding in particular. Those characters who survive the best are the ones who have cultivated a certain sense of negative capability. The ability to accept simultaneously two opposing ideas or modes of behavior becomes a means of survival. Those characters who do not have this capability end up exiled from the web of relationships established at Pamplona. Hence it is Cohn and Romero, those representatives of the traditional male role, who are ultimately excluded from any relationship with Brett, the object of their desires. Rigidity of values and, since these two men were Brett's lovers a corresponding rigidity of erectile tissue, are not what keeps Brett. Jake, it seems, wins again.

Book III opens with Jake's observation that "it was all over." Ostensibly referring to the fiesta, Jake's statement is also an assessment of the condition of the web of relationships woven in the previous two hundred pages. It is in shreds. Brett has taken off with Romero, Cohn has been left in disgrace, Jake is blind drunk for the first time in the novel, and Mike, as we presently discover, is penniless. Book III is, initially, a book of departures, but by the close of the book Jake and Brett have reunited, thus reconstructing the web. Jake and Brett have no parting scene; her departure with Romero, like Cohn's departure, takes place under cloak of night. We do see, however, the partings of Mike and Bill. Each has a different destination: Mike for Saint Jean de Luz, Bill for Paris and points west, and Jake for San Sebastian. We have no clue as to when these gentlemen will meet again, if at all.

Both Bill and Jake are visibly irritated at Mike for deceiving them into thinking he had money. When he learns that Mike is broke, "Bill's face sort of changed." And after learning from Mike that Brett paid his hotel bill, Jake questions him repeatedly about Brett's financial well-being: "She hasn't any money with her . . . Hasn't she any at all with her?" Clearly, Mike has become persona non grata. We're less sure on what terms Bill and Jake part. Their relationship has always been catch-as-catch-can, each going his separate way then reuniting in a burst of intimacy. Their parting words still exude that good-old-boy camaraderie first heard during their reunion at the beginning of Book II, but something is curiously missing from this final good bye. As they part in private, neither of them knowing when they will meet again, neither man mentions past events. Bill, who very consciously encourages Jake to get drunk at the end of Book II in order to "Get over your damn depression," now has nothing to say. No words of encouragement, compassion, or advice, though he knows full well the extent of Jake's involvement with Brett and therefore the pain he must be suffering. Clearly, Bill makes no attempt at intimacy as a departing gesture. Unfortunately, Hemingway is predictably silent about how Bill's behavior impresses Jake. We are not told, either overtly or by facial expression, how Jake feels when Bill tells him "I have to sail on the 17th" and will not be in Paris when Jake returns. We are not told if Jake or Bill waves as the train pulls out, only that "Bill was at one of the windows." We can not know if this scene represents the ordinary way two male friends say good bye, or if it represents a deeper rent in their friendship. What we do know, however, is that once Jake is alone his thoughts turn to friendship. He likes France because money will buy friends; in France "No one makes things complicated by becoming your friend for any obscure reason."

But we also know by now that such thoughts are only partial truths. Jake, perhaps more than any other character, knows how obscure and unfathomable friendship can be. He knows that few situations and even fewer relationships offer up a fixed set of truths; as he states halfway through the book: "I did not care what it was all about. All I wanted to know was how to live in it."

In San Sebastian Jake takes long, solitary swims, and hides behind irony and sarcasm in an attempt to recover from the events at Pamplona. We realize how damaged Jake has been by these events through his attitude towards others. Not only does he put friendship on a monetary basis by deciding which waiters he wants for "friends," but he discourages any form of bonding with men of his own station. He purposely snubs the bicycle team manager. This uncharacteristic but telling action is a good measure of Jake's suffering when we recall how easily and eagerly he bonded with Wilson-Harris and Montoya. Now, not even the purely masculine comradeship between fellow sportsmen appeals to Jake.

But the habit of loving is a most difficult one to break. Though Jake responds to Brett's telegram with his by now characteristic sarcasm, he nonetheless reserves a seat on the Sud Express and whisks off to Madrid. Their reunion exhibits all the tenderness and caring one wishes Bill had exhibited at his departure. Jake not only physically comforts Brett by holding and kissing her, but he solicits her words: "Tell me about it," he says. And when Brett rambles on with her story despite her refrain of "let's not talk about it," Jake is still attentive and caring. Though his answers are one word responses this does not necessarily indicate a lack of concern on Jake's part, but rather an instinct that less is more. When one friend is hurting, sometimes the best thing another friend can do is listen. Jake does exactly this. But not without a price.

Involvement, of course, means pain. Jake could have just as easily wired Brett some money; he knew already she was broke. But their friendship cannot be measured in monetary terms. Later at the bar and the restaurant, Jake begins to show the effects of his rescue mission. . . . The amount of food and alcohol he consumes seems to keep his mouth full so he won't have to talk, to speak what's on his mind. When Brett admonishes him that he doesn't have to get drunk, Jake replies, "How do you know." She backs off, he finishes one more glass and they go for a taxi ride.

In effect they are back at the beginning when they took their first taxi ride together. But however similar the two scenes seem, something has changed. The web has begun to mend. Friendship is renewed. Jake, by rescuing Brett, reaffirms his love for her, and Brett, by recognizing her own faults and deciding not to be a bitch, recognizes the danger of passion for passion's sake. This realization, taking place as it does outside the narrator's scope of vision, can only be measured by its after effects. Brett's tears, her trembling, her sudden smallness, her hesitation in feeling proud for deciding not to be

"one of these bitches that ruins children," are completely believable, as is her heretofore uncharacteristic refusal of alcohol at dinner. Her concern at dinner that Jake not get drunk is genuine, almost motherly, what any good friend would do.

Hemingway has said that the more applicable epigraph for his novel is the one from Ecclesiastes and not the one attributed to Gertrude Stein. We must take the author's word on some things; the very title bears this out. If this novel exhibits traits of Stein's lost generation, it also exhibits the cyclical nature of friendship, its rhythm of disintegration and renewal. Brett's and Jake's relationship may have been dealt a cruel blow by fate or the First World War, but it is anything but lost, sadistic, and sick. It, and the bullfights, are the only lasting things in the book. Contrary to what many readers believe, Brett Ashley is a positive force, a determined yet vulnerable woman who makes an attempt to live honestly. (pp. 88-96)

Hemingway broke with convention by creating a brilliant example of the New Woman and dismantled nineteenth century gender lines by uniting love with friendship. His masculine ego did not suffer one iota in the process. He, unlike many of his critics, believes as Jake Barnes does: "In the first place, you had to be in love with a woman to have a basis of friendship." (pp. 96)

Sibbie O'Sullivan, "Love and Friendship/Man and Woman in 'The Sun Also Rises'," in Arizona Quarterly, *Vol. 44, No. 2, Summer, 1988, pp. 76-97.*

FURTHER READING

Atherton, John. "The Itinerary and the Postcard: Minimal Strategies in *The Sun Also Rises*." *ELH* 53, No. 1 (Spring 1986): 199-218.
    Examines how Hemingway uses travel and tourism as a metaphor in *The Sun Also Rises*.

Bier, Jesse. "Jake Barnes, Cockroaches, and Trout in 'The Sun Also Rises'." *The Arizona Quarterly* 39, No. 2 (Summer 1983): 164-71.
    Maintains that "Jake Barnes's impotence in *The Sun Also Rises* is a psychological and moral condition as well as a physical one."

————. "Liquor and Caffeine in 'The Sun Also Rises'." *American Notes and Queries* XVIII, No. 9 (May 1980): 142-44.
    Examines the thematic implications of two short passages in *The Sun Also Rises* concerning these substances.

Budick, E. Miller. " 'The Sun Also Rises': Hemingway and the Art of Repetition." *The University of Toronto Quarterly* 56, No. 2 (Winter 1986-87): 319-37.
    Explores the evolution of Jake's narration from adolescent rage to mature restraint.

Daiker, Donald A. "The Affirmative Conclusion of 'The Sun Also Rises'." In *Modern American Fiction: Form and Function,* edited by Thomas Daniel Young, pp. 39-56. Baton Rouge: Louisiana State University Press, 1989.
    Refutes earlier pessimistic interpretations of Jake's mental state in Book III.

Rudat, Wolfgang E. H. "Cohn and Romero in the Ring: Sports and Religion in 'The Sun Also Rises'." *The Arizona Quarterly* 41, No. 4 (Winter 1985): 311-18.

Submits that "Hemingway did indeed cast Romero as a Jew and that he portrayed Romero and Cohn as having more in common than is usually realized.

—————. "Mike Campbell and 'The Literary Chaps': Palimpsestic Narrative in 'The Sun Also Rises'." *Studies in the Novel* XX, No. 3 (Fall 1988): 302-15.
    Argues that in *The Sun Also Rises* "Hemingway's prose is in its deceptive leanness richly suggestive and his style full of almost Joycean complexities."

—————. "Jake's Odyssey: Catharsis in 'The Sun Also Rises'." *The Hemingway Review* IV, No. 1 (Fall 1984): 33-6.
    Asserts that Jake demonstrates heroism in the closing scene of *The Sun Also Rises*.

Scott, Arthur. "In Defense of Robert Cohn." *College English* 18, No. 6 (March 1957): 309-14.
    Regards Robert Cohn's romanticism as superior to the cynicism of such characters as Jake and Brett.

Strychacz, Thomas. "Dramatizations of Manhood in Hemingway's 'In Our Time' and 'The Sun Also Rises'." *American Literature* 61, No. 2 (May 1989): 245-60.
    Maintains that Hemingway possessed a complex concept of manhood as evidenced by the male characters of *In Our Time* and *The Sun Also Rises*.

Thorn, Lee. " 'The Sun Also Rises': Good Manners Make Good Art." *The Hemingway Review* VII, No. 1 (Fall 1988): 42-9.
    Traces Hemingway's attempt to construct an aesthetic upon etiquette rather than upon ethics in *The Sun Also Rises*.

Wagner-Martin, Linda M. "Hemingway's Search for Heroes, Once Again." *The Arizona Quarterly* 44, No. 2 (Summer 1988): 58-68.
    Examines how Hemingway contemporizes legends and myths of heroism in *The Sun Also Rises*.

Wedin, Warren. "Trout Fishing and Self-Betrayal in 'The Sun Also Rises'." *The Arizona Quarterly* 37, No. 1 (Spring 1981): 63-74.
    Explicates the symbolic function of Jake's fishing trip to Burguete in *The Sun Also Rises*.

Zora Neale Hurston

1891-1960

American novelist, folklorist, short story writer, autobiographer, essayist, dramatist, librettist, and anthropologist.

The following entry presents criticism on Hurston's novel *Their Eyes Were Watching God* (1937). For discussions of Hurston's complete career, see *CLC,* Vols. 7, 30.

Hurston is considered among the foremost writers of the Harlem Renaissance, a period of great achievement in African-American art and literature during the 1920s and 1930s. Her fiction, which depicts relationships among black residents in her native Southern Florida, was largely unconcerned with racial injustices. While not well known during her lifetime, Hurston's works have undergone substantial critical reevaluation, particularly since the advent of the black protest novel and the rise to prominence of Richard Wright, Ralph Ellison, and James Baldwin during the post-World War II era. Hurston's present reputation and popularity are evidenced by the reissuing of several of her works, including *Their Eyes Were Watching God,* in the late 1980s. In addition to having published four novels, three nonfiction works and numerous short stories and essays, Hurston is acknowledged as an important collector and publisher of black American folklore. Lillie P. Howard stated: "[Hurston's] works are important because they affirm blackness (while not denying whiteness) in a black-denying society. They present characters who are not all lovable but who are undeniably and realistically human. They record the history, the life, of a place and time which are remarkably like other places and times, though perhaps a bit more honest in the rendering."

Hurston was born in Eatonville, Florida, the first incorporated black township in the United States and the setting for most of her fiction. At the age of fourteen, she left home to work as a maid with a traveling Gilbert and Sullivan theatrical troupe. In 1923, Hurston entered Howard University, a black college in Washington, D.C., where she published short stories in *Stylus,* the university literary magazine, and attracted the attention of noted sociologist Charles S. Johnson. With Johnson's encouragement, Hurston moved to New York City in 1925 and subsequently secured a scholarship to Barnard College with the assistance of Annie Nathan Meyer, a white philanthropist and well-known supporter of Harlem Renaissance artists. While at Barnard, Hurston studied anthropology under Franz Boas, one of the most renowned anthropologists of the era, and, after her graduation in 1928, she continued her work with Boas as a graduate student at Columbia University.

With the aid of fellowships and a private grant from Mrs. Rufus Osgood Mason, a New York socialite interested in "primitive Negro art," Hurston returned to the South to collect folklore. She traveled to Alabama, Louisiana, and Florida, living among sharecroppers and workers lodged in labor camps whose primary form of entertainment consisted of telling tall tales, or "lies." In 1935, Hurston compiled *Mules and Men,* a collection of African-American folktales that expanded upon her academic studies and anthropological field work. In addition to tales and descriptions of voodoo practices and

beliefs, *Mules and Men* includes work songs, legends, rhymes, and lies, all of which contained hidden social and philosophical messages considered essential to survival in racist society. African-American folklore forms a basis for all of Hurston's writing, including what critics refer to as her greatest novel, *Their Eyes Were Watching God.* Largely unappreciated at the time of its publication, the novel is now considered, as James Robert Saunders described it, "a cornerstone in literary history."

Thought to be essentially autobiographical, *Their Eyes Were Watching God* is the story of a woman's search for self-definition in sexist Southern society of the early 1900s. Janie Crawford is a beautiful, light-skinned black woman who is unable to discover her true self until she begins to take charge of her life. The oral narrative employed to relate Janie's quest implies that her strength and identity grow as she becomes more attuned to her black heritage; the telling of tales is as integral a part of black culture as the tales themselves. Similarly, Janie's account is a story within a story, told in flashback to her good friend Pheoby Watson. Hurston's narrative recreation of Southern black rural dialect has been consistently praised by critics. George Stevens asserted: "[The] narration is exactly right, because most of it is in dialogue, and the dialogue gives us a constant sense of character in action.

No one has ever reported the speech of Negroes with a more accurate ear for its raciness, its rich invention, and its music."

Janie's story begins with her childhood and ends with her return at age forty to Eatonville, Florida, after the tragic death of her third husband. As a child, Janie lives with her grandmother, Nanny, an ex-slave who was raped repeatedly by her white master and is determined that her grandchild will live a better life than the one she endured. Raised on the farm of the white family that employs Nanny, Janie is unaware that she is black until, at age six, she sees a photograph of herself. Her confusion is complicated by Nanny, whose old-fashioned diatribes promote the attainment of that which she herself never enjoyed—leisure, wealth, property, and, most of all, security. She explains to Janie: "De nigger woman is de mule uh de world so fur as Ah can see. Ah been prayin' fuh it tuh be different wid you," and marries her off, at sixteen, to a middle-aged farmer named Logan Killicks, whose sixty acres of land ensure a stable future. However, the ebullient Janie finds Logan boring and farm life suffocating. Critics have noted that Nanny, for all her good intentions, cannot understand that love is essential to happiness. Nanny's colloquial expression becomes ironic when Logan begins to treat Janie like a servant and purchases a mule so that she can plow the fields. Although a romantic, Janie eventually realizes that no matter how much she tries, she will never love Logan. Hurston writes: "She knew now that marriage did not make love. Janie's first dream was dead, so she became a woman."

When a handsome young man named Jody Starks passes by the secluded farm, Janie offers him a drink of water and they strike up a conversation. Jody is ambitious and bound for the newly established, all-black town of Eatonville with visions of grandeur. Immediately taken with Janie's beauty and unconcerned with her marital status, Jody asks her to be his bride. To Janie, Jody is, quite literally, a knight in shining armor who offers an escape from her loveless marriage and the drudgery of the farm and promises her a new lifestyle: "A pretty doll-baby lak you is made to sit on de front porch and rock and fan yo'self." Wooed by his charms but indifferent to the young man's plans and the prospect of great wealth, Janie leaves Logan for a fun and adventurous new life. Janie's apron, the mark of her servility to Logan, becomes symbolic of her freedom, too, when she happily unties it and flings it into a bush as she leaves with Jody. Immediately upon reaching Eatonville, Jody begins to realize his plans; he buys the general store and becomes the town's self-proclaimed mayor, a position no one else saw a need to establish. Soon Eatonville's wealthiest citizen, he builds a beautiful, enormous white house that makes the rest of the town resemble servant's quarters. Jody, like Nanny and much of white society around them, is obsessed with materialism and status. He treats Janie not as an equal, but as a jewel he can display to the common folk. Jody forbids her to mingle with the crowds and join in the most popular local form of entertainment, the telling of tall tales and lies, on the front porch of the general store. Many critics concur that the passages set here are among the most vivid in the book and are the most representative of the vibrant, folkloric culture Hurston evokes. Janie loves listening to the stories while working at the store, but being unable to join in, she is denied a rich influence of black history and folklore. Several critics have compared Janie's quest with the journey of Ralph Ellison's protagonist in his novel *Invisible Man:* both feel the pull of white society's powerful influences, but must reject them to attain self-realization.

Throughout their twenty-year marriage, Jody stifles Janie's individuality and growth, chiefly because he is intensely jealous. He insists that she wear a headrag to bind her beautiful hair, but doesn't explain it is because he has seen other men admiring her. Janie understands only that she must conceal a part of herself. While forbidding his wife to take part in storytelling, Jody himself often plays "the dozens," an extremely popular, traditional folk game which consists of a verbal exchange of insults between players. Frequently, his target is Janie, whom he humiliates and ridicules in the general store. After one especially aggravating session in which Jody has mocked her age yet again, Janie defies her husband and plays the dozens herself: "You big bellies round here and put out a lot of brag, but 'tain't nothin' to it but yo' big voice. Humph! Talkin' 'bout *me* lookin' old! When you pull down yo' britches, you look lak de change uh life." With his impotency thus revealed to the citizens Jody has heretofore lorded over, his bombastic facade is shattered, his spirit is broken, and he soon dies. At his death bed, Janie vents the anger that has been quelled for twenty years in a scene many critics have deemed heartless. Others consider Janie's outrage justifiable, for she has survived two decades of indignity while Jody's fragile ego collapses after one round of the dozens. After the funeral, Janie burns all her headrags, a symbolic gesture of freedom that echoes her emancipation from Logan.

At thirty-seven, Janie is a very attractive, wealthy widow. Several friends urge her to marry again, but she has no desire to live as a second-class citizen. Janie continues to work at the general store, where she meets a man named Vergible "Tea Cake" Woods. Much younger than Janie, he is vibrant, loving, and accepting, and she soon enters into the most rewarding relationship of her life. Hurston based the romance of Tea Cake and Janie on the emotions fueled by her own affair with a twenty-three year old West Indian when she was forty. Hurston wrote: "The plot was far from the circumstances, but I tried to embalm all the tenderness of my passion for him in *Their Eyes Were Watching God*." In the store, Tea Cake invites Janie to play checkers, something Jody forbid her to do, and she is warmed by his presumption of equality. Their whirlwind romance is looked upon skeptically by the gossip-hungry villagers: most believe that the devil-may-care Tea Cake, who is not averse to gambling, is after Janie's money. But Tea Cake's intentions prove far more honorable. He encourages Janie to live for herself and helps her to find her self-respect and her true voice. Previously silenced by Nanny, Logan, and Jody, Janie finally learns the power and joy of her ancestral language.

Tea Cake and Janie marry, leave Eatonville, and move to the Florida Everglades. Janie finds greater happiness toiling as a bean-picker and living in a migrant workers camp than she had in her prestigious house in Eatonville. As her apron and headrag are symbolic of her past confinement, the overalls Janie now regularly wears are an expression of her freedom. The newlyweds' house becomes the chief gathering place for parties and conversation, and it is here that Janie, with her fledgling voice, discovers her talent for storytelling. The harmony Janie is beginning to feel with her black heritage is symbolized in her growing connection with oral folklore and in her disgust with black people who emulate whites. The couple are happily married for two years, until tragedy strikes: a hurricane hits the Everglades, and the couple are caught in the ensuing flood. Risking his life to save Janie, Tea Cake is bitten on the cheek by a mad dog. He contracts rabies and slides into a paranoid state. Crazed and jealous, Tea Cake tries to shoot Janie, and she must kill him in self-defense. After a perfunctory murder trial, Janie returns to Eatonville alone, amid whispers and rumors. Although grief-stricken, she is more at peace with herself than ever before because of her personal growth and newfound strength. Janie chooses to tell her story only to her best friend Pheoby. This act of story-telling, which is the book itself, illustrates the success of Janie's search for identity and affirmation of her culture. Mary Jane Lupton asserted: "*Their Eyes Were Watching God* is a novel of life, power, and survival. . . . It is difficult to discover, either in Afro-American tradition or in any other literary tradition, the kind of adventuresome, defiant, and triumphant womanhood achieved by Janie Crawford. . . .

[No] woman in fiction exhibits so strongly as Janie those strengths associated with the Homeric epic hero—bravery, the completion of a voyage, the endurance of trials, mastery in battle, acceptance in the community, self-definition, survival."

From the initial publication of *Their Eyes Were Watching God,* critics have debated Hurston's ostensible disregard of the issue of racism. Many of Hurston's black contemporaries considered her an opportunist who catered to white benefactors, and early reviewers believed her book to be an attempt at escapism. However, other commentators note that Janie's dilemmas are not with racism but sexism, a concern for all women during the 1920s. While there are very few Caucasian characters in *Their Eyes Were Watching God,* white values are presented in Nanny, Jody, and Mrs. Turner, a black Everglades neighbor who hates her culture. All three cause grief for Janie and deny themselves the richness of their heritage. Most contemporary critics argue that Hurston concentrates on strength and affirmation in the black community, and not the denial and anger racism often evokes. Another issue of intense debate concerning *Their Eyes Were Watching God* is the death of Tea Cake. Most reviewers agree that it is essential to Janie's quest that she return to Eatonville alone, but many question whether it was necessary for Tea Cake to be sacrificed for Janie to obtain her sense of identity. The novel's ironic ending is generally considered representative of Hurston's beliefs in her writing and her life, in which she challenged conventional norms. Although Janie finds happiness with Tea Cake, Hurston depicts a greater intrinsic joy in the completion of her individual quest for self-definition: "Here was peace. She pulled in her horizon like a great fish-net. . . . So much of life in its meshes! She called in her soul to come and see."

(See also *Black Writers, Contemporary Authors,* Vols. 85-88, and *Dictionary of Literary Biography,* Vol. 51.)

PRINCIPAL WORKS

NOVELS

Jonah's Gourd Vine 1934
Their Eyes Were Watching God 1937
Moses, Man of the Mountain 1939; also published as *The Man of the Mountain,* 1941
Seraph on the Suwanee 1948

SHORT FICTION COLLECTIONS

Spunk: The Selected Stories of Zora Neale Hurston 1985

PLAYS

Color Struck 1926
The Great Day 1932
Polk County: A Comedy of Negro Life on a Sawmill Camp [with Dorothy Waring] 1944

OTHER

Mules and Men (folklore) 1935
Tell My Horse (folklore) 1938; also published as *Voodoo Gods: An Inquiry into Native Myths and Magic in Jamaica and Haiti,* 1939
Dust Tracks on a Road (autobiography) 1942
I Love Myself When I Am Laughing . . . and Then Again When I Am Looking Mean and Impressive: A Zora Neale Hurston Reader (fiction and nonfiction) 1979
The Sanctified Church (essays) 1981

GEORGE STEVENS

Whether or not there was ever a town in Florida inhabited and governed entirely by Negroes, you will have no difficulty believing in the Negro community which Zora Neale Hurston has either reconstructed or imagined in this novel [*Their Eyes Were Watching God*]. The town of Eatonville is as real in these pages as Jacksonville is in the pages of Rand McNally; and the lives of its people are rich, racy, and authentic. . . .

The central character is Janie, born to love and to look for love through three marriages. She escapes from the first marriage, with a steady but middle-aged and unsympathetic farmer, to run away with Joe Starks, an unusual and delightful Negro go-getter with something in him of Babbitt and a little of the Emperor Jones. How Joe becomes mayor, boss, and plutocrat of Eatonville, is a good story, humorous, eventful, and full of character. Rewarding as Joe is to the reader, he is a disappointment to Janie; when he becomes too successful he doesn't love her any more; and Janie, though she is cowed by public opinion, eventually goes off with Tea Cake, a shiftless, warm-blooded gambler who leads her a chase but makes her happy. The rest of the story is of their life and work together on a Florida plantation, until a hurricane brings on a melodramatic, but credible, conclusion.

The only weak spots in the novel are technical; it begins awkwardly with a confusing and unnecessary preview of the end; and the dramatic action, as in the story of the hurricane, is sometimes hurriedly and clumsily handled. Otherwise the narration is exactly right, because most of it is in dialogue, and the dialogue gives us a constant sense of character in action. No one has ever reported the speech of Negroes with a more accurate ear for its raciness, its rich invention, and its music. In many ways *Their Eyes Were Watching God* recalls Lyle Saxon's recent *Children of Strangers;* both of them are love stories of women with mixed blood; and in both there is an undertone, never loud enough to be isolated, of racial frustration. But *Their Eyes Were Watching God* has much more humor in it; and paradoxically—possibly because the author is writing unselfconsciously of her own people—it is more objective. It never comes to the verge of conscious, sentimental "sympathy." A simple and unpretentious story, but there is nothing else quite like it.

George Stevens, "Negroes by Themselves," in The

Saturday Review of Literature, *Vol. XVI, No. 21, September 18, 1937, p. 3.*

LUCY TOMPKINS

[*Their Eyes Were Watching God* is] Zora Hurston's third novel, again about her own people—and it is beautiful. It is about Negroes, and a good deal of it is written in dialect, but really it is about every one, or at least every one who isn't so civilized that he has lost the capacity for glory.

"When God made The Man, he made him out of stuff that sung all the time and glittered all over." But, in the name of love, Janie's grandmother took "the biggest thing God ever made, the horizon . . . and pinched it into such a little thing that she could tie it about her granddaughter's neck tight enough to choke her." So it was a long time before Janie found her "shine." Her grandmother had been a slave. So she wanted Janie, born in freedom, to have advantages. In Janie, she figured, the Lawd had given her a second chance. . . . And she thought she could die easy if she knew neither white men nor black could use Janie the way she'd been used. What she wanted for Janie was protection. So when she saw her kissing a "trashy nigger" over the gatepost she figured Janie had come on her womanhood, and married her off straightway to a widower who spelled security.

But Janie found that marriage didn't compel love, neither didn't it "end the cosmic loneliness of the unmated." So she married Jody Sparks and went off with him to a town made all out of colored folks. Jody soon ran the town, and being Mayor went to his head. But being Mrs. Mayor didn't go to Janie's head: it hung round her like a stone. She had had something quite different in her mind's eye when she was 16. She had wanted "flower dust and springtime sprinkled over everything" and all she got on her second try was position and a one-tracked husband who was so busy being boss to the town and her that he thought of nothing else. All the folks of the town, of course, envied Janie. Her place looked like heaven to them. And as for Jody, he thought he'd done quite enough to make a fine lady out of her. Finally she told him, "all dis bowin' down, all dis obedience under yo' voice—dat ain't whut ah rushed off down de road to find out about you." But Jody, like the Emperor Jones, changed everything, and unlike the Emperor, nothing ever changed him.

So Janie had her old age first, and when shortly before she was 40 Jody died and Tea Cake came along she wasn't too spent and disillusioned to live as sooner or later all creatures ought. How different the story would have been if a sophisticated woman stood, at 40, in Janie's shoes, scores of novels already testify!

The story of Janie's life down on the muck of Florida Glades, bean picking, hunting and the men shooting dice in the evening and how the hurricane came up and drove the animals and the Indians and finally the black people and the white people before it, and how Tea Cake, in Janie's eyes the "son of Evening Son," and incidentally the best crap shooter in the place, made Janie sing and glitter all over at last, is a little epic all by itself. Indeed, from first to last this is a well-nigh perfect story—a little sententious at the start, but the rest is simple and beautiful and shining with humor. In case there are readers who have a chronic laziness about dialect, it should be added that the dialect here is very easy to follow, and the images it carries are irresistible.

Lucy Tompkins, "In the Florida Glades," *in* The New York Times Book Review, *September 26, 1937, p. 29.*

STERLING A. BROWN

[In *Their Eyes Were Watching God*] Janie's grandmother, remembering how in slavery she was used "for a work-ox and a brood sow," and remembering her daughter's shame, seeks Janie's security above all else. But to Janie, her husband, for all his sixty acres, looks like "some old skull-head in de graveyard," and she goes off down the road with slick-talking Jody Sparks. In Eatonville, an all-colored town, Jody becomes the "big voice," but Janie is first neglected and then browbeaten. When Jody dies, Tea Cake, with his contagious high spirits, whirls Janie into a marriage, idyllic until Tea Cake's tragic end. Janie returns home, grief-stricken but fulfilled. Better than her grandmother's security, she had found out about living for herself.

Filling out Janie's story are sketches of Eatonville and farming down "on the muck" in the Everglades. On the porch of the mayor's store "big old lies" and comic-serious debates, with the tallest of metaphors, while away the evenings. The dedication of the town's first lamp and the community burial of an old mule are rich in humor but they are not cartoons. Many incidents are unusual, and there are narrative gaps in need of building up. Miss Hurston's forte is the recording and the creation of folk-speech. Her devotion to these people has rewarded her; *Their Eyes Were Watching God* is chock-full of earthy and touching poetry.

> Ah don't want yo' feathers always crumpled by
> folks throwin' up things in yo' face. And ah can't
> die easy thinkin' maybe de menfolks white or black
> is makin' a spit cup outa you: Have some sympathy
> fuh me. Put me down easy, Janie, Ah'm a cracked
> plate.

Though inclined to violence and not strictly conventional, her people are not naive primitives. About human needs and frailties they have the unabashed shrewdness of the Blues. It is therefore surprising when, in spite of her clear innocence, all the Negroes turn away from Janie at her murder trial.

But this is not *the* story of Miss Hurston's own people, as the foreword states, for *the* Negro novel is as unachievable as the Great American Novel. Living in an all-colored town, these people escape the worst pressures of class and caste. There is little harshness; there is enough money and work to go around. The author does not dwell upon the "people ugly from ignorance and broken from being poor" who swarm upon the "muck" for short-time jobs. But there is bitterness, sometimes oblique, in the enforced folk manner, and sometimes forthright. The slave, Nanny, for bearing too light a child with gray eyes, is ordered a terrible beating by her mistress, who in her jealousy is perfectly willing to "stand the loss" if the beating is fatal. And after the hurricane there is a great to-do lest white and black victims be buried together. To detect the race of the long-unburied corpses, the conscripted grave-diggers must examine the hair. The whites get pine coffins; the Negroes get quick-lime. "They's mighty particular how dese dead folks goes tuh judgment. Look lak they think God don't know nothin' 'bout de Jim Crow law." (pp. 409-10)

Sterling A. Brown, " 'Luck Is a Fortune','" in The

Nation, *New York, Vol. 145, No. 16, October 16, 1937, pp. 409-10.*

LARRY NEAL

Among the literary figures that emerged from the all too brief, black-cultural upsurgence of the Harlem Renaissance, Zora Neale Hurston was one of the most significant and, ironically, one of the least well known. She was one of the first black writers to attempt a serious study of black folklore and folk history and, as such, was a precursor of the interest in folkways that shapes much of contemporary black fiction. Her comparative present-day anonymity, then, is surprising, but is perhaps explained by the complexity of her personality and the controversy that attended her career.

Writing in the May, 1928, edition of the *The World Tomorrow,* Zora Neale Hurston made the following observation about herself: "Sometimes, I feel discriminated against, but it does not make me angry. It merely astonishes me. How can anyone deny themselves the pleasure of my company!" This is the kind of remark that one came to expect from Miss Hurston, who is remembered as one of the most publicly flamboyant personalities of the Harlem literary movement. She was very bold and outspoken, an attractive woman who had learned how to survive with native wit. She approached life as a series of encounters and challenges; most of these she overcame without succumbing to the maudlin bitterness of many of her contemporaries. (p. 11)

Zora Neale Hurston was born in . . . [1891] in the all-black town of Eatonville, Florida. This town and other places in Florida figure quite prominently in much of her work, especially her fiction. Her South was, however, vastly different from the South depicted in the works of Richard Wright. Wright's fictional landscape was essentially concerned with the psychological ramifications of racial oppression, and black people's response to it. Zora, on the other hand, held a different point of view. For her, in spite of its hardships, the South was Home. It was not a place from which one escaped, but rather, the place to which one returned for spiritual revitalization. It was a place where one remembered with fondness and nostalgia the taste of soulfully prepared cuisine. Here one recalled the poetic eloquence of the local preacher (Zora's father had been one himself). For her also, the South represented a place with a distinct tradition. Here one heard the best church choirs in the world, and experienced the great expanse of green fields.

When it came to the South, Zora could often be an inveterate romantic. In her work, there are no bellboys shaking in fear before brutal tobacco-chewing crackers. Neither are there any black men being pursued by lynch mobs. She was not concerned with these aspects of the Southern reality. We could accuse her of escapism, but the historical oppression that we now associate with Southern black life was not a central aspect of her experience.

Perhaps it was because she was a black woman, and therefore not considered a threat to anyone's system of social values. One thing is clear, though: unlike Richard Wright, she was no political radical. She was, instead, a belligerent individualist who was decidedly unpredictable and perhaps a little inconsistent. At one moment she could sound highly nationalistic. Then at other times she might mouth statements that, in terms of the ongoing struggle for black liberation, were ill conceived and even reactionary.

Needless to say, she was a very complex individual. Her acquaintances ranged from the blues people of the jooks and the turpentine camps in the South to the upper-class literati of New York City. She had been Fannie Hurst's secretary, and Carl Van Vechten had been a friend throughout most of her professional career. These friendships were, for the most part, genuine, even if they do smack somewhat of opportunism on Zora's part. For it was the Van Vechten and Nancy Cunard types who exerted a tremendous amount of power over the Harlem literary movement. For this element, and others, Zora appears to have become something of a cultural showcase. They clearly enjoyed her company, and often "repaid" her by bestowing all kinds of favors upon her.

In this connection, one of the most interesting descriptions of her is found in Langston Hughes's autobiography, *The Big Sea:*

> In her youth, she was always getting scholarships and things from wealthy white people, some of whom simply paid her just to sit around and represent the Negro race for them, she did it in such a racy fashion. She was full of side-splitting anecdotes, humorous tales, and tragicomic stories, remembered out of her life in the South as the daughter of a traveling minister of God. She could make you laugh one moment and cry the next. To many of her white friends, no doubt, she was a perfect "darkie," in the nice meaning they give the term— that is a naive, childlike, sweet, humorous, and highly colored Negro.

According to Mr. Hughes, she was also an intelligent person, who was clever enough never to allow her college education to alienate her from the folk culture that became the central impulse in her life's work.

It was in the field of folklore that she did probably her most commendable work. With the possible exception of Sterling Brown, she was the only important writer of the Harlem literary movement to undertake a systematic study of African-American folklore. The movement had as one of its stated goals the reevaluation of African-American history and folk culture. But there appears to have been very little work done in these areas by the Harlem literati. There was, however, a general awareness of the literary possibilities of black folk culture—witness the blues poetry of Langston Hughes and Sterling Brown. But generally speaking, very few writers of the period committed themselves to intensive research and collection of folk materials. This is especially ironic given the particular race consciousness of the twenties and thirties. (pp. 13-15)

In terms of the consummate uses of the folk sensibility, the Harlem movement leaves much to be desired. There was really no encounter and subsequent grappling with the visceral elements of the black experience but rather a tendency on the part of many of the movement's writers to pander to the voguish concerns of the white social circles in which they found themselves. But Zora's interest in folklore gave her a slight edge on some of her contemporaries. (p. 16)

Her second novel, ***Their Eyes Were Watching God*** (1937), is clearly her best novel. This work indicates that she had a rather remarkable understanding of a blues aesthetic and its accompanying sensibility. Paraphrasing Ellison's definition of the blues: this novel confronts the most intimate and brutal aspects of personal catastrophe and renders them lyrically. She is inside of a distinct emotional environment here. This is a passionate, somewhat ironic love story—perhaps a little too rushed in parts—but written with a great deal of sensitivity to character and locale.

It was written in Haiti "under internal pressure in seven weeks," and represents a concentrated release of emotional energy that is rather carefully shaped and modulated by Zora's compassionate understanding of Southern black life styles. Here she gathers together several themes that were used in previous work: the nature of love, the search for personal freedom, the clash between spiritual and material aspiration and, finally, the quest for a more than parochial range of life experiences.

The novel has a rather simple framework: Janie, a black woman of great beauty, returns to her home town, and is immediately the subject of vaguely malicious gossip concerning her past and her lover Tea Cake. Janie's only real friend in the town is an elderly woman called Pheoby. It is to her that Janie tells her deeply poignant story. Under pressure from a strict grandmother, Janie is forced into an unwanted marriage. Her husband is not necessarily a rich man; however, he is resourceful and hard-working. In his particular way, he represents the more oppressive aspects of the rural life. For him, she is essentially a workhorse.

After taking as much as she can, she cuts out with Jody Starks, whose style and demeanor seem to promise freedom from her oppressive situation. She describes him:

> It was a citified, stylish dressed man with his hat set at an angle that didn't belong in these parts. His coat was over his arm, but he didn't need it to represent his clothes. The shirt with the silk sleeve-holders was dazzling enough for the world. He whistled, mopped his face and walked like he knew where he was going. He was a seal-brown color but he acted like [white benefactor] Mr. Washburn or somebody like that to Janie. Where would such a man be coming from and where was he going? He didn't look her way nor no other way except straight ahead, so Janie ran to the pump and jerked the handle hard while she pumped. It made a loud noise and also made her heavy hair fall down. So he stopped and looked hard, and then he asked her for a cool drink of water.
>
> (pp. 17-18)

She later leaves her husband, and takes up with Jody Starks, who is clearly a man with big ideas. He has a little money, people love him and he is an excellent organizer. But Janie does not really occupy a central emotional concern in Jody's scheme of things. She is merely a reluctant surrogate in his quest for small-town power and prestige. Jody is envied by everyone for having so much organizational and economic ability. But his lovely wife, who represents an essential aspect of his personal achievements, is basically frustrated and unloved. After several years, Jody Starks dies. The marriage itself had died years ago. She had conformed to Jody's idea of what a woman of influence and prestige should be. But again, she had not been allowed to flower, to experience life on her own terms.

The last third of the novel concerns Janie's life with Tea Cake, a gambler and itinerant worker. Tea Cake represents the dynamic, unstructured energy of the folk. He introduces her to a wider range of emotional experience. He is rootless, tied to no property save that which he carries with him, and he is not adverse to gambling that away if the opportunity presents itself. But he is warm and sensitive. He teaches her whatever she wants to know about his life and treats her with a great deal of respect. In spite of the implicit hardship of their lives, she has never lived life so fully and with such an expanse of feeling. And here is where Zora introduces her characteristic irony.

While working in the Everglades, they are nearly destroyed by a mean tropical storm. They decide to move to high ground and are forced to make their way across a swollen river. (The storm is described in vivid details that bear interesting allusions to Bessie Smith's "Backwater Blues.") A mad dog threatens Janie, and while protecting her Tea Cake is bitten. He contracts rabies, and later is himself so maddened by the infection that he begins to develop dangerous symptoms of paranoia. He threatens to kill Janie, and in self-defense she is forced to kill him. This is the story that she tells Pheoby.

But there is no hint of self-pity here. Just an awesome sense of the utter inability of man to fully order his life comparatively free of outside forces. Zora Neale Hurston was not an especially philosophical person, but she was greatly influenced by the religious outlook of the black Church. So that this novel seems often informed by a subtle, though persistent kind of determinism. She has a way of allowing catastrophe to descend upon her characters at precisely the moment when they have achieved some insight into the fundamental nature of their lives. She introduces disruptive forces into essentially harmonious situations. And the moral fiber of her characters is always being tested. Usually, in a contest between the world of flesh and the world of spirit, she has her characters succumb to the flesh.

However, she has no fixed opinions about relationships between men and women. She can bear down bitterly on both of them. She will allow a good woman to succumb to temptation just as quickly as a man. And when such things occur with couples who genuinely love each other, she has a way of illustrating the spiritual redemption that is evident even in moral failure. She is clearly a student of male/female relationships. And when she is not being too "folksy," she has the ability to penetrate to the core of emotional context in which her characters find themselves. In this regard, she was in advance of many of her "renaissance" contemporaries. There are very few novels of the period written with such compassion and love for black people. (pp. 18-19)

> *Larry Neal, "Eatonville's Zora Neale Hurston: A Profile," in* Black Review, *No. 2, 1972, pp. 11-24.*

S. JAY WALKER

The primary goals of the major American Liberation movements, Black Lib, Women's Lib, and Gay Lib, are in such affinity that it seems on the surface almost incredible that the three should not long since have formed an effective working alliance. In general terms, each demands, essentially, three things: definition of self, ending of oppression, and acceptance by society of the group's own goals and standards regarding itself.

Yet it is obvious that this alliance neither exists, nor is, beyond *pro forma* expressions of mutual sympathy, likely to exist. For whereas the generalized goals may be similar, the priorities and the applications of priority are different. (p. 519)

There have been mutual interchanges of concern and regard: Huey Newton has publicly acknowledged Gay and Women's groups as part of the general liberation struggle, whereas John Murray and Gloria Steinem have recognized that while racism remains pervasive in society there can be no real freedom for anyone. Yet Gay Lib and Women's Lib remain primarily white, middle-class organizations, and Black Lib remains virtually totally black. (pp. 519-20)

A 1971 *Ebony* article reported the majority of its black female respondents at best indifferent and at worst hostile to Women's Lib, with opinions ranging from the idea that the struggle with racism is enough for any black's energies to the belief that the last thing needed by black men at this time is being put down by black women, ("We should stand behind our men, not against them"), to the assertion that Women's Lib is a game being played by bored middle-class white women whose toilets are being cleaned by working-class, black women: you have to be in a Doll's House to want to get out of one.

The thrust of the Black Nationalist organizations, too, taken largely, one feels, from the leadership of the Black Muslims, is heavily male-oriented. It is seldom expressed with the brutality of Stokeley Carmichael's reported response to the question of what should be the "proper position" of women in the struggle—"Prone," he said. . . . Black Liberation makes a point of respecting, even revering, black women, but they are respected or revered *in their place,* a place perhaps best defined by Amina Baraka (a.k.a. Mrs. LeRoi Jones). The duty of black women, she writes, is "to inspire our men, educate our children, and participate in the social development of our nation." The accepted role, then, is clearly that of an auxiliary.

Thus it comes as something of a shock to discover that Zora Neale Hurston's neglected 1937 masterpiece, *Their Eyes Were Watching God,* deals far more extensively with sexism, the struggle of a woman to be regarded as a person in a male-dominated society, than racism, the struggle of blacks to be regarded as persons in a white-dominated society. It is a treatment virtually unique in the annals of black fiction, and in her handling of it, Ms. Hurston not only shows an aching awareness of the stifling effects of sexism, but also indicates why the feminist movement has failed, by and large, to grasp the imaginations of black womanhood.

Janie Killicks Starks Woods, the heroine of the novel, is followed through three marriages, the first of which brings her safety, the second wealth and prestige, and the third love. On the surface, it sounds indistinguishable from the women's-magazine fiction which has been denounced as the most insidious form of sexism. Yet a great deal goes on beneath the surface of Hurston's novel, leading to a final interpretation of love that denies not sexuality but sex-role stereotypes. The love that completes the novel is one that the previous marriages had lacked because it is a relationship between acknowledged equals. Janie and "Tea Cake," her husband, share resources, work, decisions, dangers, and not merely the marriage bed.

It is something less than a primer of romanticized love. At one point, Tea Cake, jealous of a suspected rival, beats Janie; at another, Janie, having the same suspicion, beats Tea Cake. Each has weaknesses, fears; but in the final analysis each re-

spects the other as a person, and it is that respect that allows them to challenge the world's conventions and to find each other, and themselves.

Hurston has a technical problem in maintaining this intensely personal vision during the desperate period, 1883-1923, in which the novel is set, without betraying herself into a Catfish Row fantasy of black life. She solves it by the simplest of devices: for the major exploration of the sexist theme, the second marriage, she removes her characters from the white world, establishing them in Eatonville, Florida, an all-black village (and one in which the author herself grew up) in which Janie's husband, Starks, is Mayor and owner of the general store, thus freeing them from contact with or economic dependence upon the white world.

It is within this society, secure both in person and prestige, that Janie ruminates to her crony, Pheoby Watson, on her personal desires as opposed to those of the grandmother who had reared her, and on the limitations of security and prestige:

> She [the grandmother] was borned in slavery times when folks, dat is black folks, didn't sit down anytime dey felt lak it. So sittin' on porches lak de white madam looked lak uh mighty fine thing tuh her. Dat's whut she wanted fuh me—don't keer whut it cost. Git up on uh high chair and sit dere. She didn't have time tuh think whut tuh do after you got up on de stool of do nothin'. . . . So Ah got up on de high stool lak she told me, but Pheoby, Ah done nearly languished tuh death up dere. Ah feel lak de world wuz cryin extry and Ah ain't read de common news yet.

And Pheoby answers, "Maybe so, Janie. Still and all Ah'd love to experience it for just one year. It look lak heben tuh me from where Ah'm at."

The distinction here is clearly drawn. Janie is the mayor's wife, but Pheoby is a worker, one of those Eatonville citizens described as becoming human only when "the sun and the bossman were gone." Her life is dominated almost entirely by the struggle to survive, and her tedious round between field and kitchen makes Janie's "stool of do nothing" appear a throne.

A *Black Scholar* article, "The Black Movement and Women's Liberation," by Linda La Rue sums up the ordinary class/race distinction between blacks and whites in a single question: "Is there any logical comparison between the oppression of the black woman on welfare who has difficulty feeding her children and the discontent of the suburban woman who has the luxury to protest the washing of the dishes on which her family's full meal has been consumed?"

This is the dichotomy—class, not race—which Hurston explores. Janie seeks to expand her experience, her understanding, her personality. Pheoby replies for all the black women who have never been admitted to the Doll's House. And who are not flocking into Women's Lib.

The path to that dissatisfied eminence has been a long one for Janie. It began with her grandmother, feeling that she was soon to die, seeking safety for the sixteen-year-old girl, threatening her with the dangers awaiting the unprotected black woman. . . . (pp. 520-22)

The safety envisioned by the grandmother is marriage to Logan Killicks, an elderly man who is "prosperous" in that he owns a sixty-acre farm. But the grandmother warns even against Killicks. ". . . de white man throw down de load and tell de nigger man tuh pick it up. He pick it up because he have to, but he don't tote it. He hand it to his womenfolks. De nigger woman is de mule of de world so fur as Ah can see."

One of the few favorable responses to the *Ebony* article echoed this "we are the slaves of slaves" sentiment: "It is not enough for black men to be free—black women cannot afford to wait . . . to deal with our oppression as women."

Janie's response to this warning is, in fact, to establish firmly the sex-oriented roles in their marriage. When her husband calls to her to come to assist him in the barn, she calls back from the kitchen, "You don't need no help out dere, Logan. Youse in yo' place and Ah'm in mine." And when Killicks grumbles that she might at least carry the firewood into the kitchen, pointing out that his first wife had even chopped it, Janie hurls at him the essential *kinder, küche, und kirche* putdown: "Ah'm just as stiff as you is stout. If you can stand not to chop and tote wood Ah reckon you can stand not to get no dinner. 'Scuse my freezolity, Mist' Killicks, but Ah don't mean to chop de first chip."

Killicks doesn't give up easily; he makes plans to buy a second mule, one that a woman can handle. Nor does Janie. She is preparing to fight for her place in the kitchen rather than behind the plow when she realizes that, even winning that fight, she will lose. For whereas Killicks can give her safety and respectability and a modicum of comfort, he cannot give her love.

Love seems to be offered by Joe Starks, the ambitious, debonair stranger who passes en route to Eatonville and who stays to court her with a new vision of what life can be: "A pretty doll-baby lak you is made to sit on de front porch and rock and fan yo'se'f."

She thinks over his words for several days, and then one morning, while quarreling with Killicks and cooking his breakfast, she walks out of the house and, with a fine symbolic gesture, unties her apron, flings it over a low bush, and runs away with Starks. (It is also perhaps symbolic of the identification of form with respectability that she and Starks marry the same evening, without either considering the matter of divorce.)

If the marriage to Killicks constitutes the "kitchen" era of Janie's existence, the marriage to Starks constitutes the "porch" era. Arrived in Eatonville, Starks takes charge of the growing community. He buys additional land and increases the settlers. He builds the store; he establishes the post office; he erects the first street-light; he arranges for the village's incorporation, and, inevitably, he becomes Mayor Starks.

Janie is "Mrs. Mayor Starks," and she finds the experience somehow disquieting. She tells Starks:

> "Youse always off talkin' and fixin' things and Ah feels lak Ah'm just markin' time. Hope it soon gits over." "Over, Janie?" [he replies.] . . . "Ah ain't even started good. Ah told you in de very first beginnin' dat Ah aimed tuh be a big voice. You oughta be glad, 'cause dat makes uh big woman outa you." . . . A feeling of coldness and fear took hold of her. She felt far away from things and lonely.

It is at this point that Hurston begins to develop her theme.

Clearly it is not enough for Janie to be made a big woman by her husband's being a big man. Sitting on the porch and fanning herself, watching the endless checker games of the village men and listening to their conversations, in neither of which she is expected to participate, Janie is merely "marking time." What is more, the "place" for which she had so doggedly fought Killicks now seems stultifying. Starks' "pretty doll-baby" is just that: his toy, his possession; and he emphasizes his ownership by insisting that Janie wear a turban, a "head-rag," in public, so that the sight of her beautiful hair can be enjoyed by no one other than himself. (pp. 522-24)

But perhaps even more galling than the possessiveness of Starks is his demand that Janie leave every decision to him. When she is invited to make a speech at one of the village celebrations, Starks replies for her:

> " . . . mah wife don't know nuthin' 'bout no speech-makin'. Ah never married her for nothin' lak dat. She's uh woman and her place is in de home."
>
> Janie made her face laugh after a small pause, but it wasn't too easy. She had never thought of making a speech and didn't know if she cared to make one at all. It must have been the way Joe spoke out without giving her a chance to say anything one way or another that took the bloom off things.

Starks also insists that she maintain her caste, above and separate from the common people of Eatonville: "He didn't want her talking [with] . . . trashy people. 'You're Mrs. Mayor Starks, Janie. . . . Ah can't see what uh woman uh yo' [class] would want tuh be treasurin' all dat gum-grease from folks dat don't even own de houses dey sleeps in.' "

Essentially, what Janie is deprived of is the company of other women, of the sisterhood of those with common experiences and common problems, and she begins to fight a lonely battle against Starks', and man's, definition of women:

> Starks. "Somebody got to think for women and chillun and chickens and cows. . . . they sho' don't think none themselves."
>
> Janie. "Ah knows a few things, and womenfolks thinks sometimes, too!"
>
> Starks. "Ah naw they don't. They just think they thinkin'. When Ah sees one thing Ah understands ten. You see ten things and don't understand one."

The attitude is a red flag waved before Janie's eyes, and she becomes, almost unwillingly, the Eatonville spokesman, if not for women's liberation, at least for women's dignity. It is an unwilling decision because she, too, is trapped into a pattern of thinking which makes her status dependent upon her husband's. (pp. 524-25)

But even lying, maintaining the façade of Mrs. Mayor Starks, she bursts out again and again at the casually disparaging remarks of her husband and his cronies:

> "Sometimes God git familiar with us womenfolks too and talks His inside business. He told me how surprised He was 'bout y'all turnin' out so smart after Him makin' yuh different; and how surprised y'all is agoin' tuh be if you ever find out you don't know half as much 'bout us as you think you do. It's so easy to make yo'self out God Almighty when you ain't got nothin' tuh strain against but women and chickens."

"You gettin' too moufy, Janie," Starks told her. "Go fetch me de checker board and de checkers."

The marriage is at an end, even though it drags on for years, and it is only when Starks is on his deathbed that Janie is able to force him to listen to her assessment of the emptiness of her life:

> Ah ain't here tuh blame nobody. Ah'm just tryin' tuh make you know what kind a person Ah is befo' it's too late. . . . You wasn't satisfied wid me de way Ah wuz. Nah! Mah own mind had tuh be squeezed and crowded out tuh make room for yours in me. . . . All dis bowin' down, all dis obedience under yo' voice—dat ain't whut Ah rushed off down de road tuh find out about you.

Starks dies, and Janie makes another symbolic gesture. Just as she had untied her apron and "flung it on a low bush" when leaving Killicks, now, "before she slept that night she burnt up every one of her head-rags and went about the house next morning with her hair in one thick braid swinging well below her waist."

It is another step, and the penultimate one, towards emancipation. She has left Killicks; she has defied and finally outlived Starks. Now she must combat both society and conventional wisdom. Janie is forty years of age, and when "Tea Cake" Woods, twelve years her junior, comes to court her, both the village and a deep caution within herself warn that he can be after nothing except her money. The village has a "suitable" third husband selected for her: a middle-aged undertaker with money, and whereas Janie quickly rejects that association with death, she cannot easily accept the association with life that Tea Cake offers to her.

It is simply too foreign to her experiences, and yet its foreignness is delightful. The checkerboard, that symbol of masculine exclusiveness and dominance, becomes an early indicant of what Tea Cake is to mean. He invites her to play and, when she confesses ignorance of the game, offers to teach her. "She found herself glowing inside. Somebody wanted her to play. Somebody thought it natural for her to play."

And from there they move through a series of small but significant challenges to the-way-things-ought-to-be. They dig worms at midnight and fish until dawn; they rent an automobile and drive to the nearest city to watch baseball games. . . . [Against] the advice of friends, legends of the sad fates of others, and her own forebodings, she agrees to follow Tea Cake to Jacksonville and marry him there. It is for her the ultimate expression of her thoughts after Starks' death:

> She had been getting ready for her great journey to the horizons in search of *people;* it was important to all the world that she find them and they find her. But she had been whipped like a cur dog, and run off down a back road after *things.*

It is important to note that in one respect Hurston diverges here from the radical feminists of the 1970's. Janie's search for *people* can only be accomplished through a *person,* a man. In this sense of an individual being incomplete without an individual, personal love, Hurston returns, in effect, to the romantic tradition of reciprocal passion, a tradition as old as Charlotte Brontë and George Eliot, and it is in terms of that tradition that finally she views the relationship between Tea Cake and Janie. Janie herself recognizes that personal love is

the cement of her life, and is uncaring that the world will not understand or approve it:

> Dey gointuh make 'miration 'cause mah love didn't work lak they love, if dey ever had any. Then you must tell 'em dat love ain't somethin' lak uh grindstone dat's de same thing everywhere and do de same thing tuh everything it touch. Love is lak de sea. It's uh moving' thing, but still and all, it takes its shape from de shore it meets, and it's different with every shore.

And certainly her love and Tea Cake's is "different." If the apron was symbolic of her life with Killicks and the head-rag of her life with Starks, overalls are the symbol of her life with Tea Cake, for she dons them and goes into the fields to work side by side with him as a migrant laborer in the Everglades.

It may seem a strange "liberation," particularly for the girl who didn't "mean to chop de first chip" for Killicks, but it *is* a liberation; it grows neither out of need nor greed but simply of the desire of Janie and Tea Cake to be together, to share all their experiences, "to partake wid everything," as Tea Cake puts it. And the sharing is genuine: after their day in the fields, Tea Cake helps to get supper. There is no longer the "youse in yo' place and Ah'm in mine" because there are no longer separate places, and it is that blurring of "places," essentially the blurring of sex-role stereotypes within an intensely sexual relationship, that constitutes the liberation and happiness of Janie Killicks Starks Woods.

It is significant that only in this portion of the novel does Hurston shift into what is ordinarily the primary theme of the black novelist: the exploration of racism and black reactions to it. The experiences of racism, as they occur here, are experiences that Janie and Tea Cake can meet and master because they meet them side by side.

As they await the onslaught of the hurricane which is, indirectly, to kill Tea Cake, he questions her about their life: "Ah reckon you wish now you had of stayed in yo' big house 'way from such as dis, don't yuh?" And she replies,

> Naw. We been tuhgether round two years. If you kin see de light at daybreak, you don't keer if you die at dusk. It's so many people never seen de light at all. Ah wuz fumblin' round and God opened de door.

Following Tea Cake's death, Janie returns to Eatonville, still wearing her overalls, to live out her life as she sees fit and to tell her story to her friend Pheoby. There is an ironic indication in the final pages of the novel that Janie, in her own liberation, has become a subversive influence, one that the village arbiters will be hard-pressed to cope with. For, as she concludes her story to Pheoby, her friend, who little more than two years earlier had been one of the strongest backers of the "respectable undertaker" marriage, breathes out shock and admiration:

> Lawd! Ah done growed ten feet higher from jus' listenin' tuh you, Janie. *Ah ain't satisfied wid mahself no mo'.* Ah means tuh make Sam take me fishin' wid him after this. (Italics mine.)

Women's Lib has come to Eatonville, Florida, and Sam Watson, Pheoby's husband, and the other men, will probably find that it takes a little getting used to, just as the world of 1975 finds that the various Liberation groups take a little getting used to.

But in the final analysis, they will probably make it, for as Zora Neale Hurston recognized, the real enemy of progress is not hostility; it is mental inertia, masquerading as hostility or ridicule.

Joe Starks' initial plan for a post office in Eatonville, for instance,

> irritated Hicks and he didn't know why. He was the average mortal. It troubled him to get used to the world one way and then suddenly have it turn different. He wasn't ready to think of colored people in post offices yet. He laughed boisterously.

Yet the laughter notwithstanding, Eatonville got its post office, and the world, and even Hicks, were none the worse for it. (pp. 525-27)

> S. Jay Walker, "Zora Neale Hurston's 'Their Eyes Were Watching God': Black Novel of Sexism," in Modern Fiction Studies, Vol. 20, No. 4, Winter, 1974-75, pp. 519-27.

MARIA TAI WOLFF

In the opening paragraphs of *Their Eyes Were Watching God,* the narrator presents two models for evaluating life:

> Ships at a distance have every man's wish on board. For some they come in with the tide. For others, they sail forever on the horizon, never out of sight, never landing until the Watcher turns his eyes away in resignation, his dreams mocked to death by Time. That is the life of men.
>
> Now, women forget all the things they don't want to remember, and remember all the things they don't want to forget. The dream is the truth. Then they act and do things accordingly.

Men, it seems, stoically watch what reality presents, accepting that which life reveals to them. While they may wish or dream, their inner hopes can be fulfilled only by factors beyond human control; events and circumstances are the "ships at a distance." Men are controlled by Time; if it does not favor their dreams, it will "mock" them, destroy them. "That is the life of men": Life is given, not made. Women, on the other hand, create their own lives from their interpretations of reality. This involves a selective process of willed forgetting and remembering, and it leads to the formulation of a personal image of life, a "dream." On this "truth" of life, women base their actions, living their dreams. Time has less power here; in this process the past is re-shaped and brought into the present, contributing to the acts of the future.

Before introducing the protagonist of the novel, the narrator reveals that this will be a woman's story: "So the beginning of this was a woman. . . . " "This" is the narration of life as lived by a woman, the creation of a "dream as truth." It is also the presentation of a model of reading, of understanding an oral or written text.

Ralph Freedman describes the movement of a lyrical novel as evidencing a "qualitative progression" rather than the temporal progression usually found in a novel. In a lyrical novel, the "fictional world" is "conceived not as a universe in which men display their actions but as a poet's vision fashioned as a design. The world is reduced to a lyrical point of view." The novel works, then, not as a historical account or narrative of events alone, but as the lyric formulation of a personal vision—or dream. Examining the effects of lyric language on narrative, Freedman writes, "Actions are turned into scenes which embody recognitions."

This transformation of events or actions into elements of a lyrical point of view takes place on several levels in *Their Eyes Were Watching God.* The descriptions of certain crucial scenes, and their repetitions, turn them into emblems or symbols. Yet the transformation of the outside world into a personal vision, of "actions" into self-recognitions, is also the theme of the novel.

A large part of the text is the story of Janie's life; the narrator presents it as Janie tells it to Pheoby. And Janie speaks "full of that oldest human longing—self revelation." It is she who reveals her past to her friend as she speaks, but, in a sense, Janie also narrates the manner in which her identity has been revealed to her. The story is structured around successive scenes of self-recognition which are Janie's repeated attempts to create a clear, satisfying picture of who she is. The events of the narrative, and the other characters, function within this structure. Janie is lead to form her own dream, her own truth, from what she has lived.

Beyond this, though, the text inspires the reader to formulate his or her own personal image of it. The story of Janie is a "revelation" to the reader as well, since the narrative presents a series of perceptions for our evaluation. In hearing, or, indeed, in living, Janie's adventures, the reader is led to reconsider the text within his or her own experience, and to "act and do things accordingly."

The first episode that Janie narrates presents the problem which will structure the series of recognitions in the novel. When she sees herself in a photograph, Janie sees for the first time that she is black. She becomes aware that there are two possible perceptions of her: the intrinsic, natural image she has of herself, and the image held by the rest of the world. . . . The outside world has also attached its perceptions to her as names, although with no consistency: " 'Dey all useter call me Alphabet 'cause so many people had named me different names.' " She is what she has been called. Until a moment just before the death of Joe Starks, Janie will be unable to separate and evaluate these two perceptions, to understand her own identity.

Janie's "conscious life," and the real beginning of her efforts to know herself, begin when she first becomes aware of her sexuality. On the first occasion of this, the narrator, in a lyric passage, uses several images which will recur whenever Janie meets a new suitor. These symbols are the "blossoming pear tree" and the spreading pollen of spring. The perception of these elements in nature responds to certain forces within Janie:

> The rose of the world was breathing out smell. It followed her through all her waking moments and caressed her in her sleep. It connected itself with other vaguely felt matters that had struck her outside observation and buried themselves in her flesh. Now they emerged and quested about her consciousness.

Janie has "been summoned to behold a revelation." These two passages show an essential passivity of her experiences: The world will present itself to her. "She felt an answer seeking her, but where?"

Yet Janie's perception of the world will become an active,

transforming one. . . . [She] must make a mirror of her consciousness, transforming the "revelation" into part of herself. She must structure her experiences and create or find the answer. In ***Their Eyes Were Watching God,*** Janie's search for identity is not a temporal, progressive process, but involves the representation and evaluation of a series of experiences or images. These include various "mirrors," or portraits of Janie herself, presented by others or viewed by the heroine. From these, she must choose. In a sense, she learns to make a lyrical formulation of the world—with the text presenting the material for the process of formulation as well.

Janie must select from or reconcile material from two different sources: the information about herself she receives from others, and her own feelings and experiences. In a sense, these are two texts, which often conflict. The first, which comes from the spoken opinions of others and corresponds to the "outside" image of her, is almost forced on Janie. The second is less easily explained: It is something she knows and is always capable of possessing, but it must be brought out and valued.

Janie's grandmother is the first to impose a role on the girl. Noting that Janie is aware of men, she announces to the girl, " 'Janie, youse uh 'oman now. . . . ' " Yet Janie is, supposedly, without knowledge of the world and is deemed incapable of making her own decisions: " 'Dat's what makes me skeered. You don't mean no harm. You don't even know where harm is at.' " So her grandmother makes it possible for Janie to fulfill the old woman's own " '*dreams* of what a woman *oughta be and to do*' " (emphasis added). She marries Janie to a well-to-do farmer. (pp. 29-30)

At first, Janie has no experience of love and marriage: "Janie had had no chance to know things, so she had to ask." Common opinion substitutes for and suppresses her own feelings. . . . Yet she becomes increasingly disillusioned with Logan Killicks; for her role as a married woman does not correspond to her dreams or images: " ' Ah wants things sweet wid mah marriage lak when you sit under a pear tree and think,' " she says.

The narrator uses lyric imagery to present Janie's inner world, including her implicit dissatisfaction with her role or "text":

> . . . when the pollen again gilded the sun and shifted down on the world she began to stand around the gate and expect things. What things? She didn't know exactly. Her breath was gusty and short. She knew things that nobody had ever told her.

The last sentence of this passage presents the dialogue between Janie's thoughts, what she "knows," and what she has been told. Her own experiences must give her something to counter the voices of others. Indeed, this first marriage brings about one development: "She knew now that marriage did not make love. Janie's first dream was dead, so she became a woman." Only experience has made her a "woman"; her grandmother's announcement of the change has been undermined.

There are several episodes in which Janie withdraws into the inner world of her thoughts to evaluate received "texts." Before she leaves Logan Killicks, for instance, Janie isolates herself for a moment: "Janie . . . turned wrongside out just standing there and feeling. When the throbbing calmed a little she gave Logan's speech a hard thought and placed it be-

side other things she had seen and heard." The received text, Killick's definition of her role as his wife, is reconsidered. It is made part of her system of experiences, what she has "seen and heard." And it is left behind.

Nevertheless, when Janie marries Joe Starks, she has not found a fulfillment of her inner desires, since Joe has his own plan for life:

> Every day after that they managed to meet in the scrub oaks across the road and talk about when he would be a big ruler of things with her reaping the benefits. Janie pulled back a long time because he did not represent sun-up and pollen and blooming trees, but he spoke for far horizon. He spoke for change and chance.

He has also planned her role in his world: "with her reaping the benefits." Although he does not seem to offer what Janie needs, he presents the possibility of new experiences, "speaking" for a new life. She feels, somehow, that her feelings will find a way outside: "Her old thoughts were going to come in handy now, but new words would have to be made and said to fit them."

Yet Joe does not permit Janie's desires to find their words. His aim is to be "a big voice" in the town, and he comes to speak for all of Eatonville. His life, though, becomes nothing more than a series of orders given to others. . . . (p. 30)

Again, Janie withdraws into herself, experiencing a moment of self-recognition. . . . She looks at her past and reevaluates it, discovering what had been forgotten and "turning her back" on her illusions. At this point, she makes a clear distinction between her own "feelings"—her "inside"—and the outer self which she presents to the world. The experience needed to fulfill the former—a "man she had never seen"—must be awaited. She resumes her role as Jody's wife, but only by making a conscious "bow to the outside of things." And, especially after she and Jody have moved definitively apart, "new thoughts had to be thought and new words said."

Throughout the marriage, Joe has attempted to force a premature, false aging on her. He tells her repeatedly that she is as " 'old as Methusalem' " and creates a story about her age and unattractiveness. Yet, at Joe's death, Janie's self-examination in a mirror produces a visual recognition which undermines the image Joe's text had created: "Years ago, she had told her girl self to wait for her in the looking glass. It had been a long time since she had remembered. Perhaps she'd better look. . . . The young girl was gone, but a handsome woman had taken her place." Here, Janie's own image replaces that which others have made for her. It is a true mirror, and her own eyes, not the verbal mirror of others, show her what she is. Again, the transition in her life from girlhood to womanhood is shown not merely to be an effect of time, but a change in consciousness. Recalling the earlier description of Janie's becoming a woman at the death of her dreams, the reader of this passage observes a more knowledgeable and more secure woman.

After Joe's death, Janie does a series of "re-readings" of her past. She discovers, for example, that "she hated her grandmother and had hidden it from herself all these years under a cloak of pity." She recognizes, as well, her own desires to seek out experiences, to make "a great journey to the horizons," rather than be attached to defined roles, "things." She knows, also, that it is "all according to the way you see things. Some people could look at a mud-puddle and see an ocean with ships." Life may be a "revelation," but it is the acceptance or interpretation of this revelation which is important. Each person must formulate his or her own "way of seeing." Her grandmother had forced on her one perception in the "name of love." Janie, however, recognizes that another's ideas are never adequate. The only truths she will now accept are those derived from her own experience: "This freedom feeling was fine. These men didn't represent a thing she wanted to know about. She had already experienced them through Logan and Joe."

While both of her husbands and her grandmother have imposed a role on Janie, in telling her what she should be, the man she next becomes involved with, Tea Cake, tells her only what she is capable of becoming: " '. . . you got good meat on yo' head. You'll learn.' " It seems that Tea Cake is not part of the outside world, but part of her own, personal being: "Seemed as if she had known him all her life." The lyrical language which has heretofore invoked only desire is now used to describe one person: "He could be a bee to a blossom—a pear tree blossom in the spring." Rather than telling her who or what she is, he directs her only to recognize it for herself: " 'Ah betcha you don't never go tuh de lookin' glass and enjoy yo' eyes yo'self.' " He becomes a mirror for her, but one which refers her back to her own experience. (p. 31)

Tea Cake seems to share Janie's awareness of the importance of "how one sees things." It is "thought," or evaluation, which makes age important—or unimportant. This is the contrary of Joe's view. Tea Cake offers Janie the role of his wife—a role which is not a role:

> "So yuh aims tuh partake wid everything, hunh?"
>
> "Yeah, Tea Cake, don't keer what it is."
>
> "Dat's all Ah wants tuh know."

Theirs is a text as yet unwritten, a text to be created out of "everything." Tea Cake gives Janie the world, from which they will make a "dream" together. He offers her experience.

From her grandmother, Logan Killicks, and Joe Starks, Janie receives a ready-made text, a definition of her role. She is expected to conform to it. From Tea Cake, on the other hand, she receives an invitation to live a text, to formulate a role. In the narrative of Janie's life, knowledge accepted from a prepared text—one that is told—is opposed by knowledge gleaned from experience. And it is the second which is most satisfying, most "true"—although experience includes the hearing and evaluation of others' stories. Janie comes to know herself only after she has carefully examined others' stories, and "put them beside" her own perceptions.

A reader might be led, however, to question the position of *Their Eyes Were Watching God* within this structure. Does it not, after all, present a story told, one which must be accepted completely by the reader, one which limits the reader to passive acceptance? A careful examination of the kinds of "telling" presented in the novel, and a consideration of the modes of narration employed, will answer this question.

Logan Killicks, Joe Starks, and Nanny all claim a certain power or truth for what they say. With their words, they impose opinions on Janie, constrain her actions. Throughout the text, there are scenes in which words are used as weapons. In these, as in Joe's orders to Janie, the teller tries to control or wound another person. . . . [When] Janie returns to Eatonville, her neighbors make "burning statements with ques-

tions, and killing tools out of laughs. It was mass cruelty. A mood come alive. Words walking without masters. . . ." Talking becomes a kind of performative language, a curse or a constraint. (pp. 31-2)

There is . . . another kind of telling, which is both more and less related to experience. It is telling for its own sake, for the listener's and teller's enjoyment. Sam and Hicks' conversation about the latter's powers over women is an example. Hicks seems to describe this playful talking when he remarks that women " 'loves to hear me talk because dey can't understand it. Mah co-talkin' is too deep.' " This kind of talking is a game or a drama, in which all participate: "The girls and everybody else help laugh. They know it's not courtship. It's acting-out courtship and everybody is in the play."

While this narration for narration's sake is less didactic and has less claim to "truth" than do more "serious" passages in the novel, it is more evocative and exciting. We are allowed to hear the "big picture talkers," who use "a side of the world for a canvas. . . ."

After Janie has married Tea Cake, she, too, learns to "tell big stories." Indeed, her entire story to Pheoby could be so classified. It is not an example of the other, forceful telling; Janie does not concern herself with answering the accusing voices of the porch-sitters. Her story has another purpose: It is both a presentation of experience and an encouragement to experience—an experience in itself. Janie tells Pheoby, " 'If they wants to see and know, why don't they come kiss and be kissed? Ah could then sit down and tell 'em things.' " Janie does not claim to have found any joy which all can or must achieve in the same way. Love, for example, must be found by each individually. . . .

Often talking, or listening to such talk, seems only to be a substitute for experience: " '. . . talkin' don't amount tuh uh hill uh beans,' " remarks Janie, " 'when yuh can't do nothin' else. And listenin' tuh dat kind uh talk is jus' lak openin' yo' mouth and lettin' de moon shine down yo' throat. It's uh known fact, Pheoby, you got tuh *go* there tuh *know* there.' " Every text, especially an oral one, directs the listener to go outside or beyond it, to live and to know for oneself. Unless it is done with memory of experience, talking or listening can be only a consolation. . . .

Nonetheless, when one can "do something else," there is a certain amount of pleasure to be taken in listening or reading. For the teller and the listener, there comes a kind of participation: We are told, for instance, that, in the Everglades, Janie " . . . could listen and laugh and even talk some herself if she wanted to. She got so she could tell big stories herself from listening to the rest. Because she loved to hear it, and the men loved to hear themselves, they would 'woof' and 'boogerboo' around the games to the limit." Between the teller and the listener there is almost a dialogue, the latter being called in to evaluate the teller's story. Yet the teller must present the story in such a way that the listener can "live through" it. As Janie tells Pheoby: " '. . . 'tain't no use in me telling you somethin' unless Ah give you de understandin' to go 'long wid it. Unless you see de fur, a mink skin ain't no different from a coon hide.' " The listener must form an "understanding." Yet telling must become experience in order for this to happen; the listener must "see" the story.

As they discuss women, Sam says to Hicks, " 'Ah's much ruther see all dat than to hear 'bout it.' " For telling to be successful, it must become a presentation of sights with words.

The best talkers are "big picture talkers." In this way, the opposition between listening or reading and experience is broken down—or reading is brought as close to living as possible.

The narrator of **Their Eyes Were Watching God** is, one might say, a "big picture talker" as well, who employs lyrical language in order to allow the reader to make a visual and sensual expression of the text. . . . The narrator presents Janie's story as a series of episodes and pictures. Indeed, nearly all of her story is presented in the third person; in it Janie herself narrates the basic problem she must resolve. The following episodes contain images and experiences which she must organize with reference to her own problem. The reader or listener, on the other hand, is free to form his or her own evaluation from the material presented, to individually "integrate" the world. Pheoby, Janie's listener, is asked only " 'for a good thought' "—a sympathetic, active listening. (p. 32)

The narrator uses a variety of narrative stances and techniques to render the text more sensually and visually immediate. I have already noted the sensual language which evokes Janie's inner language. An interior monologue is often introduced to evoke Janie's thoughts and perceptions: "She knew the world was a stallion rolling in the blue pasture of ether. She knew that God tore down the old world every evening and built a new one by sun-up." At times, though, the narration shifts to the direct address of an implied reader: "Daisy is walking a drum tune. You can almost hear it by looking at the way she walks." The narration can also take on the diction of oral language: "Joe Starks was the name, yeah Joe Starks from in and through Georgy. Been workin' for white folks all his life." The book's narration, it seems, is deliberately flexible; it takes on the qualities suitable to the situation it describes. The narrator has many voices. It is not consistent representation which is served, but presentation, or revelation. The text is presented to the "active" and "creative" reader.

The truth of the tale is not at issue so much as its effect on the teller and as its telling. The narrator and Janie are both "tellers"; in fact, one might imagine that they are occasionally as unreliable as Lige or Sam. The situation of their tale is perhaps the same as that of the story Tea Cake tells Janie about his day's absence. Neither she nor the reader have any assurance of its "truth." Yet Janie desires only to share in the adventure—and, ultimately, in the telling: " 'Looka heah, Tea Cake, if you ever go off from me and have a good time lak dat and then come back heah tellin' me how nice Ah is, Ah specks tuh kill yuh dead.' "

The episode of the buzzards' funeral for the mule, for example, could be interpreted as a challenge to the reader. It is presented in the same way that the other narrated incidents are. Yet it is, obviously, a fantasy. The scene takes place at the end of the mule's funeral, an event which Janie, whom Joe has left at home, does not witness. The funeral itself is a comedy; the people "mocked everything human in death." And the buzzards' funeral is a further parody of this parody, narrated with absolute seriousness. The last sentence of the episode is: "The yaller mule was gone from the town except for the porch talk, and for the children visiting his bleached bones now and then in the spirit of adventure." There is no witness to the scene of the buzzards; one might imagine that this tale is "porch talk," presented for the reader's enjoyment, and his or her rejection or acceptance. Within Janie's tale, told to Pheoby, it might be a story that she has heard and in-

tegrated into her own story. And, in the entire text, it points out that the narrator has chosen material to include by following a method other than strict representation, an idea I will return to later.

Near the end of the novel, Janie says, " 'Ah done been tuh de horizon and back and now Ah kin sit heah in mah house and live by comparisons.' " Having seen the world, she can now evaluate it, perhaps forgetting what she does not wish to remember and remembering what she does not want to forget. Her reading of the past is a selective, personal one. . . . Her past becomes, at last, something that she can possess. The world is reduced to an image, to be "draped over her shoulder." It is a dream which she has created for herself and in which she can live: "She called in her soul to come and see," This image and her own small room are much larger than Eatonville or Logan Killicks' sixty acres. And her image will allow her to live in the outside world as well, bringing it back to her own thoughts and dreams. . . .

While a text presents a reader with a new set of experiences, it can also lead one to re-evaluate his or her own experiences, or "formulate oneself." In a sense, then, every text teaches something. In reading it, one learns how to read, or even how to live. The opening paragraphs of **Their Eyes Were Watching God** certainly have a didactic element, stating flatly two models of reading. They also lend an allegorical tone to the text; Janie is, after all, an example of a "woman." The text, the story, is the narrator's: Through Janie's story, the narrator tells another, a story about reading, and living.

Yet the narrator chooses a model that presents, in a sense, a non-lesson, or a lesson that readers are left to formulate for themselves. The reader's own experiences and dreams will lead him or her to interpret the text in an individual way, to transform it into a personal image. And every image will be the "true" text. Beyond this, though, the text may bring one to re-consider his or her own life, and to live it more fully. If the example of Janie's life teaches anything, it is that nothing can truly be "taught." The truth, the text, comes from, and ends in, the reader's or the liver's own perception. And there are " 'two things everybody's got tuh do fuh theyselves. They got tuh go tuh God, and they got tuh find out about livin' fuh theyselves.' " What Janie says of "livin' " can be said of reading as well. (p. 33)

Maria Tai Wolff, "Listening and Living: Reading and Experience in 'Their Eyes Were Watching God'," in Black American Literature Forum, Vol. 16, No. 1, Spring, 1982, pp. 29-33.

GAY WILENTZ

[*The essay excerpted below was originally presented as a paper at a conference held at Hofstra University in Fall, 1982.*]

Aspects of Afro-American culture in the U.S. have been formed by a necessity of those in the oppressed group to confront and in some way control the oppressor from the white slave masters to the later dominant white culture. "With tongues cocked and loaded," folktales were "the only killing tool they [were] allowed to use in the presence of white folks." The folktales and the folk culture provided the black folks with a source of "power and knowledge alternative to those existing within the world of the master class." Therefore, for blacks, the God of the white man takes on a sinister role in contradistinction as well as in addition to the savior

God of the community church. Within the context of an oppressive society, "God" is viewed ironically, if often surreptitiously, as the strict slave master determined to keep the dominated culture in its place. (p. 285)

[In *Their Eyes Were Watching God,* Zora Neale Hurston weaves a] folktale of the white man as a false "god" who must eventually be defeated. The novel is about Janie, an independent black woman, who does not, as her community does, watch God; she is looking elsewhere. Janie fights her way out of the constricting conventions of the dominant culture and, through her quest for self-determination, comes to find her own values in life. These spiritual values are paramount to Janie's growth and well-being, unlike the materialistic, middle-class values imposed on a group which by color alone cannot realize the "ideal." At each stage of Janie's development, certain characters pressure her to deify the white culture. First there is her grandmother Nanny's materialism; later, her husband Jody's bourgeois aspirations; and finally, Mrs. Turner's worship of white features. As the pressure of this imposing white culture increases, the ability of each character involved to exert influence over Janie decreases as she progresses towards what is real. What is *real* in this novel are Janie's self-determination, her love for Tea Cake, and the folk culture.

Hurston has received criticism, from both black and white critics, for ignoring racial issues in her novels. It is true that she does not document the tragic history of social injustice as did Richard Wright (who compared Hurston to Jane Austen and said she did not look at race or class struggles). Yet by the very absence of explicit racial conflict, the pressure of the dominant culture on the thoughts and actions of the all-black community of Eatonville as well as blacks as a whole, is detailed throughout the novel. Robert Hemenway, in his biography of Hurston [see Further Reading list], states that Hurston "triumphs over the racist environment without political propaganda but by turning inward and turning around the folktale. . . . " By breaking away from the racist atmosphere in which she was brought up, Janie loses a false god and finds herself. And Hurston, through the medium of the folk culture, creates a world in which Janie defeats the oppressor.

The title of the novel strikes us as strange when it becomes apparent that the story is about one woman rather than the "they" mentioned in the title. The reference to the title comes when there is a hurricane on the "muck" (the Florida everglades). The seasonal workers in the community are debating whether or not to leave the area: "They seemed to be staring in the dark, but their eyes were watching God." I am not suggesting that the "God" of the passage is the white man; certainly the concept of a supreme being governing humanity is present in the novel. But Hurston gives us a second reading of "God" which indicates that it may refer not only to an absolute spirit but to the white hegemony. In the section describing the hurricane in the everglades, numerous references are made to God as "bossman" and "Ole Massa." God appears at times at capricious slave master whose whims and dangerous acts are incontrollable. Yet Hurston constantly keeps us aware of the duality of the Christian God for the black folks as they make their decision to leave the muck: "The time was past for asking the white folks what to look for outside that door. Six eyes were questioning God." Therefore, the title and the word "God" incorporates a double, yet contradictory meaning: There is the God to whom we look for answers and pray for help and there is the other god, the cruel, false god who definitely needs watching.

As a young girl, Janie is confronted with her grandmother's desires that Janie have everything she did not have. This is the first stage of Janie's development when she is totally under Nanny's control. Janie doesn't understand why she is marrying ancient Logan Killicks but listens to her grandmother. To Nanny, "being married is just being like white folks." It will protect Janie and help her to achieve certain middle-class values, particularly since Logan has 60 acres of land and will not beat her. (pp. 285-87)

Nanny dies before Janie runs off with Jody Starks, but it is he who secures and even furthers Nanny's dream for Janie. Nanny's basic materialism is transformed into Jody's bourgeois aspirations. Jody is an example of the "Black Bourgeoisie" who believed that acquisitions of wealth and status would in some way make them closer to the white culture which thought them inferior. In the all-black community of Eatonville, Jody quickly rises to success. . . . It is important to note that Janie did not leave Logan for Jody because of any material gains; she went because of a sense of adventure and because she was sure "the change was bound to do her good." At this point, Janie begins to make choices concerning her own life.

Jody is a hard-working, ambitious person and basically good-natured, but he is bourgeois and conventional in the way that he sees the world. He gains many possessions, the finest of these being his wife. He believes, as Nanny did, that the life for Janie is one in which she can "class off." Jody is confused by Janie's desire to thwart his attempts to put her "on the porch." The notion is that Janie, being the mayor's wife, should act more like a white woman. Jody, like the Black bourgeoisie "who strove to make themselves over in the image of the white man," wanted to change his community into one which would be comparable to the white town up the road. The "white" imagery in the Eatonville section is striking. Jody builds a "gloaty, sparkly white" house in the tradition of the old plantations and a large white porch for Janie to sit on. He buys a street lamp for the town and keeps it on show for a week. It was the first "light" brought to the colored town although some felt it a useless notion. He does not understand Janie's disillusionment with their relationship because he did what he promised—made a "big woman" out of her. Although at this stage Jody has a greater identification with white middle-class values than Nanny did, his power over Janie is less complete.

Janie's values are different from Jody's and what she wants is a spiritual partnership which has nothing to do with material things: "She got nothing from Jody except what money could buy, and she was giving away what she didn't value." Janie realizes that the life determined for her by Nanny which she lived with Jody was not for her. . . . [She] has been living a life that was not her choice and with the death of Jody, she is determined to follow her own judgment. She has found out what love is not and that leads her to make a positive step towards Tea Cake and spiritual fulfillment.

Even after Janie goes with Tea Cake to the muck—which unlike the town is rich and black and big and free—she still must deal with the white world seen through the eyes of the mulatto Mrs. Turner. This woman exemplifies the final stage of white identification: idol worship. Of the three characters, Mrs. Turner has the least effect on Janie; her main function is to show how warped an individual can become when she chooses the white man as her god. Janie's caucasian features, which are incidental to her, become paramount to Mrs. Turner. She separates Janie and herself from dark ones like Tea Cake. Janie does not understand why this is important and in answer to Mrs. Turner's suggestion that they "class off," Janie replies, "Us can't *do* it. We'se a mingled people and all of us got black kinfolks as well as yaller kinfolks." Mrs. Turner is horrified that Janie lets her whiteness be "defiled" by Tea Cake's blackness, because Mrs. Turner had deified white features and now is prepared to worship them in anyone who fits this description:

> Anyone who looked more white folkish than herself was better than she was in her criteria, therefore it was right that they should be cruel to her at times, just as she was cruel to those more negroid than her in direct ratio to their negroness. . . . Once having set up her idols and built altars to them it was inevitable that she would worship there. It was inevitable that she should accept any inconsistency and cruelty from her deity as all good worshippers do from theirs. All gods who receive homage are cruel. All gods dispense suffering without reason. Otherwise they would not be worshipped. . . .

> Mrs. Turner, like all other believers had built an altar to the unattainable—Caucasian characteristics for all. Her god would smite her, would hurl her from pinnacles and lose her in deserts. But she would not forsake his altars.

Even though Mrs. Turner's views "didn't affect Tea Cake and Janie too much" ironically, it is Mrs. Turner's brother who is the object of Tea Cake's jealousy when he goes mad at the end.

After Janie and Tea Cake leave the muck during the hurricane, they end up in Palm Beach. Since Tea Cake has been bitten by a dog (they do not know it's rabid) while saving Janie from the flooding waters, they remain in a hotel for a few days attending to Tea Cake's wounds. Finally Tea Cake wanders out to find out what has happened to his friends. While he is out on the streets of Palm Beach, he encounters two white men with guns who *force* him to recover and bury the victims of the flood. When he objects, one man shoves the rifle in his face and says, "Git on down de road dere, suh! Don't look out somebody'll be buryin' you!" The Palm Beach incident, which has been viewed as an isolated example of racial injustice, appears in light of this analysis to be a concrete representation of what has been happening all along: the imposition of a dominant culture on an oppressed group, whether the oppression be physical or psychological. [In *Black Fiction*], Roger Rosenblatt notes that Tea Cake and Janie flourish only when they avoid the white world. This world implies white cultural values as well. When Janie and Tea Cake are pushed off the bridge in the storm to make room for the white folks and later in Palm Beach when Tea Cake is forced to throw the black corpses in a pit while he buries the white ones, we see their lives violated by the white world; yet, equally destructive to their sense of well-being are the Mrs. Turners and the materialistic considerations in the Eatonville community. Janie resists these pressures and looks to Tea Cake and their love so that her soul can crawl out of its hiding place.

Life on the muck is very different from life in Eatonville. Janie has left her "white" house and all the trappings of the false "white" god and has gone to find her own values in the rich, black soil, the stories and the folk tales, and the warm feeling of friendship shared there. Janie, through the rejection of the white values, becomes self-determining:

> Sometimes Janie would think of the old days in the big white house and the store and laugh to herself. What if Eatonville could see her now in her blue denim overalls and heavy shoes? The crowd of people around her and a dice game on her floor! She was sorry for her friends back there and scornful of the others. The men held arguments here like they used to do on the store porch. Only here she could listen and laugh and even talk some herself if she wanted to.

Through their love and spiritual partnership, Tea Cake and Janie find an alternative to the white culture which is not only hostile and unattainable, but also sterile and confining. They are not like Mrs. Turner; they make no distinctions concerning the folks. They bring the West Indians into their group of friends, and their house is a center of activity. Unlike the big, white house in Eatonville which became a center by power and fear, Tea Cake and Janie's place on the muck is a center fashioned from love. Even as the storm threatens to break up this close-knit community, Janie and Tea Cake retain allegiance to the folk culture and the black world. As their Bahamian friend Lias leaves the glades, he tells them "If Ah never see you no mo' on Earth, Ah'll meet you in Africa." They will not meet in the cold, hard heaven of the white man; they will find each other in the rich, black fields of their African heaven.

The story makes it clear that the heaven which is controlled by the white man does not include black folks. We see this in Janie's thoughts about help from God when Tea Cake is dying. Since he was bitten by a rabid dog while trying to save her from drowning, Janie realizes that he will "die for loving her."

Janie, questioning their fate, looks up into the "blue ether" of the sky and waits for a sign. Like the cold, blue eyes of the slave master, "the sky stayed hard looking and quiet so she went into the house. God would do less than He had in His heart." Janie sees no recourse in the "god" of the white man nor in the dominant culture. Certainly the white doctor who tells her how dangerous Tea Cake is, never sends the medicine to make Tea Cake's dying easier for him and less threatening to Janie. After Janie is forced to kill the rabid Tea Cake in self-defense, she thanks him "wordlessly for giving her the chance for loving service." (pp. 287-90)

When Janie returns to Eatonville after Tea Cake's death, without him and without the "fine clothes" she left with, she feels no need to justify herself to the community. Perhaps they think Tea Cake stole her money and left her for another woman (which happened to one woman who turned her back on the community), but Janie is satisfied that she knows the truth. She comes back in her overalls to a house once filled with the loneliness of Jody's dreams and now filled with the rich memory of Tea Cake's love. She shares this with Pheoby, not to explain her position to the community but because Pheoby is her friend. And Pheoby hears and learns. . . . The community of Eatonville showed her what love was *not,* but by looking into herself, she found what it was. Janie's advice to the town is that they better stop watching "god" and find out what their own lives are about before they go to God. "Two things everybody's got tuh do fuh themselves. They got tuh go tuh God, and they got tuh find out about livin' fuh theyselves."

Janie does just that. She finds her humanity against all odds. . . . And Janie pays a price for finding her humanity. She loses Tea Cake and is alone at the end. But by negating a false system of values, she becomes one of the few women characters in early Afro-American fiction to emerge whole. "Here was peace. She pulled in her horizon like a great fish-net. Pulled it from around the waist of the world and draped it over her shoulders. So much of life in its meshes! She called her soul to come and see."

Robert Bone in *The Negro Novel in America* states, "In true [Negro] Renaissance spirit, it is the folk culture, through Tea Cake, which provides the means of spiritual fulfillment." Folk tales often have a moral at the end to point out quirks in human nature or to give a new perspective on an old problem. If we look at *Their Eyes Were Watching God* as a broader type of folk tale, or perhaps folk novel, Hurston's moral is that black folks can be proud of their cultural heritage, presented in this novel by the folk culture, tales and language, and should not look to the false "gods" of the white world. And Hurston herself seems to have taken on the role of the folk trickster: She tricks the white readership by her own positive resistance—her ability to negate the values of the dominant culture in this novel without once saying it outright.

For finally, this is a novel of resistance. It is not negative in tone but it details Janie's fight for self-determination by negating the values imposed by the white culture. And although Janie's own values are not concretely articulated in the novel, they are real and fluid creations of self. Janie's resistance to the dominant culture is in itself a positive step, a life-affirming process which has evolved from the folk culture—a culture which has sought to keep its humanity in a hostile and life-opposing world. (pp. 290-91)

> *Gay Wilentz, "Defeating the False God: Janie's Self-Determination in Zora Neale Hurston's 'Their Eyes Were Watching God'," in* Faith of a (Woman) Writer, *edited by Alice Kessler-Harris and William McBrien, Greenwood Press, 1988, pp. 285-91.*

MICHAEL G. COOKE

Zora Neale Hurston has been regarded as a daughter or heir of the Harlem Renaissance. It is truer to think of her as a fully grounded and amply evolved post-Depression figure, and to think of the Harlem Renaissance as an explosive but foiled striving in the fissure between the First World War and the Depression. In the main, characters of the 1920s . . . have about them a sort of self-exhausting mobility, a rootlessness in time or space. Langston Hughes's *Not Without Laughter* may be said to resist this tendency, but at the ironic cost of merely breeding up a black bourgeois. They are as it were unwittingly *in transition*. Hurston's Janie is as subject to circumstances, as much in motion as they, but bears with her a brooding power of inevitable development. The more she is threatened, the more resourceful she becomes. The more she is deprived, the more self-sufficient she becomes. That inner stability and outer indomitability mark her off from anything that has gone before; these traits will not appear again before Alice Walker's *Meridian* in the 1970s. The confinement of this phenomenon to women's hands is perhaps telling itself, showing the capacity to bear not just children,

or the continuance of life, but to bear life itself. It is a rare phenomenon, even among women.

The story of Janie Crawford in *Their Eyes Were Watching God* (1937) is the record of black development from materialism and passivity (her grandmother's belief that money and/or white patronage are the essence of a good life) to self-respect, self-reliance, and (qualified) self-realization. Janie is said to be "full of that oldest human longing—self-revelation." The difficulty of getting a bead on that self is severe enough. Hurston renders the stock scene of racial discovery with rare delicacy, complexity, and resonance. Not social prejudice or personal meanness but *affection* leads to Janie's discovery that she is black. Without distinction, along with the white children of the family her grandmother works for, she has lived and played and been naughty and gotten "a good lickin' "; and in that spirit she is included in a photograph of the group. She looks for herself in the picture and where she is supposed to be sees only "a real dark little girl with long hair," whom she does not recognize. "Where is me? Ah don't see me," she complains. She has taken the image, perhaps the imprint, of her white companions.

It is a poignant rather than a wrenching or crushing scene; "everybody laughed" at her failure to tell herself. Her reaction to instruction ("Aw, aw! Ah'm colored") evokes further laughter. In this unusual rendition there is little of the trauma of repudiation, and a good dash of humor and consolation. But Hurston reinforces the "discovery" scene with what we may term the *nemo* syndrome: the little girl who doesn't know her own face also doesn't know her own name. "Dey all useter call me Alphabet," Janie recalls, " 'cause so many people had done named me different names." As a nickname Alphabet implies something both extravagant and defective, the elements of any name or all names without the shape or strength of one. Janie's grandmother sets forth her ambition for the child: "Ah wanted you to look upon yo'self. Ah don't want yo' feathers always crumpled by folks throwin' up things in yo' face." But Janie, as the photograph proves, can't look upon herself with recognition or confidence. In the burgeoning tradition of Afro-American literature, her grandmother's desire to see her "safe in life" resounds ominously. The desire to be "safe" has undermined every value and underscored every disaster for Irene Redfield, in Nella Larsen's *Passing.*

The source of confidence and safety her grandmother contrives harks back to the materialism we have identified in black literature, here in the form of marriage to the old farmer Logan Killicks. The deadliness of that age-old materialism, though, is intuitively grasped by Janie, who sees Killicks as "some ole skullhead in de grave yard." It is not clear whether Killicks, destroying Janie's sense of sunup and blossoming pear trees, is destroying Janie's spirit or her sexuality. The two perhaps intertwine for her. Some naturalistic romance of beginning summons her; and Killicks, who "don't take nothin' to count but sow-belly and corn-bread," can only detain and thwart her with his sixty acres of "seed p'taters" and "manure." Johnson's millionaire has shown us abstract materialism, his money detached from work or any particular source; Logan Killicks brings materialism down to earth, and shows it is not only deadly but dreary and foul.

At first blush Janie's resistance to Logan Killicks's needs and ways must seem like the old May-January pattern, and more so as she quits her kitchen to run off (bigamously) with dapper Joe Starks. But much more is afoot. Not only does Janie

Crawford-Killicks not cancel herself in the interest of materialism, but she puts materialism on the defensive. Logan Killicks is made to feel that he has no leg to stand on, and soon to feel ugly and impotent. He reacts by redoubling rather than revising his materialism, trying to make Janie into a surrogate mule on the grounds that the farm requires more and more work. When she refuses, he makes a gesture that embodies the philosophical weakness and functional despotism of the materialistic way: Logan Killicks threatens to take an ax to Janie and kill her.

With Joe Starks, Janie enters the terra incognita beyond materialism. Two pieces of data furnish preliminary clues to this world. First, Joe Starks appeals to Janie's yearning for the "far horizon," without touching her feeling for "sun-up and pollen and blooming trees," which is to say that he probably won't be able to satisfy her deepest, primary needs. And second, Joe Starks takes overnight, where Logan Killicks took at least a few weeks, to stop "making speeches with rhymes" to Janie, which is to say he probably won't be out to satisfy those needs. As things develop, Joe publicly prevents Janie from speaking in public ("her place is in de home"), and has so much to do as "Mayor-postmaster-landlord-storekeeper" of the "colored town" of Eatonville (incidentally the name of Hurston's birthplace in Florida) that he has neither time nor thought for her. "You oughta be glad," he intones, "'cause dat makes uh big woman outa you." In short, Janie finds herself in a world of paradox, where to be neglected and belittled is to become "big,"

Materialism, which in its own terms means access to possessions and comfort and luxury, has yielded to political power as a goal. (This is a notable turning point; as late as 1933, Jessie Fauset's *There is Confusion* and *Comedy, American Style* had shown materialism's tenacity.) Joe Starks's profits prove secondary to his control over other people. He will not let Janie, or anyone else, near that power, but what he is offering to Janie alone is the opportunity to be the beneficiary rather than a victim of materialism (as the other people of Eatonville are victims, disliking and even mistrusting Joe Starks but putting up with him and admiring him in return for creature comforts like street lights and a provisioned store).

Though in terms of social history what Joe Starks is doing may look necessary and desirable, the way he does it changes from bold to coercive and cold before our eyes. (William Melvin Kelley in *A Different Drummer* brings Tucker Caliban, like a Moses, to the stage where one would expect the founding of a black township, but does not delineate any way in which Eatonville's pitfalls might be avoided.) An ominous quality clings to Joe Starks's work both publicly and domestically, and Janie has neither instinct nor argument—as with Logan Killicks—to protect herself against him. Nothing brings out more sharply the harmful development of Starks's town than the images of metamorphosis that grow up around him.

The first metamorphosis is cumulative and has to do with Joe Starks's appurtenances. The townspeople see him turning into a white man, or a cento of white men, with a "promenading white" house like that of "Bishop Whipple, W. B. Jackson and the Vanderpool's," a desk "like Mr. Hill or Mr. Galloway over in Maitland," and a "gold-looking" spittoon like "his used-to-be bossman used to have in his bank . . . in Atlanta." We recall in fact that when Joe Starks first appears "he acts like [white] Mr. Washburn . . . to Janie." She intuits at once what the townsfolk will only slowly and obliquely rec-

ognize. But she is not bred to act on her intuitions. The second metamorphosis goes beyond trappings into the basic makeup of the character: "It was like seeing your sister turn into a 'gator." Strictly, this is analogy rather than metamorphosis, but the townspeople are representing a moral and social passage in Joe Starks from one state of being to another, and representing equally—such is the consciousness of analogy—a change in their own attitude.

What they do defensively and passively to Joe Starks, to keep some perspective and self-esteem, he eventually does to Janie in a forthright and hostile way. He metamorphoses her into a barnyard animal, again not literally, but as a way of expressing a social judgment: "Somebody got to think for women and chillun and chickens and cows." In point of fact, Janie has been reduced to a projection of Joe Starks's ambition, without substance or activity of her own. It is striking how little of the Eatonville section of the novel deals with her, as her existence falls into a pattern of seeing others as real, and seeming rather than being an individual.

If Janie has escaped materialism, or being "run off down a back road after *things,*" she has not advanced very far. She has attached herself to a believer in images, and it seems truer to say that she has herself become, than that she has developed, an image. Her lack of self-image in the photograph scene entailed at least a poignant humor. Her capitulation to the Killicks order of images has a grim, stifling air. Thus it is important that when Joe Starks slaps her around for presenting him a "tasteless mess" of a meal, "her image of [him] tumbled down and shattered." This clears the way for a further stage of development. She has seen mere substance in Killicks, illusory substance in Starks. Now Hurston alerts us to another level of experience in Janie by reinvoking, and exorcising, Janie's naturalistic romance:

> She had no more blossomy openings dusting pollen
> over her man, neither any glistening young fruit
> where the petals used to be. She found that she had
> a host of thoughts she had never expressed to him,
> and numerous emotions she had never let Jody
> know about.

The change that occurs in Janie is at first internal, secret; she bears her new realization a long time before she is driven, by Joe's carping insults, to retort it against him: "You big-bellies round here and put out a lot of brag, but 'tain't nothin' to it but yo' big voice. . . . Talkin' about *me* lookin' old! When you pull down yo' britches, you look lak de change uh life." As she says this in the presence of townsfolk, the whole world of illusion evaporates. In that moment, the text draws a distinction between power and possessions on the one hand and personhood on the other. Joe Starks feels that Janie has "cast down his empty armor before men. . . . They'd look with envy at *the things* and pity *the man*" (italics added). We may note the blunt assault on Joe Starks here, as opposed to the metaphorical distancing in the townsfolk's judgment. They refer to their "sister" as a "'gator" and only thus convey their shock and distress at Joe Starks's transformation. Attention is called to the transformation more strictly than to Joe himself, and they retain at least a baffled sympathy: "You keep seeing your sister in the 'gator and the 'gator in your sister, and you'd rather not." But Janie holds Joe directly before us, not so much transformed as *exposed,* and exposed as an unmanned being in a state of decay; the "change of life" pertains to a woman whose fertility is past. She not only unmans but feminizes Joe Starks.

If the townsfolk were addressing Joe, they might be said to be signifying. Janie has all but lost the patience or style to signify. She puts her husband down, and out, sexually and socially. Indeed, she does not even address Joe Starks, she *categorizes* him in the merciless synecdoche of the verb "big-bellies." The townspeople might have set the example in unmanning Joe Starks, but they use the term "big-belly" *of* rather than *to* him, and at least retain enough of a sense of human relationship to adopt the indirection of signifying and think of him as a metamorphosed sister. They say Janie is "really playin' de dozens"; in fact there is little verbal play on Joe's part, and on Janie's a deadly bluntness that seems to crash through signifying and into denunciation. She is rectifying an imbalance of power, as signifying fundamentally sets itself to do. But she is working head on, whereas signifying leads the mind to an awareness of entities and forces and values not explicit in the actual words used. The signifying gesture instigates a conclusion that it does not itself reach. To illustrate, the word *abraxas* is significant of the supreme power, yet still observes the law that the supreme power must go unnamed. The monkey never goes up into the lion's face, but signifies at a distance, from the trees.

Joe Starks experiences her action as a deliberate attempt to kill, though she only means him to live in another light. It takes him a good second to realize what her retort amounts to, and that is an omen of his unwillingness or inability to change. In imputing to her a desire to kill, he is indicating that he will die to hold on to his position. Change would be tantamount to death. He is wholly accustomed to putting her down with impunity; she takes him, and herself, by surprise when she rises up to keep from being psychically *put away*. For all her long-suffering, for all her willingness to present herself in his image, Janie will not be cancelled. Her attitude here poignantly anticipates her confrontation with the maddened, deadly, beloved Tea Cake.

It gives proof of *her* mind's going beyond images, beyond credulity, that when Joe Starks calls in a conjure man she can withstand that worthy's manipulation of the townspeople's minds. Both materialism and image-bearing are past for Janie. Before she announces Joe Starks's death to the waiting townspeople (the conjurer can neither harm Janie nor help her husband, unlike the Chesnutt pattern of a scant four decades earlier), Janie looks at herself in the mirror, and recognizes herself, though changed, and approves of herself. For the first time in her life, from the childhood photograph through the dreaminess under the pear tree to the coercive facade of life as Joe Starks's mate, image and substance fuse, so that image as such loses its force. When she lets down her rich hair that Joe had jealously obliged her to bind up, she is asserting not only the rightness of her beauty and her confidence in it, but also the rightness of her self. Janie takes a place in the long tradition, from the Bible to *La Femme du Boulanger,* of expressing inner freedom by freeing the confined hair. To evaluate this freedom, let us look at what Janie has been through.

Despite the marked differences in manner and purpose among them, the three principal persons in Janie's life to this point, her grandmother, her aged-farmer husband and then her entrepreneur-politician husband, all make the same demand on her: to cancel herself. She appears to yield to her grandmother's devotion and emotion, and again to Joe Starks's presence and rhetoric, but at bottom she holds fast to something as unknown as indomitable.

That "something" is her freedom, or her ability as a forty-year-old widow who has been largely silenced and set aside to move with eloquence and direction into the town and beyond it into the future. Let us note that she is not bursting out afresh and full of vigor from a comatose state, like the sleeping beauty. Rather she has been tacitly prepared to cope by her entire experience since puberty, in that her experience with her grandmother and both her husbands has been one of essential *solitude*. She has not joined or shared with anyone. Her life has been an unconscious preparation for being by herself. Only now she is aware of it, and herself links freedom and solitude: "She liked being lonesome for a change. This freedom feeling was fine."

At this stage Janie's solitude is simple, that is, uncomplicated by desire or deficiency, and her freedom is rudimentary—it is freedom from falsehood or obstacles, but without any positive expression or form. Her relationship with Vergible Woods, "Tea Cake," first gives Janie to herself by confirming and eliciting her powers, physical and social and moral. There is a dash of sentimentality or hyperbole in the treatment . . . but Janie and Tea Cake share something with all the propriety of what is genuine and all the unorthodoxy (in relative age, wealth, position) of what is original. The upshot of the relationship is to give form to Janie's freedom while paradoxically also giving depth and force to her solitude.

Janie and Tea Cake occupy a world of applied pastoral, with a dash of the Wife of Bath—that is, their feelings are elevated and lovely, but their setting is a rather realistic environment of gambling and railroad workers and "money and fun and foolishness." In this situation Janie, who has withstood two husbands and considerable social pressure, submits herself wholly to Tea Cake, the way Chaucer's Wife gives "maistrie" to her devoted, young, fifth husband. Like the Wife of Bath, Janie fulfills herself by surrendering herself, in that surrendering to one who surrenders to her causes the fiction of domination to disappear. . . . (pp. 71-9)

The violence and unpredictability that from the outset dwell on the edge of the relationship between Janie and Tea Cake slowly close in, culminating in the hurricane and Tea Cake's being bitten by a rabid dog from which he is trying to save Janie. They learn too late that he has been infected. It is a cruel irony that he, who had a pattern of abrupt disappearances and who has taught Janie a legitimate faith in him absent, cannot stand to have her out of his sight. The symptom of his illness is the symptom of his love gone mad. A sense of irony becomes almost overwhelming when Tea Cake, paranoid in illness, comes at Janie with a gun and is shot in horrified self-defense by the woman he has lovingly taught to shoot. And yet the final air of the novel is neither tragic nor melodramatic.

Beginning in accidental solitude with her grandmother, and passing to accepted solitude with Logan Killicks and Joe Starks, Janie ends in what may best be called accomplished solitude. Tea Cake, part bean-planter and part happy-go-lucky gambler, has shown her not only the far horizon Joe Starks promised but also sunup and pear trees in bloom, which her instinctive mind had desired: "he could be a bee to a . . . pear-tree blossom in the spring." Life has shown her the rest, including the need to kill even the beloved for the sake of life. Above all, Tea Cake and life together have shown her herself, *Janie* (Crawford and Killicks and Starks and Woods are inadequate surnames, appendages). And Janie is a woman with (1) the strength to survive and to even forgive the slanderers (first Tea Cake's friends in "De Muck" and then her own friends back in Eatonville) who would belie and befoul her time with Tea Cake; and (2) the command and lucidity before experience to see that "Love is lak de sea. It's uh movin' thing, but still and all, it takes its shape from de shore it meets, and it's different with every shore."

Finally, Janie is a woman with power enough to transcend her two greatest ambitions: to have a man like Tea Cake and to have the gift of ready speech. Perhaps she has the first transcendence forced upon her, but that takes little away from the merit of being able to sit, grieving over killing and being nearly killed by Tea Cake, and thanking him "for giving her the chance for loving service." She is . . . seeing things steadily and seeing them whole. The second transcendence, of silence, is again bathed in paradox: even as she resorts to words to tell her story, Janie can say of the word-mongers:

> Talkin' don't amount tuh uh hill uh beans when
> yuh can't do nothin' else. And listenin' tuh dat kind
> uh talk [the slanderers] is jus' lak openin' yo' mouth
> and lettin' de moon shine down yo' throat.

(pp. 80-1)

To say that Janie has reached a state of accomplished solitude is to recognize both the progress she has made in personal development and the denial she encounters in the social sphere. Her home is a symbol of her condition, free and proud and yet radically unshared. She is not disposed to come out to the community, and the townsfolk are in one sense afraid and in another unfit to come in to her. Pheoby (whose name, as a variant of Phoebus, may be meant to convey light) comes in, but she does not carry word, or light, back out. The reverence she comes to feel for Janie will if anything baffle the community, since her very reverence will prevent her from profanely broadcasting the story. Pheoby confirms rather than offsets Janie's solitude. Hers has become an inner world, where all light concentrates on Janie: "The light in her hand was like a spark of sun-stuff washing her face in fire."

Janie's transcendence of Joe Starks's image-world is tacitly reaffirmed in the closing scenes of *Their Eyes.* She remains wholly unconcerned about the image the townsfolk have of her. She neither courts nor defies their opinion. Her life is beyond that. Pheoby will not be a sunrise for the new Janie, for that Janie, while unable to express herself at large, cannot be reduced to a superficial image. (p. 84)

> *Michael G. Cooke, "Solitude: The Beginnings of Self-Realization in Zora Neale Hurston, Richard Wright, and Ralph Ellison," in his* Afro-American Literature in the Twentieth Century: The Achievement of Intimacy, *Yale University Press, 1984, pp. 71-109.*

DONALD R. MARKS

In Zora Neale Hurston's second novel, *Their Eyes Were Watching God,* Janie, the central character, is involved in four consecutive love relationships: her first sexual encounter with Johnny Taylor, her first marriage to Logan Killicks, and her subsequent marriages to Joe Starks and Vergible "Tea Cake" Woods. These successive relationships provide the novel's structure, for each new lover brings about both a change in setting and a new stage in the story of Janie's life. Though each of the relationships is different from the others,

there are two in which Janie is passionately involved, her short-lived romance with Johnny Taylor and her marriage to Tea Cake, and two in which she is restricted and unhappy, her marriages to Logan Killicks and Joe Starks. Thus, Janie's four loves fall into two categories: those of passion and those of control.

Each category is characterized by particular tropes and sign structures. To the passionate relationships Hurston attaches metaphors of natural fertility and sexuality, whereas she associates control relationships with physical deformity, decay, and technological, non-sexual productivity. Also, the two different types of relationships allow Janie two kinds of interaction with her community. These are signified by the opposing categories of work and play. Johnny Taylor and, more significantly, Tea Cake represent opportunity for Janie to play: in other words, to move out from herself and participate meaningfully in an organic community. Logan Killicks and Joe Starks remove her from genuine communal activity and require her to work, or to support the class distinctions of bourgeois capitalism.

Ultimately, Janie's relationships of passion and control are themselves sign structures signifying two conflicting ideological positions. The ideology signified by her passionate relationships endorses an essentially organicist vision of society. In the novel, this vision takes the form of Tea Cake's community "on the 'Glades." Though it occurs within a hierarchical order, this organic community retains a high degree of autonomy and is free of the legislative power structures characteristic of a mechanistic society. The other ideological position, signified by Janie's relationships of control, reinforces the dominant social structure, placing value on social mechanisms, technological progress, and the accumulation of wealth and power. It is this mechanistic ideology which informs Hurston's portrayal of Joe Starks' Eatonville.

Hurston clearly accepts the organicist ideology of romantic pastoralism over the mechanistic one of bourgeois capitalism, for it is with Tea Cake in the community "on the muck" that Janie is most content. Yet both ideological positions are undercut by the violence the author finds inherent in the heterosexual relationships she uses to represent them. Even in what Hurston considers the most viable organic community, sexual violence is accepted and justified as a sign of passion. It is not until Janie has killed Tea Cake and all of her lovers are out of the novel that she is able to find real peace and independence. (p. 152)

In the love relationships which signify a mechanistic political ideology, tropes of organic decay and technological progress are attached to men who achieve places of respect in their communities parallel to those considered respectable by the capitalistic white society. To Janie, Logan Killicks " 'look like some old skullhead in de grave yard.' " The very thought of marrying him is "desecrating" to Janie's association of love with the pear tree blossom. Killicks even smells as though he were decaying; Janie would " 'ruther be shot wid tacks then tuh turn over in de bed . . . whilst he is in dere.' " Yet, as far as Janie's grandmother is concerned, Killicks is a highly respectable man. Her grandmother considers the marriage as an opportunity for Janie to take an upward step on the local social ladder: " 'If you don't want him you sho oughta. Heah you is wid de onliest organ in town, amongst colored folks, in yo' parlor. Got a house bought and paid for and sixty acres uh land right on de big road. . . .' " Killicks is an acceptable husband not because Janie is in love with him, but because he is landed and financially sound and has begun to acquire possessions which are somewhat technologically sophisticated.

Joe Starks presents the opportunity for Janie to escape from Logan Killicks, but his subsequent relationships with her is one of control rather than passion. . . . Starks, like Killicks, is associated with death and decay. Using "the distended belly" of Matt Bonner's mule for his "platform," Starks presides, mayorally, over the animal's mock funeral. And Hurston, in turn, connects the mule's death with the mayor's, and the mayor and his social system with a flock of buzzards that descends, hierarchically, on the mule's carcass, each bird waiting for the leader to perform a mock funeral, just as Starks has done with the people of his town. The buzzards proclaim that the mule's death was caused by " 'Bare, bare fat.' " Ironically, this is Starks' condition before his death. . . . Starks' death of festering stagnation sets his way of life and the ideology he both espouses and signifies in direct opposition to Janie's vision of love as a fertile, blossoming, organic process.

Like Killicks, Starks holds a position of power and respect in his community. Immediately upon his arrival in Eatonville, he establishes himself as mayor and begins to structure a town centered around himself and his store. . . . In addition to social mechanisms, Starks brings technological advances to Eatonville, the most exemplary being the street lamp which signifies his attempt to govern natural processes. Yet the townspeople frequently compare his achievements and his powers to those of the whites rather than to those of the prophets. " 'All he got he done made it offa de rest of us,' " Sim Jones says. " 'He didn't have all dat when he come here.' " When Starks orders that a ditch be dug to drain the street in front of his store, the townspeople "murmur hotly about slavery being over," and his residence makes the rest of the town look "like servants' quarters surrounding the 'big house.' " Hurston clearly considers the kind of social system Starks establishes to be as oppressive and economically unbalanced as that imposed by white society.

Janie's relationships of control with Logan Killicks and Joe Starks require her to base her life on labor and material production rather than on play and sexuality. They force her to withdraw from the community in which she lives to a position of "honor and respect." This removal is, ultimately, a form of imprisonment which leads to her loneliness and desire to be free of the men with whom she is involved. Killicks takes " 'nothin' to count but sow-belly and corn-bread.' " He places more importance on maintaining the farm than on sustaining his marriage. " 'A whole lot of mens will grin in yo' face,' " he tells Janie, " 'but dey ain't gwine tuh work and feed yuh.' " Though Killicks provides for both Janie and himself during the first months of their marriage, he gradually begins to expect her to do a share of the labor.

> Long before the year was up, Janie noticed that her husband had stopped talking in rhymes to her. He had ceased to wonder at her long black hair and finger it. Six months back he had told her, "If Ah kin haul de wood heah and chop it up fuh yuh, look lak you oughta be able tuh tote it inside. Mah fust wife never bothered me 'bout choppin' no wood nohow. She'd grab dat ax and sling chips lak uh man. You done been spoilt rotten."

Before Janie leaves him for Joe Starks, Killicks proposes that she, like him, could run a plow: " '. . . Ah needs two mules

dis yeah. Taters is goin' tuh be taters in de fall. Bringin' big prices. Ah aims tuh run two plows, and dis man Ah'm talkin' 'bout is got uh mule all gentled up so even uh woman kin handle 'im.' " Though Killicks considers what he has done to improve Janie's social and economic status a favor, claiming that he has taken her from " 'de white folks back-yard,' " his lack of play and passion makes her feel isolated and confined. Janie is removed from her home and the community centered around her grandmother in order to work on Killicks' land. For her, "It was a lonesome place like a stump in the middle of the woods where nobody had ever been."

Joe Starks also expresses an intolerance for playfulness and places more value on social position and monetary gain than on romance. He complains that his people should " 'get mo' business in 'em and not spend so much time on foolishness.' " His emphasis on work and his desire to provide Janie with a position of respect within the community inhibits the couple's sexuality:

> When it was all over that night in bed Jody asked Janie, "Well, honey, how you lak bein' Mrs. Mayor?"
>
> "It's all right Ah reckon, but don't yuh think it keeps us in uh kinda strain?"
>
> "Strain? You mean de cookin' and waitin' on folks?"
>
> "Naw, Jody, it jus' looks lak it keeps us in some way we ain't natural wid one 'nother. You'se always off talkin' and fixin' things, and Ah feels lak Ah'm jus' markin' time. Hope it soon gits over."
>
> "Over, Janie? I god, Ah ain't even started good. Ah told you in de very first beginnin' dat Ah aimed tuh be uh big voice. You oughta be glad, 'cause dat makes uh big woman outa you."
>
> A feeling of coldness and fear took hold of her. She felt far away from things and lonely.

Joe's behavior feels unnatural to Janie and makes her life seem as empty and mechanical as "markin' time." Later in their marriage, Joe's unceasing demand for her submission stifles the couple's sexuality completely:

> He wanted her submission and he'd keep on fighting until he felt he had it.
>
> So gradually, she pressed her teeth together and learned to hush. The spirit of the marriage left the bedroom and took to living in the parlor. . . . The bed was no longer a daisy-field for her and Joe to play in. It was a place where she went and laid down when she was sleepy and tired.

Starks' quest for marital and social dominance also deprives Janie of meaningful communal interaction. When the townspeople gather outside his store, Janie is forbidden to join in the conversation or tell stories of her own; as the mayor's wife she is to remain above the activities of the commoners:

> Janie loved the conversation and sometimes she thought up good stories on the mule, but Joe had forbidden her to indulge. He didn't want her talking after such trashy people. . . . when Lige or Sam or Walter or some of the other big picture talkers were using a side of the world for a canvas, Joe would hustle her off inside the store to sell something. Look like he took pleasure in doing it.

Aside from Joe's overt efforts to separate Janie from the townspeople, the very fact that she holds a position of authority in a hierarchical social structure divides her from the remainder of the community: "The wife of the Mayor was not just another woman as she had supposed. She slept with authority and so she was part of it in the town mind. She couldn't get but so close to them in spirit."

Hurston clearly finds the materialistic, capitalistic ideology which Starks represents to be destructive of life and love. For Janie, her work in the store is a "waste of time and life." The "head-rag" which "irk[s] her endlessly" and which Starks insists she wear while working, signifies Janie's confinement both in the store and in her marriage.

Janie's two passionate relationships, which signify Hurston's organicist ideology, are characterized by tropes of new life and natural fertility. The men with whom Janie is passionately involved, Johnny Taylor and Tea Cake, are considered "shiftless" and irresponsible by other members of the community. Neither has property or social power or possesses the kind of ambition exhibited by Logan Killicks and Joe Starks. Since Janie's encounter with Johnny Taylor is extremely short-lived, an analysis of the relationships in this category must rely almost wholly on an understanding of Janie's life with Tea Cake. Tea Cake, unlike Killicks or Starks, is not associated with social order, but rather with rituals of disorder, such as gaming, fighting, gambling, and celebrating. These rituals of disorder take place within a hierarchically ordered social system, the feudalistic landowner-tenant laborer system of the Everglades. Rather than signifying revolutionary action, the rituals distance Tea Cake, Janie, and the community with which they are involved from the broader hierarchical structure within which they exist. Janie's relationship with Tea Cake allows her the freedom to live meaningfully in a community which is not concerned with emulating the social mechanisms of a capitalistic society. . . .

Janie's first romantic relationship is described through an extension of the garden metaphor: "Through the pollinated air she saw a glorious being coming up the road. In her former blindness she had known him as shiftless Johnny Taylor, tall and lean. That was before the golden dust of pollen had beglamored his rags and her eyes." (p. 154)

Both Johnny Taylor and Tea Cake are characterized by a physical and natural beauty which, for Janie, is mythic in its power. Yet other members of her community do not consider these men to be either powerful or respectable. Janie herself has always thought of Johnny Taylor as "shiftless," and before his clothes are "beglamored" with the "pollinated air," he is dressed in rags. Janie's grandmother complains that Johnny Taylor is beneath her granddaughter in the community's social hierarchy: " 'Ah don't want no trashy nigger, no breath-and-britches, lak Johnny Taylor usin' yo' body to wipe his foots on.' " The people of Eatonville assume that Tea Cake is " 'spendin' on her now in order tuh make her spend on him later.' " Sam and Pheoby Watson would prefer that Janie marry a well-to-do undertaker—another symbol of death attached to bourgeois social values—in order to protect the estate Starks has built for her.

Tea Cake's behavior is antithetical to Logan Killicks' and Joe Starks'; he is interested in play rather than work, in spending and dispersing any wealth he has rather than accumulating more. When he finds his new wife has two hundred dollars, Tea Cake, instead of buying land or saving the money, uses it to throw a barbecue and dance party: " . . . pretty soon he made up his mind to spend some of it. He never had had his hand on so much money before in his life, so he made up his mind to see how it felt to be a millionaire. They went on out to Callahan round the railroad shops and he decided to give a big chicken and macaroni supper that night, free to all.' " Tea Cake not only distributes his newly acquired wealth, he also spends it on himself. . . . He spends the money on a guitar, an instrument of play to be used for gatherings and dances. Rather than accumulating property and distinguishing himself from the remainder of society, Tea Cake concerns himself with active participation in communal rituals of disorder. He even earns money through an anti-structural means, gambling: " ' . . . round four o'clock,' " he tells Janie, " 'Ah had done cleaned 'em out complete—all except two men dat got up and left while dey had money for groceries, and one man dat wuz lucky. Then Ah rose tuh bid them good-bye agin. None of 'em didn't lak it, but dey all realized it wuz fair. Ah had done give 'em a fair chance.' " By living off his dice Tea Cake subverts the work-based economic structure of capitalist society and sets up his own structure based on the rules of play: " 'it wuz fair.' " Tea Cake is no revolutionary, but he does not subscribe to the work ethic in the way that Joe Starks and Logan Killicks do.

Tea Cake's liberality allows Janie greater freedom to participate in her community than do her more rigid relationships with Killicks and Starks. Starks believes his people should spend less time on "foolishness." Tea Cake offers Janie the opportunity to be "foolish" and to break the constraints which Starks and his position of authority impose upon her. The first service Tea Cake performs for Janie is to teach her how to play checkers: "He set it up and began to show her and she found herself glowing inside. Somebody wanted her to play. Somebody thought it natural for her to play. That was even nice." Janie's life with Tea Cake in the Everglades is centered around leisure and festivity as opposed to work and commerce.

> Sometimes Janie would think of the old days in the big white house and the store and laugh to herself. What if Eatonville could see her now in her blue denim overalls and heavy shoes? The crowd of people around her and a dice game on her floor! . . . The men held big arguments here like they used to do on the store porch. Only here, she could listen and laugh and even talk some herself if she wanted to. She got so she could tell big stories herself from listening to the rest. Because she loved to hear it, and the men loved to hear themselves, they would "woof " and "boogerboo" around the games to the limit. No matter how rough it was, people seldom got mad, because everything was done for a laugh.
>
> (pp. 154-55)

The community "on the 'Glades," though it exists within the essentially feudalistic framework of the landowner-tenant laborer system, is not itself hierarchically structured. People do not establish permanent residences or aspire to attain positions of political power. The community is in a constant state of flux; the people are "permanent transients with no attachments." At the start of the working season, "they came in wagons from way up in Georgia and they came in truckloads from east, west, north and south." At the close of the season the " . . . people went away like they had come—in droves." Economic stability and technological progress are less important to the people "on the muck" than "dancing, fighting, singing, crying, laughing, winning and losing love every hour."

Work all day for money, fight all night for love." . . . This is the life "on the muck," and it is this life which Janie's passionate relationship with Tea Cake affirms. Hurston romanticizes the community on the Everglades as a kind of brotherhood that is free of the constraints and class divisions imposed by a mechanistic, capitalistic society like that of Eatonville.

The fact that the farming and, to an extent, the lives of the workers "on the 'Glades" are directed by white overseers is a notable absence in the text. It appears that Hurston does not indict the bosses and landowners because the community she is concerned with is almost oblivious to them: "Men made big fires and fifty or sixty men slept around each fire. But they had to pay the man whose land they slept on. He ran the fire just like his boarding place—for pay. But nobody cared. They made good money, even to the children. So they spent good money. Next month and next year were other times. No need to mix them up with the present." The people in the community, and Hurston herself, do not seem concerned with the inequity of the economic situation, but rather with the possibilities for play and interaction found on the Everglades. The last lines of the above quotation seem to be a particularly euphemistic way of saying that the people "on the muck" have no future.

Hurston does have a tendency to romanticize agrarian communities according to a pastoral ideal. In her autobiography *Dust Tracks on a Road,* she rationalizes away even the racism of a white man who obviously stands for her version of that ideal: "I knew without being told that he was not talking about my race when he advised me not to be a nigger. He was talking about class rather than race. He frequently gave money to Negro schools." In spite of the man's blatant racism, Hurston attributes mythic powers and "virtues" to him:

> He was an accumulating man, a good provider, paid his debts and told the truth. Those were all the virtues the community expected. Any more than that would not have been appreciated. He could ride like a centaur, swim long distances, shoot straight with either pistol or guns, and he allowed no man to give him the lie to his face. He was supposed to be so tough, it was said that he once was struck by lightning and was not even knocked off his feet, but the lightning went off through the woods limping. Nobody found any fault with a man like that in a country where personal strength and courage were the highest virtues. People were supposed to take care of themselves without whining.

This man actively participates in the community, bringing the Hurstons food and helping to deliver Zora. However, in endorsing the man and the rugged, non-mechanistic social order he supports, Hurston implicitly accepts his racist views. Relatedly, she does not mention that the feudalistic landowner-tenant laborer system "on the muck" is inherently racist and as economically unbalanced as the capitalism of Joe Starks, which she actively derides.

The organicist ideology signified by Janie's expansive love for Tea Cake is clearly Hurston's, and the community of the 'Glades corresponds to the kind of social order she apparently endorses, yet the novel's drama does not stop there. Janie and Tea Cake, though they are very much in love, have a series of violent quarrels fueled by jealousies. When Tea Cake is bitten by a rabid dog and madness inflames his already violent temper, Janie is forced to kill him in order to survive. In

doing this, Janie achieves for the first time independence from a heterosexual relationship and, subsequently, her lasting, personal peace.

In her "Foreword" to the novel, Sherley Anne Williams argues that "Zora was evidently unable to satisfactorily define herself in a continuing relationship with a man, whereas such definition is the essence of Janie's romantic vision. . . ." I would argue that Janie, as well as Hurston, is unable to come to terms with the violence Hurston finds inherent in heterosexual relationships. However, I would agree that such a relationship is essential to "Janie's romantic vision." A heterosexual relationship is also an essential signifier of the natural process in Hurston's organicist vision; and this, in part, accounts for the novel's metaphoric resolution.

Throughout the novel Hurston links sexuality with the threat of violence. When Janie first becomes aware of love and marriage in her grandmother's garden, she feels "a pain remorseless sweet." Her first kiss with Johnny Taylor is described as "lacerating." Joe Starks, at one point in their marriage, slaps Janie's face "until she had a ringing sound in her ears." When Tea Cake accompanies her home from Starks' store for the first time, Janie, becomes keenly aware of the danger involved: "Janie was halfway down the palm-lined walk before she had a thought for her safety. Maybe this strange man was up to something! But it was no place to show her fear there in the darkness between the house and the store. He had hold of her arm too."

For Hurston, violence is an ever-present, imminent possibility in passionate love relationships. In *Dust Tracks on a Road,* she presents the following account of a violent quarrel with her lover:

> The terrible thing was that we could never leave each other alone, nor compromise. Let me seem too cordial with any male and something was going to happen. Just let him smile too broad at any woman, and no sooner did we get inside my door than the war was on! One night (I didn't decide this) something primitive inside me tore past the barriers and before I realized it I had slapped his face. That was a mistake. He was still smoldering from an incident a week old. A fellow had met us on Seventh Avenue and kissed me on my cheek. Just one of those casual things, but it had burned up A.W.P. So I had unknowingly given him an opening he had been praying for. He paid me off then and there with interest. No broken bone, you understand, and no black eyes. I realized afterwards that my hot head could tell me to beat him, but it would cost me something. I would have to bring head to get head. I couldn't get his and leave mine locked up in the dresser-drawer.

This passage is rife with rationalizations and justifications for violent behavior. "Something primitive inside" Hurston is the cause for her striking him. She attributes the instability of heterosexual relationships to forces beyond the control of the people involved. "No broken bone, you understand, no black eyes" sounds very much like the justification given for Tea Cake's beating of Janie: "No brutal beating at all." Though she attempts to minimize its gravity, Hurston clearly does find an inherent violence in passionate love relationships. The incident which excites their fight seems triflingly small, and her lover has been "smoldering" for a week, looking for an "opening," a reason to justify an act of violence. As Hurston says at the close of the chapter entitled "Love" in *Dust Tracks on a Road,* "maybe the old Negro folk rhyme tells all there is to know: 'Love is a funny thing; Love is a blossom; If you want your finger bit, poke it at a possum.' "

For Hurston to romanticize Tea Cake's love for Janie, to make it free of the violence she observes in sexuality, would be to give the lie to her own experience of male-dominated, periodically violent love relationships. Yet the violence of Janie's relationships does not allow her to be at peace with herself and the world. Also, the tension it produces undercuts Hurston's vision of community as a harmonious organic process. Thus, the author rationalizes Tea Cake's violence into an appropriate form of behavior through the acceptance of the supposition that it is not committed out of malice but out of love or madness. When Tea Cake, spurred on by the insinuations of Mrs. Turner, beats Janie out of jealousy, Hurston justifies it as a way for Tea Cake to relieve his anxieties: "When Mrs. Turner's brother came and she brought him over to be introduced, Tea Cake had a brainstorm. Before the week was over he had whipped Janie. Not because her behavior justified his jealousy, but it relieved that awful fear inside him. Being able to whip her assured him in possession. No brutal beating at all. He just slapped her around a bit to show he was boss." Hurston further rationalizes Tea Cake's behavior by having other characters, both men and women, enviously view the beating as something erotic, as a sign of passion and strength they themselves do not have: "Everybody talked about it the next day in the fields. It aroused a sort of envy in both men and women. The way he petted and pampered her as if those two or three face slaps had nearly killed her made the women see visions and the helpless way she hung on him made men dream dreams."

The bite from the rabid dog and Tea Cake's ensuing illness are plot contrivances Hurston uses in order to justify his final fit of jealousy and his death. To have Tea Cake become enraged to the point of killing Janie without the factor of madness would make all hetrosexual unions seem impossible, just as would Janie's killing or leaving him for a more mundane reason. As it happens, Hurston can remove the threat of violence and, through the use of metaphor, provide both an aesthetic and ideological resolution for the novel: "Tea Cake with the sun for a shawl. Of course he wasn't dead. He could never be dead until she herself had finished feeling and thinking. The kiss of his memory made pictures of love and light against the wall. Here was peace." Janie achieves her lasting peace in the abiding (figurative) presence of Tea Cake, who lives on in her consciousness, and Hurston retains the possibility of heterosexual union which is essential to the organicist vision she endorses.

There is, however, one condition other than freedom from the violence Hurston finds in heterosexual relationships which must be met in order for Janie to attain her lasting peace. She must leave the community "on the muck" and return alone to her own room in her own house to live within her own world, indeed, within her own consciousness. Janie's withdrawal from the community is necessitated by Hurston's own inability to find an adequate physical locus for her organicism. Of the social structures represented in the novel, the community "on the muck" is the one which Hurston portrays as the most acceptable and "natural." It supports a meaningful folk culture and provides Janie with the freedom to live rather than the duty to work. Yet it is also a community which "fights all night for love," and which finds a husband's beating of his wife to be romantic and erotic. Thus, if Janie retains a "romantic vision" of a non-violent heterosexual relationship, she must do so out of the context of even the most viable folk community. A nonviolent heterosexual relationship, which for Janie is the ideal state and for Hurston the signifier of an organic process, is not found, ultimately, in a particular kind of community but in a particular kind of consciousness.

Janie is unable to remain in the Everglades after Tea Cake's death because, for her, meaning has been shifted from the external world to her feelings and memories: "They begged her to stay on with them and she had stayed for a few weeks to keep them from feeling bad. But the muck meant Tea Cake and Tea Cake wasn't there. So it was just a great expanse of black mud." Tea Cake, once relegated to Janie's memories, comes to signify a harmonious heterosexual relationship free of violence. He and what he signifies now abide only in Janie's thoughts and feelings. For Janie, all meaning has been divorced from the landscape and can now be found only in her consciousness. The only possession Janie carries with her when she leaves the 'Glades is a packet of seeds. The metaphorical connection with Hurston's organicism is obvious, but what is more important is Janie's motivation for taking them:

> She had given away everything in their little house except a package of seed that Tea Cake had bought to plant. . . . The seeds reminded Janie of Tea Cake more than anything else because he was always planting things. She noticed them on the kitchen shelf when she came home from the funeral and had put them in her breast pocket. Now that she was home, she meant to plant them for remembrance.

The seeds are significant because they function as a remembrance; they are not important in and of themselves but only in their relationship to Janie's consciousness.

When Janie returns to Eatonville she does not attempt to integrate herself into the community once defined by Joe Starks. Rather, after telling her tale to Pheoby, she chooses to dwell alone. Upon her arrival in Eatonville, she does not stop to join the group of men and women on the Watsons' porch as "they became lords of sounds and lesser things. They passed nations through their mouths." "When she got to where they were she turned her face on the bander log and spoke. They scrambled a noisy 'good evenin' ' and left their mouths setting open and their ears full of hope. Her speech was pleasant enough, but she kept walking straight on to her gate. The porch couldn't talk for looking." Though Janie would once have longed to join this kind of "lyin' session," similar to the ones which take place at Joe Starks' store, she continues on alone.

After Janie tells Pheoby her story, she cautions her not to be too harsh on the people of the community for what they say, for they do not speak from experience and in the way that Janie herself does. . . . Janie, unlike "de rest of 'em," has *been* there and *knows.* She has found out about living for herself and now holds her experience within her consciousness as knowledge. This separates her and the story she tells from the people of the community and the tales they create. After this counsel there is a "finished silence" between Pheoby and Janie. She has told her tale, and there is nothing left to say. When Pheoby leaves, Janie makes sure that "everything around downstairs was shut and fastened." Her means of communicating with others is closed, and she retreats to her bedroom: "Now, in her room, the place tasted fresh again. The wind through the open windows had broomed out all the fetid feeling of absence and nothingness. She closed in and sat down. Combing the road-dust out of her hair. Thinking." With the rest of the world shut out in this way, Janie communes with her "living" memory of Tea Cake. In her solitude she discovers and relives her past: "She pulled in her horizon like a great fish-net. Pulled it from around the waist of the world and draped it over her shoulder. So much of life in its meshes! She called in her soul to come and see." The expanse of Janie's life, "her horizon," is metaphorically "pulled in" and wrapped about her. Her meaningful communication from this point on will be with herself, her feelings, her memories, and her soul.

Janie's achievement of a personal vision, a sort of organic wholeness existing only in consciousness and divorced from any physical locus, is a device which provides both an aesthetic and ideological resolution for the novel. However, it provides an ideological resolution only in the sense that it disguises Hurston's own ideological dilemma.

Rather than endorse a revolutionary ideology that would produce a vision of society in which a nonviolent, heterosexual relationship would be possible, Hurston endorses the reactionary organicist ideology, then relegates the signifier of this ideology (Tea Cake) to (Janie's) consciousness. As a result of this transposition, meaning in Janie's life exists solely in her consciousness, distinct from any outside community. This metaphoric resolution provides Hurston with the heterosexual relationship which is necessary for her view of the world as a harmonious organic process. At the same time, this synthetic resolution mystifies Hurston's inability to find an ideological position that will produce a vision of community not predicated upon violence and male domination. In place of a more viable vision of society than either capitalism or romantic pastoralism can provide, Hurston asserts that human beings can find their ultimate peace outside the physical world. For Janie, the locus for this peace is the isolated, experienced consciousness. (pp. 155-57)

> *Donald R. Marks, "Sex, Violence, and Organic Consciousness in Zora Neale Hurston's 'Their Eyes Were Watching God',"* in Black American Literature Forum, *Vol. 19, No. 4, Winter, 1985, pp. 152-57.*

CLAIRE CRABTREE

Critics have largely neglected or misunderstood Hurston's conscious use of traditional or "folk" materials in . . . [*Their Eyes Were Watching God*]. Further, most readers find the ending of the novel dissonant and see it as weakening the work; while a recognition of the uses Hurston intended for traditional materials will not thoroughly justify her authorial decisions, it can help to explain the apparent weakness of the ending and to show that the novel presents a rhetoric of authenticity—an implicit assertion that it represents "real" black life—introduced initially by the storytelling frame and reinforced by various techniques throughout the novel.

It may be useful to delineate four aspects of the transformation of folk material into the body of the tale of Janie Crawford's journey through three marriages to a final position of self-realization. They are: Hurston's use of the storytelling "frame" of the story as well as of other conventions from oral

tradition; her use of the language, metaphor and symbol of a specific rural community; her incorporation of certain kinds of gaming and other performances as incidents within the narrative; and her attempt to situate the narrative voice in a collective folk consciousness toward the end of the book. Folklore is, in fact, so thoroughly integrated into the fabric of the novel as to be inextricably bound to the themes of feminism and Black self-determination which Hurston is exploring. The value of the folk experience is itself as strong an assertion of the novel as the need of Blacks for self-determination and the right of women to be autonomous.

The story of Janie Crawford's journey to autonomy and spiritual liberation is told to her friend Pheoby in the form of a reminiscence when, as the book opens, Janie returns to her home after an absence of a year and a half and the recent death of her third husband, Tea Cake. Janie is the tale-teller and her telling of the story is a consciously artistic act, one in which she imposes order and meaning on the material of her life. The story Janie tells is an intimate communication between the two friends, with Janie depending on Pheoby "for a good thought," that is, for a sympathetic hearing, on the basis of their having been "kissin' friends for twenty years." It is understood that Pheoby will later interpret Janie's story for the curious and not entirely well-meaning townspeople in whom Janie disdains to confide. Janie had left the town with her younger husband over a year before and now, returning in overalls, she finds the townspeople ready to think she has been thrown over by her husband.

Hurston presents Janie's story within a storytelling frame, but equally significant, as a story that is designed to be repeated. In folkloristic terms, Janie's story is a memorate or true experience narrative placed within a fictional framework but nonetheless privileging itself and asserting its own authenticity. The form of a folktale is in part determined by its replicability; it must be developed through a series of events that can be recalled and reconstructed by various tellers. Janie starts her story with events from her early life and traces her life journey through specific, clearly delineated events. For each situation and feeling state there is a symbol which is both commonplace and rich with meaning, such as Tea Cake's guitar and Janie's apron, headrag and overalls. Such symbols are easy to recall and, like the elements of folktales, serve as pegs upon which the teller and listener can each hang the narrative strands. Since Hurston was a skilled folklorist, it seems likely that her use of the storytelling frame is part of a rhetorical strategy through which she attempts to persuade her readers that the novel does in fact duplicate the experience of Black life, including oral traditions of specific Black communities. The novel both approaches and avoids the novelistic technique of the story within a story: it is self-reflective in that it draws attention to the process of telling, yet deflects the reader's attention from the writing process to the telling process and thus from an awareness of its fictional nature to an illusion of immersion in "real" folk experience. The reader is implicitly discounted as the audience of the novel in favor of the "real" audience, Pheoby and the townspeople. The material of Janie's narrative will become part of the gossip that enlivens the front porch talk sessions that form the backbone of the town of Eatonville's social life.

Hurston begins Janie's narrative a few pages into the book with her first-person account of incidents from Janie's early childhood. But after the initial incidents, Hurston eases into a third-person narrative:

Pheoby's hungry listening helped Janie to tell her story. So she went on thinking back to her young years and explaining them to her friend in soft, easy phrases while all around the house, the night time put on flesh and blackness.

She thought awhile and decided that her conscious life had commenced at Nanny's gate.

This narrative explanation replaces part of the story. The author reframes the story by intruding and in so doing comments on the importance of the listener to the event.

Within the storytelling frame Janie's life is depicted as a spiritual journey, in Janie's words, a journey to the horizon and back as "a delegate to de big 'ssociation of life . . . De Grand Lodge, de big convention of livin.' " Janie follows a pattern familiar to folklorists of a young person's journey from home to face adventure and various dangers, followed by a triumphant homecoming. Like the hero of a folktale, Janie Crawford leaves home behind her, meets strangers who become either allies or enemies, expresses the transformations she undergoes through costumes and disguises which are invested with special significance, experiences reversals in her perceptions of individual people and events, and returns cleansed, enlightened and alone. The folktale's repetition of events in a series of three is duplicated in Janie's three marriages, as well as by her movement out of the rural community of Nanny, her grandmother, and her first husband, to the town where she keeps a store with Joe Starks, and finally to the "muck" of the Everglades where she experiences joy and bereavement through Tea Cake, her third husband.

The three marriages and the three communities in which Janie moves represent increasingly wide circles of experience and opportunities for expression of personal choice. Nanny, Janie's grandmother, had in fact been a slave and had borne a child to her master. The marriage Nanny forces upon Janie represents a practical arrangement which brings with it another kind of servitude. Feminist themes fuse with themes of Black self-determination as Janie discards her apron, historically the badge of the slave woman as well as of the docile wife, and goes off with Joe Starks. Hurston justifies Janie's abandonment of her first marriage, not on the grounds that Janie feels no love for Killicks, who "look like some ole skull-head in de graveyard," but because Killicks decides to buy a mule for Janie to work the fields with—since she has borne him no heir. Janie needs freedom and an expansion of her horizons more than she needs love—a theme which will surface again, particularly when the novel's ending deflates the romanticism of the relationship with Tea Cake and excises the romantic hero from the heroine's life yet leaves her stronger rather than weaker. Here Hurston consciously rejects the happy ending of the traditional novel.

The second marriage to a man of higher ambitions puts Janie in touch with a larger world, that of the all-Black town which Joe founds, but leaves her stifled and controlled by Joe's white-inspired values. Like Killicks, Joe dictates Janie's work and prevents her from being a full participant in the social life of the town. Only after Joe's death does Janie find the freedom and spontaneity which she values and seeks, in her marriage to Tea Cake. (pp. 54-7)

Janie's recounting of the story to the listening Pheoby closes with storms, a flood, and finally the death of Tea Cake and Janie's return to Eatonville. As at the start of the book, Hurston shifts persons, this time from the third-person narrator to Janie's own direct communication with the listening Pheoby:

> Now, dat's how everything wuz, Pheoby, jus' lak Ah told yuh. Ah'm back home agin and Ah'm satisfied tuh be heah. Ah done been to de horizon and back and now Ah kin set heah in mah house and live by comparisons. Dis house ain't so absent of things lak it used tuh be befo' Tea Cake come along. It's full uh thoughts, 'specially dat bedroom.

The story is thus framed by the scene of the two women sitting on Janie's back porch as darkness descends, the frame itself enclosed by the lyric third-person prose in which Hurston writes the first and last few paragraphs of the novel. The power of the storytelling event demands the switch back to the first person, thus giving authority to Janie by marking the end of the communication with her own words. This passage does not suggest that memories of Tea Cake are *all* Janie has left—the bedroom is full of thoughts, not just of Tea Cake, but of Janie's journey. Later, Janie will assert that her *soul* is the subject of her meditations.

In recent years critics have been unanimous in praising the vitality of Hurston's language: Hurston is a master at transforming the language of a folk group, in this case the West Florida Blacks of the town in which she herself grew up, into convincing dialogue. The authenticity of the language, although documented, is much less important as a "slice of life" than as an implicit claim of authority about Black life. The success of Hurston's novel depends upon the melding of folkloric and fictional elements in such a way as to create characters whose speech is both reflective of the language of the folk and highly individualized. Hurston's novel asserts itself as a statement that goes beyond the limitations of the local color story because her characters and their speech are plausible, individualized and enduringly interesting.

Those who consider the tall tale sessions and courting rituals that Hurston depicts in the course of the narrative to be extraneous or digressive are perhaps misreading *Their Eyes Were Watching God* or reading it as if it were a wholly conventional novel. The novel is conventional, but some of the conventions it relies upon are derived not from the novel genre but from the folktale and from oral tradition. Certainly the incidents on the porch of Joe's store, such as the parody of the courting rituals or the telling of "tall tales," do not serve to advance the obvious action of the narrative as incidents in a more typical novel might be expected to do. They are important, however, both thematically and symbolically. On the one hand, Janie's exclusion from active participation in the "lyin' sessions," and Joe's reluctance to have her even serve as a spectator to the performance events portrayed both serve to elaborate the theme of Janie's desire to transcend the role she has been relegated to as a Black woman. On the other hand, these performance events serve as metaphors for the kind of active and spontaneous interpersonal exchanges which Tea Cake will make available to Janie later in the novel. (pp. 58-9)

Both the unselfconscious use of metaphoric language and the more performance oriented forms of expression found in the novel represent men's and women's use of imagination to enliven and elaborate upon the events of their lives. The very limitation and deprivation of life in rural areas and among poor people can produce, as Hurston knew from her work as a folklorist and anthropologist, a flowering of highly imaginative modes of thought and expression. If Hurston had sought simply to preserve the oral culture of this region of West Florida through her novel, she would not have produced a successful novel, but rather an ethnography. However, she instead has transformed folk materials into fiction. Specific performances in the novel symbolize for Janie the kind of active participation in life which has been denied to Blacks, women, and the poor by society and circumstance. The mock funeral of Matt Bonner's mule is linked in the reader's mind with Nanny's notion of woman as "de mule of the world," who carries the burdens laid on her by whites and by Black males. The political statements implicit in the courting rituals enacted in front of Joe Starks' store suggest the sexual politics operative in Janie's marriage to Joe, as well as in her earlier marriage to Logan Killicks. In each of the instances, the woman is seen as valuable only as long as she hesitates; once she is won over and possessed in some way, she ceases to arouse interest or be perceived as valuable. The mule becomes a motif linked to Nanny, Killicks and Starks. It was, in fact, Killicks' decision to put Janie to work behind a mule which set the stage for her elopement with Starks. (p. 59)

Tea Cake's role in the novel is that of both character and exemplar of the spontaneity and self-determination Hurston holds up for the reader's admiration; he constantly uses imaginative expressions, whether playing his "box" or guitar or inventing imaginary onlookers for his conversations with Janie. Above all, Tea Cake is associated with vitality and freedom and is unhampered by the orientation toward white values which is the flaw of characters like Starks, Nanny and Mrs. Turner.

Nanny is paradoxical; the reader first views her sympathetically because of her devotion to the young Janie, the pathos of her history, and her powerful use of metaphor and vividly imagistic language. Later, however, Hurston forces the reader to reevaluate Nanny in the light of Janie's realization after Joe's death that Nanny's notion of what Janie should strive for is not only insufficient—it is destructive. Born a slave, Nanny wants her granddaughter to go beyond the limitations she herself suffered: "Ah wanted yuh to school out and pick from a higher bush and a sweeter berry." . . . While Nanny encourages Janie's aspirations for a better life, she insists on defining what those aspirations should be. She defines them only in terms of economic security, a definition which belies the rich imagery of her language. The stolid Logan Killicks is far from the "sweet berry" that Janie will eventually find in the aptly nicknamed Tea Cake.

Nanny's aspirations derive from a distrust of life, a distrust of men both white and Black, and a negative attitude toward Blackness and femininity. Because her use of language makes Nanny a sort of "poet of the folk" she, like Tea Cake, brings together the strands of folk expression, Black self-determination, and women's equality. A close look at Nanny's dialogue reveals deeply negative views which inform her poetic use of language. For example, while Janie in her sexual awakening has viewed herself as a pear tree in blossom, Nanny unconsciously deflates this fantasy by identifying Janie and herself with a more sterile version of the same sort of image: "You know, honey, us colored folks is branches without roots and that makes things come round in queer ways." Further, Nanny's negative vision creates negative realities. She takes on the qualities of a tree for the narrator; her head and face look "like the standing roots of some old tree that had been torn away by storm." A veteran of male exploitation, having borne a child to her white master and

later having seen that daughter's life destroyed by the rape that produced Janie, Nanny sees Janie's first kiss as a defilement and a prophecy of disaster. Johnny Taylor is seen through Nanny's eyes as "lacerating" Janie with his kiss. She tells Janie, "Ah don't want no trashy nigger . . . usin' your body to wipe his foots on." As the Black woman is economically a mule, she is sexually a "spit cup" for both white and Black males. (pp. 60-1)

Nanny is a poet whose vision is antagonistic to Janie's yearning for pleasure and freedom. The very poetic nature of Nanny's language gives it authority, but the process of self-development requires that Janie discard values and attitudes Nanny expresses in her seductively beautiful language. Nanny lacks experience with the larger world and is therefore unable to make connections between the "scraps" of her negative experience with men and with the world beyond her own experience which holds a potential for positive relationships, such as Janie's with Tea Cake. . . .

Joe Starks seems initially to represent escape for Janie from the limitations of her grandmother's dream for her. Joe does, in fact, rescue her from the deadening isolation of her marriage to Killicks, and brings her to Eatonville, where he becomes mayor of the first all-Black town incorporated in the United States. In terms of Janie's autonomy and personal growth, however, the second marriage is hardly less stultifying than the first. Essentially Janie exchanges one form of servitude for another, despite the broader range of experience and interactions with people that life in the town offers. As Killicks had planned to put Janie to work behind a mule, Starks insists that Janie work in his store and makes her cover her beautiful hair with a headscarf. The headrag provides an ironic counterpoint to the portrayal of Starks as a progressive entrepreneur, for his insistence on her covering her hair suggests his need to belittle Janie, despite his protestations of her high stature as a lady. (p. 62)

Joe Starks, Mayor of Eatonville and thus a symbol of Black self-determination, is in fact a man who takes his values from white societal models. Janie, though she lives in a white house that appears to be surrounded by servants' quarters, works behind a counter waiting on customers rather than rocking on her porch. Significantly, when authentic communication takes place between Janie and Pheoby at the start and finish of the novel, it is on the back porch rather than the public front porch.

From the point of view of Black self-determination, it is not the front porch of the white house, but rather the porch of Starks' store that best exemplifies the strengths of Eatonville and its people. If Janie's front porch represents empty pretensions and the back porch intimate conversation, it is the porch of the store that provides the middle ground between public and private worlds. For here people congregate to tell tales and talk about such local characters as Matt Bonner and his yellow mule. Although Joe does not permit Janie to join in the folk performances and prefers that she remain aloof from these common activities, as befits her status as Mrs. Mayor Starks, Janie loves these sessions:

> When the people sat around on the porch and passed around the pictures of their thoughts for the others to look at and see, it was nice. The fact that the thought pictures were always crayon enlargements of life made it even nicer to listen to.

The tales and mock rituals of Lige, Sam and the other "regulars" make of routine life something larger which, through Hurston's narrative tone, becomes rhetorically linked to universal experience. Thus, the pathetic neglect by Bonner of his mule leads to high comedy, an act of compassion, and eventually, upon the mule's death, to a mock heroic funeral: Janie sees the "big picture talkers" in large terms, as "using a side of the world for a canvas." Although Joe sits and laughs at the mule-talk and even makes the fine gesture of buying the mule so it can live out its last days in ease, Joe, like Nanny, sees humans as small. Telling Janie that the folktellers are unworthy of her company, he calls them "jus' some puny humans playin' round de toes uh Time." Even Joe is capable of poetic language at times but, like Nanny, he sees much of the world in a negative light. For Janie, on the other hand, "lyin' sessions" and performances lend vividness and a sense of universality and connectedness to life.

Through the incorporation of the figurative language of the folk into the narration itself, Hurston emphasizes the widening of Janie's mental horizons through her experiences on Joe's porch. Thus the narrator uses images based upon folk expressions and beliefs in describing Janie's world, particularly after Janie goes off with Tea Cake and lives through the storm and flood which indirectly take Tea Cake's life:

> Every morning the world flung itself over and exposed the town to the sun.
>
> The sun was gone, but he had left his fingerprints in the sky. The storm woke up Okechobee and the monster began to roll in his bed. Began to roll and complain like a peevish world on a grumble.
>
> And then again Him-with-the-square-toes had gone back to his house . . . His pale white horse had galloped over waters, and thundered over land. The time of dying was over. It was time to bury the dead.

Hurston's use of a narrative voice that parallels and reinforces Janie's expanding view of the world makes it clear that folklore is integrated into all levels of the text. In fact, the narrative voice, always close to but not identical with Janie's consciousness, becomes more prominent toward the end of the book, as if to suggest that the folkloric material is directly relevant to Janie's final achievement of harmony and peace. Folklore is a thematic element, as well as a component of the themes of Janie's search for identity and self-determination as a Black and as a woman.

If folklore is simply one way for men and women to order and interpret their lives and environments, then the title, whose relevance to the book as a whole is not transparent, becomes more accessible. The eyes of the folk watch God and the elements for signs of safety and indications of where and how each one fits into society and the world. *Their Eyes Were Watching God* is a book about a woman's journey of self-discovery, but also about a woman's exploration of the physical and social worlds available to her. If it were a simple tale of romantic love, . . . Janie's loss of Tea Cake at the end would be a tragedy, depriving her life of the meaning she had finally found. But this is not the case; Tea Cake represents something more to Janie than the presence of a single man. He is represented as a wanderer who shows Janie who she is and can be and who magically remains present to her even after his death.

Tea Cake combines a sense of his own identity as a Black and a concomitant ability to set his own standards for himself with a natural acceptance of and faith in Janie, which enables her to define her own standards for herself. The heart of the life that Janie so much enjoys in the Florida "muck" is folk expression in the form of playing and gaming in the fields or singing and tale-telling in the cabin and "jook."

The flood and Tea Cake's death toward the end of the novel are problematic from a traditional critical point of view. Janie's shooting of Tea Cake after he has been maddened by a bite from a rabid dog during the flood seems implausible. A traditional female protagonist would be happily placed in an appropriate marriage at the end of the book, or else would experience the loss of her man as a tragedy. Again Hurston challenges conventional norms by integrating the expectations of a folktale with the form of the novel, for Janie returns from her adventure into the big world with Tea Cake much as a young male character in a folktale returns home both richer and wiser than he left. Further, she has struggled with the giant—that is, with storms and death—and returned victorious. In the folk tale, the magical teacher is dispensed with as the hero triumphs, and so is Tea Cake left behind on Janie's journey. The flood serves to remove the characters from the life of social interaction in Eatonville and later in the Everglades and puts them into the elemental struggle of natural disaster. Here the narrative voice becomes strong and increasingly suggestive of a sort of collective, choric voice. Storm, flood and death are personified. The effect of this shift is an emphasis on the universal nature of Janie's experience.

When the narrator says of Janie, Tea Cake and their friends as they wait out the storm, "They seemed to be staring at the dark, but their eyes were watching God," Hurston is speaking of the universal human situation as well as of the specific plights of these characters. Aspects of performance and folk culture are portrayed by Hurston as an expression of courage and creativity in the face of everyday realities such as poverty and deprivation, as well as catastrophe and imminent death. The book's title suggests that men and women, confronting "dark" unknowns such as loss and death, create or recognize a force behind reality that makes sense out of it.

In telling her story to Pheoby after Tea Cake's death, Janie assumes the role of artist and sense-maker. Her experiences with Tea Cake have endowed her with an ability to transform experience so that at the end of the novel she can return to Eatonville and the kind of life that appears to belong to the aspirations of Nanny and Joe Starks, but which is, because of her own inner harmony, no longer stifling or unsatisfying . . . . The apparent weakness of the ending of the novel is perhaps explained by the possibility that Hurston, as a feminist, did not want Janie to find fulfillment in a man, but rather in her new-found self, and thus tried to reorient the form towards the traditional story of the young male. There is a suggestion of the literary theme of the birth of the artist, as well as of the folk theme of the triumphant young male. (pp. 62-5)

[Rather] than living on her memories of Tea Cake, Janie is centering on herself, her life and her "soul." Her ability to transform routine reality and even tragedy into something beautiful, a quality evidenced in the fantasy of the pear tree but suppressed by Nanny, Killicks, and Starks, has been revived and nurtured by her associations with Tea Cake and the "big convention of livin'." *Their Eyes Were Watching God* is a novel of self-definition, feminism and Blackness expressed through the folk experience. (p. 66)

Claire Crabtree, *"The Confluence of Folklore, Feminism and Black Self-Determination in Zora Neale Hurston's 'Their Eyes Were Watching God',"* in The Southern Literary Journal, *Vol. XVII, No. 2, Spring, 1985, pp. 54-66.*

ALICE REICH

I like to think that Zora Neale Hurston would be happy to be an anthropologist today, that she would come to our feminist studies with the same energy and skepticism that she brought to her studies of folklore, that she would feel affirmed by what we are doing and prod us to go beyond that. I wondered particularly, as I read *Their Eyes Were Watching God,* what she would think of the work of Nancy Chodorow, Carol Gilligan (and many others now) who point the way to a model of female development that is very different from male development, to a female myth that does not look so much like the journey of Odysseus as the growth patterns of a tree or the phases of the moon. And I hope she would indulge me as I attempt to read the story of her Janie as a particularly female myth, for I do this with respect not only for all I can see in Janie, but also for all I cannot see.

In a book rich with imagery and black oral tradition, Zora Neale Hurston tells us of a woman's journey that gives the lie to Freud's assertion that "the difficult development which leads to femininity seems to exhaust all the possibilities of the individual." On the contrary, Janie finds her self and her voice by working through and finally transcending the limiting images of woman as servant, as wife, as romantic lover. She finds herself through relationship with others and she finds her voice, finally, through "Pheoby's hungry listening."

Janie's self is a given, a jewel inside her that is there from the beginning, as it is in all people:

> When God had made The Man, he made him out of stuff that sung all the time and glittered all over. Then after that some angels got jealous and chopped him into millions of pieces, but still he glittered and hummed. So they beat him down to nothing but sparks but each little spark had a shine and a song. So they covered each one over with mud.

Janie's journey is her struggle against the forces that cover her jewel with mud and silence her singing, and the forces ranged against her are the obstacles encountered both by black people in their historical struggle and by women in our individual struggle. For a time, these forces silence her and subvert her sensuality into subordination.

Janie first awakens to her sensuality early in the novel in an orgasmic communion with nature as she lies dreaming beneath a pear tree; and ever after she "saw her life like a great tree in leaf." But at this first shine of her jewel, Janie's grandmother, seeing the danger of a bad marriage, or a pregnancy without marriage, transfers Janie to her first husband, Logan Killicks, a steady, economically independent man. Thus, *Their Eyes Were Watching God* is a chronicle of sanctioned attempts to silence Janie's voice and her sense of herself. Janie is first silenced as black women in slavery were silenced. She is redefined not as a pear tree, but as "branches without roots"; Janie's grandmother "wanted to preach a great sermon about colored women sittin' on high, but they wasn't no pulpit for me." . . . Janie tries to tell her grandmother that "the vision of Logan Killicks was desecrating the pear tree, but Janie didn't know how to tell Nanny that."

So Janie marries not a man but sixty acres and protection. . . . She waits "a bloom time, and a green time and an orange time," but discovers "that marriage did not make love." . . . Little better than a farm animal, she is fed and not mistreated so long as she works.

Janie and Killicks do not speak much to one another at all. She talks to falling seeds, and she looks up the road. Down the road comes Joe Starks, not "pollen and blooming trees" but "far horizon . . . change and chance." She leaves Logan Killicks and goes off with Joe, hoping to revive her first feelings of herself. . . . In his material success and political power as storeowner and mayor of the all-black community of Eatonville, Joe Starks represents another real step up from slavery. However, in his bourgeois life, a man must have (own) a wife to display his success. Janie is there to receive material things ("Joe didn't make many speeches with rhymes to her, but he bought her the best things"); she is an object in his store. With Killicks, Janie had had no place ("You ain't got no particular place. It's wherever Ah need yuh"); with Joe Starks, "she's uh woman and her place is in de home."

What Janie likes best about Eatonville are the gatherings around words, the speech-making, sermonizing, story-telling, singing, and "woofing," but Joe forbids her participation. His is the big voice in his community and it defines and silences Janie. . . . Janie comes to know the dual consciousness of the wife, the woman who has feelings but no voice to express them. "She didn't change her mind but she agreed with her mouth." And, "gradually, she pressed her teeth together and learned to hush," losing her "petal-openness":

> She had no more blossomy openings dusting pollen over her man, neither any glistening young fruit where the petals used to be. . . . She had an inside and an outside now and suddenly she knew how not to mix them.

Janie intends to stay in her marriage in spite of its costs to her, in spite of her knowledge that it does not have anything other than a public meaning anymore. She says, "Maybe he ain't nothin' . . . but he is something in my mouth. He's got to be else Ah ain't got nothin' to live for. Ah'll lie and say he is." Because her life and her outside voice are a lie, the injustice of her situation finally drives her to use her own true voice: Joe teases her about her age and looks and she returns the barb in front of other men. When she stops reflecting back to him his own magnified image, Joe is shattered: "Joe Starks didn't know the words for all this, but he knew the feeling." And he sickens and dies, believing that Janie has poisoned him. Though she comes to understand some of the difficulties of his life, she never sees how they could have been resolved: "She thought back and forth about what happened in the making of a voice out of a man." And at the same time she remembers that there is a free girl self still in her, and this self rollicks "with the springtime across the world" while she sends her face to Joe's funeral.

There remains one major adventure that Janie has not had, one relationship to work through before she can claim her self. "She was saving up her feelings for some man she had never seen." Janie now has the "luxury" of romantic love. She has never found a man who might be to her as "a bee to a blossom—a pear tree blossom in the spring." She knows that she is not interested in any of the Eatonville men who come to court the well-to-do widow and she enjoys her freedom, even her loneliness. But in the store "it always seemed to her that she was still clerking for Joe and that soon he would come in and find something wrong that she had done." And Janie cannot free herself from that. She needs a man, but not just any man. She needs a man who will not merely repeat what her first two husbands have done, to use her solely for their own ends; she needs a man who will free her by loving the hidden parts of her self. And along comes Tea Cake, who wants her to play, to sing, to tell stories. (pp. 163-66)

Janie leaves Eatonville with Tea Cake, explaining to her friend Pheoby that it may not make "business" sense, but it is love; that she has lived the life her Grandmother wanted for her, and it is now time to live her own. . . . Tea Cake is a route to herself for Janie. He embodies all that she had to silence to survive as Joe Starks' wife; dreaming and living his dreams, the antithesis of a materialist, he is life and joy; Janie loves him. But Janie's love for Tea Cake poses the contradiction that all women in patriarchal society find in heterosexual love. Her grandmother has warned her "Dat's de very prong all us black women gits hung on. Dis love!" But for Janie it is only with this "self-crushing love" that "her soul crawled out from its hiding place."

Tea Cake takes Janie to the Everglades where she finds a freedom she has never known, a classless society based on manual labor and good times. Janie and Tea Cake's love is blissful. She works with him, not for him; she joins in the story-telling and is no longer silent; her feelings and her words, her self and her man are all unified. But Janie herself never sees the limitations in the way he defines her, though they are there for the reader to see. She is so in love with him that her place is wherever he wants it to be, that she is able to let him slap "her around a bit to show he was boss," that she waits for him at home or goes with him to work, as he wishes. With Tea Cake, Janie has found the love she has dreamed of (and its contradictions, of which she remains unaware). With Tea Cake, Janie finds a way to herself, but it is not until she no longer has Tea Cake that Janies finds her self.

Into the unity of "the muck" comes the chaos of a hurricane, confounding the categories of human and animal, life and death, love and hate. As Janie and Tea Cake are trying to escape, he is bitten by a rabid dog, a dog who "wuzn't nothin' all over but pure hate. Wonder where he come from?" The mad dog of hate transforms Tea Cake and in his madness he attacks Janie, who kills him in self defense. She loved him, but she is not at all paralyzed by his loss. She goes to her trial where she tells her story and "make[s] them see." She arranges his funeral where, in contrast to her experience at Joe's funeral, "She was too busy feeling grief to dress like grief." And she returns to Eatonville where, in her story to Pheoby, which constitutes the bulk of the book's narrative, her life, her thoughts, her feelings, and her words are finally unified.

Janie had been angry at her grandmother for having "taken the biggest thing God ever made, the horizon . . . and pinched it in to such a little bit of a thing that she could tie it about her granddaughter's neck tight enough to choke her." Through following her own dreams however, she has been "tuh de horizon and back." And she ends with that horizon over her shoulder "like a great fishnet. . . . So much of life in its meshes! She called in her soul to come and see." Janie finds herself through other people and is, in this, very female. Her living through first her grandmother's dream for her, then the dream of a materialistic society, and finally her own dream of love is not a sign of weakness, but of a female

way of being in the world that emphasizes attachment and relationship rather than separation and achievement. (pp. 167-68)

Alice Reich, "Pheoby's Hungry Listening," in Women's Studies, *Vol. 13, Nos. 1 & 2, 1986, pp. 163-69.*

ELIZABETH A. MEESE

Through her novel *Their Eyes Were Watching God,* Zora Neale Hurston presents a forceful resistance to black women's oppression in a sexist and racist society. She does so by means of her own artistic accomplishment, which she shares with her character Janie Crawford. The work has attracted varied attention since it was first published in 1937. June Jordan called it the greatest novel of Blacklove ever written. Alice Walker has explored its place in Hurston's presentation of herself as a role model for black women artists. A host of critics have discussed the significance of Janie as a black woman who creates herself in her own image. Not all of the commentary, however, has been positive. Ignoring her critique of sexual politics, some writers have criticized Hurston's political views, comparing her unfavorably with Richard Wright and Ralph Ellison and describing her as an opportunist and a reactionary. While we have finally developed a fuller understanding of Hurston's work, critics still feel obliged to begin their discussions by reconstructing the author's life and works, continually reestablishing their right to undertake the more specialized literary analysis this black feminist writer deserves. Few critics have talked at any length about the literary value and construction of meaning in *Their Eyes Were Watching God,* one of the century's finest works of fiction.

Hurston remains something of an enigma. She incited jealousy, dedication, love, and anger in her friends and associates; later writers have shared these responses in varying degrees. Certainly no one is immune to them because Hurston's position . . . refuses a one-dimensional reduction. Her defiant individualism frequently displays itself in the bias, equivocation and obliquity of her critics' commentaries. In her exceptional essay, "On Refusing to Be Humbled by Second Place in a Contest You Did Not Design: A Tradition by Now," which serves as the Dedication to the Feminist Press edition of Hurston's selected writings [see Hurston's entry in *CLC,* Vol. 30], Alice Walker summarizes the puzzle surrounding the author and her work:

> Is *Mules and Men* racist? Or does it reflect the flawed but nonetheless beautiful creative insights of an oppressed people's collective mythology? Is **"Gilded Six-Bits"** so sexist it makes us cringe to think Zora Neale Hurston wrote it? Or does it make a true statement about deep love functioning in the only pattern that at the time of its action seemed correct? Did Zora Neale Hurston never question "America" or the status-quo, as some have accused, or was she questioning it profoundly when she wrote phrases like "the arse-and-all of Democracy"? Is Janie Crawford, the main character in *Their Eyes Were Watching God,* light-skinned and silken-haired because *Hurston* was a colorist, as a black male critic has claimed, or because Hurston was not blind and therefore saw that black men (and black women) have been, and are, colorist to an embarrassing degree?

Is Hurston the messenger who brings the bad news,
or is she the bad news herself? Is Hurston a reflection of ourselves? And if so, is that not, perhaps,
part of our "problem" with her?

Through the use of countervailing questions, Walker defends
the writer against her critics and provides us with a badly
needed corrective in her re-membering of Hurston. Walker
concludes her litany of questions by cautioning us to restrict
our comments to Hurston's artistry. (pp. 41-2)

Over the years, critics have commented variously on the central theme of *Their Eyes Were Watching God.* [In "Zora
Neale Hurston: A Woman Half in Shadows," Mary Helen]
Washington argues that the novel's most powerful theme "is
Janie's search for identity, an identity which finally begins to
take shape as she throws off the false images which have been
thrust upon her because she is both black and woman in a society where neither is allowed to exist naturally and freely."
Hurston expresses this theme, Washington maintains,
through the images of the horizon and the pear tree, the former symbolizing Janie's personal, individual quest, the latter,
her search for fulfillment through union with another. Ann
Rayson argues similarly [in her "The Novels of Zora Neale
Hurston"] that Hurston chooses "becoming" rather than
"being" as the principal focus of her fiction, suggesting a parallel with Ellison's protagonist, who says, "the end is the beginning." While Rayson's comment reveals her sensitivity to
Hurston's choice of narrative strategy, she does not examine
that sense of circularity or the reasons underlying Hurston's
choice. This question of creating form through narrative
technique, which serves as the basis for Janie's deconstruction of the effects of power, provides the focus for my discussion of *Their Eyes Were Watching God* and offers one way
of relating this work to those of other feminist writers.

The puzzle of the novel's structure is inseparable from considerations of its theme. . . . Hurston employs a narrative
strategy that is culturally, philosophically, and aesthetically
complex. This complexity reveals itself through Hurston's
decision to re-tell the story rather than to tell it. Barbara
Christian makes an important observation about this choice,
which the scope of her book [*Black Women Novelists*] does
not permit her to develop: "*Their Eyes Were Watching God*
is a story within a story. Janie Starks tells the story of her
childhood, her life, and her loves to her best friend, Phoebe
[*sic*], and to the community to which she has just returned.
This aspect of the novel is critical to its substance, for Janie
Starks is not an individual in a vacuum; she is an intrinsic
part of a community, and she brings her life and its richness,
joys, and sorrows back to it. As it has helped to form her, so
she also helps to form it." Lillie Howard, however, [in her
Zora Neale Hurston; see Further Reading list], finds fault
with Hurston's method and maintains that "the story is rather awkwardly told by both the heroine, Janie Crawford, and
an omniscient narrator, and is revealed, for the most part, in
a flashback to Janie's best friend, Pheoby Watson. The narrative is awkward in some places because much of what Janie
tells Pheoby, Pheoby must already know, partly because she
is Janie's best friend, and partly because Pheoby was a part
of Eatonville just as Janie was." It is neither through accident
nor uncalculated device that Janie's story is re-told rather
than told. Why does Hurston choose to do this when, as
Howard correctly observes, Pheoby—the audience for the
fiction within the fiction—surely knows much of the story she
is being told? The value of the approach as strategy exists in
what Hurston accomplishes through its use; here as well rests
much of the novel's significance for feminist readers today.

Hurston's artistic method displays a keen awareness of the
performative quality of fiction as it emerges from the tradition of oral narrative, as well as a clever consciousness of the
storyteller/writer's role in constructing the history of a people through language. Her brilliant use of dialect, specifying
pride and ownership, lends credibility to the novel's claim as
a work for the black community. It is a testament to the
power and beauty of blackness. Hurston is culturally and artistically at ease with the narrative convention of re-telling
the tale, just as her character Janie has grown used to an audience: "Pheoby's hungry listening helped Janie to tell her
story." . . . Hurston's aim is textuality—the process of producing a text through the transformation of other texts—and
through this textuality, a form of feminist self-definition. By
transforming Janie's orality—Hurston's intertexts—into textuality, the writer creates both herself as a writer and her own
story, while Janie creates her life through language. Creator
and character fuse in Hurston's description of Janie's motivation for relating the story that follows: "that oldest human
longing—self-revelation." All the events of the novel's one
long evening find their center in the act of telling the tale.

To understand the effects of the novel's frame, the embodiment of Hurston's narrative strategy, it is useful to suspend
consideration of that device for the moment in order first to
examine the story Janie tells. The frame consists only of the
first chapter and the final three pages of the novel's twentieth
and last chapter. Since the story within the story comprises
much of the novel, it always commands the greatest critical
attention. Here Hurston offers the tale of Janie Crawford's
development from puberty to womanhood as a model of
black female development. The story begins in the home of
her grandmother, moves to the homes of her two husbands,
Logan Killicks and then Joe Starks, and concludes with the
death of her third husband and lover Vergible "Tea Cake"
Woods. Janie orders the story in such a way that she chronicles her progress from dependence to independence, while
Hurston gives us the story of Janie's development from silent
"object" to speaking "subject."

At the beginning of the story within the story, Janie receives
her sense of definition from others. She is woman as object
under the control of a racist, patriarchal culture. Failing to
recognize herself as the one black child in a photograph, she
begins her story without name or color: " 'Dey all useter call
me Alphabet 'cause so many people had done named me different names.' " Initially she reconciles herself to the received
wisdom, the history of black women's place in the prevailing
power structure as imparted by Nanny, her grandmother. . . . Nanny projects a stereotypical identity (wife)
and a secure future (house and land) for Janie based upon
what she knows, which is limited by the historical constraints
of what she has seen of the white man's power over blacks
and the black man's relationship to the black woman. Thus,
she explains to Janie: " 'Ah was born back due in slavery so
it wasn't for me to fulfill my dreams of whut a woman oughta
be and to do. Dat's one of de hold-backs of slavery.' "

Nanny arranges Janie's marriage to Logan Killicks and his
sixty acres of land, thereby "desecrating" Janie's vision from
the pear tree of idyllic union. [In "This Infinity of Conscious
Pain," Lorraine] Bethel explains Nanny's behavior as a protective measure: "She is attempting to adjust Janie to the prevailing sexual and racial milieu, and her protectiveness

emerges as violence directed against Janie. Nanny attempts to explain to Janie the historical and social forces that make her innocent actions so serious. . . . " Bethel sees in this cross-generational relationship the pattern of black women's victimization by oppressive racial and sexual forces. "In this sense," she concludes, "Janie and her grandmother illustrate the tragic continuity of Black female oppression in white/male America" [See Further Reading list]. While it is true that the oppression continues, it is also evident that Hurston makes Janie differ from Nanny in some important ways. Part of what the character learns is to place her grandmother's words in perspective—to understand how Nanny's recounting of experience shaped what Janie was later able to see. In this respect, Hurston stages a break with the oppressor's culture and points to the sexual and racial liberation of women.

The grandmother's gift of a life different from her own permits Janie to pursue dreams and visions beyond those that Nanny, " 'a cracked plate' " damaged by slavery, could have projected. Janie creates her own future, the way to her individual happiness, at the same time that Hurston constructs a new legacy through the tale Janie tells. The story Janie tells Phoeby and the narrative the reader receives are vastly different from the shaping and socializing story Nanny tells Janie. In a sense, Nanny is the unreconstructed past, and Janie her fulfillment through a newly constructed present. Although the grandmother's narrative power has been repressed into further silence, Nanny still envisions the story she longed to tell: " 'Ah wanted to preach a great sermon about colored women sittin' on high, but they wasn't no pulpit for me' "; but silence distorts this story to the point where the horizon of women's potential is constricted to the private sphere of domestic life. Through Janie, Hurston exposes the crack in the plate and preaches the liberating and defiant sermon that Nanny was never able to deliver and that black women, indeed all women, have been waiting to hear. Janie's story can be read as a new (hi)story constructed out of love and passed from one black woman to another.

The process of Janie's freedom from oppressive roles entails several steps and engenders predictable male opposition. Logan Killicks expresses his complaint about Janie's independence in racial terms: " 'You think youse white folks by de way you act.' " Joe Starks brings Janie closer to racial/cultural autonomy by escaping the control of white hegemony. His desire to be a "big voice" in a place beyond the authority of white men suggests change, chance, and the far horizon to Janie, although from the outset she realizes that Starks does not completely embody her vision: "He did not represent sun-up and pollen and blooming trees." From the day she rides off with him in a hired rig, sitting in a seat "like some high, ruling chair," Janie confronts the delimiting structures of language: "Her old thoughts were going to come in handy now, but new words would have to be made and said to fit them." Hers is a new life beyond the limits of the imagined, demanding the creation of a new story for its expression.

Their Eyes Were Watching God is a novel about orality—of speakers and modes of speech: Joe's "big voice" wields power modeled on white culture; the grandmother speaks the language of slavery time; the store porch hosts "mule-talkers" and "big picture talkers"; and each town has its complement of gossips. Here, as everywhere, language produces power and knowledge as well as constraint; it is the ability to inter-

pret and to transform experience. The townspeople perceive the equation of word and law, how Joe's big voice commands obedience: " 'You kin feel a switch in his hand when he's talkin' to yuh' "; " 'he's de wind and we'se de grass. We bend which ever way he blows.' " Commenting on this effect, Howard makes the clever observation that "It is no mistake that he [Joe] often prefaces his remarks with 'I, god.' " Just as the town chorus is alienated by Joe's power of speech, they also note Janie's silence. In this world of lively speakers, Janie lives a speechless existence. At the town's dedication ceremony, Joe speaks when Janie is asked to say a few words. Although he robs her of this opportunity, she sees and reflects upon her loss: "She had never thought of making a speech, and didn't know if she cared to make one at all. It must have been the way Joe spoke out without giving her a chance to say anything one way or another that took the bloom off of things." Janie discovers the emptiness of class status, and especially of status by affiliation—the territory of women. In particular, she grows to understand the loneliness of silence, how orality is required for community. She loves the mule stories people tell on the store porch and creates her own tales in silence, but Joe restricts Janie's personal autonomy by prohibiting her participation in discourse. She can neither tell stories nor serve as a member of an audience—the folk community required for the telling.

Through the novel, Hurston also exposes phallocentrism and instructs her readers in the terms of discourse. By means of their oral skills, the porch speakers demonstrate the powerful effects of logocentrism: "They are the center of the world." As in white patriarchal culture, language serves as a locus for social control through its centrality within an order of meaning. Robert Hemenway and Roger Abrahams both comment on the importance of "negotiating respect" through verbal skill in the black community. In "Are You a Flying Lark or a Setting Dove?" Heminway remarks that "negotiating for respect is not a static process dependent upon the institutions or instrumentalities offered to a woman by society—marriage, the home, the church—but a dynamic response to events growing out of a woman's capacity for self-expression." Phallocentrism is so fundamentally pervasive that it is difficult to conceive of one's self, actions, and meaning outside of its system of control. To attempt to escape its constraints, Janie must use power in order to have power. By transforming her characteristic silence into speech, she stands a chance of establishing a different relationship with Joe, that is, a relationship based on acknowledging difference and accommodating change. Eventually she tires of his endless verbal disputes designed to bring about submission. Her silence in the external world reflects her internal repression until the hollow image of Joe Starks crashes from the shelf in her mind, and she discovers her emotional silence: "She had a host of thoughts she had never expressed to him, and numerous emotions she had never let Jody know about. Things packed up and put away in parts of her heart where he could never find them. She was saving up feelings for some man she had never seen."

The three places in the text where Janie speaks publicly are marked in the novel. When Joe implements Janie's idea by freeing a persecuted mule—the analogue of black slaves, and especially of black women ("de mule uh de world")—Janie praises him. She gives a speech in which she compares Joe with Abraham Lincoln. The townspeople note her skill: " 'Yo' wife is uh born orator, Starks. Us never knowed dat befo'. She put jus' de right words tuh our thoughts.' " In the second instance, Hurston herself, through the omniscient narrative voice, underscores Janie's incursion into orality: "Janie did what she had never done before, that is, thrust herself into the conversation." This time, instead of presenting an oblique defense of women through the suffering mule, Janie . . . gets "too moufy" and preaches her sermon on women (the one Nanny never could deliver) to the men on the porch: " 'Sometimes God gits familiar wid us womenfolks too and talks His inside business. He told me how surprised He was 'bout y'all turning out so smart after Him makin' yuh different; and how surprised y'all is goin' tuh be if you ever find out you don't know half as much 'bout us as you think you do. It's so easy to make yo'self out God Almighty when you ain't got nothin' tuh strain against but women and chickens.' " The final instance of Janie's mastery that ultimately establishes her power occurs when, in retaliation for Joe's verbal abuse, she humiliates him in front of his male friends. She seizes his authority—language—and leaves him speechless. (pp. 43-8)

Constructing another course for black women, Hurston directs Janie's language toward the discovery of a discourse of emotion, a language she learns through her relationship with Tea Cake who fulfills the bee and blossom imagery of the novel's opening. He demands a union of speech and feeling, and she asks that he speak "with no false pretense." He is the master linguist of "otherness"; as Janie tells Pheoby in the story within the story, " 'So in the beginnin' new thoughts had tuh be thought and new words said. After Ah got used tuh dat, we gits 'long jus' fine. He done taught me de maiden language all over.' " This "maiden" language defies the social construction of difference and permits new perspectives to emerge from narrative action. For example, Janie rejects being "classed off," separated from other black people through her imprisonment in Joe's house and store as "his showpiece, his property." To a degree, she frees herself from his story, another constriction of her horizon, and shares her perception with Pheoby: " 'And Ah'd sit dere wid de walls creepin' up on me and squeezin' all de life outa me.' " Janie rejects the "race after property and titles" in favor of "uh love game." Recognizing that the exclusion of others is the repression of differences within one's self, she merges her life with the life of the black community, telling big stories, listening to them, working along with the other women, and rejecting Mrs. Turner's politics of color—a pecking order that privileges white features over black. (pp. 48-9)

One of Janie's greatest lessons about language centers on its power to deconstruct and to construct, to kill or to give life. When she is on trial for Tea Cake's murder, she recognizes this potential in the black members of the audience: "They were there with their tongues cocked and loaded, the only real weapon left to weak folks. The only killing tool they are allowed to use in the presence of white folks." This passage recalls the frame's opening segment in which Hurston describes the townspeople sitting on their porches at night: "They became lords of sounds and lesser things. They passed nations through their mouths. They sat in judgment." Adopting the traditional means of defense against gossip, Janie selects Pheoby, a trusted member of the community network, to whom she can provide an account of her behavior. In addition to this pragmatic motive for narration, Janie uses language to give life and memory to feeling. Following the death of the mule, for example, it is memorialized in story by the porch talkers, just as the life of the black woman in slavery is fixed in Nanny's discourse when contrasted with Janie.

Thus, according to the conventions of their discursive fields, Janie's story enters oral tradition while Hurston's novel passes into literary tradition. Through her character's discovery, the writer gives us a story of how language outwits time and exclusively patriarchal determinations of meaning, and the reader finds new significance in the frame's opening commentary comparing men, "whose dreams [are] mocked to death by Time," and women: "Now, women forget all those things they don't want to remember, and remember everything they don't want to forget. The dream is the truth. Then they act and do things accordingly."

Although the novel's work is conducted primarily through Janie's story, much of its significance rests in and in relationship to the narrative frame. The importance of the frame is that it permits Hurston to tell her story through a reconstituted subject. Hurston holds to this even at the expense of creating anomalies in Janie's story—the places where Pheoby is mentioned in the third person, dialogues between Pheoby and Janie in which Pheoby is presumably a participant in the telling, since Janie addresses her remarks to her friend. The story we receive is not constituted until Janie returns, changed. She arrives as the witness to a new epistemology: "you got tuh *go* there tuh *know* there." Through Janie's story, Hurston presents an alternative conception of power as it operates in black female discourse. Rather than replicating verbal power as oppression, its form among whites and blacks imitating whites, Hurston espouses a form of narrative authority indigenous to black tribal tradition. . . . Janie operates according to a system whereby you don't say what you don't know, and you can't know something until you experience it. . . . Having gone there, you are changed, and the story you have to tell is a different story. The interpretations of the phallocentric hegemony are called into question rather than assumed. This move wrests the control of meaning from a sexist, racist culture and locates the potential for change within the individual.

Besides the significance of how the story is changed by the fact that Janie has gone and returned, it is additionally important that Janie returns as a "speaking subject" to bring her story to the people. At this point, the changed Janie, Janie the storyteller, fuses with the author. Hurston designates the end of Janie's story with the novel's only authentic silence—one that is elected rather than imposed, and is as natural as the sounds that mark the ending: "There was a finished silence after that so that for the first time they could hear the wind picking at the pine trees." With the full resonance of the parallel, *Their Eyes Were Watching God* might well be understood as a "Portrait of the Artist as a Black Woman."

Through the overarching and elusive meaning of her title, Hurston confronts the dilemma of the phallocentric ground of determinate meaning. At the most critical moments in the novel, Janie and others scrutinize the heavens for a sign of God's intention. Like their African ancestors (and the Puritan interpreters), they are seeking a way through nature to unlock and interpret the meaning of events. They act out the reader's effort to interpret the text. In the novel's opening frame, we encounter the Watcher, an Everyman waiting for the ship of dreams to come in and trying to outwit Death who was "there before there was a where or a when or a then." Following Janie's sensual awakening, she desires validation for her dreams: "She was seeking confirmation of the voice and vision, and everywhere she found and acknowledged answers. A personal answer for all other creations except herself. She felt an answer seeking her, but where? When? How?" Only once does there seem to be a sign—the arrival of Tea Cake, which Janie invests with referential power taking us back to the blossoming pear tree and the bee: "He looked like the love thoughts of women. He could be a bee to a blossom—a pear tree blossom in the spring. He seemed to be crushing scent out of the world with his footsteps. Crushing aromatic herbs with every step he took. Spices hung about him. He was a glance from God."

While Janie accepts Tea Cake as a sign, his presence cannot resolve the problem of interpretation—the signification of events. When the hurricane is imminent, people consider God's purpose: "They sat in company with the others in other shanties, their eyes straining against crude walls and their souls asking if He meant to measure their puny might against His. They seemed to be staring at the dark, but their eyes were watching God." The only answer given is the storm itself, suggesting that the people's question, as related by the narrator, contained its answer, that this was indeed a contest of force. The hurricane and Tea Cake's love for Janie ultimately contribute to his death, so that on a symbolic level, it would seem that what was once responsible for his presence is in the end responsible for his absence. Through the compelling imagery of the frame, Hurston refuses this simple dichotomy by rejecting the bipolar logic of absence: "Tea Cake, with the sun for a shawl. Of course he wasn't dead. He could never be dead until she herself had finished feeling and thinking. The kiss of his memory made pictures of love and light against the wall. Here was peace. She pulled in her horizon like a great fish-net. Pulled it from around the waist of the world and draped it over her shoulder. So much of life in its meshes! She called in her soul to come and see." (pp. 50-3)

Hurston offers a particular concept of presence—the presence of a present—through Janie's re-telling. The only present is its illusion in narration, occasioned by and filling in for absence. Bringing the past into the present, Hurston gives both dimensions a particular reconstructed value, and propels the past, itself a former present, toward a future that exists only as an anticipated possibility for black women. Thus, these elements of time remain fluid, each containing traces of the other. As storytellers, as speaking subjects, Janie and Hurston don't escape phallocentrism. Rather, they stage a critique from what [Jacques] Derrida calls "a certain inside of logocentrism. But it is an inside that is divided enough and tormented enough and obsessed enough by the other, by contradictions, by heterogeneity, for us to be able to say things about it without being simply 'outside of it.' And we say them within the grammar, within the language of logocentrism while allowing the alterity or the difference which obsesses this inside to show through." By extricating herself from cultural control, Janie/Hurston creates culture. Through the retelling of Janie's story, orality becomes textuality. Textuality is produced by Janie's learned orality, her participation in the oral tradition of the culture. She learns to be one of the people; thus, this is a story of her acculturation into black womanhood and her artistic entitlement to language. By chronicling Janie's development, Hurston transforms the status of narrative from the temporality characteristic of oral tradition to the more enduring textuality required to outwit time's effect on memory. In doing so, she presents feminist readers with a map of a woman's personal resistance to patriarchy, and feminist writers—in particular Alice Walker—with the intertext for later feminist works. (p. 53)

Elizabeth A. Meese, "Orality and Textuality in Zora Neale Hurston's 'Their Eyes Were Watching God'," in her *Crossing the Double Cross: The Practice of Feminist Criticism, The University of North Carolina Press, 1986, pp. 39-53.*

JENNIFER JORDAN

In 1970 Alice Walker began a study of black folklore to authenticate some information on voodoo that she wanted to incorporate into the short story "The Revenge of Hanna Kemhuff." Her research led her to **Mules and Men,** a collection of Southern folklore, compiled by Zora Neale Hurston, the noted Harlem Renaissance writer and folklorist, and to an almost obsessive campaign to reconstruct and reaffirm the life and work of a woman whose existence seemed somehow to validate Walker's own artistic and personal struggles as a beginning writer. According to Walker, Hurston was an auspicious discovery because every author needs a role model "in art, in behavior, in growth of spirit and intellect."

But the very qualities that made Hurston so admirable to Walker as an emerging young writer, both black and female, made her an anomaly in her own time, for Hurston was an outrageous and aggressive woman who was as comfortable in the ivy-covered halls of academe as she was in the jook joints of the Southern backwoods. She was a lover and shaper of art and ideas and a black writer whose works reflect a cultural awareness that Walker so aptly calls "racial health; a sense of black people as complete, complex *undiminished* human beings." Hurston was also an artist and anthropologist who pursued her work and her pleasure with an intense dedication and with little regard for the conventional restrictions society placed on both her sex and her race.

Alice Walker was shocked to discover that the early critics of Afro-American literature did not share her enthusiasm for Hurston. Instead, these critics—Hurston's contemporaries—found her aggravatingly contradictory and amazingly complex. They responded with negative commentary that Alice Walker condemns as "misleading, deliberately belittling, inaccurate, and generally irresponsible attacks." Often these "attacks" were fueled by Hurston's own ambivalences about race and class and by her pragmatism, which bordered on opportunism. Darwin Turner in *In a Minor Chord* accuses her of being "obsequious toward her supposed superiors," a conclusion that does not seem unreasonable given Hurston's unctuousness in her dealings with Mrs. Rufus Osgood Mason, a wealthy New Yorker who subsidized not only Hurston's work, but also that of Langston Hughes and the Harlem Renaissance painter Aaron Douglass. Hurston, perhaps out of financial necessity and a sincere need for the mothering that the tyrannical Mrs. Mason provided, stooped to bothersome levels of sycophancy in her letters to Mrs. Mason, referring to her patron as " 'the immaculate conception' " and " 'a glimpse of the holy grail.' "

Hurston's pragmatism also prevented her from being a racial and political militant despite her cultural chauvinism. In her autobiography, **Dust Tracks on a Road,** she admits she was disturbed when a black man tried to integrate the whites-only barbershop in Washington where she worked as a manicurist. His insistence on service was problematic because it was a threat to her livelihood as well as to that of the black man who owned the segregated business. Such statements and an attempt in **Dust Tracks** to cast herself as a person above the troublesome limitations of racialism resulted in Hurston's being branded a racial conservative by some and a traitor to the race by others. (pp. 105-06)

Despite her lack of veracity, critics like Alice Walker, Robert Hemenway, and Mary Helen Washington have managed to maintain both a certain objectivity about Hurston's weaknesses and a respectful fondness for her daring and talent. This same openmindedness and tolerance for ambivalence are not always reflected in the critical responses to her greatest work, *Their Eyes Were Watching God.* Hurston's independence, her refusal to allow her love interests and marriages to hamper her career, and her adventuresomeness in confronting the dangers of anthropological research in the violent turpentine camps of the South and in the voodoo temples of Haiti make her a grand candidate for feminist sainthood. Difficulties arise, however, when critics transfer their narrow conception of Hurston's personal attitudes and history to their readings of *Their Eyes Were Watching God,* a novel that reflects Hurston's ambiguity about race, sex, and class. The result is the unsupportable notion that the novel is an appropriate fictional representation of the concerns and attitudes of modern black feminism. (pp. 106-07)

One of the major issues in the redefinition of black womanhood is the role of individualism in a minority literature that has from its inception emphasized group development and salvation. (p. 107)

[The] new emphasis on self-fulfillment in the literature of black women writers has not eliminated from black feminist discourse the sixties' insistence on the political accountability of literature and the demand for the inclusion in the literature of a racial tradition of communalism. The nature of that accountability for black feminist writers and critics, however, has changed. First of all, there has been a call for a literature in which women "have pivotal relationships with one another," achieve a feminine bonding, and arrive at "liberation through [their] sisters." Black feminists, at the same time, have insisted that the sororal nexus not result in an isolation from one's racial culture and community. Ultimately, the liberation of black women from sexism and racism is to transform all black people and American society. Thus black feminist theory balances any perceived egocentrism with the cultural and political reintegration of transformed women into a revitalized society. Such mergence of individual and group needs makes for the happy ending of Alice Walker's *The Color Purple.*

The attempts of black feminists to accommodate the often conflicting imperatives of individual transformation, feminine bonding, and racial communalism have had a powerful effect on the reinterpretation of Hurston's *Their Eyes Were Watching God.* The novel is seen as a vehicle of feminist protest through its condemnation of the restrictiveness of bourgeois marriage and through its exploration of intraracial sexism and male violence. It is seen as a quest through which the heroine, Janie Killicks Starks Woods, achieves a sense of identity as a self-fulfilled woman and, through her own self-realization, becomes a leader of women and of her community. Although *Their Eyes Were Watching God* provides a most effective examination of the stultification of feminine talent and energy within traditional middle-class life, it ultimately belittles the suffering of the majority of black women whose working-class existences are dominated by hard labor and financial instability. Furthermore, Janie's struggle for identity and self-direction remains stymied. She never defines

herself outside the scope of her marital or romantic involvements and, despite her sincere relationship with her friend Pheoby, fails to achieve a communal identification with the black women around her or with the black community as a whole. As the novel ends, Janie chooses isolation and contemplation, not solidarity and action.

Even though *Their Eyes Were Watching God* does not meet the black feminist demand that a heroine achieve both self-definition and social commitment, it does skillfully expose, through its delineation of Janie's marriage to Jody Starks, the devaluation and aloneness of the middle-class woman whose sole purpose is to serve as an ornament and symbol of her husband's social status. . . . Although the Depression had decimated that burgeoning middle class, it had not destroyed the race's yearning for the trappings of bourgeois American life—an urge much fueled by the black periodicals of the Harlem Renaissance like *The Crisis, Opportunity,* Garvey's *Negro World,* and *The Messenger,* which constantly reinforced "middle class expectations of women" and focused on the role of the woman as a helpmate in the home. Hurston's novel exposes the domestic bliss of middle-class America as an empty dream.

Through the first half of the novel, Janie struggles to free herself from the expectations of her slave grandmother, who sees marriage as a haven from indiscriminate sexual exploitation (as opposed to the particular abuse of a loveless marriage) and as a shelter from financial instability. Janie escapes the marriage to Logan Killicks, which provides neither affection nor comfort. Her second marriage to Jody Starks is, at first, not devoid of emotional gratification, but ultimately Jody reduces Janie to an enviable possession that advertises his superior status to less fortunate men. As a possession she is denied any self-defined goals and even the expression of her own opinions. She is publicly humiliated and physically abused. (pp. 107-09)

Janie's marriage to Tea Cake is paradoxically interpreted by various critics either as a continuation of male domination that is overcome through Janie's killing of Tea Cake or as a marriage of true and equal minds in which Janie arrives at self-expression and self-esteem. Those who explain Janie's involuntary shooting of the rabid Tea Cake as a blow for personal freedom argue that his death is the result of his physical abuse of Janie. Alice Walker, [in *In Search of Our Mothers' Gardens*], contends that the beating "is the reason Huston *permits* Janie to kill Tea Cake" and that Janie is aware that "she has been publicly humiliated." [In "Zora Neale Hurston and the Survival of the Female"], Mary Jane Lupton also interprets Tea Cake's death as the result of a sexual war in which the male receives his comeuppance [see Further Reading list]. For Lupton, Tea Cake's rescue of Janie during the flood is a male/female battle for dominance, ending in the destruction of the males (Tea Cake and the mad dog) and the triumph through endurance of Janie and the cow. Lupton, ignoring the fact that Janie's escape from danger has nothing to do with her own abilities, proclaims Janie's survival and her ability to outshoot the sick Tea Cake as Hurston's proof of female superiority and dominance in a Darwinian world. (p. 109)

There is little evidence for the revenge theory in the text of *Their Eyes Were Watching God.* Janie at one point slaps Tea Cake when she suspects him of flirting with the fieldhand Nunkie, and the two engage in a ritualized struggle that is simply sexual foreplay. The narrative voice in *Their Eyes* dismisses Tea Cake's later violence by stating that it is "no brutal beating." The assault, which some critics use to emphasize Tea Cake's viciousness, is described as "two or three face slaps" resulting in Tea Cake's pampering of Janie and her clinging to him in a "helpless way." Not a single word implies than Janie harbors any resentment; at most, Hurston uses the beating to emphasize Tea Cake's insecurity.

Diane Sadoff argues [in her "Black Matrilineage: The Case of Alice Walter and Zora Neale Hurston"] that Janie kills Jody metaphorically with her tongue and Tea Cake literally because "Hurston has motivated her narrative, perhaps unconsciously, to act out her rage against male domination and to free Janie, a figure for herself, from all men." Whatever Hurston's attitude toward male dominance, she accepts as commonplace a certain type of physical violence between the sexes. In her autobiography, *Dust Tracks on a Road,* she describes an altercation between herself and A. W. P., the young lover who she says inspired the writing of *Their Eyes Were Watching God.* During their argument she slaps him and he returns the blow. She writes,

> He paid me off then and there with interest. No broken bones, you understand, and no black eyes. I realized afterwards that my hot head could tell me to beat him, but it would cost me something. I would have to bring head to get head. . . .
>
> Then I knew I was too deeply in love to be my old self. For always a blow to my body had infuriated me beyond measure. . . . But somehow, I didn't hate him at all. . . . He went out and bought some pie and I made a pot of hot chocolate and we were more affectionate than ever.

Hurston's personal attitude about violence in the battle of the sexes makes it unlikely that Tea Cake's death is a punishment for his treatment of Janie. His death is instead a typical resolution of the tale of courtly love in which the young troubadour or knight engages in an all-consuming passion with a lady of high rank. Tea Cake, the young bluesman and Janie's social inferior, falls in love with a lady, dedicates himself to making her happy, and sacrifices his life fighting the dragon, a kind of mad cow/dog/monster. Hurston creates an alliance of pure romance, a life of adventure and sexual union in a kind of Eden. But in the tradition of the western romance this love affair does not survive in a temporal realm. Denis de Rougemont in *Love in the Western World* argues that romantic love is often terminated by death but that the romancer uses death not to destroy love but to heighten its passion. Love is sweeter because of the partings and obstructions, and death is the ultimate obstruction, the greatest enhancer of an epic obsession.

So Tea Cake's death allows Janie to hold on to her paradise and to a dream of a perfect love. She can choose to remember the passion and the good times rather than sickness, death, the return of racism. She can cherish Eden rather than the world of the fall. In *Dust Tracks* Hurston contends she wrote *Their Eyes Were Watching God* to "embalm all the tenderness of [her] passion" for A. W. P., whom she gave up, she argues, because he did not approve of her career. Inherent in the word "embalm" are the notions not only of death but also of preservation, an attempt to counteract the ravages of time, to cherish something intact and unspoiled. Tea Cake's death eternalizes not only a love affair but also the novel by rescuing it from the pulp-level mediocrity of a they-lived-happily-ever-after ending.

The school of thought that sees the marriage to Tea Cake as a liberating and consciousness-raising experience focuses on the supposed equity of sexual roles. . . . Janie learns to use a rifle and goes to work in the field. Tea Cake, after she starts working, even helps with the cooking. But Hurston creates a dream relationship that allows Janie freedom to do the things that are amusing and to avoid the burdens of responsibility. She works much harder in Joe Starks's store. On the muck she goes to the fields primarily to be with Tea Cake, and the two of them spend a great deal of time "romping and playing." For Janie, stoop labor is the equivalent of two weeks at summer camp. When they arrive on the muck, Tea Cake carefully picks the only place that has a bathtub and makes sure that the work in the bean fields never gets oppressive. After they meet the Bahamans and start sponsoring all-night jump-ups behind their house, he does not "let her go with him to the field. He wanted her to get her rest." The day of the hurricane Janie stays home because it is too hot. Furthermore, although Janie is wealthy in comparison to Tea Cake, she has no financial responsibilities. Tea Cake insists that she live on what he makes. " 'Ah no need no assistance tuh help me feed mah woman.' " Janie in effect gets to eat her cake and have it too.

Ultimately, Janie's quest for excitement and pleasure in the Florida Everglades does not lead to an independent, self-fulfilled womanhood. She never learns to shape her destiny by making her own choices. It is Tea Cake who frees her, and until he becomes ill with rabies, she is dependent upon him for those things she craves—adventure, play, and erotic love. Janie acknowledges her dependency when she says, " 'He kin take most any lil thing and make summertime out of it when times is dull. Then we lives offa dat happiness he made till some mo' happiness come along.' " She tells Tea Cake after he saves her during the flood, " 'You come 'long and made somethin' outa me. So Ah'm thankful fuh anything we come through together.' "

The reversal created by Tea Cake's illness and death provides Janie with the opportunity for self-direction and control over her life. She is able to choose self when forced to save her life by killing Tea Cake, but she moves immediately into a new position of dependence. It is unfortunate that Hurston chooses a group of well-to-do white women as Janie's mentors. Why Janie finds them simpatico is not clear, but immediately she is determined to "make *them* know how it was.". . . The white women see in her a black representative of their class, and they serve to shield her, not from the white, male court system that treats her with kid gloves and acquits her in five minutes, but from the unruly blacks who call for her head. After the acquittal, "the judge and everybody up there smiled with her and shook her hand. And the white women cried and stood around her like a protecting wall and the Negroes, with heads hung down, shuffled out and away."

Janie's brief relationship with the white women who come to her aid grows out of expediency; there is little indication that she forms a strong bond with any community of women. (pp. 109-12)

Janie's allegiance to other women of any class is minimal. She has not one real female friend on the muck and associates only with the racist Mrs. Turner to whom she is indifferent. She ultimately has little in common with the rest of the women around her, who remain mules of the world. Even her good friend Pheoby finds it difficult to identify with her struggle to get down from the "high chair" of privilege. Pheoby says to her " 'Ah'd love tuh experience it for just one year. It look lak heben tuh me from where Ah'm at.' " Hurston writes *Their Eyes Were Watching God* to prove the emptiness of the middle-class woman's isolation and the falseness of her seeming social elevation. it is true that Janie in several interchanges with Jody also defends the status and dignity of all women, but in the long run her story makes light of the fate of the majority of black women in the thirties by turning migrant labor into fun and games and wife beating into a prelude to sexual ecstasy. (p. 112)

Janie's return to Eatonville has evoked elaborate critical discussion. A number of critics insist on the transcendent nature of her experience and proclaim her a returning teacher, elder, and artist, who in the role of storyteller conveys a message of liberation to black women and to her community. But Janie returns to Eatonville because she cannot continue her quest for excitement without Tea Cake and has demonstrated no ability to survive alone. Eatonville is the home of her only real friend, Pheoby, and the site of her house and of the rental property that is the source of her livelihood.

The claim that Janie's growing abilities to express her feelings and to tell a story make her an artist is tempered by the narrative structure of *Their Eyes Were Watching God.* Janie's voice is not the one that weaves the magic of the novel. We see her in chapter one telling Pheoby about her life. But chapter two is taken over by a third-person narrator, who relates a number of events in which Pheoby is an active participant. Janie and Pheoby returns as teller and listener only in the last chapter. At moments when Hurston could have given Janie the chance to prove her skill as a wordsmith, we are not allowed to hear her voice. Supposedly, while on the muck with Tea Cake, Janie "got so she could tell big stories herself," but we never hear her tell one. We also never experience the eloquence with which she defends herself and her love for Tea Cake in the courtroom after his death. Instead we are presented a synopsis of that defense. Hurston does not give Janie a fully fleshed-out character independent of her role as lover, nor does she create for her a voice that carries her tale.

The broader social implications of Janie's story are also debatable. The women of Eatonville seem unlikely recipients of any message she might convey and relish what they perceive as her diminished state. They see her return in overalls and without her man as "a weapon against her strength, and if it turned out of no significance, still it was a hope that she might fall to their level some day." Janie, of course, is glad to see Pheoby because they have always loved each other, but she is motivated to recount her adventures, not out of some magnanimous and pompous desire to drop pearls of wisdom to the masses but out of what Hurston explicitly calls "the oldest human longing—self revelation." If Janie is an artist, she is an aesthete, one whose art serves individual rather than communal purposes. She gives Pheoby permission to retell her story to the others because she does not want them to denigrate Tea Cake and her love for him. But she has little faith that the women of Eatonville will understand and appreciate her experiences. Her final comment on them is antagonistic. She says, " 'Dem meatskins [gossiping women] is *got* tuh rattle tuh make out they's alive.' " Hurston also seems to reject the notion that art or the telling of the story can transform people's lives. (pp. 113-14)

The contention that Janie becomes an activist and leader in the community is also not supported by the text. The imagery of the ending of the novel connotes the very opposite of activism and involvement. Janie is portrayed not as a self-defined, aware woman who will take charge of her own and others' destiny. Instead Hurston presents her as a woman whose life has passed, who has seized one bright moment by surrendering herself to the right man, and who will end that life commemorating that brief happiness. (pp. 114-15)

Their Eyes Were Watching God is a novel that examines with a great deal of artistry the struggle of a middle-class woman to escape the fetters of traditional marriage and the narrow social restrictions of her class and sex. But Janie Killicks Starks Woods never perceives herself as an independent, intrinsically fulfilled human being. Nor does she form the strong female and racial bonds that black feminists have deemed necessary in their definition of an ideologically correct literature. The novel fails to meet several of the criteria defined by black feminist criticism. Perhaps the acceptance and glorification of this novel as the bible of black women's liberation speak to the unconscious conflicts about emotional and financial dependence, sexual stereotyping, intraracial hostilities, and class interests inherent within the black feminist movement. In its very ambivalences Hurston's *Their Eyes Were Watching God* may serve as a Rorschach test by which these conflicts are revealed and thus is an appropriate manifesto for black feminism.

But the novel's success or failure as an ideological document does not diminish its aesthetic worth. It remains one of the great novels of black literature—a novel that is laughing outloud funny, that allows black people to speak in their own wonderful voices, and that portrays them in all their human nobility and pettiness. (p. 115)

Jennifer Jordan, "Feminist Fantasies: Zora Neale Hurston's 'Their Eyes Were Watching God'," in Tulsa Studies in Women's Literature, *Vol. 7, No. 1, Spring, 1988, pp. 105-17.*

KLAUS BENESCH

When *Their Eyes Were Watching God* was first published in 1937, two earlier books had already proved Zora Neale Hurston's particular interest in black oral culture: *Mules and Men* (1935) and *Jonah's Gourd Vine* (1934). Hurston had collected the material for *Mules and Men,* a compilation of folk tales, folk songs, folk speech, conjure formulas, root prescriptions, and various voodoo rituals, during a two-year stay in Florida under the supervision of Franz Boas, then one of the leading anthropologists in the United States. This book, dealing for the first time with Afro-American folklore from the perspective of the black rural community, is notable because it ties together the numerous stories in an overall narrative structure and thus gives the reader a sense of the original context that produced them. But although this leads to a certain fictionalization of the text, *Mules and Men* still retains an anthropological approach. It was not until *Jonah's Gourd Vine* that Zora Neale Hurston tried to embed her experience of black *oral* culture in an elaborate *literary* form, the modern novel.

Both *Jonah's Gourd Vine* and *Their Eyes Were Watching God* are set in Eatonville, Florida, Hurston's birthplace, which, in the words of Robert Hemenway, was "a proud, self-governing, all-black village that felt no need of integration and, in fact, resisted it, so that an Afro-American culture could thrive without interference." Furthermore, both texts are in some ways related to incidents and persons in Hurston's life. Although this autobiographical impulse is less perceptible in *Their Eyes,* she tells us in *Dust Tracks on a Road* that after receiving a Guggenheim Fellowship and leaving for Jamaica, she took the opportunity to come to grips with a muddled love-affair and wrote a new novel: "So I sailed off to Jamaica and pitched into work hard on my research to smother my feelings. But the thing would not down. The plot was far from the circumstances, but I tried to embalm all tenderness of my passion for him in *Their Eyes Were Watching God.*" The result, however is no ordinary love-story. Janie not only struggles against the anxieties and expectations of a slave-born grandmother who raised her, but also tries to resist the violent attempts of her later husbands to break her will to self-determination and to restrict her behavior to traditional female roles. Only with Tea Cake, her third husband, is Janie able to arrive at something like romance. But even this relationship, far from being harmonious all the time, is not free from oppression and violence. Finally, after shooting Tea Cake in self-defense, Janie returns to Eatonville where she sits down on the veranda to tell her story to Pheoby, an old friend.

At first glance, it looks as if *Their Eyes* is the story of a woman's resistance to male oppression and of her search for identity. If it were not for the abundant use of Black English, which in itself ties the text to a specific cultural background, *Their Eyes* might as easily be taken for the story of a white woman and thus to refer to ubiquitous problems of human existence. Yet, numerous textual oppositions show that there is more at stake here than a confrontation of gender-related interests: oppositions such as people versus things, communication versus isolation, blackness versus whiteness.

Mary Helen Washington argues [in her "Zora Neale Hurston: The Black Woman's Search for Identity"] that "the black frame of reference is achieved in Ms. Hurston's novel in three ways: 1. the language is the authentic dialect of black rural life; 2. the characters are firmly rooted in black culture; and 3. Janie's search for identity is an integral part of her search for blackness" [see Further Reading list]. Blackness, represented in the text by the various forms of black folklore and black culture, functions as a kind of barometer for Janie's development. Ultimate emancipation for her means far less to renounce the traditional male-female relationship than to claim active participation in the oral traditions of her environment. It is on the level of language that the reader first encounters this tradition. Dialogue and oral communication are heavily emphasized, and authorial voice, using a so-called standard English, is frequently reduced to a mere introductory function while meaning and content are constituted in the subsequent conversation rendered in a transcription of black rural speech:

> Some of them thought Starks ought not to have done that. He had so much cane and everything else. But they didn't say that while Joe Starks was on the porch. When the mail came from Maitland and he went inside to sort it out everybody had their say. Sim Jones started off as soon as he was sure that Starks couldn't hear him.

> "It's uh sin and uh shame runnin' dat po' man way from here lak dat. Colored folks oughtn't tuh be so hard on one 'nother." . . . "You kin feel a switch in his hand when he's talkin' to yuh," Oskar Scott complained. "Dat chastisin' feelin' he totes sorter gives yuh de protolapsis uh de cutinary linin'."

> "He's a whirlwind among breezes," Jeff Bruce threw in. "Speakin' of winds, he's de wind and we's de grass. We bend which ever way he blows," Sam Watson agreed, "but at dat us needs him. De town wouldn't bc nothin' if it wasn't for him. He can't help being sorter bossy. Some folks needs thrones, and ruling-chairs and crowns tuh make they influence felt. He don't. He's got a throne in de seat of his pants."

The figurative and metaphorical qualities of Black English are evident in this passage. Verbal play and rhetorical improvisation ("speakin' of winds" et cetera) dramatize the oral-aural orientation of the black community of Eatonville and demonstrate their linquistic virtuosity, of which Zora Neale Hurston once said, "who knows what fabulous cities of artistic concepts lie within the mind and language of some humble Negro boy or girl who has never heard of Ibsen."

But Black English and its specific characteristics are also thematically involved in the text. The conflict between Janie and her second husband Joe Starks culminates in an act of speech. As Henry Louis Gates, Jr. points out [in his *Black Literature and Literary Theory*], Janie not only participates in the rituals of the signifying but "is openly signifying upon her husband's impotency." To Stark's taunting insinuations about her being too old now to mingle with all the men in his shop, she answers with self-confidence:

> Naw, Ah ain't no young gal no mo' but den Ah ain't no old woman neither. Ah reckon Ah looks mah age too. But Ah'm uh woman every inch of me, and Ah know it. Dat's uh whole lot more'n *you* kin say. You big-bellies round here and put a lot of brag, but 'tain't nothin' to it but yo' big voice. Humph! Talkin' 'bout *me* lookin' old! When you pull down y' britches, you look lak de change uh life.

After his impotence is publicly exposed, Starks's physical strength declines rapidly. From now on he will not leave his bed, and even the intensive efforts of a root-doctor cannot prevent him from dying soon afterwards. Whether or not his "kidney-failure" is as Gates argues, only a pun of sorts, a hidden allusion to the 'actual' cause of his death, to be 'kid-ded' upon, remains unclear. Yet, without doubt, by supplying Janie with the specific technique of signifying at the point of her utmost resistance to banishment from the center of public communication Hurston draws our attention to the preeminent role of oral speech in Afro-American culture. Even more than Langston Hughes, who frequently uses Black English in his fiction and poetry, she emphasizes the cultural autonomy of the Black vernacular, which for her is a language that even the poorest and least educated blacks master and which should not flinch from comparison with any other language, be it American English or the classical European languages. (pp. 627-29)

Although *Their Eyes* omits any direct confrontation between blacks and whites, a distinct opposition of whiteness and blackness pervades all levels of the text. Janie's search for identity turns out to be primarily a search for blackness, a coming to terms with the various forms of Afro-American folk and oral culture. In her teens Janie had to face the anxieties and demands of a grandmother whose attitudes toward life still reflected the experience of slavery. Completely deprived of self-determination and free will, Nanny directed all her ambitions toward her children, and after the raping of her own daughter, toward Janie:

> You can't beat nobody down so low till you can rob'em of they will. Ah didn't want to be used for a work-ox and a brood-sow and Ah didn't want my daughter used dat way neither. It sho wasn't mah will for things to happen lak they did. Ah even hated de way you was born. But, all de same Ah thank God, Ah got another chance. . . . Ah been waitin' a long time, Janie, but nothin' Ah been through ain't too much if you just take a stand on high ground like Ah dreamed.

This vision of Nanny, to "take a stand on high ground," is one of the earliest efforts in the text to exclude and isolate Janie from interaction with her black community or, to modify an epithet of Langston Hughes's, from "the ways of the black folks." Of course, Nanny's plans for her granddaughter are not in line with the blatant imitation of white behavior exhibited by Killicks, Starks, or Mis' Turner. However, as a major impulse throughout Janie's life, they do not prove ineffectual. . . . Nanny is certainly molded by her experience as a black woman, "de mule uh de world," as she herself puts it, and also manifests in many ways what Ralph Ellison, talking about the blues, once called a "sheer toughness of will." Yet, wanting "protection" for Janie, she finally pushes her into the loveless marriage with Logan Killicks, a representative of a rather 'white' value system.

Without any considerable contact with members of the black community, Janie's early life is primarily distinguished by its lack of personal communication. With Killicks she is about to experience for the first time that "to be safe" (which in itself, in the sense of a depository, connotes seclusion) to her means isolation from the bustling life of black culture in favor of at least questionable, white middle-class aspirations. However, it is in the all-black community of Eatonville that this tension reaches its climax. Starks's store-porch, "where people sat around . . . and passed around the pictures of their thoughts for the others to look at and see," is *the* central meeting-place for the town folks, a true forum for Afro-American folklore. Here tale telling and lying sessions take place, courtship rituals are acted out and every conceivable business of the town is talked over. In these passages Hurston's representation of black rural life is at its most vivid and brilliant. Since she grew up in Eatonville herself, the intimate knowledge of this milieu enables her to render the various folk forms in their genuine cultural context and to transcribe spoken language with a sensitivity rarely achieved since. She defies all efforts to view black oral culture as a mere reaction to repressive conditions. For her, the playful and artistic use of language is a natural gift, more often than not motivated by sheer pleasure:

> "It takes money tuh feed pretty women. Dey gits uh lavish uh talk."

> "Not lak mine. Dey loves to hear me talk because dey can't understand it. Mah co-talking is too deep. Too much co to it."

Joe Starks, the "citified, stylish dressed man" who came to Eatonville, as Hurston puts it ironically, to become "a big voice," is set off from the very beginning against the community's bent for idleness and communication. In a town where fixed political structures are totally unknown, he starts out to persuade the people of the need for a mayor and to enthrone himself in that position. His rigorous way of "buyin' in big" soon raises him to the top and, as the most powerful man in Eatonville, he begins to signify on every level his 'otherness' and superiority:

> Take for instance that new house of his. It had two stories with porches, with banisters and such things. The rest of the town looked like servants' quarters surrounding the "big house." And different from everybody else in town he put off moving in until it had been painted, in and out. And look at the way he painted it—a gloaty, sparkly white. The kind of promenading white that the houses of Bishop Whipple, W. B. Jackson and the Vanderpool's wore. It made the village feel funny talking to him—just like he was anybody else.

His "golded-up spitting pot" and somewhat smaller "lady-size" one for Janie are additional examples of his grotesque ambitions to copy and even exaggerate emblems of the white upper class. But the most striking caricature of Starks as a representative of whiteness is yet to come. Ironically, one of his first public acts as mayor of Eatonville is the installment of a street lamp. During a barbecue preceding the occasion, he says: "Dis occasion is something for us all tuh remember tuh our dyin' day. De first street lamp in a colored town. Lift yo' eyes and gaze on it. And when Ah touch de match tuh dat lamp-wick let de light penetrate *inside* of yuh, and let it shine, let it shine" (my emphasis). In his attempt to bring 'light' into the 'darkness' of Eatonville, Starks is evoking a two thousand year-old investment of blackness with negative and whiteness with exclusively positive attributes. . . . In *Their Eyes*, Starks's notion of illumination and enlightenment(!) from 'within,' that is the internalizing of the 'white' point of view, is ingeniously set off against the vision of the spiritual expression of 'black' experience and tradition: "We'll walk in de light, de beautiful light / Come where the dew drops of mercy shine bright / shine all *around* us by day and by night / Jesus, the light of the world" (my emphasis). Here, light as a metaphor is applied to envisioned conditions, things 'outside' an individual self, which are supposed to guarantee freedom and peace for all people, regardless of either race or color. By signifying upon Starks's preoccupation with light, Hurston succeeded in challenging, by way of connotation, an ancient and firmly established stereotype.

It is no surprise, then, that Starks gradually withdraws from the store-porch, the center of black oral tradition. He rarely talks ("Saving his breath on talk . . . weakened people"), and his role in the "mule-talking" and "lying sessions" is confined to listening and occasional laughter: "Janie noted that while he didn't talk the mule himself, he sat and laughed at it." This smug reticence as well as his continuing endeavors to acquire an aura of being 'white' and thus different are subjected to the most subtle but at the same time extremely effective caricature. In chapter six, the longest in the book, we are invited to eavesdrop on the talking and the performances on the store-porch. At first, the full-length representation of a folk tale, a "contest in hyperbole," and the playful courtship rituals seem unintegrated into the rest of the plot and may appear as flaws in the novel. At the forefront of those who have used this argument against *Their Eyes*, Darwin Turner illustrates a general tendency in criticism and at the same time accentuates the pivotal role this chapter plays in the context of Hurston's efforts to apply oral folklore to literary texts: "Digressive and unnecessary, the chapter merely suggests that Miss Hurston did not know how to integrate the folk material which she considered essential for local color." [See Hurston's entry in *CLC,* Vol. 30]. Yet, considering the opposition of whiteness versus blackness which can be traced throughout the rest of the text, I wish to suggest that this chapter is more than a clumsy and slightly exaggerated accumulation of "local color."

The beginning and the end of the chapter demonstrate two important stages in Janie's search for blackness. Having been assigned to tend her husband's store, she is frequently exposed to the performances of Afro-American folklore, acted out on the store-porch. Before long Janie begins to enjoy the ever-new and fancy stories of her customers, yet her own active participation in the telling is vehemently vetoed by Starks: "Janie loved the conversation and sometimes she thought up good stories on the mule, but Joe had forbidden her to indulge. He didn't want her talking after such trashy people." Some thirty pages later, however, Janie, for the first time, gains her own 'voice.' Joining the tale-telling on the store-porch, she not only challenges a taboo established by her husband but publicly corroborates her affiliation with black folk traditions: "Janie did what she had never done before, that is, thrust herself into the conversation."

Prior to this event, we witness the "lying" and talking on the store-porch. The so-called "mule talk" is one of the favorites: "He [the mule] was next to the Mayor in prominence and made better talking." "Brazzle's ole yaller mule," a popular and widely known legend in Eatonville, and which Hurston also used for *Mule Bone*, the play she co-authored with Langston Hughes, was a fixed part of the general repertoire. Yet, these stories do not function as "local color." Hurston again confronts the reader with the imagination and verbal versatility of people like Sam, Lige, and Walter, and by rendering their stories with the least narrative distance, she elucidates the different modes of *oral* and *literary* tale-telling. (pp. 629-32)

But the "mule talk" . . . points to another frame of reference, which exceeds the context of Eatonville. The comparable condition of mules and slaves—both are considered workhorses and, more often than not, treated in similar ways—made the mule a favorite symbol of Afro-American folklore, a prominent object of identification for many black people, even long after Emancipation. Mules are not only bought and sold, driven to work and, most of the time, malnourished, but are also strong, stubborn, and unpredictable. By way of a double-voiced strategy, the black story-teller and his audience were able to play the role of the workhorse, which was imposed on them by their white masters, and at the same time to use the story as an act of resistance, by stressing the potential obstinacy of the mule:

> "Ah does feed'im. He's jus' too mean tuh git fat. He stay poor rawbony jus' fuh spite. Skeered he'll hafta work some."

> "Yeah, you feeds'im. Feeds'im offa 'come up' and seasons it wid raw-hide."

> "Does feed de ornery Varmint! Don't keer whut Ah do Ah can't git long wid 'im. He fights every inch in front uh de plow, and even lay back his ears tuh kick and bite when Ah go in de stall tuh feed him."

To be sure, the identification of 'mules and men' is no longer the main impetus for the tale-tellers in an all-black community like Eatonville. Yet, by using such stories in *Their Eyes*, Hurston not only signifies on a collective past but also, in alluding to Nanny's earlier remark that "de nigger woman is de mule uh de world," signifies on the role of black women

as well as on the male-female relationships. This technique of implying two or more levels of possible meaning is most evident in the mule's "mock burial." Here, the lines between a particular incident in the history of Eatonville (the death of Mat Bonner's "yaller mule"), the fictional device (the satirical exposing of Starks's 'alienated' behavior), and the traditional folk tale (a part of the general repertoire of black oral culture), are blurred together. And even more explicitly than before, the mule is invested with human features: "Out in the swamp they made great ceremony over the mule. They mocked everything human in death. Starks led off with a great eulogy on our departed citizen and the grief he left behind him, and the people loved the speech." Although his "eulogy" makes him "more solid than building the schoolhouse had done," Starks becomes again the main target of irony. At the end of the burial, when the carcass is left to the buzzards, the animals, in a kind of call and response, not only mock his greediness and voracity but anticipate on the level of the plot, his own death: " 'What killed this man?' The chorus answered, 'Bare, bare fat.' "

Already before this, Starks has been ridiculed through his role in the "mule talk." To stop the store-porch crowd from playing tricks on Mat Bonner's mule, he purchases the animal and, supplying his food, allows him to rest as a "free mule" in the streets of Eatonville. Yet, notwithstanding the general approval of his deed, a mocking note in Janie's remarks is hard to miss: "Freein' dat mule makes uh mighty big man outa you. Something like George Washington and Lincoln. Abraham Lincoln, he had de whole United States tuh rule so he freed de Negroes. You got uh town so you freed uh mule. You have tuh have power tuh free things and dat makes you like uh king uh something." Again, it is extremely difficult to separate the 'real' incident, as part of the plot, from one of the mule-stories. Hurston's constant skipping between two different levels of narration generates a creative tension which, by sarcastically signifying on Starks, gradually directs our sympathies toward the black folk traditions. (pp. 632-34)

Janie's third relationship is sharply set off against her former marriages. Like a true blues hero, Tea Cake is deeply rooted in traditional folk behavior. He performs the old courtship rituals, indulges in crap-shooting and razor fighting, plays the dozens and the blues. Unlike Killicks and Starks, he prefers communication and people to 'things': "So us goin' off somewhere and start all in Tea Cake's way. Dis ain't no business proposition, and no race after property and titles. Dis is uh love game." "Down in the muck," where their house is "a magnet, the unauthorized center of the 'job,' " Janie, having so far been denied involvement in Afro-American oral culture, feels free to join the notorious "lying" and tale-telling sessions whenever she wants to: "She got so, she could tell big stories herself from listening to the rest." Yet, even with Tea Cake, she has to face occasional crises and physical violence. S. Jay Walker has argued that Hurston betrays Janie's gradual resistance to traditional role stereotypes by confining her for a third time to the traditional pattern of the male-female relationship. [See Walker's excerpt above]. However, according to my own argument, Janie's development is above all a function of her meaningful participation in black folk traditions, and only secondarily depends on the opposition of a woman to gender-related expectations. Therefore, *Their Eyes* closes neither with an idealized love-affair nor with a feminist challenge to male hubris and arrogance. Back in Eatonville, Janie does what might be considered as the essential subtext of the whole book: she tells her story. This final emphasis on communication and community is representative not only of Zora Neale Hurston's affirmative attitude toward Afro-American oral culture, but also of a frequently misunderstood narrative strategy: the merging of *literary* and *oral* style. (p. 634)

Klaus Benesch, "Oral Narrative and Literary Text: Afro-American Folklore in 'Their Eyes Were Watching God'," in Callaloo, Vol. 11, No. 3, Summer, 1988, pp. 627-35.

JAMES ROBERT SAUNDERS

Referring to Zora Neale Hurston's **Their Eyes Were Watching God** (1937), Alice Walker asserts, "There is no book more important to me than this one." Added to that statement of memorial is a poem composed by Walker dedicated to the main protagonist of that Hurston novel, a work that has rapidly become recognized as a modern classic. Included in her collection of poems entitled *Good Night, Willie Lee, I'll See You in the Morning* (1977), Walker writes:

I love the way Janie Crawford
left her husbands
the one who wanted to change her
into a mule
and the other who tried to interest her
in being a queen.
A woman, unless she submits,
is neither a mule
nor a queen
though like a mule she may suffer
and like a queen pace the floor.

Within the context of that poem, Walker has accurately interpreted much of the message in Hurston's novel. Understandably, Janie is not satisfied in her marriage to Logan Killicks, especially once she discovers that he plans to work her in the fields. Yet the more subtle psychological brutality exercised by Janie's second husband Joe is equally offensive: just after having been elected mayor of Eatonville, he can be found proclaiming, "She's uh woman and her place is in de home." Upon having just met Janie, one of his initial responses to her cascading hair and light skin had been to say that "a pretty doll-baby lak you is made to sit on de front porch and rock and fan yo'self and eat p'taters dat other folks plant just special for you." It would become Starks' intention to make a lady out of one who had in his estimation been gifted with physical beauty and, hopefully, a submissive disposition.

It is worth noting that in her poem Walker indicates Hurston's heroine "left her husbands." Yet while Janie does actually leave Killicks, she forsakes Joe Starks in a much different way. Having traveled some distance to take advantage of the newly developing all-black town, that second husband soon finds himself holding all of the town's most prominent positions, including those of storekeeper, postmaster, and mayor. However, as his responsibilities begin to mount, he finally is forced to let his wife help him operate the general store. Before long, Steve Mixon, from the Eatonville community, comes into that store to get some chewing tobacco, whereupon Janie finds herself in the position of having to cut out a plug for him. She fails to do this properly, whereupon Joe issues scathing criticism and then orders, "Don't stand dere rollin' yo' pop eyes at me wid yo' rump hangin' nearly to yo' knees!" Janie is personally humiliated, but as Hurston further

writes, there was in addition "laughter at the expense of women." Men milling about the store begin desecrating womanhood in general, insinuating through their hideous laughter that no woman can do things as well as men. This marks a turning point in the novel because it is the point at which Janie decides to relinquish what had been loyalty to Joe and stand up for herself. It is as though the author herself became a character in her fiction as "Janie took to the middle of the floor to talk right into Jody's face, and that was something that hadn't been done before." Thus Janie retaliates:

"Stop mixin' up mah doings wid mah looks, Jody. When you git through tellin' me how tuh cut uh plug uh tobacco, then you kin tell me whether mah behind is on straight or not."

"Wha—whut's dat you say, Janie? You must be out yo' head."

"Naw, Ah ain't outa mah head neither."

"You must be. Talkin' any such language as dat."

"You de one started talkin' under people's clothes. Not me."

"Whut's de matter wid you, nohow? You ain't no young girl to be gettin' all insulted 'bout yo' looks. You ain't no young courtin' gal. You'se uh ole woman, nearly forty."

"Yeah, Ah'm nearly forty and you'se already fifty. How come you can't talk about dat sometimes instead of always pointin' at me?"

"T'ain't no use in gettin' all mad, Janie, 'cause Ah mention you ain't no young gal no mo'. Nobody in heah ain't lookin' for no wife outa yuh. Old as you is."

"Naw, Ah ain't no young gal no mo' but den Ah ain't no old woman neither. Ah reckon Ah looks mah age too. But Ah'm a woman every inch of me, and Ah know it. Dat's uh whole lot more'n *you* kin say. You big-bellies round here and put out a lot of brag, but 'tain't nothin' to it but yo' big voice. Humph! Talkin' 'bout *me* lookin' old! When you pull down yo' britches, you look lak de change uh life."

In this verbal exchange much of our attention is drawn to the unorthodox spellings, double negatives, and folk expressions making up black dialect. But the most important point Hurston wishes to make has to do with the manner in which Janie has responded to Joe's efforts to confine her to "her place." After twenty years of his mental abuse, she finally rejects the premise upon which he had conceived their marriage. Only in this sense has Janie actually left him, and unable ever to recover from the shock of her assertiveness, he dies from what the author tells us is some kind of kidney trouble. (pp. 1-3)

At the beginning of her collection of essays entitled *In Search of Our Mothers' Gardens,* Walker astutely offers her own list of alternative definitions for the term "womanist." The most essential explanation is that the word refers to "outrageous, audacious, courageous or *willful* behavior." The emphasis is on "willful" because for so long, so many black women have not been considered to be in possession of their own free wills, and no small part of the problem has resided in the psyche of black men. While many of her attitudes about the role of women in society are indeed outdated, Janie's grandmother, in *Their Eyes Were Watching God,* is not wholly out of date when she tells her ward:

> Honey, de white man is de ruler of everything as fur as Ah been able tuh find out. Maybe it's some place off in de ocean where de black man is in power, but we don't know nothin' but what we see. So de white man throw down de load and tell de nigger man tuh pick it up. He pick it up because he have to, but he don't tote it. He hand it to his womenfolks. De nigger woman is de mule uh de world so fur as Ah can see.

Nanny warns Janie about racism and sexism, but the grandmother is more specifically concerned about the position of black women at the bottom of the totem pole. In spite of this entreaty, though, Janie has to learn the lesson for herself, experiencing two marriages that resemble what life would be like in a prison. (pp. 4-5)

It is rather difficult to believe that the similarities in . . . [Hurston's novel] are mere coincidence. Born in Eatonville, Florida, at some unidentified point near the turn of the century, Hurston describes in her autobiographical *Dust Tracks on a Road* (1942) how she "used to climb to the top of one of the huge chinaberry trees which guarded our front gate, and look out over the world." Young Zora Neale was anxious to behold all that a full life might afford the individual. Further on in that autobiography the author tells us, "It grew upon me that I ought to walk out to the horizon and see what the end of the world was like." Similarly, in the very first line of her novel we are provided with the reflection that "Ships at a distance have every man's wish on board." Hurston then goes on to explain how some of those ships come in with the tide while others "sail forever on the horizon, never out of sight." Even those men who do not attain their dreams have at least at some point in their lives been able to envision themselves fulfilling their fantasies. At sixteen, that age when the search for identity is most profound, Janie slips out of her grandmother's house and imagines, "Oh to be a pear tree— *any* tree in bloom!" Janie envisions complete fulfillment; however, it must be noted that she identifies not with another person, but with a part of nature. As a "tree" she will be in possession of great strength, awesome beauty, and communion with the natural world. (p. 5)

In the foreword to Robert Hemenway's *Zora Neale Hurston: A Literary Biography,* Walker writes of her efforts to locate and mark Hurston's grave. "It was, rather, a duty I accepted as naturally mine—as a black person, a woman, and a writer—because Zora was dead and I, for the time being, was alive" [see Further Reading list]. Walker's action in finding and marking Hurston's grave is comparable to the dead artist's own devotion to her craft in spite of many obstacles. (p. 6)

In another era Hurston might have been a literary legend in her lifetime; instead, she died in relative obscurity at a Florida welfare home, based on what Walker has been able to ascertain, from either malnutrition or a stroke. Commenting on a rejection letter received by Hurston after she had submitted one of her later manuscripts, Hemenway laments that it "indicates the personal tragedy of Zora Neale Hurston: Barnard graduate, author of four novels, two books of folklore, one volume of autobiography, the most important collector of Afro-American folklore in America, reduced by poverty and circumstance." It is not so difficult to understand why Walk-

er was compelled to find the whereabouts of Hurston's final resting place. . . .

Walker mentions that when looking for Hurston's grave, she searched and searched before finally reaching a point where there was "only one thing to do." In the midst of that desolate Florida setting, it occurred to Walker that having come this close she need only cry out for acknowledgement. "Zo-ra!" she screamed and suddenly her "foot sinks into a hole." Perhaps by some act of supernatural intervention, Hurston had "reached out" to join in communion with one who was of the same mind as she. This brings us to the point of once again considering the poem that Walker wrote in memory of Hurston's Janie Crawford. It has been noted that the poem's heroine left Logan Killicks, but her departure from Joe Starks was much more profound than mere physical leavetaking. However, even more peculiar is the fact that Hurston's character Tea Cake is not mentioned as the poet Walker tells how Janie "left her husbands." Nevertheless Tea Cake is the most significant male in Hurston's novel, being the type of natural man who seems to love Janie for herself. He and Janie work and play together, sharing their lives almost completely. Still, this presumably perfect man can strike his wife, and so she has to kill him in the end, although Hurston has made the development ambiguous by first having a rabid dog bite this third husband, causing him to go insane. Hurston has forced us, through Janie's act of self-defense, to take in the fact that some married women have had no recourse but to save themselves by violent reaction. (p. 7)

It is most appropriate to remember Hurston as both a folklorist and a novelist. Her first collection of folklore, entitled *Mules and Men,* was published in 1935, and Hemenway comments, "Its publication was historically important, the first book of Afro-American folklore collected by a black American to be presented by a major publisher for a general reading audience." (pp. 9-10)

Nevertheless, it is the awe-inspiring *Their Eyes Were Watching God* that has sealed Hurston's place in arts and letters. The tale of Janie Crawford is one that was not fully appreciated during the 1930s when women were to a large extent still controlled by chauvinistic attitudes. Now, however, this landmark novel is accepted for what it is—a cornerstone in literary history. . . .

What Hurston had advocated in *Their Eyes Were Watching God* was the right of women to choose directions for themselves. "Perhaps the most important choice," say sociologists Joan Huber and Glenna Spitze, "is the ability to leave a man who will not do his share." Regardless of the changing times, there are many women who remain helplessly bound in unfulfilling matrimony. Financial dependence entraps some while others simply believe that any man is better than no man at all. It is this latter psychological phenomenon against which Hurston railed the most as she wrote her portrayal of Crawford's three fateful unions. (p. 10)

James Robert Saunders, "Womanism as the Key to Understanding Zora Neale Hurston's 'Their Eyes Were Watching God' and Alice Walker's 'The Color Purple'," in The Hollins Critic, Vol. XXV, No. 4, October, 1988, pp. 1-11.

FURTHER READING

Awkward, Michael. " 'The Inaudible Voice of It All': Silence, Voice, and Action in *Their Eyes Were Watching God*." In *Studies in Black American Literature: Black Feminist Criticism and Critical Theory*. Edited by Joe Weixlmann and Houston A. Baker, Jr., pp. 57-109. Greenwood, Fla.: The Penkevill Publishing Co., 1988.
  Critically regarded as "arguably, the most insightful essay yet written" on *Their Eyes Were Watching God*, Awkward's work examines Hurston's successful blend of voice and action.

Bethel, Lorraine. " 'This Infinity of Conscious Pain': Zora Neale Hurston and the Black Female Literary Tradition." In *All the Women Are White, All the Blacks Are Men, But Some of Us Are Brave: Black Women's Studies*. Edited by Gloria T. Hull, Patricia Bell Scott, and Barbara Smith, pp. 176-88. Old Westbury, N.Y.: The Feminist Press, 1982.
  Feminist appreciation and reevaluation of Hurston.

Bloom, Harold, ed. *Zora Neale Hurston*. Modern Critical Views. New York: Chelsea House Publishers, 1986, 192 p.
  Contains nineteen biographical and critical essays on Hurston, including pieces by Langston Hughes, Fannie Hurst, Larry Neal, and Alice Walker.

Carr, Glynis. "Storytelling as *Bildung* in Zora Neale Hurston's *Their Eyes Were Watching God*." *CLA Journal* XXXI, No. 2 (December 1987): 189-200.
  Chronicles Janie's maturity and increasing mastery of storytelling.

Ferguson, SallyAnn. "Folkloric Men and Female Growth in *Their Eyes Were Watching God*." *Black American Literature Forum* 21, Nos. 1 & 2 (Spring-Summer 1987): 185-97.
  Charts Janie's growth through her three marriages and examines the novel's folkloric influences.

Giles, James R. "The Significance of Time in Zora Neale Hurston's *Their Eyes Were Watching God*." *Negro American Literary Forum* 6, No. 2 (Summer 1972): 52-3, 60.
  Discusses Hurston's use of time to accentuate the conflict between goodness and hedonism.

Hemenway, Robert E. *Zora Neale Hurston: A Literary Biography*. Chicago: University of Illinois Press, 1977, 371 p.

Biographical information and criticism of Hurston's works. See excerpt in *CLC*, Vol. 30.

Howard, Lillie P. *Zora Neale Hurston*. Boston: G. K. Hall & Co., 1980, 192 p.
  Contains literary criticism, biographical information and extensive bibliography.

Kalb, John D. "The Anthropological Narrator of Hurston's *Their Eyes Were Watching God*." *Studies in American Fiction* 16, No. 2 (Autumn 1988): 169-80.
  Explores the crucial roles of folklore and dialect toward the understanding of Hurston's narration.

Kubitschek, Missy Dean. " 'Tuh de Horizon and Back': The Female Quest in *Their Eyes Were Watching God*." *Black American Literature Forum* 17, No. 3 (Fall 1983): 109-15.
  Interprets Janie's search for identity as an individual quest that enriches the community of Eatonville upon its completion.

Lupton, Mary Jane. "Zora Neale Hurston and the Survival of the Female." *The Southern Literary Journal* XV, No. 1 (Fall 1982): 45-54.
  Discusses the tenacity of Hurston's female protagonists in the novel *Their Eyes Were Watching God* and the short story "Sweat."

Pondrom, Cyrena N. "The Role of Myth in Hurston's *Their Eyes Were Watching God*." *American Literature* 58, No. 2 (May 1986): 181-202.
  Interprets the influence of Greek mythology in Hurston's novel.

Walker, Alice. "In Search of Zora Neale Hurston." *Ms* III, No. 9 (March 1979): 74-9, 85-9.
  A reflection on Hurston's later life, Walker's essay recounts a trip to Eatonville, Florida, Hurston's hometown and the inspiration for many of her writings.

Washington, Mary Helen. "Zora Neale Hurston: The Black Woman's Search for Identity." *Black World* XXI, No. 10 (August 1972): 68-75.
  Examines the roles of black dialect and culture in Janie's quest for identity.

Jack Kerouac

1922-1969

(Born Jean-Louis Lebris de Kerouac) American novelist, poet, and essayist.

The following entry presents criticism on Kerouac's novel *On the Road* (1957). For discussions of Kerouac's complete career, see *CLC,* Vols. 1, 2, 3, 5, 14, 29.

Kerouac is a key figure of the artistic and cultural phenomenon of the 1950s known as the Beat Movement, which began simultaneously in Greenwich Village and San Francisco as a reaction to the conservatism of post-World War II America. Kerouac coined the term "Beat," meaning both "beaten down," or outcast, and "beatific," or full of spiritual joy, to describe the condition of his generation. His best-known novel, *On the Road,* depicts the counter-culture lifestyle of the Beats, which was marked by impulsive travelling and experimentation with sex and drugs. Some passages in this book are considered early examples of the "spontaneous prose" method Kerouac developed in an effort to escape the strictures of grammar and syntax. Consequently, *On the Road* moves with the same frenetic energy as its characters, chronicling numerous road trips and drunken episodes without extensive characterization or plot development. Most of the early reviews of *On the Road* emphasized the lifestyle depicted rather than the novel's literary qualities. As early as 1959, however, *On the Road* began receiving measured critical attention from literary scholars interested in tracing the novel's inspiration and influences. *On the Road* is said to have inspired the youth of the 1960s. The continuing popularity of this novel and the proximity of Kerouac's philosophy to that of such honored American writers as Walt Whitman and Henry David Thoreau have garnered Kerouac a place in the canon of contemporary American authors.

Born in a French-Canadian community in Lowell, Massachusetts, Kerouac was raised a Catholic and educated in parochial schools. An outstanding athlete, he received a football scholarship to Columbia University but withdrew from school during the fall of his sophomore year. He joined the Navy in 1943 and was released after six months for psychological reasons. Kerouac worked the remainder of World War II as a merchant seaman and associated with the bohemian crowd around Columbia that included Allen Ginsberg and William Burroughs, two prominent Beat writers who would feature in his fiction. The publication of *On the Road* in 1957, based on events that occurred in the late 1940s, brought Kerouac sudden notoriety. Eight of his books were produced during the next few years as publishers rushed to capitalize on his popularity. Kerouac's natural shyness, however, kept him from enjoying his fame; he was known to arrive at interviews intoxicated and failed in his sporadic attempts to withdraw from society to concentrate on writing. A sincere patriot and Catholic, Kerouac became increasingly bewildered by and alienated from his bohemian fans in the 1960s. He returned to the place of his birth in 1966, and died of alcoholism in 1969.

Kerouac considered his novels a series of interconnected autobiographical narratives of the type Marcel Proust pub-

lished at the turn of the century. The novels that compose "The Legend of Duluoz," as Kerouac called the totality of his works, include *Visions of Gerard,* which pictures Kerouac's childhood as overshadowed by the death of his revered brother Gerard at age nine; *Doctor Sax: Faust Part Three,* a surrealistic depiction of Kerouac's boyhood memories and dreams; *Maggie Cassidy,* which recounts Kerouac's first love; and *Vanity of Duluoz: An Adventurous Education 1935-46,* which chronicles Kerouac's years of playing football at prep school and Columbia. In *On the Road,* Kerouac wrote about the late 1940s, focusing on the years of traveling and socializing with Neal Cassady, Allen Ginsberg, and William Burroughs. *Visions of Cody,* viewed by many critics as a late revision of *On the Road,* retells the story in spontaneous prose. Kerouac wrote about his love affair in 1953 with an African-American woman in *The Subterraneans,* and his adventures on the West Coast learning about Buddhism from the poet Gary Snyder are chronicled in *The Dharma Bums. Desolation Angels* covers the years just prior to publication of *On the Road,* while *Big Sur* displays the bitterness and despair Kerouac experienced in the early 1960s and his descent into alcoholism. Kerouac and his friends have a variety of pseudonyms in these novels, and styles range from the relatively traditional to the almost surreal effects of spontaneous prose.

Together these novels portray the birth, education, and eventual disillusionment of an American idealist.

The controversial history of *On the Road* begins with the lack of consensus regarding the number of drafts Kerouac wrote during the years when he was trying unsuccessfully to have this novel published. There is also disagreement concerning the degree to which Malcolm Cowley and other editors at Viking Press altered Kerouac's version of *On the Road* before publishing it. A barely fictionalized portrait of the late 1940s when Kerouac and his friends travelled back and forth across the United States, *On the Road* was not universally perceived as literature upon publication. David Dempsey, for example, remarked: "Jack Kerouac has written an enormously readable and entertaining book but one reads it in the same mood that he might visit a sideshow—the freaks are fascinating although they are hardly part of our lives." Sal's enthusiastic description of the manic adventures that make up the plot of this novel, including stealing, drunkenness, purposeless travel, drug use, and sexual promiscuity, convinced other critics that the lifestyle depicted in *On the Road* signalled the moral demise of Kerouac's generation. Gilbert Millstein, representing the opposing view, decreed that the publication of *On the Road* was an "historic occasion" and the immoderate lifestyle of the Beats was a "search for belief." Critics who shared this attitude focused on the spiritual quest theme of *On the Road,* which, along with its picaresque narrative, made this novel a descendent of American "road literature," represented by such works as Mark Twain's *Adventures of Huckleberry Finn.* Although *On the Road* was said to inspire the peripatetic Hippie generation of the 1960s, later critics paid greater attention to Sal's disillusionment with the road at the conclusion of the novel. Some now view *On the Road* as depicting the conflict within Sal between the contemplative life of a writer and spiritually-oriented person and the gregarious, adventurous life on the road.

For reasons of libel, Kerouac was asked to invent pseudonyms for himself and the friends who populated his works. In *On the Road* Kerouac is called Sal Paradise; Sal's friend Dean Moriarty is the real-life Neal Cassady whose lifestyle inspired several of Kerouac's works; the poet Allen Ginsberg appears as Carlo Marx; and William Burroughs—whose notorious novel, *Naked Lunch,* Kerouac helped type—is Old Bull Lee, a heroin addict in Denver. The female characters in Kerouac's novels are also largely based on the women in Kerouac's life and the lives of his friends, although these are generally minor roles.

On the Road is widely recognized, if begrudgingly by some, as an important contribution to American literature. Considerable interest has been shown in Kerouac's "spontaneous prose" method as a variation on the "stream of consciousness" technique favored by the Modernists. Many critics have examined the novel in terms of the literary tradition known as "road literature," picaresque narratives in which the travel experiences of real or fictional characters embody a spiritual quest. Critics have also examined the impact of Kerouac's interest in jazz and Buddhism on *On the Road;* the Beats' relation to other social outcasts, including racial minorities, drug addicts, and jazz musicians; and the novel's conventional depiction of women.

(See also *Contemporary Authors,* Vols. 5-8, rev. ed., Vols. 25-28, rev. ed. [obituary]; *Dictionary of Literary Biography,* Vols. 2, 16; *Concise Dictionary of Literary Biography 1941-1968;*

and *Dictionary of Literary Biography Documentary Series,* Vol. 3.)

PRINCIPAL WORKS

NOVELS

The Town and the City   1950
On the Road   1957
The Subterraneans   1958
The Dharma Bums   1958
Doctor Sax: Faust Part Three   1959
Maggie Cassidy   1959
Big Sur   1962
Visions of Gerard   1963
Desolation Angels   1965
Vanity of Duluoz: An Adventurous Education 1935-1946   1968
Visions of Cody   1972

OTHER

Mexico City Blues   (poetry)   1959
The Scripture of the Golden Eternity   (nonfiction)   1960
Book of Dreams   (nonfiction)   1961

GILBERT MILLSTEIN

On the Road is the second novel by Jack Kerouac, and its publication is a historic occasion in so far as the exposure of an authentic work of art is of any great moment in an age in which the attention is fragmented and the sensibilities are blunted by the superlatives of fashion (multiplied a million-fold by the speed and pound of communications).

This book requires exegesis and a detailing of background. It is possible that it will be condescended to by, or make uneasy, the neo-academicians and the "official" avant-garde critics, and that it will be dealt with superficially elsewhere as merely "absorbing" or "intriguing" or "picaresque" or any of a dozen convenient banalities, not excluding "off-beat." But the fact is that *On the Road* is the most beautifully executed, the clearest and the most important utterance yet made by the generation Kerouac himself named years ago as "beat," and whose principal avatar he is.

Just as, more than any other novel of the Twenties, *The Sun Also Rises* came to be regarded as the testament of the "Lost Generation," so it seems certain that *On the Road* will come to be known as that of the "Beat Generation." There is, otherwise, no similarity between the two; technically and philosophically, Hemingway and Kerouac are, at the very least, a depression and a world war apart.

Much has been made of the phenomenon that a good deal of the writing, the poetry and the painting of this generation (to say nothing of its deep interest in modern jazz) has emerged in the so-called "San Francisco Renaissance," which, while true, is irrelevant. It cannot be localized. (Many of the San Francisco group, a highly mobile lot in any case, are no longer resident in that benign city, or only intermittently.) The "Beat Generation" and its artists display readily recognizable stigmata.

Outwardly, these may be summed up as the frenzied pursuit

of every possible sensory impression, an extreme exacerbation of the nerves, a constant outraging of the body. (One gets "kicks"; one "digs" everything, whether it be drink, drugs, sexual promiscuity, driving at high speeds or absorbing Zen Buddhism.)

Inwardly, these excesses are made to serve a spiritual purpose, the purpose of an affirmation still unfocused, still to be defined, unsystematic. It is markedly distinct from the protest of the "Lost Generation" or the political protest of the "Depression Generation." . . .

As John Aldridge has put it in his critical work, *After the Lost Generation,* there were four choices open to the post-war writer: novelistic journalism or journalistic novel-writing; what little subject-matter that had not been fully exploited already (homosexuality, racial conflict), pure technique (for lack of something to say), or the course I feel Kerouac has taken—assertion "of the need for belief even though it is upon a background in which belief is impossible and in which the symbols are lacking for a genuine affirmation in genuine terms." . . .

That is the meaning of *On the Road.* What does its narrator, Sal Paradise, say?

> . . . The only people for me are the mad ones, the ones who are mad to live, mad to talk, mad to be saved, desirous of everything at the same time, the ones who never yawn or say a commonplace thing, but burn, burn, burn like fabulous yellow roman candles. . . .

And what does Dean Moriarty, Sal's American hero-saint say?

> And of course no one can tell us that there is no God. We've passed through all forms. . . . Everything is fine, God exists, we know time. . . . God exists without qualms. As we roll along this way I am positive beyond doubt that everything will be taken care of for us—that even you, as you drive, fearful of the wheel . . . the thing will go along of itself and you won't go off the road and I can sleep.

This search for affirmation takes Sal on the road to Denver and San Francisco; Los Angeles and Texas and Mexico; sometimes with Dean, sometimes without; sometimes in the company of other beat individuals whose ties vary, but whose search is very much the same (not infrequently ending in death or derangement; the search for belief is very likely the most violent known to man).

There are sections of *On the Road* in which the writing is of a beauty almost breathtaking. There is a description of a cross-country automobile ride fully the equal, for example, of the train ride told by Thomas Wolfe in *Of Time and the River.* There are the details of a trip to Mexico (and an interlude in a Mexican bordello) that are, by turns, awesome, tender and funny. And, finally, there is some writing on jazz that has never been equaled in American fiction, either for insight, style or technical virtuosity. *On the Road* is a major novel.

> *Gilbert Millstein, in a review of "On the Road," in* The New York Times, *September 5, 1957, p. 27.*

CARLOS BAKER

The seeing eye of Jack Kerouac's second novel *On the Road*

is a young novelist named Salvatore Paradise who is filled with transcontinental dreams, will do anything for "kicks," has evidently read *The Adventures of Augie March* and *A Walk on the Wild Side,* attends Columbia College, has a book partly done, and lives with his aunt in Patterson, N. J.

But Sal is restless. By page 37, he has reached Denver, 3200 miles from Paterson, and is staying with another writer named Roland Major, who lives in a "really swank apartment" belonging to someone else (all the artifacts in this book belong to someone else), and enjoys fine wines "just like Hemingway." Roland is an all-right fellow but Sal really takes to the wild ones: a poet named Carlo Marx and a "saint" named Dean Moriarty who is simultaneously servicing two girls named Marylou and Camille. They really dig Denver, these "fine gone daddies," and after they are through digging Denver, the dig the old mining town called Central City where the two girls Babe and Betty cook them up a fine snack of franks and beans and they have a wonderful beer party with bottles rolling all over the floor. Next day Sal walks around Denver, but it is no good any more. "Beyond the glittering street was darkness, and beyond the darkness the West. I had to go." (p. 19)

That's the way it goes with an itching foot. Sal and Dean ferry furniture between Testament, Va., and Paterson, N. J., barreling along at seventy miles an hour in a 1949 Hudson; they dig the great jazz pianist George Shearing in his great 1949 days "before he became cool and commercial"; they go to big parties in the West Nineties; Dean works in a parking-yard to earn some jack. But it is too cool in New York and they bowl down to New Orleans, hitting the dull bars in the French Quarter and the Negro jazz-shacks among the oil-flats, while Marylou samples everything in the books ("tea, goofballs, benny, and liquor") just for kicks. Their host Old Bull Lee takes his evening fix in the bathroom, using his neck-tie as a tourniquet and "jabbing with the needle into his woe-some arm with the thousand holes." Up in the Pecos Canyon country on the way home, they all take their clothes off and sit side by side in the front seat while Dean cries, "Yass, yass. . . . If I lived around here I'd go be an idjit in the sagebrush. . . . I'd look for pretty cowgirls—hee-hee-hee-hee! Damn! Bam!" For that is the way Dean talks, whether they are stumbling out of a bus in Detroit or getting high on marijuana in Old Mexico. It is said to be sad and blank when Dean's huge hunger for "life" begins to shows signs of appeasement.

But what is really sad and blank is Kerouac's American landscape. *On the Road* contains evidence that he can write when he chooses. But this dizzy travelogue gives him little chance but to gobble a few verbal goofballs and thumb a ride to the next town. (pp. 32-3)

> *Carlos Baker, "Itching Feet," in* Saturday Review, *Vol. XL, No. 36, September 7, 1957, pp. 19, 32-3.*

DAVID DEMPSEY

On the Road belongs to the new Bohemianism in American fiction in which an experimental style is combined with eccentric characters and a morally neutral point of view. It is not so much a novel as a long affectionate lark inspired by the so-called "beat" generation, and an example of the degree to which some of the most original work being done in this country has come to depend upon the bizarre and the off-beat for its creative stimulus. Jack Kerouac has written an enormously readable and entertaining book but one reads it in the same mood that he might visit a sideshow—the freaks are fascinating although they are hardly part of our lives.

The story is told—with great relish—by Sal Paradise, a young college student who satisfies, through his association with a character named Dean Moriarity, his restlessness and search for "kicks." Moriarity, a good-natured and slap-happy reform-school alumnus, is pathologically given to aimless travel, women, car stealing, reefers, bop jazz, liquor and pseudo-intellectual talk, as though life were just one long joy-ride that can't be stopped. He is Mr. Kerouac's answer to the age of anxiety—and one of the author's real accomplishments is to make him both agreeable and sympathetic. . . .

The incessant and frenetic moving around is the chief dynamic of *On the Road,* partly because this is one of the symptoms of "beatness" but partly, too, because the hot pursuit of pleasure enables Mr. Kerouac to serve up the great, raw slices of America that give his book a descriptive excitement unmatched since the days of Thomas Wolfe.

Unlike Wolfe, Nelson Algren or Saul Bellow (there are trace elements of all three writers here), Mr. Kerouac throws his characters away, as it were. His people are not developed but simply presented; they perform, take their bows and do a hand-spring into the wings. It is the difference between a vaudeville act and a play. The hedonism, the exquisite pointlessness of Moriarity's way of life is not so much the subject of *On the Road* as a sightseeing device.

The non sequiturs of the beat generation become the author's own plotless and themeless technique—having absolved his characters of all responsibility, he can absolve himself of the writer's customary attention to motivation and credibility. As a portrait of a disjointed segment of society acting out of its own neurotic necessity, *On the Road* is a stunning achievement. But it is a road, as far as the characters are concerned, that leads nowhere—and which the novelist himself cannot afford to travel more than once.

David Dempsey, "In Pursuit of 'Kicks'," in The New York Times Book Review, *September 8, 1957, p. 4.*

THOMAS F. CURLEY

Since he belongs to the beat generation, the narrator [of *On the Road*], Sal Paradise by name, is not light-hearted; he is out for kicks, out to dig everything under the tutelage of the hero, Dean Moriarty, a beat saint, a Major Hoople hipster (Dean talking, "Hmm, ah, yes, excellent, splendid, harrumph, egad!") who "knows about time." *On the Road* is a mirror of the American roadway, a representation of our obsession with time and with movement, a song of our restless soul. It reminds one of Celine, yes, but also of Whitman sounding his barbaric yawp that spanned a continent and of a little-known book by Wyndham Lewis, *America and Cosmic Man.*

Lewis wrote that the America of the atomic era was not a place but a time. Kerouac has imagined this. That, I think, explains *On the Road*'s lack of plot. To plot, to impose on events the order of beginning, middle and end, is to falsify. In Kerouac's vision, man does not control time, time controls man. At the beginning of one of the many trips, Paradise

comments "We were all delighted, we all realized we were leaving confusion and nonsense behind and performing our one and noble function of the time, *move.*" This is not mere youthfulness; it is an acute perception of the power of time accompanied by an equally acute recognition of an entire culture's doubt that time is rooted in eternity. The normal man gets dizzy trying to imagine such a world; he needs security and standards outside of or transcending time. Only Dean Moriarty and a few others know time, know that man and all his works are by-products of process.

Reason is the formal principle of human vitality. But in Kerouac's vision, reason itself is subservient to time. Thus all our certainties, moral, scientific and metaphysical, become the slaves of process. Everything moves, but nothing is alive. That is why the people in *On the Road* drink and eat, fornicate, marry, divorce and dance in a chaos of mechanical ecstasies; they remind you of the man with the rope around his neck in *Waiting for Godot.* Of all of them, however, only Dean Moriarty fully and consciously knows time and thus abandons himself completely to the pendulum of impulse.

The narrator, Sal Paradise, does not. That's why he is human and Dean is a monster. It is Paradise, therefore, who enters into the one meaningful human relationship in the novel.

Quite early in the book, Paradise is alone on a bus going from San Francisco to Los Angeles. He meets a Mexican girl, Terry, who has just left her husband and baby. (One must remember that traditional morality is not a norm in *On the Road.*) They strike up a conversation, go to L.A. together and get a room. But unlike other such acts in the book, this adultery is not casual; it develops into a genuine love affair. First they wander about L.A. trying to find money for their "kicks" and for bus fare to New York. Then they go back North where Terry picks up her little boy. The three live together. Sal Paradise finds work as a cotton picker at a dollar and a half a day and they manage not to starve. But fall comes on; it gets cold and the going gets rough.

> "Go back to your family," I said. "For God's sake, you can't be batting around tents with a baby like Johnny; the poor little tyke is cold."

But concern for the child is only an excuse, for a few lines later Paradise writes, "I could feel the pull of my own life calling me. I shot my aunt a penny postcard across the land and asked for another fifty." (pp. 595-96)

I think Kerouac's handling of this episode is the book's major flaw. The episode itself is one of the best parts of the book but when it is over Paradise goes zooming across the land again quite as if he had never met and loved Terry. Not long after this affair Paradise tells Dean Moriarty that he is tired of jumping around, that he wants to marry a girl so that he can rest his soul with her. Dean, of course, does not take him seriously, and neither can the reader. He had that girl and he left her. Throughout the remainder of the book, Paradise remembers Terry only once.

But Kerouac's bravura style pulls him through more than one ticklish situation. Indeed he is a natural writer, equalled, among the younger American novelists I've read, only by the Saul Bellow of *Augie March* and the William Styron of *The Long March.* But style is not enough; it does not hide forever the hollowness of the narrator's pathos and his ultimate lack of seriousness. At times, one suspects that Kerouac is using his gift for hyperbole to burlesque his narrator's feverish emotions. Words like "God," "holy," "soul," "saint," and "love," are thrown around almost as if the people meant them. They don't, they can't. All that Paradise has, all that any of the many other people in *On the Road* have (always excepting Dean Moriarty) are exacerbated instincts, a frenzied need for love and order without the strength or the faith to make the love that would create the order.

This is an exciting book to read; it meets head-on all the difficulties which confront the novelist today and surmounts them. It provokes admiration as well as disagreement. The episode of Sal Paradise and Terry shows that Kerouac can imagine a genuine human love, but he shut it off too abruptly. Yeats, who knew as well as anyone all the ignominy of flesh and bone," could counter that ignominy with:

> And when through all the town there ran
> The servants of your enemy,
> A woman and a man,
> Unless the Holy Writings lie,
> Hurried through the smooth and rough
> And through the fertile and waste,
> Protecting, till the danger past,
> With human love.

(pp. 596-97)

> *Thomas F. Curley, "Everything Moves, but Nothing Is Alive," in* The Commonweal, *Vol. LXVI, No. 24, September 13, 1957, pp. 595-97.*

GENE BARO

Every generation in every society in every age produces that kind of social dissident for whom ordinary modes of self-expression and development are insufficient. These men and women reject existing social values largely through misunderstanding them; in the social sense, they are infantile, perversely negative or indifferent. They want from their everyday experiences something that will give them an exalted, intensified sense of life—that will make them "live," that will make life "real"; they want to transcend, not their actual limitations, but their *sense* of limitation. In point of fact, they are mystics, and their mystique is the self.

[In *On the Road*] Jack Kerouac writes of a "group" of young dissidents in post-war America. Dean Moriarty and his friends cross and re-cross the continent, "living it up," "getting their kicks." They measure themselves against one another; the maddest and least predictable is the most admired. Sexually promiscuous, drink-and-drug ridden, thieving, lying, betraying, they belong to volatility, to movement, to sensation. They spend themselves gladly and savagely; their joys are hysterical and obsessive, their sorrows sentimental or incoherent. They are the shaped, not the shapers; something has been "done" to them, and what has been done justifies what they now do. They disclaim all responsibility for the world; yet if they are, so to speak, "out of society," they cannot be thought of, nor can they think of themselves seriously, in any other context than in the cities of mid-twentieth century America—in its "jazz joints," cheap hotels, bars, and roadhouses.

Indeed, the intense love of life of Dean Moriarty and his friends is a disguised love of death: the ultimate limit of sensation is annihilation—the mystical ecstasy where the individual merges with "life" itself. Curiously, the "hipsters" and "crazy cats" of this novel have some intuition that the road

they travel so frantically leads only back upon itself. Time serves worst those who live by the will alone. . . .

Quite apart from its characterizations, which are given and illustrated rather than developed, the chief distinction of this novel is its sentimental emotion. Certainly, *On the Road* is a romantic treatment of delinquency and, as such, is of considerable interest.

> *Gene Baro, "Restless Rebels in Search of—What?" in* New York Herald Tribune Book Review, *September 15, 1957, p. 4.*

BEN RAY REDMAN

Jack Kerouac's publisher tells us that he is the voice of "The Beat Generation," a product of World War II. But, far from being "beat," the central characters of [*On the Road*] are possessed of a demoniacal energy and an insane compulsion that drive them back and forth across the North American continent, from coast to coast, from city to city, anywhere at all, for no sane reason at all, in search of they know not what.

They travel as hitchhikers, by bus, by automobile—sometimes stolen—and wherever they find themselves they "live it up" according to their crazy lights. They "dig" everything everywhere, everything they do is strictly for "kicks," and they think of themselves as perfectly wonderful people. . . .

Instead of talking they yell, shout, scream, howl, moan, groan, and sing. They go into spastic ecstasies. They sweat—how they sweat! They ride naked along the highway. Their favorite word is "mad," and it is a word of highest praise.

Their story is told by Sal Paradise, a writer in his middle twenties. At the center of the action is Dean Moriarty—worshiped by Sal—a lunatic who says "Yes" to everything in life, provided it makes no sense, and whose battle cry is "Damn! I gotta go!" . . .

Kerouac possesses a powerful talent, but it is as yet completely uncontrolled. He can slip from magniloquent hysteria into sentimental bathos, and at his worst he merely slobbers words. His best, however, makes it clear that he is a writer to watch. But, if this watching is to be rewarded, he must begin to watch himself.

> *Ben Ray Redman, "Living It Up with Jack Kerouac," in* Chicago Tribune, *October 6, 1957, p. 4.*

HERBERT GOLD

"Whoee, I told my soul." This urgent message from Jack Kerouac to his soul contains most of the sense which emerges from his frantic tirade in the form of a novel, *On the Road,* and it is his ability to make such stuff hip, cool, beat and frantic, all at once, which has earned him a title more valued nowadays than that of "novelist": He is a Spokesman.

For what this time? Kerouac has appointed himself prose celebrant to a pack of unleashed zazous who like to describe themselves as Zen Hipsters—poets, pushers and panhandlers, musicians, male hustlers and a few marginal esthetes seeking new marginal distinctions. They have a center in San Francisco, another in Greenwich Village, and claim outposts in Tangiers, on merchant vessels, in Chicago, a fragment among the fragments in New Orleans, a fringe of the fringe in Mexico City. Despite all wandering, however, their loneliness for the herd sends them eagerly trumpeting back into each other's arms after brief periods of saying whoee to their souls among the outlanders. At least two of them happen to be talented—Allen Ginsberg, a poet of shock and wild wit, whose blathering *Howl* really does contain some of the liveliest epithets in contemporary verse; and Jack Kerouac, whose mammoth journal has been edited into the form of a novel by The Viking Press. One of the heroes of *On the Road,* of course, is Allen Ginsberg (under the name of Carlo Marx), just as one of the heroes of *Howl* is Jack Kerouac (under the name of Jack Kerouac). (p. 349)

On the Road carries the ensign of the hipster with considerable humor and vitality, much awe, and a little of the literary hipster's prevalent social disease, the faked-up pretension that these are underground intellects who know all about Zen Buddhism, St. John of the Cross, Proust, and good bad old Charlie Parker, and could tell us if they only cared to. The awe breaks to happy moments of lucidity which are those of a real writer. Kerouac then sees the hipster, agape and bedazzled, mumbling about the world-historical significance of bop—but only mumbling. What he tells, he tries to tell true enough according to his lights. At times he almost seems to understand that Charlie Parker blew fine horn, but was not God.

However, there is a structural flaw in this contemporary revival of the literary-criminal or ecstatic-delinquent underground which makes Jack Kerouac's book a proof of illness rather than a creation of art, a novel. In the first place, Villon Rimbaud and Jean Genet really lived by their criminal passivity and wits. They showed their rumps to society because they were caught from behind. These Americans, however, are *literary* in their coolness, hipness, beatness, and they are unauthentic exactly to the degree that they are literary. The hipster-writer is a perennial perverse bar mitzvah boy, proudly announcing: "Today I am a madman. Now give me the fountain pen." The frozen thugs gathered west of Sheridan Square or in the hopped-up cars do not bother with talk. That's why they say "man" to everyone—they can't remember anybody's name. But Ginsberg and Kerouac are *frantic.* They care too much, and they care aloud. "I'm *hungry.* I'm *starving, let's eat right now!*" That they care mostly for themselves is a sign of adolescence, but at least they care for something, and it's a beginning. (p. 350)

When Kerouac wails about "many and many a lost night, singing and moaning and eating the stars and dropping the juices drop by drop on the hot tar," he is in a respectable literary tradition, and the tradition's name is Thomas Wolfe. This is not hipster talk. When he passes through Fresno, sees an Armenian and thinks: "Yes, yes, Saroyan's town," he has some of that aging bucko's freewheeling self-love—and just as literary. When he hints at orgy, his real daddy is the daddy of all the living boheems, Henry Miller, though he practices a conciseness of sexual rhetoric which probably derives from the publisher's timidity rather than from any cool indifference. Sometimes he writes the purest straight-and-true Hemingway, as when he meets a Mexican girl: "Her breasts stuck out straight and true." Later his friend Dean is driving a car no-hands, but "it hugged the line straight and true."

This is not beat. This is not cool. This is not hip. This is the Columbia College boy vacationing on his G.I. Bill money, reading Papa. But despite all the bookish derivations,

Kerouac retains a stubborn integrity: "I had nothing to offer anybody but my own confusion."

He has something more to offer. I would guess, writing before publication, that the bookselling business is not yet ready for a particular blend of nihilism and mush which might someday take its place in the gassy world of bestsellerdom. When Kerouac mentions the Bomb, he makes us blush: he doesn't mean it, it's pure stylishness, and we resent the fact that the great disaster of contemporary history should be used in passing to let us know that a poet "cares." However, beyond the pretense, the derivations, the plotless rambling, the grate of vacant noise, Kerouac somehow achieves communication of a happy sense for the humor of car-stealing and marital confusion, for the insanity and pomp of addicts, for the joys of being tormented. And he gives us a fascinating tape recording of the skinny bunyanesque car-thief, Dean Moriarty, craving intellect, wives, fast travel and bop, emitting fiery nonsense from the tail of his hurtling nuttiness:

> But of course, Sal, I can talk as soon as ever and have many things to say to you in fact with my own little bangtail mind I've been reading and reading this gone Proust all the way across the country and digging a great number of things I'll never have TIME to tell you about and we STILL haven't talked of Mexico and our parting there in fever—but no need to talk. Absolutely, now, yes?

He balances the crazed Dean with a certain wryness about himself, whom he calls Sal Paradise:

> She was a nice little girl, simple and true. . . .

Oh-oh, Hemingway again.

> . . . and tremendously frightened of sex. I told her it was beautiful. I wanted to prove this to her. She let me prove it, but I was impatient and proved nothing. She sighed in the dark, "What do you want out of life?" I asked, and I used to ask that all the time of girls.

Here he enlists both our indulgence and our sympathy for poor impatient Sal, and does it with wit and feeling and imaginative detachment. But at other places he is capable of the melodrama of the purebred dormitory genius:

> I would be strange and ragged and like the Prophet who has walked across the land to bring the dark Word, and the only Word I had was "Wow."

At still another juncture he forgets that he is the Prophet of Wow and informs us that his word is Mad. There are other words in his sack, too.

But wha hoppin?

Nothin' hoppin, man.

Dean Moriarty is brilliantly transcribed, not rendered as a man through time and desire, despite all his velocity. He begins mad, he stays mad, he concludes mad: he is a stripped, tormented, dancing celluloid doll, burning fast, without a gesture that can surprise us although he says and does exactly what he would say and do. Kerouac is loyal to him. In garlands of prose, the words *mad, madness, madly* are the stems to which the buffeted reader can look for a principle of organization. It is the end of the philosophy for which the hungering boy traveler yearns, the great death-in-life to fill the boredom. He is fading away because of boredom, since nothing can make him happy, nothing can enlist him for more than a few spasmodic jerks, and the mad ones seem in his eyes to have an inner purpose. They are driven, while he is hung up. Unfortunately for communicative purpose, after many repetitions of the phrase, "It was *mad*," we hear not the trumpets of Blake nor the divine flap of Antonin Artaud, but rather an interior decorator describing last night's binge. "As in a dream," he adds—because he wants to make life a mad dream and so pronounces MAD and DREAM at us over and over—"we made the bed bounce a half hour." The precise report of the time arouses our suspicion. *Why was he looking at his watch?* Such modest journalism does not imply a dreamlike transport.

Kerouac's people rarely talk, respond, exchange warmth with each other. They split their guts to cross the continent, say, "Hello, whooee, wow, Charlie Parker, soul" to their friends, get a quick divorce, make a quick marriage, and rush back to San Fran to a first or second or third wife, bringing along a girl from Denver. They zoom up and down the continent for no reason but bored impulse, though they call it "find our souls." Then they write 18,000-word letters explaining why they never had that good long talk. Words fly, but they cannot communicate. They "tell" each other things: "Went for a walk in the middle of the night and came back to my girl to tell her what I thought about during my walk. I told her a number of things."

Even the wonderful chatter of the run-on hero, Dean Moriarty, which is the strongest thing in the book, tells us only one thing: He began as a psychopath and ended as a psychotic. Though lively along the way, this is not much of a journey, and tells little of anyone's life—including the real life of Moriarty.

On the Road asks us to judge the lives of its characters; it requires no real-life acquaintance with them to see that they are "true" projections—that is, the book represents Kerouac's attempt to do justice to his friends. This is a very different matter from the artist's attempt to project meaningful people through the medium of his imagination onto the medium of the imaginations of readers: characters who will be true to possibility, not necessarily to fact. *On the Road* reads right along—it contains, essentially, some lively rambling conversation about the exploits of big bad boys—but it is deeply insular in its intentions. Kerouac has not faced an important decision about whom he is writing for—his "soul" (to prove that he has one), his friends (to prove that he is worthy of them), or the public at whom his editor and publishers aim the book. He seems to be confused by the difference between writing a novel about hipsters—a legitimate stunt in an age of anti-heroes—and becoming a hipster in order to leave a track of paper. (pp. 351-53)

I take the Ginsberg of *Howl* and the Kerouac of *On the Road* to be typical of their little boystown at its rare best, serious, convinced and trying hard. Through them, one can ask what this clan of superfrantic subhipsters wants. Are they bringing a scout's message, a Word? Do they represent a new style of American? Will they provide a bracing antidote to the chronic headache of American culture?

They seem to be more a wounded shrilling and shrinking than an angry and vital reaction. Curiously enough their command performance of ecstatic rituals has misled them; they feel no ease in the expense of impulse; puzzled, they withdraw from pleasure. Madness is the penultimate escape,

which seems both to allow joy and illumination and to oil over the troubling itch of responsibility. It seems so, that is, to the broody tourist, traveling home to his mother's suburb to describe his friends to his notebook, and then justifying them to his editors. I am sure that from within madness is different, and less delightful. They are ascetics of excess. They yearn for the annihilation of sense through the abuse of the senses. They look for a society of unchanging virtue in which the risks of possibility have been removed; pure love will reign, green marijuana will be discovered in the mad glove compartments of every straight and true stolen car, Saroyan will live at peace in Fresno, souls will tell each other things. The terms of heaven have changed, but all this is very familiar. The ultimate goal is that single small step beyond madness.

What Kerouac wants is what the mystics driven by fright in all ages want, "the complete step across chronological time into timeless shadows . . . the stability of the Intrinsic mind." Such unhappy nonsense, such droopy-jeaned naysaying to the blessed facts of time and change! There are other possible mysticisms, but Kerouac models his heaven on Marie Stopes's elegant, Swedenborgian, impossibly weary orgasm, saying "wow!" in advance just because he hopes to describe it as "MAD." No wonder all the fireworks. The experience he craves is simple, dark and in any case inevitable to all of us sooner or later—immolation. He is not content to wait. Mortality terrifies him; better death at once than the long test of life. He expresses this fantasy with convulsive violence, trying to disguise the truth from himself and from the reader, using breathlessness as a surrogate for energy. But he is compelled. The jitters are not an active state of being. He puts to the service of his rockabye dream of oblivion all the violence, sex, drink, dope, and the batty babbling buddies with whom he populates his heaven, anything, every easeful and bitter experience, even that of turning to rot in the Mexican jungle:

> The jungle takes you over and you become it. . . .
> The dead bugs mingled with my blood; the live
> mosquitoes exchanged further portions. . . . Soft
> infinitesimal showers of microscopic bugs fanned
> down on my face as I slept, and they were extreme-
> ly pleasant.

It would help Jack Kerouac if he could find within himself the strength to stop writing about Love, Life and Death (with a dot dot dot between these stylish abstractions) and remember the real boy who enjoyed midget auto races. He might then discover that he knows something about death, life and love. At present he is a wolf of the hotrod age, Thomas and Virginia melted together into a damp creature from which even Aristophanes, who loved hybrids, would turn away. This wolf bays at the hipster moon, but howls for the Helen of someone else's youth; it ravens down the raw streets of America, taking gladness in the fact that the Mississippi has lived up to its advance notice in Mark Twain, describing one haunt after another as "storied," literary as literary can be, raised on the great books, as aren't we all? Where Thomas Wolfe broke his head butting against the world of New York intellectual highlife, Jack Kerouac is butting but unbroken against the world of the hipsters, a party that never quite pleases its adherents, no matter how much marvelous wild partying foreplay. Despite its drag race of words and gestures, *On the Road* does nothing, thinks nothing, acts nothing, but yet manages to be a book after all—a loving portrait of hip Dean Moriarty and his beat, cool friends as they run

110 miles an hour in order to stand still. It's a frantic book, and for that reason there is hope for Jack Kerouac.

Pseudo-Hipster, You Can't Run Further.

Meta-Hipster, You Can't Yell Louder.

Hipster, Go Home. (pp. 354-55)

> Herbert Gold, "Hip, Cool, Beat—and Frantic," in The Nation, New York, Vol. 185, No. 16, November 16, 1957, pp. 349-55.

RALPH GLEASON

> "As he was the illegitimate son of the Lost Generation, the Hipster was really *nowhere*. And, just as amputees often seem to localize their strongest sensations in the *missing* limb, so the Hipster longed, from the very beginning, to be *somewhere*. He was like a beetle on its back; his life was a struggle to get *straight*. But the law of human gravity kept him overthrown, because he was always of the minority—opposed in race or feeling to those who owned the machinery of recognition."—Anatole Broyard, "Portrait of the Hipster."

The central character in Jack Kerouac's **On the Road** is no hipster, even if the literary critics may call him one. That is, he is no hipster in the jazz musician sense. But he is a hipster in the Broyardian sense of trying to get somewhere. His motivation is the same and it carries with it the identification with jazz. The entire book is, on more than one level, the account of postwar youth trying madly to get somewhere, somehow.

And despite the fact that there is actually very little about jazz in this book—and where there is, it is usually a reflection of the European critical view of entrenched primitivism (*i.e.*, crow-jim)—it is still a jazz novel in that it reflects, immediately and vividly, to those who have been stricken with the jazz virus, a knowledge and expression of their own struggle to get straight, like Mr. Broyard's beetle. . . .

In an early passage of **On the Road** Kerouac refers to "that sound in the night which bop has come to represent for all of us." This is the whole point. Faced with a society which he considers has rejected him (and the fact that he believes this makes it real, if not a fact), the young intellectual has come to identify himself in a great degree with jazz music because this is also the position of the jazz artist. It has aspects of a cult, to be sure. But it also has something much more than that. It has a culture. Put him down anywhere and the jazz fan finds himself at home as soon as he finds the inevitable brother jazz fan. . . .

Kerouac writes from this point of view. His book assumes a knowledge of the language and litany of jazz. He is able, through adroit use of the jazz slang, to express ideas and situations which, if depicted in ordinary English prose, would raise the temperature in Boston and have him swung from the Golden Gate. But there is no profanity in the ordinary sense in this book. Instead there is the explicit, vivid vocabulary of jazz. . . .

Even though Kerouac himself—and many of his admirers—speaks of "the beat generation," this is not true. To be beat means to be "beat to the socks," down and out, discouraged and without hope. And not once in **On the Road**, no matter how sordid the situation nor how miserable the people, is

there no hope. That is the great thing about Kerouac's book and, incidentally, this generation. They swing. And this, in the words of Father Kennard, a Catholic commentator on jazz, means to affirm. Kerouac himself points out (through the medium of his autobiographical character and narrator, Sal Paradise), "All my New York friends were in the negative, nightmarish position of putting down society—this can't go on all the time—all this franticness and jumping around. We've got to go someplace, find something."

Be somewhere, in other words.

Later in the book Kerouac asks, "What's your road, man? Holyboy road, madman road, rainbow road . . . it's an anywhere road for anybody, anyhow." And, unlike a member of a generation that is really beat, Kerouac leaves you with no feeling of despair, but rather of exaltation.

This is really the quality we get from jazz, even from the lowest of low-down blues. Ellington's lyric "The saddest tale on land or sea is the tale they told when they told the truth on me" has exaltation in it. And **On the Road** certainly has. Locked in the perpetual struggle against the formality of what has been accepted (just as jazz is struggling for its own tradition) the post-war generation can be "cool" or "beat" or whatever you want to call it. But it is only a passing stage. Like the character in Bernard Wolfe's *The Late Risers* who says, "Don't be fooled. I'm really not cool. I just don't know what else to be," the jazz generation is marking time, being cool, waiting, disengaged, if you must, looking for somewhere to be. Meanwhile, writers like Kerouac and music like jazz are its voice.

> Ralph Gleason, "Kerouac's 'Beat Generation'," in Saturday Review, Vol. XLI, January 11, 1958, p. 75.

GEOFFREY NICHOLSON

[In England] the received idea at present is that writers should stay at home and cultivate their neighbours. In America, on the evidence of Jack Kerouac's **On the Road,** a kind of nomadic bohemianism is very much the thing with the post-war, the 'beat' generation. The narrator, a writer by the name of Sal Paradise, tells us about his friends who, each spring, take the road west or south from New York looking for 'kicks': girls, liquor, drugs, stealing, progressive jazz, restless movement for its own sake. They live it up to prove they are alive.

The ultimate in their mode of life is Dean Moriarty, an ex-reform-school boy, who comes to New York so that Chad, the poet of the group, can 'teach him all about Nietzsche and all the wonderful intellectual things that Chad knew,' and who talks like this: 'Man, wow, there's so many things to do, so many things to write! How to even *begin* to get it all down and without modified restraints and all hung up on like literary inhibitions and grammatical fears. . . .' He is a crazy man, an *aficionado* of madness in others, with as few restraints as it needs to keep alive and out of jail. The rest, Paradise especially, look on him as a saint, an angel.

Certainly [**On the Road**] contains a lot of special pleading, but it is not easily dismissed on that account. These people are worth knowing about, and it is unlikely that anyone but an insider who accepted their attitudes could have described them as knowledgeably. Kerouac is fluent in their sub-bop idiom. He has a keen sense of what it means to be a native of a country that is almost a continent. If he is easy to parody and patronise, so is Hemingway. When all the sentimentality and mannerisms of both have been discounted, it must be said that both writers expressed the mood of a post-war generation with considerable understanding, and for the reason that they identified themselves with it.

Geoffrey Nicholson, "All This Franticness," in The Spectator, *Vol. 200, No. 6778, May 23, 1958, p. 666.*

FREEMAN CHAMPNEY

[Kerouac's] name has come to be associated with something which is going on in American life and which involves, or shocks, or intrigues a sufficient number of people to create a market for books about it. This something is known as the "beat generation" and Kerouac is known as its spokesman and celebrant.

To the outsider, fitting this beat generation into any coherent or familiar scheme of American culture takes quite a bit of doing. It has been said that this group is not so much in revolt from society as in permanent secession. And perhaps we should leave the job of interpretation to field-work teams of anthropologists and linguists. Either you dig it or you don't. But these overage youths and assertively unglamorous women of the cities and campuses may be our neighbors or our children; they grew out of American life and their existence is a fact to be lived with. What they have to say—directly, in the words of Kerouac, or just by being here—should be listened to.

Kerouac's most sustained exposition of his group was in **On the Road,** which had a reputation even before it was published in 1957. Its characters "danced down the streets like dingledodies, and I shambled after . . . the only people for me are the mad ones, the ones who are mad to live, mad to talk, mad to be saved, desirous of everything at the same time, the ones who never yawn or say a commonplace thing, but burn, burn, burn. . . . " There is plenty of burning in this book. It has something in common with the hard, gemlike flame which consumed a previous generation, though often it is more like the explosion of a tar bucket. Keeping the flames leaping high calls for a great deal of speed, sex, alcohol, "that sound of night which bop has come to represent," marijuana, and yahooing around the appropriate nightspots.

It is not easy to look at the external and public nuisance aspects of the beat generation without lining up with the censorious elders. These young "haters of everything" can seem nothing more than spoiled brats, rejecting a civilization they have not bothered to understand and done nothing to deserve, wrecking lives and other peoples' Cadillacs with equal relish and for no reason at all, sponging on relatives they despise, and pretending a superiority which is only a big brag of loudmouthed nastiness. . . . But this is not listening to what they have to say.

Each of Kerouac's quarrels with American culture—or with what he thinks American culture is—is tied to a positive value. He thinks middle-class life is dull, anxious, and pointless: "not enough ecstacy for me, not enough life, joy, kicks, darkness, music, not enough night." (This one is mixed up with the wish that he were one of "the happy, true-hearted ecstatic Negroes of America.") He has had a bellyfull of "tedious intellectualness" and contrasts it with Dean Moriarity

(his "new kind of American saint") and his "wild yea-saying overburst of American joy." Life should be more alive, more spontaneous. It should break through its cautious negations and its purse-mouthed string-saving to caper in the present—the great shouting intensities of direct experience and heightened sensation.

Well, gee whizz, who's arguing? We all want to be more alive, more free, more aware. What holds us back? Mostly a stubborn set of facts about human life. That it is *human,* to begin with: our standard factory equipment is inadequate for living until it has been shaped and tuned up by interacting in a human way with other people. And we go on living with other people, including ourselves. We can't live purely in the present and be human beings. The same is true of living purely for sensation, or purely within the single self. We aren't made that way. And because we aren't, we have all this baggage from the past—all these customs and laws and institutions. All of it is there because we made it, because we needed it or thought we did. At any given time, of course, much of it is junk. Rebellious generations have always led in the endless job of clearing out the junk, but Kerouac's boys and girls seem to want, not a clean house, but no house at all.

The test of the beat way of life, like any other, is in the way it works out. And even though Kerouac's rebellion may not be particularly new or intelligent, he rates high marks for honesty in following his new saints through their odysseys and reporting on the results. In fact, this honesty makes the celebration of Dean Moriarity in **On the Road** a very ambiguous achievement. The intention seems to have been to say: here is a "Holy Goof" whose life is a mess by all respectable criteria but who has "got the secret that we're all busting to find" and represents "the ragged and ecstatic joy of pure being." Which is the one supreme value. There is a climactic scene in which Moriarity is told off by his buddies and their disillusioned wives. He has meant trouble for them all and as they reject him he is shown

> standing in front of everybody, ragged and broken and idiotic, right under the lightbulbs, his bony mad face covered with sweat and throbbing veins, saying 'Yes, yes, yes,' as though tremendous revelations were pouring into him all the time now, and I am convinced they were, and the others suspected as much and were frightened. He was BEAT—the root, the soul of Beatific.

So there we have it, and Kerouac's Sal Paradise is moved to be loyal to this beatific hero and they take off on one of their mad cross-country dashes. But the only heroism, the only saintliness visible in Moriarity is his frenzy of activity. His quoted conversation is babble; his rocketing from woman to woman, with an accidental child here and there, is not freedom but compulsiveness. He steals and cheats and lies. His one saleable talent is as "the most fantastic parking lot attendant in the world." We have only Kerouac's word to indicate that there is any "joy of pure being" involved here. The evidence shows little but desperation and mania and a beatness too overwhelmingly beatific for even his fellow madmen.

If it is hard to see what is admirable—on any terms, or by any measure—in this Kerouac hero, it is even harder to see the beat way of life as holding much joy for its women. They have a very rough time. Their only real functions are as audience and as erotic furniture (sometimes as providers and meal tickets). They may come along for the ride, but they don't dig the deeper secrets of life, and their demands for attention and consideration can be a real nuisance. And they turn out badly. They flip and they suicide; they become whores. Or they turn into nagging shrews who challenge the very basics of beatness by demanding regular hours and incomes from their men.

Kerouac's honesty about woman's place in the beat culture is devastating to his whole crusade for "a shining now-ness" which is to carry "America like a shining blanket into that brighter nowhere Already." Much of his gospel might seem a male revolt against the gracious-living quest of the middle-class woman, with her smooth certainties and her pitiful vulnerability. Some questioning of the viability of this kind of life is audible in the more literate suburbs, as some of these women go most ungraciously to pieces while their men hover helpless and wonder where they lost the way. Kerouac seems to speak to this unease when Japhy Ryder prescribes [in *The Dharma Bums*]: "get a friendly smart sensitive human-being gal who don't give a shit for martinis every night and all that dumb white machinery in the kitchen." But on the evidence in Kerouac's books, the beat way of life is even more of a trap for women than the suburbs. (pp. 114-17)

As a people, we have been trying to come to terms with industrial civilization for better than a hundred years. And even though Kerouac drops names right and left to show that he has been through all of human culture and left it behind him, he and his buddies show no understanding whatever of where we have been in this struggle. No one has told them about the Great Depression, for one thing—when the horizons of life contracted to do you have a job, any kind of job? Such notions as freedom and self expression were remote and irrelevant beside the tightening paralysis of the early Thirties. (Did Kerouac ever hear about the woman whose family finally went on relief and who went out every morning with her broom and swept the sidewalks of her entire city block?) (p. 118)

There is irony in the fact that it is our lush abundance which enables a beat generation to avoid imprisonment in the "system of work, produce, consume." They get by on pickings from the system's leftovers, and on handouts from imprisoned relatives, while they shout their obscenities at the horror of it all. (pp. 118-19)

Unarguably, there is work to be done to find ways of living with industrialism which enrich and fulfill. The basic disciplines of the industrial process (time, impersonality, and coordination) are not to be avoided, but the human involvement in the process is changing all the time. The inhumanities which, a generation ago, were being charged to The Machine have been eased by further mechanization and by union organization. Today's working stiff has an easier, more abundant life than many semiprofessionals. Today's crying human indignities seem to center in marketing and all the hoopla it has come to require. Once the basic knowhow of making and moving is functioning, there is, in truth, nothing very humanly substantial in the process itself. Life has to get its bite and flavor elsewhere and if we have to learn this from Kerouac and his pals, we should be grateful for being told.

As the Alger-book eager beaver fades as a folk hero, and life looks less like pure individual grabbing, we are increasingly concerned with each other. You can sneer at this as "other-directedness" or you can see it as clear gain in understanding. All sorts of factors enter in: the diffusion of the psychological approach (or at least the diffusion of the jargon); the welfare state and its institutionalizing of personal difficulties; the dissolution of the patriarchal family into togetherness; a population increasingly on the move; the effect of universal television, and so on. This heightened interacting is a fact and is also reflected in the beat credo. Though the more popular forms of this interacting are beneath beat contempt, there is much talk in Kerouac about "really communicating." The examples given are not very convincing (there is a polyphony of monologue but no one seems to listen), but it is notable that at their maddest his crowd do not actually knock each other's physical brains out, as a bystander might expect. They blunt their conflicts in drink and drugs and what passes for a great sad common compassion. (pp. 119-20)

[Kerouac's] writing is intended to be larger than the simply rational and didactic, and it often succeeds in what David Dempsey called "a descriptive excitement unmatched since the days of Thomas Wolfe" [see excerpt above]. At its best it has zest and vitality and a fine blaring poetry. At its worst it is blah pure and undefiled. Kerouac believes in "spontaneous writing" or Pouring It All Out. The trouble is he leaves it there, all, as poured. Capturing in words some approximation of the full flow of consciousness is no mean achievement. But to empty a mind on the counter like a lady's handbag creates only a jumble of knickknacks unless the mind happens to be a first-rate one.

There is a built-in conflict in Kerouac's writing. He celebrates pure sensation, timeless absorption in the living Now, and direct mindless experience. But he tries to do this by writing words on paper—inescapably a cerebral, laborious, lonely operation. People who really live in the present don't write books. One of the ways in which Kerouac meets this dilemma is to write badly. Meanings are ignored, syntax is garbled, and form sprawls. (It is impossible to parody Kerouac; he has done it himself beyond improvement.) This negation of mind and language does sometimes suggest a great undefined Something, which may be what he is after. But a muted trumpet does it better.

So we've got problems. And life is seldom up to what we demand. This is new? Well, it is new the first time you come upon it. And if the beat generation doesn't see that this is an ongoing process, that we have come a long way, and that we are all part of the procession, maybe we haven't kept in touch with them (telling them too many ceremonial lies, hiding our own failures, shielding them from small troubles). Is their choice only between sterile respectability and more sterile self-destruction? This seems nonsense on the face of it, but that the question comes up at all is disturbing. We owe Kerouac some thanks for raising it for his fellows—though Kerouac himself is old enough to know better. (pp. 120-21)

Freeman Champney, "Beat-Up or Beatific?" in The Antioch Review, *Vol. XIX, No. 1, Spring, 1959, pp. 114-21.*

WARREN TALLMAN

It is always an implicit and frequently an explicit assumption of the Beat writers that we live, if we do at all, in something like the ruins of our civilization. When the Second World War was bombed out of existence in that long-ago '45 summer, two cities were in literal fact demolished. But psychically, all cities fell; and what the eye sees as intact is a lesser truth than what the psyche knows is in ruins. The psyche knows that the only sensible way to enter a modern city is Gregory Corso's way, very tentatively, 'two suitcases filled with despair'. This assumption that the cities which live in the psyche have all gone smash is one starting point of Beat.

But if our cities are in something like ruins, there have been survivors. Those have survived who had the least to lose, those whose psychic stance in face of modern experience had already been reduced to minimum needs: the angry Negro, the pathological delinquent, the hopeless addict. These outcasts had already fought and *lost* the battle each of us makes to establish his psyche within the social continuum. The Negro who feels that integration offers worse defeats than those already suffered at hands of the segregation to which he has long-since adjusted; the delinquent who realizes that continued irresponsibility is the only effective physician to the ills which previous irresponsibilities have brought upon him; the addict who knows that the extent to which he is hooked by his habit is as nothing alongside the extent to which he is hooked by the social purgatory he must endure in order to feed that habit—these advanced types of the social outcast have long since had to forego the psychic luxuries available to those of us who are not outcasts. Crucially, they have had to give up that main staple of psychic continuity, Ego. . . . The outcast knows that ego, which demands self-regard, is the enemy that can trap him into kinds of social commitment which his psyche cannot afford. Ego is for the squares. Let them be trapped. To be released from the claims of ego is to be released from the claims of others, a very necessary condition for survival if you happen to be an outcast. But the consequences can be devastating. For when ego vanishes, the continuity of one's existence is likely to vanish with it. (pp. 58-9)

It is an axiom of the human spirit that whosoever wanders into purgatory will attempt to escape. With luck, with courage, with ingenuity, some succeed. The solution of the outcast who has given up a large part of his ego has been to fall back not upon the mercy of society—for society has long since been committed to the merciless proposition that only certain men are brothers—but upon, or rather into the moment. The moment becomes the outcast's island, his barricade, his citadel. Having lost his life in the social continuum, cast out and cyphered, he finds it again within the moment. But when the social outcast takes over the moment as his province, he is faced with yet another problem. He must make it habitable. How unsuccessful most such outcast efforts have been can best be seen in any skid-road district, where men come to their vacant pauses within what Ginsberg describes as 'the drear light of Zoo.' However, some of the animals in the skid road and slum zoos have long since rebelled. Up from the rhythms and intensities which animate the Negro, the delinquent, and the addict have risen the voices that dig and swing on the Beat streets in the North American night, a music and a language, Jazz and Hip.

First the language. Strictly speaking, a hipster is an addict and hip talk is the addict's private language. But it has become much more. Granting many exceptions in which addiction is incurred accidentally, it is almost axiomatic that the addict is an outcast first and acquires his habit in an effort to escape from the psychic ordeal of being brotherless, unable to exert claims upon anybody's love. But once hooked, he is necessarily a man living from moment to moment, from fix to fix. The intervals between become a kind of purgatorial school in which one learns to care about less and less: not sur-

roundings, not status, not appearance, not physical condition, not even crimes, but only for the golden island ahead where one can score, then fix, then swing. To swing is to enter into full alliance with the moment and to do this is to triumph over the squares who otherwise run the world. For to enter the moment, you must yield to the moment. The square person can never get the camel caravan of his ego-commitments through the eye of the needle which opens out upon hipster heaven. Excluded from the moment and consequently seeking it out ahead in a future which never has been and never will be, all that the square person can dig is his own grave. The hip person knows that the only promised land is Now and that the only way to make the journey is to dig everything and go until you make it and can swing.

Hip talk, then, is Basic English which charts the phases, the psychology, even the philosophy of those persons who live for, with and—when they can—within the moment. It is in fact less a language than a language art in which spontaneity is everything. The words are compact, mostly monosyllabic, athletic: dig, go, make it, man, cat, chick, flip, goof, cool, crazy, swing. In his very suggestive essay, 'The White Negro', Norman Mailer argues that the basic words of hip form a nucleus which charts and organizes the energies of the hipster into maximum mobility for his contentions with the squares, as indeed with other hipsters, for the sweets of this world. Mailer's emphasis upon the endless battle between hip and square is true, I think, but not true enough because less vital than is the hipster's even deeper need to establish a new continuity for his life. The most severe ordeal of his constantly emphasized isolation is not loss of the social sweets but loss of the moment. It is against this fate that he has evolved his cryptic language art. The talented hipster is as sensitive to the nuances and possibilities of his language as he necessarily is to the nuances and possibilities of the moment. Which is why the real hip cat who can dig and swing with the other cats in hipland has such close affinities with the aristocrat among such outcasts, the jazzman.

Jazz swings in and with the moment. The universal name for a good group is "a swinging group', one in which each individual is attuned to all of the others so that improvisation can answer improvisation without loss of group harmony. . . . Jazz played in this way can be a spontaneous, swinging poem in which the group first creates the shape, the musical metrics of the given moment. Then individuals begin to improvise . . . or the talented soloist to move his sound out into the possibilities of the moment. When this happens the jazzman and the hip person who can swing with him experience release into the moment that is being created, as Kerouac notes, 'so he said it and sang it and blew it through to the stars and on out.' Since such release is the hip person's deepest need and desire, the jazzman becomes the hipster hero who has moved among the mountains of the moment and in so doing has conquered the most vindictive of their enemies, time. In jazz the moment prevails.

But sounds die out. And are replaced by other sounds. Where jazz was factory whistles will be when Daddio Time turns on tic toc dawn to light the hipman and the jazzman home. And the square eye of morning tells both what each had been trying to forget, that when you fall out of the moment and happen to be an outcast you are back among the ruins in a world where only certain men are brothers. At which point the Beat writers appear on the scene, chanting Holy, Holy, Holy—but with a Bop beat.

BOP: In a conventional tune the melody moves along not quite like but something like an escalator, steadily and as the feet would expect, so that the good children of this world can keep their eyes fixed upward for the sign that says: TOYS. But the restless outcast children in the department store of this world know that the journey is NOW. As their jazz escalator goes at a syncopated beat from level to level, the outcast children dip into the toy shop of the moment and come up with little hops, skips, and jumps that are answered back by other hops, skips, and jumps, until, by the time the syncopated escalator reaches the top level, everybody is hopping and jumping about, together and as individuals, and this of course is improvisation—the life of jazz. However, this dual progression in which the syncopated beat of the melody escalator carries the spontaneous action of the improvisations from level to level has given way, with the advent of Bop, to a music which seems to travel from level to level on the improvisations alone. That is, the melody (the escalator) has been assimilated into the pattern of improvisations (hop, skip, jump) and the improvisations—always the life impulse of jazz—have dominated in this merger. At best Bop has freed jazz from the tedium of banal melodies. It has also given emphasis to a principle of spontaneous creative freedom which has been taken over by the Beat writers in ways likely to have a strong influence upon North American poetry and fiction.

In old-style fiction the narrative continuity is always clearly discernible. But it is impossible to create an absorbing narrative without at the same time enriching it with images, asides, themes and variations—impulses from within. It is evident that in much recent fiction—Joyce, Kafka, Virginia Woolf, and Faulkner are obvious examples—the narrative line has tended to weaken, merge with, and be dominated by the sum of variations. Each narrative step in Faulkner's work is likely to provoke many sidewinding pages before a next narrative step is taken. More, a lot of Faulkner's power is to be found in the sidewindings. In brief, what happens in jazz when the melody merges with the improvisations and the improvisations dominate, has been happening in fiction for some time now. (pp. 59-64)

There have been a number of attempts, heroic in their singlemindedness, to confront with language the increasing deviousness of meanings, notably those of Joyce, Eliot, and Faulkner. But the result has been a fiction and poetry so difficult as to require years-long efforts of explication—which is to communicate the slow way. We are put in the odd position of honouring men whom we cannot understand. Moreover, efforts to understand their writings have usually dwindled into the sterility, the word games, the intellectual tea times which make up so large a part of modern criticism. The result for most people has been a distinct breakdown of any vital connection with our best literature. To the fact of this breakdown the Beat writers bring a new solution.

Their solution is to be Beat. To be Beat is to let your life come tumbling down into a humpty-dumpty heap, and with it, into the same heap, the humpty-dumpty meanings which language attempts to sustain. There are fewer things beneath heaven and earth than our present-day multiple-meaning philosophers would have us believe. From the ruin of yourself pick up yourself (if you can) but let the meanings lie. Now cross on over to the outcast side of the street to where the hip folk and the jazz folk live, for the way your life is now is the way their lives have been for years. Step right in through the Open Door to where the tenor man is crouching with the bell mouth of his horn down in the basement near his feet, reaching for the waters of life that come rocking up through the debris of the day that dawned over Hiroshima everywhere long 1945 ago. The sound you hear is life, 'the pit and prune juice of poor beat life itself in the god-awful streets of man'. And life is Holy. And this is the meaning of words. Life is holy, and the journey is Now.

Kerouac's sound starts up in his first novel, **The Town and the City,** and anyone who grew up with or remembers the sentimental music of the 1930s will recognize what he is doing. The New England nights and days of his childhood and youth are orchestrated with slow violins, to which sound the children whose lives he chronicles are stirred into awareness as the stars dip down and slow breezes sweep along diminishing strings towards soft music on a farther shore. It is the considerable achievement of the novel that Kerouac is able to sustain the note of profound sentimentality his style conveys even as he is tracing, with remorseless intelligence, the downfall of the New England family, the Martins, who try to sustain their lives on this tone. The sound bodies forth their myth—soft music on a farther shore—while the action brings both myth and sound down in ruins. (pp. 64-6)

I think it is evident that in creating this testimonial to a gone childhood, Kerouac is also breaking with that era. How decisively he does break becomes plain in his second published novel, **On the Road,** where the sounds become BIFF, BOFF, BLIP, BLEEP, BOP, BEEP, CLINCK, ZOWIE! Sounds break up; and are replaced by other sounds. The journey is NOW. The narrative is a humpty-dumpty heap. Such is the condition of NOW. The ruins extend from New York City, down to New Orleans, on down to Mexico City, back up to Denver, out to San Francisco, over to Chicago, back to New York—six cities at the end points of a cockeyed star. The hero who passes from star-point to star-point is Dean Moriarity, the mad Hamlet of the moment, shambled after by Sal Paradise, who tells the story. And all that Sal can say is, 'Yes, he's mad,' and 'Yes, he's my brother.' Moriarity is the hero-prince of all Beat people, a 'madman angel and bum' out to con the North American nightmare of a chance for his soul to live. Nothing that his tormented hands reach for will come into his hands except the holiness which comes rocking up direct from the waters of life upon the jazz rhythms with which Kerouac pitches his cockeyed star of wonder about.

Moriarity is a Denver jailkid who does not have to wait for his life to come down in ruins. It begins that way. His mother 'died when Dean was a child' and his wino father is so indistinguishable from all the other winos in all the skid-road districts where Dean thinks he may find him that 'I never know whether to ask.' Kerouac provides only enough details about 'all the bitterness and madness' of Dean's Denver childhood to make it clear that the social forms to which all good children go for their bread of life (or so they think) were made forbidden areas for Dean by reason of rejection, guilt, shame, rage, hatred—the dreadful emotions likely to orchestrate the secret lives of children who one day wake up Beat. Hence the car-stealing frenzies in which he turns himself into a car so that his thwarted energies can come 'blasting out of his system like daggers'. On the maddest night of the novel he climaxes one such (five-car) binge by stealing a police detective's auto (inviting punishment) which he abandons in front of the house where he then passes out in peace and calm of mind—drunk—all passion spent.

An even more definite sign of Moriarity's inability to live

within existing social forms consists in the insane doubling-up of those relationships from which he does seek satisfaction, brotherhood, love. No sooner does he dig Sal Paradise the very most than he must rush into an even more intense relationship with Paradise's friend, Carlo Marx. No sooner does he set up housekeeping with his first wife, Marylou, than he must arrange an elaborate time-schedule in order to set up parallel housekeeping with his second, interchangeable wife, Camille. The Denver bohemia must be matched by bohemian San Francisco. His life on the west coast is a process of creating the complications which will be resolved by flight to the east coast. Tormented by almost complete inability to live within even the relaxed bohemian life-forms, Moriarity turns again and again to the one form in which his energies find something like release and fulfilment—the road.

In a car on the road, surrounded by darkness, the existing forms vanish and with them vanishes the distraught, guilt-tormented self. Speed, strangeness and space, dark forests, heavy-shouldered mountains and open prairies bring new transient forms, semi-forms, even formless forms, rushing into place. All of these are fleetingly familiar, for all of these are life. And because life is holy, the soul moves in behind the wheel and 'every moment is precious' as the mad city Hamlet gives way to a road-going Quixote who cares only for the soul's journey, the one sweet dreadful childhood could not steal from him. Thus 'It was remarkable', Sal Paradise tells us, 'how Dean could go mad and then continue with his soul . . . calmly and sanely as though nothing had happened.' The mad self blends into the speeding car as the sane soul continues down the one road of life on the only journey which 'must eventually lead to the whole world'.

An apotheosis of sorts is achieved briefly in Mexico on the strangest yet most strangely familiar of all the roads Moriarity and Paradise take, on a womb-like jungle night, 'hot as the inside of a baker's oven'. Here the travellers are taken over by 'billions of insects' until 'the dead bugs mingled with my blood'. Time, self, and history are temporarily annihilated and there is only the 'rank, hot and rotten jungle' from which a prophetic white horse, 'immense and phosphorescent', emerges to pace majestically, mysteriously past Moriarity's for-once sleeping head. When they waken from this dream of annihilation and rebirth it is to enter mountains where 'shepherds appeared dressed as in the first time'. And Moriarity 'looked to heaven with red eyes', aware that he has made it out of orbit with the cockeyed star of NOW into orbit with 'the golden world that Jesus came from'. But if this Beat angel journeys through the jazz of the North American night finally to reach a semblance of creation day morning time in the Mexican mountains of the moment, he is much too mad to more than distractedly glimpse, and giggle, and give a wristwatch to a Mexican creation-day child, inviting her to enter time. 'Yes, he's mad,' says Sal, and so Quixote gives way to Hamlet as Dean Moriarity ends with stockings down-gyv'd—'ragged in a moth-eaten overcoat'—a parking-lot attendant in New York—which is no way for a con man to live—silent—'Dean couldn't talk any more'—with only his sad Horatio, Sal, to tell his brother's story.

The jazz is in the continuity in which each episode tells a separate story—variations on the holiness theme. And it is in the remarkably flexible style as Kerouac improvises within each episode seeking to adjust his sound to the resonance of the given moment. Some moments come through tinged with the earlier *Town and City* sentimentality. Others rock and sock

with Moriarity's frenzy, the sentences jerking about like muscles on an overwrought face. Still others are curiously quiescent, calm. And the melody which unifies the whole and lifts the cockeyed star up into the jazz sky is the holiness of life because this for Kerouac is the meaning of words, the inside of his sound. Dean Moriarity is sweet prince to this proposition. To read *On the Road* with attention to the variations Kerouac achieves is to realize something of his very impressive talent for meshing his sound with the strongly-felt rhythms of many and various moments. It is not possible to compare him very closely with other stylists of note because his fiction is the first in which jazz is a dominant influence. (pp. 66-9)

Warren Tallman, "Kerouac's Sound," in The Tamarack Review, *No. 11, Spring, 1959, pp. 58-62, 64-74.*

MELVIN W. ASKEW

It is, perhaps, a matter of dispute whether or not there is space in serious journals for the Prince of the Beats, Jack Kerouac, and doubtless there are some assured suspicions that there are matters of more moment to be discussed and explored in them. Few, certainly, would hesitate to dismiss a full-scale review of *On the Road* from consideration, for it is not a good novel as one ordinarily understands excellence in novels: it is neither exciting, illuminating, or enduring. As a matter of fact, almost by page one hundred and seventy-five one is so sick of parties in Denver that he is reluctant to have another, if, indeed, he does not put the book aside in adamant refusal. In addition, *On the Road* demonstrates almost every treacherous and tedious aspect of the fallacy of imitative form. So it is not my intention here either to extoll the novel or even to analyze it, for that matter.

Curiously, though, the briefest examination of *On the Road* reveals that it is intimately related to two distinct and particular traditions peculiar to the American novel—evidence, incidentally, that the beats are not really something new under the sun. That this novel, however, is not ennobled by its relationship to these traditions almost goes without saying, but it does nevertheless reveal these traditions in clearer perspective and it indicates in its none-too-eloquent prose, in its shabby realization of scenes, and in its frightening actualization of motive and meaning, the tempo, drift, and quality of our culture both in literature and society. (p. 231)

On the Road is vitally involved with two literary traditions which were determined and conditioned by the actual historical facts of American settlement, independence, and expansion. It is, in its way, a compendium of the thrill and promise of such slogans as "Manifest Destiny," "54-40 or Fight"; it is a testament of the lingering spirit of Lewis and Clark and Pike. Thus it becomes a modern expression of what Professor R. W. B. Lewis calls the hero in space, an expression of the moving, wandering American character. But it is also an expression of the proto-typical American settler who came to this continent with a fervent and abiding trust in a deeply spiritual but very remote Father, of the settler who subsequently went to war to assert his independence from a historical father and who later wrote a great deal of literature describing his search for another. Represented in literature, then, these two motifs are the hero who pursues his quest in space and the hero who pursues his quest for the surrogate father. In *On the Road* these two traditions merge, and their merging represents the coordination of two historical facts and their two representations in literature. Both should be traced at some length.

After colonies had been established along the eastern seaboard, there was no direction for movement but West, and movement was necessary for both economic and social reasons. . . . They were on the move for the promise of more fertile pasture beyond the next range of hills, for the promise of gold or silver buried in greater quantity and greater purity in the next mountain range that defined the horizon, for the furs that brought money and whiskey in the settlements, or for the adventure they were sure to meet beyond the limits of civilization. But first and last they were on the move, and like the movement in **On the Road,** they started from the extreme East and moved westward, but unlike the confused and wandering characters in that novel, they did not, when they finally made their way to California, meet themselves coming.

But from this pattern of historical circumstances there was born the hero in space, the hero who like the archetypal cowboy had no need to come to terms with exigencies of the heart, of society, or of time—who could always move, who could always ride to the horizon and wave as he disappeared. Thus Natty Bumpo avoids the proposals of all females and with lingering pleasure but irrevocable determination retreats to the woods with his Indian friend, Chingachgook. On the move. And after him came the hosts of American characters who resort to the same flight. Hester Prynne in *The Scarlet Letter* admonishes Arthur Dimmesdale that all space is available to them; that they need not abide in the village which knows their ignominy; that they can retreat deeper into the woods or fly across the sea. Ishmael, in *Moby Dick,* disgruntled and at odds with society and himself, does not need to remain behind and subtilize his experience, or live with it, or assimilate it; he can fly to the space of the ocean and in his baptism of sperm or water leave it all behind him. Huckleberry Finn, escaping the prison-house of the reforming women or the prison-house of his unregenerate father, can idle down the Mississippi, and when the adventure is over, "light out" for the new Territory. Or more recently, Lieutenant Henry, when trapped by the birth of a "skinned rabbit with an old man's face" and with a mistress who (had she survived) would probably not have been satisfactory any more for the "good kind of destruction," can walk—dismally, of course—down the rain-drenched and baptismal streets of Geneva and leave it all behind him.

Dean Moriarty of **On the Road** is obviously a close kinsman of these American fictional characters, and, though he is perhaps degenerate and deformed, he is nevertheless recognizable. With his succession of Marylous—they are, of course, all Marylou done over with different jobs, different hair, and different smiles—he can have his succession of disastrously ungratifying affairs, suddenly, relentlessly, and meaninglessly, and then take his rented, stolen, or borrowed car and leave all behind him; plunge to the promise of richer things in Galveston; plunge to the promise of greater excitement and adventure in Harrisburg, Virginia; plunge to the more meaningful things in Denver. So Natty Bumpo, Hester Prynne, Ishmael, Huckleberry Finn, and Lieutenant Henry form the literary matrix out of which Dean Moriarty emerges. (pp. 231-33)

The last paragraph in **On the Road**—in addition to isolated references scattered throughout the text—identifies this novel

and its principals with a second literary tradition in America: the search for the father.

> So in America when the sun goes down and I sit on the old broken-down river pier watching the long, long skies over New Jersey and sense all that raw land that rolls in one unbelievable huge bulge over to the West Coast, and all that road going, all the people dreaming in the immensity of it, . . . and nobody, nobody knows what's going to happen to anybody besides the forlorn rags of growing old, I think of Dean Moriarty, I even think of Old Dean Moriarty, the father we never found, I think of Dean Moriarty.

It is, of course, senseless to suggest that the quest for the father was an invention in American literature. It wasn't. It has for centuries been the property of folklore and legend and it became a literary property at least twenty-five centuries ago when Telemachus knocked on Helen's and Menelaus's door and asked for his daddy. But again for historical reasons this motif is poignantly and characteristically American. In the first place, as I suggested earlier, the awesome metaphorical quest for the Father was made by the earliest Puritan writers, by the Mathers and Anne Bradstreet and Jonathan Edwards who sought the Father in their hearts and meditations. And when their successors put their Jesus on the shelf in favor of money, commerce, and industry, they tapped in their writings this tradition of the quest, enhanced it, and ultimately gave it shape in actual movement in search for the father. (pp. 233-34)

Hawthorne's short tale, "My Kinsman, Major Molineux," is, perhaps, the fullest fictional account of precisely this procedure. Here, it will be remembered, appears Robin, dressed in characteristic American costume and engaged in characteristic endeavor: seeking his fortune. Having left his actual and temporal father (who, it may be worth remembering, is a preacher and pray-er), and obviously, by the time the story closes, deprived of returning to him, Robin appears in the little town to find the aid, protection, and security offered by his kinsman, Major Molineux, who is a European and in the employ of the British government. But his futile and sometimes humiliating search for this surrogate father ends when he discovers Molineux tarred and feathered and banished from the village. Allegorically, then, it is clear that the Revolutionary War deprived young America of its father figure and left it to search out another, just as Robin finds a surrogate father in the gentleman who befriends him at the end of the story and encourages him to try his fortune there.

The pattern of the search for the father—as well as historical implications of this search—as it is established here, is carried through American literature and forms one of its traditions. Thus Redburn, in what is perhaps one of the happiest tropes in any literature, tries with frustration and dismay to discover Liverpool with the aid of his father's guidebook and notes. Huckleberry Finn, as some contend, finds the surrogate father in Jim. But more recently in Sherwood Anderson's "I Want To Know Why," the kid tries to find a father figure in the race-track dandy who visits and kisses low-type women who live in suspicious houses: he finds the father and loses him. Even though Thomas Wolfe knew that you can't go home again, there is nevertheless the same impulse in Eugene Gant, who, in spite of his own very colorful and actual father, moves restlessly to find another. And, more recently still, there are all the homeless and fatherless youths in the fiction of J. D. Salinger who run away or drift in search of the surrogate.

So it is with Dean Moriarty and with Sal of *On the Road:* they make the search for the father. And here the two traditions of movement and questing, and the search for the father figure, join. Just as those literary figures mentioned before, from Cooper to Hemingway, were free to move in space, so too are Robin and Redburn, the kid in "I Want to Know Why," Eugene Gant, Holden Caulfield, Dean Moriarty, and Sal free to move away from authority, or revolt against it and to search for other authority and security vested elsewhere.

Kerouac, Cooper, and Hawthorne; Kerouac, Melville, and Salinger. No matter how they are put together, the name of Kerouac seems to leave a smirch on the configuration of classic American literature. But there they are, similar in fundamental respects: on the move, on the road for the promise of better things; on the move to escape entanglements with time and the heart; on the move and on the road for the promise of the father figure, the authority, the security somewhere. There are, however, some fundamental differences, essential differences, and an exploration of these indicates not only how far the literature of the beats (and of Kerouac especially) diverges from the literature of traditional American letters, but also defines the drift and disintegration of values and humanity in American society and literature.

The demonic and break-neck circling about the United States in *On the Road* is a merging of two very similar literary circling rituals: the movement of Eliot's Hollow Men about the prickly pear at four o'clock in the morning and the circling orgy-porgy game that the citizens of *Brave New World* play to get their sexual satisfaction. But there is again a fundamental difference between these two more famous and more artistically successful rituals and the one recorded in *On the Road:* both Eliot and Huxley allow the "meaningless" actions to be played out against the backdrop of religious tradition and the values represented in *The Divine Comedy* (which furnishes the principal imagery of "The Hollow Men") and, as in the case of *Brave New World,* against the backdrop of an orderly but spontaneous and independent society of individuals that we like to believe remains in our historical traditions. In *On the Road,* however, the meaninglessness of the action described is compounded by the meaninglessness of the backdrop against which it is played out, that is, the meaninglessness of Denver, New York or 'Frisco society. Thus, the meaninglessness of the action in "The Hollow Men" or of the citizens of *Brave New World* is only apparent (since it takes dimensions of meaning from the framework of assumptions and imagery in which it occurs), while the meaninglessness of the action of the characters in *On the Road* is full, whole, and real. This is the source, circumstance, and result of the fallacy of imitative form mentioned previously.

In terms, however, of the total implications of the language, form, and content of *On the Road,* the obvious meanings which do emerge from the novel are much more frightening and sinister than a simple matter of faulty aesthetics and artistic structure. These meanings are clearly two: the total loss of personal goals, the hopeless quest for the father notwithstanding, and the total loss of personal values. And clearly these are precisely the crucial losses which divorce *On the Road* from the two literary traditions of which, as we have seen, it is so much a part. Moreover, that this novel has been enormously popular—not only among adolescents but also among "adults"—that it has defined and described reality for

so many, indicates the dimensions which this loss of values and loss of goals has assumed in American society.

Values, certainly, are not easily defined: they have something to do with caring, with the involvement of conscious and subconscious, of attitudes toward right and wrong, of conscience and motive, but most importantly of all, with the *personal* experiential quality of these. Although values are not easily defined, they are easily illustrated, and it might be added, they are illustrated in the literature recalled here to define American literary traditions. But by way of demonstrations, note briefly [a] justifiably memorable and famous [passage] from *Huckleberry Finn:*

> . . . I couldn't rest easy till I could see the ferry-boat start. But take it all around, I was feeling ruther comfortable on accounts of taking all this trouble for that gang, for not many would 'a' done it. I wished the widow knowed about it. I judged she would be proud of me for helping these rapscallions, because rapscallions and dead-beats is the kind the widow and good people takes the most interest in.

> Well, before long here comes the wreck, dim and dusky, sliding along down! A kind of cold shiver went through me, and then I struck out for her. She was very deep and I see in a minute there warn't much chance of anybody being alive in her. I pulled all around her and hollered a little, but there wasn't any answer; all dead still. I felt a little bit heavy-hearted about the gang but not much, for I reckoned if they could stand it I could.

Here the demonstration of values is fairly evident. In the first place, the action is—as the psychologists say—person-oriented. The principal character sees himself in distinct relationship to other distinctly human beings: people who are sick, who are dead-beats, and bad people or good people. But, what is still more important, Huckleberry responds to these other people in the world and he responds to himself self-consciously; that is to say, he is aware of his own feelings, recognizes them and expresses them, as in the instance of the wry or bitter or *consciously* careless humor at the end. . . . These feelings and these responses in terms of oneself or of other people, it seems to me, are the indications of personal and individual values, and these values have been the norm of literature until very recent times. But with Hemingway and the host of imitators who followed him something new and terrible happened in literary form and human values: all values, all attitudes, and all feelings were drained from the prose, and only those impersonal and apparently un-valuable things that a dispassionate camera eye could catch were caught by the eye of the observer—only, that is to say, the places, numbers, and things. (pp. 234-37)

This omission of value words represents one step in the departure of a man from his feelings, from the integration of his vision and his awareness with his response. This manner of writing—or representing action and things—puts a man at one remove from himself: he indeed sees clearly what is happening (and he perhaps responds to these happenings), but his feelings, his attitudes, or, more succinctly, the *value for him* of what he sees is not embodied or expressed in his representation of it.

In *On the Road* Kerouac takes this process one step further. . . . [Not] only are all values—in terms of response—drained from his prose, but he portrays Sal reporting on himself *as if he were reporting on someone else.* Values for himself no longer exist. Avoiding such obvious and numerous banalities as "I lit a woodfire on the cement floor of the barn to make light. We made love on the crates. Terry got up and cut right back to the shack . . . " or "We went back to the barn; I made love to her under the tarantula. What was the tarantula doing?" note in this regard the following passage which is not entirely devoid of literary merit.

> . . . The picture was Singing Cowboy Eddie Dean and his gallant white horse Bloop, that was number one; number two double-feature film was George Raft, Sidney Greenstreet, and Peter Lorre in a picture about Istanbul. We saw both of these things six times each during the night. We saw them waking, we heard them sleeping, we sensed them dreaming, we were permeated completely with the strange Gray Myth of the West and the weird dark Myth of the East when morning came. All my actions since then have been dictated automatically to my subconscious by this horrible osmotic experience. I heard Peter Lorre make his sinister come-on; I was with George Raft in his paranoiac fears; I rode and sang with Eddie Dean and shot up the rustlers innumerable times. People slugged out of bottles and turned around and looked everywhere in the dark theatre for something to do, somebody to talk to. In the head everybody was guiltily quiet, nobody talked. In the gray dawn that puffed ghostlike about the windows of the theatre and hugged its eaves I was sleeping with my head on the wooden arm of a seat . . .

Here Sal's conception of himself is simply not in human terms. Indicative of this are such phrases as "we were permeated completely," "this horrible osmotic experience," "automatically dictated," and "paranoiac fears." The conception, in short, is in the language of machinery and science—physical science and psychology. Now the worst of this conception as a statement of the deterioration of humanity and the disintegration of a human being is not this. It is finally in the total loss of volition, of personality, of human values which is implied in the following series of associations: I was with George Raft, Peter Lorre, Sidney Greenstreet, and Eddie Dean; all my actions since then have been dictated automatically to my subconscious by this horrible osmosis; people slugged out of bottles. More explicitly still, Sal identifies with the actors on the screen; as they are automatically contrived, as they move automatically and inevitably, so are all his actions automatic and contrived and beyond his volition or *valuation;* and, finally (there is no transition from the actors on the screen to the people in the theatre) all the people in the all-night theatre are just as void of volition, just as automatic, and just as un-valuable as he, Sal, and the actors. Thus there is no conscious experience of self and there is no conscious experience of others.

Therefore in *On the Road* there are hundreds of episodes and actions, but not one experience. Many of the actors tremble and quiver, but not one has nerves; many are struck in the face or torn in body or hung over, but no one responds with pain; many of them sleep together, but no one experiences pleasure, or feeling, or fun. There is nowhere in the novel human failure or human success; there is nowhere a system or a hint of what we understand as human values. Now, as the human being and his system of responses, feelings, and affects disappear from a work, the work as literature suffers proportionately. If this were not so, then there would have been long since a tradition of literature based on actual mari-

onettes, robots, or mechanical devices. On the contrary, however, as in R U R, for example, where the greatest number of agents actually are robots and mechanical devices, these *things* become interesting, engaging, and meaningful only as they approach a distinctly human condition. What happens, though, in Kerouac, and in the literature of the beats generally, is precisely this: the "human" agents approach the condition of the machine and, as they do, the work suffers commensurately as *literature*. Thus, even though a certain cleverness or imagination reveals itself in the episode of the all-night movie house, it fails finally to be good art and certainly enduring art because it occurs in a context that leaves it meaningless, and, one suspects, not *worth* reporting.

The vision of the decline and deterioration of human values in our society is, of course, not a recent one. Obviously the poets—like Eliot—saw it earlier, and subsequently it has been explored psychologically, sociologically and scientifically. Even the causes of this deterioration are not difficult to find: simple human experience is not a marketable commodity; it purchases no status; it leads to no easy retirement. Further, in an age of machines and science, feelings, passions, and experience are conceived in the terms of machinery or logic; we ignore the obvious fact that the heart has its logic as well as its reasons. Human experience and values, then, which are remarkable constants in literature, when measured against the expanding and elongating index of scientific, material, and intellectual growth and achievement, appear to diminish, and increasingly, in the practical execution of one's social conduct and employment, they do actually diminish. For some, precisely those who, like Kerouac, produce the literature of the beats, and precisely those for whom these works stand as a definition of reality, the essential human values and the essential worth of human experience and feeling grow so worthless that it is not, as in *On the Road,* worth telling about or being conscious of.

For reasons that should now be clear, I cannot believe that the literature of the beats, and especially the work of Jack Kerouac, has any intrinsic value, either literary or human. But it is nonetheless significant, and it is nonetheless subject matter for the consideration of responsible individuals and responsible literary scholars. To the responsible citizen it points up the texture and quality of the human ingredient in the society he assimilates and produces; it points up his ostensible value and the value of his experience to the organization of his fellows. To the serious student of literature this work points up in clear and summary perspective some of the principal American literary traditions from which it not only borrows but to which it will also undoubtedly add. And finally it points up to both simultaneously the values and lack of values which constitute our contemporary world and the reflection of that world in contemporary literature. (pp. 237-40)

> *Melvin W. Askew, "Quests, Cars, and Kerouac,"*
> *in* The University of Kansas City Review, *Vol.*
> *XXVIII, No. 3, March, 1962, pp. 231-40.*

FREDERICK FEIED

It was the political significance of the hobo that [John] Dos Passos undertook to explore in the pages of *U.S.A.;* it was his economic significance that [Jack] London chiefly stressed at a time when vast economic disturbances triggered by the crises of industrial capitalism threw large numbers of men out of work and onto the road. In both periods, the existence of a serious hobo problem stimulated an interest in the hobo that was sociological as well as literary. By the late 1940's, however, following a period of war and unparalleled prosperity, the hobo was no longer a factor of any proportions in American political life, and scarcely an economic one. Railroad spokesmen were agreed that the days were gone "when nearly every freight train was infested with tramps. . . ." Literature devoted to the subject of the migrant, as recorded in the various indices, had diminished to a trickle, and an affluent and self-satisfied society seemed to have eliminated the conditions which in earlier times had given rise to a hobo problem and to a literature concerned with the hobo. Yet, despite all this, the theme of the tramp and the hobo (neither category completely covers the case) found expression in two of the most widely read and controversial novels of the 1950's—*On the Road* and *The Dharma Bums.*

Perhaps the reason the theme of the hobo could arouse widespread interest in such a period is that the hoboes of the 1940's and 1950's appeared as one of the first concrete manifestations of a movement of wholesale rejection of contemporary values, and Kerouac's use of the theme dramatized the sense of alienation of large numbers of his contemporaries. For although hoboes of the type he describes were few in number, their presence attested to the existence of a condition that was fairly widespread. They reflected a growing uneasiness in America, a gnawing sense that all was not well in the richest land in the world. Their frantic flights across country, their rootless and disaffected behavior, but above all their profound sense of disaffiliation, testified to a growing spirit of discontent. In going on the road they gave expression, in the clearest and most direct way possible, to all the repressed longings and vague dissatisfactions abroad in the populace at large. (pp. 57-9)

Dynamic obsolescence—planned waste—is one form of madness which contributes to this sense of uneasiness. One of the characters of *On the Road* expresses something of this feeling when he says:

> "They prefer making cheap goods so's everybody'll have to go on working and punching timeclocks and organizing themselves in sullen unions. . . ."

Another is the threat of nuclear destruction. At one point in *On the Road* the narrator gives vent to this feeling when he sees a group of Indians who

> had come down . . . to hold forth their hands for something they thought civilization could offer, and they never dreamed the sadness and the poor broken delusion of it. They didn't know that a bomb had come that could crack all our bridges and railroads and reduce them to jumbles, and we would be as poor as they someday, and stretching out our hands in the same, same way.

For Kerouac's hoboes the very act of going on the road amounts to a kind of protest, inasmuch as it represents a symbolic turning of one's back on society as constituted. In the era of "the great McCarthy hysteria," flight is the only means they have of expressing their dissent, and flight here functions as a substitute for more direct forms of protest which "had been closed for some time." In both *On the Road* and *The Dharma Bums* this fugue, or flight, is portrayed on the realistic level as an attempt to escape from an intolerable personal or social situation, and on the symbolic level as a search for

values or for inner light and understanding, a search for the road, the way to spiritual truth, in short, a search for God.

But, despite the difference in motivation between Kerouac's hoboes and those of the past, the two characters whose adventures and philosophies are described in *On the Road* and *The Dharma Bums* can be seen, in one light at least, as counterparts of the types encountered in the works of London and Dos Passos. Dean Moriarty of *On the Road* is an unconscious caricature of Nietzsche's superman, and Japhy Ryder of *The Dharma Bums* is a natural descendant of the vanishing wobbly. Kerouac's first-person narrator, called Sal Paradise in *On the Road* and Ray Smith in *The Dharma Bums,* treks back and forth across the country in tutelage to these two characters. He is "digging" American life and apparently attempting to formulate some sort of philosophy out of the ideas and attitudes of his tutors. Though Kerouac's two heroes are strikingly different, the road as a way of life looms large in both their philosophies.

In the first of the two books, *On the Road,* it is an encounter with Dean Moriarty, a road-kid of the 1940's just out of a New Mexico reform school, that sends Sal Paradise off to "dig" the West.

> With the coming of Dean Moriarty began the part of my life you could call my life on the road. . . . Dean is the perfect guy for the road because he actually was born on the road, when his parents were passing through Salt Lake City in 1926, in a jalopy, on their way to Los Angeles.

Dean had spent a good part of his childhood, during the Depression, bumming around with his father and his father's drinking cronies. When the book opens, however, Dean's days as a railroad bum are far behind him. In the affluent society of the 1940's there is always a car to be come by in some fashion, whether it be a second-hand borrowed jalopy or a late-model stolen car. It is Sal Paradise, middle-class, college-educated romantic, who hitchhikes, hops freights, and waxes poetic over hobo life in *On the Road.*

The book deals with the period from the winter of 1947 to the late fall or winter of 1950. In that brief span Paradise, alias Kerouac, treks back and forth across the American continent no less than five times. Each journey is progressively more feverish, more frantic, and more "beat" in character than the preceding. The action boils over in a score of American cities where the fugitives pause in their flight only long enough to replenish their resources and wear out their welcome. Numerous side trips and a final junket to Mexico lace up the continent from east to west and north to south.

Paradise's first journey west is almost leisurely in pace by comparison with later trips when he travels with Dean Moriarty, and in the beginning he is anything but knowing about the ways of the road. After "poring over maps of the United States in Paterson for months, even reading books about the pioneers," he finally sets out, he tells us, "filled with dreams" of what he would do "in Chicago, Denver and then finally in San Fran." But instead of thumbing his way west, he indulges a notion to head due north to Route 6, which "was one long red line . . . that led from the tip of Cape Cod clear to Ely, Nevada, and then dipped down to Los Angeles." Route 6 turned out to be a little-used road through the Catskills, however, and on his first night out Sal Paradise is stranded in Bear Mountain in the middle of a rainstorm. "It was my dream that screwed up," he admits, "the stupid hearthside idea that it would be wonderful to follow one great red line across America instead of trying various roads and routes." He winds up taking a bus to Chicago and renting a room at the Y.M.C.A., but despite this inauspicious start he does succeed in hitchhiking part of the way across the continent. Twice more before he arrives at his destination, however, he resorts to the bus lines.

Each ride, each adventure along the way, is duly recounted and described, for this is the stuff of Kerouac's novels—experiences and encounters reported upon for their own sakes. If there is an occasional suggestion of the flight motif at this point, it does not yet emerge as anything like a theme. Sal Paradise is primarily "digging America," he is "reading the American Landscape," and nothing is too trivial to be breathlessly recounted—cold and hunger, the meals eaten in restaurants or over campfires, discomfort and dullness, sunsets and dawns and the excitement of new towns and cities. Sal Paradise ingests it all, consumes it with his senses. This is not the satisfaction of obstacles surmounted, of hardships overcome, that one finds in London. It is, rather a sensuous devouring of every new experience like a child gorging himself on sweets. He parades before us an array of mid-century American types as varied and exhaustive as anything to be found in Chaucer: motherly, middle-aged women in tidy coupés, blond young Minnesota farmers in trucks who pick up every hitchhiker on the road, truckdrivers and salesmen, waitresses and cowboys, criminals and con-men, Mexican field hands, hoboes, prospectors, Hollywood pimps, nature-boy saints and religious zealots, Arkies and Oakies, homosexuals and dope addicts in an unending procession. To these he adds portraits of intellectuals of the incipient beat generation.

Among those he describes with great zest are the other hoboes and hitchhikers he meets on the road. The first is a young New Yorker, a heavy drinker, whom Paradise suspects is fleeing the law. He is as much a novice on the road as Paradise himself.

> We didn't know how to hop a proper chain gang; we'd never done it before; we didn't know whether they were going east or west or how to find out or what boxcars and flats and de-iced reefers to pick, and so on. So when the Omaha bus came through just before dawn we hopped on it. . . .

Memories of the hoboing of the 1930's are evoked when a cowboy who gives Paradise a ride tells him:

> "During the depression . . . I used to hop freights at least once a month. In those days you'd see hundreds of men riding a flatcar or in a boxcar, and they weren't just bums, they were all kinds of men out of work and going from one place to another and some of them just wandering. It was like that all over the West. Brakemen never bothered you in those days. I don't know about today."

Kerouac is constantly haunted by visions of lost bums, solitary figures tramping their rounds from one end of the States to the other. He is filled with a poignant awareness of their loneliness, their isolation, both spiritual and physical. London did not make much of this theme of isolation. His tramp is satisfied if he can escape the crushing horrors of existence in the Social Pit. If warm and well-fed, he is not likely to be concerned over the fact that he is a thousand miles from anywhere. Dos Passos' characters have a sense of participating in a movement. They find their fellow workers everywhere.

It is only when they are removed from the arena of class struggle that they are likely to feel isolated.

All the types that Kerouac catalogues seem to reveal a chronic restlessness, an uneasiness that manifests itself, no matter where they are, in a desire to get going and keep moving. They do not always have a destination in mind. " 'You boys going to get somewhere, or just going?' " a carnival owner asks Paradise at one point. "We didn't understand his question, and it was a damn good question." This quality becomes more exaggerated as the chronicle progresses. Everyone Paradise meets is just starting out, just arriving, or making plans to depart. Each one offers different reasons, but they all add up to dissatisfaction with the conditions of their lives, and the theme of mass flight slowly begins to make itself felt. Whatever their motivation, Kerouac "digs" them all, but the person he digs the most is the clawing, flapping, demonaic Dean Moriarty.

Paradise is attracted to Dean because he feels that he is different from his old friends and college buddies who

> were in the negative, nightmare position of putting down society and giving their tired bookish or political or psychoanalytical reasons. . . . Dean just raced in society, eager for bread and love; he didn't care one way or the other. . . .

Even his criminality, Paradise tells us, "was not something that sulked and sneered; it was a wild yea-saying overburst of American joy. . . . "

Dazzled by Moriarty's pyrotechnics, Paradise confesses:

> I shambled after as I've been doing all my life after people who interest me, because the only people for me are the mad ones, the ones who are mad to live, mad to talk, mad ones who never yawn or say a commonplace thing, but burn, burn, burn burn like fabulous yellow roman candles exploding like spiders across the stars and in the middle you see the blue centerlight pop and everybody goes to be saved, desirous of everything at the same time, the "Awww!" What did they call such young people in Goethe's Germany?

Moriarty is a truly awesome figure, a personification of the wasteful spirit of our age. He uses up objects at an astonishing rate. He steals cars, or a series of cars, runs them at top speed and leaves them beat-up and battered at the side of the road. He uses up people in much the same way. He runs everything at top speed, including himself. He leaps from friend to friend, from mistress to mistress, in the same way that he leaps from one stolen car to another.

> Dean had never seen his mother's face. Every new girl, every new wife, every new child was an addition to his bleak impoverishment.

There is no sating his appetites, no way to halt his flight. Motion is the rule and guide of his life. His soul "is wrapped up in a fast car, a coast to reach, with a woman at the end of the road. . . . " When Paradise begins to travel with Dean, the pace of the novel becomes more frantic.

Paradise sees Dean and others like him "rising from the underground, the sordid hipsters of America, a new beat generation that I was slowly joining." Dean's frantic pursuit of the road is to him symbolic of the plight of thousands of others who have nothing to do, nowhere to go, nobody to believe in, or who cross and recross the country every year because they have no place they can "stay in without getting tired of it and because there was nowhere to go but everywhere. . . . "

The death of Dean's mother when he was just a child had left the elder Dean Moriarty and his son without a hub to their universe. Dean's father had become a cook-shack tramp, a down-and-out bum, drinking himself unconscious at every opportunity. Dean had grown up on the rods and had been on the move ever since, "surrounded by the battered suitcases of his motherless feverish life across America and back numberless times, an undone bird."

One of the few things in the book which humanizes Moriarty and sets him before us in a way that we can feel sympathy with is the search for his father. This theme, which seems to have deep significance for Kerouac, is one which recurs again and again. Ever since the death of his mother, Dean's life on the road has accentuated his double loss as he follows his father from one skid row to another, through one debauch after another, seeking the love, guidance, and understanding that his father, in his demoralized state, could not give. (pp. 60-8)

As Paradise contemplates their frantic balling and bumming across "ole tumbledown holy America" it comes to represent for him, as for the others, the only meaningful act that is permitted them. In taking to the road they are "leaving confusion and nonsense behind and performing our one and noble function of the time, *move*." The pattern of restless, unprovoked and aimless flight gradually begins to take on the aspect of a pilgrimage. Through a kind of motivational metamorphosis, flight becomes transformed into its opposite—a search for values, for something to do, somewhere to go, someone to believe in.

More and more as the novel progresses the talk turns on religion—God. Every happening of any possible religious consequence is examined for any significance it may possess. At one point they pick up a mad Jew named Hyman Solomon, who "walked all over the USA, knocking and sometimes kicking at Jewish doors and demanding money: 'Give me money to eat, I am a Jew.'" They "carried Solomon all the way to Testament"—a small Southern town where Paradise's brother lived. Dean finds in this coincidence sure proof of the existence of God:

> "Now you see, Sal, God does exist, because we keep getting hung-up with this town, no matter what we try to do, and you'll notice the strange Biblical name of it, and that strange Biblical character who made us stop here once more, and all things tied together all over like rain connecting everybody the world over by chain touch. . . . "

In the course of their search the old bum Dean Moriarty, the tinsmith, becomes the tramp equivalent of the mendicant Jesus, the carpenter.

> Where was his father?—old bum Dean Moriarty the Tinsmith, riding freights, working as a scullion in railroad cookshacks, stumbling, down-crashing in wino alley nights, expiring on coal piles, dropping his yellowed teeth one by one in the gutters of the West.

The road is equated with the Tao, the way:

> "Someday you and me'll be coming down an alley together at sundown and looking in the cans to see."
> "You mean we'll end up old bums?"

"Why not, man? Of course we will if we want to, and all that. There's no harm ending that way. You spend a whole life of non-interference with the wishes of others, including politicians and the rich, and nobody bothers you and you cut along and make it your own way." I agreed with him. He was reaching his Tao decisions in the simplest direct way. "What's your road, man?—holyboy road, madman road, rainbow road, guppy road, any road. It's an anywhere road for anybody anyhow. Where body how?"

In a sense, ***On the Road*** is a twentieth-century restatement of *The Pilgrim's Progress*. Sal and Dean are on the road, the holyboy road, and the road is life. Like Christian and Faithful their goal is the Celestial City, but Sal has a premonition that they will never make it. He has a dream about a Shrouded Traveler:

> . . . a strange Arabian figure that was pursuing me across the desert; that I tried to avoid; that finally overtook me just before I reached the Protective City. . . . Something, someone, some spirit was pursuing all of us across the desert of life and was bound to reach us before we reached heaven.

It's an anywhere road and the road is the way to eternal life, but what emerges from their search at last is a perverse religion compounded of all the sick elements of mid-century America.

Sal and Dean want to be good, they talk of Jesus, they refer to God, they try to be tender, they seek to love, but somehow it all turns to kicks, somehow everyone who comes in contact with them gets hurt in the process. They steal another car and race away in another direction, or a fifty-dollar bill from the aunt back East and the call of the middle-class life lures them away from the path of the mendicant Jesus. Though they love Negroes and "Japs" and especially Mexicans in Mexico, and though they hate their own sick culture, they end up sick, diseased, and crippled, revealing in exaggerated form all the vulgarity and grossness from which they allege themselves to be fleeing.

Kerouac's hoboes are seeking escape—escape not only from the threats of a hostile society, but escape from their own inadequate personalities and unsatisfactory human relationships. They seek to make good their escape in moment-to-moment living, digging everything, pursuing their kicks with a kind of desperate energy that passes for enthusiasm. Narcotics, jazz, sexual experimentation are the vehicles of their escape. Fast cars and all-night talk jags are a part of the play, but the road always turns back on itself, and the talk never leads anywhere. Their religion ends up in a fetishism of jazz, their love in a debauch of sex. The communicants line up to receive God, but the wafer has lost its transubstantiating power, and the host is impotent to bring the holy vision of God without the intercession of Benzedrine or "H." The "connection to the starry dynamo in the machinery of night" turns out more often to be a connection with a dirty needle in the arm, for God has made a fair-trade pact with the pushers, and refuses to show his face for free.

The plight of Kerouac's hipster hoboes is in some ways more desperate than that of the submerged tenth of London's experience or the most persecuted of Dos Passos' wobblies. In the war-deranged culture of the 1940's, Kerouac's characters live in a value void, a mores nihilism. It is this void that they seek to fill with bizarre and frantic activity or a wistful seeking for something in which to believe, but there is no voice crying to them from out of the wilderness; John the Baptist has been bugged for observation at Rockland, and Moloch reigns unchallenged, God of the establishment. (pp. 69-73)

Frederick Feied, "Chapter Three," in his No Pie in the Sky: The Hobo as American Cultural Hero in the Works of Jack London, John Dos Passos, and Jack Kerouac, The Citadel Press, 1964, pp. 57-80.

JACK KEROUAC [INTERVIEW WITH TED BERRIGAN]

[Berrigan]: *Why don't we begin with editors. How do you . . .*

[Kerouac]: O.K. All my editors since Malcolm Cowley have had instructions to leave my prose exactly as I wrote it. In the days of Malcolm Cowley, with **On the Road** and **The Dharma Bums,** I had no power to stand by my style for better or for worse. When Malcolm Cowley made endless revisions and inserted thousands of needless commas like, say, Cheyenne, Wyoming (why not just say Cheyenne Wyoming and let it go at that, for instance), why, I spent $500 making the complete restitution of the **Bums** manuscript and got a bill from Viking Press called "Revisions." Ha ho ho. And so you asked about how do I work with an editor . . . well nowadays I am just grateful to him for his assistance in proofreading the manuscript and in discovering logical errors, such as dates, names of places. For instance in my last book I wrote Firth of Forth then looked it up, on the suggestion of my editor, and found that I'd really sailed off the Firth of Clyde. Things like that. Or I spelled Aleister Crowley "Alisteir," or he discovered little mistakes about the yardage in football games . . . and so forth. By not revising what you've already written you simply give the reader the actual workings of your mind during the writing itself: you confess your thoughts about events in your own unchangeable way . . . well, look, did you ever hear a guy telling a long wild tale to a bunch of men in a bar and all are listening and smiling, did you ever hear that guy stop to revise himself, go back to a previous sentence to improve it, to defray its rhythmic thought impact . . . If he pauses to blow his nose, isn't he planning his next sentence? and when he lets that next sentence loose, isn't it once and for all the way he wanted to say it? Doesn't he depart the thought of that sentence and, as Shakespeare says, "forever holds his tongue" on the subject, since he's passed over it like a part of the river flows over a rock once and for all and never returns and can never flow any other way in time? Incidentally, as for my bug against periods, that was for the prose in **"October in the Railroad Earth,"** very experimental, intended to clack along all the way like a steam engine pulling a 100-car freight with a talky caboose at the end, that was my way at the time and it still can be done if the thinking during the swift writing is confessional and pure and all excited with the life of it. And be sure of this, I spent my entire youth writing slowly with revisions and endless rehashing speculation and deleting and got so I was writing one sentence a day and the sentence had no FEELING. Goddamn it, FEELING is what I like in art, not CRAFTINESS and the hiding of feelings.

What encouraged you to use the "spontaneous" style of **On the Road?**

I got the idea for the spontaneous style of **On the Road** from seeing how good old Neal Cassady wrote his letters to me, all first person, fast, mad, confessional, completely serious, all detailed, with real names in his case however (being letters). I remembered also Goethe's admonition, well Goethe's prophecy that the future literature of the West would be confessional in nature; also Dostoevsky prophesied as much and might have started in on that if he'd lived long enough to do his projected masterwork, *The Great Sinner.* Cassady also began his early youthful writing with attempts at slow, painstaking, and-all-that-crap craft business, but got sick of it like I did, seeing it wasn't getting out his guts and heart the way it *felt* coming out. But I got the flash from his style. It's a cruel lie for those West Coast punks to say that I got the idea of **On the Road** from him. All his letters to me were about his younger days before I met him, a child with his father, et cetera, and about his later teenage experiences. The letter he sent me is erroneously reported to be a 13,000 word letter . . . no, the 13,000 word piece was his novel *The First Third,* which he kept in his possession. The letter, the main letter I mean, was 40,000 words long, mind you, a whole short novel. It was the greatest piece of writing I ever saw, better'n anybody in America, or at least enough to make Melville, Twain, Dreiser, Wolfe, I dunno who, spin in their graves. Allen Ginsberg asked me to lend him this vast letter so he could read it. He read it, then loaned it to a guy called Gerd Stern who lived on a houseboat in Sausalito California, in 1955, and this fellow lost the letter: overboard I presume. Neal and I called it, for convenience, the *Joan Anderson Letter* . . . all about a Christmas weekend in the poolhalls, hotel rooms and jails of Denver, with hilarious events thoughout and tragic too, even a drawing of a window, with measurements to make the reader understand, all that. Now listen: this letter would have been printed under Neal's copyright, if we could find it, but as you know, it was my property as a letter to me, so Allen shouldn't have been so careless with it, nor the guy on the houseboat. If we can unearth this entire 40,000 word letter Neal shall be justified. We also did so much fast talking between the two of us, on tape recorders, way back in 1952, and listened to them so much, we both got the secret of LINGO in telling a tale and figured that was the only way to express the speed and tension and ecstatic tomfoolery of the age. . . . Is that enough?

How do you think this style has changed since **On the Road?**

What style? Oh, the style of **On the Road.** Well as I say, Cowley riddled the original style of the manuscript there, without my power to complain, and since then my books are all published as written, as I say, and the style has varied from the highly experimental speedwriting of **"Railroad Earth"** to the ingrown toenail packed mystical style of **Tristessa,** the *Notes-from-the-Underground* (by Dostoevsky) confessional madness of **The Subterraneans,** the perfection of the three as one in **Big Sur,** I'd say, which tells a plain tale in a smooth buttery literate run, to **Satori in Paris** which is really the first book I wrote with drink at my side (cognac and malt liquor) . . . and not to overlook **Book of Dreams,** the style of a person half awake from sleep and ripping it out in pencil by the bed . . . yes, pencil . . . what a job! bleary eyes, insaned mind bemused and mystified by sleep, details that pop out even as you write them you don't know what they mean, till you wake up, have coffee, look at it, and see the logic of dreams in dream language itself, see? . . . and finally I decided in my tired middle age to slow down and did **Vanity of Duluoz** in a more moderate style so that, having been so esoteric all these years, some earlier readers would come back and see what ten years had done to my life and thinking . . .

which is after all the only thing I've got to offer, the true story of what I saw and how I saw it. (pp. 64-7)

What is that state of "Yeatsian semi-trance" which provides the ideal atmosphere for spontaneous writing?

Well, there it is, how can you be in a trance with your mouth yapping away . . . writing at least is a silent meditation even though you're going 100 miles an hour. Remember that scene in *La Dolce Vita* where the old priest is mad because a mob of maniacs have shown up to see the tree where the kids saw the Virgin Mary? He says, "Visions are not available in all this frenetic foolishness and yelling and pushing; visions are only obtainable in silence and meditation." Thar. Yup. (p. 68)

Why do you think Neal [Cassady, the model for Dean Moriarty] doesn't write?

He has written . . . beautifully! He has written better than I have. Neal's a very funny guy. He's a real Californian. We had more fun than 5000 Socony Gasoline Station attendants can have. In my opinion he's the most intelligent man I've ever met in my life. Neal Cassady. He's a Jesuit by the way. He used to sing in the choir. He was a choir boy in the Catholic churches of Denver. And he taught me everything that I now do believe about anything that there may be to be believed about divinity.

About Edgar Cayce?

No, before he found out about Edgar Cayce he told me all these things in the section of the life he led when he was on the road with me—he said, We know God, don't we Jack? I said, Yessir boy. He said, Don't we know that nothing's going to happen wrong? Yessir. And we're going to go on and on . . . and hmmmmmm ja-bmmmmmmm. . . . He was perfect. And he's always perfect. Everytime he comes to see me I can't get a word in edgewise.

You wrote about Neal playing football, in **Visions of Cody.**

Yes, he was a very good football player. He picked up two beatniks that time in blue jeans in North Beach Frisco. He said I got to go, bang bang, do I got to go? He's working on the railroad . . . had his watch out . . . 2:15, boy I got to be there by *2:20.* I tell you boys drive me over down there so I be on time with my train . . . So I can get my train on down to—what's the name of that place—San Jose? They say sure kid and Neal says here's the pot. So—"We maybe look like great bleat beatniks with great beards . . . but we are cops. And we are arresting you."

So, a guy went to the jailhouse and interviewed him from the New York Post and he said tell that Kerouac if he still believes in me to send me a typewriter. So I sent Allen Ginsberg one hundred dollars to get a typewriter for Neal. And Neal got the typewriter. And he wrote notes on it, but they wouldn't let him take the notes out. I don't know where the typewriter is. Genet wrote all of *Our Lady of the Flowers* in the shithouse . . . the jailhouse. There's a great writer, Jean Genet. He kept writing and kept writing until he got to a point where he was going to come by writing about it . . . until he came into his bed—in the can. The French can. The French jail. Prison. And that was the end of the chapter. Every chapter is Genet coming off. Which I must admit Sartre noticed.

You think that's a different kind of spontaneous writing?

Well, I could go to jail and I could write every night a chapter

about Magee, Magoo, and Molly. It's beautiful. Genet is really *the* most honest writer we've had since Kerouac and Burroughs. But he came before us. He's older. Well, he's the same age as Burroughs. But I don't think I've been dishonest. Man, I've had a good time! God, man, I rode around this country free as a bee. But Genet is a very tragic and beautiful writer. And I give them the crown. And the laurel wreath. I don't give the laurel wreath to Richard Wilbur! *Or* Robert Lowell. Give it to Jean Genet and William Seward Burroughs. *And* to Allen Ginsberg and to Gregory Corso, especially. (pp. 77-8)

What about jazz and bop as influences rather than . . . Saroyan, Hemingway and Wolfe?

Yes, jazz and bop, in the sense of a, say, a tenor man drawing a breath and blowing a phrase on his saxophone, till he runs out of breath, and when he does, his sentence, his statement's been made . . . that's how I therefore separate my sentences, as breath separations of the mind . . . I formulated the theory of breath as measure, in prose and verse, never mind what Olson, Charles Olson says, I formulated that theory in 1953 at the request of Burroughs and Ginsberg. Then there's the raciness and freedom and humor of jazz instead of all that dreary analysis and things like "James entered the room, and lit a cigarette. He thought Jane might have thought this too vague a gesture . . . " You know the stuff. As for Saroyan, yes I loved him as a teenager, he really got me out of the 19th century rut I was trying to study, not only his funny tone but his neat Armenian poetic I don't know what . . . he just got me . . . Hemingway was fascinating, the pearls of words on a white page giving you an exact picture . . . but Wolfe was a torrent of American heaven and hell that opened my eyes to America as a subject in itself.

How about the movies?

Yes, we've all been influenced by movies. Malcolm Cowley incidentally mentioned this many times. He's very perceptive sometimes: he mentioned that **Doctor Sax** continually mentions urine, and quite naturally it does because I had no other place to write it but on a closed toilet seat in a little tile toilet in Mexico City so as to get away from the guests inside the apartment. There incidentally is a style truly hallucinated as I wrote it all on pot. No pun intended. Ho ho.

How has Zen influenced your work?

What's really influenced my work is the Mahayana Buddhism, the original Buddhism of Gotama Sakyamuni, the Buddha himself, of the India of old . . . Zen is what's left of his Buddhism, or Bodhi, after its passing into China and then into Japan. The part of Zen that's influenced my writing is the Zen contained in the haiku, . . . the three line, seventeen syllable poems written hundreds of years ago by guys like Basho, Issa, Shiki, and there've been recent masters. A sentence that's short and sweet with a sudden jump of thought in it is a kind of haiku, and there's a lot of freedom and fun in surprising yourself with that, let the mind willy-nilly jump from the branch to the bird. But my serious Buddhism, that of ancient India, has influenced that part in my writing that you might call religious, or fervent, or pious, almost as much as Catholicism has. Original Buddhism referred to continual conscious compassion, brotherhood, the *dana paramita* meaning the perfection of charity, don't step on the bug, all that, humility, mendicancy, the sweet sorrowful face of the Buddha (who was of Aryan origin by the way, I mean of Persian warnor caste, and not Oriental as pictured) . . . in original Buddhism no young kid coming to a monastery was warned that "here we bury them alive." He was simply given soft encouragement to meditate and be kind. The beginning of Zen was when Buddha, however, assembled all the monks together to announce a sermon and choose the first patriarch of the Mahayana church: instead of speaking, he simply held up a flower. Everybody was flabbergasted except Kasyapa, who smiled. Kasyapa was appointed the first patriarch. This idea appealed to the Chinese like the Sixth Patriarch Hui-Neng who said, "From the beginning nothing ever was" and wanted to tear up the records of Buddha's sayings as kept in the sutras; sutras are "threads of discourse." In a way, then, Zen is a gentle but goofy form of heresy, though there must be some real kindly old monks somewhere and we've heard about the nutty ones. I haven't been to Japan. Your Maha roshi yoshi is simply a disciple of all this and not the founder of anything new at all, of course. On the Johnny Carson show he didn't even mention Buddha's name. Maybe his Buddha is Mia. (pp. 83-5)

What about ritual and superstition? Do you have any about yourself when you get down to work?

I had a ritual once of lighting a candle and writing by its light and blowing it out when I was done for the night . . . also kneeling and praying before starting (I got that from a French movie about George Frederick Handel) . . . but now I simply hate to write. My superstition? I'm beginning to suspect that full moon. Also I'm hung up on the number 9 though I'm told a Piscean like myself should stick to number 7; but I try to do 9 touchdowns a day, that is, I stand on my head in the bathroom, on a slipper, and touch the floor 9 times with my toe tips, while balanced. This is incidentally more than Yoga, it's an athletic feat, I mean imagine calling me "unbalanced" after that. Frankly I do feel that my mind is going. So another "ritual" as you call it, is to pray to Jesus to preserve my sanity and my energy so I can help my family: that being my paralyzed mother, and my wife, and the ever-present kitties. Okay?

You typed out On the Road *in three weeks,* The Subterraneans . . . *in three days and nights. Do you still produce at this fantastic rate? Can you say something of the genesis of a work before you sit down and begin that terrific typing—how much of it is set in your mind, for example?*

You think out what actually happened, you tell friends long stories about it, you mull it over in your mind, you connect it together at leisure, then when the time comes to pay the rent again you force yourself to sit at the typewriter, or at the writing notebook, and get it over with as fast as you can . . . and there's no harm in that because you've got the whole story lined up. Now how that's done depends on what kind of steeltrap you've got up in that little old head. This sounds boastful but a girl once told me I had a steeltrap brain, meaning I'd catch her with a statement she'd made an hour ago even though our talk had rambled a million lightyears away from that point . . . you know what I mean, like a lawyer's mind, say. All of it is in my mind, naturally, except that language that is used at the time that it is used. . . . And as for On the Road *and* The Subterraneans, no I can't write that fast any more . . . Writing the Subs in three nights was really a fantastic athletic feat as well as mental, you shoulda seen me after I was done . . . I was pale as a sheet and had lost fifteen pounds and looked strange in the mirror. What I do now is write something like an average of 8,000 words a sitting, in the middle of the night, and another about a week

later, resting and sighing in between. I really hate to write. I get no fun out of it because I can't get up and say I'm working, close my door, have coffee brought to me, and sit there camping like a "man of letters" "doing his eight hour day of work" and thereby incidentally filling the printing world with a lot of dreary self-imposed cant and bombast . . . bombast is Scottish word for stuffing for a pillow. Haven't you heard a politician use 1500 words to say something he could have said in exactly three words? So I get it out of the way so as not to bore myself either. (pp. 88-90)

What about the influence of Ginsberg and Burroughs? Did you ever have any sense then of the mark the three of you would have on American writing?

I was determined to be a "great writer," in quotes, like Thomas Wolfe, see . . . Allen was always reading and writing poetry . . . Burroughs read a lot and walked around looking at things. . . . The influence we exerted on one another has been written about over and over again . . . We were just three interested characters, in the interesting big city of New York, around campuses, libraries, cafeterias. A lot of the details you'll find in Vanity . . . in On the Road where Burroughs is Bull Lee and Ginsberg is Carlo Marx . . . in Subterraneans, where they're Frank Carmody and Adam Moorad respectively, elsewhere. In other words, though I don't want to be rude to you for this honor, I am so busy interviewing myself in my novels, and have been so busy writing down these self-interviews, that I don't see why I should draw breath in pain every year of the last ten years to repeat and repeat to everybody who interviews me what I've already explained in the books themselves. . . . (Hundreds of journalists, thousands of students.) It beggars sense. And it's not that important. It's our work that counts, if anything at all, and I'm not proud of mine or theirs or anybody's since Thoreau and others like that, maybe because it's still too close to home for comfort. Notoriety and public confession in literary form is a frazzler of the heart you were born with, believe me. (pp. 97-8)

What was it that brought all of you together in the 50's? What was it that seemed to unify the "Beat Generation?"

Oh the beat generation was just a phrase I used in the 1951 written manuscript of On the Road to describe guys like Moriarty who run around the country in cars looking for odd jobs, girlfriends, kicks. It was thereafter picked up by West Coast leftist groups and turned into a meaning like "beat mutiny" and "beat insurrection" and all that nonsense; they just wanted some youth movement to grab onto for their own political and social purposes. I had nothing to do with any of that. I was a football player, a scholarship college student, a merchant seaman, a railroad brakeman on road freights, a script synopsizer, a secretary . . . And Moriarty-Cassady was an actual cowboy on Dave Uhl's ranch in New Raymer Colorado . . . What kind of beatnik is that?

Was there any sense of "community" among the Beat crowd?

That community feeling was largely inspired by the same characters I mentioned, like Ferlinghetti, Ginsberg; they are very socialistically minded and want everybody to live in some kind of frenetic kibbutz, solidarity and all that. I was a loner. Snyder is not like Whalen, Whalen is not like McClure, I am not like McClure, McClure is not like Ferlinghetti, Ginsberg is not like Ferlinghetti, but we all had fun over wine anyway. We knew thousands of poets and painters and jazz musicians. There's no "beat crowd" like you say . . . what about Scott Fitzerald and his "lost crowd," does that sound right? Or Goethe and his "Wilhelm Meister crowd?" The subject is such a bore. Pass me that glass.

Well, why did they split in the early 60's?

Ginsberg got interested in left wing politics . . . like Joyce I say, as Joyce said to Ezra Pound in the 1920's, "Don't bother me with politics, the only thing that interests me is style." Besides I'm bored with the new avant-garde and the skyrocketing sensationalism. I'm reading Blaise Pascal and taking notes on religion. I like to hang around now with nonintellectuals, as you might call them, and not have my mind proselytized, ad infinitum. They've even started crucifying chickens in happenings, what's the next step? An actual crucifixion of a man . . . The beat group dispersed as you say in the early 60's, all went their own way, and this is my way: home life, as in the beginning, with a little toot once in a while in local bars. (pp. 101-03)

> *Jack Kerouac and Ted Berrigan, in an interview in* The Paris Review, *Vol. 11, No. 43, Summer, 1968, pp. 60-105.*

GEORGE BOWERING

Jack Kerouac's **On the Road** has never fared well with the American critics. The early reviews treated it as a piece of pop culture, a "bible of the Beat Generation," in the way that nineteen-fifties TV shows used girls with lank black hair and white makeup for "beatnik" comedy or dance numbers. The majority of articles that treated the novel either alone or as part of the Beat phenomenon, downgraded it as plotless and without serious literary ideas. Lately there has been little discussion of Kerouac's second novel, at least in the literary magazines.

Many critics & teachers tend to think of Kerouac, especially of **On the Road,** more as a symptom than a part of our literature. It would seem to them to be something thrown up from the turmoil underlying the Eisenhower-Doris Day decade, to be recorded as a footnote to American mainstream literature. I don't quite know where it is, but there's an inconsistancy in there. The fact that **On the Road** is a novel (I take it as a fact, because Kerouac calls it a novel—I don't want to fight about definitions) & that it has had a large effect on style since its time, living style & writing style, lead me to believe that the novel offers ideas that may indeed be called literary, or further philosophical. Maybe philosophical in a comfortable, liveable, American context. Kerouac is not Pascal, not yet.

Norman Podhoretz [see excerpt in *CLC*, Vol. 1] makes it clear in his condescending language that he finds the idea of Kerouac as a literato unappealing. He tries to explain the success of **On the Road** on sociological grounds, saying that Americans feel guilty about being suburbanites & need a little Bohemian flogging in their reading time. He laments the appearance that the Beats' idea of bohemianism makes its way known not in terms of morality but in terms of spirituality, somehow suggesting that the latter won't get anything done to better Man's condition. He had no way of knowing it, but he presaged the complaint heard from the Old Left on viewing the semi-mysticism & electicism of the New Left. It is ironic in this context that Podhoretz reads the famous passage about Sal Paradise's envy for the Black soul:

> At lilac evening I walked with every muscle aching

among the lights of 27th and Welton in the Denver colored section, wishing I were a Negro, feeling that the best the white world had offered was not enough ecstasy for me, not enough life, joy, kicks, darkness, music, not enough night.

and calculates that Kerouac is updating the plantation-owner's rationalizations. Podhoretz is thinking sociologically, & missing the point. In *Soul on Ice,* Eldridge Cleaver says that that same Kerouac passage was a message (unheeded) to an older generation that the postwar disaffiliated, black & white, were trying to get together, & that they would get together by virtue of their being closer to their individual souls.

It is probably because of the sociological blinders that Podhoretz also bemoans Kerouac's failure to describe anything in words. Description is the social scientist's procedure, & its limitations in literature should by this time be well recognized. Here, look instead for personal testament, or Pound's *increment of association,* because we have here poetry, not case history, a life in America, not history. The road does not reach its importance when it may be described by the moving writer's ego, as object of his writing intention, but when it enters the story by way of the writer; where he has had it inside him as other people carry their internal clocks, waking up before the alarm goes off:

> As a seaman I used to think of the waves rushing beneath the shell of the ship and the bottomless deeps thereunder—now I could feel the road some twenty inches beneath me, unfurling and flying and hissing at incredible speeds across the groaning continent with that mad Ahab at the wheel. When I closed my eyes all I could see was the road unwinding into me.

But Podhoretz bemoans his finding that in the book "nothing that happens had any dramatic reason for happening."

There is his blindness. He wants Kerouac to set them up & knock them down, the way Bernard Malamud would, I suppose. He complains that the Beat writer & or character rebels, but not "against anything so sociological and historical as the middle class or capitalism or even respectability." The buggers just will not settle into the old-time bohemian mold. Instead, Kerouac retreats to such atavistic rebellion as that against the crushing of human soul, sensitivity, and communicability of warmth. He doesn't show the capitalist as stomping on the fingers of the worker's children, but as a tourist driving nervously thru the American West; terrified of hitchhikers and of driving away from the red line on the gas station map in the hands of the middle-aged woman on the seat beside him. Or look at a scene in which Sal Paradise & Terry the Mex-chick are trying to hitchhike away from Los Angeles:

> We stood under a roadlamp, thumbing, when suddenly cars full of young kids roared by with streamers flying. "Yaah! Yaah! we won! we won!" they all shouted. Then they yoohooed us and got great glee out of seeing a guy and a girl on the road. Dozens of such cars passed, full of young faces and "throaty young voices," as the saying goes. I hated every one of them. Who did they think they were, yaahing at somebody on the road just because they were little high-school punks and their parents carved the roast beef on Sunday afternoons? Who did they think they were, making fun of a girl reduced to poor circumstances with a man who want-

ed to belove? We were minding our own business.
And we didn't get a blessed ride.

Mercy, Pity, Peace, & Love, are the human qualities in which one encounters God, Blake advised. But Blake, as the LA highschoolers were likely told, was mad. In his vision of *America* he saw people freed from their chains, lighting off across the New World on its brandnew roads. He advised the ogres of crown & pulpit to look at their own bodies to find the human form divine. Kerouac gets ridiculed by the English teachers for taking Blake seriously instead of taking him as literature.

But Podhoretz blithely misses the point, maintaining that Kerouac supports all youth, including "young savages in leather jackets . . . with their switch-blades and zip-guns" against older folk. Kerouac objected to this bastard image of Beatdom in some TV interviews, but he need not have if people like Podhoretz had read passages such as the above. Podhoretz drags a red herring across the road when he says that Kerouac is "against intelligence itself." Kerouac & Ginsberg, for goodness' sake, are consistently praising intelligence, but an intelligence freed from the confines of the human brain, an intelligence that can, for instance, be known at the fingertips, as Robert Duncan has said, a mind that throws down its spears, making war no more on the body.

Of course, Norman Podhoretz' opinions about Kerouac's writings are easy to align with his other public feelings. We should also look at a typical response to *On the Road* as tendered by someone we don't know, writing in an abscure magazine most likely to be encountered in a university reading room. Melvin W. Askew is the author of an essay in *The University of Kansas City Review* entitled "Quests, Cars and Kerouac" [see excerpt above]. Askew first makes clear his idea that as literature, *On the Road* is not to be taken seriously. Askew doesn't go on to explain why then he wrote and submitted the article, but he does take a certain academic tack that entails finding the novel's tradition among American frontier-travel fiction, & search-for-the-father epics. The next step in the exercise is, as ever, to show that if the novel doesn't succeed well as a member of the family the academician has pickt for it, it is doomed to abject failure. University professors are addicted to the idea of literature's "succeeding" or "failing". Books are a bit like junior executives.

But Askew doesn't give Kerouac's story & its people much of a chance. He calls the book's story "shabby" & its hero "degenerate and deformed." The word "deformed" is a tip-off. It suggests an approved form, & that any deviation from it is ugly or evil. The "human form divine" had better be sociologically approved, & critically, too. Askew says that the name of Kerouac alongside those of Cooper, Hawthorne, Melville & Salinger, "seems to leave a smirch on the configuration of classic American literature." Seldom has an important American literato received so much name-calling & emotional vilification from the men who write for magazines supported by universities & business.

But we are tipt off again. The same critic who can use the idea of formlessness can use the idea of meaninglessness. When Askew says that the Kerouac sub-societies of New York, Denver & San Francisco are "meaningless," we understand that he means they are foreign to him, that he can't draw from them the meanings he prefers. There is no meaningless human action; there are only those people who shrink from receiving meaning from certain actions. When forced to face

the great popularity of *On the Road,* Askew opines that it reflects a great loss of personal values amongst readers in American society. For "loss" read "change," & you will get your sensibility past the prof & toward Eldridge Cleaver, the changemaker.

So when Askew says that in the novel there is no "hint of what we understand as human values", he is probably right, but he doesnt realize that the group he refers to as "we" is smaller than he would think & as he consistently states that the American novel can mainly be understood as it reflects American consciousness, we may conclude that his failure to recognize familiar human values in the novel runs parallel to the inability of fathers these days to understand their children. Kerouac's book is, after all, quite autobiographical. The famous "generation gap" is made possible because the older generation has squatted in the suburbs, somewhere between the Negro streets of the city & the song of the open road. (pp. 191-93)

Generally the heroes or antiheroes of the novels about alienation show a man alienated intellectually & morally from his immediate & generalized society, though he himself may be working robot-like within it, as professor or cost-accountant or whatever. Kerouac deals with a world in which the people are not alienated on an abstract level—they are physically & socially shunted aside, into prison, ghetto, or as Ginsberg had shown, onto their knees for the whole subway ride from the Battery to the Bronx. But as the alienated hero may clam up except to his psychiatrist or notebook, Kerouac's people are still looking for the contact high with other folk. As Sal Paradise says, introducing the figure of Dean Moriarty alighting on the concrete island:

> . . . the only people for me are the mad ones, the ones who are mad to live, mad to talk, mad to be saved, desirous of everything at the same time, the ones who never yawn or say a commonplace thing, but burn, burn, burn like fabulous yellow roman candles exploding like spiders across the stars and in the middle you see the blue centerlight pop and everybody goes "Awww!"

But they survive their oppression, just as the children do in Blake's *Songs of Innocence.* Just as the chimney sweep and the orphan kid shine with a radiance all their own, shining thru the grime of industrial moneymaking Empire centering City of London, so Dean, parking cars in NYC:

> His dirty workclothes clung to him so gracefully, as though you couldn't buy a better fit from a custom tailor but only earn it from the Natural Tailor of Natural Joy.

According to the sociologically-oriented critic, Dean is one of the dispossest of the American urban jungle, & should be bitter & hopeless. But Kerouac ascribes, at least in this early book, to the oldfashioned ideal of a man's soul, & to the idea that his worth & possible salvation are to be found in his closeness to his soul. That is why the simple, able men in rural America of the West join the underground people of the city in their vitality & their virtue. They dont seem to be afraid. They can, & often do, spend their last dollar on food, without fearing the next month's budget.

That lack of fear is necessary to the kindness Kerouac calls for, & natural to the generosity he finds in his most welcome characters. The novel countless times returns to the people who come together openly, to give to each other, including hitchhiking strangers, cigarettes or information or encouragement, to share visions, to do favors, to explain the particulars found in new experiences. They are all each others' parents, & replace the lost father of Dean Moriarty. Those hardened big city critics who deplore the sentimentality in Kerouac's writing seem willing to miss the point that the sentimentality is always seen in these acts of generosity. & the sentimentality is always casual & simple, as if natural. A portion of *The Scripture of the Golden Eternity* tells why:

> "If someone will simply practice kindness," said Gotama to Subhuti, "he will soon attain highest perfect wisdom." Then he added: "Kindness after all is only a word and it should be done on the spot without thought of kindness."

Thus love doesn't just belong to two people—it is a thing visited upon you in your generosity. "They had no cigarettes. I squandered my pack on them, I loved them so," says Sal Paradise of a couple of casually-met hitchhikers. Or of the first sight of Terry, the Mexamerican chick: "A pain stabbed my heart, as it did every time I saw a girl I loved who was going the opposite direction in this too-big world." That's casual & sentimental. That's natural in godlight. Blake said he could not see another's woe & not feel sorrow too. So when Sal Paradise is working in the cottonfield of California to support Terry & her child, & he senses animosity from some other folk, he refers to the threat "we Mexicans" have to face.

Work, as well as love, is approacht casually & simply. It is seen as a source, not the basis of a philosophy. Rather than holding a *belief* in work, the Kerouac hero knows it as a necessary thing you do in order to get a little money for eating & traveling. . . .

Work is not necessarily good for the spirit, as Americans, getting to the West Coast had been told. The spirit finds its image in the other human being approacht nakedly. He may recognize holiness in the gestures of freedom—dancing in the streets of Denver, hiking in the hills of Marin County, parking cars in Manhattan garage, making love under the harmlessly dangling spider under the barn roof. & Sal Paradise wants to travel on the road, watching the gestures of the holy: "If you keep this up you'll both go crazy, but let me know what happens as you go along," he says to his friends, the bluejean dervishes.

Those gestures are not the gestures of the union folk in Farrell's novels. They arent socially conceived, & should not be sociologically described. But they are still a deviation from over-programmed American society, a baring of brains under the El, an exploration of the shared soul that is not allowed for in the program:

> Boys and girls in America have such a sad time together; sophistication demands that they submit to sex immediately without proper preliminary talk. Not courting talk—real straight talk about souls, for life is holy and every moment is precious.

So when casual love & casual work come into conflict, the proper values are not hard to fall toward, as we may see in the lovely scene in which Sal Paradise has a job as private armed policeman guarding the muster station of men going to work in America's Asian frontier. Sal cant bring himself to do the oppressive cop job, & instead gets drunk with all the randy guys he's supposed to be calming. (pp. 194-96)

As a matter of fact, Sal Paradise substitutes another fabled

American virtue for the work ethic, & that is simple self-sufficiency, natural Thoreau's way of staying in accord with the cosmos while living next to public America. In later books Kerouac finds his Tathagata Walden as fire lookout on top of Cascades mountains, but in Los Angeles Sal Paradise finds his on a low cement wall in back of a Hollywood parking lot, where he makes salami-&-mustard sandwiches for a bus trip to New Jersey, one dollar left in his pocket, great Hollywood premier searchlights waving across the sky nearby. Hitchhiking itself is an odd combination of self-sufficiency & dependence on strangers' good-will or friendliness, that other virtue found on the road. Both may be found anywhere, wherever the road goes, thru holy forest of Pennsylvania or mudflats of Oklahoma. The wilderness is not only in the western half of the continent. But there is also proof everywhere that you may have to search for goodness:

> That night in Harrisburg I had to sleep in the railroad station on a bench; at dawn the station masters threw me out. Isn't it true that you start your life a sweet child believing in everything under your father's roof? Then comes the day of the Laodiceans, when you know you are wretched and miserable and poor and blind and naked, and with the visage of a gruesome grieving ghost you go shuddering through nightmare life.

The *Songs of Experience* make the *Songs of Innocence* believable. Sal Paradise doesnt lose himself completely any more than Conrad's Marlow does. He has half his mind opened to brilliance by Dean & the road, but he still recognizes his longing for marriage & comfort & some other destiny than the one shimmering in the haze of the golden city at the end of the highway. In the middle of snowy Texas:

> Comfortable little homes with chimneys smoking appeared along the road at intervals. I wished we could go in for buttermilk and beans in front of the fireplace.

Time is a road as much as US66 is, & as much as the travelers seem to escape its socialized limitations, as we may see in the famous dream of the shrouded traveler (Also see Allen Ginsberg's poem, "The Shrouded Stranger," 1949) who overtakes Sal just before he reaches the Protective City. "Naturally, now that I look back on it, this is only death: death will overtake us before heaven." Death is both feared & desired for its dream-suggested pre-natal peace, a hint of the religious direction that Kerouac's later writings will take. In fact, Sal later sees a vision of Dean as the Shrouded Traveler.

But death behind you, pushing you to the end of time, is met by IT in front of you, teasing you out of time. Dean Moriarty pursues enchanting IT just as Shelley sought holy ecstasy, or as a more optimistic Wordworth no longer mourning the inevitable loss of "visionary gleam." Traditional hipsters look for it with drugs, the old Time-dissolvers; excitable Moriarty, who has "done" time, finds it also where the next-second artist improvises:

> "Now, man, that alto man last night had IT—he held it once he found it; I've never seen a guy who could hold so long." I wanted to know what "IT" meant. "Ah well"—Dean laughed—"now you're asking me impon-de-rables—ahem! . . . Time stops. He's filling empty space with the substance of our lives, ... everybody knows it's not the tune that counts but IT— . . .

Doing time or keeping time or marking time are routines for

this vegetative world, just as description is. The thing you're after may lie around the bend of the next second, time slain. The thing you're after may remain always abstract, while verb, that which you may not own, takes over from noun in the new America:

> We were all delighted, we all realized we were leaving confusion and non-sense behind and performing our one and noble function of the time, *move*. And we moved!

In the continuum, America is not an object, but space becomes as time—there is only you in the present:

> What is that feeling when you're driving away from people and they recede on the plain till you see their specks dispersing?—it's the too-huge world vaulting us, and it's good-by. But we lean forward to the next crazy venture beneath the skies.

Beyond that, forward time & backward time dropt away, you in the present quivering under the blessed beak of Eternity, beyond that is further movement, by way of visions, *beyond* time, to the abode where the immortals are (the master theme of *Howl*), as Sal eventually realizes in a vision on the street in San Francisco:

> And for just a moment I had reached the point of ecstasy that I always wanted to reach, which was the complete step across chronological time into timeless shadows, and wonderment in the bleakness of the mortal realm, and the sensation of death kicking at my heels to move on, with a phantom dogging its own heels, and myself hurrying to a plank where all the angels dove off and flew into the holy void of uncreated emptiness, the potent and inconceivable radiancies shining in the bright Mind Essence, innumerable lotuslands falling open in the magic mothswarm of heaven. I could hear an indescribable seething roar which wasn't in my ear but everywhere and had nothing to do with sounds. I realized that I had died and been reborn numberless times but just didn't remember especially because the transitions from life to death and back to life are so ghostly easy, a magical action for naught, like falling asleep and waking up again a million times, the utter casualness and deep ignorance of it.

For the confessional writer, such a vision must be a teaching, & must be at the source of the writer's words for the world. Thus Sal/Jack does not criticize the world sociologically, as Podhoretz would have him do, but because of the vision & the movement he speaks of, he thinks of his own inner struggle between desire for comfort brought by school-competition & the contrary open moment of the road. Looking at a neighborhood baseball game in the dusk of Denver, he realizes the Time-scourged alienation of his bourgeois (if you like) youth that competitive ambition:

> Never in my life as an athlete had I ever permitted myself to perform like this in front of families and girl friends and kids of the neighborhood, at night, under lights; always it had been college, big-time, sober-faced; no boyish, human joy like this.

& so the famous passage about his wanting on lilac evening to change his own place to that over the Denver Negroes & Mexicans, to get closer to his soul. (pp. 197-99)

Imagine again the difference between the ever-circling, numbered clock, with its arms pointing out a man's regular route of bed-kitchen-subway-office-chair, & it's alternative, the road, that white ribbon there, & the ever-subtle changing of the film, or more than that, how it can enter a man as other men are entered by their clocks so that they wake up a second before the alarm goes off. With Dean tittering maniacally at the wheel, at one point, Sal lies on the floor in front of the back seat, & experiences the Romantic external made internal, the magic entering & defining the soul: "When I closed my eyes all I could see was the road unwinding into me."

But the argument is still going on within Sal. He is still at times, usually when physically weak, brought down by the constant following of the white line. Nobody, after all, has said that the way West will always be lit by the glow of the city of gold:

> I realized I was beginning to cross and recross towns in America as though I were a traveling salesman—raggedy travelings, bad stock, rotten beans in the bottom of my bag of tricks, nobody buying.

But these moments are only the lowest alienated useless feeling moments. Dean was not exaggerating when he said that the road leads to the whole world. The Pacific Ocean is not the end of the road if you believe that America as well as the highway takes up room inside the human soul, wherever that is. So Dean & Sal decide to travel south into Mexico, new road, another chance to outrace Time hurtling thru their capillaries:

> I couldn't imagine this trip. It was the most fabulous of all. It was no longer east-west, but magic *south*. We saw a vision of the entire Western Hemisphere rockribbing clear down to Tierra del Fuego and us flying down the curve of the world into other tripics and other worlds. "Man, this will finally take us to IT!" said Dean with definite faith. He tapped my arm. "Just wait and see. Hoo! Whee!"

—another opportunity to rescue America for themselves. As soon as they cross the Mexican border, Sal's first time there, they finally find, he says, "the magic land at the end of the road and we never dreamed the extent of the magic." "This road drives *me!!*" says Dean, himself entered as never so deeply before.

In Mexico, along the as-yet uncommercialized highway, Sal finds the people he's been looking for in the United States, people close to their souls as Terry was, none alienated because none yet turned around by steel clocks. Dean remarks on the open-faced brown folks along the road:

> "There's no *suspicion* here, nothing like that. Everybody's cool, everybody looks at you with such straight brown eyes and they don't say anything, just *look*, and in that look all of the human qualities are soft and subdued and still there. . . .

Maybe most important, "Nobody's ever alone in this country," he adds, & Sal remembers that "his eyes were redstreaked and mad and also subdued and tender—he had found people like himself."

To Kerouac that means people who have not abstracted Time & made an abstract god of it, but people who still measure themselves in accordance with the sun & the earth, who were accused falsely of selling Manhattan to the concrete barons, who stand silently by the roadway during dude frontier days in Cheyenne, who abide in tents alongside the cotton fields of California:

These people were unmistakably Indians and were not at all like the Pedros and Panchos of silly civilized American lore—they had high cheekbones, and slanted eyes, and soft ways; they were not fools, they were not clowns; they were great, grave Indians and they were the source of mankind and the fathers of it.

The whole of chapter 6 in Part Four, telling of the country between Texas and Mexico City, is a rhapsody to a place free of Time, the shepherds in the golden world where Jesus came from, eyes of Mary looking from under shawls in the mountains, old volcanoes nestling towns built on centuries-old configurations. Once again Kerouac neglects or refuses or naturally disdains to characterize the Mexindian folks sociologically. He sees in them the promise the road has always been holding out, that if you keep driving & drive far enough, you will find a human being who will offer an unpracticed smile & in his hand whatever simple & beautiful stone he was able to find on the sunlight part of the earth.

A long way from these angels on the slopes of Mexican volcanoes to the TV images of Kerouac Beat heroes with leather & knives, as falsely perpetuated by so many of the University critics. But who now reads, except for amusement, the English critics who reviled Shelley as a ravening sexual fiend & supporter of assassins? Here, too, it is advisable to read Kerouac's story of possible angels before reading the critics who can call his heroes "degenerate and deformed." (pp. 199-201)

> *George Bowering, " 'On the Road': & the Indians at the End," in* Stony Brook, *Nos. 3 & 4, 1969, pp. 191-201.*

CAROLE GOTTLIEB VOPAT

Nothing has been published about Jack Kerouac for seven years. Most of what has been written is either hostile or condescending or both. While it may perhaps be true, as Melvin W. Askew suggests [see excerpt above] that to speak of Jack Kerouac in the same breath with Melville, Twain and Hawthorne is "to leave a smirch on the configuration of classic American literature," Kerouac has, as they have, provided an enduring portrait of the national psyche; like Fitzgerald, he has defined America and delineated American life for his generation. Certainly, Kerouac is not a great writer, but he is a good writer, and has more depth and control than his critics allow. *On the Road* is more than a "crazy wild frantic" embrace of beat life; implicit in Kerouac's portrayal of the beat generation is his criticism of it, a criticism that anticipates the charges of his most hostile critics. For example, Norman Podhoretz' assertion [see excerpt in *CLC*, Vol. 1] that "the Beat Generation's worship of primitivism and spontaneity . . . arises from a pathetic poverty of feeling," parallels Kerouac's own insights in *On the Road.*

In that novel Kerouac makes it clear that Sal Paradise goes on the road to escape from life rather than to find it, that he runs from the intimacy and responsibility of more demanding human relationships, and from a more demanding human relationship with himself. With all their emphasis on spontaneity and instinct, Sal and his friends are afraid of feeling on any other than the impassive and ultimately impersonal "wow" level. For Sal especially, emotion is reduced to sentimentality, roleplaying and gesture. His responses are most often the blanket, indiscriminate "wow!" or the second-hand raptures gleaned from books and movies; he thrills to San Francisco as "Jack London's town" and melodramatically describes leaving his Mexican mistress: "Emotionlessly she kissed me in the vineyard and walked off down the row. We turned at a dozen paces, for love is a duel, and looked at each other for the last time . . . ". Sal is continually enjoying himself enjoying himself, raptly appreciating his performance in what seems more like an on-going soap-opera than an actual life: "She'd left me a cape to keep warm; I threw it over my shoulder and skulked through the moonlit vineyard. . . . A California home; I hid in the grapevines, digging it all. I felt like a million dollars; I was adventuring in the crazy American night."

Sal's self-conscious posturing undercuts his insistence on the life of instinct and impulse, and indicates his fear of emotions simply felt, of life perceived undramatically and unadorned. He responds to experience in a language of exaggeration; everything is the saddest or greatest or wildest in the world. Although on page 21 he meets a "rawhide oldtime Nebraska farmer" who has "a great laugh, the greatest in the world," a few pages later he encounters Mr. Snow "whose laugh, I swear on the Bible, was positively and finally the one greatest laugh in all this world." Reality is never good enough; it must be classified, embroidered and intensified; above all, the sheer reality of reality must be avoided. Sal's roleplaying shelters him from having to realize and respond to actual situations, and to the emotions and obligations, whether of others or of himself, inherent in those situations. He is protected from having to face and feel his own emotions as well as from having to deal with the needs and demands of other people. What Sal enthuses over as "a California home" Kerouac reveals as a place of poverty, frustration, anger and despair, but Sal's raptures cushion him from recognizing the grimness of the existence to which he is carelessly consigning his mistress and her small son, a child he had called "my boy" and played at fathering. By absorbing himself in the melodramatics of a renunciation scene, Sal is protected from the realities of Terry's feelings or her future, nor must he cope with his own emotions at parting with her. (pp. 385-87)

Kerouac's characters take to the road not to find life but to leave it all behind: emotion, maturity, change, decision, purpose, and, especially, in the best American tradition, responsibility; wives, children, mistresses, all end up strewn along the highway like broken glass. Sal refuses responsibility not only for the lives of others but for his own life as well. He does not want to own his life or direct his destiny, but prefers to live passively, to be driven in cars, to entertain sensations rather than emotions. A follower, Sal is terrified of leading his own life; he is, as Kerouac points out, "fearful of the wheel" and "hated to drive;" he does not have a driver's license. He and Dean abdicate self-control in a litany of irresponsibility: "It's not my fault, it's not my fault . . . , nothing in this lousy world is my fault." Both of them flee from relevance and significance, telling long, mindless stories and taking equally pointless trips. They avoid anything—self-analysis, self-awareness, thinking—which would threaten or challenge them, for with revelation comes responsibility for change and, above all, they do not want change. They demand lives as thin and narrow as the white lines along the road which so comfort and mesmerize them, and are content with surfaces, asking for no more. Thus they idolize Negroes as romantic and carefree children, seeing in the ghetto not the reality of poverty and oppression, but freedom from responsibility and, hence, joy.

Sal and his friends are not seeking or celebrating self, but are rather fleeing from identity. For all their solipsism, they are almost egoless. They do not dwell on the self, avoid thinking or feeling. They run from self-definition, for to admit the complex existence of the self is to admit its contingencies: the claims of others, commitments to society, to oneself. Solipsism rather than an enhancement of self is for them a loss of self, for the self is projected until it loses all boundaries and limits and, hence, all definition. Sal in the Mexican jungle completely loses his identity; inside and outside merge, he becomes the atmosphere, and as a result knows neither the jungle nor himself. For Sal and Dean, transcendentalism, like drugs, sex, liquor, and even jazz, leads not to enlightenment but to self-obliteration. Erasing both ego and world, nothing remains save motion and sensation, passive, self-effacing and mechanical. Only the sheer impetus of their frantic, speeding cars holds their scattered selves together.

Their selves have no definition and their lives no continuity. Nothing is related, neither self nor time; there is no cause and effect, life is not an ongoing process. Rather, there is only the Eternal Now, the jazz moment, which demands absolutely nothing. Their ideals are spontaneity and impulse because both are independent of relation to what has gone before and what may come after. Spontaneity and impulse are the ethic of disjunction, recognizing neither limit, liability or obligation. Their emphasis on spontaneity is a measure of their fear of life. In their cars they are suspended from life and living, as if in a capsule hurtling coast-to-coast above the earth. They seek out not truth nor values but this encapsulated almost fetal existence as an end in itself, an end that is much like death.

For even their much touted ideal of Freedom is in reality a freedom from life itself, especially from rational, adult life with its welter of consequences and obligations. Dean is utterly free because he is completely mad. He has defied maturity and logic, defied time with its demands that he grow up to responsibility. Like Nietzsche's superman, he is beyond good and evil, blame and expectation, nor must he justify his existence through work and duty, a state Sal sorely admires: "Bitterness, recriminations, advice, morality, sadness— everything was behind him, and ahead of him was the ragged and ecstatic joy of pure being." Sal's own longing for freedom is embodied in a mysterious Shrouded Traveler, a figure who unites the road and death. In many avatars, he pursues Sal in his headlong flight down the highway, offering, through solitary travel, the "lost bliss" which is the death of the self: "The one thing that we yearn for in all our living days, that makes us sigh and groan and undergo sweet nauseas of all kinds, is the remembrance of some lost bliss that we probably experienced in the womb and can only be reproduced (though we hate to admit it) in death."

"Free love" is rather freedom from love and another route down that same dark deathwish. For Sal the lovebed is "the deathbed," where he goes to obliterate himself and to find the safe "lost bliss" of the womb, "blindly seeking to return the way he came." But Sal is only able to find this particular version of "lost bliss" when he has reduced his partner to the non-threatening role of fellow child. He has trouble succeeding with adult women; he fills Rita with nothing but talk and is convinced Theresa is a whore until he discovers with relief that she is only a baby, as fragile and vulnerable as he:

> I saw her poor belly where there was a Caesarian scar; her hips were so narrow she couldn't bear a child without getting gashed open. Her legs were like little sticks. She was only four foot ten. I made love to her in the sweetness of the weary morning. Then, two tired angels of some kind, hung-up forlornly in an LA shelf, having found the closest and most delicious thing in life together, we fell asleep . . .

Sex here is not a wild explosion but the desperate, gentle solace two babes in the woods haltingly offer each other. . . . Sal says he ought to be seeking out a wife, but his true search is, as is Dean's, not for lover but for father, for someone to shelter him from life and responsibility. He turns to Terry not for ecstasy or even sensation, but as a respite from his search, an escape from the demands of life: "I finally decided to hide from the world one more night with her and morning be damned."

In short, for all their exuberance, Kerouac's characters are half in love with easeful death. And this Sal Paradise and his creator well know. Neither is deceived about the nature of beat existence. Kerouac is able to step back from his characters to point out their follies; to show, for example, Dean's pathetic justification of life on the road. . . . Sal himself is able to articulate his own fear of feeling and responsibility and his resultant, overwhelming emptiness:

> Well, you know me. You know I don't have close relationships with anybody anymore. I don't know what to do with these things. I hold things in my hand like pieces of crap and don't know where to put it down. . . . It's not my fault! It's not my fault! . . . Nothing in this lousy world is my fault, don't you see that? I don't want it to be and it can't be and it *won't* be.

He realizes that he has "nothing to offer anybody except my own confusion," and marks the deaths of his various illusions with the refrain, "Everything is collapsing."

Kerouac further points out that the shortcomings of his characters parallel the shortcomings of the country to which they are so intimately connected. Kerouac's response to America is typically disillusioned. America is a land of corruption and hypocrisy, promising everything and delivering nothing, living off the innocence and opportunity, the excitement and adventure of the past. In particular Kerouac indicates America for failing to provide his searching characters with any public meaning or communal values to counteract the emptiness of their private lives. Sal looks to America much as he looks to Dean, to provide him with direction, purpose and meaning, to offer him a straight line, an ordered progression to a golden destination, an "IT" of stability and salvation. But IT never materializes, and the straight line itself becomes an end; the going, the road, is all. Dean's response to continual disillusionment is to forsake the destination for the journey: "Move!" Sal follows his leader but eventually becomes disgusted with the purposeless, uncomfortable jockeying from coast to coast, just as he becomes disgusted with Dean. Unlike Dean, Sal is able to recognize and identify his despair and, ultimately, to act on the causes of it; where for Dean change is merely deterioration, Sal undergoes true development.

In addition to Sal's growing insight, Kerouac equips his narrator with a double vision, enabling Sal to comment on the people and events of the novel as he saw them when they happened, and as he views them now that they are over, a sadder-but-wiser hindsight which acts as a check upon his naive, undiscriminating exuberances and provides a disillusioned alternative view of the beatifics of the beat generation.

While the younger Sal idolized Dean upon first meeting him, the older Sal reminds the reader that "this is all far back, when Dean was not the way he is today . . . ", and notes that "the whole mad swirl of everything that was to come began then; it would mix up all my friends and all I had left of my family in a big dust cloud over the American night." He observes the sad effect of Time upon his old friends who once "rushed down the street together, digging everything in the early way they had, which later becomes so much sadder and perceptive and blank." He corrects himself when his earlier view of Dean intrudes upon the more precise voice of his older self: "Dean . . . had finished his first fling in New York. I say fling, but he only worked like a dog in parking lots." Sal continually checks and repudiates his youthful self, and deflates his naive view of Dean and life on the road: "I could hear a new call and see a new horizon, and believe it at my young age; and a little bit of trouble or even Dean's eventual rejection of me as a buddy, putting me down, as he would later, on starving sidewalks and sickbeds—what did it matter? I was a young writer and I wanted to take off." (pp. 388-93)

Sal's double vision does more than correct his impulses. It projects the reader forward in time and provides the sense of continuity the disjunctive characters, including the younger Sal, lack. This older voice offers relations and connections, causes and effects, connects past with present and projects into the future. It firmly anchors reader and narrator to the familiar world of change and conjunction. It knows the discrepancy between appearance and reality and realizes sadly that Time eventually captures even frantically speeding children. It is the view of a man who has, in Dean Moriarty's words, come to "know Time," it prepares the reader for Sal's eventual disillusionment with beat life and "the sordid hipsters of America."

Sal's double vision is proof of his eventual recapitulation to time and change, a recapitulation which he battles for most of the novel. It is this battling, perhaps, so constant and monotonous, which has infuriated readers used to traditional novels of development and makes them wonder, indeed, whether anything happens to anyone in the novel at all. Sal alone of the characters continually perceives the futility and insanity of his journeys, yet continually makes them, always with the same childlike innocence and expectation, always to follow the same pattern of hopefulness ending in disillusionment as he learns and relearns the same weary lessons about America and Dean Moriarty. Nonetheless, Sal does finally accept the obligations of his insights and revelations, decides to bear the heavy weight of change and responsibility, and grows up to understand, evaluate and finally repudiate Dean Moriarty, the American Dream, and life on the road. (pp. 393-94)

Dean offers Sal more than direction and meaning; he simultaneously provides both a quest and an escape, a hiatus from adult life and adult feelings, a moratorium on maturity. Sal associates Dean with his own childhood: ". . . he reminded me of some long-lost brother . . . , made me remember my boyhood. . . . And in his excited way of speaking I heard again the voices of old companions and brothers under the bridge . . . ".

Indeed, although Sal is older than Dean, he regards Dean at first not so much as "long lost brother" but as Father whom he passively follows, trusting to be protected, loved and directed. Sal is disenchanted with Dean at the end of Part Two not because Dean has proven himself a poor friend, but because he has turned out to be yet another bad father: "Where is Dean and why isn't he concerned about our welfare?" (pp. 395-96)

Sal's emotional maturation is evident in his first "lover's quarrel" with Dean. Enraged by Dean's casual reference to his growing old ("You're getting a little older now"), Sal turns on him, reducing him to tears, but immediately afterwards realizes that his anger is directed at aging rather than at Dean: "I had flipped momentarily and turned it down on Dean." He takes responsibility for hurting Dean, and apologizes to him, humbly and lovingly: "Remember that I believe in you. I'm infinitely sorry for the foolish grievance I held against you . . . ". He sees that his present anger springs from sources buried in his youth ("Everything I had ever secretly held against my brother was coming out . . . "). This insight into himself helps him to understand Dean, who is, like him, mired in a past whose anger and frenzy he is compelled to act out, but, unlike Sal, without benefit of apology or insight: "All the bitterness and madness of his entire Denver life was blasting out of his system like daggers. His face was red and sweaty and mean." Regarding his friend without desperate idealism, Sal sees that Dean's frantic moving and going is not a romantic quest for adventure or truth but is instead a sad, lost circling for the past, for the home and the father he never had. He sees that both he and Dean are as frightened and lost as "the Prince of Dharma," going in circles in the dark lost places between the stars, searching for that "lost ancestral grove." The road on which they run is "all that old road of the past unreeling dizzily as if the cup of life had been overturned and everything gone mad. My eyes ached in nightmare day." True to his vow, he takes Dean back to New York with him, yet knows that for them a "permanent home" is impossible. Their marriage breaks down; Dean returns to his crazy welter of wives and children, Sal to his aunt and his disillusionment. (pp. 401-02)

In Mexico Sal hopes to escape from the self, civilization, and their discontents. At the bottom of his primitivism is a desire to confront the primal sources of pure being, to discover life as it was—shapeless, formless, dark—before being molded into self or society; in short, to find once and for all the womb he has been seeking all his life. If nothing else, he hopes to search out his final, true and ultimate parents among the Indians who are "the source of mankind and the fathers of it."

But the "strange Arabian paradise we had finally found at the end of the hard, hard road" is only "a wild old whore house" after all. The Indians are coming down from the mountains drawn to wristwatches and cities. They and the Mexicans welcome Sal and Dean not as brothers or fellow children, but as American tourists to be exploited. The brothel where they converse for their ultimate mind-and time-blowing fling is a sad, frantic, desperate place, full of eighteen-year-old drunks and child whores, "sinking and lost," "writhing and suffering." . . . Their great primitive playground is no more than "a sad kiddy park with swings and a broken-down merry-go-round . . . in the fading red sun . . . ". And in that "sad kiddy park" Sal leaves behind his faith in the possibility of an infantile paradise and, with it, his faith in Dean.

Dean first induced Sal to accompany him over the border with the happy announcement that " . . . the years have rolled severally behind us and yet you see none of us have really changed . . . ". In Mexico Sal finds this denial of time not a reprieve but a condemnation. Dean cannot change and he cannot rest, not even in "the great and final wild uninhibited Fellahin childlike" Mexico City. Wedded forever to his terrible, changeless compulsions, not the love of his friend nor the possibility of paradise can stay him from his rounds. He leaves the "delirious and unconscious" Sal to return to "all that again," for, as he himself announces, "the road drives *me*." Sal understands and pities him ("I realized what a rat he was, but . . . I had to understand the impossible complexity of his life, how he had to leave me there, sick, to get on with his wives and woes", realizing his friend is the least free of anyone. Dean leads not a primitive life of spontaneity and instinct but instead a sorry, driven existence of joyless "sweats" and anxieties. Sal has a "vision" of Dean not as sweet, holy goof but as the Angel of Death, burning and laying waste whatever he touches. . . . (pp. 402-04)

Returning to America, Sal meets up once more with the Shrouded Traveler, a symbol of the fatal lure of the road and the restless, nomadic beat life. Sal wonders if this "tall old man with flowing white hair . . . with a pack on his back" is a sign "that I should at last go on my pilgrimage on foot on the dark roads around America." He wonders, in short, if he ought to become the Ghost of the Susquehanna, to enter the darkness from which the old man appeared and into which he vanished. He responds to the romance of this suggestion, but is haunted by its loneliness. Later, in New York, he calls out his name in the darkness and is answered by Laura, "the girl with the pure and innocent dear eyes that I had always searched for and for so long." Settling his dreams of paradise and salvation in her, he gives up the road. (pp. 404-05)

In a sense, Sal's growth as an adult can be measured through his responses to Dean and in the changing aspects of their relationship. Sal moves from idolatry to pity, from a breathless, childlike worship of Dean as alternately Saint and Father, to a realization of Dean's own tortured humanity, marked by Sal's attempt to be brother, then Father, to his friend, sensitive to Dean's needs without melodrama, facing responsibility and decision, allowing himself to feel blame and love, yet, eventually, for the sake of his own soul, rejecting, deliberately and sadly, his lost, perpetually circling friend.

When Dean arrives to rescue him once more from the world of age and obligatiaon, Sal refuses to go. He discards Dean's plan to leave for San Francisco before he himself is absolutely ready ("But why did you come so soon, Dean?"), and, deciding that he "wasn't going to start all over again ruining [Remi's] planned evenings as I had done . . . in 1947," he pulls away from Dean and leaves him behind. (pp. 405-06)

In the course of his scattered journeys Sal has learned, perhaps to his regret, what rather tentatively might indeed finally matter, and to this tenuous value he cautiously decides to commit himself, giving up the ghost of the Shrouded Traveler, of Dean Moriarty and Old Dean Moriarty and dead America, and accepting in their place feeling, responsibility, and roots—not in a place but in another person, Laura. Sal's relationship with Dean has served as an apprenticeship during which he has learned how to accommodate to intimacy, as his disillusionment with America has prepared him to look beyond the road for salvation and paradise. Neither America nor Dean can successfully order his life, provide him with direction or meaning. Neither can father him; ultimately, he

must father himself, must look inward for purpose and belief. For America has lost hcr innocence and her sense of purpose just as Dean has and, like Dean, is continually making bogus attempts to pretend it still has all the potential and grace of its youth. . . . (pp. 406-07)

On the Road ends with an elegy for a lost America, for the country which once might have been the father of us all, but now is only "the land where they let children cry." Dean Moriarty is himself America, or rather the dream of America, once innocent, young, full of promise and holiness, bursting with potential and vitality, now driven mad, crippled, impotent ("We're all losing our fingers"), ragged, dirty, lost, searching for a past of security and love that never existed, trailing frenzy and broken promises, unable to speak to anybody anymore. (p. 407)

Carole Gottlieb Vopat, "Jack Kerouac's 'On the Road': A Re-Evaluation," in The Midwest Quarterly, *Vol. XIV, No. 4, Summer, 1973, pp. 385-407.*

WILLIAM BLACKBURN

Many of Jack Kerouac's critics resemble the members of his family, as he describes them in his work, in refusing to take seriously either his writing or his Buddhism. In the opinion of John Ciardi, "Whether or not Jack Kerouac has traces of a talent, he remains basically a high-school athlete who went from Lowell, Massachusetts, to Skid Row, losing his eraser en route." Alan Watts, though he finds "something endearing about Kerouac's personality as a writer" in *The Dharma Bums,* notes that "Kerouac's own Buddhism is a true beat Zen which confuses 'anything goes' at the existential level with 'anything goes' on the artistic and social levels." Even one of his most sympathetic critics and biographers, Ann Charters, concludes that Kerouac's "Buddhism was a tangled and personal matter, but its most immediate appeal to him was that it served as a defense and as a philosophic way of justifying his suffering to himself." The conviction that Kerouac is really just a failed Catholic after all, and that his Buddhism is too emotional and too eccentric to merit serious consideration, discourages any attempt to explore the place of Buddhism in the pattern of his fiction. And yet, as a careful reader of Kerouac's major novels will find, Buddhism has a central place in both the structure and meaning of what Kerouac called the Legend of Duluoz.

We know that Kerouac became seriously interested in Buddhism "early in 1954 at a time when he was feeling most lost and alone." Whatever the precise reason for this interest, it seems likely that Kerouac responded to certain elements in the life of Prince Siddhartha, who

> for twenty-five years . . . saw only the beautiful and pleasant. About this time the sorrows and sufferings of mankind affected him deeply, and made him reflect on the problem of life. Impelled by a strong desire to find the origin of suffering and sorrow and the means of extirpating them, he renounced at the age of twenty-nine all family ties and retired to the forest. . . .

Kerouac, obsessed as he was with the lost innocence of his childhood, with his piercing awareness of human suffering, and with his sense of himself as a holy wanderer seeking an end to this suffering, seems to have found in the career of

Prince Siddhartha (later the Buddha) both an emblem of his own life and a pattern for his major fiction.

It is true that Siddhartha is only the first of many characters with whom Buddhism informs Kerouac's fiction. Such later figures as Han Shan and Japhy Ryder are more elaborately studied, but Prince Siddhartha is the first in the series of Buddhist models Kerouac's heroes encounter. Though Buddhism is not otherwise prominent in Kerouac's second published novel, *On the Road* (1957), the basic elements of alienation, exile, and quest are present in the career of the hero, as they are present in the life of Prince Siddhartha. Sal Paradise begins his wanderings "not long after my wife and I split up. I had just gotten over a serious illness that I won't bother to talk about, except that it had something to do with the miserably weary split-up and my feeling that everything was dead." The quest on which Sal Paradise has embarked in response to his "feeling that everything was dead," is two-fold. He wishes to establish "close relationships," of the kind he has not known since childhood, and he wishes to find wisdom. His search for relationships is concentrated in his association with Dean Moriarty; at one point he tells Dean "you know I don't have close relationships with anybody any more—I don't know what to do with these things," and admits "I wanted to know Dean more . . . because somehow, in spite of our difference in character, he reminded me of some long-lost brother."

That Sal's travelling is also a quest for wisdom is suggested in his faith that "somewhere along the line I knew there'd be girls, visions, everything; somewhere along the line the pearl would be handed to me." On his first cross-country trip, Sal has a vision of "Denver looming ahead of me like the Promised Land." His chance of reaching this Promised Land seems to be contingent upon a complete breaking of the ties with his previous life. Just as Prince Siddhartha left home, wife, and family to live the life of a homeless ascetic, so Kerouac's hero leaves everything behind in his search for a new life; after a day's exhausted sleep in an Iowa hotel,

> I woke up as the sun was reddening; and that was the one distinct time in my life, the strangest moment of all, when I didn't know who I was—I was far away from home, haunted and tired with travel . . . and I looked at the cracked high ceiling and really didn't know who I was for about fifteen strange seconds. I wasn't scared; I was just somebody else, some stranger, and my whole life was a haunted life, the life of a ghost. I was halfway across America, at the dividing line between the East of my youth and the West of my future. . . .

The nature of the hero's dual quest is clearly defined, but, as Kerouac's critics have never been slow to point out, the hero's travels apparently lead nowhere. Sal Paradise finally reaches San Francisco, but fails to find his Promised Land: "Here I was at the end of America—no more land—and now there was nowhere to go but back." Subsequent trips appear equally vain: "This can't go on all the time—all this franticness and jumping around. We've got to go someplace, find something." Sal Paradise's wanderings, instead of leading to wisdom and deliverance, become one more image of the confusion of modern America: "What is the meaning of this voyage . . . ? What kind of sordid business are you on now? I mean, man, whither goest thou? Whither goest thou, America, in thy shiny car in the night?"

For half the novel, Kerouac's hero remains happily ignorant

of the fundamental contradiction of his dual quest. He has not yet realised that he cannot simultaneously pursue wisdom and the kind of frenzied and confused immersion in the world which his friendship with Dean demands. Dean's soul is "wrapped up in a fast car, a coast to reach, and a woman at the end of the road," and such worldly entanglements only hinder the seeker of enlightenment. This is brought home to Kerouac's reader, if not to Kerouac's hero, in an episode at the centre of the novel. Sal, "Out of my mind with hunger and bitterness," has been abandoned by his girl-friend Marylou and his "brother" Dean. His sense of himself as an orphan is deepened when he slinks into a hashery and has a vision of a mother repudiating her son: "It suddenly occurred to me this was my mother of about two hundred years ago in England, and I was her footpad son returning from gaol to haunt her honest labours in the hashery." In the grip of this vision, Sal completes the pattern; his enforced isolation, like the voluntary isolation of Prince Siddhartha, is the necessary precursor to illumination and the understanding of one's true being:

> I stopped frozen with ecstasy on the sidewalk. I looked down Market Street. I didn't know whether it was that or Canal Street in New Orleans, it led to water, ambiguous, universal water. . . . And for just a moment I had reached the point of ecstasy that I always wanted to reach, which was the complete step across chronological time into timeless shadows . . . where all the angels dove off and flew into the holy void of uncreated emptiness, the potent and inconceivable radiancies shining in bright Mind Essence, innumerable lotus-lands falling open in the magic mothswarm of heaven. . . . I realized it was only because of the stability of the intrinsic Mind that these ripples of birth and death took place, like the action of wind on a sheet of pure, serene, mirror-like water.

Kerouac's readers might well share Sal's feeling of being "too young to know what had happened." One of the things Sal does not seem to know about is the relationship between his temporary solitude and his moment of insight. He does not see—perhaps he does not care to see—that the pursuit of wisdom is apparently incompatible with the life he has been living. Prince Siddhartha's break with the world and its temptations was complete. Kerouac obviously understands, as Sal Paradise fails to understand, that a worldly life lived in accordance with wisdom is almost an impossibility. Dean lures Sal back into the old round, and, less than a page after Sal's ecstatic decision to return to the world, he "was sick and tired of everything, and so was Dean." Sal returns to New York, having failed in his quest once more: "What I accomplished by coming to Frisco I don't know. . . . We were all thinking we'd never see one another again and we didn't care."

The novel's habit of alternating immersion and withdrawal asserts itself once again, as Sal Paradise finds himself no more capable of living alone than he found himself capable of sharing Dean's frenzied life in the world. Encouraged by the customary omens and portents, he sets out on the road to *Nirvana* once more. Sal continues to think of himself as a religious wanderer, leaving everything behind and going forth to the homeless life as a seeker after wisdom, but the reader has long since realised that Sal's renewed association with Dean can lead him only to further bewilderment and frustration. Sal sees the stars in the Colorado night "as lonely as the Prince of the Dharms who's lost his ancestral grove and journeys across the spaces between points in the handle of the Big Dip-per trying to find it again," but refuses to believe that the solitude of that other seeker is an essential condition of the spiritual quest. He continues on the road with Dean.

The climax of the novel is their trip into Mexico, which Sal imagines as a search for the Holy City in the mountains, at once the goal of his spiritual searching and also a place where he can find the sense of community which has so constantly eluded him in his travels with his "long-lost brother." Crossing the border at Laredo, Sal observes "We were longing to rush right up there and get lost in those mysterious Spanish streets. It was only Nuevo Laredo but it looked like Holy Lhasa to us." They celebrate their arrival with some marijuana in one of the whorehouses of "Holy Lhasa," until Sal's money runs short and he has to leave, "remembering I was in Mexico after all and not in a pornographic hashish daydream in heaven." They stumble on, apparently near the end of their journey at last:

> We had reached the approaches of the last plateau. Now the sun was golden, the air keen blue, and the desert with its occasional rivers a riot of sandy hot space and sudden Biblical tree shade. . . . The shepherds appeared, dressed as in first times, in long flowing robes, the women carrying golden bundles of flax, the men staves. . . . "Man, man," I yelled to Dean, "wake up and see the shepherds, wake up and see the golden world that Jesus came from, with your own eyes you can tell!"

Sal believes that he has finally found the goal of all his seeking in Mexico City: "All Mexico was one vast Bohemian camp. . . . This was the great and final wild uninhibited Fellahin-childlike city that we knew we would find at the end of the road."

But now the pattern of the novel asserts itself once more. What Sal finds here is not enlightenment, but oblivion, not a cure for his ills, but another disease: "I got fever and became delirious and unconscious." Like Denver, like San Francisco, like New York, Mexico City cannot be home for Sal and Dean. Kerouac has used the formal elements of the religious quest ironically; Sal and Dean reach the Holy City, but cannot live there: "Gotta get back to my life," as Dean says when he abandons Sal. Sal Paradise is no Prince Siddhartha; his quest has brought him neither lasting wisdom nor lasting relationships. At the novel's close we see him withdrawn from the world once again, his voyaging done, an orphan twice over, having found neither his "long-lost brother" nor the lost father:

> So in America when the sun goes down and I sit on the old broken-down river pier watching the long long skies . . . and sense all the raw land that rolls in one unbelievably huge bulge over to the West Coast, and all that road going, all the people dreaming in the immensity of it . . . and nobody, nobody knows what's going to happen to anybody besides the forlorn rags of growing old, I think of Dean Moriarty, I even think of old Dean Moriarty, the father we never found, I think of Dean Moriarty.

On the Road is probably Kerouac's most successful novel; critics of the lost-eraser school too often fail to appreciate the aesthetic distance Kerouac maintains between himself and Sal Paradise. However Kerouac may be thought to resemble his hero, there can be no question about his successful dramatization of Sal Paradise's dilemma. Sal's attempt to imitate

Siddhartha, and to reconcile his conflicting impulses to immerse himself in life on the road and to withdraw from it in contemplative detachment determine the structure of the novel and give it thematic unity. Critics who sneer at Kerouac because "Zen Buddhism has spread like the Asian flu" likewise fail to realise both how sincere Kerouac was about his Buddhism and how successfully he employed it in his fiction. (pp. 9-13)

William Blackburn, "Han Shan Gets Drunk with the Butchers: Kerouac's Buddhism in 'On the Road,' 'The Dharma Bums,' and 'Desolation Angels,'" in Literature East & West, Vol. XXI, Nos. 1-4, January-December, 1977, pp. 9-22.

TIM HUNT

This past year marked the twenty-fifth anniversary of *On the Road*'s publication and, with it, seemingly yet another revival of interest in Kerouac's work. Graduate schools have gradually come to allow Kerouac as a dissertation topic, and professional meetings have now been held to honor him. . . . But it may be that the more things seem to change, the more they are really just staying the same. However much it may seem like the time has come to start discussing such issues as whether Spontaneous Prose is best understood as stream of consciousness or stream of attention, the relative merits of *Doctor Sax* and *Big Sur,* or the impact of Buddhism on Kerouac's nature writing, these issues are still premature. Whatever Kerouac revival there may be is still largely concerned with Kerouac as a public figure and with *On the Road* as pop culture and largely unconcerned with anything else. (p. 29)

We normally think of *On the Road* as a book written in three weeks of high speed, "spontaneous" work by an intensely charismatic man with an unfortunate tendency to get drunk and say semicoherent or foolish things about writing—an "avatar," as an early reviewer phrased it, of the Beat Generation (whatever that was). But *On the Road* was a book of the late 1950s only in its publication date and the public controversy that became associated with it. The events of the book are from the late 1940s, and the book itself was begun in 1948. From 1948 to 1952, the book went through five distinct phases or versions, progressing from a relatively traditional, omniscient third-person narrative to a limited third-person narrative to a first-person narrative using a child persona to the first-person narrative of what we now call *On the Road* to the series of voice experiments of what we now call *Visions of Cody.*

This process itself suggests that Kerouac's interest in point of view and craft was more intense and sustained than the stereotype of "King of the Beatniks" has suggested. It also calls into question the centrality of *On the Road* and suggests the importance of *Visions of Cody,* a more experimental, less autobiographical, and more literary work than *On the Road. On the Road* will likely continue to be Kerouac's best-known work because the way it evokes and examines cultural types makes it a kind of 1950s *The Great Gatsby,* but the book that Kerouac originally meant to give us as *On the Road,* that is *Visions of Cody,* is a better indication of Kerouac's project and his significance as a writer.

Several factors have obscured the place of *Visions of Cody* in Kerouac's career. For one, it wasn't published until 1972, after Kerouac's death and fifteen years after *On the Road.*

Second, when it was published, few realized its status as the fifth and final version of *On the Road.* Third (and most important), the stereotype of Kerouac as an energetic but thoughtless and unskilled naïf was so firmly entrenched that few were willing to consider that *Visions of Cody*'s difficulty might come from Kerouac's literary ambition and sense of experiment rather than careless solipsism. Few, that is, could credit that Kerouac might be an experimental writer rather than a simple reporter of his own life and thoughts.

The fascination with Kerouac as "King of the Beatniks" might have been inevitable given the media attention to the Beat Generation, but Kerouac certainly confused matters and made the misperception of his own seriousness more likely. When Kerouac suddenly found himself a celebrity in the late 1950s and found himself, moreover, under attack as a semiliterate barbarian for *On the Road* and his "beatness," he tried to defend himself by explaining his project as a writer in terms of his theory of Spontaneous Prose, but Spontaneous Prose was only partly reflected in the book everyone was reading and discussing, *On the Road.* By 1957, Kerouac had already drafted *Visions of Cody, Doctor Sax, The Subterraneans,* "Railroad Earth," *Tristessa,* and others, but none of these had been published. And when Kerouac claimed his writing was "experimental" on the basis of his largely traditional novel, he encouraged people to assume that what he meant by "spontaneity" was "speed" of composition and disregard of craft—assumptions that encouraged people to think of Kerouac and *On the Road* as pop phenomena and dismiss both as semiliterary at best. (As Truman Capote sneered, "That's not writing, that's typewriting.")

We need to realize that Kerouac did not mean speed-writing when he talked about Spontaneous Prose, and we also need to recognize that *On the Road* was not written spontaneously. What Kerouac meant by Spontaneous Prose, or "sketching" as he originally termed it, was developed after what is now *On the Road* was drafted, and the discovery of sketching was the reason Kerouac decided to set aside the traditionally fictional book we know as *On the Road* and begin again with the draft that became the experimental *Visions of Cody.* (p. 30)

In 1958, Kerouac catalogued the principles of sketching in **"Essentials of Spontaneous Prose,"** explaining that one sketches from the memory of "a definite image-object" which is used to generate a "free deviation (association) of mind" as one writes "outwards swimming in sea of language to peripheral release and exhaustion." Perhaps most importantly, to Kerouac, sketching was a matter of "beginning not from preconceived idea of what to say about image but from jewel center of interest in subject at moment of writing." (pp. 31-2)

From the time he "discovered" sketching until *On the Road*'s publication in 1957, Kerouac was largely concerned with the kind of writing typified by *Visions of Cody.* This makes it particularly ironic, and unfortunate, that most readers and critics have understood Kerouac's work as primarily a matter of narrative, and autobiographical narrative at that. Kerouac's work throughout clearly derived from the events and situations of his own life, but Kerouac at his best did not use this material for the purpose of creating plots. Rather, he used this material from his life to provide the occasion for the narrator to meditate on a series of thematically and tonally related images that become, as they repeat, vary, and evolve, the structure and action of the books. As I've tried to suggest, some of the reasons for the impression that Kerouac's work

is primarily autobiographical narrative are inadvertent or accidental. Kerouac's charisma, his actual experiences, and the Beat Generation controversy all helped divert attention from his writing and its nature. In addition, two other factors contributed to the general impression of Kerouac's work. First, the two Kerouac novels that first received wide circulation and attention, *On the Road* and *The Dharma Bums,* were both largely narrative in their emphasis. Even though these two novels bracketed the period of Kerouac's most intense creativity (*On the Road* immediately preceding it and *The Dharma Bums* following it, marking Kerouac's first attempt to carry on with his work after becoming a public figure) and even though the books are actually quite dissimilar except in both being primarily narrative and both portraying the actions of nonconformists, most critics and readers perceived them as of a piece thematically and stylistically. By the time Kerouac's books from 1952 to 1956, books like *Visions of Cody* and *Doctor Sax,* began to appear and be discussed, the general sense of Kerouac as a kinetic but superficial teller of his own story was well established. Second, the few books that Kerouac did manage to write after becoming a celebrity, like *The Dharma Bums* and *Big Sur,* are much more clearly autobiographical narratives than the work written before *On the Road*'s publication. Moreover, some of Kerouac's key attempts to describe his overall project as a writer stress the "confessional" and "autobiographical" basis of his work.

If writers were consistently the best commentators on their work and consistently reliable, not much more would need to be said; we could safely conclude that Kerouac's work is what the general consensus says it is. But writers don't have such a good track record when it comes to these matters, and a closer look at some of the statements Kerouac made in the later years of his life about the books he'd written shows that even these statements are not as simple and consistent as they at first seem. In the preface to *Excerpts from Visions of Cody* that Kerouac revised and reused for the 1962 novel *Big Sur,* Kerouac writes:

> My work comprises one vast book like Proust's except that my remembrances are written on the run instead of afterwards in a sick bed. . . . [The books] are just chapters in the whole work which I call *The Duluoz Legend.* . . . The whole thing forms one enormous comedy seen through the eyes of poor Ti Jean (me), otherwise known as Jack Duluoz, the world of raging action and folly and also sweet gentleness seen through the keyhole of his eye.

This passage is often cited to support the contention that Kerouac's work is one grand narrative of his life, but the passage really suggests something else. Characterizing the work as Proustian "remembrances" and stressing that the books deal with what Ti Jean has "seen," rather than done, is actually more consistent with the sketching aesthetic of image-centered work like *Visions of Cody* than plot-centered work like *The Dharma Bums.* The primary evidence in the passage for Kerouac having regarded his work as autobiographical narrative is his title for the "whole work": *The Duluoz Legend,* but even this does not really justify organizing Kerouac's texts into a single narrative of his life. To do so means that books as radically different in style, tone, and intention as *Visions of Gerard, Doctor Sax, Maggie Cassidy,* and *Vanity of Duluoz* must form the earliest chapters simply because they draw events, characters, and images from the earliest parts of Kerouac's life. Rather the preface justifies seeing the books as one ongoing process of perception and imagination, and if that suggests or requires that the books be ordered into a larger entity, the obvious order is the order of the individual book's composition, and this would mean regarding *Doctor Sax* as an early chapter, *Vanity of Duluoz* as the last chapter, and the other two books as intermediate chapters. Then *The Duluoz Legend* would present the "history" of the world as "seen through keyhole of [Ti Jean's] eye." And then perhaps we would realize that Kerouac, the "word man," was at his best involved in something much like the modern long poem structured by collage, one reason why he has consistently been taken most seriously by poets such as Ginsberg, Duncan, Creeley, and Snyder.

Perhaps if the time comes when Kerouac finally acquires readers to replace his fans, we will come to appreciate the poignance of an anecdote reported by Marjorie Perloff in her book *Frank O'Hara: Poet Among Painters*. She writes that Joe LeSueur, a friend of O'Hara's, "recalls an evening at the Cedar Bar in the Village, c. 1960, when Kerouac, very drunk, came up to O'Hara and said: 'I thought you liked me.' O'Hara replied: 'It's not you I like, it's your work,' a remark that pleased Kerouac very much." (pp. 32-3)

> Tim Hunt, "The Misreading of Kerouac," in The Review of Contemporary Fiction, *Vol. III, No. 2, Summer, 1983, pp. 29-33.*

ADAM GUSSOW

The publication history of *On the Road* begins in controversy. According to Kerouac's biographer Dennis McNally, Kerouac sat down at his typewriter one day early in April 1951, cranked in a long roll of art-paper sheets Scotch-taped together, and by April 25th had pounded out *On the Road* in one unbroken 175,000-word paragraph. Kerouac insists in **"Origins of the Beat Generation"** that he wrote the book in May, not April; McNally says that the May draft, on teletype paper, was the second. Critic Tim Hunt argues that Kerouac began his *Road* book in 1948 and had written five primary versions by 1952, while Kerouac's first biographer, Ann Charters, asserts that the book was "rewritten and revised countless times."

All accounts agree on one point, however: from the beginning, in *whatever* draft, *On the Road* received precious little editorial sympathy. In May 1951 Kerouac submitted the teletype draft to Robert Giroux, then an editor at Harcourt Brace. Giroux, who had published Kerouac's first novel *The Town and the City,* "was deaf to Jack's explanations of a breakthrough and shocked by the form of *On the Road*," according to Kerouac biographers Gifford and Lee; "[he] recoiled simply at the look of the thing." Kerouac's friend John Clellon Holmes gave the manuscript to his literary agent, Rae Everett. She returned it, McNally reports, "with a great deal of carping criticism."

"The Beats," as John Tytell observes in *Naked Angels: The Lives and Literature of the Beat Generation,* "saw themselves as outcasts, exiles within a hostile culture . . . rejected artists writing anonymously for themselves." At no point until the very end of his career did Kerouac feel more rejected than during the early 1950's. When he had given up an athletic scholarship and withdrawn from Columbia in 1944 to become a writer, his father Leo had angrily disowned him; but he had gained fatherly approval and the beginnings of a literary reputation when Giroux published *The Town and the City* in 1950. Now, having written what seemed to him clearly his best work to that point, he was being denied both approval and success. For consolation he turned to the same friends who had served as subject matter for his fiction, particularly Allen Ginsberg. Ginsberg had also had a troubled relationship with his father—a poet and college English professor of conservative tastes who strongly disapproved of his son's experiments with freer poetic forms—and during this period the two young rejected artists exchanged countless long impassioned letters in which they vilified the older literary men who had rejected them. In 1954, Seymour Lawrence at Little, Brown was to turn down *On the Road* with the usual complaints about lack of craftsmanship, and Mark Van Doren, a poet-critic and Columbia professor whom Jack admired deeply, would dismiss his newest work, *Doctor Sax,* as "monotonous and probably without meaning in the end." (pp. 293-94)

In March of 1953, Kerouac first met Malcolm Cowley. Several months earlier, Cowley had been sent a copy of *On the Road* by Phyllis Jackson, Kerouac's agent at the time. "I think it came into Viking marked for my attention," Cowley remembered in a recent letter to me. "I was surprised, impressed, and talked about it at a Tuesday editorial meeting. But others read it and turned thumbs down." In March, as a way of returning Kerouac's manuscript, Cowley took the neglected young writer out to lunch. On July 3rd, Ginsberg, who had replaced Jackson as Kerouac's agent, wrote to Cowley telling him that Kerouac was working on another version of *On the Road* and asking him whether he was interested in seeing it. On 14 July 1953 Cowley responded with a letter that seems in retrospect even more astonishing than it must have seemed at the time to the two young Beats:

> You are right in thinking that I am interested in Kerouac and his work. He seems to me the most interesting writer who is not being published today—and I think it is important that he should be published, or he will run the danger of losing that sense of the audience, which is part of a writer's equipment. But the only manuscript of his that I have read with a chance of immediate book publication is the first version of *On the Road.* As much of the second version as I saw contained some impressively good writing, but no story whatsoever.

Cowley's complaint about the lack of "story" in *On the Road* would return to plague Kerouac throughout his relationship with the stubborn editor. But Cowley's evident admiration for Kerouac's writing and his concern for Kerouac's career stand in striking contrast to the editorial neglect Kerouac had received to this point. *On the Road,* clearly, is at the heart of the matter: how do we explain Cowley's unabashedly favorable response to a work that had thus far produced little more than anger and incomprehension in other leading editorial minds of the day? The answer lies, among other places, deep in Cowley's own literary past.

"Since most critics had never experienced anything like the *Road,*" argues Dennis McNally, "they denied its existence as art and proclaimed it a 'Beat Generation' tract of rebellion, then pilloried it as immoral." This is true—up to a point— but Cowley was a critic with the soul of a storyteller. He had not merely experienced something like *On the Road* but had created, in *Exile's Return,* a road narrative about his own rebellious, "lost" generation. Published in 1934 (and revised for re-publication just two years before Cowley first read

Kerouac's novel), *Exile's Return* is Cowley's first-person account of the exploits of a group of rootless and high-spirited young Americans during the decade following the Great War. Like *On the Road, Exile's Return* moves back and forth nervously along an East-West axis: Paris-New York in Cowley's case, New York-San Francisco in Kerouac's. Like *On the Road* it swerves south several times for pilgrimages to spiritual fathers and for binges facilitated by favorable foreign exchange rates. These structural parallels are less important, however, than the common sensibility that had produced them—one that Cowley could not possibly have failed to perceive. Coming of age in two different postwar worlds, both Cowley and Kerouac had been driven to write honest reports about their own uprooted lives and in so doing had helped define (Cowley more retrospectively than Kerouac) two radically new generations. Both men—and both generations—had rebelled against inherited values and taken to the road in pursuit of a separate peace. In Malcolm Cowley and Jack Kerouac, it might fairly be said, the Lost Generation and the Beat Generation were meeting for the first time—and discovering in each other an unexpected resemblance. (pp. 295-96)

That Cowley found in Kerouac a way of reconnecting with his own past is hinted at by his statement to an interviewer:

> I remember one night Jack and I went out on the town. I wanted him to show me the new dives in Greenwich Village with which I was totally unfamiliar, not having been a Villager for twenty years. And he took me down.

What Cowley saw in Kerouac and Kerouac's novel, I suggest, was the sort of impatient young man in love with life and language that Cowley had been when he was Kerouac's age. "[T]he only people for me are the mad ones, the ones who are mad to live, mad to talk, mad to be saved, desirous of everything at the same time, the ones who never yawn or say a commonplace thing, but burn, burn, burn," Sal Paradise had cried at the beginning of *On the Road,* and his words—Kerouac's self-portrait, as it were—are, surprisingly enough, an apt description of young Malcolm Cowley. . . . But if the Dada-inspired freneticism of Cowley's early years and his experiments with lyrical prose made him sympathetic with Kerouac's attempts to capture the texture of postwar life among the young, I suspect that he was struck still more forcibly by something else: Kerouac's vision of a rootless generation bound by spoken language into a self-sustaining community.

Cowley had been trying to recover precisely such a communal life since the days of *Exile's Return,* when he first formulated his myth of diasporactive exile as a way of explaining the Lost Generation. His own life and the lives of his friends, he wrote in that book, had been marked by "a long process of deracination," a progressive destruction of all ties to place and to human community: "[O]ur whole training was involuntarily directed toward destroying whatever roots we had in the soil, toward eradicating our local and regional peculiarities, toward making us homeless citizens of the world." *Exile's Return,* in which Cowley depicts his generation's scattering, is full of descriptions of provisional communities held together by one unending dialogue. "[O]n Sunday nights [in the Village] there were poker games played for imaginary stakes and interrupted from moment to moment by gossip, jokes, plans," he wrote. "[E]verything in those days was an excuse for talking." Kerouac's sense of homelessness was no less keen than Cowley's; John Clellon Holmes has called him

"the seeker after continuity who, no matter how rootless his life may seem, has always known that our anguish is uprootedness." And it is a striking aspect of *On the Road* that while *written* literature per se plays only a small role in the lives of the Beats, *oral* literature—the recounted story—literally holds their lives together. "[W]e headed for Mexico, telling our stories," cries Sal Paradise, "O sad American night! All the way from Amarillo to Childress, Dean and I pounded plot after plot of books we'd read into Stan, who asked for it because he wanted to know. . . . Stan talked and talked; Dean had wound him up the night before and now he was never going to stop." In "What Writers Are and Why," an essay published in 1954, Cowley characterized writers as "[people who] tell stories that become the myths of the tribe." This broad-minded conception of the writer's role and the communal function of language, I suggest, made it possible for Cowley to value the mad storytellers portrayed by Kerouac—indeed, to value Kerouac himself—in a way that other editors and critics evidently could not.

Norman Podhoretz was perhaps the best known of those unsympathetic critics in 1958 when he remarked in "The Know-Nothing Bohemians" that

> the unveiling of the Beat Generation was greeted with a certain relief by many people who had been disturbed by the notorious respectability and "maturity" of postwar writing. This was more like it—restless, rebellious, confused youth living it up instead of thin, balding, buttoned-down instructors of English composing ironic verses with one hand while changing the baby's diapers with the other. [see excerpt in *CLC,* Vol. 1]

It is a fascinating point of literary history that Cowley, the editor responsible for bringing *On the Road* into print, was also the critic who worked hardest during the 1950's to foster precisely the sort of dissatisfaction with "mature" postwar fiction that might lead the public to greet Kerouac's book with relief. . . . In 1953 and 1954 [Cowley] wrote a series of polemical essays for general-interest magazines on "the literary situation," most of which were republished late in 1954 in a book by that name. It was in March of 1953, near the beginning of this project, that he first read *On the Road.*

What becomes clear when we read Cowley's essays of the period is the extraordinary degree to which Kerouac's novel met the specifications Cowley was demanding of contemporary fiction. . . . In his "Invitation to Innovators," published the following year in *Saturday Review,* Cowley complained that young novelists were content to imitate

> the asthmatic, comma-dotted style of [Henry James's] later years—as if [they] were tired expatriates who had to pause for breath after speaking two or three words, instead of being young stay-at-homes bursting with energy. . . . [T]he [novel] form might decongeal and, instead of novels like funerary monuments, we might have loosely conceived narratives that carried one or many heroes through a variety of adventures.

That the young stay-at-home Kerouac was on Cowley's mind as he delivered this exhortation goes without saying: earlier in the article he had referred to "John Kerouac's unpublished long narrative" as "the best record of [the] lives of the Beat Generation."

But if Cowley had a number of reasons for thinking so highly of *On the Road,* The Viking Press did not. "[I] got a couple more readings for it," he told an interviewer, "but no, they wouldn't publish. It was very much a matter on my mind. I thought, here is something new. Here is something that ought to get to people. A way has to be prepared for it." Cowley had been rejected by Viking's conservative editorial board in similar fashion when he first proposed *The Portable Faulkner.* He had responded by writing a long essay on Faulkner's work and then doing what he called "beefing." it—publishing it in sections in several different magazines, using his independent critical voice to give Faulkner's name enough public currency so that Viking was finally forced to take a second look. He used a variation on that strategy to pave the way for *On the Road.* Not only did he praise Kerouac's fiction in print, but he convinced a reluctant Kerouac that "beefing" his novel was the surest way of persuading Viking to publish it. When Cowley wrote Kerouac in the summer of 1954 to ask if he might send an excerpt of the book to Arabelle Porter at *New World Writing,* Seymour Lawrence at Little, Brown had just rejected the book. Kerouac raged at Lawrence in a letter to Allen Ginsberg dated 30 July, but he praised Cowley repeatedly, invoking his name like a mantra. He willingly gave Cowley the go-ahead. On August 6th he received word from Miss Porter that **"Jazz Excerpts"** had been accepted, and he wrote a short, ecstatic letter of gratitude to Cowley. He had begun to lose heart, he said, but this gave him a lift toward further effort.

The lift was short-lived. By Christmas, E. P. Dutton had turned down *On the Road,* and Joe Fox, Editor-in-Chief at Alfred Knopf, sent it back with a comment that Kerouac characterized in a letter to Ginsberg as "contemptuous." Kerouac grew increasingly desperate during the early months of 1955, his intense need for the approval of his literary elders counterbalanced by his disgust with a publishing world that refused to recognize his genius on its own terms. (pp. 297-301)

On 12 July 1955, Cowley wrote to Kerouac's new agent, Sterling Lord, and asked to have another look at *On the Road.* Viking had recently hired Keith Jennison, a young editor who was familiar with Kerouac's work, and when he read the manuscript he quickly became convinced that Cowley was right in wanting to publish it. But although Jennison's name subsequently began to turn up in Kerouac's letters to Ginsberg, Cowley remained Kerouac's principal connection with Viking. For a variety of reasons, including Kerouac's unstable personality and a fundamental difference in literary values, the editorial process became one long exercise in frustration.

The first thing Cowley did after securing Jennison's backing was to write Kerouac a letter describing the obstacles that would have to be surmounted if *On the Road* were to be published. According to Viking's attorneys, said Cowley, the present manuscript was both libelous and obscene. Cowley himself wasn't bothered by Kerouac's over-honest language, but he did feel that the narrative had structural problems and he later described the editorial suggestions he had made:

> I thought there should be some changes to make it more of a continuous narrative. It had swung back and forth between East Coast and West Coast like a huge pendulum. I thought that some of the trips should be telescoped. . . . All the changes I suggested were big ones, mostly omissions. I said why don't you boil down these two or three trips and keep the mood of the content.

Cowley's intent, clearly, was to have Kerouac rearrange his narrative of lived experience into something more closely resembling a "story," while retaining the sense of life of the original. That narrative literature should tell stories had been a near-sacred principle for Cowley throughout his career. (pp. 302-03)

When Kerouac received Cowley's initial suggestions for editorial changes in *On the Road,* he was too happy with the prospects of seeing his novel in print to argue. In a letter dated 20 September 1955 he agreed to work with Cowley on the twin problems of libel and obscenity, and he said that he was ready to assist Cowley in rearranging the narrative as the editor saw fit. He was never to speak this generously to Cowley again. In fact, he was later to turn on him, much as Thomas Wolfe had turned on Maxwell Perkins, bitterly criticizing him for damaging the structure and texture of his novel. His charges were later picked up and transformed into myth by Allen Ginsberg, who bemoaned

> the sadness that [*On the Road*] was never published in its most exciting form—its original discovery—but hacked and punctuated and broken—the rhythms and swing of it broken—by presumptuous literary critics in publishing houses.

The true source of Cowley's dispute with Kerouac lay not so much in Cowley's insistence on *story,* but in a second, more fundamental principle: his insistence on *craft.* Perhaps it was inevitable that an editor who once confessed, "I hate to write and love to revise" would end up at loggerheads with an impatient young writer whose own poetic was summed up in a manifesto entitled **"Essentials of Spontaneous Prose."** The irony of the conflict is that the two men were in far greater accord on the matter than they were subsequently willing to admit. A combination of pride, stubbornness, and sheer happenstance led them to force each other into extreme positions.

Kerouac, despite his later insistence that the writer remove all "literary, grammatical, and syntactical inhibition," felt no qualms about revising his own early drafts of *On the Road* prior to submission. What he opposed, as Tim Hunt has pointed out, was others' cutting material out of his manuscript. Even so, his Whitmanesque aesthetic of spontaneity—

> tap from yourself the song of yourself, *blow!*— *now!*—*your* way is your only way—"good"—or "bad"—always honest, ("ludicrous"), spontaneous, "confessional," interesting because not "crafted"—

was formulated explicitly only *after* the publication of *On the Road,* when he had an image of uncompromising artistry to protect. And although Cowley had always insisted that art should be "crafted," he was anything but a rigid formalist: he regarded inspiration and radical experimentation as equally crucial components of the artistic process. In fact, he described Whitman's composition of "Song of Myself" in his 1959 introduction to that poem in terms that might equally well have expressed his vision of *On the Road:* "It . . . bears the marks of having been conceived as a whole and written in one prolonged burst of inspiration, but its unity is also the result of conscious art, as can be seen from Whitman's corrections in the early manuscripts." Yet in later years, thrown on the defensive by Kerouac's attacks, Cowley cynically disparaged the idea that inspiration was the only source of Kerouac's art:

Well, Jack did something that he would never admit to later. He did a good deal of revision, and it was very good revision. Oh, he would never, never admit to that, because it was his feeling that the stuff ought to come out like toothpaste from a tube and not be changed, and that every word that passed from his typewriter was holy. On the contrary, he revised, and revised well.

In light of Norman Podhoretz's complaint that *On the Road* is "patently autobiographical in content. . . . Nothing that happens has any dramatic reason for happening"—a criticism echoed even by some of Kerouac's admirers—it would seem hard to fault Cowley on principle for having pressured Kerouac to bring out the "story" in his narrative. But what revisions actually were made? Kerouac later bragged to Ginsberg that the "revision" he gave to Viking was substantially unchanged: he had simply "purged all material not directly related to Cassady, and had accepted . . . Cowley's suggestion to fuse the various trips for the sake of focus." Yet in a letter he wrote to Ginsberg on 21 July 1957, shortly before publication, Kerouac made a fascinating assertion: Don't be upset, he told Ginsberg, by the passage Cowley wanted put in on page six about your "intellectualism." A reader who turns to that page in a hardcover copy of *On the Road* comes upon the following passage:

> In those days [Dean Moriarty] really didn't know what he was talking about; that is to say, he was a young jailkid all hung-up on the wonderful possibilities of becoming a real intellectual, and he liked to talk in the tone and using the words, but in a jumbled way, that he had heard from "real intellectuals"—although, mind you, he wasn't so naïve as that in all other things and it took him just a few months with Carlo Marx [Ginsberg] to become completely *in there* with all the terms and jargon.

Podhoretz undoubtedly had this passage in mind when he accused the Beat Generation of "an anti-intellectualism so bitter that it makes the ordinary American's hatred of eggheads seem positively benign." That the tone of Kerouac's jibe is obviously lighthearted rather than bitter is less to the point, however, than Kerouac's suggestion that the jibe may not have been his idea at all. The circumstantial evidence for Cowley's involvement is tantalizing. . . . If conclusive proof that Cowley persuaded Kerouac to add the passage mocking the "terms and jargon" of "real intellectuals" is lacking, it seems clear at the very least that Kerouac found in the civic critic a sensibility uniquely responsive to his own low regard for the systematic mind divorced from life.

Despite such shared attitudes, however, Kerouac's nascent editorial relationship with Cowley began to sour almost as soon as it had begun—and for a thoroughly mundane reason. Cowley had received an appointment to teach creative writing during the winter quarter at Stanford, and on 8 November 1955 he wrote to Kerouac at Allen Ginsberg's place in Berkeley, where Jack was spending the fall, telling him that he and Mrs. Cowley would be in Palo Alto by January 2nd. "Of course I plan to see you then if you are still in San Francisco," he told him. But Kerouac, itinerant as always, was in Rocky Mount, North Carolina by the time Cowley's letter reached Ginsberg's Milvia Street apartment. Kerouac traveled up to New York after Christmas, expecting to work with Cowley on revisions of *On the Road,* and when he discovered his editor's absence he felt abandoned. By the time he made it back to California in April of 1956, the quarter at Stanford

was over and Cowley had returned to New York. Angry and insecure, Kerouac decided to exploit what seemed to him a legitimate grievance with the way Cowley had treated him. On 9 May he wrote the editor and proposed a new project: an historical novel about the Zapotec Indians of Mexico, complete with Kerouacian descriptions of their legendary sex orgies. All Cowley had to do, insisted Kerouac, was write to the Mexican patron that Kerouac had lined up and assure him that he, Cowley, would be interested in publishing such a work—subject, of course, to the approval of the Viking editorial board. Kerouac followed this demand by complaining that he was penniless and ragged, and that Cowley had broken his heart by neglecting him. He begged for some kind of news.

Cowley responded immediately. He apologized for the delay with *On the Road*—he had been loaded down with "rush jobs" after returning from Stanford—and he sent Kerouac a copy of the letter he had written to Kerouac's patron. "I don't think it is the book you should be writing at this moment," he told him. "But if Mr. Garver is willing to stake you to grub and lodging, I approve of that part of the operation." Kerouac was to remind Cowley repeatedly of a truth the editor knew from his own early days as a freelance critic, that "money is the central problem of a young writer's life." That July, in fact, Kerouac wrote him threatening to withdraw his book unless Cowley came through with a firm contract and an advance. Cowley could do little to hasten the editorial process at Viking, but he did manage to "beef" two more sections of the script—one of them to his old friend George Plimpton at *Paris Review.* And he used his influence at the National Institute of Arts and Letters to secure Kerouac a $300 grant. Delighted, Kerouac wrote Ginsberg that Cowley had assisted the "helpless angels."

In mid-December 1956, almost four years after Cowley had first read *On the Road* in an early draft, Viking accepted Kerouac's novel for publication. Libel remained a problem—Viking's attorneys didn't clear the manuscript until late in March—but with Keith Jennison's help Cowley had managed to persuade Viking's editors that the book was a sound investment. (pp. 303-08)

Contrary to popular myth, Kerouac never complained about having to change the names of his friends in *On the Road* and otherwise cooperating with demands made by Viking's libel lawyers. But he felt increasingly testy about the whole idea of editorial changes. On 4 July 1957, with book publication only two months away, Kerouac sent Cowley a copy of his essay **"October in the Railroad Earth,"** from the latest issue of *Evergreen Review.* Here, he kidded Cowley, was spontaneous prose as it should be, untouched by editorial hands. He added a biblical postscript:

> "Take no thought beforehand what ye shall speak, neither do ye premeditate; but whatsoever shall be given to you in that hour, that speak ye; for it is not ye that speak, but the Holy Ghost."

Underneath the note, in case Cowley had missed his point, he typed the words "spontaneous prose." Cowley took the bait, responding on July 16th:

> That's a fine quotation from Mark 13.11. If the Holy Ghost is speaking through you, fine, fine, let him speak. Sometimes he turns out to be the devil masquerading as the Holy Ghost, and that's all right too. Sometimes he turns out to be Simple

Simon, and then you have to cut what he says. A good writer uses his subconscious mind and his conscious mind, one after the other, and uses them both as hard as they can be used.

Looking to the future, Cowley also told Kerouac he thought **Doctor Sax** was "the best of the present manuscripts," and he suggested that Kerouac lengthen it by writing in some new scenes about his boyhood.

Kerouac received Cowley's letter on July 21st, along with a boxful of advance copies of his book. Because of time constraints he had never been sent any galley proofs, and he now discovered, much to his chagrin, that additional cuts and changes had been made in the story without his approval. The record does not reveal what changes were made and who made them, although Cowley insisted in a recent letter to me that he hadn't seen the additional changes and that those which Kerouac complained about were made by an in-house editor with whom Cowley had been working on the book. Kerouac was in no doubt about the culprit, however; he dashed off a quick, angry letter to Allen Ginsberg. "Crafty Cowley" had asked him to write more scenes for **Doctor Sax,** he told Ginsberg, and he was sure that the editor would yank the fantasy section out of **Sax** without his permission, just as he had yanked material out of **On the Road.** At least **On the Road,** he grumbled, was "undecimatable," unlike **Sax.** (pp. 308-09)

The next day he wrote Cowley from Mexico City. The long letter was an exercise in pure duplicity. He told Cowley he thought the edition of **On the Road** was excellent and he praised the "few cuts" Cowley had made—now it would fit into pocket editions, and anyway the story was "well-nigh undecimatable." Then . . . he pleaded with Cowley to send him money. He had only $33 in his pocket, the advance for **On the Road** had been small, and Malcolm—he called him Malcolm six times—would *have* to send him $80 or $100 more. He was trying, he said, to write the new scenes Cowley had requested by recreating the conditions under which the bulk of **Doctor Sax** had been written; he mentioned an adobe hut and candlelight, but said nothing about his nonstop consumption of marijuana. He ended by telling Cowley that he was completely at his mercy.

The ploy worked: Cowley quickly arranged through Kerouac's agent, Sterling Lord, to have money cabled to Jack in Mexico. "Good luck on your Mexican venture," Cowley wrote him on July 23rd. "I am looking forward to reading the expanded version of **Doctor Sax,** and I hope that the new chapters will fit perfectly into what you have written already." Kerouac received the money and wrote the new chapters, but a bad case of the flu sent him staggering home to his mother's house in Florida. After his nightmarish month in Mexico, and with publication less than two weeks away, the accumulated tensions of his relationship with Cowley and literary New York burst through the surface. On August 20th he wrote a despairing letter to his friend Alan Anson. He was so sick and tired of the self-satisfied silence of wise men that he could kill them, he said. God save us, he added—in an obvious reference to Cowley—from the wise man puffing on his pipe. Two weeks later a new wise man, Gilbert Millstein of *The New York Times,* praised **On the Road** lavishly in a widely read review [see excerpt above], and Kerouac was literally an overnight success. Except for two glancing references, he never again mentioned Cowley in his letters. (pp. 309-10)

Adam Gussow, "Bohemia Revisited: Malcolm Cowley, Jack Kerouac, and 'On the Road'," in The Georgia Review, *Vol. XXXVIII, No. 2, Summer, 1984, pp. 291-311.*

SVEN BIRKERTS

I first read Jack Kerouac's **On the Road** when I was a junior in high school—a little more than twenty-one years ago. Someone had given my mother a copy of the book; I immediately "borrowed" it, consumed it, and started it circulating among my friends. Soon we were all obsessed—hitchhiking everywhere we could, trying to be like the characters in the novel.

Our every late-adolescent desire for movement, escape, *action* was brought to a blaze. Not that much fanning of sparks was needed. After all, it was 1968. If it hadn't been Kerouac, it would soon have been someone else.

Though Kerouac had begun writing **On the Road** in 1948, and it had first been published in 1957, the book could not have felt more present tense. Kerouac had caught hold of a spirit we understood; he raised a call to arms. What for me had been just inchoate turmoil and longing had now been set down in words. I grew restless and excited when the book's narrator, Sal Paradise, announced:

> . . . the only people for me are the mad ones, the ones who are mad to live, mad to talk, mad to be saved, desirous of everything at the same time, the ones who never yawn or say a commonplace thing, but burn, burn, burn like fabulous yellow roman candles exploding like spiders across the stars and in the middle you see the blue centerlight pop and everybody goes "Awww!"

That was it right there: madness, excess, something nonstop and feverish to hold against the blandness of our suburban childhoods.

When I went off to college, I found that we had not been unique: everyone, it seemed, had been reading Kerouac. And Ginsberg and Corso and Burroughs and Kesey (and Wolfe *on* Kesey). This was our non-curricular education. These were the spirits who conferred their benediction upon us, upon our efforts to live differently—more intensely—than our parents had. (p. 74)

I decided that I would commemorate the passing of two decades by re-reading **On the Road.** I knew, of course, that everything would be different. How could it not? In 1968 it had been a book whose title promised *discovery.* Now the cover blurb announced that I was about to read "the book that turned on a generation." Braced as I was, however, I still got a terrible jolt. There is simply no adequate protection against the ways we grow and change.

The novel, *qua* novel, is not really much at all. Kerouac's alternately matter-of-fact and ebullient prose tracks Sal Paradise through his far-flung travels. The pattern is simple: About once a year, Sal gets restless in his secure lodgings with his aunt (the *mémère* to whom Kerouac remained neurotically attached all his life) and launches forth from New Jersey to the beckoning West. Each time, he hooks up with Dean Moriarty, his "mad" mentor, the aging juvenile delinquent who represents (to him) velocity, kicks, and enlightenment. Others join up and disperse, moving about like molecules of a boiling liquid. The American highway system is the spice route of their dreams. "Somewhere along the line," says Sal as he first sets out, "I knew there'd be girls, visions, everything; somewhere along the line the pearl would be handed to me."

Kerouac is sequential, at times almost diaristic. On the first trip West—perhaps because it *is* the first—every movement is tabulated. We follow Sal from the bus rides that get him started, to the long, "careening" (a favorite Kerouac word) rides that come once he gets west of Chicago and puts out his thumb. (p. 75)

"Wild" and "lyrical" are two more favorite Kerouac words—they crop up in most of his more energized riffs, especially through the first half of the book. It's as if Sal can't kick the language up quite as high as he wants it—he makes these loosely deployed adjectives carry so much of the freight of the inexpressible. But once—for me at least—they did carry it. When I first read *On the Road,* no one needed to tell me how a night, or a town, or a train, or a bum, could be "lyrical"— they just were. Kerouac's scattershot words and phrases accorded perfectly with my jumbled-up feelings about life. Now, for whatever reason, I seem to crave more precision—a passage like that no longer delivers.

On Sal's first trip West, he wants to "dig" everything. And everything is there to be dug. When he gets to Denver, his first real layover, a gang of friends and friends of friends is waiting. There follow rampaging nights with the hard-partying Bettencourt sisters and the Rawlins clan: "We started off with a few extra-size beers. There was a player piano. Beyond the back door was a view of mountainsides in the moonlight. I let out a yahoo. The night was on."

New sights and the promise of good times are, of course, part of what lures Sal away from home again and again; but the real draw is Dean—the outlaw, the limit-breaker. Sal wants to be near him as much as possible. Dean steals cars, he tears between the coasts in nonstop driving binges, he loves every "gal" in every diner along the way. He is Sal's "yellow roman candle," his life force; he is the catalyst that helps Sal break through his essential passivity.

Sal and Dean have one of those eternally boyish American friendships. Though women are desired, discussed, and dallied with, they are also always in the way—nagging, getting pregnant, threatening to stop the fun. Leslie Fiedler long ago identified the homoerotic nature of the bond (yes, Ishmael and Queequeg, Huck and Jim . . .) in *Love and Death in the American Novel.* And biographers of Kerouac now bear out that his friendship with Cassady did extend to some hesitant, experimental sex.

In any event, what weaves together the separate travel episodes is the unfolding history of a friendship—a history which begins with Sal's enchantment with the charismatically amoral Dean Moriarty and which ends with his pained disillusion. In an early, blinded description, Sal writes: "And a kind of holy lightning I saw flashing from his excitement and his visions, which he described so torrentially that people in buses looked around to see the 'overexcited nut.'" But after he has been deserted and betrayed enough times, Sal finds his perceptions shifting. Dean's mad avidity is not so much heroic as desperate. He is fleeing his own inner void— the legacy of his rummy father, who abandoned him among the bars and poolhalls of Denver when he was a young boy.

By the end of the book, Sal's "thin-hipped" hero has become a figure of profound sadness. In the very last scene, when Sal is on his way to a concert, riding in the back of a hired Cadillac, he looks out at his friend : "Dean, ragged in a motheaten overcoat he brought specially for the freezing temperatures of the East, walked off alone . . . " He then adds this valedictory cadenza: " . . . nobody knows what's going to happen to anybody besides the forlorn rags of growing old, I think of Dean Moriarty, I even think of Old Dean Moriarty the father we never found, I think of Dean Moriarty."

It is probably a mistake to go back to the decisive books of one's youth. They are causes; the reader has long since become, in part, their effect. Clear vision is just not possible. I feel myself in a position somewhat like Sal's. It was not so much that Dean had changed from what he was—more that Sal had watched the vivid mantle of desires and dreams that he had created around Dean slowly dissipate. So, too, has the magic of *On the Road* dissipated for me.

Reading this book at sixteen, my friends and I wanted nothing so much as to be like Dean and Sal—close to the ground, connected, in motion, "paying our dues." We aspired to the "beat" ideal, with its double connotation of "worn-out" and "beatific." And when it led, as it inexorably did, to the hippie ethos of turning on, tuning in, and dropping out (how quaint it sounds!), many of us followed. But that next step was also a kind of last step—the premises of hippiedom were quickly consumed on the pyre of its excesses. Thus, once again, effects had come around to swallow their causes; henceforth, "beat" would also mean something like "proto-hippie."

All of this went through my mind as I re-read *On the Road.* Indeed, at some point I realized that I was not so much reading a book as taking stock—of those times, of these times, of myself in both. For me, the hardest thing was to see past the jadedness and cynicism of the '80s—to remember even a little of what life felt like back then. I don't know that I was able to, finally. The notes were as scored, sure, and the sounds were the same. But I kept feeling as if I were listening to a party record the morning after the party. It sounded sad, nothing like the way it had sounded while I was dancing to it. (pp. 75-6)

Sven Birkerts, "On the Road to Nowhere: Kerouac, Re-Read and Regretted," in Harper's, *Vol. 279, No. 1670, July, 1989, pp. 74-6.*

FURTHER READING

Bartlett, Lee. "The Dionysian Vision of Jack Kerouac." In *The Beats: Essays of Criticism,* edited by Lee Bartlett, pp. 115-26. Jefferson, N. C., and London: McFarland, 1981.

> Utilitizes psychoanalyst C. G. Jung's theories to illuminate the connection Lee asserts Kerouac makes between the jazz musician and the Dionysian writer.

Burns, Jim. "Kerouac and Jazz." *The Review of Contemporary Fiction* III, No. 2 (Summer 1983): 33-41.

> Explicates the references to jazz pieces and musicians in *On the Road* and other Kerouac works.

Charters, Ann. *Kerouac: A Biography.* San Francisco: Straight Arrow, 1973, 419 p.

 The earliest biography available on Kerouac.

Duffey, Bernard. "The Three Worlds of Jack Kerouac." In *Recent American Fiction: Some Critical Views,* edited by Joseph J. Waldmeir, pp. 175-84. Boston: Houghton Mifflin, 1963.

 Brief survey of Kerouac's novels as representative of the spirit and art of the Beat generation.

French, Warren. *Jack Kerouac.* Boston: Twayne Publishers, 1986, 147 p.

 Analyzes the novels that comprise "The Duluoz Legend" as an extended effort by Kerouac to recast his life in the form of a literary legend analogous to the Stephen Daedalus novels of James Joyce.

Holmes, John Clellon. "The Philosophy of the Beats." *Esquire* 99, No. 6 (June 1983): 158-60, 162-64, 166-67.

 Early analysis originally published in the February, 1958 issue of *Esquire* that emphasizes the importance of the spiritual quest to the Beats.

Huebel, Harry Russell. *Jack Kerouac.* Edited by Wayne Chatterton and James H. Maguire. Boise, Idaho: Boise State University, 1979, 48 p.

 Biography focusing on the years Kerouac was writing. Huebel summarizes plots and critical response to Kerouac's major works and includes a selected bibliography.

———. "The 'Holy Goof': Neal Cassady and the Post-War American Counter Culture." *Illinois Quarterly* 35, No. 4 (April 1973): 52-61.

 Combines a short biography of Cassady, the real-life model for Dean Moriarty, with information from fictional portraits of him created by Kerouac and others in order to gain insight into the "nature of the bohemian-left community."

Hunt, Tim. *Kerouac's Crooked Road: Development of a Fiction.* Hamden, Conn.: Archon, 1981, 262 p.

 Delineates the complicated textual history of *On the Road* based on Kerouac's correspondence and his 1948-1949 work journal.

Jones, Granville H. "Jack Kerouac and the American Conscience." In *Lectures on Modern Novelists,* by Arthur T. Broes, et. al., pp. 25-

39. 1963. Reprint. Freeport, New York: Books for Libraries Press, 1972.

 Defines the individualistic philosophy Kerouac advocated in his fiction and life as a distinctly American phenomenon.

McDarragh, Fred W. *Kerouac and Friends: A Beat Generation Album.* New York: William Morrow, 1985, 338 p.

 Selection of newspaper and magazine articles and essays from the 1950s, reprinted along with McDarragh's photographs of major and minor Beat figures.

McNally, Dennis. *Desolate Angel: Jack Kerouac, the Beat Generation, and America.* New York: St. Martin's, 1978, 400 p.

 Discusses the general historical background of Kerouac and the Beats.

Nicosia, Gerald. *Memory Babe: A Critical Biography of Jack Kerouac.* New York: Grove Press, 1983, 767 p.

 Comprehensive biography based on interviews, correspondence, and other documents from Kerouac's friends and family.

Nisonger, Thomas Evans. "Jack Kerouac: A Bibliography of Biographical and Critical Material, 1950-1979." *Bulletin of Bibliography* 37, No. 1 (January-March 1980): 23-32.

 Restricted to English-language material with some Western European-language citations.

Sheed, Wilfrid. "Beat Down and Beatific." In his *The Good Word and Other Words,* pp. 110-15. New York: E. P. Dutton, 1978.

 Describes the atmosphere in which the Beat Generation worked and played in New York.

Weinreich, Regina. *The Spontaneous Poetics of Jack Kerouac: A Study of the Fiction.* Carbondale and Edwardsville, Illinois: Southern Illinois University Press, 1987, 180 p.

 First full-length treatment of Kerouac's prose style in *The Country and the City, On the Road, Visions of Cody,* and *Desolation Angels.* Includes a selected bibliography.

Werner, Craig Hansen. "The Many Mirrors: Joyce's Techniques." In his *Paradoxical Resolutions: American Fiction Since James Joyce,* pp. 33-119. Urbana: University of Illinois Press, 1982.

 Compares the structure of *On the Road* to that of James Joyce's *Portrait of the Artist as a Young Man.*

Stephen King

1947-

(Born Stephen Edwin King; has also written under pseudonyms Richard Bachman and John Swithen) American novelist, short story writer, scriptwriter, nonfiction writer, autobiographer, and author of children's books.

King is a prolific and immensely popular author of horror fiction. In his works, King blends elements of the traditional
gothic tale with those of the modern psychological thriller,
detective, and science fiction genres. His fiction features colloquial language, clinical attention to physical detail and
emotional states, realistic settings, and an emphasis on contemporary problems, including marital infidelity and peer
group acceptance, that lend credibility to the supernatural elements in his fiction. King's wide popularity attests to his
ability to create stories in which he emphasizes the inability
to rationalize certain facets of evil in seemingly commonplace
situations.

King's interest in the demonic and the paranormal is usually
reflected in his protagonists, whose experiences and thoughts
serve to reveal psychological complexities and abnormalities.
His first novel, *Carrie,* concerns a socially outcast teenage girl
whose emotional insecurities lead her to take violent revenge
on taunting classmates by means of telekinetic powers. In
The Shining, malevolent spirits in a remote resort hotel manipulate a recovering alcoholic caretaker into attempting to
murder his wife and child. Similarly, a haunted car in *Christine* gains control of an alienated teenage boy. Other works
in which paranormal events recur include *The Dead Zone*
and *Firestarter.*

Some of King's novels offer variations on classic stories of
fantasy and horror. *'Salem's Lot,* for example, is a contemporary version of Bram Stoker's novel *Dracula* set in an isolated
New England town. In this work, a young writer and an intelligent youth combat a small group of vampires that turns out
to include an increasing number of the town's residents.
King's apocalyptic epic *The Stand* is close in structure to
J. R. R. Tolkien's *The Lord of the Rings* in its tale of a deadly
virus and the resulting battle between the surviving forces of
good and evil. *Pet Sematary,* a version of W. W. Jacob's classic short story "The Monkey's Paw," tells of a physician who
discovers a supernatural Indian burial ground where the dead
return to life and succumbs to temptation after his child is
killed. *The Talisman,* written in collaboration with English
horror writer Peter Straub, also recalls *The Lord of the Rings*
in its evocation of a fantasy world in which a boy searches
for a cure for his mother's cancer. *The Dark Tower: The Gunslinger* and *The Dark Tower: The Drawing of the Three* are
two in a series of episodes previously published in periodicals
and inspired by Robert Browning's poem "Childe Roland to
the Dark Tower Came." These books focus on a gunslinger
who pursues a mysterious man in black toward the Dark
Tower, "the linchpin that holds all of existence together."

King has admitted to writing five novels under the pseudonym Richard Bachman to avoid overpublishing under his
own name. These novels seldom contain elements of the supernatural or occult, focusing instead on such themes as

human cruelty, alienation, and morality. In *Rage,* a psychopath shoots a schoolteacher and holds a classroom hostage,
singling out one pupil for physical and mental torture. *The
Long Walk* and *The Running Man* focus on near-future societies in which people compete to the death in ritualistic
games. *Roadwork* explores a man's reactions after observing
his family, work, and home destroyed by corporate and governmental forces beyond his control. *Thinner* describes the
fate of an obese man who begins to lose weight following a
gypsy's curse.

It is intended as a compendium of horror that King has identified as concluding his treatment of children and supernatural monsters. Set in the fictional community of Derry, Maine,
the novel focuses on a self-proclaimed "Losers Club" consisting of seven outcasts who successfully fought off a supernatural threat living below the town's sewer system in 1958, unaware that It resurfaces every twenty-seven years to control
individuals and kill children as a sacrifice for adult sins. An
amalgam of fears, It may appear as whatever frightens an individual, as a vampire or werewolf, or less melodramatically,
in the form of crime, racial and religious bigotry, or domestic
violence. When It telepathically recalls the Losers Club in
1985, the group's members must rediscover their childhood
humor and courage to counter the limitations of adulthood.

Although many reviewers considered the novel overlong, Robert Cormier commented: "King still writes like one possessed, with all the nervous energy of a young writer seeking his first big break. He never cheats the reader, always gives full measure. . . . He is often brilliant, and makes marvelous music, dark and sinister."

King's recent fiction is often semiautobiographical in subject. *Misery* focuses on Paul Sheldon, a pseudonymous author of popular historical romances featuring an indomitable heroine known as Misery Chastain. After writing his first "literary" novel, Sheldon stages a funeral for his alias but suffers an automobile accident and awakes to find himself the invalid prisoner of a psychotic nurse who forces him to resurrect Misery by writing another book. Christopher Lehmann-Haupt commented: "[Unlike] much of Mr. King's fiction, this novel is more than just a splendid exercise in horror. . . . Not only must Paul create under pressure a story he doesn't particularly want to tell, but he must also make it plausible, even inspired, for Annie Wilkes is a shrewd connoisseur of storytelling, what one might call the ultimate editor and critic. Under her tutelage the experiences of meeting a deadline and being cut take on terrifyingly literal meanings." *The Dark Half* revolves around Thaddeus Beaumont, a writer who as a child experienced headaches resulting from the incompletely absorbed foetus of a twin lodged in his brain. Although Thad decides to give up his pseudonymous identity as an author of thrillers, his alter ego returns, intent on revenge and forcing Thad to teach him the craft of writing by holding his wife and child hostage. George Stade called *The Dark Half* "a parable in chiller form of the popular writer's relation to his creative genius, the vampire within him, the part of him that only awakes to raise Cain when he writes."

King has also written two short story collections, *Night Shift* and *Skeleton Crew,* comprised of detective, science fiction, and horror tales. *Stephen King's Danse Macabre* includes autobiographical essays and a critical history of the horror genre in films, television, and literature. *Different Seasons* consists of four novellas which, like the Bachman novels, focus on the terrors of everyday existence. King has also written screenplays for several films. These include *Creepshow* and *Cat's Eye,* which consist of horror vignettes presented in a humorous, comic-book style; *Silver Bullet,* an adaptation of an earlier novel, *Cycle of the Werewolf;* and *Maximum Overdrive,* an expansion of the short story "Trucks," which King himself directed. In this film, a passing comet inexplicably causes motor vehicles to come alive and hold a group of people captive in a highway diner.

(See also *CLC,* Vols. 12, 26, 37; *Contemporary Authors,* Vols. 61-64; *Contemporary Authors New Revision Series,* Vol. 1; *Something about the Author,* Vols. 9, 55; and *Dictionary of Literary Biography Yearbook: 1980.*)

PRINCIPAL WORKS

NOVELS

*Carrie 1974
*'Salem's Lot 1975
*The Shining 1977
**Rage 1977
The Stand 1978
The Dead Zone 1979
**The Long Walk 1979

Firestarter 1980
Cujo 1981
**Roadwork 1981
**The Running Man 1982
The Dark Tower: The Gunslinger 1982
Christine 1983
Cycle of the Werewolf 1983; also published as *Silver Bullet,* 1985
Pet Sematary 1983
The Talisman (with Peter Straub) 1984
**Thinner 1984
IT 1986
Misery 1987
The Tommyknockers 1987
The Dark Tower: The Drawing of the Three 1987
The Dark Half 1989

SHORT FICTION COLLECTIONS

Night Shift 1978
Creepshow (comic book adaptation) 1982
†Different Seasons 1982
Skeleton Crew 1985

SCREENPLAYS

Creepshow 1982
Cat's Eye 1984
Silver Bullet 1985
Maximum Overdrive 1986

OTHER

Stephen King's Danse Macabre (nonfiction) 1981
The Eyes of the Dragon (juvenile novel) 1984
My Pretty Pony (children's novel) 1989

---

*These books were republished in 1981 under the title *Stephen King.*

**These books were originally published under the pseudonym Richard Bachman and republished in 1984 as *The Bachman Books.*

†Contains the novellas *Rita Hayworth and the Shawshank Redemption, Apt Pupil, The Body,* and *The Breathing Method.*

CHRISTOPHER LEHMANN-HAUPT

The drain. Things down there in the drain. Things down there in the drain that might reach up and get you. The awful necessity of having to go down the drain to face those things. These are the essential fantasy-fears that underlie *It,* Stephen King's latest, longest and most complicated novel of terror to date. If drains ever bothered you, then *It* is going to suck you right in. If not—well, the story's other compensations may or may not suffice.

It all begins in 1958, when a 6-year-old boy named Georgie Denbrough floats a little paper boat down the gutter of a thoroughfare in the city of Derry, Me. When the boat disappears into a storm drain, Georgie peers down disconsolately and spies a merry clown holding the boat in one hand and a bunch of brightly colored balloons in the other. Would Georgie like his boat back and a balloon into the bargain? Sure. Georgie reaches out. Shrill screams attract passers-by. Moments later the Denbrough child is found dead in the gutter, with a gaping wound where his arm was once attached to its socket.

Flash forward now to 1985. Stanley Uris, a successful Atlanta accountant, gets an after-dinner phone call from a friend in Derry that prompts him to go upstairs, run a bath, climb into it, and slice his wrists with a razor blade, scrawling on the wall the bloody word "IT" as his dying act. But five other former Derry residents reluctantly accept telephoned reminders of a promise they once made as children. They immediately set out for their hometown.

What can be so terrifyingly compelling? It seems that whatever got little Georgie Denbrough back in 1958 is acting up again—indeed that it has been acting up every 27 years or so since anybody can remember, and that whatever the gang of seven did in 1958 to stop it will have to be done again, as the gang once vowed in a ritual of blood. So home go the six to Derry, and forward goes Mr. King's narrative, jumping back and forth between 1958 and 1985 until we can hardly distinguish the horror of then from the horror of now.

Mr. King's huge novel is about a multitude of things. *It* involves the guilts and innocences of childhood and the difficulty for adults of recapturing them. *It* questions the difference between necessity and free will. *It* also concerns the evil that has haunted America from time to time in the forms of crime, racial and religious bigotry, economic hardship, labor strife and industrial pollution.

It is a museum filled with the popular culture of the 1980's; brand names, rock 'n' roll songs and stars, the jokes and routines of childhood in that era. *It* explores fairy tales, language and literature. One of the six who go back is Georgie Denbrough's older brother, Bill, who has surmounted his family's tragedy—or maybe harnessed it—to become a successful writer of horror fiction. "It" is not only the unknown monstrosity hiding beneath the city of Derry; "It" is also excrement, the dark, the unconscious, the sex act, and everything else that is frightening or inconceivable to children.

The novel is filled with every sort of scary set piece that Mr. King is so adept at contriving: nightmarish chases; trips into cellars where monstrous creatures may be lurking; a photograph album that bleeds; a bathtub drain that cackles hideously and "gouts" blood. (I don't know offhand if it was Mr. King who first revived and revised the verb form of "gout"—whose obsolete meaning, according to the Oxford English Dictionary, was "to drop" or "to gutter"—but blood in these pages gouts everywhere like water gushing from a fire hose.)

Such set pieces help to hold our interest in this epic of coprophilia. So do Mr. King's raw powers as a yarn spinner of horrors—his sense of pace and scene, his almost adolescent affinity for the gross and vulgar. But he has met himself two formidable plot challenges: one is to produce something terrifying enough to justify Stanley Uris's decision to commit suicide rather than face whatever is lurking in the sewers of Derry; the other is to explain what moved the children to pledge their lives to the city on that fateful day of the blood oath.

In neither of these challenges does Mr. King quite succeed. Nothing ever explains why Uris cuts his wrists or why the gang has to reunite. The story moves along, but for all its awesome stage effects, it huffs and puffs and creaks and clanks. It lacks the political vision of *The Dead Zone.* It misses the logic of *Firestarter* and *Cujo.* It wants the brooding,

ominous mood of *The Shining;* It has nothing like the funereal oppressiveness of *Pet Sematary.* It tries too hard; it reaches for too much; it's too damn complicated.

Or maybe you simply have to have a thing about drains for *It* to terrify you the way it was obviously meant to.

Christopher Lehmann-Haupt, in a review of "It," in The New York Times, *August 21, 1986, p. C21.*

ROBERT CORMIER

Yes, of course, Stephen King is the acknowledged master of the modern horror story—so what else is new? Maybe this: he is perhaps the ultimate Young Adult novelist who also writes terrific children's books, although very evil and very corrupt. (But since when did fairy tales suddenly become pure and innocent?) Stephen King, then, has two kinds of horror going for him—first, the horror that haunts old Colorado hotels, classic 1958 Plymouths, neglected cemeteries and entire Maine towns; second, the everyday horror found in the acned hearts of adolescents and in the perilous lives of children between the ages of, say, 5 and 10. He knows precisely their longings and agonies, their follies and fancies, just as he knows every foul impulse of his imagined monsters.

There's little doubt that Stephen King's intention always has been to scare the daylights out of us but he has also, with the help of serendipity perhaps, created a gallery of unforgettable young people. Stephen's kids.

Remember Carrie White and the excruciating moment in the school shower when that shy and perennially embarrassed girl-child discovers blood gushing between her legs while her classmates hoot and howl? And what about Arnie Cunningham, innocent prey of bullies, who falls in love with and succumbs to, of all things, a decaying and evil Plymouth? Or Charlie Tomlinson, that incendiary 10-year-old who breaks a reader's heart because she is, first of all, not a firestarter but a child very like the reader's very own or the little girl next door? Five-year-old Danny in *The Shining.* Four-year-old Tad Trenton in *Cujo.* Twelve-year-old Mark Petri in *Salem's Lot.* These are not just names from King's novels but real, living kids to thousands of readers who cared about them. Maybe that's why the terror of those novels is so great—we care about the victims.

If Stephen King's kids have one thing in common, it's the fact that they are all losers. In a way, all children are losers, of course—how can they be winners with that terrifying adult world stacked against them? Maybe they ring so true because so many of us carry the heavy baggage of childhood around most of our lives. In his latest novel, *It,* a massive and mesmerizing odyssey of terror and childhood, King adds to his roster of memorable children, outdoing himself this time by presenting seven young protagonists, all of them losers, all of them about 10 years old, poised on the edge of adolescence but still too young to say goodbye to childhood.

Losers? Bill Denbrough stutters and Eddie Kaspbrak suffers from psychosomatic asthma. Ben Hanscom is too fat and Beverly Rogan is abused by a violent father. Richie Tozier's quick mouth spews wisecracks to hide his insecurities. Mike Hanlon is black and Stan Uris is a Jew which makes both of them instant outsiders in the Wonder Bread world of rural Maine. In Stephen King's hands, they rise above their Central Casting origins, however, and become painfully real as they confront not only the bullies who always gang up on losers but the unspeakable evil that slithers and slides and finally emerges from the sewers and drainpipes of Derry, Maine to claim their sanity and their lives. "It"—the biggest bully of them all.

Derry is not the bucolic community one glimpses driving north on Route 7. Something strange has been going on there for years. Mysterious fires and explosions that take countless lives. Children who disappear into thin air. The townspeople don't know that the town is haunted by an evil presence which slumbers for decades and then awakens to feed on the town, particularly its children. In the summer of 1958, the monster intends to feed on our band of losers but they close ranks and after a harrowing encounter somehow bring an end to the horror. Or do they?

Twenty seven years later, they learn that "It" has survived and is on the prowl again. (pp. 1, 6)

A summary can't possibly convey the experience of *It,* because the novel itself is a kind of monster, swelling to more than 1,100 pages, feeding upon its own excesses. There is too much of everything—blood, terror, agony, fires, storms, explosions, nightmares come true. "It" is everywhere and becomes the thing you fear most—a werewolf or a mummy or even Frankenstein's monster. Horror piles upon horror and there is a numbing repetition as the events of 1958 are played out all over again in 1985.

And yet. And yet. King still writes like one possessed, with all the nervous energy of a young writer seeking his first big break. He never cheats the reader, always gives full measure. (Full measure? Hell, this book overflows with the stuff of a dozen novels). He is often brilliant, and makes marvelous music, dark and sinister, for instance, when he enters the mind of "It" and speculates on the secret of belief's "second edge"—

> If there are ten thousand medieval peasants who create vampires by believing them real, there may be one—probably a child—who will imagine the stake necessary to kill it. But a stake is only stupid wood, the mind is the mallet which drives it home.

In *It,* we have seven children who drive that mallet home. Stephen King is the mind that created them. And stuttering Bill, wheezing Eddie, bruised Beverly and their friends join Carrie White and Arnie Cunningham in that gallery of memorable children Stephen King has given us these last dozen years or so. (p. 6)

> Robert Cormier, "Stephen King and the Monsters Within," in Book World—The Washington Post, August 24, 1986, pp. 1, 6.

WALTER WAGER

Where did Stephen King, the most experienced crown prince of darkness, go wrong with *It?* Almost everywhere. Casting aside discipline, which is as important to a writer as imagination and style, he has piled just about everything he could think of into this book and too much of each thing as well. While the legendary kitchen sink does not appear, there is a bathroom sink that spouts blood, a toilet that explodes and an entire municipal sewer system that is awash with ravaged corpses and the bones of many local children whom It has eaten over several centuries.

Unfortunately, that's only a small sampling. Determined to keep the shocks appearing every 20 pages or so, Mr. King has conscientiously spiced his story with deadly flying leeches, an awful eye slightly larger than a beer truck, a homicidal bird with the wingspan of a jet fighter and other lethal lollapaloozas created by the enormously powerful mind-body of It. . . .

In these pages young is good and old is bad, and neither breaks any new ground. Previously Mr. King scored with such lively killers as a fiendish automobile and a hotheaded girl who could think fires into happening. Though bigger and stronger than either of those, It turns out to be kind of old-fashioned. That's not because It has been around so long that it boasts it is eternal. The sad truth is that a 15-foot spider just doesn't frighten the way it did 20 years ago.

Shrewdly recognizing this, the author has given us an advanced, super-duper spider. How about a really rotten spider that can change itself into any shape it wants? A werewolf? No problem. A limb-rending clown? You got it. The entity called It can also control human minds, even from great distances. One reason that adults in Derry, Me., ignore the disappearances of children and other atrocities over the centuries is that It governs their thinking. It can even get them to unite to lynch individuals and murder groups.

So you still don't shudder? O.K., It isn't *actually* a spider. That shape is the closest to the entity's reality that humans can comprehend. And where did this thing come from long ago? Outer space—a drearily shop-worn idea. The entity is pretty tired itself, awakening only every 27 years to gorge itself on Derry's children, whose pure fear is the primary nourishment for It.

Nothing stops It until 1958, when the virtuous outsiders, who are being brutally abused by a gang of semi-retarded bullies, discover It and how to fight it. The war is basically mental. If the good children believe in nice birds, Santa Claus, the Tooth Fairy and such, they can resist the entity. If they tell it jokes or speak in funny voices doing parodies, that spider will be hurt. It has to be feared. When these kids figure out that their belief, humor and courage are their best weapons, Old Creepy is in deep trouble.

With the exception of the black boy, who goes to work in the Derry library, the other "losers" scatter and prosper. Then It telepathically calls them back 27 years later to try to destroy them. If that belief routine shows that Mr. King has read *Peter Pan,* the rest of the novel reveals a familiarity with *Animal Farm.* All seven kids are equal, and all have prospered, but one is more equal than the others.

Now here's the imaginative part. Mr. King has given us a semi-autobiographical horror novel. The stuttering boy grew up to attend the University of Maine, where his nonintellectual and straight-ahead stories were derided as junk. So he wrote a novel to defy the snide faculty scoffers and sent it off to a New York publishing company because he liked the firm's logotype. It was Viking. Mr. King grew up in a Maine city of 30,000, went to that state's university and has had all his novels published by Viking. The leader of the children turns out to be the now rich and famous writer.

> Walter Wager, "More Evil Than a 15-Foot Spider," in The New York Times Book Review, August 24, 1986, p. 9.

LLOYD ROSE

To someone who isn't sensitive to King's particular talents, his popularity is mystifying. He's an awkward stylist and he overwrites (he won't settle for one vampire if he can have a whole townful). His characters are flat. He overdoes his effects. But it's not as if his fans don't know this. They admit it. What matters is that King frightens them. He slips past all the adult censors—rationality, skepticism, contempt for a low-rent literary form like the horror story—to yell "Boo!" at the little kid inside who wants to be scared.

Horror fiction and films can move us because they're often the symbolic depiction of our common experience. King takes ordinary emotional situations—marital stress, infidelity, peer-group-acceptance worries—and translates them into violent tales of vampires and ghosts. He writes supernatural soap operas. In *Carrie* the heroine's problem (aside from lethal telekinesis) is that she isn't popular at school. The crazed dog in *Cujo* is an embodiment of revenge on bad spouses—the abusive husband is castrated and killed; the adulterous wife loses her child. *The Shining* is basically the story of a writer snowed in with his wife and child who develops a rather extreme case of cabin fever (one thinks of King, who lives in Maine, writing through those long winters . . .). King can make everyday experience not merely the setting for but also the subject of his horror. This is probably what contributes most to his popularity.

But even a reader whom King doesn't scare can appreciate his energy and obsessiveness, his total commitment to bringing out the darkest elements in his material. His major question to himself as a writer appears to be, How much worse can it get? and the gleeful answer is always, Lots. He has the innocent, grisly curiosity of a child: What if grass grew out of your eyeball? What if a woman were decapitated while giving birth? Then what? Huh? He seems driven to explore any awful possibility that occurs to him. When you finish one of his books, you know you've spent time with someone: he's *in* his work.

Sometimes he can give the impression that he's stuck there. There's rarely any release in King's books: they're claustrophobic, blocked up, a trap enclosing him and the reader. His characters live in the worst possible moral universe: you're punished if you do wrong and you suffer if you're innocent. It's like the world of a child with crazy parents—whatever you do, they'll beat you, and you'll never know why. The confusion and rage at the center of this view of the world have a primal power that has nothing to do with King's hokey plots and monsters and that, boiling under them, gives them disturbing heat.

King is particularly sympathetic to the fears of children (he wrote an excellent essay on childhood fear and anger for the *Washington Post's Book World* a few months back). His best writing comes when he dwells on their helplessness, their dependence on fallible or malicious adults. And he's frank about the ambivalence of parents toward their children: their impatience and sometimes brutal rages. In his newest novel, which bears the superbly to-the-point title *It*, the indifferent, destructive parents are represented by a whole town—Derry, Maine—and the heroes are adults who overcome the monstrous It by recovering the imagination that they had as children. (pp. 102-03)

It starts high: in the first sixty-one pages there are two ghastly supernatural murders, a graphic description of a body eaten by fish, and a suicide in which the victim leaves the word *It* scrawled in blood on the bathroom tiles. After this things slow down, but the book goes on for another 1,083 pages. Whether this is a problem depends on the reader. For me, King's most effective novel is the relatively short *Pet Sematary;* I like the dark, remorseless logic of its story. But while I was bored with the Elks convention of ghosts that check into the hotel in *The Shining,* most people I know consider it King's scariest book. For them, 1,144 pages may be too short. Or they may find it distracting and beside the point when King attempts to go beyond the usual limits of a horror story—to describe the dull awfulness of small-town life or capture the magical period just before childhood becomes adolescence. King has some of the interests of a "serious" novelist—how our experiences as children shape us, what we lose and gain in growing up, how the places where we grow up can drive us away yet compel our nostalgia—and he indulges them fully in *It.* Unfortunately, this works against him. He doesn't really have the literary strengths necessary for straight novel-writing. And although he does a credible job with Derry—at times it's like Lake Wobegon with dry rot—the more convincing Derry is, the less believable is the creature haunting its sewers. And when we face the creature, the town becomes unconvincing and far away. Rather than blending, the real world and the supernatural one keep elbowing each other out. And the real world—with its racists, homophobes, wife-beaters, and sadistic teenage bullies—is the scarier of the two. The reader begins to welcome the appearance of It, since on the way to menacing the blameless it frequently takes a little side trip to squash one of Derry's human monsters.

This is the pleasure of the book—the vindication of the adolescent heroes and the destruction of their enemies. Like *Carrie, It* is a revenge-of-the-nerds fantasy, but in *It* the nerds (except for two who die—one from cowardice, the other from heroism) not only survive, they triumph. They become fulfilled, prosperous adults, while their persecutors, even before their destruction, are losers. In a sense *It* is King's autobiography, a fictional rendering of his journey from poor and picked-on kid to major American success. What he has learned on the way is the message of *It:* facing horror can be not only terrible but also liberating; weakness as well as strength has its uses; the strongest adults are those who never quite forsake their childhood selves; and, of curse, he who laughs last laughs best. King's is the happy laughter of a winner, and *It* is, finally, an optimistic novel with a fairy-tale ending of lovers restored to each other. A sweet book, really—but King hasn't let success dull his sense of what his public wants. He still manages to serve up a Chinese meal in which the fortune cookies contain not fortunes but . . . *something gross!!!* Let the reader beware. (p. 103)

Lloyd Rose, "The Triumph of the Nerds," in The Atlantic Monthly, *Vol. 258, No. 3, September, 1986, pp. 102-03.*

THOMAS R. EDWARDS

Stephen King's books contain much that is childish, even infantile, but that alone is no scandal. We have all been children, and we hold the hidden signs of that ordeal—even a serious interest in art begins in childish make-believe. King seems to have no other subject than the ways by which childhood conceives of itself, and his resolute loyalty to that subject seems finally a little sad. It is also rewarding: at thirty-nine he is said to have sold fifty million copies of his twenty books. Yet his work avoids a cynical or exploitative note. I would judge that he believes in what he does, that he writes not just to make money but to exorcise demons, his and ours.

It begins, demonically enough, in 1957, when a six-year-old boy has his arm torn off by what appears to be a circus clown lurking down a storm drain. This happens in Derry, Maine, where similarly dreadful things have been recorded, at intervals of about twenty-seven years, since 1741, when the entire settlement, some three hundred Yankee souls, simply vanished. . . .

King organizes the tale as two parallel stories, one tracing the activities of seven unprepossessing fifth-graders ("The Losers' Club") who discovered and fought the horror in 1958, the other describing their return to Derry in 1985 when the cycle resumes. In their youth the Losers were a sorry crew, but time has consoled them. Their leader, "Stuttering Bill" Denbrough, has become a famous horror novelist and married a movie star. Ben Hanscomb, the lonely fat kid who played with his erector set and hung out at the public library, is now trim and handsome, and also (according to *Time*) "perhaps the most promising young architect in America." Richie Tozier, the wise-cracking rock-and-roll nut who wore glasses and got good grades, is a big-time disc jockey in Los Angeles. Beverly Marsh, the tomboy from the wrong side of the tracks, is a sexy Chicago fashion designer. Eddie Kasprak, the asthmatic mama's boy who survived on vitamin pills and nasal sprays, now owns a limo company in Manhattan. Stanley Uris, the class Jew, runs his own accounting firm in Atlanta. Only Mike Hanlon stayed in Derry, to work as a librarian. Mike is black, King tells us rather late in the novel, and so most of the precincts of childhood "otherness" eventually report in.

As children they all had in common unpopularity, various special talents (Ben could build things, Eddie had an uncanny sense of direction, etc.), a fascination with horror movies and fantasy fiction, and a fatal allure as victims for a vicious set of schoolyard bullies. . . .

For readers of earlier fantasists like H. P. Lovecraft, J. R. R. Tolkien, or E. Nesbit (King's tale seems a kind of ghastly commentary on Nesbit's cheerful *Five Children and It*), the story thus far is unsurprising. An evil something from beyond the stars has been haunting Derry since long before its European settlement, indeed since before the Ice Age. "It" now inhabits the town's sewer system, emerging from hibernation every twenty-seven years in various guises—as Mr. Bob Gray, aka Pennyworth the Dancing Clown, as a syphilitic hobo who lurks in the cellar of an abandoned house and offers fellatio to passing schoolboys, or as the Creature from the Black Lagoon, Rodan, or whatever other popular monstrosity It's victims are most deeply scared by. It feeds on "the chemicals of fear," and having acquired unrecognized power over most of Derry, It aspires to a larger dominion over (gulp!) the whole world. Only brave and imaginative children, or adults who learn to remember and honor their childish selves, can hope to foil It, as the Losers finally do in 1985.

But if the story of *It* is negligible, what sells all those books? King is not simply pandering to a mass audience that's too stupid to see the absurdity of his stories. His novels are usually long and organized with some complexity, plainly but not badly written, and you need to know more than comic books and movies to enjoy them. In fact it helps to have read some

serious literature: the sections of *It* carry epigraphs taken not only from old rock-and-roll lyrics but from W. C. Williams, George Seferis, Virgil (in Latin), Emily Dickinson, Karl Shapiro, and Dickens.

King tries to conflate cultural material that teachers, critics, and other squares urge young people to keep distinct; his is the sort of brash mixing of high and low that *Mad* magazine was doing heavy-handedly before writers like Pynchon, Barthelme, and Coover did it much more elegantly. King is closer to *Mad* than to Pynchon, to be sure, but he has his moments. I'm amused and touched when in *It* Mike Hanlon sees his face in the mirror as being that of "a bank teller in a Western movie, the fellow who never has any lines, the one who just gets to put his hands up and look scared when the robbers come in." (That the teller's face was always white and Mike's is black adds a complexity that King doesn't spell out.) If not exactly amused, I'm startled when, at the moment the Losers finally destroy It down in the sewers, the toilets of Derry suddenly explode, killing among others an unfortunate woman "who was sitting on the john at the time and reading the current Banana Republic catalogue." And I like the remark about Hanlon's diary of the horrors by an anonymous commentator who knows King's methods: "One supposes the thought of popular publication had done more than cross Mr. Hanlon's mind."

King has a nice eye for the weaknesses of the commercial culture (including horror fiction itself) that is his primary connection with most of his audience, and his dislikes, which are not necessarily those of all his readers, do him credit: racism, homophobia, anti-Semitism, child abuse, *machismo,* social snobbery, and Middle American narrowness in general. But for him such present evils are only aspects of a larger and older one, for which It is the mighty metaphor. . . . (p. 58)

No time is a good time to grow up in, but King's people have had to live with an unusually nasty world, what with Vietnam, pollution, drugs, social and sexual revolutions, apartheid, mass murders, and terrorism, yuppies and AIDS and the moral majority. "It" is not just a large, pregnant, spiderlike monster swimming in our waste products ("They all had, after all, seen spiders before," King remarks); It is a mindless wasting of human substance and possibility which we know about without reading Stephen King.

King's message is welcome, and its gothic wrappings can easily be discarded. But in *It* and King's other books there's something that makes one uneasy, less a message than an unresolved anxiety. At one point Richie Dozier the disc jockey reflects about the power of rock and roll to make "all the skinny kids, fat kids, ugly kids, shy kids—the world's losers, in short" feel "bigger, stronger, more *there.*" No doubt it does, and King, whose love of rock is open and endearing, clearly hopes that his books have similar power. But so do uglier things like heroin and crack, or beating up smaller or weaker losers. What kind of power are we talking about, and what does it want to do? What *can* it do?

For King, the adult world is It, the devourer of imagination and of life itself. The parents of the Losers are similar: Eddie's father died before the story begins, Ben's is mysteriously absent, Bill's is remote and indifferent, Beverly's is a blue-collar tyrant with incest on his mind; the other three fathers are fair to good, but two of them die of cancer before the story ends; the mothers, if generally more available, are smothering or ineffectual. The Losers themselves have no children, nominally because It wants no new generation of such enemies, but effectively, perhaps, because King needs them to remain young enough at heart to destroy It once and for all—it's hard to be a child and a parent at the same time. For the book's *bad* children, the dull-witted bullies who do some of It's work and for whom family life is much harder and sadder than it is for the Losers, King strangely expresses no sympathy at all. When the worst of them actually murders his truly monstrous father, I sense a pattern that King either isn't clearly aware of or chooses not to acknowledge. This might have private meaning—King's own father left home when his son was two, and was not heard from again, but whatever the case, the "imagination" that King would have his readers preserve from the virus of adulthood contains grim images of hostility and aggression between the generations.

It makes some sense to say, as King does, that art and life were Stephen King novels before he ever wrote one. Places like Derry—and all towns are a little like Derry—have had their Jew-baiters and gay-bashers and child-molesters all along. It's all very well to say that the Bible is horror fiction, that Idi Amin and Jim Jones prove that monsters are real and come cheap, that one of childhood's great truths is that *"Grownups are the real monsters."* But having said this, what then? Some part of everyone grows up, learns a more complex idea of justice and obligation than children have, and suffers for having learned it. When Bill Denbrough, at age ten, sees that by persuading his comrades to believe in and oppose It he is risking their lives to serve himself, he despises himself: *"Oh Christ,* he groaned to himself, *if this is the stuff adults have to think about I never want to grow up."* But the joke's on him—he will grow up all right, to think and write about this stuff, just like Stephen King, and along with the philosophic mind, the years will bring him a cure for his stuttering, a beautiful and loving wife, and $800,000 a year.

It is King's immortality ode. To his young enthusiasts he keeps saying, rather loudly, Don't ever change!, even while he whispers to those who already have changed, The best is yet to be. At the end Bill Denbrough drowsily thinks: *"It is good to be a child, but it is also good to be grownup and able to consider the mystery of childhood."* It's not such wisdom that makes *It,* or earlier and better books of King's like *Carrie, Salem's Lot,* and *The Shining,* so unexpectedly (if only intermittently) interesting. King's sober truths are striking only when they are entangled in the popular paraphernalia which he can so deftly and affectionately manipulate. (p. 59)

Thomas R. Edwards, "Gulp!" in The New York Review of Books, *Vol. XXXIII, No. 20, December 18, 1986, pp. 58-60.*

GEORGE STADE

It's no use condescending to writers of popular fiction, spitting into the wind. The stuff is irresistible, if you're all there. The person to whom none of the popular genres appeal has got a hole in the head, right where his fantasy life should be. Surely characters like Dracula, Sherlock Holmes, Tarzan, Rebecca and Sam Spade, or their derivatives, occupy as much space in our collective imaginations as do Achilles, the Wife of Bath, Hamlet or Mrs. Dalloway. What is more, a really good entertainment, one that realizes the potentials of its genre, a novel such as *The Exorcist, The Godfather* or *Red Dragon,* is harder to come by than the kind of novel that wins the yearly book awards. Writers like Ross Macdonald and

Daphne Du Maurier are scarcer than writers like John Hawkes and Susan Sontag, and arguably more valuable. Popular fiction is read not just by people who never read anything else but also by people who read or write or talk about books for a living. (p. 258)

The genre most condescended to is the chiller. People read horror fiction as they used to read pornography, on the sly. Reviewers with intellectual pretensions titter in print. Academic critics distance themselves with donnish humor or ponderous scholarship. The prevailing tone of the scant discourse about horror fiction is an amused derision that cuts both ways—at the chiller, for being what it is, at the discourser, for his interest in it. And yet there is now a body of decent critical writing, free of embarrassed self-consciousness, about Westerns, romances, whodunits, thrillers, science fiction and adventure. Recent critics, some of them very highbrow, have worked at tidying up overlapping concepts like the grotesque, the uncanny and the fantastic. But what we mean when we use the word "horror" remains unclear.

One explanation may lie in certain oddities about the emotion of horror, if an emotion is what it is. Horror, to cite one oddity, is typically a response to something that is not there. Typically, that is, it attends such things as nightmares, phobias, art and literature, hallucinations, delusions. It also attends apparitions of the supernatural, of course, but for me the whole realm of the supernatural is a delusion, alas—although the horror is real. Horror can be distinguished from terror, which is sudden fright in the presence of a material cause, a charging lion, say. Material threats can be dissipated by material cures, a well-placed shot from a .450 Nitro Express, say. But horror is sudden dread in the presence of an immaterial cause. The frights of nightmares, daymares and nightmarish literature cannot be dissipated by a bullet, unless the bullet is silver, unless it is invested with magical, that is, delusory, properties.

Phobias at first glance seem to have material causes. But if you have a phobia of earmuffs or peaches, of toadstools or dripping faucets, of dirt on your hands or red-haired men, it is because they remind you of what horrifies you, and not because of what materially they are. Situations that should theoretically produce terror, like premature burial or shrinking rooms, can turn horrifying if you invest them with psychological meaning, as Poe did.

There are indeed times when a sinister conspiracy of coincidences seems to echo or expose our thoughts, or worse, seems produced by them—when, that is, the effect of horror is caused by something actually there. I gather from the accounts of those who have recovered, or from the recorded speech of those who have not, that paranoid schizophrenia is a condition of sustained horror. The whole world becomes your phobia, as though you were a character in a story by Kafka, as though you were Leopold Bloom in the "Circe" episode of *Ulysses.* Madness, in spite of those who champion it as the higher sanity, is almost always horrifying, in literature and in life, to the victim and to the witness.

A second oddity of horror, as distinct from terror or disgust, is that what evokes it is frequently as attractive as it is repulsive; there is as much fascination as dread. The apparitions of horror are attractive because they represent wishes; they are dreadful because the wishes are taboo. In that respect the vampire baring his teeth for a kiss is exemplary. (p. 259)

What horror does for us is a question worth trying to answer.

We can make the plausible assumption that our emotions were once good for something, that they helped us survive. My guess is that horror evolved as the emotional concomitant to the breaking of a taboo. The emotion of horror, then, would be a signal that we are indulging actually or imaginatively in something we have forbidden ourselves, usually for the sake of the group. The bodily weakness, loss of focus, sense of suffocation and inability to move prevent us from indulging ourselves further.

Thinking big, we can suggest a social function for horror fiction. On the one hand, it stimulates imaginative indulgence in activities we forbid ourselves in the flesh. To that extent the chiller is morally subversive. On the other hand, the indulgence is depicted as monstrous, and the monsters who do all the indulging are finally defanged by the good guy or nice girl or sacrificial hero. To that extent the chiller is ethically conservative. Other things being equal, the composer of chillers who performs his social function best will be one whose conscious values coincide with those of his group, whose phobias are also taboos—with the understanding that where there are taboos, there is an itch to violate them. The violation arouses a compulsion to restore them.

On the evidence, Stephen King is the writer of chillers who at the moment performs his social function best, the prodigy of a flourishing school. According to one critic, the current boom in horror fiction, now of twenty years' duration, is an aftershock of the baby boom immediately following World War II. "Family horror fiction is a collective autobiography of a generation's psyche," says Ann Douglas in a study of 117 representative chillers written between 1963 and 1983. The chillers of Stephen King, born in 1947, are full of reminders that his generation was born with the bomb, took in strontium 90 with its milk. It was toilet trained during the most puritanical period of twentieth-century America. It began to look around when for the last time movies and comic books were plentiful and cheap, when pre-Beatles rock was on the verge of transforming popular music entirely (very different values are implied by a preference for Elvis and Little Richard over Bing Crosby and Perry Como). It went to school when middle-class parents became hysterical about teen-age rebels without a cause, when working-class "hoods" flashed switchblades in schoolyards, when everybody had or wanted a car, and not just to get out of the suburbias and small towns that had become spooky with fading self-confidence. The collective psyche of Stephen King's generation came of age when American politics turned psychopathic, or at least paranoid, when a sexual revolution overturned the life-denying decencies of the 1950s. The venerable prejudices that governed relations between men and women, husbands and wives, parents and children, were all shook up, while the literate middle class stroked itself with a reverse racism that turned every Afro-American into the unlikely combination of sexual savior and saint (saintly black saviors feature prominently in three of King's novels). All the while, the divorce rate rose. Families in the chillers of King's generation tend to be unhappy in the same way: fathers absent or brutal, mothers desperate or smothering, the children dreadful. The horrors in King's fiction are transmogrifications of one or another of these episodes in the collective biography of his generation.

It, for instance, is a transmogrification of all of them at once. The 1,138 pages of *It* comprise an encyclopedia or anatomy of horror, King's summing up, his valedictory performance in the genre, according to what he told one interviewer. The stuff of his earlier novels is all there: a local apocalypse, a chosen remnant, sexual shudders, paranoid politics, a black saint, schoolyard bullies, inadequate parents, haunted children. Through allusions on every page, we get something like an inventory of the pop cult clutter of 1958, when most of the novel is set, when King's seven protagonists are 11 years old, a baby-boom Our Gang. Their shape-shifting antagonist, It itself, appears variously as a possessing alien from outer space, a clown, a demonic child, the Frankenstein monster, a werewolf, a mummy, a gigantic spider, a crawling eye and a big bird that looks suspiciously like Rodan the Flying Monster.

This polytropic Thing arrives on earth before the age of mammals, a refugee from some spaceless, timeless otherwhere. It carries with it into the present the stench of Paleozoic slime, which oozes from the pores of Derry, Maine, the small city that grew over the site of its landing as toadstools might sprout on a grave. It collects in the sewer system, from which it wells up every twenty-seven years or so to raise hell. (p. 260)

King's Thing, then, is primitive, an ingredient of the evolutionary soup that still simmers in our veins. It is sex, thinks one character, "some unrealized undefined monster . . . full of the unknown's eternal power." The It is *das Es.* But It is also the spirit of American Gothic, the evil that in a half dozen of King's novels pervades isolated New England communities such as the one he grew up in. It is also each man's particular devil, for It appears to each man in the shape of his most abject fears and longings. Above all, It is the biggest of those many bullies who occupy disproportionate verbal space throughout King's fiction.

The schoolyard bullies of *It* drive King's prepubescent monster-mashers into one another's arms, as though some providence were scheming to derive good from bad. The bullies, who have names like Belch Huggens and Boogers Taliendo, are loutish, dumb, racist, sexist, cowardly, working class and unbelievable. Their victims are sensitive and intelligent misfits, outsiders, nerds, the makings of a Losers Club, which is what they come to call themselves. . . . In 1958, by virtue of some semimystic bond of innocent love that holds the Losers together, they defeat It and its bully boys. . . . [In 1985, possessing only] the diminished imaginative resources of adults, the Losers must again face up to the It within them and the It without, and they must evade a cadre of bullies, some new, some the old ones resurrected by It.

In rapid succession the events of 1958 and 1985 alternate until the two climactic battles occur almost simultaneously on the page. All that is skillfully managed. But although there are effective episodes, as when a respectable Swedish lady turns into a ghoul shouting obscenities, the horror in the novel as a whole does not come off. The novel is not scary. It does not arouse the frightful longings that constitute horror—the uncanny recognitions, the sinister allure. One reason is that literary monsters, those werewolves and vampires and lurching humanoids, are not scary in themselves; they are made horrific by the contexts that charge them with meaning. The Frankenstein monster, for example, depends for its effect upon the corpses of which it is constituted, upon the idealistic and fanatical doctor who constructs it, upon its murderous innocence, upon its violations of nature and domesticity, upon its source in the Prometheanism of science, which has exposed our collective gizzards to vultures. Similarly, the werewolf only gets to us when we are made to sympathize with the decent guy who wears this dog beneath his skin, when there is a logic to his predations, when the werewolf's victims are objects of the decent guy's repressed lust and rage. Again, the monsters of postwar Japanese films, like Rodan, depend for their effect upon the encompassing allegory of a nuclear cataclysm in part feared, in part desired, and worst of all, just possibly deserved. But in *It*, King's many monsters scrape each other clean of the contexts that once made them scary; what's left is camp and nostalgia. Further, too many hairsbreadth escapes too close together, so much blood, mud, slime, sewage, vomit, urine, feces and oozing flesh soon become funny. The spendthrift elaboration and gargantuan iteration are more appropriate to the genius of comedy than to the spirit of horror, which is anal and claustrophiliac.

Finally, bullies are not horrifying unless you see around them, unless you see in them what you deny in yourself. In real life, nerds have mixed feelings about bullies. They feel about them as Isaac Babel felt about Cossacks: yes, they are loutish and dangerous, but they also have an enviable prowess, freedom, rebelliousness, style and erotic allure. In King's other parables about the relations between bullies and nerds, in *Carrie* (1974) and *Christine* (1983), for example, the nerds are the source of the horror, as they should be. Behind every nerd is a Victor Frankenstein. But *It* too often reads like the endlessly elaborated fantasy of a neurasthenic child: My parents are unsatisfactory and bullies are mean to me, but someday I'll show them, just you wait. The scariest thing about King's bullies is the savagery with which he exacts revenge on them on behalf of his male and female leads. Unless there is love mixed in with the loathing, there is no horror. (pp. 260-62)

> *George Stade, "The Big Chiller," in* The Nation, *New York, Vol. 244, No. 8, February 28, 1987, pp. 258-62.*

JOHN KATZENBACH

[*Misery*] is the midyear offering from the prolific bard of Bangor . . . and, as such, *Misery* will undoubtedly perform as other Stephen King novels have—cresting to the top of the best-seller lists, splashing heavily with the Book-of-the-Month Club, weighing down the corners of thousands of beach blankets this summer.

All of which, in an odd way, is unfortunate. Success has a way of diminishing value and obscuring actual worth. The numbers attached to a book (one million copies first printing, $400,000 promotional budget) gain more attention than the words the book contains. It is easy to lose sight of the realization that *Misery* is a novel that would probably demand considerable interest even were it not from the writing phenomenon that is Stephen King.

Mr. King has been justifiably acclaimed as a modern master of the horror story; he fills his work with demons, ghosts, vampires, beasts and seemingly ordinary folk who control extraordinary powers. His books stem from the traditions of Poe, Lovecraft, perhaps a bit of Ambrose Bierce. *Misery*, however, seems to belong to a different genre. To begin with, it contains only two characters: Paul Sheldon, a best-selling author, and Annie Wilkes, a psychotic, utterly deranged former nurse. The story takes place within the limited confines

of a single house—indeed, almost exclusively in one room—in a rural part of the Colorado mountains.

The protagonist, Sheldon, has just completed what he considers a "literary" novel—far different from the 19th-century historical potboilers that have made him an immense commercial success. Those books have featured a plucky, beautiful, indomitable young woman named Misery. In the last of the series, Sheldon, to his great delight, finally killed her off.

Or wanted to.

In drunken celebration of his new, contemporary book, he runs his car off a road in the midst of a snowstorm. He awakens, legs mangled, rescued—a word one uses gingerly—from death by the insane nurse. She is, by coincidence, a devoted fan. So devoted that she will not countenance Misery's literary demise, and through drugs and torture she forces the hapless Sheldon to write a resurrection of Misery. A private edition, Sheldon thinks. With a first and only printing of exactly one.

The standard King fan will warm up to the gruesome nature of this relationship. Blood flies. The nurse has an unfortunately gory habit of lopping off important (but not essential) appendages belonging to her captive. Can the hero-writer survive? Will he escape? Will he turn on his tormentor? This book is built on a single cliff and hangs there throughout its length.

But the novel functions as well on a more sophisticated level. Mr. King evokes the image of Scheherazade. He muses on the literature of possession and the idea that art is an act in which the artist willingly becomes captive. He delves deeply into the psychology of creation, and it is to his credit that much of the tension in the book stems from the devilish dilemma the author-hero discovers: his book based on psychotic demand is actually quite good, by far the best he has written. He is, in a wonderful touch, compelled to finish it—and to save it, as well as himself, from destruction. For all writers who have faced the torture of a blank page, this is a delicious irony: that real torture can solve the problems of writer's block.

Sheldon is well drawn and we see the entire story from his perspective: we willingly go along with him as he searches for a way out of his problems, those of his literary creation and those created by his captor. Nurse Wilkes is seen only through his eyes. She alternates between childish glee and ax-wielding madness. She hasn't much depth but remains a single-dimensional hulking horror throughout the book.

Wilkes is expected to provide the terror that traditional King fans demand. Is she the type of character who frightens us so much that we can't turn off the light until the book is finished, and who then lurks first in shadows, then in subsequent nightmares? I do not know if she is successful on that score.

Ultimately, I think *Misery* is probably far less viscerally frightening than most of Mr. King's offerings. There will be no sweaty palms, no tightened throats while reading this book. That will probably disappoint some fans.

It shouldn't.

Even if *Misery* is less terrifying than his usual work—no demons, no witchcraft, no nether-world horrors—it creates strengths out of its realities. Its excitements are more subtle. And, as such, it is an intriguing work.

> *John Katzenbach, "Sheldon Gets the Ax," in* The

New York Times Book Review, *May 31, 1987, p. 20.*

CHRISTOPHER LEHMANN-HAUPT

In the opening pages of *Misery,* the protagonist wakes up from a coma in excruciating pain and tries to take stock:

> He was Paul Sheldon, who wrote novels of two kinds, good ones and best-sellers. He had been married and divorced twice. He smoked too much (or had before all this, whatever 'all this' was). Something very bad had happened to him but he was still alive.

What had happened, it gradually dawns on Paul, is that he had been out celebrating the completion of a "good" novel, *Fast Cars.* . . . He had gotten high on champagne, gone driving in a Colorado snowstorm, skidded on a mountainside, and flipped his car.

Now he is in bed in a farmhouse somewhere. His legs are smashed and screaming with pain. He is being nursed by a large blank-gazed woman, who feeds him drugs periodically to kill the pain. The woman introduces herself as Annie Wilkes, the No. 1 fan of his Misery series. She found him in his wreck, recognized him and brought him home to her remote farmhouse. She doesn't like *Fast Cars,* the manuscript of which she found in his traveling bag. It's confusing and the language is profane. She's extremely upset about the death of Misery Chastain, the paperback account of which she's just finished reading. She wants Paul to get well and write a book bringing Misery back to life.

In fact she insists on it.

Now this situation might seem to have the makings of a comedy, but in Stephen King's hands, it isn't the least bit funny. With mounting anxiety, Paul realizes that he can't use his legs and that he's hooked on pain-killers, completely cut off from civilization and wholly dependent on this rather peculiar woman, who, to punish him for the language in *Fast Cars,* makes him wash down his pills with the soapy water she's just used to clean his room, and then forces him to burn his only copy of the manuscript.

Bit by bit, he comes to understand that Annie Wilkes is not only peculiar but "dangerously crazy." He will have to write a new Misery book just to save his life. On the other hand, she'll probably kill him as soon as he finishes. So he must write and write, just like Scheherazade.

The portrait Mr. King draws of this madwoman is diabolical. She's exquisitely logical yet altogether unpredictable. No matter how far ahead Paul Sheldon schemes, she's always one jump ahead of him, waiting to inflict more punishment. Indeed the lengths to which she goes to torture Paul will prove too much for some readers, and could be considered gratuitously sadistic if the subject of *Misery* were nothing more than terror and violence.

But unlike much of Mr. King's fiction, this novel is more than just a splendid exercise in horror. Its subject is not merely torture, but the torture of being a writer. Not only must Paul create under pressure a story he doesn't particularly want to tell, but he must also make it plausible, even inspired, for Annie Wilkes is a shrewd connoisseur of storytelling, what one might call the ultimate editor and critic. Under her tute-

lage the experiences of meeting a deadline and being cut take on terrifyingly literal meanings.

On top of the pressure to create, Paul runs into other obstacles. The ancient Royal typewriter Annie has bought for him is missing its "n," so the manuscript has to be gone over by hand. Soon the machine throws its "t" and "e," the two most common letters in the English language. Added to this inconvenience, Paul suffers the usual perverse moods of writerly despair. "The *truth,*" he tells himself when the new Misery book begins to go well,

> was that the increasing dismissal of his work in the critical press as that of a 'popular writer' (which was, as he understood it one step—a small one—above that of a "hack") had hurt him quite badly. It didn't jibe with his self-image as a Serious Writer who was only churning out these . . . romances in order to subsidize his (flourish of trumpets, please!) REAL WORK! Had he hated Misery? Had he really? If so, why had it been so easy to slip back into her world?

In other words, for all her craziness, Annie Wilkes becomes Paul Sheldon's literary muse, and as muses go she probably isn't too much worse than average, her main fault being a tendency to punish more literally than most muses do. In fact, considered as a metaphor, the whole story of *Misery* is really not much more than the struggle to write a novel, from the pain of confinement, to the sense of being drugged, to the anticlimax of completion. . . .

Of course a lot of blood gets spilled in the denouement, but then, in the struggle between a muse and a writer, somebody's going to have to die in the end. Even with all the violence, justified or not, *Misery* is one of Mr. King's best. All things considered, it's a winner.

> *Christopher Lehmann-Haupt, in a review of "Misery," in* The New York Times, *June 8, 1987, p. C17.*

CAROLYN BANKS

In *Danse Macabre,* Stephen King, discussing grist for the writer's mill, talks about a dream that plagues him when he's stressed. It's about a homicidal madwoman inhabiting a house in which he is busily writing. Sooner or later, he says, "the sound of my typewriter will cause her to come after me." When she finally comes it is "like a horrid jack from a child's box, all gray hair and crazed eyes, raving and wielding a meat-ax." Well, there, in a nutshell, is the plot of this, Stephen King's latest, most heavily autobiographical and funniest work [*Misery*]. Here, though, it isn't a matter of causing the madwoman to come after the writer; she's got him from the start. King gleefully acknowledges his debt to earlier versions of this captivity plot: *A Handful of Dust; Whatever Happened to Baby Jane?, The Collector.* (p. 1)

The set-up is that Annie found Paul after he'd crashed his Camaro in a Colorado blizzard. Paul writes historical romances and Annie has read all but his latest. In fact, the garble that Paul has been hearing is Annie Wilkes' declaring herself his number one fan.

Annie doesn't know that Paul despises not only the genre that has won her heart but its devotees as well, the "hundreds of thousands of . . . people across the country—ninety percent of them women—who could barely wait for each new five-hundred-page episode in the turbulent life of the foundling who had risen to marry a peer of the realm." And not only that, but Paul hates his own lead character, Misery Chastain, enough to have circulated among friends an obscene April Fools' Day parody called *Misery's Hobby,* featuring Misery and her husband's favorite Irish setter. Lucky for Paul that Annie Wilkes hasn't stumbled onto a copy of that one!

Because when Annie reads that last official volume of the Misery series and discovers that Paul has killed poor Misery off, she goes from mad to madder. And as the scrapbook she keeps will attest, Annie isn't someone to cross. She's a nurse. She keeps news of former patients in that book: their obituaries.

Annie is as round a character as they come, riddled with believable contradictions. She's cruel, yes, but also, as Paul describes her, "strangely prim." She won't take money from his wallet, for instance, but will hand it to him instead. And her objection to Paul's new manuscript—the one that Paul thinks of as a real novel, book award material, the one that's going to free him from the whole historical romance biz—is that "Every other word is that effword!" Annie herself says things like, "You dirty bird." Her favorite adjective is "cockadoodie." Annie proves positive King's dictum (again in *Danse Macabre*) that humor is implicit in horror.

If any of the above might lead you to believe there isn't anything really scary in all of this, you're wrong. Stephen King proves his power, in part with what he himself has called "the gross out factor," but also in more respectable ways, through solid character delineation and terrifying insight. Paul's examples of "radical reader involvement" with fictional characters are superb examples of both. Here, Paul remembers a fan who creates a room for Misery, and who supplies a 10-page letter about the furnishings and 40 Polaroid shots of them. This admirer follows up with five more letters, "(the first four with additional Polaroids) before finally lapsing into puzzled, slightly hurt silence." But Annie is the real downside, the fan beyond whom all others, no matter how wacked out, are benign indeed.

But back to Stephen King. In addition to being able to scare the reader breathless, he is able, in this book, to say a tremendous amount about writing itself, about its "deep and elemental drawing power," its letdowns, its challenges.

In the letdown category, we learn that finishing a book is

> always the same, always the same—like toiling up-hill through jungle and breaking out to a clearing at the top after months of hell only to discover nothing more rewarding than a view of the free-way—with a few gas stations and bowling alleys thrown in for good behavior, or something.

On the challenges—or maybe I should say the triumphs—we have Paul's confession cum boast:

> There's a million things in this world I can't do. Couldn't hit a curve ball, even back in high school. Can't fix a leaky faucet. Can't roller-skate or make an F-chord on the guitar that sounds like anything . . . I have tried twice to be married and couldn't do it either time. But if you want me to take you away, to scare you or involve you or make you cry or grin, yeah. I can. I can bring it to you and keep bringing it until you holler uncle. I am able. I CAN.

Paul also provides a better lesson on plot than the reader is likely to get in any accredited college. The writer of *Misery* so clearly delights—and we do too—in his own virtuosity. Like the writer in *Misery,* he can bring it to you and keep bringing it to you and there isn't a one of us anywhere near to hollering uncle. (pp. 1, 14)

> *Carolyn Banks, in a review of "Misery," in* Book World—The Washington Post, *June 14, 1987, pp. 1, 14.*

KIM NEWMAN

More than any other contemporary horror writer, Stephen King comes across as the sum of his influences. He is as capable of borrowing from Grace Metalious or John Steinbeck as from Bram Stoker or H. P. Lovecraft, and has therefore brought a weird, '50s-Technicolor vitality to a genre too often strangled by gothic cobwebs. He has also, paradoxically, managed to create his own, distinctive, recognisable world out of what are essentially leftovers.

His success has gone a long way towards legitimising, if not plagiarism, then the brand of *hommage* which has long been acceptable in the cinema. If it's all right for Steven Spielberg to borrow from Hitchcock, *Moby Dick* and *The Creature From the Black Lagoon* in filming *Jaws,* then surely it must be equally all right for King to play variations, in *Salem's Lot,* on *Dracula* and *Peyton Place,* or, in *The Stand,* on *Lord of the Rings* and George Stewart's *Earth Abides.* Unfortunately, the side effect of this has been that, in his recent books, King has tended to disappear behind the second-hand conventions he has chosen to live by and turned out an increasingly bloated, predictable and unscary series of novels.

With **Misery,** he is not only back on form, but near the top of it. Along with *Apt Pupil,* another long novella from *Different Seasons,* it is the best thing he has written. Like that earlier work, it foresakes the world of sentient killer cars, pyrokinetic teenagers and zombie cats for a more straightforward world of human psychosis and cruelty. Originally, the author had intended to publish it under his Richard Bachman pseudonym, a secret identity he created to allow him to escape from the pressures of being Stephen King, but with the exposing of the imposture he has allowed it to come out under the King imprimatur.

It's not entirely without its borrowings—John Fowles' *The Collector,* which is gratefully acknowledged in the text, but also Joan Aiken's short story "Marmalade Wine", which isn't—but, as always, it's the use King makes of his plot that counts, not the plot itself. Paul Sheldon, a successful author who makes a fortune with a series of slushy historical romances about a 19th-century foundling called Misery Chastain, but who really wants to write gritty, realistic novels about New York lowlife, is injured in a car crash and comes to in the house of ex-nurse Annie Wilkes. Annie is Paul's number one fan, but also a touch crazy, and she has opted to keep him prisoner on her isolated farm. What follows is a writer's nightmare: upon finishing the latest Misery Chastain novel, in which her creator has succumbed to the lure of the Reichenbach and killed Misery off, Annie is so enraged that she forces Paul—by witholding the painkillers on which he has become dependent—to burn the only copy of his newly-written masterpiece of modern urban angst, *Fast*

Cars, and then provides him with a typewriter and reams of paper so that he can write, just for her, *Misery's Return.*

There are obvious parallels with King's own well-publicised feelings that his chosen genre has been eating him alive, and it is perhaps significant that the novel Sheldon writes for Annie turns out a lot better than he had expected, the desperate circumstances surrounding its creation adding to the book as it comes to life. One of the most pertinent criticisms of King's recent fiction is that he has become too rich and successful to be scared of anything any more and has thus lost his power to communicate fear to the reader: in **Misery** he opens up a whole new area of potent neuroses and complexes that make the novel the most shatteringly horrid he has ever done. Also, in Annie Wilkes, he has created his most monstrous of monsters: Ultimate Evil as Ultimate Banality. (p. 30)

Kim Newman, "Body Snatcher," in New Statesman, Vol. 114, No. 2947, September 18, 1987, pp. 30-1.

CHRISTOPHER LEHMANN-HAUPT

The hero of Stephen King's latest bloodboiler, **The Tommyknockers,** is, believe it or not, a drunk. He is a poet named Jim Gardener, or Gard, as his only friend, the novelist Roberta (Bobbi) Anderson, calls him.

In the opening chapters of **The Tommyknockers,** he falls off the wagon while on a poetry-reading tour, and, in an episode quite entertaining for its rage and excess, makes a scene at a party that gets him banned from poetry readings for life. Eight days later, he comes to lying on a stone breakwater at Arcadia Beach, N.H., recalling little of the time since the party. He feels so hopeless he decides to jump into the ocean. But then something tells him Bobbi Anderson needs him. So instead of killing himself he hitchhikes to her house in the woods near Haven, Me. There he finds bad enough trouble to drive him right back off the wagon.

By the end of what follows you come to identify closely with drunken Jim Gardener. Partly this is because he is about the only decent man in a crowd of very ugly characters. But mostly it's because if you've read to the end of **The Tommyknockers** it means you've got problems with addiction almost as serious as Jim Gardener's.

I freely confess to being an addict of Stephen King. I got hooked by his good novels—**The Shining, Pet Sematary** and **Misery.** So I keep on reading the ones that are not so good. **Christine, The Talisman** (which he wrote with Peter Straub) and **It.** This latest one is impressively bad. It shamed me into realizing just how far gone I am.

The plot declines pretty steeply after that rollicking faculty-party scene. The trouble that Bobbi Anderson is in is that she's tripped over something made of metal that is sticking out of the ground in the woods near her house, and whatever it is has taken possession of her, reminding her of the nursery rhyme:

> Late last night and the night before,
> Tommyknockers, Tommyknockers,
> Knocking at the door.
> I want to go out, don't you know if I can.
> 'cause I'm so afraid
> of the Tommyknocker man.

Somehow this isn't particularly scary. Nothing about Tommyknockers—which, according to Mr. King's research, are either tunneling ogres or ghosts that hadn't deserted mines or caves—is particularly scary.

Nevertheless, at the climax of an early scene in the novel, Bobbi telepathically communicates the jingle to her friend.

And: "Jim Gardener screamed."

Eek?

From this point on, we are subjected to repetition, implausibility, an illogically switching point of view, manipulative narrative leaps forward and backward in time, countless teeth dropping out as the citizens of Haven begin to "become" whatever has seized control of them, and a tiresome amount of bleeding and vomiting. A lot of vomiting.

What the novel finally boils down to is mostly green slime. It is about as real and horrifying as that glop for children celebrated in Saturday morning television ads for being yukky. If they make a movie out of it they're going to use up all the plastic.

And yet like Gard in his cups, one keeps going back for more. It's hard to resist the sheer energy of the storytelling. When Mr. King backs up to fill you in on a development, he not only disappears over the horizon, he also circles the globe and returns with every gruesome oddity under the sun. The tasks that he undertakes, like showing the effect of Bobbi's discovery on an entire town, might exhaust many writers. But Mr. King succeeds in dreaming up nearly endless variations of the horror and in making his town fairly teem with his grotesques. It doesn't hurt that he knows Maine life and that he can sketch its types with malicious humor.

One keeps trying to swear off the stuff. After all, as Mr. King himself points out through the mouth of one character in **The Tommyknockers** his friend and sometime collaborator Peter Straub undertook more or less the same fictional exercise in his horror novel *Floating Dragon,* about a cloud of poison gas that gets loose and drives an entire town nuts. But darn it, when Mr. King attempts even a tired stunt, he does it so much better than the other fellows do.

So I guess what **The Tommyknockers** proves is that Stephen King can do anything he wants to. We already knew he could grip us with good horror stories and so-so horror stories. Now he has shown that he can grip us with a lousy horror story as well.

Anybody who can make me read a book called **The Tommyknockers** has to be some kind of genius.

Christopher Lehmann-Haupt, in a review of "The Tommyknockers," in The New York Times, November 5, 1987, p. C33.

DAVID NICHOLSON

[Early in **The Tommyknockers**], a writer of pulp westerns modifies her battered Underwood manual typewriter (under the guidance of an alien presence from space) with four D-cell batteries and a radio circuit board so that she can simply *think* the words onto the paper. Relieved of the tedium of typing, she writes a 400-page novel in three days, much of it while she sleeps. Given the number of his novels and the regularity with which he publishes them, one wonders whether

Stephen King might not also have a "thought writer" at his disposal.

Readers of *The Tommyknockers* only get to read the first four paragraphs of *The Buffalo Soldiers,* the novel by Roberta "Bobbi" Anderson, the hapless writer who discovers an alien spaceship in the woods near her Maine farmhouse. But four paragraphs is enough, for *The Buffalo Soldiers* just isn't very good. In that regard, it's got a lot in common with *The Tommyknockers,* which isn't very good either. It might have been; somewhere inside this bloated, self-indulgent hulk of a novel is a taut thriller, tribute perhaps to low-budget science fiction movies of the 1950s and '60s like *Invasion of the Body Snatchers.* The pity is that King never lets that taut thriller get out.

The Tommyknockers starts out promisingly enough with Bobbi Anderson literally stumbling over an exposed edge of the buried spaceship. Something about the ship draws her to it, and Bobbi becomes obsessed with digging it up. As more of the ship's hull is exposed, and it oxidizes, the airborne molecules begin to have a peculiar effect on Bobbi and the people of Haven, the nearest small town.

Meanwhile, Bobbi's friend and former lover, an alcoholic poet and sometime anti-nuclear activist is in the midst of a binge that gets him thrown off the New England Poetry Caravan tour. A few mornings after, Gardener wakes up feeling that Bobbi's in trouble and needs him. Heeding his intuition, Gardener makes his way to Haven. . . .

The people of nearby Haven, changing as Bobbi is changing, all seem to be inventing things too—the village postmistress devises a machine that sorts letters, even misaddressed ones; the postman's wife rewires the television to electrocute her husband (who's been having an affair with the postmistress); and a 10-year-old boy intent on learning how to perform magic tricks makes his little brother disappear. Permanently.

Under the influence of the ship and whatever it carries, Bobbi and the people of Haven are all becoming Tommyknockers, as Gard decides to call them. He himself is not completely immune to the ship, though a metal plate implanted in his head after a skiing accident spares him most of the effects. And though Gard is horrified at what is happening to Bobbi—she's losing her teeth and undergoing other physical changes best not discussed in a family newspaper—he agrees to help her dig up the ship.

Just why Gard decides to stick around and help isn't quite clear—it has something to do with his love for Bobbi and with his half-formed conviction that there might be something in the ship that could be used for the good of humanity—and that points to some of the problems with *The Tommyknockers.*

Gard's motivations, and those of many of the other characters, are unclear. Moreover, the novel seems without a center. Bobbi is on stage for the first 50 pages, then Gard for twice that, then the people of Haven in a series of momentum-derailing portraits. It's as if King couldn't decide whose story it was, and the result is a series of disjointed vignettes involving cardboard characters. These episodes are occasionally entertaining, but more often filled with flatulence, feces and menses (as well as more traditional blood and gore) and pointlessly horrific.

Perhaps more than other kinds of fiction, fantasy, horror and science fiction demand the reader's willing suspension of belief. Not only are the things that happen improbable, they are, after all, things we would not *admit* wanting to happen. The onus is on the writer, then, not merely to create an irresistible inevitability in his plot, but to furnish a plausible world and plausible characters with whom the reader can identify, no matter how implausible the things that happen to them there.

For the most part, King's work—whatever its lack of subtlety—has always been possessed of energy and power. In his last book, *Misery* (a trim middleweight compared to this obese opus), a writer is kidnapped by one of his fans and forced to revive the killed-off heroine of the romance series that made him famous. (p. 9)

King pulls out all the stops—besides the alcoholic everyman doing his best in an extreme situation, there are the kindly grandfather, the lost little boy, and the tough, but honest, cop. None ever really comes alive on the page. And despite his use of the honorable tricks of the trade—weaving together three or more stories and interrupting a section of the narrative just before the climactic moment—the book lacks intensity. Instead of being swept up in the flow of events and carried by the rush of the narrative, the reader plods on, occasionally excited, more often disappointed, continuing in the hope that *The Tommyknockers* will hit its stride and turn out to be the kind of story he's learned to expect from King after all.

It never does. Worse, it presents evidence that King has begun to take himself seriously in the worst way. It's not just that the novel could have used a firm editor to trim a third of its bulk, but King's attempted to create a kind of bargain basement Yoknapatawpha County. There are references to other of his novels—*The Dead Zone* and to the movie version of *The Shining;* the clown who was It in *It* makes an appearance, as does a character from *The Dead Zone.* And King refers to himself as "that fellow who lived up in Bangor" who wrote novels "all full of make-believe monsters and a bunch of dirty words."

That fellow's still writing them, but more and more they don't seem quite as good as they used to. (pp. 9-10)

> David Nicholson, "Stephen King and Strange Happenings in Haven, Maine," in Book World—The Washington Post, *November 29, 1987, pp. 9-10.*

AREND FLICK

[In *The Tommyknockers*], a 37-year-old writer of Westerns named Robert Anderson stumbles on a piece of metal protruding from the ground. It's not a discarded bean can, she soon discovers. For one thing, she's unable to wiggle it out of the soil; for another, it vibrates faintly to the touch. Unable to let well enough alone, Bobbi returns with digging equipment and starts an excavation that reveals the curved shell of an enormous space ship crashed to Earth millions of years ago.

Since this is a King novel, we hold out little hope that this communion with space visitors will lead to anything as pleasant as flying our bikes with them against the full moon. And we're right. By the time Bobbi's closest friend (and occasional lover) Jim Gardener looks in on her three weeks later—called to her by a telepathy King loves to use when friends are in trouble—Bobbi has lost 30 pounds and is nearly catatonic. . . . Horrified, fascinated, Jim joins Bobbi in her effort to unearth the saucer's hatch and gain entrance.

Maybe we sometimes look too hard for allegory in science fiction novels and movies as a way of justifying our liking them. And sometimes when allegory is clearly intended, the freighter isn't substantial enough to bear the cargo. But you don't need the critical equivalent of a backhoe to uncover the moral of *The Tommyknockers.* It's a blatant parable of technology run amok, an expression of King's mistrust of man's capacity to control machines to serve his nobler purposes.

King scorns one machine in particular here: the nuclear reactor. The Tommyknockers' ship becomes a metaphor for nuclear fuel; it's superficially a "dream of endless power," actually a demon of mass destruction. And the "becoming" itself results from the presence of "an alien and inimical atmosphere" around Haven—Gardener thinks "becoming" resembles getting "caught in a great big messy Atomic meltdown." King also wants us to draw parallels between the loss of individuality that is "becoming" and the collective lie that is "safe" nuclear power.

I don't want to make *The Tommyknockers* sound dourer or more pretentious than it is. It's got politics in its hold and strapped all over its deck, but the ship still floats. Partly this is due, I think, to King's humor. Like Vonnegut, he seems to find our faith in machines less an evil to be feared than an idiocy to be laughed at. The novel's jokes often misfire, but the wacky colloquialisms (for which King has been criticized) usually made me laugh—as when a villager at the dig site is compared to "a rube Druid (on) his first trip from the boonies to see Stonehenge." There's also a great comic homage to *Dr. Strangelove* near the novel's end involving one of 20th-Century America's most ubiquitous technological icons.

King's fans will find familiar pleasures as well. The moments of intense horror are rarer here than earlier, but perhaps all the more effective for that. (Ruth's death in the tower is preceded by a gross-out encounter with bats that is vintage King, and something dreadful happens to Bobbi's basset hound.) The novel also effectively evokes the banality of small-town American life in ways that remind me of Flannery O'Connor.

Why has King been so popular? There probably isn't a single answer to this question, any more than there is a single explanation for why everybody got Rubik's Cubes as gifts in 1981. The appeal of horror in an age like ours is pretty obvious. But what seems to me to set King apart from some of his lesser colleagues is his credible exploration of *power* in his fiction— as something most of us don't have, secretly want, but could probably not use wisely if we were ever to get it.

Writing of Lee Harvey Oswald, King once expressed his fascination that "one nerd with a mail order gun was able to change the entire course of world history in just 14 seconds or so." In a sense, all King's protagonists tend to be latter-day Oswalds in their initial powerlessness. (Jim Gardener is a mediocre poet with a drinking problem before he gets the opportunity to save the world.) King's morality—and popularity— lies in the fact that his heroes often find better things to do with their sudden power than wipe chicken grease from their hands and take aim on a passing limousine. (pp. 1, 12)

Arend Flick, "Stephen King as Nerd's Best Friend," in Los Angeles Times Book Review, *December 20, 1987, pp. 1, 12.*

NINA AUERBACH

It doesn't matter that in [*The Tommyknockers*] a flying saucer—not vampires, telekinesis, Wendigos or a demonic clown in the drains—invades Stephen King Country; nor does it matter that this small Maine town is called Haven instead of Jerusalem's Lot or Derry. The science fiction trappings only add a new décor to the nightmare Stephen King tells over and over: something terrible comes Down Home and draws all its inhabitants, whether we like them or not, into its power. The story is frightening each time because the likable characters are so appealing they seem incorruptible. But then. . . .

The Tommyknockers live in a giant spaceship buried for eons in the backyard of self-sufficient Bobbi Anderson, who writes westerns. Bobbi feels compelled to dig it out; her dog becomes strangely revitalized; she digs some more; she turns into a mechanical genius. Then her former lover Jim Gardener, known as Gard, turns up. He is an alcoholic poet crazed by visions of nuclear disaster and thinks the ship might contain an alternate power source that will save the world. . . .

The first third of *The Tommyknockers* is wonderful. With his usual eerie effortlessness, Mr. King attaches us to Bobbi and Gard, taunting us with menace neither they nor we can define. When evil starts gobbling Haven with a vengeance, swollen prose and comic-book grue spurt out one authentic gem (a little boy's magic show) and instill in us a creeping terror of good country folks. The last third of the novel is Armageddon, as is usual with Mr. King.

In his early novels, Stephen King certified his authenticity by dropping brand names, but now instead of Flair pens and Marvel Straight cigarettes he pours out torrents of literary allusion. H. G. Wells, Stephen Jay Gould, James Dickey, Doris Lessing, Mother Goose, Stephen King himself (shamelessly), Herman Melville and The Who are only some of the people woven into this fat book. (Toward the end, Gard mutters: "It's hard to spend such a long time thinking you're . . . Homer. . . . and discover you were . . . Captain Ahab all the time.")

It's hard to take such epigrams seriously; it's virtually impossible to take seriously the cumbersome machinery whereby the Tommyknockers do or don't do their murkily defined mission. But Mr. King's presumption that we are afraid of everything makes him a great and terrible storyteller—even when he is saying "EEEEOOOOOOARRRHMMMMM-MM!" or *"Hurts! It hurrrrr—."* Whether he is making these noises or quoting *Moby-Dick,* we believe him.

Nina Auerbach, "Not with a Bang but an EEEOOO-OARRRHMM!" in The New York Times Book Review, *December 20, 1987, p. 8.*

MICHAEL R. COLLINGS

Reading *IT,* one becomes more aware of how completely the novel functions as a compendium of horror, a self-reflexive work that looks back not only to literary traditions but to film, folklore, and to King's own novels and stories.

On one level, *IT* is intensely autobiographical. Certainly the fact that King was eleven in 1958 (as are most of his characters) explains much of the power of the novel—and much of its historical fascination for me, since I was also eleven in 1958. One of the central characters, Bill Denbrough, is a successful writer of horror novels, several of which have been turned into films; his early experiences with creative writing in college sound as if they might parallel King's own. . . . The passages describing Denbrough's struggles do not, of course, project King's own experiences exactly; instead, they suggest and tantalize, while carrying a distinctive ring of authenticity that deepens Denbrough's character and prepare him for the test to come.

In fact, connections between King, his world, and his novel are at times so close that one of the minor characters who suffers a dramatic death by dismemberment, Eddie King, not only carries a variant on King's name (Stephen *Ed*win King) but is described as a bearded man wearing glasses almost as thick as his stomach. Several episodes reflect actual occurrences in Bangor; [according to King], the murder of a homosexual in "After the Festival" is "almost literally true . . . the names have been changed to protect the innocent (not to mention the guilty. . . .), but what happened in Derry happened in Bangor two summers ago." (pp. 13-14)

More intriguingly, however, *IT* incorporates references to many of King's major fictions, particularly in the central characters. Stan Uris lives in Atlanta, close enough to the locale of *Firestarter* to be suggestive. Richie lives as an adult in California and is part of the "in" culture of rock 'n roll, just as was Larry Underwood in *The Stand* ("Stan Underwood" appears briefly at the end of the novel). Ben Hanscomb lives near Gatlin and Hemingford Home, Nebraska, familiar as the setting for **"Children of the Corn."** Eddie Kraspback is from New York, also important in *The Stand.* And Bill Denbrough's temporary home in England suggests *The Talisman,* although peripherally—Peter Straub was living in England when he and King first met and discussed collaborating. In an additional layering, *IT* reflects the recurrent evil portrayed in Straub's *Floating Dragon;* some readers have in fact mentioned *Floating Dragon,* **The Talisman,** and *IT* as comprising a triptych of horror. . . .

About a third of the way through *IT,* King moves back in time to 1930 and the burning of a black servicemen's club. To one alert to the reflexive nature of the novel, it comes as no surprise that one hero of the disaster—credited with saving many lives—is a young army cook [who appears in *The Shining* and] who somehow seems to *know* what to do and when to do it . . . named Dick Hallorann. The monstrous black bird that plays a key role in the episode may be a visual parallel to the manta-like black form that erupts from the Presidential Suite of the Overlook Hotel. And it may be particularly significant that only Dick Hallorann sees it. (p. 15)

On a more abstract, thematic level, *IT* continues the exploration of childhood and maturity begun in such stories as *The Body* and **"The Raft"**; of the conflict between childhood and the adult world implicit in such works as *Rage, The Long Walk,* **"Here There Be Tygers,"** and **"Cain Rose Up"**; of the inimical relationships between parent and child at the center of *Carrie, Cujo,* and *Pet Sematary;* and of childhood beliefs in monsters come true, as in *'Salem's Lot* and *Cycle of the Werewolf.*

This last also suggests the wide-ranging experimentation in *IT,* as King introduces virtually every horror monster— literary and filmic—that has found place in our culture. The werewolf appears (*I Was a Teenage Werewolf*), along with the Mummy, the walking dead, Lovecraftian horrors from distant places (*The Colour Out of Space*), a crawling eye (*The Crawling Eye*), and assorted giant birds, piranha, parasites,

etc. Images from the film *Alien* appear, as do a number of the 1950's films King has noted as influential in his development. (p. 16)

Shirley Jackson receives attention in a reference to Hill House; similarly, H. P. Lovecraft provides much of the underlying imagery for It. Indeed, *IT* may be one of King's most Lovecraftian novels. Although the monster also suggests Tolkien's Shelob at critical moments, It also brings to mind Lovecraft's alien species. References to alien, non-Euclidian geometry, to "rugose horrors," and to entities from a larger universe at best disinterested in (at worst inimical to) humanity illustrate King's deep debt to Lovecraft.

IT also continues King's exploration of important themes, especially his reconsideration of the sacrificial child. A number of critics have traced this theme in virtually everything King has written: the child forced to confront the adult world without any support or understanding. Beginning with *Rage,* King has continually pitted the innocent world of the child against the harsh, cynical, hypocritical world of adults . . . usually to the detriment of the child, as in *Carrie, Cujo, The Body, Apt Pupil,* **"The Raft,"** and others.

In *IT,* however, King's fictional children grow up. There is certainly sacrifice aplenty, in 1958, 1985, and the other years in which the cycle of horror crests. Throughout the bloody history of It in Derry, children have been the primary target; It feeds on them, literally as It consumes their flesh and figuratively as It absorbs their fear and terror. But in this novel— really for the first time in a novel-length work from King— the sacrifice succeeds.

In earlier fictions, there was a lingering sense that the death or threatened death of the child was ultimately of little value. Nothing changes after Carrie White's death; a final scene suggests that the telekinetic powers are already at work again, presumably destroying other innocents. In *'Salem's Lot,* the best one can hope for is to escape; the ostensible heroine dies and the child loses family and heritage. In *The Stand,* one of the closest to an optimistic novel King has yet written, there is renewed peace; but the Dark Man still exists, as do those bombs and weapons of destruction left deserted. (pp. 16-17)

Only rarely does the child become instrumental in restoring order. It might be argued that *The Shining* concludes optimistically—although even there Danny Torrance is just beginning to break free of his experience, and the other levels of sacrificial children (the Gradys, even Jack and Wendy themselves) have brought forth little good. More critically, however, the *source* of evil is not destroyed, as Hallorann realizes when the great black shape emerges from the Presidential Suite just before the Overlook explodes. As happens so often in King's fiction, [as Collings has mentioned elsewhere], "the horrific elements, though displaced, survive, and in their survival lies the kernal of future horror." (pp. 17-18)

IT breaks with the typical pattern in King's prose. Instead of irresolute closure, there is a clear sense that evil has indeed been destroyed. On a literal level as well as a symbolic level, King is careful to point out that It has been defeated; while the mechanisms of It's defeat are not new to King's fictions, the *fact* of it is.

In part, the sense of absolute closure relates to two key developments: first, King overtly acknowledges an "Other" to counter the force of evil; and second, he has finally reconciled the worlds of children and adults—paradoxically by having children act as adults (a common motif elsewhere in his fiction) *and* by having adults become as children. Their return to the sewers beneath Derry signals their acceptance of adult responsibility and of childhood faith combined into an irresistible force.

Because of It's relationship to the children-become-adults, Pennywise the Clown stands among King's most ambitious "monsters." Like Satan in Milton's *Paradise Lost,* the character is ubiquitous, powerful, seductive, and fatally convincing in It's many guises. And, also like Satan in the poem, It receives much of King's attention. Although the multiple manifestations do tend toward the expected (given the length of the novel and the many appearances It makes, however, that sense is almost inevitable), often described in similar terms (but again, how many ways are there to express absolute horror?), they form the core of the novel. As the children discover the nature of their enemy, and their adult selves *re*-discover it, Pennywise grows into a monster strong enough and secure enough in It's evil to provide more than a strawman or cardboard opponent. There may be a momentary drop in horror as we discover It's "real" form, since for some readers the spider-entity may seem stereotypic and trite. Still, King had to select a single manifestation for the climactic confrontation; and since any one he chose might prove less frightening than others for some of his readership, a lessening of emotional conviction may be inevitable. But that drop is more than made up for as King takes us into the mind of It and reveals It's relation to the "macrouniverse."

Unfortunately, that revelation leads King into the same difficulty Milton faced in *Paradise Lost:* the threat that his villain might become larger than the hero. King counters the threat by setting seven characters opposite It—seven being a mystical number of great potency. Later, the number drops to five, less powerful than seven but still a number with mystical/magical significance. The important point, though, is that the heroic role is divided and each character plays a critical part in destroying It. Milton resolved his dilemma by dividing his later attention between the Son and Adam and Eve in the Garden; King largely restricts his interest to human spheres, so the further subdivisions become necessary. Still, given the intensively re-created backgrounds King gives us for each of the seven, we believe that they *will* in fact be a match for It . . . almost.

That "almost" is important because in *IT* (again, for almost the first time in King's fiction) King overtly acknowledges the presence of an Other to counter evil. There is no "deus ex machina," no rabbit pulled out of a hat at the end to restore universal order. Instead, King plays it very carefully. In the first three-fourths of the novel, there are only a few enigmatic references to the "Turtle"; and when we finally encounter that entity, it is surprisingly static. It barely moves. The Turtle does not act to save the children; instead it answers questions and by doing so enables the children to save themselves. Yet it is clear that It and Turtle are of the same order of creation, so to speak. In spite of It's pretensions to immortality, omniscience, and omnipresence, It is (again like Milton's Satan) a secondary creation. In spite of It's overwhelming power in this world and It's apparently commensurate (if not greater) power in the macrouniverse, It is only a creation. And the Turtle, we discover, is even more subject to the laws of time and mortality.

What makes *IT* different from anything else King has written, except perhaps **"The Reach,"** is the intrusion of the Other into the struggle. Evil is powerful, but Good is not without its advocate. In *The Stand,* for example, Randall Flagg seems almost to destroy himself; his precipitous actions confound his own plans. Some force for good may be involved, but we never perceive that force directly. In *IT,* the Other speaks—admittedly in King's down-home dialect but recognizably parallelling the Biblical "Behold my beloved son, in whom I am well pleased." The "son" is no deity, however, but a human who has opened himself to the promptings of the Other.

This additional layering of power helps keep *IT* from being merely an exploration of Lovecraftian horror or yet another variant on any of several folkloric patterns. Instead *IT* approaches the mythic, a sense that increases as the adult/children themselves draw closer to their final meeting with It. In describing that meeting, King almost ignores physical violence and force to allow the battle to take on a psychological, emotional, and spiritual nature.

In addition, King also resolves the longstanding conflict he has frequently delineated between the worlds of childhood and of adulthood. Initially *IT* suggests his earlier works. Children are victims, not only of monsters but of adults and of other children. George Denbrough dies violently in the opening pages, the precursor to literally hundreds of deaths implied or described. Many are at the hands of Pennywise the Clown; others result from the adult world as it impinges upon the child's. In some instances something even worse happens as, through their experiences with the adult world, children become insane, crippled spiritually until they become It's willing tool in destroying other children. Frequently, the deaths are graphic and chilling; to this extent, *IT* carries many of King's distinctive trademarks. But there are also essential differences.

First, many deaths do *not* occur. Pennywise and It's minions wonder what is happening; in spite of their best efforts, they are unable to destroy certain of their enemies: the seven, while undergoing physical and mental stress, seem unaccountably charmed.

And second, the seven achieve what few of King's characters even understood that they must strive for. They *blend* child and adult. On one level, this seems an extension of the "sacrificial child" motif. Eddie figuratively marries his mother; mother and wife are archetypal Kingesque "monstrous women," a figure almost as pervasive in his fiction as the too-adult child. (pp. 18-21)

On another level, however, the blending gives *IT* unique power. The twenty-seven-year cycle of death roughly recapitulates a single generation; It's hope is that the seven, as adults, will be incapable of generating the force necessary to confront and destroy It. . . . Later, King makes even more explicit the relationship between child-like faith and the destruction of the monster. It realizes that the children had

> discovered an alarming secret that even It had not
> been aware of: that belief has a second edge. If there
> are ten thousand medieval peasants who create
> vampires by believing them real, there may be
> one—probably a child—who will imagine the stake
> necessary to kill it. But a stake is only stupid wood;
> the mind is the mallet which drives it home.

What actually occurs is that the characters must re-capture the essence of childhood, an action symbolized by King's narrative structure. Moving with increasing frequency from

1958 to 1985 and back, he does not complete either narrative independently. Instead, the adult parallels the child in each of the seven (soon to be six) as they *remember* as adults at precisely the same pace they had *experienced* as children. (pp. 21-2)

They become adult/children. They must recapture their innocence, their willingness to believe implicitly in what they know experientially about Pennywise the Clown. The characters attempt to return to that state of belief, bolstered this time by adult strength and perseverance.

King's attitudes toward sexuality demonstrate this merging of the two worlds. Initially, again, there seems to be little change from his earlier works. The first suggestions of sexuality focus on homosexuality; one of the first victims of the new cycle of terror is a gay man set upon by "straights," who throw him into the canal—and into the waiting arms of It. As elsewhere, King's attitudes toward homosexuality are ambivalent. The theme occurs frequently in his fiction; it is often overtly negative as in **"Children of the Corn"** and the opening scene of **"Nona,"** but also frequently ambivalent, as in *The Long Walk.* In *IT* the treatment of homosexuality becomes more openly vicious than ever. Not only do the characters react negatively and strongly to the suggestion of homosexuality, but the narrative links (i.e., the narrator's voice itself) continue that harsh, stereotypic attitude. The gay man killed never rises above the slickest of stereotypes, nor do reactions to his death ever overcome the hurdle of his sexual orientation.

King explains this orientation in terms of events during Bangor's sesquicentennial celebration, culminating in the death of a young asthmatic gay man thrown into the Kenduskeag Stream by three other young men and his subsequent death by asphyxiation. "I took notes on the police interrogation," King writes, and even though the official records were never used in court and were later destroyed, he says that

> a lot of the conversation in the chapter is reputedly what was said. It is, in fact, what I believe to be true. The ritual nature of the killing—at least when placed in the context of a summer festival—and the cross-connection to Eddie's asthma made it just too good to drop. So I used it to bookend George Denbrough's death. If the chapter strikes you as homophobic, please remember that this is a case of "We don't make the news, we just report it."

In spite of these connections with external events, the novel does, however, focus on homosexuality as sub-theme. Much later in the narrative, even the hint of a homosexual relation is sufficient to drive one character into insanity; the text explicitly connects his subsequent actions with that single moment of crisis. Other elements in his family and background certainly moved him toward insanity, but King carefully notes that one action makes the insanity inevitable.

There is a certain justification for this attitude in the novel. By its nature, homosexuality opposes heterosexuality, the linking of man and woman in the deepest emotional bonds. And that intense bonding lies at the center of *IT.*

In earlier novels, sexuality had been almost invariably a threat to King's characters. Carrie dies because menstruation (and potential sexuality) triggers powers she is incapable of handling. The vampire in *'Salem's Lot* is a traditional image of threatening sexuality—particularly developed in the death of Susan Norton. The perverted sexuality of Nadine Cross

and Harold Lauder in *The Stand* inhibits either of them from developing as mature adults; only the birth of a child to Frannie Goldsmith comes close to establishing a sense of sexuality as regenerative. (pp. 22-4)

With *IT,* that negative emphasis changes. At first, of course, sexuality remains a mystery and a threat. Boys do not quite understand the mechanics of the sex act (also referred to as doing "it," with connections to the monster that are anything but accidental—sexuality *is* an unknown and potentially deadly monster for children). Girls understand a bit more, but refuse to handle the realities other than through giggles and self-conscious embarrassment.

The It/it dichotomy develops most strongly in the passage where King finally allows his characters to move from childhood to adulthood. In a powerful scene, sexuality binds the seven—not the physical act of having sex but the emotional commitment of deeply binding and adult love. Sexuality becomes the key to survival, in a way that would have been impossible for almost any of King's earlier characters. The moment is handled as indirectly as possible; obviously the physical element of the act is critical, since those involved are eleven or twelve years old and none fully understands what it entails. Yet King continually emphasizes the *emotional* effects, not the physical. And in doing so, he transcends himself, to create a conclusion that is more positively emotionally stirring than anything else—again, with the possible exception of **"The Reach."**

In a recent letter [to Collings], King wrote that *IT* culminates his treatment of children and monsters; he would not return to it again (3 March 1986). What is appropriate, since in *IT* his fictional children finally mature on their own, embracing the adult world consciously and willingly. They integrate the two levels of experience, and in doing so make possible the defeat of evil.

Put in those terms, *IT* sounds almost mythic. And it is. The conclusion is as powerful as myth or archetype; the narrative is an extended rite of passage, with externalized monster that represents (literally) the deepest fears of childhood that must be faced and overcome before the adult can develop into an independent and healthy individual. When I read King, I expect a strong ending. Rarely am I disappointed. In novel after novel, he adds just the right touch to confirm the narrative: *Pet Sematary* epitomizes the strength of his conclusions. The single word *"Darling"* chills the reader to the zero point.

What I do not expect—and what *IT* gave me—is an intensely emotional awareness of the rightness of things, a quality that transcends fiction to touch upon the archetypal patterns we respond so deeply to. When I read such a novel (and they are rare), the power is so intense that words are inadequate—words, in fact, come between me and the experience.

This happened with *IT.* Although it has its share of crudities and harsh language, violence, and stylistic infelicities (including repetitions that may simply be inevitable in a novel, the manuscript for which is, as King puts it, bigger than his own head), at the end, *IT* transcends itself, to stand as the most powerful novel King has yet written. (pp. 24-5)

Michael R. Collings, in his The Stephen King Phenomenon, *Starmont House, Inc., 1987, 144 p.*

TONY MAGISTRALE

Stephen King's largest and one of his most ambitious novels to date embodies many of the core themes and issues that I have raised in preceding chapters of this book. A tale of monsters and threatened children, *It* is also a story of endurance and loyalty. And once again, as we have traced throughout King's fictional canon, the central conflict in this novel is between American adult society and the children who are neither understood nor appreciated. The five adults who survive their quest to do battle against It manage to do so because all of them are, in a manner of speaking, still children maintaining the mutual bond of love that has united them against adversity—both human and supernatural—since the time of their shared adolescence. (p. 109)

In the Smoke-Hole Ceremony, two members of the Losers' Club, Mike and Richie, go back to the origins of the earth in order to witness the conception of evil, the latter coinciding with the arrival of It in the center of Derry, Maine: " 'It landed right where the downtown part of Derry is now. . . . It's *always* been here, since the beginning of time . . . sleeping, maybe, waiting for the ice to melt, waiting for the people to come'." Mike highlights the importance of It's relationship to the mortal world; the creature lies dormant until humans arrive to wake it from a dark slumber. It is what the first puritan settlers might have called original sin, the principle of evil that they felt was an omnipresent component in the moral arrangement of the cosmos. As we have seen operation elsewhere in King's fiction, this principle nourishes itself on human sin, growing ever more powerful as the individual (and his community) moves further from the status of childhood and toward the corruption of adulthood.

Perhaps the greatest link that ties King to the late nineteenth-century naturalists—Crane, Dreiser, Norris, London—whose work so captivated King as an undergraduate, is a sense of the city as a place where human waste and confinement has reached a level in which crime and violence become its "natural" manifestations, like mold on stale bread. In his November 6, 1986 address at the University of Maine, Orono, King acknowledged that *It* specifically owed much to William Carlos Williams and Charles Dickens insofar as "the novel is an epic poem of the city as an organism." Pennywise, the clown that haunts the canals, deserted trainyards, and, most frequently, the Derry sewer system, preying on the children while inciting adults to greater levels of mayhem and violence, is the collective representation of the town's adult crimes and darkest impulses. The sewer system of any city contains the wastes of its populace; Derry's accumulative moral wastes coalesce into Pennywise. (pp. 109-10)

Every twenty-seven years Derry's " 'unusually high rate of every violent crime we know of, not excluding rape, incest, breaking and entering, auto theft, child abuse, spouse abuse, assault'," reaches a point in which the clown is either strong enough (or Derry weak enough) to reactivate Pennywise. Following a particularly gruesome outburst of communal violence, the clown resurfaces to stalk Derry's children, suggesting that this town, like the America portrayed in **"Children of the Corn,"** must somehow compensate for its past moral transgressions by sacrificing a part of its future. Derry is indeed "a feeding place for animals," possessing all the unsavory aspects of modern America found elsewhere in King's canon. (pp. 110-11)

Like Faulkner's examination of Yoknapatawpha County,

King's elaborate and dark history of Derry, Maine chronicles many of the most brutal and inhumane events which have occurred during the past three centuries. And also like Faulkner, King uses specific and interrelated histories of his seven protagonists to detail the horrors that transpire daily in this closed society. Consequently, the creature that inhabits the Derry sewer system seems as much related to the environment of the town itself as Percy Grimm, Sutpen, or Flem Snopes emerge as products of Faulkner's South. The real evil in Faulkner's fiction, like King's, is social: the individual in Jefferson's society is forced to define his or her identity according to rigid distinctions of race, color, geographic and family origins. These distinctions, created and nurtured by man, become the progenitors of a caste system that defines individuals principally by means of social identification. Those who can neither fit nor be fitted into the convenient categories that have been established by the people of Faulkner's towns, must be destroyed or banished from the society whose patterns of belief are threatened.

In King's fiction, the children are more often than not the outcasts, threatening the adult community—its pervasive systems of regulation and deceit. Derry's adults profess a love for their progeny, but aside from imposing an early evening curfew, there are no concrete examples of adult panic or concern surrounding the disappearance of so many young people. Indeed, the adults in this novel are most conspicuous by their absence; in the midst of Pennywise's slaughter, children remain unattended and are permitted to play in the secluded Barrens. The town has come to accept the loss of its children as a price for conducting daily business. . . . As Mike informs the other members of the Losers' Club upon their return to Derry, the demise of so many town children has not appeared on national news because neither the city nor the creature that feeds upon it wants the information revealed.

Hawthorne and his puritan ancestors would have understood most thoroughly Pennywise's relationship with the town of Derry. They knew evil as an element that pervades everything human—from the community itself to the individuals who guide it. Anytime any act of violence or cruelty occurs in Derry, Pennywise is present to celebrate it, to participate in it, and to reap the power accrued from the act itself. When the Bradley gang is slaughtered in the center of town by the citizens of Derry, the clown is a member of the righteous mob, emptying her own bullets from a smoking rifle. Similarly, when the Black Spot is torched by a legion of racial bigots, Pennywise is there in the guise of a giant bird of prey, " 'big bunches of balloons tied to each wing, and it floated'."

The spontaneous explosion of the Kitchener Ironworks that results in the deaths of many unsuspecting children who are searching for Easter eggs within its bowels is tied to Derry and the clown that punishes the city at the same time as it represents it. Both the ironworks disaster and Pennywise herself prey upon the vulnerability of children. Under the veneer of Pennywise's games and promises lurks the reality of deception and slaughter. The adult citizens of Derry mirror this very tendency in their daily behavior toward their children. Bev's father, for example, abuses his daughter in physical beatings that barely mask his repressed incestuous urges. He has done permanent psychological damage to her, as her eventual choice of marriage to Tom is simply a continuation of the violent pattern that originated with her father and extends beyond him to Pennywise the Dancing Clown. . . . Like the adults in King's novella *The Body,* Derry's grown-ups don't really "see" their own children, or if they do, it is only long enough to abuse them; ironically, Derry's children are the only ones capable of seeing Pennywise and the gory remains of her victims.

King's choice of a clown as a unifying symbol for the various creatures representing It is masterful: what better lure for a child than the carnival clown—an adult in elaborate make-up—who is capable of disguising monstrous intentions. When Stan encounters Pennywise for the first time as a child, he is attracted to the creature by the sound of calliope music. As the boy draws nearer to the steel Standpipe, "the calliope music had gotten suddenly louder, as if to mask the sound of footsteps." The word "mask" is important here as it appropriately signifies the role of the clown throughout the novel: her viciousness is "masked" under the promise of false joy. Pennywise attracts all children to her by preying upon the youthful recollections of summer carnivals, "conjuring up trace memories which were as delightful as they were ephemeral." In actuality, however, the clown, mirroring the spirit of the town she embodies, scorns innocence; her real purpose, like the "Heaven" described in Emily Dickinson's own poem on carnivals "I've known a Heaven, like a Tent," is to deliver only death and negation. . . . (pp. 111-13)

It is not one of Stephen King's finest novels; the book possesses neither the thematic and philosophical depth of *The Stand,* the concise focus of *Pet Sematary,* nor the sustained terror of *The Shining.* But *It* does represent one of King's most ambitious stylistic endeavors. As early as *Carrie,* King evinced an interest in experimenting with narrative forms. *The Stand's* multiple story lines, which produce an initial sense of confusion in the reader, eventually coalesce into a single theme: the allegorical battle between good and evil. In many of his fictional works, King freely uses experimental stylistic devices—the stream of consciousness, interior monologues, multiple narrators, and a juggling of time sequences—in order to draw the reader into a direct and thorough involvement with the characters and events of the tale.

In a 1986 interview with Burton Hatlen, King's former professor informed me that as an undergraduate King was intrigued with the novels of William Faulkner and that "he spent one year reading everything he (Faulkner) ever wrote." I have already mentioned a possible Faulknerian influence in *It's* portrait of a regional evil and the generational corruption that is associated with It, but an awareness of the Southern writer is also apparent in King's stylistic efforts. In *The Sound and the Fury,* perhaps Faulkner's best work in terms of stylistic innovations, the writer eclipses a traditional succession of events by the careful interplay of leitmotifs that serve to disrupt the logical passage from one moment to another. He chooses to dispense with the typical characteristics that are found in conventional narratives—a linear plot development and chronological character growth—in order to show the internal workings of the mind. The demise of the Compson family is told backwards through a series of recollections, reflections, and remembrances, instead of through a logical pattern of rising actions.

King employs a similar interrupted narrative style throughout *It,* as the history of the Losers' Club and the monster that is the town of Derry is slowly and thoroughly made clear for the reader in a series of dramatic childhood flashbacks and recapitulations. The actions of the present are held in suspension for the length of long clarifying flashbacks in a way that vividly recalls Faulkner's techniques of stylistic experimenta-

tion. The inversion of the years 1958 and 1985 reflects King's structural efforts throughout the novel to juxtapose past with present. As the quest to destroy It intensifies, forcing the six adults to recall their adolescent encounters with the monster, the specific time frames of 1958 and 1985 blur, becoming nearly inseparable. Indeed, the last quarter of the book mirrors this focus as the varying time references of individual chapters literally flow into one another making memory and reality synonymous.

In attempting to penetrate the myth of a complicated Southern past, Quentin Compson and his friend Shreve in *Absalom, Absalom!* must synthesize the diverse and subjective interpretations of Miss Rosa, Quentin's father, and his grandfather. Quentin is forced into such an intimate involvement with the flow of words and concepts that he, like the reader, becomes almost unaware of time sequence or the chronological relativity of events. In King's novel, a similar process is at work as the individual members of the Losers' Club struggle to piece together a collective twenty-seven year memory that none of them understands completely. King highlights their quest in a series of clarifying flashbacks that bridges the gap of history. Aside from establishing the timelessness of It as well as the timelessness of childhood fears, King's experimentation with spatial relationships is also meant to underscore the only hope these child-adults possess in their struggle against Pennywise: that their link to one another and a collective adolescent imagination can be re-established quickly enough to destroy the creature. . . . (pp. 114-15)

Ben Hanscom's favorite recollection of his childhood in Derry is the public library. Not only do his memories of pleasant days within its doors contrast with his larger perspective of life in the town, but the physical structure of the place itself—especially the glassed-in corridor that connects the child and the adult sections of the library—has exerted a profound influence over Hanscom's architectural career. The glass corridor served as an inspiration for his first major office building, constructed in London. But even more relevant to the return of Ben and his friends to Derry is the use of the corridor image as a metaphor for the novel's quest to recapture the past.

> He walked across the library lawn, barely noticing that his dress boots were getting wet, to have a look at that glassed-in passageway between the grown-ups' library and the Children's Library. It was also unchanged, and from here, standing just outside the bowed branches of a weeping willow tree, he could see people passing back and forth. . . . The magic was that glowing cylinder of light and life connecting those two dark buildings like a lifeline, the magic was in watching people walk through it across the dark snowfield, untouched by either the dark or the cold. It made them lovely and Godlike. . . . The force of memory almost dizzied him for a moment as he stepped into the mild light of the hanging glass globes. The force was not physical—not like a shot to the jaw or a slap. It was more akin to that queer feeling of time doubling back on itself that people call, for want of a better term, *deja-vu.* Ben had had the feeling before, but it had never struck him with such disorienting power; for the moment or two he stood inside the door, he felt literally lost in time, not really sure how old he was. Was he thirty-eight or eleven?

Analogous to the manner in which this fragile glass conduit bridges the gap between the adult and child sections of the library, in the course of this novel the members of the Losers' Club move between the two worlds of their remembered childhood and present adulthood to re-establish their own "magic lifeline." Just as the observed rainbow in William Wordsworth's "My Heart Leaps Up" serves as a connecting point between "when my life began / So it is now I am a man," Hascom's passageway represents the possibility for adult self-renovation that is available in the recollection of adolescent memories. . . . [The] passageway from innocence to experience is a crucial one for many of [King's] characters; those who pass through this symbolic corridor to sever completely their connection to childhood are doomed to the isolated sterility of adulthood. The ideal condition, as King symbolizes in the above excerpt, seems to be within the individual's ability for keeping open the passageway that connects adolescence to adulthood. This is, of course, why Ben and his long-lost friends must return to Derry: to defeat It once and for all the Losers' Club must reopen their personal and collective conduits to childhood.

Although each of the Losers is highly successful financially (except for Mike, who has chosen to remain in Derry), their childless marriages have allowed them to maintain a connection to "'some sort of group will'" associated with their shared adolescence. Their recollected loyalty, coupled with a willingness to sacrifice individual volitions and, as it turns out, lives for the welfare of each other, insulates these five men and one woman from the traits of selfishness and immorality that are usually synonymous with King's descriptions of adulthood. (pp. 115-17)

Just as Pennywise gains a kind of supernatural energy from the sins of Derry's adults, the potency of their collective love allows the Losers to perform courageous acts against forces more powerful than their individual selves. . . . [There] is a power in love that is stronger than the malevolent energies King associates with evil. In *It,* Mike Hanlon's father imparts to his son the same sense of continuity, courage and hope that the latter will employ in order to re-establish the bond of love among the Losers. Mike's father is certainly an illustration of how an adult might maintain a loving and positive link to his children as well as to his own childhood. In this sense, Mike's relationship with his father—and by extension, his father's recollections of Dick Hallorann's bravery the night The Black Spot burned—become the models upon which the Losers will base their own selfless commitment to one another. The act of sexual intercourse that Beverly shares with each member of the Losers' Club after their initial battle against It in the summer of 1958 cements their union; she becomes the center of their magic circle, and serves as an effective feminine force to counterbalance the evil of the female It. Although Beverly is childless, her friends become her surrogate children; she protects and comforts each of them throughout the book. When Eddie Kaspbrak dies at the end of the novel, it is in her arms, and she offers him a final repose in imagery reminiscent of the Pietà. In contrast to Beverly, It is pregnant, but her children are doomed. As It flees from Bill and Richie, eggs are discarded haphazardly, left to be crushed under the bootheels of Ben Hanscom. Evil dies as it chooses to live: without regard for anyone or anything beyond itself. (pp. 117-18)

On two separate occasions a young boy fearlessly rides his skateboard in front of Bill while pointing out that "'you can't be careful on a skateboard'." Bill and his friends come to employ the same spirit of adolescent abandonment in their assault against It. They are inspired by a child's righteous indignation toward the monster's callous actions. As a result of their spontaneous concern for each other, they overcome the adult fear that results in Stan's suicide and produces their own initial apprehensiveness upon returning to Derry. His renewed contact with the recuperative powers of childhood also enables Denbrough to rescue his wife from a catatonic state after her encounter with It. Dressed in clothes that are reminiscent of his youth, Bill rides with Audra on his bicycle "to beat the devil" one last time. Just as his adolescent friends have helped him to retrieve his past to defeat It, Bill's renewed commitment to "the mystery of childhood" allows him to partake of the mystical energy Ben Hanscom first perceived in the glass-domed corridor of the library.

King's belief in the spiritual importance of adults maintaining a child-like faith in the magic of life is directly relevant to the many references to rock music which appear in *It.* Throughout King's fiction it is possible to trace a strong association among adolescence, automobiles, and rock music. In *Christine,* for example, each chapter heading makes use of rock lyrics from songs written about cars. Until *It,* however, King's frequent references to this music usually appear to highlight or foreshadow sinister events; as Christine becomes more diabolical, the lyrical allusions reflect the novel's impending doom, becoming darker, more ominous. In *It,* on the other hand, King employs rock and roll as yet another means to illustrate the dynamism of youth. A fundamental premise of rock music is its commitment to sustaining the magic of adolescence, even into adulthood. This concern has been a guiding force in rock since its inception, and it is especially prevalent in songs by The Who, The Doors, and Bruce Springsteen, all of whom are some of King's favorite artists. (pp. 118-19)

Richie "Records" Tozier's role in *It* is interesting in light of this discussion, as his contact with rock music extends from his association with the Losers to his current adult occupation as an L.A. disc jockey. His connection to music has allowed him to maintain a fresh and dynamic perspective on life. Indeed, he possesses the same bravado and self-assertiveness that are characteristic of the rock era; and these elements are not only instrumental to the final destruction of It, they also help Richie to survive. In contrast to the adults of Derry, who, like Richie's and Bill Denbrough's mothers, are "death on rock and roll," Richie obtains a strength from the music that ties him not only to the world's losers, but also to the world's children: "There was a power in that music, a power which seemed to most rightfully belong to all the skinny kids, fat kids, ugly kids, shy kids—the world's losers, in short." For Richie, as well as for King, rock music is more than a good beat; it is a means of communicating a sense of personal and collective disenfranchisement, of identifying with a source of power, and of transcending the self's limitations on a current of rhythm and energy: "In it he felt a mad hilarious voltage which had the power to both kill and exalt." In essence, Richie's response to rock and roll parallels Ben Hascom's magic corridor. It is therefore no mere coincidence that Bill Denbrough's transformation at the novel's conclusion, which allows him to rescue Audra at the same time as he rescues his nexus to youth, is subtly aligned with the mysterious energies of rock and roll. . . . (pp. 119-24)

In "Tintern Abbey," "Ode: Intimations of Immortality," and *The Prelude,* William Wordsworth advises the adult to retain an active memory of his childhood in order to cope with the "evil tongues, / Rash judgments, the sneers of selfish men . . . where no kindness is." Though no longer a child, it is possible for the adult to watch and hear with sympathetic eyes and ears. Moreover, the adult may not share the uncomplicated joys of childhood, but he can find moral strength in retaining the values learned as an adolescent.

The neo-Wordsworthian vision of hope that animates the entire girth of *It* reaffirms the pattern for survival we have traced in King's novels and tales. In one of his diary entries, Mike Hanlon argues that "It protects Itself by the simple fact that as the children grow into adults, they become either incapable of faith or crippled by a sort of spiritual and imaginative arthritis." This position is certainly in evidence throughout King's work, but so is its antithesis: that adult perspectives do not have to narrow; that faith in the magic of life, which makes both life and magic possible, does not have to disappear with the loss of childhood. It seems equally clear, however, that to sustain the metaphor of Ben Hanscom's "glowing cylinder of light and life," adults need to maintain their connection to adolescence—especially the capacity to accept and give love. As Wordsworth tells us in the First Book of *The Prelude,* "my hope has been, that I might fetch / Invigorating thoughts from former years."

King's romantic perception of childhood offers to light the way to moral excellence by helping man to distinguish between, and understand the nature of, good and evil. As Bill Denbrough comes fully to understand at the conclusion of *It,* the imaginative faith of childhood was given to man to guide him through life. It can help him envision the moral constitution of the world; it can explain the nature of the human animal and its natural imperfections; it can even lead him to the threshold of recreating his personality and identity.

Stephen King grew up without a father, and the absence of this relationship in his real life may have given impetus to the fictional creation of his "alternative families." However, if these non-traditional families—the Losers' Club, and the pairings of Jack and Speedy, Danny and Hallorann—were simply autobiographical statements of the writer's broken childhood, the recollection of what these characters mutually experienced would not continue to endure for the reader. Abandoned by governmental bureaucracies and the nuclear family itself, King's small non-traditional alliances represent the light in the darkness of his social landscape. His heroes and heroines establish character unions that embody the spiritual essence of Ben Hascom's symbolic corridor, as the relationships which endure in King's world most often appear to consist of a melding of child with adult. The resulting synthesis produces individuals who possess the courage to vanquish worldly evil because of their sustained association with the magical powers of youth. While traditional families and societal relationships may not endure in King's landscape of fear, his protagonists arc cndowcd with altcrnativcs to thcsc fractured institutions that represent not only the hope for survival, but also the dream of salvation. (pp. 120-21)

> *Tony Magistrale, in his* Landscape of Fear: Stephen King's American Gothic, *Bowling Green State University, 1988, 132 p.*

RICHARD FULLER

[The protagonist of *The Dark Tower: The Gunslinger*] wears two guns as he pursues a mysterious man in black across "the apotheosis of all deserts." But before you think of Clint Eastwood, you should know that he earned those guns in combat, armed only with a hawk, with his larger, older, presumably stronger teacher; that his land is called New Canaan, and that his name is Roland. Ambiguity is all in this yarn about Good versus Evil, which mixes its genres—the western, science fiction—as well as its metaphors. ("Sudden terror dawned in Kennerly's eyes, like twin moons coming over the horizon.") Is the man in black the personification of Evil? He raises someone from the dead in the town of Tull, while the pursuing gunslinger mows down everybody in town. This mass murderer is the hero? The gunslinger follows the man in black through five stories, picking up a character called young Jake along the way for more ambiguity. . . . The gunslinger at last meets up with the man in black, who calls the gunslinger "the world's last adventurer" and then talks of "The Dark Tower," the overall title of an epic series that may reach an even more epic 3,000 pages, according to the afterword; Stephen King describes it as a "stairway, perhaps, to the Godhead itself." The whole thing was inspired by Browning's poem "Childe Roland to the Dark Tower Came," which Mr. King read in his sophomore year of college. Mr. King the college graduate would later learn to unmix the metaphors and the genres and get on with unpretentious page-turners. But this undergraduate-style goulash, which was first published in a limited edition in 1982, is, alas, merely sophomoric. (pp. 22-3)

> *Richard Fuller, in a review of "The Dark Tower: The Gunslinger," in* The New York Times Book Review, *January 8, 1989, pp. 22-3.*

TOM EASTON

Between 1978 and 1981, Stephen King published in F&SF a number of rather cryptic tales of a distant, dusty, fin-de-siècle future. The time was long after our civilization had vanished into dust and relics. The protagonist was Roland, a young man fleeing the fall of his ancestral home to revolution, carrying his holy six-guns, pursuing some ineffable villain. The Gunslinger, hot on the trail of the Man in Black, his eyes intent on a Black Tower at the nexus of all space and time. The impetus, as King writes, was "a sense that it was time to stop goofing around with a pick and shovel and get behind the controls of one big great God a'mighty steam shovel, a sense that it was time to try and dig something big out of the sand, even if the effort turned out to be an absymal failure." The result was the five segments of *The Gunslinger*. . . .

Is it the failure King feared? Well . . . King grants that it *is* pretty blatantly modeled on the coming of Childe Roland to the Black Tower. It is also too heavily and obviously freighted with symbolism, and too self-conscious a shot at "literature," to be a complete success. But it's quite readable, even on second exposure. (p. 185)

> *Tom Easton, "Anadems," in* Analog Science Fiction/Science Fact, *Vol. CIX, No. 6, June, 1989, p. 185.*

GEORGE STADE

[*The Dark Half* is not the first work in which] Stephen King has written a dark allegory of the fiction writer's situation. *Misery* (1987) is a parable in chiller form of the popular writer's relation to his audience, which holds him prisoner and dictates what he writes, on pain of death. Mr. King's new novel, **The Dark Half**, is a parable in chiller form of the popular writer's relation to his creative genius, the vampire within him, the part of him that only awakes to raise Cain when he writes, the fratricidal twin who occupies "the womblike dungeon" of his imagination.

Thaddeus Beaumont is the writer in question. At age 11 he writes his first story. Around the same time he begins to get excruciating headaches, which culminate in a convulsion. Surgery reveals something startling—first an eye, the other small fragments of an incompletely absorbed twin that's lodged in his brain. This sort of "*in utero* cannibalism," according to his doctor, is not unusual, although rarely is anything left undigested, as it is in Thad Beaumont's case.

The operation is a success, and Thad grows up to be a mild-mannered professor of creative writing, a doting husband and the father of twins, a modestly successful writer of novels with titles like *Purple Haze*. But under the pen name of George Stark he is the best-selling author of ferocious thrillers like *Sharkmeat Pie*, the protagonist of which is named Alexis Machine because he kills like one.

Circumstances force Thad to own up to his pseudonym, which in any case has become irksome. He has decided to go it on his own, to lay his fictional self to rest. He and his wife even hold a mock burial service for George Stark, papier-mâché tombstone and all. But one morning a man-sized cavity is discovered at the site. Footprints lead away. Very soon, people begin to die horribly, in particular everybody associated with Thad's decision to bury George Stark, whose prose style governs the graphic and gruesome descriptions of the murders. For George Stark has materialized. As Stark himself puts it, "The word became flesh, you might say."

But George Stark is not content to be merely undead. He wants to be alive entirely. He wants Thad to begin another novel under Stark's name. . . .

On the whole, Mr. King is tactful in teasing out the implications of his parable—never mind an author's note that acknowledges a debt to "the late Richard Bachman," Mr. King's own pseudonym, without whom "this novel could not have been written." No character in the novel comes right out and says, for example, that writers exist (at least to readers) only in their writing, that each person (at least to himself) is his own fiction, that the writer's imagination can feel alien to him, a possessing and possessive demon, a Dracula arisen to prey on the whole man and his family. Nor does anyone in the novel say outright that reality inevitably leaks fiction, which then floods reality, that reality and fiction feed on and feed each other, that they are at war yet they are twins—so identical that attempts to say which is which only lead to more fictions. Such things are better left unsaid, anyhow. Stephen King is not a post-modernist.

He is, however, a very good storyteller. **The Dark Half** mostly succeeds, as both parable and chiller, in spite of occasional clichés of thought and expression and bits of sophomoric humor (the F.B.I. is "the Effa Bee Eye," marijuana is "wacky tobaccy"). At the end, the decent family man wins out, but at a cost—which is how it should be. Most readers, I believe, will want decency and reality to triumph, but only with some reluctance, only after their most monstrous imaginings, like George Stark, have been unearthed and indulged. And few writers around are better than Stephen King at giving readers what they want.

George Stade, "His Alter Ego Is a Killer," in The New York Times Book Review, *October 29, 1989, p. 12.*

JOHN SKOW

[With **The Dark Half,** another] Stephen King blood leaker is loosed upon the world, this one in a record first printing of 1.5 million copies. The ghost of Gutenberg, calling feebly for beer from the gridiron of some Germanic hell, must be wondering whether movable type was really a good idea.

That is snobbery, of course, and a reader addicted to another sort of trash—detective stories, say—must distrust his instinct to ridicule horror novels. But in each genre there is good trash and bad trash, and King's does not seem very good. Mention this to a fan—young, intelligent, well read—and the reply is the same as is heard, above the level of pop lit, when one more dismal fiction by Joyce Carol Oates appears: "Yes, but you should read the early books."

In his new thunderation, the first of four in a reported $30 million to $40 million publishing deal, the author plays with a twist of the old good-twin, bad-twin theme. Novelist Thad Beaumont, who lives in Maine (as does King), collided with writer's block a few years ago and rescued his career by writing four novels under the pseudonym of George Stark (just as King has written five novels as Richard Bachman). These tales, unlike Beaumont's, were violent, brutal and very successful. Now Beaumont, writing on his own again, wants to bury Stark.

No dice. Stark, actually the ghost of Beaumont's fetal twin, who was incompletely absorbed *in utero* (the medical horror here is the book's only high-voltage shocker), comes to life as a cunning psychopath who, somewhat ludicrously, is determined to keep on writing. He slices up Beaumont's agent and editor and several other innocents with a straight razor, in scenes so lovingly detailed they would be called pornographic if the author had given the same attention to sex.

As usual, King's prose is fast, simple and sloppy. He has young Beaumont in 1960 use the current slang "get off on," meaning enjoy, and lets an elderly English professor say he will "loan" the hero a car (old pedants say "lend"). The climax has the brutish Stark absurdly trying to write another novel to keep his ectoplasm from sloughing away in rivulets of goo. Characterization is perfunctory, with an odd exception: Beaumont's eight-month-old twin babies are vividly and charmingly described. For King fans this may be the sort of thing that sustains the myth that "he writes so well." (pp. 105-06)

John Skow, "Slice of Death," in Time, New York, *Vol. 134, No. 21, November 20, 1989, pp. 105-06.*

FURTHER READING

Collings, Michael R. *The Annotated Guide to Stephen King: A Primary and Secondary Bibliography of the Works of America's Premier Horror Writer.* Mercer Island, Wa.: Starmont House, 1986.

————. *The Films of Stephen King.* Mercer Island, Wa.: Starmont House, 1986, 201 p.

Compares adaptations of King's novels for film with the original works up to 1985. Collings also analyzes adaptations and original screenplays written by King and provides a filmography.

————. *The Many Facets of Stephen King.* Mercer Island, Wa.: Starmont House, 1985, 190 p.

Collection of essays on King's role as a critic and social phenomenon. Includes a primary and secondary bibliography.

————. *Stephen King as Richard Bachman.* Mercer Island, Wa.: Starmont House, 1985, 168 p.

Individual examination of King's five novels written under the pseudonym Richard Bachman. See excerpt in *CLC,* Vol. 37.

————. *The Stephen King Phenomenon.* Mercer Island, Wa.: Starmont House, Inc., 1987, 144 p.

Examines various aspects of King and his work to identify the author's status as a figure in mass culture. See excerpt above.

Collings, Michael R., and Engebretson, David A. *The Shorter Works of Stephen King.* Mercer Island, Wa.: Starmont House, 1985, 202 p.

Focuses on the author's uncollected stories and short fiction collections; includes a checklist of King's short fiction and poetry.

Egan, James. "Apocalypticism in the Fiction of Stephen King." *Extrapolation* 25, No. 3 (Fall 1984): 214-27.

Analysis of King's treatment of world destruction in his horror fiction.

————. "'A Single Powerful Spectacle': Stephen King's Gothic Melodrama." *Extrapolation* 27, No. 1 (Spring 1986): 62-75.

Examination of King's blend of Gothic elements and melodrama.

————. "Technohorror: The Dystopian Vision of Stephen King." *Extrapolation* 29, No. 2 (Summer 1988): 140-52.

Analysis of anti-technological aspects of King's fiction.

Grant, Charles L.; Morrell, David; Ryan, Alan; and Winter, Douglas E. "Different Writers on *Different Seasons.*" In *Shadowings: The Reader's Guide to Horror Fiction, 1981-1982,* edited by Douglas E. Winter, pp. 38-43. Mercer Island, Wa.: Starmont House, 1983.

Features individual responses to King's novellas *Rita Hayworth and the Shawshank Redemption, Apt Pupil, The Body,* and *The Breathing Method.*

Horstling, Jessie. *Stephen King at the Movies.* New York: Signet/Starlog, 1986.

Contains several interviews and sixty color photographs, centering on King's responses to adaptations of his films.

Indick, Ben P. "Stephen King as an Epic Writer." In *Discovering Modern Horror Fiction,* pp. 56-67. Edited by Darrell Schweitzer. Mercer Island, Wa.: Starmont House, 1985.

Examines King's novels *The Stand* and *The Dark Tower: The Gunslinger* according to the epic tradition exemplified by J. R. R. Tolkien's *The Lord of the Rings.*

Kimberling, Ronald C. "The Audience and Popular Art." In his *Kenneth Burke's Dramatism and the Popular Arts,* pp. 69-92. Bowling Green, Oh.: Bowling Green State University Popular Press, 1982.

Examines King's ability to overcome reader skepticism in his novel *The Dead Zone.*

Magistrale, Tony. *Landscape of Fear: Stephen King's American Gothic.* Bowling Green Oh.: Bowling Green State University Popular Press, 1988, 132 p.

Collection of new and previously published essays on such subjects as King's treatment of technology and social phenomena.

Schweitzer, Darrell, ed. *Discovering Stephen King.* Mercer Island, Wa.: Starmont House, 1985, 219 p.

Includes essays on general themes by Ben P. Indick, Michael R. Collings, and other commentators, as well as a bibliography.

Underwood, Tim, and Miller, Chuck, eds. *Fear Itself: The Horror Fiction of Stephen King.* New York: New American Library/Signet, 1982, 286 p.

Collection of general essays and observations by such critics and practitioners of the horror genre as Peter Straub, Fritz Leiber, Charles L. Grant, and George A. Romero. Includes a bibliography.

————. *Kingdom of Fear: The World of Stephen King.* New York: New American Library/Signet, 1987.

Contains seventeen essays on King's fiction by various critics, including Leslie Fiedler, Ben P. Indick, and Chuck Miller.

————. *Bare Bones: Conversations on Terror with Stephen King.* New York: McGraw-Hill Book Company, 1988, 211 p.

Collection of interviews previously published in such periodicals as *Playboy, Rolling Stone College Papers,* and *Heavy Metal.*

Winter, Douglas E. *Stephen King: The Art of Darkness.* New York: New American Library, 1984, 252 p.

Favorable analysis of King's life and career up to 1984. Features overviews of King's individual works, an appendix of his short fiction and of film adaptations of his books, and a bibliography.

Michel Leiris

1901-

(Born Michel Julien Leiris) French autobiographer, poet, essayist, anthropologist, and novelist.

A distinguished anthropologist and Surrealist poet, Leiris is perhaps most respected for his autobiographical writings, which critics agree have expanded the boundaries of confessional literature. In his acclaimed memoirs, including *L'age d'homme* (*Manhood: A Journey from Childhood into the Fierce Order of Virility*) and the four-volume work *La règle du jeu* (*The Rules of the Game*), Leiris recounts in unsparing detail his obsessions, fears, inadequacies, and longings. By revealing personal deficiencies, Leiris hopes to purge inhibitions that he believed were ruining his life and to express the ultimate meaning of his existence. While some critics designated Leiris's works as mere exercises in self-therapy, many noted that much of his writing possesses insights of universal interest.

In 1924, Leiris became involved in Surrealism, an influential artistic movement dedicated to examining irrational and subconscious aspects of the human mind. This involvement inspired Leiris to write the poems collected in his first volume of verse, *Haut mal,* as well as his only novel, *Aurora.* A heavily autobiographical work, *Aurora* concerns Leiris's obsession with decrepitude and mortality as well as his debilitating anxiety over love and life. By 1929, the subjects covered in *Aurora* began to overwhelm Leiris, and he suffered a nervous breakdown, accompanied by impotence. Following a year of psychoanalysis, Leiris developed an interest in anthropology and soon landed a position as curator of the Musée de l'Homme in Paris. As part of his job, Leiris traveled to Africa in 1931, documenting the experience in *L'Afrique fantôme de Dakar a Djibouti, 1931-1933.* Leiris returned frequently to Africa and published several volumes of ethnographical writings and art criticism. In a review of *African Art,* J. B. Donne praised Leiris's "enlarging of the whole concept of African art."

The idea behind Leiris's first memoir, *Manhood,* originated during psychoanalysis. Generally regarded as his finest literary achievement, this work differs from most autobiographies in its emphasis on the author's shortcomings rather than his life history. *Manhood* chronicles Leiris's hypochondria, sexual fantasies, inferiority complex, and, above all, cowardice. In the prefatory essay, "De la littérature considérée comme une tauromachie," Leiris states that one should write as if he were a bullfighter risking impalement. Leiris attains a feeling of danger by abolishing inhibitions common to autobiographers. While some critics questioned Leiris's absolute frankness because he omitted mention of his marriage and job as curator, most agreed that he had created an original and poignant work of literature. Susan Sontag observed: "[It] is precisely through *Manhood*'s unstated rejection of the rationalist project of self-understanding that Leiris makes his contribution to it." *Nuits sans nuit et quelques jours sans jour* (*Nights as Day, Days as Night*), which is generally considered an adjunct to *Manhood,* is a memoir comprising dream fragments and conscious meditations covering forty years of Leiris's life.

Written in the form of prose poems, these entries reveal his thoughts on Surrealism, anthropology, and World War II.

Leiris continues his self-analysis in the four volumes of *The Rules of the Game* he wrote over a period of three decades. In these works, Leiris rejects chronology and instead recreates facets of his past through memories triggered by words and ideas. The first volume, *Biffures,* was begun during the German occupation of France in World War II but remained unpublished until 1948. Here Leiris recounts important episodes from his childhood in relation to his discovery that language is not his private possession but belongs to others as well. In the second book, *Fourbis,* Leiris resumes his struggle to overcome his fixation with the horror of death and to establish a means to merge the poetic life with the social. The next volume, *Fibrilles,* discusses Leiris's 1958 suicide attempt and his guilt over his political inactivity. The concluding work, *Frêle bruit,* is a disjointed collection of notes and ideas that illustrates Leiris's perception of the fragmentary nature of existence. In a related volume of autobiography, *Language tangage; ou, Ce que les mots me disent,* Leiris continues his quest for meaning by exploring the significance of common words through their sound.

(See also *Contemporary Authors,* Vols. 119, 128.)

PRINCIPAL WORKS

AUTOBIOGRAPHY

L'age d'homme 1939
 [*Manhood: A Journey from Childhood into the Fierce Order
 of Virility,* 1963]
Nuits sans nuit et quelques jours sans jour 1945
 [*Nights as Day, Days as Night,* 1988]
*Biffures 1948
*Fourbis 1948
*Fibrilles 1966
*Frêle bruit 1976
Language tangage; ou, Ce que les mots me disent 1985

POETRY

Haut mal 1934
Vivantes cendres, innommées 1961

OTHER

Aurora (novel) 1934
L'Afrique fantôme de Dakar a Djibouti, 1931-1933 (travel
 journal) 1934
Miroir de la tauromachie (essay) 1938
African Art (art criticism) [with Jacqueline Delange]
 1968
Francis Bacon: Face et profil (art criticism) 1983
 [*Francis Bacon: Full Face and in Profile,* 1983]

_____

*These books form a multi-volume work often referred to as *La règle
du jeu* [*The Rules of the Game*].

_____

CLAUDE MAURIAC

Michel Leiris described himself in *L'Age d'homme* (The Age
of Man) as "a specialist, a maniac for confession." He
thought he had to specify in the course of the same work that
"if confession has an irresistible attraction for him, it is as a
vehicle of humiliation, shame and exhibitionism." If confession appears so fascinating to the author of *La Règle du jeu*
(Rule of the Game) it is, as he noted in the first volume, *Biffures* (Deletions), because he cannot bear to be judged for
what he is not:

> Like the lover anxious to be loved only "for him-
> self," it is myself such as I am—and not as a strang-
> er—that I wish to be accepted. In no way would it
> help to use counterfeit money in settling this ac-
> count, in no way would it help to short-change any-
> one: I shall literally have to *pay with my person* if
> I conclude this bargain, which is a trade with my-
> self as much as a transaction with others.

From book to book (I was going to say: from mirror to mirror—but never did Narcissus look at himself with less self-
satisfaction) Michel Leiris probes his face and his whole
physical appearance. The baldness with which he was threatened at the age of thirty-four, when he was writing the first
pages of *L'Age d'homme,* reappears, as was foreseeable, in
one of the last pages of . . . *Fourbis.* Here also he describes
the inflammation of the eyelids mentioned in the first portrait. Michel Leiris admits in several places in his works that
he attaches a certain importance to the way he dresses. A
concern for elegance which reached the point of coquetry in
his youth is preserved today only in the form of an indispensable correctness. The reason for this fastidiousness in clothing is a form of self-defense. For Leiris it is not so much a
matter of being handsome as of overcoming the weakness and
ugliness of which he suspects himself. In *Aurora,* written at
thirty, an imaginative work scintillating with personal avow-
als, we find the following revelation: "I looked on my own
body only with disgust; I tried all possible ways of giving it
a granitelike aspect, and often I remained motionless, for
hours on end, thinking that thereby I could bring myself in
some measure to be a statue."

What is important to Michel Leiris is not his body but what,
without any metaphysical implication, we may call his soul.
He is sensitive about his outer appearance only in so far as
it betrays his inner disposition. Thus, for example, the clumsiness he so often attributes to his limbs "is only his lack of decision translated into physical terms." In *L'Age d'homme* as
in the two volumes of *La Règle du jeu,* which recently appeared (and already, although to a lesser degree, in *L'Afrique
fantôme* [Phantom Africa], we find innumerable observations
relative to the author's character (he would say rather his
lack of character).

Attaching the greatest value to *precise biographical references,* Michel Leiris permits himself no infraction of the absolute rule of perfection which was to remain his model. . . .
His object is to recount everything that concerns him, beginning with what is ridiculous to those who only go by appearances.

Even the most normal taste, the taste for comfort, he exposes
in himself in order to find fault with it, reproaching himself,
for example, "for lazily abandoning to the bullfight enthusiasts of more modest means the seats where one broils in the
sun, in order to relax, like a sybarite, in those which are in
the shade." Michel Leiris comes back twice to this modest detail about his life as an *aficionado.* But he had more serious
complaints to make about himself on this score. We know the
importance of bullfights in the personal mythology of the author of the **"Miroir de la tauromachie"** (Mirror of Tauromachy) and especially of **"De la Littérature considerée comme
une tauromachie."** In the latter work he states that for him
it is a matter of "baring certain obsessions of a sentimental
or sexual order, confessing publicly certain deficiencies or
acts of cowardice which make him feel most ashamed in
order to introduce at least the shadow of a bull's horn into
a literary work," thus depriving it, as far as possible, of its
harmlessness. Michel Leiris informs us in *Fourbis* that he
ended by "liquidating" not so much his interest in *corridas*
as his literary exploitation of them:

> What is repugnant to me now is not the thing itself
> (with its undeniable foundation of barbarousness in
> attractive trappings) but my own attitude toward
> this thing: appreciating as a dilettante a spectacle
> based on death and courage, when I myself am so
> uneasy about death and so little courageous.

There remains the real courage which he demonstrates above
all by speaking about his cowardice. What he has the courage
to call *cowardice,* a word we all fear when it comes to apply-
ing it to ourselves, is one of Michel Leiris's deepest obsessions. He sees the germ of it in the lack of energy he displayed, as a child, in the gymnasium where he was obliged
to go every week. (pp. 61-4)

From the first pages of *L'Age d'homme,* Michel Leiris calls himself "crushed by shame, feeling his whole being corrupted by this incurable cowardice." This *fear of life* made psychoanalytic treatment necessary and here the idea of writing *L'Age d'homme* was born. He exposed with as little complacence as reticence the various aspects of his disturbance. Childhood fears still dominated him, "analogous to those of a nation perpetually prey to superstitious terrors and in the power of cruel and somber mysteries." The impression that all pleasures must be paid for, especially those of love; simultaneous search for and fear of the different forms in which "suffering, failure, expiation, punishment" may be clothed. These, among many others, are some of the themes in *L'Age d'homme:*

> I always behave like a kind of "accursed man" whose punishment pursues him eternally, who suffers because of it but who wishes nothing so much as to push to its peak this cursedness, an attitude from which I have for a long time derived acute though austere joy, eroticism for me being necessarily conjoined with torment, ignominy, and, even more, terror.

Similar confessions are found in *Biffures* where he denounces "his anxieties, his narcissism, his manias"; complacency "in the padded heedlessness of an egotistic solitude"; "weakness of character going hand in hand with pusillanimity in the practice of words"; "the same stage-fright panic when facing words to be linked as before an act to be accomplished. Always beating around the bush. Wavering. Shifting. Evading." And in *Fourbis:*

> Being as stingy about myself as a miser could be about his pennies; bound by fear; reticent in love (perhaps on account of this fear of having to pay with my body which also causes me to shrink from the idea of grief); wanting to play the part of the *torero,* but without ever facing a real bull, and the part of Don Juan, without conquests or defying the Commander. . . .

Let us go no further in this inventory. The disadvantage presented by this genre of authors is that they say much more about themselves than their exegete can repeat if he does not want to take advantage of the ammunition they have provided. There is no need to read very much of Michel Leiris in order to come up with a diagnosis. "If modern explorers of the subconscious," he writes in *L'Age d'homme,* "speak (in connection with me) about Oedipus, castration, guilt feelings, narcissism, I do not think that it helps a great deal as far as the essential part of the problem is concerned (which remains, according to my way of thinking, related to the problem of death and to the apprehension of oblivion and so relates to metaphysics)." Perhaps, it would have been better to speak of sadism and masochism (examples abound in the aforementioned book) but what difference does it make? The real question lies elsewhere.

Death haunts Michel Leiris. He returns to it ceaselessly. *L'Age d'homme* opens with an evocation of it; a long chapter of *Fourbis* is dedicated to it. As he notes in *Biffures,* it is "the haunting of time and the obsession of decrepitude" that are at the source of his literary attempts, which aim at nothing less than the erection *of his own statue.* A statue that resembles the model, that does not cheat about its defects, but by the very fact that it solidifies and immobilizes them in a work of art, is a relative guarantee against annihilation and oblivion. *Overwhelmed as he is by fear of death,* Leiris writes "to

compose a veneer of beauty to hide from himself the horror of living." From the time that he depended on poetry alone to express and save himself, he held on to the conviction that "through the lyrical use of words man has the power of transmuting all." (*Transmute* is one of the words that for a long time he preferred to all others.) The qualifying adjective *lyric* is no longer necessary when he "tries to adopt autobiography as the sole means of expression." By attacking "this rather special layer of memories which he undertakes to prospect," Michel Leiris hopes *to make a quasi-scientific use of literature.* Hence "his almost maniacal interest in minute and not easily verifiable facts resulting from what goes on in his innermost self." Hence his patient, somewhat monotonous, and often seemingly pathological way of *churning himself up.*

The essence for Michel Leiris does not lie so much in the picturesque biographical detail as in what he can identify as fundamental in both his past and present, neither existing without the other. Both are aspects of the same continuous and continued reality. Thus, the reality of his own life still in progress is provisionally saved from oblivion by its older manifestations which are less exhumed than recovered alive in the present. It would be unjustifiable to assemble this material except from the double point of view of ethics and aesthetics. The reward he anticipated was to live and write better and thus, through an ennobling work, to make his life worthwhile. (pp. 64-7)

Biffures had been completed on a note of pessimism and what's-the-use which we find again at the end of *Fourbis.* A cyclothymic rhythm of relative euphoria and total despair which all artists experience to some extent: relatively reassured as long as they are constructing their work, uneasy as soon as the last wisps are dissipated, those last embellishing, exalting, anesthetizing wisps of creative intoxication, when they consider with what they believe to be objectivity (which is a new form of subjectivity) the little that they have done. Concerning *Biffures* (which was not much of a success), Michel Leiris writes in the beginning of *Fourbis* that "this book was nothing but an empty gesture compared with what he had hoped from it": to succeed, thanks to it, *in existing more profoundly,* through its medium to take *revenge on a life with which he was not satisfied,* for "it was less a question of defining himself in retrospect than of taking stock of himself in order to go beyond himself." (pp. 67-8)

Already in the last pages of *Biffures,* Michel Leiris had reached the point of doubt about the future of his prospecting. The method of investigation which he announces as far back as *L'Age d'homme* appears to be, however, of an inexhaustible fecundity. We find it hard to understand that he can fear "mental bankruptcy," from which, working indefinitely on the same stock of memories, he might be able to present nothing more than "a weaker and a more diluted rehash." In fact, it is not like a vein of ore that we follow to its end. The more we dig into our past, especially into our childhood, the more discoveries we make and continue to live and to live better, let us hope, thanks to the exploitation we make of these shrouded images.

What Michel Leiris wishes to clarify is that particular being, irreducible, obscure to himself, which he seeks in his most distant past and thoughts: for example in the substratum of language, a trap in which are caught from infancy the mysterious but instructive elements of our personal mythology, an irrationality where perhaps our reason for living is hidden. These are difficult to reach, a humble but fruitful way of coming to the remembrance of things past. Even in the balancing of certain of his sentences (more often, it is true, inspired by the master of his surrealist youth, André Breton), the influence of Proust is evident. Leiris, unconcerned about any possible ridicule, follows right through with his game of words. (pp. 68-9)

Leiris, like Joyce, is master of his means. His manias, and whatever is incontestably pathological in his behavior, far from reducing interest in his research, give it significance. Whoever meditates on the repetitive words of Michel Leiris must agree: there does not exist, there never did exist, there will not exist in the future, a more reasonable man. We are all madmen at large adjusting ourselves as best we can to our monsters by putting our best foot forward in order to fool people. We are all in terror and despair for days on end, our only moments of respite being those when we succeed in distracting ourselves from our obsessions, in particular, from the haunting fear of death. Hence that fever of activity to which most men abandon themselves, that more or less vain agitation by which they are duped in the end, especially when they attain the goal of the less illusory playthings, endowed with concrete material reality, money and power.

We find in this monograph [*Biffures*], then, a being who is exceptionally vulnerable, unprotected, lost, who, while he judges himself with cruel lucidity, remains fascinated by his most ridiculous obsessions. This is a monograph about the Abnormal which could also no doubt be about the Normal, since nothing is more widespread than that crushed attitude toward life, that weakness, the panic of existing, the horror of knowing oneself to be mortal. Such confessions dealing with humble and everyday things may seem ridiculous to persons who tend to dissociate themselves from what they really are. Thus Michel Leiris's courage is all the greater. (p. 70)

What Michel Leiris can never express exaggeratedly enough is the vertigo of living. An existentialist anxiety, this manifests itself in his simplest gestures as well as his most insignificant thoughts. This is easy to recognize since, although it may take a different form, it is analogous to our own. Hence the paradoxical comfort of knowing that we are not as alone as we may think. Not only do we find a brother in Michel Leiris, but the similarity of our experience permits us to infer a more extensive fraternity, which really includes the entire human race. (p. 72)

Michel Leiris reproaches himself for by-passing, more or less voluntarily, the great experiences of man: those of giving up life, risking death. Without suspecting that the one who gives up his life finally discovers a reason for risking it, he writes: "With a bitterness that I never suspected before I have just realized that all that I need in order to save myself is a certain fervor, but that this world lacks anything for which I would give my life" [*L'Age d'homme*]. In *Fourbis:* "If there is nothing in love—or taste—for which I am ready to face death, I am only stirring up empty space and everything cancels itself out, myself included."

In this it seems to him lies the failure of his existence. Only a literary work, by describing his life, can turn it into a kind of success. Incapable of conquering his obsessions, he enumerates and labels them, following the advice of Jacques Rivière, who made it a rule *to consolidate his position with his reverses.*

His testimony has not been in vain: "If I should reach the point of contributing, no matter how little, to enable humani-ty, by throwing aside old teachings in favor of more fraternal behavior, to attain a kind of maturity, what difference should it make to others if my fate—considered simply as a work of art—is not a masterpiece?" (p. 73)

Claude Mauriac, "Michel Leiris," in his The New Literature, *translated by Samuel I. Stone, George Braziller, Inc., 1959, pp. 61-73.*

THE TIMES LITERARY SUPPLEMENT

Now that *Fibrilles* has been added to *Biffures* (1948) and *Fourbis* (1955), Michel Leiris's patient and profound essay in autobiography, *La Règle du jeu,* is complete. He had intended to write a fourth volume, *Fibules,* which was to tie everything together in a supreme act of reconciliation between the muddle of his life and the mythical patterns of his books, but he now seems to have achieved this reconciliation where it matters more, in the world of action as opposed to that of imagination. It is in fact the subtle traffic between these two tragically divided worlds which provides the substance of *La Règle du jeu,* and M. Leiris's own honesty and intelligence in recording it which makes all three volumes so sympathetic and original.

The repeated *f*s and *b*s of his chosen titles are a first indication that he sees the chronology of a life as of much less interest than its assonances. Chronology is logical, anonymous and an unpleasant reminder of mortality, and M. Leiris rejects it outright, choosing instead to re-create certain aspects of his past by the simple association of words, or ideas. During the 1920s he was for some years an accredited Surrealist and for some months the patient of a psychoanalyst and his autobiography owes everything to these two experiences, because it is a prolonged exercise in auto-analysis, intended not only to inform the reader but also to help the writer, who has always suffered from a profound sense of inadequacy as a human being.

M. Leiris begins, therefore, not with the formation of his limbs but with that of his language, and in *Biffures* he recalls certain crucial episodes of his early childhood, when he first became aware that his own language was also partly that of other people. The key word here is "partly", because he has never been foolish enough to put away these childish things and suppose that any two people use precisely the same language. *La Règle du jeu* recognizes above all that all words face both inwards and outwards, and that certain words crackle with an emotional charge which is an irresistible invitation to self-examination for the person feeling it. From one point of view these books constitute a dictionary of such privileged words, arranged not alphabetically but affectively, as M. Leiris works to reveal to himself and to others the associations which they have suddenly or gradually acquired for him. It is inevitable that a large part of his research should lead him back to his childhood, and the years before words and things were wholly one. . . .

In an influential essay called **"De la littérature considérée comme une tauromachie"** published soon after a war which made very few demands on his courage, M. Leiris stressed that writing would be pointless so far as he was concerned if it did not involve him in taking risks. What he wanted to be able to do was to see the sheet of paper as a bull-ring and himself as a matador, performing the ritual gestures of his trade. The obvious difficulty is to find a suitable pair of horns over which a sedentary writer can bend with the illusion of danger, and the solution once again was supplied by language, by the phrase "the moment of truth", used of that instant of time when it is most possible to judge how fully the bull-fighter is prepared to commit himself to the rules of his "game". The writer who wants to pursue "moments of truth" in public can only hope to do so by overcoming the normal inhibitions of autobiographers, and this is what Michel Leiris has done. The risks which he takes in *La Règle du jeu* are those of self-revelation, but they are taken in full knowledge of their essentially theatrical nature, since these are acrobatics performed above a safety-net. To say that these three volumes are completely frank is certainly not the same thing as saying that in them M. Leiris spares nobody and nothing. About certain aspects of his life, notably his marriage, he is very reticent; what he has achieved is an unheroic honesty which never once topples over into self-abasement and never once asks for our pity as opposed to our complicity.

But it is clear that the risks he was prepared to take in print could never finally have reconciled M. Leiris to the intimate hesitations which have marked his life. When he set out on *La Règel du jeu,* during the German occupation of France, it was with the conviction that somewhere he could find the philosopher's stone which would enable him to make sense of his life, but the mythical organization he managed now and again to impose on it remained stubbornly imprisoned in his writing, and cast no golden glow over his living. The two divergent tendencies of his nature refused to be brought together.

In *Fibrilles* these tendencies are embodied for the last time, as what M. Leiris calls his "Mao-side" and his "Kumasi-side", the first standing for a sense of community and for positive action, the second for withdrawal into the self and for nostalgia. Yet just when things seem darkest he at last takes the risk which brings poetry into his life, having spent so long trying to turn life into poetry. The risk was an attempt at suicide and the scar left in his throat by the tracheotomy which saved his life is now Michel Leiris's *fibule,* an emblem of unity which he once thought could be nothing better than the title of a book.

"*À la Recherche du Temps,*" in The Times Literary Supplement, *No. 3407, June 15, 1967, p. 536.*

D. J. ENRIGHT

Michel Leiris's short self-exposure [*Manhood*] manages to seem long, obsessive, intellectually over-heated and emotionally cold—especially cold. It is totally free of prurience, as far-removed as possible from the pornographic, and empty of any common or garden kind of vanity. It was first published in France in 1939, and presumably its appearance in English owes something to the current taste for the life-story which 'tells all'. In fact, though it tells with extreme clarity, *Manhood* tells very little.

Essentially Leiris is (or was) a highly intellectual masochist—except perhaps that he doesn't enjoy suffering. In this book he is forever paying in advance for goods which never seem to arrive, which makes him a masochist of a superior and peculiarly absolute sort. He is a much travelled man, a distinguished anthropologist specialising in Africa, and he must have had a great deal of 'life' which doesn't appear in this book and isn't in any way predicted by it. What this book tells us is that its author was afraid of life.

Manhood is ineffably literary. Like some other literary intellectuals, Leiris is an authority on bull-fighting, and the reader who experiences a low tolerance towards metaphors drawn from the *corrida* would be well advised to skip the introduction, 'The Autobiographer as *Torero*', were it not that this essay strikes a note which sounds throughout the book. The young Leiris wishes to be sincere and lucid, to avoid artifice, neither gilding nor blackening the picture, but this (he says) is not enough. To save his confessions from being no more than the graceful movements of a ballerina, he must ensure the presence of an element of danger. He is to be matador rather than dancer: 'To expose certain obsessions of an emotional or sexual nature, to admit publicly to certain shameful deficiencies or dismays was, for the author, the means—crude, no doubt, but which he entrusts to others, hoping to see it improved—of introducing even the shadow of a bull's horn into a literary work.' Having made heavy weather over this tauromachic parallel, Leiris is then obliged to make heavy weather over the obvious differences between autobiographer and matador. The former runs a moral risk, he can hurt friends or alienate them, he can (as we say) get himself a bad name, but 'unless he has committed an offence whose admission makes him liable to capital punishment', he is unlikely to risk his life. These confessions were written before the war, when Leiris was a relatively young man of 34 and more susceptible to social or professional damage, but even so it is difficult to envisage the reading public as a bull of much weight or ferocity. Yet Leiris retains the metaphor of bull-fighting as ritual, the whole confrontation having 'a *sculptural* character'. It is the discipline, the 'classicism', of the *corrida* that he finally wishes to keep for his confessions.

Manhood can be said to be 'classical' in various senses of this well-nigh senseless word. For instance, in that it is not romantic in any simple sense of that word, and Leiris talks of himself as if (which he hardly ever does) he were talking of someone else. Emotionally he is severe, even Spartan, but intellectually he permits himself the somewhat frigid convolutions of the French mind turned in upon itself. (pp. 309-10)

The women who have dominated his imagination, 'Lucrece the cold, and Judith the sword-wielder', followed by Salome, Carmen, Delilah, Cleopatra, have one thing in common: either they suffered through love or they caused suffering through love. . . . There is certainly a classical consistency about it all.

Classical too are the women in the book, in that they are mostly myths or statues. Leiris mentions an 'absolutely hideous' bronze of a snake-charmer, naked but for a turban, which his father considered very chaste, though (says Leiris) 'I have more than once indulged in contestable behaviour because of this statue, having first fingered the entire body at great length.' . . . Along with a love of statues went an early love of allegory, irrespective of the allegorical significance, for 'all I ever saw was a beautiful statute'—presumably 'statue' is meant—'as in the parks, the portrait of a goddess as alluring as Deceit or fair as Truth.' Outside the stone or bronze variety, there is very little sense of *woman* in *Manhood,* only brief, spectral and rather unfeeling references to the partners of several painful amours and an old-fashioned (and none the worse for that) allusion to 'the woman who shares my life'. This latter topic, left undeveloped, makes one wonder about the tendentiousness of confessions so severely delimited as these, and also whether Leiris may not have found a sort of happiness nonetheless, out of which he was unable to create literature, allegory, myth or symbol.

The humans adumbrated here have no more personal presence or independent existence than do the scissors with which Leiris lacerates himself during the one protracted affair other than his marriage in what he calls 'an extremely poor emotional life', or the fists of the prostitutes whom he asks to beat him up. The poverty of the dramatis personae detracts, I would say, from the persuasiveness of Leiris's insistence that the writer must seek to tip the scales 'towards the liberation of *all* men, without which none can achieve his own'.

But the self-analysis ends in self-understanding at least. . . .

What is best in this book arises out of Leiris's honesty, self-pitilessness and avoidance of self-excuse. What is worse comes from his fearfully self-conscious insistence on symbolic connections of an extremely tenuous kind—and from his avoidance of self-excuse. Never to seek to excuse or extenuate is a sort of callousness, or incompleteness. It is too easy for the literary man to forget that his path is set among human beings, not among myths, alas. It is difficult to describe Leiris's detailed self-portraiture without sounding censorious or at least impatient. And such a response is not much to offer by way of a bull's horn, or even its shadow! (p. 310)

> *D. J. Enright, "The Shadow of a Bull's Horn," in*
> The Listener, *Vol. LXXIX, No. 2032, March 7,*
> *1968, pp. 309-10.*

MARTIN SEYMOUR-SMITH

[Michel Leiris's *L'Age d'homme* is] one of the most interesting books of the century. Strictly speaking, this is not a novel; but, in an age one of whose preoccupations is the true nature and, therefore, direction of fiction, it will exercise its greatest influence in this sphere. One would expect nothing less of a French work described by its author as 'the negation of a novel.'

Leiris is an anthropologist by profession, as well as a littérateur and surrealist poet. But *Manhood*, the first version of which he completed in 1935, is neither anthropological nor literary in intention: it is an attempt by the author to write a book about himself so sincere that, in Baudelaire's words, the paper would shrivel and flare at each touch of the writer's fiery pen. By exposing 'certain obsessions of an emotional or sexual nature,' and admitting publicly to 'certain shameful deficiencies or dismays' Leiris hoped to achieve a catharsis, 'a vital fulfilment.' He wanted, by involving himself in a positive danger, to attain the freedom of 'self-realisation as a whole man.'

This could easily have become a pretentious project, but in Leiris's hands it is quite the opposite. *Manhood* is an account, traced with a unique objectivity, of his sexual life; though rather less of its facts than of the motivation behind them: of the coldness of his temperament, his incapacity to feel carnal pleasure except when it is accompanied by 'superstitious terror' (a theme that has been fully explored in English poetry, hardly at all in English fiction) and an absence of the reproductive instinct, and the obsession of his imagination with two images of women—the suicide Lucretia and the murderess Judith.

Leiris's sexuality is, of course, peculiar to himself; but its in-

gredients are common to all men. This self-exploration is astonishing in its maturity; Leiris is one of the very few modern writers to demonstrate how a book can be an act as well as a gesture. (p. 299)

> *Martin Seymour-Smith, "Great Powers," in* The
> Spectator, *Vol. 220, No. 7289, March 8, 1968, pp.*
> *299, 301.*

RICHARD WOLLHEIM

Manhood contains much that would, I imagine, scandalise the ordinary cultivated reader. It contains—and I stay with this word, for the book is supremely a receptacle—many, many accounts of adventures with women, masturbation phantasies, evocations of childhood eroticism, carefully laid plans for failure and self-destruction, grandiose visions of bisexuality, and innumerable references, direct and oblique, to impotence and boredom, and worse still, to the fear of impotence and to the fear of boredom. And if we are to some degree habituated to these things in modern fiction or in the confessions of the self-confessed outsiders, it is another thing to be asked to confront them in the autobiography of someone who incontrovertibly belongs to the world of high bourgeois culture. *Manhood* is a record of those thoughts which Prufrock would have kept even from himself. (p. 350)

Leiris, at the age of 34, half-way through life, starts his autobiography by considering himself as a body seen naked in a glass. The light brown hair cut short to prevent baldness; the broad bulging forehead with projecting veins; the habitually inflamed eyelids; the shiny skin, and the tendency to blush—the style of depiction is set, and it remains constant as we move from the body to the mind and its contents. But if the portrait is harsh or unflattering, the painter, who is also the sitter, is loving of the strokes that make up the portrait. It is from this superimposition of love upon contempt, of concern upon indifference, as well as of detachment upon a kind of frenzy that can turn equally into abasement or into exaltation, that the pervasive beauty of Leiris's fragment derives.

There are two main characters to the book, and many background figures, nearly all women, lightly identified but also totally recalled. To the two heroines Leiris remains faithful: the book is indeed the story of his devotion. The subsidiary women, the dramatis personae, constitute the fashion in which he is faithful: the objects of his sexual passion—had either in the body or, more frequently, in the mind, in solitary pleasure—they are the means by which he shows his devotion. These subsidiary women are real women—streetwalkers, barmaids, party-goers, the inhabitants of brothels, women in momentary distress, companions in boredom, waifs. The two great loves, on the contrary, are mythological figures, most memorably recorded in a great double portrait by Cranach, which forms the frontispiece to the book. Both are naked, both armed, both fresh from a sexual experience—Lucrece who stabs herself after being raped, Judith who cuts off the head of the man she has made her lover.

How are we to read this book? We are to read it, of course, by starting at page one and reading through till we reach the end. But when we reach the end we will find that the book has re-formed itself into another shape. When we take stock of this shape, it dissolves, and another takes its place; or we are left with the text. We are not to resist this process. I have mentioned Freud, and there is obviously a link between Leiris and Freud which goes deeper than Leiris's own rejection of certain psychoanalytic interpretations, or indeed of the touch of psychoanalysis upon himself. For, in the first place, the way of understanding upon which the book rests is clearly connected with the pursuit of associations, with the following up of concatenated images and scenes: for that is how the book is constructed. And, secondly, the aim of understanding, which the book pursues, has no finality to it. Nothing, it is true, is quite what it seems to be: but nor is it anything else definitive, anything that can be exhaustively characterised. The forces of condensation and displacement are constantly at work.

Suppose we start, for instance, in the middle of the book, with an incident from the age of 12, when Leiris cut his head on the schoolyard wall, and on regaining consciousness felt the blood flowing, and thought: 'How can I make love?' Besides the thought explicitly expressed, we can find two other thoughts expressed here, each of which has its complex history recorded in *Manhood,* and each of which conditions or leads to its own understanding of Leiris's two loves.

The first is: How can I make love if *she* will bleed? From his sexual tastes Leiris explicitly exempts pregnant women: indeed, it is the very first thing that we learn about these tastes. To the horror of pregnancy Leiris associates a childhood belief about how the Christmas toys came to arrive on the hearth. The toys did not, he believed, come down through the narrow shaft of the chimney, but omnipotent God created them where he found them. As to his own birth, he could not believe—or, as he puts it, he never had the idea—that anything erotic ever occurred between his parents. And it is probably to sexual curiosity, so deflected, that we are to attribute the young Leiris's fascination with the theatre, into which his sister, the earlier-born, initiated him. For we may think of the theatre as a kind of bland image at once for the mother's body and for the child's frightened mind; Leiris's particular enthusiasm, he tells us, was for plays where there was something to 'understand'. Set against the belief, thus elaborated, that the woman is and must remain intact, the figures of Lucrece and Judith now take on a special and shared significance. We must look to their hands and see what they carry: the instruments of their own satisfaction. The women are self-contained objects, women of marble, and in front of them, under their shadow, Leiris can only run after whores or try, magically, hubristically, to emulate their completeness.

And the second thought is: How can I make love if *I* will bleed? The thought here is, of course, among the most familiar to a distinctively modern consciousness or sensibility. But what is strange to observe is how, under the pall of these oedipal fears, Lucrece once again assimilates herself to Judith: for, by a piece of anatomical *trompe-l'oeil,* the dagger, as it passes between the breasts, can be seen to penetrate not the woman but the man. So the horror completes itself. For, despite the duality of his love, at no moment is there choice open to him. At one moment it is all virginity, at another all death.

And then between the lines of *Manhood,* or in the twines of Leiris's own mind, a compromise suggests itself. In many descriptions, in many adventures, we glimpse, beside the woman who excludes the man and the woman who admits him only to a fatal embrace, the shadow of another woman: the woman who can contain him. She can hold him without damage to her or revenge upon him. Traces of this woman,

the woman of living marble, are distributed widely across this book, embodied in many figures. At one point she shrinks, becomes depersonalised, she is now the white basin into which the whore spits after the man has defiled her. And then we find her again, writ large, for she is the book itself, which can, as I have said—and now we can see why I said it—be seen as a vast receptacle. At this point the theme, the style, the intention of the book fuse into a haunting, magical perfection.

Rereading Leiris's book in this light, we will then be struck by a distinctive feature: what might be called the lingering character of the images, the fantasies, the way they remain pebble-like in the stream of disclosed consciousness. A thought encountered by chance in the act of composition, like a woman casually acquired on a nocturnal walk, remains imperishably distinct, perhaps (and perhaps this is a criticism) inadequately worked into the texture of the book. In the last resort **Manhood,** for all its sophistication, its sadness, its subtlety, is like a child showing us his toys: allowing us a momentary glimpse at the brightly coloured contents of his box, at objects cherished beyond himself. Leiris's book establishes, once more, the absurdity of the category of innocence. More important still, even as it stands, even in the present wretched translation, it refutes the narrower criticism by revealing the beauty, the poignancy, the momentary glory, that can be achieved by a book written totally outside the hierarchy of moral values. (pp. 351-52)

> *Richard Wollheim, "On Self-Exposure," in* The Listener, *Vol. LXXIX, No. 2033, March 14, 1968, pp. 350-52.*

GERMAINE BRÉE

The case of Leiris seems, at first glance, simple. A 1955 table of his works raises no question as to genre: it lists voyages, essays, poetry, novel. In 1960, another listing substitutes the rubric "autobiographical *écrits*" (pieces) for essays, and adds a new category, "aesthetics." But Leiris' volumes themselves carry no such classification, even when, like **Mots sans mémoire** (1969), most of the pieces collected therein had at some previous time been published as poetry.

Leiris himself raises the question of the literary genre. In his 1946 preface to **L'Âge d'homme** (1939), he situates that work among the "autobiographical novels, private diaries, souvenirs, confessions" which, he adds, "have had so extraordinary a vogue in the past years (as if the factor of creation was being neglected in the literary work envisaged only from the point of view of expression)." The remark itself contains an implied criticism, and toward the end of his preface he returns to the topic, noting that where the "academic genres are concerned," he had "gone in a completely different direction." "I distinguish in literature a kind of genre which I consider *major . . .* and . . . to the degree only that no rule of composition can be detected in regard to it other than the one which served the author as his Ariadne's thread in the abrupt explication he was carrying out . . . with himself; [only to this degree] can work of this type be considered literarily 'authentic.' "

To illustrate his meaning, he uses the analogy of the bullfight that made the preface—and possibly Leiris himself—famous: "literature considered as a bullfight." The analogy can be almost indefinitely developed; but, in brief, a bullfight is a ritualized ceremonial killing which involves the risk of death for the matador. The "genre" Leiris dreams of would comprise "those works in which the horn [of the bull] is present in one form or another: a direct risk assumed by the author either of a confession or of an *écrit* [piece] with a subversive content." It is not the place here to discuss Leiris' conception of literature as "self-exposure," but merely to emphasize his description of a type of work which corresponds to no type, and by that very character defines itself as "authentic literature," of which, Leiris adds, poetry is a pure form. One thinks of Blanchot who, also in the realm of narrative, aspires to "a new mode which is neither novel, nor *récit* nor essay," a "genre that has no name."

A look, however brief, at Leiris' autobiographical work is enlightening. *L'Âge d'homme* begins, in a traditional manner consonant with the genre, as a linear narrative in the first person: "I'm just thirty-four, half a life-time. Physically, I'm of medium height, on the short side. . . ." But after about four pages, the linear development is broken. The work is then organized first around certain general themes—old age and death, the supernatural, the infinite. This would then suggest a certain modality of the genre—the essay à la Montaigne. But the categories become more and more disparate and discontinuous: Carmen, Lucretia and Judith, "a wounded foot, a bitten buttock, a split head," etc. Sections begin with long quotations, accounts of dreams are sporadically introduced, connections are established only, though not always, within the separate fragments of text, not from one fragment to another. As a result the "I"—the narrator and protagonist—becomes composite, and the surface characteristics which we expect to be present in an autobiography are destroyed.

When we move from volume to volume, the fragmentation is accentuated. *Biffures* (*Deletions*), the first volume of *La Règle du jeu,* offers unconnected developments on certain words, on the letters of the alphabet, etc.; there appears to be no logic to the development of the book and no purpose or clear design in the material collected; it seems to propose no meaning in terms of Leiris' life. The titles indicate the general movement away from sustained narrative—*Biffures, Fourbis, Fibrilles, Fibules.*

Leiris, at the start of his autobiographical enterprise, as he explains it, had the compelling urge to talk about himself which also characterized Rousseau, and also the drive to speak the truth; he uses the same vocabulary as Bataille: to disrobe publicly, to present himself in his "nudity." This desire in his case was accompanied by belief in literary expression as a form of art which the bullfight metaphor conveys. As an ethnologist and a writer, he gave himself a code establishing the "rules" of the game: to deal exclusively with elements whose veracity was unquestionable and which had a "documentary" value that seemed in some way significant—memories, anecdotes, dreams, impressions. The literary effort was to transcribe them exactly in the most "condensed" language, with no attempt at transposition, so as to achieve the quality he called "authenticity"—the negation of fictional verisimilitude—a kind of absolute realism both psychic and social, free of rationalization, interpretation, teleological intent. This is what he called the "canon" of composition. He was in fact conducting an ethnographer's research project, an investigation of himself through all the modalities of his psychic life in search of a possible pattern—a central myth, perhaps underlying all the mythical patterns unconsciously set up, but which his ethnographer's eye detected. His search was for some inherently related structure that would emerge from the material

itself and so would not be fictional, that is, not imposed by him upon the data from outside, nor by any chronological or logical pattern. He calls these "filing-cards," "une série d'écrits," fragments. What traditionally defined autobiography as a genre becomes in his hands a kind of alphabet or perhaps a "glossary."

I am not concerned here with the logic or results of Leiris' literary "bullfight"—but merely with its disintegration of one of the prose genres here discussed. Most typical perhaps of this activity is the small volume entitled *Nuits sans nuit et quelques jours sans jour.* The autobiography has become a kind of widely spaced journal: a succession of usually short accounts of dreams, carefully dated, interspersed with a few accounts of experiences occurring in "demi-sommeil" or "lived," spanning the years 1923-1960. These Leiris refers to as "poetry"—that is, in his terms, "authentic" literature, which he equates with strangeness. Perhaps we might use for them the Pongian term "proems." The "composite" subject confronts the archetypal dreamer, but no mythical narrative spans the whole, transforming the fragments into the "block" Leiris had assumed would emerge out of his investigation, and which would interrelate them all.

The whole effect of the work is different from Bataille's; their writing seems situated at polar opposites, but the same characteristics appear; an abundance of disparate "écrits" in which at times a fragmentary order, non-logical in kind, asserts itself; a subject who is present, yet, as a writer, posits his own strict exclusion from involvement in the structure of what he is writing; a serious concern for what is fundamental in their experience, respect for a reality that cannot be reduced: this is a mimetic use of language, but in relation to the *psychic* world.

The register is different: Bataille's "bullfight" concerns a "wild," "exorbitant" area of experience which he claims language cannot encompass, but can to a certain extent mime: void, madness, horror, ecstasy, outrage, mystic trance. The impulse is toward the "inordinate," which is the major Bataille theme and which the erotic literally "embodies." Leiris, with meticulous precision, deals with the daily life. But both speak of the strangeness of the reality disclosed as they "expose" themselves through a discourse that seeks to dissociate life from meaning: and they call that effect of strangeness "poetry" when they succeed in translating it into language. (pp. 9-12)

Germaine Brée, "The Break-up of Traditional Genres: Bataille, Leiris, Michaux," in Bucknell Review, *Vol. XXI, No. 2, Fall, 1973, pp. 3-13.*

JOHN STURROCK

[Michel Leiris] became an autobiographer not long after he had tried psychoanalysis and got little or nothing from it. Psychoanalysis he had come to through Surrealism, a doctrine which, like other lapsed members of André Breton's chapel, Leiris has never altogether disowned. He would have been wrong to do so: some parts of it have helped greatly to make him an exemplary autobiographer.

He has preserved above all a faith in the cognitive powers of language; he believes that language has secrets, to penetrate which is to learn something about the world, and about oneself. As an autobiographer Leiris lends his attention as much to language as to life, concentrating on certain salient words or groups of words in the certainty that these will show themselves to be privileged points of entry into his past. He uses as an autobiographical program what Freud offers as a description of psychic dynamics: "In order that thought-processes may acquire quality, they are associated in human beings with verbal memories, whose residues of quality are sufficient to draw the attention of consciousness to them and to endow the process of thinking with a new mobile cathexis from consciousness."

Freud of course wanted to understand not the process of remembering but the process of forgetting, and the signs in consciousness which teach us when and where to recognize the subconscious. The Freudian technique that Leiris chooses has as its premise that what most matters in a potential autobiography is what has been censored. Leiris goes very much further, in fact, than Stephen Spender had even planned to go. Not only does he organize his volumes of autobiography by association of ideas (and sometimes of words) instead of by chronology, but he deliberately follows those networks of association which will cause him the greatest unease. Autobiography, by this new dispensation, becomes an exercise in self-therapy. Leiris began writing about himself to try to rationalize certain, as he believed, crippling weaknesses in his personality. The books were intended to have a practical result, which was to cure him of particularly tenacious inhibitions by making a public spectacle of their etiology. They failed, perhaps for the reason advanced in Jeffrey Mehlman's helpful if fiercely Lacanian essay on Leiris in *A Structural Study of Autobiography*, which is that language is never the possession of any individual so that to employ it is to be alienated from the self. Leiris, in this interpretation, is a victim of convention, his hopes dashed by the realization that even a total sincerity must yield to protocol if it is to become words. His failure is the one foreseen by Diderot's "homme au paradoxe" in the *Paradoxe sur le comédien*, who recognized that his real-life *sensiblerie*, which caused him to become tongue-tied, confused, and eventually speechless, would never do for a portrayal of *sensiblerie* on the stage, which needed to be articulate. Leiris' success in performance is beyond question; what has been sacrificed is his private failure.

His mistake, we can agree with Mehlman, was to believe that the autobiographer might possess not only his own past but also his native language. That was his only mistake: he was right to ignore the usual conventions of autobiography. His most pointed rebuff to them comes right at the start of the very first volume, *L'Age d'homme*, ["Old Age and Death"] whose opening section has the title "Vieillesse et mort." Such are the provocations of Surrealism. Under this heading, never before deemed possible for an autobiographical volume, Leiris in fact groups together images, memories, and reflections connected with those two themes. He is being ostentatiously morbid launching his autobiography with these terminal concerns, but at the same time identifying the particular phobia—the fear of annihilation—which he blames for so much of what has been unsatisfactory about his life.

Old age and death are succeeded, as rubrics, by other imposing abstractions: "The Infinite," "The Soul," "Subject and Object," in a series which becomes more and more idiosyncratic, to culminate in such inimitable groupings as "Stories of Injured Women" and "Stories of Dangerous Women." The arrangement is ambitious; Leiris sets out to make a book from his thoughts instead of from his acts and proves, finally, that, contrary to a common prejudice, in true autobiography words speak louder than actions. As an autobiographer, he belongs, it could be said, to the *Annales* school, working to recreate his own "mentalité," not to the older school for whom autobiography remains "événementiel."

Autobiography of this kind is not without a sense of direction. The narrative of *La régle du jeu* is one of the accumulation of self-knowledge and the establishment of order—the autobiographer's own order—in the past. Once chronology has been given up, the autobiographer is lost and must take his bearings by writing. He knows, as it were, nothing of his life until he has seen what he puts. The power of association, of bringing into the light mnemonic instead of temporal contiguities, has infinitely more to tell us about our permanent psychic organization than the power of chronology. The autobiographer, like the analysand, needs therefore to cultivate states of heightened receptivity, so that the censorship is outflanked and he is free to register as fully as he can what Leiris calls, in a central definition of his method, "ces noeuds de faits, de sentiments, de notions se groupant autour d'une expérience plus colorée que les autres et jouant le rôle d'un signe ou d'une illustration assez frappante pour me servir de repère."

The notion of the writer ceding the initiative to words is at least as old as Mallarmé, but it has been taken, *when* it has been taken, as a recommendation exclusively for poets or writers of lyrical, unworldly prose, not for autobiographers, who are classed with the writers of narrative and realism and forbidden to cede the initiative at all. The thought that an autobiography might be the exploration of its author's language rather than his life will seem eccentric to many and offensive to some. But the language and the life support one another; all that is at stake is which we see as coming first. The biographer is surely correct to produce a book in which the narrative appears to have dictated the narration; the autobiographer would do well to achieve the opposite effect, of a book where the narration appears to have dictated the narrative.

This is what Leiris has done and what many of his predecessors in autobiography might have done, given more courage. Autobiography is a form which has long appealed to poets, who will have grasped, even if they have largely failed to tap, its possibilities for that specifically poetic activity of realizing verbal paradigms. What they feared perhaps was the strain and emotional expense of such a procedure, maintained not over the quite short period of time it takes to work on a poem but over the months or years it takes to write an autobiography; what they may have feared even more was the resistance of their readers, who tolerate the blatant artifice and abstention from chronology in poems only because poems are known to be verbal constructs offering verbal satisfactions.

Readers will need reconditioning to think of autobiography in the same way. Books like the three volumes of *La régle du jeu* will not seem rectilinear to those whose fixed idea of a straight line is the straight line of chronology. Yet these books, like all books, *are* rectilinear; they are written as a succession of words and read as one. The straight line we are asked to follow is the one the writer traces as he writes. A large element of convention remains even so: that line is only apparently straight and unbroken, the books having been written intermittently and, in Leiris' case, over a number of years. The writer's stream of consciousness does not flow at the same speed or with the same intensity as the talker's. The writer has to write things down, and he can write things down only as fast as he can write things down; there is a brake on his will to associate. He is, moreover, on his own and must do without the guidance—the explanations, encouragement, the fatherly presence—of a psychoanalyst. His one interlocutor is a phantom: the audience for his work represented as yet entirely by himself. And being alone the writer also misses that useful obligation we generally feel in company not to fall wholly silent; in writing composition stands in for compulsion. The associative autobiography is thoroughly conventional, but its conventions seem to me to make better sense than the traditional ones.

As a literary innovation it should be classed with those other twentieth-century innovations which have introduced the writer explicitly into his text, and which have allowed linguistic accident—homophones, alliteration, rhyme—to fix the direction that the text is to take. . . . Recollection exceeds commentary I would guess in *La règle du jeu* and fairly lengthy episodes from the past are narrated chronologically; no autobiographer could follow up every association that came to him as he wrote. His text should be a compromise between intention and improvisation.

La règle du jeu does not add up to a history of Leiris' life; its coverage of the past would be strikingly incomplete even supposing its contents could be recombined into a rough chronological sequence. But if these books are not a history, what then are they? A description would be one answer, or a diagram of the autobiographer. Where orthodox narrative is temporal, this other sort is spatial, bearing in mind, though, that all verbal messages are extended in time. In some typologies of autobiography I do not doubt that Leiris would be disallowed, as having failed to satisfy certain elementary requirements, and notably the requirement of Starobinski "qu'il y ait précisément narration et non pas description." What fails, by this test, to qualify as autobiography, is confined to being a "self-portrait."

Here there is a bias against "description," which is what happens in novels when narration stops. Description, traditionally, is a respite from the story, a stopping of the clock. But in the kind of autobiography we are talking about, that clock has never been started, description and narration have merged and description can now be seen for what it is, that is to say, consecutive and mobile. A "self-portrait" is a misnomer, applied to a literary work, because it implies the instantaneous production of a likeness of the author. It may be a convenience to call a book a "self-portrait" once it is complete, but it is highly misleading to call it that while it is being written. The term loses sight altogether of the business of writing and helps to reinforce the mistaken view that the process of narration is subsumed in the events narrated. (pp. 58-62)

It is a paradox that Leiris' own profound, revolutionary autobiography should have had as its most urgent aim the negation of time. It was his intense fear of death and the extinction of his ego which led him away from chronology and to the belief that he might, through his alternative method of recovering the past, immunize himself against the fatal passage of time. He imagined, as a once loyal Surrealist no doubt should, that he might apprehend his past no longer as filiform but as a three-dimensional solid, inside which he could wander at will, safe from reminders of mortality. The structure of his autobiography was conditioned by his psychology; it is the wonderfully intelligent sublimation of his fears. But the innovations Leiris has made in autobiography are now available to everyone, and there is no reason why those autobiog-

raphers who decide to follow him should do so only because they share his fears.

The compulsion to which Leiris admits is, one might claim, a neurotic exaggeration of the wish behind all autobiography, to encompass one's life as a single, thoroughly meaningful whole and insure it against oblivion. But *La règle du jeu,* which began as an attempt at self-therapy, is both a literary triumph and a personal fiasco. Leiris expelled from his books what was to him the most unwelcome of conventions, that of chronology, only to be made cruelly aware that it is not chronology which kills us but time, and for the writer time is measured out by the movement of his pen. (p. 62)

John Sturrock, "The New Model Autobiographer," in New Literary History, *Vol. IX, No. 1, Autumn, 1977, pp. 51-63.*

GERMAINE BRÉE

One could consider Michel Leiris's literary work, or even his work in its entirety, as a single autobiographic text. Interrupted at intervals, on occasion espousing different generic masks (poetry, novel, ethnographic studies, prefaces to various literary or artistic volumes), it comes to a halt rather than ends with each successive volume, only to start off again with the next. I shall refer here, however, only to that part of his work that belongs properly to the autobiographic mode in a more limited sense: to the volumes predicated upon a deliberate and sustained (though idiosyncratic) autobiographic project—to the four volumes grouped under the title *The Rule of the Game,* preceded by the prefatory **Manhood.** Leiris warns us that with *Frêle bruit* (Frail Sound, 1976) that project has drawn to a close. *Frêle bruit* is his "last word." At seventy-five he is playing his last cards as autobiographer. He has laid out like a deck of cards the fragmentary passages that make up the volume: "dealing them out, displacing them, grouping them as one lays out cards for a game of patience." The word Leiris uses here is *réussite.* It designates both the game of patience he specifically evokes and an act or project successfully brought to completion.

Leiris is not a man who uses words without weighing their implications. But if a *réussite* there is, for him it can be understood in no ordinary sense of the word, whether in terms of Leiris's life as he sees it, or in terms of a literary success:

> Failure everywhere: as a writer, because almost unable to go beyond the scrutiny of self he had only rarely acceded to poetry and, furthermore, knew that he was not made of the same timber as those whose fate is hanging, madness, or a definitive departure; as a rebel, since he had never abandoned bourgeoise comfort, and after stubborn revolutionary impulses, he had to admit that averse to violence as much as to sacrifice, he was not of the stuff of which militants are made; as a lover, since his sentimental life had been of the most banal and his sensual ardour had soon cooled down; as a traveller, since, confined to a single language, his mother tongue, he had perhaps been less apt than anyone else to feel at ease with people and things, even in his own clime. From his profession as ethnographer, he had, concretely, drawn very little: highly specialized work in the language of initiates in the Sudan and on ritual possessions in Ethiopia; work on 'negro art' based on secondary sources and, without much significance, in spite of high-

minded intentions, other works with an anti-racist bias; finally (and this was, he would think in his blackest hours, what was most worthy of mention) a few articles manifesting his will to put ethnography at the service, not of Western science, but of the peoples of the third world, a naive will, it is true, since those peoples are concerned with quite other things.

Leiris's sharply reductive balance sheet (which sets the sternly judgmental observer apart from the objectified "he," temporarily displacing the subjective "I") calls for some interpretation. For, if seen from outside with only its surface patterns visible, Leiris's long and respectable life could hardly be called a "failure." From the outset, he has lived in a privileged stratum of society, participating more fully than most in the sophisticated intellectual and artistic life of Paris. The roster of his friends from Raymond Roussel and Max Jacob, both of whom he knew as an adolescent, to André Masson, Sartre, Simone de Beauvoir, Camus, Picasso, and Giacometti among many others, could in itself have furnished abundant material for traditional memoirs. The list of his works and their variety are far from negligible; and he has consistently lived through the difficult years of his adult life (the years of the German occupation included) with more than average dignity. His reductive balance sheet, couched as it is in terms of the grandly romantic roles he failed to live up to, strikes one as being rather suspect. The mask does not entirely fit what one knows of the man. It reads like a set piece. And it is perhaps designed specifically to cast doubt upon itself, in the writer's eyes as well as in the readers'. Leiris's "simple confession," as he once called it, is indeed never a simple affair.

That the positive aspects of his existence are absent from the *bilan* is symptomatic, for they are just as absent, on the whole, from his entire autobiographic work. In *Manhood* and more sparsely and fragmentarily in the successive volumes, we catch sight of his childhood and adolescent world, later of the traveller and of his abortive love affairs, sometimes too of the poet involved in his word games and word associations. But only rarely do we get a glimpse of his married life, of the social or professional man. Leiris gives us very little information on the outer, factual surfaces of his life. They obviously do not concern his project. But it is notable that in his survey of his failures, he does not mention the twelve hundred-odd pages of *Manhood* and *La règle du jeu.* Perhaps in his eyes these represent the *réussite* and the counterweight to those other lacks and "failures."

Until recently Leiris has received scant attention from either readers or critics. Only the first section of his "immense monologue," *Manhood,* has reached what one might call a reading public. Consequently, and particularly in the English-speaking world, since it is the only volume available in English, *Manhood* has often been considered the exemplification of Leiris's use of the autobiographic medium. Nothing could be more misleading. As Leiris moves from volume to volume he approaches his material differently. The modification of the form that his investigation into his existence takes is not only central to this "autobiographical quest" but it is in fact its "raison d'être." (pp. 194-97)

From the outset Leiris was not content to equate autobiography with retrospective narrative, since it was his intent to use the autobiographic mode as a vehicle, not as an end. In the course of many years of practice he defined many times not only the nature and complexities of his task but also his will to proceed with the maximum honesty. It became a major—perhaps the major—theme of his writing. One fairly late definition seems to subsume most others: to pursue "the written formulation of that immense monologue that in a sense is given me, since all its substance is drawn from that which I have lived, but which in another sense obliges me to a constant effort of invention, since I must introduce an order in that indefinitely renewed substance, churn up its elements, adjust them, refine them until I manage in some measure to grasp their significance" (*Fibrilles*). The card game turns into a game of Tarot.

Leiris distinguishes several components he must take into account: that which has been or is being lived (indefinitely renewed); the continuous inner but apparently not as yet worded soundless monologue carried on with himself; the formulation in writing that imposes its invented order upon the fluid inner substance and monologue; and the decoding of the emergent pattern whereby that which was lived becomes readable. An osmosis takes place as existence is translated into writing, a phenomenon Mehlman accurately discerned when he defined Leiris's "autobiographic quest" as the attempt "to become alive (*bio*) to oneself (*auto*) in what the French call the elusive realm of *l'écriture* (*graphie:* writing)." This is not an easy position to hold. It posits a series of tensions: first, between the indefinitely renewed stuff of existence with its accompanying inner discourse and the writing that seeks to arrest and circumscribe it; second, between the slow tempo of the act of writing and the tempo of the life meanwhile continuing to develop; third (and as a consequence), the discrepancy between the self in the mobile present and the always anachronistic work of self-presentation or representation involved in the writing.

In the first instance, a "metadiscourse" underlies the effort of selection and organization required by the writing of a text. It puts the autobiographer's task in double jeopardy: the slippage into a tautological reduplication of its premises will disconnect it from the reality it was to reveal; it will then both replace and mask that reality it was meant to bring to the surface. In the second and third instances the complicated meshings of heterogenous time patterns that the autobiographic effort of self-display sets in motion compromise the hope of a self-discovery that would open up a perspective not only on the past but on the future. This Leiris set up as one of his goals: "Who is that I," he asks, "that self of mine around which everything is articulated?" Ethnographer that he is, he seeks in the materials of his life the central symbolic order that could give them significance. In terms of that *hors-texte*—the reality beyond the text that is his life—the project "to establish one's portrait in writing will remain illusory if one proposes to portray in his interiority he who, at that moment, is holding the pen and not another whom one already knows only through memory when he projects himself upon the page." Then "the inevitable discrepancy" between the moment in which one writes and the moment one would describe may turn into a "crying dissonance." The "time of the book" and the "time of life" fail to coincide; another such gap opens between the time span of the writer writing and the time span during which he turns into the reader—and possibly the rectifier—of his text (*Fibrilles*).

In this labyrinthine situation the status of the text itself is open to question. The pathway that the act of writing was to "invent" twists and turns upon itself. Leiris's determination not to be caught in the trap of a rhetoric that would contaminate the authenticity of his investigation inevitably leads him to try new methodical prospections. From volume to volume and sometimes within a single volume, he has, he states, tried "one after the other various trails and tunnels" (*Fourbis*). The image of the maze, although never fully explicated, surfaces here, each path opening up on another in a multiple itinerary that is interminable in the full sense of the word. The only way to terminate is to stop. No final resolution takes place. A Leiris-Daedalus refuses to be led to the center of the maze he has built to entrap himself, and he simultaneously seeks to escape it by acquiring the clear sense of its design. My analogy here is not altogether gratuitous; for the function of the maze in the first place seems to have been in great part to prevent anyone from reaching its center.

Leiris of course did not start out with the full sense of the problematics in which he had become involved. But the reader-critic (myself) may surmise that the *réussite* to which he alludes in the opening page of the last volume to date of his autobiographic quest is that he has eluded the temptation to answer his question. At one time it had been his intent to do so. A projected title, *Fiburles* (the clasps holding together the Roman toga), notified the reader that Leiris was to assemble into a single garment the fragmentary materials provided by the preceding volumes. The project did not materialize. *Frêle bruit* is composed of fragments between which, in the layout of the pages themselves, interstices open up into a kind of void. Admittedly Leiris fears and loathes the fact and idea of death. The deferment of any resolution to his quest leaves open the question of the presence of that inner self; it implies that the center around which all else is articulated cannot be reached by language, belongs then perhaps to the enigmatic realm of "the sacred" to whose exploration he had dedicated himself at the outset. Failure to reach it would consequently be a manner of success. For as we are apprised on the back cover of *Frêle bruit,* Leiris's investigation has yielded him as self-knowledge only the sense of being motivated by a few rather generally shared inner drives: ". . . an aspiration to the marvelous, the will to commitment in the struggle against social inequity, the desire for a universality that led him to establish contacts with other civilizations. . . ." While possessed by "horror" of death, in that "horror" the "sacred" most surely still haunts Leiris's world; and, in counterpoint, even in his old age the elusive sense of an absent center maintains its status as a never circumscribed exigency of creativity. On every level and in this same fashion Leiris continually balances and keeps alive conflicting hypotheses.

One could roughly classify the successive volumes as follows: *Manhood,* the investigation of formative personal and cultural myths, rooted in a childhood world in which the marvelous and the sacred coincide. *Biffures* elucidates the associations embedded in both the poetic and the private use of a shared language with their charge of the "marvelous," his natural ambience or "clime" as poet. With *Fourbis,* in the context of the war and its aftermath, Leiris investigates his aspirations to overcome the horror of death by moving beyond the closed circle of his subjectivity toward the glamorous "other." The movement reveals his need of an ethic that would allow him to sustain the poetic life within the societal. *Fibrilles* is his book of voyage and return in space and across time, not the least of which is the account of Leiris's journey toward death in attempted suicide. Of *Frêle bruit,* one might conclude that in relation to *Manhood,* the book of his thirties, it is the book of old age, a kind of post-face to the rest, all passion spent.

What is lost in this classification is the close interaction between experience, memory, and analysis that through the labor of writing and via the network of language binds each volume to the others in what Leiris speaks of as a form of symphonic orchestration and which I prefer to compare to a carefully built maze. For while the maze leaves one in uncertainty as to which path inward one should take, it is also a maze that reshapes itself continually, within an inevitable circularity. This is more particularly true of the three central volumes, *Biffures, Fourbis,* and *Fibrilles.* In each of these works, what changes is the criterion adopted for the written ordering of the text. This turns the reader who attempts to define Leiris's procedures as autobiographer into a meta-meta-critic; the initial meta-critic is always Leiris himself. Seen in this perspective and as a whole, *The Rule of the Game* has the elusive contours of mobile sculptures projected in space by a play of light or of mirrors.

Manhood, the initial volume in the autobiographic project, offers an insight into the process whereby Leiris's material acquires a kind of plasticity. Furthermore, it was in the course of writing this book that Leiris evolved the famous analogy between the *tauromachia* and the practice of literature as he understood it, deducing therefrom the poetic or "rule of the game" that he seeks to apply in the succeeding volumes. This is Leiris's first attempt at dealing with the problematics of the genre that on finishing *Manhood* he thought he had solved: for *Manhood* was first conceived as a "meta-autobiography," a consciously structured narrative whose episodes revealed, as in Sartre's later *The Words,* an underlying, comprehensible pattern that determined the book's organic structure. Leiris's organizing pattern was, of course, quite different from Sartre's. (pp. 198-202)

Of all the autobiographic volumes, *Manhood* comes closest to the traditional narrative model as analyzed by Philippe Lejeune: from a given point in time and in achievement (Leiris's access to "manhood"), the autobiographer retrospectively and in chronological sequence tells how he got there. And indeed *Manhood* goes back to the usual though fragmented scenes of childhood and moves on through a stormy adolescence in the post World War I years to 1929. The narrative is not linear in the sense that no apparent effort has been made to link the fragments in a continuous discourse. Often introduced by quotations, the successive chapters appear as vertical juxtapositions, laid out side by side, a technique of montage and collage reproduced within each section. The book as a whole gives an impression of both enigmatic strangeness and yet unity. For the reader, *Manhood* is certainly the most intensively fascinating volume in Leiris's sometimes tedious autobiographic itinerary.

Leiris proceeds methodically and on two levels: the selection of his materials and his reading of them. To the first level—what we might call the selected deck of cards extracted from his archives—he has given us the key: "If I assemble all those facts borrowed from what was, when I was a child, my daily life," he wrote, after a brief listing of the main episodes recounted in the first chapter of *Manhood,* "I see taking shape little by little an image of what is, for me, the sacred . . . something which, in sum, I cannot conceive very well except as marked, one way or another, by the supernatural." The terrain of his autobiographic quest was defined by the combination of the surrealist myth with the anthropological research of Mauss (one of Leiris's masters) into the origin and function of the sacred and the taboo in the life of collectivities. And at the time this was also a major preoccupation of Georges Bataille and Maurice Blanchot with whom Leiris was fairly closely connected. (A certain almost obsessional fascination for the sacred was a minor cultural phenomenon of the thirties.) Leiris's investigation was directed toward the exploration of what "sacralized" these episodes in his life, whether individual or cultural. His parents' addiction to opera had fostered his early, fascinated absorption in the theatrical representations of opera which, at this stage of his investigation, he saw as having shaped his sexual mythology and expectations, the inner theater of his latent erotic desires. Freudian psychoanalysis, which postulated that erotic desire with its escort of repression and symbolic transferences was the key to personal behavior, suggested the hypotheses that gave the episodes that Leiris had selected their unity and meaning. It turned his otherwise insignificant adventure into an erotic script, finally epitomized symbolically in two figures, Cranach's Judith and Lucretia. Leiris recognized that these figures had "perhaps" been charged by him with an arbitrary allegorical significance in which love, cruelty, and death dramatically combined. But by elucidating his own myths, Leiris hoped to be able to objectively examine the modalities of his sexual behavior as texts to be rationally decoded. He would thus presumably be able to confront reality, understand and control his erotic drives, and become at last an initiate in "the fierce order of virility," while giving the erotic drives aesthetic validity as had Cranach.

His revolt against the culture that had imposed upon him the fear and repression of these erotic drives explodes violently in *L'Afrique fantôme.* In *Manhood,* such emblems as Judith, Lucretia, Holofernes, and *The Raft of the Medusa* exteriorize and demythify Leiris's childhood sublimations. But the writing yields its own mythology, a personal language that Leiris will then bring under scrutiny. And indeed the next step Leiris took (in *Biffures*) was to explore the associations at work in his language, only to find that the verbal networks he thus established were mere fantasy. And so it would be with each new tentative at organizing his *fiches.*

This is where the allegory of the *tauromachia* takes on its multiple meanings. That in his role as autobiographer Leiris aspires to function with the bullfighter's qualities of skill in performance, courage, and mastery in self-exposure is the more evident of its connotations, and the strict ritual of the combat as the toreador confronts the unpredictable assault of brute violence is what seems most to attract him in the image. For the autobiographer, the chaotic assault of the adversary seems to embody the brute substance upon which he works. That some intimation of the quasi-physical struggle inherent in the act of writing should reveal at least the "shadow" of the bull's horn—that is, the threat of mutilation, wound, or death—seems to Leiris the guarantee that the writing meshes into a real *hors-texte* and is not functioning merely as yet another verbal, that is "mythic," construct.

Only much later in *Fibrilles* will Leiris spell out in detail a large list of the self-imposed rules of the game his bullfight image embodies, rules that sharply constrain the autobiographer's "performance" of the autobiographic act. Curiously the code developed is largely negative: not to lie, not to promise what you can't execute; not to use words lightly, not to get caught in a rhetoric. Leiris sought to compose a rhetoric, an ethic, and a tactics for the autobiographer that would be binding for both the societal man responsible to others for what he reveals of their lives and for the writer responsible

for the use he makes of language. All the rules he formulates spell out the meaning he ascribes to the word "authenticity." Here Leiris becomes a kind of Boileau of autobiography, albeit only in regard to himself. In brief, in Leiris's codification the exigency of complete and objective truth is qualified by a rule of respect for others, including the reader: therefore the absence of any allusion—except fleetingly—to the most intimate relations in his life; thence too the absence of the sensational and shocking, at least in the linguistic texture of the discourse. To the "taboos of conduct" Leiris added the "taboos of writing": the elimination of jargon and gratuitous lyricism, the search for a strict adherence to the most accurate expression. As he considered it anew in *Fibrilles,* he realized much later that the formalistic code implicit in the allegory of the *tauromachia* was a mistake. He corrected it by an act of faith: "It is man that counts with the use he makes of language, eventually what he thinks about it and not language itself." This reverses the attitude implicit in the allegory of the *tauromachia,* summarizing his thirty-year itinerary and situating him clearly among the literary humanists in the cultural topography of his time. (pp. 203-06)

The reader who has followed Leiris, the "lost-promeneur who tries to make his way out by reconstructing his itinerary," may find the process tedious. But in effect Leiris has thoroughly dramatized and explored the quasi-insoluble conflicts at work in the very postulation that autobiogrpahy is a generic and definable literary category. In this sense, *The Rule of the Game* presents an exemplary act of "deconstruction." And Leiris knows this: he states that he has left us with the assembled materials for writing the autobiography rather than with the autobiography itself, thus suggesting that critic-readers will produce the unifying schemas that escaped him. Leiris's strategy as autobiographer, geared to his horror of annihilation in death, would then qualify the notion of failure, though it would not perhaps appear as a victory. (p. 206)

Germaine Brée, "Michel Leiris: Mazemaker," in Autobiography: Essays Theoretical and Critical, *edited by James Olney, Princeton University Press, 1980, pp. 194-206.*

CHRISTOPHER ROBINSON

From the poetry of his surrealist period in the late twenties it can already be seen how Leiris delights in the notion of words as a system of symbols or metaphors whose formal relationships disguise an inner secret. In the autobiographical works this notion is extended to the belief that by exploring the associations raised by inter-connections of language, the writer can assemble or create the essential elements of his own consciousness. *L'Age d'homme* is a step towards this approach. It owes its existence to a course of psycho-analysis which Leiris underwent in 1929-30. This psycho-analysis, with its insistence on the importance of sexuality within his personality, allows Leiris to construct his autobiography around themes and images which draw on his memories, dreams and contemporary experiences. Autobiography here becomes self-therapy, although as he was to admit in **'De la littérature considérée comme une tauromachie',** an essay added to a later edition of **L'Age d'homme,** 'at the bottom of all introspection is a taste for self-contemplation and . . . at the bottom of all confession is a desire for absolution'. Self-explanation is attempted primarily in terms of sexual obsessions, but the image which is present at the beginning and at the end of the book, and which Leiris is unable to banish, is that of death. It emerges that what Leiris is trying to extract from his past is an *ego;* sexuality increases his awareness of death, and death consumes the ego, effacing the Narcissistic image. *L'Age d'homme* suggests the close association between personal salvation and language which the volumes of *La Règle du jeu* will follow up. The first-person voice becomes little more than a linguistic function, and preservation is seen to lie in writing, a closed domain which points to the eternal:

> a means of attaining the eternal by simultaneously escaping growing old and finding an enclosed domain.

In *Biffures* (1948), leaving behind the limiting subject of sexuality, but attempting to exclude even further the subject of other people, Leiris uses as the principle of connexion the memory of how language itself and its relation to reality imposed themselves on his childhood consciousness; chronology and event are fragmented and the various aspects of the past subordinated to the complicated process of writing itself. The act of composing the autobiography assumes priority over all previous states of the writer's consciousness. The artist's reflection becomes totally dependent upon what he writes about himself; nothing appears to be known until the word gives it existence. In describing his method as 'a process of meditation zigzagging along the line of the writing itself' Leiris places importance on the act of writing in the process of the construction of an image of the self. Nevertheless, as John Sturrock has pointed out [see excerpt above], *La Règle du jeu* though possibly a literary *tour de force* is also a personal fiasco, for with the expulsion of chronology from the autobiography, Leiris confronts the fact that it is not chronology which kills us but *time,* measured for the writer by the movement of his pen as remorselessly as by any watch. (pp. 77-9)

> Christopher Robinson, "Literature and the Self," in his *French Literature in the Twentieth Century, Barnes & Noble, 1980, pp. 52-81.

LEAH D. HEWITT

In attempting to make autobiography an act encompassing both life and literature, Michel Leiris persistently questions the definition of an event. What is worth writing must be weighed against a set of standards which measure the significance of events. From Leiris' 1939 self–portrait, *Manhood,* to his four volume autobiography, *La Règle du jeu* (finished in 1975), the significance of what I am calling the "autobiographical act," that is, what it means to write an autobiography, is measured in terms of what would constitute a major event in lived experience as well as in writing. My attempt will be to analyze the kinds of events which shape and define the autobiographical act, in order to show how the clear-cut divisions between life and writing become embroiled, for Leiris, in a game where acts are both real and fictive, beautiful and loathsome, authentic and false, serious and ironic . . . where autobiography hesitates between performance, description and interpretation.

When writing about one's self, the question of value becomes crucial in two ways. First, the events chosen must be considered sufficiently important to warrant their narration. This implies that: a) the autobiographer has ascertained what moments in his life have caused him to become what he is (becoming); b) his "life" is worthy of being published for others to read. If these criteria are taken at face value, autobiography appears as an unproblematic description of "faits accom-

plis": near the end of a productive life, one sits back to contemplate and then to recount the significant events from one's experience. But this marginal (passive) position of autobiography with respect to literature and to life is put into question when one considers the second way in which value becomes an issue in writing about personal experience. Leiris deems that autobiography should be thought of as an activity in its own right and is a constant reworking and rethinking of itself. This ultimately suggests that in its relationship to literature and to life, autobiography includes an unending process of re-evaluation which has repercussions for future living (and writing).

In speaking of an "autobiographical act," it is implied that the autobiographer is performing an action, is *doing* something with words.

> To write a book that is an act—such is, broadly, the goal that seemed to be the one I must pursue when I wrote *Manhood.* An act in relation to myself, since I meant, in writing it, to elucidate by this very formulation certain still obscure things to which my psychoanalysis, without making them entirely clear, had drawn my attention. An act in relation to others, since it was apparent that despite my oratorical precautions, the way in which I would be regarded by others would no longer be what it had been before publication of this confession. An act, finally, on the literary level, consisting of a backstage revelation that would expose, in all their unenthralling nakedness, the realities which formed the more or less disguised warp, beneath surfaces I had tried to make alluring, of my other writings.

Leiris' act would thus be comprised of a self-transformation brought about through the relationship with his readers. But Leiris' attempts to tell the truth are always subject to a game of reinterpretation which forces him to wonder about his choice of material, the way he (re)activates it and what the act he has accomplished actually means. Let us consider the perimeters he selects in framing his events.

There are two conceptions of the major event which operate most often in *Manhood* and *La Règle du jeu,* and each conception corresponds to a live version and to a literary one. In the first conception of the event, the individual's experiences are evaluated with respect to history on a world scale. The cataclysms of World Wars I and II establish the criteria for measuring personal worth. The heroes of war, those who have risked their lives, leave Leiris with the feeling that he has not really lived. In the literary realm, the great works of tragedy offer bigger-than-life models of action in confronting destiny. The majestic figures created by such literature make Leiris nostalgic for beautiful, intense moments of a legendary past. Stylistically, tragedy also serves as a model for dramatic intensity of which Leiris feels his work lacking. In the context of these real and literary events, Leiris' life and writing acquire the status of non-events.

It quickly becomes clear, in this first definition of the event, that it is death which confers value and meaning on life for Leiris. Death is the capital event proclaimed in war and in literary tragedy. It also represents—figuratively and literally—the point at which the autobiographical narrative would find its end and completion. A literal death would, of course, stop the process, but it is also clear that for Leiris, the successful end of the autobiographical project could mean that he had arrived at the point where writing was no longer necessary. Life would lie on the other side, ready to be experienced to the fullest, without the "crutch" of introspection.

When Leiris begins to compose his self–portrait in the thirties, he turns to writing as a remedy for the fact that he has experienced life as painfully vain and empty because it has been devoid of a lethal risk. Like many young men of his generation, he feels that he has never proven himself because he was too young to take part in World War I. Thus in choosing to divulge his sexual deficiencies and obsessions in the self-portrait, he hopes to infuse his literature with risks similar to those a bullfighter takes in the arena. In the "prière d'insérer" to *Manhood,* Leiris stresses that the bullfighter's work must adhere to a rigorous formal code, as well as include a lethal risk. The characteristics of the bullfight combine Leiris' requirements for life and literature in a significant act. But at the time of publication in 1939, the potential success of writing one's manhood was undermined by the prospect of another war and Leiris realized that the risks of confessional writing bore little resemblance to what he will call in 1946 "that authentic horn of the war." (pp. 485-87)

Leiris' essential lack of a true or real experience is directly related to his preoccupation with death as the capital event. Clearly, one can never tell one's death and to speak of it never renders it present. Only the feelings of anguish persist and are in themselves difficult to translate. For Leiris the horror of death is such that any possibility of representing this horror suggests that the experience must not have been an authentic one. In Volume II of *La Règle du jeu* he describes the dilemma in the following way:

> What is the value . . . of the experiences I speak of if it is understood that in order to speak of them, and even to remember them with enough lucidity, it is necessary for them to have been sufficiently anodyne for me to live through them without losing lucidity?

The violence of the real event—one in which death's presence is felt—is so overwhelming that it constitutes the unutterable (unrepresentable), thereby condemning the autobiographer to write about inessentials. The traumatic cannot be pronounced because it does not reach consciousness in intelligible form. It is therefore not surprising that when Leiris does recount his experiences as a soldier in 1940 in Volume I of *La Règle du jeu,* he presents himself as one who acts out heroic stances, *playing* at soldier instead of being one. Even those acts which *can* be narrated are problematic because of their equivocal nature. Performing and acting always imply a repetition which blurs the distinction between the feigned and the authentic. (pp. 487-88)

As a French soldier in the North African desert in 1940, Leiris experienced the war as an uneventful waiting period. It seemed inauthentic because it did not measure up to its own supposed standards. Leiris found himself in its immediacy and yet the fight was still being deferred. The uneventful war turned into the long wait of the Occupation when Leiris began writing *La Règle du jeu.* The Occupation was in fact the real war for Leiris, more frightening than anything he had experienced as a soldier, and its absence in the first chapters of Volume I silently records his inability to confront it in writing because it was so overwhelming. Again, the real event is that which can never be narrated in its immediacy. Writing is only a shadow of the real, incapable of (re)presenting a true experience.

In the opening chapters of Volume I of *La Règle du jeu,* Leiris shuts out contemporary events of the Occupation to return to the protected past of his childhood. It is here that the second definition of the event comes into play. This is what Leiris calls the "Sacred in Everyday Life." These events are made up of minute occurrences which, to the individual experiencing them, are just as resounding as an awesome event on a world scale. In literature, this is the domain of poetry which, for Leiris, harbors all the surprises of language which the poet communicates to his readers. This second kind of event differs from the first in that Leiris lays no claim to a present risk in writing. Instead he explores the minute events of his early discoveries in language, the way words and ideas resonate and bounce off each other or slide unwittingly into others. For example, Leiris chooses the word "verglas," and develops its various meanings and their relationship to moments of his past. He is particularly interested in the way he has misheard or misread certain words or expressions as a child. Language will thus provide the guiding thread through the labyrinth of the past.

Volume I opens with a childhood drama in which the young boy Michel is corrected by an adult in the pronunciation of the word "heureusement." The child is dumbfounded when he learns that the word is not "reusement" but rather "heureusement." This constitutes the crucial discovery that language is not the boy's private possession but rather a social object belonging to no one and everyone. In this framework the event includes an element of surprise, an unexpected alteration or interruption in a previous code or system. It is the point where, as Leiris says, one loses one's footing. This discovery is crucial for the adult remembering it because it reminds him of his own accountability as autobiographer. But Leiris' goal in Volume I is not simply to recount such experiences in language. It is more a matter of making literature an act, with true experiences taking place in the movement or transition between the childhood accounts. . . . Does the repetition of a discovery constitute another discovery *in writing?* What is, in fact, the experience discovered? The situation has become doubly complicated. In the bullfight metaphor, literature was unable to become an act and was inexorably detached from real experience (that is, the war). And yet now a representation of a true experience becomes indistinguishable from the latter. Leiris' clear intentions become confused by virtue of the experience's repeatability, by its refusal to remain within one unique context. The "artificial" supplement of the literary formulation is woven into the true experience. Writing does indeed become an act here, engendering in Leiris (the reader) the very effects which he sought in the real event, but it has been cut off from the wholeness of an intentional present. The author lives the event of writing as an impossible choice between past and present, between literature and life. Both reality and literature now confirm the experience of losing one's footing, that is, of experiencing something crucial. (pp. 488-90)

Leiris' events consist in the concurrent creation and destruction of lived myths in an act which must be both experiential and interpretative, timeless and historical. The autobiographical act hovers between opposing poles, but in matters of value these poles are always penetrated by their opposites. Tragedy and history often serve to criticize the autobiographical enterprise, as well as its specific content. And yet tragedy provides Leiris with the sense of an enriched esthetic in personal experience, while history and its on-going movement open up *future* possibilities for meaning. On the other hand, the "sacred in everyday life" has the potential to alter rigid systems and codes which inhibit the multiplicity of life. The radical doubt of the autobiographer as to the meaning of his act is precisely the interval where we, as Leiris' readers, lose our footing in the incessant game of interpretation. (p. 493)

Leah D. Hewitt, "Events in Life and Writing: The 'Autobiographical Act' of Michel Leiris," in The Romanic Review, Vol. LXXIV, No. 4, November, 1983, pp. 485-93.

ALLAN STOEKL

We have already seen the importance of puns and double (or multiple) meanings in the writings of Raymond Roussel; Roussel's "writing machine" was made possible by the steadily elaborated mutations of words and by the "ordering" of those mutations into a narrative. Michel Leiris, in his four-volume series of autobiographical writings [*La Règle du jeu*], takes Roussel's writing procedure one step further: rather than ordering his autobiography in a simple chronological progression (from his birth to the impossible recording of his own death), Leiris structures his memories around the experience of certain privileged words. In Leiris, the various metamorphoses of a single word act as magnets that accumulate personal memories: these memories in turn illustrate the personal importance to Leiris of the word itself. Thus, quite often, the event recounted is Leiris's childhood memory of the oral permutations of certain words, and the free associations that these permutations generated.

An excellent example of this procedure can be found in the chapter entitled "Perséphone," in *Biffures* [*Erasures*], the first volume of *La Règle du jeu* [*Rules of the Game*]. Of course Persephone is the goddess of spring, who is yearly captured by Hades and brought to the depths of the underworld, and who yearly escapes and passes through the crust of the earth to cause the rebirth of nature. Leiris associates a number of images that involve piercing, spirals, "circonvolutions," and so on with the name—and sound—of "Perséphone." The twists of a corkscrew, the turns of a drunk, the spirals of the tendrils of a grape vine, as well as the spit curl on the cheek of a prostitute and the decorations of the entrances to the Métro—and many others—are conjured up by the idea of the spiraling growth of springtime, as well as by the penetration of the spiral through the earth, the passage from the subterranean realm of death and seed to the realm of solar illumination.

From "Perséphone" Leiris derives the word "perce-oreille," French for that most Joycean of creatures, the earwig. "Percer" means "to pierce," and the earwig is said to be able to pierce the ear of a sleeper and enter his brain. Indeed "perce-oreille" (literally "pierce-ear") is a kind of double play on "Perséphone": "perce" is derived from the identical sound—but different meaning—of the first syllable of "Perséphone," whereas "oreille" is different in sound from "phone," but related in meaning, for it is the ear that is sensitive to phonic signals. The transformation of "Perséphone" into "perce-oreille" indicates in itself the double aspect of the generation of the transformation of words in Leiris. One aspect is phonic, dependent on the ear (this is the association of "Persé"/"perce"); the other is figural, dependent on associations of elusive signifieds rather than signifiers (hence "phone" and "oreille" are associated, despite the fact that the two words do not sound the same). This second kind of association could be said to be essentially written, because associations on this level could best be fully developed through recourse to written compendia of definitions, histories, analyses, as well as dictionaries and encyclopedias. Ironically enough, it is the syllables "Persé"/"perce," which indicate writing (for they indicate the piercing of paper by pen and pencil), that are linked phonetically, whereas the syllables that indicate sound ("phone"/"oreille") are linked through their meaning, and thus depart from the phonic.

This is certainly a significant variation on Roussel's writing machine, because here the whole problem of the relation of sound to writing in the mutations of words (in the constitution of narrative) is figured in the machine itself. In the "Perséphone" chapter Leiris presents us with a machine that—much like Roussel's weaving/writing machine—serves as a master metaphor for the constitution of his narrative. Leiris's machine, however, takes into account both the written and the phonic: it is his father's phonograph, or more properly, his "Graphophone."

When Leiris was a small boy his father owned a deluxe Edison "Graphophone," which had the capability of both making home recordings on wax cylinders and playing back either the home recordings, or commercially produced cylinder recordings. The process of recording, which Leiris recounts in detail, involves the same conjunctions of sound and writing, piercing and spiraling, above and below ground, that were associated with Persephone: . . . "the trace, in wax, of this long tight helicoid in which the succession of sounds was transcribed." As the recording needle pierces the wax, it leaves both the spirals of its sound/writing, and the spirals of the excess wax gouged out of the virgin surface of the cylinder.

When in turn a recording is listened to, the chthonian or underground realm is reached by the piercing needle: it is the sound track. The fact that Leiris's system of figural "turns" or spirals enables us to make the association "realm of the dead"/"origin of sound" indicates that it is precisely as an inscription that sound must be considered here. Indeed, Leiris presents the reproduced sounds from the inscribed roll as "cadavres resuscités" as well as "céréales mûres"; the reproduced sound must always be considered as already a corpse, as well as a living grain. Death accompanies germination, just as writing accompanies sound in this "Graphophone," a device that seems to favor the "graph" over the "phone," contrary to the usual order of things ("phonograph").

Just as Roussel's weaving machine had an unknowable "black box" that both guaranteed its operation and was radically exterior to it, so Leiris's "Graphophone" is fitted with a "diaphragme" whose membrane both is the origin of the sounds emitted by the phonograph and is alien to them: . . . "the action of the sensitive membrane of the diaphragm seems incapable of explaining by itself the budding of all these vocal notes." Rather than being a mere passive receptor of sound, this mysterious diaphragm seems to conjure up out of its inner depths not only music, but the jarring crackles that common sense tells us are the result of interferences in the musical inscription of the cylinder; the diaphragm itself seems to be the origin of these crackles: . . . "tearing them out of its bowels rather than receiving them from the outside, acting thus as a separate cause of the disorder rather than as a passive instrument." In the diaphragm, then, in the space of "origin" of sound, the phonic and the crackles (products of the decay of the inscription) are coterminous. In the diaphragm the crackles and breaks of inscribed reproduction —the marks of the resuscitated cadaver of sound—appear simultaneously with the contours of the "original" sound.

The diaphragm/mechanical union of the continuities of sound and the fragmentary breaks of inscription is clearly a figure of the unknowable yet necessary mechanism behind Leiris's autobiographical project. As the impossible embodiment of irruption and constitution, the diaphragm is "in itself" a fragment: . . . "I have some difficulty, in fact, picturing to myself the word 'diaphragm' without imagining it maintaining a strict etymological link with 'fragment,' which the existence of the same compact block of sounds in each of these substantives seems to demonstrate irrefutably."

Also associated with the diaphragm—and for that reason with the operation of Leiris's text—is the word "anfractuosité," defined by the *Petit Robert* dictionary as a "deep and irregular cavity." While the phonic resemblance of this word to "fragment" is clear enough, it is also a kind of mirror image of "fragment," because it indicates not a discrete and solid entity, but instead a hollow that might remain after a fragment has been removed. Associated with "anfractuosité" are not only the cracks or hollows in rocks, but the crackling noises of splitting stone, the "fracas" that brings us back to the crackling of the diaphragm. And through "an*fract*uosité"—through its associations with rocks, fracas, and the noise of cracking—we come not only to "dia*phrag*me" but to the ear: . . .

> The word "anfractuosity"—as it is situated in my vocabulary—thus hides a paradox, since it serves me here by evoking at the same time as the sharpness and the impenetrable hardness of rock, the auricular opening through which I would now believe that the mineral world interferes with me, that which is, in other words, the most irreducible and the most foreign to me.

We have now come full circle, from the crackling associated with writing (the interference in the diaphragm) to the primacy of the aural and phonic. But it is not that simple. The ear opens out, but not simply to sound; it opens itself to what is "foreign" or "irreducible," namely to the solidity of rocklike fragments, the sharpness and impenetrable hardness of a diamond stylus.

If the fragmentary diaphragm is opened to sound or if, conversely, the phonic ear of the diaphragm is opened to its opposite, sharp rock, then in both cases we have a metaphor for the functioning of the text: the diaphragm, offspring of Roussel's "black box," opens itself to what is *other* (solid/splitting writing is opened to sound, and vice versa). The "neutral space" of Leiris's writing—if we can carry over this term from our discussion of the constitutent element of Roussel's machine—is not simply the point of incompatibilities of strata of writing, but is the point of interference between the written and the phonic, neither of which can be logically or temporally prior. The diaphragm in Leiris's textual machine signals a radical break indeed: it departs not only from simple writing or simple speech, but (impossibly) from what Derrida has called the "Western metaphysical tradition" of phonocentric and hence logocentric thought.

Without contemplating this radicality of *Biffures* as an "urtext" of deconstruction—we will return to the radicality

of the writing/speech interference later—we might consider what the "radically exterior" is for Leiris as a theme in *Le Règle du jeu*. As figured in his autobiography, to what *other* is the textual machine—the ear—open? To what does the long arm of the diaphragm—the needle—reach? What does that stylus hear?

Leiris does not spell out the answer to this question, precisely because the answer is a function of a language that is not associable with a single, stable signified; the "bifur" (a pun on the title of the first volume of his autobiography, *Biffures*), the bifurcation that is a split and a knot in meaning or concentration, in turn refers to other splits, other doublings. The bifurcations generate an experience of being situated "en porte à faux", of losing one's footing, of finding oneself suddenly on another level: . . . "the individual (undergoing bifurcations) feels himself thrown into a peculiarly acute state and (the losses of footing and jumps in level) apparently making the limits crack, open up the horizon."

A breaking of the limits of existence, an opening of the horizon; both of these expressions indicate the moving across, or piercing, of a barrier, and the reaching of what is beyond. It seems, however, that beyond this framework, there is only (always again) a heightened experience of other "bifurs," and so on to infinity. Is this a progression or a vicious circle?

Leiris over and over throughout the four volumes of his autobiography does provide one other "exterior" that should—indeed must—be reached: the realm of society, of other people. And the terms in which he presents the movement outward from elite aesthetic project to social concern are much the same as those used to indicate the movement through the breach in language—through the trace, through the auricular opening or solid fragment (which itself breaks open the smooth flow of sound)—to the "bifur" and beyond.

In the "Perséphone" chapter Leiris already broaches the problem that will become more and more important as one volume follows another of *La Règle du jeu*—the necessity of breaking open or piercing through the screen of words to the "reality" that lies behind it: . . . "the same screens separate me from reality". In this context, "reality" is associated with "nature," but that nature, as we will see shortly, cannot be simply separated from a conception of society. In *Fourbis* [*Thingamabob*], the second volume of *La Règle du jeu,* Leiris writes of his intact body . . . "which, never risked, seems to me unfinished as if, in spite of my age, I were still a preadolescent." The fact that he has never been wounded—that the screen of his skin has never been pierced by a projectile—strikes Leiris as an indication of his isolation from the great social upheavals of his time, such as (and especially) the Liberation of Paris in 1944. Finally, in the third volume (*Fibrilles*) [*Fibrils*], Leiris reflects back on the opening chapter of *Biffures* and sees in it an event that represents the breaking out of a closed personal space and an attainment of the social realm through the accession to language: . . .

> I had discovered, learning that it is "heureusement" ["fortunately"] and not " . . . reusement" as the brat that I was had just said, the existence of language as exterior reality going beyond me: from which it is necessary to infer that *one does not speak completely alone* (the others, even absent, were implicated in the act of speaking since it is their words that one uses).

The "external" reality, the breaking open of frames, the penetration of limits or screens—all this recalls the image that we saw at the beginning of our reading of "Perséphone," namely the needle or pen piercing a surface and reaching, after traversing or chiseling a hollowed-out passage, a submerged or subterranean "pit" ("ce puits central"). Leiris presents this cavelike opening as belonging to a "chthonian deity," perhaps Hades himself, or one of the other earth deities who could be put in opposition to the brilliant (and reasonable) power of a monotheistic God.

Absurd as it might seem, this piercing through to the chthonian must be seen as a move to formulate a political strategy for the autobiographer and his text. Leiris was involved with Georges Bataille in a study group, the Collège de Sociologie in the late 1930s. Bataille (in the Acéphale group of the same period, to which Leiris did *not* belong) promoted a kind of political cult that would, he hoped, bring off a revolution in more than just the sphere of relations of production: he hoped that a subversive group, by reinstituting virulent myth in everyday life, would rejuvenate society. The myth of the headless man, like that of the chthonian earth deities, implied a "base materialism" of orgiastic expenditure and sacrificial dread. In opposition to the solar God of reason and conservation, the chthonian god embodied loss, death, and mutilation.

In a letter to Bataille in 1939, Leiris objects that many of Bataille's formulations in his lectures for the Collège de Sociologie—and by implication, in his writing for the cult-organ *Acéphale*—deviated from the anthropological theories of Durkheim. (It must be recalled that Leiris was a trained anthropologist, and Bataille was not.) Perhaps what Leiris objected to in Bataille was less Bataille's lack of theoretical rigor than his insistence on the need for a small, active revolutionary group that would light the fuse for a revolutionary rebirth of myth. In a text published in the *Nouvelle Revue Française* in 1938 (along with texts by Bataille and Caillois) entitled **"Le Sacré dans la vie quotidienne,"** Leiris presents an intimate portrait of his childhood, using scenes that will reappear later in *La Règle du jeu.* These childhood scenes are meant to indicate that myth *already exists* in everyday life, that the subversion of Bataille's mythic chthonian figures can be seen in the linguistic experiences of a middle-class Parisian childhood. In opposition to Bataille's (at least theoretically) violent sect, Leiris presents himself, alone, as a singularly cerebral, nonphysical child, yet as a child whose verbal experimentation will (or already results) in chthonian mythical revolution.

In this early version of *La Règle du jeu,* then, we see a bizarre political project—the subversion by the chthonian or mythic—rewritten as an individual autobiographical experience. This is the central paradox of Leiris's project: how can the writing of an autobiography—necessarily an individual task played out between a writer and his language—move *beyond* words and have a constructive, revolutionary purpose in society? This is the final problem posed by the diaphragm as a metaphor for Leiris's text: how can the diaphragm embody not only the impossible interpenetration of writing and speech, but the conjunction of the writing/speech dyad—and its "subject"—with an external social "reality"?

Leiris's project specifically equates taking heroic risks in the realm of political action with the act of writing the autobiography itself. The auricular breach opens out to the bifurcations of language—hence to the text itself—as well as to the social realm "outside" the solipsistic literary games of the child or adult. In the (at least desired) unification of these two

tendencies—or their complementary bifurcation—the heroic task of the individual writer supplanting the collectivity as the most subversive "mythical" revolutionary is brought off. Leiris alone in his room, writing, supplants the theatrical rituals of Bataille's Acéphale group. As we will see, however, the risk taken by the text, its breach, soon reverses itself into an extremely stable form of adaptability. It is the how and why of this reversal that we must now investigate.

One aspect of Leiris's project that critics seem to have ignored is its function as a confession. Leiris manages to fill his text with everything that has ever happened to him, down to the most minute and most recent detail. His writings are certainly the polar opposite of the narratives of Blanchot, from which virtually all narrative—and autobiographical—detail has been stripped. This will to say all must be considered as a confession and as a desire for absolution. (pp. 51-8)

In **"De la littérature considérée comme une tauromachie,"** written immediately after World War II and published as a preface to Leiris's autobiographical essay *L'Age d'homme* [*Manhood*], Leiris posits the act of writing an autobiography in which no details will be spared the reader—this as a kind of "engagement," analogous to the risk of death (or of being punctured by horns) faced by the bullfighter in the "corrida"—or, as suggested by its resonances with the term "littérature engagée," by the politicized Sartrean intellectual when he takes a stand and refuses to relinquish his freedom and be appropriated by regressive political forces. This often-cited piece by Leiris is a strange amalgam of the continuation of, on the one hand, the valorization of solely individual experience (such as the various sexual experiences Leiris recounts in *L'Age d'homme*) and, on the other, an affirmation of the collective action that Sartre at the time was promoting as "engagement" (indeed a chapter of *Biffures,* "Dimanche" ["Sunday"] was originally published shortly after the war in Sartre's *Les Temps Modernes*). The way out of this potentially troublesome internal bifurcation (Leiris himself writes of his "mauvaise conscience") is to pose the writing of the autobiography itself as a kind of risk, analogous to the risking of life by the bullfighter (facing the "horn of the bull") and, by implication, by "L'homme engagé." Indeed, Leiris conflates bullfighter and autobiographer when he points out that they both follow strict rules, which in turn lead to greater risk (although, of course, the nature of the risks run is different in the two cases).

Writing, that sedentary occupation par excellence, can be compared to fighting bulls or fascists to the extent that the writer takes a risk when he exposes *all* of his life in his work, even the most seedy or disgraceful details. By making this move, Leiris opens the hermetic activity of writing to the risks run in society and politics. By writing everything, Leiris's pen pierces the screen of writing and reaches society.

But there is a problem in this. What if the writer must confess not only his sexual peccadilloes and fears, but his own guilt in the form of the betrayal of a just political cause? Could he then claim that he is taking a mortal risk somehow analogous to political engagement by confessing his betrayal of that same engagement?

This is essentially what concerns Leiris in *Fourbis,* the second volume of *La Règle du jeu,* but with an added twist. Not only is his text an embodiment of risk through a confession of guilt, but it risks its isolation as an autonomous text by affirming its solidarity with progressive political movements.

Thus it bifurcates, risking the security of its author in two opposing ways: it presents him as politically compromised and as a committed radical.

It should be noted, however, that if the confession of guilt and the proclamation of commitment are less than thoroughgoing, the status of the text as the author's total and even death-defying risk will be put into question. . . . "A certain desire to state the maximum": of all the chapters of *La Règle du jeu*, "Les Tablettes sportives" ["Sporting Notes"] is the most concerned with a frank portrayal of Leiris's inadequacies; the chapter opens with a description of the idolization of jockeys by Leiris and his brothers—and, of course, their fantasies of themselves as jockeys. Leiris then goes on to present himself as a completely nonathletic youth, the kind who fails at all sports after making only perfunctory efforts: . . .

> To give up from the beginning, not even to try (from fear of not succeeding or from simple apathy): a mixture of pessimism and laziness, each one at the basis of the other, resulting in a vicious circle.

The great irony is that, while nonathletic, Leiris also imagines himself a great jockey; in fact his only resemblance to a jockey is that, like a true dandy, he wears colorful clothes, just as the jockeys wear the colors of their stables. He even tries to play rugby as a youth after World War I, not because he wants to be an athlete but because he wants the image of an athlete: . . . "in sum I played at being someone who plays rugby." It would seem that behind this facade there is nothing genuine; a genuine physical development, perhaps the most authentic thing to the one who is incapable of achieving it, is replaced by a mere facade, a screen of dandyism that evokes not the substance of physical prowess, but merely its signs.

But coupled with this surface ornamentation, this "parure," there is a tendency in Leiris (according to Leiris) to absolute, withering honesty—an ability to see beyond the decorations, to see their uselessness, and finally to see their ultimate irrelevance in situations of extreme danger, of *real* physical risk. . . . (pp. 58-60)

Later in this chapter Leiris transposes this paradigm (facade/honesty) onto his experiences in Occupied France. Beyond the facade, the screen, the "tricherie" ["cheating"] there is always the question: what is it to risk death, how would Leiris stop being a spectator, and become "engagé."

He recounts a number of his experiences under the Nazis, and in the liberation of Paris. At the outset he makes it clear that he never really risked the smooth surface of his skin in the war and that this lack of involvement is reminiscent of his refusal to involve himself in physical activities. Indeed, each incident that he recounts indicates goodwill toward the forces fighting the Nazis, but a complete lack of physical involvement in the struggle. He joins a partisan group but his sole act is giving some bullets (left over from his father's gun, which he gave to the German authorities at the beginning of the Occupation) to a man named "Marc"; he occupies the Comédie-Française briefly, then leaves it to occupy the Musée de l'Homme (the museum of ethnography where Leiris worked). He fails to carry out an adventurous mission involving a pickup of arms at the Place de la République; finally, hoping there will be more action in the sixth arrondissement where he lives, he returns home, but never quite gets involved in the project of moving a garbage truck that blocks the street. His conclusions: . . . "Thus, during the in-surrection, as during the war, I limited myself to a few gestures, none of which led to anything, and which I carried out, moreover, as pure formalities." He explicitly compares his activity to his performance in the gym as a child, when he made only a show ("de mimique rituelles") of doing the exercises that had been assigned to him. Even in the war, then, he wore a facade—and now it is his critical, ruthless gaze that pierces through it (beyond it there is impotence and guilt) as he writes his autobiography.

As in **"De la littérature considérée comme une tauromachie,"** the grave risk that is never confronted under the Occupation is encountered here, in the act of confession. The revelation of one's own guilt is the true risk, the true "horn of the bull" faced by the matador.

One of the most striking things about Leiris's guilt, however, is its innocuousness. If Leiris is not heavily involved in the Resistance, it is not out of sympathy for the Germans, but out of fear of being tortured or killed—certainly a fear with which any reader can sympathize. Indeed, in the postwar notes to *L'Age d'homme,* he writes: . . . "I am still . . . certain that, if I had ever been put in the position of being tortured, I never would have had . . . the strength not to speak." The only time under the Occupation when Leiris actually faces death is when, on his bicycle, he is inadvertently caught between a squad of Germans and their bleeding victim; here, however, he is once again an innocent bystander whose worst crime is a certainly justifiable self-preservation, as he quickly pedals away.

It hardly seems that one will risk death, or even censure, for the kind of details Leiris recounts. If there is no risk in recounting them, and if, as is the case, Leiris does not indicate that (after the war) his "indecision"—thus his refusal to get involved, his clinging to facades—is behind him, it is likely that his confession is less a mortal risk, the opening up of his skin or screens to fenestration, than it is the alternative to risk, that is, another facade, another jockey's costume.

What is behind this facade? In the very act of confessing and recognizing a guilt, Leiris has made it minor; the recognition of one (petty) guilt implicitly rules out the possibility of another, all-corroding but still passive, guilt. Caught for a moment on his bicycle between victim and Nazis, Leiris can feel threatened, his life in the balance, his skin vulnerable to a hail of gunfire. Then he rides away. The point here is certainly not to see in Leiris (or Leiris as he has written himself, for we are not analyzing or judging here the "actual historical Leiris: we are not writing a biography) any active guilt—it is no crime to have survived the Occupation. And no one could or should argue that he or she would have behaved differently in this emblematic and terrifying situation. Perhaps Leiris's very innocence, and concomitant moderation, is itself guilty. The paradox, which is probably as painful today in contemporary America as it was in Occupied France, is that one's moderation, one's simple attempt to continue living, becomes guilty through the very fact that working, eating and sleeping cannot be dissociated from collaboration. Perhaps there is no real way to resist effectively. One does not resist, one only continues to go reluctantly along with things, and in this one is profoundly guilty. This deeper but still passive guilt is never recognized or admitted in Leiris's text, except perhaps in the very hollow of its elision, through the recounting of these events.

By recognizing and affirming minor guilt, then, the text elides this other more general and thoroughgoing guilt. The same phenomenon occurs toward the end of "Les Tablettes sportives" as well, but on the opposite end of the political spectrum. At this point we are exposed not to Leiris's guilt, but to his liberalism. He finds himself in Dakar, Senegal, on V-E Day. To condense a long story: wanting desperately to celebrate the end of the war, Leiris breaks away from a stodgy group of whites and, by now very drunk, decides to impose himself on three blacks (whom he does not know) and walk with them. Leiris is full of noble sentiments: . . . "I affirmed my wish for a better understanding between the races, my love for Africa . . . and the Africans, people closer to the true life than are the Europeans." These sentiments are rewarded when Leiris is beaten by the blacks; his shoes and wallet are stolen as well. Finally he punches not one of his assailants—who have disappeared—but a white seaman who can only imagine that Leiris was looking for sexual relations with his assailants. Leiris is finally knocked out by the white.

Once again Leiris must tell all; his mea culpa consists of exposing the liberal naïveté in what, in another context, might have been a resolute "engagement," a willingness to risk injury fighting for what one believes in (the rights and dignity of blacks). But Leiris (at least as he portrays himself, in 1945) has not made the effort to understand why the blacks might resent the aggressive drunken friendliness of a white stranger.

Just as Leiris would present himself as an innocent bystander whose guilt is passive and innocuous, so he now presents himself, ironically, it is true, as a liberal whose politics are well meaning but naive and harmless. By getting into fights, Leiris certainly risks his skin to prove he is liberal. But what is he risking through his confession? Certainly not his political beliefs; throughout *La Règle du jeu* he has proclaimed himself a "progressive" who is nevertheless opposed to forms of left-wing dogmatism. Nor is Leiris risking his position in society, let alone his life; there is nothing risky about confessing that one is naive.

If there is no risk, once again we face the possibility that this confession is a façade. Just as before an innocuous guilt displaced a deeper and perhaps more universal one, so here ineffective liberalism replaces a more thoroughgoing and rigorous—but also more threatening and dangerous—politics. In the presentation of China or Cuba Leiris displays his sympathy for the regimes of Mao and Castro without ever risking a "dogmatic" statement that might discredit him. Instead, his appreciation of these regimes is largely sentimental and aesthetic. In much the same way as the nineteenth-century novel tended to both exile or condemn the police while at the same time embodying the functions of the police in its narrative strategy, so Leiris both exiles any pretense of innocence, while at the same time embodying innocence in his text through his endless confessions of harmless guilt or innocuous liberal "radicalism."

Leiris in "Les Tablettes sportives" has managed to cover both ends of the political spectrum: the left and the right. Between these two alternatives there is a "bifur" that is not a "bifur," a simulacrum of saying all that can be said, of finally reaching an absolute knowledge of confession (no matter how "contradictory" it might be) from which, nevertheless, all the really guilty or dangerous positions are implicitly exiled and through which the author is vindicated because he is a moderate. Indeed it is the exile of these dangerous positions that makes the safe confession—the screen, the façade—possible. Leiris's confession is for that reason still dependent on those

more radical positions, but only negatively. The outline of those missing positions is indicated through their very rejection, when Leiris is read critically.

Interestingly enough, the same exile of radical alternatives takes place when Leiris confesses his impotence in the writing of his autobiography. Writing of his method of writing—the elaboration of a complex network of associations and contraries ("bifurs"), which he builds up through the coordination of a vast collection of notecards—Leiris argues for a freedom of experience that the interplay of his notecards makes possible: . . .

> Everything free and living that can enter into my work [will become], finally, a question of links or transitions and these will [gain] density as I advance, to the point where they represent the true experiences.

On the other hand, *Biffures* ends on something of a note of defeat because the project of coordinating notecards and writing the autobiography has become little more than the work of an archivist, the review of the fragmentary remains of once vibrant experiences and associations: . . .

> Soon nothing was left of the "bifurs" but the name. . . . So I bogged down in my job as polisher of notecards, and I find a more and more bitter taste in this perpetual reexamination of observations.

In these metastatements on his own writing, we once again have a kind of false "bifur" between two alternatives. Leiris covers here the entire spectrum of his writing—from its radically liberating side to is stuffy, archival, and egocentric side. Yet each of these sides by its recognition or confession of a phenomenon manages to bracket something else that is more excessive. Recognizing the liberating aspect of the play of associations, he neglects precisely what we saw to be the most radical implication of his writing: the interpenetration of the phonic and written, and the corresponding possibility of an "originary" *writing*. Similarly, in recognizing himself as guilty of the mere collecting of dead cards, he sets aside the more serious guilt that may arise from his (confessed) indecisiveness. He "says all" concerning his guilt when it comes to writing boring confessions; we are meant to excuse him because he has been honest, he has taken his risk. . . .

In attempting to write everything there is to write about his own writing, Leiris exiles its most excessive gestures: its radicality as writing, and the implicit threat of its radicality as a doubled political position (in complicity with right and left) that could only be seen as a betrayal from the point of view of the reigning "moderate" or "commonsense" political alternatives. (This latter radicality is indicated only negatively, by a text that outlines certain extreme political realms by rejecting them—just as, perhaps, the outline of the "fragment" can be determined by examining the surfaces of the "anfractuosity.") But the coming together of these excesses was implied in the "Perséphone" chapter when the stylus pierced a surface and came into contact with a chthonian revolutionary underground. It was there that writing acceded to a mythical political position based not on conservation but on death, the excessive element in any closed economy. In order for it to constitute itself as a total, honest confession, however, Leiris's autobiography had to omit any text that touched on the interpenetration of the realms of writing and chthonian politics. This is not to say that Leiris never wrote such a text, but only that his autobiography had to exile anything that would call into question its integrity, its completeness as the account of the *life* of a comfortably excessive, moderate man. (pp. 60-5)

We must face the curious fact that the autobiography that confesses all—even its own ultimately lovable naïveté, impotence, and guilt—precisely cannot say (or write) everything. Yet the second, doubled autobiography—the diaphragm (like the "black box")—had to be written as well, but could never be a part of the autobiography. The very heterogeneity of this second autobiography ("Le rêve est une seconde vie") ["Dream is a second life"] is perhaps founded on the fact that not only do elements seemingly banished from *La Règle du jeu* come together in it, but that they come together in a repetitive *point;* the autodestruction of the author at the moment of the meeting of the phonic and the written. Unlike the "main" autobiography that continues to grow by accretion as its author slowly grows older, this para-autobiography "says" everything in a point, in an impossible and repetitive instant—which is a "bifur," and also a canceling or erasing, a "biffure" (to the extent that the "main" text must always cancel it, or make it unknowable, in order to go on). (pp. 68-9)

Allan Stoekl, "Leiris's Unwritten Autobiography," in his Politics, Writing, Mutilation: The Cases of Bataille, Blanchot, Roussel, Leiris, and Ponge, *University of Minnesota Press, 1985, pp. 51-69.*

LAWRENCE R. SMITH

It is hard to ascribe a genre to Michel Leiris' *Nights as Day, Days as Night*. . . . It is a book made up of dream episodes, and a few waking reveries, which have been compiled over almost 40 years of a man's life. But is it an autobiography? Are these dream episodes really surrealist prose poems in disguise? Is it a history of the French imagination from the early '20s until the early '60s, including the Nazi occupation? The fact that it is all of these simultaneously, and many other things as well, is what makes this book so fascinating. . . .

[Leiris] believed that the recollection of and meditation on dreams constituted a kind of serious scientific research—and he maintained this notion, as this book testifies, throughout his life. But what he actually does with these dreams is as difficult to define as the genre of the total work. He sometimes offers them to us as "prose poems," occasionally with dazzling virtuosity. For instance, consider this dream from 1954:

> In need of money, I hire myself out as a bull in a corrida. As the papers are being signed, the impresario insists that I undergo an inspection to make sure that I indeed have the five horns stipulated by the contract; he has after all guaranteed that he will furnish a 'bull with five horns.' Two of these horns are supposedly on my head; two more are protrusions of my shoulder blades which the impresario verifies by touching them. My wife is present, and I tell her it gives me the chills to be touched there, just below my nape, on the very spot where the death-blow will fall. She says to me: 'It's just a lousy morning you'll have to get through. Once it's all over, you'll feel fine. . . .' I get incensed. 'Once it's over, I'll be dead!' Beside myself with rage, I shout at both of them: 'I'm not going to fall for this!' And I add: 'I'd rather take my chances as a

> bullfighter!' The contract will not be signed and the dream ends there.

> Almost everybody to whom I have recounted this dream has asked me where my fifth horn was located.

The combination of the ludicrous (but fatal) situation, the mystery of the creature he has become, and the emotional narrative (with its wonderful final turn) make for a richly evocative piece. This has the profoundity and ineffable quality of great surrealist art.

However, most of the dreams are not in this form. The typical format, if it can be said there is one, since there is so much variety, is the recounting of the dream and a few words of analysis. Although Leiris, like all the surrealists, was well-versed in Freudian psychology, he refuses, with the exception of one dream, to indulge in such analysis. He retains (and values) the mystery of the dream world, its coexistence on an equal footing with the world of waking reason. Many of these dreams seem to have the weight of political prophesy, or of second sight, or "objective change," as Bréton termed it. And yet Leiris makes no total statement. He simply recounts and analyzes or elaborates on these dream-texts, as if they were separate cultural objects, like the artifacts he studied as a professional ethnographer. What results is much less unified and dramatic than the visions of Bréton in *Nadja* and Aragon in *Paysan de Paris;* the poetic fireworks of the unconscious are missing. But Leiris' scientific distance makes these texts appear less self-consciously literary, less contrived, and finally more real and mysterious.

Above all, *Nights as Day, Days as Night* stands as a companion piece to Leiris' great work, his memoirs (*L'age d'Homme*). The existence of both books establishes a stunning assertion, that the dream life of a person is as valid and telling as the more usual memoirs. In fact, Leiris seems to be suggesting that only when the unconscious mind and the conscious mind are seen together, and the network of connections between politics, sexuality, fear, the exotic and the mundane, is reconstructed in all of its mystery, can the person begin to be known. Somewhere we begin to see the total life of a person come into view, like the metamorphic vision of a paradisal dream city that recurs throughout this book. It is the surrealist New Jerusalem, where the rational and irrational come together to produce the "supreme point," the place of final knowing.

Lawrence R. Smith, "Perchance to Dream: A Literary Experiment," in Los Angeles Times Book Review, *July 17, 1988, p. 3.*

AMY EDITH JOHNSON

[In *Nights as Day, Days as Night,* Leiris] collects nocturnal dreams, waking dreams and dreamlike incidents of waking life, all meticulously recorded over four decades. "Dream—a scintillating mirage surrounded by shadows—is essentially *poetry,*" Mr. Leiris asserts; and each brief prose episode simultaneously displays his poetic lyricism and his scientific detachment. The incidents and images are largely uninterpreted, although some readers will find the pensive essay, here published as a foreword, in which Maurice Blanchot reflects on Mr. Leiris's text to be the gem of this volume. Many of the pieces themselves are pedestrian, and the author is uncomfortably faithful to the solemnity and self-dramatization that often color dream experience. But arresting images do emerge. True to his epigraph from Gérard de Nerval—"Dream is a second life"—Mr. Leiris cherishes all evidence of experience, waking or sleeping, and reserves his intolerance for a post-surgical occasion of anesthesia-induced oblivion. "It was not so much the void that bothered me, but rather the gaping fault-line represented by this truly *dead time* that had been cut out of my life by the stroke of an axe."

Amy Edith Johnson, in a review of "Nights as Day, Days as Night," in The New York Times Book Review, *August 7, 1988, p. 20.*

IRVING MALIN

In this odd, profound book [*Nights as Day, Days as Night* Leiris] offers a series—a discontinuous one?—of dreams and realities over a period of forty years. He never precisely alerts us to the differences between dreams and real life—although he gives us dates or "real-life" entries—because he assumes that it is the fragmentation and fiction-making of reality which dislocates us.

When we move from one fragment to another, we begin to see Leiris's point of view. There is not any verifiable difference between dreams and realities. We are situated in a hallucinatory world in which we can never be quite sure that we *know* things. We are trying to put fragments together, to concretize life, but we are surrounded by blankness. (p. 265)

[If] we follow the course of the book, we find that we are trapped in spaces. The very whiteness of the page begins to assume meaning; the whiteness, the space, the opening—this non-written area is, as we think about it, as real as the typeface. If we were to construct our lives, we would have to omit events. We cannot remember everything; we are not complete recorders of life. Our lives—as we write or speak them—consist largely of the unspoken, routine events which occur to us. Perhaps, then, every life is a fiction because we choose to remember and shape merely "important" experiences. But the *untold* may be as meaningful as the narrated.

Leiris gives us a book—an autobiographical fiction—which disturbs us. It informs us that we really don't know what *forms* us or what we *form*. Life, art—these are open to question. . . .

We must read this book before we decide exactly the difference between night and day, completion and incompletion, fiction and non-fiction. (p. 266)

Irving Malin, in a review of "Nights as Day, Days as Night," in The Review of Contemporary Fiction, *Vol. 9, No. 1, Spring, 1989, pp. 265-66.*

DAVID COWARD

Nights as Day and Days as Night (1961), translated with due elegance by Richard Sieburth, is a collection of Leiris's dreams spanning forty years. Other people's dreams are a bore, but these are prose poems of gossamer spun in such a way that they become part of the collective awareness. Leiris's autobiographical work has always set out to divest the confessional of self-aggrandizement, self-abasement and the distortions of the literary. He sees writing as a form of tauromachy which leads him to the moment of truth—his truth made general. The "I" of his dreams is not even our

"we", although we recognize the signs, but an extension of that "impersonal enunciation" which leads us all, collectively, to a recognition of the sacred, oneiric myths which unite us. Roger Shattuck reckons in a foreword that "Leiris is our Montaigne". Perhaps. But few would disagree that in a world clamorous with memoirs and confessions, Leiris sets about the task of communal self-discovery with a passionate detachment which is as rare as it is illuminating.

David Coward, "The Apostles of Anguish," in The Times Literary Supplement, *No. 4505, August 4-10, 1989, p. 857.*

CHRISTINE SCHWARTZ

Brisées: Broken Branches, a collection of essays written between 1925 and 1965, is a good introductory selection of Leiris's literary and critical *morceaux,* as well as a look back at the time when Europe—Paris in particular—was the center of the intellectual and artistic world. Most of the 52 essays in *Brisées* constitute a commentary on Leiris's life and intellectual progress. His belief in using literary experimentation to produce a language both personal and universal was progressively refined. In 1927, he was a young surrealist, excited by the "irrationality" of 16th century astrologers (**"The Hieroglyphic Monad"**). Ten years later, his intense involvement in the art world resulted in his formulation of art as a bullfight: **"Spain, 1934-1936"** explains that "art's crucial point" is "the inexpiable war between the creator and his work, between the creator and himself, and between the subject and the object; a fecund dichotomy, a bloody joust in which the entire individual is engaged, a last chance for man—if he is willing to risk his very bones for it—to give form to something *sacred.*" (p. 5)

[Leiris's] development can be followed throughout *Brisées.* We begin with young Leiris hoping to escape the alleged dreariness of his own culture (**"Phantom Africa,"** 1934). He later experiences the qualms of a leftist ethnographer, aware that his desire to empower the recently independent peoples he studies depends on economic forces neither he nor they control (**"The Ethnographer Faced with Colonialism,"** 1950). Finally, in **"Through *Tristes Tropiques*"** (1956), Leiris subscribes to Lévi-Strauss's pessimism about anthropology, quoting the conclusion of *Tristes Tropiques:* "Every effort to understand destroys the object we had attached ourselves to . . . until we reach the only enduring presence, which is that in which the distinction between meaning and absence of meaning disappears: that from which we started out." In anthropology as in literature, Leiris is oddly preoccupied with the lacks and failures that lay behind the brightest appearances of success—in the 1950s he was at the top of his career.

Leiris's reviews are militant and poetic, precise in description and analysis. In **"Alberto Giacometti (on a Postage Stamp or Medallion),"** written as the sculptor was being awarded the Grand Prix de Sculpture at the Venice Biennial in 1962, Leiris sees the grace and tension of Giacometti's work springing from his attempt to "approach art as though it had not yet been invented and, as much a stranger to feigned naïveté as to deliberate primitivism, to recreate, day after day, the immemorial invention that will always remain to be created." Schoenberg, Satie, Picasso, Miró, Arp, Duchamp: Leiris reviewed all of them, often taking risks in defending their introduction to the French public, often befriending the artists soon after. His essays remind us how bold those artists were, and how indebted today's art world is to them.

Reading **Brisées** is a trying experience, because what stays with the reader, more than anything, is the pathos of Leiris's intellectual life. Between the lines, a schizoid image takes shape—of an idealist seduced by existentialism, a formalist attracted by all kinds of rebellions, a master of an uncertain science, and a perpetual student of the arts—the true picture of a tortured thinker, and not a comfortable one to contemplate. After following him through four decades, it is clear that in 1965 (as in his 1989 collection of aphorisms, **Images de Marque**), Leiris was still struggling to find an authentic language of his own. In **"A Look at Alfred Métraux"** (1963), he credits his friend and fellow ethnographer with teaching him that "nothing is worth more than the combination of . . . a fierce ardor for life joined to a relentless awareness of the absurdity of this ardor," and with showing him what a genuine poet is: "someone who strives for an absolute understanding of that in which he lives and who breaks through his isolation by communicating this understanding." Leiris's obsession, which may seem trivial or pointlessly deluded to postmodern generations, flows beneath most of his reviews. Striving for an ideal that he found in the work of others but not in his own, Leiris leaves us with an aftertaste of self-hatred and depression, artfully concealed in a series of brilliant, "broken" pieces. (pp. 5-6)

Christine Schwartz, in a review of "Brisées: Broken Branches," in VLS, No. 84, April, 1990, pp. 5-6.

FURTHER READING

Hewitt, Leah D. "Historical Intervention in Leiris' Bif(f)ur(e)s." *French Forum* 7, No. 2 (May 1982): 132-45.
    Examines the impact of historical events on Leiris's authorship of his first volume of autobiography, *Biffures.*

Leigh, James. "The Figure of Autobiography." *MLN* 93, No. 4 (May 1978): 733-49.
    Detailed study of Leiris's unconventional approach to autobiography.

Matthews, J. H. "Michel Leiris." In his *Surrealism and the Novel,* pp. 107-23. Ann Arbor: The University of Michigan Press, 1966.
    Exegesis of the novel *Aurora.*

Mehlman, Jeffrey. "Reading (with) Leiris." In his *A Structural Study of Autobiography,* pp. 65-150. Ithaca: Cornell University Press, 1974.
    Analysis of Leiris's autobiographical works, in which Mehlman maintains that no author has gone further in exploring the boundaries of the genre.

Terry McMillan

1951-

American novelist and short story writer.

McMillan earned critical praise for her first novel, *Mama,*
which follows the turbulent passage of a black American
family through the 1960s and 1970s. Set initially in a small
industrial town in Michigan and later in Los Angeles, the
novel centers on Mildred Peacock, a poverty-stricken, twen-
ty-seven-year-old mother of five who strives to support her
children despite her son's drug addiction, her own alcoholism, and her husband's violent temper. Some reviewers
deemed *Mama* flawed, citing uneven prose quality, lack of
narrative focus, and overt sociological commentary; most,
however, commended the novel's remarkably realistic description and its hardy, zestful heroine. Michael Awkward
observed: "In its purposely stark, unlyrical delineation of an
unredeemed and unrepentant female character . . . , *Mama*
stands boldly outside the mainstream of contemporary black
women's fiction. . . . [What *Mama* provides], in its largely
episodic depictions of the travails of Mildred and her family,
is a moving, often hilarious and insightful exploration of a
slice of black urban life that is rarely seen in contemporary
black women's fiction."

McMillan continues her inquiry into urban black life in *Disappearing Acts,* an account of a tempestuous love affair between Zora, a college-educated music teacher living in New
York City who longs to become a professional singer, and
Franklin, a sporadically employed construction worker who
never finished high school. Initially passionate and warm, the
alliance sours when Zora becomes pregnant and Franklin
turns abusive due to his frustration over frequent unemployment. Reviewers commented that McMillan's novel skillfully
investigates difficulties in relationships between black profes-
sionals and those of the working class. While most critics objected to the novel's excessive profanity, many concurred that
like *Mama, Disappearing Acts* features complex, authentic
characters and intelligent humor. David Nicholson commented: "McMillan deserves applause. She has refused to
perpetuate the well-worn conventions of black women's writing. And, in fact, she may have created a whole new category—the post-feminist black urban romance novel."

(See also *CLC,* Vol. 50.)

PRINCIPAL WORKS

NOVELS

Mama 1987
Disappearing Acts 1989

WILL BLYTHE

For the sassy, unsinkable Mildred Peacock, the men come
and go as quickly and sweetly as the paychecks. She boots out

her first husband, Crook, in the winter of 1964, leaving her
with five children and only one regret—the man who had fathered them. Mildred is the hero—protagonist is too weak a
word—of Terry McMillan's first novel [*Mama*], a chronicle
of a poor black family's gritty passage through the 60's into
the 70's.

Point Haven, Mich., offers its citizens few opportunities beyond drinking, but Mildred not only drinks, she also hustles
ceaselessly to sustain her family. She works in a salt factory
and a Prest-o-Lite spark plug plant, cleans houses, throws
rent parties, draws welfare and endures a brief stint as a prostitute.

Such labors don't spare her children from misfortune. Her eldest daughter, Freda, is raped at the age of 14; Money, her
only son, shoots heroin and ends up in jail. Mildred relies
more on the help of family and friends than religion in coping
with each crisis. "It ain't that I don't believe in God, I just
don't trust his judgment," she says.

In its inexorable movement toward economic doom, *Mama*
distinguishes itself by its exuberant comic sensibility, proving
that dignity can't be carried in a wallet. When life presses in
on Mildred in the form of bill collectors, police and nosey
neighbors, she presses right back. Indeed, in the vernacular

of this fine novel, Mildred Peacock slaps the forces of economic determinism clean upside their hoary heads.

Will Blythe, "Hustling for Dignity," in The New York Times Book Review, February 22, 1987, p. 11.

MICHAEL AWKWARD

Terry McMillan's first novel, *Mama,* opens with the elaborate plans of its memorable title character, Mildred Peacock, to defend herself against an attack from her alcoholic husband Crook. Mildred's self-protective scheme, almost militaristic in its multiple options and tactical flexibility, serves as an accurate reflection of the survivalist mentality that compels her subsequent adventures and misadventures. . . . *Mama* delineates Mildred's ultimate rejection of a fearful existence as victim of an abusive man, her resilience in the face of much—perhaps too much—adversity, her ability to fend for herself and her five children in both the urban wasteland of Point Haven, Michigan, and in a materially seductive Los Angeles, and her general resolve to gather her rosebuds whenever the opportunity presents itself.

If viewed in a cursory way, McMillan's novel seems, in its figuration of an unquestionably resourceful black female protagonist, consistent with the impulses of the emerging black women's literary tradition. However, *Mama* is, in the final analysis, more accurately read as what Hortense Spillers's essay "Cross-Currents, Discontinuities: Black Women's Fiction" calls a moment of "discontinuity" in the tradition, one in which the author "reaches behind her most immediate writing predecessor[s]" and embraces not the lyrical mode of contemporary Afro-American women writers such as Paule Marshall, Toni Morrison, and Alice Walker, but the clearly realistic models of black female precursors such as Ann Petry. In its rather self-conscious rejection of the examples of these immensely influential writers, McMillan appears intent on protecting herself from unjustified considerations of indebtedness to these contemporaries.

In its purposely stark, unlyrical delineation of an unredeemed and unrepentant female character (whose most significant psychological transformation is her ability to tell her oldest child Freda that she loves her), *Mama* stands boldly outside of the mainstream of contemporary black women's fiction. Unlike the tradition's most representative texts, *Mama* offers no journeys back to blackness, no empowering black female communities, no sustained condemnation of American materialism or male hegemony. What it does provide, in its largely episodic depictions of the travails of Mildred and her family, is a moving, often hilarious and insightful exploration of a slice of black urban life that is rarely seen in contemporary black women's fiction.

McMillan's goals are infinitely less grand than recent works such as *The Color Purple* and *Praisesong for the Widow* which offer female protagonists whose lives as abused or bourgeoise figures which, although quite different from one another, seem intended in some respect to represent large classes of Afro-American women. Mildred Peacock is no transendent or unquestionably triumphant exemplar of "the black woman's experience," but an alcoholic, nerve-pill popping, frequently self-centered character whose strength is manifested in her ability to survive (sometimes barely) the difficulties which fate—and her own, often thoughtless, actions—brings her way.

At times *Mama* might leave readers perplexed about the larger narrative and/or thematic purpose of certain incidents because of an apparent failure to explore their potential psychological consequences more fully. The eldest child Freda's molestation by a family friend named Deadman, for example, may prove, in its relative lack of clearly delineated ramifications for the young female character, particularly puzzling for readers accustomed to more symbolic figurations of rape which occur in texts such as *The Bluest Eye* and *The Women of Brewster Place*. Much of the point of McMillan's novel, however, seems to be that painful experiences come as a consequence of living in the world, that living means learning how to survive such incidents and steel one's self for subsequent challenges.

Pain—as a result of male abuse, poverty, petty jealousy, neglect, or the inability to cope successfully with one's own seeming unimportance—is such an omnipresent aspect of the world McMillan delineates that to assign to any specific incident a larger metaphorical implication is to suggest that its source can be fully comprehended and ultimately transcended. McMillan provides no such localized—locatable—evil. Instead, *Mama* offers characters capable of only small victories over their particular difficulties.

It is in her depictions of her characters' seemingly small triumphs, like the obviously cathartic demonstration of affection between Mildred and Freda which concludes the novel, that McMillan's *Mama* most clearly succeeds. Their loving embrace is a mutually beneficial interaction that suggests forgiveness for the painful effects of Mildred's earlier emotional distance and inaugurates a higher level of emotional supportiveness between mother and daughter. . . . Mildred's and Freda's deftly sketched individual journeys have provided them with the knowledge that they can find support for life's travails in one another. (pp. 649-50)

Michael Awkward, "Chronicling Everyday Travails and Triumphs," in Callaloo, Vol. 11, No. 3, Summer, 1988, pp. 649-50.

PUBLISHERS WEEKLY

McMillan's first novel *Mama* was highly praised; critics compared the author to Zora Neale Hurston. Naming the heroine of [her second novel, *Disappearing Acts,* "Zora"] may have been intended as an homage to that also gifted and black writer, but despite an abundance of flash and energy, this book lacks the depth and breadth to which McMillan aspires. This is a love story between Zora, an independent, aspiring singer . . . and Franklin, a sometimes-employed carpenter. . . . Life has been unkind to these star-crossed lovers, but they're both survivors. McMillan threads her politics through the narrative and her characters occasionally lapse into dialogue more appropriate for a position paper than conversation. In that sense, and it's not necessarily a bad one, this is an old-fashioned kind of novel, the kind with a Message. But in her effort to achieve authenticity, the author bombards readers with four-letter words, and the effect is both irritating and distancing. Though, indeed, real people talk that way, the question is: Do we want to read a novel with such relentlessly scatological dialogue? In the end, however, readers who are willing to immerse themselves in this gritty slice of life will count it an edifying experience.

A review of "Disappearing Acts," in Publishers Weekly, Vol. 235, No. 24, June 16, 1989, p. 56.

LOUISE BERNIKOW

Sometimes a very simple novel can be beautiful and easy to get lost in. This one is. **Disappearing Acts** is a love story told alternately by a man and woman who, to the astonishment of people who know them, fall in love.

She is Zora, a teacher who wants to be a singer. When Zora moves into a new apartment, Franklin is there, fixing up the place. She's respectable and responsible; he's thwarted, hasn't finished high school. Neither wants to be involved. The rest is nearly four hundred pages of accommodation to loving.

For her feisty, tough black heroines, McMillan has been compared to Alice Walker and Gloria Naylor. Zora surely joins that lineup of indomitable women, but the stunning achievement here is the creation of Franklin, whose voice on the page rings with authenticity, whose intimidation, anger, even violence are unforgettable. Watch Terry McMillan. She's going to be a major writer.

Louise Bernikow, in a review of "Disappearing Acts," in COSMOPOLITAN, Vol. 207, August, 1989, p. 42.

VALERIE SAYERS

Terry McMillan's new novel is a love story waiting to explode. The lovers of **Disappearing Acts** are both intelligent and good-looking, both possessed of dreams—but Zora Banks is an educated black woman and Franklin Swift is an unschooled black man. It's Brooklyn, it's 1982, and it's clear from page 1 that the two of them are sitting in a mine field and something's going to blow.

Ms. McMillan's first novel, **Mama,** was original in concept and style, a runaway narrative pulling a crowded cast of funny, earthy characters. **Disappearing Acts** is also full of momentum, and it's a pleasurable, often moving novel. In this intricate look at a love affair, Ms. McMillan strikes out in a whole new direction and changes her narrative footing with ease. But **Disappearing Acts** is also a far more conventional popular novel than **Mama** was. Despite its raunchy language and its narrative construction (Franklin's voice and Zora's alternate), its descriptions, its situations, even its generic minor characters are often predictable. I say this with some surprise, because it seems to me that Terry McMillan has the power to be an important contemporary novelist.

Much of the predictable feel of the story has to do with Zora Banks's narrative. Zora, who reaches her 30th birthday in the book, has come to New York from Ohio; she is a musician who makes her living teaching in a junior high school but feeds her soul by writing songs. She dreams of landing a recording contract, and seems on her way to that goal when she falls hard for Franklin Swift, separated and the father of two, who is working on the renovation of her apartment building. The progress of their love affair is punctuated by construction layoffs for Franklin: as his resentment escalates, so does Zora's frustration. She becomes pregnant, and by the time their son is born they are both enraged and near desperation.

Zora's voice, though generally likable, has a bland quality (Franklin's son says she "talk like white people"), and her narrative is sometimes written in a pop-magazine style that has her forever reminding her readers how handsome Franklin is. She applies the same gushing descriptions to her friends. . . . That voice makes me wince, and so does the one that compares her emotions to the most banal symbols of pop culture. . . . She's sure Franklin is intelligent because he plays a mean game of Scrabble and beats her at "Wheel of Fortune." *"Wheel of Fortune"*?

This shallow voice seems incongruous when you consider that Ms. McMillan's heroine is named for Zora Neale Hurston, who knew how to make imagery streak and crackle across a hot dark sky. Zora puts Hurston's great novel *Their Eyes Were Watching God* on the bookshelf next to a picture of her dead mother—giving Hurston the role of literary mother—but despite her admiration (and some intriguing parallels between Zora's love affair and the affair Hurston describes in her autobiography, *Dust Tracks on a Road*), this Zora's voice is way too flat. Even her profanity gets boring.

Franklin's profanity also gets old, but his voice is hot and electric; when he's talking, the narrative sparks. Franklin Swift is smart, bigoted, passionate, loving, generous, mean-spirited, ignorant, intractable, forgiving, resentful. His voice is far grittier than Zora's and it's genuine. In addition, Ms. McMillan takes some real chances not only with Franklin's voice but with his life. Summarized, his history makes him sound like a loser: he's a high school dropout who's played with drugs and seen the inside of a prison; a man who despises his mother and his wife; a father who sees and supports his two children sporadically; a lover who sometimes asks for sex in a repellent, coarse whine; an expectant father so frustrated by his dealings with the white construction world that he hits a pregnant Zora—and later does worse. Much worse.

The miracle is that Ms. McMillan takes the reader so deep into this man's head—and makes what goes on there so complicated—that his story becomes not only comprehensible but affecting. The reader comes to see why Zora loves him, and why she kicks him out. Franklin is a more compelling character than Zora because he's allowed his moments of childishness and even wickedness: he's a whole person. Ms. McMillan's portrayal of this man may well be controversial (anybody looking for a successful, strong-but-gentle African-American male won't find him here), but it's undeniably alive.

I have my doubts about the ending of **Disappearing Acts,** but I'm a hardhearted reader; I leave you to your own conclusions. Nevertheless, I admire the risks Terry McMillan has taken in making Franklin Swift come to such intense life. I imagine she'll make a long and challenging career of taking such chances.

Valerie Sayers, "Someone to Walk Over Me," in The New York Times Book Review, August 6, 1989, p. 8.

DAVID NICHOLSON

For the past decade or more, books by black women have appeared in such numbers as to constitute almost a separate genre within an all too frequently ghettoized American literature. Surely, however, this second novel by Terry McMillan [**Disappearing Acts**] must be one of the few to contain rounded, sympathetic portraits of black men and to depict relationships between black men and black women as something more than the relationship between victimizer and victim, oppressor and oppressed.

For that, and for daring to create a heroine who, though disappointed in love, does not condemn all men or retreat to militant homosexuality, McMillan deserves applause. She has refused to perpetuate the well-worn conventions of black women's writing. And, in fact, she may have created a whole new category—the post-feminist black urban romance novel.

The novel concerns the two-year affair of Franklin Swift, a high school dropout in his 30s who works intermittently doing construction, and Zora Banks (yes, she *is* named after the novelist, anthropologist and free spirit of the Harlem Renaissance), a junior high school music teacher who wants to become a singer. Having decided to move from Manhattan to Brooklyn, Zora meets Franklin at her new apartment where he is at work on the renovating crew.

The two fall in love, almost literally at first sight. . . . Soon, the two are involved and then living together, but there are problems. . . . They are both fearful of their future together because of their past failures in love. Their biggest problem, however, is the difference in their backgrounds.

That last device is, of course, one of the oldest in literature, but the specifics here are of particular relevance to black Americans. Professional black women complain of an ever-shrinking pool of eligible men, citing statistics that show the number of black men in prison is increasing, while the number of black men in college is decreasing. Articles on alternatives for women, from celibacy to "man-sharing" to relationships with blue-collar workers like Franklin have long been a staple of black general interest and women's magazines.

To some extent, though, McMillan stacks the deck. Franklin is no ordinary construction worker. He may be a high school dropout, but he has taken pains to educate himself. . . .

Despite the "equal time" given Franklin and the sympathetic way in which he is portrayed, this is, I think, a women's novel. I can't imagine most men liking it, in part because of the hard truths Zora and her friends have to tell (in the female equivalent of lockerroom bull sessions) about men they've known. Mostly, though, it's that there is a sweetness about *Disappearing Acts;* it is really an old-fashioned love story, albeit a sincere one.

If, in the end, Franklin and Zora are not entirely credible (Zora is a maddeningly passive character, and I would prefer to believe that most black women are not so desperate as to suffer abuse such as Franklin's), then it is also true that we are, initially at least, caught up in their lives and pulling for them and their success together. The minor characters . . . are well drawn and the dialogue is authentically rendered black urban folk speech. What's troublesome is the abundant profanity—as much as one obscenity every other line on some pages—so much that it soon becomes neither funny nor shocking, but merely tedious.

For all that is good about this novel, however, I like it more for what it represents than for what it achieves, and I think McMillan deserves congratulations for what she has attempted, not for what she has accomplished.

The house of fiction has many mansions, but each technical decision involves tradeoffs. Telling the story from alternating first person viewpoints gives us different sides of the same story but also leaves the book without the center that a novel of this length demands. This is not, after all, a slim poetic novel where feelings are traced as delicately as a pencil line on paper, but an attempt to render the world concretely and realistically. But whose voice are we to trust in this recounting of a series of ordinary events whose extraordinariness is never revealed? And where does the author stand?

McMillan's tight focus is suffocating, rather than intimate or revealing, and the book is too long. For all that we have these people talking to us for 384 pages, curiously they remain unknown to us when the novel ends. And too much of the book is a repetition of certain themes or issues: Franklin's continuing refusal to take responsibility for his life, blaming instead racism and "the white man"; Zora's dithering about her music career. The two analyze their relationship, over and over and over again. After a while, we want to scream at them, "Oh, just shut up and *do* something. Anything. Just do *some*thing!" Scenes that include other characters . . . are a welcome relief from the mutual navel-gazing in Franklin and Zora's apartment.

There is a beer commercial aimed at black buyers, and seemingly designed with full knowledge of the troublesome demographics of the black community, where a young, obviously professional black woman walks past a man laboring over a jackhammer. Their eyes meet, and she walks on. A moment later, we see her in a nightclub with friends. She looks up onstage and sees the same man, now dressed in a sportscoat and open-collared shirt, playing the saxophone. The commercial ends with him coming over to her table.

Disappearing Acts reminds me of that commercial. The book deserves to be read, and I hope it will be, but I think that McMillan, for all her exploration of interiors has (like that commercial) illuminated only exteriors.

David Nicholson, "Love's Old Sweet Song," in Book World—The Washington Post, *August 27, 1989, p. 6.*

THE NEW YORKER

If Ntozake Shange, Jane Austen, and Danielle Steel collaborated on a novel of manners, this blunt and entertaining book [*Disappearing Acts*] might be the result. It is narrated in alternating chapters by Franklin Swift and Zora Banks, two weary veterans of the black singles wars, as their Brooklyn love affair shifts from struggling alliance to misalliance and back again, and as they try to find the right measure of each other's worth through elation and suspicion, career breakthroughs and setbacks, and, ultimately, childbearing and the possibility of a lasting truce. Class differences as well as gender play a part: Zora is a schoolteacher with a college degree; Franklin is a high-school dropout who is unsteadily employed as a carpenter and construction worker. The vulnerability and complexity of black male self-esteem and the precariousness of black middle-class existence are powerfully dramatized. Less successful are the supporting characters, who generally conform to type, and a maternal villain who is used to explain away far too much; but the insistent, profane, and honest voices of Franklin and Zora win the reader over.

A review of "Disappearing Acts," in The New Yorker, *Vol. LXV, No. 39, November 13, 1989, p. 147.*

NEIL McKENNA

Heady doses of social realism and sexual explicitness invade an essentially schmaltzy black version of the archetypal New York love story in Terry McMillan's second novel, *Disappearing Acts.* Although the story is set for no obvious reason in 1983, the distance of seven years lends no enchantment and little illumination to this conventional tale of love triumphant.

Like all the worst and the best New York love stories, *Disappearing Acts* begins outside a newly converted brownstone but this time it's Brooklyn rather than Manhattan. Sassy, feisty Zora is 29 and teaches school, but one day she will be a great singer. She has two major weaknesses—tall black men and the consumption of food, and she's trying to cut down on both. That is, until she meets tall, black Franklin outside the brownstone and it's love at first sight.

But is love (and steamy sex) enough to keep the gathering storm clouds of social realism at bay? What with Franklin's drink problem, unemployment and low self-esteem *and* Zora's eating disorder, epilepsy and musical ambitions (let alone a lesbian lunge from best friend Marie) things don't look too good.

The night, as convention dictates, is darkest before the dawn, while saccharine endings and terminal blandness are just two blocks away.

> *Neil McKenna, "The Serpent Spirals of Desire," in*
> The Observer, *February 4, 1990, p. 60.*

Mary Lee Settle

1918-

American novelist, memoirist, nonfiction writer, and dramatist.

Settle is best known for *The Beulah Quintet,* a series of five novels set over a three-hundred-year period that illustrate the development of American cultural identity. Beginning in 1649, the Beulah saga recounts the histories of three families whose common ancestor, Jonathan Church, was executed at the age of sixteen for refusing to bow before General Oliver Cromwell during England's Civil War. Church's American descendants, settlers in the fictitious region of Beulah, West Virginia, embody the soldier's defiant, democratic spirit. In each of these novels, a protagonist advocates humanistic ideals in a malevolent Southern society composed variously of emigrant farmers, soldiers, plantation owners, coal miners, and debutantes. As the *Quintet* follows these families through such events as frontier settlement, the American Revolution, antebellum slave-ownership, the American Civil War, and the coal strikes of the early twentieth century, Settle emphasizes the disastrous effects of racial and class-oriented bigotry. Commenting on *The Beulah Quintet*'s relation to the historical novel, Brian Rosenberg remarked: "[Settle] adapts a tradition largely European and conservative to subjects American and revolutionary. For though historical fiction of this depth and extensiveness had been written before, never had it been by an American author attempting to define the characteristically American historical experience."

Settle was born into patrician Southern society, the daughter of a civil engineer and coal mine owner who moved his family from Kentucky to Florida to West Virginia. Settle initially attended Sweet Briar College, a women's school, but left after two years to pursue an acting and modeling career in New York City. There she met and married an Englishman whom she later followed to London, where she joined the women's division of the Royal Air Force during World War II. After the war, she divorced and remarried, living in both the United States and England. In addition to contributing articles to American magazines, Settle wrote several plays that went unpublished. In England, Settle researched and wrote her first full-length works, *Kiss of Kin* and *The Love Eaters,* two contemporary novels set in the fictional town of Canona, West Virginia and featuring families who later appear in *The Beulah Quintet.* Many reviewers in America and Britain considered the novels well-detailed and indicative of a fresh talent.

In 1954, Settle began research in London's British Museum for *O Beulah Land,* a historical novel that she originally envisioned as the leading work in the "Beulah Land Trilogy." Spanning twenty years between the French and Indian War and the American Revolution, *O Beulah Land* chronicles hardships encountered by settlers in the region of the Ohio River Valley that would later become West Virginia. After Hannah Bridewell, a transported London prostitute, escapes her Indian captors, she meets and marries Jeremiah Catlett, a fugitive bondsman from the Virginia colonies. Although the couple is later killed in an Indian ambush, their son survives to marry the daughter of Jonathan Lacey, a Virginia gentleman descended from English aristocrats. *O Beulah Land,*

which set the foundation for *The Beulah Quintet,* initially received little notice; however, several commentators later contended that this and subsequent volumes of the *Quintet* were neglected due to a prevalent critical disdain for the historical novel.

Beulah, the community founded by Hannah and Jeremiah in *O Beulah Land,* is the setting for Settle's next novel, *Know Nothing,* which explores the events that led to the American Civil War. Spanning the years 1837 to 1861, the novel follows the Laceys and Catletts, focusing on Jonathan Catlett, the son of a wealthy slave-owner, who becomes a disenchanted Confederate soldier fighting against his abolitionist brother, Lewis. Settle has commented that in *Know Nothing* she strived to uncover the true past beneath popular romantic myths about Southern culture before the Civil War. Aaron Latham observed: "[*Know Nothing*] is about the zenith of antebellum civilization in Beulah and shows the author at the zenith of her powers." The next work in Settle's *Beulah* series, *Fight Night on a Sweet Saturday,* received largely negative reviews. Intended to link *Know Nothing* with the contemporary period, Settle's first manuscript for *Fight Night* contained sections later excised by her publisher depicting the violent mine strikes of the early twentieth century. The resulting novel features an embittered and indigent Jake Catlett who kills his wealthy distant cousin, Jonathan McKarkle. Settle later replaced *Fight Night on a Sweet Saturday* with *The Killing Ground,* a subsequent novel that investigates similar themes.

Distressed by what she perceived as the inconclusive nature of the trilogy, Settle resolved to extend the saga backwards, to delve into the historical basis of the revolutionary ideals she finds essential to the American character. *Prisons* chronicles the 1649 execution of Jonathan Church, a young soldier in Oliver Cromwell's Puritan Army during the English Civil War. Church, who was inspired by Cromwell's rage against the English monarchy, becomes disillusioned at the commander's increasingly imperious manner and refuses to vow his allegiance. Executed as a rebel for his democratic idealism, Church leaves behind an illegitimate son who is raised as a member of the aristocratic Lacey family. Descended from this child are the Laceys, Catletts, and McKarkles of other *Beulah* novels. While some critics deemed the novel's subject obscure and its style monotonous, others lauded Settle's evocative depiction. Jane Gentry Vance remarked: "In all five novels, and particularly in *Prisons,* Settle uses the raw material of a near-lost history that she unearths and pieces together to create a vast, magical, instructive fictional world. Her research methods and her creative processes . . . are keys to the uniqueness of her accomplishment."

Expanding upon the omitted sections of *Fight Night on a Sweet Saturday,* Settle developed *The Scapegoat,* a novel set in the first decades of the twentieth century that recounts bloody disputes between coal mine owners and miners struggling to form a labor union. *The Scapegoat* features a female protagonist named Lily Lacey, the daughter of a mine owner, who empathizes with the impoverished miners. After an appearance by the historical labor organizer Mother Jones, whose speech Settle resurrected from court documents, the novel follows Lily to France, where she is killed while serving as a nurse in World War I. Although some critics objected to the novel's profusion of characters, most considered it scrupulously detailed and dramatically engaging.

To conclude *The Beulah Quintet,* the novel *The Killing Ground* presents Settle's families in a contemporary setting. Hannah McKarkle, an established novelist, returns to a small town in West Virginia for the funeral of her brother, Johnny. A wealthy *bon vivant* who is controlled by his mother, Johnny is inadvertently killed in a fist fight with a stranger, who proves to be his distant cousin Jake Catlett. Hannah, author of four novels with the titles *Prisons, O Beulah Land, Know Nothing,* and *The Scapegoat,* contemplates the town's history, including the familial relationship between Johnny McKarkle and Jake Catlett. She regards her brother as heir to the tradition of rebellious and hardy Beulah pioneers, but mourns his unglorious death as a symptom of life in a modern era corrupted by wealth and ease.

After spending twenty-six years on her *Beulah* epic, Settle began the contemporary novel *Celebration.* Set in London, Hong Kong, Turkey, and Africa, *Celebration* relates the love affair of Teresa, a recently-widowed American in London recuperating from an operation for uterine cancer, and Ewen, a Scottish geologist studying at the British museum. Their many friends, including an African Jesuit priest and a heartbroken homosexual recently returned from Hong Kong, provide eclectic subplots. While some critics disliked the novel's digressive style, others lauded Settle's generous scope. William Boyd observed: "[*Celebration*] is about triumphing over

adversity, about holding on to what is good, beautiful and true in this cruel and chaotic time we have on earth. One can only applaud such sentiments."

Settle is also the author of *Blood Tie,* winner of the 1978 National Book Award. This novel, a portrait of the cultural clashes between seven American expatriates living in Turkey and the country's repressive government, is informed by Settle's own experiences in that country, where she lived while writing *Prisons.* Critics esteemed the novel's accurate depictions of deep-sea diving and archaeological explorations, as well as its intricate characterizations. Settle's other works include *The Clam Shell,* an autobiographical novel set at a Southern college similar to Sweet Briar, and *All the Brave Promises: The Memories of Aircraft Woman 2nd Class 2146391,* a nonfiction memoir concerning Settle's World War II service in the British signals corps.

[See also *CLC,* Vol. 19; *Contemporary Authors,* Vols. 89-92; *Contemporary Authors Autobiography Series,* Vol. 1; and *Dictionary of Literary Biography,* Vol. 6.]

PRINCIPAL WORKS

NOVELS

The Love Eaters 1954
The Kiss of Kin 1955
O Beulah Land 1956
Know Nothing 1960
Fight Night on a Sweet Saturday 1964
The Clam Shell 1971
Prisons 1973; also published as *The Long Road to Paradise,* 1974
Blood Tie 1977
The Scapegoat 1980
The Killing Ground 1982
Celebration 1986

NONFICTION

All the Brave Promises: The Memories of Aircraft Woman 2nd Class 2146391 1966
The Story of Flight (juvenile) 1967
The Scopes Trial: The State of Tennessee v. John Thomas Scopes 1972

JONATHAN YARDLEY

[*The Killing Ground*] is the concluding volume of Mary Lee Settle's ***Beulah Quintet,*** a saga that is centrally concerned with the clash between labor and capital as it takes place over many generations in the coal-mining country of West Virginia, with side excursions to other settings in this country and overseas. ***The Killing Ground*** is an intelligent novel, searchingly introspective about the needs and motives that drove Settle to write the ***Quintet;*** but for precisely that reason it is also an unusually self-preoccupied novel, and it seems likely to be of interest primarily to those readers who, through the previous four books, have developed a consuming interest in the valley of Beulah and its people.

The Killing Ground begins in June 1978, with the return of

Hannah McKarkle to her West Virginia home town of Canona. She is 48 years old and has been away for nearly two decades, since the death of her beloved brother Johnny in an incident that, for the town and her family, remains cloaked in mystery. During that period she has become an accomplished and admired novelist, the author of books that carry the same titles as Mary Lee Settle's and that deal with the same themes; with what some will regard as courage and others as narcissism—I suspect some of both are involved—Settle has unabashedly placed herself directly at the center of the novel, under the very thinnest of disguises, and has made it a meditation upon her own reasons for writing fiction. . . .

The novels of the *Quintet* are the "books of my search" for the meaning of Beulah's past, or, as she puts it later: "In the truncated churchyard I knew that I was reaching into caves of memory, recognitions that could be rung against what I had learned for the adultery of nostalgia or shame or pride, burn off the rust of all the evasions, and see that what had happened rang true." These words . . . are a concise statement of the fundamental purpose of the historical novel: to reach an understanding of the past and its legacy, to grapple with "the long battalioned ghosts of old wrongs and shames that each generation of us both inherits and creates"—words from Faulkner that Settle takes as the novel's epigraph.

The focus of this attempt at understanding the past is her obsession with her brother's death, her determination "to shake the single event that had started it all, the smash of an unknown fist against an unknown face." She sees her brother as heir to an honored tradition: "Brother Jonathan, the eighteenth-century archetype of the revolutionary soldier. Brother Jonathan, Johnny Reb, Johnny Appleseed, a character once as familiar as Uncle Sam, fades in and out of our history . . . " But the more she explores the past that she and Johnny shared, the more she comes to believe that his rebellion, like hers, was corrupted by the relative wealth and ease they were granted by a weak father and a manipulative mother. Johnny, the beloved Johnny, was not a revolutionary but a man-child who played at life. . . .

Eventually she discloses that the "unknown fist" that struck Johnny was that of a distant relative, a member of the yeoman branch of the family. Whatever the exact impulse that drove Jake Catlett to smash his fist against her brother as they occupied a crowded drunktank, she sees it as at heart an expression of class hatred and rivalry, a consequence of "unknown scars" with origins deep in Beulah's past. And in it she finds "the armature, an ambiguity of steel, on which I have built my book," the conflict

> between democrat and slave holder, a dilemma all the way to our founding, that seemed so often to have no place in the pragmatic surviving days of living, but yet had had a place, had built a country, fused dreams into cities, seeking always the illusive balance, sometimes almost imperceptible, but even then it had so often left behind a residue of spirit, like an old campfire, gone cold but potent with clues.

This is good if slightly overwrought writing, and the point it makes is eminently sound. But evocative prose and stimulating ideas do not, of themselves, make interesting, engaging fiction. What the novel lacks is what it needs most: life and heart. Mary Lee Settle is obviously in the grip of deep and important emotions, but she fails to convey them to the reader; she is content to tell rather than show, with the predictable

result that the reader simply does not respond to the feelings she describes. Her previous work has shown her to be an accomplished storyteller, but *The Killing Ground* is less story than recitation. It has too many characters, too few of whom emerge from the crowd as distinct individuals and too many of whom seem to exist solely as objects of Settle's contempt.

Mary Lee Settle must always be taken seriously, which can be said of lamentably few American novelists, and in *The Killing Ground* her tough intelligence is a formidable presence. But as a work of fiction, *The Killing Ground* falls considerably short of the rest of the *Beulah Quintet*—and it is as a work of fiction, of course, that a novel must ultimately be judged.

> Jonathan Yardley, "Mary Lee Settle Concludes the Beulah Quintet," in Book World—The Washington Post, *June 13, 1982, p. 3.*

GAIL GODWIN

The Killing Ground opens with novelist Hannah McKarkle returning home to the mining town of Canona, West Virginia, where she has been invited to lecture on her work at the old country club on the hill. Though a pariah in the eyes of "the best people" among whom she was raised (Hannah marched against the war in Vietnam; worse, she "exposed" her family and region in her novels), she is "the only famous person" who will consent to be the star attraction for this important fundraiser for the town's new art museum. "All that's left to us is the arts," bewails one member of the hanging committee, as the four ladies drive Hannah to her lecture. "You have to understand . . . that this audience is not really intellectual or literary like you're used to," the same lady tells Hannah as the Cadillac climbs the hill and we, the readers, receive capsule histories of the "pathetic, redundant" lives of these four women who do hope Hannah will keep her remarks light and amusing. . . . These women are, Hannah concludes to herself, in a little ecstasy of hatred, "in one of the bloodiest centuries of the Christian era, women to whom nothing has happened that is not personal."

But personal things have a way of happening whenever Hannah comes home, and this time is no exception. While she is presenting a high-minded and technically sophisticated lecture on how she went about tracing the history of this community through novels (which, incidentally, have the same titles as Mary Lee Settle's *Beulah Quintet,* of which *The Killing Ground* is the conclusion), word spreads round the hall that a popular bachelor in town has hanged himself. The crowd disperses with alacrity; the dinner party for Hannah is canceled on the spot as the "hanging committee" transfers its interest from art to the deceased. The personal has, if you will, avenged itself on Hannah, who is left alone with her memories of another homecoming, eighteen years ago, when she arrived just in time for the freakish death of another popular Canona bachelor: her beloved brother Johnny.

The circumstances surrounding this death, caused by a blow from a resentful hill kin's fist against the face of white-dinner-jacketed Johnny during a Saturday night sojourn in the jailhouse drunk tank, were what galvanized Hannah McKarkle into becoming a novelist. (p. 30)

The impact of her promising, attractive brother's wasteful death, and the social and historical questions that lie behind it, impel Hannah to begin a fictional quest that will take her all the way back to 1649 to an ancestor, also named Johnny, a soldier in Cromwell's army who is shot for refusing to doff his hat to authority. From England she will begin her imaginative recreation of the collective consciousness of the people who settled the hills and valleys of Canona, instilling into their descendants a "genetic sense of loss," some dim racial memory of being kicked out, of having to leave home. Through four novels, Hannah will trace the paradoxical, ornery seam that runs through her people, or perhaps all Americans, making them fight their oppressors to the death for freedom, yet imitate the pretensions of these oppressors once they've got it. It is this central paradox that provides the themes and the tensions in Hannah's (and Mary Lee Settle's) Beulah books: we see generation after generation struggling out of poverty, anonymity, danger, only to achieve the house on the hill and start aping the very oppressors who threw out their ancestors.

Until her ill-fated lecture at the old country club, Hannah thought her project was almost done: *Prisons, O Beulah Land, Know Nothing,* and *The Scapegoat* were to be the great act of imagination which would set her free to live in the present. Now she realizes that the quartet must be a quintet, and the last book must deal with what's closest to home: *The Killing Ground* will be the personal story behind the historical, fictionalized ones. In it, Hannah must come full circle back to her own time, her immediate family, the wasted Johnny of her own generation, and her own struggle to leave home without getting trapped by the old fears and hatreds.

It is perhaps Hannah's grimness as she shoulders the last burden of this huge, protracted task she has set for herself that gives this final volume of the series its joyless, duty-ridden tone. ("My God, I have traced us through four books, and still it wasn't over, paid my dues and been charged again.") Unfortunately, this tone of a writer/protagonist being overawed by her own Grand Design interferes with the enjoyment of the work. Every time we begin to be eased into the stream of fiction, the voice of Hannah pulls us back with an interpretation of the events we are witnessing, the characters we are getting to know, quite well, on our own. Settle ought to trust her vivid, discriminating eye, her accurate ear more: what people do and how they express themselves reveal much in this society Settle evokes for us. . . . But Hannah is too often at our elbow, reminding us how these people are generic as well as personal, or assuring us mid-description, how much she condemns them, even though she is one of them. . . .

[A] startling insight into kindly Uncle Ephraim, the gentleman farmer, loses half its impact because of Hannah's untimely infusion of hate. It's hard to see a character clearly when you are rushing to his defense. Just as, when Hannah brought the weight of the Christian centuries down on those ladies with their spotted hands in the Cadillac, I felt suddenly more sympathetic toward them than I'm sure Hannah meant me to feel.

Maybe it was part of Mary Lee Settle's plan to make Hannah, her mouthpiece and alter ego, difficult to like; perhaps she thought it would be unfair, making "herself" lovable while drawing such relentlessly devastating portraits of Hannah's family and friends. (Hannah's mother is a monster of Southern respectability; her sister a cornucopia of small-minded bitcheries.) Whatever happened here, Settle is capable of creating more appealing heroines: the headstrong, passionate Lily Lacey, the mine owner's daughter in *The Scapegoat,* who was, like Hannah, an idealist, an activist, but also

charming. I'm also thinking of that tough, brave, elegant young woman in *All the Brave Promises,* Settle's fascinating and moving memoir of her time in the Royal Air Force in World War II. It is because I loved this book so much that I felt so impatient with the voice in *The Killing Ground.* The voice of the memoir is compassionate, perceptive, warm. I kept wondering why Settle had denied her alter ego in *The Killing Ground* a fuller range of the tones she had in her to draw on.

Although I could not love the book, or lose myself in it, I was compelled, with Hannah, to pursue the "mystery" of brother Johnny's needless death. It is a mystery in the philosophical sense. We know who felled this last male hope of the McKarkles, but we must learn, through Hannah's tireless researches into family secrets, what it is in a society that breeds dangerous "feral twins." Hannah finally tracks down her brother's destroyer on a final trip home to the funeral of an eccentric old aunt who has been sitting on the information Hannah needs for her epilogue. It is with a grudging acceptance that Hannah has been right all along in her thesis that we discover Johnny's killer diligently struggling up through the layers of Canona society—trying to become Johnny.

During her country club lecture, Hannah tells her Canona audience that she has been trying

> to trace the clues to both the failure of a dream and its persistence in our innate dissatisfaction with things as they are, that is our constant undercurrent, and breaks sometimes into revolt . . .

She accomplishes this task to her own satisfaction at the end of *The Killing Ground.* As her plane circles higher above Canona, she feels she carries away something deeper than the land whose history and people have enthralled her for so long. The single legacy she chooses to keep from her heritage is "the choice to choose, to be singular, burn bridges, begin again, whether in a new country or a new way of seeing or a new question. . . ."

We come away admiring her ambitious undertaking and her stamina to complete it; we cannot help but hope her future choices will earn her that eventual larger freedom whose ripest fruit is compassion. (pp. 30-2)

> *Gail Godwin, "An Epic of West Virginia," in* The New Republic, *Vol. 186, No. 24, June 16, 1982, pp. 30-2.*

AARON LATHAM

Mary Lee Settle, the novelist of the West Virginia coal country, writes books that are as good and as bad as the mines themselves. Though she sometimes pollutes her fiction with waste words and waste characters and waste subplots, just when it appears time to close the mine she strikes a rich vein that makes the work of digging through so many words seem worthwhile.

Her new novel, *The Killing Ground,* completes a five-book cycle that she calls *The Beulah Quintet,* a series of interconnecting tunnels stretching back and down 300 years. In this volume, at last, the story arrives in the present. *The Killing Ground* fits the pattern of the rest of the cycle, being part slag but part good, sturdy, useful black gold.

The first half of this novel takes place during a ladies' literary luncheon, which is just as dull as one might imagine. The guest speaker is a novelist named Hannah McKarkle who talks about writing a series of books entitled *Prisons, O Beulah Land, Know Nothing* and *The Scapegoat,* which just happen to be the first four books of **The Beulah Quintet.**

Once the endless luncheon breaks up, something very like literature actually begins to happen in **The Killing Ground.** Miss Settle begins to examine why Hannah McKarkle wrote her books. She traces the original motive, the original obsession, the original compulsion back to the death of Hannah's brother, Johnny. Her life is as purposeless as her brother's until he dies violently. Then, in trying to discover why his life meant so little, her own life and work and words take on meaning. (p. 1)

Hannah McKarkle mourns in print for her lost brother, Johnny, by resurrecting in writing his ancestors dating all the way back to 1649. This task has occupied 20 years. "It has taken," Miss Settle (writing in the first person as McKarkle) says in **The Killing Ground,** "a long time to give them back their lives." In *Prisons,* Miss Settle tells the story of Johnny Church, who is executed during Oliver Cromwell's Roundhead Revolution. In *O Beulah Land,* she writes of Jonathan Lacey, who is killed in the American Revolution. In *Know Nothing,* she gives us Johnny Catlett, who dies in the Civil War. In *The Scapegoat,* her "Johnny" is a young woman named Lily Lacey who loses her life while serving as a nurse in World War I.

Miss Settle's poor Johnny in modern dress gets killed fighting not in a war but in a jail's drunk tank on a Saturday night. **The Killing Ground,** once it finally gets started, is about how this Johnny makes his way to that cell. So the quintet, which begins with a book called *Prisons,* ends in jail. One of the themes stitching all of the novels together is Miss Settle's hatred of all that imprisons us, from Cromwell's church to Johnny McKarkle's country club. Johnny is "caged" by his class, by other people's expectations, by his lovers, by his family—and by his mother, who in a sense encompasses all the others. Miss Settle seems to be saying that the weak often rule the strong, that dependents compromise the independence of those on whom they depend, that the unliberated deprive others of liberty, that slaves enslave their masters. Politically and socially, she is a modern Harriet Beecher Stowe who would free us all.

"So we sat, the women Johnny had let pull his heart and hamstrings until he was small enough to live with us," she writes, "we the slave owners who had inherited the punishment unto the third generation, that of having to rule, but having no one to rule but each other; need and training turned inward, slave and master one."

In the end, Johnny McKarkle, the heir to all the Johnny Rebs, dies rebelling against all the petty things that imprison him, but especially against his mother. He gets drunk to escape her for a little while and gets his head broken to escape from her for good. He dies a diminished death in a diminished age, but in a sense the author of this death seems to be trying to convince herself that his dying is inevitable since he is descended from a long line that died either in prison or trying to escape from one. He had violent death in his genes. One also senses that the author is trying to free herself from her own death dreads, making novels out of death the way Mahler made a game out of death, to exorcise her fear of that final prison.

In a strange—and unintended—sense, the evolution of Mary Lee Settle's novels echoes the history of the land they are about. *O Beulah Land* (1956) begins hopefully, as did the early settlers, then gets lost in the wilderness, as did her ancestors, and then finishes strong, as did the hardiest of the pioneers. *Know Nothing* (1960) is about the zenith of antebellum civilization in Beulah and shows the author at the zenith of her powers. After her pre-Civil War novel, Miss Settle knew no more about which way to turn than did her own postwar ancestors. The civilization, the valley's land and the family's blood seemed almost worn out. As though afraid of the future, Miss Settle plunged even more deeply into the past, writing *Prisons* (1973), which is set in the time of Cromwell and is as dull as a Roundhead Sunday sermon. *The Scapegoat* (1980) takes place on the eve of World War I and shows a further thinning of the novelistic blood.

So one enters **The Killing Ground** with some trepidation, fearing more tired blood, more overcultivated soil—a stripmined valley. And at first one is horrified to find one's self in just such a reverse Eden.

But when Miss Settle finally finds a vein in the middle of this valley that takes her beneath the surface, **The Killing Ground** turns out to be worth mining after all. What I believe Miss Settle should do now is sift out the slag and reduce her **Beulah Quintet** to a single long novel. This volume should include the beginning and end of *O Beulah Land,* all of the wonderful *Know Nothing,* none of the preachy *Prisons,* none of the scapegrace *Scapegoat* and the last half of **The Killing Ground.** Such a diminished novel would, I believe, be a diminished American classic. In such a resurrected Beulah Land, Mary Lee Settle's dear, doomed Johnnys might well be immortal. (pp. 20-1)

Aaron Latham, "The End of the Beulah Quintet," in The New York Times Book Review, *July 11, 1982, pp. 1, 20-1.*

J. D. O'HARA

Boxing has given us lots of useful terms: knockout, out for the count, taking a dive and—heartwarming phrase—a clean break. Life affords us far too few clean breaks. Listen to country music: someone's always hanging on for dear life, unable to let go and walk away. Mary Lee Settle's **The Killing Ground** takes its story from that situation.

Hannah McKarkle is the product of a number of West Virginia families, most of them involved in coal mining, who have moved downriver from the Beulah Valley to the town of Canona, where they mingle with the other nouveau riche families that form the town's elite. Like her sister, Melinda, and her brother, Jonathan, Hannah was raised to continue the existence of her family and her class by doing what everyone else did. But she and Johnny couldn't or wouldn't fit in, and in the 1960s she left for New York City. Johnny stayed home but refused to marry, took pointless jobs, bedded many local women, drank too much and was killed in a jailhouse brawl. Back in Canona for his funeral, Hannah found what many find on similar homecomings: she hadn't broken clean after all.

To understand her complicated relationships with her family, the town and the whole area, Hannah looks deep into the past. Where Canona is now, a prehistoric town once stood. According to legend, a mother goddess inhabited a sacred circle upriver, and fathers offered her the blood of sons or substitutes. Today, on the site of that ancient killing ground, "the spire of All Saints, the Episcopal church, pierces the sky, and on Sundays the chalice is passed discreetly." . . . But, as Hannah learns, the sacrifices are still going on, though now the mother goddesses frequent the country club.

Most sons capitulate without bloodshed. They join the family firms, wear the right clothes, live the properly ritualized lives, marry the cosmetically blushing brides . . . and why not? Settle is wonderful in evoking "the seduction of duty and comfort and compliance." (p. 150)

The novel begins with Hannah back in town and looking forward to a ride with her old "friends": "The Cadillac door will close on me. It will fit with a slight puff, a lady fart." As the "girls" in the car bitch at one another, we hear their thoughts. Kitty Puss Baseheart, "once the fastest girl in her crowd," thinks of Johnny and other lovers: "Lover was a fine word, but it ended up where it began, in a motel room." Another thinks about children: "You did everything in the world for them and what did you get in return?"

This concern with profit and loss, with pride and humiliation, evokes a major theme in Settle's treatment of women: theirs is the calculating, self-centered tyranny of the weak. Their weapons are the swoon, the silence, the troubled withdrawal, the snub, the sick headache and, of course, the appeal to propriety. At every crisis we hear "not now," "not here," "at a time like this," "today of all days," "now is not the time."

Settle has an ear for the vernacular—the fake genteel diction of Canona's elite, the rough back-country speech of its lower classes—that would have delighted Mark Twain. . . . As these voices create a complex counterpoint, we find an unpleasant world, disturbingly like our own, rising up around us. West Virginia, coal-mining mama, takes us home. *The Killing Ground* is fine entertainment; it will make you hope for rainy weather and a chance to read it slowly.

But that's not the half of it. Mary Lee Settle won the National Book Award in 1978 for *Blood Tie,* a fine, serious novel set in Turkey, but her central work has been the livelier, even more serious and often raucously funny *Beulah Quintet: Prisons, O Beulah Land, Know Nothing, The Scapegoat* and now *The Killing Ground.* The first four novels trace the movement of immigrants from England to North America in the 1600s; the settlement of West Virginia; the Civil War years; the development of the coal industry in the Beulah Valley; and the industry's sellout to "outside interests" during the depression of 1907.

Once in Canona, the well-off survivors of the depression set about remaking their lives and their history. In *The Killing Ground,* a women's cultural committee has taken over "the old beer joint, the Wayfaring Stranger," and has turned it into "a doll's house, San Francisco style," to house an art gallery. The gallery is intended to counteract the museum. "The state took over the museum," one woman explains sadly. "It's awful. . . . You know, models of coal mines and a lot of stuff about early man. I wouldn't call that taste. We're the hanging committee, so we have control over taste." The deadly hanging committee does what it can. But the *Beulah Quintet* is like the state museum: it offers unprettified reality, including coal mines and early man. (pp. 150-52)

In *The Killing Ground,* the patterns of the past have been disrupted and distorted. Mining companies have stripped the

land down to hardpan and rock. Canona society, as the gentrification of the Wayfaring Stranger bar suggests, is sterile and false, its life based on money—coal mining money. We frequently hear that this or that item "cost an arm and a leg," and among the working class, we meet those who paid—the substitute sacrifices—shorn of a limb by a mining accident.

The Beulah Valley is a fearful and dangerous world, but Settle preaches no simple rebellion against its history. Our country was settled by "people who for three hundred years had left home because they had to," says Hannah, who left home herself. But she also realizes that "our country was made by people who had no place else to go." Since they cannot break clean, Settle's rebels must make their home in this alien world—"perhaps a place to leave without guilt and return to without regret, and there the seeking ends."

Have I made the *Beulah Quintet* sound like a five-volume sermon? It is not. Settle is far too lively and witty a writer to preach. At the end of *The Killing Ground* she pays a quick tribute to "Cassandra, an eminently sensible girl, the first novelist." No one ever believed Cassandra's warnings. No one may ever heed Settle's wisdom. But if you know any literate young person whom you wish well, you might buy him or her a copy of *The Killing Ground* when you buy your own. (p. 52)

J. D. O'Hara, "The Last of Beulah Valley," in The Nation, New York, Vol. 235, No. 5, August 21-28, 1982, pp. 150-52.

NANCY CAROL JOYNER

Her literary ancestor is William Faulkner; her Yoknapatawpha is Beulah Valley, West Virginia. She tacitly acknowledges her debt to Faulkner by using his words as the epigraph for her most recent novel, *The Killing Ground:* "We are fighting, as always, the long battalioned ghosts of old wrongs and shames that each generation of us both inherits and creates." Through nine of Mary Lee Settle's ten novels, she has recorded the wrongs and shames and the battles against them in her little postage stamp of the world, which in her case is situated on two continents and spans three centuries.

Her most sustained work is what is now called the *Beulah Quintet,* which begins in 1956 with a single novel, *O Beulah Land.* The book takes place in Virginia between 1754 and 1774, dramatically recreating General Braddock's defeat in 1755 and introducing the early English and Scotch settlers. Hannah and Jeremiah Catlett, Jonathan and Sally Lacey, and Solomon McKarkle are among the most prominent of the characters whose descendants are to reappear in later volumes. *Know Nothing,* published in 1960, covers the years 1831-61, when Peregrine Catlett, grandson of both the Laceys and the Catletts of the earlier work, is master of Beulah and master of many slaves. His two sons, Jonathan and Lewis, enlist in opposing armies when the Civil War begins. *Fight Night on a Sweet Saturday,* published in 1964, originally constituted the concluding volume of *The Beulah Trilogy.* Set in 1960, it records the family's reaction to the death of Johnny McKarkle, who is killed during a brawl in a jail cell by his cousin, Jake Catlett. Shortly after the presumed completion of the series, Settle explained to interviewer Roger Shattuck, "I saw that the trilogy had not yet done what I wanted it to do. A whole part of our being American was missing, our revolutionary sense." She then published *Pris-*

ons in 1973, a novel set in seventeenth century England, in which the narrator, Jonathan Church, is executed by Cromwell in 1649. At age 16 Johnny Church has fathered an illegitimate child named Jonathan Lacey, by implication the ancestor to the Virginia pioneer. In 1980 *Scapegoat* appeared, a novel involving a coalminers' strike at Beulah in 1912. The owner of the mine, Beverly Lacey, is opposed by his cousin, Jake Catlett, one of the miners. *The Killing Ground,* published in 1982, might be called the sixth volume of the quintet, for it is a revision and expansion of *Fight Night on a Sweet Saturday.* Taken as a whole, the series is elaborately detailed, carefully constructed, and extremely complex in its connections.

Settle's saga does not end with the *Beulah Quintet,* however, for three of her four other novels are set in Canona, West Virginia (presumably Charleston), as is *The Killing Ground,* thus making a lateral connection among those books. *The Kiss of Kin* (1955) takes place in a house close to the Canona River, and two other novels, *The Love Eaters* (1954) and *The Clam Shell* (1971), are set in the town of Canona and include many of the same characters that appear in *The Killing Ground,* such as the Dodds, the Potters, the Slingsbys, and Charlie Bland. With a single exception, *Blood Tie* (1977), set almost exclusively in Turkey, (and, somewhat ironically, her single winner of the National Book Award), Mary Lee Settle has spent most of her career of nearly thirty years in creating her Canona Saga.

Critical response to Settle's work has not reflected her downright awesome accomplishment. Generally favorable reviews for each of her ten novels have appeared in American and British publications, but despite positive reactions to her individual volumes, Settle's literary reputation remains obscure, and scholarly attention to her work has been conspicuously and mysteriously absent. (pp. 33-4)

Critical attention is, however, gradually burgeoning. Both Roger Shattuck and Granville Hicks have written introductions for the Ballantine editions of the Beulah series. . . . [But essays] that do something other than provide a general introduction to her work or assess individual volumes are rare.

In fact, a minor backlash appears to have occurred before there was much of a forward motion in criticism of the *Beulah Quintet.* When *The Killing Ground* appeared in the summer of 1982, Aaron Latham went on record on the front page of the *New York Times Book Review* [see excerpt above] to say he found Settle's powers diminishing over the last twenty years and feared he would find "a stripped mine" in her latest book, only to discover "ore worth mining." Nonetheless, he thought Settle could profitably "remove the slag" from the five novels in the series and compress them into a single volume. In a recent article in the *Appalachian Journal* on the *Quintet,* William J. Schafer announces at the outset that he sees Settle as "an ambitious, accomplished, and impressive writer" but goes on to compare her technique pejoratively with that of E. M. Forster, Stephen Crane, and Tolstoy, and concludes that she lacks a panoramic view of history. Commonly one sees such negative criticism in response to inflated praise or extreme popularity, two literary situations that Settle has never enjoyed. Surely her work merits more critical analyses than it has so far received.

The critics who have dealt with the *Beulah Quintet* inevitably attempt to find common threads within the five novels that

link them to one another. Even Schafer, after he has examined the series and found it wanting, identifies four such threads: recurring prison imagery, the presence of war, "the inextricable complexities of family structure," and changes in the land. While these elements are not in each novel, they occur in four of the five and are legitimate linking devices. But these four categories are not exhaustive; other linking elements occur. The Biblical source for the name Beulah (Isaiah 62:4) or a quotation from the nineteenth century hymn "O Beulah Land" appears in each of the five novels. Classical allusion, such as the Narcissus myth, abounds throughout, with particularly heavy emphasis on the Antigone legend, which Settle told an interviewer was the controlling myth for the series. At least one prominent historical figure appears in each of the novels, from Oliver Cromwell to J. F. Kennedy. Some objects that are first discussed in *O Beulah Land,* a silver handle of a riding crop and a deep red stone found by Hannah Bridewell in the wilderness and variously referred to as a ruby and a garnet, are traced through subsequent novels until they are held as family heirlooms in *The Killing Ground.* Aside from the requisite family connections in the five Beulah novels, then, Settle consciously and conscientiously has included many other kinds of links in the series.

Settle uses these linking devices to reinforce one of her major themes in the *Quintet,* class consciousness and the resultant conflict such awareness engenders. She does this through a cluster of images relating to dress and the decoration of houses, as well as through statements concerning status and wealth. Because critics have heretofore tended to ignore this particular set of connections, an examination of some of the instances in which these images and attitudes are present should be useful in determining the quality of Settle's art.

In *Prisons* Johnny Church's earliest memory is of the Christmas of 1634, when he goes to visit the estate of his Royalist uncle, Valentine Lacy. His mother dresses him in a black velvet suit to indicate his family's Puritan predilections. The five year old Johnny is especially impressed with the yule log and the silver punch bowl from which he is offered a drink of wassail. When Sir Valentine pays attention to the "Little preacher," Johnny reports "I sat upon his lap and saw, for the first time, my new black clothes against the soft white satin sash he wore." The distinctions between the two adjoining estates are more profound than habits of dress, of course, but the description of dress symbolizes those differences in religious belief, political affiliation, and social prominence. Johnny studies with his cousin Peregrine's tutor until they both go to Oxford, an exhilarating experience. . . . When Johnny argues with his father and goes off to fight in the Civil War with Cromwell, he stops by Lacy House, where he has an illicit tryst with his aunt. She asks to see what provisions he has for his journey, and they have the following conversation:

> "No money. . . . These saints that make themselves God in their houses and will not let their children free. Now hark it, my Johnny, money is freedom."
> "Freedom's more than that." I did not like to hear such words from her lips.
> "Aie, money's the oil of it, though."

Because *Prisons* is primarily about Johnny at war, relatively little is mentioned about clothes, decoration of houses, or money. Nevertheless, the themes are included.

Class distinctions are more domestically presented in *O Beulah Land.* Hannah Bridewell, a convicted thief transported from London, is found after wandering in the wilderness for forty days following her escape from the indians. Her benefactor is Jeremiah Catlett, an indentured servant who had run away into the wilderness after having found religion and having escaped his master. When he stumbles upon the unconscious Hannah he first notes "a gray shred of linsey" and sees the "ludicrous remains of her clothing." He takes her home to his small, one-roomed, dirt-floored hut, dominated by a rock fireplace on one end and his hog, Hagar, on the other. The clothes he first provides the woman who eventually becomes his wife consist of deer skins and a panther fur.

In sharp contrast to the Catletts are the founders of the Beulah community, Jonathan and Sally Lacey, who have moved there from the eastern shore of Virginia. When Jonathan brings Sally to the house he has built for her, the arduous trip is marked chiefly by the accident in which all but one of her "blue and white Cheeny plates, all sent from England," are lost. The remaining plate becomes a symbol for prosperity and culture thereafter, being displayed on the chimney ledge. When Sally invites the other women in for hot chocolate (which none knows how to drink), she allows each to hold the plate briefly and tells them that once she had five others. . . . (pp. 35-7)

Jonathan is dismayed beyond anger at Sally's behavior and tries to explain her new position in life: "Now listen to me, ye poor leetle gel. There's a mighty lot ye've got to leave behind ye, over the mountains. . . . Tomorrow morning ye're goin to take a hoe over your shoulder, and ye're goin down to the stockade field and ye're goin to work all day like a Negrew to show ye're one with the rest of us." The other women, however, save her from that fate, for they convince Jonathan that her hands are far too delicate for such strenuous work. Thus we see that in the frontier society members of the lower class actively maintain class distinctions.

Because Jonathan's land holdings exceed those of his neighbors, he is considered the wealthiest and most powerful of the settlers, and Sally rigidly maintains her position as the society leader in the community she insists upon calling "Cicero" instead of Beulah. She is so unsatisfied with her house, the finest in the settlement, that she encourages everyone who passes by the river bank to bring home one rock so the outside might eventually boast a stone veneer. When her daughter marries beneath her, as inevitably she must, Sally is unable to cope with the strain. . . . One reason for her dismay is that the groom, Ezekial Catlett, comes dressed for his wedding in a buckskin outfit Hannah has made for him "that had taken nearly the winter to make fine enough." In the description of the wedding, then, Settle dramatically presents the conflicting social norms present in the frontier society.

Sally, with all her airs, is presented as a comic figure, made ironic in light of the Lacey's actual financial and social background. . . . Earlier in the novel there are indications that Sally's family had lost its social and financial status. When she goes west with her husband she apparently does so because she has nothing left of the comfortable situation in which she grew up except a few household furnishings—and two slaves.

In *Know Nothing,* the novel that begins in the 1830s, slaves play an important role, as do the Catletts, the current first family of Beulah. In the first scene another Sally Lacey, from the eastern branch but in financial straits, is on her way to see her western cousins. Her husband, Brandon Lacey, calls

them their "backwoods Catlett kin" but Sally admonishes him: "they are Virginians even if they are transmontane." When they arrive they admire the new three story brick house and the furnishings in the parlor. . . . The backwoods kin are as conscious of fashion as their Tidewater relatives, and, by the mid-nineteenth century, their position as members of the upper class has become as substantial as the Victorian elegance of their house.

Know Nothing might be considered a sort of Appalachian *Gone With the Wind,* with its deliberately romantic scenes of match-making and sociability. The middle and longest section of the book is set primarily at Egeria Springs, where the family vacations in hopes of finding suitable husbands for the marriageable girls. On the day the trip begins, Peregrine stops his horse to watch them: "Far way down the path toward the carriage, the three bell-shaped women swayed, the heads of the girls up and expectant, as if in the first excitement of going they were practicing their gliding strut, working out like two fillies down the course of the walk." (pp. 38-9)

The need for money to maintain the life style of these upper class Catletts and Laceys is an important motif of *Know Nothing.* Peregrine Catlett is reduced to selling some of his slaves because of his financial difficulties, and Brandon Lacey, in dire straits, presumably commits suicide: he "took the only way out a gentleman could take under the circumstances, gone through with everything, even his people and Sally's jewels knocked down to his creditors." Sally is desperate to make a good match for her regrettably plain daughter and does her best to train her properly. At one point she says, "Don't talk about money, Sara. It ain't genteel. My stars, nobody talks about money but Yankees." Sara, "having heard her mother talk about nothing else since her father's death," does not demur. In *Know Nothing,* the false gentility of the women reflects the increasingly frantic attempts to disguise a weakening economy.

While the Catletts and the Laceys are on more or less equal footing in society in *Know Nothing,* such is not the case in Settle's post-Civil War novel, *The Scapegoat,* for in 1912 Jake Catlett, Peregrine's grandson, lives west of Beulah at Lacey Creek, where he is employed by his distant cousin, Beverly Lacey, owner of the Seven Stars Coal Mine. On the same day that Beverly entertains men who have come in their private train to discuss the threat of unionization, Jake entertains Mother Jones, who has come by coach to help organize. Jake's wife, Essie, is the Lacey's cook, for Ann Eldridge Lacey will have none of the black Laceys inside her house. Although the house is not described in detail, the reader knows that it is sufficiently elegant to boast a tower room . . . ; a library with a large plaster copy of Victory of Samothrace; a wine cellar (which Beverly will allow no one but himself to enter because he doesn't want anybody to see how poorly stocked it is); and a large front porch. Of particular interest when the book opens is the Gatling gun that has just been installed on the porch. Jake's house, in contrast, is actually the cabin his father Lewis built on property he claimed through squatter's rights. The furniture is cast-off from the Lacey house. When the novel opens, a tent city has been established in his front yard, a refuge for coal miners who have been evicted.

Clothes in this novel are important symbols of status. Essie wears her hat instead of her poke bonnet every day when she goes to the Laceys "to help out" because "it showed every one of them that she wasn't no servant." The men who have been brought in to guard the mine dress in black, as does Mother Jones. In contrast, Beverly Lacey has taken to wearing an old ill-fitting white suit, because "it made him feel rich again." His daughters were also in white. The middle daughter, Althea, reports "Papa insisted, by the calendar, that his girls greet the May, as he called it, in white dresses. He made a little ceremony out of it." When the eldest daughter, Lily, leaves suddenly for New York, her mother gives her the dress she had been saving for her birthday: "Look at your new dress. Crepe de chine, with gold fringe. It's all the rage. *Vogue* says so. . . . You might have need of it. Besides, you have to look rich. It's a great protection in this world." Many other references to clothes appear in the novel, but these examples should be sufficient to show the variety of symbolic purposes with which choice of dress is imbued. The preceding brief examples, however, do not do justice to Settle's stylistic mastery in description of clothes. The following passage illustrates her ability to create a complex of moods while she is indicating another set of symbols emanating from the description. Althea, the most iconoclastic of the daughters, remembers the events in 1912 from the vantage point of a day in 1927:

> Oh I was the loveliest thing when I was a girl. Mother had bought me a hat in the Via Condotti in Rome. It was the loveliest thing you ever saw and it cost the earth, pale gray clouds of georgette with pink rosebuds faint behind them. I can still smell that smell of a costly hat before the Great War, smell of tissue paper, silk, and straw and hear the sound of the weightless lifting of it, a rustle and a falling breeze of tissue paper, and it had no weight at all and I moored it to my head with my best hatpin, filigreed gold, oh absolutely lovely, and I sallied out to meet my dear one who had followed us all the way from Lausanne. We were madly in love. Shit. I don't even remember his name. But I do remember the black trees, and the old, old shade, and I remember the hat, perched on the grass like a gray dove and I lost my cherry in the Borghese Gardens.

In this case the hat does much more than indicate class consciousness; it symbolizes Althea's lost youth, lost wealth, and lost innocence.

Althea figures prominently in the final volume of the Quintet, for, as Hannah McKarkle's oldest living relative, she is one of the agents by which the protagonist searches for the secrets of her family's past which will help her discover her own identity, the principal theme of *The Killing Ground*. The most experimental of all of Settle's books, this one presents the fictitious Hannah, twelve years younger than Settle herself, as the author of the other Beulah novels. The book begins in 1978, when the distinguished author, Hannah, returns to her home town to deliver a speech. While she is lecturing news of Charlie Bland's suicide reaches the audience, and when Hannah hears of it she is vividly reminded of the accidental death of her brother Johnny, which brought her back to Canona in 1960. She retraces the events surrounding his death and her search for her own roots at the time (the subject of *Fight Night on a Sweet Saturday,* the original fifth volume of the Quintet that *The Killing Ground* supercedes). The book ends with an epilogue, set in 1980, when Hannah returns for her Aunt Althea's funeral and finally straightens out the tangled threads of her background—Hannah's connections with the past. (pp. 40-2)

As in the earlier novels, clothes play a significant role, but in *The Killing Ground* the emphasis is on the dress of the upper class. Hannah remembers Johnny in his rented morning suit at their sister's wedding, in his black tails during the first grown-up dance she attends, in the habitual white dinner jacket for the boring dances at the country club. She remembers her own exaltation and dismay when she wore her white organdy for Melinda's wedding and the green taffeta with the torn ruffles at her first dance. (p. 43)

But it is money—the awareness of having it, of having had it and lost it—that most informs the book. When the women of Hannah's country club set take her to her lecture in the essential luxury of a Cadillac Seville, one of the women thinks, "there was . . . nearly ten million dollars riding in the car, and a fat lot of good it did any of them." Hannah herself grew up in an affluent household, untroubled by money or the lack of it, but her mother, having come from a family in which the fortune was lost, is overly conscious of both possessions and appearances. . . . Sally Brandon, for her part, has never recovered from her father's losing their property in Beulah. Once she tells Hannah:

> We were haunted by money. Money money money! The drains said money, don't run out of money. Money makes the mare go, don't marry for money but marry where money is; pride and patches and no money. That's what I lived with. I would climb up the pear tree and think about money when I wanted to be thinking of higher things.

This fixation with money and the position it confers is partially responsible for making Sally Brandon McKarkle, as Gail Godwin calls her in *New Republic* "a monster of Southern respectability" [see excerpt above]. She is that and more, for, when Hannah refuses to come back to Canona to fill the vacuum left by Johnny's death, Sally disinherits her.

When Sally McKarkle wonders to Hannah "Do you think . . . they'll put it in the paper? All that business about Jake Catlett being a distant relative? After all, everybody has a less fortunate branch of the family . . . ," and when she later snubs Jake Catlett at Johnny's funeral, she is echoing the behavior of the Sally Laceys of *O Beulah Land* and *Know Nothing.* In doing so she confirms Hannah's thoughts about her own disinheritance: "I would, through the years, have a genetic inheritance more powerful than money; slave, slave owner, slave in turn. I would trace the tap of my mother's bare foot back to poor little genteel Sal who carried with her over the mountains, imitation of an oppressor she did not know, a camouflage." Hannah also realizes that she has inherited an impulse to rebel as well as the impulse to conform. But, she goes on to say, "most of all I would carry that itch for balance between them, a quality that quarrels with itself, poised between democrat and slave owner."

The Killing Ground represents a deliberate attempt to connect the *Beulah Quintet,* to make coherent the diverse styles and stories of the other novels. Because the book is a gloss on the other novels, it is impossible to appreciate without having read the entire series. And because the final novel explicitly states the comprehensive theme and draws connections among the preceding books, it is at times unfortunately self-conscious and redundant, especially in light of the connections of images, of which dress and decoration of houses are only two of many; and implicit themes, of which attitudes about money, class consciousness and family connections are only three of many, are already present. Nevertheless, the *Beulah Quintet* is a stunning achievement. With it, Mary Lee

Settle has made a major contribution to American fiction. (pp. 43-4)

Nancy Carol Joyner, "Mary Lee Settle's Connections: 'Class and Clothes in the Beulah Quintet'," in The Southern Quarterly, *Vol. XXII, No. 1, Fall, 1983, pp. 32-45.*

DORIS BETTS

At the heart of [*Celebration*] is a Jesuit named Pius, 6'9", originally a prince in his native Dinka tribe, a nigger in the city surrounding Georgetown University where he studied, a nignog in the book's setting of London, but "priest everywhere. He clung to that, as he clung to that old rugged cross till its burden at last he could lay down. That had been the first song he had learned in Washington, D.C., the first time he had been invited anywhere." Besides Pius, there is an intangible "black monk" who lives in the mind of Teresa Cerrutti—a figure composed of psychic fragments from her own Jungian animus, Chekhov's story, a remembered childhood friend, a foreshadowing of the real Pius, and what we might call her own soul-voice or conscience.

Such a reverberation from natural to supernatural is typical of *Celebration,* in which real events in 1969 ripple until they merge first into biography, then history, at last mythology. . . .

[As the novel opens], Teresa Cerrutti and her husband Michael, anthropologists, are on a dig in Kurdistan, where sacred objects are buried in layers of collapsed civilizations, and where the locals have learned to "salt" the territory with counterfeits. Michael descends into a tabooed well he believes is a shrine and dies from its real taboo—a tangle of poisonous snakes at the bottom. On the plot-surface, these mistranslations of reality continue. Russian and American agents in Turkey play chess while trying to reduce an ancient world to cold-war terms. When the widowed Teresa has healed her grief and moved to London, she is spied upon by a C.I.A. agent who interprets her international circle of friends as a Communist cell.

But apparent reality, to Settle, is almost comic relief. The real story is one which Jung, E. M. Forster, Sir James George Frazer and Mircea Eliade have continued to read below the surface of written history and which the priest Pius identifies at a joyous party celebrating America's first moon-landing, spinning a globe as he talks: ". . . like this globe, this room contains a world, a globe you can't see. It was in this room that we stepped on the moon and saw ourselves blue in space, a little pendant orb, and here tonight we celebrate a wedding of each other, a wedding of the soulscapes that in this room make up that world. I knew a man once who called it the country behind his eyes. You . . . have in your soulscape the mountain where Noah landed." (p. 211)

At a time when the novel as a form seems often the size of one solipsistic psyche—sometimes the narrator's, sometimes the novelist's—Mary Lee Settle has steadily moved the boundaries of her region out to encompass the human spirit. Early critics said she had made Virginia her Faulknerian Yoknapatawpha, traced it and the nation's history through recurring characters. Instead of giving us full details of suburban car pools and women's rooms, Settle has extended her early process to the scale of what Eliade calls in his subtitles "archaic realities." Like E. M. Forster's, her crisp prose always telegraphs her empathy for people displaced or misunderstood. She takes her readers into a worldwide Marabar Cave of her own, but unlike Mrs. Moore, she does not agree that "everything exists, nothing has value." *Celebration,* which ends with two ceremonies, a funeral and a wedding, leaves no uncertainty about Settle's recognition of death and her celebration of life. Even the book's cover shows the mythical snake and Michael's death-snake juxtaposed against the mythical flower-mandala of fruition and life. In the end, Teresa has accepted Pius's conviction that "you lived within other people, in what he called their soulscapes . . . she felt full of light and constructed by the love she had been given, and held within her."

"Only connect," E. M. Forster advised. Mary Lee Settle has followed his advice in novel after novel until her connections have grown very large and generous, while still respecting mystery. (pp. 211-12)

Doris Betts, in a review of "Celebration," in America, *Vol. 156, No. 10, October 18, 1986, pp. 211-12.*

WILLIAM BOYD

[*Celebration*] opens with intriguing power. Teresa Cerrutti, recently widowed, recently operated on for uterine cancer, tries to face a fragile future with some hope and confidence:

> She stood there naked, thirty years old, with an angry red line from her navel to where her pubic hair had been. "You must face bravely the physical loss of your sex; but remember, there are compensations for not having children," Dr. Dangle had said . . . and she answered aloud, naked in the morning, "You're goddam right there are, mister."

She quits her post at her university and leaves America for London. The year is 1969. . . .

[Once in London], Teresa is suspected of being a subversive. In the past, her anthropological studies have taken her to the interior of Turkey, close to the Russian border. Her Turkish friends are politically dubious, with leftist affiliations, and a faculty snoop at her university has alerted the Central Intelligence Agency. Teresa's file follows her to London and is passed on to the local C.I.A. man, and Turkish expert, there—friendly Frank Proctor, who, moreover, has had [her] sublet flat comprehensively bugged.

Frank falls in love with Teresa, vainly and wordlessly, as it turns out. Thanks to his hidden microphones he soon learns all he needs to know about Teresa's life. Most hurtful to him is the fact that she meets and falls in love with a Scottish geologist (they are both doing halfhearted research in the British Museum) called Ewen McLeod. Ewen moves in with her, and soon we become acquainted with the other dwellers in the neighboring apartments and the couple's small circle of friends. These are unusually eccentric and heterodox. There is Noel, a languid, aristocratic homosexual; Pius, an immensely tall African Jesuit priest; a squabbling bourgeois husband and wife whose marriage is in its terminal phase; Zephyr, a beautiful Turkish girl with lots of money; and Artemesia Ambler, a strident, hard-swearing editor of pornographic magazines.

The year moves on. . . . Teresa and Ewen fall deeper in love. The process is slow and somewhat fraught. Both are recovering from illnesses and both are emotionally scarred. Poor

Ewen is even temporarily impotent after a heavy bout of malaria contracted in central Africa. Under these strains, things turn sour, and then, one night, Ewen unburdens himself and confesses a crime he committed in Africa to Teresa. This clearing of the air reunites them, their happiness marred only by the senseless death of one of their friends.

If this summary makes the narrative line of *Celebration* seem less than engrossing, that is because much of the book is taken up not so much with the present but with the characters' pasts. In the context of Teresa and Ewen's love story we get many other stories—pre-eminently Noel's (the history of a bitter love affair in Hong Kong); Pius's (his calling and religious education); Ewen's (an adventure in Africa, where he is inveigled by his uncle into becoming a mercenary) and Teresa's (the story of an anthropological trip to Kurdistan and of the death of her husband). Between these shorter narratives we return to London and the tenderness and gentle comedy of the curious community at Battestin House.

However, this adumbration of the structure of *Celebration* makes it seem more sturdy than the experience of reading it warrants. In fact, this longish book is rambling and not a little dull. Certain technical decisions made by the author exacerbate these tendencies. Although Teresa is at the novel's center, the story is only infrequently told from her point of view. Instead we have a form of omniscient narration, with the author free to enter the head of any character she chooses. But at the same time, the stories told by the respective figures are related in monologue, between quotation marks and in the first person. Monologues of this length are very hard to sustain within the general context of objective omniscient narration in the third person. It breaks down particularly in Ewen's story, where the narrative moves randomly between his voice (he's telling the story to a dozy Teresa) and an orthodox third-person account. There is nothing wrong with choosing such an ambitious narrative scheme, but it seems to me there's no purpose in it if it is not done consistently or to some clear dramatic purpose. Neither of these aims is achieved or even postulated in *Celebration* and the consequent haphazard effect only serves to accentuate the untidiness of the whole. The novel may be a loose baggy monster when it comes to content, but its form demands tighter control.

Celebration, as its title implies, sets out to be a yea-saying book. It is about triumphing over adversity, about holding on to what is good, beautiful and true in this cruel and chaotic time we have on earth. One can only applaud such sentiments. At the novel's end Teresa and Ewen achieve real happiness in the midst of tragic events, and that's enough to bring a lump to anyone's throat. But the novel does not lead us naturally to these conclusions; it's undone and they are thwarted by the confused narration, a multitude of variously rendered voices and patches of uncertain style. We visit five continents and encounter a dozen nationalities. The conception is bold, but in the end one has to ask if it was wise. Passages that convince with their authority (such as the Kurdistan episode, reminiscent of the Turkish setting of Miss Settle's *Blood Tie*) consort uneasily with episodes, accents, nationalities, idioms and ideologies that seem only partly grasped: ' "You see," he explained . . . 'when you are born a Scot, a boy, and not the first-born, there is a thing you know right from the start. You see it in the hard granite, and in the braes, where only the heather grows. There is no room for you in Scotland.' "

Well, frankly, and speaking as a Scot, I think this is nonsense.

I know what Miss Settle is getting at, but people simply don't talk this way, and the effect achieved is the opposite of the one intended. And that is what finally disappoints in the novel. For all the topographical exactness, the tone in which the places, characters and dialogue are rendered edges perilously close to the precious and coy, as if the effort to deliver a resounding "Yea!" in the face of life's unfairness and indifference has fogged Mary Lee Settle's normally clear vision with heavy tints of rose.

William Boyd, "Teresa Cerrutti Can Take It," in The New York Times Book Review, *October 26, 1986, p. 14.*

FRANCES TALIAFERRO

Celebration's epigraph is also its premise: "The real knowledge of death is sudden and certain. It takes different people different ways. After that crossing to the less naive side of the river Styx . . . nothing is taken for granted." Each of *Celebration*'s four major characters has been intimately acquainted with death; each of them finds that knowledge the most compelling reason for joyously embracing life.

Their four lives converge in London in 1969—an uneasy time of hippie ascendancy and Vietnam protests, but also the hopeful year of the moon landing. Teresa Cerrutti and Ewen McLeod have each been painfully bereaved. They meet in the reading room of the British Museum and fall quickly, chastely in love. . . .

Teresa is an American anthropologist who first encountered death in the mountains of Turkey, where she and her husband Michael had gone to study the Yezidi, a Kurdish subtribe. . . . With a professional archeologist's skeptical curiosity, Michael investigated a forbidden site; he died a needless and horrible death. Now, four years later, Teresa has left academic life, survived her own cancer operation, and come to London as a young widow, hoping to live rather than grieve.

At first we know very little of her lover Ewen except that he is a Scottish geologist fascinated by sand and that he is still recovering from the malaria he contracted in Africa. . . . Ewen survived, thanks to an unlikely rescuer.

This guardian angel is Pius Deng, a black man close to seven feet tall who is both a prince of the Sudanese Dinka tribe and a Jesuit priest educated at Catholic University. He has seen his own people ravaged. In Africa he saved Ewen's life; now in London, Pius is helping Ewen come to terms with the blood-guilt that haunts his malarial hallucinations. Pius is merry, wise and good: a lovely man.

The fourth major character, Noel, is Teresa's long-lost childhood friend and first love, a British peer, for years an ardent homosexual. Noel's story takes us to Hong Kong, where he loved and was bereft of his one great passion, a young Chinese man. . . .

The reader of this review may find it difficult to keep up with four major characters of four different nationalities whose converging lives have brought them to London via Kurdistan, the Scottish Highlands, the Sudan and Hong Kong. Mary Lee Settle has always been attracted to a broad canvas and a large cast of characters, as in the admired *Beulah Quintet,* a series of novels set in West Virginia from Revolutionary times to the present. In *Celebration,* a jet-age *Decameron,* she skillfully manages the flashbacks that constitute most of the narrative, but a disaffected reader might complain that these are properly three or four separate novels: Teresa's tragic exploration of Kurdish culture, Noel's poignant homosexual idyll in Hong Kong, and Ewen's salvation, by Pius Deng, from the heart of darkness.

Suffering has strengthened these four people, and the interweaving of their lives makes it clear that we are all part of Providence's larger pattern. The weakness of the novel is the profusion of small narrative threads and fringes. The "present" sections, which take place in London in 1969, are cluttered with little plots, including the capture of Noel's deserted town house by revolutionary squatters and the theft of a small Cezanne from the National Gallery by two nice IRA boys. In addition, each inmate of the house where Teresa and Ewen live has some little tic of personality. . . .

Other vivid, superfluous characters are Artemesia Ambler, the "high-booted, mini-skirted, Afro'ed and beaded" editor of an outrageous magazine with a four-letter name, and a Mr. Evans-Thomas, who appears in full Cavalier fig on feast days of the Society for the Restoration of the Stuart Monarchy. These are colorful, even charming satirical sketches, but after a while the reader gets tired of keeping track of the huge cast of characters and yearns for a more concentrated narrative. The most absorbing—and strangely beautiful—section of *Celebration* is the story of Ewen's African ordeal and his rescue by Pius Deng, the Dinka Jesuit. One wishes these two had the novel to themselves.

Frances Taliaferro, "Mary Lee Settle and the Wisdom of the Heart," in Book World—The Washington Post, *November 9, 1986, p. 7.*

EDITH MILTON

Mary Lee Settle's writing is generally epic in scale and substance, and generous in spirit. At the very least, one puts down her books with a sense of having been well-nourished.

At first, though, *Celebration* looks like a modest book, a romance about Teresa, a young American, who meets a Scot named Ewen in the Reading Room of the British Museum. The time is 1969. She is an anthropologist, in flight from her past and convalescing from a sequence of losses: her husband's death, her own nearly fatal cancer, and a growing sense of anomy. He is a geologist, beset by recurrent malaria and some hidden sorrow which we assume, correctly as it turns out, involves a deep personal guilt. Together they move into a flat off the Prince Albert Road in a house inhabited by a United Nations Assembly of eccentrics.

Its the perfect set-up for a Barbara Pym novel: educated minds, nurtured in the anthropology section of the British Museum library, observing uneducated hearts, nurtured in the anthropological fields of North London. And Settle plays sporadically with that paradox: the ambience, story, and design of *Celebration* often labor to remind us of that long tradition of English fiction, through Austen back to pastoral comedy, that delights in ironies of perception and misconception and rejoices in the grandeur of the banal. But Settle has very little feeling for what she has worked to evoke; her writing is quintessentially American, impatient with style, ambitious for meaning, prodigal with symbol, flirting with the occult. I wondered more than once in the course of reading the novel why its London setting and tone should so contradict

its American scale. Or why its characters, whose humble lives are circumscribed by the mundane, should carry baggage clearly intended for other climates and a larger world.

I suppose you could ask the same questions of *War and Peace,* and certainly *Celebration* means its ordinary, English present to act as a lens in which to focus the time and space beyond. Through its characters' memories it enters a far past; through their travels and the diversity of their acquaintances, it reaches the four corners of the earth. In fact, what *Celebration* most celebrates may be variety. I rather admired the book's frequent shifts in perspective: from omniscient narrator to first-person monologue, from limited third-person viewpoint to stream of consciousness. Though there seems no particular need for all the shifts, they do lend the book an engaging sense of spontaneity, of coming about unsought.

And the styles in which the novel is written are extraordinarily varied: Teresa's memory of her months in a remote Turkish village is lyrical; Ewen's talk of his bleak Highland childhood is simple and intense, while his account of gunrunning in East Africa is in the dark suspense mode of a modern spy novel. Noel, a British peer and Teresa's long-lost friend, speaks with sophisticated self-mockery: the best passage of the book is his deeply felt account of homosexual love and attrition which is, on its own, a gem of a short story.

Indeed, Settle's ear for her characters' language is usually exact and her social observations through their eyes are often exquisite. Teresa's terminally snobbish landlord, for instance, says of the English that "embarrassment . . . is the only truly killing emotion we have." . . .

Still something is missing: so many ingredients should add up to more than the final result which is *Celebration.* Perhaps the novel's surface, the London present, is not powerful enough or sure enough to unify the multiplicities into their proper totality. Or perhaps the novel's central themes—how far its people have come from their points of origin and how much detritus they still carry with them—are often too explicit to interest us. When an account of the moon landing follows directly on Pius's tale of a visionary experience in his tribal youth, one is aware of the artifice of the juxtaposition, and hears no echo between the two events.

In the end, for all its perception and the courage of its intention, *Celebration* remains an engagingly intricate patchwork quilt. It collects its pieces from a very wide world, but stitched together they never come close to achieving the profound illusion of reality. Given the possibilities, that is a shame.

Edith Milton, in a review of "Celebration," in Boston Review, *Vol. XI, No. 6, December, 1986, p. 30.*

GEORGE GARRETT

Taken together in their finally established chronological sequence, rather than in the sequence of creation and publication, the novels of [*The Beulah Quintet*] offer a considerable variety within the unity that binds them all together. *Prisons* is the first-person story of twenty-year-old Johnny Church, beginning on his birthday in April of 1649 and continuing up to the very last instant of his life ("There are no words. I am empty. / I stretch wide my arms. / I step forward") just as the firing squad executes him in the churchyard in Burford. But that first-person tale, strictly adhered to, is bracketed with a functional "Foreword" by the author (as well as an epigraph from *The Revolution Betrayed* by Leon Trotsky) and a short "Afterword." These elements are more than decorative. . . . Beyond the value of "Foreword" and "Afterword" in furnishing enough historical fact to "place" the story for the reader whose detailed knowledge is sketchy, these sections have a larger function. For, set as the first and last word of *Prisons,* they help by ironic contrast to vivify the fiction of Johnny Church's narrative. One can see by demonstration how conventional historical prose, based upon fact and abstraction, is wholly inadequate to contain the story of this young man. And yet, also by this demonstration, that is in truth the case. Church's vivid, living and breathing (and dying) story comes, in the present, out of plain factual history. And in the end his story fades first into journalism and then into further exposition. So that one of the things which Settle is showing, essential to her subject and the themes of the quintet, is how history, when it is accurate, is always based on what happened in the lives of people, known and unknown, of flesh and blood. That it is the *imagined* characters (not imaginary; for their names, at least, were known) who live most fully in *Prisons* makes another complex comment on the inadequacy of conventionally abstract, factual discourse to re-create very much reality.

Once past the establishing exposition of the "Foreword," the reader is at once plunged into the narrative account, in first person, of the life of the protagonist—Jonathan Church. First-person storytelling offers several strong advantages at this point. It allows for a voice, and a language for that voice to use, to be efficiently and directly established. And first-person narration offers some traditional strengths. Authenticity is one of these. To overcome the contemporary reader's ignorance of the past, particularly this confused and partly forgotten part of history, there is nothing more instantly immediate than a speaker from the time who is fully alive as an imaginary character. Witnesses and narrators are trusted, in fiction at least, until they definitively prove themselves to be unreliable or, at any rate, severely limited. The farther removed in time, space, or common reality, the more important the character of the reporting witness becomes. Which is why so many stories of fantasy and ghost stories, for example, avail themselves of the powers of first-person narration. Johnny Church was credibility and authority. He is acutely sensitive, all five senses adroitly evoked by the author so that what happens to him is "real" in the sense that a body, flesh and blood, enjoys or endures it all. By the same token his voice, in the language Settle has created to echo the language of his times, works in two ways. First, by its distinct difference from our own written and spoken language it establishes a certain distance between the reader and the narrator and other people and the events of the time, making them all, at first and appropriately, somewhat alien. Alien and mildly exotic they may be, but must never be merely quaint; for that would diminish everything. Meantime the substance, the events and memories, though they may be in details different from contemporary experience, must also seem to be part of the shared and universal pulse of things. And the sensory affective experience must become powerfully immediate. Then, gradually, as readers accustom themselves to the rhythms and habits of the language, as in a foreign language composed of close cognates, it becomes more and more familiar, thus more transparent. What is happening, then, is that readers are having experiences and developing memories out of this material. To support this, Jonathan's story begins in the present tense as he rides in the rear guard of the Parliamentary army, together

with his close friend Thankful Perkins, half asleep, nodding, remembering. He remembers his own childhood in vivid images (and in a contrasting past tense). One comes to know him and his times through his memories as much as his present experiences.

All of this works well and strongly in the isolated context of *Prisons,* as a single novel in and of itself. But in the larger sense of the whole design it is urgently important that this, the very first voice, offer an even stronger memory pattern which will haunt all five books and all of the characters in them, though they, unlike readers, can never be consciously aware of the ghosts, ideas and images as well as people with voices, who haunt them.

Essentially the story he tells of himself is how he grew up in a strict Puritanical household, strongly in contrast to the household of Lacy House, ruled over by his uncle, Sir Valentine Lacy, and Nell Cockburn Lacy, his aunt. . . . Johnny Church is torn between his own limited understanding and vision of his father's house, Henlow, built upon an ancient ruin, and Lacy House only six miles away. (pp. 43-8)

[At Henlow], Johnny elected on his sixteenth birthday to rebel against his father over a particular act of insensitive cruelty. He went off to Lacy House, where he discovered Sir Valentine dying (and with him the old England of the old country aristocracy). He was, without difficulty and no shame at the time, seduced by his aunt. Outfitted with money and equipment from the Lacys, who honored his conscience ("Kin and neighbors are a damn sight closer than politics," Sir Valentine had said), he rode off to find the wars. (p. 48)

Thereafter the story follows Church and his friends, Gideon and especially Thankful Perkins, a good and simple man of great faith, through his first major battle at Naseby—as fine a piece of writing of the first confused experience of combat, as felt and witnessed by a raw recruit, as any we have, including its great model, *The Red Badge of Courage.* (p. 49)

The gradual disintegration of the army follows . . . , and the gradual triumph of authority, Cromwell, over conscience and idealism. . . . Thankful and Jonathan Church are elected Agitators for their regiments, an honorable, representative post, for which they must later suffer to intimidate the others. Cromwell will not negotiate with them ("Must I quarrel with every dog in the street that barks at me?"). The last pages, leading up to the execution of Thankful and Johnny, are a great debate between authority and conscience. Johnny Church, being educated and from good family, is given a chance to live if he will use his influence with the disaffected to persuade them to follow their leader obediently. He makes the free and tragic choice of conscience and dies for it. (pp. 49-50)

Thus, in the first book of the series there is a clear outline of what the basic subject and basic themes of the quintet will be: that it will be an accounting of history in terms of the never-ending conflict between liberal conscience, the youthful dream of liberty, and the power of authority; that it will be played out in violence and on the edge of violence, but always in terms of family and kinship, of bloodlines, known and unknown; that what is good and true, exemplary, will be knowledge and understanding and the acceptance of duty; that those who are good and worthy, to one degree or another, are those "who quest, who wander, who question;" that those who are wicked and unworthy (to one degree or another) are those who are cruel or overprivileged and too comfortable or too weak to hold to any serious beliefs. And together with family names and any number of image clusters which will recur in various patterns, linking the separate stories, there is the central classical myth which holds the whole quintet together—the story of Antigone and Creon. (pp. 50-1)

There are many classical allusions and parallels in the quintet, but the strongest single myth is the story of Antigone.

The next book of the series, *O Beulah Land,* is set a full century later in time; located, at least at the outset, in the wilderness of the new continent; already in another kind of English language, changed through time and by the natural reticence and the lack of education of most of the characters. It is a tale with a very different method of storytelling—a third-person, omniscient, chiefly scenic and dramatic narration, a kind of narration that is ideal to focus concentration, with considerable objectivity, on events. Much happens and sometimes very quickly. It is, then, a large tale; the cast of important, principal characters is large, and their interconnections are complex. And the time scheme, rather than being the kind of straightforward chronology of a few deeply intense days in the middle of May in 1649, enriched and enlarged by the personal memories of a single protagonist, Jonathan Church, is a full twenty years, almost generational. In fact, Hannah Bridewell and Jeremiah Catlett, the first people met in the "Prologue" (Hannah is almost nineteen at the time) and who die violently in the last sequence, an Indian attack, leave behind a son, Ezekiel, who is almost as old as Hannah had been at the beginning. A full lifetime has fallen in between.

The tone of the whole book is determined and dominated by its "Prologue," four short chapters and roughly fifty pages of virtuoso writing around the theme of survival against enormous odds. It begins with a high, distant, almost abstract (except that the language is wonderfully concrete) view of a woman lost and alone in the wilderness, "a haunted, chased creature mindless with panic" and "kept alive only by some boundless miracle that lets the nervous fawns live, or the silly, vulnerable fish." "I saw her stripped down to nothing," Settle has said in conversation, "but life and survival. She had no memory. She had a direction and that was all. Because what I realized that I was doing was tracing the genesis of our being in this country. And instead of trying to write social history, I was putting it in terms of single people. A woman was lost in the Endless Mountains, and I wanted the reader and myself to experience the pure luxury of having *any* kind of food and *any* kind of shelter."

In terms of single people. The narrator circles and observes, then suddenly comes down and joins Hannah physically in her hunger, her bone-weariness, her panic, as she survives her forty days and forty nights in the wilderness. Most of the allusions and parallels here are biblical, for the characters, even the illiterate ones, know their scripture. And it is in scriptural terms that they see their experience having meaning, making any sense. The reader follows her reduction to the purity of a surviving (barely so) animal. And there comes this moment when, sleeping in a cave to escape the chill rain, she finds she is not alone there: "But she woke, frozen, when she felt movement, felt the great, living, damp, soft pelt beside her, and knew that whatever beast it was, tired to death too, had crept close to her for her pathetic warmth, and still purred, drifting to sleep, meaning no harm."

Much later—years later in the life of Hannah—readers will learn how she happened to be present, as were so many other

characters in this story, at the crushing defeat of the army of British General Braddock, in July of 1755, by the French and Indians, near Fort Duquesne. How she was taken captive and held by the Indians. How she escaped to come here.

She is found and saved and slowly nursed back to health by Jeremiah Catlett, equally alone, living alone in a hut with his sow Hagar. As Hannah heals, she learns his story—how he was sold into indentured servitude from Liverpool at the age of five, suffered much, fell in with an itinerant preacher, was converted and ran away to be with him. And now he lives alone like a religious hermit until he is sorely tempted by the presence of the young woman, strong now, who lives with him. (pp. 51-4)

Here then, in Settle's version, are America's Adam and Eve: Hannah Bridewell, who is a transported whore from London, and Jeremiah Catlett, fugitive indentured servant, coming together with a wordless animal passion in a dirt-floored hut in the Endless Mountains. . . .

[Following her union with Jeremiah, Hannah tends the cabin fire; the] familiar literary convention is that the fire flares up to symbolize passion. Here, in peace, the peace of the contented sow with her piglets, Hannah builds up the fire to symbolize something more—joy, satisfaction, energy, life. The shadows of flames on the wall become their wedding dance and end their loneliness. It is a brilliant and overwhelming moment. No wonder that before *Prisons* became part of the background of this story, some readers and critics tended to lose sight of the basic and larger political theme. One aspect of social statement comes across emphatically, however. In later volumes the descendants of these earliest settlers will often have either forgotten the truth of where they come from, where and how it began, or, in the false lights and colors of the imagination, they will paint a beautified picture of the past, prettier, but far less vital and powerful. And, indeed, that is another strong thematic thread in the whole quintet— the power, for good and/or ill, of the imagination to transmute raw material into myth. The imagination can find and tell truth or lies. If the imagination settles for lies, the results, no matter how briefly comforting, will be severely crippling. (pp. 55-6)

The seeds of what may follow are planted in *O Beulah Land,* though it ends with some hope for the future, if only with the hope of some of the most prescient characters—like the marvelously drawn Jarcey Pentacost, scholar and printer and free spirit—that the American Revolution is close at hand.

Know Nothing, jumping ahead almost another century of time, concerns among other things the coming on of the Civil War. It opens with the image Settle described, with (on 29 July 1837) the next Johnny, Johnny Catlett, being thrown by his father into the Great Kanawha river to sink or swim. He swims and, as if in tribal rite, is accepted by his father, Peregrine Lacey Catlett, master of Beulah. Who begins to tell him:

> "God in his Providence saw fit to give your family bottom-land along the river, and put our people under our care." . . .
>
> He liked the way Minna told him that better. She said, "Listen here, Marse Johnny, we owns this here valley. We owns the mose people, and the mose horses, and the mose cows, and the mose land. We ships the best salt and we got the mose plates and furniture. I knows, I done been a heap

of places and seed. So don' you go actin like po whites ain't got nothin." That made him feel like the Knights of Old.

Minna is accurate in her description of where Beulah stands at the beginning of the story—a peak of seeming power and affluence, the land already radically changed from the hard wilderness Johnny's grandparents knew. (pp. 57-8)

Know Nothing becomes primarily the story of the obligation, settled, at the outset and again in the final section, on Johnny Catlett as if it were his bounden duty, to protect and to defend, to *conserve* the already threatened way of life the inhabitants of Beulah Land have come to since the hard and perilous times of Hannah and Jeremiah. So much has happened in such a short time. The land has been taken and tamed for profit, but requires slaves to maintain it. Even the stories of the past have changed. Perry Lacey, the murderous and disinherited son of Jonathan Lacey, is now honored in memory as Colonel Peregrine Lacey, "this great Injun fighter and glorious hero of the Revolution, . . . an American hero and patriot." And even the Catletts have acquired the patina of a false history. . . . (pp. 58-9)

The language has changed. Now there seems to be a firm separation, a dichotomy between the living speech spoken by Minna, a slave, and a more "literary" language which is at once romantic and nostalgic, based, Settle says, on the fiction of Walter Scott. Thinking in that language transmutes present reality into false myth, "Knights of Old." Johnny Catlett, at the beginning, is more than a little like Tom Sawyer. And the world of *O Beulah Land,* almost wholly forgotten by most of the principal characters, has turned upside down. In such a little time the women, who had mostly been hard survivors, equal sharers of the wilderness and the frontier, are turned into variations not on the original model of Hannah, but much more on the lines of the poor deluded Sally Lacey. They are at best decorative dependents; so much so that when Johnny's father dies, near the end of the story, he can, in dying advice, offer his son this counsel: "Be good to them. Poor innocent things. I've always taught you that, ain't I, Johnny? Women and niggers. They ain't fitten to look after theirselves." The women of the family, including various unattached kinfolk, are trapped not only by the manners, habits, and circumstances of the times, but in the terms of a false myth. And the best of them are intelligent enough to know it and to resent it bitterly even as they patiently live out their own form of servitude. In what is, in fact, the longest sustained section in the book, the family goes to the resort spa at Egeria Springs (modeled on White Sulphur Springs) in an attempt to engage in the complex mating rituals of the times, hoping to find eligible husbands for the marriageable women. Here there is a fascinating picture of the clothing and the manners of the period.

The story, told not in a "floating point of view" but rather, in the manner of *O Beulah Land,* in a straightforward, third-person, omniscient manner, moving within that freedom from one limited third-person point of view to another, is mainly centered around the young life of Johnny Catlett. He grows up into a tragic figure of quite different dimension, indeed almost opposite to his long-lost and long-forgotten true ancestor—Johnny Church—although he in fact shares much also, including some real courage, sensitivity, compassion, and finally the wisdom of self-knowledge. The story shows him growing up into manhood, shows him learning, at the University of Virginia, later in a hard life out West and in the terrible times in Kansas in 1856. He becomes someone, far from guiltless, but after all honorable and worthwhile; and, at the end, just as the Civil War is beginning, a war he knows, rationally, has doomed his side, his way of life, and is wrong and unjust, but in which he must serve, must kill and perhaps be killed, all out of a sense of familial duty, a living obligation freely, if wearily, undertaken and, finally, beyond right and wrong. Just at the end of things in this story, as he is surrounded by many names familiar to the quintet reader (there is even the latest Gideon McKarkle to take and to tend his horse), Johnny Catlett has a brief bright moment of pure witness: "As in other moments of his life, he knew complete stillness, the stillness of the woods, of sorrow, of night—just for a moment, acting on him. He knew it had begun and the luxury of questioning was over, thrown away." And so he must step forward and do his duty, even as once Johnny Church had taken his last tragic step. But in a sense Catlett's action is sadder, more classically tragic in that this performance of his duty lacks even the assurance of good conscience. The one act of the martyrdom of conscience is performed by a minor character, a preacher named Charles McAndrews, who recognizes Johnny in Missouri and asks Johnny to carry the message to his mother in Virginia that he has gone to preach love and liberty in bloody Kansas. . . . [In] a sense it is McAndrews in this brief meeting who absolves him in advance, saying: "Perhaps you are the kind loyalty's more important to. Greater love hath no man. . . . A man like you caint live a heartless life."

Johnny Catlett's last act before going out into the confusion of the first skirmish of the war is a brief prayer that says it all: " 'Oh God,' he prayed, 'forgive us our sins and don't let me have to kill my brother.' "

His brother is Lewis, a preacher and an abolitionist who is also cruel, obsessed, utterly uncharitable and abstracted from his own humanity. The reader can be sure, safe in the knowledge of what was to come to pass, that he will prove to be an implacable, indefatigable enemy.

Since the next volume of the quintet, *The Scapegoat,* leads into the twentieth century and a different sort of historical memory, it is important to pause here long enough to acknowledge what sort of history Settle created in the first three volumes of the series, what she has added or changed from the conventional view. *Prisons* surprises with its accurate and contemporary understanding of how early and how fully certain ideals now taken for granted were planted in the Anglo-American consciousness. It likewise revises conventional thinking about the revolutionary period of the middle seventeenth century. Much of that, a revolution within a revolution which ended with the Restoration, has been lost to Americans. *O Beulah Land,* in large part because of the accuracy and authenticity of its details, presents eighteenth-century, pre-Revolutionary America in a harder, tougher, more endangered time and place than many with hindsight have chosen to remember. There is something of vision she shares with the very different novelist Kenneth Roberts, but he wrote of Maine. The South had not been so accurately and starkly presented. With *Know Nothing,* while nothing there mitigates the crimes of the antebellum South, much serves to make the beginning of the Civil War as tragic for the region as it was for her character Johnny Catlett. The system and the society were dying from the inside, anyway, rotten at the core. But she has remarkably presented good men and true who were caught by conflicting forces larger than any man, as doomed as any dynastic figures in a Greek tragedy. In one sense *Know Nothing* might be seen in part as Creon's side of the story.

The Scapegoat tells the story, from various angles and in several styles, of the beginning of a coal strike in West Virginia (Beulah Land was still a part of Virginia in *Know Nothing*) in 1912. Tightly plotted, and complex in its own terms as well as in relation to the rest of the quintet, *The Scapegoat* is a large novel, not a *long* novel, without sprawl or prolixity. Its cast of characters is both extensive and various, ranging from mine owners to native mountaineers and coal miners, from an English geologist and a Scottish engineer to the immigrant families newly arrived to dig out the coal. There are "ladies" and mountain women, and there is a wonderful rendering of an amazing historical figure, the union organizer Mother Jones. People of all ages are treated and developed sympathetically. (pp. 59-64)

For this novel Settle has noted moving into the zone of her own historic memory. Her mother and aunts were alive in 1912. They carried the language of their childhood with them. She had heard it all her life. Moreover there were more commonplace things than family treasures, antiques and relics to touch and use. . . . The research, including trial transcripts of the period and talks with people who had seen Mother Jones in fact and flesh, was easier and more assured. And, part of the ease and assurance behind the whole book, it should be remembered that she began to put *The Scapegoat* together in the confident awareness that at last, at the age of 60 with *Blood Tie,* she had been recognized and had earned for herself a place at the high table of the literary establishment.

The Scapegoat has some surprises for the reader who has followed the quintet from its beginning. There is the matter of primary narrative time. *O Beulah Land* covers twenty years, 1754-1774. *Know Nothing* deals with 1837-1861. And while it is true that the main line of action of *Prisons,* at least in the central narrative of Johnny Church, is confined to a few days (12-17 May 1649), the character of the first-person narration is to create an immediacy and freedom in time well beyond the imposed limits of "actual" time. The time of any first-person story is all present and simultaneous, the time of the telling. Told in four precisely timed and identified sections, *The Scapegoat* begins at 3:00 p.m. on Friday, 7 June 1912 and ends at 8:00 a.m. on Saturday, 8 June 1912. There is a good deal of freedom within the boundaries of this apparently strict time scheme. There are gracefully executed background exposition and personal memories, seeming to derive naturally out of present action and reaction in the story. For example, there is the necessary Italian, old-country background of the Pagano family, originally from Perugia. Much more unusual, however—and in fact daring in surprising audacity—are Settle's use of flash forwards in time, presenting action that will take place later as part of the line of this story. (pp. 64-6)

One of the values gained from this surprising introduction of future time within the context of present, forward-moving time in this story is another perspective on the events of the story. *The Scapegoat* is, on the basic narrative level, held together by the suspense generated by the coming of the 1912 coal strike with its considerable potential for violence and personal tragedy. There are moments of real sorrow, and violence claims the life of one innocent man, the "scapegoat" of the title. But even the worst of the violence in West Virginia,

potential as well as realized, fades into puny insignificance measured against the incredible fire storm of violence to come. There is a huge difference. And yet there is a real connection also. After all, the genesis of the story began in the author's mind, and likewise begins as a narrative, with a Gatling gun, a machine gun, incongruous and menacing, shiny and unloaded, on the front porch of the Lacey house. That particular gun causes no damage here. A few years later Lily must deal with the results of the military use of this relatively new weapon—the machine gun. Among other things it kills young Englishman Neville Roundtree, who figured in the events of 1912 as an agent and employee of the absentee English mine owners. (pp. 66-7)

Another technical surprise in *The Scapegoat,* another example of an audacious confidence and authority, is the way Settle uses point of view to tell her story. Considering the expository narrative, the "Foreword" and "Afterword" which bracket Jonathan Church's first-person story in *Prisons,* her method had always been fully omniscient. But in *The Scapegoat* she carries the power of that strategy to a new level. Just as within the stated time frame she allows herself great freedom, so here she shifts rapidly and deftly in and out of first-person and third-person narration, giving herself the opportunity and occasion to shift and blend language, often on the same page, sometimes in the same paragraph (for a *character,* in the first-person mode, may shift into a limited third-person accounting of actions witnessed or imagined), the language of speech and the written language. This allows every principal character at least two kinds of language, written and spoken, simultaneously; at the same time, paradoxically, it puts the author, hand in glove with the reader, in total control. Settle points the camera where she chooses when she is ready, turns on or off the sound system as she pleases. (pp. 68-9)

With *The Scapegoat,* Settle and her series of novels had at last arrived. It remained to see how she would transform *Fight Night on a Sweet Saturday* and bring the quintet to a close.

In the beginning of section 2 of *The Killing Ground* Hannah McKarkle says this: "Thankful Perkins had called the road I was traveling the long road to Paradise. If his road had ended in the genes of people in Beulah valley, for me it had begun there, too. I had, at last, to go back to the event, the act that had begun my search, the fury of one unknown fist hitting an unknown face."

In the creation of *The Killing Ground,* Settle chose to develop a surprising (astonishing would not be too strong a word) narrative strategy. She wanted, of course, to revise and to retell the story of the death of Johnny McKarkle in the drunk tank following the Labor Day dance of 1960 and the quest of his sister, Hannah, to find how it had happened and somehow to lay his restless spirit to rest. It had been what the whole sequence of books had pointed toward since she began *O Beulah Land* in about 1954. And this story had been previously completed, albeit in edited and truncated form, in *Fight Night on a Sweet Saturday* (1964). There had been the addition of two full-length books, *Prisons* and *The Scapegoat,* to the series, and there had been twenty years of contemporary history, some of which—especially the later 1960s, after the death of the fictional Johnny McKarkle and after the completion and publication of *Fight Night on a Sweet Saturday*— had, in her view, radically changed the psychic climate of America. Already *Fight Night* was historical, a full generation behind herself and the times. There had been, she believed, another revolution. Perhaps it was now again the age of the Thermidore. But in any case the earlier novel was conceived by her as inadequate. She had to find a way, a story of something larger, with more apt contemporaneity into which the story of Johnny McKarkle could be incorporated, still central, crucial, but more intricately related to past and future than it had ever been. Whatever the new book, new version or vision, would be, it must do two things at once—stand as a single story in and of itself, at least on one level, a level Settle has described in conversation as "without the irony"; and at the same time it must do something to bring the whole series to a natural, acceptable, and credible conclusion.

What Settle chose to do, a daring and risky choice yet wonderfully efficient, was to make Hannah McKarkle a writer like herself. And something more. Not any writer, but the author of the four previous novels of the Beulah quintet, by name and title. In the opening section, "The Return: June 1978," Hannah has been asked back to Canona to help at a fund-raiser by giving a lecture. The book opens with someone musing about the prehistoric, three-thousand-year-old archaeology of the region, the bones of seven-foot giants found in an ancient burial/killing ground. And she easily refers to Johnny Church, to Lily, to the Hannah of *O Beulah Land,* and others from the quintet. She also summons up the dominant classical myth which informs the quintet: "I know, if anyone does, why Antigone had to bury the evasive Polynices. She buried an obsession so it would not haunt her. She had to bless him who was unblessed. At last, at last, she must have told herself, grief-stricken and relieved, I will know where he is." Soon enough she is being introduced to her audience: "Uh, she is the author of numerous works of fiction including *Prison* I mean *Prisons O Beulah Land Know Nothing.* She is working on a novel about the coal business in 1912 called *The Scapegoat.*"

Just as there is throughout the quintet a subtle and reciprocal relationship between fact—historical, political, geographical, social, and personal—and fiction, so the creation of the fictional character Hannah McKarkle at once supported and justified Settle's relationship with her own fiction. But there were simpler and more practical reasons and values for this overt transmutation. For one thing, she wanted Hannah to be younger than herself, to be of a slightly different generation, the Eisenhower generation, which had missed the full impact of the experience of World War II. She wanted more innocence to drive Hannah's curiosity about herself and the world than she, Settle, could legitimately muster. Hannah could write the books without really knowing as much as Settle did. Moreover, with Hannah younger, she could actively participate in the young people's revolution in the 1960s and not be, as Settle had been, an enthusiastic witness, a supporter, to be sure, but more witness than actor. And, above all, as the writer of the four previous books of the series, she could be conscious, even acutely self-conscious, about her literary as well as her personal intentions. She could simply and directly make connections between the actions and discoveries of *The Killing Ground* and the other books. And yet there would be some things—as, indeed, there prove to be—that Hannah could not know, but which Settle and perhaps an acutely engaged reader could not help knowing. Hannah is aware of that imaginary reader, too: "The unknown giant, and Johnny Church, shot at Burford, my namesake Hannah, and lovely dangerous Lily are in lost graves, forgotten, except by me and a lone reader who has not been able to sleep either,

who is bringing them to life from the books of my search. It has taken us both a long time to give them back their lives."

The split between Settle and Hannah, and with it the establishment of Settle's clear-cut omniscience, is resolved easily enough by having this story told in the same multiple points of view that have come to be characteristic of the entire series—sometimes in third person, both limited and omniscient, and here, especially, often in first person; usually in Hannah's voice and view, though often others tell lengthy first-person stories as well. The story is put together so that Hannah can act and react as a character and, at one and the same time, legitimately comment on the action and on herself, in terms of the whole quintet. (pp. 70-4)

The Killing Ground is a series of circlings around events, held together with ritual funerals for the dead, told in four separate units: "The Return: June 1978," "Before The Revolution: 1960," "The Beginning: 1960-1980," and an "Epilogue: January 1980." It has an enormous cast of characters; not only are most of the major characters of the first four novels of the quintet remembered and refurbished, but also characters from other fictions of Canona jostle with and against Hannah and the reader. And given time and scrutiny, characters change. (p. 75)

The "Epilogue: January 1980" is Althea's funeral and Hannah's final trip home. She has already come far and learned much. She knows now, for example, why her first version of the story of Johnny McKarkle had not worked, "not knowing yet that forgiveness comes only when the facts are faced, all the way to the font of tears and hope." "It was then that I tried for the first time to set down Johnny's death in words," she (Hannah) continues. "It was too soon. I failed then because I knew too little of the past. The vision was a lie. It lacked distance and empathy. I had not yet seen my father, Mooney, as a tentative boy, or the killing pride of Captain Dan Neill. I had not caught Lily's blind yearning, or seen the child, my mother, in the speckled mirror, become her isolated self." She knows that for herself, as for Settle, the change of heart and direction came in the churchyard at Burford. The quest was renewed. It all ends, finally, at the limits of knowledge, at Althea's funeral, where Hannah stands side by side with Jake Catlett, who killed her brother Johnny all those years ago in jail, and is now a "dressed-up well-upholstered hillbilly in his Buick, who I had last seen caged behind bars in the county jail, desperate and skinny." And some of the simple, factual mystery is solved by what Jake tells Hannah:

> She marched right up there, little skinny woman,
> I never even knew her, and she posted my bond and
> I walked out between her and Pa, out on bail. I remember standing there in the sun in front of the
> courthouse and I never knew which way to turn.
> All she said was, "This has gone far enough."

It is Aunt Althea, then, whose act of justice and love saved the life of Jake Catlett and now ends the quest of Hannah. (pp. 75-6)

[*The Killing Ground*], full of sorrow and surprises, ends with tears for the dead at a graveside and with a vision of the new, the next generation of these families, there in the cemetery where so many of the honored dead, Catletts, Neills, and Laceys, lie buried beneath inappropriately pompous epitaphs. . . . It needs to be said that in this rich book, with its "stratum on stratum of connection," the wisdom and peace of the brief epilogue is earned. Not only earned, but essential. The length and depth of the quintet demand it. And, intricately, it comes down to something that urgently simple. "Deep within us there had been instilled an itch," Hannah/Settle says at the end, "a discontent, an unfulfilled promise, perpetually demanding that it be kept. Johnny and Thankful, and all of us, would always fail and always win, and eternal vigilance and our sense of loss, of being unblessed, were the price of freedom." (pp. 77-8)

The place of the whole extraordinary quintet, and the place of *The Killing Ground* within it, remain to be fully known and understood. Time will tell. Meantime the five volumes illustrating and exemplifying our history stand as a remarkable achievement, already recognized by some as a major contribution to the literature of the time.

William F. Ryan has a strong reasonable basis for the claim he makes for her work: "Mary Lee Settle may well be remembered as the 20th-century American novelist who most splendidly recorded the passion and ideals of our history." (pp. 78-9)

> *George Garrett, in his* Understanding Mary Lee Settle, *University of South Carolina Press, 1988, 187 p.*

JANE GENTRY VANCE

Mary Lee Settle's claim to be a major contemporary novelist rests on *The Beulah Quintet* (*Prisons,* 1973; *O Beulah Land,* 1956; *Know Nothing,* 1960; *The Scapegoat,* 1980; and *The Killing Ground,* 1982), the epic story of Beulah Valley in West Virginia. Subtract that work from her ten novels and those remaining (*The Love Eaters,* 1954; *The Kiss of Kin,* 1955; *The Clam Shell,* 1971; *Blood Tie,* 1977; and *Celebration,* 1986) are narratively accomplished, thematically wise, but still not remarkably cohesive or substantial as a body of work. In the quintet the destinies of several pioneer families of divergent backgrounds (indentured servants from London, illegitimate and/or younger sons of gentry, the Scotch-Irish, Irish, German, and, later, Italian) meet, and their lives inextricably intertwine to form a microcosm of American experience.

The quintet traces the forces that bring Beulah into being, sustain its brief flowering, and dissipate quickly as old manners and values catch up with the frontier and take root in new ground. Conjuring images that carry the reader back through 350 years of lived experience, the novels recreate the passions, actions, and ideas that undergird the ideology of America. Beginning in 1649 in *Prisons,* with the ideals of social, political, and religious liberty of Johnny Church, a twenty-year-old Leveler in Cromwell's New Model Army during the English Civil Wars, Settle discovers in his rhetoric the formative American vision of freedom. She follows as his illegitimate son by his aunt migrates to Virginia and as his descendant, Capt. Jonathan Lacey, in *O Beulah Land,* settles at Beulah, where he briefly realizes Church's dreams of social equality and freedom. She picks up Lacey's descendants, intermarried now with the families of other settlers at Beulah, in *Know Nothing,* as they shape Beulah into a large plantation blighted by slavery and as Johnny Catlett, master of Beulah Plantation, bows to family pressure and fights for the Confederacy. The descendants of the original families, mixed still further in *The Scapegoat,* participate in the preliminary conflicts of the Mine Wars at the Laceys' Seven Stars Coal Mine. Finally, in *The Killing Ground,* the families, now thoroughly intermingled after almost 200 years, attempt to come to terms with the technological age and struggle to recover a sense of identity and liberty in post-industrial West Virginia.

Chronologically, the narrative comes forward from seventeenth-century England through the five books to present-day Canona (a city much like Charleston), near Beulah. However, the impetus of emotion and of suspense, both for writer (by her own account) and for reader, runs backward in time rather than forward. In *The Killing Ground,* novelist Hannah McKarkle comes home in 1980 to speak about her work to a group of old friends. She intends also to investigate the death of her brother, Johnny McKarkle, in 1960 in the drunk tank of the Canona jail, where he was struck by his distant cousin, Jake Catlett. According to Settle [in her essay **"Recapturing the Past in Fiction"**], her fantasy in 1954 of that blow bloomed into the great flower of the quintet. Obsessed with the vision of this scene, Settle felt compelled to discover the forces that brought the two men together in the cell and made them enemies in their ignorance of themselves and of each other. She set out to correct the failures of collective memory that kept Jake and Johnny from knowing that, literally, they spring from the same seed. For in the quintet, as in *Oedipus Rex,* the real drama lies in the step-by-step acquisition of the truth of a lost past. Hannah McKarkle's recovery of her family's story creates the energy and the movement of the whole quintet. And its mystery is the Oedipal mystery: the heroes turn out to be the culprits, and the "solutions" lie in the heroes' discovery of their own true identity.

Essentially, then, the quintet takes the prototypical American consciousness back through time, uncovering layer after layer of willfully forgotten experience until the reader arrives at Johnny Church, who, at the point of his execution by Cromwell, realizes his identity as it is formed by his past as the son of his particular father and mother. The various later protagonists carry the remnant of Church's epiphany as it waxes again briefly at Beulah before the Revolutionary War and then wanes gradually until, in the eighties, it is finally grasped again by Hannah McKarkle who, in the story of the quintet, writes the novels. But Church's reality as a character and the persuasiveness of his vision of his own wholeness and of the ideal of liberty are enhanced greatly by the reader's previous knowledge of Hannah McKarkle, his twentieth-century incarnation. Actually, she is his daughter many times removed, and more important, she is his sister, his Antigone, in rebellion against the social and spiritual constraints that kill. "Of all the volumes," Settle says, "the most truly autobiographical, the most urged on me by present circumstances, was *Prisons.* . . . Out of fear, and a hope that blasted hopes survive the hopeful, I found *Prisons* and Johnny Church. I am Johnny Church." Hannah McKarkle and Mary Lee Settle both find their identities as novelists, as recoverers of lost histories.

The quintet is best read backward, beginning with *The Killing Ground* and concluding with *Prisons.* One reason the quintet has not been widely appreciated is that most readers naturally start with *Prisons,* which seems fragmentary, difficult to get into, without benefit of the context of the other four novels. But read last, *Prisons* discovers in fitting crescendo the family situations, the personalities, the emotional, economic, and political forces that are the seeds of Hannah and the story she is to write within the story, that of Jake Catlett and Johnny McKarkle. Settle unearths the taproot of American ideas of liberty in Church's voice, which she makes so audible to the reader's ear through her imaginative absorption of the extensive research she did in the actual pamphlets written by soldiers during the Civil War. Each of the other novels, too, gains emotional and intellectual impact from being read in the context of the books that succeed it in actual historical time, for that is the direction of the development of Settle's vision.

Because Settle works, then, from the particular to the general, from the present to the past, and not the other way around as is often the case with historical novelists, the psychological immediacy of her characters is the hallmark of her fiction. In digging for the sources of American experience, the richest vein she mines is her characters' voices. She calls herself "an archaeologist of language"; she probes in newspapers, letters, pamphlets, and popular drama of all the periods she treats to get to the bone of individual character, the voices and gestures that will bring back to the present the lived ideas and emotions. She begins with the gesture of Jake Catlett's blow to Johnny McKarkle in the Canona jail, that "carried within it abandoned hopes, old hates and a residue of prejudices. To trace them," she says, "I knew that I was going to have to travel back to when the hates were new, the hopes alive, the prejudices merely contemporary fears."

Settle explains her own theory of historical fiction better than any critic. Like Georg Lukacs she believes that "historical fidelity" and inclusiveness arise most often out of the dramatization of "the outwardly insignificant events, the smaller (from without) relationships." Thus, the Beulah novels are set mainly in the periods preceding the great turning points of history: *Prisons,* before Cromwell's eleven-year dictatorship; *O Beulah Land,* in the thirty years before the Revolutionary War; *Know Nothing,* mainly in the decades before the American Civil War; and *The Scapegoat,* in 1912 just before the labor movement became a dominant force in American life.

[In **"Recapturing the Past in Fiction"**], Settle quotes Nicola Chiaromonte to explain why she writes fiction to "learn something real about individual experience. Any other approach is bound to be general and abstract." And fiction, to function as recreated experience, must be predominantly specific and concrete. "Both time and space are distances, and they work for historians and novelists in the same way—not as a gulf, but as a psychic focus. Hindsight—which revises, tears down, discovers trends and explains by concept—has little place in fiction. To try to see, to hear, to share a passion, to become contemporary, is its task." She aims, then, to dramatize "what people thought was happening during the times they lived in, rather than what historians tell us was really happening." (pp. 213-16)

Most reviewers of *Prisons* objected to Settle's abdication of what William J. Schafer calls "the large interpretive role of the historical novelist." But she writes:

> There is a generation whose taproot was cut somewhere in each American past, whether by poverty, diaspora or land enclosure. It is the generation that had to leave home. We inherited from it a sense of loss. . . . We seek a personal identity, and sometimes, with more luck than perseverance, when the memory has been truly evoked, we find it, a historic déjà vu. We have been there somehow and we are there again. It is a way of facing the old, cold passions, the fears, the notions that seemed once to be

fact—things that can form nodules deep within the present as black as manganese.

The dramatic evocation of these "nodules" is the pulsing heart of Settle's Beulah books. "The fictional process," she writes, "is a mixture of nonchalance, memory, choice, subjective and sensuous vision, formed in the unconscious and raised into reality."

One of the purest of these realizations comes to Johnny Church in the crystalline moment when he stands before Cromwell's firing squad. Now he knows why he cannot doff his hat as his father had demanded and as Cromwell now demands. He sees why he must be able to say, "I am freeborn and bow to no man nowhere." When he defies his father and joins the army, he chooses disinheritance, as all Settle's visionary characters must, as Hannah McKarkle does 300 years later in order to be able to rediscover the history that connects her to Johnny Church and tells her who she is. At the end of *The Killing Ground,* Hannah asks, "How far back could the unknown scars go? How deep was the anger behind Jake Catlett's fist?" Recovering her beginnings in Johnny Church empowers Hannah McKarkle to live freely as an authentic self, as the artist who can write the quintet.

Other characters, who fail to undertake or to complete this quest for identity (Johnny Catlett, in *Know Nothing,* who bows to family pressure and fights for slavery; Beverly Lacey, in *The Scapegoat,* who clings to outmoded paternalistic attitudes toward labor in the family coal mines; and Johnny McKarkle, in *The Killing Ground,* who cannot wrest himself away from his mother), make "the sad incestuous choice" of conformity to procrustean family expectations and social pressures. Even Hannah strongly feels "the seduction of duty and comfort and compliance, the deep training of a place I had not asked for, earned or prepared." The opposite extreme poses equal danger: she must withstand the "impotent seduction of the rebels, the wild boys like Doggo Cutwright. . . ." She carries "that itch for balance between the two extremes, a quality that quarrels with itself, poised between democrat and slaveowner, a dilemma all the way to our founding, that seemed so often to have no place in the pragmatic surviving days of living, but yet had had a place, had built a country, fused dreams into cities seeking always the elusive balance." This balance, Hannah says, is "the ambiguity of steel, on which I have built my book."

This understanding is the bedrock of Hannah's identity, and of Johnny's and Jake's had they not been cut off from the community of memory. Memory saves; in the possession of history lies the only possibility for a future. "Know thyself," the Beulah books say, seeing the same destruction outside that knowledge as did the Delphic Oracle. Not to know who you are, like Oedipus, to have lost your history, places you in jeopardy of destroying yourself and those whose lives you touch. In Settle's vision the original ideal of America offered the opportunity to establish a political and social context in which the individual would be free to develop toward full realization of self. (pp. 216-18)

[Like] Jesus (whose initials he carries and to whom Settle draws explicit parallels at the end of *Prisons*) and like Socrates, Johnny chooses to die rather than to compromise his conviction of the psychological and political necessity of freedom. Cromwell, manipulating through both his psychological and his political power, identifies himself with God. (p. 218)

In *Prisons* Johnny dies victorious, as Jesus and Socrates do, and his vision generates the energy of the development of Beulah, which is to follow. He sees in a dream that "all that sets men apart from the beasts is the act without hope of reward." He chooses death because he understands that life without freedom to grow and to be is not life. . . .

The American amnesia sets in several generations after Church's death, when the English sense of class rears its head in the new world, as the various families begin to want to forget their origins, to shed their own true history. In Beulah Valley, Settle's microcosm of the American experience, the corruption of Church's vision can be exactly dated to 1765, the year Johnny Lacey brings Sally Mason, his aristocratic wife, to the frontier station, where before her arrival all the settlers of various backgrounds (German, Scotch-Irish, English; rich and poor) work together harmoniously for their survival in the wilderness and to create a new order in which they will all be better off than under European manners. But when Sal introduces her silly corruptions of traditional gentility, the snake slithers into Eden. (p. 219)

[Johnny and Sal's] house, lovingly built by Jonathan in preparation for Sal's coming, deeply disappoints her pretensions. Her dismay at its lack of finish hardens Johnny's happy pride into foreboding. . . . In the form of this house, Sal sees the hopelessness of her position as a wife on the frontier, where traditional ideas of breeding and manners, her only real values, are unimportant. Within hours the disheartened Jonathan understands her limitations for the first time and senses that they are ruinous to his dreams for Beulah. God cannot "marry the land in blessedness" if Sal's divisive values have any place there. (p. 220)

This, then, is the source of the dangerous forgetting: these beginnings of class consciousness in theoretically classless America. In the quintet the new social mobility distorts the various families' sense of historical continuity, preventing the evolution of truthful community tradition. As the families leave behind humble origins and poverty for status, wealth, and political power, they wish to erase the memory of hard times, of powerlessness, and, sometimes, of criminality. . . . This all too typical amnesia both springs from and feeds family pride. The resulting sense of aristocracy, misplaced and ludicrous on the frontier, today remains repressive to less privileged family groups in American society. (pp. 220-21)

Beginning in *O Beulah Land* and on down through *Know Nothing, The Scapegoat,* and *The Killing Ground,* Settle's characters are to various degrees vulnerable to the ill effects of these manners and this willful forgetting of a past that nevertheless keeps intruding. The nonrebellious, conventional women in Settle's vision guard and perpetuate treacherous family myths. Their motherly and wifely voices urge their kin to procrustean beds of pretentious attitudes and country club manners. In *Know Nothing* old Mrs. Catlett, a Lacey from Virginia, descendant of Johnny Lacey and grandmother of Confederate officer Johnny Catlett, derives her identity from a farfetched family history. . . . Partly she lies out of her own need to prettify, and partly she merely passes on the distortions of previous family suppressions. . . .

Settle sees establishment women, like Mrs. Catlett, as destructive to psychic growth and creative being. They, in collusion with the men, transmit inaccurate stories of who they are and how they came to be. (p. 221)

From *O Beulah Land* on through the remaining three novels,

this repressive sense of position, based on false history and corrupted memory, dominates increasingly, until in *The Killing Ground,* it destroys Johnny McKarkle, whose existence is choked by his mother's sense of class and the restrictions it lays on his life. He is struck and killed in the Canona jail by his poor relation, Jake Catlett, who knows him, but whom he does not know since Jake is socially inferior. . . . Ultimately, Johnny is rich and Jake is poor because one's ancestor inherited bottomland at Beulah where coal was discovered and the other inherited higher ground where it was not.

While the repressive social forces eviscerate the men in the last two novels of the quintet, the women's voices take on strength and promise anew the freedom for which the earlier men like Johnny Church and Johnny Lacey have fought. One of the strongest voices in the novels belongs to Mother Jones, the real-life union organizer, who comes to the Beulah coalfields in 1912, looking like "somebody's grandmother." . . . Mother Jones's voice is one of Settle's most significant archaeological finds and most imaginative creations. No records of any speeches of hers were extant until Settle unearthed a deposition that included a transcript of one. Her voice, as Settle extrapolates it, carries the vision of freedom that began with Johnny Church and that the Beulah men have lost. Settle makes immediate the reality of Mother Jones's personality and the power of her voice to inspire.

At the end of *The Killing Ground,* Hannah McKarkle, heir of the voice of Johnny Church, finds her power in having recovered the memory of who she is. The voice she discovers, the true voice of her families' history, becomes the narrative of *The Beulah Quintet.* Hannah becomes the novelist who resurrects Johnny Church and late in the twentieth century recovers his idea of freedom from the buried past that determines the present they all live. The search carries her back 350 years. "How the past goads us! We move toward tomorrow but the past informs us," thinks Johnny Church as he begins to know what fate awaits him as Cromwell surrounds Burford village in the Cotswolds. Without memory there is no real identity, personal or communal. Without identity there is no self. Without self there is no being. In *The Beulah Quintet,* the process of fiction is lifesaving.

As history inspires and shapes the Beulah novels, so myth inspires and shapes *Blood Tie* and *Celebration.* Although *Blood Tie* dramatizes the relation between the ancient mythic world and the modern workaday one and *Celebration* deftly interweaves the stories of its four middle-aged main characters struggling toward lives and minds of their own, still these two best of Settle's other five novels lack the vision and insight of the Beulah epic. But the two pose the same questions as the quintet and are well crafted and wise.

Blood Tie takes place in the early seventies in Turkey, in what was ancient Greek Ionia. The symbolism of the novels centers on Mt. Latmos where the grave of Endymion and a temple to the fertility moon goddess, Artemis, are somewhat hidden. The characters, caught in webs of power that reach back into that mythic past, know themselves and these forces only superficially, and several are destroyed by their lack of awareness. Like the quintet, *Blood Tie* asks, "How far back did the accident that had taken her (a character who drowns) go?" Since no event in Settle's world is accidental, she traces the causes back through the lives of the characters to the end of the Caliphate in 1923 and ultimately into the prehistorical era of the origins of the Endymion myth. The characters who learn from suffering and who come to know, as Ataturk said, that earth, "this hell, this heaven is ours" know what Settle calls "the ambiguity of steel." Ariadne, the pivotal figure in the story, says this knowledge "costs too much," this rare and most worthwhile human achievement.

Celebration, too, celebrates the power of the Great Goddess, the moon in all her phases, ageless symbol of "the power and beauty and indifference of God." A less successful novel than *Blood Tie, Celebration*'s four separate stories share backgrounds of myth: Greek, African, Middle Eastern, and Chinese. Settle pulls tricks out of the old bag of narrative devices to get all these stories told, relying too heavily on flashbacks and hallucination. Because of these mechanisms, Teresa, the earth character, the center of the story, does not come alive convincingly, and the magnetism that Settle claims for her remains an attribution. Similarly, the perspective on issues of social class, so central to Settle's focus, is not clear as it is in the quintet and in *Blood Tie,* where upper-class manners and arrogance are unambiguously oppressive and divisive. While Settle attributes to Teresa the rejection of upper-class values, she undercuts this claim by the extent to which Teresa's life is shaped and guarded by these values. In the end the Goddess, the moon, dropping her light on murdered and murderers alike, embodies the knowledge of both death and the simultaneous immortality we can experience through the living whole in which we are individual dying parts. This ambiguity dominates this novel as well. And the voices of the characters, reaching back into their own experience and into the mythic past, struggle to articulate this hard-won understanding.

Mary Lee Settle is a writer who believes in words, in language, in voice: the power of words to name, the power of language to teach, and the power of voice to create freedom, articulate memory, and express identity. She sees history and its telling as essential for the health (i.e., the wholeness) of the self and the community. She is a novelist whose phrases ring unabashedly, who knows she is doing well, whose vision bravely confronts the fundamental ambiguity of the human condition, its lack of any comforting absolutes. Understanding is Settle's primary value—understanding of the oneness of all individuals; of the fluidity of past, present, and future; and of the necessity for freedom to become oneself within the limits of the ambiguities. She sums up her aims best at the end of **"Recapturing the Past in Fiction."** "In our bewildered time, when we feel powerless, perhaps we need to recognize through looking at the past that doubt is timeless, change the only norm and accepted 'facts' too often passing notions. We can learn to trust to understanding instead of the frozen certainties we yearn for, and for which we might surrender the birthright earned by nameless people through the 300 years of our becoming." (pp. 222-24)

Jane Gentry Vance, "Mary Lee Settle: 'Ambiguity of Steel'," in American Women Writing Fiction: Memory, Identity, Family, Space, *edited by Mickey Pearlman, The University Press of Kentucky, 1989, pp. 214-29.*

FURTHER READING

Bach, Peggy. "The Searching Voice and Vision of Mary Lee Settle." *The Southern Review* 20, No. 4 (October 1984): 842-50.
      General biographical and critical introduction to Settle's works.

Rosenberg, Brian. "Mary Lee Settle and the Critics." *Virginia Quarterly Review* 65, No. 3 (Summer 1989): 401-17.
      Traces the critical reception of Settle's works and argues that reviewers neglected the *Beulah Quintet* because the literary establishment considers the historical novel a debased form.

————. "Mary Lee Settle and the Tradition of Historical Fiction." *The South Atlantic Quarterly* 86, No. 3 (Summer 1987): 229-43.
      Discusses the place of Settle's works within the traditions of the English and American historical novel.

Settle, Mary Lee. "The Search for Beulah Land." *The Southern Review* 24, No. 1 (Winter 1988): 13-26.
      Settle describes the origin and evolution of *The Beulah Quintet.*

Vance, Jane Gentry. "Historical Voices in Mary Lee Settle's *Prisons:* 'Too Far in Freedom.'" *Mississippi Quarterly* XXXVIII, No. 4 (Fall 1985): 391-413.
      Analyzes Settle's vision of Johnny Church in *Prisons* and postulates that Church's ideal of liberty resonates throughout the *Quintet.*

May Swenson

1919-1989

American poet, translator, author of children's books, dramatist, and critic.

Respected for her colorful and perceptive observations of natural phenomena and human and animal behavior, Swenson playfully experimented with poetic language, form, and sound, making extensive use of such devices as metaphor, alliteration, assonance, and dissonance. Critics often compare Swenson's poetic style with those of Marianne Moore, Elizabeth Bishop, and e e cummings; like Moore and Bishop, Swenson used richly evocative language and exacting detail in descriptions of the complexities of nature, and, like cummings, she displayed a penchant for wordplay. Swenson's poems are typically related in an objective, detached voice that approaches everyday human concerns, scientific topics, and nature with a sense of curiosity and wonder. Dennis Sampson described Swenson as "mischievous, inquisitive in the extreme, totally given over to the task of witnessing the physical world."

Many of the poems in Swenson's first three volumes, *Another Animal, A Cage of Spines,* and *To Mix with Time: New and Selected Poems,* are carefully structured in sound patterns. Critics praised her verbal ingenuity, clear images, and skillful use of internal rhyme, all of which contribute a fresh perspective on human and animal characteristics, death, sexuality, and the art of poetry. Sven Birkerts commented upon Swenson's early work: "The complexities of animal life and natural form are eagerly seized upon, while the intricacies of the social order and the human emotions are not so much overlooked as proscribed. It is as if the greater part of Swenson's psychic endowment has been channeled into the sense organs, which then become capable of the most precise registrations." Swenson examined the worlds of nature and science in *Half Sun Half Sleep* and *Iconographs.* The latter title is the word Swenson used to describe typographically distinct pieces, including her "shape poems," which are rendered in visual form and syntactical structures associated with the subjects or objects being discussed. For example, the poem "Stone Gullets" is divided into three sections by vertically curving lines, providing a visual image to accompany words that describe the ebb and flow of water in a rocky seascape.

Visual and aural elements of language are prominent concerns in *New and Selected Things Taking Place* and *In Other Words,* which collect many poems originally published in periodicals, including Swenson's frequent contributions to *The New Yorker.* The subject matter of these poems ranges from such ordinary activities as going to the dentist to contemplations of animals, trees, and landscapes. Swenson's continuing interest in science is reflected in poems about an eclipse and the passing of Halley's comet; the five-part "Shuttles" discusses the launches of these spaceships and concludes with ruminations on the *Challenger* shuttle disaster of 1986. While several critics stated that Swenson adopted a more self-conscious voice in her later work that lessened the exuberance of her experiments with poetic form and language, and others commented on the lack of emotion and social consciousness throughout her writings, she is generally praised

for her technical abilities and explorations of the challenges and possibilities of language. Mary Jo Salter commented: "Swenson provides comedy in two senses: marrying her words off in one happy ending after another, she makes us laugh as she does so. But whether she writes in jest or earnest, she belongs to that rare company of poets who convert the arbitrary correspondences among the sounds of words into what seems a preexisting order."

(See also *CLC,* Vols. 4, 14; *Contemporary Authors,* Vols. 5-8, rev. ed.; *Something about the Author,* Vol. 15; and *Dictionary of Literary Biography,* Vol. 5.)

PRINCIPAL WORKS

POETRY

Another Animal 1954
A Cage of Spines 1958
To Mix with Time: New and Selected Poems 1963
Half Sun Half Sleep 1967
Iconographs 1970
New and Selected Things Taking Place 1978
In Other Words 1988

BOOKS FOR CHILDREN

Poems to Solve   1966
More Poems to Solve   1971
The Guess and Spell Coloring Book   1976

RECORDINGS

The Poetry and Voice of May Swenson   1976

BABETTE DEUTSCH

The poetry of the '50s tends to fall roughly into two groups. There are those makers who write with a deliberate grace, a sly wit, that seem almost willfully obtrusive. And then there are those who rage against the folly and knavery of the world, or try to take heaven by violence. The fewest produce poems that call attention to themselves rather than to the author. Among these few is May Swenson. She looks at her pluriverse with avid perceptiveness. Whether she greets its inhabitants blithely or gravely, her response is generous. With a happy impartiality she will turn a microscope on the minuscule, a telescope on the grand. [In *A Cage of Spines,* her] ability to relate the one to the other is evidenced in the opening poem, **"Almanac,"** which begins: "The hammer struck my nail, instead of nail./A moon flinched into being. Omen-black,/It began its trail. Risen from horizon/on my thumb (no longer numb and indigo)/it waxed yellow, waned to a silver that now/sets white, here at the rim I cut tonight." The lines that follow trace the progress of the slight bruise and the prodigious events that accompany its disappearance. . . . The poem demands to be read in its entirety, but these excerpts indicate Miss Swenson's scope and method. The accurate verb, the hidden pun, the inner rhyme, the quiet tone that actualize the ordinary, are characteristic. But these lines can only hint at the quality of a book that offers such a rich sense of being. The object that catches Miss Swenson's attention may be an egg at breakfast, a child's game, a tree, a portrait in the making, or she may deal with such perennial themes as time and death. As she handles them, each is given a fresh gloss, in both senses of that word.

A craftsman, Miss Swenson enjoys experimenting with metaphor, stanza pattern, typography. Some of her experiments fail, but all are stimulating. She is an imagist with a metaphysical approach to what she so precisely depicts. Delighting in the physical body, whether animal, vegetable or mineral, she enjoys the life of the mind, and her book enhances both for her readers.

> Babette Deutsch, "Poems Generous and Quiet," in New York Herald Tribune Book Review, October 5, 1958, p. 6.

WILLIAM MEREDITH

The poet differs from other people in the significance he attaches to mere words, and in the pleasure he takes from them. In fact the *mereness* of a word, the unique and living energy which is something like its soul and often quite unlike its definition, is what he exploits. Words for him are not counters for the expression of thoughts and feeling but the very causes of thought and feeling.

May Swenson's original and charming poems seem to start from the premise that nothing is commonplace until matter-of-fact language and attitudes make it so. [In *A Cage of Spines,* she] leads the reader into fresh experience by riddles, a form of word-play where the recognition of familiar things is delayed and insisted on. "Roused from napping in my lap/ this nimble animal or five-legged star/ parts its limbs sprat-wide." (Answer: her hand).

Miss Swenson uses the sounds of words slyly. Her rhymes and echoes are often incomplete and internal, supplying (as we learned from her earlier book) [**Another Animal**] organic rather than merely formal connections.

She has a distinct tone of voice that conveys muttered astonishment at what she sees and hears in the world. Her wizardry is sometimes diminished by private or precious associations. The poem called **"Parade of Painters,"** for instance, is built of lines like "Titian heron leather pimento": what was sibylline elsewhere is pixie here. But *A Cage of Spines* is a very successful book and maintains great verbal originality.

> William Meredith, "Familiar Things Freshly Observed," in The New York Times Book Review, February 8, 1959, p. 10.

RICHARD MOORE

May Swenson seems to disagree with Robert Frost that a poem should begin in delight and end in wisdom. She seems to think it ought to have delight all the way through and, like Homer, leave the wisdom to the reader, if he has any. Her best poems are all haunting specifics — done with a fanciful brilliance of physical perception which reminds one at times of Emily Dickenson, at times of Elizabeth Bishop, but has a quality found in neither. Like Georg Trakl she pursues a skepticism so absolute that it distrusts abstractions of any kind. With her, perception itself is a mystique, and it is only in recent poems [in *To Mix with Time: New and Selected Poems*] that she attempts to explain it. Of these perhaps the best is **"The Universe,"** which is no explanation at all, but a comedy of unanswered questions echoing one another like a cat chasing its tail.

Many a poet today can tell us endlessly that red wheelbarrows are important. Not many can actually make us feel in our flesh *why* they are. Only the vivid vision can prove it; and when we have seen Miss Swenson's "bleeding triangles of pie" at a lunch counter, her "sails as slow as clouds" that "change bodies when they come about," or her doorways at night "dark as sockets," we are in business. What other poet today could run into the sunflowers in Provence which Van Gogh painted and, instead of shrinking in terror or squeezing out three or four logic-chopping stanzas in self-defense, make you feel that poetry can outdo painting? —

> Like eclipses of the sun,
> Their plate-heads, almost black, spun
> within the yellow aureoles. . . .

The book floats on such uncanny evocations. A few more tourists like this, one feels, and cameras would be recognized as the hoaxes they are.

If one believes that there are grave poets and frivolous ones, Miss Swenson can be disconcerting. She presents us with the play of an outrageous fancy, and her poker face and voice seem to say, "There's truth for you!" Her poems sometimes have an outlandish quality which reminds one of the mythologies of Australian aborigines; and her queer alternation of verbal brilliance, chantlike repetition, awkwardness both apparent and real, and even flat prose, enhance the impression. The opening stanzas of the remarkable poem, **"Landing On The Moon,"** actually make the reader feel like a bushman puzzling the night sky. In fact the visible world which Miss Swenson seeks and presents tends to keep the primitive duplicity it has before our philosophical or practical consciousness decides what it is. It is a part of us, she says in a poem significantly titled **"The Primitive,"** and we are indistinguishable from it; but at the same time it is implacably and completely unconcerned with us. Nothing can be known by seeing, and yet by seeing alone can one know all the wonders that the world is full of. What makes this meaningful is that we see and hear the wonders in the poems.

Miss Swenson gives us plenty of lapses as well. Poems like **"Downward"** seem bare, flat statements; and with neither a firm meter, regular rhymes nor rhetoric to cling to, she dissipates sometimes into prosy formlessness. Especially in her earlier pieces she lacks denouement and variety of tone; and her intermittent fascination with typographical tiddlywinks occasionally tricks her into thinking that a collection of sputters is a poem. But there is hair-raising poetry in this book. (pp. 76-7)

Richard Moore, "One Knows by Seeing," in The Nation, *New York, Vol. 197, No. 4, August 10, 1963, pp. 76-7.*

PETER DAVISON

Poetry of late has been aiming itself in new directions. With the disappearance from the scene, within the last several years, of most of the senior American poets, an era has ended. Robert Frost, William Carlos Williams, E. E. Cummings, Theodore Roethke have died within the last eighteen months, and Robinson Jeffers and Wallace Stevens preceded them by not long. T. S. Eliot and Ezra Pound have all but stopped writing. Of the veterans only Conrad Aiken, it seems, continues in the full strength of his poetic powers. In the meantime, poets who only a year ago were thought of as "younger" suddenly find themselves, in their forties, the movers and shakers whom the younger poets look up to: Robert Lowell, Richard Wilbur, Howard Nemerov, Robert Duncan. . . .

Like the poets of a generation ago, perhaps of any generation, these younger poets must challenge themselves to seek out a style of their own—a rhetoric competent to register the full range of their inchoate feelings, yet one which will collect these feelings into a clarity. A poet's style is more than an answer to a question; it is even more than "the man himself." The interaction between a poet's style and his subject matter is itself part of what he confronts in the world around him. How does this tree, this grief, this sunlight embody itself in language—*my* language? I cannot know experience except through language; and if my language is inadequate to my experience, must I change the warp of my language, or must certain realms of experience pass forever into darkness for me? This very dilemma can work its way into the stuff of poetry: the interchange between language and feeling, between sunlight and fog. (p. 82)

[May Swenson] is, to my personal taste, one of the most ingenious and delightful younger poets writing today (*To Mix with Time: New and Selected Poems*). She has, at any rate,

probably the best eye for nature. What does she not see? A snake:

> Mud-and-silver-licked, his length—a
>   single spastic muscle—
> slid over stones and twigs to a snuggle
>   of roots, and hid.

A bird:

> And a grackle, fat as burgundy,
> gurgles on a limb.

> His bottle-glossy feathers
> shrug off the wind.

A cat:

>   Not a hair
> in the gap of his ear moves.
> His clay gaze stays steady.

Her attention to nature gives May Swenson's poems a directness of gaze that is sometimes lacking when she turns to other, apparently broader subjects. She needs, perhaps, the concreteness of things close at hand in order to see deeply; it is as though language, in her hands, responded naturally only to the actual and palpable. She has a staggering poetic equipment: visual acuity, a sense of form, a fine ear for rhythm and the colloquial. Among her recent poems there are too many with high pretensions, in the shapes of arrows or zigzags or earthquakes, dealing with the Scheme of Things. A series of travel poems—with the exception of one about a bullfight—strikes me as terribly selfconscious, as though someone had been Taking Notes. But even if, in her straining for fresh ways of saying things, this poet's sureness sometimes deserts her, she just cannot go wrong with her nature poems. They are *seen;* the husks and kernels of nature are *there.* And sometimes, at moments of great simplicity, her poems go almost as far in eloquence as poems can—as in a favorite of mine called **"Question."**

> Body my house
> my horse my hound
> what will I do
> when you are fallen

> Where will I sleep
> How will I ride
> What will I hurt

> Where can I go
> without my mount
> all eager and quick
> How will I know
> in thicket ahead
> is danger or treasure
> when Body my good
> bright dog is dead

A poem like this, in its simple lyricism, makes us forget all questions about the direction of poetry, about schools and generations. It is, after all, a song; and songs hold their own secrets. This one may hold the secret of long life. (pp. 84-5)

Peter Davison, "Books and Men: New Poetry," in The Atlantic Monthly, *Vol. 212, No. 6, December, 1963, pp. 82-5.*

KARL SHAPIRO

The poet's joy is in the writing. When the writing is joyous enough, it carries over to the reader and becomes contagious, like laughter.

A. R. Ammons's poems in [*Northfield Poems*] are joyless and depressing. . . . Unable, apparently, to face the joy of language, he can only parry it and assert his indifference. Talented or not, he sends a cold shiver through the reader.

In high contrast, May Swenson [in *Half Sun, Half Sleep*] leaps to the love of language and has a ball. It hardly matters what her subject is. Her concentration on the verbal equivalent of experience is so true, so often brilliant, that one watches her with hope and pleasure, praying for victory all the way. Whether it's a trip to the dentist or the trip of the latest rocket to the moon, flowers in a city garden, somebody's eyelashes, sunrise over the sea, her watch, anything—what difference does it make? She draws everything into her ken, into a sharp focus which is inescapable. And the reader laughs with joy that she has done it. How beautiful it is, that eye on the object look, Auden once wrote (or words to that effect). May Swenson is a true artist, giving the object its due and trying to flirt it down.

Quotation commonly is mutilation, the more so with a poet whose every word is so cherished that none can be removed. (p. 8)

[In **"The Watch"** the] words in the rhyme position are almost all personal pronouns; the poet is on one side, the fixer on the other and the watch in the middle. It is a play and the play on words opens the door to the heart, as in Hopkins's poem about his own watch. May Swenson's poem is very much in the high baroque fashion of our time, and she is so much at home in it as to be one of its masters.

The whole volume is an album of experiments—but experiments that pay off. It is strange to see the once-radical *carmen figuratum*, the calligraphic poem, spatial forms, imagist and surreal forms—all the heritage of the early years of the century—being used with such ease and unselfconsciousness. Miss Swenson has truly assimilated the lessons of the old craftsmen. She shows how well the idiom is established; she is completely in phase with it. All that technique which was once so wild and shocking is now domesticated and put at ease.

And being at ease in this poetic language, she is at ease in her world. Her book is a far cry from the poetry of complaint and terror to which we have become accustomed and perhaps insensitive. And it is a far cry from the howl of personal anguish and accusation. Hers is a book of pleasures, and most of all the pleasures of the artist at work in the medium she loves. (p. 34)

Karl Shapiro, "A Ball with Language," in The New York Times Book Review, *May 7, 1967, pp. 8, 34.*

CHAD WALSH

May Swenson and Robert Creeley have both reached that perilous stage for poets, their 40s. Each has published several widely acclaimed volumes. Each is solidly a part of the current poetic establishment. And each is being watched by the literary arbiters of taste who are equally quick to deplore "stagnation" and "unfortunate departures from his early gift and style."

Half Sun Half Sleep reveals Miss Swenson continuing to do with brilliance what she was already doing in her previous book, *To Mix with Time*. Louis Untermeyer has called her an Emily Dickinson who has read D. H. Lawrence. I see more of the Dickinson than the Lawrence. And of the Dickinson I recognize especially the sharp and loving eye for specific detail, and more rarely the metaphysical flashes. In most of Miss Swenson's poems the sheer thingness of things is joyfully celebrated. At times even objects seem unimportant; color itself, in an abstract pattern, takes over, as in a poem called **"Colors without Objects"**:

> Colors without objects—colors alone—
> wriggle in the tray of my eye,
> incubated under the great flat lamp
> of the sun:
> bodiless blue, little razor-streak,
> yellow melting like a firework petal,
> double purple yo-yo
> in a broth of murky gold.

The poet par excellence of sights and colors, Miss Swenson can pause at any spot and fix it in words as though she were doing a sketch for a very high-class souvenir postcard.

Imagination powerfully supplements direct observation, as in **"August 19, Pad 19,"** one of the most vivid space-travel poems yet written:

> 8 days without weighing anything.
> Not knowing up from down.
> Positioned for either breach birth
> or urn burial. My mission the practice
> of catching up by slowing down,
> I am the culmination of a 10-storey bottle,
> in 3 disconnectable parts,
> being fueled with seething vapor

At times Miss Swenson's poetic high spirits lead her to wild typographical experiments—poems shaped like their subject, or simply made to look like interesting doodles. Generally she carries it off with a graceful touch, though occasionally it becomes merely cute. Finally, the book contains translations from the work of contemporary Swedish poets, a welcome set of bridges across a linguistic frontier rarely crossed in poetry.

Chad Walsh, "The Sense of Delight," in Book Week—The Washington Post, *June 4, 1967, p. 5.*

ROBERT PACK

I take it that the goal of experimentation is to find something: experimentation is not an end in itself. If a poet invents new forms or breaks down old ones, he still must be judged by familiar criteria: Do his words have the thrust to move the reader in fresh ways? Do they have the power to inspire speculation and meditation? May Swenson is experimental in the sense that she has found patterns of speech that allow her to distinguish her own voice from the chaos of today's political rhetoric and from the mere formlessness of most contemporary poetry (which is rationalized, of course, in the name of freedom). The freedom May Swenson earns is that of making hard, not easy, choices.

Iconographs is a book of remarkable wittiness, not only because Miss Swenson's poems amuse and delight, but also because they possess her unique kind of inventiveness. Her typological tricks are not gimmicks or a stylistic eccentricity that she relies on for the essential effect of the poem. Rather, they support the poem's verbal life, heightening sensations that are already there, imitating a meaning inherent in the words themselves. For example, in **"How Everything Happens (Based on a study of the Wave)"** regard how the eye and the mind of the reader perform the same game:

<pre>
                                            happen.
                                        to
                                    up
                            stacking
                                is
            something
    When nothing is happening

    When it happens
            something
                            pulls
                                back
                                    not
                                        to
                                            happen.
</pre>

There is a range of voices within which May Swenson is comfortably herself, varying from the casual and the colloquial ("At the Army Surplus Store. I bought an old field jacket") to the decorative and playful ("Later, a pale blue VW, running on poetry,/ weaves down Park Avenue, past yellow/ sprouts of forsythia, which, due to dog-do/ and dew, are doing nicely . . . ") to the grim, an effect achieved by selecting an unlikely persona, as in the poem **"Bleeding"** ("Stop bleeding said the knife./ I would if I could said the cut"). But for the most part her voice is conversational, informed often by metaphors of current scientific knowledge or the reading of the daily newspaper. Yet Miss Swenson's meditations and her talk are almost always grounded in or linked to precise and careful observation. She has a marvelous eye for the ordinary and the giveaway detail.

Nearly all of the poems in this book are interesting in one way or another: for their verbal play, for their clear images, for their intelligence. But the best are gripping because of their compassion. Such a poem is **"Feel Me,"** which recalls the mysterious words spoken by the poet's father on his deathbed: "Feel me to do right, our father said." In the exploration of the possible meanings of these words, there emerge both an idea of "right" and a powerful feeling that describes the relationship between father and daughter, between "feeling" in a tactile sense and in an emotional sense.

May Swenson's iconographs are experiments that find true poems.

> *Robert Pack, in a review of "Iconographs," in Saturday Review, Vol. LIV, No. 34, August 21, 1971, p. 29.*

MAY SWENSON [INTERVIEW WITH KARLA HAMMOND]

Karla Hammond: *Women writing from the Thirties and Forties onward seem more preoccupied with nature, pastoral scenes, elegy, and praise (as common themes in their work); whereas today's women poets, in large part, view poetry as a means of psychological/confessional investigation, exploration of sexual identity and nationalistic consciousness, and as a vehicle of social commentary. Certainly there are exceptions in either case, but is it a fair assessment, and if so, do the culture, the media, and socialization alone determine what people will concern themselves with?*

[May Swenson]: For me, nature includes everything: the entire universe, the city, the country, the human mind, human creatures, and the animal creatures. Nature is the big construct; so if I'm called a nature poet then I'm happy about that. It isn't simply the birds, the bees, and the butterflies.

If culture, the media, and socialization determine what people concern themselves with, it means that they are certainly over-civilized. Animals aren't human beings, but human beings are animals. They aren't only animals. They are human, but the human arises out of the animal nature. The animal is instinctive. It's the quality which makes it possible for us to live with the earth, with the universe, with nature. People should not lose their animal nature. I mean they will, but it's too bad. The media, socialization, and culture can turn people into artificial things.

Real poets don't follow the trend. They may be *with* the trend. They may be leading the trend, but they aren't hooked up to it. Psychological/confessional? Today some of the poetry within that vein will live and go on, but not merely because it's psychological/confessional poetry. It will have to have some added *art* value.

How is poetry humanizing?

Not only poetry, but all the arts. In the article in which I discuss this, I wondered what might happen as technology goes on. For, while I venerate science, I'm also afraid of it in its technological aspects. Cloning is talked about. What will be the next step in evolution? Will it be toward stereotypy, toward man and mechanism combined? It takes a person, a personality, to produce art. Conversely, art as an influence creates personhood. It humanizes—humanizes the one who makes it, as well as all the others who enjoy it.

Elizabeth Bishop is one of the few poets mentioned in your work (your letter poem for her). Do you think of her work as humanizing? And do you feel an influence from her?

Almost everything that E. B. has written stays with me. I will not say that she is a great *woman* poet. I'll say that she is a great poet. These days many people agree with that; so I'm not making a new discovery. Of course, she is humanizing.

Have I been influenced by her? Not necessarily, although neither of us writes confessional poetry. E. B. has always stayed with the objective, the large view, the impersonal which contains the personal if you look into it deeply. I have this tendency, but not because of any influence of hers. I think we share some of the same basic perceptive equipment.

Is it plausible to speak of influences?

My earliest poetry wasn't influenced by anyone because I didn't read poetry when I first began writing. When I discovered Marianne Moore's and Cummings' work, I was intrigued. I was interested in Marianne Moore's subject matter, her objectivity; she wasn't writing about her emotions. As to Cummings, I liked his playfulness. I was attracted by the way he made words actual on the page—pages of poetry that looked different from the ordinary. Language for the poet is what pigment is for the painter. Part of my pleasure in a painting is to notice just how the colors are applied, or placed, by brush or palette knife.

Your poems frequently emphasize "things" as opposed to people. Have you "felt" Rilke's, Williams', or Ponge's influence in this regard?

That title of my latest book, **Things Taking Place,** is an old one. It's been in my mind for a couple of decades, and finally I'm using it. If I've been influenced by other poets, it's been subconscious. It's seldom that reading poetry stimulates me to write. Rather I could say that I've felt affinities with the work of certain painters, for instance with Milton Avery, with Georgia O'Keeffe, with the constructions of Marcel Duchamp that he called "Ready-Mades." I once played a game of chess with Duchamp. It was a thrill. He was a guest at the MacDowell Colony for a week one summer that I was there. This was shortly before he died. We played billiards, too.

Writing in the latter half of the Twentieth Century, do you consider yourself a feminist?

I think I began to be a feminist at age three-and-a-half [laughs] . Certainly long before that word took on the meaning it has today. I don't actually like the word very much if it means to cut out the male. Male and female exist in every person. The world is made up of male, female, and combinations thereof. If the word means "I am Feminine and that's all I need," I disagree—that's extreme. It all depends on definition. I've always felt complete within myself as a person, but sometimes felt that some of the rest of the world didn't find me as complete or capable as if I had been born male. This has annoyed me.

I raised the question because of your poem "Women," although I realize the comic irony intended.

"Women" wasn't written to be a feminist poem, but call it that, if you like. It was first published in **Iconographs** and it's one of my shaped poems. Its shape might remind you of a rocking platform, which is a visual metaphor for what the poem is saying. Were you to take it literally, you wouldn't realize that it really means the opposite of what it's saying. Why, it could be *anti*-feminist [laughs] if you were to take it simply as a statement, and you had no sense of humor. (pp. 60-2)

Your work reveals many interests—some in science and evolution. In an article several years ago you said, "Sometimes I long to remember my life as a cephalopod under the sea, and cannot." Are you suggesting a belief in reincarnation?

No. I can't believe in reincarnation because I have no evidence for it. As for "cephalopod," I'm just talking about evolution, and that I'd like to know the origins of the human being and experience those origins. Do *you* believe in reincarnation? The people who do can't explain it, can't tell you *how* it happens, how it works. (p. 64)

You have said: "Poetry doesn't tell; it shows. Prose tells." Is this because poetry deals with the inner landscape of the human being—the subconscious and psyche, because it is an implicit and symbolic language as opposed to exposition, explanation, or description?

What I meant was that poetry doesn't talk *about* something. It presents the thing to your senses, so that it can be grasped whole. At least, this is what makes it poetry for me. My own feelings are that poetry doesn't talk about it; it doesn't tell about it. It isn't a story. There is a narrative poetry, of course, but I want to *build* a poem with language as the material. My way of showing goes farther than even the presenting of images (which many poets do). I think of a poem as a mobile, almost a construct, something you can look around, that moves, that is concrete. You can almost hold it in your hand.

I think of it as projecting to the reader something more actual, more graspable by his senses than just words on the page. This has led me into the iconographic poem. I don't do this much anymore, but I did make a whole book of **Iconographs.** That's a made-up word meaning picture-writing.

Could you explain the difference between concrete poetry and your iconographics?

Apollinaire was one of the early concrete poets in France. Some good American concrete poets are Mary Ellen Solt and John Hollander. There are others who do nothing except show you one word, an abstract word, at that, taken apart on the page. That's just tricky and trivial. It doesn't give anything. Poetry has to give more than one aspect, more than one dimension. Less is not more when you get down to zero. (A Danish poet, Vagn Steen, published a book titled *Write It Yourself,* all the pages of which were blank.) But the main difference is this. The concretist starts out with his arrangement and he fits the words into this arrangement. My iconographs are never designed until I have the poem absolutely finished and every word set. I never change a word in order to fit it into the frame. You see, it's the difference between the frame and the painting. Of course the painting must be major, not the frame. In fact, in the "Selected" section of **Things Taking Place** I've reprinted some iconographs without their "frames"—gone back to conventional arrangements.

*Would you say that your earlier reference to the eye's primacy in poetry foreshadowed the visual achievement of **Iconographs?***

Oh yes. My eyes have been primal from the very beginning. It starts with my being nearsighted. It seems odd that a defect in one's eyes should make one visual; but being nearsighted, I look at everything more carefully close up, and notice details. I think that this comes into my work. For me the eyes are the main sense, although all of the senses should come into play simultaneously, if possible. (pp. 65-7)

You've said that poetry "is done with words; with their combination, sometimes with their unstringing." Do you regard revision as part of that "unstringing"?

In saying that, I might have been thinking of my poem about Robert Frost (**"R. F. at Bread Loaf His Hand Against A Tree"**) where the words are actually pulled apart to show words inside of themselves.

Why don't we just think of revision as what the word actually means: to re-view, to re-vise, have a vision again, to make it more exact. Revision means making the thing closer to what you first experienced, what prompted you to write the poem. It's important in that you want your first vision to still be there. It's not that you discard that vision and substitute something else, because the beginning impulse of a poem, the vision, for me, is primary. It contains the germ of what made me want to write in the first place. I want to keep that in, because if I removed it, I'd get something else: probably something mechanical, rather than what I started out with.

Do you ever research material for a poem?

Yes. I try to be exact, and when I'm uncertain about something factual I look it up. When I was writing my space poems I researched material because I wanted to be factually accurate.

*In **"Things I Can Do In My Situation"** you mention: "when*

I began/ these notes . . . " Does a poem generally begin with notes?

There's one other poem that actually has "Notes" in the title: **"Notes Made in the Piazza San Marco."** I was sitting at a cafe table in Venice in the Piazza when I began to set down my impressions. It really was notes in a notebook. In revision I let the poem stay rather rough like the notes. That's why I kept the title.

You don't keep a journal?

Yes I do. I don't keep one with the specific notion of using it for poetry, though things have come out of it for poetry. Sometimes I record a dream. My daybook generally begins with the weather. It has a lot of weather in it [laughs]. Weather, and how I feel inside that morning. It's a private record of my inner moods more than anything else—not really a poetic journal. (pp. 68-9)

In your **New and Selected** *book, have you changed many of the poems from earlier books?*

I tried not to. I don't like to tamper with my earlier self very much. When I see poems that need to be improved extensively, I leave them out in making a selection. It isn't a good idea to impose your older self on your younger self because you've become a different person. What you produced when you were young had better stay in that form or else be discarded. Sometimes I'll make a small change, but I usually try not to do that.

The title, **Things Taking Place**—*Is that because many poems deal with events?*

Yes, partly. And then it refers to their objectivity. I think of my poems as "things" rather than messages made of words. That title is a common phrase—my poems often use commonplace experiences—and also, I like the idea of subject and object linked by the verb. "Things" (the poems) are taking their "places" on the pages. As actors do on a stage, for instance.

One of your more recent poems, **"The Pure Suit of Happiness"** *in the following lines: "It has its own weather,/ which is youth's breeze,/ equilibrated by the ideal/ thermostat of maturity," reminds me of Stanley Kunitz' statement that youth is not a state of genius but a biological condition.*

"The Pure Suit of Happiness" is a central poem for me because in addition to being about me, in a funny way, the imagery was derived from astronaut suits. Remember, I was fascinated by the space program.

"The pure suit of happiness,/ not yet invented . . . " Of course it's a pun on the pursuit of happiness. "How I long/ to climb into its legs,/ fit into its sleeves, and zip/ it up, pull the hood/ over my head." "Pull the hood/ over my head" indicates that I'm really laughing at myself for wanting to hide. "It's got/ a face mask, too, and gloves/ and boots attached. It's/ made for me. It's blue. It's/ not too heavy, not too/ light. It's my right./ It has its own weather,/ which is youth's breeze,/ equilibrated by the ideal/ thermostat of maturity,/ and, built-in to begin with,/ fluoroscopic goggles of/ age. I'd see through/ everything, yet be happy./ I'd be suited for life. I'd/ always look good to myself."

This is a typical poem of mine in that it's simultaneously serious and funny. It ties in with science and relates to an attitude about myself. Critics have pointed out, and it's true, that my poems are generally very objective and only more subtly subjective. Of course you can't help talking about yourself if you're writing (unless you're under assignment from a publisher to write a trash book or something). If you're really writing, you're writing about yourself regardless of what you're saying in your writing. Art *is* confessional, it *is* autobiographical after all. Always has been.

Maxine Kumin said you're writing about yourself in that what you write is "invested with self."

That's a good way to put it. I like her pun there, too. (pp. 70-1)

Would you talk about one or two of your other, newer poems?

I could say this about **"October,"** a seven-part quite long one. Each of its sections was written in one day in a given week in October, here in Sea Cliff, Long Island.

I was alone for that week and I gave myself the assignment of writing the poem in that way. I wrote first thing every morning, before breakfast. I'd sit down at my desk and make a first draft. The revisions came later. It is, however, unusual for me to set myself projects. That hasn't been my habit in writing, but I did it for this particular poem. (p. 72)

In **"October"** *you speak of your "little desk of cherry wood" where you wrote your first poems. When did you start writing?*

My Dad was a cabinet maker. He taught mechanical engineering at the college I graduated from. Mechanical engineering is a fancy term for wood-working. He taught house-building, wood-carving, pattern-making. He made most of the furniture in our house: the dining-room table (mentioned in an early poem, **"Lion"**), a buffet in the dining room, and chairs. He was a wonderful craftsman and a great designer. In fact, I have a cellaret (for holding wine) left to me in his will. He designed it, constructed it, and carved the door on it, for which he won a prize in his youth.

As to your question, though, he made me a small desk of cherry wood that I mention in **"October."** That desk is lost, I'm sorry to say. I left it in Salt Lake City with a friend, who moved and left it with someone else. It was a beautiful little desk. The lid of it came down; I wrote in longhand on it. It had little cubbyholes and little drawers. Some of my first poems were made on that desk. I began writing at thirteen. I didn't know that I was writing poems. But when I'd type them out, their arrangement was instinctive, and I'd say to myself, "This must be a poem. It doesn't look like a story."

Can you give me another recent example from **Things Taking Place?**

"Ending"—written perhaps a year ago—is about death. It's one of these funny/serious poems. In *Things Taking Place* there are a number of rather dark old-age and death poems in the first section; all newer poems are in the front. I've arranged the sequence backwards, as I usually do my books, the opposite of chronological. **"Ending"** is at the end of the new-poems section. The idea is one of those wishes: if only physical death were not the end. As far as any evidence I have, physical death is the end to human life. I wish that I could imagine how it could not be so. So here I'm taking this idea of the soul (which used to be thought of as inhabiting the body) being able to escape from the body and move into another environment [laughs]. I call this soul a "me." "Maybe there *is* a Me inside of me/ and, when I lie dying, he/ will

crawl out. Through my toe./ Green on the green rug . . . ''
This little soul, Me inside of me, is like a chameleon that
changes color by what it walks on. "Green on the green rug,
and then/ white on the wall, and then/ over the window sill,
up the trunk/ of the apple tree, he/ will turn brown and
rough and warty/ to match the bark. But you'll be/ able to
see—(*who* will be/ able to see?)" See, I'm not there anymore.
I'm dead. So that's amusing to contemplate. Or, I should say,
bemusing. Well, the poem goes on, and it *is* ironic, imagining
that I could escape death by having my soul become an "ar-
chaeopteryx"—early in evolution, a tiny lizard that had
wings but didn't fly.

It's an interesting contrast to **"On Its Way."**

Yes, it is, in its tone and technique. **"On Its Way"** is an autumn lyric. Rhythmic. Elegiac. A nature poem!

As I said before, each poem is a thing in itself. After you've
accumulated enough work, you can see threads that move
through and connect, but my poems are separate constructs—autonomous—which may explain why I have a
gamut of treatments and styles.

*You've spoken of the impulses of the scientist and poet being
parallel. Are the impulses of the dancer or the choreographer
and the poet parallel?*

All the arts are like each other in what they attempt, I think.
Many years ago, E. M. Forster, the British novelist (one of
my pets), said that "Art for art's sake" is the right attitude.
That was at a time when that attitude was questioned sharply. It's still questioned, I suppose. I believe that the poem, the
dance, the painting, whatever, is valid enough to be made for
its own sake. In fact, that's the best way to make it—not hitch
it on to something else, or require it carry something else, be
a vehicle.

Has science given us a vernacular applicable to poetry?

If you look at poetry of the past, you find a different vernacular from poetry of the present. In the future you'll see more
differences in the vernacular. We use the language that we
read, we speak, we hear. Science is relatively late in the life
of mankind. Science wasn't always there. Its language came
into our lives and, of course, it's been filtered down into art.
This is to be expected. Scientists aren't actually giving us our
vernacular. We just pick it up like we pick up slang or other
language around us. It's just part of our lives. If there's a
glitch in this interview when you've got it finished, it'll be
your fault—O.K.?

*[laughs] I remember in your analogy between the scientist and
the poet, you spoke of the insatiable curiosity of both, and the
use of language as a medium.*

Of course there are differences between the artist and the scientist, but they're each on a search. In that comparison I was
just talking about myself, because I'm on a search, although
I didn't deliberately set out to make a search in poetry. I have
a philosophical bent which harks back to a religious background that I abandoned. Other poets may not be on any
search other than into their own selves. But I've been on a
search into the universe and the human mind.

My intuition is the only launching pad I have, but scientists
probably take off from intuition, too.

*You've spoken of the poetic experience as one of "constant curi-
osity, skepticism, and testing—astonishment, disillusionment,*

*renewed discovery, re-illumination." Would you add any other
qualities to this list?*

Yes, darkness. For every blazing galaxy, a black hole. I wrote
the original list long ago. That's still the experience, but add
to that: darkness. When I say "for every blazing galaxy, a
black hole," I'm usurping an astronomical image. Astrono-
mers think they have discovered black holes in between the
blazing galaxies. Similarly there is a new psychological discovery that occurs as one ages. (pp. 72-5)

*May Swenson and Karla Hammond, in an inter-
view, in* Parnassus: Poetry in Review, *Vol. 7, No. 1,
1978, pp. 60-75.*

DAVE SMITH

May Swenson's ***New and Selected Things Taking Place*** collects nearly thirty years of her remarkable poetry. At sixty,
she may well be the fiercest, most inquisitive poet of her generation; certainly few are more brilliant or more independent
of mien. Her poems, through six collections since 1954, are
characterized by an extreme reticence of personality, an
abundant energy, and an extraordinary intercourse between
the natural and intellectual worlds. She has always been as
formal as poets come, demonstrating early and late a skilled
employment of traditional verse as well as a passion for invented patterns. There are two central obsessions in her
work: the search for a proper perspective and the celebration
of life's embattled rage to continue. Her poems ask teleological questions and answer them, insofar as answers are ever
possible, in every conceivable poetic strategy: she writes narrative, catalog, image, concrete, interrogatory, and sequence
poems (often mixing these in a single work). Her language is
generally sonorous, remarkable for its Anglo-Saxon stress, alliteration, extensive word fusions, and a devotion (now declining, it appears) to rhyme. She has made language an instrument for pursuit of ideas, but always ideas discoverable
only in things of the experiential world. She believes, apparently, that the world functions according to some hidden
final purpose, and furthermore that a right apprehension ultimately reveals a Coleridgean interconnectedness of all parts.
A section from **"Order of Diet,"** an early poem, suggests her
belief and her cadences, both essentially unchanged though
refined:

> Ashes find their way to green;
> the worm is raised into the wing;
> the sluggish fish to muscle slides;
> eventual chemistry will bring
> the lightning bug to the shrewd toad's eye.
> It is true no thing of earth can die.

Nothing so excites Swenson's imagination or reveals her poetic investigation as that image of flight. In poems about air-
planes, birds, insects, and especially space exploration, she
celebrates the joy of flight. Motion is both her subject and her
image, being life itself. Flight, however, rarely means escape;
it is her means for exploration, penetration, for travel to and
through the world; it is what humans cannot naturally do
("light pierces wings of jays in flight: / they shout my grief ")
but what becomes the passage toward and into vision. In this
book's earliest poem, Swenson wrote "all that my Eye encircles I become" and risked an Emersonian cartoon. Vision,
seeing, looking, recording are so pervasive in her poems that
one almost forgets how active she makes all the senses in the
service of penetrating surfaces. Flight is not only the revela-

tion of human bondage, it is also the vehicle of imaginative and intellectual possibilities. As she writes in **"Distance And A Certain Light,"** speaking of her poetics, "No contortion / without intention, and nothing ugly." Never a poet of ennui or cynicism, though often a poet of elegiac grief, she believes that all is beautiful if seen properly: "Rubbish becomes engaging shape—/ you only have to get a bead on it . . . " And:

> From an airplane, all
> that rigid splatter of the Bronx
> becomes organic, logical
> as web or beehive. . . .
>
>   (pp. 291-92)

Swenson's emphasis on flight and perspective, always in the context that "earth will not let go our foot," extends from her conception of the primary tension of existence: "The tug of the void / the will of the world." By will she means the rage to survive and flourish which is continually contested by absence, death, and the void, hence "Though devious and shifty in detail, the whole expanse / reiterated constancy and purpose." Swenson's effort has been and is to make felt the nature of that purpose. (p. 292)

"October," a new poem, shows she means to fly into the world, not out of it. Here she emphasizes the search for vision, not its verbal contrivance:

> . . . Stand still, stare
> hard into bramble and tangle,
> past leaning broken trunks,
> sprawled roots exposed. Will
> something move?—some vision
> come to outline? Yes, there—

Swenson, however, seems not to have come to any definitive identification of a teleological purpose. She has found or accepted no answer except her intuited conviction that all is interconnected and rooted in love. Her temperament, always religious and never orthodox, causes her to caution: "I do not mean to pray." Yet her newest poems seem prayerful, perhaps in the increased awareness of the void's tug, which makes her note, "Too vivid / the last pink / petunia's indrawn mouth." More acutely now she feels what age reveals, "the steep / edge of hopelessness," and writes more intimately of what's been loved: family, flowers, landscapes and seascapes, birds, and vibrant colors. Perhaps no poet since Wallace Stevens has so reveled in colors; they name poems, accrue into image patterns, are ingested as objects. For May Swenson, life is motion and *color*. Yet the colors of new poems are slightly less brilliant, are the colors of seasonal decline. Staring into the bramble thicket, she writes "Better here / in the familiar, to fade."

If Swenson's new poems are more attentive to the inevitable void, she remains at least as interested in chronicling what is happening as what has happened. Her sixty-two new poems evidence still a vigorous curiosity, a compulsive meticulousness, and a passionate sense of life which forces us toward poetry's accomplishment, renewed vision. She has plenty to write about, including Navaho rugs, bison, rodeos, western mountains, the sea, swamps, income tax, fashion, Georgia O'Keefe, baseball and football, an outhouse, parents, a junkyard dog, Mormonism, Nanook the Eskimo, and an aviary (there can hardly be a poet who has written more about birds or about more birds!). And writing of July 4th fireworks, she says:

> And we want more: we want red giant, white dwarf,
> black hole, extinct, orgasmic, all in one!

Dedicated as they are to angles of vision, avoiding autobiography and personality, Swenson's poems necessarily emphasize structure—sometimes to the point of mannerism. Often enough they possess a wonderful lyricism that celebrates; but primarily they nominate, and this occasionally leads to an annoyingly indiscriminate series of similes: a thing looks like this. Or this, or this. This mannerism reveals a kind of "scientific" attitude in her work, an attitude also marked by often esoteric and technical terminology—not in itself a problem though it helps create the impression of a dispassionate stance when there is passion present and the need to show it. Swenson's reticence may sometimes mean the difference between a powerful experience and no experience, as in riddles or dry humor. Indeed, one of Swenson's characteristics is a wry wit which sometimes trails off into whimsy, into the glib and clever. For me she has too strong a willingness to keep work marked by visual puns (particularly from *Iconographs*), work less felt and sustaining than contrived and biodegradable. Such work does disservice to her significant accomplishment, though some "readers" will doubtless applaud her gamesmanship and experimenting. For them, here is a stanza of **"MAsterMANANiMAL":**

> ANiMAte MANANiMAL MAttress of Nerves
> MANipulAtor Motor ANd Motive MAker
> MAMMAliAN MAtrix MAt of rivers red
> MortAL MANic Morsel Mover shAker

Swenson's interest in this sort of visual word-play extends to poems carved in zigzags, curves, a snail's shape (among others), and multiple, often opposed columns of print. Sometimes charming, sometimes bitingly effective as in **"Women"** and **"Orbiter 5 Shows How Earth Looks From The Moon,"** the poems too often depend on a gimmickry that wears quickly thin. In **"Look,"** for example, a poem about two people before a mirror, the right hand column of print uses a form of "look" twenty-two times, and one wants as much as anything not to look.

Neither are all of Swenson's more traditionally executed poems free from excess that may be attributed to her high and democratic spirit. She betrays a tendency to telegraph conclusions in some of the image poems. In **"The Solar Corona"** the sun's enormous ring becomes a pizza that "is 400 times / larger than the moon. / Don't burn your lips!" Here, we can only say Ouch! And we cringe when in a love poem, **"Poet To Tiger,"** she writes "You put your paws in your armpits / make a tiger-moo." Because there is a strain of the highly impressionistic in this eclectic poet, there is a scattering of poems of which the closest readings scarcely dislodge either subject or meaning or both so that poems such as **"Written While Riding The Long Island Rail Road"** and **"O'Keefe Retrospective"** remain interesting and baffling.

Any collection as rich and massive as this one must have, however, its weaknesses and I would hope they do not obscure the book's dominant strength. Swenson's voracious imagination makes her an extremely social and adventurous writer who turns poetry into a living, if idealized, human speech. From previous collections she has trimmed more than fifty poems and has reordered most of what remains, in effect creating not merely a Collected Poems but a freshly ordained and perpetual world of poetry. Among the new poems, I would cite for their excellence **"Bison Crossing Near Mt. Rushmore," "Staying At Ed's Place," "The Wil-**

lets," "That The Soul May Wax Plump," "Scroppo's Dog," "October," and "Dream After Nanook" in particular. Among the previous collections there is such an abundance of splendid, welcome old friends that it is impossible and nearly invidious to choose for citation. . . .(pp. 293-95)

If Swenson sometimes generates consternation and dismay, that fault is born of a poetry urgently trying to tell us that everything matters, a poetry so affirmative that we cannot escape knowing we matter. Even random reading here produces surprise, delight, love, wisdom, joy, and grief. May Swenson transforms the ordinary little-scrutinized world to a teeming, flying first creation. Bother such words as *great* and *major*—she is a poet we want in this world for this world is in her as it is in few among us ever. I have been told she hasn't a great readership. Not in size or, perhaps, intensity. Too often we accuse our poets of inattention when the fault is in ourselves. That she deserves readers as intense, as scrupulous, as intelligent, and as rewarding as May Swenson is seems to me as plainly true as the continually unfurling world of her *New And Selected Things Taking Place.* Twenty years ago she wrote of her relationship with the reader and called it "the lightning-string / between your eye and mine." The first poem in this eminent new collection, **"A Navaho Blanket,"** re-engages that paradigmatic image and serves better than any reviewer's words to introduce what she does, who she is, why we are compelled to echo her and cry we want more!

> Eye-dazzlers the Indians weave. Three colors
> are paths that pull you in, and pin you
> to the maze. Brightness makes your eyes jump,
> surveying the geometric field. Alight, and enter
> any of the gates—of Blue, of Red, of Black.
> Be calmed and hooded, a hawk brought down,
> glad to fasten to the forearm of a chief.
>
> You can sleep at the center,
> attended by the Sun that never fades, by Moon
> that cools. Then, slipping free of zigzag and
> hypnotic diamond, find your way out
> by the spirit trail, a faint Green thread that
> secretly crosses the border, where your mind
> is rinsed and returned to you like a white cup.

(pp. 295-96)

Dave Smith, "Perpetual Worlds Taking Place," in Poetry, Vol. CXXXV, No. 5, February, 1980, pp. 291-96.

SVEN BIRKERTS

Reverse chronology appears to be enjoying a vogue among publishers of collections of poetry. I can't see the logic of it myself. If the poet in question has improved over the years, shedding bad habits, widening the reach, then we are apt to get increasingly demoralized as we turn the pages. If, on the other hand, the poet has declined, then the arrangement scarcely serves his best interests—though, admittedly, when that's the case any policy other than self-censorship is a bad one. And if the poet has not so much progressed or declined, has simply changed? Well, then the result can be be quaint, like watching the dog running backward over the lawn while the ball arcs back into the hand; or, provided our study is motion and change, instructive.

May Swenson's *New & Selected Things Taking Place* has been put together in just such a fashion. I read it, as I'd been

trained, in the Christian manner—proceeding from left to right, top to bottom, front to back—and after a time I realized that I was participating in a most curious event: an eclipse of personality. Section by section, I felt voice and expressiveness yielding ground to formal precision. Subject matter was increasingly framed and distanced. I was disappointed, not because I couldn't enjoy the poems themselves, but because I'd missed the experience of the real process behind the career. Where I should have felt some of the exalting sensations of struggle and self-liberation, I traced only diminution. Any transposition I make now is intellectual and *a posteriori.*

Not every reader, I suspect, will agree that the changes in Swenson's poetry represent positive growth. Those with a bias toward strict form might argue that her poems have declined from purity. The early work has a structural self-containment largely absent from recent offerings; artifice is prized. Those who value poetry as a vehicle for personal expression, on the other hand, will want to praise the human event: here is a poet who has, with patience and determination, made her way from a detached fascination with otherness to an increasingly subjective recognition of the self as an agent in the chaotic here and now. The inevitable question arises—what do we cherish more, technical excellence or voice? In Swenson's poetry the latter has been achieved to some extent at the price of the former.

The transformation I would chart is a gradual one, and there are exceptions to the pattern everywhere. I can locate free-spoken lines in *Another Animal,* the earliest included selection, and formal austerities in *Things Taking Place,* the latest. But the overall steady displacement of aesthetic distance by personal involvement seems incontestable. A few sample poems might make my distinction clearer. Here, from *Another Animal,* is "Horse and Swan Feeding":

> Half a swan a horse is
>   how he slants his muzzle to the clover
>   forehead dips in a leaf-lake
>   as she the sweet worm sips
>   spading the velvet mud-moss with her beak
> His chin like another hoof he plants
>   to preen the feathered green
> Up now is tossed her brow from the water-mask
> With airy muscles black and sleek
>   his neck is raised curried with dew
> He shudders to the tail delicately
>   sways his mane wind-hurried
> Shall he sail or stay?
> Her kingly neck on her male
>   imperturbable white steed-like body
>   rides stately away

Note the control. In almost every line the natural flow of the language is subverted, either syntactically, through subject-predicate reversal, or through the elided pronoun ("forehead dips in a leaf-lake"). Persistent artifice, grafted upon the mythic conceit, gives the poem an autonomous character; it is something fashioned *out of* language, not discovered *in* it. The horse has been seen with astonishing accuracy, and the diction expertly serves its ends ("His chin like another hoof he plants" or "Up now is tossed her brow from the water-mask"), but its animal life is passed to us through a mesh woven, at least in part, of the cadences and imaginings of Marianne Moore. Compare it with the first stanza of Moore's "No Swan So Fine":

> "No water so still as the

dead fountains of Versailles." No swan,
with swart blind look askance
and gondoliering legs, so fine
   as the chintz china one with fawn-
brown eyes and toothed gold
collar on to show whose bird it was.

Moore announces her aestheticism, struts it; Swenson is less flamboyant. But in both poems the attention is less focused upon the intrinsic merits of subject, more upon the delays and revelations possible through careful clause manipulation.

Now, from the front of the book, from *Things Taking Place* (and we might remark the two respective titles, the one— *Another Animal*—signaling modest detachment, the other a more embracing sense of activity), [there] is a poem called **"The Willets."** . . .

That Swenson's diction has loosened is obvious immediately. The lines, still tensed, are now open to the event, and the literary nimbus has been blown off. A word like "curried" would be as out of place in this poem as "stupid" would be in its predecessor. But the most fundamental change is of vision. Though both poems belong to the same genre—nature observed—they are are unlike as can be. In **"Horse and Swan Feeding,"** nature has been entirely appropriated by art. **"The Willets,"** while it acknowledges the poet's projections ("in fear she wouldn't stand? . . . "), does not varnish or transform the real event. What's more, it embodies a wisdom, a note of mature reconciliation, that the earlier poem does not. The limitations of language are implicit—we can reflect upon the world around us, but we cannot penetrate its strangeness. What a difference between "white steed-like body/ rides stately away" and "She/ animated. And both went back to fishing." Diction is the least of it. The conceptual gulf is as wide as that between Tennyson and Auden.

Swenson's aesthetic has always been exclusionary. We sense, especially in the early poems, that every choice of subject also involves the deliberate avoidance of other subjects. And in this, I think, her debt to Marianne Moore and the early Elizabeth Bishop is most conspicuous. (One cannot but wonder in what ways aesthetic reticence is bound up with the privacies of sexual preference, whether the line between private and public is not differently drawn.) The complexities of animal life and natural form are eagerly seized upon, while the intricacies of the social order and the human emotions are not so much overlooked as proscribed. Perception sustained; feeling overruled. It is as if the greater part of Swenson's psychic endowment has been channeled into the sense organs, which then become capable of the most precise registrations. The early sections are filled with *tour de force* lines and images, and playful imaginings that are in no way held by the gravitational field of the emotions. In the poem **"At East River,"** for instance, Swenson artfully turns floating gulls into "ballet slippers, dirty-white," points out how a plane "Turns on its elegant heel:/ a spark, a click/ of steel on blue," and concludes by describing Brooklyn as "a shelf of old shoes/ needing repair."

These early poems, outward-looking though they might be, are not all of a kind. Self-exempted from the hazards of voicing emotion, Swenson is free to try on different styles. (Or is this a polite way of saying that she has not yet forged her own distinctive idiom?) In the opening lines of **"Two-Part Pear Able"** (from *A Cage of Spines*), we see her making use of a lucent, Williams-like diction:

In a country where
every tree is a pear tree
it is a shock to see
one tree
(a pear tree undoubtedly
for its leaves are the leaves
of a pear)
that shows no pears

It is a fairly tall tree
sturdy
capable looking
its limbs strong its leaves glossy
its posture in fact exceptionally
pleasing

The play of long "ee" sounds against sharply articulated consonants leaves a vivid impression of etched branches. The very same section, however, also finds her using these clotted lines to characterize a squirrel:

Furry paunch, birchbark-snowy, pinecone-brown back,
   a jacket with sleeves to the digits.
Sat put, pert, neat, in his suit and his seat, for a minute,
   a frown between snub ears—bulb-eyed head
   toward me sideways, chewed.
                            (from **"News From the Cabin"**)

Which would we say is the definitive Swenson? Or should we look instead to the shaped quickness of **"Fountain Piece"**?:

A bird
   is perched
         upon a wing

         The wing
   is stone
   The bird
is real

This is where the perspectives of hindsight turn out to be useful. If we read from the vantage of Swenson's later *Iconographs* phase, then **"Fountain Piece"** is the more prophetic. If, on the other hand, our ear is more attuned to the most recent work, then the cadences, as well as the relaxed presence of the first-person pronoun, of a poem like **"Waiting For It"** will seem to be the truest heralds:

My cat jumps to the windowsill
and sits there still as a jug.
He's waiting for me, but I cannot be
coming, for I am in the room.

His snout, a gloomy V of patience,
pokes out into the sun.
The funnels of his ears expect
to be poured full of my footsteps.

The lines are vigilant and precise, hovering at the edge of humor. The language is transparent, stripped of excess vowels and consonants; the living creature fills the space exactly. Swenson may have tossed human nature out with a pitchfork, but it has found a way in through the back window. The non-human order vibrates at a frequency very near that of the human. A charming domesticity results.

The natural world in Swenson's early poetry is delicately perceived, and its hierarchies are carefully set out. If the household cat reigns over the near end of the spectrum, its counterpart roars at the other:

In the bend of your mouth soft murder
   in the flints of your eyes

the sun-stained openings of caves

(from **"Lion"**)

In the intervals between we come upon pigeons, owls, butterflies, horses, and monkeys, to name a few. Here, though, is one way in which Swenson differs from Moore. Moore would pounce upon the peculiarities of nature, allowing her observations to coax her language to the idiosyncratic extreme. Swenson is more intent upon charting the distance between creature and human; peculiarity is merely a by-product. Thus, the cat is in intimate alliance ("He's waiting for me"), while the squirrel occupies a middle ground—in nature, but wearing "a jacket with sleeves to the digits"—and the lion is emphatically Other: "in the flints of your eyes/ the sun-stained openings of caves."

The animal kingdom is just one part of Swenson's subject. Geographical and geological environments are of nearly equal importance. Her poetry moves freely among the different kinds of urban habitat, but it annexes just as avidly the less-tenanted places—mountains, plains, shores, and waters. She finds poetic material wherever the eye can discover movement or form. And, I might add, the nuances that she fastens upon are predominantly visual; the delicate measuring tool of the ear works to underscore the masses and details of the seen world. One could put together quite an anthology of kinds of settings, moving from city [**"Distance and a Certain Light"**]: . . . to garden [**"A City Garden in April"**]: . . . to lakes [**"A Lake Scene"**]: . . . to the sea (and note here the remarkable interiorization of the imagery):

Slowly a floor rises, almost becomes a wall.
Gently a ceiling slips down, nearly becomes a floor.
A floor with spots that stretch, as on a breathing
animal's hide. It rises again with a soft lurch.

(from **"A Hurricane at Sea"**)

Nor is Swenson content to observe the limits of the terrestrial. There are poems that survey landscape from the air, poems that observe clouds from the windows of a plane, and then, with increasing frequency, poems about the sun, the moon, the galaxies. In more recent work the landing of the Apollo astronauts becomes a topic of some fascination. Swenson delights in rendering the technological penetration of the unearthly in terms of the most archaic human images:

A nipple, our parachute
covers the capsule: an
aureole, on a darker aureole

like the convex spiral of
a mollusc, on a great breast:

(from **" 'So Long' to the Moon from the Men of Apollo"**)

The more adventurously Swenson ranges among the outer universe of images in these poems, the more conspicuous is her rejection of the human subject. So successful is she at keeping her gaze trained outward, that one begins to wonder if she is not in some way using the whole natural world as a correlative for the psyche and its processes. Indeed, couldn't we argue that the psyche is bound to represent itself, its repressed contents, in whatever images it selects, whatever rhythms it convokes? Or is the dissociation of self a better explanation? Eliot, of course, maintained that the progress of the artist was a "continual extinction of personality." But then Eliot did not foresee that posterity would read his poetry with a watchful eye on the individual conspicuously positioned behind the arras of his words. I am not going to debate here whether dissociation or psychic determinism is the key

to interpretation. But Swenson's work, as we shall see, makes the question a live one.

In her contribution to a volume entitled *The Contemporary Poet as Artist and Critic* (1964), in her discussion of fellow formalist Richard Wilbur, Swenson wrote:

The modern lyric is autonomous, a separate mobile, having its own private design and performance. It may be little on the page, yet project a long and versatile dance in the mind. Its total form and gesture is not a relative, it is an absolute, an enclosed construct.

This would have been written at about the time that Swenson published *To Mix With Time: New and Selected Poems* (1963). Her description is striking, for it joins together the precise fixities of something constructed and the fluidity of dance—form and freedom. Certainly she had her own work in mind. As it happens—and as the phrase "a separate mobile" suggests—Swenson was beginning to develop an interest in the semantic possibilities of a poem's appearance. A number of poems in that collection explore the relationship between the look of a poem and its meaning. Some even put the visual and phonic elements on an equal footing, trusting that the disjunction between the seeing and hearing would set up an unexpected propulsion of parts:

They said there was a	Thing
that could not	Change
They could not	Find
it so they	Named
it	God
They had to	Search
so then it must be	There

(from **"God"**)

To my mind, any attempt to subvert the aural foundation of poetry is doomed to failure. Not only is the natural integrity of the genre compromised—for no effective oral performance is possible—but our own allegiances are strained. A poem like this asks us to admire its concept even more than its verbal reality. It is, in a sense, the ultimate attempt to pry poetry loose from the spoken idiom. To make of words "an enclosed construct" is to follow the formalist impulse for its own sake; and pure form, as Hans Castorp discovered on the Magic Mountain, is death.

Swenson continued for a time to move in this direction. Some time after the 1963 collection came *Iconographs,* in which, as is obvious from the title, the visual aspects of the poems were dominant. Some of the artifacts, typographically too complex to be reproduced here, were clearly to be considered as artistic shapes in their own right. Poem and world, form and idiom, were set into opposition.

If we were to draw a figure (how à propos) representing Swenson's poetic development, *Iconographs* would mark—according to bias—either an apogee or a nadir. By insisting that the poem function visually, she drew the elastic to its limit. Since that time, obedient perhaps to the laws of elasticity (otherwise known as "dialectics"), she has been moving decisively in the opposite direction, toward a poetry of natural diction. The change in orientation could not be more complete. I will not presume to theorize about the deeper causes of this change, but a closer look at the shape of some of the *Iconographs* poems might give us some idea about the tensions involved.

400

Let us accept, for argument's sake, that poetry—indeed, any mode of expression—is entirely determined by the forces of the unconscious. We could agree, then, that both the linguistic and visual choices in these poems were responses to specific psychic pressures—in which case, the iconographic features would be most telling. Now, even a glance at the poems in this collection will reveal that a great number of them are in some way fissured or fractured, that their layout strains against the unity implicit in our conception of poetry. . . .

> Stop bleeding   said the knife.
> I would if I   could said the cut.
> Stop bleeding   you make me messy with this blood.
> I'm sorry   said the cut.
> Stop or   I will sink in farther said the knife.
>
> Don't   said the cut.
>
> (from **"Bleeding"**) (pp. 317-27)

Of course, not all of the poems are iconographically split—some essay other effects—but the tendency is pronounced enough to give pause. There is, as I see it, a fundamental contradiction at the heart of the matter. The dominant impulse sponsoring the visual construction is a formal one; it is a desire for aesthetic wholeness and self-containment. Swenson certainly described her lyric ideal unambiguously enough in the sentences I quoted. How is it then that the artifacts themselves are so often emblems of rupture? Does it seem too far-fetched to say that the tension between form-making and form-destroying forces determines this phase of Swenson's career? Or that the obvious movement away from "enclosed construct(s)" in the subsequent poetry marks a victory for the deeper—repressed—demands of the self? The poems in *Things Taking Place* are, with few exceptions, repudiations of the credo cited above. It is almost as if *Iconographs* allowed Swenson to discharge her own imperatives once and for all, as if the artifacts self-destructed out of their own inner necessity, freeing her to move in a new direction.

Things Taking Place, comprising mainly work from the 1970s, is an uneven collection. In some ways it is like a first book, exhibiting that on-off quality that often accompanies a new poet's search for voice. But with this important difference: that the poems that do achieve that expressive synthesis of subject and tone are unquestionably the work of a mature and sophisticated artist. Though there is a paradox here, it shouldn't be too perplexing. For in one very important sense this is a debut. In a long lifetime of writing, Swenson has never before tried to bring her own self forward.

The change is conspicuous, but not dramatic. Readers familiar with Swenson will find many of her customary subjects—there are poems on landscape, animals, the moon landing, and even a few more formal exercises that hearken back to earlier work. But then, alongside this archive of the known, Swenson has included a dozen or so longer pieces that are different from anything she has done before. Not only does she take her own experience as a central subject, but she allows a stubborn and distinctive personal voice to emerge. Restraint has not vanished—hers is not a declamatory "I"—but the ideal of a pure and autonomous poetry has been left behind.

The austerities of observation, once central, are now placed in the service of the voice. Swenson uses the first-person pronoun without coyness or artifice; formerly this could not have happened. Here is a section from an earlier poem called **"Riding the 'A' "**:

> I ride
> the 'A' train
> and feel
> like a ball-
> bearing in a roller skate.
> I have on a gray
> rain-
> coat. The hollow
> of the car
> is gray.

The "I" is a situating device, utterly opaque. Compare this with the opening lines of the recent **"Staying at Ed's Place"**:

> I like being in your apartment, and not disturbing any-
>   thing.
> As in the woods I wouldn't want to move a tree,
> or change the play of sun and shadow on the ground.
> The yellow kitchen stool belongs right there
> against white plaster. I haven't used your purple towel
> because I like the accidental cleft of shade you left in it.

Measured against the best work of a generation of autobiographical poets, this sort of expression does not command special attention. When compared to Swenson's previous work, however, the departure is quite startling.

Swenson begins *Things Taking Place* with a series of poems about travels in the American West. (As she was born in Utah, this could be interpreted as a gesture of homecoming.) Her description of spaces, mountains, and natural detail is calm and loving. Though their subjectivity is tentative, they diverge from previous efforts in that the perceptions are not rendered out of omniscient objectivity, but are controlled by the vantage of the speaker:

> Great dark bodies, the mountains.
> Between them wriggling the canyon road,
> little car, bug-eyed, beaming, goes
> past ticking and snicking of August insects,
> smell of sage and cedar, to a summit of stars.
> Sky glints like fluorescent rock.
> Cloth igloo erected, we huff up our bed,
> listen to the quaking of leaf-hearts
> that, myriad, shadow our sleep.
>
> (from **"The North Rim"**)

The lines have a casual, intimate fall. I would even say that they stray over into cuteness—with the punning "bug-eyed, beaming," and the oddball pairing of "ticking and snicking." Nature is not so much the fierce and fabulous architect as a friendly—though still bewitching—presence. The poet herself, as part of the "we," has moved forward into the middle distance. She is not exactly confessional, but she is *there*.

Throughout *Things Taking Place,* we feel Swenson looking for a comfortable way to lodge herself in her settings. Her most successful mode, and the one that she resorts to most often, is both personable and precise. She gives us the human element, but her incessant detailing keeps us at arm's length from intimacy, even when the situation is relatively "unbuttoned":

> When, squint-eyed from the flashing river,
> we climbed into farmyard shade, I spied
> the squeaking door of a little privy
> of new pine board, among trees beyond
> where the blond horse crops. The bright
> hook worked like silk. One seat, and no wasps,
> it was all mine. An almanac, the pages Bible-thin,
> hung by a string through a hole made with an awl.
> Outside, steady silence, and in

the slit-moon-window, high up, a fragrant
tassel of pine. Alone, at peace, the journey done,
I sat. Feet planted on dependable planks, I sat.
Engrossed by the beauty of the knothole panel before me,
I sat a nice long time.

(from **"The Beauty of the Head"**)

Earlier parts of the poem have set up the relentless swaying of the boat; the square solidity of the privy comes to seem like the very image of heaven—or haven. The delicacy of the description ("The bright/ hook worked like silk." and "An almanac, the pages Bible-thin,/ hung by a string through a hole made with an awl." yields beautifully to the flat, emphatic repetitions of "I sat." My delirious ear hears "satisfaction" and "satiety"; my Swiftian self bids I add: "shat."

Emotion is still problematic for Swenson. While she has begun to address herself and her fellows as subjects, protocols of reserve are studiously observed. When she does allow her gaze to settle on another person, it is generally from a distance, either literal, as in [the] painterly composition [**"Captain Holm"**]: . . . or, as in this poem on the death of her mother, through the scrim of a conceit:

> Mother's work before she died was self-purification,
> a regimen of near-starvation, to be worthy to go
> to Our Father, Whom she confused (or, more aptly, fused)
> with our father, in Heaven long since. She believed
> in evacuation, an often and fierce purgation,
> meant to teach the body to be hollow, that the soul
> may wax plump. At the moment of her death, the wind
> rushed out from all her pipes at once. Throat and rectum
> sang together, a galvanic spasm, hiss of ecstacy.

(from **"That the Soul May Wax Plump"**)

This conflation of the spiritual and profane senses of *pneuma* is not my idea of an emotional farewell. It achieves a note of liberation, but precisely because it bypasses the expected pieties. Swenson's extreme detachment keeps her hovering between the exacerbated directness of Villon and the nervous tittering of Monty Python.

In **"Poet to Tiger,"** Swenson attempts a good-humored love poem. But even here, she cannot free herself for apostrophe before she has turned the object of her affections into a hyperbolic dream-creature. . . .

Still, this is a less restrained Swenson than we're used to seeing. The active pressure of the lines—not to mention their content—shows a woman's determination to assert herself more vigorously. The to-and-fro modulations between dream and wakefulness make it clear that the contest is, at least in some sense, between the unconscious and conscious parts of the self.

Much as I approve Swenson's effort to present more of herself in her poetry, I do not find that she has fully mastered her new voice. For one thing, there are a number of instances—like the mother poem—where she cannot align her address with her subject. She is skillfull when the narration is centered upon material surfaces, but often irritating and unconvincing when [as in **"Watching the Jets Lose to Buffalo at Shea"** and **"Fashion in the 70's"**] she tries her techniques on popular or topical subjects. . . . (pp. 327-32)

This brings me to the heart of my complaint about Swenson. She is a poet of obvious gifts, among them a lively imagination and a most delicate sensory apparatus. But I rarely find her gifts working on behalf of her full sensibility. The material has always been thought through or imagined through; it

has seldom been felt through. The eye does work that the heart should be doing. I cannot speak for everyone, naturally, but I find that poetry not fundamentally rooted in the tears of things is quickly forgotten and seldom, if ever, returned to. Entirely too many of these pieces are of this stamp.

To be fair, though, there are several praiseworthy exceptions; poems, indeed, that distinguish themselves by striking a balance between the inner claim and the external detail. And, as it happens, they tend to be the very poems that take aging and death as their subject. Swenson's reticence and her way with natural images stand her in good stead. In **"October,"** for instance, one of the finest lyrics in the book, she allows the images to hew to the track of the unstated emotion. The yield is an unaffected and clear-sighted eloquence. . . .

The clean observation, always a feature of Swenson's poetry, is no longer serving strictly aesthetic ends. The images, carried by a steady voice, take their place naturally in a procession that is simultaneously outward and inward. We do not have to be told that the landscape is itself *and* the correlative for the past as it presents itself to the memory. The hard-won calm that suffuses the lines could never have been manufactured; the daring of that single "Chuck" certifies that we are in the hands of a genuine poet. I have but one quarrel: that the poem itself belies the final adjuration. Its strength and its grasp of the surrounding world point less to fading than to that singing that comes with the tatters of the mortal dress. Passionate proclamation may yet be in the cards. (pp. 332-34)

Sven Birkerts, "A Versatile Dance in the Mind," in Parnassus: Poetry in Review, *Vols. 12 & 13, Nos. 1 & 2, 1985, pp. 317-34.*

MARY JO SALTER

[May Swenson's new book *In Other Words*] is a welcome addition to a paradoxical oeuvre. Few writers who on occasion strongly remind us of others have created so fully recognizable and inimitable a world. A playful spirit for whom writing is a (very exacting) game—as even the titles of *Poems to Solve* and *More Poems to Solve* suggest—she has in her typographical and syntactical ingenuity recalled, and often surpassed, e.e. cummings. Her penchant for scientific subjects, and her scientist's patience for documentation, evoke Marianne Moore and W. H. Auden. More surprisingly, this very modern poet who exuberantly breaks lines, and rules, in unexpected places takes one back to the 17th century—to the far sterner-minded George Herbert—to find another poet so dedicated to fashioning the right form for the fresh occasion each poem presents.

The poet whose presence we most sense behind the shoulder of *In Other Words,* however, is Swenson's friend, the late Elizabeth Bishop. The first poem, **"In Florida,"** immediately—and deliberately, one assumes—draws one back to the lushness and lists of Bishop's "Florida." (Bishop catalogs seashells; Swenson, flowers.) In the elegiac **"In the Bodies of Words,"** Swenson walks a beach—a favorite Bishop setting—and meets the bird of Bishop's "Sandpiper" reincarnated, as it were: "your pipers, Elizabeth!" If Swenson's **"Waterbird"** (perhaps an oblique homage to Bishop's waterbirds), too, shows how much these two poets shared—a keen visual perception, particularly of the natural world; a passion for the exotic; a capacity for self-effacement—it also points to some ingrained differences.

Few readers would dispute Bishop's ultimate superiority: with an unassuming dexterity similar to Swenson's, she achieved a much wider and darker range of feeling, often in a single poem. Yet credit must go where it is due. Bishop, whose ear was as fine-tuned as Swenson's, but who shied from superfluity, would probably not have rhymed "otter" with "water" twice in an 18-line poem, as Swenson does successfully here. Indeed, the word "water" actually appears as an end word three times, and the repetitive effect is heightened by internal rhymes: "her cry,/ a slatted clatter . . . " Swenson—like the poet she frequently resembles more than she does Bishop, Gerard Manley Hopkins—combines a fine sense of musical proportion with a conviction that excess can sometimes only be justified by further excess. If this high-spirited musical density, in which melody is written not in single notes but in chords, robs Swenson of the "naturalness" of tone Bishop so skillfully cultivated, one can only observe that Swenson rarely wishes to cultivate the natural. By the time **"Waterbird"** ends, we are entirely hers, entrapped in a net of aural cross-references:

> She flaps up to dry on the crooked, look-dead limb
> of the Gumbo Limbo, her tan-tipped wing fans
> spread, tail a shut fan dangled.

In Other Words offers scores of equally felicitous word couplings and triplings. Repetition means not monotony but enhancement, as in "a white pontoon plane / putt-putts, puts down / into choppy furrows / of the bay" or "My clever Cockatoo, too, had a parrot's / longevity." The neat classifications of assonance, consonance, rhyme, and off-rhyme blur into virtual uselessness; often in a single instance, Swenson conflates three or four of them. Take, for instance, the finale of another poem (whose title is a sonic illustration of what's to come), **"Goodbye, Goldeneye"**:

> And goodbye, oh faithful pair of
> swans that used to glide—god and goddess
> shapes of purity—over the wide water.

Goodbye/glide/god/goddess are all cousins; but so are glide/wide and (cousins two lines removed) pair/purity. Note too how "glide" enacts its meaning on the current of the long dash that follows it. (p. 40)

Because Swenson's poems are so beautiful to listen to, one is continually surprised, and relieved, that they are rarely "pretty." . . . Even the most admiring reader, however, might reasonably wish that a poet of Swenson's enviable powers would apply them to loftier or deeper subjects than she customarily chooses. There are slight poems here about a blood test, about a houseful of bear rugs and teddy bears, even about the quality of the wrapping string on a package. Such poems, despite the pleasure individual lines afford, sit uncomfortably beside a small lyric that enlarges the spirit such as **"Waterbird."**

And yet whenever Swenson turns her hand to more "ambitious" poems (or at least lengthier ones), the results suggest that she is, for better or worse, more the poet of the well-wrought phrase than of the well-developed idea. *In Other Words* extends the Swenson tradition of writing about astronomy and space travel—large subjects indeed—but I found myself more taken with her chanting in the brief **"Comet Watch on Indian Key"** ("Halley's Comet . . . Comet / coming. Coming again") than with the extensive, reportorial, five-part **"Shuttles,"** which ends with the disastrous launch of the Challenger. Written on the occasion of five shuttle launches from 1981 to 1986 (there were actually six, but "I

missed the third," she admits engagingly), the poem seems less shaped than accreted; while one shudders at the final line (*"They were alive. They knew."*—her italics), one's discomfort may well result more from recollections of the event than from this retelling.

Another long poem, **"Some Quadrangles,"** written for the 1982 Phi Beta Kappa exercises at Harvard, falls flat when it attempts moral uplift. . . . And the longest, concluding poem, **"Banyan,"** a bizarre and imaginative speculation on the newspaper story of a cockatoo that disappeared from its cage and then, apparently, locked itself up again, is richer in manner ("this necromancer / proliferating like a cancer") than in matter ("The purpose of life is / To find the purpose of life").

Ambition is large but does not necessarily, in a poet, take long to prove. Swenson sometimes best demonstrates her ambition and accomplishment in poems that are not only short but light. A section modestly called "Comics" contains some of the finest work in the book. . . . (pp. 40-1)

We have too few comic poets. Swenson provides comedy in two senses: marrying her words off in one happy ending after another, she makes us laugh as she does so. But whether she writes in jest or in earnest, she belongs to that rare company of poets who convert the arbitrary correspondences among the sounds of words into what seems a pre-existing order. *In Other Words* confirms that there are no words other than her own, exactly, for what the language discovers in May Swenson, or for what she gives back to it. (p. 41)

> Mary Jo Salter, "No Other Words," in The New Republic, Vol. 198, No. 10, March 7, 1988, pp. 40-1.

DENNIS SAMPSON

Nobody writes poetry quite like May Swenson anymore. She is a genuine anomaly: mischievous, inquisitive in the extreme, and totally given over to the task of witnessing the physical world. In **"Goodbye, Goldeneye"** from [*In Other Words*], . . . she mourns the intrusion of rude humanity on one of her favorite haunts, the shore facing the ocean:

> So, goodbye, goldeneye, and grebe and
>   scaup and loon.
> Goodbye, morning walks beside the tide
>   tinkling
>
> among clean pebbles, blue mussel shells
>   and snail
> shells that look like staring eyeballs.
>   Goodbye,
> kingfisher, little green, black crowned
>   heron,

> snowy egret. And, goodbye, oh faithful pair of
> swans that used to glide—god and goddess
> shapes of purity—over the wide water.

Swenson's remorse is genuine, as is her deep and abiding fondness for all living creatures. Her most obvious precursor is Marianne Moore. Unlike Moore, she rarely makes literary allusions (she does have a fine poem here addressed to Elizabeth Bishop upon hearing of her death), yet she shares Moore's enthusiasm for detail, especially as it pertains to nature.

Never solemn or self-indulgent, eschewing the big finale,

Swenson is intent on noticing everything around her while preferring herself to remain in the wings. Sometimes she subjugates the self to such an extent that it may seem on the verge of disappearing altogether from the poem. But her language is so sensuous and her eye so exacting, one instead comes away from her writing feeling one has been in the presence of a mind as comprehensive as Darwin's, as chimerical as Herbert's or Dickinson's, as felicitous as Donne's. When the self does emerge, the effect can be fairly startling, as in **"A New Pair,"** where presumably two swans are being described. Near the end of the poem she says,

> One tall neck dips, is laid along the other's back,
> at the place where an arm would embrace.
>
> A brief caress. Then both sinuous necks arise,
> their paddle feet fall to water. As I stare,
> with independent purpose at full sail, they steer
> apart.

A person from another planet reading her poetry might believe there were no wars on Earth and that death and the postmortem realm do not receive here the kind of attention we in fact spend on them. Only infrequently do we get to see the darker side of Swenson, as in this passage from an otherwise unsuccessful poem about the recent space shuttle catastrophe:

> One morning, on the beach near Canaveral, a navy
>   blue sock
> washed up. In it, a fragment of bone and human tissue.
> Evidence without connection . . .

And in the penultimate stanza of **"In Florida,"** having provided the reader with a lush description of the landscape, she pans in on a litter of kittens underneath the porch:

> To behold the tableau, get on your knees,
> put an eye to the widest crack between boards,
>   where Polar
> in the half-dark with her brood patiently endures.

Other poems experiment with shape, there is a quirky novel of four pages written in verse, a mock prose-poem of some length—yet no matter where you open this book you find the authentic voice of the poet, unashamedly translating the world. (pp. 387-88)

> *Dennis Sampson, in a review of "In Other Words,"*
> *in* The Hudson Review, *Vol. XLI, No. 2, Summer,*
> *1988, pp. 387-88.*

LINDA GREGERSON

"The soul in paraphrase" was Herbert's happy paraphrase for the devotional discipline he called "prayer" and the poetry we call "metaphysical." May Swenson has called her latest book **In Other Words,** thus reinscribing the poetry of paraphrase and conspicuously gesturing toward that prior book whose words are the originals of humanity's "others." Bacon called that prior book the book of nature. May Swenson might be prepared to call it that as well. Certainly the better half of her poems devotedly inventories the sensuous and sensible aspect of things. And this work is dense with a double materiality: that of language—heavily paratactic, maximally alliterative—and that of the observable world. In her descriptive mode, the poet's insistent treatment of sounds as things—her heaping up of syntactical and metrical abut-

ments, of echoing vocables, of appositional metaphors—seems quite palpably to be an act of invocation. . . . (p. 233)

The soul in paraphrase is the soul at risk, the soul out on a limb. And in the final section of **In Other Words,** the poet takes to the branches of a banyan tree for a 33-page allegorical sojourn. The tree the poem is named for sends out a parasitic sprawl of root and branch: the poem propagates analogously, by means of sprawling high-and low-cultural spoofs. Its narrator, who assumes the contours of a woolly monkey for the duration of the fable, takes as her consort a white cockatoo, whom she acquires by jailbreak from a cage in the municipal library in Coconut Grove, Florida. These heroines, Tonto and Blondi, make a mixed marriage of the sort that used to unfold in comic strips when wives were always buxom or on prime time when a masked white man was sure to command loyalty among the nobler specimens of a primitive race. The mission of the poem, however, is neither domestic subversion nor freelance outback justice but a sequestered meditation on "the purpose of life." The cockatoo, fresh from its library, provides an endless stock of literary tags: the fable makes glancing allusion to famous plots from that of *Paradise Lost* to that of "The Murders in the Rue Morgue." In a climactic mirror vision, the cockatoo and the monkey are revealed to be two of the Ages of Woman, the one (the bird) an old-fashioned, new-minted child of two, the other (the primate) a figure of brutal decrepitude:

> Her stomach poked out and sagged, partly hiding
>   her slumped,
> hairless pudenda, and her flattened breasts hung,
>   the left longer
> than the right. . . . Arms and lower legs were thin,
>   but the
> flaccid thighs, the buttocks and the coil of fat at the
>   waist hung
> in jelly-like bags.

The poem's mild-mannered deployment of cultural cliché and cultural satire only feebly prepares us for this harsh naysaying to vanity's wish for transcendence. And as coda to this vision, Halley's comet appears, the span between its anticlimactic returns just the length of a human being's decline into age. Clipped-winged, the cockatoo returns to its cage and succumbs to genre, intoning its new tag phrase oracularly: "The purpose of life is/ To find the purpose of life." This collapse into tautology is meant to resonate with the achieved tenor of spiritual quest: the chastened spirit recording its dilemma in a partial breakdown of language. But the breakdown of language here is something more mundane than a crisis of faith would account for, and the poem's ironic strategies do not quite solve the tonal problems of prolonged self-dramatization. (pp. 233-34)

Despite her title, and despite her devotion to banyan, cockatoo, saguaro, and egret, Swenson does not submit her "other words" as a form of deference to some prior order. Taking the world of nature and the world of words for her twin playgrounds, she flaunts poetic conceit and poetic prerogative. A thing is so because she's taken a fancy to saying it's so. The waterbird's tail may be "a shut fan dangled," a family of egrets may be "Three White Vases," snow may be "an ermine floor," and saguaro may be shamelessly anthropomorphized ("Flowers come out of their ears"). Metaphor in these poems is a celebratory exercise in ingenious ornament, immoderate, unreclaimed. In their sprightly disregard for decorum, these ornaments resemble the metaphysical conceit but, unlike the metaphysical conceit, they exhibit no strenuousness and no catalytic capacity. Swenson has no interest in the labor that makes of metaphor an argument or metamorphosis. Hers are frictionless conceits for the most part, the mind's eye eyeing its own pleasure; poetic figure delightfully embellishes but does not alter or explicate the underlying object of regard. There are exceptions, of course, as in **"Eclipse Morning,"** where the sequence of mixed and overdetermined metaphors both mimics and manifests the difficulty of accommodating solar eclipse to the scale of earthly comprehension, or in **"A Day Like Rousseau's *Dream*,** where the female genitalia, "a pod of white unpainted canvas," are at once the center of revery and the space that eludes it. For the most part, Swenson's poetic project finds its fable in **"A Thank-You Letter,"** where the gift consists of its wrapping—a "cradle of string" and its durable transformations—not in any posited "inside." Stanza after pleasurable stanza, Swenson's poems find shapeliness in self-reference and pure assertion: well-wrought vases made from a glimpse of egrets.

There are dangers in this imperturbable refusal to measure the figural imagination by its service to argument. When image fails in its magic, the language quite simply misfires. While **"Shift of Scene at Grandstand"** doggedly pursues its inert equation of seasonal change and theatrical scene shift, more delicately nuanced observation is overwhelmed. Though **"Shuttles"** does eventually marshall a fairly lively indictment of the phallic imperialism embodied in the American space program, it first bogs down in a great deal of ill-regulated jargon: "All systems are Go" and so forth. In **"Strawberrying,"** a late-season excursion to the berry fields is glossed with the language of violence and predation (the picker's hands are "murder red"; gray berries are "families smothered as at Pompeii"), but the metaphoric subplot, for all its hyperbole, remains inconsequent. (pp. 235-36)

[In **"Blood Test"**] Swenson records a scene of strictly contextualized intimacy between two persons of different sex, race, and professional expertise, his on display in the phlebotomy lab, hers in the poem that renders it. Amidst this quiet negotiation of curiosity and power and vulnerability, the "Big Paw" and the "black chamois wrist" are not trespasses in any simple sense, but neither are they retrieved from trespass by the expressed desire to be a bearcub "in his arms." Immersed in the transcription of her home-spun phenomenology, the poet, like her kindred, the tourist and the colonialist and the ethnographer, casts a proprietary eye on the spectacle of cultivated estrangement. And though the implications of its own methodology are actively ignored in this poem, poetic conceit is by nature an appropriative move. In this instance, the subject with whom metaphoric liberty is taken is neither a cactus nor a waterbird but a member of the race whose own liberties have been, repeatedly and to our shame, conspicuously abridged; this subject, moreover, belongs to a professional class (he is a medical technician) whose authority is all too easily overridden by the retrospective authority of the poet.

The clichés of estrangement, including the ameliorative fantasy of desire with which the poem closes, have an extrapoetical history and an extrapoetical politics of which this poem pretends to be innocent. But look what innocence produces: the artificial and unconvincing sequestration of politicized subject and poetic method allow cliché to hold uncontested sway. And between the races, between the classes, between the sexes, as history has taught us, cliché is a dangerous thing. Innocence will not always serve. I am sorry to say it.

Where Swenson's methods *are* transformative, and delightfully so, is in the territory she modestly refers to as "comics." In a Halloween poem, Swenson renders the season's propitiatory masking by pursuing a child's game of switched consonants: "The roldengod and the soneyhuckle,/ the sack eyed blusan and the wistle theed" work their sweet mischief in **"A Nosty Fright,"** where the "nasty fright" we summon for pleasure's sake lurks very obligingly behind the "frosty night." And when has the ghost of Gertrude Stein been more happily heard from? In **"Giraffe,"** which the poet calls *"A Novel,"* she sets language before us in all its emphatic thingness: "Giraffe is the first word in this chapter. Is is the second word," and so forth. The project that appears so frontal soon becomes sly: "Is is the second word is the second sentence in the first chapter," for instance. That sentence appears at first to be a misprint for its equally accurate but more facile second cousin ("Is is the second word *in* the second sentence in the first chapter"), but it is we, not the typesetters, who have faltered. The more fully the poem turns its back on the world of conventional signifying, the more fully it claims to be a world unto itself. As long as the layers of self-reflection and reification are backward looking, the poem called a novel still safely endorses our expectations of referentiality. But with **"Chapter 7"** ("This is the first word in this chapter and the third and seventy-fifth word in the tenth chapter") the reification becomes anticipatory. Summarizing the past and the future in a single arc, the poem completes its divorce from the world of referents and wraps itself in imperturbable closure.

The rigors here, as must be clear, are of the sort that animate a ledger sheet: the playfulness is not calculated to inspire affection. **"Giraffe"** works in territory that has been very cumbersomely theorized of late: it works with the simplest of tools and with immutable composure. And its virtuosity lies in this, that the poem's "other words" are the only ones sufficient to its cause. What is the measure of truth in these sentences? Self-reference alone, except for that supernumerary, the giraffe—the useless one, the beautiful, the one with nothing to graze upon, the one with the lofty view. (pp. 237-38)

Linda Gregerson, "A Cradle of String," in Poetry, *Vol. CLIV, No. 4, July, 1989, pp. 233-38.*

Sue Townsend

1946-

English novelist, dramatist, scriptwriter, and essayist.

Townsend's plays and novels are humorous social commentaries that often focus on the sense of inferiority she believes is felt by England's lower classes. Described by Jonathan Keates as "larky, sparky, and demotic to her fingers' ends," Townsend treats bleakness in everyday life with a blend of satire and pathos that effectively conveys hope rather than melancholy. She stated: "In a sense, I'm only interested in writing about deeply sad and important things. But I have this curse that I can only express it through humour." Related primarily from a feminist perspective, Townsend's concerns of liberation and independence are rooted in her deeply unhappy childhood and early marriage. Her father passed away when she was eight years old, and his death was not explained to Townsend and her two sisters. Three years later, their mother remarried and maintained that the children's stepfather was their real father. Townsend left school at fourteen, was soon married, and bore three children. Her husband deserted the family when Townsend was in her twenties. Accordingly, the males in Townsend's plays and novels are often weak and ineffectual, while the women are vibrant and strong.

Although Townsend was relatively unfamiliar to the British public before the enormous success of her novel *The Secret Diary of Adrian Mole, Aged 13 ¾* and its sequel, *The Growing Pains of Adrian Mole,* she originally wrote tragicomic plays concerning contemporary social ills. Her first play, *Womberang,* tackles Great Britain's socialized medicine program. Neglected in a hospital waiting room, several gynecological patients are rallied by Rita Onions, a boisterous, irrepressible woman, who inspires them to overpower hospital authorities and to take command of their own lives. The farcical, highly acclaimed *Bazaar and Rummage* revolves around a self-help group of agoraphobics and their efforts to hold a garage sale. With compassion and irony, Townsend illustrates how a social worker's lust for control leads her to exploit the group's anxieties to fulfill her own neurotic needs. *Groping for Words,* also critically praised, examines adult illiteracy. In this play, uneducated characters concoct elaborate ruses to hide their handicap before learning of literacy's liberating potential.

Townsend's most famous creation, the long-suffering, melodramatic adolescent Adrian Mole, became a phenomenon in England after being introduced in a thirty-minute radio script titled *Nigel Mole's Diary.* The two novels known as the *Adrian Mole Diaries* have sold over five million copies in England alone, have been translated into twenty-two languages, and have spawned two television series and a stage musical. Much of the humor in these works derives from Adrian's deadpan, naive reactions to life. Critics have compared the personality and widespread popularity of Townsend's young protagonist to Holden Caulfield, the misunderstood voice of youth in J. D. Salinger's *The Catcher in the Rye.* Like Holden, Adrian is an emotionally neglected idealist seeking stable personal relationships. The first Mole book, *The Secret Diary of Adrian Mole, Aged 13¾,* chronicles approximately a year of the boy's daily life up to his fifteenth birthday. Most of Adrian's

musings consist of normal, adolescent angst: his unrequited love for Pandora, a classmate of higher social status; his worries about the length of his penis and his plethora of pimples; and his terror of the neighborhood bully, Barry Kent. Adrian writes: "I don't see how there can be a God. If there was surely he wouldn't let people like Barry Kent walk about menacing intellectuals? . . . When I go to university I may study the problem. I will have my thesis published and I will send a copy to Barry Kent. Perhaps by then he will have learnt to read." Believing he is an undiscovered poetic genius, Adrian sends horrid poems to the British Broadcasting Corporation, receiving kind but firm rejections from the BBC head of drama, John Tydeman, who actually wrote his own replies for the book. Adrian joins the Good Samaritans club at school and is assigned to care for Bert Baxter, a surly, hard-drinking octogenarian who, along with Adrian's austere grandmother, give the youth the stability he desperately needs. Adrian is the child of an unhappy marriage, and it is his parents' precarious relationship and extramarital affairs that constitute the core of the novel's informal plot. Townsend implements role reversal, portraying Adrian as a worrisome, responsible character striving for competency and obsessive about health and ethics, while the adults, children of the 1960s, are permissive and hedonistic.

Both *The Secret Diary* and its sequel, *The Growing Pains of Adrian Mole,* are scathing satires of England under Margaret Thatcher's leadership. A critic for *The Listener* observed: "Adrian Mole is no real lad . . . but a comic yet revelatory distorting mirror of adult preoccupations and problems in the emasculated Eighties." In *The Growing Pains of Adrian Mole,* rising unemployment rates and the declining welfare state both play crucial roles in the family's despair. Adrian's father is laid off and unable to find another job. Adrian becomes more frustrated with the state of his country, and such concerns as the Falklands War and the bigotry experienced by a neighborhood Pakistani family are discussed in his diary. In an early record, Adrian is joyous over the royal wedding of Prince Charles and Lady Diana: "We truly lead the world when it comes to pageantry! I must admit to having tears in my eyes when I saw all the cockneys who had stood since dawn, cheering heartily all the rich, well-dressed, famous people going by in carriages and Rolls-Royces." Approximately a year later, however, when his class greets the school headmaster's servile announcement of the birth of Prince William with sarcasm and anger, Adrian begins to realize the irony of working-class support of the monarchy. Eventually, Adrian's persistent love for Pandora is finally requited, and his poems, containing lines such as "Norway! Land of difficult spelling / Hiding your beauty behind strange vowels," are steadily rejected. His rebelliousness grows as he defies his school's dress code, supports a teacher who writes "Three million unemployed" upon the cleavage in a portrait of Thatcher, and helps his pregnant mother deal with the rigidness of the Department of Health and Social Services. William Grimes asserted: "What makes the diaries something more [than harmless fun] is their sharply observed social realism, which gives, in quick takes, a picture of shabby lower-middle-class life in the English Midlands. It succeeds brilliantly in conveying the texture of life among Britain's 'nouveau poor' (as Adrian's mother refers to the Mole family)."

Rebuilding Coventry, Townsend's first novel after the Mole books, also makes use of diary entries as a narrative technique. Coventry Dakin, a British housewife, invents an alterego, Lauren Skye, to overcome the boredom in her life. Lauren authors a secret diary in which she refers to Coventry's husband and children as "the drearies." Coventry's life undergoes a drastic change when she accidentally crushes her loutish neighbor's soft skull with an Action Man doll and must flee a murder charge. Coventry escapes to London, where picaresque adventures free her from her vapid, domestic life. Receiving mixed reviews, the novel was faulted for grossly exaggerated characterizations while winning praise for acute observations. Anne Smith commented: "[In Coventry, Townsend] has found the perfect character through which to express not only her humorous view of the human condition, but also her cut-the-shit perceptions of contemporary Britain." She added: "Everything in *Rebuilding Coventry* is done with ruthlessly satisfying economy. This is satire in the best, Jonsonian tradition, with nothing and no one spared."

Townsend has also published a collection of essays and short fiction, *True Confessions of Adrian Albert Mole, Margaret Hilda Roberts, and Susan Lilian Townsend,* in which she discusses her trip to the Soviet Union and offers glimpses of Adrian at age twenty-one. Still living at home, he has been fired from the public library for shelving Jane Austen's works in the Light Romances section and is infatuated with Sarah Ferguson, the Duchess of York. Maintaining her concern

with Great Britain's unjust class system, Townsend's recent play, *Ten Tiny Fingers, Nine Tiny Toes,* examines a futuristic England where only certain socio-economic groups are allowed to procreate.

(See also *Contemporary Authors,* Vols. 119, 127 and *Something about the Author,* Vols. 48, 55.)

PRINCIPAL WORKS

PLAYS

Womberang   1980
Dayroom   1981
The Ghost of Daniel Lambert   1981
Bazaar and Rummage   1982
Captain Christmas and the Evil Adults   1982
Are You Sitting Comfortably   1983
Groping for Words   1983
The Great Celestial Cow   1984
The Secret Diary of Adrian Mole, Aged 13 ¾   1984
Ten Tiny Fingers, Nine Tiny Toes   1989

NOVELS

The Secret Diary of Adrian Mole, Aged 13 ¾   1982
The Growing Pains of Adrian Mole   1984
The Adrian Mole Diaries   1985
Rebuilding Coventry   1988

OTHER

Nigel Mole's Diary   (radio script)   1982
Bazaar and Rummage   (television play)   1983
Bazaar and Rummage, Groping for Words, Womberang: Three Plays   (play collection)   1984
The Secret Diary of Adrian Mole   (television series)   1986
CounterBlasts No. 9: Mr. Bevan's Dream   (essays)   1989
True Confessions of Adrian Albert Mole, Margaret Hilda Roberts and Susan Lilian Townsend   (essays, short fiction)   1989

MARION GLASTONBURY

At last: a wit to touch the hearts of three generations. [In Sue Townsend's *The Secret Diary of Adrian Mole, Aged 13 ¾*], Adrian Mole, poet, Dinner Monitor and pensioner's friend, suffers from an irritable, low-income father who neglects his appearance, and a newly assertive mother whose disregard of nutrition undermines her family's health. Worse, she turns 'wanton' and goes off with a neighbour, leaving a broken home to the ministrations of a stalwart grandmother and a neurotic dog.

In the long run, this trauma does everyone good. Adrian reads Orwell and Germaine Greer, unblocks drains and acquires other domestic skills, enlists the Samaritans' help with his homework, encounters doctors, vets, youth workers and officials from the Electricity Board, and covers the Noddy wallpaper in his bedroom with black vinyl paint. At school, he edits an unmarketable magazine, acts Joseph in an experimental Nativity play, and campaigns against uniform-socks, with the support and inspiration of Pandora who joins the

Women's Group at which his reformed father manages the crèche.

On occasion, the Midland Moles resemble Posy Simmonds's Londoners: the timeless truths of desire and jealousy are presented in a similarly topical context. Parental gloom persists despite news of the Royal pregnancy; and Adrian fails a geography test when he claims that the Falklands belong to Argentina. The author's accuracy and comic timing left me wincing with pleasure and strengthened in the belief that Adrian's dauntless peers will successfully withstand current assaults, not least the phasing out of hot meals at midday: 'Perhaps Mrs Thatcher wants us to be too weak to demonstrate in years to come.'

Marion Glastonbury, "Against All Odds," in New Statesman, Vol. 104, No. 2697, November 26, 1982, p. 26.

JOHN LAHR

When she was a schoolgirl in Leicester, England, Sue Townsend made people laugh for 3p each. Always a reluctant exhibitionist, Townsend learned early that being manic was the best way to hide panic. At school, the kids queued to hear her and a friend send up their teachers. Twenty-two years on, having written secretly until 1978, her wit is an event drawing bigger crowds. Townsend's *The Secret Diary of Adrian Mole Aged 13 ¾* has made her a kind of comic phenomena. . . . (p. 474)

Townsend's laughter, like her face, is etched in pain. Abandoned in her twenties with three children under five and hospitalised with various ailments including tuberculosis of the stomach, Townsend "expects pain—it feels normal to me." But courage wants to laugh; and Townsend's humour comes out of her inheritance of aggression and fear. She is that oddest of theatrical hybrids—a female trickster capable of throwing her voice into the persona of a teenage chauvinist like Mole (the final image in his diary is the trickster's emblem of anarchy—a penis made from birthday balloons) or creating a comic whirlwind like Rita Onions in *Womberang* (1978) who turns a gynaecological clinic upside down. All her plays culminate in some sort of mayhem. "I like to have a go at everybody," she says, "especially the trendy left who are only interested in the marxist poor."

This appetite for combat is part of a comedian's chemistry, a vindictive triumph in play over the forces of personal oppression. Townsend's childhood was so strange and unsettling in its fierce repressions that she still gets nervous talking about it. "I was always fearful of authority. I was in a constant state of fear. I think I had the earliest nervous breakdown known to child or woman."

Her father died when she was eight, but none of the three children were told. Friends assembled at the house but the children were sent to school. Afterwards, no mention was made of the father's absence and no emotion shown. When Townsend was eleven, her mother remarried. Again, the children weren't told. "There was a wedding cake on the table when we got up one morning, and the same people who were at the funeral were at the wedding."

To this day, Townsend's mother and stepfather maintain the fantasy that the three sisters are his real children. The conspiracy of parental silence left its mark on Townsend. Even now the thought of breaking the parental taboo to talk about her family scares her. She lights another cigarette. "I grew up thinking you couldn't trust adults. The whole thing was a lie. Fear kept me from speaking out. It was written into the atmosphere of family life that you didn't ask questions."

Womberang, Townsend's first play, is a daydream of mastered fear; and her heroine, Rita Onions, acts out the trickster's ambition to be lethal. Rita is a catalyst for action and change. Ignored by the hospital clerk, she pulls a bell out of her bag and rings it. "Don't you know it's bad manners to ignore people?" she says. Rita pronounces herself loudly to the world and gets the other timid clinic patients around her finally to do the same.

"I never exhibit the kind of freedom Rita does," says Townsend, whose first husband never knew she wrote and who was so timid about showing *Womberang* to the Phoenix Arts writers' group in Leicester that she waited six weeks before submitting the play, written in block capitals and held together with a nappy pin.

Rita is Townsend's notion of pure freedom, the "epitome of relaxation" who puts others at ease and gives them courage to face themselves. She literally intoxicates the women in the waiting room, getting them to remove their burdens from corsets to husbands, getting them to dance, to admit their failure to talk. "All I do is speak my mind," she says.

The activity goes to the heart of Townsend's anxiety, allowing her stage surrogate to accomplish what she could never do in life: say the unsayable. Rita breaks the conspiracy of silence. The hospital staff see her as "the agent of the devil"; but she rightly calls herself an "activist." Her real liberation is a clown's victory: the liberation from fear.

"Womberang," says Townsend, "is saying you don't have to be pushed around; you can talk back; you can have some control over your life." But in her life Townsend wasn't practising what she preached. "I was reacting to things. I was a leaf in the wind." That year she wrote a list of the things that made her unhappy and that she was determined not to be scared of: Typing/Driving/Heights/Water. She stopped typing and driving. She went on a mountaineering course and a white-water canoeing course which she's now qualified to teach. On the course, she also met the man with whom she now lives, who encouraged her to show her writing.

"I never thought I'd be a writer," says Townsend. . . . "We lived in a prefab. My parents were on the buses. I left school at 15. How could you want to write a book? You didn't hope or dream because you didn't want to be disappointed. Sometimes I feel like two different people."

What Townsend calls "the sense of inferiority that comes with class" stokes the terror and farce behind the situations she's drawn to write about: a lower middle class boy with social ambitions, a self-help group of agoraphobics, the subterfuge of adult illiterates trying to evade the judgment of the bourgeois world. Sitting in a Hampstead kitchen, there is no hint of her working class background in the educated tones of her voice. "I hate myself because it's gone, going," she says. But at her children's comprehensive, where her work is not known, teachers still condescend to her. She doesn't disabuse them: being between two worlds feeds the mischievousness of her comic voice.

In her early life, Townsend detached herself from the judgment of others by her obsessive reading and by imagining the sources of anxiety as tiny specks in the universe. Now laughter creates that distance, deflating fear while exposing the patterns that create it. Mole's diary is *secret,* as Townsend's writing was for so long, a means by which a brittle ego can assert its longings, fears and angers, and dummy-up a sense of destiny without being discounted.

An adolescent Pooter, Mole's diary also helps him sustain the illusion that he's in detached control of the confusing things that happen around him. Using the memory of her own arrogant teenage voice, Townsend teases Mole's ignorance ("Nigel said the end of the world is coming. He said the moon is having a total collapse") and the poignance of his social pretentions with his father on the dole:

"*Sunday 27 February:* Had egg and chips and peas for Sunday dinner! No pudding! Not even a proper serviette. My mother says we're the *nouveau poor.*"

"I didn't want too many bizarre things in the book. I wanted very dull, ordinary things," Townsend says of Mole's life, which consists mostly of his unrequited love of Pandora, his parents' on-again, off-again marriage and a chronic case of acne. "I wanted it to be comforting." By dramatising fear, Townsend encourages people to see problems not as personal failures but as part of a larger social pattern.

In *Womberang,* Townsend shows how institutions infantalise people; and in her excellent *Bazaar and Rummage* (1982), a play with music about agoraphobics lured out of their isolation to run a jumble sale, Townsend shows how volunteer social workers manipulate their clients' panic for their own neurotic needs.

"You've got to do what Gwenda says. She's in charge of us," says the ex-singer Katrina who has taken to her house after being pelted by plastic pineapples at a gig some years before. Gwenda is the Malvolio of Townsend's talented dissection of panic. An hysteric "who absolutely adores crisis," Gwenda's social life is this collection of walking wounded whom she keeps in place with put-downs and pills. "They're extremely effective on naughty children and unhappy women," Gwenda says of tranquilisers to the widow she's aptly dubbed Bell-Bell.

Townsend's sense of anger moves the play inevitably towards farce, a genre to which all her work aspires. "I'm incredibly aggressive. I don't like to admit it or show it," she says of herself. She lets laughter take revenge for her. She skewers Gwenda in a few lines of inspired dialogue. "Oh, I'm so tired," says Gwenda. "I've been on the go since six. My teasmade ejaculated prematurely." Gwenda has colonised the women, keeping them apart and talking to each other on the phone. Face to face, they give each other courage and information. Gwenda loses control over them.

Townsend invents a hilarious mini-opera as a first act finale for the ladies while they set out their jumble, and engineers a second act transformation for a foul-mouthed "troublemaker" called Margaret as she's decked out in one of Katrina's slinky frocks to face the world. The brilliant theatricality of these scenes shows women finding the energy to impose themselves on life.

At the finale, the ladies take their first tentative steps outside the hall. "The public can be so fickle once they turn," says Katrina as she exits. The stage directions insist the ladies "are

not cured of their agoraphobia." But they are learning to be free of fear and the judgment of others. And that is their liberation. The play's last line is comedy's eternal grace note of hope: "Cheer up."

In 1977, unable to escape the pressure of living up to other people's expectations on the showcase estate of Eyres Mansell, Townsend moved into the more "neutral" black and poor white estate of Highfields. "People there can't quite figure out what I do for a living. A lot think I'm a prostitute because I come and go to the railway station at odd hours."

In *Groping for Words,* a powerful play . . . about adult literacy and the tragic/comic ruses with which illustrates hide their handicaps, Townsend examines this terror of social judgment as a means of keeping the working class in its place. "They don't want us to read! There ain't room for all of us, is there?" says the young caretaker, Kevin . . ., who can't even read the letter firing him from his job.

Townsend understands education as a form of social control. "I'm not unique," she says. "Those kids I used to work with were quick, bright, inquisitive, witty. Where did it go? It used to go into the factories and warehouses. Now it goes nowhere." In *Groping for Words,* she lets George, the vagrant who wants to read and write so he can keep in touch with his daughter in Australia, express her sense of impotence and waste. "We've never been able to choose," he tells the naive, newly-trained middle class matron who instructs him. "We've always done as we're told."

A farceur in embryo, Townsend is still groping for a proper structure in which her tremendous sense of fun can coalesce with her social insights. Built around the comedy of people with a secret compounding their lies in order to save face, *Groping for Words* pulls back from exploiting the frenzy of farce and settles for ferment. "I felt very emotionally involved with the play," she says. "Keeping the knowledge from people, keeping the words from people because words are power."

Townsend certainly has the words, and the increasing confidence to use them with the comedian's full potential for mayhem. In time, she will find the right metaphor to marry her sense of terror and elation. But her mission is clear. "Apart from making love," she says, "laughter is the most pleasant occupation I know." (pp. 474-75)

John Lahr, "A Female Trickster," in New Society, *Vol. 63, No. 1062, March 24, 1983, pp. 474-75.*

NATALIE BABBITT

Sue Townsend's *The Secret Diary of Adrian Mole, Aged 13 ¾,* if taken at face value, paints a dreary life indeed. Adrian describes, first person, a home life in which he is sorely neglected by a melancholy, out-of-a-job father and a frivolous, selfish mother who runs away with the man next door. The house is a mess, and often there isn't enough to eat. But Adrian is resourceful, and his voice is adult, witty, ironic. The result is like a series of scripts for a sit-com in which the wiseguy child actor has all the good lines: "I was racked with sexuality but it wore off when I helped my father put manure on our rose bed." A lot of different things happen over the year and a half covered by the diary—Adrian is 15 by the end of it—including a tonsillectomy; a trip to Scotland with mother and her lover; ups and downs with girlfriend Pandora; and a relationship with Bert Baxter, aged 89, whom Adrian has volunteered to look after as a member of a group called the Good Samaritans. . . .

[**Adrian Mole**] is so liberal with its Britishisms that it may sometimes mystify young American readers. If they hang in long enough, they will see that "dead" means 'very,'" for instance, or that a "removal lorry" is a moving van. But I never did figure out which part of a car is the "big-end." Aside from that, and over-frequent references by Adrian to his "thing" (quotation marks and euphemism Adrian's), it's a modestly entertaining story—a best seller in England—with all more or less resolved in the end. The feeling persists, however, that Adrian is Gary Coleman in disguise and that you've seen it all before on the telly.

> *Natalie Babbitt, "Writings of Passage: The Young and the Restless," in* Book World—The Washington Post, *May 13, 1984, p. 18.*

BRYN CALESS

[Sue Townsend's] **Bazaar and Rummage** is set in a 'multi-purpose' town hall, and concerns the attempts of a volunteer social worker, Gwenda, to persuade a group of agoraphobics to emerge and face the world. The playlet is witty and sharp, with a slick dialogue and some memorable exchanges. Gwenda is a domineering, bossy woman of the Lady Bountiful stereotype, who in fact wants to keep the group dependent on her. Fliss, the trainee social worker, opposes such enslavement and forces the group to recognize and come to terms with its problems. The play ends hopefully with each character stepping out into the night.

Groping for Words is a superb piece of theatre. It concerns the faltering attempts of a group of diverse characters to learn to read. The 'gropers' are adult illiterates who are helped by Joyce to learn how literacy will liberate them. **Womberang** is set in a hospital out-patients' waiting-room, and involves a group of women, all with gynaecological problems of some kind, in a conflict with the mindless hospital authorities.

Sue Townsend has a fine grasp of the conflict that must underlie all good drama. Her plays are contemporary, urban, and community-based; her attitudes are radical-chic and feminist, her focus is upon social problems and dilemas created by society. Her solutions, such as they are, concern education, liberal tolerance and humanity. All this is worthy, sensible and edifying, even if one balks at the simplicity of the answers to complex questions. The stock working-class character with a heart of gold and a ready tongue is too obviously Townsend's sentimentalized ideal, and I can't accept such saintly figures as Fliss without suspending more disbelief than I'm prepared to.

> *Bryn Caless, in a review of "Bazaar and Rummage," "Groping for Words" and "Womberang," in* British Book News, *August, 1984, p. 500.*

FRANCIS WHEEN

My, how he's grown. At the start of [Sue Townsend's] predecessor to this volume Adrian Mole was, famously, 13 ¾. By the end of the book he was 15 and *The Growing Pains of Adrian Mole* takes our hero to his 16th birthday, on which he wins the legal right to buy cigarettes, have sex, ride a

moped and live away from home. 'Strangely,' he muses, 'I don't want to do any of them.'

But he always was different from other children. Let us never forget that Adrian is an intellectual, who submits his poems to the BBC and comments thoughtfully on the issues of the day. 'It was with great pleasure that I saw Mr Roy Hattersley on television tonight,' he writes in June 1982. 'Once again I was struck by his obvious sincerity and good vocabulary.' Adrian is a thoroughly responsible pundit. His diary entry for 18 January reads: 'Lord Franks has published his report on the Falklands War. I will make no further comment until I have studied today's *Guardian* editorial on the matter. *10.30 p.m.* Can't find *Guardian:* it's not in its usual place in the dog's basket.'

Adrian's diary is not confined to his observations on public affairs. Private affairs are well reported, especially his father's continuing dalliance with the woman known as Stick Insect and his mother's canoodlings with Mr Lucas. Adrian's own romance with Pandora is as troublesome as ever, but I blame the parents. Pandora's mum has joined the Social Democratic Party; Adrian's has been to Greenham Common and is reading *Living Without Men—A Practical Guide* with a strange glint in her eye. As if that were not enough, Adrian also has to put up with acne, a new baby sister, ungrateful old Bert Baxter, the smelly and psychopathic Alsatian Sabre, the mad master 'Pop-Eye' Scruton, the delinquent Barry Kent, a holiday *en famille* at the Rio Grande Boarding House in Skegness, a blind date at a roller disco . . . Life's no fun for an adolescent intellectual. For the reader—as you'll know anyway if you've read the first volume—it's a hoot.

> *Francis Wheen, in a review of "The Growing Pains of Adrian Mole," in* New Statesman, *Vol. 108, No. 2788, August 24, 1984, p. 24.*

ELIZABETH WINTER

The difficulty of having parents is often underestimated. Traditionally, it is the children who get into scrapes, experiment adventurously and cause anxiety. . . . [In **The Growing Pains of Adrian Mole** however, Adrian], for all his pubescent worries, is constantly being upstaged by the delinquent behaviour of a mother who has belatedly discovered feminism and a father who has been made redundant from his job as an electric radiator salesman.

Not that Adrian always grasps immediately what is going on. Much of the comic effect of his diaries, indeed, relies on his stolid inocence. Why should Mr Lucas (his mother's lover) insist on having a blood test when baby sister Rosie is born? Why does his father go pale when Doreen Slater, looking unusually fat, unbuttons her coat? Some of these jokes will inevitably be over the head of a young reader, but the more knowing teenager will enjoy being drawn into an amiable conspiracy against the bookish (but not very bright) Adrian.

The register of his daily jottings (now covering two-and-a-half years, from the age of 13 ¾ to 16¼) wavers as violently and uncontrollably as his breaking voice—from the ponderous, pompous, multi-syllabic cliché to colloquial playground slang. We are also given samples of his more ambitious efforts—poems he submits to the BBC in the hope of instant fame, and the odd school essay of which he is particularly proud. Sue Townsend's feeling for language is acute, and we are treated to pastiches of Philip Larkin, Jack Kerouac and others, as Adrian temporarily falls under the their influence. Townsend's ear for dialogue is also excellent, and some of the more memorable characters (Bert Baxter, eighty-nine and a veteran of the trenches, or Courtney Elliot, the elegant postman who left his academic job "after a quarrel in the university common room over the allocation of chairs") come to life through their speech, transcribed with an accuracy which no teenage boy could maintain. Topical references and details of encounters at school, at the Department of Health and Social Services, in hospital, add up to a vivid picture of the social turmoil behind the family's immediate problems. Loss of faith in the welfare state is the background to the "nouveau poor" Mole family in their cul-de-sac in the Midlands. Only the monarchy, the BBC and Grandma seem to offer any continuity and stability.

Adrian's own little rebellion—joining a gang of skinheads for a few boring sorties then running away from home to spend his sixteenth birthday at Manchester railway station—is soon put to rights and the second volume ends on a fairly optimistic note. So far, Adrian Mole has turned out rather better than expected.

Just before his revolt, Adrian makes the following entry in his diary:

> During the month of March 1982 it would seem that both my parents were carrying on clandestine relationships, which resulted in the birth of two children. Yet my diary for that period records my childish fourteen-year-old thoughts and preoccupations.
>
> I wonder, did Jack the Ripper's wife innocently write:
>
> 10.30 pm Jack late home. Perhaps he is kept late at the office.
>
> 12.10 am Jack home covered in blood; an offal cart knocked him down.

Adrian has lost his innocence, and the device on which these diaries depended has been blown.

Elizabeth Winter, *"Late Entries,"* in The Times Literary Supplement, *No. 4261, November 30, 1984, p. 1382.*

NIGEL ANDREW

There are bestsellers and there are Phenomena. Bestsellers are just books that sell an awful lot of copies—the latest Jeffrey Archer, say, or Stephen King. Phenomena are something else: their origins are invariably obscure and their beginnings modest; their success comes as a surprise, but quickly develops an overwhelming momentum, not only ensuring continuous domination of the bestseller lists but demanding the creation of a virtual industry in spin-offs and adaptations. The Phenomenon of the late 1970s was *The Country Diary of an Edwardian Lady*—the book of the tea-towel—and the Phenomenon of the mid-1980s is, undoubtedly, *Adrian Mole.*

The beginnings were just right for a Phenomenon. Sue Townsend, playwright and former social worker (to say nothing of early school-leaver, petrol-pump attendant, mother of four), was on a bursary as Writer in Residence at the Phoenix Arts Centre in Leicester. At the annual meeting of the Phoenix Writers' Workshop in 1980, an actor 'tore out of her sticky fingers' a manuscript which purported to be a month's diary written by one Nigel Mole, aged 14 ¾. The actor, Nigel Bennett, performed this as a stage show at the Phoenix, and a 30-minute radio script was then sent to Radio Birmingham, who turned it down. But the Phenomenon thrives on rejection: Bennett tried it on John Tydeman, Assistant Head of Radio Drama at the BBC, and after leaving it unread for a month, he read, liked, accepted. Meanwhile the idea of a book of the diary had been enthusiastically accepted. . . .

John Tydeman's radio production of *Nigel Mole's Diary* was broadcast in January 1982, and was well received. This was followed by a change of name—to protect the justly sacred memory of Nigel Molesworth, prep-school hero of the 1950s—and a lowering of age to the celebrated 13 ¾. (p. 17)

The rest is history. Latest sales figures for the paperback *Secret Diary of Adrian Mole Aged 13 ¾* are in excess of 1.9 million (the hardback sold more than 90,000), and the follow-up, *The Growing Pains of Adrian Mole,* which was also ushered in by radio extracts in August 1984, sold over half a million in hardback, followed by a million on paperback publication and a further 250,000 or so since. With combined sales presently running at something over 1,000 a day, the record books are, as they say, being rewritten. The mania is now such that it cannot be confined to the book trade and Radio 4. There was a stage musical of *Mole* in Leicester last year, the transfer of which is packing them in at Wyndham's Theatre in London, and now Thames Television is running a six-part adaptation of *The Secret Diary,* brilliantly cast, cleverly produced, scripted by the author—and bound to whip up yet more *Mole* frenzy. We should perhaps be grateful that this particular Phenomenon doesn't lend itself to tea-towels and furnishing fabrics—and still more grateful for Sue Townsend's firm resolve not to publish any more *Mole* material until her creation is a young man of 26 or so.

The interesting thing about a Phenomenon is seldom the book itself—hands up all those who *read* the Country Diary—but rather what it tells us about the culture which gives it birth. It is always the less than 'literary' book—and especially the Phenomenon—that is the most informative index of the spirit of the times: send not to know who won the Booker Prize, rather look what they're reading on the commuter train. Of course what they are reading is *Adrian Mole*—but who are *they?* Overwhelmingly . . . they are women—and that seems to me to be a fact of some significance in itself. (Interestingly, it was also true of the Country Diary.)

Every Phenomenon offers one thing above all—reassurance, a comfortable feeling that, despite everything, all's well with the world. How then does the fictional diary of an adolescent boy offer this—and why particularly to women? Adrian Mole might be said to represent male sexuality in a tame, manageable and somewhat absurd form—and that is something which seems to have a deep appeal. Just look at the image of the male—more particularly the husband and father—projected in any number of television commercials: invariably he is portrayed as a lovable buffoon, a desexed wally. And advertisers know what they're doing. There is something in the air, a kind of cultural vapidity which is reflected in such diverse phenomena (small p) as Next clothes shops—designed specifically to enable women to dress their men to their own tastes—and the witless, substanceless pop videos which dominate all 'young people's' television. Adrian Mole is an apt totem for a society—or rather a large segment of it—that seems (sorry, ladies) to have mislaid its balls.

But that is only part of the story. The humour of *Mole* is of a particularly knowing kind, and consists largely in young Adrian's half-innocent, half-informed interpretation and misinterpretation of the adult world around him. For the most part, in fact, the subject matter is not Adrian Mole's growing pains but the pains and idiosyncrasies of the various adult characters, comically refracted in Mole's dawning consciousness. This adolescent is no Holden Caulfield of the 1980s, and the *Mole* books are as different from *The Catcher in the Rye* as the Eighties from the Fifties. Their subject—and this is the key to understanding the Phenomenon—is not male adolescence at all. It is adult life.

Consider these books as plausible, comically heightened versions of what a pubescent boy might actually confide to his diaries, and they are for the most part woefully wrong (a fact probably not very apparent to their female audience). Compared to the real agony, shame, frustrated yearning and furtive anxiety of adolescence, the growing pains of A. Mole are so much good, healthy fun. The real-life male adolescent inhabits a dark world hermetically sealed off from that of his parents, and his posture is one of surly defiance. Not so Mole. It is his parents' world that is sealed off from him, while his personality is essentially open, confiding and eager to please. Certainly there are features that are recognisably drawn from nature—the emotional lability, the intellectual pretensions, the puppy love, etc. But these are presented ready shaped for adult laughter: Mole is an eager accomplice in the joke against himself.

What the *Mole* phenomenon provides to its adult audience is a particular kind of reassurance about a wide range of distressing and difficult subjects. Chiefly it is about the break-up or radical distortion of marriage and family life. It is also about feminism, sexual irregularity, divorce, redundancy, lack of money. In fact it is about hard times—the hard times which we all sense to be just around the corner, waiting for us to collapse into them, if we have not already. But all of this is filtered through the pseudo-adolescent consciousness of Adrian Mole, and in the process is sanitised, softened, sentimentalised and shaped into a mode of comic reassurance.

Mole offers its audience a way of coping with anxieties which are very close to home, and most of which are of particular concern to women, they being the ones who are usually left to pick up the pieces. With soaring divorce rates, high unemployment and rapid changes in family life, the England of the early 1980s was ripe for *Adrian Mole.*

Central to its Phenomenal success is the reversal of roles whereby Adrian is essentially the adult of the family, while the supposed 'grown-ups' behave most of the time like naughty children. This reversal has great symbolic potency—most of Dickens's novels are based around some form of it—and perhaps it is especially powerful at this particular time. We are still, to a great extent, living in the fall-out from the upheavals of the 1960s—but we are in radically changed social and economic circumstances. Our instincts may still be hedonistic, permissive, regressive, but there are harsh imperatives and responsibilities to be faced, and life is hard. How are the children of the Sixties to grow up, to become adults? For many people, I suspect, *Adrian Mole* is—underneath the laughter—giving some sort of answer to that question.

When the social history of the 1980s comes to be written, the *Mole* books—astonishing though it may now seem—will probably be considered as key texts. (pp. 17-18)

Nigel Andrew, "Diary Makes Dead Good Social History!!!" in The Listener, *Vol. 114, No. 2929, October 3, 1985, pp. 17-18.*

PETER CAMPBELL

Squawks are heard all over London these days from newly-fledged birds being pushed off the twig. The reasons for not leaving home multiply: no money, no job, rents high, flats scarce. With the decay of the old custom of not fornicating under the parental roof the strongest reason for having a place of your own has gone. Forced contiguity is exacerbated by the New Frankness. The children of the Sixties (the ones born then) have a view of the infantile passions, the neurotic insecurity, and the vulnerability, of their parents which might accompany a severe scepticism about all human relationships. Have age and experience done *nothing* for these parents? they ask. Their younger brothers and sisters, born in the Seventies, have even worse cases to manage. But at least they now have a laureate.

The immense success of the two *Mole* books . . . is a tribute to self-awareness. The public, like a man who finds his symptoms are no mere concatenation but a syndrome, need no longer suspect itself of hypochondria. Sue Townsend's descriptions ring true, the word is out: kids, parents, pets and geriatrics are all in this mess together.

Children take to the books partly, I gather, because the disgusting details of Adrian's spots, the mention of his wet dreams and of his regular measuring of his 'thing', break taboos. But more because—despite his hypochondria, his naff intellectual ambitions, his deeply untrendy tastes—he is a hero who suffers as they suffer. Just at the moment when it has, to an unparalleled degree, become open to inspection, the adult world turns out to have nothing to offer but pain, betrayal and embarrassment. The epigraph to *The Secret Diary* is taken from [D. H. Lawrence's novel] *Sons and Lovers:* 'Paul walked with something screwed up tight inside him . . . yet he chatted away with his mother. He would never have confessed to her how he suffered over these things and she only partly guessed.' The worst insults, the ones which start fights and feuds, are still slights on your family—above all, on your mother's virtue. For boys who have to keep fatally embarrassing facts about home and parents secret, Adrian's torments are cathartic.

These are children's books in which the real characters are adults. It showed up in the television adaptation. Adrian's mother, his Granny, his father, Bert (the pensioner Adrian is issued with to practice good samaritanism on): they are the round characters. Adrian and Pandora, his priggish girlfriend, the cardboard foils. . . . The children strive for an appearance of competence, the adults achieve anarchy. Because there are jokes on every page the bleak facts take a little time to emerge; and the very excellence of the television acting tended to make one miss them. Consider Adrian's lot: his father is made redundant, and gets a job from the Manpower Services Commission cleaning a canal bank which every morning is strewn again with garbage. His mother runs off with, and back from, Mr Lucas ('rat fink Lucas'). Mrs Mole's unexpected pregnancy (she is 37—much too old in Adrian's eyes even to be thinking of having children) may have been caused by George Mole or by Lucas. Doreen Slater ('Stick Insect') is certainly pregnant by George Mole. By the end of the second book Adrian has witnessed his sister's—half sister's?—birth, a death and a cremation. He has taken his mother to the National Insurance office to fight officials. He has witnessed, or guessed at, the scenes of verbal violence and sexual reconciliation which mark the progress of his parents' marriage. Near the end of **Growing Pains** he retires to bed with nervous exhaustion.

Adrian may not shape up perfectly to life's problems, but put a few heroes of the received canon of children's literature in his place, and how do they get on? E. Nesbit's children would sympathise with his poverty, and do at least as well as he does in looking after Bert, but they would find the feckless self-indulgence of the Mole parents beyond comprehension. Their world recognises the bottomless pit of poverty; but never admits there might be no moral bottom to life. Others would be too good-mannered to notice things which embarrass Adrian. In the world of Arthur Ransome's children parents hardly figure as characters. Their role is to establish the absolute security outside the plot which can make the adventures within it seem both realistic and safe. No possible turn of a Ransome story would allow John, Roger, Susan and Titty to be embarrassed by their mother's breasts showing through a tight sweat shirt. Many heroes are a cut above Adrian in talent. K. M. Peyton's Pennington is a rough diamond and gets into trouble with the police, but he is also a concert pianist. None of these characters would be any help to Adrian. . . .

Adrian Mole is immensely popular: most library copies are nicked. . . . His observation that Pandora's chest bounces, read in class or out of it, causes explicable glee. But removing a taboo on description gives no larger appreciation of the thing described or how you use it in real life. A teacher I talked to compared the writing a class did in Mole mode, which was imitative and not very good, to what they wrote about the characters in Stan Barstow's novel *Joby*. This book, set in the late 1930s, tells of a bad year: Joby's mother goes to hospital with cancer and has a breast removed, his best friend goes to a different school, he is thrown out of the cinema (and misses the last episode of *Flash Gordon*) because of someone else's misbehaviour, and his father becomes infatuated with another woman. Along the way he learns about sex and sees its consequences in a forced marriage. The book ends with Joby on a canal bank, persuading his father (who Joby thinks is suicidal though he probably only wants some time to himself) to come home. A large proportion of the boys, asked to describe what life might be like in Joby's family after all this, wrote of the wounded feelings, doubt and uneasiness of families in which trust has been abused. Only one boy tacked on a fairy-tale ending of reconciliation.

Those teachers who loathe Mole and all his works do so because they encourage ribaldry in the face of problems which are far from funny. But books like *Joby*, which look with more feeling at the same kinds of problem, are rare: the best hope for anyone worried about Mole's nihilism is that his contemporaries will copy out his library list: Eliot, Amis and Waugh should reawaken any moral parts the **Diary** has anaesthetised.

Peter Campbell, "Adrian," in London Review of Books, Vol. 7, No. 21, December 5, 1985, p. 18.

WALTER CLEMONS

Adrian Mole, a pimply lower-middle-class Britisher who keeps a diary of his day-to-day scrapes from the age of 13 ¾ to 16, has become a craze in England over the past four years. Sue Townsend, a former Leicester homemaker, wrote a half-hour radio play about Mole that was followed by two best-selling books, a London musical, a TV series and a spinoff industry of T shirts, games and accessories rather like the '70s mass-marketing of John Irving's T. S. Garp in the United States. *The Adrian Mole Diaries* is a combined American edition of two books that together have sold 5 million copies at home.

Adrian, an aspiring intellectual who mails awful poems to the BBC, is a fastidious, persnickety critic of his layabout father and slatternly mother—who cries, "For God's sake, Adrian, this room is like a shrine! Why don't you leave your clothes on the floor like *normal* teenagers?" He nurses a frustrated passion for his classmate Pandora and writes rude entries about the scruffy, dispirited England of the '80s: "It has just been on the news that a man has been found in the Queen's bedroom. Radio Four said that the man was an intruder and was previously unknown to the Queen. My father said: 'That's her story'." The gags are often mechanical ("I am reading the *Mill on the Floss* by a bloke called George Eliot"), but they come several to a page and make broad, undemanding entertainment. Can *The Adrian Mole Diaries* repeat its British success in this country? I doubt it, but I was mistaken about Garp.

Walter Clemons, "A Mole Surfaces," in Newsweek, Vol. CVII, No. 18, May 5, 1986, p. 76.

THE NEW YORKER

[*The Adrian Mole Diaries*], which were received with great enthusiasm in England several years ago, begin with Adrian's New Year's resolutions ("I will not start smoking. . . . I will help the poor and ignorant") and his grim comments on the previous evening's festivities ("My father got the dog drunk on cherry brandy at the party last night. If the RSPCA hear about it he could get done"). Adrian Mole, at thirteen and three-quarters, is an avid diarist, and the reader quickly learns that he is also an only child, a romantic ("Goodnight Pandora my treacle-haired love"), a hypochondriac, and an intellectual ("Finished *Animal Farm*. It is dead symbolic. . . . From now on I shall treat pigs with the contempt they deserve. I am boycotting pork of all kinds"). Adrian's short entries include a familiar yet unpredictable cast of characters, among them his ever-quarrelling parents; their new, intensely patriotic Anglo-Indian neighbors, the Singhs; and Bert Baxter, a crafty Marxist pensioner whom Adrian meets through Good Samaritans. Sue Townsend is rarely off the mark; she manages to be consistently clever without being precious. The diaries were originally published in two volumes, and this overlong edition does them a disservice. Nevertheless, American readers will be happy to make Adrian Mole's acquaintance under any circumstances.

A review of "The Adrian Mole Diaries," in The New Yorker, Vol. LXII, No. 13, May 19, 1986, p. 120.

TIME

"I was racked with sexuality but it wore off when I helped

my father put manure on our rose bed." There, in 20 words, is the essence of **The Adrian Mole Diaries,** a novel composed of entries by an English adolescent. Poor Adrian is beset with millstones: acne, parents and an indifferent world. When the family must move in order to make room for a baby, he fumes, "Babies hardly take any space at all. They are only about 21 inches long." But sometimes he is merry: The headmaster "said that somebody had entered his office and drawn a moustache on Margaret Thatcher and written 'Three million unemployed' in her cleavage." For a mildly diverting twit, Adrian has enjoyed a remarkable career. Five million copies of the book have been sold in Britain, and a TV series has been optioned in the U.S. As the boy says of a chap who natters too long about his passions. "I'm all for a man having outside interests, but this is ridiculous."

A review of "The Adrian Mole Diaries," in Time, *New York, Vol. 127, No. 20, May 19, 1986, p. 100.*

NORMA KLEIN

When is a young adult novel not a young adult novel? **The Adrian Mole Diaries,** published in two volumes in Britain for adults, deals with the growing pains of an aspiring intellectual boy who ages from 13 to 16. Funny, poignant, sardonic but also compassionate, the diaries deserve at least some portion of the attention they received in their native country. The acclaim was nothing short of extraordinary: five million copies sold, a 1984 stage play with music, a television series, even the inevitable excrescences of our modern age—Adrian Mole computer games, pencil cases, writing pads and diaries. *The Listener* wrote, "When the social history of the 1980s comes to be written, the 'Mole' books—astonishing as it may seem now—will probably be considered as key texts" [see Nigel Andrew's excerpt above].

What is astonishing about all this is not only that it happened to two books in the literary mold but that, unlike young adult heroes in the United States, Adrian Mole and his angst, described with humor by Sue Townsend, a playwright, were taken seriously by an adult audience. Is this even possible in America? It was when *Catcher in the Rye* was published in 1951, because the young adult category had not been discovered. Many good things have come from having young adult literature considered as a separate field, but one of the unfortunate results has been to segregate books that under other circumstances would certainly appeal to adults as well as teen-agers. My fear for Adrian Mole in America is that, like his American equivalents, he will be perceived as falling between two stools, too radical and shocking for teen-agers, at least as they are seen by the library establishment, but uninteresting to adults by virtue of being under college age. Yet it is hard to conceive of anyone of either age group with even a passing interest in the best contemporary fiction who will not find the diaries a delight.

Some first-person books about adolescents can be as solipsistic as their narrators; one feels locked inside a world of narrow experience and shallow reflections about reality. It is Sue Townsend's gift that she portrays not only Adrian's life, including his battery of rejections from the BBC, to which he keeps sending his hilariously solemn poetry, but the lives of his parents, his old-age pensioner friend, Bert Baxter, and his schoolmates, assorted punks, radicals and everyday kids struggling with O-level exams. Indeed, **The Adrian Mole Diaries** are as vivid a satire on Margaret Thatcher's England as

can be found in recent fiction. Adrian's father's unemployment, the stabs at radical behavior at his school (the students wear red socks for a day and are almost expelled) and the sense of domestic chaos engulfing his parents extend the range of the books. Through Adrian's eyes we see what he sees and more: what emerges is as sad and devastating as it is laugh-out-loud funny.

The central plot is the story of Adrian's parents, who are hanging on to a middle-class existence by their toes. That they are allowed center stage so often and that their affairs are described so unsparingly make this all the more a novel whose purpose is to analyze adult as well as adolescent relationships. Adrian's mother, inspired by a newly discovered feminism, runs off with the pathetic next-door neighbor, Mr. Lucas, whose own wife has left him for another woman. In her absence, Adrian's father takes up with Doreen Slater, an unmarried woman already burdened with a young son. (Adrian persists in referring to Doreen as the Stick Insect.)

The cumulative effect of these and other traumas causes Adrian to leave home, an event that is almost unnoticed by his self-absorbed parents. But eventually things sort themselves out. Thinking about his impending O-levels, Adrian muses, "My overriding problem is that I'm *too* intellectual: I am constantly thinking about things, like: was God married? and: if Hell is other people, is Heaven empty?" Part Woody Allen, part a kindred spirit to the heroes of Philip Roth's early novellas, Adrian is a fictional character who inspires in the reader a rare affection and warmth. I hope he will return as an adult, never losing his gimlet-eyed clarity about the world in which he and all of us live.

Norma Klein, "I Was a Teen-Age Intellectual," in The New York Times Book Review, *May 25, 1986, p. 9.*

WILLIAM GRIMES

Toward the end of Sue Townsend's [**Adrian Mole Diaries**], . . . the narrator, an English adolescent, draws a line down the middle of a piece of paper. On one side he lists "Reasons for living"; on the other, "Reasons for not living." Category Two totals seven items, leading off with the unanswerable "You die anyway." Category One contains but a single entry: "Things might get better." Meet Adrian Mole, worrier, miser, hypochondriac, obsessive, depressive, and, in his own way, hero.

Adrian, age 13 and three-quarters when the book begins, suffers from the usual assortment of adolescent ills. Morbidly self-conscious, he monitors all bodily changes with scientific rigor: his pimples come under minute scrutiny, their waxings and wanings recorded daily. He has a limitless capacity for embarrassment, rooted in the dead certainty that all eyes are on him at all times. "We went to Sainsbury's [grocery store] in the afternoon," reads one diary entry. "My father chose a trolley that was impossible to steer. It also squeaked as if somebody was torturing mice. I was ashamed to be heard with it." On a seaside holiday, his father sports a "Kiss Me Quick, Squeeze Me Slowly" hat; Adrian puts on dark glasses and walks 10 feet behind him.

Adrian's self-absorption is nearly total. If his mother falls ill, he wonders whether she'll be able to iron his school uniform in the morning. He enjoys looking at himself as the suffering hero in a tragic drama. After taking part in neighborhood caroling, he confides to his diary: "I must say that I presented a touching picture as I stood in the snow with my young face lifted to the heavens, ignoring the scenes of drunken revelry around me." Far from sympathizing with his father's employment difficulties, Adrian blames him for failing to provide the cushy lifestyle some of his friends enjoy:

> This weekend with Nigel has really opened my eyes! Without knowing it I have been living in poverty for the past 14 years! I have had to put up with inferior accommodation, lousy food and paltry pocket money. If my father can't provide a decent standard of living for me on his present salary, then he will just have to start looking for another job.

All this is harmless fun. What makes the diaries something more is their sharply observed social realism, which gives, in quick takes, a picture of shabby lower-middle-class life in the English Midlands. It succeeds brilliantly in conveying the texture of life among Britain's "nouveau poor" (as Adrian's mother refers to the Mole family), all of whom appear to have bought the book. . . . The book's crowning achievement is Adrian himself, a thoroughly contemporary youth whose natural confidence has been sapped by an era of consumer protection, truth in advertising, and health-consciousness. He is a worried old man. He frets about his poor diet at home and constantly pushes information about vitamins under the noses of his indifferent parents. At the grocery store, he sneaks health food into the cart whenever their backs are turned. Almost every human activity seems to him fraught with peril. When his girlfriend leaves for a vacation in Tunisia, he broods about metal fatigue in the airplane, then checks an atlas to make sure she will not be flying over the Bermuda Triangle. Hearing friends of his parents propose a dawn climbing expedition, he reacts with horror, then delivers a stern lecture: "I pointed out to them that they were blind drunk, too old, unqualified, unfit and lacking in any survival techniques, had no first-aid kit, weren't wearing stout boots, and had no compass, map or sustaining hot drinks."

Though knowing and cynical about adult relationships, Adrian sustains a pedantic, lawyerlike faith in the rules. He can never quite believe it when his father smokes on the bus, a policeman curses, or the mailman reads postcards before delivering them. When a classmate reports that he has seen their headmaster smoking cigarettes confiscated from a student, Adrian writes: "Surely this can't be true?" When he is not in a state of dread lest a member of the family be dragged away by the police, he is preparing a denunciation to the authorities.

The dark shadow that falls across Adrian's life is his parents' turbulent marriage, which propels the novel's casual plot. Entangled in adulterous affairs, hard-pressed by unemployment, George and Pauline Mole lose track of their son. The miseries of the Mole household lend pathos to what would otherwise be trivial adolescent whining. Adrian's love of appointments with doctors, clergymen, counselors—anyone who will listen, really—is both funny and painful. His plight does not seem to be unique. When kind Mr. Lambert invites students to talk over their troubles with him, virtually every kid in the school signs up for a little chat. Within a week Mr. Lambert has aged visibly and has begun biting his nails.

Adrian seeks calm, order, and stability—everything his parents have failed to provide. He keeps his room immaculate ("a bloody shrine," his mother calls it) and takes pains to present a neat appearance. Above all, Adrian looks for permanent relationships. Unlike his parents, he works hard at them. Ninety-year-old Bert Baxter, a charity case, finds in Adrian a steady companion and a reliable friend. Adrian may gripe, but he's there when things get tough for the old man.

The most important person in Adrian's life is Pandora Braithwaite, whom he pursues throughout the novel and eventually wins. He remains patient as she flirts with militant feminism, left-wing politics, and other boys. Perseverance is rewarded, and at the end of the novel, with dreaded exams approaching, Adrian achieves something resembling mental calm: "If I don't pass my exams it won't matter. I have known what it is to have the love of a good woman."

William Grimes, "Drear Diary," in The Village Voice, *Vol. XXXI, No. 22, June 3, 1986, p. 45.*

HOLLY THOMAS

If you're a teenager, or remember what it's like, you'll enjoy [*The Adrian Mole Diaries,* a] light and funny look at adolescence through the eyes of a fictional British teenager named Adrian Mole.

Adrian keeps faithful entries in his "secret diaries," which begin when he's thirteen and three quarters. Nothing is immune to Adrian's scrutiny. He chronicles his parents' soap opera marriage, from his mother's affair with an insurance salesman to the liaison his father has in retaliation. Then there's his own sometimes-torrid relationship with an "older woman" named Pandora (she's three months his senior). He even finds room for comments on Lady Diana's wedding and the war with Argentina. He does volunteer work for an 89-year-old man with a fierce Alsatian dog. The Moles' own nameless family dog is constantly being taken to the vet after eating lumps of coal or walking through wet cement. Adrian thinks he might be a veterinarian himself some day, although he's barely passing biology. Meanwhile, he struggles under the weight of being a self-proclaimed intellectual and submits poems to the BBC.

Originally published in England, where it was first a radio program, the book now makes its American debut with lots of advance hype. Jacket blurbs compare it to *Catcher in the Rye,* but I wouldn't go that far. It's too light to be that deeply affecting. Adrian may dramatize his own problems ("Two-and-a-half hours of homework! I will crack under the strain."), but he manages to keep a certain warped perspective on things ("I hope Bert doesn't die. Apart from liking him, I have got nothing to wear to a funeral."). With comments like these, it's hard to take him too seriously.

For an adult, this will all sound familiar. For a teenager, it should provide a new opportunity to laugh at the sort of crises that seem so monumental at the time. For all his self-indulgence—or rather, because of it—we all recognize a little of ourselves in Adrian Mole.

Holly Thomas, in a review of "The Adrian Mole Diaries," in West Coast Review of Books, *Vol. 12, No. 2, July-August, 1986, p. 35.*

CYNTHIA RIEBEN

The Adrian Mole Diaries chronicle two-and-a-half years in the fictional life of a modern British adolescent making his precarious way through public school, puberty and parental strife assisted by his girlfriend, Pandora. Naivete gives way to knowledge as Adrian is swirled about in the turbulence of his parents' relationship. It is a rapidly maturing young man who scribbles, "I am just sick and tired of adults! They have the nerve to tell kids what to do and then they go ahead and break all their own rules." There is scarcely a topic left unturned as Adrian remarks upon the trivial (the number of spots on his face) to the historic (the wedding of Prince Charles and Princess Diana). The tone ranges from the mildly humorous to the hysterically outrageous and is occasionally reminiscent of Paula Danziger's *The Cat Ate My Gymsuit* and Judy Blume's *Are You There, God? It's Me, Margaret.*

Adrian Mole has been a huge success in Great Britain, and we may soon see him in a television mini-series. However, his appeal for the American young adult librarian, English teacher and teenager has facets beyond his appeal in Great Britain.

To begin with, as part of the English-speaking world, we ought to have on hand a copy of a British bestseller, if it is appropriate reading for teenagers, so that they can get an idea of what the British find funny. Second, it is enlightening to learn how a British teenager might feel about peer pressure, family turmoil, the Falklands crisis and Americans, although the author may have exaggerated a point or two. Third, the flexibility and mutability of our common language is strikingly illustrated in the myriad colloquialisms Adrian uses. In fact, this third reason for putting the book on the shelf may also be one of its chief drawbacks. What is a "poofter"? What does it mean if an apartment is "dead grotty"? I did guess that a "call box" is a telephone, but what are "the pips"? What does it mean "to go off" someone, and what do you do when you go out "conkering"? . . .

However, it's not just adolescent slang that is a problem. The off-handed references to politics, grocery products, popular literature and music, vacation spots and social agencies make some entries very puzzling. While the author did provide a glossary for Americans, it by no means elucidates all the references to things particularly British.

I found that the diary format lent itself well to the *non sequitar* asides and sudden revelations, but this may be an obstacle for our teen readers. Some are immediately turned off by a diary format, while others do appreciate the absence of tedious description. Another drawback for me was the bathroom and bedroom humor which was a bit raw and tiresome after awhile, even if it is "real life." However, if that can be overlooked, the *Diaries* do introduce us to a most memorable young man.

> Cynthia Rieben, in a review of "The Adrian Mole Diaries," in Voice of Youth Advocates, Vol. 9, No. 5, December, 1986, p. 222.

ANNETTE CURTIS KLAUSE

One of the funniest young adult books that I've read lately is *The Adrian Mole Diaries.* It's a real laugh-out-loud, read-to-your-husband, make-all-your-colleagues-take-it-home book. It's a combination of two novels by Sue Townsend that have become best sellers in Britain for good reasons. It's hard to decide whether the humor has immediacy for teens, or whether it's funnier for an adult looking back at being a teenager. I think it's a bit of both. Adrian's diary entries take him from 13 ¾ to 16, and contain his observations on his parents'

marital troubles, the way his body won't behave, and his friendships with the desirable Pandora and a scrungy, foulmouthed, old-age pensioner named Bert. His callous attitude toward adults is embarrassingly recognizable when compared to my own teen diaries, and he writes with such naiveté about his life, while readers are often hilariously aware of what is really going on. Adrian is worried about the lack of morals in society, and is afraid of turning into an intellectual. "It must be all the worry. . . . A bad home, poor diet, not liking punk. I think I will join the library and see what happens." He sends poems to the BBC with lines like "Norway! Land of difficult spelling," and "Do you weep, Mrs. Thatcher, do you weep?" Yet the poem he writes as an obituary for Bert's wife manages to be very funny and poignant at the same time.

Nothing goes right for Adrian. An example is when he is tempted to sniff glue while making a model airplane:

> I put my nose to the undercarriage and sniffed for five seconds, nothing happened, but my nose stuck to the plane! My father took me to Casualty to have it removed, how I endured the laughing and sniggering I don't know.

Poor Adrian—love, he says, is the only thing that keeps him sane. (p. 35)

> Annette Curtis Klause, "So What's So Funny, Anyway?" in School Library Journal, Vol. 33, No. 6, February, 1987, pp. 34-5.

JOHN J. O'CONNOR

The Secret Diary of Adrian Mole is a seven-episode British production being offered as a series for young viewers. It is not, be assured, your ordinary fare for youngsters. A clue to the tone and style can be detected when Adrian, age 13 ¾ tells us his mother is "not like the moms on TV."

Adapted from her own book by Sue Townsend, the series begins on New Year's morning. While his parents are still recovering in bed from the previous night's partying, Adrian is gazing into a mirror and discovering a pimple on his cheek. "Just my luck," says the chronically forlorn young man. He accuses his mother, Pauline, of not giving him enough vitamin C. "Well, go buy an orange then," she groans.

On the surface, Adrian is a very ordinary lad, sort of your basic nerd. He's small for his age and wears glasses. He makes a perfect target for the bullies at school. Within, though, in his secret world, Adrian is in total control, convinced that his is the only sane voice in a world sinking into fatal eccentricities. Apparently fated to being an intellectual, Adrian knows he will have to pay a price even as he squirrels away his profound impressions of life in a diary.

The supporting players include his grandmother, who visits and flits through the house occasionally, muttering about how disgustingly dirty it is. Or there is the old-age pensioner whom Adrian knows through a good Samaritan program he has joined at school. Living in a dingy room with a terrible smell, the old codger insists that the boy shouldn't be disturbed just because his poetry was rejected by the BBC. "It's a well-known fact," says the old man, "that everybody that works there is a drug addict." . . .

The Secret Diary of Adrian Mole manages to capture the

pains and absurdities of adolescence without being patronizing or terminally cute. Adrian can be hilarious and exasperating, often simultaneously. When his mother announces that she is going to get a job, Adrian warns that "I could wind up a delinquent." When his parents totter on the edge of divorce, he groans that "I'm going to be an official statistic." Little wonder that Mom and Dad begin arguing about who *doesn't* get custody of Adrian.

While Adrian goes through the nasty rituals of growing up, the other people in his life don't simply stand still. His mom, Pauline . . . is positively dizzying. Obviously having an affair with a smarmy neighbor, Pauline is in the process of liberating herself. Returning from a class in assertiveness training, she announces triumphantly to husband and son that "the worm has turned." For some women, she confides to Adrian, "marriage is like a prison." The boy concedes that Mom is "a bit melodramatic."

On top of everything else, Adrian thinks he might be falling in love with the stunningly poised Pandora, a classmate from a posh background that includes riding lessons. It is little wonder that Adrian wonders why he couldn't have been born Prince Edward. The world is caving in on him, and he hasn't even reached his 14th birthday. "Oh my God," he cries, looking in the mirror again, "and now my rotten skin has gone to pot."

John J. O'Connor, " 'The Secret Diary of Adrian Mole,' on Channel 13," in The New York Times, June 19, 1987, p. C34.

SIMON BRETT

Sue Townsend virtually colonised the best-seller lists with her brilliant Adrian Mole books, and ***Rebuilding Coventry*** is her first novel since those successes. Like its predecessors, it is wonderfully readable and the relative cheapness of its price suggests [the publishers are] anticipating further huge sales.

I think they could be right, though this book doesn't have the Adrian Mole ingredient of appeal across the generations. ***Rebuilding Coventry*** is an adult novel, and a very strange one at that. It is about a woman called Coventry Dakin, whose committing of a murder forces her to leave her boring family life in the Midlands and flee to London. There she experiences the stresses of poverty and meets a picaresque selection of contemporary types until her problems are resolved in an unlikely climax at Gatwick Airport.

The style of the book is naive and cartoonlike. Short scenes follow each other like comic strips. Characters are grotesquely exaggerated. Upper-class people say things like, "Git owl of my harse, you detty little commie!"

There seem to be points about politics—and sexual politics—the North/South divide and life in Thatcher's Britain being made, but the level of satire is about that of the [comic book] *Beano*. It's all very odd. ***Rebuilding Coventry*** is not literary. And it will probably sell in huge numbers to a readership which is not literary either. (p. 52)

Simon Brett, "A Wesleyan Hymn," in Punch, Vol. 295, September 2, 1988, pp. 51-2.

ANNE SMITH

[The title character in Sue Townsend's ***Rebuilding Coventry***] is a housewife in her thirties. She lives on a grey estate in the Midlands with her tortoise-fancying husband Derek and her teenage son and daughter. One day she accidentally kills her beer-bellied macho neighbour Gerald, who has been boasting in the pub about having an affair with her, by caving in his skull with an Action Man doll as he is busy strangling his wife.

Coventry becomes a fugitive from justice, living in London's Cardboard City in a box Dodo, an upper-class refugee from insanity: "Some time ago Dodo had a nervous breakdown. She *used* to think that she was the chief constable of Manchester: God told her she was, and she believed God."

Before the dramatic change in her circumstances, Coventry had been a fastidious housewife some of the time, planning her life in advance with daily lists of what she must do—for example:

> Post Noreen's birthday card.
> Has Bella got my big whisk?
> Ask doctor if I'm going mad.
> Light bulbs.

The third item refers to what Coventry does the rest of the time, in her *alter ego* as art student Lauren Skye. Her son discovers this in her secret diary after she has run away. Lauren's contempt for the people Coventry lives with is savage: "Hello, I'm back. The drearies are at work, school and college"; "Lauren could not attend her first lesson today because one of the drearies has a temperature of 101 and is in bed."

Sue Townsend is just irresistibly funny, and in Coventry she has found the perfect character through which to express not only her humorous view of the human condition, but also her cut-the-shit perceptions of contemporary Britain. Her funniest asides have a cutting edge: "I dreamt of being in prison. I was sharing a cell with Ruth Ellis. We were very jolly and plucked each other's eyebrows." The characters are sketched in with a sure hand—Coventry's parents . . ., the god-awful and totally credible Detective Sly, the equally awful and credible Derek, "Podger" the Cabinet Minister and his antics at an upper-crust dinner-party, and the party itself: "You can say what you like about Hitler, but he knew . . . how to *prioritise.*"

Along the way there are a professor of forensics and his psychiatrist wife, the Willoughby D'Esterbys, with their nonexistent housekeeping and a mad hermit son living off pigeons in the attic, all wonderfully funny examples of the hopeless impracticability of high-flown theories of behaviour, comfortably cocooned in the intellectual meritocracy. There is also, and by no means incidentally, a quietly poignant dramatisation of what it is like to be a woman alone, dirty and hungry, in London.

Everything in ***Rebuilding Coventry*** is done with ruthlessly satisfying economy. This is satire in the best, Jonsonian tradition, with nothing and no one spared.

Anne Smith, "The Secret Diary of Lauren Skye," in New Statesman & Society, Vol. 1, No. 14, September 9, 1988, p. 39.

SHENA MACKAY

Some years ago . . . [a seal of approval was given] to Action Man because the now-defunct, scar-faced, sexless mannikin catered to the desire of little boys to dress and undress dolls without incurring accusations of sissiness. [In *Rebuilding Coventry*] Sue Townsend's heroine, Coventry Dakin, putting him to more macho use, brings Action Man down on the head of an unpleasant neighbour, Gerald Fox, who has been spreading false rumours, in the local theme pub, that he is her lover. Fox's skull was preternaturally thin and his body was a cardiac and arterial time bomb set to explode, but neither Coventry nor the police know this, and Coventry flees, Inter-City, from her home on a Midlands council estate to London.

The author is, of course, best known for the *Secret Diary* and *The Growing Pains of Adrian Mole* (the new book's pun may well be lost on many of her thousands of young fans), and her latest work contains references to both those titles; Coventry's Moleish son discovers his mother's secret diary, written by her assumed *alter ego,* the painter Lauren Skye, and we witness her growth into the beautiful self who has always lurked in the sensible shoes and skirts she wears. Coventry was repressed as a child by her parents, known as Tennis Ball and Bread Knife, and we are given to suppose might have been named more appositely Bristol. That notwithstanding, her schoolmates make much of her name.

That the mass of women lead lives of quiet desperation is one of Sue Townsend's recurrent themes, and their liberation from boring or violent men one of her favourite fantasies. Gerald Fox beats up his wife, who is dully grateful for his demise, and Coventry's husband is a bore. As a bore, Derek is convincing, and touching too when shunned by his workmates at the firm's annual dinner dance. When, in a desperately lonely bid to recall his lost wife, he dresses up in her clothes, Derek is perceived as a possible poofter by the odious Inspector Sly who is investigating the murder, and his appearance in drag and lipstick, scented with *Tramp,* hints at a hidden side to his character, but he has been cast as a bore and must stay within the confines of his role. It is in his characterization that the author makes two serious mistakes: the first is her use of his pet tortoises, as any cheloniaphile would agree, as exemplars of his drabness, and the second is that no true tortoise-lover would, even to prevent their theft, paint the reptiles' names in luminous paint on their shells.

When Coventry, dressed in pale blue polyester bell-bottoms (and soot-streaked because she was cleaning her chimney at the time of the alleged murder), hits London, the novel becomes picaresque as she embarks on a series of bizarre adventures; once she wore *Tramp,* now she has become one. The narrative, while making some Martian observations of London through provincial eyes, and some acute social and sartorial comments—though it seems fairly unlikely that she could have bought a pair of leather boots for under £20—is an uneasy synthesis of reality and fantasy. It might be what Fay Weldon would call a fairy-tale for grown-ups: thus when Coventry takes up residence in Cardboard City and is befriended by a bag lady, her rescuer turns out not to be the sort who pisses herself and gets turned off buses, but an aristocrat in disguise; in other words, the Good Fairy.

Eventually, by dint of blackmail in High Places, the two of them fly off from Gatwick into the blue yonder, leaving the subplot behind. Coventry, rebuilt, has her cake and eats it: she is reunited briefly with the children she adores but depict-ed in her diary as "Drearies"—and they are rather—and born skivers; she *is* Lauren Skye. Derek and the tortoises live happily ever after.

Shena Mackay, "Lady into Tramp," in The Times Literary Supplement, *No. 4459, September 16-22, 1988, p. 1012.*

ALAN RUSBRIDGER

Dear Diary. Have just finished reading *Rebuilding Coventry* by Sue Townsend. Didn't take long—about a morning. Only about 150 pages, with short chapters. Dust jacket says it's her first work of fiction since coining it with Adrian Mole (well, sort of), that it's provocative and utterly original and that it turns "a brilliant spotlight on some dark corners of English Society". You could have fooled me!

Adrian Mole is a hard act to follow, of course. Danger is, once you start writing in diary form difficult to get out of. Don't think Sue's really managed it with this! Really just a series of short episodes strung together with flimsy plot to give it all some sort of coherence. Padded out with lots of dialogue of sort you overhear on buses and jot down in your diary for later use. Quite funny to begin with, but gets a bit irritating after while.

Book's full of quite amusing one-liners, but doesn't really go anywhere. Characters a bit irritating, too. Nearly all of them fruitcakes. Lot of silly names and silly jobs. Tone veers between Moleish *faux naif* and straightforward patronising. Not successful combination in grown-up book.

Story's basically about this provincial housewife (with silly first name: Coventry) who kills a neighbour more or less by accident (never really explained) then goes on the run to London. Dosses around a bit, stays with a barmy prof and his wife (silly names: Prof Willboughby D'Eresby and Letitia) who wears no clothes (the wife, not the prof) and son, Keir, who is also a nutter and only eats pigeons he strangles on windowsills. Housewife goes dossing again. Ludicrous bit where she gets mixed up with Cabinet minister. Chased by policeman with silly name (Inspector Sly). Plot peters out towards end. Chapters alternate between diary-like entries by housewife and third-person narrative.

Just re-read this and wonder if a bit harsh. One or two nice little perceptions in amongst all this, and some sharp, fleeting Moleish observations. But not really a novel. A bit thin, really. And so to lunch.

Alan Rusbridger, "Nowhere Like Coventry," in Manchester Guardian Weekly, *October 9, 1988, p. 29.*

ANDREW STEPHEN

So who, they asked me, do you think is the best-selling author of the Eighties? Whose book has been translated into 20 languages—Serbo-Croat, Russian, Japanese, and so on—and has sold more copies in this country than any other work? Plus hundreds of thousands of hardbacks in the Soviet Union? Who has had to be protected by police from over-enthusiastic fans at book-signing sessions in Yugoslavia?

I would probably be surprised by the answer, they went on. It was not Jeffrey Archer. Nor Catherine Cookson. Not Barbara Cartland. No, not Frederick Forsyth. It wasn't even John Le Carre, either.

Last week I finally discovered the answer for myself. Britain's best-selling author this decade looks set to be a 43-year-old mother-of-four who left school at 15, lives in Leicester, and only started writing professionally less than 10 years ago. Her name is Sue Townsend, and *The Secret Diary of Adrian Mole Aged 13 ¾* has already sold more copies than Archer's *Kane and Abel,* Audrey Eyton's *The F-Plan Diet* or any other smash-hit of the Eighties. And the third best-selling book of the decade just happens to be *The Growing Pains of Adrian Mole*—by the same Sue Townsend.

It was publication date of her latest book in London last Thursday. . . .

That morning a smart-aleck review in the *Times* had said she did not 'cerebrate' in her books:

> I felt that was odd. You may not have the brightest brain in the world, but a certain amount of thinking has to go into writing *anything.* Michael Billington called me the Douanier Rousseau of British drama, and when I read that I thought how can that be? I understood it and knew the reference. If I'd been naive I wouldn't have understood it.

What much of London's literary, cognoscenti have failed to realise is that besides creating Mole (as she describes the genre) Ms Townsend has also written several serious stage and television plays as well as a successful novel. . . .

But somehow the lightweight image still persists; she does not even rate a mention in the 1989 *Who's Who.* 'People don't see me as a literary writer,' she explains.

> There are a few comic writers—people like Alan Bennett—who have a foot in each camp. But then he writes for the *London Review of Books,* doesn't he? I think I'm seen in some establishments as quite a vulgar sort of person—a nouveau-riche upstart, a flash in the pan.

Her absence from *Who's Who,* she believes, 'illustrates perfectly a lot of things—about class, and about how humour is perceived'. She is 'obsessed' with class, she says: 'It's because I was so conscious of it as a child. I think it's got a stranglehold on this country. It's a huge dampener. It ghetto-ises people, keeps them apart. There's a sort of fear of middle and upper-class people.' And she shares that fear? 'Yes, I do. I think there are certain middle-class people who just take up too much *room.'* . . .

For a long time, she says, her children used to deny to their friends that she was their mother.

And the egregious but world-famous Adrian Mole is most definitely *not* based on either of her two sons Sean (aged 24½) or Daniel (aged 19 ¾), she adds—nor on the youths she used to work with at an adventure playground. 'It's something to do with my own personality and psyche.' Could she not more easily have written the diaries of a teenage girl, then? 'No.'

She has tried to analyse why she has such a devastating insight into the mind of pubescent masculinity, sometimes with the help of Jung 'in a bumbling, amateurish way'. But not with formal Jungian analysis? 'No. God, no. Penguin paperback Jung.' She believes that boys and girls at 13 are more similar than is generally believed. 'They have so much in

common at that stage—overpowering, emotional turmoil. Then their paths start to diverge.'

She chain-smokes, despite heart trouble and diabetes. She has known other unhappinesses too: her first husband, a sheet-metal worker, left her and three children for a younger woman. In the creation of the pretentious but pathetic Adrian Mole, is there not a hint of sexism, of the reverse of misogyny?

'Yes,' she replies unhesitatingly.

> He started out to be an anti-hero. When I started to write it I was extremely interested in feminism and still am. I wanted to illustrate certain points and use him. But then I actually sort of fell for the character. Which is what a lot of good women do— they fall for a bloke.

In her latest book, there are brief glimpses of Mole at 21—working in dead-end jobs in a library and then the Department of the Environment. But she says she will not write another major Mole epic until 1992: 'The publishers won't like this, but he'll be an adult then. He'll be 24, 25. We're into a completely different ball game.'

The comedy, presumably, will by then be turning into tragedy as Mole's adolescent dreams fade and his hopes and ambitions remain unrealised? 'This is the constant dilemma of my work. In a sense, I'm only interested in writing about deeply sad and important things. But I have this curse that I can only express it through humour. That's a word I hate.' . . .

Ninety-eight miles south in London, Sue Townsend's publishers are frantically distributing her latest book: doubtless another best-seller. Her latest stage play *Ten Tiny Fingers, Nine Tiny Toes*—set in a Britain of the future where certain socio-economic groups are allowed to have babies and other not—is about to go into rehearsal.

What would Britain's best-selling author of the Eighties most like to be remembered for, though? As a serious playwright? Novelist? Adrian Mole? 'Before I die I just want to do an excellent piece of writing,' she says, stubbing out her umpteenth cigarette. 'I would just like a rave review in the *London Review of Books.* Really.'

> *Andrew Stephen, "Growing Pain of a Literary Outsider," in* The Observer, *September 3, 1989, p. 35.*

JONATHAN KEATES

English writers spend an inordinate amount of time pretending not to be literary, and an entire subspecies has evolved of women who see it as a distinct advantage to go on being taken for the dizzy *ingenues* they never were.

Alice Thomas Ellis, Beryl Bainbridge, Pam Ayres and Wendy Cope are shrewd variants of the type. So is Sue Townsend. Her Leicester schoolboy Adrian Mole has made it to the GCSE list, up there in the big league with *Romeo and Juliet* and *The Mayor of Casterbridge.*

But our Sue is still our Sue, larky, sparky and demotic to her fingers' ends, not one to have her head turned by Dame Fame. 'What, me a writer?' says she to herself as she jaunts off to Russia with the likes of Alan Bennett and Craig Raine, a trip relived with many a breathless ebullition of cachinnation in this latest harvest of fugitive pieces, [*The True Confes-*

sions of Adrian Albert Mole]. The vagabond scribes feast off twiglets, liquorice allsorts and lemon vodka, Sue suspects Sakharov is wearing Max Factor panstick but it turns out to be not enough bran in his diet, and Paul Bailey turns the literati of Orel into a bunch of groupies by hinting that La Townsend is *une femme louche.*

The other items are decidedly curate's-eggy. There's a truly—blushmaking little outburst on **"Why I Like England"** written in the sort of Lego-kit, neo-infantile prose much favoured by the *ingenues.* Sue's thumbnail sketch of **"Writing For Television"**, on the other hand, is a classic chart of professional pitfalls, from the arm-twisting lunch to the jeremiads of the producer's wife against the pinkos at the Beeb.

To give the Adrian Mole treatment to the Leaderene, *Margaret Hilda Roberts aged 14½* was a neat idea, but only half the jokes really catch fire. Reading *Intermediate Chemistry* for fun and helping the Alderman to water down the dandelion-and-burdock at 5am is indeed hideously plausible, as is her mother staying in bed with *Madame Bovary* and a packet of violet creams, but the 'smelly, working-class oiks' called Ginger Shinnock and Roy Batterfree—oh per-*lease!*

And what about our Adrian, you ask? Sixteen going on 17 and, if anything, more convincing than his former avatar. Shall we live to see him drawing his pension? The single jarring note is the survival of the dreadful Pandora: such constancy in adolescent boys is seldom found. But at her best Sue doesn't 'arf make you larf.

Jonathan Keates, "Mole Among the Soviets," in The Observer, September 3, 1989, p. 46.

THE TIMES EDUCATIONAL SUPPLEMENT

Dear Mole. He is, for me, one of the key literary characters of our time. His words have a terrible ineluctable truth. His stoicism in the face of family life is almost unbearably touching. As is his almost total lack of a sense of humour: like all the best comic characters, he has no idea that he's in a comedy. I was hooked from the very first entry in the *Secret Diary:* "My father got the dog drunk on cherry brandy at the party last night. If the RSPCA hear about it he could get done." It has the inevitable rightness of something by Kafka, hasn't it? When things start to fall apart and the centre cannot hold, one of the first signs will be inebriation and riot among the family pets. She knows, you know.

Despite the enormous success that Sue Townsend has enjoyed, I think her literary achievement has been underrated. It *looks* easy enough to do, but none of her imitators has come anywhere near her. And in the *Growing Pains* she managed to write a sequel that took bigger risks and was even more rewarding to read than the *Secret Diary.*

The new book [*True Confessions of Adrian Albert Mole*] is, I guess, essential reading for Mole-followers, but it has its anxiety-inducing aspects. Mole is, at 16, still worrying away about life, but he has developed a rather flatulent style to do it in, and his insights seem less sharp and bleak, even a little bit, well, boring: "My present domestic abode is a semi-detached house in a suburban cul-de-sac in the Midlands. Yes, like many of my fellow-Britons, I live with a party wall between me and another family's intimate secrets. I will never understand why it is called a party wall because when our next-door neighbours throw a party every celebratory sound is heard." Every celebratory sound, eh? Hmm.

At 17, Mole falls heavily for Sarah Ferguson: "I know the dog and you will get along" he says in desperation: he knows he's on a loser. It is a temporary aberration; Pandora is on holiday in Russia at the time. At 20, his heart still belongs to Pandora, but his thing appears to belong to Sharon Botts, who measures 30 inches round the tops of her thighs. But Mole at the age of 20 is not to be thought about. Even by Sue Townsend, who abandons him abruptly on page 66. We also get some extracts from *The Secret Diary of Margaret Hilda Roberts aged 14½:* "Walking to school I was almost knocked down by a horrid working-class man on a bicycle." A Mr Tebbit, it turns out to be, looking for work. Margaret reflects that his sort ought to be forbidden to breed. It's a brilliant idea and I could have done with more than 18 pages of it, which is all we get. There are also some bits by Sue Townsend as herself, which, which . . . fill up another 30 pages.

"Still Muddling On," in The Times Educational Supplement, No. 3822, September 29, 1989, p. 32.

PENELOPE FITZGERALD

Sue Townsend's *The Secret Diary of Adrian Mole aged 13 ¾* came out at much the same time as John Pocock's *The Diary of a London Schoolboy 1826-30.* John Pocock, 12 ¾, decisively a real person, was a builder's son who lived on the edge of Kilburn, two miles out of London. In his journal, written on the empty pages of an old bankbook, he notes that on 23 May 1826 he walked to school: 'Old Monk drinks like a fish.' At 14 he feels it is 'high time for me to be learning some trade or profession', and at 15 he is alone at his father's deathbed, holding 'the cold clammy hand'. At 16 he ships for Australia as an apprentice surgeon. His experiences were hard enough. But although his diary was so private that he had to write part of it (particularly when his father was arrested for debt) in cipher, he makes no mention of his adolescent spots, his wet dreams, or the anxieties of measuring his Thing. Adrian Mole's diary, which does, made an instant appeal to six million readers as being truer to life.

The *Diary* and the *Growing Pains* are catalogued by the publishers under Teens and Humour, but their genre is really that of the ironic-innocent child's confession. Probably the first of these to appear was *The Life of Lazarillo de Tormes* in 1554. Lazarillo is an orphan boy who faces starvation in the hard streets of Salamanca. His first master, a blind man, beats him and wrenches open his jaws to smell whether he has eaten the last piece of turnip. But Lazarillo holds fast, he tells us, to his dying mother's advice: 'keep close to good people, in order to become one of them.' The irony of his struggle to do this lies, of course, in the word 'good'. A more orderly world, but not so very much gentler, is the Late Victorian private school of Eden Philpotts's classic, *The Human Boy.* There is 'an element of autobiography' in it, Philpotts said, and the speaker was to be 'a fair specimen of the commonplace, idiotic, eager, human boy'—not, like Adrian Mole, an intellectual. That sort of thing is left to the school poet, who makes the surprisingly high charge of twopence a line. The editors begged for a *Human Girl,* but Philpotts replied that 'all that the human boy knows of the human girl will be found in my stories concerning him; it is not very much.'

All these three—Lazarillo, the Human Boy and Mole—have

compassionate hearts, the priceless gift of nature. . . .When the Doctor makes a disastrous mistake, as headmasters in fiction tend to do, the Human Boy is shocked to see him for a moment looking 'old and haggard and queer'. Adrian Mole, in his turn, notes that when the electricity is cut off for non-payment his feckless father looks 'sad and old'. Later in life Adrian has a narrow escape from the Sunshine People, who guarantee world peace for a £20 subscription. 'I will get the money somehow. Nothing is too expensive where peace is concerned.' In spite of his overwhelming anxieties, he has sympathy to spare for Jesus on the Cross, for a horse standing alone in a field—it must be 'dead bored'—for his dog, for his wayward mother, for the maverick old age pensioner allocated to him by the Samaritans. As to the anxieties themselves, they are intensely comic, but Sue Townsend's epigraph is from *Sons and Lovers:* 'Paul walked with something screwed up tight inside him . . . yet he chatted away with his mother. He would never have confessed to her how he suffered over these things and she only partly guessed.' Sue Townsend is the mother who wholly guessed.

What is to become of Mole? In *The Growing Pains* he widens his political and literary horizons ('Tuesday, April 6th. The nation has been told that Britain and Argentina are not at war, we are at conflict . . . I am reading *Scoop* by a woman called Evelyn Waugh'). There are steps forward, too, into adult experience. He runs away from home, getting as far as Manchester, although his disappearance seems to cause no stir—nothing about him on the Six O'Clock News—and he has to write a card addressed to himself: 'Come home, son. Without you the house is devoid of love and laughter.' He goes to a cremation. He visits his mother in the pre-natal ward and is allowed (rather improbably) to watch the birth of his baby sister. He knows, too, that the baby's father is the next-door neighbour, Mr Lucas. At school he has his own girlfriend, a little older and a good deal cleverer and better-off than himself, the feminist with treacle-coloured hair, Pandora. Pandora is at one with him as an intellectual, but will not let him see her nipples, and Mole's situation, at the age of 16, is in perilous balance. Sue Townsend had the alternative of abandoning him altogether, or letting him grow up. Adrian could not, in any case, stay unchanged, since time and adolescence are at the heart of the situation. By 1988 he is 20. He could become corrupt—as Lazarillo does, marrying the arch-priest's daughter in exchange for a job as town crier—or he could, against all expectations, succeed.

The *True Confessions of Adrian Albert Mole, Margaret Hilda Robert and Susan Lillian Townsend* never quite find their direction. Gone, of course, are the days when Mole dreamed of being an intellectual road-sweeper who would amaze the litter-louts by quoting Kafka. Still living dismally at home, he has been fired from his job at the library for shelving Jane Austen in the Light Romances section. Sex is no longer an urgent problem, since he is on close terms with Sharon Botts, 'a provincial dullard working in a laundry'. But alas, they bore one another, and there is a distressing feeling that Mole has been defeated in his gallant struggle against a cultureless, boil-in-a-bag society.

More spirited are the diaries of Margaret Hilda Roberts, a grocer's daughter, who spends her evenings studying chemistry and helping her father to water down the dandelion and burdock, while by day she relentlessly organises everyone about her. The diaries are thought to date from the 1930s, but unfortunately, we are told, nothing is known as to what became of the writer. Sue Townsend also includes some of her own travel notes from Majorca and Russia, where she went as a guest of the GB-USSR Association. These are written with great good nature, but confirm the facts that it is not much fun to be on your own in Spain, and that writers are at their very worst in an organised group. She is frankly not sorry to be back again, although 'the England I love best is, of course, the England of childhood, where children could play in the streets without the neighbours getting up a petition.' Given the choice between death and exile, she says: 'I'd choose exile every time, but I'd be very, very unhappy to leave the club.'

Sue Townsend's playground in the Forties was the pavements of Leicester, and she was born (and rescued from pneumonia) by courtesy of the Welfare State. In *Counter Blasts No. 9: Mr. Bevan's Dream* she takes as a starting-point the first principle of the Beveridge Report: 'that the wishes of any one section of the community are not given undue weight against any other section.' She can't and won't, she says, present a formal argument ('I have fallen back on the traditional working-class method for expressing ideas—the anecdote') and these stories, from high-rise blocks and DHSS queues and understaffed hospitals, give her all the force she needs to protest against the dream's ten-year decline. Her case might have been even stronger if she had left out her colourful characters—an insane headmaster who shadow-boxes with all comers, a drunken pork-butcher. She is speaking, after all, on behalf of the overlooked and uncolourful.

Penelope Fitzgerald, "Human Boys," in London Review of Books, *Vol. 11, No. 23, December 7, 1989, p. 24.*

George F. Walker

1947-

Canadian dramatist and scriptwriter.

An important force in contemporary Canadian drama, Walker is associated with the rise of alternative theater in Toronto during the 1970s and 1980s. His extensive use of elements associated with the Theater of the Absurd and popular culture have helped expand the scope of Canadian drama, which had been traditionally dominated by naturalistic plays concerning rural and small town life. Walker's satirical farces feature black humor and language dominated by irony, non sequiturs, and pseudopsychological jargon, and he often draws upon and parodies comic strips, film noir, and detective novels. His depictions of the struggles of individuals in a corrupt world, which frequently involve stock characters representing good or evil, are extended symbolically and metaphorically through nonlinear plot development and various theatrical devices Walker employs to blur distinctions between reality and fantasy. Jerry Wasserman identified Walker's abiding concerns as "corruption, obsession, power, [and] the apocalyptic struggle between the forces of good and evil, order and chaos."

Born and raised in Toronto's east end, where he has set some of his plays, Walker held numerous odd jobs after dropping out of high school. While driving a taxicab he noticed an advertisement inviting submission of scripts to the Factory Theatre Lab, a forum for alternative drama. Walker responded with a script, thus initiating a successful association with the Lab and its artistic director, Ken Gass. Walker served as playwright-in-residence at the Factory Lab from 1971 to 1974, and many of his works were initially staged by this group, including his first play, *The Prince of Naples,* which he wrote after noticing the ad. An examination of youth-oriented popular culture, this drama depicts an inverted student-teacher relationship in which the younger member assumes power. Critics often detect the influences of such playwrights as Eugène Ionesco and Samuel Beckett in Walker's early plays, particularly in his use of surreal and absurdly comic incidents. For example, the main character in *Ambush at Tether's End* is the corpse of an embittered poet who has committed suicide and left notes that urge his peers to confront reality by performing similar unequivocal actions. *Sacktown Rag* focuses on a schoolboy beset by representative adolescent problems that are exaggerated by caricatures of his parents and teachers.

Critics agree that Walker established his own approach to drama with his next three works, *Bagdad Saloon, Beyond Mozambique,* and *Ramona and the White Slaves,* all of which parody B-movies and are collected in *Three Plays. Bagdad Saloon* consists of a series of brief sketches featuring heroes of American popular culture who have been kidnapped by Arabs attempting to divine the secret of popular success. *Beyond Mozambique* parodies jungle movies while exploring the decline of Western civilization. Set on a colonial estate in a jungle, this play features a mad scientist and his hunchbacked assistant among six stock characters; in an ironic twist of B-movie plots, the characters's reliance on technology and Western values undermines their ability to survive. *Ramona*

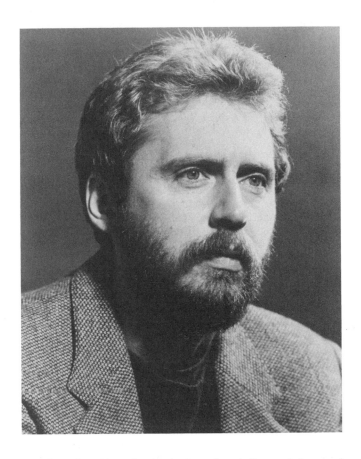

and the White Slaves begins in the opium-influenced dream of Ramona, the madam of a brothel in Hong Kong. Distinctions between reality and dream remain obscure throughout the play while Walker explores the obsessive personality of the madam.

Walker achieved international recognition with *Zastrozzi, The Master of Discipline.* Based, according to Walker, on his reading of a description of Percy Bysshe Shelley's novel, *Zastrozzi,* this play centers on a master criminal who embodies extreme evil. Set in various locales in nineteenth-century Europe, the play follows the title character's pursuit of an idealist and moralist named Verezzi, whom Zastrozzi holds responsible for his mother's death. While perpetrating violence and bloodshed on innocent characters, Zastrozzi is foiled in his attempts to capture Verezzi by Victor, a lapsed priest. Toying with symbolism, character identification, and melodramatic elements of B-movies, Walker explores the nature of good and evil. As is typical in Walker's work, the evil character is disciplined and decisive while the representative of good is plagued by self-doubt and ineffectiveness. This trait is further elaborated in such plays as *Gossip, Filthy Rich,* and *The Art of War,* which were collected and published in *The Power Plays.* At the center of these three works is Tyrone M. Power, a bungling private investigator and failed writer who attempts to uphold truth and justice amid political corruption. The protagonist's inefficiency is contraposed with resolute and uncompromising authority figures who maintain power by manipulating political bureaucracies.

Three of Walker's works, published together as *The East End Plays,* are set in a working-class section of Toronto and concern conflicts among members of several families. *Criminals in Love,* which won the Governor General's Award, centers on teenage lovers Junior and Gail who are torn apart by the criminal activities of the young man's family. *Better Living,* written after but set before *Criminals in Love,* contrasts the values and strengths of females in Junior's family with those of obsessed, weak, or criminal males, a theme further elaborated in *Beautiful City.* A satire on urban decay, this play depicts competing families using all of their resources in a fight for possession of property. Jerry Wasserman observed: "The battles fought within and between family groups (there are four of them) in *Beautiful City* are battles for the soul of the city and the fate of urban man." Walker won a second Governor General's Award as well as several drama prizes in Toronto for *Nothing Sacred.* Based on Ivan Turgenev's midnineteenth-century novel *Fathers and Sons, Nothing Sacred* centers on a nihilistic, self-styled rebel determined to help overthrow the existing social order. Romance, class struggles, and differing values among the characters become sources of conflict, culminating in a duel between the nihilist and a foppish, humanistic aristocrat. *Nothing Sacred* was a popular and critical success in regional theaters throughout North America.

(See also *CLC,* Vol. 44; *Contemporary Authors,* Vol. 103; *Contemporary Authors New Revision Series,* Vol. 21; and *Dictionary of Literary Biography,* Vol. 60.)

PRINCIPAL WORKS

PLAYS

Prince of Naples   1971
Ambush at Tether's End   1971
Sacktown Rag   1972
Bagdad Saloon   1973
Beyond Mozambique   1974
Ramona and the White Slaves   1976
Gossip   1977
Zastrozzi, the Master of Discipline   1977
Filthy Rich   1979
Rumours of Our Death   1980
Theatre of the Film Noir   1981
The Art of War   1983
Criminals in Love   1984
Better Living   1986
Nothing Sacred   1988

BRYAN JOHNSON

[*The article excerpted below originally appeared in the* Globe and Mail, *November 3, 1977.*]

As swift and clean as a rapier through the guts—and just about that lethal. That's *Zastrozzi.* . . .

Subtitled *The Master of Discipline,* the play is a sort of Gothic tragedy with a gift for farce. . . .

Zastrozzi is an impossible character, a mythical devil who destroys whole cities, ravages their women, kills mediocre artists "just to prove that even artists must answer to someone".

You hesitate to use a word like joy in describing a play whose inevitable climax is a bloodbath which kills off everyone except the hero-devil. But unless I'm a closet sadist, I don't know how else to explain the exhilaration the play gives.

That kind of praise makes it sound like a masterpiece. But, for all its good points, *Zastrozzi* is hardly that. For one thing, none of its other five characters is anywhere near the hero's class—and one or two are badly flawed, in fact. And though Walker has seeded his play with a number of sharp, insouciant quips, the . . . cast had a heck of a time delivering them.

The play—which Walker based on a capsule description of the Shelley novel, *Zastrozzi*—centres on the master criminal's search for revenge on Verezzi, who apparently committed some atrocity on Zastrozzi's mother years ago. The way Walker sees him, Verezzi has become a raving religious lunatic in the meantime, full of messianic delusions. . . . [As] a whining, silly weakling, he's about the last man in the world with whom an audience can identify.

The effect, naturally, is to take away any conflict there might have been. Zastrozzi is a fascinating, extraordinary evil dynamo. His intended victim is a little fop we'd just as soon see dead. Who cares, therefore, about the deadly bond between them?

That weakens the play greatly. But, fortunately, there's a cast of vastly more interesting side characters for Zastrozzi to deal with. There's Matilda, for one, who plays master seductress to his master criminal. . . . [Victor is] the brains behind Verezzi, an ex-priest who rises to challenge the villain's sword.

Then there's the huge [Bernardo], a near-cartoon as the henchman who "strives hard to be Zastrozzi's shadow", and Julia, also a caricature of the young, blond virgin who is trampled by the unstoppable evil.

Walker has, as I say, given them all a sort of dramatic-comic duality. When the temptress Matilda tells Julia she hates her, for example, because "women like you make me feel like a tart", the virgin replies innocently: "Nonsense. It's the way you dress".

And though there are lots of funny lines like that, [the director] hasn't been able to integrate them properly. No matter who's saying them, the delivery is inevitably deliberate and obvious. The actors are painfully aware of the quips, and handle them like grenades, dropping them as if afraid they will blow up in their faces.

That's more than a tiny quibble, but it's not nearly enough to defeat *Zastrozzi.*

Bryan Johnson, in a review of "Zastrozzi," in Canadian Drama/L'Art dramatique canadien, *Vol. 11, No. 1, 1985, pp. 142-43.*

TERRY CURTIS FOX

George F. Walker is one of those people who writes comedies

because he cannot bear the indifference of the universe. A moralist who hides behind a stream of mock-camp dialogue, Walker is finally coming into his own, both in his native Canada and in the United States. . . .

"Fame is the artist's only excuse for existence," declares Ahrun, the Arab collector of American immortals in *Bagdad Saloon,* [collected in] *Three Plays.* . . . It is a major theme in Walker's work. His world is peopled by uncontrollable egocentrics who are capable of only passing glances toward their victims. When Friedrich, the paraplegic piano player of *Ramona and the White Slaves* (1976), suddenly appears with a new set of legs, his mother, watching him fall after a first clumsy attempt to use them, dismissively notes, "If it was a miracle, would he be lying on the floor?" When Friedrich finally does manage his new appendages, they are nothing more than an annoyance: "Walking. Walking," another character declares. "That's all you ever think about these days." Pain, miracles, art are all too dangerous for Walker's characters to acknowledge. Other people's emotions get in the way of the self; suffering does not lead to compassion or empathy, it breeds competition.

Unlike these earlier plays, *Gossip* (1977) takes place in a remotely recognizable city, but its subject is quite the same. Walker knows his audience and he knows his own self: he'd no more write a play entitled *Illegal Activities of Canadian Parliamentarians* than we would come to see one. So when T. (for Tyrone) M. Power declares that he can't stand gossip and wants his political column back, it's a bit hard for the audience to stand up and cheer journalistic integrity. Power's vulgar, foppish, father-obsessed publisher Baxter is right: *Gossip* is exactly what we want to hear, even when it's about people we don't know.

Most of the people in *Gossip* are guilty of at least one murder, crimes uncovered by Power in his search not for the truth but for a way of getting his column back. Like the reporter-hero, both guilty and innocent are highly unpleasant, potentially violent, or nearly deranged. The nearly deranged is Power's girlfriend, who happens to be the sister and lover of that corrupt member of parliament not mentioned in the title. In the course of the play, crusading reporter Power mercilessly pushes the girl over the edge. He even waits for the proper moment to drive the girl nuts: until he's got all the facts for his story, he shouts "Later" whenever she shows signs of breaking down. She obliges by holding off her madness until the climactic scene, at which time Power no longer cares what she does. *Gossip* is a farce with a cyanide grin. (p. 90)

Terry Curtis Fox, "Unexaggerated Rumors," in The Village Voice, *Vol. XXIV, No. 14, April 2, 1979, pp. 90-1.*

CHRIS JOHNSON

It is now ten years since the Factory Theatre Lab opened its first season in a makeshift theatre above an auto-body shop on Dupont Street in Toronto. Theatre Passe Muraille had been in operation for two years, and Tarragon Theatre and Toronto Free Theatre were to join the new Toronto "alternative theatre scene" shortly. Together, the four theatres played a major role in encouraging the upsurge in interest in Canadian drama whose impetus we are still feeling. The renewed burst of theatrical activity in Toronto, this time with a distinct Canadian accent, encouraged increased interest in Ca-

nadian drama, and a number of Canadian writers who had been exerting their productive energy in a theatrical direction for several years, among them Robertson Davies, John Herbert, George Ryga, and James Reaney, acquired an increased importance in the eyes of those interested in the development of Canadian culture. . . . With the added efforts of Passe Muraille, Factory Lab, Tarragon, Toronto Free Theatre, and the writers associated with these companies, Canadian drama was seen for the first time as an "entire enterprise," a suddenly more impressive whole whose parts deserved more attention. (p. 87)

As well as being one of the most accomplished writers to emerge from Ken Gass's [Factory Theatre Lab], Walker is a writer with a long and close connection with the theatre: his first play was produced in 1971 in the company's second season, he was for a number of years the Factory Lab's resident playwright, and he served for a brief period as the theatre's Artistic Director. He wrote his first play, *Prince of Naples,* in response to the Factory Lab's ubiquitous posters calling for new scripts; until then, he had only dabbled in verse and short fiction. The one-act piece, and the full-length play which followed shortly after, *Ambush at Tether's End,* are both clearly the work of a writer new to theatre, of a writer of urban and cosmopolitan sensibility looking to established writers for models in the form new to him. (p. 89)

Prince of Naples concerns a relationship familiar to every North American, that of student and teacher, and draws extensively on the perspectives of a contemporary urban world, simultaneously literate and electronic. The work shows its literary ancestry through its form: in its use of language, transforming pat phrases into extended and volcanic passages of nonsense, in its heavy dependence on a central theatrical image, and in its concerted effort to include the audience within the emotional event the characters are experiencing, the play models itself after the Theatre of the Absurd in general and after Ionesco's *The Lesson* in particular. Walker reverses the usual power structure in the educational process, making the young the instructor of the old, to examine a social phenomenon, the cult of the young and the supposedly liberated, associated with the sixties, and in the process questions the new credo of relativity:

> Now the word insane has been reapproached by the wide-eyed armies of time and given a new meaning. The word has been dragged out of the dampness of our mental basement and placed high on the clouds of our consciousness.

The method of employing a form to question ironically the ideas underlying the form became characteristic of Walker's work.

Ambush at Tether's End was Walker's second exercise in the theatrical techniques of the Absurd: this time, the most important model appears to be Samuel Beckett's *Waiting for Godot.* The central character in the play is a corpse (an echo of Ionesco's *Amédée, or How to Get Rid of It?*), a poet-philosopher who has hanged himself and who has left a series of notes attacking the values of his friends, challenging them to confront "reality" as he has with a "definitive act" equal to his. While there are similarities linking the friends to Beckett's tramps, Walker has localized the situation, and has made from the dichotomy depicted by Vladimir and Estragon a more North American opposition of obsessions, those of the ambitious businessman and the sexual athlete. If those who wait are diminished, so too is that for which they wait.

Max, the moralizing corpse, endangers his own authenticity through his posthumous showmanship, and the philosophical life is discredited by the dead man's petty rivalry with a colleague. While Galt and Bush are, predictably, destroyed by the dilemma in which they find themselves, there is little to recommend an alternative to their views if Max is the representative of that alternative. Walker sees both the society he satirizes and the modish and pseudo-romantic challenge to that society as inadequate, and in the play constructs a theatrical model of the intellectual quandary in which many of his generation found themselves. (pp. 89-90)

The Theatre of the Absurd has remained largely a European phenomenon: American playwrights have had as much difficulty transplanting its insights and techniques to a North American *milieu* and audience as have had the Canadians. . . . Martin Esslin [in *The Theatre of the Absurd*] attributes the difficulty to history:

> [The] convention of the Absurd springs from a feeling of deep disillusionment, the draining away of the sense of meaning and purpose in life, which has been characteristic of countries like France and Britain in the years after the Second World War. In the United States there has been no corresponding loss of meaning and purpose.

While the statement is undoubtedly less true than it was when it was first written, it is significant that most of the American playwrights whose work had close affinities to the European avant-garde of the fifties and early sixties have subsequently developed in different directions. Thomas Porter advances a more commercial explanation in *Myth and Modern American Drama*. While mainstream American drama consistently portrays the failure of the American Dream, that which has maintained the illusion of "meaning and purpose," the American theatre-going public has an aversion to the next step, a dramatic form which not only discusses but reflects the disintegration of the Dream. In consequence, American attempts to transfer the technique as well as the message have been stillborn. The American playwrights who have most successfully communicated to an American audience those insights usually associated with the Theatre of the Absurd have been those, like Jean-Claude van Itallie or Sam Shepard, who have taken particular care to couch these insights in an American idiom, who have employed the disjointed nature of American popular culture to display a fragmented theatrical vision of lost "meaning and purpose." Shepard, whose work is most clearly relevant to a consideration of Walker's, has proven particularly adept at employing the trivia of American society as a means of both celebrating the vulgar vitality of that society and suggesting an emptiness beyond.

In Walker's third play, *Sacktown Rag,* he draws on North American pop culture in a manner somewhat similar to Shepard's, and in turning to more autobiographical subject matter, discards some of the literary self-consciousness which intrudes in the earlier plays. The structural technique is that of the cartoon: the schoolboy protagonist experiences the traumas of growing up in a world sometimes realistic and sometimes drawn in the lurid colours of the comic strip. While the caricatures of parents and teachers sometimes have the gleeful and scatological energy of schoolboy graffiti, Walker does not entirely trust his conventions and chooses to explain them away with an unconvincing memory frame: the play subsequently loses the impact of the cartoon without gaining

enough in psychological insight to compensate. It is probably the least satisfying of Walker's published work.

In *Bagdad Saloon,* first produced in 1973 and subtitled "a cartoon," Walker does not dilute his pop art conventions: the result is a bawdy, sprawling collage of short scenes, music, and *coups de théâtre*. The cartoon figures are less personal than the graffiti of *Sacktown Rag;* characters drawn from American high and low culture, Gertrude Stein, Henry Miller, Doc Halliday, have greater resonance, and extend the implications of the piece beyond itself.

The incident which precipitates the action of the play is the kidnapping of the American legends by a pair of improbable Arabs who want to learn the secret of mythic immortality. The attempt, of course, is futile: Halliday and Miller are frauds, and Stein, while she has visions, proves incapable of communicating what she sees. The American saloon is grafted onto fabled Bagdad, and Aladdin decks himself out as a dime store cowboy in pursuit of a new and neon mythology, even while the efficacy of any myth in staving off the chaos is put in question:

> AHRUN: Fame is a fickle commodity. Not bad, mind you. Just fickle.
> DOC: So what?
> STEIN: Exactly.
> AHRUN: It needs to be guided, so to speak. And if it's guided in the right direction, it can create things. Purpose. Glamour. Mystique. (*Pause*) Artists. Or folk heroes. All things which we find very scarce around here.
> STEIN: What happens then?
> AHRUN: Folk-lore.
> STEIN: And then?
> AHRUN: More folk-lore.
> STEIN: And then?
> AHRUN: And then . . . and you can—and then there's always . . .
> STEIN: Yes?
> DOC: What?
> (*Ahrun shakes his head violently. Turns. Leaves. . . .*)

So much for identity, Arab, Canadian, or otherwise. (pp. 91-2)

[The] first movement of the play constructs the saloon and decorates it in all its crass glory, while the second movement destroys and discredits the structure. Unfortunately, the process is unduly protracted and Walker is often distracted by his fascination with the decoration; the piece is theatrically inefficient. Still, in *Bagdad Saloon* Walker shows increased control of his new medium, and develops further the talent for stage metaphor revealed in the earlier plays: the image of the all-American hero, sportsman, and pop singer as pathetic, speechless grotesque is an image that lingers long after memories of the irritating meanderings have faded.

It is a commonplace that, particularly in matters of structural convention, theatre has been drawing for the last two or three decades on popular electronic forms, especially film, reclaiming the debt that art form owes theatre in general and August Strindberg in particular. (pp. 92-3)

[Film] also provides, especially through the so-called B-movies, a rich source of images, plot models, and a set of stock characters not unlike those used in melodrama or Commedia dell'Arte, an iconography available to the contemporary playwright to be employed as he sees fit. While Walker uses a number of cinematic structural devices in *Bagdad Saloon,* he makes comparatively little use of filmic iconography; *Beyond Mozambique* (1974) marks the beginning of extensive recourse to the raw material of the B-movie, material characteristic of all his subsequent work. In employing stock characters and situations as the vehicles for insights and ideas beyond the capacity of the popular form from which they were drawn, Shepard in *Mad Dog Blues* or *Angel City* and Walker in *Beyond Mozambique* and *Ramona and the White Slaves* follow well-established theatrical practice: Beckett and Ionesco draw from music hall and film comedy; Pirandello, Chekhov, and Ibsen drew from melodrama; and, of course, Molière made use of the characters and conventions of Commedia dell'Arte.

The B-movie also provides an ironic mode, an element acquired through the almost accidental manner in which the older B-movies were reintroduced into the mainstream of popular art through late-night movies on television and hence into the imaginations of the generation shaped by television. In this way, trivial work which would otherwise have perished, as do novels unworthy of reprinting or plays not worth reviving, lead an extended life; the extension, the survival of artifacts meant to be disposable, frequently leads to levels of meaning not intended by their creators. The B-movies of the forties and fifties present a vision of life so simple and naive that the effect is comic, while the rapidity of shifts in popular taste gives the films a quaintness which emphasizes the naiveté and heightens the comic effect.

In adapting the world of the B-movie for the stage there are two dangers. The first is that an audience might accept that world at face value, despite the integral irony of a topical perspective out of context. The second pitfall is the temptation to revel in the exuberant awfulness of it all: the result, here, is usually described as "camp." . . . In *Beyond Mozambique* and subsequent plays, Walker circumvents the perils through the addition of elements from other modes, hyperbole, and explicit comment on the theatrical context.

Beyond Mozambique is a jungle movie, but contrary to the opinions of several first-night critics, it is not just a jungle movie. Set on the porch of a decaying colonial mansion in the jungle, the play throws together six disparate characters, in the best "ship of fools" tradition, and allows these figures, or "masks" as Richard Horenblas describes them [in *Scene Changes,* October 1975], to enact for us the decline and disintegration of western civilization; while its mode is that of the B-movie, its content is not: technology does not triumph over nature, white heroines are not pure, white heros are not all-powerful, and while the embattled whites are not overwhelmed by the forces of "savagery" drumming in the bush, they do succumb to the chaos within, and it is the drumming of that threat which provides the play's rhythm and central theatrical metaphor. (pp. 93-4)

[The play's central character] is that most twentieth-century of archetypes, the mad scientist. Rocca combines the familiar B-movie archetype and hints of concentration camp "medical experiments," sadism disguised as a quest for knowledge, or, perhaps, the quest for knowledge undisguised; he is both the historical nightmare and the popular rendition of the obsessions in part responsible for those nightmares: in the face of impending disintegration, he can think only of pressing on with his experiments and of acquiring the necessary subjects. While he is horrifying, Rocco is, in Walker's wry view, the most positive character in the play; he has a Kurtz-like integrity which compels him to define, to defy chaos even if in a perverse way, a drive often expressed in gloriously B-movie lines: "There's something about committing crimes against humanity that puts you in touch with the purpose of the universe." Parody makes the line funny; history, and the terrifying possibility that Rocco may be right, given an Absurdist vision of the universe, make it not funny.

Rocco is accompanied by the requisite hunch-backed assistant, Tomas, who is primarily responsible for acquiring the experimental subjects and initiating a one-man crime wave. Tomas says very little, and much of that in Greek (a sardonic combination of classical heritage and bestiality personified), but his presence brings onstage a manifestation of the savagery by which the central characters feel themselves threatened, and makes explicit the erotic and racist implications of all those glistening dark bodies in B jungle movies. As the whites decline, non-white Tomas ascends, expropriating for himself the style and trappings of power. Later in the play, we encounter a third B-movie personage, the failed priest; again the element of parody is present, as Liduc does not go to the ends of the earth to redeem himself, but has been sent by a Church which sincerely hopes he will never be heard from again. His presence makes possible the introduction of the pseudophilosophical observations so characteristic of the B-movie as a form, and which Walker gleefully deflates and redirects: "Jesus doesn't mind losers but he has no patience for idiots."

To these refugees from a jungle movie, Walker adds figures from other worlds, but worlds no less threatened by the surrounding chaos. Olga, Rocco's wife, is obsessed with the world of Chekhov's plays to the point where she believes that she is the character of the same name from *The Three Sisters,* complete with a sentimental attachment to the artistic traditions of the *ancien régime* (represented in the play by a treasured Renoir which she employs as a talisman against the forces of the jungle), a determination to preserve social form at all costs, and the obligatory yearning for Moscow. . . . The introduction of a Chekhovian character points the pattern of non-communication and obsession in the piece, gives an added significance to the manner in which characters are isolated from each other, and adds a dream-like memory of bitter-sweet against which Walker can contrast his more garish effects.

Corporal Lance, formerly of the R.C.M.P., brings a distinctly Canadian contribution to the model apocalypse; we, too, get a share in the fall of the West. The Corporal is the only explicitly Canadian character in Walker's work (although [*Gossip* and *Filthy Rich*] are nominally set in Toronto) and it is a reflection of Walker's views on what Canadian theatre ought to be that the character is a very crafty parody: the Corporal is inept (natives have dismantled his motorcycle and he can't put it together again), naive, apparently clean-living, and very Canadian—in the grip of malarial hallucinations, he sees wheat. The character is a good example of Walker's growing ability to manipulate audience expectations. The Corporal is at first merely a comic mountie, who, as we would expect, fails to understand what is happening in the sophisticated world of decadent allusion, worries about not having anything formal to wear but his scarlets ("Am I over-dressed?"), and gives his wholesome all to the battle against subversion. But this quintessentially Canadian joke, which makes possible the uniquely Canadian pleasure of being self-deprecatory and self-congratulatory simultaneously and which therefore neatly disarms a Canadian audience's defence mechanisms, acquires an uglier, more sinister quality as the play progresses: he is so distressed by misery that he puts to death all who suffer, hence making his Canadian wholesomeness an agent of the final destruction. The acute but unkind comment about our national personality is administered while we are still distracted by the reassuring cartoon.

The last of this stranded crew of expatriate whites is both of the world of B-movies and not of that world, thus providing a bridging device and a means of comment. Rita is a porn-movie star engaged in jungle smuggling operations in an attempt to raise the money to finance a legitimate movie and realize her dreams of respectable stardom: "This one is going to be a classic. It'll have sex. But it'll be sex with class." A classic definition of the romantic B-movie, or, for that matter, B jungle movies. Rita is the character most fully aware of the theatrical and cinematic elements of their plight, and the one most given to consciously dramatizing the situation; through her, Walker adds to the devices of hyperbole and film the technique of explicit comment which makes *Beyond Mozambique* more than an exercise in nostalgia and parody. . . . (pp. 95-6)

Beyond Mozambique is a much more disciplined play than is *Bagdad Saloon*. . . . *Beyond Mozambique* has tighter focus, and a clearer sense of direction, in part created by Walker's continued progress in the creation of the single, unifying stage image, the device which gives Theatre of the Absurd much of its trenchant force. The split between Walker's manic sense of humour and his more serious concerns is effectively healed; *Beyond Mozambique* is splendid black comedy, combining the comic and the grotesque to produce Jonsonesque social comment. And Walker completed, in this play, an important step toward developing an efficient personal style. (p. 97)

Having used this lens to bring social comment into focus in *Beyond Mozambique,* in *Ramona and the White Slaves* (1976) Walker directs his new instrument on the problems of characterization, an area of dramatic endeavour notoriously weak in much Canadian drama. Set in what is apparently a brothel in a turn of the century, impossibly decadent and chaotic Hong Kong, the play shows us the Madam/Mother, Ramona, and her convoluted relationships with her daughters, their lovers, her crippled son, and a man who may be her pimp, her missing husband, or both. Two frameworks are provided: the piece begins with Ramona's opium dream in which she is raped by a lizard—and there is a strong possibility that the entire play is an opium dream (a drug induced state of mind is another "lens" to which Walker sometimes resorts)—while commentary is provided by a detective ostensibly attempting to solve a murder, one of many, which occurred in the street outside the brothel. The detective (a device Walker also employs in *Gossip,* 1977, and *Filthy Rich,* 1979) has a long history as a useful dramatic device, and in addition provides the B-movie lens. Cook's inquiries do not produce the answers he sets out to find, nor do they reveal much biographical information about Ramona, for most spectators guess early in the play the bizarre secret of the ex-nun's history. The search, however, takes us through a tour of Ramona's psyche, the obsessions which compel her to devour her children and which make her, simultaneously, a powerful and compelling figure, a B-movie Medea. Her character provides one of the most rewarding roles for an actress in Canadian drama, a striking presentation of the mother/whore dichotomy so central to Western erotic fantasy, and the play makes an extraordinarily effective use of eroticism.

Walker's growing skills as a social satirist and his developing expertise in portraiture are both brought to bear on *Zastrozzi* (1977). . . . *Zastrozzi* is certainly more accessible than all but his earliest plays, and this, in combination with Walker's continued growth as a playwright, has made *Zastrozzi* his most popular work. The play is, unabashedly, a melodrama, and is subtitled as such. It pits good against evil in a plot taken from Shelley's novel, but a note in the Playwrights Co-op edition of the play informs the reader that Walker worked from a description of the novel: therefore the play is not really an adaptation of the original work. In the context of this discussion, it is important to note that there is certainly as much Errol Flynn as there is Percy Bysshe Shelley in Walker's play, and that Walker is continuing to make use of his B-movie lens.

As William Lane, the director of the original production, implies in his introduction, *Zastrozzi* is, in addition to being a melodrama, a contemporary (and tongue-in-cheek) morality play; Walker evidently believes that morality plays are rare in contemporary theatre and ought to be supplied, but is also aware that a contemporary audience is unlikely to accept a naked statement of central propositions: our defensive objectivity or superficiality or materialist disbelief must be circumvented through giving us the opportunity to laugh. "The moral centre of the play is Zastrozzi himself—the very one who never has a moral crisis." Zastrozzi, in fact, constitutes the moral centre through his implacable desire to follow the dictates of a kind of morality to that point where morality annihilates itself. "Mankind is weak. The world is ugly. The only way to save them from each other is to destroy them both." This is a logical extension of the thinking of both fundamentalist Protestantism and the playwrights of the Absurd. In the plot, Zastrozzi is the play's villain, the master criminal of Europe, and the adamant pursuer of his mother's murderer, a man turned saint or fool by the magnitude of the act. Within the play's metaphorical structure, Zastrozzi is the principle of order, standing as the last bastion against the coming of a new, liberal, "pleasantly vague" world being born at the turn of the century, the time of the play's events and the beginning of our own era. . . . He is, in short, "the master of discipline," the one who takes it upon himself to supply an absolute, a means of assuring that everyone is answerable.

Evil has great stage presence, and given the theatrical advantages ever afforded the villain, it is inevitable that the eponym seizes and holds the attention, and in some ways, the sympathy of the audience (after all, the murder of a mother is difficult to forgive, even allowing for extenuating circumstances and the fact that the lady herself · may have been a killer). . . . [Walker] deliberately presents the B-movie hero-in-white in such a way that contemporary cynicism cannot fail to judge the character a fool. The man whom Zastrozzi has pursued for three years cannot recognize the danger he is in, choosing instead to fantasize that he is a sort of messiah, complete with invisible followers; most telling stroke of all, he is a sexual flop, and we certainly don't want to identify with that. At the same time, Walker puts into the mind and mouth of a character we are sometimes invited to despise sentiments with which we know we ought to agree. At first glance, *Zastrozzi* seems to run contrary to Walker's usual practice of using a form to undermine the mode of thought behind the form: for the play, like melodrama and melodramatic B-movies, makes a clear distinction between good and evil, and gives each side the formalized statements of faith or anti-faith. However, by giving to the villain a passion for order and definition in some respects attractive to the inhabitants of chaotic times, as well as many of the best lines, and by giving to the putative hero qualities which we know cannot stand up to current events or intellectual trends, Walker encourages the wry and condescending smile with which we customarily respond to melodrama (unless it has been updated with the contemporary trappings of T.V. social drama) and with which we reject the melodramatic world of good and evil revealed. Walker's skilled evocation of the double response leads us into an old fashioned examination of the nature of good and evil; again, the theatrical hand is quicker than the eye of the audience, who thought they were just watching swashbuckling melodrama and parody of swashbuckling melodrama.

Melodramatic simplicities are further complicated by Victor. In some ways, Zastrozzi and Verezzi are opposites: Zastrozzi is a realist and Verezzi is an idealist. In other ways, they are similar; both shape their lives with absolutes. In this respect, and others, both find their opposite in Victor, servant to Verezzi and failed priest, who, in order to keep a promise does his utmost to protect the victim from the destroyer. Realistic, materialistic, pragmatic, Victor commands respect for his decency, resourcefulness, and courage. It is here that Walker's growing powers of characterization are most impressive, for despite all his decencies (and decency is notoriously boring on stage), Victor is an interesting character; he is the one who, as Lane points out, has the moral dilemma, and he responds to it in a manner with which most members of the audience would agree. He calls a madman a madman, acts instead of hypothesizing, and, alone among the characters, is possessed himself of a sense of humour. We identify with him; he is like us. And like us, he is wrong, and the error results in his death. His secular faith also has its limitations, and his balance, his moderation, is ultimately his undoing.

We therefore agree intellectually with one character, feel we ought to respond spiritually to a second, and identify most closely with a third. While B-movie conventions would lead us to expect an either/or proposition, we are given three poles, and ambivalent poles at that. Walker uses the rest of the cast of stock characters to extend the central issue, and to comment upon it. An assistant villain is present not only to facilitate the plot in the usual manner, but to demonstrate the difference between ideological evil and mere thuggery. The presence of a villainess and a purer-than-white heroine gives a sexual shape to the contest, reducing the cosmic struggle to "naughty" *vs.* "nice," and at the same time adding a strong strain of eroticism to help bring the point home, to bed. Zastrozzi's imaginary seduction of Julia is a very compelling scene indeed.

The values which emerge from Walker's work seem to be those of a small-"c" conservative, the technical trappings of the *avant-garde. Zastrozzi* ultimately asserts that evil does exist, is not the product of environment, and must be confronted. In *Prince of Naples,* the easy assumptions based on a facile acceptance of relative values are pilloried, and *Bagdad Saloon* dismantles a system of value based on the publicizing of subjective fantasy. Walker is a champion of language and definition, a concern that has increased as his career progressed, and he rejects naturalism, in part, because

it has forgotten how to reach areas of human experience accessible to older dramatic forms. In this, he resembles Eugene Ionesco, who claims not to be of the *avant-garde* at all; Ionesco dismisses much recent drama, finding "Ibsen heavy, Strindberg clumsy, Pirandello outmoded," and wants in his own work to return to the theatre of the Greeks and the Elizabethans, a larger than life theatre "concerned with the human condition in all its brutal absurdity." That is what we are left with at the end of *Zastrozzi* as the villain surveys a positively Jacobean heap of corpses, enjoying his impersonal Greek blood revenge. The form is contemporary but the clash of forces therein depicted is an old and vital one.

While *Zastrozzi* is a continuation of Walker's earlier thematic explorations (there are, for instance, striking similarities between the obsessions of Rocco and those of Zastrozzi) and of the playwright's technical development (the manner in which Victor is employed to manipulate audience expectations differs from the way in which the Corporal was used only in that the technique is elaborated in the later play), it is at the same time a meticulously constructed and highly successful piece of entertaining theatre: to be truly successful, parody must be as skilfully constructed as that which it parodies, and in this respect *Zastrozzi* is a literary in-joke—poker-faced, Walker demonstrates that he is perfectly capable of writing a well-made play, and does so without sacrificing his personal, non-documentary vision.

This new concern with "generosity" is evident in Walker's other recent plays. *Gossip* and *Filthy Rich* appear to be detective B-movies, and can be enjoyed at that level, but they are really contemporary comedies of manners, high comedy revived. *Rumours of Our Death,* first produced in 1980 and published in the *Canadian Theatre Review,* No. 25, is, on the surface, a Ruritanian romance-*cum*-spy movie, and was given punk rock treatment in the original Factory Lab production, but it introduces politics through a tantalizing political fable which at times seems to apply to Canada, and at others (no doubt as a result of the playwright's intention) snatches the easy and national answer away by interrupting the pattern. Walker is using popular forms, primarily B-movies, as a means of exploring old dramatic verities. . . . (pp. 97-101)

The man who appears to be among Canada's most abstruse and esoteric playwrights has, in fact, a thorough grasp of populist techniques, and can use the forms of popular theatre as both popular vehicle and as a means of sharing with a broader audience a more demanding dramatic view. In this ability to speak to a more general audience, Walker resembles the populist docu-dramatists of Passe Muraille or the Tarragon playwrights, who address a popular, middle-class audience within the conventions it knows best, and in the process, he gives them some penetrating analysis of themselves. The tendency to commercialism in recent Canadian drama and commercialism in the artistic policies of many Canadian theatres has been decried, as it should be, but commercialization should not be confused with a movement underway in Canada for some time, a movement whose aim has been to take theatre to a larger audience, abandoning the coterie audiences of the regionals and attempting to reach instead an audience previously unaccustomed to attending formal, legitimate theatre. The venture, should it prove successful, could help to change the status of theatre as mere social status symbol, to which it has unfortunately so often been relegated in twentieth-century North America, and to restore to the theatre the power of broad appeal which has traditionally given drama an edge over other literary forms. This increased ability to reach out to an audience is one of the directions which theatre has taken in response to Esslin's question, "After the Absurd, what?" And it is a direction to which Canadian drama has been a major contributor. Seen in the context of these larger movements, Walker and the Factory Lab are not mavericks at all, but the source of one of the most theatrically potent streams within the new Canadian drama. (pp. 101-02)

Chris Johnson, "George F. Walker: B-Movies Beyond the Absurd," in Canadian Literature, No. 85, Summer, 1980, pp. 82-103.

RAY CONLOGUE

[*The review excerpted below originally appeared in the* Globe and Mail, *February 24, 1983.*]

George F. Walker seems to be pioneering a new form of entertainment: the fascist two-step, or, play it again, Fritz.

That seems to be the only way to avoid concluding that **The Art of War** . . . is either part of a continuing investigation into the nature of evil (which is ponderous) or a playwright spinning his wheels (which is tempting, but unfair; the show is still entertaining).

Let's say it's a symmetrical three-on-three encounter on the edge of a provincial park. In this corner is a retired Canadian general, his psychopathic bodyguard, and the beautiful daughter of a third world dictator. They have the guns.

In the other corner is a drunken investigative journalist, a kid who hangs around with him, and the daughter (cute but not beautiful) of the local farm news publisher. They have the morals.

The show answers the question: What does a murderous commando with a steel plate in his brain do to "kill time" on guard duty? Answer: He sings "getting to know you, getting to feel free and easy". Or: What can you do to really upset a mad general who has just killed your best friend? Answer: transplant his roses so they get brown petals.

Nobody would deny that George Walker has a wickedly assured sense of humor. But there's an eleventh-hour quality about the humor in **Art of War;** the eleventh hour of a long evening in a bar, that magical moment when you've had enough to loosen the flow of wit but not yet enough to slur your words. That slaphappy moment when you know that whatever you believe in, if it wins, will for sure be corrupted. So you have that last drink, and you slur your words.

Walker was slurring when he had . . . [Tyrone M. Power], the feckless humanist of a journalist, stand up at the general's table and blurt out: "Any idiot can make the trains run on time! The hard part is to have a society where people get on the train for any other reason than that they're terrified of whoever made them run on time!" Whew. Now that's earnest. It's the earnestness of the poor guy who believes that goodness is weak, and strength wouldn't be caught dead hanging around with it.

C. S. Lewis once dramatized the banality of evil by showing his villain plucking feathers out of a living bird while reciting a nonsense verse. Walker does that, too. Unfortunately, his good guys recite nonsense verses too, even if they're only plucking feathers out of dead birds. Everybody is enervated.

But even when he is coasting, Walker demonstrates a certain assurance. The play, after all, is about a general who has been transferred from the Ministry of Defence to the Ministry of Culture ("his idea of a cultural event is bombing an opera house") where all kinds of timely swipes at arts cutbacks and the interviewing techniques of Barbara Frum can be giddily admixed with speculation on the nature of creation. The whole thing is so loosely assembled that the scenes sometimes feel like cabaret skits. You expect the cast to return swinging parasols in unison after a blackout. In fact, it actually ends with—but that would be telling.

Ray Conlogue, in a review of "The Art of War," in Canadian Drama/L'Art dramatique canadien, Vol. 11, No. 1, 1985, p. 222.

BOYD NEIL

George Walker has admitted two things important to understanding his plays: "I don't have any wisdom" and "sometimes I replace what is a normal dramatic conflict with conflict between two obsessions". The first saves those of us who agree from the embarrassment of resorting to *ad hominen* arguments in reviews; the second gets to the heart of what is so disturbing about his work. . . .

The battle lines [in **The Art of War**] are obvious, even too familiar, to regular Walker watchers. They aren't, however, the two obsessions which replace the natural dramatic conflict Walker talks about. Those really belong to General Hackman and the playwright himself—the general's obsession is for the culture of order, the playwright's is with the knocking knees of the well-intentioned.

Fair enough. We do have something to fear from the ineffectual dithering of people of good will. But Walker's *idée fixe* makes for unwholesome and single-tracked drama. He so disarms his benevolent characters with indecisiveness, irrationality and softness that they are just unlikeable twits. I'd much rather spend an evening with Karla Mendez—as distasteful as her ideas are—than Power's friend Heather Masterton because Mendez is at least passionate. (If Walker truly wants us to prefer the company of fascists in his play, then his ideas are more dangerous than I thought.)

None of this troubles Walker's fans who love his unlikely wit. His comedy comes from the timeless pleasure of enjoying unavoidable human foibles. His special flair is for the SCTV sort of comedy—off-beat, contemporary cynicism that leaves middle class intellectual poseurs content in the knowledge that *they* would never stoop to being well-intentioned.

Boyd Neil, in a review of "The Art of War," in Canadian Drama/L'Art dramatique canadien, Vol. 11, No. 1, 1985, p. 224.

L. W. CONOLLY

Although the three plays in [**The Power Plays: Gossip, Filthy Rich, The Art of War**] have all been previously published, there are particular benefits (in addition to convenience) in bringing them together in [one volume]. Given a unifying link by their central character, Tyrone M. Power, the plays form a natural trilogy, thereby inviting comparison with other major trilogies in contemporary Canadian drama—James

Reaney's Donnelly plays and David French's Mercer trilogy. There are some significant

Part of the fascination of these plays lies in witnessing the extended development of situation and character that the length of each trilogy allows. There is, to be sure, a similar fascination in **The Power Plays,** but it has fewer dimensions. The subject matter of the third of the Power plays—**The Art of War**—is quite significantly removed from that of **Gossip** and **Filthy Rich,** and its level of seriousness is on an altogether higher plane. The two early plays amuse us with their convoluted murder plots, whereas **The Art of War,** while still amusing, poses troublesome questions about the nature of "liberalism" in the face of autocratic power. **Gossip** and **Filthy Rich** are clever plays; **The Art of War** is an intelligent play, and it doesn't sit easily with the other two. (pp. 110-11)

If the plays have a significant coherence, it comes from [the character T. M. Power]. Power is one of the most intriguing characters in recent Canadian drama. An unsuccessful journalist, failed novelist, and (until **The Art of War**) reluctant private detective, Power bungles his way through life in traditional anti-hero fashion. He looks the part ("middle-aged and balding. Walrus mustache. Thick-rimmed glasses. A bit overweight"); he behaves the part ("Why can't we do anything properly. It's so goddamn depressing"). Cynical, frequently devious, he is yet a moralist, seeking out truth and justice with dedication and inefficiency. His ultimate triumphs in solving murder cases in **Gossip** and **Filthy Rich** are not matched in **The Art of War,** where political manipulation and corruption are shown as too strong for Power's good intentions. Walker creates a rich array of characters in **The Power Plays**—the portrait of John Hackman, militaristic adviser to the Minister of Culture in **The Art of War** is striking—but Power remains the principal focus.

Walker's imagination is eclectic; and it is unevenly realized in **The Power Plays.** As in his earlier work, the influence of Absurdism and second-rate movies is evident, though the influence brings mixed blessings. While it is amusing, for example, to recognize parodies of B-movie situations, this device too often seems to be an end in itself. Walker finds some easy targets and easy jokes (about actors, for example, in **Gossip**), and the humour is at times merely self-indulgent. He opts for comfortably familiar situation comedy, as in Power's entrance (in darkness) in scene four of *Gossip:* "Hello? Is anyone here? [*Lights a match. Keeps moving. Suddenly trips over something. Falls. Match goes out. Darkness.*] Ah, for Christ's sake." Maybe this is intentional parody; maybe it says something about life imitating bad art. Whatever the purpose, the effect is tiresome. Tiresome, too, are Power's drowsy aphorisms—"Do you know what life is? Life is a series of apparent coincidences contrived by mysterious forces to make sane men like me crazy"—but these are happily relieved by extensive passages of sharp, literate dialogue, particularly in **The Art of War.** (pp. 111-12)

Walker's wit, dialogue, and idiosyncratic view of life sparkle especially brightly in **The Art of War.** But the failure of **Gossip** and **Filthy Rich** to reach the level of **The Art of War** denies the trilogy the stature of Reaney's and French's achievements. (p. 112)

L. W. Conolly, "Dramatic Trilogies," in Canadian Literature, *No. 112, Spring, 1987, pp. 110-12.*

JOHN BEMROSE

Russian writer Ivan Turgenev first popularized the term "nihilist" in his great 1862 novel, *Fathers and Sons.* He used the word to describe his protagonist, Bazarov, a haughty, self-styled rebel who believes in destroying all established order. Turgenev despised what Bazarov stood for, but sympathized enough with the character to turn him into one of the most vivid creations of Russian literature. In **Nothing Sacred,** . . . Canadian playwright George F. Walker has caught the novel's broad sympathies and subtle play of ideas in a brilliant stage version. Although he amplifies the gentle humor of Turgenev's tragicomedy to near-farcical levels, the result is still spellbinding.

As in the novel, Bazarov first appears in the company of Arkady Kirsanov, who is bringing his fellow student home for a visit to his family's estate. Walker's Bazarov loves to make frontal assaults on middle-class gentility. Strutting arrogantly in his Byronesque black cloak, he lectures his listeners with such pronouncements as "I look at the world and think of ways of taking it all apart." He soon clashes with Arkady's foppish uncle, Pavel, whose conservative views reflect Turgenev's own. . . .

By the time [Bazarov and Pavel] meet in a climactic pistol duel, the play has achieved that paradoxical mixture of portentous weight and utter lightness of the best drama. . . . *Nothing Sacred* is easily one of the finest Canadian productions of this or any other season.

John Bemrose, "Dance of the Dialectic," in Maclean's Magazine, *Vol. 101, No. 5, January 25, 1988, p. 53.*

MEL GUSSOW

Since its premiere last January in Toronto, **Nothing Sacred** has become one of the most popular new plays in American regional theaters. . . . In the program, Mr. Walker announces that this is not an adaptation [of Ivan Turgenev's novel, *Fathers and Sons,*] but a play inspired by the novel, adding, "I think you can't approach these dead guys with unreserved reverence." One would have hoped at least for a little reserved reverence. . . .

[*Nothing Sacred* is] close enough in outline as to make the playwright's disclaimer ingenuous. His iconoclastic view is summarized by the title of his play, borrowed from the 1937 Fredric March-Carole Lombard film.

Despite his statement that **Nothing Sacred** is a "Canadian comedy not a Russian tragedy," it takes place in the novel's time and place. The playwright refers to the characters—the ones he retains—by their original names and they share relationships as in Turgenev.

The novel, Turgenev's acknowledged masterpiece, focuses on the character of Bazarov, the proud nihilist (and doctor) who challenges traditional values—those held by his parents, by the father of his acolyte, Arkady, and in particular by Arkady's Uncle Pavel, a Russian dandy irrepressibly infatuated with Western culture.

In Mr. Walker's version, Bazarov becomes a diabolical clown as well as something of a vulgarian and Pavel a ridiculous fop. Both characters veer into caricature. In the novel, Pavel challenges Bazarov to a duel, in which the older man is superficially wounded. In the play, Pavel kills Bazarov in that duel, and Bazarov's body is thrown on the trash heap (an accumulation of broken tables, wheels and spare parts that line the open stage like an automobile graveyard).

Dying such a fool's death robs Bazarov of his tragic dimension and vitiates the political weight of the novel. It also eliminates one of the most moving death scenes in all literature.

The tragedy of Bazarov is that he—a confirmed skeptic—succumbs to an unfulfilled romantic love for a wealthy widow and later pays the price for his own awakened idealism. He dies of an infection contracted while treating peasants for typhoid fever. Mr. Walker's changes include the suggestion that Bazarov's relationship with the widow is an affair that precedes the events of the play by several years. The playwright has also elected to keep Bazarov's parents offstage, weakening the generational conflict between fathers and sons.

In quest of comedy, he moves his play dangerously close to whimsy. Flowers repeatedly sprout on cue through the floorboards of the stage and at one point a character proclaims, "I ain't going up against the wood demon," as if the adapter had momentarily confused Turgenev with a cowboy version of Chekhov. Though Mr. Walker's exact purpose remains undefined, one might surmise that his interest is at least partly deflationary.

The play is effective in two respects: in showing the alliance between Bazarov and Arkady (they wander through the landscape like Rosencrantz and Guildenstern) and in picturing the subjugation of servants, who are beset by social as well as physical abuse. . . .

It was Isaiah Berlin who said that by exploring man's moral predicament Turgenev's novels, especially *Fathers and Sons,* are basic documents "for the understanding of the Russian past and of our present." In his eccentric dramatization. Mr. Walker has made Turgenev seem remote.

Mel Gussow, "Turgenev, with License," in The New York Times, January 13, 1989, p. C5.

JUDITH RUDAKOFF

In many ways, Gina Mae Sabatini is the character who provides the key to understanding survival, the primary objective of the quirky inhabitants of George F. Walker's remarkable East End trilogy: *Criminals in Love, Better Living* and *Beautiful City* [collected in *The East End Plays.*]

"I want a throbbing, connecting, living creature neighbourhood," she declares. In her working-class neighbourhood, those who wantonly give themselves to the raw basics of *life* and embrace its "Life Force," Gina Mae's "simple, ugly truth," may yet survive.

In a world in which everything is relative (as William proclaims in *Criminals In Love* and Nora echoes in *Better Living*), survival is as easy as breathing in. And then remembering to breathe out. It is a society in which nothing can be assumed. Destiny, the paranormal, and even witchcraft are debunked, while the minutiae of daily existence (oranges and bananas?) are imbued with almost magical properties. Mundane and empty ceremonies are elevated to the level of ritual: the handshakes in *Beautiful City* and the peremptory kisses in *Criminals in Love* become oaths sworn to seal pacts of mythic proportion. . . .

And what of the traditional anchors of contemporary society—home, love, and mom? In Walker's East End Toronto, home is more a war zone than a haven, love functions largely as a weapon, and mom . . . well, mom varies from cosmic communicator to karmic castrator. The cardinal rule in all three plays of Walker's East End trilogy is abundantly clear: if you sever yourself from the "Life Force" (the collective unconscious, the microcosm, the balance of yin and yang, the mother ship, whatever you want to call it) part of you dies. Whether you retreat to the artificial mall-world of *Beautiful City*'s Raft Family, or Nora and Tom/Tim's mole-world sanctuary in *Better Living,* the result is the same: you isolate yourself and you wither away. And dying isn't really the primary issue; it's the slow leaking out of the Life Force that is the unforgivable waste.

In The East End trilogy as well as in Walker's other recently published playscript, the award-winning *Nothing Sacred,* the glorious orchestration of ideas and words reads as well as it plays. Walker's characters, from the ferociously ardent to the timidly uncertain, are genuine, memorable, and always in some way recognizable. Even when they are based on the characters who populate Turgenev's novel of 19th-century Russia, *Fathers and Sons.*

In *Nothing Sacred,* a comedy filled with serfs and nihilists, class barriers and even a duel, Walker is surprisingly successful in synthesizing the contemporary and the archaic. . . .

Whether the plays are set in Walker's own era and in his own backyard, or in some exotic locale in a far-off time, the folks that populate Walker's neighbourhoods have the power to connect to each other *and* to us.

Judith Rudakoff, "War Zone," in Books in Canada, Vol. 18, No. 2, March, 1989, p. 28.

IRENE N. WATTS

George F. Walker is one of Canada's most innovative playwrights. His work has been produced abroad and with increasing frequency in Canada. . . .

In *Criminals in Love,* young urban lovers must cope with a small-time crook father who insists on implicating them in the plots of a neurotic terrorist uncle. In *Better Living,* Mother is digging under the foundations for a better future, Uncle Jack has lost his faith, three daughters with a variety of problems return home, and the new lodger may or may not be their deceased father. Murder seems a viable solution. In *Beautiful City,* two families fight for possession of property, assets and each other in this satire on the decay of urban life and morals.

Unlike many earlier writers in Canada who wrote lovingly of rural conditions and problems, Walker creates characters bred of the decaying wasteland of the inner city in which they are completely at home. They draw us immediately into the landscape of school yards, alleys and seedy homes and seem to make even the most grotesque and bizarre situation plausible.

Walker is a brilliant and highly imaginative writer of dialogue and of broadly theatrical characters. The women are particularly well drawn. . . .

Both narrative and characters are always on the brink of violence that threatens to errupt, and the plays have the cliff-hanging suspense of a 1940 B movie. Frequently, there is a filmlike quality to many of the episodes. Plots are complex, involved and riveting—a wonderful mixture of realism and soaring imagination.

There is never a dull moment. Walker writes of obsessions, anxiety, family break-up, and odd loyalties, of corruption, decay and love with a comedic and theatrical imagery that captivates and stimulates the audience to awareness of what is chaotic in our society.

> *Irene N. Watts, in a review of "The East End Plays: Criminals in Love, Better Living, Beautiful City," in* CM: Canadian Materials for Schools and Libraries, *Vol. XVII, No. 4, July, 1989, p. 199.*

JERRY WASSERMAN

Existential comedy strung out along the border between the serious and the bizarre has for two decades been the specialty of George F. Walker, a writer whose career progress is demarcated by semi-official trilogies. The first, **Three Plays** (1978), marked Walker's evolution from derivative absurdism to exotic B-movie extravaganzas like **Beyond Mozambique** and **Ramona and the White Slaves** in which he established his own distinct dramatic signature. **The Power Plays** (1984) epitomized Walker's *film noir* phase. Still distanced by their generic flavour and cinematic frame, these plays showed Walker moving from other times and places to the more or less here and now. His concerns remained the same—corruption, obsession, power, the apocalyptic struggle between the forces of good and evil, order and chaos—but the modern city was the new setting. Tyrone M. Power, investigative reporter and private eye, is an ordinary man swimming against the current of slime in which he barely stays afloat, ultimately kept buoyant by that other constant of Walker's work, his marvellous deadpan comic voice. (p. 71)

[A third Walker trilogy, **The East End Plays,** contains] **Criminals in Love, Better Living,** and **Beautiful City.** Though the back cover says that these plays of the mid-eighties 'do not constitute a trilogy,' they share common characters, themes, and terrain. The east-end setting, though not explicitly identified in any of the plays, seems to mark another phase in Walker's movement closer to home: the east end where he grew up, Toronto where he still lives. The family is the field on which the primal Walkeresque battle is joined this time. More than in any of his previous plays common people are involved in the fight. For them the prize is simple happiness and the trilogy shows a steady progress towards the ability to imagine that goal. As usual the plays are shot through with Walker's bleak epigrammatic humour.

In **Criminals in Love,** the only play of the three previously published, a pair of teenage lovers, Gail and Junior, struggle against destiny (variously described as the abyss, the call of the pit, the hanging shadow) in the form of Junior's degenerate criminal family. Junior fears that he's doomed to follow his pathetic father to prison, and when demented 'Aunt' Wineva turns up to force them to join Uncle Ritchie's gang things look grim. The lovers are assisted by a Kafkaesque alcoholic philosopher-bum named William K. who suggests numerous strategies of resistance, including dressing in a new suit:

> The suit is the answer. It is the cruise missile of social conflict. It exerts power. We need power. We

must go on the offensive. To the disgusting underclass of society the suit is like garlic to Dracula. It makes them grab their genitals. It's an inbred reflex action based on years of grovelling.

But when Wineva involves them in her revolutionary action to destroy the world ('If you'd been in Chicago in '68 you'd understand'), William is less sanguine:

> Some people would tell you just to think positively. These are people, of course, who have been able to spend all their summers outdoors. Probably their grandmothers had a lot of money. Others would tell you to pick yourselves up by the bootstraps. These are people who have forgotten anything they might have known about life. . . . I've taken this trip before. At a certain point you just hold your breath till you reach the destination. The bottom, so to speak.

About to be hauled off to prison at the end, Junior crawls back under Gail's sweater, the position of passive infantile security we found him in at the start. The terrifying illogic of the apparently inevitable proves overpowering. Legacy, as Junior feared, seems indeed to be destiny.

Though Wineva carries the ball for the forces of evil and William's ideas power what little resistance is available to the forces of good, the play's fundamental opposition is between a destructive patriarchy and a constructive feminine *eros* symbolized by what lies beneath Gail's sweater. In **Better Living,** a prequel to **Criminals in Love,** Walker pushes this feminist argument a lot further. The family in this play is constituted as a community of women (Nora and her three daughters including Gail). Junior, courting Gail about a year before **Criminals in Love,** is little more than a cipher. Also on board is Uncle Jack, a familiar Walkeresque failed priest. ('I haven't lost my faith. I've just lost my enthusiasm. And that won't kill me, it will just make me pathetic.') This good father is impotent in the face of the real family patriarch, Tom, an ex-cop whom daughter Mary Ann thinks of as 'the principal, the crossing-guard, the premier, the president, the executive director, the person with the key, the one who signs the cheques.' Abusive and destructive, Tom had been driven away by the family years earlier but has now returned with a vision of 'the total shit future' and a fascist program with which he organizes them, Charles Manson-like, into a paranoid defensive shell. When daughter Elizabeth tells him he's insane he replies, 'I *am* insane. But I love you. I love this family. . . . The love of an insane man is priceless in the total shit future.'

The lives of all four women have been badly shaken by the chaos Tom's insane love leaves in its wake. Nora spends most of the play tunnelling rooms underneath the house in a kind of comic-literal descent into another level of being which she calls better living (maybe her version of Gail's sweater). Gail is looking for a stable domestic life—the simple happiness that Walker's nightmare of a nuclear family won't allow—but is still ambivalently attracted to her father. ('She's a criminal conservationist,' Nora complains.) Lawyer Elizabeth willingly surrenders her strength and competence in Tom's presence. And poor neurotic Mary Ann intuits from her broken family a cosmic principle. . . . Things take a turn for the better at the end. Gail and Uncle Jack drive Tom away (though with suspect methods: a gun and Junior's criminal father for persuasion). Life returns to the wasteland. There will be babies. Windows in the underground rooms. Wallpaper. 'I've decided happiness is the thing we should all work towards,' Nora says as the lights fade—and Tom reappears at the door. A skirmish has been won but the war for better living will rage on.

Both these plays, for all their wit and weirdness, are overwritten and essentially static. Without the exotica of earlier Walker to sustain interest, their tendency to go over and over the same abstract ground leaves us with unaccustomed stretches of dramatic listlessness. With *Beautiful City* Walker shifts gears, pushing the trilogy towards its macro-comic conclusion by returning to the elaborate plotting and social concreteness of *The Power Plays.*

The battles fought within and between family groups (there are four of them) in *Beautiful City* are battles for the soul of the city and the fate of urban man. Paul, an architect who has sold out to the developers, is sick from lack of contact with the life-force. It takes a mother-daughter combination to cure him. The mother, Gina Mae, is a witch who works at Bargain Harold's. She explains the reality principle:

> If you don't get better you won't be able to work, you won't have any money, soon you won't have any friends. You'll be on welfare. They'll cut you off welfare. You won't be able to eat properly. You won't have a place to live. No clothes. You'll sleep in doorways. . . . In the winter you'll freeze. Being naked and freezing and starving is hell. The simple ugly truth is metaphysical.

Gina Mae is William K. of *Criminals in Love* with a difference: along with the will she has the power to change things. She takes responsibility for rehabilitating her scummy brother-in-law and his scummier son. She faces down the elegant criminal matriarch Mary Raft and her obsessive developer son who builds mega-malls based on 'indigenous anxiety' ('Family and safety. Everything indoors.'). Gina Mae succeeds in getting her own agenda: parks, social housing, shelters for the homeless, 'big bright wonderful stores where people get useful products at reasonable prices'—in short 'a throbbing, connecting, living, creative neighbourhood.'

It should be evident that *Beautiful City* is not so much comedy as romance, albeit in the distinctive Walker mode. After the appropriate rewards and punishments have been dished out with the help of a female cop (the first woman among Walker's many purveyors of justice), we even get an unashamedly classic resolution, a proposal of marriage between the putative hero and heroine. But over it all still looms the dark shadow. Mary's parting words echo through many of Walker's plays:

> Enjoy your fantasy while you can. But don't assume that the people around here, your so-called victims, were put on this earth for any other reason than to serve the needs of the powerful. And don't assume that this natural state of affairs won't return eventually.

The struggle continues.

In Canadian drama's Year of the Family it seems appropriate that the play of the year is an adaptation of *Fathers and Sons.* In *Nothing Sacred,* winner of the Chalmers, Dora, Governor-General's, and Canadian Authors Association awards, Walker picks up the key thematic threads of *The East End Plays* and draws them back through nineteenth-century Russia. The struggle here has concrete historical form. Begun with the emancipation of the serfs, it will climax sixty years later in a revolution that shakes the world. But in both Turgenev's novel and Walker's play the struggle is also for happiness. Will there be a place for love in the brave new world just dawning in 1859?

The central debate in the play pits the cold rationalism of the nihilist Bazarov ('He's not a man. He's a primal force.') against the budding humanism of his friend and disciple Arkady ('a primal force in training'). At first the battle-lines appear to be political and generational: the progressive young, Bazarov and Arkady, oppose the conservative old, Arkady's landowner father Kirsanov and dandyish uncle Pavel. But Arkady soon chafes at the smug gospel according to Bazarov which scoffs at kindness and other such minor virtues. Bazarov's attitude is relentlessly scientific. 'I simply base my conduct on what is useful. . . . You take the conditions. And measure them against the facts.' When Arkady asks about pity, Bazarov's response is blunt and well rehearsed: 'No time for that. Pity excuses weakness.'

The crux of the matter is love, a weakness that bridges the old and new orders. Liberal-minded Kirsanov loves Fenichka, the servant girl who has borne their child, but his traditional class-consciousness prevents him from marrying her. Pavel has had a destructive lifelong passion for the mother of Anna, the beautiful anarchist whom he now loves. Bazarov scorns all that as 'romantic bilge' but eventually professes to love Anna too, as does Arkady. Bazarov says he loves Gregor, a freed serf and one of the degraded hundred million whose rehabilitation constitutes Bazarov's revolutionary project. Finally Arkady, whose emotional journey forms the backbone of the play, realizes how much he loves his father and the estate that symbolizes the old order. 'The truth is I might belong here . . . forever.'

The conservative sensibility of *Nothing Sacred* originates with Turgenev. But as *The East End Plays* reveal, Walker himself seems to have come around to the idea that better living has more to do with mundane domesticity than apocalyptic transformation. (In the preface he notes that he's now forty and a father himself.) It may be no coincidence that the most interesting character in the play—certainly the show-stopper in performance—is not the charismatic Bazarov but the reactionary Pavel. Resplendent (or ridiculous) in English suits and pink nail-polish, Pavel is never the buffoon one might expect in a satiric comedy of manners like this, nor the cartoon he might have been in Walker's earlier work. The emotional sympathy Walker allows Pavel is symptomatic of Walker's affinity with Turgenev's novel. He has basically grafted his play onto the novel and assumed its point of view, its strong story line and characterization. With his normal excesses thus held in check Walker has written a well-made play, his most rigorously constructed to date but also one of his tamest. The contemporary wit and verbal gamesmanship are identifiably his own; the play of ideas mostly Turgenev's. The kinks that make Walker so attractive are rarely in evidence here. Eccentric leaps of imagination are relatively few. And I have to admit I miss them just a little.

Even if *Nothing Sacred* is not The Great Canadian Play that its success might lead us to believe, it is a strong and provocative work. (pp. 71-5)

Jerry Wasserman, in a review of "The East End Plays," in University of Toronto Quarterly, *Vol. LIX, No. 1, Fall, 1989, pp. 71-9.*

FURTHER READING

Bemrose, John. "Urban Survival." *Maclean's Magazine* 102 (October 23, 1989): 76-7.

Review of *Love and Anger* and discussion of Walker as a major figure in contemporary Canadian drama following the success of *Nothing Sacred.*

Johnson, Chris. "George F. Walker Directs George F. Walker." *Theatre History in Canada* 9 (Fall 1988): 157-72.

Based on rehearsals of the 1987 Factory Theatre Lab production of *Zastrozzi, the Master of Discipline,* Johnson examines Walker's casting choices and directing techniques to explore his "language of the stage" as a complement to the language of his script and to determine his current interpretation of the play.

Johnston, Denis W. "George F. Walker: Liberal Idealism and the 'Power Plays.'" *Canadian Drama* 10, No. 2 (1984): 195-206.

Discusses the theme of good people in conflict with corrupt society as developed in the "Power Plays"—*Gossip, Filthy Rich,* and *The Art of War.*

O'Hara, Jane. "The Odd Man Out in Canadian Theatre." *Maclean's* 95 (8 March 1982): 16, 19-20.

Profile of Walker, blending biographical information with descriptions of the conception, plots, and reception of his plays.

Sinclair, Gregory J. "Live from Off-Stage." *The Canadian Forum* LXVI (August/September 1986): 6-11.

Traces Walker's career and examines how experimental playwrights Walker, Tom Walmsley, and Judith Thompson have greatly influenced contemporary Canadian drama.

Wynne-Jones, Tim. "Acts of Darkness." *Books in Canada* 14 (April 1985): 11-14.

Feature article on Walker as well as analysis and description of his plays.

☐ Contemporary Literary Criticism

Indexes

Literary Criticism Series
  Cumulative Author Index
Cumulative Nationality Index
Title Index, Volume 61

This Index Includes References to Entries in These Gale Series

Contemporary Literary Criticism

Presents excerpts of criticism on the works of novelists, poets, dramatists, short story writers, scriptwriters, and other creative writers who are now living or who have died since 1960.

Twentieth-Century Literary Criticism

Contains critical excerpts by the most significant commentators on poets, novelists, short story writers, dramatists, and philosophers who died between 1900 and 1960.

Nineteenth-Century Literature Criticism

Offers significant passages from criticism on authors who died between 1800 and 1899.

Literature Criticism from 1400 to 1800

Compiles significant passages from the most noteworthy criticism on authors of the fifteenth through eighteenth centuries.

Classical and Medieval Literature Criticism

Offers excerpts of criticism on the works of world authors from classical antiquity through the fourteenth century.

Short Story Criticism

Compiles excerpts of criticism on short fiction by writers of all eras and nationalities.

Children's Literature Review

Includes excerpts from reviews, criticism, and commentary on works of authors and illustrators who create books for children.

Contemporary Authors Series

Encompasses five related series. *Contemporary Authors* provides biographical and bibliographical information on more than 95,000 writers of fiction, nonfiction, poetry, journalism, drama, motion pictures, and other fields. Each new volume contains sketches on authors not previously covered in the series. *Contemporary Authors New Revision Series* provides completely updated information on active authors covered in previously published volumes of *CA*. Only entries requiring significant change are revised for *CA New Revision Series. Contemporary Authors Permanent Series* consists of updated listings for deceased and inactive authors removed from the original volumes 9-36 when these volumes were revised. *Contemporary Authors Autobiography Series* presents specially commissioned autobiographies by leading contemporary writers. *Contemporary Authors Bibliographical Series* contains primary and secondary bibliographies as well as analytical bibliographical essays by authorities on major modern authors.

Dictionary of Literary Biography

Encompasses four related series. *Dictionary of Literary Biography* furnishes illustrated overviews of authors' lives and works and places them in the larger perspective of literary history. *Dictionary of Literary Biography Documentary Series* illuminates the careers of major figures through a selection of literary documents, including letters, notebook and diary entries, interviews, book reviews, and photographs. *Dictionary of Literary Biography Yearbook* summarizes the past year's literary activity with articles on genres, major prizes, conferences, and other timely subjects and includes updated and new entries on individual authors. *Concise Dictionary of American Literary Biography* comprises six volumes of revised and updated sketches on major American authors that were originally presented in *Dictionary of Literary Biography*.

Something about the Author Series

Encompasses three related series. *Something about the Author* contains heavily illustrated biographical sketches on juvenile and young adult authors and illustrators from all eras. *Something about the Author Autobiography Series* presents specially commissioned autobiographies by prominent authors and illustrators of books for children and young adults. *Authors & Artists for Young Adults* provides high school and junior high school students with profiles of their favorite creative artists in the mediums of print, film, television, drama, song lyrics, and cartoons.

Yesterday's Authors of Books for Children

Contains heavily illustrated entries on children's writers who died before 1961. Complete in two volumes.

Literary Criticism Series
Cumulative Author Index

This index lists all author entries in the Gale Literary Criticism Series and includes cross-references to other Gale sources. References in the index are identified as follows:

AAYA: *Authors & Artists for Young Adults,* Volumes 1-3
CAAS: *Contemporary Authors Autobiography Series,* Volumes 1-11
CA: *Contemporary Authors* (original series), Volumes 1-130
CABS: *Contemporary Authors Bibliographical Series,* Volumes 1-3
CANR: *Contemporary Authors New Revision Series,* Volumes 1-29
CAP: *Contemporary Authors Permanent Series,* Volumes 1-2
CA-R: *Contemporary Authors* (revised editions), Volumes 1-44
CDALB: *Concise Dictionary of American Literary Biography,* Volumes 1-6
CLC: *Contemporary Literary Criticism,* Volumes 1-61
CLR: *Children's Literature Review,* Volumes 1-21
CMLC: *Classical and Medieval Literature Criticism,* Volumes 1-5
DC: *Drama Criticism,* Volume 1
DLB: *Dictionary of Literary Biography,* Volumes 1-92
DLB-DS: *Dictionary of Literary Biography Documentary Series,* Volumes 1-7
DLB-Y: *Dictionary of Literary Biography Yearbook,* Volumes 1980-1988
LC: *Literature Criticism from 1400 to 1800,* Volumes 1-13
NCLC: *Nineteenth-Century Literature Criticism,* Volumes 1-28
PC: *Poetry Criticism,* Volume 1
SAAS: *Something about the Author Autobiography Series,* Volumes 1-9
SATA: *Something about the Author,* Volumes 1-59
SSC: *Short Story Criticism,* Volumes 1-6
TCLC: *Twentieth-Century Literary Criticism,* Volumes 1-37
YABC: *Yesterday's Authors of Books for Children,* Volumes 1-2

A. E. 1867-1935 .... TCLC **3, 10**
See also Russell, George William
See also DLB 19

Abbey, Edward 1927-1989 ...... CLC **36, 59**
See also CANR 2; CA 45-48;
obituary CA 128

Abbott, Lee K., Jr. 19??- .... CLC **48**

Abe, Kobo 1924- .... CLC **8, 22, 53**
See also CANR 24; CA 65-68

Abell, Kjeld 1901-1961............ CLC **15**
See also obituary CA 111

Abish, Walter 1931-.............. CLC **22**
See also CA 101

Abrahams, Peter (Henry) 1919- ..... CLC **4**
See also CA 57-60

Abrams, M(eyer) H(oward) 1912-... CLC **24**
See also CANR 13; CA 57-60; DLB 67

Abse, Dannie 1923-............ CLC **7, 29**
See also CAAS 1; CANR 4; CA 53-56;
DLB 27

Achebe, (Albert) Chinua(lumogu)
1930- .... CLC **1, 3, 5, 7, 11, 26, 51**
See also CLR 20; CANR 6, 26; CA 1-4R;
SATA 38, 40

Acker, Kathy 1948- .... CLC **45**
See also CA 117, 122

Ackroyd, Peter 1949-.......... CLC **34, 52**
See also CA 123, 127

Acorn, Milton 1923-.............. CLC **15**
See also CA 103; DLB 53

Adamov, Arthur 1908-1970 ...... CLC **4, 25**
See also CAP 2; CA 17-18;
obituary CA 25-28R

Adams, Alice (Boyd) 1926- ... CLC **6, 13, 46**
See also CANR 26; CA 81-84; DLB-Y 86

Adams, Douglas (Noel) 1952- ... CLC **27, 60**
See also CA 106; DLB-Y 83

Adams, Henry (Brooks)
1838-1918 .... TCLC **4**
See also CA 104; DLB 12, 47

Adams, Richard (George)
1920- .... CLC **4, 5, 18**
See also CLR 20; CANR 3; CA 49-52;
SATA 7

Adamson, Joy(-Friederike Victoria)
1910-1980 .... CLC **17**
See also CANR 22; CA 69-72;
obituary CA 93-96; SATA 11;
obituary SATA 22

Adcock, (Kareen) Fleur 1934-...... CLC **41**
See also CANR 11; CA 25-28R; DLB 40

Addams, Charles (Samuel)
1912-1988 .... CLC **30**
See also CANR 12; CA 61-64;
obituary CA 126

Adler, C(arole) S(chwerdtfeger)
1932-...................... CLC **35**
See also CANR 19; CA 89-92; SATA 26

Adler, Renata 1938-............ CLC **8, 31**
See also CANR 5, 22; CA 49-52

Ady, Endre 1877-1919 .... TCLC **11**
See also CA 107

Agee, James 1909-1955 .... TCLC **1, 19**
See also CA 108; DLB 2, 26;
CDALB 1941-1968

Agnon, S(hmuel) Y(osef Halevi)
1888-1970 .... CLC **4, 8, 14**
See also CAP 2; CA 17-18;
obituary CA 25-28R

Ai 1947-..................... CLC **4, 14**
See also CA 85-88

Aickman, Robert (Fordyce)
1914-1981 .... CLC **57**
See also CANR 3; CA 7-8R

CLC Cumulative Nationality Index

CLC-61 Title Index

Title Index